The South African
OXFORD
SCHOOL
DICTIONARY

The South African

OXFORD
SCHOOL
DICTIONARY

Compiled by Joyce M. Hawkins

OXFORD
UNIVERSITY PRESS

OXFORD

UNIVERSITY PRESS

Great Clarendon Street, Oxford OX2 6DP

Oxford University Press is a department of the University of Oxford.
It furthers the University's objective of excellence in research, scholarship,
and education by publishing worldwide in

Oxford New York

Athens Auckland Bangkok Bogotá Buenos Aires Calcutta
Cape Town Chennai Dar es Salaam Delhi Florence Hong Kong Istanbul
Karachi Kuala Lumpur Madrid Melbourne Mexico City Mumbai
Nairobi Paris São Paulo Singapore Taipei Tokyo Toronto Warsaw

with associated companies in Berlin Ibadan

Published in South Africa
by Oxford University Press Southern Africa, Cape Town

The South African Oxford School Dictionary
ISBN 0 19 571414 8

First edition published 1996
Eighth impression 2000

Commissioning editor: Helen Laurenson
South African editor: Julie-Anne Justus
Copy editors: Sharon Hughes and Inge du Plessis
Designer: Peter Burgess

Published by Oxford University Press Southern Africa
PO Box 12119, N1 City, 7463, Cape Town, South Africa

Set in Helvetica Monotype Ariel and Adobe Utopia by Compleat Typesetters,
Fish Hoek, Cape Town and Photoprints Limited, Cape Town
Cover reproduction by RJH, Cape Town
Printed and bound by CTP Book Printers (Pty) Ltd, Caxton Street, Parow 7500, Cape Town

The Publishers would like to thank Raj Mesthrie, of the University of Cape Town
Linguistics Department, for commenting on the pronunciation of the South
African entries
Adapted material from *The Oxford Advanced Learner's Dictionary*,
Fifth Edition, 1995 by permission of Oxford University Press

Contents

Preface

This dictionary has been specially written for senior primary and secondary school students. Students will find it an invaluable aid for classroom work. It combines a clear easy-to-use layout with the detailed information and the large number of headwords students will need.

The dictionary is easy to use because it avoids abbreviations and special symbols. The typeface used is fairly large, and the entries are set out in a clear way. Tenses of verbs (e.g. *benefited/benefiting, preferred/preferring*), plurals of nouns, and comparatives and superlatives of adjectives and adverbs are usually spelt out in full unless their formation is very straightforward. Pronunciation of difficult words is given in a simple look-and-say system without special symbols. Definitions are clearly expressed, with careful explanations of difficult concepts (e.g. *hindsight, hypothesis, irony*), and many examples of words in use are provided. There are a number of notes on correct usage, grammatical points, and opposites or similar terms are sometimes indicated (e.g. *maximum/minimum, optimist/pessimist, libel/slander*).

An important feature of this dictionary is that it includes key words and phrases used in school subjects at the senior primary and secondary levels. Entries have been selected from a range of disciplines such as physical science, biology, agriculture, business economics, and art.

The South African Oxford School Dictionary includes many words that are used exclusively in South Africa (e.g. *toyi-toyi, kraal, songololo*). We have also tried to show that language changes over time by including words or phrases that are considered new. Words such as *glasnost, greenhouse effect*, and *ghetto-blaster* make the dictionary interesting as well as informative.

The English language

English is the chief language of Britain, the USA, Australia, and a number of other countries. More than 300 million people speak it as their first or only language, and millions more in all parts of the world learn it as a foreign language for use in communicating with people of other nations. It is the official language used between airline pilots and their air traffic controllers in all countries, and in shipping, and the main language of international business, science, medicine, and computing.

All languages have a history: they are constantly changing and evolving. It is probable that nearly all the languages of Europe came from one ancient community. As people moved away they lost contact with each other and developed new and different life-styles. Naturally their language needs changed too. They invented new words and forgot old ones, and the grammar of the language also changed. Many varied languages grew from the original parent tongue, until the time came when people with the same ancestors would no longer have understood each other.

Invasions and conquests complicated the process, as the outline on the following page shows. The earliest form of English, now called **Old English**, arose out of Anglo-Saxon and Old Norse, and bears little resemblance to the English we know today. For example, *Faeder ure, þu þe eart on heofonum* means 'Our Father, who art in heaven'.

In 1066, England was invaded by the Normans, who spoke French. English life was greatly changed in the years that followed, and the language changed too, so much so that, with a little practice, we can now fairly easily read and understand the language of that time. These lines, for example, were written in about 1390: *This carpenter hadde wedded newe a wyf, Which that he lovede moore than his lyf.* We call this language **Middle English** to distinguish it from Old English.

From about 1500 onwards the English language continued to change and develop. It adopted words from other languages with which people came into contact through trade and travel, and it was exported to other lands when English-speaking people travelled abroad. In the early seventeenth century colonies began to be established, first in North America and in India, then in the West Indies, and later in Australia, New Zealand, Hong Kong, and Africa. To each country the settlers took the English language of their own time, and in each country it changed, little by little, until it differed in various ways not only from the English of other settlements but from its parent form in Britain.

Modern English today continues to develop as it acquires words from other cultures and other languages through travel, films, radio and television programmes, and computer services such as the Internet.

The vocabulary of English

In modern English, we can often express the same idea in different words. This is because English has over the centuries absorbed words from many different languages. For example, *fear*, *terror*, *alarm*, and *fright* all have similar meanings but each came into English from a different language.

Anglo-Saxon

English developed from Anglo-Saxon (also known as Old English), the language brought to Britain by Germanic tribes (the Angles, Saxons, and Jutes) in the fifth century AD. These invaders gave England its name, 'the land of the Angles', and provided the language with many common basic terms.

man	breed	woman	house
woman	eat	work	

Latin

At the end of the sixth century, a group of monks came as missionaries from Rome to strengthen Christianity in Britain. The words which came into English from Latin at this time are mainly connected with religion and learning.

school	candle	verse
pope	minister	mass

Old Norse

In the ninth and tenth centuries, invaders came from Scandinavia and occupied a large part of eastern England. Many everyday words in modern English come from their language, Old Norse, which is related to Anglo-Saxon.

sky	dirt	take
call	leg	

French

When Britain was conquered by the Normans in 1066, French became the language of the ruling classes. Many words in modern

English which describe government and the legal system, as well as terms connected with cooking, came from French at this time.

sovereign	braise	court	veal
govern	mutton	advise	

Latin and Greek

Many words of Latin origin came into English through French, but the Renaissance of the fifteenth and sixteenth centuries brought a new interest in classical learning and an influx of words from Latin and Greek.

physics	compute	radius
architecture	educate	history

Worldwide

Latin and Greek are still used as a source of new words, particularly in the field of science, but English speakers today take words from a wide variety of other languages for phenomena that have no existing English name.

telephone	tattoo	video
tea	trek	sauna

Dictionaries of English

There are over 500 000 words in the English language, and the total is increasing all the time. Of these, about 3 000 are known and used by almost everyone whose first language is English. Most people know the meaning of at least another 5 000 words, though they may not use all of them in everyday speech or writing. In addition, those who specialize in a particular subject (e.g. music, chemistry, medicine, computers) have a wide vocabulary of words that are used by people working in that subject but are not generally known to others.

The biggest dictionary in the world is *The Oxford English Dictionary*, which fills twenty very large volumes, and it contains most of these words. (This dictionary is also published in CD-ROM format.) Small dictionaries can find room for only a fraction of the whole language; they include most of the words that are in common use, but (in order to make the book a convenient size and not too expensive) they have to miss out a considerable number of words, and a larger dictionary must be consulted for information about these.

South African English

English in South Africa

South Africa is a country with a rich linguistic heritage. This fact is recognized by our constitution, which names eleven official languages, including English. Although English is spoken as a first language by only about 8% of the population, it plays an important role in two ways.

Firstly, English (along with Afrikaans and Zulu) is a *lingua franca* or 'language of wider communication', which allows speakers of different languages to understand each other. Secondly, English is the only official language which is widely used in other countries. As such, it is an important language for international trade, academia, politics, and popular entertainment.

South African entries in this dictionary

The South African entries come from a variety of languages, showing how English has continually absorbed words to create a uniquely South African variety of English. We are indebted to William and Jean Branford's *A Dictionary of South African English* (fourth edition) and *The South African Pocket Oxford Dictionary* (eighth edition) for their selection of South African words.

Our choice of words from these sources is based on the likelihood of senior primary and secondary pupils encountering the words in general print. This means that we have not attempted to include any great number of South African slang words since these tend often to be isolated to one area or group, nor have we included words which reflect an earlier time or which teenagers are unlikely to encounter in a general context.

- Military terminology of the 1970s and 1980s such as *varkpan* and *klaar out*, for example, has been omitted.
- Neither have we included the many words which have developed around the use of alcohol (e.g. *tshwala*, *mampoer*) and drugs (e.g. *white pipe*, *zol*).
- Relatively few combined forms of words have been listed. *Boer* is included, for example, as is *boerewors* and *boeresport*, but not *boerebeskuit*, *boerekos*, or *boeremeisie*.
- Exhaustive lists of South African plants and animals have not been possible. Entries such as *disa*, *mamba*, and *stockfish* were selected on the basis of their general occurrence both geographically and in print.

Etymology

In keeping with the general principles of this edition, no etymology has been included for the South African entries.

Plural forms

Nouns in South African English tend to take the English plural rather than the plural form of the language of origin. *Velskoen*, for example, would be *velskoene* in its Afrikaans plural form, but the English user will refer more happily to *velskoens*. In such cases, both plural forms have been given.

Pronunciation

Phonetic respelling of South African words reflects the pronunciation of 'educated South Africans who speak English as their first language' (William Branford in *The South African Pocket Oxford Dictionary*).

How to use the dictionary

Finding words and definitions

Words defined are arranged in alphabetical order. The top of each page shows the letter of the alphabet covered on that page. At the top left of the left-hand page is the first word found on that page; at the top right of the right-hand page is the last word of that page.

Entries

Words with the same spelling but with a different meaning or origin are given separate entries numbered with a raised figure, e.g.:

> **peer**[1] *verb* look at something closely or with difficulty.
> **peer**[2] *noun* 1 a noble. 2 someone who is equal to another in rank or merit etc., *She had no peer.* **peeress** *noun*

Derivatives

Words derived from the main word are often included in the same entry without definitions if their meaning can easily be worked out from that of the main word. For example, the word *peeress* in the example above is a noun derived from *peer*[2] meaning 'a female noble'. Here is another example:

> **baker** *noun* a person who bakes and sells bread or cakes. **bakery** *noun*

Phrases

If you are looking for a phrase rather than a single word, look for the first important word in the phrase, e.g. *jump the queue* is found under the entry for *jump*:

> **jump**[1] *verb* ...move up suddenly from the ground into the air. ...
> **jump at** (*informal*) accept something eagerly. ...
> **jump the queue** not wait your turn.
> **jump**[2] *noun* a jumping movement.

Meanings

Many words have more than one meaning. Each meaning is numbered separately within the entry, e.g.

> **always** *adverb* 1 at all times. 2 often, *You are always crying.* 3 whatever happens, *You can always sleep on the floor.*

More information about the words

Parts of speech

These are printed in italic or sloping print (e.g. *noun, adjective, verb*) after the word and before its definition. Some words can be used as more than one part of speech, e.g.:

> **barricade**[1] *noun* a barrier, especially one put up hastily across a street etc.
> **barricade**[2] *verb* (**barricaded, barricading**) block or defend with a barricade.

Inflections and plurals

Derived forms of verbs, plurals of nouns, and comparative and superlative forms of adjectives and adverbs are usually given if they are irregular or if there might be doubt about the spelling. When only two verb forms are given, e.g.:

> **admit** *verb* (**admitted, admitting**)

the first form is both the past tense (as in 'he *admitted* it') and the past participle ('it was *admitted*'). When three forms are given, e.g.:

> **come** *verb* (**came, come, coming**)
> **freeze** *verb* (**froze, frozen, freezing**)

the first is the past tense (as in 'he *came*'; 'it *froze*') and the second is the past participle ('he had *come*'; 'it was *frozen*'). The last form given (ending in -*ing*) is the present participle.

Style labels

Some words are more suited to formal contexts (such as writing or public speaking), whereas others are more suited to informal contexts (such as chatting to a friend or writing a personal letter). Formal and informal uses of words are labelled as such, e.g.:

> **accord**[2] *verb* **1** be consistent with something. ...**2** (*formal*) give, *He was accorded this privilege.*

> **bash**[2] *noun* (*plural* **bashes**) **1** a hard hit. **2** (*informal*) a try, *Have a bash at it.*

Very informal language is called slang. It is used either for fun, or to express something in a more vivid and picturesque way than dignified words would do, or to shock people and attract their attention. Often, special slang words are used by members of a group, and they recognize others who use them as belonging to it too.

> **grub**[1] *noun* **1** a tiny worm-like creature that will become an insect; a larva. **2** (*slang*) food.

Words which might cause offence (such as racist or sexist terms and strong swear words) have been omitted.

Examples

Examples of words in use are given in italic or sloping print *like this* to help make a definition clearer, e.g.:

> **beware** *verb* be careful, *Beware of pickpockets.*

Example sentences have been supplied:
- to illustrate distinctions between literal and figurative use of words;
- to supply additional and useful information about the word;
- when the distinction between two meanings is very fine.

Usage notes

Usage notes after entries give guidance on terms often confused, as well as the appropriacy of words in formal contexts, e.g.:

> **complimentary** *adjective* **1** expressing a compliment. **2** given free of charge.
> - USAGE: Do not confuse with *complementary.*

Spelling of -ise and -ize

Words that end in **-ize** or **-ization** (e.g. *realize, realization*) may also be spelt with *s* instead of *z* (as in *realise, realisation*). Both spellings are equally correct. Words given in this dictionary with the spelling *-ise* (e.g. *advertise, surprise*) cannot be spelt with a *z*.

Proprietary terms

This book includes some words which are or are asserted to be proprietary names (e.g. *Vaseline*). The presence or absence of such assertions should not be regarded as affecting the legal status of any proprietary name or trade mark.

Pronunciation

Help is given with this when the word is difficult, or when two words with the same spelling are pronounced differently. The pronunciation is given in brackets with *say*, e.g.:

chaos (*say* kay-oss) *noun*

Words are broken up into small units (usually of one syllable), and the syllable that is spoken with most stress is shown in thick black letters. In the pronunciation guide, note the following distinctions:

ch   shows the sound as in *chin*
kh   shows the sound as in *gogga*
sh   shows the sound as in *shin*
th   shows the sound as in *thin*
th   shows the sound as in *this*
zh   shows the sound as in *vision*

a	shows the sound as in *cat*	oh	shows the sound as in *blow*
ah	shows the sound as in *park*	oo	shows the sound as in *soon*
air	shows the sound as in *bare*	or	shows the sound as in *warn*
ay	shows the sound as in *cake*	ow	shows the sound as in *house*
e	shows the sound as in *met*	oy	shows the sound as in *boy*
ear	shows the sound as in *hear*	u	shows the sound as in *hut*
ee	shows the sound as in *meet*	ur	shows the sound as in *bird*
i	shows the sound as in *pit*	uu	shows the sound as in *book*
I	shows the sound as in *eye*	y	shows the sound as in *sign*
o	shows the sound as in *pot*		

Dictionary games and activities

The following games provide you with practice in using the dictionary. They also draw on your knowledge of how English and other languages 'work'.

Alphabetical sorting

Words are arranged alphabetically in a dictionary. How good is your knowledge of the alphabet? See how quickly you are able to sort each of these lists into alphabetical order.

List 1	List 2	List 3
blesbok	greedy	shade
sugarbird	happy	sextet
crayfish	fearful	severe
perlemoen	indignant	shadow
aardvark	grasping	sexy
hake	interesting	shackle
dassie	intelligent	sewer
nyala	frightened	sexton
hyena	humiliating	several
kingklip	good	shaft
porcupine	humble	sextuplet
quagga	frightening	sexism

Finding words fast

You'll need to use your knowledge of the alphabet in order to play this game too. See who is able to find these words in the dictionary most quickly.

banana	aubergine	budget
fanfare	history	reconnoitre
volunteer	hijack	conurbation
recover	farrier	disapprove
history	plait	pseudo-

Word searches

A word that can be found in the dictionary is hidden in each of the groups of letters at the top of the next page. For example, in the first one, the word 'sensitive' can be found. See how quickly you can find each of these hidden words.

1 tergbhi<u>sensitive</u>eyagh (9 letters)
2 awyanaxagapanthusos (10 letters)
3 egtdronesolvitchia (5 letters)
4 desegeshebeenetehebev (7 letters)
5 loithoutpoetfoyt (4 letters)
6 wamacfemargarterc (6 letters)
7 dorcontactfil (7 letters)
8 donorrintheay (5 letters)
9 azgrohoibus (3 letters)
10 lyholyly (4 letters)
11 acsevtrofligcleftreng (5 letters)
12 jijpjevygieayjey (5 letters)

True or false?

Use your dictionary to help you decide whether the following statements are true or false.

1 A *pragmatic* person treats things in a practical way.
2 A *minx* is a furry animal whose pelt is used to make expensive coats.
3 The *retina* is a membrane at the back of the eyeball.
4 The Cape *southeaster* can be described as long-winded.
5 A *de luxe* meal will probably be very expensive.
6 A *curator* is a kind of doctor.
7 A *francolin* and a *hamerkop* are both kinds of reptiles.
8 You can buy *scampi* at the hardware store.
9 A state *secedes* from another if it becomes independent.
10 It's a *fallacy* that you can do well at school without applying yourself.
11 The *cornet* is a kind of building material.
12 A *likkewaan* is something that you eat on hot days.
13 Important community decisions are made at a *kgotla*.
14 A *gecko* is a member of an international spy ring.

Making up nonsensical (but grammatical) sentences

Parts of speech are printed after every word in the dictionary. These are printed in italic print (e.g. *noun, adjective, verb*). If you are not sure how each part of speech behaves, check the separate entries in your dictionary.

A simple English sentence might look something like this:

The hungry dog eats the meat quickly.
　　 (adjective) *(noun)* *(verb)* 　　 *(noun)* *(adverb)*

Words like 'the' and 'a' are called articles, and for this activity you can choose whichever article you like.

1 Choose a page in the dictionary at random, then use words *on that page only* to make a sentence. It doesn't matter if your sentence doesn't really make sense, as long as you use the parts of speech correctly.

   For example, if we look at page 48 of the dictionary, we could make the following sentence:

The	boa	bobbed	the	bluish	boerewors	boastfully.
	(noun)	*(verb)*		*(adjective)*	*(noun)*	*(adverb)*

Some sentences may not need a second noun. For example, if we choose words from page 463 of the dictionary:

The	thief	thinks	theoretically.
	(noun)	*(verb)*	*(adverb)*

In groups, take turns to call out a page number, then compare your sentence with other sentences made up from words found on the same page.

2 Make up nonsensical sentences in a language other than English, in which the main words all begin with the same letter.

The Jabberwocky – writing your own definitions

When Alice goes *Through the Looking Glass*, in the sequel to Lewis Carroll's book *Alice's Adventures in Wonderland*, she finds a poem called 'Jabberwocky' in a book. The first verse goes like this:

'Twas brillig, and the slithy toves
Did gyre and gimble in the wabe;
All mimsy were the borogoves,
And the mome raths outgrabe.

Can you find words like *brillig*, *slithy* and *mimsy* in your dictionary? Alice couldn't tell what these words meant either, because they are not real words. The lines of verse may start to make some sort of sense if you try to identify the parts of speech, just as you did in the previous activity. We know that *toves* must be a noun, for example, because the definite article (*the*) comes before it, and it is marked by the plural -*s*. The word *slithy* must therefore be an adjective, because it 'describes' the noun *toves*.

1 Identify as many parts of speech as you can in the verse above.

Later in the story Alice meets Humpty Dumpty. She asks him to explain what this poem means. He replies:

"'Brillig' means four o'clock in the afternoon – the time when you begin *broiling* things for dinner.'" 1

   "That'll do very well," said Alice: "and '*slithy*'?"

   "Well, '*slithy*' means 'lithe and slimy'. 'Lithe' is the same as 'active.' You see [...] there are two meanings packed up into one word." 5

"I see it now," Alice remarked thoughtfully: "and what are '*toves*'?"

"Well, '*toves*' are something like badgers – they're something like lizards – and they're something like corkscrews."

"They must be very curious-looking creatures."

"They are that," said Humpty Dumpty: "also they make their nests   10 under sun-dials – also they live on cheese."

"And what's to '*gyre*' and to '*gimble*'?"

"To '*gyre*' is to go round and round like a gyroscope. To '*gimble*' is to make holes like a gimblet [a gimlet]."

"And '*the wabe*' is the grass-plot round a sun-dial, I suppose?" said   15 Alice, surprised at her own ingenuity.

"Of course it is. It's called '*wabe*', you know, because it goes a long way before it, and a long way behind it –"

"And a long way beyond it on each side," Alice added.

2 The words in 'Jabberwocky' are made-up words. But with the help of Humpty Dumpty, you now know some of their meanings. Write entries for the dictionary for the following words: *brillig, slithy, toves, gyre, gimble, wabe.* Don't forget to include pronunciation, parts of speech, plural forms, inflections, and example sentences if they are relevant. (If you want to find out the meanings of the other words in the verse, you'll have to read *Through the Looking Glass.*)

3 Working with a friend, make up nonsensical words in a language other than English. Make sure that the words you invent look like real words in that language. Show your words to each other and explain what they mean.

Science vocabulary quiz

1 What new science do these expressions belong to, and what do they mean?

software	byte	e-mail
hardware	CD-ROM	

2 What do the following words mean?

acid rain	ozone layer	radioactivity
plutonium	asbestos	

3 What do the following have in common?

nylon	polystyrene	melamine
polymers	vinyl	

4 What do the following have in common?

watts	joules	Celsius
amps	hertz	

Vocabulary chains

Different school subjects have their own vocabulary. In this activity you will make chains of words associated with different school subjects.

Make a copy of this page. Then make five chains of words for five different school subjects. Use a different colour for each subject.

Each chain ends at the bottom of a column. When you have finished each chain, add a box and fill it in with the name of the subject to which the words in the chain belong. One chain has been started and finished for you.

drama		circle		cell
	ledger		climate	
budget		stanza		reproduction
	cytoplasm		equation	
osmosis		tangent		contour
	vocabulary		grammar	
shareholder		organelle		ozone layer
	hypotenuse		pollution	
barter		equator		verb
	fraction		hydrophyte	
stock		meteorology		debtor
	environment		metaphor	
bisect		carnivore		income
	urbanization		supply	
maps		market		paragraph
	calculate		respiration	
	MATHS			

Aa

a *adjective* (called the *indefinite article* and changing to **an** before most vowel sounds) **1** one (but not any special one), *Can you lend me a book?* **2** each: per, *We see it once a day* or *once an hour.*

a-¹ *prefix* **1** on; to; towards (as in *afoot, ashore, aside*). **2** in the process of (as in *a-hunting*).

a-² *prefix* (**an-** is used before a vowel sound) not; without (as in *asymmetrical, anarchy*).

aardvark *noun* an insect-eating animal with a long snout and tongue.

aardwolf *noun* a striped hyena-like animal with a mane.

ab- *prefix* (changing to **abs-** before *c* and *t*) away; from (as in *abduct, abnormal, abstract*).

aback *adverb* **taken aback** surprised.

abacus (*say* **ab**-a-kus) *noun* (*plural* **abacuses**) a frame used for counting with beads sliding on wires.

abandon¹ *verb* give up; leave something without intending to return, *Abandon ship!* **abandonment** *noun*

abandon² *noun* a casual and careless manner, *dancing with great abandon.*

abase *verb* (**abased, abasing**) humiliate.

abashed *adjective* embarrassed.

abate *verb* (**abated, abating**) make or become less; die down, *The storm had abated.* **abatement** *noun*

abattoir (*say* **ab**-at-wahr) *noun* a slaughter-house.

abbey *noun* (*plural* **abbeys**) a monastery or convent.

abbot *noun* the head of an abbey.

abbreviate *verb* (**abbreviated, abbreviating**) shorten something.

abbreviation *noun* **1** a shortened form of a word or words, especially one using the initial letters, such as S A, Dr, U C T. **2** abbreviating something, *Some abbreviation may be necessary to save space.*

abdicate *verb* (**abdicated, abdicating**) resign from a throne; give up an important responsibility. **abdication** *noun*

abdomen (*say* **ab**-dom-en) *noun* **1** the lower front part of a person's or animal's body, containing the stomach, intestines, and other digestive organs. **2** the rear section of an insect's body. **abdominal** (*say* ab-**dom**-in-al) *adjective*

abduct *verb* take a person away illegally; kidnap. **abduction** *noun*, **abductor** *noun*

abet *verb* (**abetted, abetting**) help or encourage someone to commit a crime.

abeyance (*say* ab-ay-ans) *noun* **in abeyance** suspended or postponed.

abhor *verb* (**abhorred abhorring**) detest. **abhorrent** *adjective*, **abhorrence** *noun*

abide *verb* (**abided, abiding**) **1** (*old use*; *past tense* **abode**) remain; dwell. **2** bear; tolerate, *I can't abide wasps.* **abide by** keep a promise etc.

abiding *adjective* lasting; permanent.

ability *noun* (*plural* **abilities**) **1** being able to do something. **2** cleverness; talent, *She has the ability to solve complex technological problems.*

abiotic (*say* ay-by-**ot**-ik) *adjective* inanimate, non-living, *Soil and climate are abiotic factors in a plant's environment.*

abject (*say* **ab**-jekt) *adjective* **1** wretched; miserable, *living in abject poverty.* **2** humble, *an abject apology.*

ablaze *adjective* blazing; on fire.

able *adjective* **1** having the power or skill or opportunity to do something. **2** skilful; clever, *an able worker.* **ably** *adverb*

abled *adjective* not disabled.

abnormal *adjective* not normal; unusual. **abnormally** *adverb*, **abnormality** *noun*

aboard *adverb* & *preposition* on or into a ship or aircraft or train.

abode *noun* the place where someone lives.

abolish *verb* put an end to a law or custom etc. **abolition** (*say* ab-ol-**ish**-on) *noun*

abominable *adjective* very bad; detestable. **abominably** *adverb*

abominate *verb* (**abominated, abominating**) detest. **abomination** *noun*

aborigines (*say* ab-er-**ij**-in-eez) *plural noun* the original inhabitants of a country.

aboriginal *adjective* & *noun*

Aborigines the original inhabitants of Australia.

abort *verb* put an end to something before it has been completed, *They aborted the space flight because of problems.*

abortion *noun* loss or removal of a baby from the womb before it has developed enough to survive.

abortive *adjective* unsuccessful, *an abortive attempt.*

abound *verb* 1 be plentiful or abundant, *Fish abound in the river.* 2 have something in great quantities, *The river abounds in fish.*

about¹ *preposition* 1 near in amount or size or time etc., *It costs about R20. Come about two o'clock.* 2 on the subject of; in connection with, *Tell me about your holiday.* 3 all round; in various parts of, *They ran about the playground.*

about² *adverb* 1 in various directions, *They were running about.* 2 not far away, *He is somewhere about.*

be about to be going to do something.

above¹ *preposition* over; on the top of; higher than.

above² *adverb* at or to a higher place; overhead, *the sky above.*

above-board *adjective* & *adverb* honest; without deception.

abrade *verb* (**abraded, abrading**) scrape or wear something away by rubbing it. **abrasion** *noun*

abrasive¹ *adjective* 1 that abrades things. 2 harsh, *an abrasive manner.*

abrasive² *noun* a rough substance used for rubbing or polishing things.

abreast *adverb* 1 side by side. 2 keeping up with something, *Reading the newspaper keeps me abreast of current affairs.*

abridge *verb* (**abridged, abridging**) shorten a book etc. by using fewer words, *an abridged edition.* **abridgement** *noun*

abroad *adverb* in or to another country.

abrupt *adjective* sudden; hasty. **abruptly** *adverb*, **abruptness** *noun*

abs- *prefix* see **ab-**.

abscess (*say* ab-sis) *noun* (*plural* **abscesses**) an inflamed place where pus has formed in the body.

abscond *verb* go away secretly, *The cashier had absconded with the money.*

absent¹ (*say* ab-sent) *adjective* not here; not present, *absent from school.* **absence** *noun*

absent² (*say* ab-sent) *verb* **absent yourself** stay away.

absentee *noun* a person who is absent. **absenteeism** *noun*

absent-minded *adjective* having your mind on other things; forgetful.

absolute *adjective* complete; not restricted.

absolutely *adverb* 1 completely. 2 (*informal*) yes, I agree.

absolution *noun* a priest's formal declaration that people's sins are forgiven.

absolve *verb* (**absolved, absolving**) 1 clear a person of blame or guilt. 2 release from a promise or obligation.

absorb *verb* 1 soak up; take in. 2 receive something and reduce its effects, *The buffers absorbed most of the shock.* 3 take up a person's attention or time, *Computer games absorb her.* **absorbent** *adjective*, **absorption** *noun*

abstain *verb* keep yourself from doing something; refrain, *He was advised to abstain from smoking.* **abstainer** *noun*

abstemious (*say* ab-steem-ee-us) *adjective* eating or drinking only small amounts; not greedy. **abstemiously** *adverb*, **abstemiousness** *noun*

abstention *noun* abstaining from something, such as voting, *five votes in favour of the idea, three against, and two abstentions.*

abstinence *noun* abstaining, especially from alcohol. **abstinent** *adjective*

abstract¹ (*say* ab-strakt) *adjective* 1 concerned with ideas, not with objects, *Truth is abstract.* 2 (of a painting or sculpture) showing the artist's ideas or feelings, not showing a recognizable person or thing.

abstract² (*say* ab-strakt) *verb* take out; remove, *He abstracted some cards from the pack.* **abstraction** *noun*

abstract³ (*say* ab-strakt) *noun* a summary.

abstracted *adjective* with your mind on

other things; not paying attention.

abstruse (*say* ab-**strooss**) *adjective* hard to understand; obscure.

absurd *adjective* ridiculous; foolish. **absurdly** *adverb*, **absurdity** *noun*

abundance *noun* plenty.

abundant *adjective* plentiful. **abundantly** *adverb*

abuse[1] (*say* ab-**yooz**) *verb* (**abused**, **abusing**) 1 use badly or wrongly; misuse, *abuse drugs.* 2 ill-treat. 3 say unpleasant things about a person or thing.

abuse[2] (*say* ab-**yooss**) *noun* 1 a misuse. 2 ill-treatment. 3 words abusing a person or thing; insults. **abusive** *adjective*

abut *verb* (**abutted**, **abutting**) end against something, *Their shed abuts against ours.* **abutment** *noun*

abysmal (*say* ab-**iz**-mal) *adjective* extremely bad, *abysmal ignorance.*

abyss (*say* ab-**iss**) *noun* (*plural* **abysses**) an extremely deep pit.

ac- *prefix* see **ad-**.

acacia (*say* a-**kay**-sha) *noun* a tree that has yellow or white flowers.

academic *adjective* 1 of a school or college or university. 2 theoretical; having no practical application, *a matter of academic concern.*

academy *noun* (*plural* **academies**) 1 a school or college, especially for specialized training. 2 a society of scholars or artists.

accede (*say* ak-**seed**) *verb* (**acceded**, **acceding**) 1 agree to what is asked or suggested, *accede to a request.* 2 take office; become king or queen, *She acceded to the throne.*

accelerate *verb* (**accelerated**, **accelerating**) make or become quicker. **acceleration** *noun*

accelerator *noun* the pedal that a driver presses to make a motor vehicle go faster; something that speeds things up.

accent[1] (*say* ak-sent) *noun* 1 the way a person pronounces words, *She has an American accent.* 2 emphasis; accenting part of a word, *In 'action', the accent is on 'ac-'.* 3 a mark placed over a letter to show its pronunciation, e.g. on *café.*

accent[2] (*say* ak-**sent**) *verb* pronounce part of a word more strongly than the other parts; emphasize.

accentuate (*say* ak-**sent**-yoo-ayt) *verb* (**accentuated, accentuating**) emphasize; accent. **accentuation** *noun*

accept *verb* take a thing that is offered or presented; say yes to an invitation etc. **acceptance** *noun*

acceptable *adjective* worth accepting; pleasing. **acceptably** *adverb*, **acceptability** *noun*

access[1] (*say* ak-sess) *noun* 1 a way in, *Public buildings should have wheelchair access.* 2 the right to use or approach something, *access to classified information.*

access[2] *verb* find information that has been stored in a computer.

accessible *adjective* able to be reached. **accessibly** *adverb*, **accessibility** *noun*

accession *noun* 1 acceding; reaching a rank or position. 2 an addition, *recent accessions to our library.*

accessory (*say* ak-**sess**-er-ee) *noun* (*plural* **accessories**) 1 an extra thing that goes with something. 2 a person who helps another with a crime.

accident *noun* an unexpected happening, especially one causing injury or damage. **by accident** by chance; without its being arranged in advance.

accidental *adjective* happening or done by accident. **accidentally** *adverb*

acclaim *verb* welcome or applaud. **acclaim** *noun*, **acclamation** *noun*

acclimatize *verb* (**acclimatized**, **acclimatizing**) make or become used to a new climate or new conditions. **acclimatization** *noun*

accolade (*say* ak-ol-**ayd**) *noun* praise, approval, or honour, *Being chosen to represent their country is the highest accolade for most athletes.*

accommodate *verb* (**accommodated**, **accommodating**) 1 provide room or lodging for somebody. 2 adjust or adapt to something, *accommodate yourself to new ideas.*

accommodation *noun* somewhere to live; lodgings.

accompanist *noun* a person who plays a musical accompaniment.

accompany *verb* (**accompanied, accompanying**) 1 go somewhere with somebody. 2 be present with something, *Thunder accompanied the storm.* 3 play music that supports a singer or another player etc. **accompaniment** *noun*

accomplice (*say* a-**kum**-pliss) *noun* a person who helps another in a crime etc.

accomplish *verb* do something successfully. **accomplishment** *noun*

accomplished *adjective* skilled.

accord¹ *noun* agreement; consent.
of your own accord voluntarily; without being asked or compelled.

accord² *verb* 1 be consistent with something, *Your actions should accord with your beliefs.* 2 (*formal*) give, *He was accorded this privilege.*

accordance *noun* **in accordance with** in agreement with, *This is done in accordance with the rules.*

according *adverb* **according to** as stated by, *According to him, we are stupid*; in a way that suits, *Price the apples according to their size.* **accordingly** *adverb*

accordion *noun* a portable musical instrument like a large concertina.

accost *verb* approach and speak to a person.

account¹ *noun* 1 a statement of money owed, spent, or received; a bill. 2 an arrangement to keep money in a bank etc., *have an account at a bank.* 3 a description; a report. 4 consideration, *Take it into account.*
on account of because of.
on no account certainly not.

account² *verb* **account for** make it clear why something happens.

accountable *adjective* responsible; having to explain why you have done something. **accountability** *noun*

accountant *noun* a keeper or inspector of financial accounts. **accountancy** *noun*

accounting *noun* keeping financial accounts.

accredited *adjective* officially recognized, *our accredited agent.*

accretion (*say* a-**kree**-shon) *noun* a growth or increase in which things are added gradually, *an accretion of dust.*

accrue (*say* a-**kroo**) *verb* (**accrued, accruing**) accumulate. **accrual** *noun*

accumulate *verb* (**accumulated, accumulating**) collect; pile up.
accumulation *noun*

accumulator *noun* a storage battery.

accurate *adjective* correct; exact.
accurately *adverb*, **accuracy** *noun*

accusation *noun* accusing someone; a statement accusing a person of a fault or crime etc.

accuse *verb* (**accused, accusing**) say that a person (whom you name) has committed a crime etc.; blame. **accuser** *noun*

accustom *verb* make a person become used to something.

ace *noun* 1 a playing-card with one spot. 2 a very skilful person or thing, *an ace pilot.* 3 a service in tennis that is too good for the opponent to return.

acetylene (*say* a-**set**-il-een) *noun* a gas that burns with a bright flame, used in cutting and welding metal.

ache¹ *noun* a dull continuous pain.

ache² *verb* (**ached, aching**) have an ache.

achieve *verb* (**achieved, achieving**) succeed in doing or producing something; accomplish. **achievable** *adjective*, **achievement** *noun*

acid¹ *noun* a chemical substance that contains hydrogen and neutralizes alkalis; an acid has a pH value below 7. **acidic** *adjective*, **acidity** *noun*

acid² *adjective* 1 sharp-tasting; sour. 2 looking or sounding bitter, *an acid reply.* **acidly** *adverb*
acid rain rain made acid by mixing with waste gases from factories etc.

acknowledge *verb* (**acknowledged, acknowledging**) 1 admit that something is true. 2 state that you have received or noticed something, *Acknowledge this letter.* 3 express thanks or appreciation for something. **acknowledgement** *noun*

acme (*say* ak-mee) *noun* the highest degree of something, *the acme of perfection.*

acne (*say* **ak**-nee) *noun* inflamed red pimples on the face and neck.

acorn *noun* the seed of the oak-tree.

acoustic (*say* a-**koo**-stik) *adjective* **1** of sound or hearing. **2** (of a musical instrument) not electronic, *an acoustic guitar*. **acoustically** *adverb*

acoustics (*say* a-**koo**-stiks) *plural noun* **1** the qualities of a hall etc. that make it good or bad for carrying sound. **2** the science or study of sound.

acquaint *verb* tell somebody about something, *Acquaint her with the facts*. **be acquainted with** know slightly.

acquaintance *noun* **1** a person you know slightly. **2** being acquainted, *Their acquaintance blossomed and they became good friends*.

acquiesce (*say* ak-wee-**ess**) *verb* (**acquiesced, acquiescing**) agree to something. **acquiescent** *adjective*, **acquiescence** *noun*

acquire *verb* (**acquired, acquiring**) obtain. **acquirement** *noun*, **acquisition** *noun*

acquisitive (*say* a-**kwiz**-it-iv) *adjective* eager to acquire things.

acquit *verb* (**acquitted, acquitting**) decide that somebody is not guilty. **acquittal** *noun*

acre (*say* **ay**-ker) *noun* an area of land in the imperial system measuring 4 840 square yards (0,405 hectares). **acreage** *noun*

acrid *adjective* bitter, *an acrid smell*.

acrimonious (*say* ak-rim-**oh**-nee-us) *adjective* (of a person's manner or words) sharp and bad-tempered or bitter. **acrimony** (*say* **ak**-rim-on-ee) *noun*

acrobat *noun* a person who performs spectacular gymnastic stunts for entertainment. **acrobatic** *adjective*, **acrobatics** *plural noun*

acronym (*say* **ak**-ron-im) *noun* a word or name formed from the initial letters of other words, *Nato is an acronym of North Atlantic Treaty Organization*.

across *preposition* & *adverb* **1** from one side to the other, *Swim across the river. Are you across yet?* **2** on the opposite side, *the house across the street*.

acrostic *noun* a word-puzzle or poem in which the first or last letters of each line

form a word or words.

acrylic (*say* a-**kril**-ik) *noun* a kind of fibre, plastic, or resin made from an organic acid, *Acrylic fabrics wash easily*.

act¹ *noun* **1** an action. **2** a law passed by a parliament. **3** one of the main divisions of a play or opera. **4** a short performance in a programme of entertainment, *a juggling act*. **5** (*informal*) a pretence, *She is only putting on an act*.

act² *verb* **1** do something; perform actions. **2** perform a part in a play or film etc. **3** function, *She acted as referee*. **4** have an effect, *Alcohol acts on the brain*.

action *noun* **1** doing something. **2** something done, *Her quick action saved her life*. **3** a battle; fighting, *He was killed in action*. **4** a lawsuit. **out of action** not functioning. **take action** do something.

activate *verb* (**activated, activating**) start something working. **activation** *noun*, **activator** *noun*

active *adjective* **1** doing things; moving about; taking part in activities. **2** functioning; in operation, *an active volcano*. **3** radioactive. **4** (of a form of a verb) used when the subject of the verb is performing the action. In 'The shop *sells* sweets' the verb is active; in 'Sweets *are sold* by the shop' the verb is passive. **actively** *adverb*, **activeness** *noun*

activist *noun* a person who believes in vigorous action, especially in politics.

activity *noun* (*plural* **activities**) **1** an action or occupation, *outdoor activities*. **2** being active or lively.

actor *noun* a performer in a play or film etc. **actress** *noun*

actual *adjective* real. **actually** *adverb*, **actuality** *noun*

actuate *verb* (**actuated, actuating**) activate. **actuation** *noun*

acumen (*say* **ak**-yoo-men) *noun* sharpness of mind.

acupuncture (*say* **ak**-yoo-punk-cher) *noun* pricking parts of the body with needles to relieve pain or cure disease. **acupuncturist** *noun*

acute *adjective* **1** sharp; strong, *acute pain*.

2 having a sharp mind. **acutely** *adverb*, **acuteness** *noun*

acute accent a mark over a vowel, as over *e* in *café*.

acute angle an angle of less than 90°.

AD *abbreviation* Anno Domini (Latin = in the year of Our Lord), used in dates counted from the birth of Jesus Christ.

ad- *prefix* (changing to **ac-, af-, ag-, al-, an-, ap-, ar-, as-, at-** before certain consonants) to; towards (as in *adapt, admit*).

adamant (*say* ad-am-ant) *adjective* firm and not giving way to requests.

Adam's apple *noun* the lump of cartilage at the front of a man's neck.

adapt *verb* make or become suitable for a new purpose or situation. **adaptable** *adjective*, **adaptation** *noun*

adaptor *noun* a device to connect pieces of electrical or other equipment.

add *verb* **1** put one thing with another. **2** make another remark, '*And don't be late,*' *she added.*

add up make or find a total; (*informal*) make sense; seem reasonable.

addendum (*plural* **addenda**) *noun* thing added at the end of a book.

adder *noun* a small poisonous snake.

addict *noun* a person who does or uses something that he or she cannot give up, *drug addict.* **addicted** *adjective*, **addiction** *noun*

addictive *adjective* causing people to become addicts.

addition *noun* **1** the process of adding. **2** something added. **additional** *adjective*, **additionally** *adverb*

in addition also; as an extra thing.

additive *noun* a substance added to another in small amounts for a special purpose, e.g. as a flavouring.

addled *adjective* **1** (of eggs) rotted and producing no chick after being brooded. **2** muddled; confused.

address¹ *noun* **1** the details of the place where someone lives or of where letters etc. should be delivered to a person or firm. **2** a speech to an audience.

address² *verb* **1** write an address on a parcel etc. **2** make a speech or remark etc.

to somebody, *He addressed the crowd.*

addressee *noun* the person to whom a letter etc. is addressed.

adenoids *plural noun* thick spongy flesh at the back of the nose and throat, which may hinder breathing.

adept (*say* ad-ept) *adjective* very skilful.

adequate *adjective* enough; good enough. **adequately** *adverb*, **adequacy** *noun*

adhere *verb* (**adhered, adhering**) stick to something. **adhesion** *noun*

adherent (*say* ad-**heer**-ent) *noun* a person who supports a certain group or theory etc. **adherence** *noun*

adhesive¹ *adjective* causing things to stick together, *adhesive tape.*

adhesive² *noun* a substance used to stick things together; glue.

adjacent *adjective* near; next.

adjective *noun* a word that describes a noun or pronoun or adds to its meaning, e.g. *big, honest,* and *strange* in *big house, honest person,* and *strange place.* **adjectival** *adjective*, **adjectivally** *adverb*

adjoin *verb* be next or nearest to something.

adjourn (*say* a-**jern**) *verb* **1** break off a meeting etc. until a later time. **2** break off and go somewhere else, *They adjourned to the library.* **adjournment** *noun*

adjudge *verb* (**adjudged, adjudging**) judge; give a decision, *He was adjudged to be guilty.*

adjudicate (*say* a-**joo**-dik-ayt) *verb* (**adjudicated, adjudicating**) act as judge in a competition etc. **adjudication** *noun*, **adjudicator** *noun*

adjunct (*say* **aj**-unkt) *noun* something added that is useful but not essential.

adjust *verb* **1** put a thing into its proper position or order. **2** alter so as to fit. **adjustable** *adjective*, **adjustment** *noun*

ad lib *adjective* & *adverb* as you like; freely.

ad-lib *verb* (**ad-libbed, ad-libbing**) say or do something without any rehearsal or preparation.

administer *verb* **1** give; provide, *He administered a rebuke.* **2** manage business affairs; administrate.

administrate *verb* (administrated, administrating) manage public or business affairs. **administrator** *noun*, **administrative** *adjective*

administration *noun* 1 administering. 2 the management of public or business affairs. 3 the people who manage an organization etc.; the government.

admirable *adjective* worth admiring; excellent. **admirably** *adverb*

admiral *noun* a naval officer of high rank.

admire *verb* (admired, admiring) 1 look at something and enjoy it. 2 think that someone or something is very good. **admiration** *noun*, **admirer** *noun*

admissible *adjective* able to be admitted or allowed.

admission *noun* 1 admitting. 2 the charge for being allowed to go in, *Admission is R10.* 3 a statement admitting something; a confession.

admit *verb* (admitted, admitting) 1 allow someone or something to come in. 2 state reluctantly that something is true; confess, *We admit that the task is difficult. She admitted her crime.*

admittance *noun* being allowed to go in, especially to a private place.

admittedly *adverb* as an agreed fact; without denying it.

admonish *verb* advise or warn firmly but mildly. **admonition** *noun*

ado *noun* fuss; excitement.

adolescence (*say* ad-ol-**ess**-ens) *noun* the time between being a child and being an adult. **adolescent** *adjective* & *noun*

adopt *verb* 1 take someone into your family as your own child. 2 accept something; take and use, *They adopted new methods of working.* **adoption** *noun*

adore *verb* (adored, adoring) love very much. **adorable** *adjective*, **adoration** *noun*

adorn *verb* decorate. **adornment** *noun*

adrenalin (*say* a-**dren**-al-in) *noun* a hormone that stimulates the nervous system.

adrift *adjective* & *adverb* drifting.

adroit (*say* a-**droit**) *adjective* skilful.

adulation *noun* very great flattery.

adult (*say* **ad**-ult) *noun* a fully grown or mature person.

adulterate *verb* (adulterated, adulterating) make a thing impure or less good by adding something to it. **adulteration** *noun*

adultery *noun* being unfaithful to your wife or husband by having sexual intercourse with someone else. **adulterer** *noun*, **adulterous** *adjective*

advance[1] *noun* 1 a forward movement; progress, *the army's advance.* 2 an improvement or development in something, *recent advances in medicine.* 3 a loan; payment made before it is due. **in advance** beforehand; ahead.

advance[2] *verb* (advanced, advancing) 1 move forward; make progress. 2 lend or pay money ahead of the proper time, *Advance her a month's salary.* **advancement** *noun*

advantage *noun* 1 something useful or helpful. 2 the next point won after deuce in tennis. **take advantage of** use profitably or unfairly. **to advantage** making a good effect, *The painting shows to advantage here.* **to your advantage** profitable or helpful to you.

advantageous (*say* ad-van-**tay**-jus) *adjective* giving an advantage; beneficial.

Advent *noun* the period before Christmas, when Christians commemorate the coming of Christ.

advent *noun* the arrival of a new person or thing, *the advent of computers.*

adventure *noun* 1 an exciting or dangerous experience. 2 willingness to take risks, *a sense of adventure.* **adventurer** *noun*

adverb *noun* a word that adds to the meaning of a verb or adjective or another adverb and tells how, when, or where something happens, e.g. *gently, soon,* and *upstairs* in *flows gently, come soon,* and *go upstairs.* **adverbial** *adjective*, **adverbially** *adverb*

adversary (*say* ad-ver-ser-ee) *noun* (*plural* **adversaries**) an opponent; an enemy.

adverse *adjective* unfavourable; harmful, *adverse effects.* **adversely** *adverb*, **adversity** *noun*

advertise *verb* (**advertised, advertising**)
1 make something publicly known,
advertise a meeting. 2 praise goods etc. in
order to encourage people to buy or use
them. 3 ask or offer by a public notice,
advertise for a secretary. **advertisement**
noun, **advertiser** *noun*

advice *noun* 1 a statement telling a person
what you think he or she should do.
2 a piece of information, *We received
advice that the goods had been dispatched.*

advisable *adjective* that is the wise thing to
do. **advisability** *noun*

advise *verb* (**advised, advising**) 1 give
somebody advice; recommend. 2 inform.
adviser *noun,* **advisory** *adjective*

advocate[1] (*say* ad-vok-ayt) *verb*
(**advocated, advocating**) speak in
favour of something; recommend, *We
advocate reform.*

advocate[2] (*say* ad-vok-at) *noun* 1 a person
who advocates a policy etc., *She is an
advocate of reform.* 2 a lawyer presenting
someone's case in a lawcourt.

adze (*say* adz) *noun* an axe-like tool used to
cut away the surface of wood.

aegis (*say* ee-jiss) *noun* protection; sponsorship, *The scheme is under the aegis of the
Scout Association.*

aerate (*say* air-ayt) *verb* (**aerated, aerat-
ing**) 1 add air to something. 2 add carbon
dioxide to a liquid, *aerated water.*

aerial[1] *adjective* 1 of or in or from the air.
2 of or by aircraft.
aerial view looking down on something
from above it.

aerial[2] *noun* a wire or rod etc. for receiving
or transmitting radio or television signals.

aero- *prefix* of air or aircraft (as in
aeronautics).

aerobatics *plural noun* spectacular performances by flying aircraft. **aerobatic**
adjective

aerobics *plural noun* exercises to stimulate breathing and strengthen the heart and
lungs. **aerobic** *adjective*

aerodrome *noun* an airfield.

aeronautics *noun* the study of aircraft and
flying. **aeronautic** *adjective,* **aeronautical**
adjective

aeroplane *noun* a flying machine with
wings.

aerosol *noun* a device for producing a fine
spray of a substance.

aerospace *noun* the earth's atmosphere
and space beyond it.

aesthetic (*say* iss-**thet**-ik) *adjective* of or
showing appreciation of beautiful things.

af- *prefix* see **ad-**.

afar *adverb* far away, *The din was heard
from afar.*

affable *adjective* polite and friendly.
affably *adverb,* **affability** *noun*

affair *noun* 1 a thing; a matter; an event.
2 a temporary sexual relationship between
two people who are not married to each
other.

affect *verb* 1 have an effect on, *The new
policy will affect all of us.* 2 harm.
3 pretend, *She affected ignorance.*
● USAGE: Do not confuse with the verb
effect.

affectation *noun* a pretence; behaviour
that is put on for show and is not natural.

affected *adjective* pretended; unnatural.

affection *noun* love; a liking.

affectionate *adjective* showing affection;
loving. **affectionately** *adverb*

affidavit (*say* af-id-**ay**-vit) *noun* a statement written down and sworn to be true,
for use as legal evidence.

affiliated *adjective* officially connected
with a larger organization, *We are affiliated
with the national group.*

affinity *noun* (*plural* **affinities**) attraction,
relationship, or similarity to each other,
*There are many affinities between the two
languages.*

affirm *verb* state definitely or firmly.
affirmation *noun*

affirmative *adjective* that says 'yes',
an affirmative reply. (Compare *negative.*)
affirmative action something that
is done to favour people who have been
treated unfairly, especially because of their
race or gender, *She was appointed to the
job through affirmative action.*

affix[1] (*say* a-**fiks**) *verb* attach; add in
writing, *affix a stamp*; affix your signature.

affix[2] (*say* **aff**-iks) *noun* a prefix or suffix.

afflict *verb* cause somebody distress.
affliction *noun*

affluent (*say* af-loo-ent) *adjective* rich.
affluence *noun*

afford *verb* **1** have enough money to pay for something. **2** have enough time or resources etc. to do something.

afforestation *noun* the planting of trees to form a forest.

affray *noun* fighting or rioting in public.

affront¹ *verb* insult; offend; embarrass.

affront² *noun* an insult.

afield *adverb* at or to a distance; away from home, *travelling far afield.*

aflame *adjective & adverb* in flames; glowing.

afloat *adjective & adverb* floating; on the sea.

afoot *adjective* happening, *Great changes are afoot.*

aforesaid *adjective* mentioned previously.

afraid *adjective* frightened; alarmed.
I'm afraid I regret, *I'm afraid I'm late.*

afresh *adverb* again; in a new way, *We must start afresh.*

African *adjective* of Africa or its people.
African *noun*

Africana (*say* af-ri-**kah**-na) *plural noun* valuable books, paintings, furniture, etc. from southern Africa.

Afro- *prefix* African.

aft *adverb* at or towards the back of a ship or aircraft.

after¹ *preposition* **1** later than, *Come after tea.* **2** behind in place or order, *Which letter comes after H?* **3** trying to catch; pursuing, *Run after him.* **4** in spite of, *We can come after all.* **5** in imitation or honour of, *She is named after her aunt.* **6** about; concerning, *He asked after you.*

after² *adverb* **1** behind, *Jill came tumbling after.* **2** later, *It came a week after.*

after³ *adjective* coming or done afterwards, *in after years; the after-effects.*

aftermath *noun* the conditions after something, *the aftermath of war.*

afternoon *noun* the time from noon or lunch-time to evening.

afterthought *noun* something thought of or added later.

afterwards *adverb* at a later time.

ag- *prefix* see **ad-** .

again *adverb* **1** another time; once more, *try again.* **2** as before, *You will soon be well again.* **3** besides; moreover.

against *preposition* **1** touching; hitting, *He leant against the wall.* **2** in opposition to; not in favour of, *They voted against the proposal.* **3** in preparation for, *Protect them against the cold.*

agapanthus *noun* (*plural* **agapanthuses**) a long-stemmed lily with many blue or white flowers.

agar (*say* ay-gah) *noun* a substance that can be mixed with water to make a jelly.

age¹ *noun* **1** the length of time a person has lived or a thing has existed. **2** a special period of history or geology, *the ice age.*
ages *plural noun* (*informal*) a very long time, *We've been waiting for ages.*
come of age reach the age at which you have an adult's legal rights and obligations.

age² *verb* (**aged**, **ageing**) make or become old.

aged *adjective* **1** (*say* ayjd) having the age of, *a girl aged 9.* **2** (*say* **ay**-jid) very old, *an aged man.*

age-group *noun* people who are all of the same age.

agency *noun* (*plural* **agencies**)
1 the office or business of an agent, *a travel agency.* **2** the means by which something is done, *Flowers are pollinated by the agency of bees.*

agenda (*say* a-**jen**-da) *noun* (*plural* **agendas**) a list of things to be done or discussed, *The agenda is rather long.*

agent *noun* **1** a person who organizes things for other people. **2** a spy, *a secret agent.*

agglomeration *noun* a mass of things collected together.

aggravate *verb* (**aggravated**, **aggravating**) **1** make a thing worse or more serious, *She aggravated her condition by leaving hospital too soon.* **2** (*informal*) annoy.
aggravation *noun*

aggregate (*say* **ag**-rig-at) *adjective* combined; total, *the aggregate amount.*

aggression *noun* starting an attack or war etc.; aggressive behaviour.

aggressive *adjective* likely to attack people; forceful. **aggressively** *adverb*, **aggressiveness** *noun*

aggressor *noun* the person or nation that started an attack or war etc.

aggrieved (*say* a-**greevd**) *adjective* resentful because of being treated unfairly.

aghast *adjective* horrified.

agile *adjective* moving quickly or easily. **agilely** *adverb*, **agility** *noun*

agitate *verb* (**agitated, agitating**) 1 make someone feel upset or anxious. 2 stir up public interest or concern; campaign, *They agitated for a new community centre.* 3 shake something about. **agitation** *noun*, **agitator** *noun*

aglow *adjective* glowing.

agnostic (*say* ag-**nost**-ik) *noun* a person who believes that it is impossible to know whether God exists. **agnosticism** *noun*

ago *adverb* in the past, *long ago.*

agog *adjective* eager and excited.

agony *noun* (*plural* **agonies**) extremely great pain or suffering. **agonizing** *adjective*

agrarian (*say* a-**grair**-ee-an) *adjective* of farm land or its cultivation.

agree *verb* (**agreed, agreeing**) 1 think or say the same as another person etc. 2 consent, *She agreed to come.* 3 suit a person's health or digestion, *Curry doesn't agree with me.* 4 correspond in grammatical number, gender, or person. In 'They were good teachers', *they* agrees with *teachers* (both are plural forms) and *were* agrees with *they*; *was* would be incorrect because it is singular.

agreeable *adjective* 1 willing, *We shall go if you are agreeable.* 2 pleasant, *an agreeable place.* **agreeably** *adverb*

agreement *noun* 1 agreeing. 2 an arrangement that people have agreed on, *an international agreement.*

agriculture *noun* the process of cultivating land on a large scale and rearing livestock; farming. **agricultural** *adjective*

aground *adverb* & *adjective* stranded on the bottom in shallow water.

ah *interjection* an exclamation of surprise, pity, admiration, etc.

ahead *adverb* 1 further forward; in front. 2 forwards, *Full steam ahead!*

ahoy *interjection* an exclamation used by sailors to call attention.

aid[1] *noun* 1 help. 2 something that helps, *a hearing-aid.* 3 money, food, etc. sent to another country to help it, *foreign aid.* **in aid of** for the purpose of; to help something.

aid[2] *verb* help.

aide *noun* an assistant.

Aids *abbreviation* acquired immune deficiency syndrome, a disease that greatly weakens a person's ability to resist infections.

aikona (*say* I-ko-na) *interjection* an exclamation expressing disagreement.

ailing *adjective* ill; unwell.

ailment *noun* a slight illness.

aim[1] *verb* 1 point a gun etc. 2 throw or kick in a particular direction. 3 try or intend to do something, *She aims to get a scholarship.*

aim[2] *noun* 1 aiming a gun etc. 2 purpose; intention.

aimless *adjective* without a purpose. **aimlessly** *adverb*

air[1] *noun* 1 the mixture of gases that surrounds the earth and which everyone breathes. 2 the open space above the earth, *Kick the ball into the air.* 3 a tune; a melody. 4 an appearance or impression of something, *an air of mystery.* 5 an impressive or haughty manner, *He puts on airs.* **by air** in or by aircraft. **on the air** on radio or television.

air[2] *verb* 1 put clothes etc. in a warm place to finish drying. 2 ventilate a room. 3 express, *He aired his opinions.*

airborne *adjective* 1 (of an aircraft) in flight. 2 carried by the air or by aircraft.

air-conditioning *noun* a system for controlling the temperature, purity, etc. of a room or building. **air-conditioned** *adjective*

aircraft *noun* (*plural* **aircraft**) an aeroplane, glider, or helicopter etc.

aircraft-carrier *noun* a large ship with a long deck where aircraft can take off and land.

airfield *noun* an area equipped with runways etc. where aircraft can take off and land.

air force *noun* the part of a country's armed forces that is equipped with aircraft.

airgun *noun* a gun in which compressed air shoots a pellet or dart.

air hostess *noun* a female member of the cabin crew on a passenger aircraft.

airline *noun* a company that provides a regular service of transport by aircraft.

airliner *noun* a large aircraft for carrying passengers.

airlock *noun* 1 a compartment with an airtight door at each end, through which people can go in and out of a pressurized chamber. 2 a bubble of air that stops liquid flowing through a pipe.

airmail *noun* mail carried by air.

airman *noun* (*plural* **airmen**) a man who is a member of an air force or of the crew of an aircraft. **airwoman** *noun* (*plural* **airwomen**)

airport *noun* an airfield for aircraft carrying passengers and goods.

air raid *noun* an attack by aircraft.

airship *noun* a large balloon with engines, designed to carry passengers or goods.

airstrip *noun* a strip of ground prepared for aircraft to land and take off.

airtight *adjective* not letting air in or out.

airworthy *adjective* (of an aircraft) fit to fly. **airworthiness** *noun*

airy *adjective* 1 with plenty of fresh air. 2 light as air. 3 light-hearted; insincere, *airy promises.* **airily** *adverb*

aisle (*say* I'll) *noun* 1 a passage between or beside rows of seats or pews. 2 a side part of a church.

ajar *adverb* & *adjective* slightly open, *Leave the door ajar.*

AK47 *noun* a Russian-made automatic rifle.

akimbo *adverb* **arms akimbo** with hands on hips and elbows out.

akin *adjective* related; similar.

al- *prefix* see **ad-**.

alabaster (*say* al-a-bast-er) *noun* a kind of hard stone, usually white.

à la carte (*say* ah-la-**kart**) *adjective* & *adverb* of a restaurant meal, ordered as separate items from a menu, not as a complete meal charged at a fixed price.

alacrity *noun* speed and willingness, *She accepted with alacrity.*

alarm[1] *noun* 1 a warning sound or signal; an apparatus for giving this. 2 being alarmed, *a look of alarm.*

alarm clock a clock that can be set to make a sound at a fixed time to wake a sleeping person.

alarm[2] *verb* make someone frightened or anxious.

alarmist *noun* a person who raises unnecessary alarm.

alas *interjection* an exclamation of sorrow.

albatross *noun* (*plural* **albatrosses**) a large sea-bird with very long wings.

albino (*say* al-**been**-oh) *noun* (*plural* **albinos**) a person or animal with no colour in the skin and hair (which are white).

album *noun* a book with blank pages in which to keep a collection of photographs, stamps, autographs, etc.

albumen (*say* al-bew-min) *noun* white of egg.

alchemy (*say* al-kim-ee) *noun* an early form of chemistry, the chief aim of which was to turn ordinary metals into gold. **alchemist** *noun*

alcohol *noun* 1 a colourless liquid made by fermenting sugar or starch. 2 an intoxicating drink containing this liquid (e.g. wine, beer, whisky).

alcoholic[1] *adjective* of alcohol; containing alcohol.

alcoholic[2] *noun* a person who is seriously addicted to alcohol. **alcoholism** *noun*

alcove *noun* a section of a room etc. that is set back from the main part; a recess.

alderman (*say* **awl**-der-man) *noun* (*plural* **aldermen**) the title of certain councillors and former mayors.

ale *noun* beer.

alert[1] *adjective* watching for something; ready to act. **alertly** *adverb*, **alertness** *noun*

alert[2] *noun* a warning or alarm, *a fire alert.*

on the alert on the look-out; watchful.

alert[3] *verb* warn of danger etc.; make someone aware of something.

alga (*say* al-ga) *noun* (*plural* **algae**) (*say* al-jee) a kind of plant that grows in water, with no true stems or leaves.

algebra (*say* al-jib-ra) *noun* mathematics in which letters and symbols are used to represent quantities. **algebraic** (*say* al-jib-ray-ik) *adjective*

alias[1] (*say* ay-lee-as) *noun* (*plural* **aliases**) a false or different name.

alias[2] *adverb* also named, *Robert Zimmerman, alias Bob Dylan.*

alibi (*say* al-ib-I) *noun* (*plural* **alibis**) evidence that a person accused of a crime was somewhere else when it was committed.

● USAGE: Some people consider it incorrect to use this word as if it meant simply 'an excuse'.

alien[1] (*say* ay-lee-en) *noun* a person who is not a citizen of the country where he or she is living; a foreigner.

alien[2] *adjective* 1 foreign. 2 unnatural, *Cruelty is alien to her nature.*

alien plant a plant which grows in an area that is not its natural home.

alienate (*say* ay-lee-en-ayt) *verb* (**alienated, alienating**) make a person become unfriendly or hostile. **alienation** *noun*

alight[1] *adjective* 1 on fire. 2 lit up.

alight[2] *verb* 1 get out of a vehicle or down from a horse etc. 2 fly down and settle, *The bird alighted on a branch.*

align (*say* al-I'n) *verb* 1 arrange in a line. 2 join as an ally, *They aligned themselves with the British.* **alignment** *noun*

alike *adjective* & *adverb* like one another; in the same way, *The twins are very alike. Treat them alike.*

alikreukel *noun* a kind of shellfish which is good to eat.

alimentary canal *noun* the tube along which food passes from the mouth to the anus in the process of being digested and absorbed by the body.

alive *adjective* 1 living. 2 alert, *Be alive to the possible dangers.*

alkali (*say* alk-al-I) *noun* (*plural* **alkalis**) a substance that neutralizes acids and has a pH value above 7. **alkaline** *adjective*

all[1] *adjective* the whole number or amount of, *All my books are here; all day.*

all[2] *noun* 1 everything, *That is all I know.* 2 everybody, *All are agreed.* 3 (in games) each, *two goals all.*

all[3] *adverb* completely, *She was dressed all in white.*

all-clear *noun* a signal that a danger has passed.

all over everywhere, *We looked all over for the book;* completely finished, *The competition is all over.*

all right satisfactory; in good condition; as desired; yes, I consent.

all-round *adjective* general; not specialist, *an all-round athlete.* **all-rounder** *noun*

all there (*informal*) having an alert mind.

all the same in spite of this; making no difference, *I like him, all the same.*

Allah *noun* the Muslim name of God.

allay (*say* a-**lay**) *verb* (**allayed, allaying**) calm, *to allay their fears.*

allegation (*say* al-ig-**ay**-shon) *noun* a statement made without proof.

allege (*say* a-**lej**) *verb* (**alleged, alleging**) say something without being able to prove it, *She alleged that I had cheated.* **allegedly** (*say* a-**lej**-id-lee) *adverb*

allegiance (*say* a-**lee**-jans) *noun* loyalty.

allegory (*say* **al**-ig-er-ee) *noun* (*plural* **allegories**) a story in which the characters and events represent or symbolize an underlying meaning. **allegorical** (*say* al-ig-o-rik-al) *adjective*

alleluia *interjection* praise to God.

allergic *adjective* very sensitive to something that may make you ill, *He is allergic to pollen, which gives him hay fever.* **allergy** (*say* **al**-er-jee) *noun*

alleviate (*say* a-**lee**-vee-ayt) *verb* (**alleviated, alleviating**) make a thing less severe, *to alleviate pain.* **alleviation** *noun*

alley *noun* (*plural* **alleys**) a narrow street or passage.

alliance *noun* an association formed by countries or groups who wish to support each other.

allied *adjective* 1 joined as allies. 2 of the same kind, *a union of allied trades.*

alligator *noun* a kind of crocodile.

alliteration *noun* having the same letter or sound at the beginning of several words, e.g. in *Sit in solemn silence.*

allocate *verb* (**allocated, allocating**) allot; set aside for a particular purpose. **allocation** *noun*

allot *verb* (**allotted, allotting**) distribute portions, jobs, etc. to different people.

allotment *noun* 1 a small rented piece of public land used for growing vegetables, fruit, or flowers. 2 allotting; the amount allotted.

allow *verb* 1 permit, *Smoking is not allowed.* 2 permit someone to have something; provide with, *She was allowed R100 for books.* 3 agree, *I allow that you have been patient.* **allowable** *adjective*

allowance *noun* 1 allowing something. 2 what is allowed, *an allowance of R100 for books.*
make allowances be considerate; excuse, *Make allowances for his age.*

alloy *noun* a metal formed by mixing two or more metals etc.

allude *verb* (**alluded, alluding**) mention something briefly or indirectly, *He alluded to his wealth.* **allusion** *noun*

allure *verb* (**allured, alluring**) entice; attract. **allurement** *noun*

alluvium (*say* a-**loo**-vee-um) *noun* sand and soil etc. deposited by a river or flood. **alluvial** *adjective*

ally¹ *noun* (*plural* **allies**) 1 a country in alliance with another. 2 a person who co-operates with another.

ally² *verb* (**allied, allying**) form an alliance.

almanac *noun* an annual publication containing a calendar and other information.

almighty *adjective* 1 having complete power. 2 (*informal*) very great, *an almighty din.*

almond (*say* **ah**-mond) *noun* an oval edible nut.

almost *adverb* near to being something but not quite, *almost ready.*

aloe (*say* **a**-loh) *noun* a family of plants with toothed fleshy leaves.

aloft *adverb* high up; up in the air.

alone *adjective* without any other people or things; without help.

along¹ *preposition* following the length of something, *Walk along the path.*

along² *adverb* 1 on; onwards, *Push it along.* 2 accompanying somebody, *I've brought my brother along.*

alongside *preposition & adverb* next to something; beside.

aloof¹ *adverb* apart; not taking part, *We stayed aloof from their quarrels.*

aloof² *adjective* distant and not friendly in manner, *She seemed aloof.*

aloud *adverb* in a voice that can be heard.

alpha *noun* the first letter of the Greek alphabet (= a), written A, α.

alphabet *noun* the letters used in a language, usually arranged in a set order. **alphabetical** *adjective*, **alphabetically** *adverb*

alpine *adjective* of high mountains.

already *adverb* by now; before now, *It's already been posted.*

alright *adjective & adverb* (*informal*) all right.

Alsatian (*say* al-**say**-shan) *noun* a large strong dog, often used by the police.

also *adverb* as an extra person or thing; besides; as well.

altar *noun* a table or similar structure used in religious ceremonies.

alter *verb* make or become different; change. **alteration** *noun*

altercation (*say* ol-ter-**kay**-shon) *noun* a noisy argument or quarrel.

alternate¹ (*say* ol-**tern**-at) *adjective* happening or coming in turns; first the one and then the other. **alternately** *adverb*
• USAGE: See the note on *alternative.*

alternate² (*say* **ol**-tern-ayt) *verb* (**alternated, alternating**) use or come alternately. **alternation** *noun*
alternating current electric current that keeps reversing its direction at regular intervals. **alternator** *noun*

alternative[1] *adjective* available instead of something else. **alternatively** *adverb*

• USAGE: Do not confuse *alternative* with *alternate*. If there are *alternative colours* it means that there is a choice of two or more colours, but *alternate colours* means that there is first one colour and then the other.

alternative[2] *noun* one of two or more possibilities.

no alternative no choice.

although *conjunction* though.

altimeter *noun* an instrument used in aircraft etc. for showing the height above sea-level.

altitude *noun* the height of something, especially above sea-level.

alto *noun* (*plural* **altos**) 1 an adult male singer with a very high voice. 2 a female singer with a low voice, also called a contralto.

altogether *adverb* 1 with all included; in total, *The outfit costs R60 altogether.* 2 completely, *The stream dries up altogether in summer.* 3 on the whole, *Altogether, it was a good concert.*

• USAGE: Do not confuse *altogether* and *all together.*

altruistic (*say* al-troo-**ist**-ik) *adjective* unselfish; thinking of other people's welfare. **altruist** *noun,* **altruism** *noun*

aluminium *noun* a lightweight silver-coloured metal.

alveolus (*say* al-vee-**oh**-lus) *noun* (*plural* **alveoli**) the part of the lung where gases are exchanged.

always *adverb* 1 at all times. 2 often, *You are always crying.* 3 whatever happens, *You can always sleep on the floor.*

a.m. *abbreviation* ante meridiem (Latin = before noon).

ama- *prefix* more than one, usually indicating a group of people (as in *amaXhosa, amaZulu, amaNdebele*).

amalgam *noun* 1 an alloy of mercury. 2 a soft mixture.

amalgamate *verb* (**amalgamated, amalgamating**) mix; combine. **amalgamation** *noun*

amandla *interjection* power.
amandla ngawetu power is ours.

amasi (*say* a-**mah**-see) *noun* maas.

amass *verb* heap up; collect.

amateur (*say* **am**-at-er) *noun* a person who does something as a hobby, not as a professional. **amateurish** *adjective*

amaze *verb* (**amazed, amazing**) surprise somebody greatly; fill with wonder. **amazement** *noun*

ambassador *noun* a person sent to a foreign country to represent his or her own government.

amber *noun* 1 a hard clear yellowish substance used for making ornaments. 2 a yellow traffic light shown as a signal for caution, placed between red (= stop) and green (= go).

ambi- *prefix* both; on both sides (as in *ambidextrous*).

ambidextrous *adjective* able to use either the left hand or the right hand equally well.

ambiguous *adjective* having more than one possible meaning; unclear. **ambiguously** *adverb,* **ambiguity** *noun*

ambition *noun* 1 a strong desire to achieve something. 2 the thing desired, *her sporting ambitions.*

ambitious *adjective* full of ambition.

ambivalent (*say* am-**biv**-al-ent) *adjective* having mixed feelings about something (e.g. liking and disliking it). **ambivalence** *noun*

amble *verb* (**ambled, ambling**) walk at a slow easy pace.

ambrosia (*say* am-**broh**-zee-a) *noun* 1 something delicious. 2 the food of the gods in Greek mythology.

ambulance *noun* a vehicle equipped to carry sick or injured people.

ambush[1] *noun* (*plural* **ambushes**) a surprise attack from troops etc. who have concealed themselves.

ambush[2] *verb* lie in wait for someone; attack from an ambush.

ameliorate (*say* a-**mee**-lee-er-ayt) *verb* (**ameliorated, ameliorating**) make or become better; improve. **amelioration** *noun*

amen *interjection* a word used at the end of a prayer or hymn, meaning 'may it be so'.

amenable (*say* a-**meen**-a-bul) *adjective* willing to be guided or controlled by something, *He is not amenable to discipline.*

amend *verb* alter something so as to improve it. **amendment** *noun*
make amends make up for having done something wrong; atone.

amenity (*say* a-**men**-it-ee or a-**meen**-it-ee) *noun* (*plural* **amenities**) a pleasant or useful feature of a place etc., *The town has many amenities.*

American *adjective* 1 of the continent of America. 2 of the United States of America or its people. **American** *noun*

amethyst *noun* a purple precious stone.

amiable *adjective* good-tempered, friendly. **amiably** *adverb*

amicable *adjective* friendly. **amicably** *adverb*

amid (also **amidst**) *preposition* in the middle of; among.

amino acid (*say* a-**meen**-oh) *noun* an acid found in proteins.

amiss[1] *adjective* wrong; faulty, *There is nothing amiss with the engine.*

amiss[2] *adverb* wrongly; faultily.
take amiss be offended by, *Don't take his criticism amiss.*

ammonia *noun* a colourless gas or liquid with a strong smell.

ammunition *noun* a supply of bullets, shells, grenades, etc. for use in fighting.

amnesia (*say* am-**nee**-zee-a) *noun* loss of memory.

amnesty *noun* (*plural* **amnesties**) a general pardon for people who have committed a crime.

amoeba (*say* a-**mee**-ba) *noun* (*plural* **amoebas**) a microscopic creature consisting of a single cell which constantly changes shape.

amok *adverb* **run amok** rush about in a destructive or murderous frenzy.

among (also **amongst**) *preposition* 1 surrounded by; in, *There were weeds among the flowers.* 2 between, *Divide the sweets among the children.*

amoral (*say* ay-**mo**ral) *adjective* not based on moral standards; neither moral nor immoral.

amorous *adjective* showing love, *amorous glances.*

amorphous (*say* a-**mor**-fus) *adjective* shapeless, *an amorphous mass.*

amount[1] *noun* 1 a quantity, *the amount of bread that people buy.* 2 a total, *a bill for the full amount.*

amount[2] *verb* **amount to** add up to; be equivalent to, *Their reply amounts to a refusal.*

amp *noun* 1 an ampere. 2 (*informal*) an amplifier.

ampere (*say* am-**pair**) *noun* a unit for measuring electric current.

ampersand *noun* the symbol & (= and).

amphi- *prefix* both; on both sides; in both places (as in *amphibian*).

amphibian *noun* 1 an amphibious animal; an animal (e.g. a frog) that at first (as a tadpole) has gills and lives in water but later develops lungs and breathes air. 2 an amphibious aircraft or tank etc.

amphibious *adjective* able to live or move both on land and in water.

amphitheatre *noun* an oval or circular unroofed building with tiers of seats round a central arena.

ample *adjective* 1 quite enough, *ample provisions.* 2 large. **amply** *adverb*

amplifier *noun* a device for making something louder.

amplify *verb* (**amplified, amplifying**) 1 make louder or stronger, *to amplify sound.* 2 give more details about something.

amplitude *noun* 1 the maximum departure of the value of an alternating current or wave from the average value. 2 largeness; abundance.

amputate *verb* (**amputated, amputating**) cut off by a surgical operation. **amputation** *noun*

amuse *verb* (**amused, amusing**) 1 make a person laugh or smile. 2 make time pass pleasantly for someone. **amusement** *noun*

an *adjective* see **a**.

an-[1] *prefix* see **a-**[2].

an-[2] *prefix* see **ad-**.

ana- *prefix* up; back (as in *analysis*).

anachronism (*say* an-**ak**-ron-izm) *noun* something wrongly placed in a particular historical period, or regarded as out of date, *Bows and arrows would be an anachronism in modern warfare.*

anaemia (*say* a-**nee**-mee-a) *noun* a poor condition of the blood that makes a person tired. **anaemic** *adjective*

anaesthetic (*say* an-iss-**thet**-ik) *noun* a substance or gas that makes you unable to feel pain. **anaesthesia** *noun*

anaesthetist (*say* an-**ees**-thet-ist) *noun* a person trained to give anaesthetics. **anaesthetize** *verb*

anagram *noun* a word·or phrase made by rearranging the letters of another, *'Trap' is an anagram of 'part'.*

anal (*say* **ay**-nal) *adjective* of the anus.

analgesic (*say* an-al-**jee**-sik) *noun* a substance that relieves pain.

analogy (*say* a-**nal**-oj-ee) *noun* (*plural* **analogies**) a partial likeness between two things that are compared, *the analogy between the human heart and a pump.* **analogous** *adjective*

analyse *verb* (**analysed, analysing**) 1 separate something into its parts. 2 examine and interpret something, *analyse the causes.* **analysis** *noun*, **analytic** *adjective*, **analytical** *adjective*

analyst *noun* a person who analyses things.

anarchist (*say* an-er-kist) *noun* a person who believes that all forms of government are bad and should be abolished.

anarchy (*say* **an**-er-kee) *noun* 1 lack of government or control, resulting in lawlessness. 2 disorder, *In the absence of their teacher, the class was in a state of anarchy.*

anatomy (*say* an-**at**-om-ee) *noun* the study of how the body is constituted. **anatomical** *adjective*, **anatomist** *noun*

ancestor *noun* anyone from whom a person is descended. **ancestral** *adjective*, **ancestry** *noun*

anchor¹ *noun* a heavy object joined to a ship by a chain or rope and dropped to the bottom of the sea to stop the ship from moving. **anchorage** *noun*

anchor² *verb* 1 fix or be fixed by an anchor. 2 fix firmly.

anchovy *noun* (*plural* **anchovies**) a small fish with a strong flavour.

ancient *adjective* 1 very old. 2 of times long past, *ancient history.*

ancillary (*say* an-**sil**-er-ee) *adjective* helping people to do something, *ancillary services.*

and *conjunction* 1 together with; in addition to, *We had cakes and buns.* 2 so that; with this result, *Work hard and you will pass.* 3 to, *Go and buy a pen.*

anecdote *noun* a short amusing or interesting story about a real person or thing.

anemometer (*say* a-nee-**mom**-i-ter) *noun* a device for measuring wind force.

anemone (*say* a-**nem**-on-ee) *noun* 1 a plant with cup-shaped red, purple, or white flowers. 2 a sea anemone.

anew *adverb* again; in a new or different way, *begin anew.*

angel *noun* 1 an attendant or messenger of God. 2 a very kind or beautiful person. **angelic** (*say* an-**jel**-ik) *adjective*

angelica *noun* a fragrant plant whose crystallized stalks are used in cookery as a decoration.

anger¹ *noun* a strong feeling that makes you want to quarrel or fight.

anger² *verb* make a person angry.

angiosperm (*say* **an**-jee-oh-sperm) *noun* a flowering plant that produces seed inside a fruit or pod.

angle¹ *noun* 1 the space between two lines or surfaces that meet; the amount by which a line or surface must be turned to make it lie along another. 2 a point of view.

angle² *verb* (**angled, angling**) 1 put something in a slanting position. 2 present news etc. from one point of view.

angler *noun* a person who fishes with a fishing-rod and line. **angling** *noun*

Anglican *adjective* of the Church of England. **Anglican** *noun*

Anglo- *prefix* English or British, *an Anglo-French agreement.*

Anglo-Boer War *noun* South African War.

Anglo-Saxon *noun* the English language from about 700 to 1150, also called Old English.

angry *adjective* (**angrier, angriest**) feeling anger. **angrily** *adverb*

anguish *noun* severe suffering; great sorrow or pain. **anguished** *adjective*

angular *adjective* 1 having angles or sharp corners. 2 (of a person) bony, not plump.

animal *noun* 1 a living thing that can feel and usually move about, *Horses, birds, fish, bees, and people are all animals.* 2 a brutish person; someone not worthy of being called human.

animate *verb* (**animated, animating**) 1 make a thing lively. 2 produce something as an animated cartoon. **animation** *noun,* **animator** *noun*

animated cartoon a film made by photographing a series of drawings.

animosity (*say* an-im-**oss**-it-ee) *noun* a feeling of hostility.

aniseed *noun* a sweet-smelling seed used for flavouring things.

ankle *noun* the part of the leg where it joins the foot.

annals *plural noun* a history of events, especially when written year by year.

annex *verb* take possession of something and add it to what you have already, *annex a neighbouring state.*

annexe *noun* a building added to a larger or more important building.

annihilate (*say* an-**I**-il-ayt) *verb* (**annihilated, annihilating**) destroy completely. **annihilation** *noun*

anniversary *noun* (*plural* **anniversaries**) a day when you remember something special that happened on the same day in a previous year.

annotate (*say* **an**-oh-tayt) *verb* (**annotated, annotating**) add notes of explanation to something written or printed. **annotation** *noun*

announce *verb* (**announced, announcing**) make something known, especially by saying it publicly or to an audience. **announcement** *noun*

announcer *noun* a person who announces items in a broadcast.

annoy *verb* 1 make a person slightly angry. 2 be troublesome to someone. **annoyance** *noun*

annual[1] *adjective* 1 happening or done once a year, *her annual visit.* 2 of one year; reckoned by the year, *our annual income.* 3 living for one year or one season, *an annual plant.* **annually** *adverb*

annual[2] *noun* 1 a book that comes out once a year. 2 an annual plant.

annuity (*say* a-**new**-it-ee) *noun* (*plural* **annuities**) a fixed annual allowance of money, especially from a kind of investment.

annul *verb* (**annulled, annulling**) cancel a law or contract; end something legally, *Their marriage was annulled.* **annulment** *noun*

annunciation *noun* the announcement by the angel to the Virgin Mary that she was to be the mother of Jesus Christ.

anode *noun* the electrode by which electric current enters a device. (Compare *cathode.*)

anoint *verb* put oil or ointment on something, especially in a religious ceremony.

anomaly (*say* an-**om**-al-ee) *noun* (*plural* **anomalies**) something that does not follow the general rule or that is unlike the usual or normal kind.

anon *adverb* (*old use*) soon, *I will say more about this anon.*

anon. *abbreviation* anonymous.

anonymous (*say* an-**on**-im-us) *adjective* of or by a person whose name is not known or not made public, *an anonymous donor.* **anonymously** *adverb,* **anonymity** (*say* an-on-**im**-it-ee) *noun*

anorak *noun* a thick warm jacket with a hood.

anorexia (*say* an-er-**eks**-ee-a) *noun* an illness that makes a person unwilling to eat. **anorexic** *adjective*

another *adjective & pronoun* a different or extra person or thing, *another day, choose another.*

answer[1] *noun* 1 a reply. 2 the solution to a problem.

answer[2] *verb* 1 give or find an answer to; reply. 2 respond to a signal, *Answer the telephone.*

answer back reply cheekily.

answer for be responsible for.

answer to correspond to, *This answers to the description of the stolen bag.*

answerable *adjective* 1 able to be answered. 2 having to be responsible for something.

ant *noun* a very small insect that lives as one of an organized group.

ant- *prefix* see **anti-**.

antagonism (*say* an-**tag**-on-izm) *noun* an unfriendly feeling; hostility. **antagonist** *noun*, **antagonistic** *adjective*

antagonize *verb* (**antagonized, antagonizing**) cause a person to feel antagonism.

Antarctic *noun* the area round the South Pole.

ante- *prefix* before (as in *ante-room*).

ant-eater *noun* an animal that feeds on ants and termites.

antediluvian (*say* an-tee-dil-**oo**-vee-an) *adjective* 1 of the time before Noah's Flood in the Old Testament. 2 (*informal*) very old or out of date.

antelope *noun* (*plural* **antelope** or **antelopes**) an animal like a deer.

antenatal (*say* an-tee-**nay**-tal) *adjective* before birth; during pregnancy.

antenna *noun* 1 (*plural* **antennae**) a feeler on the head of an insect or crustacean. 2 (*plural* **antennas**) an aerial.

anterior *adjective* 1 situated at the front or the head. (The opposite is *posterior*.) 2 earlier.

ante-room *noun* a room leading to a more important room.

anthem *noun* a religious or patriotic song, usually sung by a choir or group of people.

anther *noun* the part of a flower's stamen that bears pollen.

anthill *noun* a mound over an ants' nest.

anthology *noun* a collection of poems, stories, songs, etc. in one book.

anthracite *noun* a kind of hard coal.

anthrax *noun* a disease of sheep and cattle that can also infect people.

anthropoid *adjective* resembling a human being, *Gorillas are anthropoid apes.*

anthropology *noun* the study of human beings and their customs. **anthropological** *adjective*, **anthropologist** *noun*

anti- *prefix* (changing to **ant-** before a vowel) against; preventing (as in *antifreeze*).

anti-aircraft *adjective* used against enemy aircraft.

antibiotic *noun* a substance (e.g. penicillin) that destroys bacteria or prevents them from growing.

antibody *noun* (*plural* **antibodies**) a protein that forms in the blood as a defence against certain substances which it then attacks and destroys.

anticipate *verb* (**anticipated, anticipating**) 1 do something before the proper time or before someone else, *Others may have anticipated Columbus in discovering America.* 2 foresee, *They had anticipated our needs.* 3 expect, *We anticipate that it will rain.* **anticipation** *noun*, **anticipatory** *adjective*

● USAGE: Many people regard use 3 as incorrect; it is better to avoid it and use 'expect'.

anticlimax *noun* a disappointing ending or result where something exciting had been expected.

anticlockwise *adverb* & *adjective* moving in the direction opposite to clockwise.

antics *plural noun* comical or foolish actions.

anticyclone *noun* an area where air pressure is high, usually producing fine settled weather.

antidote *noun* something that acts against the effects of a poison or disease.

antifreeze *noun* a liquid added to water to make it less likely to freeze.

antihistamine *noun* a substance that protects people against unpleasant effects when they are allergic to something.

antimony *noun* a brittle silvery metal.

antipathy (*say* an-**tip**-ath-ee) *noun* a strong dislike.

antipodes (*say* an-**tip**-od-eez) *plural noun* places on opposite sides of the earth. **antipodean** *adjective*

the Antipodes Australia, New Zealand, and the areas near them, which are almost exactly opposite Europe.

antiquarian (*say* anti-**kwair**-ee-an) *adjective* of the study of antiques.

antiquated *adjective* old-fashioned.

antique¹ (*say* an-**teek**) *adjective* very old; belonging to the distant past, *antique jewellery*.

antique² *noun* something that is valuable because it is very old.

antiquity (*say* an-**tik**-wit-ee) *noun* ancient times.

antiquities *plural noun* objects that were made in ancient times.

anti-Semitic (*say* anti-sim-**it**-ik) *adjective* unfriendly or hostile towards Jews. **anti-Semitism** (*say* anti-**sem**-it-izm) *noun*

antiseptic¹ *adjective* 1 able to destroy bacteria, especially those that cause things to become septic or to decay, *an antiseptic ointment*. 2 thoroughly clean and free from germs, *an antiseptic bandage*.

antiseptic² *noun* a substance with an antiseptic effect.

antisocial *adjective* unfriendly or inconsiderate towards other people.

antistatic *adjective* counteracting the effects of static electricity.

antithesis (*say* an-**tith**-iss-iss) *noun* (*plural* **antitheses**) the direct opposite of something, *Slavery is the antithesis of freedom*.

antitoxin *noun* a substance that neutralizes a toxin and prevents it from having a harmful effect. **antitoxic** *adjective*

antivivisectionist *noun* a person who is opposed to making experiments on live animals.

antler *noun* the branching horn of a deer.

antonym (*say* **ant**-on-im) *noun* a word that is opposite in meaning to another, *'Soft' is an antonym of 'hard'*.

anus (*say* **ay**-nus) *noun* the opening at the lower end of the alimentary canal, through which solid waste matter is passed out of the body.

anvil *noun* a large block of iron on which a blacksmith hammers metal into shape.

anxious *adjective* 1 worried. 2 eager, *She is anxious to please us*. **anxiously** *adverb*, **anxiety** *noun*

any¹ *adjective* & *pronoun* 1 one or some, *Have you any wool? There isn't any.* 2 no matter which, *Come any day you like.* 3 every, *Any fool knows that!*

any² *adverb* at all; in some degree, *Is that any better?*

anybody *noun* & *pronoun* any person.

anyhow *adverb* 1 anyway. 2 (*informal*) carelessly, *He does his work anyhow*.

anyone *noun* & *pronoun* anybody.

anything *noun* & *pronoun* any thing; a thing of any sort.

anyway *adverb* whatever happens; whatever the situation may be.

anywhere¹ *adverb* in or to any place.

anywhere² *pronoun* any place, *Anywhere will do*.

aorta (*say* ay-**or**-ta) *noun* the great artery carrying blood away from the left side of the heart.

ap-¹ *prefix* see **ad-** .

ap-² *prefix* see **apo-** .

apace *adverb* quickly.

apart *adverb* 1 away from each other; separately, *Keep your desks apart*. 2 into pieces, *It fell apart*. 3 excluded, *Joking apart, what do you think of it?*

apartheid (*say* a-**part**-hayt) *noun* the policy of keeping people of different races apart.

apartment *noun* 1 a set of rooms, *self-catering holiday apartments*. 2 (*American*) a flat.

apathy (*say* **ap**-ath-ee) *noun* lack of interest or concern. **apathetic** (*say* ap-a-**thet**-ik) *adjective*

ape¹ *noun* any of the four kinds of monkey (gorillas, chimpanzees, orang-utans, gibbons) that do not have a tail.

ape² *verb* (**aped**, **aping**) imitate; mimic.

aperitif (*say* a-**perri**-teef) *noun* an alcoholic drink taken before a meal to stimulate the appetite.

aperture *noun* an opening.

apex (*say* **ay**-peks) *noun* (*plural* **apexes**) the tip or highest point.

aphid (*say* **ay**-fid) *noun* (*plural* **aphids**) a tiny insect (e.g. a greenfly) that sucks the juices from plants.

aphis (*say* **ay**-fiss) *noun* (*plural* **aphides** (*say* **ay**-fid-eez)) an aphid.

aphorism (*say* af-er-izm) *noun* a short witty saying.

apiary (*say* ay-pee-er-ee) *noun* (*plural* **apiaries**) a place with a number of hives where bees are kept. **apiarist** *noun*

apiece *adverb* to, for, or by each, *They cost five cents apiece.*

aplomb (*say* a-**plom**) *noun* dignity and confidence.

apo- *prefix* (changing to **ap-** before a vowel or h) from; out or away (as in *Apostle*).

apocalypse (*say* a-**pok**-a-lips) *noun* **1** a violent or destructive event. **2** a revelation about the end of the world.

apocryphal (*say* a-**pok**-rif-al) *adjective* untrue; invented, *This account of his travels is apocryphal.*

apologetic *adjective* making an apology. **apologetically** *adverb*

apologize *verb* (**apologized, apologizing**) make an apology.

apology *noun* (*plural* **apologies**) **1** a statement saying that you are sorry for having done something wrong or badly. **2** a poor specimen, *this feeble apology for a meal.*

apoplexy (*say* **ap**-op-lek-see) *noun* sudden loss of the ability to feel and move, caused by the blocking or breaking of a blood-vessel in the brain. **apoplectic** *adjective*

Apostle *noun* any of the twelve men sent out by Christ to preach the Gospel.

apostrophe (*say* a-**poss**-trof-ee) *noun* the punctuation mark ' used to show that letters have been missed out (as in *I can't* = I cannot) or to show possession (as in *the boy's book*; *the boys' books*).

apothecary (*say* a-**poth**-ik-er-ee) *noun* (*plural* **apothecaries**) (*old use*) a chemist who prepares medicines.

appal *verb* (**appalled, appalling**) fill with horror; shock somebody very much.

apparatus *noun* the equipment for a particular experiment or job etc.

apparel *noun* (*formal*) clothing.

apparent *adjective* **1** clear; obvious. **2** seeming; appearing to be true but not really so. **apparently** *adverb*

apparition *noun* **1** a ghost. **2** something strange or surprising that appears.

appeal[1] *verb* **1** ask for something earnestly or formally, *They appealed for funds.* **2** ask for a decision to be changed, *She appealed against the prison sentence.* **3** seem attractive or interesting, *Cricket doesn't appeal to me.*

appeal[2] *noun* **1** the action of appealing for something or about a decision; an earnest or formal request. **2** attraction; interest, *The new fashion soon lost its appeal.*

appear *verb* **1** come into sight. **2** seem, *She appears to have many friends.* **3** take part in a play, film, or show etc.

appearance *noun* **1** appearing, *The appearance of the policeman scared the thief away.* **2** what somebody looks like; what something appears to be.

appease *verb* (**appeased, appeasing**) calm or pacify someone, especially by giving in to demands. **appeasement** *noun*

appellation *noun* a name or title.

append *verb* add at the end; attach.

appendage *noun* something added or attached; a thing that forms a natural part of something larger.

appendicitis *noun* inflammation of the appendix.

appendix *noun* **1** (*plural* **appendixes**) a small tube leading off from the intestine. **2** (*plural* **appendices**) a section added at the end of a book.

appetite *noun* a desire, especially for food.

appetizing *adjective* stimulating the appetite. **appetizer** *noun*

applaud *verb* show that you like something, especially by clapping your hands. **applause** *noun*

apple *noun* a round fruit with a red, yellow, or green skin.
   the apple of your eye a person or thing that you love and are proud of.

appliance *noun* a device, *electrical appliances.*

applicable (*say* **ap**-lik-a-bul) *adjective* able to be applied; suitable; relevant.

applicant *noun* a person who applies for something.

application *noun* **1** the action of applying. **2** a formal request, *a passport application.* **3** the ability to apply yourself, *Success at* *school requires great application.* **4** use, *has many applications.*

applied *adjective* put to practical use, *applied science.*

appliqué (*say* a-**plee**-kay) *noun* needlework in which cut-out pieces of material are sewn or fixed ornamentally on another piece.

apply *verb* (**applied, applying**) **1** put one thing on another, *apply the glue to the paper.* **2** start using something, *apply common sense to the problem.* **3** concern; be relevant, *This rule does not apply to you.* **4** make a formal request, *apply for a job.*
apply yourself give all your attention to a job; work diligently.

appoint *verb* **1** choose a person for a job. **2** arrange officially, *They appointed a time for the meeting.*

appointment *noun* **1** an arrangement to meet or visit somebody at a particular time. **2** choosing somebody for a job. **3** a job or position.

apportion *verb* divide into shares; allot. **apportionment** *noun*

apposite (*say* **ap**-o-zit) *adjective* (of a remark) suitable; relevant.

apposition *noun* placing things together, especially nouns and phrases in a grammatical relationship. In *my friend Thandi,* 'my friend' is in apposition to 'Thandi'.

appraise *verb* (**appraised, appraising**) estimate the value or quality of a person or thing. **appraisal** *noun*

appreciable *adjective* enough to be noticed or felt; perceptible. **appreciably** *adverb*

appreciate *verb* (**appreciated, appreciating**) **1** enjoy; value. **2** understand, *I appreciate your problem, but I don't think I can help you.* **3** increase in value. **appreciation** *noun,* **appreciative** *adjective*

apprehend *verb* **1** seize; arrest. **2** understand.

apprehension *noun* **1** fear, *filled with apprehension.* **2** understanding. **3** arrest. **apprehensive** *adjective*

apprentice[1] *noun* a person who is learning a trade or craft by a legal agreement with an employer. **apprenticeship** *noun*

apprentice[2] *verb* (**apprenticed, apprenticing**) place a person as an apprentice.

approach[1] *verb* **1** come near. **2** go to someone with a request or offer, *They approached me for help.* **3** set about doing something or tackling a problem.
approachable *adjective*

approach[2] *noun* (*plural* **approaches**) **1** approaching. **2** a way or road. **3** a technique, *try a new approach.*

approbation *noun* approval.

appropriate[1] (*say* a-**proh**-pree-at) *adjective* suitable. **appropriately** *adverb*

appropriate[2] (*say* a-**proh**-pree-ayt) *verb* (**appropriated, appropriating**) take something and use it as your own. **appropriation** *noun*

approval *noun* approving somebody or something.
on approval received by a customer to examine before deciding to buy.

approve *verb* (**approved, approving**) say or think that a person or thing is good or suitable.

approximate[1] (*say* a-**proks**-im-at) *adjective* almost exact or correct but not completely so. **approximately** *adverb*

approximate[2] (*say* a-**proks**-im-ayt) *verb* (**approximated, approximating**) make or be almost the same as something.

apricot *noun* a juicy orange-coloured fruit with a stone in it.

apron *noun* **1** a garment worn over the front of the body, especially to protect other clothes. **2** a hard-surfaced area on an airfield where aircraft are loaded and unloaded.
apron stage a part of a theatre stage in front of the curtain.

apropos (*say* ap-rop-**oh**) *adverb* concerning, *Apropos of tennis, who is the new champion?*

apse *noun* a semicircular part projecting from a church or other building.

apt *adjective* **1** likely, *He is apt to be careless.* **2** suitable, *an apt quotation.* **3** quick at learning, *an apt pupil.* **aptly** *adverb,* **aptness** *noun*

aptitude *noun* a talent or skill.

aqualung *noun* a diver's portable

breathing-apparatus, with cylinders of compressed air connected to a face-mask.

aquamarine *noun* a bluish-green precious stone.

aquarium *noun* (*plural* **aquariums**) a tank or building in which live fish and other water animals are displayed.

aquatic *adjective* of, on, or in water, *aquatic sports*.

aqueduct *noun* a bridge carrying a water-channel across low ground or a valley.

aquiline (*say* ak-wil-I'n) *adjective* hooked like an eagle's beak, *an aquiline nose*.

ar- *prefix* see **ad-** .

Arab *noun* a member of a people living in Arabia and other parts of the Middle East and North Africa. **Arabian** *adjective*

arabesque (*say* a-rab-**esk**) *noun* **1** (in dancing) a position with one leg stretched backwards in the air. **2** an ornamental design of leaves and branches.

Arabic[1] *adjective* of the Arabs or their language.
  arabic figures the symbols 1, 2, 3, 4, etc.

Arabic[2] *noun* the language of the Arabs.

arable *adjective* suitable for ploughing or growing crops on, *arable land*.

arachnid (*say* a-**rak**-nid) *noun* a member of the group of animals that includes spiders and scorpions.

arbiter *noun* a person who has the power to decide what shall be done or used etc.

arbitrary (*say* **ar**-bit-rer-ee) *adjective* chosen or done on an impulse, not according to a rule or law, *an arbitrary decision*. **arbitrarily** *adverb*

arbitration *noun* settling a dispute by calling in a person or persons from outside to make a decision. **arbitrate** *verb*, **arbitrator** *noun*

arboreal (*say* ar-**bor**-ee-al) *adjective* of trees; living in trees.

arboretum (*say* ar-ber-**ee**-tum) *noun* a place where trees are grown for study and display.

arbour (*say* **ar**-ber) *noun* a shady place among trees.

arc *noun* **1** a curve; part of the circumference of a circle. **2** a luminous electric current passing between two electrodes.

arc lamp or **arc light** a light using an electric arc.

arcade *noun* a covered passage or area, especially for shopping.

arcane *adjective* secret; mysterious.

arch[1] *noun* (*plural* **arches**) **1** a curved structure that helps to support a bridge or other building etc. **2** something shaped like this, *The raised part of the foot between the sole and the heel is called the arch.*

arch[2] *verb* form into an arch; curve.

arch[3] *adjective* pretending to be playful, *an arch smile.* **archly** *adverb*

arch- *prefix* chief; principal (as in *arch-enemy*).

archaeology (*say* ar-kee-**ol**-oj-ee) *noun* the study of the remains of ancient civilizations. **archaeological** *adjective*, **archaeologist** *noun*

archaic (*say* ar-**kay**-ik) *adjective* belonging to former or ancient times.

archangel *noun* an angel of the highest rank.

archbishop *noun* the chief bishop of a province of the Church.

archdeacon *noun* a senior priest ranking next below a bishop.

arch-enemy *noun* the chief enemy.

archer *noun* a person who shoots with a bow and arrows. **archery** *noun*

archetype (*say* **ark**-i-typ) *noun* the original form or model from which others are copied.

archipelago (*say* ark-i-**pel**-ag-oh) *noun* (*plural* **archipelagos**) a large group of islands, or the sea containing these.

architect (*say* **ark**-i-tekt) *noun* a person who designs buildings.

architecture *noun* **1** the process of designing buildings. **2** a particular style of building, *Greek architecture.* **architectural** *adjective*

archives (*say* **ark**-I'vz) *plural noun* the historical documents etc. of an organization or community.

archivist (*say* **ar**-kiv-ist) *noun* a person trained to deal with archives.

archway *noun* an arched passage or entrance.

Arctic *noun* the area round the North Pole.

arctic *adjective* very cold, *The weather was arctic.*

ardent *adjective* full of ardour; enthusiastic. **ardently** *adverb*

ardour (*say* ar-der) *noun* great warmth of feeling.

arduous *adjective* needing much effort; laborious. **arduously** *adverb*

area *noun* 1 the extent or measurement of a surface. 2 a particular region, *desert areas.*

arena (*say* a-reen-a) *noun* the level area in the centre of an amphitheatre or sports stadium.

aren't (*mainly spoken*) are not.
aren't I? (*informal*) am I not?

argosy *noun* (*plural* **argosies**) (*poetic*) a large merchant ship; a fleet of ships.

arguable *adjective* 1 able to be asserted; likely to be correct, *It is arguable that we would be more efficient if we were computerized.* 2 able to be doubted; not certain, *This statement contains many arguable points.* **arguably** *adverb*

argue *verb* (**argued, arguing**) 1 say that you disagree; exchange angry comments. 2 state that something is true and give reasons.

argument *noun* 1 a disagreement; a quarrel. 2 a reason put forward; a series of reasons, *accept an argument.*

argumentative *adjective* fond of arguing.

aria (*say* ar-ee-a) *noun* a solo in an opera or oratorio.

arid *adjective* dry and barren.

arise *verb* (**arose, arisen, arising**) 1 come into existence; come to people's notice, *Problems arose.* 2 (*old use*) rise; stand up, *Arise, Sir Lancelot.*

aristocracy (*say* a-ris-tok-ra-see) *noun* people of the highest social rank; members of the nobility.

aristocrat (*say* a-ris-tok-rat) *noun* a member of the aristocracy. **aristocratic** *adjective*

arithmetic *noun* the science or study of numbers; calculating with numbers. **arithmetical** *adjective*

ark *noun* 1 the ship in which Noah and his family escaped the Flood. 2 a wooden box in which the writings of the Jewish Law were kept.

arm[1] *noun* 1 either of the two upper limbs of the body, between the shoulder and the hand. 2 a sleeve, *the arm of my jacket.* 3 something shaped like an arm or jutting out from a main part; the raised side part of a chair. **armful** *noun*

arm[2] *verb* 1 supply with weapons. 2 prepare for war.

armed forces or **armed services** a country's military forces; the army, navy, and air force.

armada (*say* ar-mah-da) *noun* a fleet of warships.

armadillo *noun* (*plural* **armadillos**) a small burrowing South American animal whose body is covered with a shell of bony plates.

armaments *plural noun* the weapons of an army etc.

armature *noun* 1 the current-carrying part of a dynamo or electric motor. 2 the 'keeper' of a magnet.

armchair *noun* a chair with arms.

armistice *noun* an agreement to stop fighting in a war or battle.

armour *noun* 1 a protective covering for the body, formerly worn in fighting. 2 a metal covering on a warship, tank, or car to protect it from missiles. **armoured** *adjective*

armoury *noun* a place where weapons and ammunition are stored.

armpit *noun* the hollow underneath the top of the arm, below the shoulder.

arms *plural noun* 1 weapons. 2 a coat of arms (see *coat*[1]).

arms race competition between nations in building up supplies of weapons.
up in arms protesting vigorously.

army *noun* (*plural* **armies**) 1 a large number of people trained to fight on land. 2 a large group, *an army of ants.*

aroma (*say* a-roh-ma) *noun* a smell, especially a pleasant one. **aromatic** (*say* a-ro-mat-ik) *adjective*

aromatherapy *noun* a therapy which uses fragrant oils and plant extracts.

around *adverb* & *preposition* all round; about.

arouse *verb* (**aroused, arousing**) rouse.

arrange *verb* (**arranged, arranging**)
1 put into a certain order; adjust.
2 form plans for something, *We arranged to be there.* 3 prepare music for a particular purpose. **arrangement** *noun*

arrant *adjective* thorough and obvious, *Arrant nonsense!*

array[1] *noun* 1 a display. 2 an orderly arrangement.

array[2] *verb* (**arrayed, arraying**) 1 arrange in order, *trophies arrayed on the shelf.* 2 clothe; adorn.

arrears *plural noun* 1 money that is owing and ought to have been paid earlier. 2 a backlog of work etc.
in arrears behindhand.

arrest[1] *verb* 1 seize a person by authority of the law. 2 stop a process or movement, *arrest the spread of the disease.*

arrest[2] *noun* 1 arresting somebody. 2 stopping something, *cardiac arrest.*

arrive *verb* (**arrived, arriving**) 1 reach the end of a journey or a point on it. 2 come, *The great day arrived.* **arrival** *noun*

arrogant *adjective* proud and dictatorial in manner. **arrogantly** *adverb*, **arrogance** *noun*

arrow *noun* 1 a pointed stick to be shot from a bow. 2 a sign with an outward-pointing V at the end, used to show direction or position. **arrowhead** *noun*

arsenal *noun* a place where weapons and ammunition are stored or manufactured.

arsenic *noun* a very poisonous metallic substance.

arson *noun* the crime of deliberately setting fire to a house or building etc. **arsonist** *noun*

art *noun* 1 producing something beautiful, especially by painting or drawing; things produced in this way. 2 a skill, *the art of sailing.*

arts *noun* subjects (e.g. languages, literature, history) in which opinion and understanding are very important, as opposed to sciences where measurements and calculations are used.

the arts painting, music, and writing etc. considered together.

artefact *noun* an object made by a person or people.

artery *noun* (*plural* **arteries**) 1 any of the tubes that carry blood away from the heart to all parts of the body. (Compare *vein.*) 2 an important road or route. **arterial** (*say* ar-**teer**-ee-al) *adjective*

artesian well *noun* a well that is bored straight down into a place where water will rise easily to the surface.

artful *adjective* crafty. **artfully** *adverb*

arthritis (*say* arth-**ry**-tiss) *noun* a disease that makes joints in the body stiff and painful. **arthritic** (*say* arth-**rit**-ik) *adjective*

arthropod *noun* an invertebrate with a segmented body and jointed limbs, e.g. insects, spiders, crabs, and centipedes.

artichoke *noun* a kind of plant with a flower-head used as a vegetable.

article *noun* 1 a piece of writing published in a newspaper or magazine. 2 an object, *articles of clothing.*
definite article the word 'the'.
indefinite article the word 'a' or 'an'.

articulate[1] *adjective* able to express things clearly and fluently.

articulate[2] *verb* (**articulated, articulating**) 1 say or speak clearly. 2 connect by a joint. **articulation** *noun*
articulated vehicle a vehicle that has sections connected by a flexible joint.

artifice *noun* a piece of trickery; a clever device.

artificial *adjective* not natural; made by human beings in imitation of a natural thing. **artificially** *adverb*, **artificiality** *noun*
artificial respiration helping somebody to start breathing again after their breathing has stopped.

artillery *noun* 1 large guns. 2 the part of the army that uses large guns.

artisan (*say* art-iz-**an**) *noun* a skilled worker.

artist *noun* 1 a person who produces works of art, especially a painter. 2 an entertainer, *a trapeze artist.* **artistry** *noun*

artistic *adjective* 1 of art or artists.

2 showing skill and good taste. **artistically** *adverb*

artless *adjective* simple and natural; not artful. **artlessly** *adverb*

arum lily (*say* **air**-um) *noun* a kind of plant with large white funnel-shaped flowers.

as¹ *adverb* equally; similarly, *This is just as easy.*

as² *preposition* in the character or function etc. of, *Use it as a handle.*

as³ *conjunction* **1** when; while, *She slipped as she got off the bus.* **2** because, *As he was late, we missed the train.* **3** in the way that, *Leave it as it is.*

as for with regard to, *As for you, I despise you.*

as it were in some way, *She became, as it were, her own enemy.*

as well also.

as- *prefix* see **ad-**.

asbestos *noun* a soft fireproof material.

ascend *verb* go up.

ascend the throne become king or queen.

ascendancy *noun* being in control, *They gained ascendancy over others.*

ascendant *adjective* rising.

in the ascendant rising, especially in power or influence.

ascension *noun* ascending.

Ascension Day the 40th day after Easter, when Christians commemorate the ascension of Christ into heaven.

ascent *noun* **1** ascending. **2** a way up; an upward path or slope.

ascertain (*say* as-er-**tayn**) *verb* find out by asking. **ascertainable** *adjective*

ascetic¹ (*say* a-**set**-ik) *adjective* not allowing yourself pleasure and luxuries. **asceticism** *noun*

ascetic² *noun* a person who leads an ascetic life, often for religious reasons.

ascribe *verb* (**ascribed**, **ascribing**) attribute.

aseptic (*say* ay-**sep**-tik) *adjective* clean and free from bacteria that cause things to become septic.

asexual *adjective* (in biology) without sex or sexual organs.

ash¹ *noun* (*plural* **ashes**) the powder that is left after something has been burned.

ashen *adjective*, **ashy** *adjective*

ash² *noun* (*plural* **ashes**) a tree with silver-grey bark.

ashamed *adjective* feeling shame.

ashore *adverb* to or on the shore.

ashram *noun* a place where Hindus go for a period of time to pray and meditate alone.

ashtray *noun* a small bowl for tobacco ash.

Asian *adjective* of Asia or its people. **Asian** *noun*

Asiatic *adjective* of Asia.

aside¹ *adverb* **1** to or at one side, *pull it aside.* **2** away; in reserve.

aside² *noun* words spoken so that only certain people will hear.

asinine (*say* **ass**-in-I'n) *adjective* silly; stupid.

ask *verb* **1** speak so as to find out or get something. **2** invite, *Ask her to the party.*

askance (*say* a-**skanss**) *adverb* **look askance at** regard with distrust or disapproval.

askew *adverb* & *adjective* crooked; not straight or level.

asleep *adverb* & *adjective* sleeping.

asp *noun* a small poisonous snake.

asparagus *noun* a plant whose young shoots are eaten as a vegetable.

aspect *noun* **1** one part of a problem or situation, *Violence was the worst aspect of the crime.* **2** a person's or thing's appearance, *The forest had a sinister aspect.* **3** the direction a house etc. faces, *This room has a southern aspect.*

asperity *noun* harshness; severity.

aspersions *plural noun* an attack on someone's reputation, *He cast aspersions on his rivals.*

asphalt (*say* **ass**-falt) *noun* a sticky black substance like tar, often mixed with gravel to surface roads, etc.

asphyxia (*say* ass-**fiks**-ee-a) *noun* suffocation.

asphyxiate (*say* ass-**fiks**-ee-ayt) *verb* (**asphyxiated**, **asphyxiating**) suffocate. **asphyxiation** *noun*

aspic *noun* a savoury jelly used for coating meats, eggs, etc.

aspidistra *noun* a house-plant with broad leaves.

aspirant (*say* **asp**-er-ant) *noun* a person who aspires to something.

aspirate (*say* **asp**-er-at) *noun* the sound of 'h'.

aspiration *noun* ambition; strong desire.

aspire *verb* (**aspired, aspiring**) have a high ambition, *She aspired to become a champion.*

aspirin *noun* a medicinal drug used to relieve pain or reduce fever.

ass *noun* (*plural* **asses**) 1 a donkey. 2 (*informal*) a stupid person.

assail *verb* attack. **assailant** *noun*

assassin *noun* a person who assassinates somebody.

assassinate *verb* (**assassinated, assassinating**) kill an important person deliberately and violently, especially for political reasons. **assassination** *noun*

assault[1] *noun* a violent or illegal attack.

assault[2] *verb* make an assault on someone.

assay (*say* a-**say**) *noun* a test made on metal or ore to discover its quality.

assegai (*say* **ass**-ig-I) *noun* an iron-tipped spear used either for throwing or stabbing.

assemble *verb* (**assembled, assembling**) 1 bring or come together, *The crowd assembled.* 2 fit or put together, *She assembled the model aeroplane.*

assemblage *noun*

assembly *noun* (*plural* **assemblies**) 1 assembling. 2 a regular meeting, such as when everybody in a school meets together. 3 people who regularly meet for a special purpose; a parliament.

assembly line a series of workers and machines along which a product passes to be assembled part by part.

assent[1] *verb* consent; say you agree.

assent[2] *noun* consent; approval.

assert *verb* state firmly. **assertion** *noun*

assert yourself use firmness or authority.

assertive *adjective* asserting yourself.

assess *verb* decide or estimate the value or quality of a person or thing. **assessment** *noun*, **assessor** *noun*

asset *noun* something useful.

assets *plural noun* a person's or firm's property, reckoned as having value.

assiduous (*say* a-**sid**-yoo-us) *adjective* working hard; persevering. **assiduously** *adverb*, **assiduity** *noun*

assign *verb* 1 allot; give. 2 appoint a person to perform a task.

assignation (*say* ass-ig-**nay**-shon) *noun* 1 assigning something. 2 an arrangement to meet someone.

assignment *noun* 1 assigning. 2 something assigned; a task given to someone, *homework assignments.*

assimilate *verb* (**assimilated, assimilating**) take in and absorb something, e.g. nourishment into the body or knowledge into the mind. **assimilation** *noun*

assist *verb* help. **assistance** *noun*

assistant[1] *noun* 1 a person who assists another; a helper. 2 a person who serves customers in a shop.

assistant[2] *adjective* helping a person and ranking next below him or her, *the assistant manager.*

associate[1] *verb* (**associated, associating**) 1 put or go naturally or regularly together, *the risks associated with drugs.* 2 work together.

associate[2] *noun* a colleague or companion; a partner. **associate** *adjective*

association *noun* 1 an organization of people; a society. 2 associating, *Association with criminals is dangerous.* 3 something associated, *Does the sea have any strong associations for you?*

assonance (*say* **ass**-on-ans) *noun* similarity of vowel sounds, e.g. in *vermin* and *furnish.*

assorted *adjective* of various sorts put together; mixed. **assortment** *noun*

assuage (*say* a-**swayj**) *verb* (**assuaged, assuaging**) soothe; make less severe, *We drank to assuage our thirst.*

assume *verb* (**assumed, assuming**) 1 accept (without proof or question) that something is true or sure to happen. 2 take on; undertake, *She assumed the extra responsibility.* 3 put on, *He assumed an innocent expression.* **assumption** *noun*

assumed name a false name.

assurance *noun* 1 a promise or guarantee that something is true or will happen.

2 life insurance. 3 self-confidence, *She spoke with assurance.*

assure *verb* (**assured, assuring**) 1 tell somebody confidently; promise. 2 make certain.

aster *noun* a garden plant with daisy-like flowers in various colours.

asterisk *noun* a star-shaped sign * used to draw attention to something.

astern *adverb* 1 at the back of a ship or aircraft. 2 backwards, *Full speed astern!*

asteroid *noun* one of the small planets found mainly between the orbits of Mars and Jupiter.

asthma (*say* ass-ma) *noun* a disease that makes breathing difficult. **asthmatic** *adjective* & *noun*

astigmatism (*say* a-**stig**-mat-izm) *noun* a defect that prevents an eye or lens from focusing properly. **astigmatic** *adjective*

astir *adverb* & *adjective* in motion; moving.

astonish *verb* surprise somebody greatly. **astonishment** *noun*

astound *verb* astonish; shock greatly.

astral *adjective* of the stars.

astray *adverb* & *adjective* away from the right path or place or course of action.

astride *adverb* & *preposition* with one leg on each side of something.

astringent *adjective* 1 causing skin or body tissue to contract. 2 harsh; severe, *astringent criticism.*

astrology *noun* the study of how the stars may affect people's lives. **astrologer** *noun*, **astrological** *adjective*

astronaut *noun* a person who travels in a spacecraft. **astronautics** *noun*

astronomy *noun* the study of the stars and planets and their movements. **astronomer** *noun*, **astronomical** *adjective*

astute *adjective* clever; shrewd. **astutely** *adverb*, **astuteness** *noun*

asunder *adverb* apart; into pieces.

asylum *noun* 1 refuge and safety; a place of refuge, *The defeated rebels sought political asylum in another country.* 2 (*old use*) a mental hospital.

asymmetrical (*say* ay-sim-et-rik-al) *adjective* not symmetrical. **asymmetrically** *adverb*

at *preposition* This word is used to show 1 position (*at the top*), 2 time (*at midnight*), 3 condition (*Stand at ease*), 4 direction towards something (*Aim at the target*), 5 level or price etc. (*Sell them at R100 each*), 6 cause (*We were annoyed at his failure*). **at all** in any way; of any kind. **at it** doing or working at something. **at once** immediately; at the same time, *It all came out at once.*

at- *prefix* see **ad-**.

atheist (*say* ayth-ee-ist) *noun* a person who believes that there is no God. **atheism** *noun*

athlete *noun* a person who is good at athletics.

athletic *adjective* 1 physically strong and active. 2 of athletes, *an athletic club.* **athletically** *adverb*

athletics *plural noun* physical exercises and sports, e.g. running and jumping.

atjar *noun* chutney or hot relish.

atlas *noun* (*plural* **atlases**) a book of maps, named after Atlas, a giant in Greek mythology, who was made to support the universe.

ATM *abbreviation* automated teller machine.

atmosphere *noun* 1 the air round the earth. 2 a feeling given by surroundings, *the happy atmosphere of the fair-ground.* **atmospheric** *adjective*

atoll *noun* a ring-shaped coral reef.

atom *noun* the smallest particle of a substance. **atom bomb** an atomic bomb.

atomic *adjective* of an atom or atoms. **atomic bomb** a bomb using atomic energy. **atomic energy** energy created by splitting the nuclei of certain atoms.

atomizer *noun* a device for making a liquid into a fine spray.

atone *verb* (**atoned, atoning**) make amends; make up for having done something wrong. **atonement** *noun*

atrocious (*say* a-**troh**-shus) *adjective* extremely bad or wicked. **atrociously** *adverb*

atrocity (*say* a-**tross**-it-ee) *noun* (*plural* **atrocities**) something extremely bad or wicked; wickedness.

attach *verb* 1 fix or join to something else. 2 regard as belonging to something, *We attach great importance to neatness.* **attachment** *noun*
attached to fond of.
attaché (*say* a-**tash**-ay) *noun* a special assistant to an ambassador, *our military attaché.*
attaché case a small case in which documents etc. may be carried.
attack¹ *noun* 1 a violent attempt to hurt or overcome somebody. 2 a piece of strong criticism. 3 sudden illness or pain.
attack² *verb* make an attack. **attacker** *noun*
attain *verb* accomplish; succeed in doing or getting something. **attainable** *adjective*, **attainment** *noun*
attempt¹ *verb* make an effort to do something; try.
attempt² *noun* an effort to do something; a try.
attend *verb* 1 give care and thought to something; look and listen, *Why don't you attend to your teacher?* 2 be present somewhere; go regularly to a meeting etc. 3 look after someone; be an attendant. **attendance** *noun*
attendant *noun* a person who helps or accompanies someone.
attention *noun* 1 attending to someone or something. 2 a position in which a soldier etc. stands with feet together and arms straight downwards.
attentive *adjective* giving attention. **attentively** *adverb*, **attentiveness** *noun*
attenuate *verb* (**attenuated, attenuating**) make a thing thinner or weaker. **attenuation** *noun*
attest *verb* declare or prove that something is true or genuine. **attestation** *noun*
attic *noun* a room in the roof of a house.
attire¹ *noun* (*formal*) clothes.
attire² *verb* (**attired, attiring**) (*formal*) clothe.
attitude *noun* 1 the position of the body or its parts; posture. 2 a way of thinking or behaving, *a helpful attitude.*
attorney *noun* (*plural* **attorneys**) a lawyer who is appointed to act on behalf of another person in business or legal matters.

Attorney-General the chief legal officer of the country.
attract *verb* 1 get someone's attention or interest; seem pleasant to someone. 2 pull something by an invisible force, *Magnets attract metal pins.* **attraction** *noun*, **attractive** *adjective*, **attractively** *adverb*, **attractiveness** *noun*
attribute¹ (*say* a-**trib**-yoot) *verb* (**attributed, attributing**) regard as belonging to or created by, *We attribute his success to hard work.* **attribution** *noun*
attribute² (*say* **at**-rib-yoot) *noun* a quality or characteristic, *Kindness is one of his attributes.*
attributive (*say* a-**trib**-yoo-tiv) *adjective* expressing an attribute and placed before the word it describes, e.g. *old* in *the old dog.* (Compare *predicative.*) **attributively** *adverb*
attrition (*say* a-**trish**-on) *noun* wearing something away gradually.
attune *verb* (**attuned, attuning**) bring into harmony.
aubergine (*say* **oh**-ber-*zh*een) *noun* the deep-purple fruit of the egg-plant, also called a brinjal.
auburn *adjective* (of hair) reddish-brown.
auction¹ *noun* a public sale where things are sold to the person who offers the most money for them.
auction² *verb* sell by auction. **auctioneer** *noun*
audacious (*say* aw-**day**-shus) *adjective* bold; daring. **audaciously** *adverb*, **audacity** *noun*
audible *adjective* loud enough to be heard. **audibly** *adverb*, **audibility** *noun*
audience *noun* 1 people who have gathered to hear or watch something. 2 a formal interview with a king or queen etc.
audio *noun* reproduced sounds. **audiotape** a sound recording on magnetic tape.
audiovisual *adjective* using both sound and pictures to give information.
audit¹ *noun* an official examination of financial accounts to see that they are correct.

audit[2] *verb* (**audited, auditing**) make an audit of accounts. **auditor** *noun*

audition *noun* a test to see if a performer is suitable for a job. **audition** *verb*

auditorium *noun* (*plural* **auditoriums**) the part of a building where the audience sits.

augment *verb* increase or add to something. **augmentation** *noun*

augur (*say* awg-er) *verb* be a sign of what is to come, *These exam results augur well*. **augury** *noun*

august (*say* aw-**gust**) *adjective* majestic; imposing.

auk *noun* a kind of sea-bird.

aunt *noun* the sister of your father or mother; your uncle's wife.

auntie (also **aunty**) *noun* 1 (*informal*) aunt. 2 a word used by children when speaking politely to a woman.

au pair (*say* oh **pair**) *noun* a young foreigner who works for a time in someone's home.

aura (*say* or-a) *noun* a general feeling surrounding a person or thing, *an aura of happiness*.

aural (*say* or-al) *adjective* of the ear; of hearing. **aurally** *adverb*
 • USAGE: Do not confuse *aural* with *oral*.

aurora (*say* aw-**raw**-ra) *noun* bands of coloured light appearing in the sky at night, the **aurora borealis** (*say* bor-ee-**ay**-liss) in the northern hemisphere and the **aurora australis** (*say* aw-**stray**-liss) in the southern hemisphere.

auspices (*say* aw-spiss-eez) *plural noun* protection; sponsorship, *under the auspices of the Red Cross*.

auspicious (*say* aw-**spish**-us) *adjective* fortunate; favourable, *an auspicious start*.

austere (*say* aw-**steer**) *adjective* very simple and plain; without luxuries. **austerely** *adverb*, **austerity** *noun*

Australasian *adjective* of the area of Australia and the islands of the south-western Pacific, or its people.

Australian *adjective* of Australia or its people. **Australian** noun

aut- *prefix* see **auto-**.

authentic *adjective* genuine, *an authentic*

signature. **authentically** *adverb*, **authenticity** *noun*

authenticate *verb* (**authenticated, authenticating**) confirm something as being authentic. **authentication** *noun*

author *noun* the writer of a book, play, poem, etc. **authorship** *noun*

authoritarian *adjective* believing that people should be completely obedient to those in authority.

authoritative *adjective* having proper authority or expert knowledge; official.

authority *noun* (*plural* **authorities**) 1 the right or power to give orders to other people. 2 a person or organization with the right to give orders. 3 an expert; a book etc. that gives reliable information, *an authority on spiders*.

authorize *verb* (**authorized, authorizing**) give official permission for something. **authorization** *noun*

autistic (*say* aw-**tist**-ik) *adjective* unable to communicate with people or respond to surroundings.

auto- *prefix* (changing to **aut-** before a vowel) self-; of or by yourself or itself (as in *autograph, automatic*).

autobiography *noun* (*plural* **autobiographies**) the story of a person's life written by himself or herself. **autobiographical** *adjective*

autocracy (*say* aw-**tok**-ra-see) *noun* (*plural* **autocracies**) despotism; rule by a person with unlimited power.

autocrat *noun* a person with unlimited power; a dictatorial person. **autocratic** *adjective*, **autocratically** *adverb*

autograph[1] *noun* a person's signature.

autograph[2] *verb* sign your name on or in a book etc.

automate *verb* (**automated, automating**) work something by automation.

automatic *adjective* 1 working on its own without continuous attention or control by people, *an automatic washing-machine*. 2 done without thinking. **automatically** *adverb*

automation *noun* making processes automatic; using machines instead of people to do jobs.

automaton (*say* aw-**tom**-at-on) *noun* a robot; a person who seems to act mechanically without thinking.

automobile *noun* (*American*) a motor car.

autonomy (*say* aw-**ton**-om-ee) *noun* self-government. **autonomous** *adjective*

autopsy (*say* **aw**-top-see) *noun* (*plural* **autopsies**) a post-mortem.

autumn *noun* the season between summer and winter. **autumnal** *adjective*

auxiliary[1] *adjective* giving help and support, *auxiliary services*.
auxiliary verb a verb used in forming tenses etc. of other verbs, e.g. *have* in *I have finished*.

auxiliary[2] *noun* (*plural* **auxiliaries**) a helper.

avail[1] *noun* usefulness; help, *Their pleas were of no avail*.

avail[2] *verb* be useful or helpful, *Nothing availed against the storm*.
avail yourself of make use of something.

available *adjective* ready or able to be used; obtainable. **availability** *noun*

avalanche *noun* a mass of snow or rock falling down the side of a mountain.

avarice (*say* **av**-er-iss) *noun* greed for gain. **avaricious** *adjective*

avenge *verb* (**avenged**, **avenging**) take vengeance for something done to harm you. **avenger** *noun*

avenue *noun* 1 a wide street. 2 a road with trees along both sides. 3 a way of approaching something, *We have explored every avenue*.

average[1] *noun* 1 the value obtained by adding several quantities together and dividing by the number of quantities. 2 the usual or ordinary standard, *Her marks are above average*.

average[2] *adjective* 1 worked out as an average, *Their average age is ten*. 2 of the usual or ordinary standard.

average[3] *verb* (**averaged**, **averaging**) work out, produce, or amount to as an average.

averse *adjective* unwilling; feeling opposed to something.

aversion *noun* a strong dislike.

avert *verb* 1 turn something away, *People averted their eyes from the accident*. 2 prevent, *We averted a disaster*.

aviary *noun* (*plural* **aviaries**) a large cage or building for keeping birds.

aviation *noun* the flying of aircraft. **aviator** *noun*

avid (*say* **av**-id) *adjective* eager, *an avid reader*. **avidly** *adverb*, **avidity** *noun*

avocado (*say* av-ok-**ah**-doh) *noun* (*plural* **avocados**) a pear-shaped tropical fruit.

avoid *verb* 1 keep yourself away from someone or something. 2 keep yourself from doing something; refrain from, *Avoid rash promises*. **avoidable** *adjective*, **avoidance** *noun*

avuncular *adjective* like a kindly uncle.

await *verb* wait for.

awake[1] *verb* (**awoke**, **awoken**, **awaking**) wake up.

awake[2] *adjective* not asleep.

awaken *verb* awake. **awakening** *noun*

award[1] *verb* give something officially as a prize, payment, or penalty.

award[2] *noun* something awarded.

aware *adjective* knowing; realizing, *Were you aware of the danger?* **awareness** *noun*

awash *adjective* with waves or water flooding over it.

away[1] *adverb* 1 to or at a distance; not at the usual place. 2 out of existence, *The water had boiled away*. 3 continuously; persistently, *We worked away at it*.

away[2] *adjective* played on an opponent's ground, *an away match*.

awe *noun* fearful or reverent wonder. **awed** *adjective*, **awestricken** *adjective*, **awestruck** *adjective*

aweigh *adverb* hanging just clear of the sea-bottom, *The anchor is aweigh*.

awesome *adjective* causing awe.

awful *adjective* 1 very bad, *an awful accident*. 2 (*informal*) very great, *That's an awful lot of money*. 3 causing awe or fear. **awfully** *adverb*

awhile *adverb* for a short time.

awkward *adjective* 1 difficult to use or deal with; not convenient, *an awkward question*. 2 clumsy; not skilful. **awkwardly** *adverb*, **awkwardness** *noun*

awl *noun* a small pointed tool for making holes in leather, wood, etc.

awning *noun* a roof-like shelter made of canvas etc.

AWOL (*say* ay-wol) *abbreviation* (*informal*) absent without leave, *The soldiers went AWOL*.

awry *adverb* & *adjective* twisted to one side; crooked; wrong, *plans went awry*.

axe[1] *noun* 1 a tool for chopping things. 2 (*informal*) being axed.
have an axe to grind have a personal interest in something and want to take care of it.

axe[2] *verb* (**axed**, **axing**) remove; reduce; abolish, *Community arts projects may be axed*.

axiom *noun* an established general truth or principle. **axiomatic** *adjective*

axis *noun* (*plural* **axes**) 1 a line through the centre of a spinning object. 2 a line dividing a thing in half, *The axis of a circle is its diameter*. 3 a fixed line for measurement (e.g. on a graph), *the horizontal axis*.

axle *noun* the rod through the centre of a wheel, on which the wheel turns.

ayatollah (*say* I-a-**tol**-a) *noun* a Muslim religious leader in Iran.

aye (*say as* I) *adverb* yes.

azalea (*say* a-**zay**-lee-a) *noun* a kind of flowering shrub.

azure *adjective* & *noun* sky-blue.

Bb

---

baa *noun* the cry of a sheep or lamb.

babble *verb* (**babbled**, **babbling**) 1 talk in a meaningless way. 2 make a murmuring sound. **babble** *noun*, **babbler** *noun*

babe *noun* a baby.

baboon *noun* a kind of large monkey.
baboon spider a large hairy spider.

baby *noun* (*plural* **babies**) a very young child or animal. **babyish** *adjective*

baby-sitter *noun* someone who looks after a child while its parents are out.

bachelor *noun* a man who has not married.
Bachelor of Arts or **Science** a person who has taken a first degree in arts or science.

bacillus (*say* ba-**sil**-us) *noun* (*plural* **bacilli**) a rod-shaped bacterium.

back[1] *noun* 1 the part furthest from the front. 2 the back part of the body from the shoulders to the buttocks. 3 the part of a chair etc. that your back rests against. 4 a defending player near the goal in soccer, hockey, etc.

back[2] *adjective* 1 placed at or near the back. 2 of the back.

back[3] *adverb* 1 to or towards the back. 2 to the place you have come from, *Go back home*. 3 to an earlier time or condition or position, *Put the clocks back one hour*.

back[4] *verb* 1 move backwards. 2 give support or help to someone, *Her parents backed her in her choice of career*. 3 bet on something. 4 cover the back of something, *Back the rug with canvas*. **backer** *noun*
back out refuse to do what was agreed.
back up give support or help to a person or thing. **back-up** *noun*

backbiting *noun* spiteful talk.

backbone *noun* the column of small bones down the centre of the back.

backdrop *noun* a painted curtain at the back of a stage.

backfire *verb* (**backfired**, **backfiring**) 1 make an explosion when fuel burns too soon in an engine or ignites in the exhaust system. 2 produce an unwanted effect, *Their plans backfired*.

backgammon *noun* a game played on a board with draughts and dice.

background *noun* 1 the back part of a scene or view etc. 2 the conditions influencing something, *background information*. 3 a person's experience and education etc.

backhand *noun* a stroke made in tennis etc. with the back of the hand turned outwards.

backhanded *adjective* 1 done with the back of the hand. 2 indirect or having two meanings, *a backhanded compliment*.

backing *noun* 1 support. 2 material that forms a support or lines the back of something. 3 musical accompaniment.

backlash *noun* (*plural* **backlashes**) a violent reaction to an event etc.

backlog *noun* an amount of work that should have been finished but is still waiting to be done.

backside *noun* (*informal*) the buttocks.

backstroke *noun* a way of swimming on your back.

backveld[1] *noun* remote country districts. **backvelder** *noun*

backveld[2] *adjective* from the backveld; not having wide experience of the world or new ideas.

backward[1] *adjective* 1 going backwards. 2 having made less than the normal progress. **backwardness** *noun*

backward[2] *adverb* backwards.

backwards *adverb* 1 to or towards the back. 2 with the back end going first. 3 in reverse order, *Count backwards.* **backwards and forwards** in each direction alternately; to and fro.

backwater *noun* 1 a branch of a river that comes to a dead end with stagnant water. 2 a place that is not affected by progress or new ideas.

bacon *noun* smoked or salted meat from the back or sides of a pig.

baconer *noun* a pig kept for its bacon.

bacterium *noun* (*plural* **bacteria**) a microscopic organism. **bacterial** *adjective*

● USAGE: Note that *bacteria* is a plural. It is incorrect to say 'a bacteria' or 'this bacteria'; correct usage is *this bacterium* or *these bacteria.*

bad *adjective* (**worse, worst**) 1 not having the right qualities; not good. 2 wicked; evil. 3 serious, *a bad accident.* 4 ill; unhealthy; diseased, *a bad back.* 5 harmful, *Sweets are bad for your teeth.* 6 decayed, *This meat has gone bad.* **badness** *noun* **not bad** quite good.

bade *old past tense* of **bid**[3].

badge *noun* a thing that you wear on your clothes to show people who you are or what school or club etc. you belong to.

badger[1] *noun* a grey burrowing animal with a white patch on its head.

badger[2] *verb* pester.

badly *adverb* (**worse, worst**) 1 in a bad way; not well. 2 severely; so as to cause much injury, *He was badly wounded.* 3 very much, *She badly wanted to win.*

badminton *noun* a game in which a light object called a shuttlecock is hit to and fro with rackets across a high net.

baffle *verb* (**baffled, baffling**) 1 puzzle or perplex somebody. 2 frustrate, *We baffled their attempts to capture us.* **bafflement** *noun*

bag[1] *noun* a flexible container for holding or carrying things. **bags** (*informal*) plenty, *bags of room.*

bag[2] *verb* (**bagged, bagging**) 1 (*informal*) seize; catch. 2 put into a bag or bags.

bagatelle *noun* 1 a game played on a board with small balls struck into holes. 2 something small of little value.

baggage *noun* luggage.

baggy *adjective* hanging loosely.

bagpipes *plural noun* a musical instrument in which air is squeezed out of a bag into pipes.

bail[1] *noun* money paid or promised as a guarantee that a person accused of a crime will return for trial if released temporarily.

bail[2] *verb* provide bail for a person.

bail[3] *noun* one of the two small pieces of wood placed on top of the stumps in cricket.

bail[4] *verb* scoop out water that has entered a boat.

bailey *noun* the courtyard of a castle; the wall round this courtyard.

bailiff *noun* a law officer who helps a sheriff by serving writs and performing arrests.

bait[1] *noun* food put on a hook or in a trap to catch fish or animals.

bait[2] *verb* 1 put bait on a hook or in a trap. 2 torment or tease by jeering.

baize *noun* thick green cloth used chiefly for covering snooker tables.

bake *verb* (**baked, baking**) 1 cook in an oven. 2 make or become very hot, *We sat baking in the sun.* 3 make a thing hard by heating it. **baked beans** cooked white beans, usually tinned with tomato sauce. **baking-powder** a chemical used in cooking to make things rise.

baker *noun* a person who bakes and sells bread or cakes. **bakery** *noun*

bakkie *noun* (*informal*) 1 a small open motor truck. 2 a container or basin.

balaclava *noun* a hood covering the head and neck and part of the face.

balance¹ *noun* 1 a steady position; having the weight or amount evenly distributed. 2 an apparatus for weighing things, with two containers hanging from a bar. 3 the difference between money paid into an account and money taken out of it. 4 the money still owing after something has been paid for, *pay the balance next week.*

balance² *verb* (**balanced**, **balancing**) make or be steady or equal.

balcony *noun* (*plural* **balconies**) 1 a platform projecting from an outside wall in a building. 2 the upstairs part of a theatre or cinema.

bald *adjective* 1 without hair on the top of the head. 2 with no details; blunt, *a bald statement.* **baldly** *adverb*, **baldness** *noun*

bale¹ *noun* a large bundle of hay, straw, cotton, etc., usually tied up tightly.

bale² *verb* (**baled**, **baling**) **bale out** jump out of an aircraft with a parachute.

baleful *adjective* bringing harm or evil; menacing, *a baleful frown.* **balefully** *adverb*

ball¹ *noun* 1 a round object used in many games. 2 a solid or hollow sphere; a round mass, *a ball of string.*

ball² *noun* a grand gathering where people dance.

ballad *noun* a simple song or poem telling a story.

ballast (*say* bal-ast) *noun* heavy material carried in a ship to keep it steady.

ball-bearings *plural noun* small steel balls rolling in a groove on which parts of a machine can move easily.

ballcock *noun* a floating device controlling the water-level in a cistern.

ballerina (*say* bal-er-**een**-a) *noun* a female ballet-dancer.

ballet (*say* **bal**-ay) *noun* a stage entertainment telling a story or expressing an idea in dancing and mime.

ballistic (*say* bal-**ist**-ik) *adjective* of projectiles such as bullets and missiles.

balloon *noun* 1 an inflatable rubber pouch with a neck, used as a toy or decoration. 2 a large round bag inflated with hot air or light gases to make it rise in the air. 3 an outline round spoken words in a strip cartoon.

ballot¹ *noun* 1 a secret method of voting by means of papers or tokens. 2 a piece of paper on which a vote is made.

ballot² *verb* (**balloted**, **balloting**) vote or allow people to vote by a ballot.

ball-point pen *noun* a pen with a tiny ball round which the ink flows.

ballroom *noun* a large room where dances are held.

balm *noun* 1 a sweet-scented ointment. 2 a soothing influence, *The gentle music was balm to my ears.*

balmy *adjective* 1 sweet-scented like balm. 2 soft and warm.

balsa *noun* a kind of very lightweight wood.

balsam *noun* 1 a kind of gum produced by certain trees. 2 a tree producing balsam. 3 a kind of flowering plant.

balustrade *noun* a row of short posts or pillars supporting a rail or strip of stonework round a balcony or terrace.

bamboo *noun* 1 a tall plant with hard hollow stems. 2 a stem of the bamboo plant.

bamboozle *verb* (**bamboozled**, **bamboozling**) (*informal*) cheat or mystify someone.

ban¹ *verb* (**banned**, **banning**) forbid something officially.

ban² *noun* an order that bans something.

banal (*say* ban-**ahl**) *adjective* ordinary and uninteresting. **banality** *noun*

banana *noun* a finger-shaped yellow or green fruit.

band¹ *noun* 1 a strip or loop of something. 2 a range of values, wavelengths, etc.

band² *noun* 1 an organized group doing something together, *a band of robbers.* 2 a set of people playing music together.

band³ *verb* form an organized group.

bandage *noun* a strip of material for binding up a wound. **bandage** *verb*

bandit *noun* a member of a band of robbers.

bandstand *noun* a platform for a band playing music outdoors.

bandwagon *noun* a wagon for a band playing music in a parade.

jump or **climb on the bandwagon** join in something that is successful.

bandy[1] *adjective* having legs that curve outwards at the knees.

bandy[2] *verb* (**bandied, bandying**) pass to and fro, *The story was bandied about.*

bane *noun* a cause of trouble or worry etc., *Exams are the bane of our lives!* **baneful** *adjective*, **banefully** *adverb*

bang[1] *noun* 1 a sudden loud noise like that of an explosion. 2 a sharp blow or knock.

bang[2] *verb* 1 hit or shut noisily. 2 make a sudden loud noise, *Something banged and all the lights went out.*

bang[3] *adverb* 1 with a bang; suddenly. 2 (*informal*) exactly, *bang in the middle.*

banger *noun* 1 a firework made to explode noisily. 2 (*slang*) a noisy old car.

bangers and mash (*slang*) sausages and mashed potatoes.

bangle *noun* a stiff bracelet.

banish *verb* punish a person by sending him or her away. **banishment** *noun*

banisters *plural noun* a handrail with upright supports beside a staircase.

banjo *noun* (*plural* **banjos**) an instrument like a guitar with a round body.

bank[1] *noun* 1 a slope. 2 a long piled-up mass of sand, snow, cloud, etc.

bank[2] *verb* 1 build or form a bank. 2 tilt sideways while changing direction, *The plane banked as it prepared to land.*

bank[3] *noun* 1 a business that looks after people's money. 2 a reserve supply, *a blood bank.*

bank[4] *verb* put money in a bank.

bank on rely on.

banker *noun* a person who runs a bank.

banket *noun* a kind of rock consisting of pebbles and gold ore.

banknote *noun* a piece of paper money issued by a bank.

bankrupt *adjective* unable to pay debts. **bankruptcy** *noun*

banner *noun* 1 a flag. 2 a strip of cloth with a design or slogan, carried on a pole or two poles in a procession etc.

banns *plural noun* an announcement in a church that the two people named are going to marry each other.

banquet *noun* a formal public meal. **banqueting** *noun*

bantam *noun* a kind of small fowl.

banter *noun* playful teasing or joking.

Bantu *adjective* of the principal language family of central and southern Africa, *Shona, Sotho, Swahili, Xhosa, and Zulu are Bantu languages.*

● USAGE: Apartheid policy-makers mistakenly used the term 'Bantu' to refer to people rather than to a language group. Because of this association, some people prefer to avoid this term and use *Sintu* instead.

bap *noun* a soft flat bread roll.

baptism *noun* baptizing.

Baptist *noun* a member of a group of Christians who believe that a person should not be baptized until old enough to understand what baptism means.

baptize *verb* (**baptized, baptizing**) receive a person into the Christian Church in a ceremony in which he or she is sprinkled with or dipped in water, and usually given a name or names.

bar[1] *noun* 1 a long piece of hard substance. 2 a counter or room where refreshments, especially alcoholic drinks, are served. 3 a barrier; an obstruction. 4 one of the small equal sections into which music is divided, *three beats to the bar.*

the Bar barristers.

bar[2] *verb* (**barred, barring**) 1 fasten with a bar or bars. 2 block; obstruct, *A man with a dog barred the way.* 3 forbid; ban.

barb *noun* the backward-pointing part of a spear or fish-hook etc.

barbarian *noun* an uncivilized or brutal person. **barbaric** *adjective*, **barbarous** *adjective*, **barbarity** *noun*, **barbarism** *noun*

barbecue *noun* 1 a meal cooked over an open fire outdoors, also called a braai. 2 a grill etc. used to cook this meal.

barbed *adjective* having a barb or barbs.

barbed wire wire with small spikes in it, used to make fences.

barber *noun* a men's hairdresser.

barbet *noun* a small brightly-coloured bird.

bar-code *noun* a code consisting of lines and spaces which can be read by a machine.

bard *noun* (*formal*) a poet or minstrel.

bare[1] *adjective* 1 without clothing or covering. 2 empty of stores etc., *The cupboard was bare.* 3 plain; without details, *the bare facts.* 4 only just enough, *the bare necessities of life.* **barely** *adverb*, **bareness** *noun*

bare[2] *verb* (**bared, baring**) uncover; reveal, *The dog bared its teeth in a snarl.*

bareback *adjective* & *adverb* riding on a horse without a saddle.

barefaced *adjective* shameless; bold and unconcealed, *It's barefaced robbery!*

bargain[1] *noun* 1 an agreement about buying or selling or exchanging something, *strike a bargain.* 2 something bought cheaply.

bargain[2] *verb* argue over the price to be paid or what you will do in return for something.

bargain for be prepared for; expect, *He got more than he bargained for.*

barge[1] *noun* a long flat-bottomed boat used especially on canals.

barge[2] *verb* (**barged, barging**) move clumsily or heavily.

baritone *noun* a male singer with a voice between a tenor and a bass.

barium (*say* **bair**-ee-um) *noun* a soft silvery-white metal.

bark[1] *noun* the short harsh sound made by a dog or fox. **bark** *verb*

bark[2] *noun* the outer covering of a tree's branches or trunk.

bark[3] *verb* scrape your skin accidentally.

barley *noun* a cereal plant from which malt is made.

barley sugar a sweet made from boiled sugar.

bar mitzvah *noun* a religious ceremony for Jewish boys aged 13.

barmy *adjective* (*slang*) crazy.

barn *noun* a building for storing hay or grain etc. on a farm. **barnyard** *noun*

barn dance a kind of country dance; an informal gathering for dancing.

barnacle *noun* a shellfish that attaches itself to rocks and the bottoms of ships.

barometer (*say* ba-**rom**-it-er) *noun* an instrument that measures air pressure, used in forecasting the weather.

baron *noun* 1 a member of the lowest rank of noblemen. 2 an important owner of an industry or business, *a newspaper baron.* **baroness** *noun*, **barony** *noun*, **baronial** (*say* ba-**roh**-nee-al) *adjective*

baronet *noun* a nobleman ranking below a baron but above a knight. **baronetcy** *noun*

baroque (*say* ba-**rok**) *noun* & *adjective* (of the) highly ornate style fashionable in the arts, particularly architecture, in Europe in the 17th and 18th centuries.

barracks *noun* a large building or group of buildings for soldiers to live in.

barracuda *noun* (*plural* **barracuda** or **barracudas**) a large predatory fish.

barrage (*say* ba-**rah**z*h*) *noun* 1 an artificial barrier; a dam. 2 heavy gunfire.

barrel *noun* 1 a large rounded container with flat ends. 2 the metal tube of a gun, through which the shot is fired.

barrel-organ *noun* a musical instrument from which you produce tunes by turning a handle.

barren *adjective* not producing any fruit, seeds, children, etc.; not fertile, *barren land.* **barrenness** *noun*

barricade[1] *noun* a barrier, especially one put up hastily across a street etc.

barricade[2] *verb* (**barricaded, barricading**) block or defend with a barricade.

barrier *noun* something that prevents people or things from getting past; an obstacle.

barrister *noun* a lawyer who represents people in the higher lawcourts, also known as an advocate.

barrow[1] *noun* 1 a wheelbarrow. 2 a small cart pushed or pulled by hand.

barrow[2] *noun* a mound of earth over a prehistoric grave.

barter[1] *verb* trade by exchanging goods for other goods, not for money.

• USAGE: This word does not mean *to bargain.*

barter[2] *noun* the system of bartering.

basalt (*say* **bas**-awlt) *noun* a kind of dark volcanic rock.

base[1] *noun* 1 the lowest part of something; the part on which a thing stands. 2 a basis, *She used her family's history as a base for her novel.* 3 a headquarters, *The company has its base in Cape Town.* 4 each of the four corners that must be reached by a runner in baseball. 5 a substance that can combine with an acid to form a salt.

base[2] *verb* (**based, basing**) use something as a basis, *The story is based on facts.*

base[3] *adjective* 1 dishonourable, *base motives.* 2 not of great value, *base metals.* **basely** *adverb*, **baseness** *noun*

baseball *noun* an American ball game rather like softball.

basement *noun* a room or rooms below ground level.

bash[1] *verb* hit hard; attack violently.

bash[2] *noun* (*plural* **bashes**) 1 a hard hit. 2 (*informal*) a try, *Have a bash at it.*

bashful *adjective* shy and self-conscious. **bashfully** *adverb*

BASIC *abbreviation* Beginners' All-purpose Symbolic Instruction Code, a computer language designed to be easy to learn.

basic *adjective* forming a basis or starting-point; very important, *Bread is a basic food.* **basically** *adverb*

basilica (*say* ba-**zil**-ik-a) *noun* a large oblong hall or church with two rows of columns and an apse at one end.

basilisk (*say* **baz**-il-isk) *noun* a mythical reptile said to cause death by its glance or breath.

basin *noun* 1 a deep bowl. 2 a washbasin. 3 an enclosed area of water. 4 the area from which water drains into a river, *the Amazon basin.*

basis *noun* (*plural* **bases**) something to start from or add to; the main principle or ingredient.

bask *verb* sit or lie comfortably warming yourself.

basket *noun* a container for holding or carrying things, made of interwoven strips of flexible material or wire.

basketball *noun* a game rather like netball.

bass[1] (*say* bayss) *adjective* deep-sounding; of the lowest notes in music.

bass[2] *noun* (*plural* **basses**) 1 a male singer with a very deep voice. 2 a bass instrument or part.

bass[3] (*say* bas) *noun* (*plural* **bass**) a fish of the perch family.

basset *noun* a short-legged dog used for hunting hares.

bassoon *noun* a bass woodwind instrument.

bastard *noun* 1 an illegitimate child. 2 (*slang*) an unpleasant or difficult person or thing. **bastardy** *noun*

baste *verb* (**basted, basting**) 1 moisten meat with fat while it is cooking. 2 tack material or a hem.

bastion *noun* 1 a projecting part of a fortified building. 2 a centre of support for a cause, *a bastion of democracy.*

bat[1] *noun* 1 a wooden implement used to hit the ball in cricket, baseball, etc. 2 a batsman, *their opening bat.* **off your own bat** without help from other people.

bat[2] *verb* (**batted, batting**) 1 use a bat in cricket etc. 2 hit.

bat[3] *noun* a flying animal that looks like a mouse with wings.

batch *noun* (*plural* **batches**) a set of things or people dealt with together.

bated *adjective* **with bated breath** anxiously; hardly daring to speak.

bath[1] *noun* 1 washing your whole body while sitting in water. 2 a large container for water in which to wash your whole body; this water, *Your bath is getting cold.* 3 a liquid in which something is placed, *an acid bath.*

bath[2] *verb* wash in a bath.

bathe *verb* (**bathed, bathing**) 1 go swimming. 2 wash something gently. **bathe** *noun*, **bather** *noun*, **bathing-suit** *noun*

bathroom *noun* a room containing a bath.

baths *plural noun* 1 a building with rooms where people can bath. 2 a public swimming-bath.

baton *noun* a short stick, e.g. one used to conduct an orchestra.

B

batsman *noun* (*plural* **batsmen**) a player who uses a bat in cricket etc.

battalion *noun* an army unit containing two or more companies.

batten[1] *noun* a strip of wood or metal holding something in place.

batten[2] *verb* fasten with battens.

batten[3] *verb* feed or grow fat on something, *Pigeons battened on the crops.*

batter[1] *verb* hit hard and often.

batter[2] *noun* 1 a beaten mixture of flour, eggs, and milk, used for making pancakes etc. 2 a batsman in baseball.

battering-ram *noun* a heavy pole used to break down walls or gates.

battery *noun* (*plural* **batteries**) 1 a portable device for storing and supplying electricity. 2 a set of similar pieces of equipment; a group of large guns. 3 a series of cages in which poultry or animals are kept close together.

battle[1] *noun* 1 a fight between large organized forces. 2 a struggle. **battlefield** *noun*, **battleground** *noun*

battle[2] *verb* (**battled, battling**) fight; struggle.

battlements *plural noun* the top of a castle wall, often with gaps from which the defenders could fire at the enemy.

battleship *noun* a heavily armed warship.

batty *adjective* (*slang*) crazy.

bauble *noun* a showy but valueless thing.

baulk *verb* 1 shirk or jib at something; stop and refuse to go on, *The horse baulked at the fence.* 2 frustrate; prevent from doing or getting something.

bauxite *noun* the clay-like substance from which aluminium is obtained.

bawdy *adjective* (**bawdier, bawdiest**) funny but vulgar. **bawdiness** *noun*

bawl *verb* 1 shout. 2 cry noisily.

bay[1] *noun* 1 a place where the shore curves inwards. 2 an alcove.

bay window a window projecting from the main wall of a house.

bay[2] *noun* a kind of laurel-tree.

bay[3] *noun* the long deep cry of a hunting hound or other large dog.

at bay cornered but defiantly facing attackers, *a stag at bay*; prevented from coming near or causing harm, *We need laws to keep poverty at bay.*

bay[4] *adjective* reddish-brown.

bayete (*say* by-**ye**-te) *interjection* a Zulu greeting for a king or other important person.

bayonet *noun* a stabbing-blade attached to a rifle.

bazaar *noun* 1 a set of shops or stalls in an Oriental country. 2 a sale to raise money for a charity etc.

bazooka *noun* a portable weapon for firing anti-tank rockets.

BBC *abbreviation* British Broadcasting Corporation.

BC *abbreviation* before Christ (used of dates reckoned back from the birth of Jesus Christ).

be *verb* (**am, are, is; was, were; been, being**) 1 exist; occupy a position, *The shop is on the corner.* 2 happen; take place, *The wedding is tomorrow.* This verb is also used 1 to join subject and predicate, *He is my teacher.* 2 to form parts of other verbs, *It is raining. He was killed.*

have been have gone or come as a visitor etc., *We have been to Zimbabwe.*

be- *prefix* used to form verbs (as in *befriend, belittle*) or strengthen their meaning (as in *begrudge*).

beach[1] *noun* (*plural* **beaches**) the part of the sea-shore nearest to the water.

beach[2] *verb* come out of or cause to come out of the water onto the shore, *a beached whale.*

beacon *noun* a light (or formerly a fire) used as a signal.

bead *noun* 1 a small piece of a hard substance with a hole in it for threading with others on a string or wire, e.g. to make a necklace. 2 a drop of liquid.

beadle *noun* 1 an official with ceremonial duties in a church or college etc. 2 (*old use*) an official of a parish.

beady *adjective* like beads; small and bright, *beady eyes.*

beagle *noun* a small hound used for hunting hares.

beak *noun* the hard horny part of a bird's mouth.

beaker *noun* 1 a tall drinking-mug, often without a handle. 2 a glass container used for pouring liquids in a laboratory.

beam[1] *noun* 1 a long thick bar of wood or metal. 2 a ray or stream of light or other radiation. 3 a bright look on someone's face; a happy smile.

beam[2] *verb* 1 smile happily. 2 send out a beam of light or other radiation.

bean *noun* 1 a kind of plant with seeds growing in pods. 2 its seed or pod eaten as food. 3 the seed of coffee etc.

bear[1] *noun* a large heavy animal with thick fur.

bear[2] *verb* (**bore, borne, bearing**) 1 carry; support. 2 have a mark etc., *She still bears the scar.* 3 endure; tolerate, *I can't bear this pain.* 4 produce; give birth to, *She bore him two sons.* **bearer** *noun*

bearable *adjective* able to be borne; tolerable.

beard[1] *noun* hair on a man's chin. **bearded** *adjective*

beard[2] *verb* come face to face with a person and challenge him or her boldly.

bearing *noun* 1 the way a person stands, walks, behaves, etc. 2 relevance, *It has no bearing on this problem.* 3 the direction or position of one thing in relation to another. 4 a device for preventing friction in a machine, *ball-bearings.*

get your bearings work out where you are in relation to things.

beast *noun* 1 any large four-footed animal. 2 (*informal*) a person you dislike. **beastly** *adjective*

beat[1] *verb* (**beat, beaten, beating**) 1 hit often, especially with a stick. 2 shape or flatten something by beating it. 3 stir vigorously, *beat the eggs.* 4 make repeated movements, *The heart beats.* 5 do better than somebody; overcome. **beater** *noun*

beat[2] *noun* 1 a regular rhythm or stroke, *the beat of your heart.* 2 emphasis in rhythm; the strong rhythm of pop music. 3 a police officer's regular route.

beatific (*say* bee-a-**tif**-ik) *adjective* showing great happiness, *a beatific smile.*

beatify (*say* bee-at-i-fy) *verb* (**beatified, beatifying**) (in the Roman Catholic Church)

honour a person who has died by declaring that he or she is among the Blessed, as a step towards declaring that person a saint. **beatification** *noun*

beautiful *adjective* having beauty. **beautifully** *adverb*

beautify *verb* (**beautified, beautifying**) make beautiful. **beautification** *noun*

beauty *noun* (*plural* **beauties**) 1 a quality that gives pleasure to your senses or your mind. 2 a person or thing that has beauty.

beaver[1] *noun* an amphibious animal with soft brown fur and strong teeth.

beaver[2] *verb* work hard, *beavering away.*

becalmed *adjective* (in sailing) unable to move because there is no wind.

because *conjunction* for the reason that. **because of** for the reason of, *He limped because of his bad leg.*

beck *noun* **at someone's beck and call** always ready and waiting to do what he or she asks.

beckon *verb* make a sign to a person asking him or her to come.

become *verb* (**became, become, becoming**) 1 come or grow to be; start being, *It became dark.* 2 be suitable for; make a person look attractive, *Her new hairstyle becomes her.*

become of happen to, *What became of it?*

bed *noun* 1 a thing to sleep or rest on; a piece of furniture with a mattress and coverings. 2 a piece of a garden where plants are grown. 3 the bottom of the sea or of a river. 4 a flat base; a foundation, *a bed of concrete.* 5 a layer of rock or soil.

bedclothes *plural noun* sheets, blankets, etc.

bedding *noun* mattresses and bedclothes.

bedlam *noun* uproar.

Bedouin (*say* **bed**-oo-in) *noun* (*plural* **Bedouin**) a member of an Arab people living in tents in the desert.

bedpan *noun* a container for use as a lavatory by a bedridden person.

bedraggled (*say* bid-**rag**-eld) *adjective* very untidy; wet and dirty.

bedridden *adjective* too weak to get out of bed.

bedrock *noun* solid rock beneath soil.

bedroom *noun* a room for sleeping in.

bed-sitting-room *noun* a room used for both living and sleeping in.

bedspread *noun* a covering spread over a bed during the day.

bedstead *noun* the framework of a bed.

bedtime *noun* the time for going to bed.

bee *noun* a stinging insect with four wings that makes honey.

beech *noun* (*plural* **beeches**) a tree with smooth bark and glossy leaves.

beef *noun* meat from an ox, bull, or cow.

beefy *adjective* having a solid muscular body. **beefiness** *noun*

beehive *noun* a box or other container for bees to live in.

beeline *noun* **make a beeline for** go straight or quickly towards something.

beer *noun* an alcoholic drink made from malt and hops. **beery** *adjective*

beerhall *noun* (*old use*) a shebeen.

beeswax *noun* a yellow substance produced by bees, used for polishing wood.

beet *noun* (*plural* **beet** or **beets**) a plant with a thick root used as a vegetable or for making sugar.

beetle *noun* an insect with hard shiny wing-covers.

beetling *adjective* prominent; over-hanging, *beetling brows.*

beetroot *noun* (*plural* **beetroot**) the crimson root of beet used as a vegetable.

befall *verb* (**befell, befallen, befalling**) (*formal*) happen; happen to someone.

befitting *adjective* suitable.

before[1] *adverb* at an earlier time, *Have you been here before?*

before[2] *preposition & conjunction* 1 earlier than, *I was here before you!* 2 ahead of; in front of, *leg before wicket.*

beforehand *adverb* earlier; in readiness.

befriend *verb* act as a friend to someone.

beg *verb* (**begged, begging**) 1 ask to be given money, food, etc. 2 ask earnestly or humbly or formally.

beg the question argue in an illogical way by relying on the result that you are trying to prove.

go begging be available.

I beg your pardon I apologize; I did not hear what you said.

beget *verb* (**begot, begotten, begetting**) (*old use*) 1 be the father of someone. 2 produce, *War begets misery.*

beggar *noun* 1 a person who lives by begging. 2 (*informal*) a person, *You lucky beggar!* **beggary** *noun*

begin *verb* (**began, begun, beginning**) 1 do the earliest or first part of something; start speaking. 2 come into existence, *The problem began last year.* 3 have something as its first element, *The word begins with B.*

beginner *noun* a person who is just beginning to learn a subject.

begone *verb* (*old use*) go away immediately, *Begone dull care!*

begonia (*say* big-**oh**-nee-a) *noun* a garden plant with brightly coloured flowers.

begot *past tense* of **beget**.

begrudge *verb* (**begrudged, begrudging**) grudge.

beguile (*say* big-**I'll**) *verb* (**beguiled, beguiling**) 1 amuse. 2 deceive, *They were beguiled into giving him large sums of money.*

behalf *noun* **on behalf of** for a person; done to help a person or charity etc. **on my behalf** for me.

behave *verb* (**behaved, behaving**) 1 act in a particular way, *They behaved badly.* 2 show good manners, *Behave yourself!* **behaviour** *noun*, **behavioural** *adjective*

behead *verb* cut the head from; execute a person in this way.

behest *noun* (*formal*) a command.

behind[1] *adverb* 1 at or to the back; at a place people have left, *Don't leave it behind.* 2 not making good progress; late, *I'm behind with my rent.*

behind[2] *preposition* 1 at or to the back of; on the further side of. 2 having made less progress than, *He is behind the others in maths.* 3 supporting; causing, *What is behind all this trouble?*

behind a person's back kept secret from him or her deceitfully.

behind the times out of date.

behind[3] *noun* (*informal*) a person's bottom.

behindhand *adverb & adjective* late.

behold *verb* (**beheld, beholding**) (*old use*) see. **beholder** *noun*

beholden *adjective* owing thanks; indebted, *We are greatly beholden to you.*

behove *verb* (**behoved, behoving**) be a person's duty, *It behoves you to be loyal.*

beige (*say* bay*zh*) *noun* & *adjective* light fawn colour.

being *noun* 1 existence. 2 a creature, *a strange being from another planet.*

belated *adjective* coming very late or too late. **belatedly** *adverb*

belch *verb* 1 send out wind from your stomach through your mouth noisily. 2 send out fire or smoke etc. from an opening, *The volcano belched out smoke and ashes.* **belch** *noun*

beleaguered (*say* bil-**eeg**-erd) *adjective* besieged; oppressed.

belfry *noun* (*plural* **belfries**) a tower or part of a tower in which bells hang.

belief *noun* 1 believing. 2 something a person believes.

believe *verb* (**believed, believing**) think that something is true or that someone is telling the truth. **believable** *adjective*, **believer** *noun* **believe in** think that something exists or is good or can be relied on.

belittle *verb* (**belittled, belittling**) make something seem of little value, *Do not belittle their success.* **belittlement** *noun*

bell *noun* 1 a cup-shaped metal instrument that makes a ringing sound when struck by the clapper hanging inside it; any device that makes a ringing or buzzing sound to attract attention. 2 a bell-shaped object.

belle *noun* a beautiful woman.

bellicose (*say* **bel**-ik-ohs) *adjective* eager to fight.

belligerent (*say* bil-**ij**-er-ent) *adjective* 1 aggressive; eager to fight. 2 fighting; engaged in a war. **belligerently** *adverb*, **belligerence** *noun*

bellow¹ *noun* 1 the loud deep sound made by a bull or other large animal. 2 a deep shout.

bellow² *verb* give a bellow; shout.

bellows *plural noun* a device for pumping air into a fire, organ-pipes, etc.

belly *noun* (*plural* **bellies**) the abdomen; the stomach.

belong *verb* have a proper place, *The pans belong in the kitchen.* **belong to** be the property of; be a member of, *We belong to the same club.*

belongings *plural noun* a person's possessions.

beloved *adjective* dearly loved.

below¹ *adverb* at or to a lower position; underneath, *There's fire down below.*

below² *preposition* lower than; under, *The temperature was ten degrees below zero.*

belt¹ *noun* 1 a strip of cloth or leather etc. worn round the waist. 2 a band of flexible material used in machinery. 3 a long narrow area, *a belt of rain.*

belt² *verb* 1 put a belt round something. 2 (*slang*) hit. 3 (*slang*) rush along. **belt up** put on a seat belt; (*slang*) be quiet.

bemused *adjective* 1 bewildered. 2 lost in thought.

bench *noun* (*plural* **benches**) 1 a long seat. 2 a long table for working at, *a work bench.* 3 the seat where judges or magistrates sit; the judges or magistrates hearing a lawsuit.

bend¹ *verb* (**bent, bending**) 1 change from being straight. 2 turn downwards; stoop, *She bent to pick it up.*

bend² *noun* a place where something bends; a curve or turn.

bene- (*say* ben-ee) *prefix* well (as in *benefit, benediction*).

beneath¹ *preposition* 1 under. 2 unworthy of, *Cheating is beneath you.*

beneath² *adverb* underneath.

benediction *noun* a blessing.

benefactor *noun* a person who gives money or other help.

beneficial *adjective* having a good or helpful effect; advantageous.

beneficiary (*say* ben-if-**ish**-er-ee) *noun* (*plural* **beneficiaries**) a person who receives benefits, especially from a will.

benefit¹ *noun* 1 something that is helpful or profitable. 2 a payment to which a person is entitled from government funds or from an insurance policy.

benefit[2] *verb* (**benefited, benefiting**)
1 do good to a person or thing. 2 receive a benefit.

benevolent *adjective* 1 kind and helpful. 2 formed for charitable purposes, *a benevolent fund*. **benevolently** *adverb*, **benevolence** *noun*

benign (*say* bin-I'n) *adjective* 1 kindly, *a benign smile*. 2 favourable. 3 (of a disease) mild, not malignant. **benignly** *adverb*

benignant (*say* bin-ig-nant) *adjective* kindly.

benison *noun* (*old use*) a blessing.

bent[1] *adjective* curved; crooked.
bent on intending to do something.

bent[2] *noun* a talent for something.

benzene *noun* a substance obtained from coal-tar and used as a solvent, motor fuel, and in the manufacture of plastics.

benzine *noun* a spirit obtained from petroleum and used in dry cleaning.

bequeath *verb* leave something to a person, especially in a will.

bequest *noun* something bequeathed.

bereaved *adjective* deprived of a relative or friend who has died. **bereavement** *noun*

bereft *adjective* deprived of something.

beret (*say* bair-ay) *noun* a round flat cap.

berg *noun* a mountain.
berg wind a hot dry wind.

beriberi (*say* berry-berry) *noun* a tropical disease caused by a vitamin deficiency.

berry *noun* (*plural* **berries**) any small round juicy fruit without a stone.

berserk (*say* ber-**serk**) *adjective*
go berserk become uncontrollably violent.

berth[1] *noun* 1 a sleeping-place on a ship or train. 2 a place where a ship can moor.
give a wide berth keep at a safe distance from a person or thing.

berth[2] *verb* moor in a berth.

beryl *noun* a pale-green precious stone.

beseech *verb* (**besought, beseeching**) ask earnestly; implore.

beset *verb* (**beset, besetting**) surround, *They are beset with problems*.

beside *preposition* 1 by the side of; near. 2 compared with.
be beside himself or **herself** etc. be very excited or upset.

besides *preposition* & *adverb* in addition to; also, *Who came besides you? And besides, it's the wrong colour.*

besiege *verb* (**besieged, besieging**)
1 surround a place with troops in order to capture it. 2 crowd round, *Fans besieged the pop star after the concert.*

besotted *adjective* infatuated.

besought *past tense* of **beseech**.

best[1] *adjective* most excellent.
best man the bridegroom's chief attendant at a wedding.

best[2] *adverb* 1 in the best way; most. 2 most usefully; most wisely, *We had best go.*

bestial (*say* **best**-ee-al) *adjective* of or like a beast; cruel. **bestiality** *noun*

bestow *verb* present. **bestowal** *noun*

bet[1] *noun* 1 an agreement that you will pay money etc. if you are wrong in forecasting the result of a race etc. 2 the money that you agree to pay in this way.

bet[2] *verb* (**bet** or **betted, betting**) 1 make a bet. 2 (*informal*) think most likely; predict, *I bet he will forget.*

beta (*say* **beet**-a) *noun* the second letter of the Greek alphabet (= b), written B, β.

betide *verb* **woe betide you** trouble will come to you.

betoken *verb* be a sign of.

betray *verb* 1 be disloyal to a person or country etc. 2 reveal something that should have been kept secret. **betrayal** *noun*, **betrayer** *noun*

betrothed *adjective* (*formal*) engaged to be married. **betroth** *verb*, **betrothal** *noun*

better[1] *adjective* 1 more excellent; more satisfactory. 2 recovered from illness.

better[2] *adverb* 1 in a better way; more, *She sings better than I do.* 2 more usefully; more wisely, *We had better go.*

better[3] *verb* 1 improve something, *We hope to better the conditions of the animals.* 2 do better than, *This achievement cannot be bettered.* **betterment** *noun*

between *preposition* & *adverb* 1 within two or more given limits, *between the walls.* 2 connecting two or more people, places, or things, *The train runs between Durban and Ixopo.* 3 shared by, *Divide this money between you.* 4 separating; comparing,

Can you tell the difference between them?
● USAGE: The preposition *between* needs the objective form of a pronoun (*me, her, him, them,* or *us*) after it. The expression 'between you and I' is incorrect; say *between you and me.*

betwixt *preposition* & *adverb* (*old use*) between.

bevel *verb* (**bevelled, bevelling**) give a sloping edge to something.

beverage *noun* any kind of drink.

bevy *noun* (*plural* **bevies**) a large group.

bewail *verb* mourn for something.

beware *verb* be careful, *Beware of pickpockets.*

bewilder *verb* puzzle someone hopelessly. **bewilderment** *noun*

bewitch *verb* 1 put a magic spell on someone. 2 delight someone very much.

beyond *preposition* & *adverb* 1 further than; further on, *Don't go beyond the boundary.* 2 outside the range of; too difficult for, *The problem is beyond me.*

bhayi (*say* by-ee) *noun* a coarsely-woven cotton cloth.

bi- *prefix* two (as in *bicycle*); twice (as in *biannual*).

biannual *adjective* happening twice a year. **biannually** *adverb*
● USAGE: Do not confuse this word with *biennial.*

bias *noun* (*plural* **biases**) 1 a feeling or influence for or against someone or something; a prejudice, *a bias in favour of classical music.* 2 an edge cut diagonally across the threads of a piece of cloth, *The skirt is cut on the bias.* **biased** *adjective*

biathlon *noun* a competition in two athletic events (e.g. cycling and running).

bib *noun* 1 a cloth or covering put under a baby's chin during meals. 2 the part of an apron above the waist.

Bible *noun* the sacred book of the Jews (the Old Testament) and of the Christians (the Old and New Testament).

biblical *adjective* of or in the Bible.

bibliography (*say* bib-lee-**og**-ra-fee) *noun* (*plural* **bibliographies**) 1 a list of books about a subject or by a particular author. 2 the study of books and their history.

bibliographical *adjective*

bicarbonate *noun* a kind of carbonate.

bicentenary (*say* by-sen-**teen**-er-ee) *noun* a 200th anniversary. **bicentennial** (*say* by-sen-**ten**-ee-al) *adjective*

biceps (*say* **by**-seps) *noun* the large muscle at the front of the arm above the elbow.

bicker *verb* quarrel over unimportant things; squabble.

bicuspid *noun* a tooth with two points.

bicycle *noun* a two-wheeled vehicle driven by pedals. **bicyclist** *noun*

bid[1] *noun* 1 the offer of an amount you are willing to pay for something, especially at an auction. 2 an attempt, *a bid for freedom.*

bid[2] *verb* (**bid, bidding**) make a bid. **bidder** *noun*

bid[3] *verb* (**bid** (or *old use* **bade**), **bid** or **bidden, bidding**) 1 command, *Do as you are bid* or *bidden.* 2 say as a greeting or farewell, *bidding them good night.*

bidding *noun* a command.

bide *verb* (**bided, biding**) wait.

bidet (*say* **bee**-day) *noun* a low washbasin to sit on for washing the lower part of the body.

biennial[1] (*say* by-en-ee-al) *adjective* 1 lasting for two years. 2 happening every second year. **biennially** *adverb*

biennial[2] *noun* a plant that lives for two years, flowering and dying in the second year.

bier (*say as* beer) *noun* a movable stand on which a coffin or a dead body is placed before it is buried.

bifocal (*say* by-**foh**-kal) *adjective* (of spectacle lenses) made in two sections, with the upper part for looking at distant objects and the lower part for reading.

bifocals *plural noun* bifocal spectacles.

big *adjective* (**bigger, biggest**) 1 large. 2 important, *the big match.* 3 more grown-up; elder, *my big sister.*

bigamy (*say* **big**-a-mee) *noun* the crime of marrying a person when you are already married to someone else. **bigamous** *adjective*, **bigamist** *noun*

bight *noun* 1 a loop of rope. 2 a long inward curve in a coast.

bigot *noun* a bigoted person.

bigoted *adjective* narrow-minded and intolerant. **bigotry** *noun*

bike *noun* (*informal*) a bicycle or motor cycle.

bikini *noun* (*plural* **bikinis**) a woman's two-piece swimming-costume.

bilateral *adjective* 1 of or on two sides. 2 of two people or groups, *a bilateral agreement.*

bile *noun* a bitter liquid produced by the liver, helping to digest fats.

bilge *noun* 1 the bottom of a ship; the water that collects there. 2 (*slang*) nonsense; worthless ideas.

bilharzia (*say* bil-**hart**-see-a) *noun* a disease caused by a parasite.

bilingual (*say* by-**ling**-wal) *adjective* 1 written in two languages. 2 able to speak two languages.

bilious *adjective* feeling sick; sickly. **biliousness** *noun*

bilk *verb* cheat someone by not paying them what you owe; defraud.

bill[1] *noun* 1 a written statement of charges for goods or services that have been supplied. 2 a poster. 3 a list; a programme of entertainment, *a horror double bill.* 4 the draft of a proposed law to be discussed by Parliament. 5 (*American*) a banknote. **bill of fare** a menu.

bill[2] *noun* a bird's beak.

billabong *noun* (in Australia) a backwater of a river.

billet[1] *noun* a lodging for troops, especially in a private house.

billet[2] *verb* (**billeted, billeting**) house someone in a billet.

billiards *noun* a game in which three balls are struck with cues on a cloth-covered table (**billiard-table**).

billion *noun* 1 a thousand million (1 000 000 000). 2 a million million (1 000 000 000 000). **billionth** *adjective* & *noun*
 • USAGE: Although the word originally meant a million million, nowadays it usually means a thousand million.

billow[1] *noun* a huge wave.

billow[2] *verb* rise or roll like waves.

billy *noun* (*plural* **billies**) a pot with a lid, used by campers etc. as a kettle or cooking-pot. **billycan** *noun*

billy-goat *noun* a male goat. (Compare *nanny-goat.*)

biltong *noun* dried and salted meat.

bimbo *noun* (*plural* **bimbos** or **bimboes**) (*slang*) an attractive but unintelligent young woman.

bin *noun* a large or deep container.

binary (*say* by-ner-ee) *adjective* involving sets of two; consisting of two parts. **binary digit** either of the two digits (0 and 1) used in the system of numbers known as binary notation or the binary scale.

bind[1] *verb* (**bound, binding**) 1 fasten material round something, *bind up a wound.* 2 fasten the pages of a book into a cover. 3 tie up; tie together, *The hostages were bound and gagged.* 4 make somebody agree to do something; oblige, *bound to secrecy.* **binder** *noun*
bind a person over make him or her agree not to break the law.

bind[2] *noun* (*informal*) a nuisance; a bore.

binge *noun* (*informal*) a lively outing or feast.

bingo *noun* a game using cards on which numbered squares are covered up as the numbers are called out at random.

binoculars *plural noun* a device with lenses for both eyes, making distant objects seem nearer.

bio- *prefix* life (as in *biology*).

biochemistry *noun* the study of the chemical composition and processes of living things. **biochemical** *adjective*, **biochemist** *noun*

biodegradable (*say* by-oh-di-**grayd**-a-bul) *adjective* (of substances) that can be made to rot by bacteria.

biography (*say* by-**og**-ra-fee) *noun* the story of a person's life. **biographical** *adjective*, **biographer** *noun*

biology *noun* the study of the life and structure of living things. **biological** *adjective*, **biologist** *noun*

biome (*say* by-ohm) *noun* a large area where certain plants and animals live, *the fynbos biome.*

bionic (*say* by-on-ik) *adjective* (of a person

or parts of the body) operated by electronic devices.

biopsy (*say* **by**-op-see) *noun* (*plural* **biopsies**) examination of tissue from a living body.

bioscope *noun* (*informal*) a cinema.

biotic (*say* by-**ot**-ik) *adjective* relating to life or to living things; of biological origin, *Plant diseases are biotic factors in a plant's environment.*

bipartite *adjective* having two parts; involving two groups, *a bipartite agreement.*

biped (*say* **by**-ped) *noun* a two-footed animal.

biplane *noun* an aeroplane with two sets of wings, one above the other.

birch *noun* (*plural* **birches**) a deciduous tree with slender branches.

bird *noun* 1 an animal with feathers, two wings, and two legs. 2 (*slang*) a person. 3 (*slang*) a young woman.
bird's-eye view a view from above.

birdie *noun* 1 (*informal*) a bird. 2 a score of one stroke under par for a hole at golf.

biriani (*say* biri-**ah**-nee) *noun* a rice dish with chicken, meat, or vegetables.

birth *noun* 1 the process by which a baby or young animal comes out from its mother's body. 2 origin; parentage, *He was Namibian by birth but later took South African nationality.*
birth control ways of avoiding conceiving a baby.
birth rate the number of children born in one year for every 1 000 people.

birthday *noun* the anniversary of the day a person was born.

birthmark *noun* a coloured mark that has been on a person's skin since birth.

birthright *noun* a right or privilege to which a person is entitled through being born into a particular family (especially as the eldest son) or country.

biscuit *noun* a small flat piece of pastry baked crisp.

bisect (*say* by-**sekt**) *verb* divide into two equal parts. **bisection** *noun*, **bisector** *noun*

bishop *noun* 1 an important member of the clergy in charge of all the churches in a city or district. 2 a chess piece shaped like a bishop's mitre.

bishopric *noun* the position or diocese of a bishop.

bismuth *noun* 1 a greyish-white metal. 2 a compound of this used in medicine.

bison (*say* **by**-son) *noun* (*plural* **bison**) a wild ox found in North America and Europe, with a large shaggy head.

bit[1] *noun* 1 a small piece or amount of something. 2 the metal part of a horse's bridle that is put into its mouth. 3 the part of a tool that cuts or grips things when twisted.
a bit a short distance or time, *Wait a bit*; slightly, *I'm a bit worried.*
bit by bit gradually.

bit[2] *past tense* of **bite**.

bit[3] *noun* (in computers) a unit of information expressed as a choice between two possibilities.

bitch *noun* (*plural* **bitches**) 1 a female dog, fox, or wolf. 2 (*slang*) an unpleasant or difficult person or thing. **bitchy** *adjective*

bite[1] *verb* (**bit, bitten, biting**) 1 cut or take with your teeth. 2 penetrate; sting. 3 accept bait, *The fish are biting.*
bite the dust fall wounded and die.

bite[2] *noun* 1 biting. 2 a mark or spot made by biting, *an insect bite.* 3 a snack, *have a bite to eat.*

bitter *adjective* 1 tasting sharp, not sweet. 2 feeling or causing mental pain or resentment, *a bitter disappointment.* 3 very cold.
bitterly *adverb*, **bitterness** *noun*

bittern *noun* a marsh bird, the male of which makes a booming cry.

bitumen (*say* **bit**-yoo-min) *noun* a black substance used for covering roads etc.
bituminous (*say* bit-**yoo**-min-us) *adjective*

bivalve *noun* a shellfish (e.g. an oyster) that has a shell with two hinged parts.

bivouac[1] (*say* **biv**-oo-ak) *noun* a temporary camp without tents.

bivouac[2] *verb* (**bivouacked, bivouacking**) camp in a bivouac.

bizarre (*say* biz-**ar**) *adjective* very odd in appearance or effect.

blab *verb* (**blabbed, blabbing**) tell tales; let out a secret.

black¹ *noun* the very darkest colour, like coal or soot.

black² *adjective* 1 of the colour black. 2 very dirty. 3 dismal; not hopeful, *The outlook is black.* 4 hostile; disapproving, *He gave me a black look.* **blackly** *adverb*, **blackness** *noun*

black belt the highest grade in judo, karate, etc.

black box an automatic device for recording details of the flight of an aircraft.

black coffee coffee without milk.

Black Consciousness a movement to promote the dignity and rights of black people.

black eye an eye with a bruise round it.

black hole a region in outer space with such a strong gravitational field that no matter or radiation can escape from it.

black magic evil magic.

black market illegal trading.

black sheep one bad character in a well-behaved group.

black spot a dangerous place.

black widow a poisonous spider.

black³ *verb* make a thing black.

black out cover windows etc. so that no light can penetrate; faint, lose consciousness. **black-out** *noun*

blackberry *noun* (*plural* **blackberries**) a sweet black berry.

blackbird *noun* a European songbird, the male of which is black.

blackboard *noun* a dark board for writing on with chalk.

blacken *verb* make or become black.

blackguard (*say* **blag**-erd) *noun* a scoundrel.

blackhead *noun* a small black spot in the skin.

blackjack *noun* a weed with black spiky seeds.

blackleg *noun* a person who works while fellow workers are on strike.

blacklist *verb* put someone on a list of those who are disapproved of.

blackmail *verb* demand money etc. from someone by threats. **blackmail** *noun*, **blackmailer** *noun*

blacksmith *noun* a person who makes and repairs iron things, especially one who makes and fits horseshoes.

bladder *noun* 1 the bag-like part of the body in which urine collects. 2 the inflatable bag inside a football.

blade *noun* 1 the flat cutting-part of a knife, sword, axe, etc. 2 the flat wide part of an oar, spade, propeller, etc. 3 a flat narrow leaf, *blades of grass.* 4 a broad flat bone, *shoulder-blade.*

blame¹ *verb* (**blamed, blaming**) 1 say that somebody or something has caused what is wrong, *They blamed me.* 2 find fault with someone, *We can't blame them for wanting a holiday.*

blame² *noun* blaming; responsibility for what is wrong.

blameless *adjective* deserving no blame; innocent.

blanch *verb* make or become white or pale, *He blanched with fear.*

bland *adjective* 1 having a mild flavour, not a strong one. 2 gentle and casual; not irritating or stimulating, *a bland manner.* **blandly** *adverb*, **blandness** *noun*

blandishments *plural noun* flattering or coaxing words.

blank¹ *adjective* 1 not written or printed on; unmarked. 2 without interest or expression, *a blank look.* 3 without an opening, *a blank wall.* **blankly** *adverb*, **blankness** *noun*

blank cartridge a cartridge that makes a noise but does not fire a bullet.

blank cheque a cheque with the amount not yet filled in.

blank verse poetry without rhymes.

blank² *noun* 1 an empty space. 2 a blank cartridge.

blanket¹ *noun* 1 a warm cloth covering used on a bed etc. 2 any thick soft covering, *a blanket of snow.*

blanket² *adjective* covering a wide range of conditions etc., *a blanket agreement.*

blare *verb* (**blared, blaring**) make a loud harsh sound. **blare** *noun*

blasé (*say* **blah**-zay) *adjective* bored or unimpressed by things because you are used to them.

blaspheme (*say* blas-**feem**) *verb*

(**blasphemed, blaspheming**) utter blasphemies.

blasphemy (*say* **blas**-fim-ee) *noun* (*plural* **blasphemies**) irreverent talk about sacred things. **blasphemous** *adjective*

blast[1] *noun* 1 a strong rush of wind or air. 2 a loud noise, *the blast of the trumpets.*

blast[2] *verb* blow up with explosives. **blast off** launch by the firing of rockets. **blast-off** *noun*

blast-furnace *noun* a furnace for smelting ore, with hot air driven in.

blatant (*say* **blay**-tant) *adjective* very obvious, *a blatant lie.* **blatantly** *adverb*

blaze[1] *noun* a very bright flame, fire, or light.

blaze[2] *verb* (**blazed, blazing**) 1 burn or shine brightly. 2 show great feeling, *He was blazing with anger.*

blaze[3] *noun* 1 a white mark on an animal's face. 2 a mark chipped in the bark of a tree to show a route.

blaze[4] *verb* (**blazed, blazing**) mark a tree or route by cutting blazes. **blaze a trail** show the way for others to follow.

blazer *noun* a kind of jacket, often with a badge or in the colours of a school or team etc.

bleach[1] *verb* make or become white.

bleach[2] *noun* (*plural* **bleaches**) a substance used to bleach things.

bleak *adjective* 1 bare and cold, *a bleak hillside.* 2 dreary; miserable, *a bleak future.* **bleakly** *adverb*, **bleakness** *noun*

bleary *adjective* watery and not seeing clearly, *bleary eyes.* **blearily** *adverb*

bleat[1] *noun* the cry of a lamb, goat, or calf.

bleat[2] *verb* make a bleat.

bleed *verb* (**bled, bleeding**) 1 lose blood. 2 draw blood or fluid from.

bleep *noun* a short high sound used as a signal. **bleep** *verb*

blemish *noun* (*plural* **blemishes**) a flaw; a mark that spoils a thing's appearance. **blemish** *verb*

blench *verb* flinch.

blend[1] *verb* mix smoothly or easily. **blender** *noun*

blend[2] *noun* a mixture.

blesbok *noun* a reddish-brown antelope with a white blaze on its face.

bless *verb* 1 make sacred or holy. 2 bring God's favour on a person or thing.

blessing *noun* 1 a prayer that blesses a person or thing; being blessed. 2 something that people are glad of.

blight[1] *noun* 1 a disease that withers plants. 2 a bad or harmful influence, *The bad weather put a blight on our holiday.*

blight[2] *verb* 1 affect with blight. 2 spoil something.

blind[1] *adjective* 1 without the ability to see. 2 without any thought or understanding, *blind obedience.* 3 (in cookery) without a filling, *bake the pastry cases blind.* 4 (of a tube, passage, or road) closed at one end. **blindly** *adverb*, **blindness** *noun*

blind date an arrangement to meet someone socially whom you have not met before.

blind spot an area which a motorist cannot see; a subject about which someone is ignorant or cannot be balanced in his or her opinion.

blind[2] *verb* make a person blind.

blind[3] *noun* 1 a screen for a window. 2 a deception; something used to hide the truth, *His journey was a blind.*

blindfold *verb* cover someone's eyes with a cloth etc.

blink *verb* shut and open your eyes rapidly. **blink** *noun*

blinkers *plural noun* leather pieces fixed on a bridle to prevent a horse from seeing sideways. **blinkered** *adjective*

bliss *noun* perfect happiness. **blissful** *adjective*, **blissfully** *adverb*

blister *noun* a swelling like a bubble, especially on skin. **blister** *verb*

blithe *adjective* casual and carefree. **blithely** *adverb*

blitz *noun* (*plural* **blitzes**) a sudden violent attack.

blizzard *noun* a severe snowstorm.

bloated *adjective* swollen by fat, gas, or liquid.

blob *noun* a small round mass of something, *blobs of paint.*

block[1] *noun* 1 a solid piece of something. 2 an obstruction, *a block in the drain.*

3 a large building divided into flats or offices. **4** a group of buildings, *go for a walk around the block.*

block letters plain capital letters.

block[2] *verb* obstruct; prevent from moving or being used. **blockage** *noun*

blockade[1] *noun* the blocking of a city or port etc. in order to prevent people and goods from going in or out.

blockade[2] *verb* (**blockaded, blockading**) set up a blockade of a place.

blond (also **blonde**) *adjective* fair-haired; fair.

blonde *noun* a fair-haired girl or woman.

blood *noun* **1** the red liquid that flows through veins and arteries. **2** family relationship; ancestry, *He is of royal blood.*

blood sport a sport involving the wounding or killing of animals.

in cold blood deliberately and cruelly.

blood-bath *noun* a massacre.

bloodhound *noun* a large dog formerly used to track people by their scent.

bloodshed *noun* the killing or wounding of people.

bloodshot *adjective* (of eyes) streaked with red.

bloodthirsty *adjective* eager for bloodshed.

blood-vessel *noun* a tube carrying blood in the body; an artery, vein, or capillary.

bloody *adjective* (**bloodier, bloodiest**) blood-stained; with much bloodshed.

bloody-minded *adjective* deliberately awkward and not helpful.

bloom[1] *noun* **1** a flower. **2** the fine powder on fresh ripe grapes etc.

bloom[2] *verb* produce flowers.

blossom[1] *noun* a flower or mass of flowers, especially on a fruit-tree.

blossom[2] *verb* **1** produce flowers. **2** develop into something, *She blossomed into a fine singer.*

blot[1] *noun* **1** a spot of ink. **2** a flaw or fault; something ugly, *a blot on the landscape.*

blot[2] *verb* (**blotted, blotting**) **1** make a blot or blots on something. **2** dry with blotting-paper.

blot out cross out thickly; obscure, *Fog blotted out the view.*

blotch *noun* (*plural* **blotches**) an untidy patch of colour. **blotchy** *adjective*

blotter *noun* a pad of blotting-paper; a holder for blotting-paper.

blotting-paper *noun* absorbent paper for soaking up ink from writing.

bloubok *noun* a small bluish-grey antelope.

blouse *noun* a garment like a shirt.

blow[1] *verb* (**blew, blown, blowing**) **1** send out a current of air. **2** move in or with a current of air, *Her hat blew off.* **3** make or sound something by blowing, *blow bubbles; blow the whistle.* **4** melt with too strong an electric current, *A fuse has blown.* **5** (*slang*) damn, *Blow you!*

blow up inflate; explode; shatter by an explosion.

blow[2] *noun* the action of blowing.

blow[3] *noun* **1** a hard knock or hit. **2** a shock; a disaster, *a shattering blow to one's pride.*

blowlamp *noun* a portable device for directing a very hot flame at something.

blowpipe *noun* a tube for sending out a dart or pellet by blowing.

blubber *noun* the fat of whales.

bludgeon (*say* **bluj**-on) *noun* a short stick with a thickened end, used as a weapon.

blue[1] *noun* the colour of a cloudless sky.

out of the blue unexpectedly.

blue[2] *adjective* **1** of the colour blue. **2** unhappy; depressed. **3** indecent; obscene, *blue films.* **blueness** *noun*

blue blood aristocratic family.

blue-collar (of people) doing practical work or work requiring physical labour. (Compare *white-collar.*)

bluebell *noun* a plant with blue bell-shaped flowers.

bluebottle *noun* a large bluish fly.

bluegum *noun* a eucalyptus tree of various kinds.

blueprint *noun* a detailed plan.

blues *noun* a slow sad jazz song or tune.

the blues a very sad feeling; depression.

bluff[1] *verb* deceive someone, especially by pretending to be able to do something.

bluff[2] *noun* bluffing; a threat that you make but do not intend to carry out.

bluff[3] *adjective* frank and hearty in manner. **bluffness** *noun*

bluff[4] *noun* a cliff with a broad steep front.

bluish *adjective*　rather blue.

blunder[1] *noun*　a stupid mistake.

blunder[2] *verb*　1 make a blunder. 2 move clumsily and uncertainly.

blunderbuss *noun*　an old type of gun that fired many balls in one shot.

blunt[1] *adjective*　1 not sharp. 2 speaking in plain terms; straightforward, *a blunt refusal.* **bluntly** *adverb,* **bluntness** *noun*

blunt[2] *verb*　make a thing blunt.

blur[1] *verb*　(**blurred, blurring**) make or become indistinct or smeared.

blur[2] *noun*　an indistinct appearance; a smear.

blurt *verb*　say something suddenly or tactlessly, *He blurted it out.*

blush[1] *verb*　become red in the face because you are ashamed or embarrassed.

blush[2] *noun*　(*plural* **blushes**) reddening in the face.

bluster *verb*　1 blow in gusts; be windy. 2 talk threateningly. **blustery** *adjective*

BMX *abbreviation*　a kind of bicycle for use in racing on a dirt track.

boa (*say* boh-a) *noun*　(also **boa constrictor**) a large South American snake that squeezes its prey so as to suffocate it.

boar *noun*　1 a wild pig. 2 a male pig.

board[1] *noun*　1 a flat piece of wood. 2 a flat piece of stiff material, e.g. a chessboard. 3 daily meals supplied in return for payment or work, *board and lodging.* 4 a committee, *the school board.* **on board** on or in a ship, aircraft, etc.

board[2] *verb*　1 go on board a ship etc. 2 give or get meals and accommodation. **board up** block with fixed boards.

boarder *noun*　1 a pupil who lives at a boarding-school during the term. 2 a lodger who receives meals.

boarding-house *noun*　a house where people obtain board and lodging for payment.

boarding-school *noun*　a school where pupils live during the term.

boardsailing *noun*　surfing on a board that has a sail fixed to it.

boast[1] *verb*　1 speak with great pride and try to impress people. 2 have something to be proud of, *The town boasts a fine park.*

boaster *noun,* **boastful** *adjective,* **boastfully** *adverb*

boast[2] *noun*　a boastful statement.

boat *noun*　a hollow structure built to travel on water and carry people etc. **in the same boat** in the same situation; suffering the same difficulties.

boater *noun*　a hard flat straw hat.

boating *noun*　going out in a boat (especially a rowing-boat) for pleasure.

boatswain (*say* boh-sun) *noun*　a ship's officer in charge of equipment and the crew.

bob *verb*　(**bobbed, bobbing**) move quickly, especially up and down.

bobbin *noun*　a small spool holding thread or wire in a machine.

bobble *noun*　a small round ornament, often made of wool.

bobotie *noun*　curried mince with a savoury custard topping.

bob-sleigh (also **bob-sled**) *noun*　a sledge with two sets of runners.

bode *verb*　(**boded, boding**) be a sign or omen of what is to come, *It bodes well.*

bodice *noun*　the upper part of a dress.

bodkin *noun*　a thick blunt needle for drawing tape etc. through a hem.

body *noun*　(*plural* **bodies**) 1 the structure consisting of bones and flesh etc. of a person or animal; the main part of this apart from the head and limbs. 2 a corpse. 3 the main part of something. 4 a group or quantity regarded as a unit, *the school's governing body.* 5 a distinct object or piece of matter, *Stars and planets are heavenly bodies.* **bodily** *adjective* & *adverb*

bodyguard *noun*　a guard to protect a person's life.

Boer (also **boer**) *noun*　(*plural* **Boers** or **boere**) 1 an Afrikaner. 2 a farmer. 3 an early Dutch inhabitant of South Africa. 4 (*slang*) a police officer. **Boer War** South African War.

boeremusiek *noun*　traditional Afrikaner dance-music.

boeresport *noun*　traditional Afrikaner games, e.g. jukskei.

boerewors *noun*　a spiced sausage.

bog *noun*　an area of wet spongy ground. **boggy** *adjective*

bogged down stuck and unable to make any progress.

boggle *verb* (**boggled, boggling**) hesitate in fear or doubt, *Our minds boggled at the idea.*

bogus *adjective* not real; sham.

bogy *noun* (*plural* **bogies**) 1 an evil spirit. 2 something that frightens people. **bogy- man** *noun*

boil[1] *verb* 1 make or become hot enough to bubble and give off steam. 2 cook or wash something in boiling water. 3 be very hot.

boil[2] *noun* 1 an inflamed swelling under the skin. 2 boiling-point, *Bring the milk to the boil.*

boiler *noun* a container in which water is heated or clothes are boiled.

boisterous *adjective* noisy and lively.

bokkems *plural noun* split dried whole fish.

bokmakierie (*say* bok-ma-kee-ree) *noun* a green and yellow bird with a distinctive call.

bold *adjective* 1 brave; courageous. 2 impudent. 3 (of colours) strong and vivid. **boldly** *adverb*, **boldness** *noun*

bollard *noun* 1 a short thick post to which a ship's mooring-rope may be tied. 2 a short post for directing traffic or keeping it off a pavement etc.

bolster[1] *noun* a long pillow for placing across a bed under other pillows.

bolster[2] *verb* add extra support.

bolt[1] *noun* 1 a sliding bar for fastening a door. 2 a thick metal pin for fastening things together. 3 a sliding bar that opens and closes the breech of a rifle. 4 a shaft of lightning. 5 an arrow shot from a crossbow. 6 the action of bolting.
a bolt from the blue a surprise, usually an unpleasant one.
bolt upright quite upright.

bolt[2] *verb* 1 fasten with a bolt or bolts. 2 run away; (of a horse) run off out of control. 3 swallow food quickly.

boma (*say* boh-ma or baw-ma) *noun* an enclosure, often of thorn bush, to protect a camp or animals.

bomb[1] *noun* an explosive device.
the bomb an atomic or hydrogen bomb.

bomb[2] *verb* attack with bombs. **bomber** *noun*

bombard *verb* 1 attack with gunfire or many missiles. 2 direct a large number of questions or comments etc. at somebody. **bombardment** *noun*

bombastic (*say* bom-**bast**-ik) *adjective* using pompous words.

bombshell *noun* a great shock.

bonanza (*say* bon-**an**-za) *noun* sudden great wealth or luck.

bond[1] *noun* 1 something that binds, restrains, or unites people or things. 2 a document stating an agreement. 3 a mortgage.

bond[2] *verb* connect or unite with a bond.

bondage *noun* slavery; captivity.

bone[1] *noun* one of the hard parts of a person's or animal's body (excluding teeth, nails, horns, and cartilage).

bone[2] *verb* (**boned, boning**) remove the bones from meat or fish.

bone-dry *adjective* quite dry.

bonfire *noun* an outdoor fire to burn rubbish or celebrate something.

bonnet *noun* 1 a hat with strings that tie under the chin. 2 the hinged cover over a car engine.

bonny *adjective* (**bonnier, bonniest**) 1 healthy-looking. 2 (*Scottish*) good-looking.

bonsella *noun* a bonus or gift.

bontebok *noun* a dark antelope with white markings.

bonus (*say* **boh**-nus) *noun* (*plural* **bonuses**) an extra payment or benefit.

bony *adjective* 1 with large bones; having bones with little flesh on them, *bony fingers.* 2 full of bones, *This fish is very bony.*

boo *verb* shout 'boo' in disapproval.

booby *noun* (*plural* **boobies**) a babyish or stupid person.
booby prize a prize given as a joke to someone who comes last in a contest.
booby trap something designed to hit or injure someone unexpectedly.

book[1] *noun* a set of sheets of paper, usually with printing or writing on them, fastened together inside a cover. **bookseller** *noun*, **bookshop** *noun*, **bookstall** *noun*

book[2] *verb* 1 reserve a place in a theatre, hotel, train, etc. 2 write something down in a book or list; enter in a police record,

The police booked him for speeding.
bookcase *noun* a piece of furniture with shelves for books.
bookkeeping *noun* recording details of buying, selling, etc. **bookkeeper** *noun*
booklet *noun* a small thin book.
bookmaker *noun* a person whose business is taking bets.
bookmark *noun* something to mark a place in a book.
bookworm *noun* 1 a grub that eats holes in books. 2 a person who loves reading.
boom[1] *verb* 1 make a deep hollow sound. 2 be growing and prospering, *Business is booming.*
boom[2] *noun* 1 a booming sound. 2 prosperity; growth.
boom[3] *noun* 1 a long pole at the bottom of a sail to keep it stretched. 2 a long pole carrying a microphone etc. 3 a chain or floating barrier that can be placed across a river or a harbour entrance.
boomerang *noun* a curved piece of wood that can be thrown so that it returns to the thrower, originally used by Australian Aborigines.
boomslang *noun* a green tree snake.
boon *noun* a benefit.
boon companion *noun* a friendly companion.
boor *noun* an ill-mannered person. **boorish** *adjective*
boost[1] *verb* 1 increase the strength, value, or reputation of a person or thing. 2 push something upwards.
boost[2] *noun* 1 an increase. 2 an upward push.
booster *noun* 1 a device for increasing electrical power. 2 a rocket that gives extra speed to a missile or spacecraft as it takes off. 3 a thing that helps or encourages somebody, *a morale booster.* 4 an extra amount of vaccine given to renew the effect of an earlier one, *a tetanus booster.*
boot *noun* 1 a shoe that covers the foot and ankle or leg. 2 the compartment for luggage in a car. **booted** *adjective*
bootee *noun* a baby's knitted boot.
booth *noun* a small enclosure.
booty *noun* loot.

booze[1] *verb* (**boozed, boozing**) (*slang*) drink alcohol.
booze[2] *noun* (*slang*) alcoholic drink.
borax *noun* a soluble white powder used in making glass, detergents, etc.
border[1] *noun* 1 the boundary of a country; the part near this. 2 an edge. 3 something placed round an edge to strengthen or decorate it, *a tablecloth with an embroidered border.* 4 a strip of ground round a garden or part of it.
border[2] *verb* put or be a border to something.
borderline *noun* a boundary.
borderline case something that is on the borderline between two different groups or kinds of things.
bore[1] *verb* (**bored, boring**) 1 drill a hole. 2 get through by pushing.
bore[2] *noun* 1 the internal width of a gun-barrel. 2 a hole made by boring.
bore[3] *verb* (**bored, boring**) make somebody feel uninterested by being dull.
bore[4] *noun* a boring person or thing. **boredom** *noun*
bore[5] *noun* a tidal wave with a steep front that moves up some estuaries.
bore[6] *past tense* of **bear**[2].
borehole *noun* a well drilled to tap water underground.
born *adjective* 1 having come into existence by birth. (See the note on *borne.*) 2 having a certain natural quality or ability, *a born leader.*
borne *past participle* of **bear**[2].
• USAGE: The word *borne* is used before *by* or after *have, has,* or *had,* e.g. *children borne by Eve; she had borne him a son.* The word *born* is used e.g. in *a son was born.*
borough (*say* **bu**rra) *noun* an important town or district.
borrow *verb* 1 get something to use for a time, with a promise to give it back afterwards. 2 obtain money as a loan. **borrower** *noun*
• USAGE: *Borrow* and *lend* are often confused. It is incorrect to say *Can you borrow me R50?* The correct form is *Can you lend me R50?* if you wish to borrow from the person you are speaking to.

bosom *noun* a person's breast.

boss[1] *noun* (*plural* **bosses**) (*informal*) a manager; a person whose job is to give orders to workers etc.

boss[2] *verb* (*slang*) order someone about.

boss[3] *noun* a round raised knob or stud.

bossy *adjective* (*informal*) fond of ordering people about. **bossiness** *noun*

botany *noun* the study of plants. **botanical** *adjective*, **botanist** *noun*

botch *verb* spoil something by poor or clumsy work.

both[1] *adjective* & *pronoun* the two; not only one, *Are both films good? Both are old.*

both[2] *adverb* **both … and** not only … but also, *The house is both small and ugly.*

bother[1] *verb* **1** cause somebody trouble or worry; pester. **2** take trouble; feel concern, *Don't bother to reply.*

bother[2] *noun* trouble; worry.

bottle[1] *noun* a narrow-necked container for liquids.

bottle bank a place for depositing bottles for recycling.

bottle[2] *verb* (**bottled**, **bottling**) put or store in bottles.

bottleneck *noun* a narrow place where something (especially traffic) cannot flow freely.

bottom[1] *noun* **1** the lowest part; the base. **2** the part furthest away, *the bottom of the garden.* **3** a person's buttocks.

bottom[2] *adjective* lowest, *the bottom shelf.*

bottomless *adjective* extremely deep.

bougainvillaea (*say* boo-gan-**vil**-ee-a) *noun* a brightly-coloured tropical plant.

bough *noun* a large branch coming from the trunk of a tree.

boulder *noun* a very large smooth stone.

boulevard (*say* **bool**-ev-ard) *noun* a wide street, often with trees.

bounce[1] *verb* (**bounced**, **bouncing**) **1** spring back when thrown against something. **2** cause a ball etc. to bounce. **3** (*slang*, of a cheque) be sent back by the bank as worthless. **4** jump suddenly; move in a lively manner, *The child bounced into the room.*

bounce[2] *noun* **1** the action or power of bouncing. **2** a lively confident manner, full of bounce. **bouncy** *adjective*

bouncer *noun* (*slang*) a person who ejects troublesome people from a club.

bound[1] *verb* jump or spring; run with jumping movements, *bounding along.*

bound[2] *noun* a bounding movement.

bound[3] *past tense* of **bind**[1].

bound[4] *adjective* obstructed or hindered by something, *We were fog-bound.*

bound to certain to, *He is bound to fail.*

bound up with closely connected with, *Happiness is bound up with success.*

bound[5] *adjective* going towards something, *We are bound for Umtata.*

bound[6] *verb* limit; be the boundary of, *Their land is bounded by the river.*

boundary *noun* (*plural* **boundaries**) **1** a line that marks a limit. **2** a hit to the boundary of a cricket field.

bounden *adjective* obligatory, *your bounden duty.*

bounds *plural noun* limits.

out of bounds where you are not allowed to go.

bountiful *adjective* **1** plentiful; abundant, *bountiful harvest.* **2** giving generously.

bounty *noun* (*plural* **bounties**) **1** a generous gift. **2** generosity in giving things, *bounty towards the homeless.* **3** a reward for doing something, *They offered bounty money for the outlaw's capture.*

bouquet (*say* boh-**kay**) *noun* a bunch of flowers.

bout *noun* **1** a boxing or wrestling contest. **2** a period of exercise or work or illness, *a bout of flu.*

boutique (*say* boo-**teek**) *noun* a small shop selling fashionable clothes.

bovine (*say* **boh**-vyn) *adjective* of or like oxen.

bow[1] (rhymes with *go*) *noun* **1** a strip of wood curved by a tight string joining its ends, used for shooting arrows. **2** a wooden rod with horsehair stretched between its ends, used for playing a violin etc. **3** a knot made with loops.

bow-legged *adjective* bandy.

bow-tie *noun* a man's necktie tied into a bow.

bow-window *noun* a curved window.

bow[2] (rhymes with *cow*) *verb* **1** bend your body forwards to show respect or as a greeting. **2** bend downwards, *bowed by the weight.*

bow[3] *noun* bowing your body.

bow[4] (rhymes with *cow*) *noun* the front part of a ship.

bowel *noun* the intestine.

bower *noun* a leafy shelter.

bowl[1] *noun* **1** a rounded usually deep container for food or liquid. **2** the rounded part of a spoon or tobacco-pipe etc.

bowl[2] *noun* a ball used in the game of **bowls** or in bowling, when heavy balls are rolled towards a target.

bowl[3] *verb* **1** send a ball to be played by a batsman; get a batsman out by bowling. **2** send a ball etc. rolling.

bowler *noun* a person who bowls.

box[1] *noun* (*plural* **boxes**) **1** a container made of wood, cardboard, etc., usually with a top or lid. **2** a compartment in a theatre, lawcourt, etc., *witness-box.* **3** a hut or shelter, *sentry-box.* **4** a small evergreen shrub.

box number the number of a pigeon-hole to which letters may be addressed in a newspaper office or post office.

the box (*informal*) television.

box[2] *verb* put something into a box.

box[3] *verb* fight with the fists.

boxer *noun* **1** a person who boxes. **2** a dog that looks like a bulldog.

box-office *noun* an office for booking seats at a theatre or cinema etc.

boy *noun* **1** a male child. **2** a young man. **boyhood** *noun*, **boyish** *adjective*

boycott *verb* refuse to use or have anything to do with, *They boycotted the buses when the fares went up.* **boycott** *noun*

boy-friend *noun* a boy that a girl regularly goes out with.

bra *noun* a brassière.

braai[1] *noun* **1** a meal cooked over an open fire outdoors. **2** an appliance on which food can be grilled outdoors.

braai[2] *verb* (**braaied, braaiing**) grill food over an open fire.

braaivleis *noun* **1** a social gathering usually outdoors for a braai. **2** the food cooked at this gathering.

brace[1] *noun* **1** a device for holding things in place. **2** a pair, *a brace of pheasants.*

brace[2] *verb* (**braced, bracing**) support; make a thing firm against something.

bracelet *noun* an ornament worn round the wrist.

braces *plural noun* straps to hold trousers up, passing over the shoulders.

bracing *adjective* invigorating.

bracken *noun* **1** a large fern. **2** a mass of ferns.

bracket[1] *noun* **1** a mark used in pairs to enclose words or figures, *There are round brackets ( ) and square brackets [].* **2** a support attached to a wall etc. **3** a group or range between certain limits, *a high income bracket.*

bracket[2] *verb* (**bracketed, bracketing**) **1** enclose in brackets. **2** put things together because they are similar.

brackish *adjective* (of water) slightly salt.

bract *noun* a leaf-like part of a plant that is often coloured like a petal.

bradawl *noun* a small tool for boring holes.

brag *verb* (**bragged, bragging**) boast.

braggart *noun* a person who brags.

Brahma *noun* the Hindu Creator.

Brahmin *noun* a member of the highest Hindu class, originally priests.

braid[1] *noun* **1** a plait of hair. **2** a strip of cloth with a woven decorative pattern, used as trimming.

braid[2] *verb* **1** plait. **2** trim with braid.

Braille *noun* a system of representing letters etc. by raised dots which blind people can read by feeling them.

brain *noun* **1** the organ inside the top of the head that controls the body. **2** the mind; intelligence.

brainwash *verb* force a person to give up one set of ideas or beliefs and accept new ones; indoctrinate.

brainwave *noun* a sudden bright idea.

brainy *adjective* clever; intelligent.

braise *verb* (**braised, braising**) cook slowly in a little liquid in a closed container.

brak[1] *adjective* brackish; alkaline.

brak[2] *noun* a mongrel dog.

brake[1] *noun* a device for slowing or stopping something.

brake[2] *verb* (**braked, braking**) use a brake.

bramble *noun* a blackberry bush or a prickly bush like it.

bran *noun* ground-up husks of corn.

branch[1] *noun* (*plural* **branches**) 1 a woody arm-like part of a tree or shrub. 2 a part of a railway, road, or river etc. that leads off from the main part. 3 a shop or office etc. that belongs to a large organization.

branch[2] *verb* form a branch.
branch out start something new.

brand[1] *noun* 1 a particular make of goods, *Which brand of toothpaste do you prefer?* 2 a mark made by branding.

brand[2] *verb* 1 mark cattle or sheep etc. with a hot iron to identify them. 2 sell goods under a particular trade mark.

brandish *verb* wave something about.

brand-new *adjective* completely new.

brandy *noun* (*plural* **brandies**) a strong alcoholic drink.

brash *adjective* confident in a rude, noisy, or aggressive way, *the brash young salesperson.*

brass *noun* (*plural* **brasses**) 1 a metal that is an alloy of copper and zinc. 2 wind instruments made of brass, e.g. trumpets and trombones. **brass** *adjective*, **brassy** *adjective*

brassière (*say* **bras**-ee-air) *noun* a piece of underwear worn by women to support their breasts.

brat *noun* (*contemptuous*) a child.

bravado (*say* brav-**ah**-doh) *noun* a display of boldness.

brave[1] *adjective* 1 having or showing courage. 2 spectacular, *a brave show of poppies.* **bravely** *adverb*, **bravery** *noun*

brave[2] *noun* an American Indian warrior.

brave[3] *verb* (**braved, braving**) face and endure something bravely.

bravo (*say* **brah**-voh) *interjection* well done!

brawl[1] *noun* a noisy quarrel or fight.

brawl[2] *verb* take part in a brawl.

brawn *noun* 1 muscular strength. 2 cold boiled pork or veal pressed in a mould.

brawny *adjective* strong and muscular.

bray *noun* the loud harsh cry of a donkey.
bray *verb*

brazen[1] *adjective* 1 made of brass. 2 shameless, *brazen impudence.*

brazen[2] *verb* **brazen it out** behave as if there is nothing to be ashamed of when you know you have done wrong.

brazier (*say* **bray**-zee-er) *noun* a metal framework for holding burning coals.

breach[1] *noun* (*plural* **breaches**) 1 the breaking of an agreement or rule etc., *a breach of contract.* 2 a broken place; a gap.

breach[2] *verb* break through; make a gap.

bread *noun* a food made by baking flour and water, usually with yeast. **breadcrumbs** *noun*
bread and butter work that provides a main source of income.

breadth *noun* width; broadness.

breadwinner *noun* the member of a family who earns money to support the others.

break[1] *verb* (**broke, broken, breaking**) 1 divide or fall into pieces by hitting or pressing. 2 fail to keep a promise or law etc. 3 stop for a time; end, *She broke her silence.* 4 change, *the weather broke.* 5 damage; stop working properly. 6 (of waves) fall in foam. 7 go suddenly or with force, *They broke through.* 8 appear suddenly, *Dawn had broken.* **breakage** *noun*
break a record do better than anyone else has done before.
break down stop working properly; collapse.
break even make neither a profit nor a loss.
break out begin suddenly; escape.
break the news make something known.
break up break into small parts; separate at the end of a school term.

break[2] *noun* 1 a broken place; a gap. 2 an escape; a sudden dash. 3 a short rest from work. 4 a change in something that has continued for a long time, *a break with tradition.* 5 (*informal*) a piece of luck; an opportunity, *a lucky break.*
break of day dawn.

breakable *adjective* able to be broken.

breakdown *noun* 1 breaking down; failure. 2 collapse of mental or physical health. 3 an analysis of accounts or statistics, *a breakdown of income or expenditure.*

breaker *noun* a large wave breaking on the shore.

breakfast *noun* the first meal of the day.

breakneck *adjective* dangerously fast.

breakthrough *noun* an important advance or achievement.

breakwater *noun* a wall built out into the sea to protect a coast from heavy waves.

breast *noun* 1 one of the two parts on the upper front of a woman's body that produce milk to feed a baby. 2 a person's or animal's chest.

breastbone *noun* the flat bone down the centre of the chest or breast.

breastplate *noun* a piece of armour covering the chest.

breath (*say* breth) *noun* 1 air drawn into the lungs and sent out again. 2 a gentle blowing, *a breath of wind*.
out of breath panting.
take your breath away surprise or delight you greatly.
under your breath in a whisper.

breathalyser *noun* a device for measuring the amount of alcohol in a person's breath. **breathalyse** *verb*

breathe (*say* bree*th*) *verb* (**breathed, breathing**) 1 take air into the body and send it out again. 2 speak; utter, *Don't breathe a word of this.*

breather (*say* **bree**-*th*er) *noun* a pause for rest, *Let's take a breather.*

breathless *adjective* out of breath.

breathtaking *adjective* very surprising or delightful.

bredie *noun* a thick stew of meat with a vegetable, *waterblommetjie bredie.*

breech *noun* (*plural* **breeches**) the back part of a gun-barrel, where the bullets are put in.

breeches (*say* **brich**-iz) *plural noun* trousers reaching to just below the knees.

breed[1] *verb* (**bred, breeding**) 1 produce young creatures. 2 keep animals so as to produce young ones from them. 3 bring up; train, *a well-bred child.* 4 create; produce, *Poverty breeds illness.* **breeder** *noun*

breed[2] *noun* a variety of animals with qualities inherited from their parents, *Saanen and Toggenberg goats are the most common breeds of milk goats.*

breeze *noun* a wind. **breezy** *adjective*

breeze-block *noun* a lightweight building-block made of cinders and cement.

brethren *plural noun* (*old use*) brothers.

breve (*say* breev) *noun* a note in music, equal to two semibreves in length.

brevity *noun* shortness; briefness.

brew[1] *verb* 1 make beer or tea. 2 develop, *Trouble is brewing.*

brew[2] *noun* a brewed drink.

brewer *noun* a person who brews beer for sale.

brewery *noun* (*plural* **breweries**) a place where beer is brewed.

breyani *noun* biriani.

briar *noun* a brier.

bribe[1] *noun* money or a gift offered to a person to influence him or her.

bribe[2] *verb* (**bribed, bribing**) give someone a bribe. **bribery** *noun*

brick[1] *noun* 1 a small hard block of baked clay etc. used to build walls. 2 a rectangular block of something, *a brick of ice-cream.*

brick[2] *verb* close something with bricks, *We bricked up the gap in the wall.*

bricklayer *noun* a worker who builds with bricks.

bride *noun* a woman on her wedding-day. **bridal** *adjective*

bridegroom *noun* a man on his wedding-day.

bridesmaid *noun* a girl or unmarried woman who attends the bride at a wedding.

bridge[1] *noun* 1 a structure built over and across a river, railway, or road etc. to allow people to cross it. 2 a high platform above a ship's deck, for the officer in charge. 3 the bony upper part of the nose. 4 something that connects things, *Cultural exchanges are a way of building bridges between nations.* 5 a card-game rather like whist.

bridge[2] *verb* (**bridged, bridging**) make or form a bridge over something.

bridle *noun* the part of a horse's harness that fits over its head.

bridle-path (also **bridle-road**) *noun* a road suitable for horses but not for vehicles.

brief[1] *adjective* short. **briefly** *adverb*, **briefness** *noun*
in **brief** in a few words.

brief[2] *noun* instructions and information given to someone, especially to an advocate.

brief[3] *verb* 1 give a brief to an advocate. 2 instruct or inform someone concisely in advance.

briefcase *noun* a flat case for carrying documents etc.

briefing *noun* a meeting to give someone concise instructions or information.

briefs *plural noun* very short knickers or underpants.

brier *noun* 1 a thorny bush, especially the wild rose. 2 a hard root used especially for making tobacco-pipes.

brigade *noun* 1 a large unit of an army. 2 a group of people organized for a special purpose, *the fire brigade*.

brigadier *noun* a brigade-commander.

brigand *noun* a member of a band of robbers.

bright *adjective* 1 giving a strong light; shining. 2 clever, *a bright idea*. 3 cheerful, *a bright smile*. **brightly** *adverb*, **brightness** *noun*

brighten *verb* make or become brighter.

brilliant *adjective* 1 very bright; sparkling. 2 very clever. **brilliantly** *adverb*, **brilliance** *noun*

brim[1] *noun* 1 the edge of a cup etc. 2 the projecting edge of a hat.
brim-full *adjective* completely full.

brim[2] *verb* (**brimmed, brimming**) be full to the brim.
brim over overflow.

brimstone *noun* (*old use*) sulphur.

brine *noun* salt water. **briny** *adjective*

bring *verb* (**brought, bringing**) cause a person or thing to come; lead; carry.
bring about cause to happen.
bring off achieve; do something successfully.
bring up look after and train growing children; mention a subject; vomit; cause to stop suddenly.

brinjal *noun* an aubergine.

brink *noun* 1 the edge of a steep place or of a stretch of water. 2 the point beyond which something will happen, *We were on the brink of war*.

brisk *adjective* quick and lively. **briskly** *adverb*, **briskness** *noun*

bristle[1] *noun* 1 a short stiff hair. 2 one of the stiff pieces of hair, wire, or plastic etc. in a brush. **bristly** *adjective*

bristle[2] *verb* (**bristled, bristling**) 1 (of an animal) raise its bristles in anger or fear. 2 show indignation.
bristle with be full of, *The plan bristled with problems*.

British *adjective* of Great Britain, the British Commonwealth, or their people.

brittle *adjective* hard but easy to break or snap. **brittleness** *noun*

broach *verb* 1 make a hole in something and draw out liquid. 2 start a discussion of something, *They broached the subject*.

broad *adjective* 1 large across; wide. 2 full and complete, *broad daylight*. 3 in general terms; not detailed, *We are in broad agreement*. 4 strong and unmistakable, *a broad hint; a broad accent*. **broadly** *adverb*, **broadness** *noun*
broad bean a bean with large flat seeds.

broadcast[1] *noun* a programme sent out on the radio or on television.

broadcast[2] *verb* (**broadcast, broadcasting**) send out or take part in a broadcast. **broadcaster** *noun*

broaden *verb* make or become broader.

broad-minded *adjective* tolerant; not easily shocked.

broadside *noun* 1 firing by all guns on one side of a ship. 2 a verbal attack, *The politician launched a broadside at her critics*.
broadside on sideways on.

brocade *noun* material woven with raised patterns.

broccoli *noun* (*plural* **broccoli**) a kind of cauliflower with greenish flower-heads.

brochure (*say* broh-shoor) *noun* a booklet or pamphlet containing information.

broekielace *noun* (*informal*) decorative wrought iron on Victorian houses.

broekies *plural noun* panties; knickers.

broeks *noun* (*informal*) trousers; pants; knickers.

brogue (rhymes with *rogue*) *noun* 1 a strong kind of shoe. 2 a strong accent, *He spoke with an Irish brogue.*

broil *verb* 1 cook on a fire or gridiron. 2 make or be very hot.

broiler *noun* a chicken bred for its meat.

broke *adjective* (*informal*) having spent all your money; bankrupt.

broken-hearted *adjective* overwhelmed with grief.

broken home *noun* a family lacking one parent through divorce or separation.

broker *noun* a person who buys and sells things for other people.

bromide *noun* a substance used in medicine to calm the nerves.

bronchial (*say* **bronk**-ee-al) *adjective* of the tubes that lead from the windpipe to the lungs.

bronchitis (*say* bronk-I-tiss) *noun* a disease with bronchial inflammation.

brontosaurus *noun* (*plural* **brontosauruses**) a large dinosaur that fed on plants.

bronze *noun* 1 a metal that is an alloy of copper and tin. 2 something made of bronze; a bronze medal, usually given as third prize. 3 yellowish-brown. **bronze** *adjective*

Bronze Age the time when tools and weapons were made of bronze.

brooch *noun* (*plural* **brooches**) an ornament with a hinged pin for fastening it on to clothes.

brood[1] *noun* young birds that were hatched together.

brood[2] *verb* 1 sit on eggs to hatch them. 2 keep thinking about something, especially with resentment.

broody *adjective* 1 (of a hen) wanting to sit on eggs. 2 thoughtful; brooding.

brook[1] *noun* a small stream.

brook[2] *verb* tolerate, *brook no delay.*

broom *noun* 1 a brush with a long handle, for sweeping. 2 a shrub with yellow, white, or pink flowers.

broomstick *noun* a broom-handle.

broth *noun* a kind of thin soup.

brothel *noun* a house in which women work as prostitutes.

brother *noun* 1 a son of the same parents as another person. 2 a man who is a fellow member of a Church, trade union, etc. **brotherhood** *noun,* **brotherly** *adjective*

brother-in-law *noun* (*plural* **brothers-in-law**) the brother of a married person's husband or wife; the husband of a person's sister.

brow *noun* 1 an eyebrow. 2 the forehead. 3 the ridge at the top of a hill; the edge of a cliff.

brown[1] *noun* a colour between orange and black.

brown[2] *adjective* 1 of the colour brown. 2 having a brown skin; sun-tanned.

brown[3] *verb* make or become brown.

Brownie *noun* a member of a junior branch of the Guides.

browse *verb* (**browsed, browsing**) 1 feed on grass or leaves. 2 read or look at something casually, *browse through a magazine.*

bruise[1] *noun* a dark mark made on the skin by hitting it.

bruise[2] *verb* (**bruised, bruising**) give or get a bruise or bruises.

brunette *noun* a woman with dark-brown hair.

brunt *noun* the chief impact or strain, *They bore the brunt of the attack.*

brush[1] *noun* (*plural* **brushes**) 1 an implement used for cleaning or painting things or for smoothing the hair, usually with pieces of hair, wire, or plastic etc. set in a solid base. 2 a fox's bushy tail. 3 brushing, *Give it a good brush.* 4 a short fight, *They had a brush with the enemy.*

brush[2] *verb* 1 use a brush on something. 2 touch gently in passing, *leaves brushed her cheek.*

brush up revise a subject.

brusque (*say* bruusk) *adjective* curt and offhand in manner. **brusquely** *adverb*

Brussels sprouts *plural noun* the edible buds of a kind of cabbage.

brutal *adjective* very cruel. **brutally** *adverb,* **brutality** *noun*

brute *noun* 1 a brutal person. 2 an animal. **brutish** *adjective*

bubble[1] *noun* 1 a thin transparent ball of liquid filled with air or gas. 2 a small ball of air in something. **bubbly** *adjective*

bubble gum chewing-gum that can be blown into large bubbles.

bubble[2] *verb* (**bubbled, bubbling**) 1 send up bubbles; rise in bubbles. 2 show great liveliness, *She was bubbling with excitement.*

bubonic plague *noun* a disease spread by rat fleas.

buccaneer *noun* a pirate.

buchu (*say* **buu**-khu) *noun* a kind of aromatic plant used as medicine.

buck[1] *noun* a male deer, rabbit, or hare.

buck[2] *verb* (of a horse) jump with its back arched.

buck up (*slang*) hurry; cheer up.

buck[3] *noun* (*slang*) 1 a dollar. 2 a rand.

buck[4] *noun* an object used in the game of poker to show whose turn it is.

pass the buck (*slang*) pass the responsibility for something to another person.

buck-passing *noun*

bucket *noun* a container with a handle, for carrying liquids etc. **bucketful** *noun*

buckle[1] *noun* a device through which a belt or strap is threaded to fasten it.

buckle[2] *verb* (**buckled, buckling**) 1 fasten with a buckle. 2 bend or crumple, *Her legs buckled under her.*

buckle down to start working hard at.

bucolic (*say* bew-**kol**-ik) *adjective* of country life.

bud *noun* a flower or leaf before it opens.

Buddhism (*say* **buud**-izm) *noun* a faith that started in Asia and follows the teachings of the Indian philosopher Gautama Buddha, who lived in the 5th century BC. **Buddhist** *noun*

budding *adjective* beginning to develop.

buddy *noun* (*plural* **buddies**) (*informal*) a friend.

budge *verb* (**budged, budging**) move slightly.

budgerigar *noun* an Australian bird often kept as a pet in a cage.

budget[1] *noun* 1 a plan for spending money wisely. 2 an amount of money set aside for a purpose. **budgetary** *adjective*

the Budget the government's statement of plans to raise money (e.g. by taxes) and to spend it.

budget[2] *verb* (**budgeted, budgeting**) plan a budget.

budgie *noun* (*informal*) a budgerigar.

buff[1] *adjective* of a dull yellow colour.

buff[2] *verb* polish with soft material.

buffalo *noun* (*plural* **buffalo** or **buffaloes**) a large ox. Different kinds are found in Africa, Asia, and North America (where they are also called bison).

buffer *noun* something that softens a blow, especially a device on a railway engine or wagon or at the end of a track.

buffer state a small country between two powerful ones, thought to reduce the chance of these two attacking each other.

buffet[1] (*say* **buu**-fay) *noun* 1 a refreshment counter. 2 a meal where guests serve themselves.

buffet[2] (*say* **buf**-it) *noun* a hit, especially with the hand.

buffet[3] *verb* (**buffeted, buffeting**) hit, knock, *Strong winds buffeted the aircraft.*

buffoon *noun* a clown; a person who plays the fool. **buffoonery** *noun*

bug[1] *noun* 1 an insect. 2 (*informal*) a germ or infection. 3 (*informal*) a secret hidden microphone.

bug[2] *verb* (**bugged, bugging**) (*slang*) 1 fit with a 'bug'. 2 annoy.

bugbear *noun* something you fear or dislike.

buggy *noun* (*plural* **buggies**) 1 (*old use*) a light horse-drawn carriage. 2 a small strong vehicle, *a beach buggy.* 3 a lightweight push-chair.

bugle *noun* a brass instrument like a small trumpet, used for sounding military signals. **bugler** *noun*

build[1] *verb* (**built, building**) make something by putting parts together.

build in include. **built-in** *adjective*

build up establish gradually; accumulate; cover an area with buildings; make stronger or more famous, *build up a reputation.*

built-up *adjective*

build[2] *noun* the shape of someone's body, *of slender build.*

builder *noun* someone who puts up buildings.

building *noun* 1 the process of constructing houses etc. 2 a permanent built structure that people can go into.

building society an organization that accepts deposits of money and lends to people who want to buy houses etc.

bulb *noun* 1 a thick rounded part of a plant from which a stem grows up and roots grow down. 2 a rounded part of something, *the bulb of a thermometer*. 3 a glass globe with a wire inside to produce electric light. **bulbous** *adjective*

bulbul *noun* a kind of songbird.

bulge[1] *noun* a rounded swelling; an outward curve. **bulgy** *adjective*

bulge[2] *verb* (**bulged, bulging**) form or cause to form a bulge.

bulk[1] *noun* 1 the size of something, especially when it is large. 2 the greater portion; the majority, *The bulk of the population voted for it.*
in bulk in large amounts.

bulk[2] *verb* increase the size or thickness of something, *bulk it out.*

bulky *adjective* (**bulkier, bulkiest**) taking up much space. **bulkiness** *noun*

bull[1] *noun* the fully-grown male of cattle or of certain other large animals (e.g. elephant, whale, seal).

bull[2] *noun* an edict issued by the pope.

bulldog *noun* a dog of a powerful courageous breed with a short thick neck.

bulldoze *verb* (**bulldozed, bulldozing**) clear with a bulldozer.

bulldozer *noun* a powerful tractor with a wide metal blade or scoop in front, used for shifting soil or clearing ground.

bullet *noun* a small lump of metal shot from a rifle or revolver.

bulletin *noun* a public statement giving news.

bullet-proof *adjective* able to keep out bullets.

bullfight *noun* a public entertainment in which bulls are tormented and killed in an arena. **bullfighter** *noun*

bullfrog *noun* a large frog with a booming croak.

bullion *noun* bars of gold or silver.

bullock *noun* a young bull.

bull's-eye *noun* 1 the centre of a target. 2 a hard shiny peppermint sweet.

bully[1] *verb* (**bullied, bullying**) 1 use strength or power to hurt or frighten a weaker person. 2 start play in hockey, when two opponents tap the ground and each other's stick, *bully off.*

bully[2] *noun* (*plural* **bullies**) someone who bullies people.

bulrush *noun* (*plural* **bulrushes**) a tall rush with a thick velvety head.

bult *noun* (*plural* **bulte**) a long ridge or hump of low hills.

bulwark *noun* a wall of earth built as a defence; a protection.
bulwarks *plural noun* a ship's side above the level of the deck.

bum *noun* (*slang*) a person's bottom.

bumble *verb* (**bumbled, bumbling**) move or behave or speak clumsily.

bumble-bee *noun* a large bee with a loud hum.

bump[1] *verb* 1 knock against something. 2 move along with jolts, *The old bus bumped along the mountain road.*
bump into (*informal*) meet by chance.
bump off (*slang*) kill.

bump[2] *noun* 1 the action or sound of bumping. 2 a swelling or lump. **bumpy** *adjective*

bumper[1] *noun* a bar along the front or back of a motor vehicle to protect it in collisions.

bumper[2] *adjective* unusually large or plentiful, *a bumper crop.*

bumpkin *noun* a country person with awkward manners.

bumptious (*say* **bump**-shus) *adjective* conceited. **bumptiousness** *noun*

bun *noun* 1 a small round sweet cake. 2 hair twisted into a round bunch at the back of the head.

bunch *noun* (*plural* **bunches**) a number of things joined or fastened together.

bundle[1] *noun* a number of things tied or wrapped together.

bundle[2] *verb* (**bundled, bundling**) 1 make into a bundle. 2 push hurriedly or carelessly, *They bundled him into a taxi.*

bundu *noun* wild or distant places.
bundu bashing travelling through rough stretches of land.

bung[1] *noun* a stopper for closing a hole in a barrel or jar.

bung[2] *verb* **bunged up** (*informal*) blocked.

bungalow *noun* a house without any upstairs rooms.

bungee jumping *noun* the sport of jumping from a high place while tied by an elasticated cord from the ankles or a harness.

bungle *verb* (**bungled, bungling**) do something unsuccessfully; spoil by being clumsy. **bungler** *noun*

bunion *noun* a swelling at the side of the joint where the big toe joins the foot.

bunk[1] *noun* a bed built like a shelf.

bunk[2] *verb* (*informal*) play truant (from), *We bunked our classes.*

bunk[3] *noun* **do a bunk** (*informal*) run away.

bunker *noun* 1 a container for storing fuel. 2 a sandy hollow built as an obstacle on a golf-course. 3 an underground shelter.

bunny *noun* (*plural* **bunnies**) (*informal*) a rabbit.
bunny chow curry in a hollowed-out half-loaf of bread.

bunting *noun* strips of cloth hung up to decorate streets and buildings.

buoy[1] (*say* boi) *noun* (*plural* **buoys**) a floating object anchored to mark a channel or underwater rocks etc.

buoy[2] *verb* 1 keep something afloat. 2 hearten; cheer, *They were buoyed up with new hope.*

buoyant (*say* boi-ant) *noun* 1 able to float. 2 light-hearted; cheerful. **buoyantly** *adverb*, **buoyancy** *noun*

bur *noun* a plant's seed-case or flower that clings to hair or clothes.

burble *verb* (**burbled, burbling**) make a gentle murmuring sound. **burble** *noun*

burden[1] *noun* 1 something carried; a heavy load. 2 something troublesome that you have to bear, *Exams are a burden.*
burdensome *adjective*

burden[2] *verb* put a burden on a person etc.

bureau (*say* bewr-oh) *noun* (*plural* **bureaux**) 1 a writing-desk. 2 a business office,
They will tell you at the Information Bureau.

bureaucracy (*say* bewr-**ok**-ra-see) *noun* (*plural* **bureaucracies**) 1 too much official routine. 2 government by officials, not by elected representatives. **bureaucratic** (*say* bewr-ok-**rat**-ik) *adjective*

bureaucrat (*say* bewr-ok-rat) *noun* an official of a bureaucracy.

burette *noun* an apparatus that is used to measure the volume of a liquid.

burgeon (*say* **ber**-jon) *verb* grow rapidly.

burger *noun* a hamburger.

burgher *noun* 1 a citizen of the early Cape Colony, not a servant of the Dutch East India Company. 2 a citizen of a Boer republic who was obliged to serve in its army.

burglar *noun* a person who enters a building illegally, especially in order to steal things. **burglary** *noun*

burgle *verb* (**burgled, burgling**) rob a place as a burglar.

burgundy *noun* 1 a rich red or white wine. 2 a purplish-red colour.

burial *noun* burying somebody.

burlesque (*say* ber-**lesk**) *noun* a comical imitation.

burly *adjective* (**burlier, burliest**) with a strong heavy body; sturdy.

burn[1] *verb* (**burned** or **burnt, burning**) 1 blaze or glow with fire; produce heat or light by combustion. 2 damage or destroy something by fire, heat, or chemicals. 3 be damaged or destroyed by fire etc. 4 feel very hot.
● USAGE: The word *burnt* (not *burned*) is always used when an adjective is required, e.g. in *burnt wood.* As parts of the verb, either *burned* or *burnt* may be used, e.g. *the wood had burned* or *had burnt completely.*

burn[2] *noun* 1 a mark or injury made by burning. 2 the firing of a spacecraft's rockets.

burn[3] *noun* (*Scottish*) a brook.

burner *noun* the part of a lamp or cooker that gives out the flame.

burning *adjective* 1 intense, *a burning ambition.* 2 very important; hotly discussed, *a burning question.*

burnish *verb* polish by rubbing.

burp *verb* (*informal*) belch. **burp** *noun*

burr *noun* **1** a bur. **2** a whirring sound.

burrow[1] *noun* a hole or tunnel dug by a rabbit or fox etc. as a dwelling.

burrow[2] *verb* **1** dig a burrow. **2** push your way through or into something; search deeply, *She burrowed in her handbag.*

bursar *noun* a person who manages the finances and other business of a school etc.

bursary *noun* (*plural* **bursaries**) a grant or scholarship awarded to a student.

burst[1] *verb* (**burst, bursting**) **1** break or force apart. **2** come or start suddenly, *It burst into flame. They burst out laughing.* **3** be very full, *bursting with energy.*

burst[2] *noun* **1** bursting; a split. **2** something short and forceful, *a burst of gunfire.*

bury *verb* (**buried, burying**) **1** place a dead body in the earth, a tomb, or the sea. **2** put underground; cover up.
bury the hatchet agree to stop quarrelling or fighting.

bus *noun* (*plural* **buses**) a large vehicle for passengers to travel in.

bush *noun* (*plural* **bushes**) **1** a shrub. **2** wild uncultivated land. **bushy** *adjective*

bushbuck *noun* a large antelope.

bushel *noun* a measure in the imperial system for grain and fruit (8 gallons or 36,4 litres).

bushveld *noun* veld with scrubby or thorny bush.

busily *adverb* in a busy way.

business (*say* **biz**-niss) *noun* (*plural* **businesses**) **1** a person's concern or responsibilities, *Mind your own business.* **2** an affair or subject, *I'm tired of the whole business.* **3** a shop or firm. **4** buying and selling things; trade.
business economics the study of how private business enterprises produce goods and services to meet human needs and wants, while making a profit.

businesslike *adjective* practical; well-organized.

busker *noun* a person who entertains people in the street. **busking** *noun*

bust[1] *noun* **1** a sculpture of a person's head, shoulders, and chest. **2** the upper front part of a woman's body.

bust[2] *verb* (**bust, busting**) (*informal*) burst.

bustle[1] *verb* (**bustled, bustling**) hurry in a busy or excited way.

bustle[2] *noun* hurried or excited activity.

bustle[3] *noun* padding used to puff out the top of a long skirt at the back.

busy[1] *adjective* (**busier, busiest**) **1** having much to do; occupied. **2** full of activity. **busily** *adverb*, **busyness** *noun*

busy[2] *verb* (**busied, busying**) **busy yourself** occupy yourself; keep busy.

busybody *noun* (*plural* **busybodies**) a person who interferes.

but[1] *conjunction* however; nevertheless, *I wanted to go, but I couldn't.*

but[2] *preposition* except, *There is no one here but me.*

but[3] *adverb* only; no more than, *We can but try.*

but[4] *noun* an objection; an argument, *There's no time for ifs and buts – you must decide now.*

butcher[1] *noun* **1** a person who cuts up meat and sells it. **2** a person who kills cruelly or needlessly. **butchery** *noun*
butcher bird Jan Fiskaal.

butcher[2] *verb* kill cruelly or needlessly.

butler *noun* the chief manservant of a household, in charge of the wine-cellar.

butt[1] *noun* **1** the thicker end of a weapon or tool. **2** a stub, *cigarette butts.*

butt[2] *noun* a large cask or barrel.

butt[3] *noun* **1** a person or thing that is a target for ridicule or teasing, *He was the butt of their jokes.* **2** a mound of earth behind the targets on a shooting-range.

butt[4] *verb* push or hit with the head as a ram or goat does.
butt in interrupt; intrude; meddle.

butter *noun* a soft fatty food made by churning cream. **buttery** *adjective*

buttercup *noun* a wild plant with bright yellow cup-shaped flowers.

butter-fingers *noun* a person who often drops things.

butterfly *noun* (*plural* **butterflies**) **1** an insect with large white or coloured wings. **2** a swimming-stroke in which both arms are lifted at the same time.

buttermilk *noun* the liquid that is left after butter has been made.

butterscotch *noun* a kind of hard toffee.

buttock *noun* either of the two fleshy rounded parts at the lower or rear end of the back.

button[1] *noun* 1 a knob or disc sewn on clothes as a fastening or ornament. 2 a small knob, *Press the button.*

button[2] *verb* fasten with a button or buttons.

buttonhole[1] *noun* 1 a slit through which a button passes to fasten clothes. 2 a flower worn on a lapel.

buttonhole[2] *verb* (**buttonholed, buttonholing**) stop somebody so that you can talk to him or her, *He buttonholed me just as I was going to lunch.*

buttress *noun* (*plural* **buttresses**) a support built against a wall.

buy[1] *verb* (**bought, buying**) get something by paying for it. **buyer** *noun*

buy[2] *noun* something bought; a purchase, *a good buy.*

buzz[1] *noun* (*plural* **buzzes**) a vibrating humming sound.

buzz[2] *verb* 1 make a buzz, *The bees buzzed around the pot of jam.* 2 be full of excited talk, activity, or ideas, *The village was buzzing with preparations for the president's visit.*

buzzard *noun* a kind of hawk.

buzzer *noun* a device that makes a buzzing sound as a signal.

by[1] *preposition* This word is used to show 1 closeness (*Sit by me*), 2 direction or route (*We got here by a short cut*), 3 time (*They came by night*), 4 manner or method (*cooking by gas*), 5 amount (*You missed it by inches*).
by the way incidentally.
by yourself alone; without help.

by[2] *adverb* 1 past, *I can't get by.* 2 in reserve; for future use, *Put it by.*
by and by soon; later on.
by and large on the whole.

bye *noun* 1 a run scored in cricket when the ball goes past the batsman without being touched. 2 having no opponent for one round in a tournament and so going on to the next round as if you had won.

bye-bye *interjection* goodbye.

by-election *noun* an election to replace a Member of Parliament who has died or resigned.

bygone *adjective* belonging to the past.
let bygones be bygones forgive and forget.

by-law *noun* a law that applies only to a particular town or district.

bypass[1] *noun* (*plural* **bypasses**) 1 a road taking traffic past a city etc. 2 a channel that allows something to flow when the main route is blocked.

bypass[2] *verb* avoid by means of a bypass.

by-product *noun* something produced while something else is being made.

byre *noun* a cowshed.

by-road *noun* a minor road.

bystander *noun* a person standing near but not taking part in something.

byte *noun* a fixed number of bits (= binary digits) in a computer, often representing a single character.

byway *noun* a by-road.

bywoner (*say* **bay**-voo-a-ner) *noun* a person who rents land etc. from somebody else and gives part of his or her crop as rent to the owner of the land.

byword *noun* a person or thing spoken of as a famous example, *Their firm became a byword for quality.*

Cc

cab *noun* 1 a taxi. 2 a compartment for the driver of a lorry, train, bus, or crane.

cabaret (*say* **kab**-er-ay) *noun* an entertainment, especially one provided for the customers in a restaurant or night-club.

cabbage *noun* a vegetable with green or purple leaves.

cabin *noun* 1 a hut or shelter. 2 a compartment in a ship, aircraft, or spacecraft. 3 a driver's cab.

cabinet *noun* a cupboard or container with drawers or shelves.

Cabinet *noun* the group of chief ministers

who meet to decide government policy.

cable *noun* 1 a thick rope of fibre or wire; a thick chain. 2 a telegram sent overseas.

cacao (*say* ka-**kay**-oh) *noun* (*plural* **cacaos**) a tropical tree with a seed from which cocoa and chocolate are made.

cache (*say* kash) *noun* hidden stores or treasure; a hiding-place for treasure or stores.

cackle *noun* 1 the loud clucking noise a hen makes. 2 a loud silly laugh. 3 noisy chatter. **cackle** *verb*

cacophony (*say* kak-**off**-on-ee) *noun* a loud harsh unpleasant sound.

cactus *noun* (*plural* **cacti**) a fleshy plant, usually with prickles, from a hot dry climate.

CAD *abbreviation* computer-aided design.

cad *noun* a dishonourable person.

cadaverous (*say* kad-**av**-er-us) *adjective* pale and gaunt.

caddie *noun* a person who carries a golfer's clubs during a game.

caddy *noun* (*plural* **caddies**) a small box for holding tea.

cadence (*say* **kay**-denss) *noun* 1 rhythm; the rise and fall of the voice in speaking. 2 the final notes of a musical phrase.

cadenza (*say* ka-**den**-za) *noun* an elaborate passage for a solo instrument or singer, to show the performer's skill.

cadet *noun* a young person being trained for the armed forces or the police.

cadge *verb* (**cadged**, **cadging**) get something by begging for it. **cadger** *noun*

cadmium *noun* a metal that looks like tin.

Caesarean section (*say* siz-**air**-ee-an) *noun* a surgical operation for taking a baby out of the mother's womb.

café (*say* **kaf**-ay) *noun* 1 a small restaurant. 2 a small shop which sells groceries.

cafeteria (*say* kaf-it-**eer**-ee-a) *noun* a self-service restaurant.

caffeine (*say* **kaf**-een) *noun* a stimulant substance found in tea and coffee.

caftan *noun* a long loose coat or dress.

cage *noun* 1 a container with bars or wires, in which birds or animals are kept. 2 the enclosed platform used to raise and lower people and equipment in a mine.

cagoule (*say* kag-**ool**) *noun* a waterproof jacket.

cairn *noun* a pile of loose stones set up as a landmark or monument.

cajole *verb* (**cajoled**, **cajoling**) coax.

cake *noun* 1 a baked food made from a mixture of flour, fat, eggs, sugar, etc. 2 a shaped or hardened mass, *a cake of soap; fish cakes.*

caked *adjective* covered with dried mud etc.

calabash *noun* 1 a bowl or pipe made from a gourd. 2 a gourd, cooked and served as a vegetable.

calamine *noun* a pink powder used to make a soothing lotion for the skin.

calamity *noun* (*plural* **calamities**) a disaster. **calamitous** *adjective*

calcium *noun* a chemical substance found in teeth, bones, and lime.

calculate *verb* (**calculated**, **calculating**) 1 find out by using mathematics; count. 2 plan something deliberately; intend, *Her speech was calculated to stir up the crowd.* **calculable** *adjective*, **calculation** *noun*

calculator *noun* a small electronic device for making calculations.

calculus *noun* mathematics for working out problems about rates of change.

calendar *noun* something that shows the dates of the month or year.

calf[1] *noun* (*plural* **calves**) a young cow, whale, seal, etc.

calf[2] *noun* (*plural* **calves**) the fleshy back part of the leg below the knee.

calibre (*say* **kal**-ib-er) *noun* 1 the diameter of a tube or gun-barrel, or of a bullet etc. 2 ability; importance, *someone of your calibre.*

calico *noun* a kind of cotton cloth.

caliph (*say* **kal**-if or **kay**-lif) *noun* the former title of the ruler in certain Muslim countries.

call[1] *noun* 1 a shout or cry. 2 a visit. 3 a summons. 4 telephoning somebody.

call[2] *verb* 1 shout or speak loudly, e.g. to attract someone's attention; utter a call. 2 tell somebody to come to you; summon. 3 wake a person up. 4 telephone somebody.

5 make a short visit. **6** name a person or thing. **caller** *noun*

call a person's bluff challenge a person to do what was threatened, and expose the fact that it was a bluff.

call for come and collect; require, *The scandal calls for investigation.*

call up summon to join the armed forces.

call-box *noun* a telephone-box.

calligraphy (*say* kal-**ig**-raf-ee) *noun* beautiful handwriting.

calling *noun* an occupation; a profession.

calliper *noun* a support for a weak or injured leg.

callipers *plural noun* compasses for measuring the width of tubes or of round objects.

callous (*say* **kal**-us) *adjective* hard-hearted; unsympathetic. **callously** *adverb*, **callousness** *noun*

callow *adjective* immature and inexperienced. **callowly** *adverb*, **callowness** *noun*

callus *noun* (*plural* **calluses**) a small patch of skin that has become thick and hard through being continually pressed or rubbed.

calm[1] *adjective* **1** quiet and still; not windy. **2** not excited or agitated, *It is important to stay calm in an emergency.* **calmly** *adverb*, **calmness** *noun*

calm[2] *verb* make or become calm.

calorie *noun* a unit for measuring an amount of heat. **calorific** *adjective*

calumny (*say* **kal**-um-nee) *noun* (*plural* **calumnies**) slander.

calve *verb* (**calved**, **calving**) give birth to a calf.

calypso *noun* (*plural* **calypsos**) a West Indian song about current happenings.

calyx (*say* **kay**-liks) *noun* (*plural* **calyces**) a ring of leaves (*sepals*) forming the outer case of a bud.

camaraderie (*say* kam-er-**ah**-der-ee) *noun* comradeship.

camber *noun* a slight upward curve or arch, e.g. on a road to allow drainage.

cambium *noun* (*plural* **cambia** or **cambiums**) a tissue in a plant's stem which contains the tiny tubes that carry water and nutrients to all parts of the plant.

cambric *noun* thin linen or cotton cloth.

camel *noun* a large animal with a long neck and either one or two humps on its back, used in desert countries for riding and for carrying goods.

camellia *noun* a kind of evergreen flowering shrub.

cameo (*say* **kam**-ee-oh) *noun* (*plural* **cameos**) **1** a small hard piece of stone carved with a raised design in its upper layer. **2** a short well-performed part in a play etc.

camera *noun* a device for taking photographs, films, or television pictures. **cameraman** *noun*

in camera in a judge's private room; in private.

camomile *noun* a plant with sweet-smelling daisy-like flowers.

camouflage[1] (*say* **kam**-off-lah*zh*) *noun* a way of hiding things by making them look like part of their surroundings.

camouflage[2] *verb* (**camouflaged**, **camouflaging**) hide by camouflage.

camp[1] *noun* **1** a place where people live in tents or huts etc. **2** a fenced field for grazing or cultivation. **campsite** *noun*

camp[2] *verb* make a camp; live in a camp. **camper** *noun*

campaign[1] *noun* **1** a series of battles in one area or with one purpose. **2** a planned series of actions, *an advertising campaign.*

campaign[2] *verb* take part in a campaign. **campaigner** *noun*

camphor *noun* a strong-smelling white substance used in medicine and mothballs and in making plastics. **camphorated** *adjective*

campus *noun* (*plural* **campuses**) the grounds of a university or college.

can[1] *noun* **1** a metal or plastic container for liquids. **2** a sealed tin in which food or drink is preserved.

can[2] *verb* (**canned**, **canning**) preserve in a sealed can. **canner** *noun*

can[3] *auxiliary verb* (*past tense* **could**) **1** be able to, *He can play the violin.* **2** have the right or permission to, *You can go.*

• USAGE: It is more formal to say *You may go.*

canal *noun* 1 an artificial river cut through land so that boats can sail along it or so that it can drain or irrigate an area. 2 a tube through which something passes in the body, *the alimentary canal.*

canary *noun* (*plural* **canaries**) a small yellow bird that sings.

cancan *noun* a lively dance in which the legs are kicked very high.

cancel *verb* (**cancelled, cancelling**) 1 say that something planned will not be done or will not take place. 2 stop an order or instruction for something. 3 mark a stamp or ticket etc. so that it cannot be used again. **cancellation** *noun*

cancel out stop each other's effect, *The good and harm cancel each other out.*

cancer *noun* 1 a disease in which harmful growths form in the body. 2 a tumour, especially a harmful one. **cancerous** *adjective*

candelabrum (*say* kan-dil-**ab**-rum) *noun* (*plural* **candelabra**) a candlestick with several branches for holding candles.

candid *adjective* frank. **candidly** *adverb,* **candidness** *noun*

candidate *noun* 1 a person who wants to be elected or chosen for a particular job or position etc. 2 a person taking an examination. **candidacy** *noun,* **candidature** *noun*

candied *adjective* coated or preserved in sugar.

candied peel bits of the peel of citrus fruits candied for use in cooking.

candle *noun* a stick of wax with a wick through it, giving light when burning. **candlelight** *noun*

candlestick *noun* a holder for a candle or candles.

candour (*say* **kan**-der) *noun* being candid; frankness.

candy *noun* (*plural* **candies**) (*American*) sweets; a sweet.

candyfloss *noun* a fluffy mass of very thin strands of spun sugar.

cane¹ *noun* 1 the stem of a reed or tall grass etc. 2 a thin stick. 3 sugar-cane.

cane² *verb* (**caned, caning**) beat with a cane.

canine¹ (*say* **kayn**-I'n) *adjective* of dogs. **canine tooth** a pointed tooth.

canine² *noun* 1 a dog. 2 a canine tooth.

canister *noun* a metal container.

canker *noun* a disease that rots the wood of trees and plants or causes ulcers and sores on animals.

cannabis *noun* hemp, especially when smoked as a drug, also called dagga.

cannibal *noun* 1 a person who eats human flesh. 2 an animal that eats animals of its own kind. **cannibalism** *noun*

cannibalize *verb* (**cannibalized, cannibalizing**) take a machine etc. apart to provide spare parts for others. **cannibalization** *noun*

cannon¹ *noun* (*plural* **cannons** or **cannon**) a large heavy gun.

cannon² *verb* (**cannoned, cannoning**) bump into something heavily.

cannon-ball *noun* a large solid ball fired from a cannon.

cannot can not.

canny *adjective* (**cannier, canniest**) shrewd. **cannily** *adverb*

canoe¹ *noun* a narrow lightweight boat.

canoe² *verb* (**canoed, canoeing**) travel in a canoe. **canoeist** *noun*

canon *noun* 1 a priest with special duties in a cathedral. 2 a general principle; a rule, *the canons of good taste.*

canonize *verb* (**canonized, canonizing**) declare officially that someone is a saint. **canonization** *noun*

canopy *noun* (*plural* **canopies**) 1 a hanging cover forming a shelter above a throne, bed, or person etc. 2 the part of a parachute that spreads in the air.

cant¹ *verb* slope; tilt.

cant² *noun* 1 insincere talk. 2 jargon.

can't (*mainly spoken*) cannot.

cantaloup *noun* a small round orange-coloured melon, also called a spanspek.

cantankerous *adjective* bad-tempered.

cantata (*say* kant-**ah**-ta) *noun* a musical composition for singers, like an oratorio but shorter.

canteen *noun* 1 a restaurant for workers in a factory, office, etc. 2 a case or box containing a set of cutlery. **3** a soldier's or camper's water-flask.

canter[1] *noun* a gentle gallop.

canter[2] *verb* go or ride at a canter.

canticle *noun* a religious song with words taken from the Bible, e.g. the Magnificat.

cantilever *noun* a projecting beam or girder supporting a bridge etc.

canvas *noun* (*plural* **canvases**) **1** a kind of strong coarse cloth. **2** a piece of canvas for painting on; a painting.

canvass *verb* visit people to ask for votes, opinions, etc. **canvasser** *noun*

canyon *noun* a deep valley, usually with a river running through it.

cap[1] *noun* **1** a soft hat without a brim but often with a peak. **2** a special head-dress, e.g. that worn by a nurse; an academic mortar-board; a cap showing membership of a sports team. **3** a cap-like cover or top, *a kneecap.* **4** something that makes a bang when fired in a toy pistol.

cap[2] *verb* (**capped, capping**) **1** put a cap or cover on something; cover. **2** award a sports cap to a person chosen as a member of a team, *She was capped twice for South Africa.* **3** do better than something, *Can you cap that joke?*

capable *adjective* able to do something. **capably** *adverb*, **capability** *noun*

capacious (*say* ka-**pay**-shus) *adjective* roomy; able to hold a large amount.

capacity *noun* (*plural* **capacities**) **1** the amount that something can hold. **2** ability; capability, *a leader with the capacity to inspire loyalty.* **3** the position that someone occupies, *In my capacity as your guardian I am responsible for you.*

cape[1] *noun* a cloak.

cape[2] *noun* a promontory on the coast.

caper[1] *verb* jump or run about playfully.

caper[2] *noun* **1** capering. **2** (*slang*) an activity; an adventure.

caper[3] *noun* a bud of a prickly shrub, pickled for use in sauces etc.

Capetonian *noun* a person who lives in Cape Town.

capillary[1] (*say* ka-**pil**-er-ee) *noun* (*plural* **capillaries**) any of the very fine blood-vessels that connect veins and arteries.

capillary[2] *adjective* of or occurring in a very narrow tube; of a capillary, *Capillary action is the rise or fall of a liquid in a narrow tube.*

capital[1] *adjective* important.

capital city the most important city in a country.

capital letter a large letter of the kind used at the start of a name or sentence.

capital punishment punishing criminals by putting them to death.

capital[2] *noun* **1** a capital city. **2** a capital letter. **3** the top part of a pillar. **4** money or property that can be used to produce more wealth.

capitalism (*say* **kap**-it-al-izm) *noun* a system in which trade and industry are controlled by private owners for profit. (Compare *Communism.*)

capitalist (*say* **kap**-it-al-ist) *noun* **1** a person who has much money or property being used to make more wealth; a very rich person. **2** a person who is in favour of capitalism.

capitalize (*say* **kap**-it-al-I'z) *verb* (**capitalized, capitalizing**) **1** write or print as a capital letter. **2** change something into capital; provide with capital (= money). **capitalization** *noun*

capitalize on profit by something; use it to your own advantage, *You could capitalize on your skill at drawing.*

capitulate *verb* (**capitulated, capitulating**) admit that you are defeated and surrender. **capitulation** *noun*

caprice (*say* ka-**preess**) *noun* a capricious action or impulse; a whim.

capricious (*say* ka-**prish**-us) *adjective* deciding or changing your mind in an impulsive way. **capriciously** *adverb*, **capriciousness** *noun*

capsize *verb* (**capsized, capsizing**) overturn, *the boat capsized.*

capstan *noun* a thick post that can be turned to pull in a rope or cable etc. that winds round it as it turns.

capsule *noun* **1** a hollow pill containing medicine. **2** a plant's seed-case that splits open when ripe. **3** a compartment that can be separated from the rest of a spacecraft.

captain[1] *noun* 1 a person in command of a ship, aircraft, sports team, etc. 2 an army officer ranking next below a major; a naval officer ranking next below a commodore. **captaincy** *noun*

captain[2] *verb* be the captain of a sports team etc.

caption *noun* 1 the words printed with a picture to describe it. 2 a short title or heading in a newspaper or magazine.

captious (*say* **kap**-shus) *adjective* pointing out small mistakes or faults.

captivate *verb* (**captivated**, **captivating**) charm or delight someone. **captivation** *noun*

captive[1] *noun* someone taken prisoner.

captive[2] *adjective* taken prisoner; unable to escape. **captivity** *noun*

captor *noun* someone who has captured a person or animal.

capture[1] *verb* (**captured**, **capturing**) 1 seize; make a prisoner of someone. 2 take or obtain by force, trickery, skill, or attraction, *He captured her heart.* 3 transfer information that is written on paper to a form that can be used on a computer.

capture[2] *noun* 1 capturing. 2 a person or thing captured.

car *noun* 1 a motor car. 2 a carriage, *dining-car.* 3 the part of a lift, balloon, cable railway, etc. that carries passengers, *a cable car.*

carafe (*say* ka-**raf**) *noun* a glass bottle holding wine or water for pouring out at the table.

caramel *noun* 1 a kind of toffee tasting like burnt sugar. 2 burnt sugar used for colouring and flavouring food.

carapace (*say* **ka**-ra-payss) *noun* the shell on the back of a tortoise or crustacean.

carat *noun* 1 a measure of weight for precious stones. 2 a measure of the purity of gold, *Pure gold is 24 carats.*

caravan *noun* 1 an enclosed carriage equipped for living in, able to be towed by a motor vehicle or a horse. 2 a group of people travelling together across desert country. **caravanning** *noun*

caravel *noun* a small light fast ship used in former times.

caraway *noun* a plant with spicy seeds that are used for flavouring food.

carbohydrate *noun* a compound of carbon, oxygen, and hydrogen (e.g. sugar).

carbolic *noun* a kind of disinfectant.

carbon *noun* 1 a substance that is present in all living things and that occurs in its pure form as diamond and graphite. 2 carbon paper. 3 a carbon copy.

carbon copy a copy made with carbon paper; an exact copy.

carbon dioxide a gas formed when things burn, or breathed out by animals.

carbon paper thin paper with a coloured coating, placed between sheets of paper to make copies of what is written or typed on the top sheet.

carbonate *noun* a compound that gives off carbon dioxide when mixed with acid.

carbonated *adjective* with carbon dioxide added, *Carbonated drinks are fizzy.*

carboniferous *adjective* producing coal.

carbuncle *noun* 1 a bad abscess in the skin. 2 a bright-red gem.

carburettor *noun* a device for mixing fuel and air in an engine.

carcass *noun* (*plural* **carcasses**) 1 the dead body of an animal. 2 the bony part of a bird's body before or after it is cooked, *a chicken carcass.* 3 a framework, e.g. of a tyre.

card[1] *noun* 1 a small usually oblong piece of stiff paper or of plastic. 2 a playing-card. 3 cardboard.

cards *plural noun* a game using playing-cards.

on the cards likely; possible.

card[2] *verb* clean and disentangle wool-fibres with a wire brush or toothed instrument called a *card.*

cardboard *noun* a kind of thin board made of layers of paper or wood-fibre.

cardiac (*say* **kard**-ee-ak) *adjective* of the heart.

cardigan *noun* a knitted jacket.

cardinal[1] *noun* a senior priest in the Roman Catholic Church.

cardinal[2] *adjective* 1 chief; most important, *the cardinal features of our plan.* 2 deep scarlet (like a cardinal's cassock).

cardinal number a whole number, e.g. *one, two, three,* etc. (Compare *ordinal.*)

cardinal points the four main points of the compass (North, East, South, West).

cardiology *noun* the study of the structure and diseases of the heart. **cardiological** *adjective,* **cardiologist** *noun*

care[1] *noun* **1** serious attention and thought, *Plan your holiday with care.* **2** caution to avoid damage or loss, *Glass – handle with care.* **3** protection; supervision, *Leave the child in my care.* **4** worry; anxiety, *freedom from care.*

care[2] *verb* (**cared, caring**) **1** feel interested or concerned. **2** feel affection.

care for have in your care; be fond of.

career[1] *noun* **1** progress through life, especially in work. **2** an occupation with opportunities for promotion, *a diplomatic career.*

career[2] *verb* rush along wildly.

carefree *adjective* without worries or responsibilities.

careful *adjective* **1** giving serious thought and attention to something. **2** avoiding damage or danger etc.; cautious. **carefully** *adverb,* **carefulness** *noun*

careless *adjective* not careful. **carelessly** *adverb,* **carelessness** *noun*

caress[1] *noun* a gentle loving touch.

caress[2] *verb* touch lovingly.

caretaker *noun* a person employed to look after a school, block of flats, etc.

cargo *noun* (*plural* **cargoes**) goods carried in a ship or aircraft.

Caribbean *adjective* of or from the Caribbean Sea, a part of the Atlantic Ocean east of Central America.

caribou (*say* ka-rib-oo) *noun* (*plural* **caribou**) a North American reindeer.

caricature *noun* an amusing or exaggerated picture of someone.

caries (*say* kair-eez) *noun* (*plural* **caries**) decay in teeth or bones.

carmine *adjective & noun* deep red.

carnage *noun* the killing of many people.

carnal *adjective* of the body as opposed to the spirit; not spiritual.

carnation *noun* a garden flower with a sweet smell.

carnival *noun* a festival, often with a procession in fancy dress.

carnivorous (*say* kar-niv-er-us) *adjective* meat-eating. (Compare *herbivorous.*) **carnivore** *noun*

carol *noun* a joyful song; a Christmas hymn. **caroller** *noun,* **carolling** *noun*

carouse *verb* (**caroused, carousing**) drink and be merry.

carousel (*say* ka-roo-sel) *noun* **1** (*American*) a merry-go-round. **2** a rotating conveyor, e.g. for baggage at an airport.

carp[1] *noun* an edible freshwater fish.

carp[2] *verb* keep finding fault.

carpenter *noun* a person who makes things out of wood. **carpentry** *noun*

carpet *noun* a thick soft covering for a floor. **carpeted** *adjective,* **carpeting** *noun*

carport *noun* a shelter for a car.

carriage *noun* **1** one of the separate parts of a train, where passengers sit. **2** a passenger vehicle pulled by horses. **3** carrying goods from one place to another; the cost of carrying goods, *Carriage is extra.* **4** a moving part carrying or holding something in a machine, *a typewriter carriage.*

carriageway *noun* the part of a road on which vehicles travel.

carrier *noun* a person or thing that carries something.

carrion *noun* dead and decaying flesh.

carrot *noun* a plant with a thick orange-coloured root used as a vegetable.

carry *verb* (**carried, carrying**) **1** take something from one place to another. **2** support the weight of something. **3** travel clearly, *Sound carries in the mountains.* **4** win; approve, *The motion was carried by ten votes to six.*

be carried away be very excited.

carry on continue; manage; (*informal*) behave excitedly; (*informal*) complain.

cart[1] *noun* an open vehicle for carrying loads.

cart[2] *verb* **1** carry in a cart. **2** (*informal*) carry something heavy or tiring, *I've carted these books all round the school.*

carte blanche (*say* kart blahnsh) *noun* complete freedom to act as you think best, *The actor gave his agent carte blanche.*

cart-horse *noun* a large strong horse used for pulling heavy loads.

cartilage *noun* tough white flexible tissue attached to a bone.

cartography *noun* drawing maps. **cartographer** *noun*, **cartographic** *adjective*

carton *noun* a cardboard or plastic container.

cartoon *noun* 1 an amusing drawing. 2 a comic strip (see *comic*). 3 an animated film, *the latest Disney cartoon.* **cartoonist** *noun*

cartridge *noun* 1 a case containing the explosive for a bullet or shell. 2 a container holding film for a camera, ink for a pen, etc.

cartwheel *noun* 1 the wheel of a cart. 2 a handstand balancing on each hand in turn with arms and legs spread like spokes of a wheel.

carve *verb* (**carved, carving**) 1 make by cutting wood or stone etc. 2 cut cooked meat into slices. **carver** *noun*

carvery *noun* (*plural* **carveries**) a restaurant or buffet with large pieces of meat displayed for carving.

cascade¹ *noun* a waterfall.

cascade² *verb* (**cascaded, cascading**) fall like a cascade.

case¹ *noun* 1 a container. 2 a suitcase.

case² *noun* 1 an example of something existing or occurring; a situation, *In every case we found that someone had cheated.* 2 something investigated by police etc. or by a lawcourt, *a murder case.* 3 a set of facts or arguments to support something, *She put forward a good case for equality.* 4 the form of a word that shows how it is related to other words. *Fred's* is the possessive case of *Fred*; *him* is the objective case of *he*.

in any case anyway.

in case because something may happen; lest.

casement *noun* a window that opens on hinges at its side.

cash¹ *noun* 1 money in coin or notes. 2 immediate payment for goods etc.

cash register a device that registers the amount of money put in, used in a shop.

cash² *verb* change a cheque etc. for cash.

cashew *noun* a kind of small nut.

cashier *noun* a person who takes in and pays out money in a bank or takes payments in a shop.

cashmere *noun* very fine soft wool.

casing *noun* a protective covering.

casino *noun* (*plural* **casinos**) a public building or room for gambling.

cask *noun* a barrel.

casket *noun* a small box for jewellery etc.

cassava *noun* a tropical plant with starchy roots that are an important source of food in tropical countries.

casserole *noun* 1 a covered dish in which food is cooked and served. 2 food cooked in a casserole.

cassette *noun* a small sealed case containing recording tape, film, etc.

cassock *noun* a long garment worn by clergy and members of a church choir.

cast¹ *verb* (**cast, casting**) 1 throw. 2 shed or throw off, *Snakes cast their skins.* 3 make a vote. 4 make something of metal or plaster in a mould. 5 choose performers for a play or film etc.

casting vote the vote that decides which group wins when the votes on each side are equal.

cast iron a hard alloy of iron made by casting it in a mould.

cast² *noun* 1 a shape made by pouring liquid metal or plaster into a mould. 2 all the performers in a play or film.

castanets *plural noun* two pieces of wood, ivory, etc. held in one hand and clapped together to make a clicking sound, usually for dancing.

castaway *noun* a shipwrecked person.

caste *noun* 1 one of the social classes into which Hindus are born. 2 a social class which excludes others.

castigate *verb* (**castigated, castigating**) punish or rebuke severely. **castigation** *noun*

castle *noun* 1 a large old fortified building. 2 a piece in chess, also called a rook.

castles in the air day-dreams.

castor *noun* 1 a small wheel on the leg of a table, chair, etc. 2 a container with holes for sprinkling sugar.

castor sugar finely-ground white sugar.

castor oil *noun* oil from the seeds of a tropical plant, used as a laxative.

castrate *verb* (**castrated, castrating**) remove the testicles of a male animal; geld. (Compare *spay*.) **castration** *noun*

casual *adjective* 1 happening by chance; not planned. 2 not careful; not methodical, *a casual glance at a book.* 3 informal; suitable for informal occasions, *casual clothes.* 4 not permanent, *casual work.* **casually** *adverb*, **casualness** *noun*

casualty *noun* (*plural* **casualties**) a person who is killed or injured in war or in an accident.

cat *noun* 1 a small furry domestic animal. 2 an animal of the same family as the domestic cat, *Lions and tigers are cats.* **let the cat out of the bag** reveal a secret.

cata- *prefix* (becoming **cat-** before a vowel; combining with an *h* to become **cath-**) 1 down (as in *catapult*). 2 thoroughly (as in *catalogue*).

cataclysm (*say* kat-a-klizm) *noun* a violent upheaval or disaster.

catacombs (*say* kat-a-koomz) *plural noun* underground passages with compartments for tombs.

catalogue¹ *noun* 1 a list of things (e.g. of books in a library), usually arranged in order. 2 a book containing a list of things available, *Christmas catalogue.*

catalogue² *verb* (**catalogued, cataloguing**) enter something in a catalogue.

catalyst (*say* kat-a-list) *noun* something that starts or speeds up a change or reaction.

catamaran *noun* a boat with twin hulls.

catapult¹ *noun* 1 a device with elastic for shooting small stones. 2 an ancient military device for hurling stones etc.

catapult² *verb* hurl or rush violently.

cataract *noun* 1 a large waterfall or rush of water. 2 a cloudy area that forms in the eye and prevents a person from seeing clearly.

catarrh (*say* ka-tar) *noun* inflammation in your nose that makes it drip a watery fluid.

catastrophe (*say* ka-**tass**-trof-ee) *noun* a sudden great disaster. **catastrophic** (*say* kat-a-**strof**-ik) *adjective*,

catastrophically *adverb*

catch¹ *verb* (**caught, catching**) 1 take and hold something. 2 capture, *Cats catch mice.* 3 overtake. 4 be in time to get on a bus or train etc. 5 be infected with an illness. 6 hear, *I didn't catch what he said.* 7 surprise or detect somebody, *caught in the act.* 8 trick somebody, *catch her with a practical joke.* 9 make or become fixed or unable to move; snag; entangle, *I caught my dress on a nail.* 10 hit; strike, *The blow caught him on the nose.* **catch fire** start burning. **catch on** (*informal*) become popular; understand.

catch² *noun* (*plural* **catches**) 1 catching something. 2 something caught or worth catching, *a huge catch of fish.* 3 a hidden difficulty. 4 a device for fastening something.

catching *adjective* infectious.

catchment area *noun* 1 the whole area from which water drains into a river etc. 2 the area from which a school takes pupils or a hospital takes patients.

catch-phrase *noun* a popular phrase.

catchy *adjective* easy to remember; soon becoming popular, *a catchy tune.*

catechism (*say* kat-ik-izm) *noun* a set of questions and answers that give the basic beliefs of a religion.

categorical (*say* kat-ig-o-rik-al) *adjective* definite and absolute, *a categorical refusal.* **categorically** *adverb*

category *noun* (*plural* **categories**) a set of people or things classified as being similar to each other.

cater *verb* provide food etc. **caterer** *noun*

caterpillar *noun* the creeping worm-like creature that will turn into a butterfly or moth.

cath- *prefix* see **cata-**.

cathedral *noun* the most important church of a district, usually containing the bishop's throne.

Catherine wheel *noun* a firework that spins round.

cathode *noun* the electrode by which electric current leaves a device. (Compare *anode*.)

Catholic¹ *adjective* 1 of all Christians, *the Holy Catholic Church.* 2 Roman Catholic (see *Roman*). **Catholicism** *noun*

Catholic² *noun* a Roman Catholic.

catholic *adjective* including most things, *Her taste in literature is catholic.*

catkin *noun* a spike of small soft flowers on trees such as hazel and willow.

catnap *noun* a short sleep.

Catseye *noun* (*trade mark*) one of a line of reflecting studs marking the centre or edge of a road.

cattle *plural noun* animals with horns and hoofs, kept by farmers for their milk and beef.

cattle track a path formed when cattle walk the same way often, causing the ground to become hard and lose its vegetation.

catty¹ *adjective* (**cattier, cattiest**) speaking or spoken spitefully.

catty² *noun* (*plural* **catties**) (*informal*) a catapult.

caucus *noun* (*plural* **caucuses**) a small group within a political party, influencing decisions and policy etc.

cauldron *noun* a large deep pot for boiling things in.

cauliflower *noun* a cabbage with a large head of white flowers.

cause¹ *noun* 1 a person or thing that makes something happen or produces an effect. 2 a reason, *There is no cause for worry.* 3 a purpose for which people work; an organization or charity.

cause² *verb* (**caused, causing**) be the cause of; make something happen.

causeway *noun* a raised road across low or marshy ground.

caustic *adjective* 1 able to burn or wear things away by chemical action. 2 sarcastic. **caustically** *adverb*

cauterize *verb* (**cauterized, cauterizing**) burn the surface of flesh to destroy infection or stop bleeding. **cauterization** *noun*

caution¹ *noun* 1 care taken so as to avoid danger etc. 2 a warning, *Proceed with caution.*

caution² *verb* warn someone.

cautionary *adjective* giving a warning.

cautious *adjective* showing caution.

cautiously *adverb*, **cautiousness** *noun*

cavalcade *noun* a procession.

cavalry *noun* soldiers who fight on horseback or in armoured vehicles. (Compare *infantry.*)

cave¹ *noun* a large hollow place in the side of a hill or cliff, or underground.

cave² *verb* (**caved, caving**) **cave in** fall inwards; give way in an argument.

caveat (*say* **kav**-ee-at) *noun* a warning.

cavern *noun* a large cave. **cavernous** *adjective*

caviare (*say* **kav**-ee-ar) *noun* the pickled roe of sturgeon or other large fish.

cavil *verb* (**cavilled, cavilling**) raise petty objections.

caving *noun* exploring caves.

cavity *noun* (*plural* **cavities**) a hollow or hole.

cavort (*say* ka-**vort**) *verb* caper about.

caw *noun* the harsh cry of a crow etc.

CBD *abbreviation* central business district.

CC *abbreviation* close corporation.

cc *abbreviation* cubic centimetre(s).

CD *abbreviation* compact disc.

CD-ROM a CD containing information which can be read by a computer.

cease¹ *verb* (**ceased, ceasing**) stop; end.

cease² *noun* **without cease** not ceasing.

cease-fire *noun* a signal to stop firing.

ceaseless *adjective* not ceasing.

cedar *noun* an evergreen tree with hard fragrant wood. **cedarwood** *noun*

cede (*say* seed) *verb* (**ceded, ceding**) give up your rights to something; surrender, *They had to cede some of their territory.*

cedilla (*say* sid-**il**-a) *noun* a mark under *c* in certain languages to show that it is pronounced as *s*, e.g. in *Moçambique.*

ceiling *noun* 1 the flat surface under the top of a room. 2 the highest limit that something can reach.

celebrate *verb* (**celebrated, celebrating**) 1 do something special or enjoyable to show that a day or event is important. 2 perform a religious ceremony. **celebrant** *noun*, **celebration** *noun*

celebrated *adjective* famous.

celebrity *noun* (*plural* **celebrities**) 1 a famous person. 2 fame; being famous.

celery *noun* a vegetable with crisp white or green stems.

celestial (*say* sil-**est**-ee-al) *adjective* 1 of the sky, *The sun and moon are celestial bodies.* 2 of heaven; divine.

celibate (*say* **sel**-ib-at) *adjective* remaining unmarried, especially for religious reasons. **celibacy** *noun*

cell *noun* 1 a very small room, e.g. in a monastery or a prison. 2 a microscopic unit of living matter. 3 a compartment of a honeycomb. 4 a device for producing electric current chemically. 5 a small group or unit in an organization etc., *a terrorist cell.*

cellar *noun* an underground room.

cello (*say* **chel**-oh) *noun* a musical instrument like a large violin, placed between the knees of a player. **cellist** *noun*

cellular *adjective* 1 of or containing cells. 2 with an open mesh, *cellular blankets.* 3 (of a telephone system) that works by radio, *cellular phone.*

cellular respiration the process by which living cells transform food into energy.

celluloid *noun* a kind of plastic.

cellulose *noun* 1 tissue that forms the main part of all plants and trees. 2 paint made from cellulose.

Celsius (*say* **sel**-see-us) *adjective* measuring temperature on a scale using 100 degrees, where water freezes at 0° and boils at 100°.

Celtic *adjective* of the languages or inhabitants of ancient Britain and France before the Romans came, or of their descendants, e.g. Irish, Welsh, Gaelic.

cement¹ *noun* 1 a mixture of lime and clay used in building, to join bricks together, etc. 2 a strong glue.

cement² *verb* 1 put cement on something. 2 join firmly; strengthen.

cemetery (*say* **sem**-et-ree) *noun* (*plural* **cemeteries**) a place where people are buried.

cenotaph (*say* **sen**-o-taf) *noun* a monument, especially as a war memorial, to people who are buried elsewhere.

censer *noun* a container in which incense is burnt.

censor *noun* a person who examines films, books, letters, etc. and removes or bans anything that seems harmful. **censor** *verb*, **censorship** *noun*
● USAGE: Do not confuse with *censure.*

censorious (*say* sen-**sor**-ee-us) *adjective* criticizing something strongly.

censure (*say* **sen**-sher) *noun* strong criticism or disapproval of something.
● USAGE: Do not confuse with *censor.*

census *noun* (*plural* **censuses**) an official count or survey of population, traffic, etc.

cent *noun* a coin worth one-hundredth of a rand, dollar, etc.

centenarian (*say* sent-in-**air**-ee-an) *noun* a person who is 100 years old or more.

centenary (*say* sen-**teen**-er-ee) *noun* a 100th anniversary. **centennial** (*say* sen-**ten**-ee-al) *adjective*

centi- *prefix* 1 one hundred (as in *centipede*). 2 one-hundredth (as in *centimetre*).

centigrade *adjective* (of a temperature scale) Celsius.

centimetre *noun* one-hundredth of a metre.

centipede *noun* a small crawling creature with a long body and many legs.

central *adjective* 1 of or at the centre. 2 most important. **centrally** *adverb*

central heating a system of heating a building from one source by circulating hot water or hot air or steam in pipes or by linked radiators.

central processing unit the principal operating part of a computer.

centralize *verb* (**centralized**, **centralizing**) bring under a central authority's control. **centralization** *noun*

centre¹ *noun* 1 the middle point or part. 2 an important place, e.g. from which things are organized; a place where certain things happen, *shopping centre.*

centre² *verb* (**centred**, **centring**) place something in or at the centre.

centre-forward *noun* the player in the middle of the forward line in soccer, hockey, etc.

centrifugal *adjective* moving away from the centre; using centrifugal force.
centrifugal force a force that makes a thing

that is travelling round a central point fly outwards off its circular path.

centurion (*say* sent-**yoor**-ee-on) *noun* an officer in the ancient Roman army.

century *noun* (*plural* **centuries**) **1** a period of one hundred years. **2** a hundred runs scored by a batsman in an innings at cricket.

cephalopod (*say* **sef**-al-o-pod) *noun* a mollusc (such as an octopus) that has a head with a ring of tentacles round the mouth.

ceramic *adjective* of pottery.

ceramics *plural noun* pottery-making.

cereal *noun* **1** a grass producing seeds which are used as food, e.g. wheat, maize, rice. **2** a breakfast food made from these seeds.

cerebral (*say* se-rib-ral) *adjective* of the brain.
cerebral palsy an illness caused by damage to the brain before birth, which makes the limbs and muscles permanently weak.

ceremonial *adjective* of or used in a ceremony; formal. **ceremonially** *adverb*

ceremonious *adjective* full of ceremony; elaborately performed.

ceremony *noun* (*plural* **ceremonies**) the formal actions carried out on an important occasion, e.g. at a wedding or a funeral.

certain *adjective* sure; without doubt.
a certain person or **thing** a person or thing that is known but not named.

certainly *adverb* **1** for certain. **2** yes.

certainty *noun* (*plural* **certainties**) **1** something that is sure to happen. **2** being sure, *There is no certainty of success.*

certificate *noun* an official written or printed statement giving information about a person etc., *a birth certificate.*

certify *verb* (**certified, certifying**) declare something formally; show on a certificate. **certification** *noun*

certitude *noun* a feeling of certainty.

cervix *noun* **1** the neck. **2** the neck of the womb. **cervical** *adjective*

cessation *noun* ceasing.

cesspit (also **cesspool**) *noun* a covered pit where liquid waste or sewage is stored temporarily.

CFC *abbreviation* chlorofluorocarbon (a chemical compound that harms the ozone layer).

chafe *verb* (**chafed, chafing**) **1** rub a person's skin to make it warm again. **2** make or become sore by rubbing. **3** become irritated or impatient, *We chafed at the delay.*

chaff[1] *noun* **1** husks of corn, separated from the seed. **2** teasing; joking.

chaff[2] *verb* tease; joke.

chagrin (*say* **shag**-rin) *noun* a feeling of being annoyed and embarrassed or disappointed.

chain[1] *noun* **1** a row of metal rings fastened together. **2** a connected series of things, *a chain of mountains*; *a chain of events.*
chain-letter *noun* a letter that you are asked to copy and send to several other people.
chain reaction a series of happenings in which each causes the next.
chain store one of a number of similar shops owned by the same firm.

chain[2] *verb* fasten with a chain or chains.

chair[1] *noun* **1** a movable seat, with a back, for one person. **2** a position of authority at a meeting, *Ms Khumalo was in the chair.*

chair[2] *verb* control a meeting, *Who will chair this meeting?*

chairperson *noun* the person who is in control of a meeting. **chairman** *noun*, **chairwoman** *noun*

chalet (*say* **shal**-ay) *noun* **1** a Swiss hut or cottage. **2** a hut in a holiday camp etc.

chalice *noun* a large goblet for holding wine, especially one used at Holy Communion.

chalk *noun* **1** a soft white or coloured stick used for writing on boards or for drawing. **2** soft white limestone. **chalky** *adjective*

challenge[1] *noun* a demand to have a contest, do something difficult, say who you are, etc.

challenge[2] *verb* (**challenged, challenging**) **1** make a challenge to someone. **2** question whether something is true or correct, *This new discovery challenges traditional beliefs.* **challenger** *noun*

chamber *noun* **1** (*old use*) a room. **2** a hall used for meetings of a parliament etc.; the members of the group using it. **3** a compartment in machinery etc.

chamber music music for a small group of players.

chamber-pot *noun* a receptacle for urine etc., used in a bedroom.

chamberlain *noun* an official who manages the household of a sovereign or great noble.

chambermaid *noun* a woman employed to clean bedrooms at a hotel etc.

chameleon (*say* kam-**ee**-lee-on) *noun* a small lizard that can change its colour to that of its surroundings.

chamois *noun* (*plural* **chamois**) **1** (*say* **sham**-wa) a small wild antelope living in the mountains of Europe and Asia. **2** (*say* **sham**-ee) a piece of soft yellow leather used for washing and polishing things.

champ *verb* munch or bite something noisily.

champagne (*say* sham-**payn**) *noun* a white sparkling wine, especially from Champagne in France.

champion¹ *noun* **1** a person or thing that has defeated all the others in a sport or competition etc. **2** someone who supports a cause by fighting, speaking, etc. **championship** *noun*

champion² *verb* support a cause by fighting or speaking for it.

chance¹ *noun* **1** a possibility; an opportunity, *Now is your chance to escape.* **2** the way things happen without being planned, *I met her by chance.*

take a chance take a risk.

chance² *verb* (**chanced, chancing**) **1** happen by chance, *I chanced to meet her.* **2** (*informal*) risk, *Let's chance it.*

chancel *noun* the part of a church nearest to the altar.

chancellor *noun* an important official.

chancy *adjective* risky.

chandelier (*say* shand-il-**eer**) *noun* a hanging support for several lights.

change¹ *verb* (**changed, changing**) **1** make or become different. **2** exchange, *I need to change these dollars into rand.* **3** put fresh clothes or coverings etc. on. **4** go from one train or bus etc. to another.

change² *noun* **1** changing; alteration. **2** coins or notes of small values. **3** money given back to the payer when the price is less than the amount handed over. **4** a fresh set of clothes. **5** a variation in routine, *Let's walk home for a change.*

changeable *adjective* likely to change; changing frequently.

changeling *noun* a child believed to have been substituted secretly for another, especially by fairies.

channel¹ *noun* **1** a stretch of water connecting two seas. **2** a way for water to flow along, *channels worn in the rock.* **3** the part of a river or sea etc. that is deep enough for ships. **4** a broadcasting wavelength.

channel² *verb* (**channelled, channelling**) **1** make a channel in something. **2** direct something through a channel or other route, *Funds will be channelled through local government.*

chant¹ *noun* **1** a tune to which words with no regular rhythm are fitted, e.g. one used in singing psalms. **2** a rhythmic call or shout.

chant² *verb* **1** sing. **2** call out words in a rhythm.

chaos (*say* **kay**-oss) *noun* great disorder. **chaotic** *adjective,* **chaotically** *adverb*

chap *noun* (*informal*) a man.

chapatti (*say* chup-**ah**-tee) *noun* (*plural* **chapattis**) a flat thin piece of a kind of bread.

chapel *noun* **1** a place used for Christian worship, other than a cathedral or parish church; a religious service in this. **2** a section of a large church, with its own altar.

chaperon (also **chaperone**) (*say* **shap**-er-ohn) *noun* an older woman in charge of a young one on social occasions.

chaplain *noun* a member of the clergy who looks after a college or hospital or regiment etc.

chapped *adjective* with skin split or cracked from cold etc.

chapter *noun* **1** a division of a book. **2** the clergy of a cathedral or members of a monastery.

chapter house the building used for the meeting of a chapter.

char[1] *verb* (**charred, charring**) make or become black by burning.

char[2] *noun* a charwoman.

character *noun* 1 a person in a story or play etc. 2 all the qualities that make a person or thing what he, she, or it is. 3 a letter of the alphabet, *Chinese characters.*

characteristic[1] *noun* a quality that forms part of a person's or thing's character.

characteristic[2] *adjective* typical of a person or thing. **characteristically** *adverb*

characterize *verb* (**characterized, characterizing**) 1 be a characteristic of. 2 describe the character of, *The novelist characterizes her hero as strong and passionate.* **characterization** *noun*

charade (*say* sha-**rahd**) *noun* 1 a scene in the game of **charades**, in which people try to guess a word from other people's acting. 2 a pretence.

charcoal *noun* a black substance made by burning wood slowly.

charge[1] *noun* 1 the price asked for something. 2 a rushing attack. 3 the amount of explosive needed to fire a gun etc. 4 electricity in something, *a negative charge.* 5 an accusation of having committed a crime, *a charge of murder.* 6 a person or thing in someone's care. **in charge** in control; deciding what shall happen to a person or thing.

charge[2] *verb* (**charged, charging**) 1 ask a particular price. 2 rush forward in an attack. 3 give an electric charge to something. 4 accuse someone of committing a crime. 5 entrust someone with a responsibility or task.

charger *noun* 1 (*old use*) a cavalry horse. 2 a device for charging a battery.

chariot *noun* a horse-drawn vehicle with two wheels, used in ancient times for fighting, racing, etc. **charioteer** *noun*

charisma (*say* ka-**riz**-ma) *noun* the special quality that makes a person popular, influential, etc.

charismatic (*say* ka-riz-**mat**-ik) *adjective* having charisma.

charity *noun* (*plural* **charities**) 1 an organization set up to help people who are poor

or have suffered a disaster. 2 giving money or help etc. to the needy. 3 loving kindness towards others; being unwilling to think badly of people, *'It's not really his fault,' she said with great charity.* **charitable** *adjective,* **charitably** *adverb*

charlatan (*say* **shar**-la-tan) *noun* a person who falsely claims to be an expert.

charm[1] *noun* 1 the power to please or delight people; attractiveness. 2 a magic spell; a small object believed to bring good luck. 3 an ornament worn on a bracelet etc.

charm[2] *verb* 1 give pleasure or delight to people, *The singer charmed her audience.* 2 put a spell on; bewitch. **charmer** *noun*

charnel-house *noun* a place in which the bodies or bones of the dead are kept.

chart[1] *noun* 1 a map for people sailing ships or flying aircraft. 2 an outline map showing special information, *a weather chart.* 3 a diagram or list etc. giving information in an orderly way. **the charts** a list of the current music that is most popular.

chart[2] *verb* make a chart of something; map.

charter[1] *noun* 1 an official document giving somebody certain rights etc. 2 chartering an aircraft, ship, or vehicle.

charter[2] *verb* 1 hire an aircraft, ship, or vehicle. 2 give a charter to someone. **chartered accountant** an accountant who is qualified according to the rules of a professional association.

charwoman *noun* (*plural* **charwomen**) a woman employed as a cleaner.

chary (*say* **chair**-ee) *adjective* cautious about doing or giving something.

chase *verb* (**chased, chasing**) go quickly after a person or thing in order to capture or catch them up or drive them away. **chase** *noun*

chasm (*say* kazm) *noun* a deep opening in the ground.

chassis (*say* **shas**-ee) *noun* (*plural* **chassis**) the framework under a car etc., on which other parts are mounted.

chaste *adjective* not having sexual intercourse at all, or only with the person to whom you are married. **chastity** *noun*

chasten (*say* **chay**-sen) *verb* discipline a person by punishing them; make someone feel subdued.

chastise *verb* (**chastised, chastising**) punish severely. **chastisement** *noun*

chat[1] *noun* a friendly conversation.

chat[2] *verb* (**chatted, chatting**) have a chat.

château (*say* **shat**-oh) *noun* (*plural* **châteaux**) a large country house in France.

chattel *noun* something you own that can be moved from place to place (distinguished from a house or land).

chatter[1] *verb* 1 talk quickly about unimportant things; keep on talking. 2 make a rattling sound, *'I'm so cold my teeth are chattering,' he said.* **chatterer** *noun*

chatter[2] *noun* chattering talk or sound.

chatterbox *noun* a talkative person.

chauffeur (*say* **shoh**-fer) *noun* a person employed to drive a car.

chauvinism (*say* **shoh**-vin-izm) *noun* prejudiced belief that your own group or country etc. is superior to others. **chauvinist** *noun*, **chauvinistic** *adjective*

cheap *adjective* 1 low in price; not expensive. 2 of poor quality; of low value. **cheaply** *adverb*, **cheapness** *noun*

cheapen *verb* make or become cheap.

cheat[1] *verb* 1 trick or deceive somebody. 2 try to do well in an examination or game etc. by breaking the rules.

cheat[2] *noun* a person who cheats.

check[1] *verb* 1 make sure that something is correct or in good condition. 2 make something stop or go slower, *check the enemy's advance.*

check[2] *noun* 1 checking something. 2 stopping or slowing; a pause. 3 a receipt; a bill in a restaurant. 4 the situation in chess when a king may be captured.

check[3] *noun* a pattern of squares. **checked** *adjective*

checkmate *noun* the winning situation in chess. **checkmate** *verb*

check-out *noun* a place where goods are paid for in a self-service shop.

Cheddar *noun* a kind of cheese.

cheek[1] *noun* 1 the side of the face below the eye. 2 impudence.

cheek[2] *verb* be cheeky to someone.

cheeky *adjective* impudent. **cheekily** *adverb*, **cheekiness** *noun*

cheer[1] *noun* 1 a shout of praise or pleasure or encouragement, especially 'hurray'. 2 cheerfulness, *full of good cheer.*

cheer[2] *verb* 1 give a cheer. 2 gladden or encourage somebody.

cheer up make or become cheerful.

cheerful *adjective* 1 looking or sounding happy. 2 pleasantly bright, *a cheerful room.* **cheerfully** *adverb*, **cheerfulness** *noun*

cheerio *interjection* (*informal*) goodbye.

cheerless *adjective* gloomy; dreary.

cheery *adjective* bright and cheerful.

cheese *noun* a solid food made from milk.

cheetah *noun* a swift-running spotted wild animal, like a leopard.

chef (*say* shef) *noun* the cook in a hotel or restaurant.

chemical[1] *adjective* of or produced by chemistry.

chemical bond a force which holds atoms together as molecules.

chemical equation a written statement which uses chemical symbols and formulae to show what happens in a chemical reaction.

chemical potential energy energy stored in the form of chemical compounds.

chemical reaction a change in a substance when chemical bonds form or break and energy is transformed.

chemical[2] *noun* a substance obtained by or used in chemistry.

chemist *noun* 1 a person who makes or sells medicines. 2 an expert in chemistry.

chemistry *noun* 1 the way that substances combine and react with one another. 2 the study of substances and their reactions etc.

cheque *noun* a printed form on which you write instructions to a bank to pay out money from your account.

chequered *adjective* marked with a pattern of squares.

cherish *verb* 1 look after a person or thing lovingly. 2 be fond of.

cherry *noun* (*plural* **cherries**) a small soft round fruit with a stone.

cherub *noun* (*plural* **cherubim** or

cherubs) an angel, often pictured as a chubby child with wings. **cherubic** (*say* che-**roo**-bik) *adjective*

chess *noun* a game for two players with sixteen pieces each on a board of 64 squares (a **chessboard**).

chest *noun* 1 the front part of the body between the neck and the waist. 2 a large strong box for storing things in.
chest of drawers a piece of furniture with drawers for storing clothes etc.

chestnut *noun* 1 a tree that produces hard brown nuts. 2 the nut of this tree. 3 an old joke or story.

chevron (*say* shev-ron) *noun* a V-shaped stripe.

chew *verb* grind food between the teeth. **chewy** *adjective*

chewing-gum *noun* a sticky flavoured substance for chewing.

chic (*say* sheek) *adjective* stylish and elegant.

chicanery (*say* shik-**ayn**-er-ee) *noun* trickery.

chick *noun* a very young bird.

chicken[1] *noun* 1 a young bird, especially of the domestic fowl. 2 the flesh of a domestic fowl as food.

chicken[2] *adjective* (*slang*) afraid to do something; cowardly.

chicken[3] *verb* **chicken out** (*slang*) withdraw because you are afraid.

chicken-pox *noun* a disease that produces red spots on the skin.

chicory *noun* 1 a plant whose leaves are used as salad. 2 its root, roasted and ground and used with or instead of coffee.

chide *verb* (**chided, chidden, chiding**) (*old use*) scold.

chief[1] *noun* a person with the highest rank or authority.

chief[2] *adjective* most important; main. **chiefly** *adverb*

chieftain *noun* the chief of a tribe, band of robbers, etc.

chiffon (*say* shif-on) *noun* a very thin almost transparent fabric.

chilblain *noun* a sore swollen place, usually on a hand or foot, caused by cold weather.

child *noun* (*plural* **children**) 1 a young person; a boy or girl. 2 someone's son or daughter.

child abuse cruel treatment of children by adults.

childhood *noun* the time when a person is a child.

childish *adjective* like a child; unsuitable for a grown person. **childishly** *adverb*

childless *adjective* having no children.

child-minder *noun* a person who is paid to look after a child.

chill[1] *noun* 1 unpleasant coldness. 2 an illness that makes you shiver.

chill[2] *verb* make a person or thing cold.

chilli *noun* (*plural* **chillies**) the hot-tasting pod of a red pepper.

chilly *adjective* 1 rather cold. 2 unfriendly. **chilliness** *noun*

chime[1] *noun* a series of notes sounded by a set of bells each making a different musical sound.

chime[2] *verb* (**chimed, chiming**) make a chime.

chimera (*say* ky-**meer**-a) *noun* 1 an imaginary animal composed of the parts of several different animals. 2 a wild or impossible idea.

chimney *noun* (*plural* **chimneys**) a tall pipe or structure that carries away smoke from a fire.

chimney-pot *noun* a pipe fitted to the top of a chimney.

chimney-sweep *noun* a person who cleans soot from inside chimneys.

chimpanzee *noun* an ape, smaller than a gorilla.

chin *noun* the lower part of the face below the mouth.

china *noun* thin delicate pottery.

chink[1] *noun* 1 a narrow opening, *a chink in the curtains*. 2 a chinking sound.

chink[2] *verb* make a sound like glasses or coins being struck together.

chintz *noun* a shiny cotton cloth used for making curtains etc.

chip[1] *noun* 1 a thin piece cut or broken off something hard. 2 a fried oblong strip of potato. 3 a place where a small piece has been knocked off something, *This mug has* *a chip in it.* **4** a small counter used in games. **5** a microchip.

a chip off the old block a child who is very like his or her father.

have a chip on your shoulder have a grievance and feel bitter or resentful.

chip² *verb* (**chipped, chipping**) **1** knock small pieces off something. **2** cut a potato into chips.

chipboard *noun* board made from chips of wood pressed and stuck together.

chipolata *noun* a small spicy sausage.

chiropody (*say* ki-**rop**-od-ee) *noun* treatment of ailments of the feet, e.g. corns. **chiropodist** *noun*

chirp *verb* make short sharp sounds like a small bird. **chirp** *noun*

chirpy *adjective* lively and cheerful.

chisel¹ *noun* a tool with a sharp end for shaping wood, stone, etc.

chisel² *verb* (**chiselled, chiselling**) shape or cut with a chisel.

chit-chat *noun* (*informal*) light conversation.

chivalrous (*say* **shiv**-al-rus) *adjective* being considerate and helpful towards people less strong than yourself. **chivalry** *noun*

chive *noun* a small herb with leaves that taste like onions.

chivvy *verb* (**chivvied, chivvying**) try to make someone hurry.

chlorinate *verb* (**chlorinated, chlorinating**) put chlorine into something. **chlorination** *noun*

chlorine (*say* **klor**-een) *noun* a greenish-yellow gas used to disinfect water etc.

chloroform (*say* **klo**-ro-form) *noun* a liquid that gives off a vapour that makes people unconscious.

chlorophyll (*say* **klo**-ro-fil) *noun* the substance that makes plants green.

chloroplast (*say* **klo**-ro-plast) *noun* a green organelle containing chlorophyll found in some plant cells.

choc-ice *noun* a bar of ice-cream covered with chocolate.

chock *noun* a block or wedge used to prevent something from moving.

chock-a-block *adjective* crammed or crowded together.

chock-full *adjective* crammed full.

chocolate *noun* **1** a solid brown food or powder made from roasted cacao seeds. **2** a drink made with this powder. **3** a sweet made of or covered with chocolate.

choice¹ *noun* **1** choosing; the power to choose between things. **2** a variety from which someone can choose, *There is a wide choice of holidays.* **3** a person or thing chosen, *This is my choice.*

choice² *adjective* of the best quality, *choice bananas.*

choir *noun* a group of people trained to sing together, especially in a church. **choirboy** *noun*

choke¹ *verb* (**choked, choking**) **1** cause somebody to stop breathing properly. **2** be unable to breathe properly. **3** clog, *dead leaves choked the drains.*

choke² *noun* a device controlling the flow of air into the engine of a motor vehicle.

chokka *noun* squid often used for bait.

cholera (*say* **kol**-er-a) *noun* an infectious disease that is often fatal.

cholesterol (*say* kol-**est**-er-ol) *noun* a fatty substance that can clog the arteries.

choose *verb* (**chose, chosen, choosing**) take one or more from among a number of people or things; select. **choosy** *adjective*

chop¹ *verb* (**chopped, chopping**) cut or hit something with a heavy blow.

chop² *noun* **1** a chopping blow. **2** a small thick slice of meat, usually on a rib.

chopper *noun* **1** a chopping tool; a small axe. **2** (*slang*) a helicopter.

choppy *adjective* (**choppier, choppiest**) not smooth; full of small waves, *a choppy sea.* **choppiness** *noun*

chopsticks *plural noun* a pair of thin sticks used for lifting Chinese and Japanese food to your mouth.

chopsuey (*say* chop-**soo**-ee) *noun* (*plural* **chopsueys**) a Chinese dish of meat fried with vegetables and rice.

choral *adjective* of or for or sung by a choir or chorus.

chorale (*say* kor-**ahl**) *noun* a choral composition using the words of a hymn.

chord¹ (*say* kord) *noun* a number of

musical notes sounded together.

chord[2] (*say* kord) *noun* a straight line joining two points on a curve.

chore (*say* chor) *noun* a regular or dull task.

choreography (*say* ko-ree-**og**-ra-fee) *noun* the composition of ballets or stage dances. **choreographer** *noun*

chorister (*say* **ko**-rist-er) *noun* a member of a choir.

chorrie *noun* (*slang*) an old car.

chortle *noun* a loud chuckle.

chorus[1] *noun* (*plural* **choruses**) **1** the words repeated after each verse of a song or poem. **2** music sung by a group of people, *the Hallelujah Chorus*. **3** a group singing together.

chorus[2] *verb* (**chorused, chorusing**) sing or speak in chorus.

christen *verb* **1** baptize. **2** give a name or nickname to a person or thing. **christening** *noun*

Christian[1] *noun* a person who believes in Jesus Christ and his teachings.

Christian[2] *adjective* of Christians or their beliefs. **Christianity** *noun*

Christian name a name given to a person at his or her christening.

Christmas *noun* (*plural* **Christmases**) the day (25 December) when Christians commemorate the birth of Jesus Christ; the days round it.

Christmas beetle a cicada that is especially noisy at Christmas time.

Christmas flower a hydrangea.

Christmas pudding a dark pudding containing dried fruit etc., eaten at Christmas.

Christmas tree an evergreen or artificial tree decorated at Christmas.

chromatic (*say* krom-**at**-ik) *adjective* of colours.

chromatic scale a musical scale going up or down in semitones.

chrome (*say* krohm) *noun* chromium.

chromium (*say* **kroh**-mee-um) *noun* a shiny silvery metal.

chromosome (*say* **kroh**-mos-ohm) *noun* a tiny thread-like part of an animal cell or plant cell, carrying genes.

chronic *adjective* lasting for a long time, *a chronic illness*. **chronically** *adverb*

chronicle *noun* a record of events in the order of their happening.

chronological *adjective* arranged in the order of happening. **chronologically** *adverb*

chronology (*say* kron-**ol**-oj-ee) *noun* the arrangement of events in the order in which they happened, e.g. in history or geology.

chronometer (*say* kron-**om**-it-er) *noun* a very exact device for measuring time.

chrysalis *noun* (*plural* **chrysalises**) a caterpillar that is changing into a butterfly or moth.

chrysanthemum *noun* a garden flower that blooms in autumn.

chubby *adjective* (**chubbier, chubbiest**) plump. **chubbiness** *noun*

chuck[1] *verb* (*informal*) throw.

chuck[2] *noun* **1** the gripping-part of a lathe. **2** the part of a drill that holds the bit.

chuckle[1] *noun* a quiet laugh.

chuckle[2] *verb* (**chuckled, chuckling**) give a chuckle.

chuffed *adjective* (*slang*) delighted.

chug *verb* (**chugged, chugging**) make the sound of an engine.

chum *noun* (*informal*) a friend. **chummy** *adjective*

chunk *noun* a thick piece of something. **chunky** *adjective*

chupatty *noun* (*plural* **chupatties**) a chapatti.

church *noun* (*plural* **churches**) **1** a public building for Christian worship. **2** a religious service in a church, *I will see you after church*.

the Church all Christians; a group of these, *The Church of the Province of South Africa is also known as the Anglican Church*.

churchyard *noun* the ground round a church, often used as a graveyard.

churlish *adjective* ill-mannered; surly.

churn[1] *noun* **1** a large can in which milk is carried from a farm. **2** a machine in which milk is beaten to make butter.

churn[2] *verb* **1** make butter in a churn. **2** stir or swirl vigorously.

churn out produce in large quantities.

chute (*say* shoot) *noun* **1** a steep channel

for people or things to slide down.
2 (*informal*) a parachute.

chutney *noun* a strong-tasting mixture of fruit, peppers, etc., eaten with meat.

ciao (*say* chow) *interjection* (*informal*)
1 goodbye. **2** hello.

cicada (*say* si-**kar**-da) *noun* a winged insect that makes a loud chirping sound.

CID *abbreviation* Criminal Investigation Department.

cider *noun* an alcoholic drink made from apples.

cigar *noun* a roll of compressed tobacco-leaves for smoking.

cigarette *noun* a small roll of shredded tobacco in thin paper for smoking.

cilium (*say* si-lee-um) *noun* (*plural* **cilia**)
1 a small hairlike structure. **2** an eyelash.

cinder *noun* a small piece of partly burnt coal or wood.

cine-camera (*say* **sin**-ee) *noun* a camera used for taking moving pictures.

cinema *noun* a place where films are shown.

cinematography *noun* the art of making films.

cinnamon (*say* **sin**-a-mon) *noun* a yellowish-brown spice.

cipher (*say* **sy**-fer) *noun* **1** the symbol 0, representing nought or zero. **2** a kind of code, *a message in cipher.*

circa (*say* **sir**-ka) *preposition* (before a date) about, *born circa 150 BC.*

circle[1] *noun* **1** a perfectly round flat shape or thing. **2** a number of people with similar interests, *They move in fashionable circles.* **3** the balcony of a cinema or theatre.

circle[2] *verb* (**circled, circling**) move in a circle; go round something.

circuit (*say* **ser**-kit) *noun* **1** a circular line or journey. **2** a motor-racing track. **3** the path of an electric current.

circuitous (*say* ser-**kew**-it-us) *adjective* going a long way round, not direct.

circular[1] *adjective* **1** shaped like a circle; round. **2** moving round a circle. **circularity** *noun*

circular[2] *noun* a letter or advertisement etc. sent to a number of people.

circulate *verb* (**circulated, circulating**)

1 go round something continuously, *Blood circulates in the body.* **2** pass from place to place. **3** send round; send to a number of people, *circulate a letter.* **circulation** *noun*

circum- *prefix* around (as in *circumference*).

circumcise *verb* (**circumcised, circumcising**) cut off the fold of skin at the tip of the penis. **circumcision** *noun*

circumference *noun* the line or distance round something, especially round a circle.

circumflex accent *noun* a mark over a vowel, as over *e* in *fête.*

circumlocution *noun* a roundabout expression, using many words where a few would do, e.g. 'at this moment in time' for 'now'.

circumnavigate *verb* (**circumnavigated, circumnavigating**) sail completely round something. **circumnavigation** *noun*

circumscribe *verb* (**circumscribed, circumscribing**) **1** draw a line round something. **2** limit; restrict, *Her powers are circumscribed by many regulations.*

circumspect *adjective* cautious and watchful. **circumspection** *noun*

circumstance *noun* a fact or condition connected with an event or person or action.

circumstantial (*say* ser-kum-**stan**-shal) *adjective* **1** giving full details, *a circumstantial account of her journey.* **2** consisting of facts that strongly suggest something but do not actually prove it, *circumstantial evidence.*

circumvent *verb* find a way of avoiding, *We managed to circumvent the rules.* **circumvention** *noun*

circus *noun* (*plural* **circuses**) a travelling show with clowns, acrobats, animals, etc.

cirrus (*say* **sir**-rus) *noun* (*plural* **cirri**) a type of wispy cloud found at a high altitude.

cistern *noun* a tank for storing water.

citadel *noun* a fortress protecting a city.

cite (*say as* sight) *verb* (**cited, citing**) quote as an example. **citation** *noun*

citizen *noun* a person belonging to a particular city or country and having certain rights and duties because of this. **citizenship** *noun*

citizenry *noun* all the citizens.

citrus fruit *noun* a lemon, orange, grapefruit, etc.

city *noun* (*plural* **cities**) a large important town.

civic *adjective* of a city or town; of citizens.

civic (association) an organization whose task is to deal with complaints and bring about reform in local government, *The civic called off the consumer boycott.*

civics *noun* the study of the way citizens and towns are governed and of the rights and duties of citizens.

civil *adjective* 1 of citizens. 2 of civilians; not military, *civil aviation.* 3 polite. **civilly** *adverb*

civil defence protection of civilians in an air raid etc.

civil rights the rights of citizens, especially to have freedom, equality, and the right to vote.

civil service people employed by the government in various departments other than the armed forces.

civil war war between groups of people of the same country.

civilian *noun* a person who is not serving in the armed forces.

civility *noun* (*plural* **civilities**) politeness; a polite act.

civilization *noun* 1 a civilized condition or society. 2 making or becoming civilized.

civilize *verb* (**civilized, civilizing**) cause to improve from a primitive stage of human society to a more developed one.

clack *noun* a short sharp sound like that of plates struck together. **clack** *verb*

clad *adjective* clothed.

claim¹ *verb* 1 ask for something to which you believe you have a right. 2 declare; state something without being able to prove it. **claimant** *noun*

claim² *noun* 1 claiming. 2 something claimed, *The insurance company paid the full claim.* 3 a piece of ground claimed or assigned to someone for mining etc.

clairvoyant *noun* a person who is said to be able to perceive future events or things that are happening out of sight. **clairvoyance** *noun*

clam *noun* a large shellfish.

clamber *verb* climb with difficulty.

clammy *adjective* damp and slimy.

clamour¹ *noun* 1 a loud confused noise. 2 an outcry; a loud protest or demand. **clamorous** *adjective*

clamour² *verb* make a loud protest or demand, *clamour for attention.*

clamp¹ *noun* a device for holding things tightly.

clamp² *verb* fix with a clamp; fix firmly. **clamp down on** become stricter about something; put a stop to it.

clan *noun* a group sharing the same ancestor.

clandestine (*say* klan-**dest**-in) *adjective* done secretly; kept secret.

clang *noun* a loud ringing sound. **clang** *verb*

clangour *noun* a clanging noise.

clank *noun* a sound like heavy pieces of metal banging together. **clank** *verb*

clap¹ *verb* (**clapped, clapping**) 1 strike the palms of the hands together loudly, especially as applause. 2 slap in a friendly way, *clapped him on the shoulder.* 3 put quickly, *They clapped him into gaol.*

clap² *noun* 1 a sudden sharp noise, *a clap of thunder.* 2 clapping; applause. 3 a friendly slap.

clapper *noun* the tongue or hanging piece inside a bell that strikes against the bell to make it sound.

claptrap *noun* insincere talk.

claret *noun* a kind of red wine.

clarify *verb* (**clarified, clarifying**) make or become clear or easier to understand. **clarification** *noun*

clarinet *noun* a woodwind instrument. **clarinettist** *noun*

clarion *noun* an old type of trumpet.

clarity *noun* clearness.

clash *verb* 1 make a loud sound like that of cymbals banging together. 2 conflict. 3 happen inconveniently at the same time, *Your party clashes with a rugby match I'm going to.* 4 (of colours) look unpleasant together. **clash** *noun*

clasp¹ *noun* 1 a device for fastening things, with interlocking parts. 2 a grasp.

clasp[2] *verb* **1** grasp or hold tightly. **2** fasten with a clasp.

class[1] *noun* (*plural* **classes**) **1** a group of children, students, etc. who are taught together. **2** a group of similar people, animals, or things. **3** people of the same social or economic level, *the middle class*. **4** level of quality, *first class*.

class[2] *verb* classify.

classic[1] *adjective* generally agreed to be excellent or important.

classic[2] *noun* a classic book, film, writer, etc.

classical *adjective* **1** of ancient Greek or Roman literature, art, etc. **2** serious or conventional in style, *classical music*.

classics *noun* the study of ancient Greek and Latin languages and literature etc.

classified *adjective* **1** put into classes or groups. **2** (of information) declared officially to be secret and available only to certain people.

classify *verb* (**classified, classifying**) arrange things in classes or groups. **classification** *noun*, **classificatory** *adjective*

classmate *noun* someone in the same class at school etc.

classroom *noun* a room where a class of children or students is taught.

clatter *verb* & *noun* rattle.

clause *noun* **1** a single part of a treaty, law, or contract. **2** part of a complex sentence, with its own verb, *There are two clauses in 'We choose what we want'.*

claustrophobia *noun* fear of being inside something.

claw[1] *noun* **1** a sharp nail on a bird's or animal's foot. **2** a claw-like part or device used for grasping things.

claw[2] *verb* grasp, pull, or scratch with a claw or hand.

clay *noun* a kind of stiff sticky earth that becomes hard when baked, used for making bricks and pottery. **clayey** *adjective*

clean[1] *adjective* **1** without any dirt or marks or stains. **2** fresh; not yet used. **3** honourable; not unfair, *a clean fight*. **4** not indecent. **cleanness** *noun*

clean[2] *verb* make a thing clean.

clean[3] *adverb* (*informal*) completely, *I clean forgot*.

cleaner *noun* **1** a person who cleans things, especially rooms etc. **2** something used for cleaning things.

cleanly[1] (*say* **kleen**-lee) *adverb* in a clean way.

cleanly[2] (*say* **klen**-lee) *adjective* taking care to be clean, *cleanly habits*. **cleanliness** *noun*

cleanse (*say* klenz) *verb* (**cleansed, cleansing**) **1** clean. **2** make pure. **cleanser** *noun*

clear[1] *adjective* **1** transparent; not muddy or cloudy. **2** easy to see or hear or understand; distinct. **3** free from obstacles or unwanted things; free from guilt, *a clear conscience*. **4** complete, *Give three clear days' notice*. **clearly** *adverb*, **clearness** *noun*

clear-cut sharply defined.

clear-headed sensible.

clear[2] *adverb* **1** distinctly; clearly, *We heard you loud and clear*. **2** completely, *He got clear away*. **3** apart; not in contact, *Stand clear of the doors*.

clear[3] *verb* **1** make or become clear. **2** show that someone is innocent or reliable. **3** jump over something without touching it. **4** get approval or authorization for something, *Clear this with the principal*.

clear away remove used plates etc. after a meal.

clear off or **out** (*informal*) go away.

clear up make things tidy; become better or brighter; solve, *clear up the mystery*.

clearance *noun* **1** clearing something. **2** getting rid of unwanted goods. **3** the space between two things.

clearing *noun* an open space in a forest.

cleave[1] *verb* (*past tense* **cleaved, clove**, or **cleft**; *past participle* **cleft** or **cloven**; *present participle* **cleaving**) **1** divide by chopping; split. **2** make a way through, *cleaving the waves*. **cleavage** *noun*

cleave[2] *verb* (**cleaved, cleaving**) (*old use*) cling to something.

cleaver *noun* a butcher's chopper.

clef *noun* a symbol on a stave in music,

showing the pitch of the notes, *treble clef*; *bass clef*.

cleft[1] *past tense* of **cleave**[1].

cleft[2] *noun* a split; a separation.

clemency *noun* gentleness or mildness; mercy.

clench *verb* close teeth or fingers tightly.

clergy *noun* the people who have been ordained as priests or ministers of the Christian Church. **clergyman** *noun*

clerical *adjective* 1 of clerks or their work. 2 of the clergy.

clerk (*say* klark) *noun* a person employed to keep records or accounts, deal with papers in an office, etc.

clever *adjective* quick at learning and understanding things; skilful. **cleverly** *adverb*, **cleverness** *noun*

cliché (*say* klee-shay) *noun* a phrase or idea that is used too often.

click *noun* a short sharp sound. **click** *verb*

client *noun* a person who gets help from a lawyer, architect, or professional person other than a doctor; a customer.

clientele (*say* klee-on-**tel**) *noun* clients.

cliff *noun* a steep rock-face, especially on a coast.

climate *noun* the regular weather conditions of an area. **climatic** (*say* kly-**mat**-ik) *adjective*

climax *noun* (*plural* **climaxes**) the most interesting or important point of a story, series of events, etc.

climb *verb* 1 go up or over or down something. 2 grow upwards. 3 go higher, *The sun climbed in the sky*. **climb** *noun*, **climber** *noun*
climb down admit that you have been wrong.

clinch *verb* 1 fasten securely. 2 settle definitely, *clinch the deal*. 3 (in boxing) be clasping each other. **clinch** *noun*

cling *verb* (**clung, clinging**) hold on tightly.

clinic *noun* a place where people see doctors etc. for treatment or advice. **clinical** *adjective*

clink *noun* a thin sharp sound like glasses being struck together. **clink** *verb*

clinker *noun* a piece of rough stony material left after coal has burned.

clip[1] *noun* a fastener for keeping things together, usually worked by a spring.

clip[2] *verb* (**clipped, clipping**) fasten with a clip.

clip[3] *verb* (**clipped, clipping**) 1 cut with shears or scissors etc. 2 (*informal*) hit, *a clip on the ear*.

clip[4] *noun* a short extract from a film, *Here is a clip from her new film*.

clipper *noun* an old type of fast sailing-ship.

clippers *plural noun* an instrument for cutting hair.

clipping *noun* a piece clipped off or out, especially from a newspaper.

clique (*say* kleek) *noun* a small group of people who stick together and keep others out.

cloak[1] *noun* a sleeveless garment that hangs loosely from the shoulders.

cloak[2] *verb* cover; conceal.

cloakroom *noun* 1 a place where people can leave outdoor clothes, luggage, etc. 2 a lavatory.

clobber *verb* (*slang*) 1 hit hard again and again. 2 defeat completely, *Our team got clobbered on Saturday*.

cloche (*say* klosh) *noun* a glass or plastic cover to protect outdoor plants.

clock[1] *noun* 1 a device (other than a watch) that shows what the time is. 2 a measuring device with a dial or showing figures.

clock[2] *verb* **clock in** or **out** register the time you arrive at work or leave work.
clock up achieve a certain speed.

clockwise *adverb & adjective* moving round a circle in the same direction as a clock's hands.

clockwork *noun* a mechanism with a spring that has to be wound up.
like clockwork very regularly.

clod *noun* a lump of earth or clay.

clog[1] *noun* a shoe with a wooden sole.

clog[2] *verb* (**clogged, clogging**) block up.

cloister *noun* a covered path along the side of a church or monastery etc., round a courtyard.

clone *noun* an animal or plant made from the cells of another animal or plant and therefore exactly like it.

close¹ (*say* klohss) *adjective* **1** near. **2** detailed; concentrated, *with close attention*. **3** tight; with little empty space, *a close fit*. **4** in which competitors are nearly equal, *a close contest*. **5** stuffy. **closely** *adverb*, **closeness** *noun*

close² *adverb* closely, *close behind*.

close³ *noun* **1** a cul-de-sac. **2** an enclosed area, especially round a cathedral.

close⁴ (*say* klohz) *verb* (**closed**, **closing**) **1** shut. **2** end.

close in get nearer; get shorter.

close⁵ *noun* end, *at the close of play*.

close corporation *noun* a form of company with one to ten members, that is easy to set up.

closet¹ *noun* (*American*) a cupboard; a storeroom.

closet² *verb* (**closeted**, **closeting**) shut away in a private room.

closure *noun* closing.

clot¹ *noun* **1** a small mass of blood, cream, etc. that has become solid. **2** (*slang*) a stupid person.

clot² *verb* (**clotted**, **clotting**) form clots.

clotted cream cream thickened by being scalded.

cloth *noun* **1** woven material or felt. **2** a piece of this material. **3** a tablecloth.

clothe *verb* (**clothed**, **clothing**) put clothes on someone.

clothes *plural noun* things worn to cover the body.

clothing *noun* clothes.

cloud¹ *noun* **1** a mass of condensed water-vapour floating in the sky. **2** a mass of smoke, dust, insects, etc., in the air.

cloud² *verb* fill or obscure with clouds.

cloudburst *noun* a sudden violent rainstorm.

cloudless *adjective* without clouds.

cloudy *adjective* (**cloudier**, **cloudiest**) **1** full of clouds. **2** not transparent, *The liquid became cloudy*. **cloudiness** *noun*

clout *verb* & *noun* (*informal*) hit.

clove¹ *noun* the dried bud of a tropical tree, used as a spice.

clove² *noun* one of the small bulbs in a compound bulb, *a clove of garlic*.

clove³ *past tense* of **cleave¹**. **clove hitch**

a kind of knot.

cloven *past participle* of **cleave¹**. **cloven hoof** a hoof that is divided, like those of cows and sheep.

clover *noun* a small plant usually with three leaves on each stalk.

in clover in ease and luxury.

clown¹ *noun* **1** a performer who does comical tricks and actions, especially in a circus. **2** a person who clowns.

clown² *verb* behave comically.

cloying *adjective* sickeningly sweet.

club¹ *noun* **1** a heavy stick used as a weapon. **2** a stick with a shaped head used to hit the ball in golf. **3** a group of people who meet because they are interested in the same thing; the premises where they meet. **4** a playing-card with black clover-leaves on it.

club² *verb* (**clubbed**, **clubbing**) hit with a heavy stick.

club together join with other people in subscribing, *club together to buy a boat*.

cluck *verb* make a hen's throaty cry. **cluck** *noun*

clue *noun* something that helps a person to solve a puzzle or a mystery.

not have a clue (*informal*) be stupid or helpless.

clump¹ *noun* **1** a cluster or mass of things, *a clump of trees*. **2** a clumping sound.

clump² *verb* **1** form a cluster or mass. **2** walk with a heavy tread.

clumsy *adjective* (**clumsier**, **clumsiest**) **1** heavy and ungraceful; likely to knock things over or drop things. **2** not skilful; not tactful, *a clumsy apology*. **clumsily** *adverb*, **clumsiness** *noun*

cluster¹ *noun* a small close group.

cluster² *verb* form a cluster.

clutch¹ *verb* grasp tightly.

clutch² *noun* (*plural* **clutches**) **1** a tight grasp. **2** a device for connecting and disconnecting the engine of a motor vehicle from its gears.

clutch³ *noun* (*plural* **clutches**) a set of eggs for hatching.

clutter¹ *noun* things lying about untidily.

clutter² *verb* fill with clutter.

Co. *abbreviation* Company.

c/o *abbreviation* care of.

co- *prefix* together, jointly (as in *coexistence*, *co-operate*); joint (as in *co-pilot*).

coach[1] *noun* (*plural* **coaches**) **1** a bus used for long journeys. **2** a carriage of a railway train. **3** a large horse-drawn carriage with four wheels. **4** an instructor in sports, *the cricket coach.* **5** a teacher giving private specialized tuition.

coach[2] *verb* instruct or train somebody, especially in sports.

coagulate *verb* (**coagulated, coagulating**) change from liquid to semi-solid; clot. **coagulant** *noun*, **coagulation** *noun*

coal *noun* a hard black mineral substance used for burning to supply heat; a piece of this. **coalfield** *noun*

coalesce (*say* koh-a-**less**) *verb* combine and form one whole thing. **coalescence** *noun*, **coalescent** *adjective*

coalition *noun* a temporary alliance.

coarse *adjective* **1** not smooth, not delicate; rough. **2** composed of large particles; not fine. **3** not refined; vulgar, *coarse humour.* **coarsely** *adverb*, **coarseness** *noun*

coarsen *verb* make or become coarse.

coast[1] *noun* the sea-shore; the land close to it. **coastal** *adjective*, **coastline** *noun* **the coast is clear** there is no chance of being seen or hindered.

coast[2] *verb* ride without using power.

coastguard *noun* a person whose job is to keep watch on the coast, detect or prevent smuggling, etc.

coat[1] *noun* **1** an outdoor garment with sleeves. **2** the hair or fur on an animal's body. **3** a coating, *a coat of paint.* **coat of arms** a design on a shield, used as an emblem by a family, city, etc.

coat[2] *verb* cover with a coating.

coating *noun* a covering layer.

coax *verb* persuade gently or patiently.

cob *noun* **1** the central part of an ear of maize, on which the corn grows. **2** a sturdy horse for riding. **3** a male swan.

cobalt *noun* a hard silvery-white metal.

cobble[1] *noun* a rounded stone used for paving streets etc. **cobbled** *adjective*

cobble[2] *verb* (**cobbled, cobbling**) make or mend roughly.

cobbler *noun* a shoe-repairer.

cobra (*say* **koh**-bra) *noun* a poisonous snake that can rear up.

cobweb *noun* the thin sticky net made by a spider to trap insects.

cocaine *noun* a drug made from the leaves of a tropical plant called *coca.*

cock[1] *noun* **1** a male bird; a male fowl. **2** a stopcock. **3** a lever in a gun.

cock[2] *verb* **1** make a gun ready to fire by raising the cock. **2** turn something upwards or in a particular direction, *The dog cocked its ears.*

cockatoo *noun* a crested parrot.

cocked hat *noun* a triangular hat worn with some uniforms.

cockerel *noun* a young male fowl.

cocker spaniel *noun* a kind of small spaniel.

cock-eyed *adjective* (*slang*) **1** crooked; not straight. **2** absurd, *a cock-eyed idea.*

cockle *noun* an edible shellfish.

cockney *noun* (*plural* **cockneys**) **1** a person born in the East End of London. **2** the dialect or accent of cockneys.

cockpit *noun* the compartment where the pilot of an aircraft sits.

cockroach *noun* (*plural* **cockroaches**) a beetle-like insect.

cocksure *adjective* very sure; too confident.

cocktail *noun* **1** a mixed alcoholic drink. **2** a food containing shellfish or fruit, *shrimp cocktail.*

cocky *adjective* (**cockier, cockiest**) (*informal*) conceited. **cockiness** *noun*

cocoa *noun* **1** a hot drink made from a powder of crushed cacao seeds. **2** this powder.

coconut *noun* **1** a large round nut that grows on a kind of palm-tree. **2** its white lining, used in sweets and cookery.

cocoon[1] *noun* **1** the covering round a chrysalis. **2** a protective wrapping.

cocoon[2] *verb* protect by wrapping.

cocopan *noun* a small truck on rails used in mining, sugar-cane farming, and construction work.

COD *abbreviation* cash on delivery.

cod *noun* (*plural* **cod**) a large edible sea-fish.

coddle *verb* (**coddled, coddling**) cherish and protect carefully.

code[1] *noun* **1** a word or phrase used to represent a message in order to keep its meaning secret. **2** a set of signs used in sending messages by machine etc., *the Morse code*. **3** a set of laws or rules, *the penal code*.

code[2] *verb* (**coded, coding**) put into code.

codicil *noun* an addition to a will.

codify *verb* (**codified, codifying**) arrange laws or rules into a code or system. **codification** *noun*

coed (*say* **koh**-ed) *abbreviation* (*informal*) coeducational.
coed school a school for boys and girls.

coeducation *noun* educating boys and girls together. **coeducational** *adjective*

coefficient *noun* a number by which another number is multiplied; a factor.

coelacanth (*say* **see**-la-kanth) *noun* a large primitive sea-fish with large fins that look like limbs.

coerce (*say* koh-**erss**) *verb* (**coerced, coercing**) compel someone by using threats or force. **coercion** *noun*

coexist *verb* exist together. **coexistence** *noun*, **coexistent** *adjective*

coffee *noun* **1** a hot drink made from the roasted ground seeds (*coffee-beans*) of a tropical plant. **2** these seeds.

coffer *noun* a large strong box for holding money and valuables.

coffin *noun* a long box in which a body is buried or cremated.

cog *noun* one of a number of projections round the edge of a wheel, fitting into and pushing those on another wheel.
cog-wheel *noun* a wheel with cogs.

cogent (*say* **koh**-jent) *adjective* convincing, *a cogent argument*.

cogitate *verb* (**cogitated, cogitating**) think deeply. **cogitation** *noun*

cognac (*say* **kon**-yak) *noun* brandy, especially from Cognac in France.

cohere *verb* (**cohered, cohering**) stick to each other in a mass. **cohesion** *noun*, **cohesive** *adjective*

coherent (*say* koh-**heer**-ent) *adjective* **1** cohering. **2** clear and reasonable; not incoherent, *a coherent argument*. **coherently** *adverb*

coil[1] *noun* something wound into a spiral.

coil[2] *verb* wind into a coil.

coin[1] *noun* a shaped piece of metal used to buy things.

coin[2] *verb* **1** manufacture coins. **2** (*informal*) make a lot of money as profit, *That new gym must be coining it*. **3** invent a word or phrase.

coinage *noun* **1** coining. **2** coins; a system of money. **3** a new word or phrase.

coincide *verb* (**coincided, coinciding**) **1** happen at the same time as something else. **2** be in the same place. **3** be the same, *My opinion coincided with hers*.

coincidence *noun* the happening of similar events at the same time by chance. **coincidental** *adjective*

coir *noun* a fibre from coconuts used to make ropes, mats, etc.

coitus (*say* **koh**-i-tus) *noun* sexual intercourse.

coke *noun* the solid fuel left when gas and tar have been extracted from coal.

col *noun* a low point in a mountain range.

col- *prefix* see **com-**.

colander *noun* a bowl-shaped container with holes for straining water from vegetables etc. after cooking.

cold[1] *adjective* **1** having or at a low temperature; not warm. **2** not friendly or loving; not enthusiastic. **coldly** *adverb*, **coldness** *noun*
cold shoulder deliberate unfriendliness. **cold-shoulder** *verb*
cold war a situation where nations are enemies without actually fighting.
get cold feet feel afraid or reluctant to do something.

cold[2] *noun* **1** lack of warmth; low temperature; cold weather. **2** an infectious illness that makes your nose run, your throat sore, etc.

cold-blooded *adjective* **1** having a body temperature that changes according to the surroundings. **2** callous; deliberately cruel, *a cold-blooded murder*.

coleslaw *noun* a salad of sliced raw cabbage with a sauce of mayonnaise etc.

colic *noun* stomach-ache.

collaborate *verb* (**collaborated, collaborating**) work together on a job. **collaboration** *noun*, **collaborator** *noun*

collage (*say* kol-**ah**zh) *noun* a picture made by fixing small objects to a surface.

collagen (*say* **kol**-a-jen) *noun* a kind of protein found in animal tissue.

collapse[1] *verb* (**collapsed, collapsing**) 1 fall down or inwards suddenly; break. 2 become very weak or ill. 3 fold up.

collapse[2] *noun* collapsing; a breakdown.

collapsible *adjective* able to be folded up.

collar[1] *noun* 1 an upright or turned-over band round the neck of a garment etc. 2 a band that goes round the neck of a dog, cat, horse, etc. **collar-bone** the bone joining the shoulder-blade and the breastbone.

collar[2] *verb* (*informal*) seize.

collate *verb* (**collated, collating**) bring together and compare lists, books, etc. **collation** *noun*

collateral *adjective* 1 parallel to something. 2 additional but less important.

colleague *noun* a person you work with.

collect[1] (*say* kol-**ekt**) *verb* 1 bring people or things together from various places. 2 obtain examples of things as a hobby, *She collects stamps.* 3 come together, *Rubbish had collected at the side of the road.* 4 ask for money or contributions etc. from people. 5 fetch, *Collect your coat from the cleaners.* **collector** *noun*

collect[2] (*say* **kol**-ekt) *noun* a short prayer of the Anglican or Roman Catholic Church.

collection *noun* 1 collecting. 2 things collected. 3 money collected for a charity etc.

collective *adjective* of a group taken as a whole, *our collective opinion.* **collective bargaining** discussions about pay, working conditions, etc. between a trade union and an employer. **collective noun** a noun that is singular in form but refers to many individuals taken as a unit, e.g. *army, herd.*

college *noun* a place where people can continue learning something after they have left school.

collide *verb* (**collided, colliding**) crash into something.

colliery *noun* (*plural* **collieries**) a coal-mine and its buildings.

collision *noun* a crash.

colloquial (*say* kol-**oh**-kwee-al) *adjective* suitable for conversation but not for formal speech or writing. **colloquially** *adverb*, **colloquialism** *noun*

collusion *noun* a secret agreement between two or more people who are trying to deceive or cheat someone.

cologne (*say* kol-**ohn**) *noun* eau-de-Cologne or a similar liquid.

colon[1] *noun* a punctuation mark (:), often used to introduce lists.

colon[2] *noun* the largest part of the intestine.

colonel (*say* **ker**-nel) *noun* an army officer in charge of a regiment.

colonial *adjective* of a colony.

colonialism *noun* the policy of acquiring and keeping colonies.

colonize *verb* (**colonized, colonizing**) establish a colony in a country. **colonist** *noun*, **colonization** *noun*

colonnade *noun* a row of columns.

colony *noun* (*plural* **colonies**) 1 an area of land that the people of another country settle in and control. 2 the people of a colony. 3 a group of people or animals of the same kind living close together, *an ant colony.*

coloration *noun* colouring.

colossal *adjective* immense; enormous.

colossus *noun* (*plural* **colossi**) 1 a huge statue. 2 a person of immense importance.

colour[1] *noun* 1 the effect produced by waves of light of a particular wavelength. 2 the use of various colours, not only black and white. 3 the colour of someone's skin. 4 a substance used to colour things. 5 the special flag of a ship or regiment. **colours** *plural noun* an award given to the best members of a sports team.

colour[2] *verb* 1 put colour on; paint or stain. 2 blush. 3 influence what someone says or believes, *Don't allow your emotions to* *colour your judgement.* **colouring** *noun*

colour-blind *adjective* unable to see the difference between certain colours.

coloured *adjective* having colour.

colourful *adjective* 1 full of colour. 2 lively; with vivid details.

colourless *adjective* without colour.

colt *noun* a young male horse.

column *noun* 1 a pillar. 2 something long or tall and narrow, *a column of smoke.* 3 a vertical section of a page, *There are two columns on this page.* 4 a regular article in a newspaper. **columnist** *noun*

com- *prefix* (becoming **col-** before *l*, **cor-** before *r*, **con-** before many other consonants) with; together (as in *combine, connect*).

coma (*say* koh-ma) *noun* a state of deep unconsciousness, especially in someone who is ill or injured.

comb¹ *noun* 1 a strip of wood or plastic etc. with teeth, used to tidy hair or hold it in place. 2 something used like this, e.g. to separate strands of wool. 3 the red crest on a fowl's head. 4 a honeycomb.

comb² *verb* 1 tidy with a comb. 2 search thoroughly, *The police combed the area.*

combat *noun & verb* (**combated, combating**) fight. **combatant** (*say* kom-ba-tant) *noun*

combination *noun* 1 combining. 2 a number of people or things that are combined. 3 a series of numbers or letters used to open a combination lock.
combination lock a lock that can be opened only by setting a dial or dials to positions shown by numbers or letters.

combine¹ (*say* komb-I'n) *verb* (**combined, combining**) join or mix together.

combine² (*say* komb-I'n) *noun* a group of people or firms combining in business.
combine harvester a machine that both reaps and threshes grain.

combustible *adjective* able to be set on fire and burn.

combustion *noun* the process of burning; a chemical process (accompanied by heat) in which substances combine with oxygen in air.

come *verb* (**came, come, coming**) This word is used to show 1 movement towards somewhere, *Come here!* 2 arrival, reaching a place or condition or result, *They came to a city. We came to a decision.* 3 happening, *How did you come to lose it?* 4 occurring, *It comes on the next page.* 5 resulting, *That's what comes of being careless.*

come by obtain.

come in for receive a share of.

come to amount to; become conscious again.

come to pass happen.

comedian *noun* someone who entertains people by making them laugh.

comedy *noun* (*plural* **comedies**) 1 a play or film etc. that makes people laugh. 2 humour, *slapstick comedy.*

comely *adjective* good-looking.

comet *noun* an object moving across the sky with a bright tail of light.

comfort¹ *noun* 1 a comfortable feeling or condition. 2 soothing somebody who is unhappy or in pain. 3 a person or thing that gives comfort.

comfort² *verb* make a person less unhappy; soothe.

comfortable *adjective* 1 free from worry or pain. 2 making someone feel comfortable; not tight or harsh. **comfortably** *adverb*

comfy *adjective* (*informal*) comfortable.

comic¹ *adjective* making people laugh.
comical *adjective*, **comically** *adverb*
comic strip a series of drawings telling a comic story or a serial.

comic² *noun* 1 a paper full of comic strips. 2 a comedian.

comma *noun* 1 a punctuation mark (,) used to mark a pause in a sentence or to separate items in a list. 2 a symbol used to represent the decimal point, *2,5 kg.*

command¹ *noun* 1 a statement telling somebody to do something; an order. 2 authority; control. 3 ability to use something; mastery, *She has a good command of Zulu.*

command² *verb* 1 give a command to somebody; order. 2 have authority over. 3 deserve and get, *They command our respect.* **commander** *noun*

commandant (*say* **kom**-an-dant) *noun*
1 an officer in charge of a military academy etc. 2 a military rank in the army or police force. 3 a commanding officer of a burgher commando in former times.

commandeer *verb* take or seize something for military purposes or for your own use.

commandment *noun* a sacred command, especially one of the Ten Commandments given to Moses.

commando *noun* (*plural* **commandos**) 1 a soldier or unit trained for making dangerous raids. 2 (in history) a group of mounted burghers acting as soldiers.

commemorate *verb* (**commemorated, commemorating**) be a celebration or reminder of some past event or person etc. **commemoration** *noun*, **commemorative** *adjective*

commence *verb* (**commenced, commencing**) begin. **commencement** *noun*

commend *verb* 1 praise, *He was commended for bravery.* 2 entrust, *We commend him to your care.* **commendation** *noun*

commendable *adjective* deserving praise.

commensalism *noun* a form of symbiosis in which one partner benefits and the other does not benefit, but is not harmed.

comment[1] *noun* an opinion given about an event etc. or to explain something.

comment[2] *verb* make a comment.

commentary *noun* (*plural* **commentaries**) a set of comments, especially describing an event while it is happening, *rugby commentary.* **commentate** *verb*, **commentator** *noun*

commerce *noun* trade and the services that assist it, e.g. banking and insurance.

commercial[1] *adjective* 1 of commerce. 2 paid for by firms etc. whose advertisements are included, *commercial radio.* 3 profitable, *The concert was a commercial success.* **commercially** *adverb*
commercial farm a farm which aims to sell its produce at a profit. (Compare *subsistence farm.*)

commercial[2] *noun* a broadcast advertisement.

commercialized *adjective* altered in order to become profitable, *a commercialized resort.* **commercialization** *noun*

commiserate *verb* (**commiserated, commiserating**) sympathize. **commiseration** *noun*

commission[1] *noun* 1 committing something. 2 authorization to do something; the task etc. authorized, *a commission to paint a portrait.* 3 an appointment to be an officer in the armed forces. 4 a group of people given authority to do or investigate something, *a commission on capital punishment.* 5 payment to someone for selling your goods etc.

commission[2] *verb* give a commission to a person or for a task etc.

commissionaire *noun* an attendant in uniform at the entrance to a theatre, large shop, offices, etc.

commissioner *noun* 1 an official appointed by commission. 2 a member of a commission (see *commission* 4).
Commissioner for Oaths a person who is authorized to administer an oath.

commit *verb* (**committed, committing**) 1 do; perform, *commit a crime.* 2 place in someone's care or custody; consign, *She was committed to prison.* 3 pledge; assign, *Don't commit all your spare time to helping him.*

committal *noun* 1 committing a person to prison etc. 2 giving a body ceremonially for burial or cremation.

committee *noun* a group of people appointed to deal with something.

commode *noun* a box or chair into which a chamber-pot is fitted.

commodious *adjective* roomy.

commodity *noun* (*plural* **commodities**) a useful thing; a product.

commodore *noun* 1 a naval officer ranking next below a rear admiral. 2 the commander of part of a fleet. 3 the president of a yacht club.

common[1] *adjective* 1 ordinary; usual; occurring frequently, *a common weed.* 2 of all or most people, *They worked for the common good.* 3 shared, *Music is their common interest.* 4 vulgar.

commonly *adverb*, **commonness** *noun*
common sense normal good sense in
thinking or behaviour.
in common shared by two or more people
or things.
common² *noun* a piece of land that
everyone can use.
commoner *noun* a member of the ordinary people, not of the nobility.
commonplace *adjective* ordinary; usual.
Commonwealth *noun* an association
of countries, *The Commonwealth consists
of Britain and various other countries,
including South Africa, Zimbabwe, and
Australia.*
commotion *noun* an uproar; a fuss.
communal (*say* **kom**-yoo-nal) *adjective*
shared by several people. **communally**
adverb
commune¹ (*say* **kom**-yoon) *noun* a group
of people sharing a home, food, etc.
commune² *verb* (**communed**, **commun-
ing**) talk together.
communicant *noun* 1 a person who
communicates with someone. 2 a person
who receives Holy Communion.
communicate *verb* (**communicated,
communicating**) 1 pass news, information,
etc. to other people. 2 (of rooms etc.) open
into each other; connect.
communication *noun* 1 communicating.
2 something communicated; a message.
communications *plural noun* links
between places (e.g. roads, railways, telephones, radio).
communication satellite a satellite that is
designed to pass on telephone calls and
broadcast programmes.
communicative *adjective* willing to talk.
communion *noun* religious fellowship.
Communion or **Holy Communion**
the Christian ceremony in which consecrated bread and wine are given to
worshippers.
communiqué (*say* ko-**mew**-nik-ay) *noun*
an official message giving a report.
Communism *noun* a political system
where the State controls property, production, trade, etc. (Compare *capitalism*.)
Communist *noun*

communism *noun* a system where property is shared by the community.
community *noun* (*plural* **communities**)
1 the people living in one area. 2 a group
with similar interests or origins.
community centre a place where a community can meet for sporting activities,
education classes, social occasions, etc.
community service work done in the
community for no pay, especially by
someone who has committed a crime.
commute *verb* (**commuted, commuting**)
1 travel a fairly long way by train, bus, or car
to and from your daily work. 2 exchange;
alter a punishment to something less severe.
commuter *noun* a person who commutes
to and from work.
compact¹ *noun* an agreement; a contract.
compact² *adjective* 1 closely or neatly
packed together. 2 concise.
compact disc a small disc from which
recorded sound etc. is reproduced by
means of a laser beam. **compactly** *adverb*,
compactness *noun*
compact³ *noun* a small flat container for
face-powder.
compact⁴ *verb* join or press firmly together
or into a small space.
companion *noun* 1 a person who accompanies another. 2 one of a matching pair of
things. 3 (in book-titles) a guidebook or
reference book, *The Oxford Companion to
Music.* **companionship** *noun*
companionable *adjective* sociable.
company *noun* (*plural* **companies**)
1 a number of people together. 2 a business
firm. 3 having people with you; companionship. 4 visitors, *We've got company.*
5 a section of a battalion.
comparable (*say* **kom**-per-a-bul)
adjective similar. **comparably** *adverb*
comparative¹ *adjective* of comparisons;
comparing a thing with something else,
They live in comparative comfort.
comparatively *adverb*
comparative² *noun* the form of an
adjective or adverb that expresses 'more',
The comparative of 'big' is 'bigger'.
compare *verb* (**compared, comparing**)
1 put things together so as to tell in what

ways they are similar or different. 2 form the comparative and superlative of an adjective or adverb.
compare notes share information.
compare with be similar to; be as good as, *Our football pitch cannot compare with Athlone Stadium.*
comparison *noun* comparing.
compartment *noun* one of the spaces into which something is divided; a separate room or enclosed space.
compass *noun* (*plural* **compasses**) a device with a pointer that points north.
compasses or **pair of compasses** a device for drawing circles, usually with two rods hinged together at one end.
compassion *noun* pity; mercy.
compassionate *adjective*, **compassionately** *adverb*
compatible *adjective* able to exist or be used together; not incompatible.
compatibly *adverb*, **compatibility** *noun*
compatriot *noun* a person who belongs to the same country as yourself.
compel *verb* (**compelled, compelling**) force somebody to do something.
compendious *adjective* giving much information concisely.
compendium *noun* a package of notepaper and envelopes, or of games.
compensate *verb* (**compensated, compensating**) 1 give a person money etc. to make up for a loss or injury. 2 have a balancing effect, *This victory compensates for our earlier defeats.* **compensation** *noun*, **compensatory** *adjective*
compère (*say* **kom**-pair) *noun* a person who introduces the performers in a show or broadcast. **compère** *verb*
compete *verb* (**competed, competing**) take part in a competition.
competent *adjective* able to do a particular thing. **competently** *adverb*, **competence** *noun*
competition *noun* 1 a game or race or other contest in which people try to win. 2 competing. 3 the people competing with yourself. **competitive** *adjective*
competitor *noun* someone who competes; a rival.

compile *verb* (**compiled, compiling**) put things together into a list or collection, e.g. to form a book. **compiler** *noun*, **compilation** *noun*
complacent *adjective* self-satisfied. **complacently** *adverb*, **complacency** *noun*
complain *verb* say that you are annoyed or unhappy about something.
complaint *noun* 1 a statement complaining about something. 2 an illness, *a heart complaint.*
complement[1] *noun* 1 the quantity needed to fill or complete something, *The ship had its full complement of sailors.* 2 the word or words used after verbs such as *be* and *become* to complete the sense. In *She was brave* and *He became a well-known dancer,* the complements are *brave* and *a well-known dancer.*
complement[2] *verb* make a thing complete, *The hat complements the outfit.*
● USAGE: Do not confuse with *compliment.*
complementary *adjective* completing; forming a complement.
complementary angles angles that add up to 90°.
● USAGE: Do not confuse with *complimentary.*
complete[1] *adjective* 1 having all its parts. 2 finished. 3 thorough; in every way, *a complete stranger.* **completely** *adverb*, **completeness** *noun*
complete[2] *verb* (**completed, completing**) make a thing complete; add what is needed. **completion** *noun*
complex[1] *adjective* 1 made up of parts. 2 complicated, *a complex poem.* **complexity** *noun*
complex[2] *noun* 1 a complex whole; a set of buildings. 2 a group of feelings or ideas that influence a person's behaviour etc., *a persecution complex.*
complexion *noun* 1 the natural colour and appearance of the skin of the face. 2 the way things seem, *That puts a different complexion on the matter.*
compliant *adjective* complying; obedient. **compliance** *noun*
complicate *verb* (**complicated,**

complicating) make a thing complex or complicated.

complicated *adjective* 1 made up of many parts, *complicated wiring.* 2 difficult through being complex.

complication *noun* 1 something that complicates things or adds difficulties. 2 a complicated condition, *I have enough complication in my life without having to deal with your problems.*

complicity *noun* being involved in a crime etc.

compliment[1] *noun* something said or done to show that you approve of a person or thing, *pay compliments.*

compliments *plural noun* formal greetings given in a message.

compliment[2] *verb* pay someone a compliment; congratulate.

● USAGE: Do not confuse with *complement.*

complimentary *adjective* 1 expressing a compliment. 2 given free of charge.

● USAGE: Do not confuse with *complementary.*

comply *verb* (**complied, complying**) obey laws or rules.

component *noun* each of the parts of which a thing is composed.

compose *verb* (**composed, composing**) 1 form; make up, *The class is composed of 20 students.* 2 write music or poetry etc. 3 arrange in good order. 4 make calm, *compose yourself.*

composed *adjective* calm, *a composed manner.* **composedly** *adverb*

composer *noun* a person who composes music etc.

composite (*say* kom-poz-it) *adjective* made up of a number of parts or different styles.

composition *noun* 1 composing. 2 something composed, especially a piece of music. 3 an essay or story written as a school exercise. 4 the parts that make something, *the composition of the soil.* 5 the way in which form, colour, line, etc. are arranged in a work of art.

compost *noun* 1 decayed leaves and grass etc. used as a fertilizer. 2 a soil-like mixture for growing seedlings, cuttings, etc.

composure *noun* calmness of manner.

compound[1] *adjective* made of two or more parts or ingredients.

compound[2] *noun* a compound substance, *Water is a compound of hydrogen and oxygen.*

compound[3] *verb* put together; combine.

compound[4] *noun* a fenced area containing buildings.

comprehend *verb* understand.

comprehensible *adjective* understandable.

comprehensive *adjective* including all or many kinds of people or things.

comprehensive school a large secondary school for all or most of the children of an area.

compress[1] (*say* kom-**press**) *verb* press together or into a smaller space.

compression *noun,* **compressor** *noun*

compress[2] (*say* kom-press) *noun* a soft pad or cloth pressed on the body to stop bleeding or cool inflammation etc.

comprise *verb* (**comprised, comprising**) include; consist of, *The pentathlon comprises five events.*

● USAGE: Do not use *comprise* with *of.* It is incorrect to say 'The group was comprised of 20 men'; correct usage is 'was composed of'.

compromise[1] (*say* kom-prom-I'z) *noun* settling a dispute by each side accepting less than it asked for.

compromise[2] *verb* (**compromised, compromising**) 1 settle by a compromise. 2 expose to danger or suspicion etc., *His confession compromises his sister.*

compulsion *noun* compelling.

compulsive *adjective* having or resulting from an uncontrollable urge, *a compulsive gambler.*

● USAGE: See *compulsory.*

compulsory *adjective* that must be done; not optional.

● USAGE: Do not confuse *compulsory* with *compulsive.* An action is *compulsory* if a law or rules say that you must do it, but *compulsive* if you want to do it and cannot resist it.

compunction *noun* a guilty feeling,

She felt no compunction about hitting the burglar.

compute *verb* (**computed, computing**) calculate. **computation** *noun*

computer *noun* an electronic machine for making calculations, storing and analysing information put into it, or controlling machinery automatically.
computer science the study of the principles and use of computers.
computer virus a hidden code in a computer program that destroys or corrupts data in a computer system.

computerize *verb* (**computerized, computerizing**) equip with computers; perform or produce by computer.
computerization *noun*

computing *noun* the use of computers.

comrade *noun* 1 a companion who shares in your activities. 2 a person who belongs to the same political group as yourself, especially a socialist or Communist group, *Comrade Sipho will address the meeting.*
comradeship *noun*

con¹ *verb* (**conned, conning**) (*slang*) swindle.

con² *noun* a reason against something, *There are pros and cons.*

con- *prefix* see **com-**.

concave *adjective* curved like the inside of a ball or circle. (The opposite is *convex*.)
concavity *noun*

conceal *verb* hide; keep something secret.
concealment *noun*

concede *verb* (**conceded, conceding**) 1 admit that something is true. 2 grant; allow, *They conceded us the right to cross their land.* 3 admit that you have been defeated.

conceit *noun* being too proud of yourself; vanity. **conceited** *adjective*

conceivable *adjective* able to be imagined or believed. **conceivably** *adverb*

conceive *verb* (**conceived, conceiving**) 1 become pregnant; form a baby in the womb. 2 form an idea or plan; imagine, *I can't conceive why you want to come.*

concentrate *verb* (**concentrated, concentrating**) 1 give your full attention or effort to something. 2 bring or come

together in one place. 3 make a liquid etc. less dilute.

concentration *noun* concentrating.
concentration camp a place where political prisoners etc. are brought together and confined.

concentric *adjective* having the same centre, *concentric circles.*

concept *noun* an idea.

conception *noun* 1 conceiving. 2 an idea.

concern¹ *verb* 1 be important to or affect somebody. 2 worry somebody. 3 be about; have as its subject, *The story concerns a group of rabbits.*

concern² *noun* 1 something that concerns you; a responsibility. 2 worry, *no cause for concern.* 3 a business.

concerned *adjective* 1 worried. 2 involved in or affected by something.

concerning *preposition* on the subject of; about, *laws concerning seat-belts.*

concert *noun* a musical entertainment.

concerted *adjective* done in co-operation with others, *We made a concerted effort.*

concertina *noun* a portable musical instrument with bellows, played by squeezing.

concerto (*say* kon-**chert**-oh) *noun* (*plural* **concertos**) a piece of music for a solo instrument and an orchestra.

concession *noun* 1 conceding. 2 something conceded, *The employer was forced to make concessions to her workers.*
concessionary *adjective*

conciliate *verb* (**conciliated, conciliating**) 1 win over an angry or hostile person by friendliness. 2 reconcile people who disagree. **conciliation** *noun*

concise *adjective* brief; giving much information in a few words. **concisely** *adverb*, **conciseness** *noun*

conclave *noun* a private meeting.

conclude *verb* (**concluded, concluding**) 1 bring or come to an end. 2 decide; form an opinion by reasoning, *The jury concluded that he was guilty.*

conclusion *noun* 1 an ending. 2 an opinion formed by reasoning.

conclusive *adjective* putting an end to all doubt. **conclusively** *adverb*

concoct *verb* 1 make something by putting ingredients together. 2 invent, *concoct an excuse*. **concoction** *noun*

concord *noun* friendly agreement or harmony.

concordance *noun* 1 agreement. 2 an index of the words used in a book or an author's works.

concourse *noun* 1 a crowd. 2 an open area through which people pass, e.g. at an airport.

concrete[1] *noun* cement mixed with sand and gravel, used in building.

concrete[2] *adjective* 1 able to be touched and felt; not abstract. 2 definite, *We need concrete evidence, not theories.*

concur *verb* (concurred, concurring) 1 agree. 2 happen together; coincide. **concurrence** *noun*, **concurrent** *adjective*

concussion *noun* a temporary injury to the brain caused by a hard knock. **concussed** *adjective*

condemn *verb* 1 say that you strongly disapprove of something. 2 convict or sentence a criminal. 3 destine to something unhappy, *condemned to a lonely life.* 4 declare that houses etc. are not fit to be used. **condemnation** *noun*

condense *verb* (condensed, condensing) 1 make a liquid denser or more compact. 2 put something into fewer words. 3 change from gas or vapour to liquid, *Steam condenses on windows.* **condensation** *noun*, **condenser** *noun*
condensed milk sweetened milk that has been thickened by evaporation. (Compare *evaporated milk.*)

condescend *verb* 1 behave in a way which shows that you feel superior. 2 allow yourself to do something that seems unsuitable for a person of your high rank. **condescension** *noun*

condiment *noun* a seasoning (e.g. salt or pepper) for food.

condition[1] *noun* 1 the state or fitness of a person or thing, *This bicycle is in good condition.* 2 the situation or surroundings etc. that affect something, *working conditions.* 3 something required as part of an agreement.

on condition that only if; on the understanding that something will be done.

condition[2] *verb* 1 put something into a proper condition. 2 train; accustom.

conditional *adjective* containing a condition (see *condition* 3); depending, *Payment of the money is conditional on the goods being acceptable.* **conditionally** *adverb*

condole *verb* (condoled, condoling) express sympathy. **condolence** *noun*

condom *noun* a sheath for the penis.

condone *verb* (condoned, condoning) forgive or ignore wrongdoing, *Do not condone violence.* **condonation** *noun*

condor *noun* a kind of large vulture.

conducive *adjective* helping to cause or produce something, *Noisy surroundings are not conducive to work.*

conduct[1] (*say* kon-**dukt**) *verb* 1 lead or guide. 2 be the conductor of an orchestra or choir. 3 manage or direct something, *conduct an experiment.* 4 allow heat, light, sound, or electricity to pass along or through. 5 behave, *They conducted themselves with dignity.*

conduct[2] (*say* kon-dukt) *noun* behaviour.

conduction *noun* the conducting of heat or electricity etc.

conductor *noun* 1 a person who directs the performance of an orchestra or choir by movements of the arms. 2 a person who collects the fares on a bus etc. 3 something that conducts heat or electricity etc. **conductress** *noun*

conduit (*say* kon-dit) *noun* 1 a pipe or channel for liquid. 2 a tube protecting electric wire.

cone *noun* 1 an object that is circular at one end and narrows to a point at the other end. 2 the dry cone-shaped fruit of a pine, fir, or cedar tree.

confabulation *noun* a chat.

confection *noun* something made of various things, especially sweet ones, put together.

confectioner *noun* someone who makes or sells sweets. **confectionery** *noun*

confederacy *noun* (*plural* **confederacies**) a union of States; a confederation.

confederate[1] *adjective* allied; joined by an agreement or treaty.

confederate[2] *noun* 1 a member of a confederacy. 2 an ally; an accomplice, *his confederate in the crime.*

confederation *noun* 1 the process of joining in an alliance. 2 a group of people, organizations, or States joined together by an agreement or treaty.

confer *verb* (**conferred, conferring**) 1 grant; bestow. 2 hold a discussion.

conference *noun* a meeting for holding a discussion.

confess *verb* state openly that you have done something wrong or have a weakness; admit. **confession** *noun*

confessional *noun* an enclosed stall where a priest hears confessions.

confessor *noun* a priest who hears confessions.

confetti *noun* tiny pieces of coloured paper thrown by wedding guests at the bride and bridegroom.

confidant *noun* (**confidante** is used of a woman) a person in whom someone confides.

confide *verb* (**confided, confiding**) 1 tell confidentially, *confide a secret to someone* or *confide in someone.* 2 entrust.

confidence *noun* 1 firm trust. 2 a feeling of certainty or boldness; being sure that you can do something. 3 something told confidentially.

confidence trick swindling a person after persuading him or her to trust you.

in confidence as a secret.

in a person's confidence trusted with his or her secrets.

confident *adjective* showing or feeling confidence; bold. **confidently** *adverb*

confidential *adjective* 1 that should be kept secret. 2 trusted to keep secrets, *a confidential secretary.* **confidentially** *adverb*, **confidentiality** *noun*

configuration *noun* 1 a method of arrangement of parts etc., *the configuration of a computer system.* 2 a shape.

confine *verb* (**confined, confining**) 1 keep within limits; restrict, *Please confine your remarks to the subject being discussed.*

2 keep somebody in a place.

confined *adjective* narrow; restricted, *a confined space.*

confinement *noun* 1 confining. 2 the time of giving birth to a baby.

confines (*say* **kon**-fynz) *plural noun* the limits or boundaries of an area.

confirm *verb* 1 prove that something is true or correct. 2 make a thing definite, *Please write to confirm your booking.* 3 make a person a full member of the Christian Church. **confirmation** *noun*, **confirmatory** *adjective*

confiscate *verb* (**confiscated, confiscating**) take something away as a punishment. **confiscation** *noun*

conflagration *noun* a great and destructive fire.

conflict[1] (*say* **kon**-flikt) *noun* a fight, struggle, or disagreement.

conflict[2] (*say* kon-**flikt**) *verb* have a conflict; differ or disagree.

confluence *noun* the place where two rivers unite.

conform *verb* keep to accepted rules or customs etc. **conformist** *noun*, **conformity** *noun*

confound *verb* 1 astonish or puzzle someone. 2 confuse.

confront *verb* 1 come or bring face to face, especially in a hostile way. 2 be present and have to be dealt with, *Problems confront us.* **confrontation** *noun*

confuse *verb* (**confused, confusing**) 1 make a person puzzled or muddled. 2 mistake one thing for another, *I confused her with someone else.* **confusion** *noun*

confute *verb* (**confuted, confuting**) prove a person or statement to be wrong. **confutation** *noun*

conga *noun* 1 a tall narrow drum that is beaten with the hands. 2 a kind of dance where the dancers line up behind each other.

congeal (*say* kon-**jeel**) *verb* become jelly-like instead of liquid, especially in cooling.

congenial *adjective* pleasant through being similar to yourself or suiting your tastes; agreeable, *a congenial companion.* **congenially** *adverb*

congenital (*say* kon-**jen**-it-al) *adjective* existing in a person from birth. **congenitally** *adverb*

congested *adjective* crowded; too full of something, *The roads were congested with holiday traffic.* **congestion** *noun*

conglomeration *noun* a mass of different things put together.

congratulate *verb* (**congratulated, congratulating**) tell a person that you are pleased about his or her success or good fortune. **congratulation** *noun*, **congratulatory** *adjective*

congregate *verb* (**congregated, congregating**) assemble; flock together.

congregation *noun* a group who have gathered to take part in worship.

Congress *noun* 1 a political society or association, *African National Congress.* 2 the parliament of the USA.

congress *noun* a conference.

congruent *adjective* 1 suitable; consistent. 2 (of geometrical figures) having exactly the same shape and size. **congruence** *noun*

conic *adjective* of a cone.

conical *adjective* cone-shaped. **conically** *adverb*

conifer (*say* **kon**-if-er) *noun* an evergreen tree with cones. **coniferous** *adjective*

conjecture *noun* a guess. **conjecture** *verb*, **conjectural** *adjective*

conjugal (*say* **kon**-jug-al) *adjective* of a husband and wife.

conjunction *noun* 1 a word that joins words or phrases or sentences, e.g. *and, but.* 2 combination, *The four armies acted in conjunction.*

conjure *verb* (**conjured, conjuring**) perform puzzling tricks. **conjuror** *noun* **conjure up** produce, *Mention of the Arctic conjures up visions of snow.*

conk *verb* (*informal*) **conk out** break down; give up; fall asleep; die.

connect *verb* 1 join together; link. 2 think of as being associated with each other, *People connect Cape Town with Table Mountain.* **connection** *noun*, **connective** *adjective*, **connector** *noun*

conning-tower *noun* a projecting part on top of a submarine, containing the periscope.

connive (*say* kon-**I'v**) *verb* (**connived, conniving**) **connive at** take no notice of wrongdoing that ought to be reported or punished. **connivance** *noun*

connoisseur (*say* kon-a-**ser**) *noun* a person with great experience and appreciation of something, *a connoisseur of wine.*

conquer *verb* defeat; overcome. **conqueror** *noun*

conquest *noun* 1 conquering. 2 conquered territory.

conscience (*say* **kon**-shens) *noun* knowing what is right and wrong, especially in your own actions.

conscientious (*say* kon-shee-**en**-shus) *adjective* careful and honest, *conscientious workers.* **conscientiously** *adverb* **conscientious objector** a person who refuses to serve in the armed forces because he or she believes it is wrong.

conscious (*say* **kon**-shus) *adjective* awake; aware of what is happening. **consciously** *adverb*, **consciousness** *noun*

conscript[1] (*say* kon-**skript**) *verb* make a person join the armed forces. **conscription** *noun*

conscript[2] (*say* **kon**-skript) *noun* a conscripted person.

consecrate *verb* (**consecrated, consecrating**) make a thing sacred; dedicate to God. **consecration** *noun*

consecutive *adjective* following one after another. **consecutively** *adverb*

consensus *noun* (*plural* **consensuses**) general agreement; the opinion of most people.

consent[1] *noun* agreement to what someone wishes; permission, *He gave his consent for the article to be published.*

consent[2] *verb* say that you are willing to do or allow what someone wishes.

consequence *noun* 1 something that happens as the result of an event or action. 2 importance, *It is of no consequence.*

consequent *adjective* happening as a result. **consequently** *adverb*

consequential *adjective* consequent.

conservation *noun* conserving; preservation, especially of the natural environment.

conservationist *noun*

conservative *adjective* **1** liking traditional ways and disliking changes. **2** (of an estimate) moderate; low. **conservatively** *adverb*, **conservatism** *noun*

conservatory *noun* a greenhouse attached to a house.

conserve[1] (*say* **kon**-serve) *noun* a fresh fruit jam.

conserve[2] (*say* kon-**serve**) *verb* (**conserved, conserving**) prevent something valuable from being changed, spoilt, or wasted.

consider *verb* **1** think carefully about or give attention to something, especially in order to make a decision. **2** have an opinion; think to be, *Consider yourself lucky.*

considerable *adjective* fairly great, *a considerable amount.* **considerably** *adverb*

considerate *adjective* taking care not to inconvenience or hurt others. **considerately** *adverb*

consideration *noun* **1** being considerate. **2** careful thought or attention. **3** a fact that must be kept in mind, *Time is an important consideration in this situation.* **4** payment given as a reward.

take into consideration allow for.

considering *preposition* taking something into consideration, *The car runs well, considering its age.*

consign *verb* hand something over formally; entrust.

consignment *noun* **1** consigning. **2** a batch of goods etc. sent to someone.

consist *verb* be made up or composed of, *The flat consists of three rooms.*

consistency *noun* (*plural* **consistencies**) **1** being consistent. **2** thickness or stiffness, especially of a liquid.

consistent *adjective* **1** keeping to a regular pattern or style; not changing. **2** not contradictory, *She left as early as was consistent with politeness.* **consistently** *adverb*

consolation *noun* **1** consoling. **2** something that consoles someone.

consolation prize a prize given to a competitor who has just missed winning one of the main prizes.

console[1] (*say* kon-**sohl**) *verb* (**consoled, consoling**) comfort someone who is unhappy or disappointed.

console[2] (*say* **kon**-sohl) *noun* **1** a frame containing the keyboard and stops etc. of an organ. **2** a panel holding the controls of equipment. **3** a cabinet for a radio or television set.

consolidate *verb* (**consolidated, consolidating**) **1** make or become secure and strong. **2** combine two or more organizations, funds, etc. into one. **consolidation** *noun*

consonant *noun* a letter that is not a vowel, *B, c, d, f, etc. are consonants.*

consort[1] (*say* **kon**-sort) *noun* a husband or wife, especially of a monarch.

consort[2] (*say* kon-**sort**) *verb* be in someone's company, *consort with criminals.*

consortium *noun* (*plural* **consortia**) a combination of countries, companies, or other groups acting together.

conspicuous *adjective* easily seen; noticeable; remarkable. **conspicuously** *adverb*, **conspicuousness** *noun*

conspiracy *noun* (*plural* **conspiracies**) planning with others to do something illegal; a plot.

conspire *verb* (**conspired, conspiring**) take part in a conspiracy. **conspirator** *noun*, **conspiratorial** *adjective*

constable *noun* a police officer of the lowest rank.

constant *adjective* **1** not changing; happening all the time, *constant interruptions.* **2** faithful; loyal. **constantly** *adverb*, **constancy** *noun*

constellation *noun* a group of stars.

constipated *adjective* unable to empty the bowels easily or regularly. **constipation** *noun*

constituency *noun* (*plural* **constituencies**) **1** a district represented by a Member of Parliament elected by the people who live there. **2** a group of voters who elect a representative.

constituent *noun* **1** one of the parts that form a whole thing. **2** someone who lives in a particular constituency. **constituent** *adjective*

constitute *verb* (**constituted, constituting**) make up or form something, *Twelve months constitute a year.*

constitution *noun* 1 the group of laws or principles that state how a country is to be organized and governed. 2 the nature of the body in regard to healthiness, *She has a strong constitution.* 3 constituting. 4 the composition of something. **constitutional** *adjective*

constrain *verb* compel; oblige.

constraint *noun* 1 constraining; compulsion. 2 a restriction, *time constraints.* 3 a strained manner caused by holding back feelings.

constrict *verb* squeeze or tighten something by making it narrower. **constriction** *noun*

construct *verb* make something by placing parts together; build. **constructor** *noun*

construction *noun* 1 constructing. 2 something constructed; a building. 3 two or more words put together to form a phrase or clause or sentence. 4 an explanation or interpretation, *They put a bad construction on our refusal.*

constructive *adjective* constructing; being helpful, *constructive suggestions.*

construe *verb* (**construed, construing**) interpret; explain.

consul *noun* 1 a government official appointed to live in a foreign city to help people from his or her own country who visit there. 2 either of the two chief magistrates in ancient Rome. **consular** *adjective*

consulate *noun* the building where a consul works.

consult *verb* go to a person or book etc. for information or advice. **consultation** *noun*

consultant *noun* a person who is qualified to give expert advice.

consultative *adjective* for consultation, *a consultative committee.*

consume *verb* (**consumed, consuming**) 1 eat or drink something. 2 use up, *Much time was consumed in waiting.* 3 destroy, *Fire consumed the building.*

consumer *noun* a person who buys or uses goods or services.

consummate¹ (*say* kon-sum-ayt) *verb* accomplish; make complete. **consummation** *noun*

consummate² (*say* kon-**sum**-at) *adjective* perfect; highly skilled, *a consummate artist.*

consumption *noun* 1 consuming. 2 (*old use*) tuberculosis of the lungs.

contact¹ *noun* 1 touching. 2 being in touch; communication. 3 a person to communicate with when you need information or help.

contact lens a tiny lens worn against the eyeball, instead of spectacles.

contact² *verb* get in touch with a person.

contagion *noun* a contagious disease.

contagious *adjective* spreading by contact with an infected person, *a contagious disease.*

contain *verb* 1 have inside, *The box contains chocolates.* 2 consist of, *A litre contains 1 000 millilitres.* 3 restrain; hold back, *Try to contain your laughter.*

container *noun* 1 a box or bottle etc. designed to contain something. 2 a large box-like object of standard design in which goods are transported.

contaminate *verb* (**contaminated, contaminating**) make a thing dirty or impure or diseased etc.; pollute. **contamination** *noun*

contemplate *verb* (**contemplated, contemplating**) 1 look at something thoughtfully. 2 consider or think about doing something, *We are contemplating a visit to Lesotho.* **contemplation** *noun*, **contemplative** *adjective*

contemporary¹ *adjective* 1 belonging to the same period, *Dickens was contemporary with Thackeray.* 2 modern; up-to-date, *contemporary furniture.*

contemporary² *noun* (*plural* **contemporaries**) a person who is contemporary with another or who is about the same age, *She was my contemporary at college.*

contempt *noun* a feeling of despising a person or thing.

contemptible *adjective* deserving contempt.

contemptuous *adjective* feeling or showing contempt. **contemptuously** *adverb*

contend *verb* 1 struggle in a battle etc. or against difficulties. 2 compete, *Two teams contended for the title.* 3 assert; declare in an argument etc., *We contend that he is innocent.* **contender** *noun*

content[1] (*say* kon-**tent**) *adjective* contented, *She was content with his explanation.*

content[2] *noun* contentment.

content[3] *verb* make a person contented.

content[4] (*say* **kon**-tent) *noun* (also **contents** *plural noun*) what something contains.

contented *adjective* happy with what you have; satisfied. **contentedly** *adverb*

contention *noun* 1 contending; arguing. 2 an assertion put forward, *It is my contention that he is wrong.*

contentment *noun* a contented state.

contest[1] (*say* **kon**-test) *noun* a competition; a struggle in which rivals try to obtain something or to do best.

contest[2] (*say* kon-**test**) *verb* 1 compete for or in, *contest an election.* 2 dispute; argue that something is wrong or not legal.

contestant *noun* a person taking part in a contest; a competitor.

context *noun* the words that come before and after a particular word or phrase and help to fix its meaning.

contiguous *adjective* adjoining.

continent *noun* one of the main masses of land in the world, *The continents are Europe, Asia, Africa, North America, South America, Australia, and Antarctica.* **continental** *adjective*

contingency *noun* (*plural* **contingencies**) something that may happen but is not intended.

contingent[1] *adjective* 1 depending, *His future is contingent on success in this exam.* 2 possible but not certain, *other contingent events.*

contingent[2] *noun* a group contributing to a larger group or gathering, *The Port Elizabeth contingent will join the conference tomorrow.*

continual *adjective* constantly or frequently recurring; always happening, *Stop this continual quarrelling!* **continually** *adverb*

● USAGE: Do not confuse *continual* with *continuous. Continual* is used when an action is repeated again and again, *There were continual interruptions. Continuous* is used when something happens without stopping, *the continuous rain.*

continuance *noun* continuing.

continue *verb* (**continued, continuing**) 1 do something without stopping. 2 begin again after stopping, *The game will continue after lunch.* **continuation** *noun*

continuous *adjective* continuing; without a break. **continuously** *adverb*, **continuity** *noun*

● USAGE: Do not confuse this word with *continual.*

contort *verb* twist or force out of the usual shape. **contortion** *noun*

contortionist *noun* a person who can twist his or her body into unusual postures.

contour *noun* 1 a line (on a map) joining the points that are the same height above sea-level. 2 an outline.

contour bank a raised wall of earth, level with a contour line, which helps to prevent soil erosion on sloping land.

contra- *prefix* against.

contraband *noun* smuggled goods.

contraception *noun* preventing conception; birth-control.

contraceptive *noun* a substance or device that prevents conception.

contract[1] (*say* kon-trakt) *noun* 1 a formal agreement to do something. 2 a document stating the terms of an agreement.

contract[2] (*say* kon-**trakt**) *verb* 1 make or become smaller, *Metals contract as they get cooler.* 2 make a contract. 3 get an illness, *She contracted measles.*

contraction *noun* 1 contracting. 2 a shortened form of a word or words. *Can't* is a contraction of *cannot.*

contractor *noun* a person who makes a contract, especially for building.

contradict *verb* 1 say that something said is not true or that someone is wrong. 2 say the opposite of, *These rumours*

contradict previous ones. **contradiction** noun, **contradictory** adjective

contraflow noun a flow of road traffic travelling in the opposite direction to the usual flow and close beside it.

contralto noun (plural **contraltos**) a female singer with a low voice.

contraption noun a strange-looking device or machine.

contrary[1] adjective 1 (say **kon**-tra-ree) of the opposite kind or direction etc.; opposed; unfavourable, contrary beliefs. 2 (say kon-**trair**-ee) awkward and obstinate.

contrary[2] (say **kon**-tra-ree) noun the opposite.
on the contrary the opposite is true.

contrast[1] (say **kon**-trahst) noun 1 a difference clearly seen when things are compared, The white blossoms make a contrast against the dark bark of the tree. 2 something showing a clear difference, This work is quite a contrast to the work you did last week.

contrast[2] (say kon-**trahst**) verb 1 compare or oppose two things so as to show that they are clearly different. 2 be clearly different when compared.

contravene verb (**contravened, contravening**) act against a rule or law. **contravention** noun

contribute verb (**contributed, contributing**) 1 give money or help etc. when others are doing the same. 2 write something for a newspaper or magazine etc. 3 help to cause something, Lack of exercise can contribute to obesity. **contribution** noun, **contributor** noun, **contributory** adjective

contrite adjective penitent.

contrivance noun a device.

contrive verb (**contrived, contriving**) plan cleverly; find a way of doing or making something.

control[1] verb (**controlled, controlling**) have the power to give orders or to restrain something. **controller** noun

control[2] noun controlling a person or thing; authority.

controversial adjective causing controversy.

controversy (say **kon**-tro-ver-see or kon-**trov**-er-see) noun a long argument or disagreement.

contusion noun a bruise.

conundrum noun a riddle; a hard question.

conurbation noun a large urban area where towns have spread into each other.

convalesce verb (**convalesced, convalescing**) be recovering from an illness. **convalescence** noun, **convalescent** adjective & noun

convection noun the passing on of heat within liquid, air, or gas by circulation of the warmed parts.

convector noun a device that circulates warmed air.

convene verb (**convened, convening**) summon or assemble for a meeting etc. **convener** noun

convenience noun 1 being convenient. 2 something that is convenient. 3 a public lavatory.
at your convenience whenever you find convenient; as it suits you.

convenient adjective easy to use or deal with or reach. **conveniently** adverb

convent noun a place where nuns live and work.

convention noun 1 an accepted way of doing things. 2 a formal assembly, a teachers' convention.

conventional adjective 1 done or doing things in the accepted way; traditional. 2 (of weapons) not nuclear. **conventionally** adverb, **conventionality** noun

converge verb (**converged, converging**) come to or towards the same point from different directions. (The opposite is diverge.) **convergence** noun, **convergent** adjective

conversant adjective familiar with something, Are you conversant with the rules of this game?

conversation noun talk between people. **conversational** adjective

converse[1] (say kon-**verss**) verb (**conversed, conversing**) hold a conversation.

converse[2] (say **kon**-verss) adjective opposite; contrary, She says he is happy,

but I believe the converse to be true.
conversely *adverb*

converse[3] *noun* an opposite idea or statement etc.

conversion *noun* converting.

convert (*say* kon-**vert**) *verb* **1** change. **2** cause a person to change his or her beliefs. **3** kick a goal after scoring a try at rugby. **converter** *noun*

convertible *adjective* able to be converted. **convertibility** *noun*

convex *adjective* curved like the outside of a ball or circle. (The opposite is *concave*.) **convexity** *noun*

convey *verb* **1** transport. **2** communicate a message or idea etc. **conveyor** *noun*

conveyance *noun* **1** conveying. **2** a vehicle for transporting people.

conveyancing *noun* transferring the legal ownership of land etc. from one person to another.

conveyor belt *noun* a continuous moving belt for conveying objects.

convict[1] (*say* kon-**vikt**) *verb* prove or declare that a certain person is guilty of a crime.

convict[2] (*say* kon-vikt) *noun* a convicted person who is in prison.

conviction *noun* **1** convicting or being convicted of a crime. **2** being convinced. **3** a firm opinion or belief, *act according to your convictions.*
carry conviction be convincing.

convince *verb* (**convinced, convincing**) make a person feel certain that something is true.

convivial *adjective* sociable and lively.

convoke *verb* (**convoked, convoking**) summon people to an assembly or meeting.

convoluted *adjective* **1** coiled; twisted. **2** complicated, *the convoluted plot.*
convolution *noun*

convolvulus *noun* (*plural* **convolvuluses**) a kind of twining plant.

convoy *noun* a group of ships or trucks travelling together.

convulse *verb* (**convulse, convulsing**) cause violent movements or convulsions.
convulsive *adjective*

convulsion *noun* **1** a violent movement of the body. **2** a violent upheaval. **3** (*plural*) uncontrollable laughter, *We were in convulsions at the play.*

coo *verb* (**cooed, cooing**) make a dove's soft murmuring sound. **coo** *noun*

cook[1] *verb* make food ready to eat by heating it.
cook up (*informal*) concoct; invent.

cook[2] *noun* a person who cooks.

cooker *noun* a stove for cooking food.

cookery *noun* the action or skill of cooking food.

cool[1] *adjective* **1** fairly cold; not hot or warm. **2** calm; not enthusiastic, *She remained cool during the crisis.* **coolly** *adverb*, **coolness** *noun*

cool[2] *verb* make or become cool. **cooler** *noun*

cooldrink *noun* a soft drink.

coon *noun* a performer in a group of entertainers at the New Year festival in Cape Town.
Coon Carnival this festival.

coop *noun* a cage for poultry.

co-op *abbreviation* (*informal*) a co-operative farm, society, or business.

co-operate *verb* (**co-operated, co-operating**) work helpfully with other people. **co-operation** *noun*

co-operative[1] *noun* a farm, society, or business that is owned and run jointly by its members, who share its profits.

co-operative[2] *adjective* working helpfully with other people.

co-opt *verb* invite someone to become a member of a committee etc.

co-ordinate[1] *verb* (**co-ordinated, co-ordinating**) organize people or things to work properly together. **co-ordination** *noun*, **co-ordinator** *noun*

co-ordinate[2] *noun* **1** a co-ordinated thing. **2** (also **coordinate**) a quantity used to fix the position of something.

coot *noun* a water-bird with a horny white patch on its forehead.

cop[1] *verb* (**copped, copping**) (*informal*) catch, *You'll cop it!*

cop[2] *noun* (*informal*) **1** a police officer. **2** capture; arrest, *It's a fair cop!*

cope[1] *verb* (**coped, coping**) manage or deal with something successfully.

cope[2] *noun* a long loose cloak worn by clergy in ceremonies etc.

copier *noun* a device for copying things.

coping *noun* the top row of stones or bricks in a wall, usually slanted so that rainwater will run off.

copious *adjective* plentiful; in large amounts. **copiously** *adverb*

copper *noun* 1 a reddish-brown metal used to make wire, coins, etc. 2 a reddish-brown colour. 3 a coin made of copper or metal of this colour. **copper** *adjective*

copperplate *noun* neat handwriting.

coppice *noun* a group of small trees.

copra *noun* dried coconut-kernels.

copse *noun* a coppice.

copulate *verb* (**copulated, copulating**) have sexual intercourse with someone. **copulation** *noun*

copy[1] *noun* (*plural* **copies**) 1 a thing made to look like another. 2 something written or typed out again from its original form. 3 one of a number of specimens of the same book or newspaper etc., *five copies of the novel.*

copy[2] *verb* (**copied, copying**) 1 make a copy of something. 2 do the same as someone else; imitate. **copyist** *noun*

copyright *noun* the legal right to print a book, reproduce a picture, record a piece of music, etc.

coquette (*say* ko-**ket**) *noun* a woman who flirts. **coquettish** *adjective*

cor- *prefix* see **com-**.

coral *noun* 1 a hard red, pink, or white substance formed by the skeletons of tiny sea-creatures massed together. 2 a pink colour.

corbel *noun* a piece of stone or wood projecting from a roof to support something.

cord *noun* 1 a long thin flexible strip of twisted threads or strands. 2 a piece of flex, *electrical cord.* 3 a cord-like structure in the body, *the spinal cord.* 4 corduroy.

cordial[1] *noun* a fruit-flavoured drink.

cordial[2] *adjective* warm and friendly. **cordially** *adverb*, **cordiality** *noun*

cordon[1] *noun* a line of people, ships, fortifications, etc. placed round an area to guard or enclose it.

cordon[2] *verb* surround with a cordon, *Police cordoned off the area where the march took place.*

cordon bleu (*say* kor-don **bler**) *adjective* (of a cook, food, etc.) of the highest standard.

corduroy *noun* cotton cloth with velvety ridges.

core *noun* 1 the part in the middle of something. 2 the hard central part of an apple or pear etc., containing the seeds.

corgi *noun* (*plural* **corgis**) a small dog with short legs and upright ears.

cork[1] *noun* 1 the lightweight bark of a kind of oak-tree. 2 a stopper for a bottle, made of cork or other material.

cork[2] *verb* close with a cork.

corkscrew *noun* 1 a device for removing corks from bottles. 2 a spiral.

corm *noun* a part of a plant rather like a bulb.

cormorant *noun* a large black sea-bird.

corn[1] *noun* 1 the seed of maize and similar plants. 2 any plant (such as maize or wheat) grown for its grain.

corn-cob the central part of an ear of maize, on which the grains grow.

corn[2] *noun* a small hard lump on the foot.

cornea *noun* the transparent covering over the pupil of the eye. **corneal** *adjective*

corned *adjective* preserved with salt, *corned beef.*

corner[1] *noun* 1 the angle or area where two lines or sides or walls meet or where two streets join. 2 a region, *a quiet corner of the world.* 3 a free hit or kick from the corner of a hockey or soccer field. 4 any of the four corners of a boxing or wrestling ring.

corner[2] *verb* 1 drive someone into a corner or other position from which it is difficult to escape. 2 travel round a corner. 3 obtain possession of all or most of something, *corner the market.*

corner-stone *noun* 1 a stone built into the corner at the base of a building. 2 something that is a vital foundation, *Courtesy is a corner-stone of our school's code of behaviour.*

cornet *noun* 1 a cone-shaped wafer etc. holding ice-cream. 2 a musical instrument rather like a trumpet.

cornflakes *plural noun* toasted maize flakes eaten for breakfast.

cornflour *noun* flour made from maize or rice, used in sauces, milk puddings, etc.

cornflower *noun* a plant with blue flowers that grows wild in fields of corn.

cornice *noun* a band of ornamental moulding on walls just below a ceiling or at the top of a building.

cornucopia *noun* a horn-shaped container overflowing with fruit and flowers; a plentiful supply.

corny *adjective* (**cornier, corniest**) (*informal*) repeated so often that people are bored, *corny jokes.*

corolla *noun* the petals of a flower.

corollary (*say* ker-**ol**-er-ee) *noun* (*plural* **corollaries**) a fact etc. that logically accompanies another, *The work is difficult and, as a corollary, tiring.*

corona (*say* kor-**oh**-na) *noun* a circle of light round something, *The sun's corona can be seen during an eclipse.*

coronary *noun* short for **coronary thrombosis**, blockage of an artery carrying blood to the heart.

coronation *noun* the crowning of a king or queen.

coroner *noun* an official who holds an inquiry into the cause of a death thought to be from unnatural causes.

coronet *noun* a small crown.

corporal[1] *noun* a soldier ranking next below a sergeant.

corporal[2] *adjective* of the body.
corporal punishment punishment by being whipped or beaten.

corporate *adjective* shared by members of a group, *corporate responsibility.*

corporation *noun* a group of people legally authorized to act as an individual in business etc.

corps (*say* kor) *noun* (*plural* **corps** (*say* korz)) 1 a special army unit, *the Medical Corps.* 2 a large group of soldiers. 3 a set of people engaged in the same activity, *the diplomatic corps.*

corpse *noun* a dead body.

corpulent *adjective* having a bulky body; fat. **corpulence** *noun*

corpuscle *noun* one of the red or white cells in blood.

corral (*say* kor-**ahl**) *noun* (*American*) an enclosure for horses, cattle, etc.

correct[1] *adjective* 1 true; accurate; without any mistakes. 2 proper; done or said in an approved way, *Casual dress is not correct for a formal occasion.* **correctly** *adverb,* **correctness** *noun*

correct[2] *verb* 1 make a thing correct by altering or adjusting it. 2 mark the mistakes in something. 3 point out or punish a person's faults. **correction** *noun,* **corrective** *adjective,* **corrector** *noun*

correlate *verb* (**correlated, correlating**) compare or connect things systematically. **correlation** *noun*

correspond *verb* 1 write letters to each other. 2 agree; match, *Your story corresponds with his.* 3 be similar or equivalent, *Their assembly corresponds to our parliament.*

correspondence *noun* 1 letters; writing letters. 2 similarity; agreement, *correspondence in our views.*

correspondence course a course of study which can be followed at home, using books and exercises sent through the post.

correspondent *noun* 1 a person who writes letters to another. 2 a person employed to gather news and send reports to a newspaper or radio station etc.

corridor *noun* a passage in a building.

corroborate *verb* (**corroborated, corroborating**) help to confirm a statement etc. **corroboration** *noun*

corrode *verb* (**corroded, corroding**) destroy metal gradually by chemical action. **corrosion** *noun,* **corrosive** *adjective*

corrugated *adjective* shaped into alternate ridges and grooves, *corrugated iron.*

corrupt[1] *adjective* 1 dishonest; accepting bribes. 2 wicked. 3 made unreliable; altered from the original, *The data on the disk is corrupt and must be checked.*

corrupt[2] *verb* 1 cause to become dishonest

or wicked. **2** spoil; cause to decay. **3** change something so that it is no longer in its original form. **corruption** *noun*, **corruptible** *adjective*

corsage (*say* kor-**saa**zh) *noun* a small bunch of flowers worn on a dress, lapel of a jacket, etc.

corsair *noun* a pirate ship; a pirate.

corset *noun* a piece of underwear worn to shape or support the body.

cortège (*say* kort-**ayz**h) *noun* a funeral procession.

corvette *noun* a small escort-vessel used by the navy.

cosecant *noun* (in a right-angled triangle) the ratio of the hypotenuse to the side opposite an acute angle.

cosh *noun* a heavy weapon for hitting people.

cosine *noun* (in a right-angled triangle) the ratio of the length of a side adjacent to one of the acute angles to the length of the hypotenuse.

cosmetic *noun* a substance (e.g. face-powder, lipstick) put on the skin to make it look more attractive.

cosmetic surgery surgery which restores or improves somebody's normal appearance.

cosmic *adjective* **1** of the universe. **2** of outer space, *cosmic rays.*

cosmopolitan *adjective* of or from many countries; containing people from many countries.

cosmos (*say* **koz**-moss) *noun* **1** the universe. **2** a plant with pink or white flowers often found growing wild.

Cossack *noun* a member of a people of south Russia, famous as horsemen.

cosset *verb* (**cosseted, cosseting**) pamper; cherish lovingly.

cossie (*say* **koz**-ee) *noun* (*informal*) a swimming-costume.

cost¹ *noun* the price of something.

cost² *verb* (**cost, costing**) **1** have a certain price. **2** (*past tense* is **costed**) estimate the cost of something.

costermonger *noun* a person who sells fruit etc. from a barrow in the street.

costly *adjective* (**costlier, costliest**) expensive. **costliness** *noun*

costume *noun* clothes, especially for a particular purpose or of a particular place or period.

cosy¹ *adjective* (**cosier, cosiest**) warm and comfortable. **cosily** *adverb*, **cosiness** *noun*

cosy² *noun* (*plural* **cosies**) a cover placed over a teapot or boiled egg to keep it hot.

cot *noun* a baby's bed with high sides. **cot-death** the unexplained death of a sleeping baby.

cotangent *noun* (in a right-angled triangle) the ratio of the length of a side adjacent to one of the acute angles to the length of the opposite side.

cottage *noun* a small simple house, especially in the country. **cottage cheese** a soft white lumpy cheese. **cottage pie** a dish of minced meat covered with mashed potato and baked.

cottager *noun* a person who lives in a country cottage.

cotton *noun* **1** a soft white substance covering the seeds of a tropical plant; the plant itself. **2** thread made from this substance. **3** cloth made from cotton thread. **cotton wool** soft fluffy wadding originally made from cotton.

cotyledon (*say* kot-a-**lee**-den) *noun* the part of the seed that contains the food supply for the embryo plant.

couch¹ *noun* (*plural* **couches**) **1** a long soft seat like a sofa but with only one end raised. **2** a sofa or settee. **couch potato** (*informal*) a person who does very little exercise; someone who spends a lot of time watching television.

couch² *verb* express in words of a certain kind, *The request was couched in polite terms.*

cougar (*say* **koo**-ger) *noun* (*American*) a puma.

cough¹ (*say* kof) *verb* send out air from the lungs with a sudden sharp sound.

cough² *noun* **1** the act or sound of coughing. **2** an illness that makes you cough.

could *past tense* of **can².**

couldn't (*mainly spoken*) could not.

coulomb (*say* koo-lom) *noun* a unit of electric charge.

council *noun* a group of people chosen or elected to organize or discuss something, especially those elected to organize the affairs of a town or county.
council house a house owned and let to tenants by a town council.
● USAGE: Do not confuse with *counsel*.

councillor *noun* a member of a local council.

counsel[1] *noun* 1 advice, *give counsel*. 2 a legal adviser or group of advisers representing someone in a lawsuit.
take counsel with consult.
● USAGE: Do not confuse with *council*.

counsel[2] *verb* (**counselled, counselling**) give advice to someone; recommend.

counsellor *noun* 1 an adviser. 2 a person who gives guidance on personal problems.

count[1] *verb* 1 say numbers in their proper order. 2 find the total of something by using numbers. 3 include in a total, *There are six of us, counting the dog.* 4 be important, *It's what you do that counts.* 5 regard; consider, *I should count it an honour to be invited.*
count on rely on.

count[2] *noun* 1 counting. 2 a number reached by counting; a total. 3 any of the points being considered, e.g. in accusing someone of crimes, *guilty on all counts.*

count[3] *noun* a foreign nobleman.

countdown *noun* counting numbers backwards to zero before an event.

countenance[1] *noun* a person's face; the expression on the face.

countenance[2] *verb* (**countenanced, countenancing**) give approval to; allow, *Will they countenance this plan?*

counter[1] *noun* 1 a flat-topped fitment over which customers are served in a shop, bank, etc. 2 a small round token used for keeping accounts or scores in certain games. 3 a device for counting things.
under the counter sold or obtained in an underhand way.

counter[2] *verb* 1 counteract. 2 counter-attack; return an opponent's blow by hitting back.

counter[3] *adverb* contrary to something, *This is counter to what we really want.*

counter- *prefix* 1 against; opposing; done in return (as in *counter-attack*). 2 corresponding (as in *countersign*).

counteract *verb* act against something and reduce or prevent its effects. **counteraction** *noun*

counter-attack *verb* attack to oppose or return an enemy's attack. **counter-attack** *noun*

counterbalance *noun* a weight or influence that balances another. **counterbalance** *verb*

counterfeit (*say* kownt-er-feet) *adjective, noun & verb* fake.

counterfoil *noun* a section of a cheque or receipt etc. that is detached and kept as a record.

countermand *verb* cancel a command or instruction that has been given.

counterpane *noun* a bedspread.

counterpart *noun* a person or thing that corresponds to another, *Britain's Chancellor of the Exchequer is the counterpart of our Minister of Finance.*

counterpoint *noun* a method of combining melodies in harmony.

counterpoise *noun & verb* counterbalance.

counter-productive *adjective* having the opposite effect to that intended.

countersign[1] *noun* a password or signal that has to be given in response to something.

countersign[2] *verb* add another signature to a document to give it authority.

counterweight *noun & verb* counterbalance.

countess *noun* (*plural* **countesses**) the wife or widow of a count or earl; a female count.

countless *adjective* too many to count.

countrified *adjective* of or like the countryside.

country *noun* (*plural* **countries**) 1 the land occupied by a nation. 2 all the people of a country. 3 the countryside.
country club a sporting and social club.
country dance a folk-dance.

countryside *noun* an area with fields, woods, villages, etc. away from towns.

coup (*say* koo) *noun* a sudden action taken to win power; a clever victory.

coup d'état (*say* koo day-**tah**) *noun* (*plural* **coups d'état**) a violent and illegal change of government.

couple[1] *noun* two people or things considered together; a pair.

couple[2] *verb* (**coupled**, **coupling**) fasten or link together.

couplet *noun* a pair of lines in rhyming verse.

coupon *noun* a piece of paper that gives you the right to receive or do something.

courage *noun* the ability to face danger or difficulty or pain even when you are afraid; bravery. **courageous** *adjective*

courgette (*say* koor-zh**e**t) *noun* a kind of small vegetable marrow.

courier (*say* **koor**-ee-er) *noun* 1 a messenger. 2 a person employed to guide and help a group of tourists.

course[1] *noun* 1 the direction in which something goes; a route, *the ship's course.* 2 a series of events or actions etc., *Your best course is to start again.* 3 a series of lessons, exercises, etc. 4 part of a meal, *the meat course.* 5 a racecourse. 6 a golf-course. **of course** without a doubt; as we expected.

course[2] *verb* (**coursed**, **coursing**) move or flow freely, *Tears coursed down his cheeks.*

court[1] *noun* 1 a lawcourt; the judges etc. in a lawcourt. 2 the royal household. 3 an enclosed area for games such as tennis or netball. 4 a courtyard.

court[2] *verb* try to win somebody's love or support. **courtship** *noun*

courteous (*say* **ker**-tee-us) *adjective* polite. **courteously** *adverb*, **courtesy** *noun*

courtier *noun* (*old use*) one of a king's or queen's companions at court.

courtly *adjective* dignified and polite.

court martial *noun* (*plural* **courts martial**) 1 a court for trying people who have broken military law. 2 a trial in this court.

court-martial *verb* (**court-martialled**, **court-martialling**) try a person by a court martial.

courtyard *noun* a space surrounded by walls or buildings.

cousin *noun* a child of your uncle or aunt.

cove *noun* a small bay.

coven (*say* **kuv**-en) *noun* a group of witches.

covenant (*say* **kuv**-en-ant) *noun* a formal agreement; a contract.

cover[1] *verb* 1 place one thing over or round another; conceal. 2 travel a certain distance, *We covered ten kilometres a day.* 3 aim a gun at somebody, *I've got you covered.* 4 protect by insurance or a guarantee, *These goods are covered against fire or theft.* 5 be enough money to pay for something, *R10 will cover my fare.* 6 deal with or include, *The book covers all kinds of farming.* **coverage** *noun*

cover[2] *noun* 1 a thing used for covering something else; a lid, wrapper, envelope, etc. 2 the binding of a book, magazine, etc. 3 something that hides or shelters or protects you, *We ran for cover when the storm began.*

coverlet *noun* a bedspread.

covert[1] (*say* **kuv**-ert) *noun* an area of thick bushes etc. in which birds and animals hide.

covert[2] *adjective* stealthy; done secretly.

covet (*say* **kuv**-it) *verb* (**coveted**, **coveting**) wish to have something, especially a thing that belongs to someone else. **covetous** *adjective*

cow[1] *noun* the fully-grown female of cattle or of certain other large animals (e.g. seal, elephant, whale).

cow[2] *verb* intimidate; subdue someone by bullying.

coward *noun* a person who shows fear in a shameful way, or who attacks people who cannot defend themselves. **cowardice** *noun*, **cowardly** *adjective*

cowboy *noun* a person in charge of grazing cattle on a ranch in the USA. **cowgirl** *noun*

cower *verb* crouch or shrink back in fear.

cowl *noun* 1 a monk's hood. 2 a hood-shaped covering, e.g. on a chimney.

cowrie *noun* a small bright shell which was used as money in parts of Africa and Asia.

cowshed *noun* a shed for cattle.

cox *noun* (*plural* **coxes**) a coxswain.

coxswain (*say* **kok**-swayn or **kok**-sun) *noun* 1 a person who steers a rowing-boat. 2 a sailor with special duties.

coy *adjective* pretending to be shy or modest; bashful. **coyly** *adverb*, **coyness** *noun*

CPU *abbreviation* central processing unit.

crab *noun* a shellfish with ten legs.

crab-apple *noun* a small sour apple.

crack[1] *noun* 1 a line on the surface of something where it has broken but not come completely apart. 2 a narrow gap. 3 a sudden sharp noise, *a crack of lightning.* 4 a knock, *a crack on the head.* 5 (*informal*) a joke; a wisecrack. 6 a drug made from cocaine.

crack[2] *adjective* (*informal*) first-class, *He is a crack shot.*

crack[3] *verb* 1 make or get a crack; split. 2 make a sudden sharp noise. 3 break down, *He cracked under the strain.*
crack a joke tell a joke.
crack down on (*informal*) stop something that is illegal or against rules.
get cracking (*informal*) get busy.

cracker *noun* 1 a paper tube that bangs when pulled apart. 2 a firework that explodes with a crack. 3 a thin biscuit.

crackle *verb* (**crackled, crackling**) make small crackling sounds. **crackle** *noun*

crackling *noun* crisp skin on roast pork.

-cracy *suffix* forming nouns meaning 'ruling' or 'government' (e.g. *democracy*).

cradle[1] *noun* 1 a small cot for a baby. 2 a supporting framework. 3 the place where something begins, *the cradle of civilization.*

cradle[2] *verb* (**cradled, cradling**) hold gently.

craft *noun* 1 a job that needs skill, especially with the hands. 2 skill, *She learnt her craft from her grandmother.* 3 cunning; trickery. 4 (*plural* is **craft**) a ship or boat; an aircraft or spacecraft.

craftsperson *noun* (*plural* **craftspeople**) a person who is good at a craft. **craftsman** *noun* (*plural* **craftsmen**), **craftsmanship** *noun*, **craftswoman** *noun* (*plural* **craftswomen**)

crafty *adjective* (**craftier, craftiest**) cunning. **craftily** *adverb*, **craftiness** *noun*

crag *noun* a steep piece of rough rock. **craggy** *adjective*, **cragginess** *noun*

cram *verb* (**crammed, cramming**) 1 push many things into a space. 2 fill very full, *The rubbish bin was crammed with papers.*

cramp[1] *noun* pain caused by a muscle tightening suddenly.

cramp[2] *verb* 1 keep in a very small space. 2 hinder someone's freedom or growth etc. **cramped** *adjective*

cranberry *noun* (*plural* **cranberries**) a small sour red berry used for making jelly and sauce.

crane[1] *noun* 1 a machine for lifting and moving heavy objects. 2 a large wading bird with long legs and neck.

crane[2] *verb* (**craned, craning**) stretch your neck to try and see something.

crane-fly *noun* a flying insect with very long thin legs, also called a daddy-long-legs.

cranium *noun* the skull.

crank[1] *noun* 1 an L-shaped part used for changing the direction of movement in machinery. 2 a person with strange or fanatical ideas. **cranky** *adjective*

crank[2] *verb* move by means of a crank.

cranny *noun* (*plural* **crannies**) a crevice.

crash[1] *noun* 1 the loud noise of something breaking or colliding. 2 a violent collision or fall. 3 a sudden drop or failure, *the stock exchange crash of 1929.*

crash[2] *verb* 1 make or have a crash; cause to crash. 2 move with a crash.

crash[3] *adjective* intensive, *a crash course.*

crash-helmet *noun* a padded helmet worn to protect the head in a crash.

crash-landing *noun* an emergency landing of an aircraft, which usually damages it.

crass *adjective* 1 very obvious or shocking; gross, *crass ignorance.* 2 very stupid.

crate *noun* 1 a packing-case made of strips of wood. 2 an open container with compartments for carrying bottles.

crater *noun* 1 a bowl-shaped cavity or hollow, *a meteorite crater.* 2 the mouth of a volcano.

cravat *noun* 1 a short scarf. 2 a wide necktie.

crave *verb* (**craved, craving**) 1 desire strongly. 2 (*formal*) beg for something.

craven *adjective* cowardly.

craving *noun* a strong desire; a longing.

crawl¹ *verb* 1 move with the body close to the ground or other surface, or on hands and knees. 2 move slowly. 3 be covered with crawling things, *The dog was crawling with fleas.* **crawler** *noun*

crawl² *noun* 1 a crawling movement. 2 a very slow pace, *The traffic moved at a crawl.* 3 an overarm swimming stroke.

crayfish *noun* (*plural* **crayfish**) a rock lobster, also called a kreef.

crayon *noun* a stick or pencil of coloured wax etc. for drawing.

craze *noun* a temporary enthusiasm.

crazed *adjective* driven insane.

crazy *adjective* (**crazier, craziest**) 1 insane. 2 very foolish, *this crazy idea.* **crazily** *adverb,* **craziness** *noun*

crazy paving paving made of oddly-shaped pieces of stone etc.

creak¹ *noun* a harsh squeak like that of a stiff door-hinge. **creaky** *adjective*

creak² *verb* make a creak.

cream¹ *noun* 1 the fatty part of milk. 2 a yellowish-white colour. 3 a food containing or looking like cream, *chocolate cream.* 4 a soft substance, *shoe-cream.* 5 the best part, *the cream of the crop.* **creamy** *adjective*

cream cheese a soft rich cheese made from cream and whole milk.

cream² *verb* make creamy; beat butter etc. until it is soft like cream.

cream off remove the best part of something.

crease¹ *noun* 1 a line made in something by folding, pressing, or crushing it. 2 a line on a cricket pitch marking a batsman's or bowler's position.

crease² *verb* (**creased, creasing**) make a crease or creases in something.

create *verb* (**created, creating**) 1 bring into existence; make or produce, especially something that no one has made before. 2 (*slang*) make a fuss; grumble. **creation** *noun*

creative *adjective* inventive; imaginative.

creativity *noun*

creator *noun* a person who creates something.

the Creator God.

creature *noun* a person or animal.

crèche (*say* kresh) *noun* a place where babies and young children are looked after while their parents are at work.

credence *noun* belief, *Don't give it any credence.*

credentials *plural noun* documents showing a person's identity, qualifications, etc.

credible *adjective* able to be believed; convincing. **credibly** *adverb,* **credibility** *noun*

● USAGE: Do not confuse with *creditable.*

credit¹ *noun* 1 honour; acknowledgement. 2 an arrangement trusting a person to pay for something later on. 3 an amount of money in someone's account at a bank etc., or entered in an account-book as paid in. (Compare *debit.*) 4 belief; trust, *I put no credit in this rumour.* 5 an educational course which counts towards a qualification.

credit card a card authorizing a person to buy on credit.

credits or **credit titles** a list of people who have helped to produce a film or television programme.

credit² *verb* (**credited, crediting**) 1 believe. 2 attribute; say that a person has done or achieved something, *Columbus is credited with the discovery of America.* 3 enter something as a credit in an account-book. (Compare *debit.*)

creditable *adjective* deserving praise. **creditably** *adverb*

● USAGE: Do not confuse with *credible.*

creditor *noun* a person to whom money is owed.

credulous *adjective* too ready to believe things; gullible.

creed *noun* a set or formal statement of beliefs.

creek *noun* 1 a narrow inlet. 2 (*American & Australian*) a small stream.

up the creek (*informal*) in difficulties.

creep¹ *verb* (**crept, creeping**) 1 move along close to the ground. 2 move quietly,

We crept past the sleeping baby. **3** come gradually. **4** prickle with fear, *It makes my flesh creep.*

creep[2] *noun* **1** a creeping movement. **2** (*informal*) an unpleasant person, especially one who seeks to win favour.

the creeps (*informal*) a nervous feeling caused by fear or dislike.

creeper *noun* a plant that grows along the ground or up a wall etc.

creepy *adjective* (**creepier, creepiest**) making people's flesh creep.

creepy-crawly *noun* (*plural* **creepy-crawlies**) (*informal*) an insect or other small animal that crawls.

cremate *verb* (**cremated, cremating**) burn a dead body to ashes. **cremation** *noun*

crematorium *noun* (*plural* **crematoria**) a place where corpses are cremated.

creosote *noun* an oily brown liquid used to prevent wood from rotting.

crêpe (*say* krayp) *noun* **1** cloth, paper, or rubber with a wrinkled surface. **2** a thin pancake with a sweet or savoury filling.

crescendo (*say* krish-**end**-oh) *noun* (*plural* **crescendos**) a gradual increase in loudness.

crescent *noun* **1** a narrow curved shape (e.g. the new moon) coming to a point at each end. **2** a curved street.

cress *noun* a plant with hot-tasting leaves, used in salads and sandwiches.

crest *noun* **1** a tuft of hair, skin, or feathers on an animal's or bird's head. **2** the top of a hill or wave etc. **3** a design used on notepaper etc. **crested** *adjective*

crestfallen *adjective* disappointed; dejected.

cretin (*say* **kret**-in) *noun* a person who is mentally undeveloped through lack of certain hormones.

crevasse (*say* kri-**vass**) *noun* a deep open crack, especially in a glacier.

crevice *noun* a narrow opening, especially in a rock or wall.

crew[1] *noun* **1** the people working in a ship or aircraft. **2** a group working together, *the camera crew.*

crew[2] *past tense* of **crow**[2].

crib[1] *noun* **1** a baby's cot. **2** a framework holding fodder for animals. **3** a model representing the Nativity of Jesus Christ. **4** something cribbed. **5** a translation for use by students.

crib[2] *verb* (**cribbed, cribbing**) copy someone else's work.

cribbage *noun* a card-game.

crick *noun* painful stiffness in the neck or back.

cricket[1] *noun* a game played outdoors between teams with a ball, bats, and two wickets. **cricketer** *noun*

cricket[2] *noun* a brown insect like a grasshopper.

crime *noun* **1** an action that breaks the law. **2** law-breaking.

criminal *noun* a person who has committed a crime or crimes. **criminal** *adjective*, **criminally** *adverb*

criminology *noun* the study of crime.

crimp *verb* press into small ridges.

crimson *adjective* & *noun* deep-red.

cringe *verb* (**cringed, cringing**) shrink back in fear; cower.

crinkle *verb* (**crinkled, crinkling**) make or become wrinkled. **crinkly** *adjective*

crinoline *noun* a long skirt worn over a framework that makes it stand out.

cripple[1] *noun* a person who is permanently lame.

cripple[2] *verb* (**crippled, crippling**) **1** make a person a cripple. **2** weaken or damage something seriously, *The business was crippled by the strike.*

crisis *noun* (*plural* **crises**) an important and dangerous or difficult situation.

crisp[1] *adjective* **1** very dry so that it breaks with a snap. **2** fresh and stiff, *a crisp R50 note.* **3** cold and dry, *a crisp morning.* **4** brisk and sharp, *a crisp manner.* **crisply** *adverb*, **crispness** *noun*

crisp[2] *noun* a very thin fried slice of potato (usually sold in packets).

criss-cross *adjective* & *adverb* with crossing lines.

criterion (*say* kry-**teer**-ee-on) *noun* (*plural* **criteria**) a standard by which something is judged.

● USAGE: Note that *criteria* is a plural. It is incorrect to say 'a criteria' or 'this criteria';

correct usage is *this criterion, these criteria.*

critic *noun* **1** a person who gives opinions on books, plays, films, music, etc. **2** a person who criticizes.

critical *adjective* **1** criticizing, *The teacher was critical of her behaviour.* **2** of critics or criticism, *The play was a critical success.* **3** of or at a crisis; very serious, *It was a critical moment in our history.* **critically** *adverb*

criticism *noun* **1** criticizing; pointing out faults. **2** the work of a critic.

criticize *verb* (**criticized, criticizing**) say that a person or thing has faults.

croak *noun* a deep hoarse sound like that of a frog. **croak** *verb*

crochet (*say* **kroh**-shay) *noun* a kind of needlework done by using a hooked needle to loop a thread into patterns. **crochet** *verb* (**crocheted, crocheting**)

crock¹ *noun* a piece of crockery.

crock² *noun* (*informal*) a decrepit person or thing.

crockery *noun* household china.

crocodile *noun* **1** a large tropical reptile with a thick skin, long tail, and huge jaws. **2** a long line of schoolchildren walking in pairs.

crocodile tears sorrow that is not sincere (so called because the crocodile was said to weep while it ate its victim).

croft *noun* an enclosed piece of land; a small rented farm. **crofter** *noun*

croissant (*say* **krwah**-sahn) *noun* a flaky crescent-shaped bread roll.

crone *noun* a very old woman.

crony *noun* (*plural* **cronies**) a close friend or companion.

crook¹ *noun* **1** a shepherd's stick with a curved end. **2** something bent or curved. **3** (*informal*) a person who makes a living dishonestly.

crook² *verb* bend, *She crooked her finger.*

crooked *adjective* **1** bent; twisted; not straight. **2** dishonest.

croon *verb* sing softly and gently.

crop¹ *noun* **1** something grown for food, *a good crop of wheat.* **2** a whip with a loop instead of a lash. **3** part of a bird's throat. **4** a very short haircut.

crop rotation planting different crops on different pieces of land each year so that the soil stays fertile.

crop² *verb* (**cropped, cropping**) **1** cut or bite off, *sheep were cropping the grass.* **2** produce a crop.

crop up happen unexpectedly.

cropper *noun* **come a cropper** (*slang*) fall heavily; fall badly.

croquet (*say* **kroh**-kay) *noun* a game played with wooden balls and mallets.

crosier (*say* **kroh**-zee-er) *noun* a bishop's staff shaped like a shepherd's crook.

cross¹ *noun* **1** a mark or shape made like + or ×. **2** an upright post with another piece of wood across it, used in ancient times for crucifixion. **3** a mixture of two different things, *A mule is a cross between a horse and a donkey.*

the Cross the cross on which Christ was crucified, used as a symbol of Christianity.

cross² *verb* **1** go across something. **2** draw a line or lines across something, *Remember to cross your cheques so that they can only be paid through a bank.* **3** make the sign or shape of a cross, *Cross your fingers for luck.* **4** produce something from two different kinds.

cross out draw a line across something because it is unwanted, wrong, etc.

cross³ *adjective* **1** going from one side to another. **2** annoyed; bad-tempered. **crossly** *adverb*, **crossness** *noun*

cross- *prefix* **1** across; crossing something (as in *crossbar*). **2** from two different kinds (as in *cross-breed*).

crossbar *noun* a horizontal bar, especially between two uprights.

crossbow *noun* a powerful bow with a mechanism for pulling and releasing the string.

cross-breed *verb* (**cross-bred, cross-breeding**) breed by mating an animal with one of a different kind. **cross-breed** *noun* (Compare *hybrid*.)

cross-country *adjective* & *adverb* across open fields etc. rather than on roads or tracks. **cross-country (race)** *noun*

cross-examine *verb* cross-question someone, especially in a lawcourt.

cross-examination *noun*

cross-eyed *adjective* with eyes that look or seem to look towards the nose.

crossfire *noun* lines of gunfire that cross each other.

crossing *noun* a place where people can cross a road, railway, etc.

cross-legged *adjective & adverb* with ankles crossed and knees spread apart.

cross-patch *noun* a bad-tempered person.

cross-pollination *noun* the transfer of pollen from one plant to another.

cross-question *verb* question someone carefully in order to test answers given to previous questions.

cross-reference *noun* a note telling people to look at another part of a book etc. for more information.

crossroads *noun* a place where two or more roads cross one another.

cross-section *noun* 1 a drawing of something as if it has been cut through. 2 a typical sample, *a cross-section of the population.*

crosswise *adverb & adjective* with one thing crossing another.

crossword *noun* short for **crossword puzzle**, a puzzle in which words have to be guessed from clues and then written into the blank squares in a diagram.

crotch *noun* the part between the legs where they join the body; a similar angle in a forked part.

crotchet *noun* a note in music, lasting half as long as a minim.

crotchety *adjective* peevish.

crouch *verb* lower your body, with your arms and legs bent.

croup (*say* kroop) *noun* a disease causing a hard cough and difficulty in breathing.

crow[1] *noun* a large black bird.
as the crow flies in a straight line.
crow's nest a look-out platform high up on a ship's mast.

crow[2] *verb* (**crowed** or **crew**, **crowing**) 1 make a shrill cry as a cock does. 2 boast; be triumphant. **crow** *noun*

crowbar *noun* an iron bar used as a lever.

crowd[1] *noun* a large number of people in one place.

crowd[2] *verb* 1 come together in a crowd. 2 cram; fill uncomfortably full, *The supporters crowded the stadium.*

crown[1] *noun* 1 an ornamental head-dress worn by a king or queen. 2 (often **Crown**) a king or queen who represents the government of a country, *This land belongs to the Crown.* 3 the highest part, *the crown of the road.* 4 the part of the tooth that can be seen.
crown jewels the crown and other royal ornaments worn or carried by the king or queen.
Crown Prince or **Crown Princess** the heir to the throne.

crown[2] *verb* 1 place a crown on as a symbol of royal power or victory. 2 form or cover or decorate the top of something, *mountains crowned with snow.* 3 reward; make a successful end to something, *Our efforts were crowned with victory.* 4 (*slang*) hit on the head.

crucial (*say* **kroo**-shal) *adjective* most important. **crucially** *adverb*

crucible *noun* a melting-pot for metals.

crucifix *noun* (*plural* **crucifixes**) a model of the Cross or of Jesus Christ on the Cross.

crucify *verb* (**crucified, crucifying**) put a person to death by nailing or binding the hands and feet to a cross. **crucifixion** *noun*

crude *adjective* 1 in a natural state; not yet refined, *crude oil.* 2 not well finished; rough, *a crude carving.* 3 vulgar. **crudely** *adverb*, **crudity** *noun*

cruel *adjective* (**crueller, cruellest**) causing pain or suffering. **cruelly** *adverb*, **cruelty** *noun*

cruet *noun* a set of small containers for salt, pepper, oil, etc. for use at the table.

cruise[1] *noun* a pleasure-trip in a ship.

cruise[2] *verb* (**cruised, cruising**) 1 sail or travel at a moderate speed. 2 have a cruise.

cruiser *noun* 1 a fast warship. 2 a large motor boat.

crumb *noun* a tiny piece of bread, etc.

crumble *verb* (**crumbled, crumbling**) break or fall into small fragments. **crumbly** *adjective*

crumpet *noun* a soft flat cake made with yeast, eaten toasted with butter.

crumple *verb* (**crumpled, crumpling**)
1 crush or become crushed into creases.
2 collapse loosely.

crunch¹ *verb* 1 crush something noisily between the teeth. 2 make a sound like crunching, *Our feet crunched over the gravel.*

crunch² *noun* crunching; a crunching sound. **crunchy** *adjective*
the crunch (*informal*) a crucial event.

crusade *noun* 1 a military expedition made by Christians in the Middle Ages to recover Palestine from the Muslims who had conquered it. 2 a campaign against something believed to be bad. **crusader** *noun*

crush¹ *verb* 1 press something so that it gets broken or harmed. 2 squeeze tightly. 3 defeat.

crush² *noun* (*plural* **crushes**) 1 a crowd of people pressed together. 2 a drink made with crushed fruit. 3 (*informal*) an infatuation.

crust *noun* 1 the hard outer layer of something, especially bread. 2 the rocky outer layer of the earth.

crustacean (*say* krust-**ay**-shon) *noun* an animal with a shell, e.g. a crab.

crusty *adjective* (**crustier, crustiest**)
1 having a crisp crust. 2 having a harsh or irritable manner, *a crusty old man.* **crustiness** *noun*

crutch *noun* (*plural* **crutches**) a support like a long walking-stick for helping a lame person to walk.

cry¹ *noun* (*plural* **cries**) 1 a loud wordless sound expressing pain, grief, joy, etc.
2 a shout. 3 crying, *Have a good cry.*

cry² *verb* (**cried, crying**) 1 shed tears; weep. 2 call out loudly.

crypt *noun* a room under a church.

cryptic *adjective* hiding its meaning in a puzzling way. **cryptically** *adverb*

cryptogram *noun* something written in cipher.

crystal *noun* 1 a transparent colourless mineral rather like glass. 2 very clear high-quality glass. 3 a small solid piece of certain substances, *crystals of snow and ice.*
crystalline *adjective*

crystal ball a glass globe used by fortune-tellers, said to be able to predict the future.

crystallize *verb* (**crystallized, crystallizing**) 1 form into crystals. 2 become definite in form. **crystallization** *noun*
crystallized fruit fruit preserved in sugar.

Cub (also **Cub Scout**) *noun* a member of the junior branch of the Scout Association.

cub *noun* a young lion, tiger, fox, bear, etc.

cubby-hole *noun* a small compartment.

cube¹ *noun* 1 something that has six equal square sides. 2 the number produced by multiplying something by itself twice, *The cube of 3 is 3 × 3 × 3 = 27.*
cube root the number that gives a particular number if it is multiplied by itself twice, *The cube root of 27 is 3.*

cube² *verb* (**cubed, cubing**) 1 multiply a number by itself twice, *4 cubed is 4 × 4 × 4 = 64.* 2 cut into small cubes.

cubic *adjective* three-dimensional.
cubic centimetre, cubic metre, etc., the volume of a cube with sides that are one centimetre or one metre etc. long.

cubicle *noun* a compartment of a room.

cuckoo *noun* a bird that makes a sound like 'cuck-oo' and lays its eggs in the nests of other birds.

cucumber *noun* a long green-skinned vegetable eaten raw or pickled.

cud *noun* half-digested food that a cow etc. brings back from its first stomach to chew again.

cuddle *verb* (**cuddled, cuddling**) put your arms closely round a person or animal that you love. **cuddly** *adjective*

cudgel¹ *noun* a short thick stick used as a weapon.

cudgel² *verb* (**cudgelled, cudgelling**) beat with a cudgel.
cudgel your brains think hard about a problem.

cue¹ *noun* something said or done that acts as a signal for an actor etc. to say or do something.

cue² *noun* a long rod for striking the ball in billiards or snooker.

cuff¹ *noun* 1 the end of a sleeve that fits round the wrist. 2 hitting somebody with your hand; a slap.

cuff[2] *verb* hit somebody with your hand.

cuisine (*say* kwiz-**een**) *noun* a style of cooking.

cul-de-sac *noun* (*plural* **culs-de-sac**) a street with an opening at one end only; a dead end.

culinary *adjective* of cooking; for cooking.

cull *verb* 1 pick out and kill surplus animals from a flock or herd. 2 select and use, *culling lines from several poems.* 3 pick, *culling fruit.* **cull** *noun*

culminate *verb* (**culminated, culminating**) reach its highest or last point. **culmination** *noun*

culpable *adjective* deserving blame.

culprit *noun* the person who has done something wrong.

cult *noun* a religion; devotion to a person or thing.

cultivar *noun* a kind of plant produced by selective breeding, *New cultivars of tomatoes stay firm for longer.*

cultivate *verb* (**cultivated, cultivating**) 1 use land to grow crops. 2 grow or develop things by looking after them. **cultivation** *noun*

cultivator *noun* a farm implement that breaks up the soil after ploughing, also used for weeding and for keeping a good tilth between crop rows.

culture *noun* 1 appreciation and understanding of literature, art, music, etc. 2 customs and traditions, *Indian culture.* 3 improvement by care and training, *physical culture.* 4 cultivating things. **cultural** *adjective*

cultured *adjective* educated to appreciate literature, art, music, etc.

cultured pearl a pearl formed by an oyster when a speck of grit etc. is put into its shell.

culvert *noun* a drain that passes under a road or railway etc.

cumbersome *adjective* clumsy to carry or manage. (Compare *encumber.*)

cummerbund *noun* a broad sash worn around the waist.

cumulative *adjective* accumulating; increasing by continuous additions.

cumulus (*say* **kew**-mew-lus) *noun* (*plural* **cumuli**) a type of rounded cloud, heaped up on a flat base.

cunning[1] *adjective* 1 clever at deceiving people. 2 cleverly designed or planned.

cunning[2] *noun* being cunning.

cup[1] *noun* 1 a small bowl-shaped container for drinking from. 2 anything shaped like a cup. 3 a goblet-shaped ornament given as a prize. **cupful** *noun*

cup[2] *verb* (**cupped, cupping**) form into the shape of a cup, *cup your hands.*

cupboard *noun* a recess or piece of furniture with a door, for storing things.

cupidity (*say* kew-**pid**-it-ee) *noun* greed for gain.

cupola (*say* **kew**-pol-a) *noun* a small dome on a roof.

cur *noun* a scruffy or bad-tempered dog.

curable *adjective* able to be cured.

curate *noun* a member of the clergy who helps a parish priest.

curative (*say* **kewr**-at-iv) *adjective* helping to cure illness.

curator (*say* kewr-**ay**-ter) *noun* a person in charge of a museum or other collection.

curb[1] *verb* restrain, *curb your impatience.*

curb[2] *noun* a restraint, *Put a curb on spending.*

● USAGE: Do not confuse with *kerb.*

curd *noun* (also **curds**) a thick substance formed when milk turns sour.

curdle *verb* (**curdled, curdling**) form into curds.

make someone's blood curdle horrify or terrify them.

cure[1] *verb* (**cured, curing**) 1 get rid of someone's illness. 2 stop something bad. 3 treat something so as to preserve it, *Fish can be cured in smoke.*

cure[2] *noun* 1 something that cures a person or thing; a remedy. 2 curing; being cured, *We cannot promise a cure.*

curfew *noun* a time or signal after which people must remain indoors until the next day.

curio *noun* (*plural* **curios**) an object that is a curiosity.

curiosity *noun* (*plural* **curiosities**) 1 being curious. 2 something unusual and interesting.

curious *adjective* 1 wanting to find out

about things; inquisitive. **2** strange; unusual, *a curious-looking dog.* **curiously** *adverb*

curl[1] *noun* a curve or coil, e.g. of hair.

curl[2] *verb* form into curls.

curl up sit or lie with knees drawn up.

curler *noun* a device for curling the hair.

curlew *noun* a wading bird with a long curved bill.

curly *adjective* full of curls; curling.

currant *noun* **1** a small black dried grape used in cookery. **2** a small round red, black, or white berry.

currency *noun* (*plural* **currencies**) **1** the money in use in a country. **2** the general use of something, *Some words have no currency now.*

current[1] *adjective* happening now; used now. **currently** *adverb*

current account a low-interest bank account which you use regularly for managing your spending money.

current affairs political, social, etc. events which are happening now.

current[2] *noun* **1** water or air etc. moving in one direction. **2** the flow of electricity along a wire etc. or through something.

curriculum *noun* (*plural* **curricula**) a course of study.

curriculum vitae (*say* ku-rĭk-yew-lum veet-I) *noun* (*plural* **curricula vitae**) a description of your education, work experience, etc. usually sent with an application for a job.

curry[1] *noun* (*plural* **curries**) food cooked with spices that taste hot. **curried** *adjective*

curry[2] *verb* (**curried**, **currying**) groom a horse with a rubber or plastic pad (called a **curry-comb**).

curry favour seek to win favour by flattering someone.

curse[1] *noun* **1** a call or prayer for a person or thing to be harmed; the evil produced by this. **2** something very unpleasant. **3** an angry word or words.

curse[2] *verb* (**cursed**, **cursing**) **1** make a curse. **2** use a curse against a person or thing.

be cursed with something suffer from it.

cursor *noun* a movable indicator (usually a flashing light) on a VDU screen.

cursory *adjective* hasty and not thorough, *a cursory inspection.* **cursorily** *adverb*

curt *adjective* brief and hasty or rude, *a curt reply.* **curtly** *adverb*, **curtness** *noun*

curtail *verb* **1** cut short, *The lesson was curtailed.* **2** reduce, *We must curtail our spending.* **curtailment** *noun*

curtain *noun* **1** a piece of material hung at a window or door. **2** the large cloth screen hung at the front of a stage.

curtsy[1] *noun* (*plural* **curtsies**) a movement of respect made by women and girls, putting one foot behind the other and bending the knees.

curtsy[2] *verb* (**curtsied**, **curtsying**) make a curtsy.

curvature *noun* curving; a curved shape.

curve[1] *verb* (**curved**, **curving**) bend smoothly.

curve[2] *noun* a curved line or shape. **curvy** *adjective*

cushion[1] *noun* **1** a bag, usually of cloth, filled with soft material so that it is comfortable to sit on or lean against. **2** anything soft or springy that protects or supports something, *The hovercraft travels on a cushion of air.*

cushion[2] *verb* **1** supply with cushions, *cushioned seats.* **2** protect from the effects of a knock or shock etc., *His woolly hat cushioned the blow.*

cushy *adjective* (*informal*) pleasant and easy, *a cushy job.*

cusp *noun* a pointed end where two curves meet, e.g. the tips of the crescent moon.

custard *noun* **1** a sweet yellow sauce made with milk. **2** a pudding made with beaten eggs and milk.

custodian *noun* a person who has custody of something; a keeper.

custody *noun* **1** care and supervision; guardianship. **2** imprisonment.

take into custody arrest.

custom *noun* **1** the usual way of behaving or doing something. **2** regular business from customers, *We lost a lot of custom when the new supermarket opened.*

customs *plural noun* taxes charged on goods brought into a country; the place at a port or airport where officials examine your luggage.

customary *adjective* according to custom; usual. **customarily** *adverb*

custom-built *adjective* made according to a customer's order.

customer *noun* a person who uses a shop, bank, or other business.

cut¹ *verb* (**cut, cutting**) 1 divide or wound or separate something by using a knife, axe, scissors, etc. 2 make a thing shorter or smaller; remove part of something, *They are cutting all their prices*. 3 divide a pack of playing-cards. 4 hit a ball with a chopping movement. 5 go through or across something. 6 stay away from something deliberately, *She cut her music lesson*. 7 make a sound-recording. 8 switch off electrical power or an engine etc.
cut a corner pass round it very closely.
cut and dried already decided.
cut in interrupt.

cut² *noun* 1 cutting; the result of cutting. 2 a small wound. 3 (*slang*) a share, *a cut of the winnings*.
be a cut above something be superior.

cute *adjective* (*informal*) 1 clever. 2 attractive. **cutely** *adverb*, **cuteness** *noun*

cuticle (*say* kew-tik-ul) *noun* 1 the skin round a nail. 2 a layer covering the surface of a leaf to prevent it from drying out.

cutlass *noun* (*plural* **cutlasses**) a short sword with a broad curved blade.

cutlery *noun* knives, forks, and spoons.

cutlet *noun* a thick slice of meat for cooking.

cut-out *noun* a shape cut out of paper, cardboard, etc.

cutter *noun* 1 a person or thing that cuts. 2 a small fast sailing-ship.

cutting *noun* 1 a steep-sided passage cut through high ground for a road or railway. 2 a clipping, *a newspaper cutting*. 3 a piece cut from a plant to form a new plant.

cuttlefish *noun* (*plural* **cuttlefish**) a sea creature that sends out a black liquid when attacked.

CV *abbreviation* curriculum vitae.

cyanide *noun* a very poisonous chemical.

cybernetics *noun* a science that compares human and animal brains with machines and electronic devices.

cycad (*say* sy-kad) *noun* a spiky plant like a palm.

cycle¹ *noun* 1 a bicycle or motor cycle. 2 a series of events that are regularly repeated in the same order, *the cycle of seasons*. **cyclic** *adjective*, **cyclical** *adjective*

cycle² *verb* (**cycled, cycling**) ride a bicycle or tricycle. **cyclist** *noun*

cyclone *noun* a wind that rotates round a calm central area. **cyclonic** *adjective*

cygnet *noun* (*say* sig-nit) a young swan.

cylinder *noun* an object with straight sides and circular ends. **cylindrical** *adjective*

cymbal *noun* a percussion instrument consisting of a metal plate that is hit to make a ringing sound.

cynic (*say* sin-ik) *noun* a person who believes that people's reasons for doing things are selfish or bad, and shows this by sneering at them. **cynical** *adjective*, **cynically** *adverb*, **cynicism** *noun*

cypress *noun* (*plural* **cypresses**) an evergreen tree with dark leaves.

cyst (*say* sist) *noun* an abnormal swelling containing fluid or soft matter.

cytoplasm (*say* sy-toh-plazm) *noun* the living content of a cell apart from its nucleus.

czar (*say* zar) *noun* a tsar.

Dd

dab¹ *noun* 1 a quick gentle touch. 2 a small lump, *a dab of butter*.

dab² *verb* (**dabbed, dabbing**) touch quickly and gently.

dabble *verb* (**dabbled, dabbling**) 1 splash something about in water. 2 do something as a hobby, *dabble in chemistry*.

dachshund (*say* daks-huund) *noun* a small dog with a long body and very short legs.

dad (also **daddy**) *noun* (*plural* **daddies**) (*informal*) father.

daddy-long-legs *noun* (*plural* **daddy-long-legs**) a crane-fly.

daffodil *noun* a yellow flower that grows from a bulb.

daft *adjective* (*informal*) silly; crazy.

dagga *noun* wild hemp (*marijuana*) that is smoked as a drug.

dagger *noun* a pointed knife with two sharp edges, used as a weapon.

dahlia (*say* **d**ay-lee-a) *noun* a garden plant with brightly-coloured flowers.

daily *adverb* & *adjective* every day.

dainty *adjective* (**daintier, daintiest**) small, delicate, and pretty. **daintily** *adverb*, **daintiness** *noun*

dairy *noun* (*plural* **dairies**) a place where milk, butter, etc. are produced or sold.

dais (*say* **d**ay-iss) *noun* a low platform, especially at the end of a room.

daisy *noun* (*plural* **daisies**) a small flower with white petals and a yellow centre.

dale *noun* a valley.

dally *verb* (**dallied, dallying**) dawdle.

Dalmation *noun* a large white dog with black or brown spots.

dam¹ *noun* 1 a wall built to hold water back. 2 a pond or reservoir with a retaining wall.

dam² *verb* (**dammed, damming**) hold water back with a dam.

dam³ *noun* the mother of a horse or dog etc. (Compare *sire*.)

damage¹ *noun* something that reduces the value or usefulness of a thing or spoils its appearance.

damage² *verb* (**damaged, damaging**) cause damage to something.

damages *plural noun* money paid as compensation for an injury or loss.

Dame *noun* the title of a woman who has been given the equivalent of a knighthood.

dame *noun* 1 a comic middle-aged woman in a pantomime, usually played by a man. 2 (*informal*) (*American*) a woman.

damn *verb* curse.

damnation *noun* being damned or condemned to hell.

damned *adjective* hateful; annoying.

damp¹ *adjective* slightly wet; not quite dry. **damply** *adverb*, **dampness** *noun*

damp² *noun* moisture in the air or on a surface or all through something.

damp course a layer of material built into a wall to prevent dampness in the ground from rising.

damp³ *verb* 1 make damp; moisten. 2 reduce the strength of something, *The defeat damped their enthusiasm.*

dampen *verb* damp.

damper *noun* 1 a metal plate that can be moved to increase or decrease the amount of air flowing into a fire or furnace etc. 2 something that reduces sound or enthusiasm etc.

damping-off *noun* a fungus disease that attacks plants at the seedling stage and causes them to die.

damsel *noun* (*old use*) a young woman.

damson *noun* a small dark-purple plum.

dance¹ *verb* (**danced, dancing**) move about in time to music.

dance² *noun* 1 a set of movements used in dancing. 2 a piece of music for dancing to, *an old dance played on the piano.* 3 a party or gathering where people dance. **dancer** *noun*

dandelion *noun* a yellow wild flower with jagged leaves.

dandruff *noun* tiny white flakes of dead skin in a person's hair.

dandy *noun* (*plural* **dandies**) a man who likes to look very smart.

danger *noun* something dangerous.

dangerous *adjective* likely to kill or do great harm. **dangerously** *adverb*

dangle *verb* (**dangled, dangling**) hang or swing loosely.

dank *adjective* damp and chilly.

dapper *adjective* dressed neatly and smartly.

dappled *adjective* marked with patches of a different colour.

dare¹ *verb* (**dared, daring**) 1 be brave or bold enough to do something. 2 challenge a person to do something risky.

dare² *noun* a challenge to do something risky, *She jumped into the river for a dare.*

daredevil *noun* a person who is very bold and reckless.

dark¹ *adjective* 1 with little or no light. 2 not light in colour, *a dark suit.* 3 having dark hair. 4 secret, *Keep it dark!* **darkly** *adverb*, **darkness** *noun*

dark[2] *noun* 1 absence of light, *Cats can see in the dark*. 2 the time when darkness has come, *She went out after dark*.

darken *verb* make or become dark.

dark-room *noun* a room kept dark for developing and printing photographs.

darling *noun* someone who is loved very much.

darn[1] *verb* mend a hole by weaving threads across it.

darn[2] *noun* a place that has been darned.

dart[1] *noun* 1 an object with a sharp point, thrown at a target. 2 a darting movement, *He made a dart for the cake*. 3 a tapering tuck stitched in something to make it fit.

dart[2] *verb* run suddenly and quickly.

darts *noun* a game in which darts are thrown at a circular board (**dartboard**).

dash[1] *verb* 1 run quickly; rush. 2 throw a thing violently against something, *The storm dashed the ship against the rocks*.

dash[2] *noun* (*plural* **dashes**) 1 a short quick run; a rush. 2 energy; liveliness. 3 a small amount, *Add a dash of brandy*. 4 a short line (–) used in writing or printing.

dashboard *noun* a panel with dials and controls in front of the driver of a car etc.

dashing *adjective* lively and showy.

dassie *noun* a rodent-like animal which lives in mountainous areas.

dastardly *adjective* contemptible and cowardly.

data (*say* **day**-ta or **daa**-ta) *plural noun* pieces of information. **databank** *noun*, **database** *noun*
• USAGE: You can use this word as a singular as well as a plural noun. Both *These data are corrupt* and *This data is corrupt* are acceptable.

date[1] *noun* 1 the time when something happens or happened or was written, stated as the day, month, and year (or any of these). 2 an appointment to meet, *She had a date last night*.

date[2] *verb* (**dated, dating**) 1 give a date to something. 2 have existed from a particular time, *The church dates from 1902*. 3 seem old-fashioned, *His lack of computer knowledge really dates him*.

date[3] *noun* a small sweet brown fruit that grows on a kind of palm-tree.

daub *verb* paint or smear something clumsily. **daub** *noun*

daughter *noun* a girl or woman who is someone's child.

daughter-in-law *noun* (*plural* **daughters-in-law**) a son's wife.

daunt *verb* make somebody afraid or discouraged.

dauntless *adjective* brave; not to be daunted. **dauntlessly** *adverb*

dawdle *verb* (**dawdled, dawdling**) go slowly and lazily. **dawdler** *noun*

dawn[1] *noun* the time when the sun rises.

dawn[2] *verb* 1 begin to grow light in the morning. 2 begin to be realized, *The truth dawned on them*.

day *noun* 1 the 24 hours between midnight and the next midnight. 2 the light part of this time. 3 a particular day, *sports day*. 4 a period of time, *in Shaka's day*.

daytime the part of the day when it is light.

day-boy *noun* a pupil who attends a boarding-school but does not board.

day-girl *noun*

daybreak *noun* dawn.

day-dream[1] *noun* pleasant thoughts of something you would like to happen.

day-dream[2] *verb* have day-dreams.

daylight *noun* 1 the light of day. 2 dawn.

dazed *adjective* unable to think or see clearly. **daze** *noun*

dazzle *verb* (**dazzled, dazzling**) 1 make a person unable to see clearly because of too much bright light. 2 amaze or impress a person by a splendid display.

de- *prefix* 1 removing (as in *defrost*). 2 down, away (as in *descend*). 3 completely (as in *denude*).

deacon *noun* 1 a member of the clergy ranking below bishops and priests. 2 (in some Churches) a church officer who is not a member of the clergy.

dead *adjective* 1 no longer alive. 2 not lively, *a dead town*. 3 not functioning; no longer in use. 4 exact; complete, *a dead loss*.

dead end a road or passage with one end closed; a situation where there is no chance of making progress.

dead heat a race in which two or more winners finish exactly together.

deaden *verb* make pain or noise etc. weaker.

deadline *noun* a time-limit.

deadlock *noun* a situation in which no progress can be made.

deadly *adjective* (**deadlier, deadliest**) likely to kill.

deaf *adjective* 1 unable to hear. 2 unwilling to hear, *She was deaf to my request.*
deafness *noun*

deafen *verb* make somebody become deaf, especially by a very loud noise.

deal[1] *verb* (**dealt, dealing**) 1 hand something out; give. 2 give out cards for a card-game. 3 do business; trade, *He deals in scrap metal.* **dealer** *noun*
deal with be concerned with, *This book deals with words and meanings*; do what is needed, *deal with the problem.*

deal[2] *noun* 1 an agreement or bargain. 2 someone's turn to deal at cards.
a good deal or **a great deal** a large amount.

deal[3] *noun* sawn fir or pine wood.

dealership *noun* a business which sells goods such as vehicles and computers.

dean *noun* an important member of the clergy in a cathedral etc. **deanery** *noun*

dear *adjective* 1 loved very much. 2 a polite greeting in letters, *Dear Sir.* 3 expensive.
dearly *adverb*, **dearness** *noun*

dearth (*say* derth) *noun* a scarcity.

death *noun* dying; the end of life.
death penalty the punishment of execution for a crime.

deathly *adjective* & *adverb* like death.

death-trap *noun* a very dangerous place.

debar *verb* (**debarred, debarring**) forbid; ban, *He was debarred from the contest.*

debase *verb* (**debased, debasing**) reduce the quality or value of something.
debasement *noun*

debatable *adjective* questionable; that can be argued against.

debate[1] *noun* a formal discussion.

debate[2] *verb* (**debated, debating**) hold a debate. **debater** *noun*

debilitating *adjective* causing debility.

debility (*say* dib-**il**-it-ee) *noun* weakness.

debit[1] *noun* an entry in an account-book showing how much money is owed. (Compare *credit.*)

debit[2] *verb* (**debited, debiting**) enter something as a debit in an account-book.

debonair (*say* deb-on-**air**) *adjective* cheerful and confident.

debris (*say* **deb**-ree) *noun* scattered broken pieces of something; rubbish left behind.

debt (*say* det) *noun* something that you owe someone.
debt collector a business (or person) paid by other businesses to collect debts that are long overdue.
in debt owing money etc.

debtor (*say* **det**-or) *noun* a person who owes money to someone.

début (*say* **day**-bew) *noun* someone's first public appearance.

débutante (*say* **deb**-yew-tant) *noun* a young woman making her first appearance in fashionable society.

deca- *prefix* ten (as in *decathlon*).

decade (*say* **dek**-ayd) *noun* a period of ten years.

decadent (*say* **dek**-a-dent) *adjective* becoming less good than it was. **decadence** *noun*

decamp *verb* 1 pack up and leave a camp. 2 go away suddenly or secretly.

decant (*say* dik-**ant**) *verb* pour wine etc. gently from one container into another.

decanter (*say* dik-**ant**-er) *noun* a decorative glass bottle into which wine etc. is poured for serving.

decapitate *verb* (**decapitated, decapitating**) behead. **decapitation** *noun*

decathlon *noun* an athletic contest in which each competitor takes part in ten events.

decay *verb* 1 go bad; rot. 2 become less good or less strong, *a society in decay.*
decay *noun*

decease (*say* dis-**eess**) *noun* death.

deceased *adjective* dead.

deceit (*say* dis-**eet**) *noun* a deception.
deceitful *adjective*, **deceitfully** *adverb*

deceive *verb* (**deceived, deceiving**) cause

a person to believe something that is not true. **deceiver** *noun*

decent *adjective* **1** respectable; proper; suitable. **2** (*informal*) kind. **decently** *adverb*, **decency** *noun*

deception *noun* deceiving someone. **deceptive** *adjective*, **deceptively** *adverb*

deci- (*say* **dess**-ee) *prefix* one-tenth (as in *decimetre*).

decibel (*say* **dess**-ib-el) *noun* a unit for measuring the loudness of sound.

decide *verb* (**decided, deciding**) **1** make up your mind; make a choice. **2** settle a contest or argument, *The magistrate decided the case.* **decider** *noun*

decided *adjective* **1** having clear and definite opinions. **2** noticeable, *a decided difference.* **decidedly** *adverb*

deciduous (*say* dis-**id**-yoo-us) *adjective* losing its leaves in autumn, *a deciduous tree, not an evergreen tree.*

decimal[1] *adjective* using tens or tenths. **decimal comma** the comma in a decimal fraction. **decimal fraction** a fraction with tenths shown as numbers after a comma ($1\frac{1}{2}$ is 1,5).

decimal[2] *noun* a decimal fraction.

decimalize *verb* (**decimalized, decimalizing**) express something as a decimal. **decimalization** *noun*

decimate (*say* **dess**-im-ayt) *verb* (**decimated, decimating**) **1** kill a large part of, *The famine decimated the population.* **2** kill every tenth man (this was the ancient Roman punishment for an army guilty of mutiny or other serious crime).

decipher (*say* dis-**I**-fer) *verb* **1** decode. **2** work out the meaning of something written badly. **decipherment** *noun*

decision *noun* **1** deciding; what you have decided. **2** determination.

decisive (*say* dis-**I**-siv) *adjective* **1** that settles or ends something, *a decisive battle.* **2** full of determination; resolute. **decisively** *adverb*, **decisiveness** *noun*

deck[1] *noun* **1** a floor on a ship or bus. **2** a level surface in various devices, *a tape deck.*

deck[2] *verb* decorate with something.

deck-chair *noun* a folding chair with a canvas or plastic seat.

declaim *verb* make a speech etc. loudly and dramatically. **declamation** *noun*

declare *verb* (**declared, declaring**) **1** say something clearly or firmly. **2** tell customs officials that you have goods on which you ought to pay duty. **3** end a cricket innings before all the batsmen are out. **declaration** *noun*

declare war announce that you are starting a war against someone.

decline[1] *verb* (**declined, declining**) **1** refuse. **2** become weaker or smaller, *declining sales.* **3** slope downwards.

decline[2] *noun* a gradual decrease or loss of strength.

decode *verb* (**decoded, decoding**) find the meaning of something written in code. **decoder** *noun*

decompose *verb* (**decomposed, decomposing**) decay. **decomposition** *noun*

decompression *noun* reducing air-pressure.

decontamination *noun* getting rid of the harmful effects caused by poisonous chemicals or radioactive material.

décor (*say* **day**-kor) *noun* the style of furnishings and decorations used in a room etc.

decorate *verb* (**decorated, decorating**) **1** make something look more beautiful or colourful. **2** put fresh paint or paper on walls. **3** give somebody a medal, *decorated for bravery.* **decoration** *noun*, **decorator** *noun*, **decorative** *adjective*

decorous (*say* **dek**-er-us) *adjective* polite and dignified. **decorously** *adverb*

decorum (*say* dik-**or**-um) *noun* decorous behaviour.

decoy[1] (*say* **dee**-koi) *noun* something used to tempt a person or animal into a trap or into danger.

decoy[2] (*say* dik-**oi**) *verb* tempt into a trap etc.

decrease[1] *verb* (**decreased, decreasing**) make or become smaller or fewer.

decrease[2] *noun* decreasing; the amount by which something decreases, *a decrease in imports.*

decree[1] *noun* an official order or decision.
decree[2] *verb* (**decreed, decreeing**) make a decree.
decrepit (*say* dik-**rep**-it) *adjective* old and weak; dilapidated. **decrepitude** *noun*
dedicate *verb* (**dedicated, dedicating**) 1 devote to a special use, *She dedicated herself to her work.* 2 name a person as a mark of respect, e.g. at the beginning of a book. **dedication** *noun*
deduce *verb* (**deduced, deducing**) work something out by reasoning. **deducible** *adjective*
deduct *verb* subtract part of something.
deductible *adjective* able to be deducted.
deduction *noun* 1 deducting; something deducted. 2 deducing; something deduced, *'A brilliant piece of deduction!' she said to the detective.*
deed *noun* 1 something that someone has done; an act. 2 a legal document.
deem *verb* (*formal*) consider, *I should deem it an honour to be invited.*
deep *adjective* 1 going a long way down or back or in, *a deep well; deep cupboards.* 2 measured from top to bottom or front to back, *a hole six metres deep.* 3 intense; strong, *deep colour; deep feelings.* 4 low-pitched, not shrill, *a deep voice.* **deeply** *adverb*, **deepness** *noun*
Deepavali *noun* a Hindu religious festival at which lamps are lit, held in October or November.
deepen *verb* make or become deeper.
deep-freeze *noun* a freezer.
deep-fry *verb* cook in deep boiling fat.
deer *noun* (*plural* **deer**) a fast-running graceful animal, the male of which usually has antlers.
deface *verb* (**defaced, defacing**) spoil the surface of something, e.g. by scribbling on it. **defacement** *noun*
defame *verb* (**defamed, defaming**) attack a person's good reputation; slander, libel. **defamation** (*say* def-a-**may**-shon) *noun*, **defamatory** (*say* dif-**am**-a-ter-ee) *adjective*
default[1] *verb* fail to do what you have agreed to do. **defaulter** *noun*
default[2] *noun* failure to do something.

defeat[1] *verb* 1 win a victory over someone. 2 baffle; be too difficult for someone, *The problem defeats me.*
defeat[2] *noun* 1 defeating someone. 2 being defeated; a lost game or battle.
defeatist *noun* a person who expects to be defeated. **defeatism** *noun*
defecate (*say* **dee**-fik-ayt) *verb* (**defecated, defecating**) get rid of faeces from your body. **defecation** *noun*
defect[1] (*say* dif-**ekt** or **dee**-fekt) *noun* a flaw.
defect[2] (*say* dif-**ekt**) *verb* desert your own country etc. and join the enemy. **defection** *noun*, **defector** *noun*
defective *adjective* having defects; incomplete. **defectiveness** *noun*
defence *noun* 1 defending something. 2 something that defends or protects, *the body's defence system.* 3 a reply put forward by a defendant.
defenceless *adjective* having no defences.
defend *verb* 1 protect, especially against an attack. 2 try to prove that a statement is true or that an accused person is not guilty. **defender** *noun*
defendant *noun* a person accused of something in a lawcourt.
defensible *adjective* able to be defended. **defensibility** *noun*
defensive *adjective* used or done for defence; protective. **defensively** *adverb*
on the defensive ready to defend yourself.
defer[1] *verb* (**deferred, deferring**) postpone, *The test was deferred.* **deferment** *noun*, **deferral** *noun*
defer[2] *verb* (**deferred, deferring**) give way to a person's wishes or authority; yield, *He deferred to his mother's wishes.*
deference (*say* **def**-er-ens) *noun* polite respect. **deferential** (*say* def-er-**en**-shal) *adjective*, **deferentially** *adverb*
defiant *adjective* defying; openly disobedient. **defiantly** *adverb*, **defiance** *noun*
deficiency *noun* (*plural* **deficiencies**) 1 a lack; a shortage. 2 a defect. **deficient** *adjective*
deficit (*say* **def**-iss-it) *noun* 1 the amount by which a total is smaller than what is required. 2 the amount by which spending

is greater than income, *a budget deficit.*

defile *verb* (**defiled, defiling**) make a thing dirty or impure. **defilement** *noun*

define *verb* (**defined, defining**) 1 explain what a word or phrase means. 2 show clearly what something is; specify, *It's hard to define what has changed.* 3 show a thing's outline. **definable** *adjective*

definite *adjective* 1 clearly stated; exact, *Fix a definite time.* 2 certain; settled, *Is it definite that we are to move?* **definitely** *adverb*

definite article the word 'the'.

definition *noun* 1 a statement of what a word or phrase means or of what a thing is. 2 being distinct; clearness of outline (e.g. in a photograph).

definitive (*say* dif-**in**-it-iv) *adjective* finally settling something; conclusive, *a definitive victory.*

deflate *verb* (**deflated, deflating**) 1 let out air from a tyre or balloon etc. 2 make someone feel less proud or less confident. 3 reduce or reverse inflation. **deflation** *noun*, **deflationary** *adjective*

deflect *verb* make something turn aside. **deflection** *noun*, **deflector** *noun*

defoliate *verb* (**defoliated, defoliating**) destroy the leaves of trees and plants. **defoliation** *noun*

deforest *verb* clear away the trees from an area. **deforestation** *noun*

deform *verb* spoil a thing's shape or appearance. **deformation** *noun*

deformed *adjective* badly or abnormally shaped. **deformity** *noun*

defraud *verb* take something from a person by fraud; cheat, swindle.

defray *verb* (**defrayed, defraying**) provide money to pay costs or expenses. **defrayal** *noun*

defrost *verb* thaw out something frozen.

deft *adjective* skilful and quick. **deftly** *adverb*, **deftness** *noun*

defunct *adjective* dead.

defuse *verb* (**defused, defusing**) 1 remove the fuse from a bomb etc. 2 make a situation less dangerous.

defy *verb* (**defied, defying**) 1 resist something openly; refuse to obey, *They defied the*

law. 2 challenge a person to do something you believe cannot be done, *I defy you to prove this.* 3 prevent something being done, *The door defied all efforts to open it.*

degenerate[1] *verb* (**degenerated, degenerating**) become worse; lose good qualities. **degeneration** *noun*

degenerate[2] *adjective* having degenerated. **degeneracy** *noun*

degrade *verb* (**degraded, degrading**) 1 humiliate; disgrace. 2 decompose, *Paper will degrade if buried.* **degradation** (*say* deg-ra-**day**-shon) *noun*

degree *noun* 1 a unit for measuring temperature. 2 a unit for measuring angles. 3 extent, *to some degree.* 4 an award to someone at a university who has successfully finished a course.

dehorn *verb* remove the horns from a young animal.

dehydrated *adjective* dried up, with its moisture removed. **dehydration** *noun*

de-ice *verb* (**de-iced, de-icing**) remove ice from a windscreen etc. **de-icer** *noun*

deign (*say* dayn) *verb* condescend, be gracious enough to do something.

deity (*say* **dee**-it-ee) *noun* (*plural* **deities**) a god or goddess.

dejected *adjective* sad; gloomy; downcast. **dejectedly** *adverb*, **dejection** *noun*

delay[1] *verb* (**delayed, delaying**) 1 make someone or something late; hinder. 2 postpone. 3 wait; linger, *Don't delay! Act now!*

delay[2] *noun* delaying; the time for which something is delayed, *a two-hour delay.*

delectable *adjective* delightful. **delectably** *adverb*

delegate[1] (*say* **del**-ig-at) *noun* a person who represents others and acts on their instructions.

delegate[2] (*say* **del**-ig-ayt) *verb* (**delegated, delegating**) 1 appoint as a delegate, *We delegated Mbali to represent us.* 2 entrust, *We delegated the work to Mbali.*

delegation (*say* del-ig-**ay**-shon) *noun* 1 delegating. 2 a group of delegates.

delete (*say* dil-**eet**) *verb* (**deleted, deleting**) strike out something written or printed. **deletion** *noun*

deliberate[1] (*say* dil-**ib**-er-at) *adjective*

1 done on purpose, intentional. **2** slow and careful, *He moved in a deliberate way.*
deliberately *adverb*
deliberate[2] (*say* dil-**ib**-er-ayt) *verb* (**deliberated, deliberating**) discuss or think carefully. **deliberation** *noun*
deliberative *adjective* for deliberating or discussing things.
delicacy *noun* (*plural* **delicacies**) **1** being delicate. **2** a delicious food.
delicate *adjective* **1** fine; soft; fragile. **2** pleasant and not strong or intense. **3** becoming ill easily. **4** using or needing great care, *a delicate situation.* **delicately** *adverb*, **delicateness** *noun*
delicatessen *noun* a shop that sells cooked meats, cheeses, salads, etc.
delicious *adjective* tasting or smelling very pleasant. **deliciously** *adverb*
delight[1] *verb* **1** please someone greatly. **2** feel great pleasure.
delight[2] *noun* great pleasure. **delightful** *adjective*, **delightfully** *adverb*
delinquent (*say* dil-**ing**-kwent) *noun* someone who breaks the law or commits an offence. **delinquent** *adjective*, **delinquency** *noun*
delirium (*say* dil-**irri**-um) *noun* **1** a state of mental confusion and agitation during a feverish illness. **2** wild excitement. **delirious** *adjective*, **deliriously** *adverb*
deliver *verb* **1** take letters or goods etc. to someone's house or place of work. **2** give a speech or lecture etc. **3** help with the birth of a baby. **4** aim or strike a blow or an attack. **5** rescue; set free, *They were delivered from their enemies.* **deliverer** *noun*, **deliverance** *noun*, **delivery** *noun*
dell *noun* a small valley with trees.
delphinium *noun* a garden plant with tall spikes of flowers, usually blue.
delta *noun* **1** a triangular area at the mouth of a river where it spreads into branches. **2** the fourth letter of the Greek alphabet (= d), written Δ, δ.
delude *verb* (**deluded, deluding**) deceive.
deluge[1] *noun* **1** a large flood. **2** a heavy fall of rain. **3** something coming in great numbers, *a deluge of questions.*
deluge[2] *verb* (**deluged, deluging**) over-

whelm by a deluge.
delusion *noun* a false belief.
de luxe *adjective* of very high quality.
delve *verb* (**delved, delving**) search deeply, e.g. for information, *delving into history.*
demagogue (*say* **dem**-a-gog) *noun* a leader who wins support by making emotional speeches rather than by careful reasoning.
demand[1] *verb* **1** ask for something firmly or forcefully. **2** need, *It demands skill.*
demand[2] *noun* **1** a firm or forceful request. **2** a desire to have something, *There is a great demand for computers.*
in demand wanted; desired.
demarcation (*say* dee-mar-**kay**-shon) *noun* marking the boundary of something.
demean *verb* lower a person's dignity, *I wouldn't demean myself to ask for it!*
demeanour (*say* dim-**een**-er) *noun* a person's behaviour or manner.
demented *adjective* driven mad; crazy.
demerara (*say* dem-er-**air**-a) *noun* light-brown cane sugar.
demerit *noun* a fault; a defect.
demi- *prefix* half (as in *demisemiquaver*).
demigod *noun* a partly divine being.
demise (*say* dim-**I'z**) *noun* (*formal*) death.
demisemiquaver *noun* a note in music, equal to half a semiquaver.
demist *verb* remove misty condensation from a windscreen etc. **demister** *noun*
demo *noun* (*plural* **demos**) (*informal*) a demonstration.
democracy *noun* (*plural* **democracies**) **1** government of a country by represent- atives elected by the whole people. **2** a country governed in this way.
democrat *noun*, **democratic** *adjective*, **democratically** *adverb*
demolish *verb* knock something down and break it up. **demolition** *noun*
demon *noun* **1** a devil; an evil spirit. **2** a fierce or forceful person. **demonic** (*say* dim-**on**-ik) *adjective*
demonstrable (*say* **dem**-on-strab-ul) *adjective* able to be shown or proved. **demonstrably** *adverb*
demonstrate *verb* (**demonstrated, demonstrating**) **1** show; prove. **2** take part

in a demonstration. **demonstrator** *noun*
demonstration *noun* 1 demonstrating;
showing how to do or work something.
2 a meeting or procession etc. held to
show everyone what you think about
something.
demonstrative (*say* dim-**on**-strat-iv)
adjective 1 showing or proving something.
2 showing feelings or affections openly.
3 (in grammar) pointing out the person or
thing referred to. *This, that, these,* and *those*
are demonstrative adjectives and pronouns. **demonstratively** *adverb,*
demonstrativeness *noun*
demoralize *verb* (**demoralized, demoral-
izing**) dishearten someone; weaken
someone's confidence or morale.
demoralization *noun*
demote *verb* (**demoted, demoting**) reduce
to a lower position or rank. **demotion**
noun
demur[1] (*say* dim-**er**) *verb* (**demurred,
demurring**) raise objections.
demur[2] *noun* an objection raised.
demure *adjective* quiet and serious.
demurely *adverb,* **demureness** *noun*
den *noun* 1 a lair. 2 a person's private
room. 3 a place where something illegal
happens, *a gambling den.*
deniable *adjective* able to be denied.
denial *noun* denying or refusing something.
denier (*say* **den**-yer) *noun* a unit for
measuring the fineness of silk, rayon, or
nylon thread.
denim *noun* a kind of strong cotton cloth.
denizen (*say* **den**-iz-en) *noun* an inhabitant, *Lions are denizens of the jungle.*
denomination *noun* 1 a name or title.
2 a religious group with a special name,
*Baptists, Methodists, and other denomina-
tions.* 3 a unit of weight or of money, *coins of
small denomination.*
denominator *noun* the number below the
line in a fraction, showing how many parts
the whole is divided into, e.g. 4 in $\frac{1}{4}$.
(Compare *numerator.*)
denote *verb* (**denoted, denoting**) mean;
indicate, *In road signs, P denotes a car park.*
denotation *noun*

dénouement (*say* day-**noo**-mahn) *noun*
the final outcome of a plot or story, revealed
at the end.
denounce *verb* (**denounced, denouncing**) speak strongly against something;
accuse, *They denounced him as a spy.*
denunciation *noun*
dense *adjective* 1 thick; packed close
together. 2 (*informal*) stupid. **densely**
adverb
density *noun* (*plural* **densities**) 1 thickness. 2 (in physics) the proportion of weight
to volume.
dent[1] *noun* a hollow left in a surface where
something has pressed or hit it.
dent[2] *verb* make a dent in something.
dental *adjective* of or for the teeth; of
dentistry.
dentine (*say* **den**-teen) *noun* the hard
bony substance inside a tooth.
dentist *noun* a person who is trained to
treat teeth, fill or extract them, fit false ones,
etc. **dentistry** *noun*
denture *noun* a set of false teeth.
denude *verb* (**denuded, denuding**) make
bare or naked; strip something away.
denudation *noun*
denunciation *noun* denouncing.
deny *verb* (**denied, denying**) 1 say that
something is not true. 2 refuse to give or
allow something, *deny a request.*
deodorant (*say* dee-**oh**-der-ant) *noun*
a substance that removes smells.
deodorize *verb* (**deodorized, deodoriz-
ing**) remove smells. **deodorization** *noun*
depart *verb* go away; leave.
department *noun* one part of a large
organization. **departmental** *adjective*
department store a large shop with
many types of goods sold in different
departments.
departure *noun* departing.
depend *verb* **depend on** rely on, *We
depend on your help;* be controlled by
something else, *Whether we can picnic
depends on the weather.*
dependable *adjective* reliable.
dependant *noun* a person who depends
on another, *She has two dependants.*
• USAGE: Note that the spelling ends in -*ant*

for this noun but *-ent* for the adjective *dependent*.

dependency *noun* (*plural* **dependencies**) 1 dependence. 2 a country that is controlled by another.

dependent *adjective* depending, *She has two dependent children; they are dependent on her.* **dependence** *noun*

depict *verb* 1 show in a painting or drawing etc. 2 describe, *The play depicts the life of homeless people.* **depiction** *noun*

deplete (*say* dip-**leet**) *verb* (**depleted, depleting**) reduce the amount of something by using up large amounts. **depletion** *noun*

deplore *verb* (**deplored, deploring**) be very upset or annoyed by something. **deplorable** *adjective*, **deplorably** *adverb*

deploy *verb* spread out; place troops etc. in good positions. **deployment** *noun*

deport *verb* send an unwanted foreign person out of a country. **deportation** *noun*

deportment *noun* a person's manner of standing, walking, and behaving.

depose *verb* (**deposed, deposing**) 1 remove a person from power. 2 make a sworn statement. **deposition** *noun*

deposit¹ *noun* 1 an amount of money paid into a bank etc. 2 money paid as a first instalment. 3 a layer of solid matter in or on the earth.

deposit² *verb* (**deposited, depositing**) 1 put down, *The flood deposited silt on the plains.* 2 pay money as a deposit. **depositor** *noun*

depot (*say* **dep**-oh) *noun* 1 a place where things are stored. 2 a headquarters. 3 a place where vehicles are kept, *a bus depot.*

depraved *adjective* behaving wickedly; of bad character. **depravity** *noun*

deprecate (*say* **dep**-rik-ayt) *verb* (**deprecated, deprecating**) say that you disapprove of something. **deprecation** *noun*

depreciate (*say* dip-**ree**-shee-ayt) *verb* (**depreciated, depreciating**) make or become lower in value. **depreciation** *noun*

depredation (*say* dep-rid-**ay**-shon) *noun* the act of plundering or damaging something. (Compare *predator*.)

depress *verb* 1 make somebody sad. 2 lower the value of something, *Threat of war depressed prices.* 3 press down, *Depress the lever.* **depressive** *adjective*

depression *noun* 1 a great sadness or feeling of hopelessness. 2 a long period when trade is very slack because no one can afford to buy things. 3 a shallow hollow in the ground or on a surface. 4 an area of low air-pressure which may bring rain. 5 pressing something down.

deprive *verb* (**deprived, depriving**) take or keep something away from somebody. **deprival** *noun*, **deprivation** *noun*

depth *noun* 1 being deep; how deep something is. 2 the deepest or lowest part. **in depth** thoroughly.
out of your depth in water that is too deep to stand in; trying to do something that is too difficult for you.

deputation *noun* a group of people sent as representatives of others.

depute (*say* dip-**yoot**) *verb* (**deputed, deputing**) 1 appoint a person to do something, *We deputed Yusuf to take the message.* 2 assign or delegate a task to someone, *We deputed the task to him.*

deputize *verb* (**deputized, deputizing**) act as someone's deputy.

deputy *noun* (*plural* **deputies**) a person appointed to act as a substitute for another.

derail *verb* cause a train to leave the rails. **derailment** *noun*

derange *verb* (**deranged, deranging**) 1 throw into confusion; disturb. 2 make a person insane. **derangement** *noun*

derelict (*say* **derri**-likt) *adjective* abandoned and left to fall into ruin. **dereliction** *noun*

deride *verb* (**derided, deriding**) laugh at with contempt or scorn; ridicule.

derision *noun* scorn; ridicule. **derisive** (*say* dir-**I**-siv) *adjective*, **derisively** *adverb*, **derisory** *adjective*

derivation *noun* 1 deriving. 2 the origin of a word from another language or from a simple word to which a prefix or suffix is added; etymology.

derivative *adjective* derived from something. **derivative** *noun*

derive *verb* (**derived, deriving**) 1 obtain from a source, *She derived great enjoyment from music.* 2 form or originate from something, *Some English words are derived from Latin words.*

dermatology *noun* the study of the skin and its diseases. **dermatologist** *noun*

dermis *noun* the layer of skin below the epidermis.

derogatory (*say* dir-**og**-at-er-ee) *adjective* contemptuous; disparaging.

derrick *noun* 1 a kind of crane for lifting things. 2 a tall framework holding the machinery used in drilling an oil-well etc.

dervish *noun* (*plural* **dervishes**) a member of a Muslim religious group who vowed to live a life of poverty.

descant *noun* a tune sung or played above the main tune.

descend *verb* go down.

be descended from have as an ancestor; come by birth from a certain person or family. **descendant** *noun*

descent *noun* descending.

describe *verb* (**described, describing**) 1 say what someone or something is like. 2 draw in outline; move in a pattern. **description** *noun,* **descriptive** *adjective*

desecrate (*say* **dess**-ik-rayt) *verb* (**desecrated, desecrating**) treat a sacred thing irreverently. **desecration** *noun*

desert[1] (*say* **dez**-ert) *noun* a large area of dry often sandy land.

desert island an uninhabited island.

desert[2] (*say* diz-**ert**) *verb* abandon; leave without intending to return. **deserter** *noun,* **desertion** *noun*

desertification *noun* the process of making an area of fertile land into a desert.

deserts (*say* diz-**erts**) *plural noun* what a person deserves, *He got his deserts.*

deserve *verb* (**deserved, deserving**) have a right to something; be worthy of something. **deservedly** *adverb*

desiccated *adjective* dried.

design[1] *noun* 1 a drawing that shows how something is to be made, *a dress design.* 2 the way something is made or arranged, *computer-aided design.* 3 lines and shapes

that form a decoration; a pattern, *a floral design.* 4 a mental plan or scheme.

have designs on plan to get hold of.

design[2] *verb* 1 draw a design for something. 2 plan or intend something for a special purpose, *The vehicle was designed for desert roads.*

designate[1] *verb* (**designated, designating**) mark or describe as something particular, *They designated the river as the boundary.* **designation** *noun*

designate[2] *adjective* appointed to a job but not yet doing it, *the bishop designate.*

designer[1] *noun* a person whose job is designing things.

designer[2] *adjective* fashionable; bearing the name or label of a famous clothes designer, *designer jeans.*

desirable *adjective* 1 causing people to desire it; worth having. 2 worth doing; advisable. **desirability** *noun*

desire[1] *noun* a feeling of wanting something very much. **desirous** *adjective*

desire[2] *verb* (**desired, desiring**) have a desire for something.

desist (*say* diz-**ist**) *verb* cease.

desk *noun* 1 a piece of furniture with a flat top and often drawers, used when writing or reading etc. 2 a counter at which a cashier or receptionist sits.

desktop *adjective* (of a computer) suitable for use at an ordinary desk.

desolate *adjective* 1 lonely; sad. 2 uninhabited, *a desolate island.* **desolation** *noun*

despair[1] *noun* a feeling of hopelessness.

despair[2] *verb* feel despair.

despatch *noun* & *verb* dispatch.

desperado (*say* dess-per-**ah**-doh) *noun* (*plural* **desperadoes**) a reckless criminal.

desperate *adjective* 1 extremely serious; hopeless, *a desperate situation.* 2 reckless and ready to do anything. **desperately** *adverb,* **desperation** *noun*

despicable *adjective* deserving to be despised; contemptible.

despise *verb* (**despised, despising**) think someone or something is inferior or worthless.

despite *preposition* in spite of.

despondent *adjective* sad; gloomy.
despondently *adverb*, **despondency**
noun

despot (*say* **dess**-pot) *noun* a tyrant.
despotism *noun*, **despotic** (*say* dis-**pot**-ik)
adjective

dessert (*say* diz-**ert**) *noun* fruit or a sweet
food as the last course of a meal.

dessertspoon *noun* a medium-sized
spoon used for eating puddings etc.

destination *noun* the place to which a
person or thing is travelling.

destined *adjective* having as a destiny;
intended.

destiny *noun* (*plural* **destinies**) fate.

destitute *adjective* left without anything;
living in extreme poverty. **destitution**
noun

destroy *verb* ruin or put an end to
something. **destruction** *noun*, **destructive**
adjective

destroyer *noun* a fast warship.

desultory (*say* **dess**-ul-ter-ee) *adjective*
casual and disconnected, *desultory talk.*

detach *verb* unfasten; separate.
detachable *adjective*, **detachment** *noun*

detached *adjective* **1** separated. **2** not
prejudiced; not involved in something,
a detached judgement.
detached house one that is not joined to
another.

detail *noun* **1** a very small part of a design
or plan or decoration etc. **2** a small piece of
information. **detailed** *adjective*

detain *verb* **1** keep someone waiting.
2 keep someone at a place, *The police
detained him for questioning.* **detention**
noun

detainee *noun* a person who is officially
detained or kept in custody.

detect *verb* discover. **detection** *noun*,
detector *noun*

detective *noun* a person who investigates
crimes.

detention *noun* detaining; being detained;
being made to stay late in school as a
punishment.

deter *verb* (**deterred, deterring**) discourage
or prevent a person from doing something.
determent *noun*

detergent *noun* a substance used for
cleaning or washing things.

deteriorate (*say* dit-**eer**-ee-er-ayt) *verb*
(**deteriorated, deteriorating**) become
worse. **deterioration** *noun*

determination *noun* **1** strong intention;
having decided firmly, *She climbed the
mountain with great determination.*
2 determining or deciding something.

determine *verb* (**determined, determining**) **1** decide, *determine what is to be done.*
2 find out; calculate, *determine the height of
the mountain.*

determined *adjective* full of determination; with your mind firmly made up.

determiner *noun* a word (such as *a, the,
many*) that modifies a noun.

deterrent *noun* something that may deter
people; a nuclear weapon that deters
countries from making war on the one that
has it. **deterrence** *noun*

detest *verb* dislike very much; loathe.
detestable *adjective*, **detestation** *noun*

detonate (*say* **det**-on-ayt) *verb*
(**detonated, detonating**) explode; cause
something to explode. **detonation** *noun*,
detonator *noun*

detour (*say* **dee**-toor) *noun* a roundabout
route instead of the normal one.

detract *verb* lessen the amount or value,
It will not detract from our pleasure.
detraction *noun*

detriment (*say* **det**-rim-ent) *noun* harm;
damage, *She worked long hours, to the
detriment of her health.*

detrimental (*say* det-rim-**en**-tal) *adjective*
harmful. **detrimentally** *adverb*

deuce *noun* a score in tennis where both
sides have 40 points and must gain two
consecutive points to win.

deurmekaar *adjective* (*informal*) confused; out of place.

devalue *verb* (**devalued, devaluing**)
reduce a thing's value. **devaluation** *noun*

devastate *verb* (**devastated, devastating**)
ruin or cause great destruction to something. **devastation** *noun*

develop *verb* (**developed, developing**)
1 make or become bigger or better. **2** come
gradually into existence, *Storms developed.*

3 begin to have or use, *They developed bad habits.* **4** use an area of land for building houses, shops, factories, etc. **5** treat photographic film with chemicals so that pictures appear. **developer** *noun*, **development** *noun*

developed country a country that is industrialized and wealthy. (Compare *developing country.*)

developing country a poor or undeveloped country that is becoming more advanced economically and socially. (Compare *developed country.*)

deviate (*say* dee-vee-ayt) *verb* (**deviated, deviating**) turn aside from a course or from what is usual or true. **deviation** *noun*

device *noun* **1** something made for a particular purpose, *a device for opening tins.* **2** a design used as a decoration or emblem.

leave someone to his or **her own devices** leave alone to do as he or she wishes.

devil *noun* **1** an evil spirit. **2** a wicked, cruel, or annoying person. **devilish** *adjective*, **devilry** *noun*

devil-may-care cheerful and reckless.

devilment *noun* mischief.

devious (*say* dee-vee-us) *adjective* **1** roundabout; not direct, *a devious route.* **2** not straightforward; underhand. **deviously** *adverb*, **deviousness** *noun*

devise *verb* (**devised, devising**) invent; plan.

devoid *adjective* lacking or without something, *His work is devoid of merit.*

devolution *noun* devolving; giving authority to another person etc.; handing over responsibility for government.

devolve *verb* (**devolved, devolving**) pass or be passed to a deputy or successor.

devote *verb* (**devoted, devoting**) give completely, *He devoted his time to sport.*

devoted *adjective* very loving or loyal.

devotee (*say* dev-o-tee) *noun* a person who is devoted to something; an enthusiast.

devotion *noun* great love or loyalty; being devoted.

devotions *plural noun* prayers.

devour *verb* eat or swallow something hungrily or greedily.

devout *adjective* earnestly religious or sincere. **devoutly** *adverb*, **devoutness** *noun*

dew *noun* tiny drops of water that form during the night on surfaces of things in the open air. **dewdrop** *noun*, **dewy** *adjective*

dexterity (*say* deks-**terri**-tee) *noun* skill in handling things.

di-[1] *prefix* two; double (as in *dioxide*).

di-[2] *prefix* *see* **dis-**.

dia- *prefix* through (as in *diarrhoea*); across (as in *diagonal*).

diabetes (*say* dy-a-**bee**-teez) *noun* a disease in which there is too much sugar in a person's blood. **diabetic** (*say* dy-a-**bet**-ik) *adjective* & *noun*

diabolical *adjective* **1** like a devil; very wicked. **2** very clever or annoying, *a diabolical trick.*

diadem (*say* **dy**-a-dem) *noun* a crown or headband worn by a royal person.

diagnose *verb* (**diagnosed, diagnosing**) find out what disease a person has or what is wrong. **diagnosis** *noun*, **diagnostic** *adjective*

diagonal (*say* dy-**ag**-on-al) *noun* a straight line joining opposite corners. **diagonal** *adjective*, **diagonally** *adverb*

diagram *noun* a kind of drawing or picture that shows the parts of something or how it works.

dial[1] *noun* a circular object with numbers or letters round it.

dial[2] *verb* (**dialled, dialling**) telephone a number by turning a telephone dial or pressing numbered buttons.

dialect *noun* the words and pronunciations used by people in one district but not in the rest of a country.

dialogue *noun* a conversation.

dialysis (*say* dy-**al**-iss-iss) *noun* a way of removing harmful substances from the blood by letting it flow through a machine.

diameter (*say* dy-**am**-it-er) *noun* **1** a line drawn straight across a circle or sphere and passing through its centre. **2** the length of this line.

diametrically *adverb* completely, *diametrically opposite*.

diamond *noun* 1 a very hard precious stone that looks like clear glass. 2 a shape with four equal sides and four angles that are not right angles. 3 a playing-card with red diamond shapes on it.

diaper *noun* a baby's nappy.

diaphanous (*say* dy-**af**-an-us) *adjective* (of fabric) almost transparent.

diaphragm (*say* **dy**-a-fram) *noun* 1 the muscular partition inside the body that separates the chest from the abdomen and is used in breathing. 2 a hole that can be altered in size to control the amount of light that passes through a camera lens.

diarist *noun* a person who keeps a diary.

diarrhoea (*say* dy-a-**ree**-a) *noun* too frequent and too watery emptying of the bowels.

diary *noun* (*plural* **diaries**) a book in which someone writes down what happens each day.

diatribe *noun* a strong verbal attack.

dice[1] *noun* (strictly this is the plural of **die**[2], but it is often used as a singular, *plural* **dice**) a small cube marked with dots (1 to 6) on its sides, used in games.

dice[2] *verb* (**diced, dicing**) 1 play gambling games using dice. 2 cut into small cubes. 3 (*informal*) race with another driver on a public road.

dicotyledon (*say* dy-kot-a-**lee**-den) *noun* a flowering plant which has two cotyledons and net-veined leaves.

dictate *verb* (**dictated, dictating**) 1 speak or read something aloud for someone else to write down. 2 give orders in an officious way. **dictation** *noun*

dictates (*say* dik-**tayts**) *plural noun* orders, commands.

dictator *noun* a ruler who has unlimited power. **dictatorial** (*say* dik-ta-**tor**-ee-al) *adjective,* **dictatorship** *noun*

diction *noun* a person's way of speaking words, *clear diction*.

dictionary *noun* (*plural* **dictionaries**) a book that contains words in alphabetical order so that you can find out how to spell them and what they mean.

didactic (*say* dy-**dak**-tik) *adjective* having the manner of someone who is lecturing people. **didactically** *adverb*

diddle *verb* (**diddled, diddling**) (*slang*) cheat; swindle.

didn't (*mainly spoken*) did not.

die[1] *verb* (**died, dying**) 1 stop living or existing. 2 stop burning or functioning, *The fire had died down*.

die[2] *noun* singular of **dice**.

die[3] *noun* a device that stamps a design on coins etc. or that cuts or moulds metal.

die-hard *noun* a person who obstinately refuses to give up old ideas or policies.

diesel (*say* **dee**-zel) *noun* 1 an engine that works by burning oil in compressed air. 2 fuel for this kind of engine.

diet[1] *noun* 1 special meals that someone eats in order to be healthy or to become less fat. 2 the sort of foods usually eaten by a person or animal, *a balanced diet*.

diet[2] *verb* (**dieted, dieting**) keep to a diet.

diet[3] *noun* the parliament of certain countries (e.g. Japan).

dietitian (*say* dy-it-**ish**-an) *noun* an expert in diet and nutrition.

dif- *prefix see* **dis-**.

differ *verb* 1 be different. 2 disagree.

difference *noun* 1 being different; the way in which things differ. 2 the remainder left after one number is subtracted from another, *The difference between 8 and 3 is 5.* 3 a disagreement, *They settled their differences*.

different *adjective* unlike; not the same. **differently** *adverb*
● USAGE: It is better to say *different from,* not *different to;* the phrase *different than* is used in America but not in standard English.

differential *noun* 1 a difference in wages between one group of workers and another. 2 a differential gear.
differential gear a system of gears that makes a vehicle's driving wheels revolve at different speeds when going round corners.

differentiate *verb* (**differentiated, differentiating**) 1 make different, *These things differentiate one breed from another.*

2 distinguish; recognize differences, *We do not differentiate between them.* **differentiation** *noun*

difficult *adjective* needing much effort or skill; not easy. **difficulty** *noun*

diffident (*say* **dif**-id-ent) *adjective* shy and not self-confident; hesitating to put yourself or your ideas forward. **diffidently** *adverb*, **diffidence** *noun*

diffract *verb* break up a beam of light etc. **diffraction** *noun*

diffuse[1] *verb* (**diffused, diffusing**) 1 spread something widely or thinly, *diffused lighting*. 2 mix slowly, *diffusing gases*. **diffusion** *noun*

diffuse[2] *adjective* 1 diffused; spread widely; not concentrated. 2 using many words; not concise, *a diffuse style*. **diffusely** *adverb*, **diffuseness** *noun*

dig[1] *verb* (**dug, digging**) 1 break up soil and move it; make a hole or tunnel by moving soil. 2 poke; push, *Dig a knife into it.* 3 seek or discover by investigating, *We dug up some facts.* **digger** *noun*

dig[2] *noun* 1 a piece of digging. 2 a poke.

digest[1] (*say* dy-**jest**) *verb* 1 soften and change food in the stomach etc. so that the body can absorb it. 2 take information into your mind and think it over. **digestible** *adjective*, **digestion** *noun*

digest[2] (*say* **dy**-jest) *noun* a summary of news, information, etc.

digestive *adjective* of digestion; digesting, *the digestive system.*

digestive biscuit a wholemeal biscuit.

digit (*say* **dij**-it) *noun* 1 any of the numbers from 0 to 9. 2 a finger or toe.

digital *adjective* of or using digits.

digital clock or **watch** one that shows the time with a row of figures.

dignified *adjective* having dignity.

dignitary *noun* (*plural* **dignitaries**) an important official.

dignity *noun* 1 a calm and serious manner. 2 a high rank.

digress *verb* stray from the main subject. **digression** *noun*

dike *noun* a dyke.

dikkop *noun* a kind of bird which lays its eggs on the ground.

dilapidated *adjective* falling to pieces. **dilapidation** *noun*

dilate *verb* (**dilated, dilating**) make or become wider or larger.

dilatory (*say* **dil**-at-er-ee) *adjective* slow in doing something; not prompt.

dilemma (*say* dil-**em**-a) *noun* a situation where someone has to choose between two possible actions, each of which will bring difficulties.

diligent (*say* **dil**-ij-ent) *adjective* working hard. **diligently** *adverb*, **diligence** *noun*

dilute[1] *verb* (**diluted, diluting**) make a liquid weaker by adding water or other liquid. **dilution** *noun*

dilute[2] *adjective* diluted, *a dilute acid.*

dim[1] *adjective* (**dimmer, dimmest**) 1 not bright or clear; only faintly lit. 2 (*informal*) stupid. **dimly** *adverb*, **dimness** *noun*

dim[2] *verb* (**dimmed, dimming**) make or become dim. **dimmer** *noun*

dimension *noun* 1 a measurement such as length, width, area, or volume. 2 size; extent. **dimensional** *adjective*

diminish *verb* make or become smaller. **diminution** *noun*

diminutive (*say* dim-**in**-yoo-tiv) *adjective* very small.

dimple *noun* a small hollow or dent, especially in the skin. **dimpled** *adjective*

din[1] *noun* a loud annoying noise.

din[2] *verb* (**dinned, dinning**) 1 make a din. 2 force a person to learn something by continually repeating it, *Din it into him.*

dine *verb* (**dined, dining**) have dinner. **diner** *noun*

ding-dong *noun* the sound of a bell or alternate strokes of two bells.

dinghy (*say* **ding**-ee) *noun* (*plural* **dinghies**) a kind of small boat.

dingo *noun* (*plural* **dingoes**) an Australian wild dog.

dingy (*say* **din**-jee) *adjective* dirty-looking. **dingily** *adverb*, **dinginess** *noun*

dining-room *noun* a room where meals are eaten.

dinner *noun* the main meal of the day, either at midday or in the evening.

dinner service a set of matching crockery

used for meals.

dinosaur (*say* **dy**-noss-or) *noun* a prehistoric lizard-like animal, often of enormous size.

dint *noun* a dent.
by dint of by means of.

diocese (*say* **dy**-oss-iss) *noun* a district under the care of a bishop. **diocesan** (*say* dy-**oss**-iss-an) *adjective*

dioxide *noun* an oxide with two atoms of oxygen to one of another element, *carbon dioxide.*

dip¹ *verb* (**dipped, dipping**) put down or go down, especially into a liquid.

dip² *noun* 1 dipping. 2 a downward slope. 3 a quick swim. 4 a substance into which things are dipped.

diphtheria (*say* dif-**theer**-ee-a) *noun* a serious disease that causes inflammation in the throat.

diphthong (*say* **dif**-thong) *noun* a compound vowel-sound made up of two sounds, e.g. *oi* in *point* (made up of 'aw' + 'ee') or *ou* in *loud* ('ah' + 'oo').

diploma *noun* a certificate awarded by a college etc. for skill in a particular subject.

diplomacy *noun* keeping friendly with other nations or other people.

diplomat *noun* 1 a person employed in diplomacy on behalf of his or her country. 2 a tactful person.

diplomatic *adjective* 1 of diplomats or diplomacy. 2 tactful. **diplomatically** *adverb*

dipper *noun* 1 a kind of bird that dives for its food. 2 a ladle.

dire *adjective* dreadful; serious, *dire need.*

direct¹ *adjective* 1 as straight as possible. 2 going straight to the point; frank. 3 exact, *the direct opposite.* **directly** *adverb* & *conjunction*, **directness** *noun*
  direct current electric current flowing only in one direction.
  direct object the word that receives the action of the verb. In *'she hit him'*, 'him' is the direct object.
  direct selling (of a producer) selling directly to a consumer without an intermediary, such as by mail order or from a farm-stall.

direct² *verb* 1 tell someone the way.

2 guide or aim in a certain direction. 3 control; manage. 4 order, *He directed his troops to advance.* **director** *noun*

direction *noun* 1 directing. 2 the line along which something moves or faces. **directional** *adjective*

directions *plural noun* information on how to use or do something.

directive *noun* a command.

directory *noun* (*plural* **directories**) a book containing a list of people with their telephone numbers, addresses, etc.

dirge *noun* a slow sad song.

dirt *noun* earth, soil; anything that is not clean.

dirty *adjective* (**dirtier, dirtiest**) 1 not clean; soiled. 2 unfair; dishonourable, *a dirty trick.* 3 indecent; obscene. **dirtily** *adverb*, **dirtiness** *noun*

dis- *prefix* (changing to **dif-** before words beginning with *f*, and to **di-** before some consonants) 1 not; the reverse of (as in *dishonest*). 2 apart; separated (as in *disarm*, *disperse*).

disa (*say* **dy**-sa) *noun* a kind of orchid indigenous to southern Africa and Madagascar.

disabled *adjective* made unable to do something because of illness or injury. (Compare *abled*.) **disability** *noun*, **disablement** *noun*

disadvantage *noun* something that hinders or is unhelpful. **disadvantaged** *adjective*, **disadvantageous** *adjective*

disagree *verb* (**disagreed, disagreeing**) 1 have or express a different opinion from someone. 2 have a bad effect, *Rich food disagrees with me.* **disagreement** *noun*

disagreeable *adjective* unpleasant; bad-tempered.

disappear *verb* stop being visible; vanish. **disappearance** *noun*

disappoint *verb* fail to do what someone hopes for. **disappointment** *noun*

disapprobation *noun* disapproval.

disapprove *verb* (**disapproved, disapproving**) have or show an unfavourable opinion; not approve. **disapproval** *noun*

disarm *verb* 1 reduce the size of armed forces. 2 take away someone's weapons.

3 overcome a person's anger or doubt, *Her friendliness disarmed their suspicions.* **disarmament** *noun*

disarray *noun* disorder.

disaster *noun* **1** a very bad accident or misfortune. **2** a complete failure. **disastrous** *adjective*, **disastrously** *adverb*

disband *verb* break up a group.

disbelief *noun* refusal or unwillingness to believe something.

disburse *verb* (**disbursed, disbursing**) pay out money. **disbursement** *noun*

disc *noun* **1** any round flat object. **2** a gramophone record. **3** (in computers, usually **disk**) a storage device consisting of magnetically coated plates.

disc jockey a person who introduces and plays recorded music.

discard *verb* throw away; put something aside as being useless or unwanted.

discern (*say* dis-**sern**) *verb* perceive; see or recognize clearly. **discernible** *adjective*, **discernment** *noun*

discerning *adjective* perceptive; showing good judgement.

discharge[1] *verb* (**discharged, discharging**) **1** release a person. **2** send something out, *discharge smoke.* **3** pay or do what was agreed, *discharge the debt.*

discharge[2] *noun* **1** discharging. **2** something that is discharged.

disciple *noun* a person who accepts the teachings of another whom he or she regards as a leader; any of the original followers of Jesus Christ.

disciplinarian *noun* a person who believes in strict discipline.

discipline[1] *noun* orderly and obedient behaviour. **disciplinary** (*say* dis-ip-lin-er-ee) *adjective*

discipline[2] *verb* (**disciplined, disciplining**) **1** train to be orderly and obedient. **2** punish, *Anyone who cheats will be severely disciplined.*

disclaim *verb* disown; say that you are not responsible for something.

disclose *verb* (**disclosed, disclosing**) reveal. **disclosure** *noun*

disco *noun* (*plural* **discos**) (*informal*) a discothèque.

discolour *verb* spoil a thing's colour; stain. **discoloration** *noun*

discomfit *verb* (**discomfited, discomfiting**) disconcert; dismay. **discomfiture** *noun*

● USAGE: Do not confuse with *discomfort.*

discomfort *noun* being uncomfortable.

disconcert (*say* dis-kon-**sert**) *verb* make a person feel uneasy.

disconnect *verb* break a connection; detach. **disconnection** *noun*

disconnected *adjective* not having a connection between its parts.

disconsolate (*say* dis-**kon**-sol-at) *adjective* disappointed.

discontent *noun* lack of contentment; dissatisfaction. **discontented** *adjective*, **discontentment** *noun*

discontinue *verb* (**discontinued, discontinuing**) put an end to something.

discord *noun* **1** disagreement; quarrelling. **2** musical notes sounded together and producing a harsh or unpleasant sound. **discordant** *adjective*

discothèque (*say* dis-ko-tek) *noun* **1** a place or party where recorded music is played for dancing. **2** the equipment for playing recorded music for dancing.

discount[1] *noun* an amount by which a price is reduced.

discount[2] *verb* ignore; disregard, *We cannot discount the possibility.*

discourage *verb* (**discouraged, discouraging**) **1** take away someone's enthusiasm or confidence. **2** try to persuade someone not to do something; dissuade; deter, *Parents should discourage watching too much TV.* **discouragement** *noun*

discourse[1] *noun* a formal speech or piece of writing about something.

discourse[2] *verb* (**discoursed, discoursing**) speak or write at length about something.

discourteous *adjective* not courteous; rude. **discourteously** *adverb*, **discourtesy** *noun*

discover *verb* **1** find. **2** be the first person to find something. **discoverer** *noun*, **discovery** *noun*

discredit[1] *verb* (**discredited, discrediting**) 1 destroy people's confidence in a person or thing; disgrace. 2 distrust.

discredit[2] *noun* 1 disgrace. 2 distrust. **discreditable** *adjective*

discreet *adjective* 1 not giving away secrets. 2 not showy. **discreetly** *adverb*
• USAGE: Do not confuse with *discrete*.

discrepancy (*say* dis-**krep**-an-see) *noun* (*plural* **discrepancies**) difference; lack of agreement, *There are several discrepancies in the two accounts.* **discrepant** *adjective*

discrete *adjective* separate; distinct from each other.
• USAGE: Do not confuse with *discreet*.

discretion (*say* dis-**kresh**-on) *noun* 1 being discreet; keeping secrets. 2 power to take action according to your own judgement, *The treasurer has full discretion.*

discriminate *verb* (**discriminated, discriminating**) 1 notice the differences between things; distinguish; prefer one thing to another. 2 treat people differently or unfairly, e.g. because of their race, sex, or religion. **discrimination** *noun*
• USAGE: Note that these words have both a 'good' sense and a 'bad' sense. A *discriminating* person can mean someone who judges carefully and well, but it can also mean someone who judges unfairly.

discus *noun* (*plural* **discuses**) a thick heavy disc thrown in athletic contests.

discuss *verb* talk with other people about a subject. **discussion** *noun*

disdain[1] *noun* scorn; contempt. **disdainful** *adjective*, **disdainfully** *adverb*

disdain[2] *verb* 1 regard or treat with disdain. 2 not do something because of disdain, *She disdained to reply.*

disease *noun* an unhealthy condition; an illness. **diseased** *adjective*

disembark *verb* put or go ashore. **disembarkation** *noun*

disembodied *adjective* freed from the body, *a disembodied spirit.*

disembowel *verb* (**disembowelled, disembowelling**) take out the bowels or inside parts of something.

disempower *verb* take authority away from someone.

disengage *verb* (**disengaged, disengaging**) disconnect; detach.

disentangle *verb* (**disentangled, disentangling**) free from tangles or confusion.

disfavour *noun* disapproval; dislike.

disfigure *verb* (**disfigured, disfiguring**) spoil a person's or thing's appearance. **disfigurement** *noun*

disgorge *verb* (**disgorged, disgorging**) pour or send out, *The pipe disgorged its contents.*

disgrace[1] *noun* 1 shame; loss of approval or respect. 2 something that causes shame. **disgraceful** *adjective*, **disgracefully** *adverb*

disgrace[2] *verb* (**disgraced, disgracing**) bring disgrace upon someone.

disgruntled *adjective* discontented; resentful.

disguise[1] *verb* (**disguised, disguising**) make a person or thing look different so as to deceive people.

disguise[2] *noun* something used for disguising.

disgust[1] *noun* a feeling that something is very unpleasant or disgraceful.

disgust[2] *verb* cause disgust. **disgusted** *adjective*, **disgusting** *adjective*

dish[1] *noun* (*plural* **dishes**) 1 a plate or bowl for food. 2 food served on a dish.

dish[2] *verb* **dish out** (*informal*) distribute, *dish out compliments.*
dish up put food on plates for serving.

dishcloth *noun* a cloth for washing dishes.

dishearten *verb* cause a person to lose hope or confidence.

dishevelled (*say* dish-**ev**-eld) *adjective* ruffled and untidy. **dishevelment** *noun*

dishonest *adjective* not honest. **dishonestly** *adverb*, **dishonesty** *noun*

dishonour *noun* & *verb* disgrace. **dishonourable** *adjective*

dishwasher *noun* a machine for washing dishes etc. automatically.

disillusion *verb* get rid of someone's pleasant but wrong beliefs. **disillusionment** *noun*

disincentive *noun* something that discourages an action or effort.

disinclination *noun* unwillingness.

disinclined *adjective* unwilling to do something.

disinfect *verb* destroy the germs in something. **disinfection** *noun*

disinfectant *noun* a substance used for disinfecting things.

disinherit *verb* deprive a person of the right to inherit something.

disintegrate *verb* (**disintegrated, disintegrating**) break up into small parts or pieces. **disintegration** *noun*

disinter *verb* (**disinterred, disinterring**) dig up something buried; unearth.

disinterested *adjective* impartial; not biased; not influenced by hope of gaining something yourself, *She gave us some disinterested advice.*

• USAGE: Do not use this word as if it meant 'not interested' or 'bored' (the word for this is *uninterested*).

disjointed *adjective* disconnected.

disk *noun* a disc.

disk drive the device which moves the disk around in a computer so that data can be written and read to and from it.

dislike¹ *noun* a feeling of not liking somebody or something.

dislike² *verb* (**disliked, disliking**) not to like somebody or something.

dislocate *verb* (**dislocated, dislocating**) 1 dislodge a bone from its proper position in one of the joints. 2 disrupt, *Fog dislocated the traffic.* **dislocation** *noun*

dislodge *verb* (**dislodged, dislodging**) move or force something from its place.

disloyal *adjective* not loyal. **disloyally** *adverb*, **disloyalty** *noun*

dismal *adjective* gloomy. **dismally** *adverb*

dismantle *verb* (**dismantled, dismantling**) take something to pieces.

dismay *noun* a feeling of surprise and discouragement. **dismayed** *adjective*

dismiss *verb* 1 send someone away. 2 tell a person that you will no longer employ him or her. 3 stop considering an idea etc. 4 in cricket, get a batsman or side out. **dismissal** *noun*, **dismissive** *adjective*

dismount *verb* get off a horse or bicycle.

disobedient *adjective* not obedient. **disobediently** *adverb*, **disobedience** *noun*

disobey *verb* (**disobeyed, disobeying**) not to obey; disregard orders.

disorder *noun* 1 untidiness. 2 a disturbance. 3 an illness, *a kidney disorder.* **disorderly** *adjective*

disorganize *verb* (**disorganized, disorganizing**) throw into confusion. **disorganization** *noun*

disown *verb* refuse to acknowledge that a person or thing has any connection with you.

disparage (*say* dis-**pa**-rij) *verb* (**disparaged, disparaging**) belittle; declare that something is small or unimportant. **disparagement** *noun*

disparity *noun* (*plural* **disparities**) difference; inequality.

dispassionate *adjective* calm and impartial. **dispassionately** *adverb*

dispatch¹ *verb* 1 send off to a destination. 2 kill, *He dispatched his attacker with a blow.*

dispatch² *noun* 1 dispatching. 2 a report or message sent. 3 promptness; speed.

dispatch-box *noun* a container for carrying official documents.

dispatch-rider *noun* a messenger who travels by motor cycle.

dispel *verb* (**dispelled, dispelling**) drive away; scatter, *Wind dispels fog.*

dispensary *noun* (*plural* **dispensaries**) a place where medicines are dispensed.

dispense *verb* (**dispensed, dispensing**) 1 distribute; deal out. 2 prepare medicine according to prescriptions. **dispensation** *noun*, **dispenser** *noun* dispense with do without something.

disperse *verb* (**dispersed, dispersing**) scatter. **dispersal** *noun*, **dispersion** *noun*

displace *verb* (**displaced, displacing**) 1 shift from its place. 2 take a person's or thing's place.

displacement *noun* 1 shifting something from its place. 2 the volume of a liquid that is displaced by an object submerged or floating in it.

display¹ *verb* show; arrange something so

that it can be clearly seen.

display² *noun* **1** the displaying of something; an exhibition. **2** something displayed, *the peacock's display.*

displease *verb* (**displeased, displeasing**) annoy or not please someone. **displeasure** *noun*

disposable *adjective* made to be thrown away after it has been used.

disposal *noun* getting rid of something. **at your disposal** for you to use; ready for you.

dispose *verb* (**disposed, disposing**) **1** place in position; arrange, *Dispose your troops in two lines.* **2** make a person ready or willing to do something, *I feel disposed to help him.*
be well disposed be friendly.
dispose of get rid of.

disposition *noun* **1** a person's nature or qualities. **2** arrangement, *the disposition of scenery on the stage.*

disproportionate *adjective* out of proportion; too large or too small.

disprove *verb* (**disproved, disproving**) show that something is not true.

disputation *noun* a debate; an argument.

dispute¹ *verb* (**disputed, disputing**) **1** argue; debate. **2** quarrel. **3** raise an objection to, *We dispute their claim.*

dispute² *noun* **1** an argument; a debate. **2** a quarrel.
in dispute being argued about.

disqualify *verb* (**disqualified, disqualifying**) bar someone from a competition etc. because he or she has broken the rules or is not properly qualified to take part. **disqualification** *noun*

disquiet *noun* anxiety; worry. **disquieting** *adjective*

disregard¹ *verb* ignore.

disregard² *noun* the act of ignoring something.

disrepair *noun* bad condition caused by not doing repairs.

disreputable *adjective* not respectable.

disrepute *noun* discredit; bad reputation.

disrespect *noun* lack of respect; rudeness. **disrespectful** *adjective*, **disrespectfully** *adverb*

disrupt *verb* put into disorder; interrupt a continuous flow, *Fog disrupted traffic.*
disruption *noun*, **disruptive** *adjective*

dissatisfied *adjective* not satisfied. **dissatisfaction** *noun*

dissect (*say* dis-**sekt**) *verb* cut something up so as to examine it. **dissection** *noun*

disseminate *verb* (**disseminated, disseminating**) spread ideas etc. widely. **dissemination** *noun*

dissent¹ *noun* disagreement.

dissent² *verb* disagree.

dissertation *noun* a long speech or piece of writing about something, especially a long essay written by a candidate for a university degree.

disservice *noun* a harmful action done by someone who was intending to help.

dissident *noun* a person who disagrees; someone who opposes the authorities. **dissident** *adjective*, **dissidence** *noun*

dissipate *verb* (**dissipated, dissipating**) **1** dispel; disperse, *The sun dissipated the mist.* **2** squander; waste; fritter away. **dissipation** *noun*

dissociate *verb* (**dissociated, dissociating**) separate something in your thoughts. **dissociation** *noun*

dissolute *adjective* living a frivolous and selfish life.

dissolution *noun* dissolving.

dissolve *verb* (**dissolved, dissolving**) **1** mix something with a liquid so that it becomes part of the liquid. **2** make or become liquid; melt. **3** put an end to a marriage or partnership etc. **4** dismiss an assembly, *Parliament was dissolved and a general election was held.*

dissuade *verb* (**dissuaded, dissuading**) persuade somebody not to do something. **dissuasion** *noun*

distance *noun* the amount of space between two places.
in the distance far away.

distant *adjective* **1** far away. **2** not friendly; not sociable, *She seemed distant before we got to know her.* **distantly** *adverb*

distaste *noun* dislike.

distasteful *adjective* unpleasant.

distemper *noun* **1** a disease of dogs and

certain other animals. 2 a kind of paint.

distend *verb* make or become swollen because of pressure from inside. **distension** *noun*

distil *verb* (**distilled, distilling**) purify a liquid by boiling it and condensing the vapour. **distillation** *noun*

distiller *noun* a person who makes alcoholic liquors by distillation. **distillery** *noun*

distinct *adjective* 1 easily heard or seen; noticeable. 2 clearly separate or different. **distinctly** *adverb*, **distinctness** *noun*

• USAGE: See *distinctive*.

distinction *noun* 1 a difference. 2 distinguishing; making a difference. 3 excellence; honour. 4 an award for excellence; a high mark in an examination.

distinctive *adjective* that distinguishes one thing from another or others, *The school has a distinctive uniform.* **distinctively** *adverb*

• USAGE: Do not confuse this word with *distinct*. A *distinct* mark is a clear mark; a *distinctive* mark is one that is not found anywhere else.

distinguish *verb* 1 make or notice differences between things. 2 see or hear something clearly, *Can you distinguish the sound of the piet-my-vrou?* 3 bring honour to, *He distinguished himself by his bravery.* **distinguishable** *adjective*

distinguished *adjective* excellent; famous.

distort *verb* 1 pull or twist out of its normal shape. 2 misrepresent; give a false account of something, *distort the truth.* **distortion** *noun*

distract *verb* take a person's attention away from something.

distracted *adjective* distraught.

distraction *noun* 1 something that distracts a person's attention. 2 an amusement. 3 great worry or distress, *driven to distraction.*

distraught (*say* dis-**trawt**) *adjective* greatly upset by worry or distress.

distress[1] *noun* great sorrow, pain, or trouble.

distress[2] *verb* cause distress to a person.

distribute *verb* (**distributed, distributing**) 1 deal or share out. 2 spread or scatter.

distribution *noun*, **distributor** *noun*

district *noun* part of a town or country.

distrust[1] *noun* lack of trust; suspicion. **distrustful** *adjective*

distrust[2] *verb* not to trust.

disturb *verb* 1 spoil someone's peace or rest. 2 cause someone to worry. 3 move a thing from its position, *Don't disturb the flower arrangement.* **disturbance** *noun*

disuse *noun* the state of not being used.

disused *adjective* no longer used.

ditch[1] *noun* (*plural* **ditches**) a trench dug to hold water or carry it away, or to serve as a boundary.

ditch[2] *verb* 1 (*informal*) bring an aircraft down in a forced landing on the sea. 2 (*informal*) abandon; discard, *She ditched her boy-friend.*

dither *verb* 1 tremble. 2 hesitate nervously.

ditto *noun* (used in lists) the same again.

ditty *noun* (*plural* **ditties**) a short song.

diurnal *adjective* of the day or daytime. (Compare *nocturnal*.)

divan *noun* a bed or couch without a raised back or sides.

dive *verb* (**dived, diving**) 1 go under water, especially head first. 2 move down quickly. **dive** *noun*

diver *noun* 1 someone who dives. 2 a person who works under water in a special suit with an air supply. 3 a bird that dives for its food.

diverge *verb* (**diverged, diverging**) go aside or in different directions. (The opposite is *converge*.) **divergent** *adjective*, **divergence** *noun*

diverse (*say* dy-**verss**) *adjective* varied; of several different kinds. **diversity** *noun*

diversify *verb* (**diversified, diversifying**) make or become varied; involve yourself in different kinds of things. **diversification** *noun*

diversion *noun* 1 diverting something from its course; an alternative route for traffic when a road is closed. 2 a recreation; an entertainment. **diversionary** *adjective*

divert *verb* 1 turn something aside from its course. 2 entertain; amuse, *He was diverted by the busker.*

divest *verb* 1 strip of clothes, *He divested*

himself of his robes. **2** take away; deprive, *They divested her of power.*

divide *verb* (**divided, dividing**) **1** separate from something or into smaller parts; split up. **2** find how many times one number is contained in another, *Divide 6 by 3* (6 ÷ 3 = 2). **divider** *noun*

dividend *noun* **1** a share of a business's profit. **2** a number that is to be divided by another. (Compare *divisor*.)

dividers *plural noun* a pair of compasses for measuring distances.

divine[1] *adjective* **1** of God; coming from God. **2** like a god. **3** (*informal*) excellent; extremely beautiful. **divinely** *adverb*

divine[2] *verb* (**divined, divining**) prophesy or guess what is about to happen. **diviner** *noun*

division *noun* **1** dividing. **2** a dividing line; a partition. **3** one of the parts into which something is divided. **divisional** *adjective*

divisive (*say* div-**I**-siv) *adjective* causing disagreement within a group.

divisor *noun* a number by which another is to be divided. (Compare *dividend* 2.)

divorce[1] *noun* the legal ending of a marriage.

divorce[2] *verb* (**divorced, divorcing**) **1** end a marriage by divorce. **2** separate; think of things separately.

divulge *verb* (**divulged, divulging**) reveal information. **divulgence** *noun*

Diwali (*say* di-**wah**-lee) *noun* Deepavali.

DIY *abbreviation* do-it-yourself.

dizzy *adjective* (**dizzier, dizziest**) giddy. **dizzily** *adverb*, **dizziness** *noun*

DJ *abbreviation* disc jockey.

DNA *abbreviation* deoxyribonucleic acid (a substance in chromosomes that stores genetic information).

do[1] *verb* (**did, done, doing**) This word has many different uses, most of which mean performing or dealing with something (*Do your best. I can't do this. She is doing well at school.*) or being suitable or enough (*This will do*). The verb is also used with other verbs **1** in questions, *Do you want this?* **2** in statements with 'not', *He does not want it.* **3** for emphasis, *I do like nuts.* **4** to avoid repeating a verb that has just been used, *We*

work as hard as they do.

do away with get rid of.

do up fasten, *Do your coat up;* repair or redecorate, *Do up the spare room.*

do[2] *noun* (*plural* **dos**) (*informal*) a party; an entertainment.

docile (*say* **doh**-syl) *adjective* willing to obey. **docilely** *adverb*, **docility** *noun*

dock[1] *noun* a place where ships are loaded, unloaded, or repaired.

dock[2] *verb* **1** bring or come into a dock. **2** (of spacecraft) join together in space.

dock[3] *noun* an enclosure for the prisoner on trial in a lawcourt.

dock[4] *noun* a weed with broad leaves.

dock[5] *verb* **1** cut short an animal's tail. **2** reduce or take away part of someone's wages or supplies etc.

docker *noun* a labourer who loads and unloads ships.

docket *noun* a document or label listing the contents of a package.

dockyard *noun* an open area with docks and equipment for building or repairing ships.

doctor *noun* **1** a person who is trained to treat sick or injured people. **2** a person who holds an advanced degree (a **doctorate**) at a university, *Doctor of Music.*

doctrine *noun* a belief held by a religious, political, or other group. **doctrinal** *adjective*

document *noun* a written or printed paper giving information or evidence about something. **documentation** *noun*

documentary[1] *adjective* **1** consisting of documents, *documentary evidence.* **2** showing real events or situations.

documentary[2] *noun* (*plural* **documentaries**) a film giving an account of something, often showing real events etc.

dodder[1] *verb* totter. **doddery** *adjective*

dodder[2] *noun* a climbing plant which is parasitic.

dodge[1] *verb* (**dodged, dodging**) move quickly to avoid someone or something.

dodge[2] *noun* **1** a dodging movement. **2** (*informal*) a trick; a clever way of doing something.

dodgem *noun* a small electrically-driven

car at a fair, in which each driver tries to bump some cars and dodge others.

dodgy *adjective* (*informal*) tricky; awkward.

dodo *noun* (*plural* **dodos**) a large heavy bird that used to live in Mauritius but has been extinct for over 200 years.

doe (*say* doh) *noun* a female deer, rabbit, or hare.

doek *noun* a scarf worn around the head; a kerchief.

doepa *noun* a love potion or charm.

doer *noun* a person who does things.

doesn't (*mainly spoken*) does not.

doff *verb* take off, *He doffed his hat.* (Compare *don.*)

dog[1] *noun* a four-legged animal that barks, often kept as a pet.

dog[2] *verb* (**dogged, dogging**) follow closely or persistently, *Reporters dogged his footsteps.*

doge (*say* dohj) *noun* the elected ruler of the former republics of Venice and Genoa.

dog-eared *adjective* (of a book) having the corners of the pages bent from constant use.

dogfish *noun* (*plural* **dogfish**) a kind of small shark.

dogged (*say* dog-id) *adjective* persistent; obstinate. **doggedly** *adverb*

doggerel *noun* bad verse.

dogma *noun* a belief or principle that a Church or other authority declares is true and must be accepted.

dogmatic *adjective* expressing ideas in a very firm authoritative way. **dogmatically** *adverb*

doh *noun* a name for the keynote of a scale in music, or the note C.

doily *noun* (*plural* **doilies**) a small ornamental table-mat.

do-it-yourself *noun* the activity of making or repairing things oneself (rather than employing professional workers to do it).

doldrums *plural noun* **1** the ocean regions near the equator where there is little or no wind. **2** a time of depression or inactivity, *The economy is in the doldrums.*

dole *verb* (**doled, doling**) distribute.

doleful *adjective* mournful. **dolefully** *adverb*

doll *noun* a toy model of a person.

dollar *noun* a unit of money in the USA and some other countries.

dolly *noun* (*plural* **dollies**) (*informal*) a doll.

dolos *noun* (*plural* **dolosse**) **1** a knuckle-bone from an animal which is thrown by diviners to foretell the future. **2** a concrete block which fits together with others to form a barrier in harbours, beaches, etc. **3** (**dolossies**) small bones used as 'oxen' by children in games.

dolphin *noun* a sea animal like a small whale with a beak-like snout.

domain (*say* dom-**ayn**) *noun* realm.

dome *noun* a roof shaped like the top half of a ball. **domed** *adjective*

domestic *adjective* **1** of the home or household. **2** (of animals) kept by people, not wild. **domestically** *adverb*, **domesticated** *adjective*

domicile (*say* dom-iss-syl) *noun* a residence; home. **domiciled** *adjective*

dominate *verb* (**dominated, dominating**) **1** control by being stronger or more powerful. **2** be conspicuous or prominent, *The mountain dominated the whole landscape.* **dominant** *adjective*, **dominance** *noun*, **domination** *noun*

dominee *noun* a minister of the Dutch Reformed Church.

domineer *verb* behave in a dominating way. **domineering** *adjective*

dominion *noun* **1** authority to rule others; control. **2** an area over which someone rules; a domain, *the vast dominions of the Roman Empire.*

domino *noun* (*plural* **dominoes**) a small flat oblong piece of wood or plastic with dots (1 to 6) or a blank space at each end, used in the game of dominoes.

don *verb* (**donned, donning**) put on, *don a cloak.* (Compare *doff.*)

donate *verb* (**donated, donating**) present money or a gift to a fund or institution etc. **donation** *noun*

donga *noun* a dry water channel; a ditch caused by erosion.

donkey *noun* (*plural* **donkeys**) an animal that looks like a small horse with long ears.

donor *noun* someone who gives something, *a blood donor*.

don't (*mainly spoken*) do not.

doodle *verb* (**doodled, doodling**) scribble or draw absent-mindedly. **doodle** *noun*

doom[1] *noun* a grim fate; death; ruin.

doom[2] *verb* destine to a grim fate.

doomsday *noun* the day of the Last Judgement; the end of the world.

door *noun* a movable barrier on hinges (or one that slides or revolves), used to open or close an entrance. **doorknob** *noun*, **doormat** *noun*

doorstep *noun* the step or piece of ground just outside a door.

doorway *noun* the opening into which a door fits.

dope[1] *noun* 1 (*informal*) a drug, especially one taken or given illegally. 2 (*slang*) a stupid person. **dopey** *adjective*

dope[2] *verb* (**doped, doping**) (*informal*) give a drug to a person or animal.

dormant *adjective* 1 sleeping. 2 living or existing but not active; not extinct, *a dormant volcano*.

dormitory *noun* (*plural* **dormitories**) a room for several people to sleep in, especially in a school or institution. **dormitory town** or **suburb** a place from which people travel to work elsewhere.

dormouse *noun* (*plural* **dormice**) an animal like a large mouse that hibernates in winter.

dorp *noun* a small country town.

dorsal *adjective* of or on the back, *Some fish have a dorsal fin*.

dosage *noun* 1 the giving of medicine in doses. 2 the size of a dose.

dose[1] *noun* an amount of medicine etc. taken at one time.

dose[2] *verb* (**dosed, dosing**) give a dose of medicine to a person or animal.

dossier (*say* **doss**-ee-er or **doss**-ee-ay) *noun* a set of documents containing information about a person or event.

dot[1] *noun* a tiny spot.

dot[2] *verb* (**dotted, dotting**) mark with dots.

dotage (*say* **doh**-tij) *noun* a condition of weakness of mind caused by old age, *He is in his dotage*.

dote *verb* (**doted, doting**) **dote on** be very fond of.

dotty *adjective* (**dottier, dottiest**) (*informal*) crazy; silly. **dottiness** *noun*

double[1] *adjective* 1 twice as much; twice as many. 2 having two things or parts that form a pair, *a double-barrelled gun*. 3 suitable for two people, *a double bed*. **doubly** *adverb*

double[2] *noun* 1 a double quantity or thing. 2 a person or thing that looks exactly like another.

double[3] *verb* (**doubled, doubling**) 1 make or become twice as much or as many. 2 bend or fold in two. 3 turn back sharply, *The lion doubled back on its tracks*.

double-bass *noun* a musical instrument with strings, like a large cello.

double-cross *verb* deceive or cheat someone who thinks you are working with them.

double-decker *noun* a bus with two decks.

doublet *noun* a man's close-fitting jacket worn in Europe in the 15th–17th centuries.

doubt[1] *noun* a feeling of not being sure about something.

doubt[2] *verb* feel doubt. **doubter** *noun*

doubtful *adjective* 1 feeling doubt. 2 casting doubt, *The weather looks doubtful*. **doubtfully** *adverb*

doubtless *adverb* certainly.

dough *noun* 1 a thick mixture of flour and water used for making bread, pastry, etc. 2 (*slang*) money. **doughy** *adjective*

doughnut *noun* a round bun that has been fried and covered in sugar.

doughty (*say* **dow**-tee) *adjective* valiant.

dour (*say* doo-er) *adjective* stern and gloomy-looking. **dourly** *adverb*

douse *verb* (**doused, dousing**) 1 put into water; pour water over something. 2 put out, *douse the light*.

dove *noun* a kind of pigeon.

dovetail[1] *noun* a wedge-shaped joint used to join two pieces of wood.

dovetail[2] *verb* 1 join pieces of wood with a dovetail. 2 fit neatly together, *My plans dovetailed with hers*.

dowager *noun* a woman who holds a

title or property after her husband has died, *the dowager duchess.*

dowdy *adjective* (**dowdier, dowdiest**) shabby; unfashionable. **dowdily** *adverb*

dowel *noun* a headless wooden or metal pin for holding together two pieces of wood, stone, etc. **dowelling** *noun*

down[1] *adverb* 1 to or in a lower place or position or level, *It fell down.* 2 to a source or place etc., *Track them down.* 3 in writing, *Take down these instructions.* 4 as a payment, *We will pay R100 down and the rest later.* **be down on** disapprove of, *She is down on smoking.*

down[2] *preposition* downwards through or along or into, *Pour it down the drain.*

down[3] *noun* very fine soft feathers or hair. **downy** *adjective*

downcast *adjective* 1 looking downwards, *downcast eyes.* 2 dejected.

downfall *noun* 1 a fall from power or prosperity. 2 a heavy fall of rain or snow.

downhill *adverb & adjective* down a slope.

downpour *noun* a great fall of rain.

downright *adjective* 1 frank; straightforward. 2 thorough; complete, *a downright lie.*

downstairs *adverb & adjective* to or on a lower floor.

downstream *adjective & adverb* in the direction in which a stream flows.

downward *adjective & adverb* going towards what is lower. **downwards** *adverb*

dowry *noun* (*plural* **dowries**) property or money brought by a bride to her husband when she marries him.

dowse *verb* (**dowsed, dowsing**) look for underground water and minerals by holding a stick or rod which dips or shakes when it comes near water etc.

doze[1] *verb* (**dozed, dozing**) sleep lightly.

doze[2] *noun* a light sleep. **dozy** *adjective*

dozen *noun* a set of twelve.
● USAGE: Correct use is *ten dozen* (not *ten dozens*).

drab *adjective* (**drabber, drabbest**) 1 not colourful. 2 dull; uninteresting, *a drab life.* **drably** *adverb*, **drabness** *noun*

draconian (*say* drak-**oh**-nee-an) *adjective* very harsh, *draconian laws.*

draft[1] *noun* 1 a rough sketch or plan. 2 a written order for a bank to pay out money.

draft[2] *verb* 1 prepare a draft. 2 select for a special duty, *She was drafted to our office in Harare.*
● USAGE: This is also the American spelling of *draught.*

drag[1] *verb* (**dragged, dragging**) 1 pull something heavy along. 2 search a river or lake etc. with nets and hooks. 3 continue slowly and dully, *Time dragged on.*

drag[2] *noun* 1 a hindrance; something boring. 2 (*informal*) women's clothes worn by men.

dragon *noun* 1 a mythological monster, usually with wings and able to breathe out fire. 2 a fierce person.

dragon-fly *noun* (*plural* **dragon-flies**) an insect with a long thin body and two pairs of transparent wings.

dragoon[1] *noun* a member of certain cavalry regiments.

dragoon[2] *verb* force someone into doing something.

drain[1] *noun* 1 a pipe or ditch etc. for taking away water or other liquid. 2 something that takes away strength or resources, *a drain on my energy.* **drainpipe** *noun*

drain[2] *verb* 1 take away water etc. through a drain. 2 flow or trickle away. 3 empty liquid out of a container. 4 take away strength etc.; exhaust. **drainage** *noun*

drake *noun* a male duck.

drama *noun* 1 a play. 2 writing or performing plays. 3 a series of exciting events, *the hijacking drama.*

dramatic *adjective* 1 of drama. 2 exciting; impressive, *a dramatic change.* **dramatics** *plural noun*, **dramatically** *adverb*

dramatis personae (*say* **dram**-a-tis per-**sohn**-I) *plural noun* the characters in a play.

dramatist *noun* a person who writes plays.

dramatize *verb* (**dramatized, dramatizing**) 1 make a story etc. into a play. 2 make something seem exciting. **dramatization** *noun*

drape *verb* (**draped, draping**) hang cloth etc. loosely over something.

draper *noun* a shopkeeper who sells cloth or clothes.

drapery *noun* (*plural* **draperies**) 1 a draper's stock. 2 cloth arranged in loose folds.

drastic *adjective* having a strong or violent effect. **drastically** *adverb*

draught (*say* drahft) *noun* 1 a current of usually cold air indoors. 2 a haul of fish in a net. 3 the depth of water needed to float a ship. 4 a swallow of liquid. **draughty** *adjective*

draughts *noun* a game played with 24 round pieces on a chess-board.

draughtsman *noun* (*plural* **draughtsmen**) 1 a person who makes drawings. 2 a piece used in the game of draughts.

draw[1] *verb* (**drew, drawn, drawing**) 1 produce a picture or outline by making marks on a surface. 2 pull. 3 take out, *draw water.* 4 attract, *The fair drew large crowds.* 5 end a game or contest with the same score on both sides. 6 move; come, *The ship drew nearer.* 7 make out by thinking, *draw conclusions.* 8 write out a cheque to be cashed.

draw[2] *noun* 1 the drawing of lots (see *lot* 2). 2 the drawing out of a gun etc., *He was quick on the draw.* 3 an attraction, *The tiger was the draw of the circus.* 4 a drawn game.
• USAGE: Do not confuse this word with *drawer.*

drawback *noun* a disadvantage.

drawbridge *noun* a bridge over a moat, hinged at one end so that it can be raised or lowered.

drawer *noun* 1 a sliding box-like compartment in a piece of furniture. 2 a person who draws something. 3 someone who draws (= writes out) a cheque.

drawing *noun* a picture or outline drawn.

drawing-pin *noun* a short pin with a flat top to be pressed with your thumb, used for fastening paper etc. to a surface.

drawl[1] *verb* speak very slowly or lazily.

drawl[2] *noun* a drawling way of speaking.

dray *noun* a strong low flat cart for carrying heavy loads.

dread[1] *noun* great fear.

dread[2] *verb* fear greatly.

dreadful *adjective* (*informal*) very bad, *dreadful weather.* **dreadfully** *adverb*

dreadlocks *plural noun* hair worn in many ringlets or plaits, especially by Rastafarians.

dream[1] *noun* 1 things a person seems to see while sleeping. 2 something imagined; an ambition or ideal, *dreams of glory.* **dreamy** *adjective*, **dreamily** *adverb*

dream[2] *verb* (**dreamt** or **dreamed, dreaming**) 1 have a dream or dreams. 2 have an ambition. 3 think something might happen, *I never dreamt she would leave.* **dreamer** *noun*

dreary *adjective* (**drearier, dreariest**) 1 dull; boring. 2 gloomy. **drearily** *adverb*, **dreariness** *noun*

dredge *verb* (**dredged, dredging**) drag something up, especially by scooping at the bottom of a river or the sea. **dredger** *noun*

dregs *plural noun* worthless bits that sink to the bottom of a liquid.

drench *verb* make wet all through.

dress[1] *noun* (*plural* **dresses**) 1 a woman's or girl's garment with a top part and skirt. 2 clothes; costume, *fancy dress.*

dress rehearsal a rehearsal at which the cast wear their costumes.

dress[2] *verb* 1 put clothes on. 2 arrange a display in a window etc.; decorate, *dress the shop windows.* 3 prepare food for cooking or eating, *dress a salad.* 4 put a dressing on a wound. **dresser** *noun*

dressage (*say* dress-ahzh) *noun* management of a horse to show its obedience and style.

dresser *noun* a sideboard with shelves at the top for dishes etc.

dressing *noun* 1 a bandage, plaster, or ointment etc. for a wound. 2 a sauce of oil, vinegar, etc. for a salad. 3 manure or other fertilizer for spreading on the soil.

dressing-gown *noun* a loose garment for wearing when you are not fully dressed.

dressmaker *noun* a person who makes dresses. **dressmaking** *noun*

dribble *verb* (**dribbled, dribbling**) 1 let saliva trickle out of your mouth. 2 move the ball forward in football or hockey with slight touches of your feet or stick.

drier *noun* a device for drying hair, laundry, etc.

drift[1] *verb* 1 be carried gently along by water or air. 2 move slowly and casually; live casually with no definite objective. **drifter** *noun*

drift[2] *noun* 1 a drifting movement. 2 a natural or artificial ford in a river. 3 a mass of snow or sand piled up by the wind. 4 the general meaning of a speech etc., *Did you get the drift of her talk?*

driftwood *noun* wood floating on the sea or washed ashore by it.

drill[1] *noun* 1 a tool for making holes; a machine for boring holes or wells. 2 repeated exercises in gymnastics, military training, etc.

drill[2] *verb* 1 make a hole etc. with a drill. 2 do repeated exercises; make people do exercises.

drily *adverb* in a dry way.

drink[1] *verb* (**drank, drunk, drinking**) 1 swallow liquid. 2 drink a lot of alcoholic drinks. **drinker** *noun*

drink[2] *noun* 1 a liquid for drinking; an amount of liquid swallowed. 2 an alcoholic drink.

drip[1] *verb* (**dripped, dripping**) fall or let something fall in drops.

drip[2] *noun* 1 liquid falling in drops; the sound it makes. 2 apparatus for dripping liquid into the veins of a sick person.

drip-dry *adjective* made of material that dries easily and does not need ironing.

dripping *noun* fat melted from roasted meat and allowed to set.

drive[1] *verb* (**drove, driven, driving**) 1 make something or someone move. 2 operate a motor vehicle or a train etc. 3 cause; compel, *Hunger drove them to steal.* 4 force someone into a state, *She is driving me crazy.* 5 rush; move rapidly, *Rain drove against the window.* **driver** *noun*

drive[2] *noun* 1 a journey in a vehicle. 2 a hard stroke in cricket or golf etc. 3 the transmitting of power to machinery, *four-wheel drive.* 4 energy; enthusiasm. 5 an organized effort, *a sales drive.* 6 a track

for vehicles through the grounds of a house.

drive-in *adjective* that you can use without getting out of your car.

drivel *noun* silly talk; nonsense.

drizzle *noun* very fine rain.

droëwors *noun* dried sausage.

droll *adjective* amusing in an odd way.

dromedary *noun* (*plural* **dromedaries**) a camel with one hump, bred for riding on.

drone[1] *verb* (**droned, droning**) 1 make a deep humming sound. 2 talk in a boring voice.

drone[2] *noun* 1 a droning sound. 2 a male bee.

drool *verb* dribble. **drool over** be very emotional about liking something.

droop *verb* hang down weakly.

drop[1] *noun* 1 a tiny amount of liquid. 2 a small round sweet. 3 a hanging ornament. 4 a fall; a decrease, *a drop in prices.* 5 a descent, *a sheer drop of 100 metres.*

drop[2] *verb* (**dropped, dropping**) 1 fall. 2 let something fall. 3 put down a passenger etc., *Drop me at the station.*

drop in visit someone casually.

drop out stop taking part in something. **drop-out** *noun*

droplet *noun* a small drop.

droppings *plural noun* the dung of birds and animals.

drostdy *noun* (*plural* **drostdies**) 1 the official residence of the landdrost in former times. 2 the landdrost's area of authority.

drought (*say* drout) *noun* a long period of dry weather.

drove *noun* a moving herd, flock, or crowd, *droves of people.*

drown *verb* 1 die or kill by suffocation under water. 2 flood; drench. 3 make so much noise that another sound cannot be heard.

drowsy *adjective* sleepy. **drowsily** *adverb*, **drowsiness** *noun*

drubbing *noun* a beating; a severe defeat.

drudge *noun* a person who does dull work. **drudgery** *noun*

drug[1] *noun* 1 a substance used in medicine. 2 a substance that affects your senses or your mind, *a drug addict.*

drug[2] *verb* (**drugged, drugging**) give a drug to someone, especially to make them unconscious.

Druid (*say* **droo**-id) *noun* a priest of an ancient Celtic religion in Britain and France.

drum[1] *noun* 1 a musical instrument made of a cylinder with a skin or parchment stretched over one or both ends. 2 a cylindrical object or container, *an oil drum*.

drum[2] *verb* (**drummed, drumming**) 1 play a drum or drums. 2 tap or thrum on something. **drummer** *noun*

drumstick *noun* 1 a stick for beating a drum. 2 the lower part of a cooked bird's leg.

drunk[1] *adjective* excited or helpless through drinking too much alcohol.

drunk[2] *noun* a person who is drunk.

drunkard *noun* a person who is often drunk.

drunken *adjective* 1 drunk, *a drunken man*. 2 caused by drinking alcohol.

dry[1] *adjective* (**drier, driest**) 1 without water or moisture. 2 thirsty. 3 boring; dull, *a dry lecture*. 4 (of remarks or humour) said in a matter-of-fact or ironical way, *dry wit*. **drily** *adverb*, **dryness** *noun*

dry cleaning a method of cleaning clothes etc. by a liquid that evaporates quickly.

dry dock a dock that can be emptied of water so that ships can float in and then be repaired.

dry ice solid carbon dioxide.

dry[2] *verb* (**dried, drying**) make or become dry.

dryad *noun* a wood-nymph.

dual *adjective* composed of two parts; double.

dual carriageway a road with a dividing strip between lanes of traffic in opposite directions.

dub[1] *verb* (**dubbed, dubbing**) 1 make someone a knight by touching him on the shoulder with a sword. 2 give a person or thing a nickname.

dub[2] *verb* (**dubbed, dubbing**) 1 change or add new sound to the sound-track of a film or magnetic tape. 2 copy a recording.

dubbeltjie *noun* a kind of weed with thorns, also called a duiweltjie.

dubbin *noun* thick grease used to soften leather and make it waterproof.

dubious (*say* **dew**-bee-us) *adjective* doubtful. **dubiously** *adverb*

ducal *adjective* of a duke.

duchess *noun* (*plural* **duchesses**) a duke's wife or widow.

duchy *noun* (*plural* **duchies**) the territory of a duke, *the duchy of Cornwall in England*.

duck[1] *noun* 1 a swimming bird with a flat beak; the female of this. 2 a batsman's score of nought at cricket. 3 a ducking movement.

duck[2] *verb* 1 bend down quickly to avoid something. 2 go or push quickly under water. 3 dodge; avoid doing something.

duckling *noun* a young duck.

duct *noun* a tube or channel through which liquid, gas, air, or cables can pass.

ductile *adjective* (of metal) able to be drawn out into fine strands.

dud *noun* (*slang*) something that is useless or a fake or fails to work.

dudgeon (*say* **duj**-on) *noun* indignation.

due[1] *adjective* 1 expected; scheduled to do something or to arrive, *The train is due in ten minutes*. 2 owing; needing to be paid. 3 that ought to be given; rightful, *Treat her with due respect*.

due to caused by.

● USAGE: Correct use is as in *His lateness was due to an accident*. Many people dislike the use of 'due to' without a preceding noun (e.g. 'lateness') to which it refers. It is best to avoid uses such as 'He was late, due to an accident' where there is no such noun. (Use *because of* or *owing to* instead.)

due[2] *adverb* exactly, *We sailed due east*.

due[3] *noun* 1 a person's right; something deserved; proper respect, *Give him his due*. 2 a fee, *harbour dues*.

duel *noun* a fight between two people, especially with pistols or swords. **duelling** *noun*, **duellist** *noun*

● USAGE: Do not confuse this word with *dual*.

duet *noun* a piece of music for two players or singers.

duffel coat *noun* a thick overcoat with a hood, fastened with toggles.

duffer *noun* a person who is stupid or not good at doing something.

dug-out *noun* **1** an underground shelter. **2** a canoe made by hollowing out a tree-trunk.

duiker *noun* a kind of small antelope which tends to move quickly into cover.

duiweltjie *noun* a dubbeltjie.

duke *noun* a member of the highest rank of nobility. **dukedom** *noun*

dulcet (*say* **dul**-sit) *adjective* sweet-sounding.

dulcimer *noun* a musical instrument with strings that are struck by two small hammers.

dull *adjective* **1** not bright or clear, *dull weather.* **2** stupid. **3** boring, *a dull concert.* **4** not sharp, *a dull pain; a dull thud.* **dully** *adverb*, **dullness** *noun*

duly *adverb* in the due or proper way.

dumb *adjective* **1** unable to speak; silent. **2** (*informal*) stupid. **dumbly** *adverb*, **dumbness** *noun*

dumbfound *verb* astonish; strike a person dumb with surprise.

dummy *noun* (*plural* **dummies**) **1** something made to look like a person or thing. **2** an imitation teat given to a baby to suck.

dump¹ *noun* **1** a place where something (especially rubbish) is left or stored. **2** (*informal*) a dull or unattractive place.

dump² *verb* **1** get rid of something that is not wanted. **2** put down carelessly.

dumpling *noun* a lump of dough cooked in a stew etc. or baked with fruit inside.

dumps *plural noun* (*informal*) low spirits, *in the dumps.*

dumpy *adjective* short and fat.

dunce *noun* a person who is slow at learning.

dune *noun* a mound of loose sand shaped by the wind.

dung *noun* solid waste matter excreted by an animal.

dungarees *plural noun* overalls made of thick strong cloth.

dung-beetle *noun* a beetle whose larvae grow in dung.

dungeon (*say* **dun**-jon) *noun* an under-ground cell for prisoners.

dunk *verb* dip something into liquid.

duodenum (*say* dew-o-**deen**-um) *noun* the part of the small intestine that is just below the stomach. **duodenal** *adjective*

dupe *verb* (**duped, duping**) deceive.

duplicate¹ *noun* **1** something that is exactly the same as something else. **2** an exact copy.

duplicate² *verb* (**duplicated, duplicating**) make or be a duplicate. **duplication** *noun*, **duplicator** *noun*

duplicity (*say* dew-**plis**-it-ee) *noun* deceitfulness.

durable *adjective* strong and likely to last. **durably** *adverb*, **durability** *noun*

duration *noun* the time something lasts.

duress (*say* dew-**ress**) *noun* the use of force or threats to get what you want.

during *preposition* while something else is going on.

dusk *noun* twilight in the evening.

dusky *adjective* dark; shadowy.

dust¹ *noun* tiny particles of earth or other solid material.

dust² *verb* **1** wipe away dust. **2** sprinkle with dust or something powdery, *The pancakes were dusted with sugar.*

dustbin *noun* a bin for household rubbish.

duster *noun* a cloth for dusting things.

dustman *noun* (*plural* **dustmen**) a person employed to empty dustbins and cart away rubbish.

dustpan *noun* a pan into which dust is brushed from a floor.

dusty *adjective* (**dustier, dustiest**) **1** covered with dust. **2** like dust.

dutiful *adjective* doing your duty; obedient. **dutifully** *adverb*

duty *noun* (*plural* **duties**) **1** what you ought to do or must do. **2** a task that must be done. **3** a tax charged on imports and on certain other things.

on duty actually doing what is your regular work.

duvet (*say* **doo**-vay) *noun* a kind of quilt used instead of other bedclothes.

dwarf¹ *noun* (*plural* **dwarfs**) a very small person or thing.

dwarf² *verb* make something seem small

by contrast, *The ocean liner dwarfed the tugs that were towing it.*

dwell *verb* (**dwelt, dwelling**) live somewhere. **dweller** *noun*

dwell on think or talk about something for a long time.

dwelling *noun* a house etc. to live in.

dwindle *verb* (**dwindled, dwindling**) get smaller gradually.

dye[1] *verb* (**dyed, dyeing**) colour something by putting it into a liquid. **dyer** *noun*

dye[2] *noun* a substance used to dye things.

dyke *noun* 1 a long wall or embankment to hold back water and prevent flooding. 2 a ditch for draining water from land.

dynamic *adjective* energetic; active. **dynamically** *adverb*

dynamite *noun* 1 a powerful explosive. 2 something likely to make people very excited or angry.

dynamo *noun* (*plural* **dynamos**) a machine that makes electricity.

dynasty (*say* din-a-stee) *noun* (*plural* **dynasties**) a succession of rulers all from the same family. **dynastic** *adjective*

dys- *prefix* bad; difficult.

dysentery (*say* dis-en-tree) *noun* a disease causing severe diarrhoea.

dyslexia (*say* dis-**leks**-ee-a) *noun* unusually great difficulty in being able to read and spell. **dyslexic** *adjective*

dyspepsia (*say* dis-**pep**-see-a) *noun* indigestion. **dyspeptic** *adjective*

Ee

E. *abbreviation* east; eastern.

e- *prefix* see **ex-**.

each *adjective* & *pronoun* every; every one, *each child; each of you.*

eager *adjective* strongly wanting to do something; enthusiastic. **eagerly** *adverb*, **eagerness** *noun*

eagle *noun* a large bird of prey with very strong sight.

ear[1] *noun* 1 the organ of the body that is used for hearing. 2 hearing-ability, *She has a good ear for music.*

ear[2] *noun* the spike of seeds at the top of a stalk of corn.

earache *noun* pain in the ear.

ear-drum *noun* a membrane in the ear that vibrates when sounds reach it.

earl *noun* a high-ranking member of the nobility. **earldom** *noun*

early *adjective* & *adverb* (**earlier, earliest**) 1 before the usual or expected time. 2 near the beginning, *early in the book.* **earliness** *noun*

earmark *verb* put aside for a particular purpose.

earn *verb* get something by working or in return for what you have done.

earnest *adjective* showing serious feelings or intentions. **earnestly** *adverb*, **earnestness** *noun*

earnings *plural noun* money earned.

earphone *noun* a listening device that fits over the ear.

earplug *noun* a piece of soft material that is put into the ear to keep out water, noise, etc.

earring *noun* an ornament that hangs from the ear.

earshot *noun* the distance within which a sound can be heard.

earth[1] *noun* 1 the planet (*Earth*) that we live on. 2 its surface; the ground; soil. 3 the hole where a fox or badger lives. 4 connection to the ground to complete an electrical circuit.

earth[2] *verb* connect an electrical circuit to the ground.

earthenware *noun* pottery made of coarse baked clay.

earthly *adjective* of this earth or our life on it.

earthquake *noun* a violent movement of part of the earth's surface.

earthworm *noun* a worm that lives in the soil.

earthy *adjective* like earth or soil.

earwig *noun* a crawling insect with pincers at the end of its body.

ease[1] *noun* freedom from trouble or effort or pain.

ease[2] *verb* (**eased, easing**) 1 make less painful or less tight or troublesome. 2 move gently or gradually, *ease it in.* **3** become less severe, *The pressure eased.*

easel *noun* a stand for supporting a blackboard or a painting.

easily *adverb* **1** without difficulty; with ease. **2** by far, *easily the best.* **3** very likely, *He could easily be lying.*

east¹ *noun* **1** the direction where the sun rises. **2** the eastern part of a country, city, etc.

east² *adjective* & *adverb* towards or in the east; coming from the east. **easterly** *adjective*, **eastern** *adjective*, **easterner** *noun*, **easternmost** *adjective*

Easter *noun* the Sunday (in March or April) when Christians commemorate the resurrection of Christ; the days around it.

eastward *adjective* & *adverb* towards the east. **eastwards** *adverb*

easy¹ *adjective* (**easier, easiest**) able to be done or used or understood without trouble. **easiness** *noun*

easy chair a comfortable armchair.

easy² *adverb* in an easy way; with ease; comfortably, *Take it easy!*

eat *verb* (**ate, eaten, eating**) **1** chew and swallow as food. **2** have a meal, *When do we eat?* **3** use up; destroy gradually, *Extra expenses ate up our savings.*

eatable *adjective* fit to be eaten.

eau-de-Cologne (*say* oh-de-kol-**ohn**) *noun* a perfume first made at Cologne in Germany.

eaves *plural noun* the overhanging edges of a roof.

eavesdrop *verb* (**eavesdropped, eavesdropping**) listen secretly to a private conversation. **eavesdropper** *noun*

ebb¹ *noun* **1** the movement of the tide when it is going out, away from the land. **2** a low point, *Our courage was at a low ebb.*

ebb² *verb* **1** flow away from the land. **2** weaken; become less, *strength ebbed.*

ebony *noun* a hard black wood.

eccentric (*say* ik-**sen**-trik) *adjective* behaving strangely or unusually. **eccentrically** *adverb*, **eccentricity** (*say* ek-sen-**triss**-it-ee) *noun*

ecclesiastical (*say* ik-lee-zee-**ast**-ik-al) *adjective* of the Church or the clergy.

echo¹ *noun* (*plural* **echoes**) a sound that is heard again as it is reflected off something.

echo² *verb* (**echoed, echoing**) **1** make an echo. **2** repeat a sound or saying.

éclair (*say* i-**klair**) *noun* a finger-shaped cake of pastry with a creamy filling.

eclipse¹ *noun* the blocking of the sun's or moon's light when the moon or the earth is in the way.

eclipse² *verb* (**eclipsed, eclipsing**) **1** block the light and cause an eclipse. **2** outshine, seem better or more important, *Her performance eclipsed all the others.*

ecology (*say* ee-**kol**-o-jee) *noun* the study of living things in relation to each other and to where they live. **ecological** *adjective*, **ecologically** *adverb*, **ecologist** *noun*

economic (*say* ee-kon-**om**-ik) *adjective* of economy or economics.

economical *adjective* using as little as possible. **economically** *adverb*

economics *noun* the study of how money is used and how goods and services are provided and used. **economist** *noun*

economize *verb* (**economized, economizing**) be economical; use or spend less.

economy *noun* (*plural* **economies**) **1** a country's or household's income (e.g. from what it sells or earns) and the way this is spent (e.g. on goods and services). **2** being economical. **3** a saving, *We made economies.*

ecosystem *noun* the living things in one place and their relationship to each other and to where they live.

ecstasy (*say* **ek**-sta-see) *noun* a feeling of great delight. **ecstatic** (*say* ik-**stat**-ik) *adjective*, **ecstatically** *adverb*

eczema (*say* **eks**-im-a) *noun* a skin disease causing rough itching patches.

eddy¹ *noun* (*plural* **eddies**) a swirling patch of water or air or smoke etc.

eddy² *verb* (**eddied, eddying**) swirl.

edge¹ *noun* **1** the part along the side or end of something. **2** the sharp part of a knife or axe or other cutting-instrument.
be on edge be tense and irritable.

edge² *verb* (**edged, edging**) **1** be the edge or border of something. **2** put a border on, *edged with lace.* **3** move gradually, *He edged away.*

edgeways *adverb* with the edge forwards or outwards.

edgy *adjective* tense and irritable. **edginess** *noun*

edible *adjective* suitable for eating, not poisonous, *edible fruits.*

edict (*say* **ee**-dikt) *noun* an official command.

edifice (*say* **ed**-if-iss) *noun* a large building.

edify *verb* (**edified, edifying**) be an improving influence on a person's mind. **edification** *noun*

edit *verb* (**edited, editing**) 1 be the editor of a newspaper or other publication. 2 make written material ready for publishing. 3 choose and put the parts of a film or tape-recording etc. into order.

edition *noun* 1 the form in which something is published, *a paperback edition.* 2 all the copies of a book etc. issued at the same time, *the first edition.*

editor *noun* 1 the person in charge of a newspaper or a section of it. 2 a person who edits something.

editorial[1] *adjective* of editing or editors.

editorial[2] *noun* a newspaper article giving the editor's comments on something.

educate *verb* (**educated, educating**) provide with education. **educative** *adjective*, **educator** *noun*

education *noun* the process of training people's minds and abilities so that they acquire knowledge and develop skills. **educational** *adjective*, **educationally** *adverb*, **educationist** *noun*

eel *noun* a long fish that looks like a snake.

eerie *adjective* (**eerier, eeriest**) strange in a frightening or mysterious way. **eerily** *adverb*, **eeriness** *noun*

ef- *prefix* see **ex-**.

efface *verb* (**effaced, effacing**) wipe or rub out. **effacement** *noun*

effect[1] *noun* 1 a change produced by an action or cause; a result. 2 an impression produced, *a cheerful effect.*

effect[2] *verb* cause; produce, *We want to effect a change.*
• USAGE: Do not confuse with *affect.*

effective *adjective* producing an effect; achieving goals. **effectively** *adverb*,

effectiveness *noun*

effectual *adjective* producing the result desired. **effectually** *adverb*

effeminate *adjective* (of a man) having qualities that are thought to be feminine. **effeminacy** *noun*

effervesce (*say* ef-er-**vess**) *verb* (**effervesced, effervescing**) give off bubbles of gas; fizz. **effervescent** *adjective*, **effervescence** *noun*

efficacious (*say* ef-ik-**ay**-shus) *adjective* able to produce the result desired. **efficacy** (*say* **ef**-ik-a-see) *noun*

efficient *adjective* doing work well; producing the maximum output from the minimum input. **efficiently** *adverb*, **efficiency** *noun*

effigy *noun* (*plural* **effigies**) a model or sculptured figure.

effort *noun* 1 the use of energy; the energy used. 2 something difficult or tiring. 3 an attempt, *This painting is a good effort.*

effortless *adjective* done with little or no effort. **effortlessly** *adverb*

effusive *adjective* making a great show of affection or enthusiasm. **effusively** *adverb*, **effusiveness** *noun*

e.g. *abbreviation* for example.

egalitarian (*say* ig-al-it-**air**-ee-an) *adjective* believing that everybody is equal and that nobody should be given special privileges.

egg[1] *noun* 1 a more or less round object produced by the female of birds, fishes, reptiles, and insects, which may develop into a new individual if fertilized. 2 a hen's or duck's egg used as food.

egg[2] *verb* encourage with taunts or dares etc., *We egged him on.*

egg-plant *noun* a plant with dark-purple fruit used as a vegetable, also called a brinjal or an aubergine.

ego (*say* **eeg**-oh) *noun* (*plural* **egos**) a person's self or self-respect.

eGoli (also **Egoli**) *noun* Johannesburg, 'a place of gold'.

egotist (*say* **eg**-oh-tist) *noun* a conceited person who is always talking about himself or herself. **egotism** *noun*, **egotistic** *adjective*

Eid (*say* eed) *noun* Eid-ul-Fitr, the Muslim festival that celebrates the end of the Ramadan fast.

eiderdown *noun* a quilt stuffed with soft material.

eight *noun* & *adjective* the number 8; one more than seven. **eighth** *adjective* & *noun*

eighteen *noun* & *adjective* the number 18; one more than seventeen. **eighteenth** *adjective* & *noun*

eighty *noun* & *adjective* (*plural* **eighties**) the number 80; eight times ten. **eightieth** *adjective* & *noun*

eina *interjection* an expression of sudden pain.

eisteddfod (*say* I-**sted**-fod) *noun* a festival for musical competitions, dance, etc.

either[1] *adjective* & *pronoun* 1 one or the other of two, *Either team can win; either of them.* 2 both of two, *There are fields on either side of the river.*

either[2] *adverb* also; similarly, *If you won't go, I won't either.*

either[3] *conjunction* (used with *or*) the first of two possibilities, *He is either ill or drunk. Either come right in or go away.*

eject *verb* 1 send out forcefully. 2 expel; compel to leave. **ejection** *noun*, **ejector** *noun*

eke (*say* eek) *verb* (**eked, eking**) **eke out** manage to make something enough.

elaborate[1] (*say* il-ab-er-at) *adjective* having many parts or details; complicated. **elaborately** *adverb*, **elaborateness** *noun*

elaborate[2] (*say* il-ab-er-ayt) *verb* (**elaborated, elaborating**) describe or work out in detail. **elaboration** *noun*

eland *noun* the largest kind of South African antelope.

elapse *verb* (**elapsed, elapsing**) (of time) pass.

elastic[1] *noun* cord or material woven with strands of rubber etc. so that it can stretch.

elastic[2] *adjective* able to be stretched or squeezed and then go back to its original length or shape. **elasticity** *noun*

elated *adjective* with raised spirits, feeling very pleased. **elation** *noun*

elbow[1] *noun* the joint in the middle of the arm.

elbow-grease (*informal*) hard physical work.

elbow[2] *verb* push with the elbow.

elder[1] *adjective* older, *my elder brother.*

elder[2] *noun* 1 an older person, *Respect your elders!* 2 an official in certain Churches.

elder[3] *noun* a tree with white flowers and black berries. **elderberry** *noun*

elderly *adjective* rather old.

eldest *adjective* oldest.

elect *verb* 1 choose by voting. 2 choose to do something; decide, *We elected to go to the beach.*

election *noun* electing; the process of electing Members of Parliament.

elector *noun* a person who has the right to vote in an election. **electoral** *adjective*

electorate *noun* all the electors.

electric *adjective* 1 of or worked by electricity. 2 causing sudden excitement, *The news had an electric effect.* **electrical** *adjective*, **electrically** *adverb*

electrician *noun* a person whose job is to deal with electrical equipment.

electricity *noun* a form of energy carried by certain particles of matter (electrons and protons), used for lighting and heating and for making machines work.

electrify *verb* (**electrified, electrifying**) 1 give an electric charge to something. 2 supply with electric power; cause to work with electricity. 3 thrill with sudden excitement, *The audience was electrified.* **electrification** *noun*

electro- *prefix* of or using electricity.

electrocute *verb* (**electrocuted, electrocuting**) kill by electricity. **electrocution** *noun*

electrode *noun* a solid conductor through which electricity enters or leaves a vacuum tube.

electrolysis (*say* e-lek-**tro**-li-sis) *noun* breaking down a substance into simpler substances by means of an electric current.

electrolyte (*say* e-lek-tro-lyt) *noun* a liquid or solution which can conduct an electric current.

electromagnet *noun* a magnet worked by

electricity. **electromagnetic** *adjective*

electron *noun* a particle of matter with a negative electric charge.

electronic *adjective* produced or worked by a flow of electrons. **electronically** *adverb*

electronics *noun* the use or study of electronic devices.

electroscope *noun* a device that measures an electric charge.

elegant *adjective* graceful and dignified. **elegantly** *adverb*, **elegance** *noun*

elegy (*say* el-ij-ee) *noun* (*plural* **elegies**) a sorrowful or serious poem.

element *noun* 1 each of the parts that make up a whole thing. 2 each of about 100 substances composed of atoms that have the same number of protons. 3 a basic or elementary principle, *the elements of algebra*. 4 a wire or coil that gives out heat in an electric fire or cooker etc. 5 a suitable or satisfying environment, *Water is a fish's element*.

the elements the forces of weather, such as rain, wind, and cold.

elementary *adjective* dealing with the simplest stages of something; easy.

elephant *noun* a very large animal with a trunk and tusks.

elephantine (*say* el-if-**ant**-I'n) *adjective* very large; clumsy.

elevate *verb* (**elevated, elevating**) lift up; put high up. **elevation** *noun*

elevator *noun* 1 something that raises things. 2 (*American*) a lift.

eleven *adjective* & *noun* the number 11; one more than ten. **eleventh** *adjective* & *noun*

elf¹ *noun* (*plural* **elves**) (in fairy-tales) a small being with magic powers. **elfin** *adjective*

elf² *noun* (*plural* **elf**) a kind of sea-fish, also called shad.

elicit (*say* ill-**iss**-it) *verb* draw out information by reasoning or questioning.

eligible (*say* el-ij-ib-ul) *adjective* qualified or suitable for something. **eligibility** *noun*

eliminate *verb* (**eliminated, eliminating**) get rid of; remove. **elimination** *noun*

elision (*say* il-**lizh**-on) *noun* omitting part of a word in pronouncing it, e.g. in saying

I'm for *I am*.

élite (*say* i-**leet**) *noun* a group of people given privileges which are not given to others.

elixir (*say* il-**iks**-er) *noun* a sweetened and flavoured liquid medicine.

Elizabethan (*say* il-iz-a-**beeth**-an) *adjective* of the time of Queen Elizabeth I of England (1558–1603). **Elizabethan** *noun*

elk *noun* a large kind of deer.

ellipse (*say* il-**ips**) *noun* an oval shape.

elliptical (*say* il-**ip**-tik-al) *adjective* 1 shaped like an ellipse. 2 with some words omitted, *an elliptical phrase*. **elliptically** *adverb*

elm *noun* a tall tree with rough leaves.

elocution (*say* el-o-**kew**-shon) *noun* speaking clearly.

elongated *adjective* made longer; lengthened. **elongation** *noun*

elope *verb* (**eloped, eloping**) run away secretly with a lover. **elopement** *noun*

eloquent *adjective* speaking fluently and expressing ideas vividly. **eloquently** *adverb*, **eloquence** *noun*

else *adverb* 1 besides; other, *Nobody else knows*. 2 otherwise; if not, *Run or else you'll be late*.

elsewhere *adverb* somewhere else.

elucidate (*say* il-**oo**-sid-ayt) *verb* (**elucidated, elucidating**) make something clear by explaining it. **elucidation** *noun*

elude (*say* il-**ood**) *verb* (**eluded, eluding**) avoid being caught by someone, *The jackal eluded the dogs*. **elusive** *adjective*

em- *prefix* see **en-**.

emaciated (*say* im-**ay**-see-ay-tid) *adjective* very thin from illness or starvation. **emaciation** *noun*

e-mail *abbreviation* electronic mail (messages sent from one user to another by means of a computer network).

emanate (*say* **em**-an-ayt) *verb* (**emanated, emanating**) come from a source, *Light emanated from a candle*.

emancipate (*say* im-**an**-sip-ayt) *verb* (**emancipated, emancipating**) set free from slavery or other restraints. **emancipation** *noun*

embalm *verb* preserve a corpse from decay

by using spices or chemicals.

embankment *noun* a long bank of earth or stone to hold back water or support a road or railway.

embargo *noun* (*plural* **embargoes**) a ban.

embark *verb* put or go on board a ship or aircraft. **embarkation** *noun*
embark on begin, *They embarked on a dangerous exercise.*

embarrass *verb* make someone feel awkward or ashamed. **embarrassment** *noun*

embassy *noun* (*plural* **embassies**)
1 an ambassador and his or her staff.
2 the building where they work.

embed *verb* (**embedded, embedding**) fix firmly in something solid.

embellish *verb* ornament something; add details to it. **embellishment** *noun*

embers *plural noun* small pieces of glowing coal or wood in a dying fire.

embezzle *verb* (**embezzled, embezzling**) take dishonestly money that was left in your care. **embezzlement** *noun*

emblazon *verb* ornament with heraldic or other emblems.

emblem *noun* a symbol; a device representing something, *The crown is a royal emblem.* **emblematic** *adjective*

embody *verb* (**embodied, embodying**)
1 express principles or ideas in a visible form, *The house embodies our idea of a modern home.* **2** incorporate; include, *Parts of the old treaty are embodied in the new one.* **embodiment** *noun*

emboss *verb* decorate with a raised design.

embrace[1] *verb* (**embraced, embracing**) hold closely in your arms.

embrace[2] *noun* embracing; a hug.

embrocation *noun* a lotion for rubbing on parts of the body that ache.

embroider *verb* **1** ornament cloth with needlework. **2** add made-up details to a story to make it more interesting. **embroidery** *noun*

embroil *verb* involve in an argument or quarrel.

embryo (*say* em-bree-oh) *noun* (*plural* **embryos**) **1** a baby or young animal as it starts to grow in the womb; a young bird

growing in an egg. **2** anything in its earliest stages of development. **embryonic** (*say* em-bree-**on**-ik) *adjective*

emerald *noun* **1** a bright-green precious stone. **2** its colour.

emerge *verb* (**emerged, emerging**) come out; appear. **emergence** *noun*, **emergent** *adjective*

emergency *noun* (*plural* **emergencies**) a sudden serious happening needing prompt action.

emery-board *noun* a small strip of wood or cardboard with a gritty coating like sandpaper, used for filing the fingernails.

emetic (*say* im-**et**-ik) *noun* a medicine used to make a person sick.

emigrate *verb* (**emigrated, emigrating**) leave your own country and go and live in another. **emigration** *noun*, **emigrant** *noun*
● USAGE: People are *emigrants* from the country they leave and *immigrants* in the country where they settle.

eminence *noun* **1** being eminent; distinction. **2** a piece of ground; a hill.
His Eminence a cardinal's title.

eminent *adjective* famous; distinguished; outstanding. **eminently** *adverb*

emir (*say* em-**eer**) *noun* a Muslim ruler.

emit *verb* (**emitted, emitting**) send out (light, heat, fumes, etc.). **emission** *noun*, **emitter** *noun*

emolument (*say* im-**ol**-yoo-ment) *noun* payment for work; a salary.

emotion *noun* a strong feeling in the mind, such as love or hate. **emotional** *adjective*, **emotionally** *adverb*

emotive *adjective* causing emotion, *an emotive issue.*

empathy *noun* identifying yourself mentally with another person and understanding him or her.

emperor *noun* a man who rules an empire.

emphasis (*say* em-fa-sis) *noun* special importance given to something.

emphasize *verb* (**emphasized, emphasizing**) put emphasis on something.

emphatic (*say* im-**fat**-ik) *adjective* using emphasis. **emphatically** *adverb*

empire *noun* **1** a group of countries controlled by one person or government.

2 a set of shops or firms under one control, *a supermarket empire.*

employ *verb* **1** pay a person to work for you. **2** make use of, *Our doctor employs the most modern methods.* **employer** *noun,* **employment** *noun*

employee *noun* a person employed by someone (who is the *employer*).

emporium (*say* em-**por**-ee-um) *noun* a large shop.

empower *verb* give someone the power to do something; authorize.

empress *noun* (*plural* **empresses**) **1** a woman who rules an empire. **2** an emperor's wife.

empty[1] *adjective* **1** with nothing in it. **2** with nobody in it. **3** with no meaning or no effect, *empty promises.* **emptily** *adverb,* **emptiness** *noun*

empty[2] *verb* (**emptied, emptying**) make or become empty.

emu *noun* (*plural* **emus**) a large Australian bird rather like an ostrich.

emulate *verb* (**emulated, emulating**) try to do as well as someone or something, especially by imitating them, *He is emulating his father.* **emulation** *noun*

emulsify *verb* (**emulsified, emulsifying**) make into an emulsion.

emulsion *noun* **1** a creamy or slightly oily liquid. **2** the coating on photographic film which is sensitive to light.

en- *prefix* (changing to **em-** before words beginning with *b, m,* or *p*) in; into; on.

enable *verb* (**enabled, enabling**) give the means or ability to do something.

enact *verb* **1** make into a law by a formal process, *Parliament enacted new laws against drugs.* **2** perform, *enact a play.* **enactment** *noun*

enamel[1] *noun* **1** a shiny substance for coating metal. **2** paint that dries hard and shiny. **3** the shiny surface of teeth.

enamel[2] *verb* (**enamelled, enamelling**) coat or decorate with enamel.

enamoured (*say* in-**am**-erd) *adjective* in love with someone.

encamp *verb* settle in a camp.

encampment *noun* a camp.

encase *verb* (**encased, encasing**) enclose in a case.

enchant *verb* **1** put under a magic spell. **2** fill with intense delight. **enchanter** *noun,* **enchantment** *noun,* **enchantress** *noun*

encircle *verb* (**encircled, encircling**) surround. **encirclement** *noun*

enclose *verb* (**enclosed, enclosing**) **1** put a wall or fence round; shut in on all sides. **2** put into a box or envelope etc., *enclose a cheque.*

enclosure *noun* **1** enclosing. **2** an enclosed area. **3** something enclosed with a letter or parcel.

encompass *verb* **1** surround. **2** contain.

encore (*say* on-kor) *noun* an extra item performed at a concert etc. after previous items have been applauded.

encounter[1] *verb* **1** meet someone unexpectedly. **2** experience, *We encountered some difficulties.*

encounter[2] *noun* **1** an unexpected meeting. **2** a battle.

encourage *verb* (**encouraged, encouraging**) **1** give confidence or hope; hearten. **2** try to persuade; urge. **3** stimulate; help to develop, *Encourage healthy eating.* **encouragement** *noun*

encroach *verb* intrude upon someone's rights; go further than the proper limits, *The extra work would encroach on their free time.* **encroachment** *noun*

encrust *verb* cover with a crust or layer. **encrustation** *noun*

encumber *verb* be a burden to; hamper. **encumbrance** *noun*

encyclopaedia *noun* a book or set of books containing all kinds of information. **encyclopaedic** *adjective*

end[1] *noun* **1** the last part of something. **2** the half of a sports pitch or court defended or occupied by one team or player. **3** destruction; death, *She had a tragic end.* **4** purpose, *She did it to gain her own ends.*

end[2] *verb* bring or come to an end.

endanger *verb* cause danger to. **endangered species** a kind of animal, plant, etc. that is in danger of extinction.

endear *verb* cause to be loved, *She endeared herself to us all.* **endearing** *adjective*

endeavour[1] (*say* in-**dev**-er) *verb* attempt.
endeavour[2] *noun* an attempt.
endemic (*say* en-**dem**-ik) *adjective*
(of a disease) often found in a certain area or
group of people.
ending *noun* the last part.
endless *adjective* 1 never stopping.
2 with the ends joined to make a continuous strip for use in machinery etc.,
an endless belt. **endlessly** *adverb*
endorse *verb* (**endorsed, endorsing**)
1 sign your name on the back of a cheque or
document. 2 make an official entry on a
licence about an offence committed by its
holder. 3 confirm or give your approval to
something, *Famous people often endorse
products in advertisements.* **endorsement**
noun
endow *verb* 1 provide a source of income
to establish something, *She endowed a
scholarship.* 2 provide with an ability or
quality, *He was endowed with great talent.*
endowment *noun*
endure *verb* (**endured, enduring**) 1 suffer
or put up with pain or hardship etc.
2 continue to exist; last, *This custom has
endured for centuries.* **endurable** *adjective,*
endurance *noun*
enemy *noun* (*plural* **enemies**) 1 one who
hates and opposes or seeks to harm
another. 2 a nation or army etc. at war with
another.
energetic *adjective* full of energy.
energetically *adverb*
energy *noun* 1 strength to do things,
liveliness. 2 the ability of matter or radiation
to do work, *electrical energy.*
enfold *verb* 1 wrap up. 2 clasp.
enforce *verb* (**enforced, enforcing**)
compel people to obey a law or rule.
enforcement *noun,* **enforceable** *adjective*
enfranchise *verb* (**enfranchised, enfran-
chising**) give the right to vote in elections.
enfranchisement *noun*
engage *verb* (**engaged, engaging**)
1 arrange to employ or use, *Engage a typist.*
2 occupy the attention of, *They engaged her
in conversation.* 3 begin a battle with, *We
engaged the enemy.* 4 (of parts of a machine
etc.) fit or lock together, *One cog-wheel*

engages with another.
engaged *adjective* 1 having promised to
marry somebody. 2 in use; occupied.
engagement *noun* 1 engaging something.
2 a promise to marry somebody.
3 an arrangement to meet somebody or
do something, *a previous engagement.*
4 a battle.
engaging *adjective* attractive; charming.
engine *noun* 1 a machine that provides
power. 2 a vehicle that pulls a railway train,
a locomotive.
engineer[1] *noun* an expert in engineering.
engineer[2] *verb* plan and construct or
cause to happen, *He engineered a meeting
between them.*
engineering *noun* the design and building
or control of machinery or of structures
such as roads and bridges.
engrave *verb* (**engraved, engraving**) carve
words or lines etc. on a surface. **engraver**
noun, **engraving** *noun*
engross *verb* occupy a person's whole
attention, *He was engrossed in his book.*
engulf *verb* flow over and cover; swamp.
enhance *verb* (**enhanced, enhancing**)
make a thing more attractive; increase its
value. **enhancement** *noun*
enigma (*say* in-**ig**-ma) *noun* something
very difficult to understand; a puzzle.
enigmatic (*say* en-ig-**mat**-ik) *adjective*
mysterious and puzzling. **enigmatically**
adverb
enjoy *verb* get pleasure from something.
enjoyable *adjective,* **enjoyment** *noun*
enkosi (*say* en-**ko**-see) *interjection*
thank you.
enlarge *verb* (**enlarged, enlarging**) make
or become bigger. **enlargement** *noun*
enlighten *verb* give knowledge to a person,
inform. **enlightenment** *noun*
enlist *verb* 1 join the armed forces. 2 obtain
someone's support or services etc., *enlist
their help.* **enlistment** *noun*
enliven *verb* make more lively.
enlivenment *noun*
enmity *noun* being somebody's enemy;
hostility.
enormity *noun* (*plural* **enormities**) 1 great
wickedness, *the enormity of this crime.*

2 great size; hugeness, *the enormity of their task.*
• USAGE: Many people regard the use of sense 2 as incorrect. It is best to avoid it and use *magnitude.*

enormous *adjective* very large; huge. **enormously** *adverb*, **enormousness** *noun*

enough *adjective* (e.g. 'enough food'), *noun* (e.g. 'I have had enough'), & *adverb* (e.g. 'Are you warm enough?') as much or as many as necessary.

enquire *verb* (**enquired, enquiring**) ask, *He enquired if I was well.* **enquiry** *noun*
• USAGE: See the note under *inquire.*

enrage *verb* (**enraged, enraging**) make someone very angry.

enrapture *verb* (**enraptured, enrapturing**) fill someone with intense delight.

enrich *verb* make richer. **enrichment** *noun*

enrol *verb* (**enrolled, enrolling**) **1** become a member of a society etc. **2** make into a member. **enrolment** *noun*

ensconce *verb* (**ensconced, ensconcing**) settle comfortably, *ensconced in a chair.*

ensemble (*say* on-**somb**l) *noun* **1** a group of things that go together. **2** a group of musicians.

enshrine *verb* (**enshrined, enshrining**) keep as if in a shrine, *His memory is enshrined in our hearts.*

ensign *noun* a military or naval flag.

enslave *verb* (**enslaved, enslaving**) make a slave of; force into slavery. **enslavement** *noun*

ensue *verb* (**ensued, ensuing**) happen afterwards or as a result.

ensure *verb* (**ensured, ensuring**) make certain of; guarantee, *Good food will ensure good health.*
• USAGE: Do not confuse with *insure.*

entail *verb* make necessary, involve, *This plan entails danger.* **entailment** *noun*

entangle *verb* (**entangled, entangling**) tangle. **entanglement** *noun*

entente (*say* on-**tont**) *noun* a friendly understanding between countries.

enter *verb* **1** come in; go in. **2** put into a list or book. **3** register as a competitor.

enterprise *noun* **1** being enterprising; adventurous spirit. **2** an undertaking or

project. **3** business activity, *private enterprise.*

enterprising *adjective* willing to undertake new or adventurous projects.

entertain *verb* **1** amuse. **2** have people as guests and give them food and drink. **3** consider, *He refused to entertain the idea.* **entertainer** *noun*

entertainment *noun* **1** entertaining; being entertained. **2** something performed before an audience to amuse or interest them.

enthral (*say* in-**thrawl**) *verb* (**enthralled, enthralling**) hold spellbound; fascinate.

enthusiasm *noun* a strong liking, interest, or excitement. **enthusiast** *noun*

enthusiastic *adjective* full of enthusiasm. **enthusiastically** *adverb*

entice *verb* (**enticed, enticing**) attract or persuade by offering something pleasant. **enticement** *noun*

entire *adjective* whole, complete. **entirely** *adverb*

entirety (*say* int-**I**-rit-ee) *noun* completeness; the total.
in its entirety in its complete form.

entitle *verb* (**entitled, entitling**) give the right to have something, *This coupon entitles you to a ticket.* **entitlement** *noun*

entitled *adjective* having as a title.

entomb (*say* in-**toom**) *verb* place in a tomb. **entombment** *noun*

entomology (*say* en-tom-**ol**-ojee) *noun* the study of insects. **entomologist** *noun*

entrails *plural noun* the intestines.

entrance¹ (*say* **en**-trans) *noun* **1** the way into a place. **2** entering, *Her entrance is the signal for applause.*

entrance² (*say* in-**trahns**) *verb* (**entranced, entrancing**) fill with intense delight; enchant.

entrant *noun* someone who enters for an examination or contest etc.

entreat *verb* request earnestly; beg.

entreaty *noun* an earnest request.

entrench *verb* **1** fix or establish firmly, *These ideas are entrenched in his mind.* **2** settle in a well-defended position. **entrenchment** *noun*

entrepreneur (*say* on-trop-a-**nur**) *noun* a person who has resourcefulness, imagination, and energy, and who applies these in setting up a business. **entrepreneurial** *adjective*, **entrepreneurship** *noun*

entrust *verb* place a person or thing in someone's care.

entry *noun* (*plural* **entries**) 1 an entrance. 2 something entered in a list or in a diary etc.

entwine *verb* (**entwined, entwining**) twine round.

enumerate *verb* (**enumerated, enumerating**) count; list one by one.

envelop (*say* en-**vel**-op) *verb* (**enveloped, enveloping**) wrap thoroughly.

envelope (*say* **en**-vel-ohp) *noun* a wrapper or covering, especially a folded cover for a letter.

enviable *adjective* likely to be envied.

envious *adjective* feeling envy. **enviously** *adverb*

environment *noun* surroundings, especially as they affect people's lives. **environmental** *adjective*

environmentalist *noun* a person who wishes to protect or improve the environment.

environs (*say* in-**vy**-ronz) *plural noun* the surrounding districts, *They all lived in the environs of Soweto.*

envisage (*say* in-**viz**-ij) *verb* (**envisaged, envisaging**) picture in the mind; imagine as being possible, *It is difficult to envisage such a change.*

envoy *noun* an official representative, especially one sent by one government to another.

envy[1] *noun* 1 a feeling of discontent aroused when someone possesses things that others would like to have for themselves. 2 something causing this, *Their car is the envy of all their friends.*

envy[2] *verb* (**envied, envying**) feel envy towards someone.

enzyme *noun* a kind of substance that assists chemical processes, but does not itself change.

epaulette (*say* ep-al-et) *noun* an ornamental flap on the shoulder of a coat.

ephemeral (*say* if-**em**-er-al) *adjective* lasting only a very short time.

epi- *prefix* on; above; in addition.

epic *noun* 1 a long poem or story about heroic deeds or history. 2 a spectacular film.

epicentre *noun* the point where an earthquake reaches the earth's surface.

epidemic *noun* an outbreak of a disease that spreads quickly among the people of an area.

epidermis *noun* the outer layer of the skin.

epiglottis *noun* a piece of tissue at the back of the tongue which covers the windpipe during swallowing.

epigram *noun* a short witty saying.

epilepsy *noun* a disease of the nervous system, causing convulsions. **epileptic** *adjective & noun*

epilogue (*say* **ep**-il-og) *noun* a short section at the end of a book or play etc.

Epiphany (*say* ip-**if**-an-ee) *noun* a Christian festival on 6 January, commemorating the showing of the infant Christ to the 'wise men' from the East.

epiphyte (*say* **ep**-i-fyt) *noun* a plant which uses the stems and branches of other plants for support, but is not a parasite.

episcopal (*say* ip-**iss**-kop-al) *adjective* 1 of a bishop or bishops. 2 (of a Church) governed by bishops.

episode *noun* 1 one event in a series of happenings. 2 one programme in a radio or television serial.

epistle *noun* a letter, especially one forming part of the New Testament.

epitaph *noun* words written on a tomb or describing a person who has died.

epithelium *noun* (*plural* **epitheliums** or **epithelia**) a layer of tissues that covers the surface of the body and the organs of the body.

epithet *noun* an adjective; words expressing something special about a person or thing, e.g. 'the Great' in *Alfred the Great.*

epoch (*say* **ee**-pok) *noun* an era. **epoch-making** *adjective* very important.

equable (*say* **ek**-wa-bul) *adjective* steady; calm, *She has an equable manner.*

equal[1] *adjective* 1 the same in amount, size, or value etc. 2 having the necessary strength, courage, or ability etc., *She was equal to the task.* **equally** *adverb*

equal² *noun* a person or thing that is equal to another, *She has no equal.*

equal³ *verb* (**equalled, equalling**) be the same in amount, size, or value etc.

equality *noun* being equal.

equalize *verb* (**equalized, equalizing**) make things equal. **equalization** *noun*

equalizer *noun* a goal or point that makes the score equal.

equanimity (*say* ekwa-**nim**-it-ee) *noun* calmness of mind or temper.

equate *verb* (**equated, equating**) say things are equal or equivalent.

equation *noun* a statement that two amounts etc. are equal, e.g. $3 + 4 = 2 + 5.$

equator *noun* an imaginary line round the earth at an equal distance from the North and South Poles.

equatorial (*say* ek-wa-**tor**-ee-al) *adjective* of or near the equator.

equestrian (*say* ik-**wes**-tree-an) *adjective* of horse-riding.

equi- *prefix* equal; equally.

equilateral (*say* ee-kwi-**lat**-er-al) *adjective* (of a triangle) having all sides equal.

equilibrium (*say* ee-kwi-**lib**-ree-um) *noun* balance, being balanced.

equine (*say* **ek**-wyn) *adjective* of or like a horse.

equinox (*say* **ek**-win-oks) *noun* (*plural* **equinoxes**) the time of year when day and night are equal in length (about 20 March in autumn, about 22 September in spring). **equinoctial** *adjective*

equip *verb* (**equipped, equipping**) supply with what is needed.

equipment *noun* the things needed for a particular purpose.

equity (*say* **ek**-wit-ee) *noun* fairness, justice. **equitable** *adjective*

equivalent *adjective* equal in importance, meaning, value, etc. **equivalence** *noun*

equivocal (*say* ik-**wiv**-ok-al) *adjective* 1 able to be interpreted in two ways, ambiguous. 2 questionable, suspicious, *an equivocal character.* **equivocally** *adverb*

era (*say* **eer**-a) *noun* a period of history.

eradicate *verb* (**eradicated, eradicating**) get rid of something; remove all traces of it. **eradication** *noun*

erase *verb* (**erased, erasing**) 1 rub out. 2 wipe out a recording on magnetic tape. **eraser** *noun*

erasure *noun* 1 erasing. 2 the place where something has been erased.

ere (*say* air) *preposition* & *conjunction* (*old use*) before.

erect¹ *adjective* standing on end; upright.

erect² *verb* set up; build. **erection** *noun*, **erector** *noun*

erf *noun* (*plural* **erven**) a building plot in an urban area.

erica *noun* a kind of shrub with small leaves and bell-shaped flowers.

ermine *noun* 1 a kind of weasel with brown fur that turns white in winter. 2 this valuable white fur.

erode *verb* (**eroded, eroding**) wear away, *Water eroded the rocks.* **erosion** *noun*

erotic *adjective* arousing sexual feelings. **erotically** *adverb*

err (*say* er) *verb* 1 make a mistake. (Compare *error.*) 2 do wrong.

errand *noun* a short journey to take a message or fetch goods etc.

errant (*say* **e**-rant) *adjective* 1 misbehaving. 2 wandering; travelling in search of adventure, *a knight errant.*

erratic (*say* ir-**at**-ik) *adjective* not reliable; not regular. **erratically** *adverb*

erroneous (*say* ir-**oh**-nee-us) *adjective* incorrect. **erroneously** *adverb*

error *noun* a mistake.

erudite (*say* **e**-rew-dyt) *adjective* having great knowledge or learning. **eruditely** *adverb*, **erudition** *noun*

erupt *verb* 1 burst out. 2 (of a volcano) shoot out lava. **eruption** *noun*

escalate *verb* (**escalated, escalating**) make or become greater or more serious, *The riots escalated into a war.* **escalation** *noun*

escalator *noun* a staircase with an endless line of steps moving up or down.

escapade (*say* eska-**payd**) *noun* a reckless adventure; a piece of mischief.

escape¹ *verb* (**escaped, escaping**) 1 get yourself free; get out or away. 2 avoid something, *He escaped punishment.*

escape² *noun* 1 escaping. 2 a way to

escape, *a fire-escape.*

escapist *noun* a person who likes to avoid thinking about serious matters by occupying his or her mind in entertainments, daydreams, etc. **escapism** *noun*

escarpment *noun* a steep slope at the edge of some high level ground.

escort[1] (*say* ess-kort) *noun* a person or group accompanying a person or thing, especially as a protection.

escort[2] (*say* iss-**kort**) *verb* act as an escort to somebody or something.

Eskimo *noun* (*plural* **Eskimos** or **Eskimo**) a member of a people living near the Arctic coast of North America, Greenland, and Siberia.

● USAGE: The Eskimos of North America prefer the name *Inuit.*

ESP *abbreviation* extra-sensory perception.

espadrille *noun* a light canvas shoe.

especial *adjective* special.

especially *adverb* specially; more than anything else.

espionage (*say* ess-pee-on-ah*zh*) *noun* spying.

esplanade *noun* a flat open area used as a promenade, especially by the sea.

espresso *noun* (*plural* **espressos**) coffee made by forcing steam through ground coffee-beans.

espy *verb* (**espied, espying**) catch sight of.

Esq. *abbreviation* (short for **Esquire**) a title written after a man's surname where no title is used before his name.

essay[1] (*say* ess-ay) *noun* 1 a short piece of writing in prose. 2 an attempt.

essay[2] (*say* ess-**ay**) *verb* attempt.

essence *noun* 1 the most important quality or element of something, *the essence of the argument.* 2 a concentrated liquid.

essential[1] *adjective* not able to be done without. **essentially** *adverb*

essential[2] *noun* an essential thing.

establish *verb* 1 set up a business, government, or relationship etc. on a firm basis. 2 show to be true; prove, *He established his innocence.*

the established Church a country's national Church, established by law.

establishment *noun* 1 establishing something. 2 a business firm or other institution.

the Establishment people who are established in positions of power and influence.

estate *noun* 1 an area of land with a set of houses or factories on it. 2 a large area of land owned by one person. 3 all that a person owns when he or she dies. 4 (*old use*) a condition or status, *the holy estate of matrimony.*

estate agent a person whose business is selling or letting houses and land.

estate car a station-wagon.

esteem[1] *verb* think that a person or thing is excellent.

esteem[2] *noun* respect and admiration.

ester *noun* a kind of chemical compound.

estimable *adjective* worthy of esteem.

estimate[1] (*say* ess-tim-at) *noun* a calculation or guess about amount or value.

estimate[2] (*say* ess-tim-ayt) *verb* (**estimated, estimating**) make an estimate. **estimation** *noun*

estranged *adjective* unfriendly after having been friendly or loving. **estrangement** *noun*

estuary (*say* ess-tew-er-ee) *noun* (*plural* **estuaries**) the mouth of a river where it reaches the sea and the tide flows in and out.

etc. *abbreviation* (short for **et cetera**) and other similar things; and so on.

etch *verb* 1 engrave a picture with acid on a metal plate, especially for printing. 2 cut or impress deeply, *The scene is etched on my memory.* **etcher** *noun*

etching *noun* a picture printed from an etched metal plate.

eternal *adjective* lasting for ever; not ending or changing. **eternally** *adverb*, **eternity** *noun*

ether (*say* ee-ther) *noun* 1 a colourless liquid that evaporates easily into fumes that are used as an anaesthetic. 2 the upper air.

ethereal (*say* ith-eer-ee-al) *adjective* light and delicate. **ethereally** *adverb*

ethical (*say* eth-ik-al) *adjective* 1 of ethics. 2 morally right; honourable. **ethically** *adverb*

ethics (*say* eth-iks) *plural noun* standards

of right behaviour; moral principles.

ethnic *adjective* belonging to a particular racial group within a larger set of people.

etiquette (*say* et-ik-et) *noun* the rules of correct behaviour.

etymology (*say* et-im-**ol**-oj-ee) *noun* (*plural* **etymologies**) 1 an account of the origin of a word and its meaning. 2 the study of the origins of words. **etymological** *adjective*

eu- (*say* yoo) *prefix* well.

eucalyptus (*say* yoo-kal-**ip**-tus) *noun* (*plural* **eucalyptuses**) 1 a kind of evergreen tree, often called a gum-tree. 2 a strong-smelling oil obtained from its leaves.

Eucharist (*say* yoo-ker-ist) *noun* the Christian sacrament in which bread and wine are consecrated and swallowed, commemorating the Last Supper of Christ and his disciples.

eulogy (*say* **yoo**-loj-ee) *noun* a piece of praise for a person or thing.

euphemism (*say* **yoo**-fim-izm) *noun* a mild word or phrase used instead of an offensive or frank one, *'To pass away' is a euphemism for 'to die'*. **euphemistic** *adjective*, **euphemistically** *adverb*

euphonium (*say* yoof-**oh**-nee-um) *noun* a large brass wind instrument.

euphoria (*say* yoo-**for**-ee-a) *noun* a feeling of general happiness.

Eurasian *adjective* having European and Asian parents or ancestors. **Eurasian** *noun*

Eurocentric *adjective* having or regarding Europe as its centre; presupposing the supremacy of Europe and Europeans.

European *adjective* of Europe or its people. **European** *noun*

euthanasia (*say* yooth-an-**ay**-zee-a) *noun* the act of causing somebody to die gently and without pain, especially when they are suffering from a painful incurable disease.

eutrophication (*say* yew-troh-fi-**kay**-shun) *noun* the effect of too much fertilizer washing into rivers, which causes aquatic animals to die from lack of oxygen.

evacuate *verb* (**evacuated, evacuating**) 1 move people away from a dangerous place. 2 make a thing empty of air or other

contents. **evacuation** *noun*

evacuee *noun* a person who has been evacuated.

evade *verb* (**evaded, evading**) avoid a person or thing by cleverness or trickery.

evaluate *verb* (**evaluated, evaluating**) estimate the value of something; assess. **evaluation** *noun*

evangelist *noun* 1 any of the writers (Matthew, Mark, Luke, John) of the four Gospels. 2 a person who preaches the Christian faith enthusiastically. **evangelism** *noun*, **evangelical** *adjective*

evaporate *verb* (**evaporated, evaporating**) 1 change from liquid into steam or vapour. 2 cease to exist, *Their enthusiasm had evaporated*. **evaporation** *noun*

evaporated milk unsweetened milk that has been concentrated by evaporation. (Compare *condensed milk*.)

evasion *noun* 1 evading. 2 an evasive answer or excuse.

evasive *adjective* evading something; not frank or straightforward. **evasively** *adverb*, **evasiveness** *noun*

eve *noun* 1 the day or evening before an important day or event, *New Year's Eve*. 2 (*old use*) evening.

even[1] *adjective* 1 level; smooth; not varying. 2 calm; not easily upset, *an even temper*. 3 equal, *Our scores were even*. 4 able to be divided exactly by two, *Six and fourteen are even numbers*. (Compare *odd*.) **evenly** *adverb*, **evenness** *noun*

even[2] *verb* make or become even.

even[3] *adverb* (used to emphasize a word or statement) *She ran even faster*. **even so** although that is correct.

even[4] *noun* (*old use*) evening.

evening *noun* the time at the end of the day before most people go to bed. **evening dress** formal clothes that are worn in the evening. **evening star** the planet Venus, which can be seen in the west after sunset.

evensong *noun* the service of evening prayer in the Church of England.

event *noun* 1 something that happens, especially something important. 2 an item in a sports contest.

eventful *adjective* full of happenings.

eventual *adjective* happening at last, *his eventual success.* **eventually** *adverb*

eventuality (*say* iv-en-tew-**al**-it-ee) *noun* (*plural* **eventualities**) something that may happen.

ever *adverb* 1 at any time, *the best thing I ever did.* 2 always, *ever hopeful.* 3 (*informal,* used for emphasis), *Why ever didn't you tell me?*

evergreen *adjective* having green leaves all the year. **evergreen** *noun*

everlasting[1] *adjective* lasting for ever or for a very long time.

everlasting[2] *noun* a shrub or bush with papery flowers, *white everlastings.*

every *adjective* each without any exceptions, *We enjoyed every minute.*

every one each one.

• USAGE: Follow with a singular verb, e.g. *Every one of them is growing* (not 'are growing').

every other day or **week** etc. each alternate one; every second one.

everybody *pronoun* every person.

everyday *adjective* ordinary; usual, *everyday clothes.*

• USAGE: Do not confuse *everyday* with *every day* = each day (see *every*).

everyone *pronoun* everybody.

• USAGE: Do not confuse *everyone* with *every one* = each one (see *every*).

everything *pronoun* 1 all things; all. 2 the only or most important thing, *Beauty is not everything.*

everywhere *adverb* in every place.

evict *verb* make people move out from where they are living. **eviction** *noun*

evidence *noun* 1 anything that gives people reason to believe something. 2 statements made or objects produced in a lawcourt to prove something.

evident *adjective* obvious; clearly seen. **evidently** *adverb*

evil[1] *adjective* wicked; harmful. **evilly** *adverb*

evil[2] *noun* something evil; a sin.

evoke *verb* (**evoked, evoking**) produce or inspire a memory or feelings etc., *The photographs evoked happy memories.* **evocation** *noun,* **evocative** *adjective*

evolution (*say* ee-vol-**oo**-shon) *noun* 1 evolving; gradual change into something different. 2 the development of animals and plants from earlier or simpler forms. **evolutionary** *adjective*

evolve *verb* (**evolved, evolving**) develop gradually or naturally.

ewe (*say* yoo) *noun* a female sheep, goat, or antelope.

ewer (*say* **yoo**-er) *noun* a large water-jug.

ex- *prefix* (changing to **ef-** before words beginning with *f*; shortened to **e-** before many consonants) 1 out; away (as in *extract*). 2 up, upwards; thoroughly (as in *extol*). 3 formerly (as in *ex-president*).

exacerbate (*say* eks-**ass**-er-bayt) *verb* (**exacerbated, exacerbating**) make a pain or disease or other problem worse.

exact[1] *adjective* 1 correct. 2 clearly stated; giving all details, *exact instructions.* **exactly** *adverb,* **exactness** *noun*

exact[2] *verb* insist on something and obtain it, *He exacted obedience from the recruits.* **exaction** *noun*

exacting *adjective* making great demands, *an exacting task.*

exactitude *noun* exactness.

exaggerate *verb* (**exaggerated, exaggerating**) make something seem bigger, better, or worse etc. than it really is. **exaggeration** *noun*

exalt (*say* ig-**zawlt**) *verb* 1 raise in rank or status etc. 2 praise highly, *The song exalted the chief.* 3 delight; elate. **exaltation** *noun*

exam *noun* (*informal*) an examination.

examination *noun* 1 a test of a person's knowledge or skill. 2 examining something; an inspection.

examine *verb* (**examined, examining**) 1 test a person's knowledge or skill. 2 inspect; look at something closely. **examiner** *noun*

examinee *noun* a person being tested in an examination.

example *noun* 1 anything that shows what others of the same kind are like or how they work. 2 a person or thing good enough to be worth imitating.

exasperate *verb* (**exasperated, exasperating**) annoy someone greatly.

exasperation *noun*

excavate *verb* (**excavated, excavating**) dig out; uncover by digging. **excavation** *noun*, **excavator** *noun*

exceed *verb* 1 be greater than, surpass. 2 do more than you need or ought to do; go beyond a thing's limits, *He has exceeded his authority.*

exceedingly *adverb* very; extremely.

excel *verb* (**excelled, excelling**) be better than others at doing something.

Excellency *noun* the title of high officials such as ambassadors and governors.

excellent *adjective* extremely good. **excellently** *adverb*, **excellence** *noun*

except[1] *preposition* excluding; not including, *They all left except me.*

except[2] *verb* exclude; leave out, *I blame you all, no one is excepted.*

excepting *preposition* except.

  ● USAGE: Use *excepting* only after *not* and *always.*

exception *noun* 1 a person or thing that is left out or does not follow the general rule. 2 exclusion; excepting, *All were pardoned with the exception of traitors.*

take exception raise objections to something.

exceptional *adjective* 1 forming an exception; very unusual, *an exceptional case.* 2 outstandingly good. **exceptionally** *adverb*

excerpt (*say* ek-serpt) *noun* a passage taken from a book or speech or film etc.

excess *noun* (*plural* **excesses**) too much of something.

excessive *adjective* too much; too great. **excessively** *adverb*

exchange[1] *verb* (**exchanged, exchanging**) give something and receive something else for it. **exchangeable** *adjective*

exchange[2] *noun* 1 exchanging. 2 a place where things (especially stocks and shares) are bought and sold, *a stock exchange.* 3 a place where telephone lines are connected to each other when a call is made.

exchequer *noun* a national treasury into which public funds (such as taxes) are paid.

excise[1] (*say* eks-I'z) *noun* a tax charged on certain goods and licences etc.

excise[2] (*say* iks-I'z) *verb* (**excised, excising**) remove something by cutting it away, *The surgeon excised the tumour.*

excitable *adjective* easily excited.

excite *verb* (**excited, exciting**) 1 rouse a person's feelings; make eager, *The thought of finding gold excited them.* 2 cause a feeling; arouse, *The invention excited great interest.* **excitedly** *adverb*

excitement *noun* a strong feeling of eagerness or pleasure.

exclaim *verb* shout or cry out in eagerness or surprise.

exclamation *noun* 1 exclaiming. 2 a word or words exclaimed expressing joy or pain or surprise etc.

exclamation mark the punctuation mark (!) placed after an exclamation.

exclude *verb* (**excluded, excluding**) 1 keep somebody or something out. 2 leave out, *Do not exclude the possibility of rain.* **exclusion** *noun*

exclusive *adjective* 1 allowing only certain people to be members etc., *an exclusive club.* 2 not shared with others, *This newspaper has an exclusive report.* **exclusively** *adverb*, **exclusiveness** *noun*

exclusive of excluding, not including, *This is the price exclusive of meals.*

excommunicate *verb* (**excommunicated, excommunicating**) cut off a person from membership of a Church. **excommunication** *noun*

excrement (*say* eks-krim-ent) *noun* waste matter excreted from the bowels, dung.

excrescence (*say* iks-**kress**-ens) *noun* 1 an outgrowth on a plant or animal's body. 2 an ugly addition or part.

excrete *verb* (**excreted, excreting**) expel waste matter from the body. **excretion** *noun*, **excretory** *adjective*

excruciating (*say* iks-**kroo**-shee-ayt-ing) *adjective* extremely painful; agonizing. **excruciatingly** *adverb*

exculpate (*say* eks-kul-payt) *verb* (**exculpated, exculpating**) clear a person from blame. **exculpation** *noun*

excursion *noun* a short journey made for pleasure, *a beach excursion.*

excusable *adjective* able to be excused.

excusably *adverb*

excuse[1] (*say* iks-**kewz**) *verb* (**excused, excusing**) 1 forgive. 2 allow someone not to do something or to leave a room etc., *Please may I be excused swimming?*

excuse[2] (*say* iks-**kewss**) *noun* a reason given to explain why something wrong has been done.

execrable (*say* **eks**-ik-rab-ul) *adjective* very bad; abominable.

execute *verb* (**executed, executing**) 1 put someone to death as a punishment. 2 perform or produce something, *She executed the somersault perfectly.* **execution** *noun*

executioner *noun* an official who executes a condemned person.

executive[1] (*say* ig-**zek**-yoo-tiv) *noun* a senior person with authority in a business or government organization.

executive[2] *adjective* having the authority to carry out plans or laws, *the executive committee of that party.*

executor (*say* ig-**zek**-yoo-ter) *noun* a person appointed to carry out the instructions in someone's will.

exemplary (*say* ig-**zem**-pler-ee) *adjective* very good; being an example to others, *His conduct was exemplary.*

exemplify *verb* (**exemplified, exemplifying**) be an example of something.

exempt[1] *adjective* not having to do something that others have to do, *Charities are exempt from paying tax.*

exempt[2] *verb* make someone or something exempt. **exemption** *noun*

exercise[1] *noun* 1 using your body to make it strong and healthy. 2 a piece of work done for practice, *a maths exercise.*

exercise[2] *verb* (**exercised, exercising**) 1 do exercises. 2 give exercise to an animal etc. 3 use, *exercise patience.*

exert *verb* use power or influence etc., *He exerted all his strength.* **exertion** *noun* **exert yourself** make an effort.

exhale *verb* (**exhaled, exhaling**) breathe out. **exhalation** *noun*

exhaust[1] *verb* 1 make somebody very tired. 2 use up something completely, *exhaust a mine.* **exhaustion** *noun*

exhaust[2] *noun* 1 the waste gases or steam from an engine. 2 the pipe etc. through which they are sent out.

exhaustive *adjective* thorough; trying everything possible, *We made an exhaustive search.* **exhaustively** *adverb*

exhibit[1] *verb* (**exhibited, exhibiting**) show in public. **exhibitor** *noun*

exhibit[2] *noun* something exhibited.

exhibition *noun* a collection of things arranged for people to look at.

exhibitionist *noun* a person who behaves in a way that is meant to attract attention. **exhibitionism** *noun*

exhilarate (*say* ig-**zil**-er-ayt) *verb* (**exhilarated, exhilarating**) make someone very happy; elate. **exhilaration** *noun*

exhort (*say* ig-**zort**) *verb* urge someone earnestly. **exhortation** *noun*

exhume (*say* ig-**zewm**) *verb* (**exhumed, exhuming**) dig up something that has been buried. **exhumation** *noun*

exile[1] *verb* (**exiled, exiling**) banish.

exile[2] *noun* 1 a banished person. 2 having to live away from your own country, *He was in exile for ten years.*

exist *verb* 1 have a place as part of what is real, *Do ghosts exist?* 2 stay alive, *We cannot exist without food.* **existence** *noun*, **existent** *adjective*

exit *noun* 1 the way out of a building. 2 going off the stage, *The actress made her exit.*

exodus *noun* (*plural* **exoduses**) the departure of many people, *the exodus of children after school.*

exonerate *verb* (**exonerated, exonerating**) declare or prove that a person is not to blame for something. **exoneration** *noun*

exorbitant *adjective* much too great; excessive, *exorbitant prices.*

exorcize *verb* (**exorcized, exorcizing**) get rid of an evil spirit. **exorcism** *noun*, **exorcist** *noun*

exotic *adjective* 1 very unusual, *exotic clothes.* 2 from another part of the world, *exotic plants.* **exotically** *adverb*

expand *verb* make or become larger or fuller. **expansion** *noun*, **expansive** *adjective*

expanse *noun* a wide area.

expatriate (*say* eks-**pat**-ree-at) *noun* a person living away from his or her own country.

expect *verb* 1 think or believe that something will happen or that someone will come. 2 think that something ought to happen, *She expects obedience.*

expectant *adjective* expecting something to happen; hopeful. **expectantly** *adverb*, **expectancy** *noun*
expectant mother a woman who is pregnant.

expectation *noun* 1 expecting something; being hopeful. 2 something you expect to happen or get.

expedient[1] (*say* iks-**pee**-dee-ent) *adjective* 1 suitable, convenient. 2 useful and practical though perhaps unfair, *Cutting student subsidies was an expedient decision.* **expediently** *adverb*, **expediency** *noun*

expedient[2] *noun* a means of doing something, especially when in difficulty, *She got her own way by the simple expedient of throwing a tantrum.*

expedite (*say* eks-pid-dyt) *verb* (**expedited**, **expediting**) make something happen more quickly.

expedition *noun* 1 a journey made in order to do something. 2 the people, vehicles, etc. making such a journey, *the South African expedition.* **expeditionary** *adjective*

expeditious (*say* eks-pid-**ish**-us) *adjective* quick and efficient. **expeditiously** *adverb*

expel *verb* (**expelled**, **expelling**) 1 send or force something out, *This fan expels stale air.* 2 make a person leave a school or country etc. **expulsion** *noun*

expend *verb* spend; use up.

expendable *adjective* 1 able to be expended. 2 able to be sacrificed in order to gain something.

expenditure *noun* expending; the spending of money or effort etc.

expense *noun* the cost of doing something.

expensive *adjective* costing a lot. **expensively** *adverb*, **expensiveness** *noun*

experience[1] *noun* 1 what you learn from doing or seeing things. 2 something that has happened to you, *a terrible experience.*

experience[2] *verb* (**experienced**, **experiencing**) have something happen to you.

experienced *adjective* having great skill or knowledge from much experience.

experiment[1] *noun* a test made in order to find out what happens or to prove something. **experimental** *adjective*, **experimentally** *adverb*

experiment[2] *verb* carry out an experiment. **experimentation** *noun*

expert[1] *noun* a person with great knowledge or skill in something.

expert[2] *adjective* having great knowledge or skill. **expertly** *adverb*, **expertness** *noun*

expertise (*say* eks-per-**teez**) *noun* expert ability.

expiate (*say* eks-pee-ayt) *verb* (**expiated**, **expiating**) atone for; make amends for wrongdoing. **expiation** *noun*

expire *verb* (**expired**, **expiring**) 1 come to an end; stop being usable, *Your season ticket has expired.* 2 die. 3 breathe out air. **expiration** *noun*, **expiry** *noun*

explain *verb* 1 make something clear to somebody else; show its meaning. 2 account for something, *That explains his absence.* **explanation** *noun*

explanatory (*say* iks-**plan**-at-er-ee) *adjective* giving an explanation.

explicit (*say* iks-**pliss**-it) *adjective* stated or stating something openly and exactly. (Compare *implicit.*) **explicitly** *adverb*

explode *verb* (**exploded**, **exploding**) 1 burst or suddenly release energy with a loud noise. 2 cause a bomb to go off. 3 increase suddenly or quickly, *Population levels have exploded in the last century.*

exploit[1] (*say* **eks**-ploit) *noun* a brave or exciting deed.

exploit[2] (*say* iks-**ploit**) *verb* 1 use or develop resources. 2 use selfishly, *Child labour was exploited in the rural areas.* **exploitation** *noun*

exploratory (*say* iks-**plo**rra-ter-ee) *adjective* for the purpose of exploring.

explore *verb* (**explored**, **exploring**) 1 travel through a country etc. in order to learn about it. **2** examine something, investigate, *We explored the possibilities.* **exploration** *noun*, **explorer** *noun*

explosion *noun* **1** the exploding of a bomb etc.; the noise made by exploding. **2** a sudden great increase, *the population explosion.*

explosive[1] *adjective* able to explode.

explosive[2] *noun* an explosive substance.

expo *noun* (*plural* **expos**) a large international exhibition.

exponent *noun* **1** a person who expounds something. **2** someone who uses a certain technique, *a martial arts exponent.* **3** the raised number etc. written to the right of another (e.g. 3 in 2^3) showing how many times the first one is to be multiplied by itself.

export[1] *verb* send goods abroad to be sold. **exportation** *noun*, **exporter** *noun*

export[2] *noun* **1** exporting things. **2** something exported, *loading exports on the ship.*

expose *verb* (**exposed, exposing**) **1** reveal, uncover. **2** allow light to reach a photographic film so as to take a picture. **exposure** *noun*

expostulate *verb* (**expostulated, expostulating**) make a protest. **expostulation** *noun*

expound *verb* explain in detail.

express[1] *adjective* **1** going or sent quickly. **2** expressed; clearly stated, *This was done against my express orders.*

express[2] *noun* (*plural* **expresses**) a fast train stopping at only a few stations.

express[3] *verb* **1** put ideas etc. into words; make your feelings known. **2** press or squeeze out, *Express the juice.*

expression *noun* **1** the look on a person's face that shows his or her feelings. **2** a word or phrase etc., *a Zulu expression.* **3** a way of speaking or of playing music etc. so as to show feeling for its meaning. **4** expressing, *this expression of opinion.*

expressive *adjective* full of expression.

expressly *adverb* **1** clearly; plainly, *This was expressly forbidden.* **2** specially, *designed expressly for children.*

expulsion *noun* expelling; being expelled. **expulsive** *adjective*

expunge *verb* (**expunged, expunging**) erase; wipe out.

exquisite (*say* eks-kwiz-it) *adjective* very beautiful. **exquisitely** *adverb*

extemporize *verb* (**extemporized, extemporizing**) speak or produce or do something without advance preparation. **extemporization** *noun*

extend *verb* **1** stretch out. **2** make something become longer or larger, *The road was extended.* **3** offer; give, *Extend a warm welcome to our friends.* **extendible** *adjective*, **extensible** *adjective*

extension *noun* **1** extending; being extended. **2** something added on; an addition to a building. **3** one of a set of telephones in an office or house etc.

extensive *adjective* covering a large area or range, *extensive gardens.* **extensively** *adverb*, **extensiveness** *noun*

extent *noun* **1** the area or length over which something extends. **2** the amount, level, or scope of something, *the full extent of his power.*

extenuating *adjective* making a crime seem less great by providing a partial excuse, *There were extenuating circumstances.* **extenuation** *noun*

exterior[1] *adjective* outer.

exterior[2] *noun* the outside of something.

exterminate *verb* (**exterminated, exterminating**) destroy or kill all the members or examples. **extermination** *noun*, **exterminator** *noun*

external *adjective* outside. **externally** *adverb*

extinct *adjective* **1** not existing any more, *The dodo is an extinct bird.* **2** not burning; not active, *an extinct volcano.*

extinction *noun* **1** making or becoming extinct. **2** extinguishing; being extinguished.

extinguish *verb* **1** put out a fire or light. **2** put an end to; destroy, *Our hopes of victory were extinguished.*

extinguisher *noun* a portable device for sending out water, chemicals, or gases to extinguish a fire.

extol *verb* (**extolled, extolling**) praise.

extort *verb* obtain something by force or threats. **extortion** *noun*

extortionate *adjective* charging or demanding far too much.

extra[1] *adjective* additional; more than is usual, *extra strength*.

extra[2] *adverb* more than usually, *We had to pay extra*.

extra[3] *noun* 1 an extra person or thing. 2 a person acting as part of a crowd in a film or play.

extra- *prefix* outside; beyond (as in *extraterrestrial*).

extract[1] (*say* iks-**trakt**) *verb* take out; remove. **extractor** *noun*

extract[2] (*say* eks-trakt) *noun* 1 a passage taken from a book, speech, film, etc.; an excerpt. 2 a substance separated or obtained from another, *beef extract*.

extraction *noun* 1 extracting. 2 descent; ancestry, *He is of Chinese extraction*.

extradite *verb* (**extradited, extraditing**) 1 hand over an accused person to the country where the crime was committed. 2 obtain such a person for trial or punishment. **extradition** (*say* eks-tra-**dish**-on) *noun*

extramural *adjective* additional to work, school, studies, etc., *extramural activities*.

extraneous (*say* iks-**tray**-nee-us) *adjective* 1 added from outside. 2 not belonging to the matter in hand; irrelevant.

extraordinary *adjective* very unusual or strange. **extraordinarily** *adverb*

extra-sensory *adjective* outside the range of the known human senses.

extra-sensory perception telepathy, clairvoyance.

extraterrestrial *adjective* of or from outside the planet Earth, *extraterrestrial creature*. **extraterrestrial** *noun*

extravagant *adjective* spending or using too much. **extravagantly** *adverb*, **extravagance** *noun*

extravaganza *noun* a very spectacular show.

extreme[1] *adjective* 1 very great or intense, *extreme cold*. 2 furthest away, *the extreme north*. 3 going to great lengths in actions or opinions; not moderate. **extremely** *adverb*

extreme[2] *noun* 1 something extreme. 2 either end of something.

extremist *noun* a person who holds extreme (not moderate) opinions in political or other matters.

extremity (*say* iks-**trem**-it-ee) *noun* (*plural* **extremities**) 1 an extreme point; the very end. 2 an extreme need or feeling or danger etc.

extricate (*say* eks-trik-ayt) *verb* (**extricated, extricating**) release from a difficult position. **extrication** *noun*

extrovert *noun* a person who is generally friendly and likes company. (The opposite is *introvert*.)

extrude *verb* (**extruded, extruding**) push or squeeze out. **extrusion** *noun*

exuberant (*say* ig-**zew**-ber-ant) *adjective* very lively. **exuberantly** *adverb*, **exuberance** *noun*

exude *verb* (**exuded, exuding**) 1 give off like sweat or a smell etc. 2 ooze out. 3 display a feeling openly, *She exuded confidence*.

exult *verb* rejoice greatly. **exultant** *adjective*, **exultation** *noun*

eye[1] *noun* 1 the organ of the body that is used for seeing. 2 the power of seeing, *She has sharp eyes*. 3 the small hole in a needle. 4 a spot or leaf-bud that seems like an eye. 5 the centre of a storm.

eye[2] *verb* (**eyed, eyeing**) look at; watch.

eyeball *noun* the ball-shaped part of the eye inside the eyelids.

eyebrow *noun* the fringe of hair growing on the face above the eye.

eyelash *noun* (*plural* **eyelashes**) one of the short hairs that grow on an eyelid.

eyelid *noun* either of the two folds of skin that can close over the eyeball.

eyepiece *noun* the lens of a telescope or microscope etc. that you put to your eye.

eyesight *noun* the ability to see.

eyesore *noun* something that is ugly to look at.

eyewitness *noun* (*plural* **eyewitnesses**) a person who actually saw an accident or crime etc.

eyrie (*say* **I**-ree) *noun* 1 the nest of an eagle or other bird of prey. 2 a high place.

Ff

fable *noun* a short story that teaches about behaviour, often with animals as characters.

fabric *noun* 1 cloth. 2 the framework of a building (walls, floors, and roof).

fabricate *verb* (**fabricated, fabricating**) 1 construct; manufacture. 2 invent, *fabricate an excuse*. **fabrication** *noun*

fabulous *adjective* 1 (*informal*) wonderful. 2 incredibly great, *fabulous wealth*. 3 told of in fables. **fabulously** *adverb*

façade (*say* fas-**ahd**) *noun* 1 the front of a building. 2 an outward appearance, especially a deceptive one.

face¹ *noun* 1 the front part of the head. 2 the expression on a person's face, *a happy face*. 3 the front or upper side of something. 4 a surface, *A cube has six faces.*

face value the value printed on money or stamps; the outward appearance of something.

face² *verb* (**faced, facing**) 1 look or have the front towards something, *Our room faced the sea*. 2 meet and have to deal with something; encounter, *Explorers face many dangers*. 3 cover a surface with a layer of different material, *The dress was faced with silk.*

facet (*say* **fas**-it) *noun* 1 one of the many sides of a cut stone or jewel. 2 one aspect of a situation or problem.

facetious (*say* fas-**ee**-shus) *adjective* trying to be funny at an unsuitable time, *facetious remarks*. **facetiously** *adverb*

facial (*say* **fay**-shal) *adjective* of the face.

facile (*say* **fas**-I'll) *adjective* done or produced easily or with little thought or care.

facilitate (*say* fas-**il**-it-ayt) *verb* (**facilitated, facilitating**) make easy or easier. **facilitation** *noun*

facility (*say* fas-**il**-it-ee) *noun* (*plural* **facilities**) 1 something that provides you with the means to do things, *There are sports facilities*. 2 easiness, *She speaks Afrikaans with surprising facility.*

facsimile (*say* fak-**sim**-il-ee) *noun* an exact reproduction of a document etc.

fact *noun* something that is certainly true.

faction *noun* a small united group within a larger one, especially in politics.

faction fight a fight between hostile clans or people who are loyal to different political parties.

factor *noun* 1 something that helps to bring about a result, *Hard work was a factor in her success*. 2 a number by which a larger number can be divided exactly, *2 and 3 are factors of 6.*

factory *noun* (*plural* **factories**) a large building where machines are used to make things.

factotum (*say* fakt-**oh**-tum) *noun* a servant or assistant who does all kinds of work.

factual *adjective* based on facts; containing facts. **factually** *adverb*

faculty *noun* (*plural* **faculties**) 1 any of the powers of the body or mind (e.g. sight, speech, understanding). 2 a department teaching a particular subject in a university, *the faculty of music.*

fad *noun* a craze.

fade *verb* (**faded, fading**) 1 lose or cause to lose colour or freshness or strength. 2 disappear gradually, *memories fade with time*. 3 make a sound etc. become gradually weaker (*fade it out*) or stronger (*fade it in* or *up*).

faeces (*say* **fee**-seez) *plural noun* solid waste matter expelled from the body.

fag *noun* 1 tiring work; drudgery. 2 (*informal*) a cigarette.

fagged out tired out; exhausted.

faggot *noun* 1 a bundle of sticks bound together especially as firewood. 2 a meat ball made with chopped liver and baked. 3 a small extra-hard brick.

Fahrenheit *adjective* measuring temperature on a scale where water freezes at 32° and boils at 212°.

fail¹ *verb* 1 try to do something but be unable to do it. 2 become weak or useless; break down, *The brakes failed*. 3 not to do something, *He failed to warn me*. 4 grade a candidate or be graded as not having passed an examination.

fail² *noun* **without fail** for certain; whatever happens.

failing *noun* a weakness; a fault.

failure *noun* 1 not being able to do something. 2 a person or thing that has failed.

faint¹ *adjective* 1 weak; not clear, not distinct. 2 exhausted; nearly unconscious. **faintly** *adverb*, **faintness** *noun*

faint² *verb* become unconscious.

fair¹ *adjective* 1 right or just; according to the rules, *a fair fight.* 2 (of hair or skin) light in colour; (of a person) having fair hair. 3 (*old use*) beautiful. 4 fine; favourable, *fair weather.* 5 moderate; quite good, *a fair number of people.* **fairness** *noun*

fair² *adverb* fairly, *Play fair!*

fair³ *noun* 1 a group of entertainments such as roundabouts and sideshows. 2 an exhibition; a market, *computer fair.*

fairly *adverb* 1 justly; according to the rules. 2 moderately, *It is fairly hard.*

fairy *noun* (*plural* **fairies**) an imaginary very small creature with magic powers. **fairyland** *noun*, **fairy-tale** *noun*

faith *noun* strong belief; trust. **in good faith** with honest intentions.

faithful *adjective* 1 loyal and trustworthy. 2 sexually loyal to one partner. **faithfully** *adverb*, **faithfulness** *noun* **Yours faithfully** see *yours.*

fake¹ *noun* something that looks genuine but is not; a forgery.

fake² *verb* (**faked, faking**) 1 make something that looks genuine, so as to deceive people. 2 pretend, *They faked illness.* **faker** *noun*

fakir (*say* **fay**-keer) *noun* a Muslim or Hindu religious beggar regarded as a holy man.

falcon *noun* a kind of hawk often used in the sport of hunting other birds or game. **falconry** *noun*

fall¹ *verb* (**fell, fallen, falling**) 1 come or go down without being pushed or thrown etc. 2 decrease; become lower, *Prices fell.* 3 be captured or overthrown, *The city fell.* 4 die in battle. 5 happen, *Silence fell.* 6 become, *She fell asleep.* **fall back** retreat.

fall back on use for support or in an emergency.

fall for (*informal*) be attracted by a person; be taken in by a deception.

fall out quarrel.

fall through fail, *plans fell through.*

fall² *noun* 1 the action of falling. 2 (*American*) autumn, when leaves fall.

fallacy (*say* **fal**-a-see) *noun* (*plural* **fallacies**) a false idea or belief. **fallacious** (*say* fal-**ay**-shus) *adjective*

fallible (*say* **fal**-ib-ul) *adjective* liable to make mistakes; not infallible, *All people are fallible.* **fallibility** *noun*

fall-out *noun* particles of radioactive material carried in the air after a nuclear explosion.

fallow *adjective* (of land) ploughed but left without crops in order to restore its fertility.

fallow deer *noun* a kind of light-brown deer.

falls *plural noun* a waterfall.

false *adjective* 1 untrue; incorrect. 2 not genuine; sham; faked. 3 treacherous; deceitful. **falsely** *adverb*, **falseness** *noun*, **falsity** *noun*

falsehood *noun* 1 a lie. 2 telling lies.

falsetto *noun* (*plural* **falsettos**) a man's voice forced into speaking or singing higher than is natural.

falsify *verb* (**falsified, falsifying**) alter a thing dishonestly. **falsification** *noun*

falsity *noun* falseness.

falter *verb* 1 hesitate when you move or speak. 2 become weaker; begin to give way, *His courage faltered.*

fame *noun* being famous. **famed** *adjective*

familiar *adjective* 1 well-known; often seen or experienced. 2 knowing something well, *Are you familiar with this book?* 3 very friendly, *on familiar terms.* **familiarly** *adverb*, **familiarity** *noun*

familiarize *verb* (**familiarized, familiarizing**) make familiar; accustom. **familiarization** *noun*

family *noun* (*plural* **families**) 1 parents and their children, sometimes including grandchildren and other relations. 2 a group of things that are alike in some way. **family planning** birth control.

family tree a diagram showing how people in a family are related.

famine *noun* a very bad shortage of food in an area.

famished *adjective* very hungry. **famishing** *adjective*

famous *adjective* known to very many people.

famously *adverb* (*informal*) very well, *They get on famously.*

fan[1] *noun* a device for making air move about so as to cool people or things.

fan[2] *verb* (**fanned, fanning**) send a current of air on something.

fan[3] *noun* an enthusiast; a great admirer or supporter.

Fanakalo (also **Fanagalo**) *noun* a pidgin language used by people working on South African mines.

fanatic *noun* a person who is very enthusiastic or too enthusiastic about something. **fanatical** *adjective*, **fanatically** *adverb*, **fanaticism** *noun*

fanciful *adjective* 1 imagining things. 2 quaint; unusual, *fanciful designs.*

fancy[1] *noun* (*plural* **fancies**) 1 a liking or desire for something, *I've taken a fancy to her music.* 2 imagination, *evil fancies.*

fancy[2] *adjective* decorated; elaborate.

fancy[3] *verb* (**fancied, fancying**) 1 believe, *I fancy it's raining.* 2 imagine. 3 have a liking or desire for something.

fanfare *noun* a short piece of loud music played on trumpets.

fang *noun* a long sharp tooth.

fanlight *noun* a window above a door.

fantasia (*say* fan-**tay**-zee-a) *noun* an imaginative piece of music or writing.

fantasize *verb* (**fantasized, fantasizing**) imagine in fantasy; day-dream.

fantastic *adjective* 1 (*informal*) excellent. 2 designed in a very fanciful way. **fantastically** *adverb*

fantasy *noun* (*plural* **fantasies**) something imaginary or fantastic.

far[1] *adverb* 1 at or to a great distance, *We didn't go far.* 2 much; by a great amount, *This is far better.*

far[2] *adjective* distant; remote, *On the far side of the river.*

farce *noun* 1 an exaggerated comedy. 2 events that are ridiculous or a pretence. **farcical** *adjective*

fare[1] *noun* 1 the price charged for a passenger to travel. 2 food and drink, *There was only very plain fare.*

fare[2] *verb* (**fared, faring**) get along; progress, *How did they fare?*

farewell *interjection* & *noun* goodbye.

farm[1] *noun* 1 an area of land where someone grows crops or keeps animals for food or other use. 2 the farmer's house. **farmhouse** *noun*, **farmyard** *noun*

farm school a school for young children on a farm that is far away from a town.

farm-stall a shop or stand where farm produce is sold directly to the public.

farm[2] *verb* 1 grow crops or keep animals for food etc. 2 use land for growing crops; cultivate.

farmer *noun* a person who owns or manages a farm.

farrier (*say* fa-ree-er) *noun* a smith who shoes horses. **farriery** *noun*

farrow *noun* a litter of young pigs.

farther *adverb* & *adjective* at or to a greater distance; more distant.

• USAGE: *Farther* and *farthest* are used only in connection with distance (e.g. *She lives farther from the school than I do*), but even in such cases many people prefer to use *further*. Only *further* can be used to mean 'additional', e.g. in *We must make further inquiries.* If you are not sure which is right, use *further.*

farthest *adverb* & *adjective* at or to the greatest distance; most distant.

fascia (*say* **fay**-sha) *noun* (*plural* **fasciae** or **fascias**) 1 the board or panel on the front of a vehicle, machine, etc. with control switches. 2 the board above a shop's entrance with the shop's name on it. 3 a flat strip of wood covering the ends of the rafters in a roof.

fascinate *verb* (**fascinated, fascinating**) be very attractive or interesting to somebody. **fascination** *noun*, **fascinator** *noun*

Fascist (*say* **fash**-ist) *noun* a person who supports an extreme right-wing dictatorial type of government. **Fascism** *noun*

fashion¹ *noun* **1** the style of clothes or other things that most people like at a particular time. **2** a way of doing something, *Continue in the same fashion.* **fashionable** *adjective*, **fashionably** *adverb*

fashion² *verb* make in a particular shape or style.

fast¹ *adjective* **1** moving or done quickly; rapid. **2** allowing fast movement, *a fast road.* **3** showing a time later than the correct time, *Your watch is fast.* **4** firmly fixed or attached, *The rope held fast.* **5** not likely to fade, *fast colours.* **fastness** *noun*

fast² *adverb* **1** quickly, *Run fast!* **2** firmly; securely, *They are fast asleep.*

fast³ *verb* go without food. **fast** *noun*

fasten *verb* fix one thing firmly to another. **fastener** *noun*, **fastening** *noun*

fastidious *adjective* choosing carefully and liking only what is very good. **fastidiously** *adverb*, **fastidiousness** *noun*

fat¹ *noun* **1** the white greasy part of meat. **2** oil or grease used in cooking. **the fat of the land** the best food.

fat² *adjective* (**fatter, fattest**) **1** having a very thick round body. **2** thick, *a fat book.* **3** full of fat, *fat meat.* **fatness** *noun*

fatal *adjective* causing death or disaster, *a fatal accident.* **fatally** *adverb*

fatalist *noun* a person who accepts whatever happens and thinks it could not have been avoided. **fatalism** *noun*, **fatalistic** *adjective*

fatality (*say* fa-**tal**-it-ee) *noun* (*plural* **fatalities**) a death caused by an accident, war, or other disaster.

fate *noun* **1** a power that is thought to make things happen. **2** what will happen or has happened to somebody or something; destiny.

fated *adjective* destined by fate; doomed, *the fated lovers, Romeo and Juliet.*

fateful *adjective* bringing events that are important and usually unpleasant. **fatefully** *adverb*

father¹ *noun* **1** a male parent. **2** (in African usage) a father or father's brother. **3** the title of certain priests. **fatherly** *adjective*

father² *verb* be the father of, *He fathered six children.*

father-in-law *noun* (*plural* **fathers-in-law**) the father of a married person's husband or wife.

fathom¹ *noun* a unit of 1,8 metres, used in measuring the depth of water.

fathom² *verb* **1** measure the depth of something. **2** get to the bottom of something; work it out. **fathomless** *adjective*

fatigue *noun* **1** tiredness. **2** weakness in metals, caused by stress. **fatigued** *adjective*

fatten *verb* make or become fat.

fatty *adjective* like fat; containing fat.

fatuous *adjective* silly. **fatuously** *adverb*, **fatuousness** *noun*, **fatuity** *noun*

fault¹ *noun* **1** anything that makes a person or thing imperfect; a flaw or mistake. **2** the responsibility for something wrong, *It wasn't your fault.* **3** a break in a layer of rock.

fault² *verb* **1** find faults in something. **2** form a fault.

faultless *adjective* without a fault. **faultlessly** *adverb*, **faultlessness** *noun*

faulty *adjective* having a fault or faults. **faultily** *adverb*, **faultiness** *noun*

faun *noun* an ancient country-god with a goat's legs, horns, and tail.

fauna *noun* the animals of a certain area or period of time. (Compare *flora.*)

favour¹ *noun* **1** a kind or helpful act. **2** approval; goodwill, *She won favour with her teacher.* **3** friendly support shown to one person or group but not to another, *without fear or favour.*

favour² *verb* be in favour of something; show favour to a person.

favourable *adjective* helpful; approving; pleasing. **favourably** *adverb*

favourite *adjective* liked more than others. **favourite** *noun*

favouritism *noun* unfairly being kinder to one person than to others.

fawn¹ *noun* **1** a young deer. **2** a light-brown colour.

fawn² *verb* try to win a person's favour or affection by flattery and humility.

fax¹ *verb* send a copy of a document, picture, etc. by an electronic system using telephone lines.

fax² *noun* 1 a system for faxing copies, *a fax machine*. 2 a copy produced in this way.

fear¹ *noun* a feeling that something unpleasant may happen.

fear² *verb* feel fear; be afraid of somebody or something.

fearful *adjective* 1 feeling fear; afraid. 2 causing fear or horror, *a fearful monster*. 3 (*informal*) very great or bad, *a fearful argument*. **fearfully** *adverb*

fearless *adjective* without fear. **fearlessly** *adverb*, **fearlessness** *noun*

fearsome *adjective* frightening.

feasible *adjective* 1 able to be done; possible. 2 likely, *a feasible explanation*. **feasibly** *adverb*, **feasibility** *noun*

feast *noun* 1 a large splendid meal. 2 a religious festival, *the Passover feast*. **feast** *verb*

feat *noun* a brave or clever deed.

feather¹ *noun* one of the very light coverings that grow from a bird's skin. **feathery** *adjective*

feather² *verb* cover or line with feathers.

featherweight *noun* 1 a person who weighs very little. 2 a boxer weighing between 54 and 57 kilograms.

feature¹ *noun* 1 any part of the face (e.g. mouth, nose, eyes). 2 an important or noticeable part; a characteristic, *a feature of the debate*. 3 a long or important film, broadcast programme, or newspaper article.

feature² *verb* (**featured, featuring**) make or be a noticeable part of something.

feckless *adjective* feeble and incompetent, irresponsible.

fed *past tense* of **feed**. **fed up** (*informal*) discontented.

federal *adjective* of a system in which several States are ruled by a central government but are responsible for their own internal affairs. **federation** *noun*

fee *noun* a charge for something.

feeble *adjective* weak; without strength. **feebly** *adverb*, **feebleness** *noun*

feed¹ *verb* (**fed, feeding**) 1 give food to a person or animal. 2 take food, *The sheep fed in a corner of the camp*. 3 supply something to a machine etc. **feeder** *noun*

feed² *noun* 1 a meal. 2 food for animals.

feedback *noun* the return of information about an event or thing; a response.

feel¹ *verb* (**felt, feeling**) 1 touch something to find out what it is like. 2 be aware of something; have an opinion. 3 give a certain sensation, *It feels warm*. **feel like** (*informal*) want.

feel² *noun* the sensation caused by feeling something, *I like the feel of silk*.

feeler *noun* 1 a long thin projection on an insect's or crustacean's body, used for feeling; an antenna. 2 a cautious question or suggestion etc. to test people's reactions, *She put out a feeler to test their response*.

feeling *noun* 1 the ability to feel things; the sense of touch. 2 what a person feels.

feign (*say* fayn) *verb* pretend.

feint¹ (*say* faynt) *noun* a sham attack or blow etc. meant to deceive an opponent.

feint² *verb* make a feint.

felicity *noun* 1 great happiness. 2 a pleasing manner or style, *He expressed himself with great felicity*. **felicitous** *adjective*, **felicitously** *adverb*

feline (*say* feel-I'n) *adjective* of cats; cat-like.

fell¹ *past tense* of **fall**.

fell² *verb* cause to fall; cut or knock down, *They were felling the trees*.

fellow¹ *noun* 1 a friend or companion; one who belongs to the same group. 2 (*informal*) a man or boy. 3 a member of a learned society.

fellow² *adjective* of the same group or kind, *Her fellow teachers supported her*.

fellowship *noun* 1 friendship. 2 a group of friends; a society.

felon (*say* fel-on) *noun* a criminal.

felony (*say* fel-on-ee) *noun* (*plural* **felonies**) a serious crime.

felt¹ *past tense* of **feel**.

felt² *noun* a thick fabric made of fibres of wool or fur etc. pressed together.

female¹ *adjective* of the sex that can bear offspring or produce eggs or fruit.

female² *noun* a female person, animal, or plant.

feminine *adjective* of or like women; considered suitable for women. **femininity** *noun*

feminist *noun* a person who believes that women should be given the same rights, opportunities, and status as men. **feminism** *noun*

femur (*say* fee-mer) *noun* the thigh-bone.

fen *noun* an area of low-lying marshy or flooded ground.

fence[1] *noun* 1 a barrier made of wood or wire etc. round an area. 2 a structure for a horse to jump over. 3 (*informal*) a person who buys stolen goods and sells them again.

fence[2] *verb* (**fenced, fencing**) 1 put a fence round or along something. 2 fight with long narrow swords (called *foils*) as a sport. **fencer** *noun*

fend *verb* **fend for** provide things for someone.

fend off keep a person or thing away from yourself.

fender *noun* 1 something placed round a fireplace to stop coals from falling into the room. 2 something hung over the side of a boat to protect it from knocks.

fennel *noun* a herb with yellow flowers.

ferment[1] (*say* fer-**ment**) *verb* bubble and change chemically by the action of a substance such as yeast. **fermentation** *noun*
• USAGE: Do not confuse with *foment.*

ferment[2] (*say* fer-ment) *noun* 1 fermenting. 2 an excited or agitated condition, *The town was in a state of ferment.*

fern *noun* a plant with feathery leaves and no flowers.

ferocious *adjective* fierce; savage. **ferociously** *adverb,* **ferocity** *noun*

ferret[1] *noun* a small animal used for catching rabbits and rats. **ferrety** *adjective*

ferret[2] *verb* (**ferreted, ferreting**) 1 hunt with a ferret. 2 search; rummage, *ferret out the truth.*

ferric (also **ferrous**) *adjective* containing iron.

ferry[1] *verb* (**ferried, ferrying**) transport people or things, especially across water.

ferry[2] *noun* (*plural* **ferries**) a boat or aircraft used in ferrying.

fertile *adjective* 1 producing good crops, *fertile soil.* 2 able to produce offspring.

3 able to produce ideas, *a fertile imagination.* **fertility** *noun*

fertility cycle the process by which nutrients move upwards from the soil into plants and are returned to the soil as decaying organic matter.

fertilize *verb* (**fertilized, fertilizing**) 1 add substances to the soil to make it more fertile. 2 put pollen into a plant or sperm into an egg or female animal so that it develops seed or young. **fertilization** *noun,* **fertilizer** *noun*

fervent (also **fervid**) *adjective* showing warm or strong feeling. **fervently** *adverb,* **fervency** *noun,* **fervour** *noun*

fester *verb* 1 become septic and filled with pus. 2 cause resentment for a long time.

festival *noun* a time when people arrange special celebrations, performances, etc.

festive *adjective* of a festival; suitable for a festival, joyful. **festively** *adverb*

festivity *noun* (*plural* **festivities**) a festive occasion or celebration.

festoon[1] *noun* a chain of flowers or ribbons etc. hung as a decoration.

festoon[2] *verb* decorate with ornaments.

feta *noun* a white cheese which is matured in brine.

fetch *verb* 1 go for and bring back, *fetch some milk; fetch a doctor.* 2 be sold for a particular price, *The chairs fetched R80.*

fête[1] (*say* fayt) *noun* an outdoor entertainment with stalls and sideshows.

fête[2] *verb* (**fêted, fêting**) honour a person with celebrations.

fetish *noun* an object supposed to have magical powers.

fetlock *noun* the part of a horse's leg above and behind the hoof.

fetter[1] *noun* a chain or shackle put round a prisoner's ankle.

fetter[2] *verb* put fetters on a prisoner.

fettle *noun* condition, *in fine fettle.*

feud (*say* fewd) *noun* a long-lasting quarrel or enmity.

feudal (*say* few-dal) *adjective* of the system used in the Middle Ages in Europe in which people could farm land in exchange for work done for the owner. **feudalism** *noun*

fever *noun* 1 an abnormally high body-

temperature, usually with an illness.
2 excitement; agitation, *election fever*.
fevered *adjective*, **feverish** *adjective*,
feverishly *adverb*

few[1] *adjective* not many. **fewness** *noun*

few[2] *noun* a small number of people or
things.

fez *noun* (*plural* **fezzes**) a high flat-topped
red hat with a tassel, worn by Muslim men in
some countries.

fiancé (*say* fee-**ahn**-say) *noun* a man who is
engaged to be married.

fiancée (*say* fee-**ahn**-say) *noun* a woman
who is engaged to be married.

fiasco (*say* fee-**as**-koh) *noun* (*plural* **fias-
cos**) a complete failure.

fib *noun* a lie about something unimportant. **fibber** *noun*, **fibbing** *noun*

fibre *noun* 1 a very thin thread.
2 a substance made of thin threads.
3 indigestible material in certain foods
that stimulates the action of the
intestines. **fibrous** *adjective*

fibreglass *noun* 1 fabric made from glass
fibres. 2 plastic containing glass fibres.

fickle *adjective* constantly changing, not
loyal to one person or group etc. **fickleness**
noun

fiction *noun* 1 writings about events that
have not really happened; stories and
novels. 2 something imagined or untrue.
fictional *adjective*

fictitious *adjective* imagined; untrue.

fiddle[1] *noun* 1 (*informal*) a violin.
2 (*informal*) a swindle.

fiddle[2] *verb* (**fiddled, fiddling**) 1 (*informal*)
play the violin. 2 fidget or tinker with
something, using your fingers. 3 (*informal*)
swindle; get or change something dishonestly. **fiddler** *noun*

fiddly *adjective* small and awkward to use
or do.

fidelity *noun* 1 faithfulness; loyalty.
2 accuracy; the exactness with which sound
is reproduced.

fidget[1] *verb* (**fidgeted, fidgeting**) 1 make
small restless movements. 2 worry. **fidgety**
adjective

fidget[2] *noun* a person who fidgets.

field[1] *noun* 1 a piece of land with grass or
crops growing on it. 2 an area or section,
recent advances in the field of science.
3 a battlefield. 4 those who are taking part
in a race or outdoor game etc., *the field of
athletes.*

field[2] *verb* 1 stop or catch the ball in cricket
etc. 2 be on the side not batting in cricket
etc. 3 put a team into a match etc., *They
fielded their best players.* **fielder** *noun*

field-cornet *noun* (in history) the local
representative of the government and
commander of burgher troops, also called
a veld-cornet.

fieldwork *noun* practical work or research
done in various places, not in a library or
museum or laboratory etc.

fiend (*say* feend) *noun* 1 an evil spirit;
a devil. 2 a very wicked or cruel person.
3 an enthusiast, *a fresh-air fiend.* **fiendish**
adjective

fierce *adjective* 1 angry and violent or
cruel. 2 intense, *fierce heat.* **fiercely** *adverb*,
fierceness *noun*

fiery *adjective* 1 full of flames or heat.
2 full of emotion. 3 easily made angry.

fife *noun* a small shrill flute.

fifteen *noun* & *adjective* 1 the number 15;
one more than fourteen. 2 a team of fifteen
players, especially in rugby. **fifteenth**
adjective & *noun*

fifth *adjective* & *noun* next after the fourth.
fifthly *adverb*

fifty *noun* & *adjective* (*plural* **fifties**) the
number 50; five times ten. **fiftieth** *adjective*
& *noun*

fifty-fifty *adjective* & *adverb* 1 shared
equally between two people or groups.
2 evenly balanced, *a fifty-fifty chance.*

fig *noun* a soft fruit full of small seeds.

fight[1] *noun* 1 a struggle against somebody
using hands, weapons, etc. 2 an attempt to
achieve or overcome something, *the fight
against poverty.*

fight[2] *verb* (**fought, fighting**) 1 have a fight.
2 attempt to achieve or overcome some-
thing. **fighter** *noun*

figment *noun* something imagined,
a figment of the imagination.

figurative *adjective* using a figure of
speech (see *figure*[1]); metaphorical, not

literal. **figuratively** *adverb*

figure[1] *noun* **1** the symbol of a number. **2** a diagram or illustration. **3** a pattern or shape; the shape of someone's body. **4** a representation of a person or animal in painting, sculpture, etc., *the stone figure of an elephant.*

figure of speech a word or phrase used for dramatic effect and not intended literally, e.g. 'a *flood* of letters'.

figure[2] *verb* (**figured, figuring**) **1** imagine. **2** work out, *Can you figure out what it will cost?* **3** appear or take part in something.

figure-head *noun* **1** a carved figure decorating the prow of a sailing-ship. **2** a person who is head of a country or organization but has no real power.

filament *noun* a thread or thin wire.

filch *verb* steal something slyly; pilfer.

file[1] *noun* a metal tool with a rough surface that is rubbed on things to shape them or make them smooth.

file[2] *verb* (**filed, filing**) shape or smooth with a file.

file[3] *noun* **1** a folder or box etc. for keeping papers in order. **2** a set of data stored under one reference in a computer. **3** a line of people one behind the other.

file[4] *verb* (**filed, filing**) **1** put into a file. **2** walk in a file, *They filed out.*

filial (*say* fil-ee-al) *adjective* of a son or daughter, *filial affection.*

filibuster *verb* try to delay or prevent the passing of a law by making long speeches. **filibuster** *noun*

filigree *noun* ornamental lace-like work of twisted metal wire.

fill[1] *verb* **1** make or become full. **2** block up a hole or cavity. **filler** *noun*

fill[2] *noun* enough to fill a person or thing.

fillet[1] *noun* a piece of fish or meat without bones.

fillet[2] *verb* (**filleted, filleting**) remove the bones from fish or meat.

filling *noun* **1** something used to fill a hole or gap, e.g. in a tooth. **2** something put in pastry to make a pie, or between layers of bread to make a sandwich.

filly *noun* (*plural* **fillies**) a young female horse.

film[1] *noun* **1** a motion picture, such as those shown in cinemas or on television. **2** a rolled strip or sheet of thin plastic coated with material that is sensitive to light, used for taking photographs or making a motion picture. **3** a very thin layer, *a film of grease.*

film[2] *verb* make a film of a story etc.

filmy *adjective* (**filmier, filmiest**) thin and almost transparent. **filminess** *noun*

filter[1] *noun* **1** a device for holding back dirt or other unwanted material from a liquid or gas etc. that passes through it. **2** a screen that allows light of a particular wavelength only to pass through, *She took the picture with a green filter.*

filter[2] *verb* **1** pass through a filter. **2** move gradually, *They filtered into the hall.*

filter feeder an animal which feeds by filtering particles of food floating in water.

filth *noun* disgusting dirt.

filthy *adjective* (**filthier, filthiest**) disgustingly dirty. **filthiness** *noun*

filtrate *noun* the part of a mixture which passes through filter paper.

fin *noun* **1** a thin flat part projecting from a fish's body, that helps it to swim. **2** a small projection on an aircraft or rocket etc., that helps its balance.

final[1] *adjective* **1** coming at the end, last. **2** that puts an end to an argument etc., *You must go, and that's final!* **finally** *adverb*, **finality** *noun*

final[2] *noun* the last in a series of contests.

finale (*say* fin-**ah**-lee) *noun* the final section of a piece of music or a play etc.

finalist *noun* a competitor in the final.

finalize *verb* (**finalized, finalizing**) put into its final form. **finalization** *noun*

finance[1] *noun* the use or management of money.

finances *plural noun* money resources; funds.

finance[2] *verb* (**financed, financing**) provide the money for something. **financier** *noun*

financial *adjective* of finance. **financially** *adverb*

finch *noun* (*plural* **finches**) a small bird with a short stubby bill.

find[1] *verb* (**found, finding**) **1** get or see something by looking for it or by chance. **2** learn by experience, *He found that digging was hard work.*

find[2] *noun* something found.

fine[1] *adjective* **1** of high quality; excellent. **2** dry and clear; sunny, *fine weather.* **3** very thin; consisting of small particles, *fine dust.* **4** in good health; comfortable, *I'm fine.* **finely** *adverb*, **fineness** *noun*

fine[2] *adverb* **1** finely, *chop it fine.* **2** (*informal*) very well, *That will suit me fine.*

fine[3] *noun* money which has to be paid as a punishment.

fine[4] *verb* (**fined, fining**) make somebody pay a fine.

finery *noun* fine clothes or decorations.

finesse (*say* fin-**ess**) *noun* clever management; artfulness.

finger[1] *noun* **1** one of the separate parts of the hand. **2** a narrow piece of something, *fish fingers.*

finger[2] *verb* touch or feel with your fingers.

fingerprint *noun* a mark made by the tiny ridges on the fingertip, used as a way of identifying someone.

fingertip *noun* the tip of a finger.

have something at your fingertips be very familiar with a subject etc.

finicky *adjective* fussy about details; hard to please.

finish[1] *verb* bring or come to an end.

finish[2] *noun* (*plural* **finishes**) **1** the last stage of something; the end. **2** the surface or coating on woodwork etc.

finite (*say* fy-nyt) *adjective* limited; not infinite, *We have only a finite supply of coal.* **finite verb** a verb that agrees with its subject in person and number, *'was', 'went', and 'says' are finite verbs; 'going' and 'to say' are not.*

fiord (*say* fee-**ord**) *noun* an inlet of the sea between high cliffs, as in Norway.

fir *noun* an evergreen tree with needle-like leaves, that produces cones.

fire[1] *noun* **1** the process of burning that produces light and heat. **2** coal and wood etc. burning in a grate or furnace to give heat. **3** a device using electricity or gas to heat a room. **4** the shooting of guns, *Hold your fire!*

fire brigade a team of people organized to fight fires.

fire extinguisher a container with chemicals, foam, etc. inside used for putting out fires.

on fire burning.

set fire to start something burning.

fire[2] *verb* (**fired, firing**) **1** set fire to. **2** bake pottery or bricks etc. in a kiln. **3** shoot a gun; send out a bullet or missile. **4** dismiss someone from a job. **5** excite, *fire them with enthusiasm.* **firer** *noun*

firearm *noun* a small gun; a rifle, pistol, or revolver.

firebrand *noun* a person who stirs up trouble.

fire-engine *noun* a large vehicle that carries firefighters and equipment to put out large fires.

fire-escape *noun* a special staircase or apparatus by which people may escape from a burning building etc.

firefighter *noun* a person whose task is to put out fires.

firefly *noun* (*plural* **fireflies**) a kind of beetle that gives off a glowing light.

fireman *noun* (*plural* **firemen**) a member of a fire brigade; a firefighter.

fireplace *noun* an open structure for holding a fire in a room.

fireside *noun* the part of the room near a fireplace.

firewood *noun* wood for use as fuel.

firework *noun* a device containing chemicals that burn attractively or noisily.

firing-squad *noun* a group ordered to fire a salute during a military funeral, or to shoot a condemned person.

firm[1] *noun* a business organization.

firm[2] *adjective* **1** not giving way when pressed; hard, solid. **2** steady; not shaking or moving, *a firm grip.* **3** definite and not likely to change, *a firm belief.* **firmly** *adverb*, **firmness** *noun*

firm[3] *adverb* firmly, *Stand firm!*

firm[4] *verb* make something become firm.

firmament *noun* the sky with its clouds and stars.

first[1] *adjective* coming before all others in

time or order or importance. **firstly** *adverb*
first aid treatment given to an injured
person before a doctor comes.
first class the best category.
first name a personal name, usually coming
before a surname.
first[2] *adverb* before everything else, *Finish
this work first.*
first[3] *noun* a person or thing that is first, *He
is the first to reach the tuck-shop every day.*
fiscal[1] *adjective* of public finances.
fiscal[2] *noun* an official with many
powers at the Cape under Dutch East India
Company control and early British rule.
fiscal shrike Jan Fiskaal.
fish[1] *noun* (*plural* **fish** or **fishes**) an animal
that always lives and breathes in water.
fish cake a small cake of fish and mashed
potato, usually fried.
fish eagle a white-headed eagle that
catches and eats fish.
fish[2] *verb* 1 try to catch fish. 2 search for
something; try to get something, *He is only
fishing for praise.*
fisherman *noun* (*plural* **fishermen**)
a person who tries to catch fish; an angler.
fishery *noun* (*plural* **fisheries**) 1 the part
of the sea where fishing is carried on.
2 the business of fishing.
fishmonger *noun* a shopkeeper who sells
fish.
fishy *adjective* (**fishier**, **fishiest**) 1 smelling
or tasting of fish. 2 (*informal*) causing
doubt or suspicion, *a fishy excuse.* **fishily**
adverb, **fishiness** *noun*
fissile *adjective* 1 likely to split. 2 capable of
undergoing nuclear fission.
fission *noun* splitting something; splitting
the nucleus of an atom so as to release
energy. **fissionable** *adjective*
fissure (*say* **fish**-er) *noun* a narrow opening made where something splits.
fist *noun* a tightly closed hand with the
fingers bent into the palm.
fisticuffs *noun* fighting with the fists.
fit[1] *adjective* (**fitter**, **fittest**) 1 suitable; good
enough, *a meal fit for a king.* 2 healthy, *Keep
fit!* 3 ready; likely, *They worked till they were
fit to collapse.* **fitly** *adverb*, **fitness** *noun*
fit[2] *verb* (**fitted**, **fitting**) 1 be the right size

and shape for something; be suitable.
2 put into place, *Fit a lock on the door.*
3 alter something to make it the right size
and shape. 4 make suitable, *Her training
fits her for the job.* **fitter** *noun*
fit[3] *noun* the way something fits, *a good fit.*
fit[4] *noun* 1 a sudden illness, especially one
that makes you move violently or become
unconscious. 2 an outburst, *a fit of rage.*
fitful *adjective* happening in short periods,
not steadily. **fitfully** *adverb*
fitment *noun* a piece of fixed furniture etc.
fitting *adjective* proper; suitable.
fittings *plural noun* the fixtures and
fitments of a building.
five *noun* & *adjective* the number 5;
one more than four.
fix[1] *verb* 1 fasten or place firmly. 2 make
permanent and unable to change. 3 decide;
arrange, *We fixed a date for the party.*
4 repair; put into working condition,
He is fixing my bike. **fixer** *noun*
fix up arrange, organize.
fix[2] *noun* (*plural* **fixes**) 1 (*informal*)
an awkward situation, *I'm in a fix.* 2 finding
the position of something. 3 (*informal*)
an addict's dose of a drug.
fixation *noun* 1 fixing something.
2 a strong interest or a concentration on
one idea etc.; an obsession.
fixative *noun* a substance used to
keep something in position or make it
permanent.
fixedly *adverb* in a fixed way.
fixity *noun* a fixed condition; permanence.
fixture *noun* 1 something fixed in its place.
2 a sports event planned for a particular
day.
fizz *verb* make a hissing or spluttering
sound; produce a lot of small bubbles.
fizzy *adjective*, **fizziness** *noun*
fizzle *verb* (**fizzled**, **fizzling**) make a slight
fizzing sound.
fizzle out end feebly or unsuccessfully.
fjord (*say* fee-**ord**) *noun* a fiord.
flaaitaal *noun* flytaal.
flabbergast *verb* astonish greatly.
flabby *adjective* fat and soft, not firm.
flabbily *adverb*, **flabbiness** *noun*
flaccid (*say* **flak**-sid) *adjective* soft and

limp. **flaccidly** *adverb*, **flaccidity** *noun*

flag[1] *noun* **1** a piece of cloth with a coloured pattern or shape on it, used as a sign or signal. **2** a small piece of paper or plastic that looks like a flag. **flag-pole** *noun*, **flagstaff** *noun*

flag[2] *verb* (**flagged, flagging**) **1** become weak; droop. **2** signal with a flag or by waving.

flagon *noun* a large bottle or container for wine or cider etc.

flagrant (*say* **flay**-grant) *adjective* very bad and noticeable, *flagrant disobedience*. **flagrantly** *adverb*, **flagrancy** *noun*

flagship *noun* a ship that carries an admiral and flies his or her flag.

flagstone *noun* a flat slab of stone used for paving.

flail[1] *noun* an old-fashioned tool for threshing grain.

flail[2] *verb* beat as if with a flail; wave about wildly.

flair *noun* a natural ability, talent.

flak *noun* shells fired by anti-aircraft guns.

flake[1] *noun* **1** a very light thin piece of something, *cornflakes*. **2** a small flat piece of falling snow. **flaky** *adjective*

flake[2] *verb* (**flaked, flaking**) come off in flakes.

flamboyant *adjective* very showy in appearance or manner.

flame[1] *noun* a tongue-shaped portion of fire or burning gas.
flame lily a red lily that grows wild.

flame[2] *verb* (**flamed, flaming**) **1** produce flames. **2** become bright red.

flamingo *noun* (*plural* **flamingoes**) a wading bird with long legs, a long neck, and pinkish feathers.

flammable *adjective* able to be set on fire. **flammability** *noun*

flan *noun* a pastry or sponge shell with no cover over the filling.

flank[1] *noun* the side of something.

flank[2] *verb* place or be placed at the side of something or somebody, *The singer was flanked by her bodyguards*. **flanker** *noun*

flannel *noun* **1** a soft cloth for washing yourself. **2** a soft woollen material.

flap[1] *verb* (**flapped, flapping**) **1** wave about.

2 (*informal*) panic; fuss.

flap[2] *noun* **1** a part that is fixed at one edge on to something else, often to cover an opening. **2** the action or sound of flapping. **3** (*informal*) a panic or fuss, *in a flap*.

flare[1] *verb* (**flared, flaring**) **1** blaze with a sudden bright flame. **2** become angry suddenly. **3** become gradually wider, *trousers flared at the ankle*.

flare[2] *noun* **1** a sudden bright flame or light. **2** a gradual widening.

flash[1] *noun* (*plural* **flashes**) **1** a sudden bright flame or light. **2** a device for making a sudden bright light for taking photographs. **3** a sudden display of anger, wit, etc., *a flash of brilliance*. **4** a short item of news.

flash[2] *verb* **1** make a flash. **2** appear suddenly; move quickly, *The train flashed past us*.

flashback *noun* going back in a film or story to something that happened earlier.

flashy *adjective* gaudy; showy.

flask *noun* **1** a bottle with a narrow neck. **2** a vacuum flask.

flat[1] *adjective* (**flatter, flattest**) **1** with no curves or bumps; smooth and level. **2** spread out; lying at full length, *Lie flat on the ground*. **3** (of a tyre) with no air inside. **4** (of feet) without the normal arch underneath. **5** absolute, *a flat refusal*. **6** dull; not changing. **7** (of a drink) having lost its fizziness. **8** (of a battery) unable to produce any more electric current. **9** (in music) one semitone lower than the natural note, *E flat*. **flatly** *adverb*, **flatness** *noun*

flat[2] *adverb* **1** so as to be flat, *Press it flat*. **2** (*informal*) exactly, *in ten seconds flat*. **3** (in music) below the correct pitch.
flat out as fast as possible.

flat[3] *noun* **1** a flat thing or area. **2** a set of rooms for living in, usually on one floor of a building. **3** (in music) a note one semitone lower than the natural note.

flatten *verb* make or become flat.

flatter *verb* **1** praise somebody more than he or she deserves. **2** make a person or thing seem better or more attractive than they really are. **flatterer** *noun*, **flattery** *noun*

flaunt *verb* display something proudly, show it off, *They flaunted the trophy*.

• USAGE: Do not confuse this word with *flout*, which has a different meaning.

flavour[1] *noun* the taste of something.

flavour[2] *verb* give something a flavour, season it. **flavouring** *noun*

flaw *noun* something that makes a person or thing imperfect. **flawed** *adjective*

flawless *adjective* without a flaw; perfect. **flawlessly** *adverb*, **flawlessness** *noun*

flax *noun* a plant that produces fibres from which linen is made and seeds from which linseed oil is obtained.

flaxen *adjective* pale-yellow like flax fibres, *flaxen hair.*

flay *verb* strip the skin from an animal.

flea *noun* a small jumping insect that sucks blood.

fleck *noun* 1 a very small patch of colour. 2 a particle; a speck, *flecks of dirt.* **flecked** *adjective*

fledged *adjective* (of young birds) having grown feathers and able to fly.
fully-fledged *adjective* fully trained, *a fully-fledged engineer.*

fledgeling *noun* a young bird that is just fledged.

flee *verb* (**fled, fleeing**) run or hurry away from something.

fleece[1] *noun* the woolly hair of a sheep or similar animal. **fleecy** *adjective*

fleece[2] *verb* (**fleeced, fleecing**) 1 shear the fleece from a sheep. 2 swindle a person out of some money.

fleet[1] *noun* a number of ships, aircraft, or vehicles owned by one country or company.

fleet[2] *adjective* moving swiftly; nimble.

fleeting *adjective* passing quickly; brief.

flesh *noun* 1 the soft substance of the bodies of people and animals, consisting of muscle and fat. 2 the pulpy part of fruits and vegetables. **fleshy** *adjective*

flex[1] *verb* bend or stretch something that is flexible, *flex your muscles.*

flex[2] *noun* (*plural* **flexes**) flexible insulated wire for carrying electric current.

flexible *adjective* 1 easy to bend or stretch. 2 able to be changed or adapted, *Our plans are flexible.* **flexibility** *noun*

flick[1] *noun* a quick light hit or movement.

flick[2] *verb* hit or move with a flick.

flicker[1] *verb* 1 burn or shine unsteadily. 2 move quickly to and fro, *Her eyelids flickered in the sunlight.*

flicker[2] *noun* a flickering light or movement.

flier *noun* a flyer.

flight[1] *noun* 1 flying. 2 a journey in an aircraft etc. 3 a series of stairs. 4 the feathers or fins on a dart or arrow.
flight-recorder a device in an aircraft that records details of a flight.

flight[2] *noun* fleeing; an escape.

flighty *adjective* (**flightier, flightiest**) silly and frivolous. **flightiness** *noun*

flimsy *adjective* (**flimsier, flimsiest**) light and thin; fragile; not strong. **flimsily** *adverb*, **flimsiness** *noun*

flinch *verb* move or shrink back because you are afraid; wince. **flinch** *noun*

fling[1] *verb* (**flung, flinging**) throw something violently or carelessly.

fling[2] *noun* 1 the movement of flinging. 2 a vigorous dance, *the Highland fling.* 3 (*informal*) a short time of enjoyment, *have a fling.*

flint *noun* 1 a very hard kind of stone. 2 a piece of flint or hard metal used to produce sparks. **flinty** *adjective*

flip[1] *verb* (**flipped, flipping**) 1 flick. 2 (*informal*) become crazy or very angry.

flip[2] *noun* a flipping movement.

flip-flops *plural noun* slip-slops.

flippant *adjective* not showing proper seriousness. **flippantly** *adverb*, **flippancy** *noun*

flipper *noun* 1 a limb that water-animals use for swimming. 2 a device that you wear on your feet to help you to swim.

flirt[1] *verb* behave lovingly towards somebody to amuse yourself. **flirtation** *noun*

flirt[2] *noun* a person who flirts. **flirtatious** *adjective*, **flirtatiously** *adverb*

flit *verb* (**flitted, flitting**) fly or move lightly and quickly. **flit** *noun*

flitter *verb* flit about. **flitter** *noun*

float[1] *verb* 1 stay or move on the surface of a liquid or in air. 2 make something float, *float the raft.* **floater** *noun*

float[2] *noun* 1 a device designed to float. 2 a vehicle with a platform used for delivering milk or for carrying a display in a parade etc. **3** a small amount of money kept for paying small bills or giving change etc.

floating voter *noun* a person who does not support any political party permanently.

flock[1] *noun* a group of sheep, goats, or birds.

flock[2] *verb* gather or move in a crowd.

flock[3] *noun* a tuft of wool or cotton etc.

floe *noun* a sheet of floating ice.

flog *verb* (**flogged, flogging**) **1** beat hard with a whip or stick as a punishment. **2** (*informal*) sell. **flogging** *noun*

flood[1] *noun* **1** a large amount of water spreading over a place that is usually dry. **2** a great amount, *a flood of requests.* **3** the movement of the tide when it is coming in towards the land.

flood[2] *verb* **1** cover with a flood. **2** come in great amounts, *Letters flooded in.*

floodlight *noun* a lamp that makes a broad bright beam to light up a stage or building etc. **floodlit** *adjective*

floor[1] *noun* **1** the part of a room that people walk on. **2** a storey of a building; all the rooms at the same level.

floor[2] *verb* **1** put a floor into a building. **2** knock a person down. **3** baffle somebody, *The question floored me.*

floorboard *noun* one of the boards forming the floor of a room.

flop[1] *verb* (**flopped, flopping**) **1** fall or sit down clumsily. **2** hang or sway heavily and loosely. **3** (*informal*) be a failure.

flop[2] *noun* **1** a flopping movement or sound. **2** (*informal*) a failure.

floppy *adjective* hanging loosely; not firm or rigid. **floppiness** *noun*

floppy disk a flexible disk holding data for use in a computer.

flora *noun* the plants of a particular area or period. (Compare *fauna.*)

floral *adjective* of flowers.

florist *noun* a shopkeeper who sells flowers.

floss *noun* silky thread or fibres. **flossy** *adjective*

flotation *noun* floating something.

flotilla (*say* flot-**il**-a) *noun* a fleet of boats or small ships.

flotsam *noun* wreckage or cargo found floating after a shipwreck.

flotsam and jetsam odds and ends.

flounce[1] *verb* (**flounced, flouncing**) go in an impatient or annoyed manner, *She flounced out of the room.* **flounce** *noun*

flounce[2] *noun* a wide frill.

flounder *verb* **1** move clumsily and with difficulty. **2** make mistakes or become confused when trying to do something, *He's floundering in his new job.*

flour *noun* a fine powder of wheat or other grain, used in cooking. **floury** *adjective*

flourish[1] *verb* **1** grow or develop strongly. **2** be successful; prosper. **3** wave something about dramatically, *She flourished the telegram above her head.*

flourish[2] *noun* (*plural* **flourishes**) a dramatic sweeping movement, curve, or passage of music.

flout *verb* disobey openly and scornfully, *They flouted the rules.*

• USAGE: Do not confuse this word with *flaunt*, which has a different meaning.

flow[1] *verb* **1** move along smoothly or continuously. **2** gush out, *Water flowed from the tap.* **3** hang loosely, *flowing hair.* **4** (of the tide) come in towards the land.

flow[2] *noun* **1** a flowing movement or mass. **2** the movement of the tide when it is coming in towards the land, *the ebb and flow of the tide.*

flower[1] *noun* **1** the part of a plant from which seed and fruit develops. **2** a blossom and its stem used for decoration, usually in groups.

flower[2] *verb* produce flowers.

flowerpot *noun* a pot in which a plant may be grown.

flowery *adjective* **1** full of flowers. **2** full of ornamental phrases, *a flowery speech.*

flu *noun* influenza.

fluctuate *verb* (**fluctuated, fluctuating**) rise and fall; vary, *Prices fluctuated.* **fluctuation** *noun*

flue *noun* a pipe or tube through which smoke or hot gases are drawn off.

fluent (*say* **floo**-ent) *adjective* skilful at speaking; using a language easily and well.

fluently *adverb,* **fluency** *noun*
fluff *noun* a fluffy substance.
fluffy *adjective* having a mass of soft fur
or fibres. **fluffiness** *noun*
fluid[1] *noun* a substance that is able to flow
freely as liquids and gases do.
fluid[2] *adjective* able to flow freely, not solid
or stiff. **fluidity** *noun*
fluke *noun* a piece of good luck that makes
you able to do something you thought you
could not do.
flummox *verb* (*informal*) baffle.
fluorescent (*say* floo-er-**ess**-ent) *adjective*
creating light from radiations.
fluorescence *noun*
fluoridation *noun* adding fluoride to
drinking-water.
fluoride *noun* a chemical substance that
is thought to prevent tooth-decay.
flurry *noun* (*plural* **flurries**) **1** a sudden
whirling gust of wind, rain, or snow.
2 an excited or flustered disturbance,
a flurry of activity.
flush[1] *verb* **1** blush. **2** clean or remove
something with a fast flow of water.
flush[2] *noun* **1** a blush. **2** a fast flow of water.
flush[3] *adjective* **1** level; without projections, *The doors are flush with the walls.*
2 having plenty of money.
fluster *verb* make somebody nervous and
confused. **fluster** *noun*
flute *noun* a musical instrument consisting
of a long pipe with holes that are stopped by
fingers or keys.
flutter[1] *verb* **1** flap wings quickly. **2** move
or flap quickly and irregularly.
flutter[2] *noun* **1** a fluttering movement.
2 a nervously excited condition.
3 (*informal*) a small bet, *Have a flutter!*
flux *noun* continual change or flow.
fly[1] *noun* (*plural* **flies**) **1** a small flying
insect with two wings. **2** a real or artificial fly
used as bait in fishing.
fly[2] *verb* (**flew, flown, flying**) **1** move
through the air by means of wings or in an
aircraft. **2** travel through the air or through
space. **3** wave in the air, *Flags were flying.*
4 make something fly, *They flew model
aircraft.* **5** move or pass quickly, *Time flies.*
6 flee from, *You must fly the country!* **flyer**

noun
fly[3] *noun* (*plural* **flies**) **1** flying. **2** the front
opening of a pair of trousers.
flying saucer *noun* a mysterious saucer-
shaped object reported to have been seen
in the sky.
flying squad *noun* a team of police or
doctors etc. organized so that they can
move rapidly.
flyleaf *noun* (*plural* **flyleaves**) a blank page
at the beginning or end of a book.
flyover *noun* a bridge that carries one road
or railway over another.
flytaal *noun* an African township jargon.
flywheel *noun* a heavy wheel used to
regulate machinery.
foal[1] *noun* a young horse.
foal[2] *verb* give birth to a foal.
foam[1] *noun* **1** froth. **2** a spongy kind
of rubber or plastic. **foamy** *adjective*
foam[2] *verb* form foam; send out foam.
fob[1] *noun* an ornament hanging from
a watch-chain; a tab on a key-ring.
fob[2] *verb* (**fobbed, fobbing**) **fob off** get rid
of someone by an excuse or a trick.
focal *adjective* of or at a focus.
focal point the most prominent or striking
part of a painting etc., meant to catch the
attention of the viewer.
focus[1] *noun* (*plural* **focuses** or **foci**)
1 the distance from an eye or lens at which
an object appears clearest. **2** the point at
which rays etc. seem to meet. **3** something
that is a centre of interest or attention etc.
in focus appearing clearly.
out of focus not appearing clearly.
focus[2] *verb* (**focused, focusing**) **1** use or
adjust a lens so that objects appear clearly.
2 concentrate, *She focused her attention
on it.*
fodder *noun* food for horses and farm
animals.
foe *noun* (*old use*) an enemy.
foefie slide *noun* a children's slide
made of a bar attached to a sloping wire or
rope.
foetus (*say* fee-tus) *noun* (*plural*
foetuses) a developing embryo, especially
an unborn human baby. **foetal** *adjective*
fog *noun* thick mist. **foggy** *adjective*

fog-horn *noun* a loud horn for warning ships in fog.

fogy *noun* (*plural* **fogies**) **old fogy** a person with old-fashioned ideas.

foible *noun* a slight peculiarity in someone's character or tastes.

foil[1] *noun* **1** a very thin sheet of metal. **2** a person or thing that makes another look better in contrast, *The dark jersey provided a perfect foil for her pearls.*

foil[2] *noun* a long narrow sword used in the sport of fencing.

foil[3] *verb* frustrate, prevent from being successful, *We foiled his evil plan.*

foist *verb* make a person accept something inferior or unwelcome, *They foisted the job on me.*

fold[1] *verb* bend or move so that one part lies on another part.

fold[2] *noun* a line where something is folded.

fold[3] *noun* an enclosure for sheep.

folder *noun* a folding cover for loose papers.

foliage *noun* the leaves of a tree or plant.

folk *noun* people.

folk-dance *noun* a dance in the traditional style of a country.

folklore *noun* old beliefs and legends.

folk-song *noun* a song in the traditional style of a country.

follow *verb* **1** go or come after. **2** do a thing after something else. **3** take a person or thing as a guide or example, *He followed the teachings of Buddha.* **4** take an interest in the progress of events or a sport or team etc. **5** understand, *Did you follow what he said?* **6** result from something. **follower** *noun*

following *preposition* after, as a result of, *Following the burglary, we had new locks fitted.*

folly *noun* (*plural* **follies**) foolishness; a foolish action etc.

foment (*say* fo-**ment**) *verb* arouse or stimulate deliberately, *foment trouble.*
● USAGE: Do not confuse with *ferment.*

fomentation *noun* **1** fomenting. **2** hot liquid used to bathe an inflamed or aching part of the body.

fond *adjective* **1** loving. **2** foolishly hopeful, *fond hopes.* **fondly** *adverb*, **fondness** *noun*

fondle *verb* (**fondled**, **fondling**) touch or stroke lovingly.

font *noun* a basin (often of carved stone) in a church, to hold water for baptism.

food *noun* any substance that a plant or animal can take into its body to help it to grow and be healthy.

food chain a series of plants and animals each of which serves as food for the one above it in the series.

fool[1] *noun* **1** a stupid person; someone who acts unwisely. **2** a jester or clown, *Stop playing the fool.* **3** a creamy pudding with crushed fruit in it, *gooseberry fool.*

fool's errand a useless errand.

fool's paradise happiness that comes only from being mistaken about something.

fool[2] *verb* **1** behave in a joking way; play about. **2** trick or deceive someone.

foolery *noun* foolish acts or behaviour.

foolhardy *adjective* bold but foolish; reckless. **foolhardiness** *noun*

foolish *adjective* without good sense or judgement; unwise. **foolishly** *adverb*, **foolishness** *noun*

foolproof *adjective* easy to use or do correctly.

foot *noun* (*plural* **feet**) **1** the lower part of the leg below the ankle. **2** any similar part, e.g. one used by certain animals to move or attach themselves to things. **3** the lowest part, *the foot of the hill.* **4** a measure of length in the imperial system, 12 inches or about 30 centimetres, *a ten-foot pole*; *it is ten feet long.* **5** a unit of rhythm in a line of poetry, e.g. each of the four divisions in *Jack / and Jill / went up / the hill.*

on foot walking.

football *noun* **1** a game played by two teams which try to kick an inflated leather ball into their opponents' goal, also called soccer. **2** the ball used in this game. **footballer** *noun*

foothill *noun* a low hill near the bottom of a mountain or range of mountains.

foothold *noun* **1** a place to put your foot when climbing. **2** a small but firm position from which you can advance in busines etc.

footing *noun* **1** having your feet placed on

something; a foothold, *He lost his footing and slipped.* **2** a status, *We are on a friendly footing with that country.*

footlights *plural noun* a row of lights along the front of the floor of a stage.

footman *noun* (*plural* **footmen**) a male servant who opens doors, serves at table, etc.

footnote *noun* a note printed at the bottom of the page.

footpath *noun* a path for pedestrians.

footprint *noun* a mark made by a foot or shoe.

footsore *adjective* having feet that are painful or sore from walking.

footstep *noun* **1** a step taken in walking or running. **2** the sound of this.

footstool *noun* a stool for resting your feet on when you are sitting.

for¹ *preposition* This word is used to show **1** purpose or direction, *This letter is for you. We set out for home.* **2** distance or time, *Walk for six kilometres or two hours.* **3** price or exchange, *We bought it for R10. New lamps for old.* **4** cause, *She was fined for speeding.* **5** defence or support, *He fought for his country. Are you for us or against us?* **6** reference, *For all her wealth, she is bored.* **7** similarity or correspondence, *We took him for a fool.*

for ever for all time; always.

for² *conjunction* because, *They hesitated, for they were afraid.*

for- *prefix* **1** away, off (as in *forgive*). **2** prohibiting (as in *forbid*). **3** abstaining or neglecting (as in *forgo, forsake*).

forage¹ *noun* **1** food for horses and cattle. **2** the action of foraging.

forage² *verb* (**foraged, foraging**) go searching for something; rummage.

foray *noun* a raid.

forbear *verb* (**forbore, forborne, forbearing**) **1** refrain from something, *We forbore to mention it.* **2** be patient or tolerant. **forbearance** *noun*

forbid *verb* (**forbade, forbidden, forbidding**) **1** order someone not to do something. **2** refuse to allow, *We shall forbid the marriage.*

forbidding *adjective* looking stern or unfriendly.

force¹ *noun* **1** strength; power; intense effort. **2** (in science) an influence, which can be measured, that causes something to move. **3** an organized group of police, soldiers, etc.

in or **into force** in or into effectiveness, *The new law comes into force next week.*

the forces a country's armed forces, services, etc.

force² *verb* (**forced, forcing**) **1** use force in order to get or do something, or to make somebody obey. **2** break something open by force. **3** cause plants to grow or bloom earlier than is normal, *You can force them in a greenhouse.*

forceful *adjective* strong and vigorous. **forcefully** *adverb*

forceps *noun* (*plural* **forceps**) pincers or tongs used by dentists, surgeons, etc.

forcible *adjective* done by force; forceful. **forcibly** *adverb*

ford¹ *noun* a shallow place where you can walk across a river.

ford² *verb* cross a river at a ford.

fore¹ *adjective* & *adverb* at or towards the front, *fore and aft.*

fore² *noun* the front part.

to the fore to or at the front; in or to a prominent position.

fore- *prefix* before (as in *forecast*); in front (as in *foreleg*).

forearm¹ (*say* **for**-arm) *noun* the arm from the elbow to the wrist or fingertips.

forearm² (*say* for-**arm**) *verb* arm or prepare in advance against possible danger.

forebears *plural noun* ancestors.

foreboding *noun* a feeling that trouble is coming.

forecast¹ *noun* a statement that tells in advance what is likely to happen.

forecast² *verb* (**forecast, forecasting**) make a forecast. **forecaster** *noun*

forecastle (*say* **foh**-ksul) *noun* the forward part of certain ships.

forecourt *noun* an enclosed area in front of a building etc.

forefathers *plural noun* ancestors.

forefinger *noun* the finger next to the thumb.

forefoot *noun* (*plural* **forefeet**) an animal's front foot.

forefront *noun* the very front.

foregoing *adjective* preceding; previous.

foregone conclusion *noun* a result that can be foreseen easily and with certainty.

foreground *noun* the front part of a scene or view etc.

forehand *noun* a stroke made in tennis etc. with the palm of the hand turned forwards.

forehead (*say* forrid or for-hed) *noun* the part of the face above the eyes.

foreign *adjective* 1 of or in another country; of other countries. 2 not belonging, unnatural, *Lying is foreign to her nature.*

foreigner *noun* a person from another country.

foreleg *noun* an animal's front leg.

foreman *noun* (*plural* **foremen**) 1 a worker in charge of a group of other workers. 2 a person acting as president and spokesperson of a jury.

foremost *adjective* & *adverb* first in position or rank; most important.

forensic (*say* fer-en-sik) *adjective* of or used in lawcourts.
forensic medicine medical knowledge needed in legal matters.

forerunner *noun* a person or thing that comes before another; a sign of what is to come.

foresee *verb* (**foresaw, foreseen, foreseeing**) realize what is going to happen.

foreseeable *adjective* able to be foreseen.

foreshadow *verb* be a sign of something that is to come.

foreshorten *verb* show an object in a drawing etc. with some lines shortened to give an effect of distance or depth.

foresight *noun* the ability to foresee and prepare for future needs.

forest *noun* trees and undergrowth covering a large area. **forested** *adjective*

forestall *verb* prevent somebody or something by taking action first.

forestry *noun* planting forests and looking after them. **forester** *noun*

foretaste *noun* an experience of something that is to come in the future.

foretell *verb* (**foretold, foretelling**) forecast; prophesy.

forethought *noun* careful thought and planning for the future.

forewarn *verb* warn someone beforehand.

forewoman *noun* (*plural* **forewomen**) 1 a woman worker in charge of other workers. 2 a woman acting as president and spokesperson of a jury.

foreword *noun* a preface.

forfeit[1] (*say* for-fit) *verb* pay or give up something as a penalty. **forfeiture** *noun*

forfeit[2] *noun* something forfeited.

forge[1] *noun* a place where metal is heated and shaped; a blacksmith's workshop.

forge[2] *verb* (**forged, forging**) 1 shape metal by heating and hammering. 2 copy something so as to deceive people. **forger** *noun*, **forgery** *noun*

forge[3] *verb* (**forged, forging**) **forge ahead** move forward by a strong effort.

forget *verb* (**forgot, forgotten, forgetting**) 1 fail to remember. 2 stop thinking about, *Forget your troubles.* 3 leave something behind, *She had forgotten her book at home.* **forget yourself** behave rudely or thoughtlessly.

forgetful *adjective* tending to forget. **forgetfully** *adverb*, **forgetfulness** *noun*

forget-me-not *noun* a plant with small blue flowers.

forgive *verb* (**forgave, forgiven, forgiving**) stop feeling angry with somebody about something. **forgiveness** *noun*

forgo *verb* (**forwent, forgone, forgoing**) give something up; go without.

fork[1] *noun* 1 a small device with prongs for lifting food to your mouth. 2 a large device with prongs used for digging or lifting things. 3 a place where something separates into two or more parts, *the fork of the road.*

fork[2] *verb* 1 lift or dig with a fork. 2 form a fork by separating into two branches. 3 follow one of these branches, *Fork left.* **fork out** (*informal*) pay out money.

fork-lift truck *noun* a truck with two metal bars at the front for lifting and moving heavy loads.

forlorn *adjective* left alone and unhappy. **forlorn hope** the only faint hope left.

form[1] *noun* **1** the shape, appearance, or condition of something, *the form of a circle. He's in good form.* **2** the way something exists, *Ice is a form of water.* **3** a class in school. **4** a bench. **5** a piece of paper with spaces to be filled in.

form[2] *verb* **1** shape or construct something; create. **2** come into existence; develop, *Icicles formed.*

formal *adjective* strictly following the accepted rules or customs; ceremonious. **formally** *adverb*

formal sector the part of the economy made up of all conventional, licensed, tax-paying businesses. (Compare *informal sector.*)

formality *noun* (*plural* **formalities**) **1** formal behaviour. **2** something done to obey a rule or custom.

format *noun* the shape and size of something; the way it is arranged.

formation *noun* **1** the act of forming something. **2** a thing formed, *the rock formation.* **3** a special arrangement or pattern, *flying in formation.*

formative *adjective* forming or developing something.

former *adjective* of an earlier period; of past times. **formerly** *adverb*
the former the first of two people or things just mentioned.

formidable (*say* for-mid-a-bul) *adjective* frightening; difficult to deal with or do, *a formidable task.* **formidably** *adverb*

formula *noun* (*plural* **formulae**) **1** a set of chemical symbols showing what a substance consists of. **2** a rule or statement expressed in symbols or numbers. **3** a list of substances needed for making something. **4** a fixed wording for a ceremony etc., *The same formula is used at graduation every year.* **5** one of the groups into which racing-cars are placed according to the size of their engines.

formulate *verb* (**formulated, formulating**) express clearly and exactly. **formulation** *noun*

forsake *verb* (**forsook, forsaken, forsaking**) abandon.

fort *noun* a fortified building.

forth *adverb* **1** out; into view. **2** onwards; forwards, *from this day forth.*
and so forth and so on.

forthcoming *adjective* **1** about to come forth or happen, *forthcoming events.* **2** made available when needed, *Money for the trip was not forthcoming.* **3** (*informal*) willing to give information.

forthright *adjective* frank; outspoken.

forthwith *adverb* immediately.

fortification *noun* **1** fortifying something. **2** a wall or building constructed to make a place strong against attack.

fortify *verb* (**fortified, fortifying**) **1** make a place strong against attack, especially by building fortifications. **2** strengthen, *Sherry is a kind of wine that has been fortified with alcohol.*

fortissimo *adverb* very loudly.

fortitude *noun* courage in bearing pain or trouble.

fortnight *noun* a period of two weeks. **fortnightly** *adverb* & *adjective*

fortress *noun* (*plural* **fortresses**) a fortified building or town.

fortuitous (*say* for-tew-it-us) *adjective* happening by chance. **fortuitously** *adverb*
● USAGE: Note that *fortuitous* does not mean the same as *fortunate.*

fortunate *adjective* lucky. **fortunately** *adverb*

fortune *noun* **1** luck; chance; fate. **2** a great amount of money, *She inherited a fortune.*
fortune-teller a person who claims to predict future events in a person's life.

forty *noun* & *adjective* (*plural* **forties**) the number 40; four times ten. **fortieth** *adjective* & *noun*
forty winks a short sleep; a nap.

forum *noun* **1** the public square in an ancient Roman city. **2** a meeting where a public discussion is held.

forward[1] *adjective* **1** going forwards. **2** placed in the front. **3** having made more than the normal progress. **4** too eager or bold, *Don't be forward!* **forwardness** *noun*

forward[2] *adverb* forwards.

forward[3] *noun* a player in the front line of a team in soccer, rugby, etc.

forward[4] *verb* **1** send on a letter etc. to a

new address. **2** help something to improve or make progress, *forward your career.*

forwards *adverb* **1** to or towards the front. **2** in the direction you are facing.

fossick *verb* rummage; search.

fossil *noun* the remains or traces of a prehistoric animal or plant that has been buried in the ground for a very long time and become hardened in rock. **fossilized** *adjective*

fossil fuel a natural fuel such as gas or coal formed from the remains of prehistoric animals or plants.

fossilize *verb* (fossilized, fossilizing) turn into a fossil. **fossilization** *noun*

foster *verb* **1** bring up someone else's child as if he or she was your own. **2** help to grow or develop. **foster-child** *noun*, **foster-father** *noun*, **foster-mother** *noun*

foul[1] *adjective* **1** disgusting; filthy; tasting or smelling unpleasant. **2** (of weather) rough; stormy. **3** unfair; breaking the rules of a game. **4** colliding or entangled with something. **foully** *adverb*, **foulness** *noun*

foul play unfair play; a violent crime, especially murder.

foul[2] *noun* an action that breaks the rules of a game.

foul[3] *verb* **1** make or become foul, *Smoke had fouled the air.* **2** commit a foul against a player in a game.

found[1] *past tense* of **find**.

found[2] *verb* **1** establish; provide money for starting, *They founded a hospital.* **2** base, *This novel is founded on fact.*

foundation *noun* **1** the founding of something. **2** a base or basis, *the foundation of her argument.* **3** the solid base on which a building is built up. **foundation-stone** *noun*

founder[1] *noun* a person who founds something, *the founder of the hospital.*

founder[2] *verb* **1** fill with water and sink, *The ship foundered.* **2** stumble; fall. **3** fail completely, *Their plans foundered.*

foundling *noun* a child found abandoned, whose parents are not known.

foundry *noun* (plural **foundries**) a factory or workshop where metal or glass is made.

fount *noun* (in poetry) a fountain.

fountain *noun* a device that makes a jet of water shoot up into the air.

fountain-pen *noun* a pen that can be filled with a supply of ink.

four *noun* & *adjective* the number 4; one more than three.

on all fours on hands and knees.

fourteen *noun* & *adjective* the number 14; one more than thirteen. **fourteenth** *adjective* & *noun*

fourth[1] *adjective* next after the third. **fourthly** *adverb*

fourth[2] *noun* **1** the fourth person or thing. **2** one of four equal parts; a quarter.

fowl *noun* a bird, especially one kept on a farm etc. for its eggs or meat.

fox[1] *noun* (plural **foxes**) a wild animal that looks like a dog with a long furry tail. **foxy** *adjective*

fox[2] *verb* deceive; puzzle.

foxglove *noun* a tall plant with flowers like the fingers of gloves.

foyer (*say* foy-ay or foy-er) *noun* the entrance hall of a theatre, cinema, or hotel.

fraction *noun* **1** a number that is not a whole number, e.g. $\frac{1}{2}$, 0,5. **2** a tiny part. **fractional** *adjective*, **fractionally** *adverb*

fractious (*say* frak-shus) *adjective* irritable. **fractiously** *adverb*, **fractiousness** *noun*

fracture[1] *noun* the breaking of something, especially of a bone.

fracture[2] *verb* (fractured, fracturing) break.

fragile *adjective* easy to break or damage. **fragilely** *adverb*, **fragility** *noun*

fragment *noun* **1** a small piece broken off. **2** a small part. **fragmentary** *adjective*, **fragmentation** *noun*, **fragmented** *adjective*

fragrant *adjective* having a pleasant smell. **fragrance** *noun*

frail *adjective* **1** (of things) fragile. **2** (of people) not strong; not robust, *a frail old man.* **frailty** *noun*

frame[1] *noun* **1** a holder that fits round the outside of a picture. **2** a rigid structure that supports something. **3** a human or animal body, *He has a small frame.* **4** a single exposure on a cinema film.

frame of mind the way you think or feel for a while.

frame² *verb* (**framed, framing**) 1 put a frame on or round. 2 construct, *They framed the question badly.* 3 make an innocent person seem guilty by arranging false evidence. **frame-up** *noun*

framework *noun* 1 a frame supporting something. 2 a basic plan or system.

franc *noun* a unit of money in France, Switzerland, and many other countries.

franchise *noun* 1 the right to vote in elections. 2 a licence to sell a firm's goods or services in a certain area.

francolin *noun* a kind of partridge found in Africa and Asia.

frank¹ *adjective* making your thoughts and feelings clear to people; candid. **frankly** *adverb*, **frankness** *noun*

frank² *verb* mark a letter etc. automatically in a machine to show that postage has been paid.

frankincense *noun* a sweet-smelling gum burnt as incense.

frantic *adjective* wildly agitated or excited. **frantically** *adverb*

fraternal (*say* fra-**tern**-al) *adjective* of a brother or brothers. **fraternally** *adverb*

fraternity *noun* (*plural* **fraternities**) 1 a brotherly feeling. 2 a group of people who have the same interests or occupation, *the medical fraternity.*

fraternize *verb* (**fraternized, fraternizing**) associate with other people in a friendly way. **fraternization** *noun*

fraud *noun* 1 a dishonest trick; a swindle. 2 an impostor; a person or thing that is not what it pretends to be. **fraudulent** *adjective*, **fraudulently** *adverb*, **fraudulence** *noun*

fraught *adjective* filled; involving, *The situation is fraught with danger.*

fray¹ *noun* a fight; a conflict, *ready for the fray.*

fray² *verb* 1 make or become ragged so that loose threads show. 2 (of tempers or nerves) become strained or upset.

freak *noun* a very strange or abnormal person, animal, or thing. **freakish** *adjective*

freckle *noun* a small brown spot on the skin. **freckled** *adjective*

free¹ *adjective* (**freer, freest**) 1 able to do what you want to do or go where you want to go. 2 not costing anything. 3 not fixed, *Leave one end free.* 4 not having or affected by something, *The harbour is free of ice.* 5 available; not being used or occupied. 6 generous, *She is very free with her money.* **freely** *adverb*

free enterprise a system in which private businesses are not controlled by the government.

free market a system in which prices of goods and services are allowed to rise and fall as a result of supply and demand, and are not controlled by the government.

free² *verb* (**freed, freeing**) set free.

freedom *noun* being free; independence.

free-hand *adjective* (of a drawing) done without a ruler or compasses etc.

freehold *noun* possessing land or a house as its absolute owner, not as a tenant renting from a landlord.

freestyle *noun* a swimming race in which any stroke may be used.

freeway *noun* a motorway.

free-wheel *verb* ride a bicycle without needing to pedal.

freeze¹ *verb* (**froze, frozen, freezing**) 1 turn into ice; become covered with ice. 2 make or be very cold. 3 keep wages or prices etc. at a fixed level. 4 suddenly stand completely still, *The lion froze at the sight of the elephant.*

freeze² *noun* 1 a period of freezing weather. 2 the freezing of prices etc.

freezer *noun* a refrigerator in which food can be frozen quickly and stored.

freight (*say* frayt) *noun* goods transported as cargo.

freighter (*say* **fray**-ter) *noun* a ship or aircraft carrying mainly cargo.

French horn *noun* a coiled brass wind instrument with a wide opening at the end.

French window *noun* a long window that serves as a door on an outside wall.

frenzy *noun* wild excitement or agitation. **frenzied** *adjective*, **frenziedly** *adverb*

frequency *noun* (*plural* **frequencies**) 1 being frequent. 2 how often something happens, *the frequency of thunderstorms in summer*. **3** the number of oscillations per second of a wave of sound or light etc.

frequent[1] (*say* freek-went) *adjective* happening often. **frequently** *adverb*

frequent[2] (*say* frik-**went**) *verb* be in or go to a place often, *They frequented the club.*

fresco *noun* (*plural* **frescoes**) a picture painted on a wall or ceiling before the plaster is dry.

fresh *adjective* **1** newly made or produced or arrived; not stale, *fresh bread*. **2** not tinned, not preserved, *fresh fruit*. **3** cool and clean, *fresh air*. **4** not salty, *fresh water*. **freshly** *adverb*, **freshness** *noun*

freshen *verb* make or become fresh.

freshwater *adjective* of fresh water not sea water; living in rivers or lakes.

fret[1] *verb* (**fretted, fretting**) worry or be upset about something. **fretful** *adjective*, **fretfully** *adverb*

fret[2] *noun* a bar or ridge on the finger-board of a guitar etc.

fretsaw *noun* a very narrow saw used for making fretwork.

fretwork *noun* cutting decorative patterns in wood; wood cut in this way.

friable *adjective* easily crumbled.

friar *noun* a man who is a member of certain Roman Catholic religious orders, who has vowed to live a life of poverty. **friary** *noun*

friction *noun* **1** rubbing. **2** disagreement, quarrelling. **frictional** *adjective*

fridge *noun* (*informal*) a refrigerator.

friend *noun* **1** a person you like who likes you. **2** a helpful or kind person or thing.

friendless *adjective* without a friend.

friendly *adjective* behaving like a friend. **friendliness** *noun*

friendship *noun* being friends.

frieze (*say* freez) *noun* a strip of designs or pictures round the top of a wall.

frigate *noun* a small warship.

fright *noun* **1** sudden great fear. **2** a person or thing that looks ridiculous.

frighten *verb* make or become afraid. **be frightened of** be afraid of.

frightful *adjective* awful; very great or bad. **frightfully** *adverb*

frigid *adjective* **1** extremely cold. **2** unfriendly; not affectionate. **frigidly** *adverb*, **frigidity** *noun*

frikkadel *noun* a fried meat ball.

frill *noun* **1** a decorative gathered or pleated trimming on a dress, curtain, etc. **2** something extra that is pleasant but unnecessary, *a simple life with no frills*. **frilled** *adjective*, **frilly** *adjective*

fringe *noun* **1** a decorative edging with many threads hanging down loosely. **2** a straight line of short hair hanging down over the forehead. **3** the edge of something, *on the fringe of the crowd*. **fringed** *adjective*

frisk *verb* **1** jump or run about playfully. **2** search somebody by running your hands over his or her clothes. **frisky** *adjective*, **friskily** *adverb*, **friskiness** *noun*

fritter[1] *noun* a slice of meat or fruit or potato etc. coated in batter and fried.

fritter[2] *verb* waste something gradually; spend money or time on trivial things.

frivolous *adjective* seeking pleasure in a light-hearted way; not serious, not sensible. **frivolously** *adverb*, **frivolity** *noun*

frizz *noun* hair formed into small tight curls. **frizzy** *adjective*, **frizziness** *noun*

fro *adverb* **to and fro** backwards and forwards.

frock *noun* a girl's or woman's dress.

frog *noun* a small jumping animal that can live both in water and on land. **a frog in your throat** hoarseness.

frogman *noun* (*plural* **frogmen**) a swimmer equipped with a rubber suit, flippers, and breathing-apparatus for swimming and working underwater.

frolic[1] *noun* a lively cheerful game or entertainment. **frolicsome** *adjective*

frolic[2] *verb* (**frolicked, frolicking**) play about in a lively cheerful way.

from *preposition* This word is used to show **1** starting-point in space or time or order, *We flew from Cape Town to Johannesburg. We work from 9 to 5 o'clock. Count from one to ten.* **2** source or origin, *Get water from the tap.* **3** separation or release, *Take the gun from him. She was freed from prison.* **4** difference, *Can you tell margarine from butter?* **5** cause, *I suffer from headaches.*

frond *noun* a leaf-like part of a fern, palm-tree, etc.

front¹ *noun* **1** the part or side that comes first or is the most important or furthest forward. **2** a road or promenade along the sea-shore. **3** the place where fighting is happening in a war. **frontal** *adjective*

front² *adjective* of the front; in front.

frontage *noun* the front of a building; the land beside this.

frontier *noun* the boundary between two countries or regions.

frontier war any of many wars fought by the Xhosa people to defend their land against colonial forces.

frontispiece *noun* an illustration opposite the title-page of a book.

frost¹ *noun* **1** powdery ice that forms on things in freezing weather. **2** weather with a temperature below freezing-point. **frosty** *adjective*

frost² *verb* cover with frost or frosting.
frosted glass glass made cloudy so that you cannot see through it.

frost-bite *noun* harm done to the body by very cold weather. **frost-bitten** *adjective*

frosting *noun* sugar icing for cakes.

froth *noun* a white mass of tiny bubbles on a liquid. **frothy** *adjective*

frown¹ *verb* wrinkle your forehead because you are angry or worried.

frown² *noun* a frowning movement or look.

frugal (*say* froo-gal) *adjective* **1** very economical and careful. **2** costing very little money; not plentiful, *a frugal meal.*
frugally *adverb*, **frugality** *noun*

fruit¹ *noun* (*plural* **fruits** or **fruit**)
1 the seed-container that grows on a tree or plant and is often used as food. **2** the result of doing something, *the fruits of his efforts.*
fruity *adjective*

fruit² *verb* produce fruit.

fruitful *adjective* producing good results, *fruitful discussions.* **fruitfully** *adverb*

fruition (*say* froo-**ish**-on) *noun* the achievement of what was hoped or worked for, *Our plans never came to fruition.*

fruitless *adjective* producing no results.
fruitlessly *adverb*

frustrate *verb* (**frustrated, frustrating**) prevent somebody from doing something; prevent from being successful, *frustrate their wicked plans.* **frustration** *noun*

fry¹ *verb* (**fried, frying**) cook something in very hot fat. **fryer** *noun*

fry² *plural noun* very young fishes.

frying-pan *noun* a shallow pan for frying things.

fuchsia (*say* few-sha) *noun* an ornamental plant with flowers that hang down.

fudge *noun* a soft sugary sweet.

fuel¹ *noun* something that is burnt to produce heat or power.

fuel² *verb* (**fuelled, fuelling**) supply something with fuel.

fug *noun* (*informal*) a stuffy atmosphere. **fuggy** *adjective*, **fugginess** *noun*

fugitive (*say* few-jit-iv) *noun* a person who is running away from something.

fugue (*say* fewg) *noun* a piece of music in which tunes are repeated in a pattern.

fulcrum *noun* the point on which a lever rests.

fulfil *verb* (**fulfilled, fulfilling**) **1** do what is required; satisfy; carry out, *You must fulfil your promises.* **2** make something come true, *It fulfilled an ancient prophecy.*
fulfilment *noun*

full¹ *adjective* **1** containing as much or as many as possible. **2** having many people or things, *full of ideas.* **3** complete, *the full story.* **4** the greatest possible, *at full speed.* **5** fitting loosely; with many folds, *a full skirt.* **fully** *adverb*, **fullness** *noun*

full moon the moon when you can see its whole disc.

full stop the dot used as a punctuation mark at the end of a sentence or an abbreviation.

full² *adverb* completely; exactly, *It hit him full in the face.*

full-blown *adjective* fully developed.

fully *adverb* completely.

fulsome *adjective* praising something too much or too emotionally.

● USAGE: This word does not mean the same as *full.* Do not say 'a fulsome report' if you mean 'a full or detailed report'.

fumble *verb* (**fumbled, fumbling**) hold or handle something clumsily.

fume[1] *noun* (also **fumes**) strong-smelling smoke or gas.

fume[2] *verb* (**fumed, fuming**) 1 give off fumes. 2 be very angry.

fumigate (*say* **few**-mig-ayt) *verb* (**fumigated, fumigating**) disinfect something by fumes. **fumigation** *noun*

fun *noun* amusement; enjoyment.
make fun of make people laugh at a person or thing.

function[1] *noun* 1 what somebody or something is there to do, *The function of a knife is to cut things.* 2 an important event or party. 3 a basic operation in a computer.

function[2] *verb* perform a function; work properly.

functional *adjective* 1 working properly. 2 practical without being decorative or luxurious. **functionally** *adverb*

fund[1] *noun* 1 money collected or kept for a special purpose. 2 a stock or supply, *a fund of knowledge.*

fund[2] *verb* supply with money.

fundamental *adjective* basic. **fundamentally** *adverb*

fundi *noun* (*informal*) an expert.

funeral *noun* the ceremony when a dead person is buried or cremated.

funereal (*say* few-**neer**-ee-al) *adjective* dark; dismal.

fungicide *noun* a substance that kills fungi.

fungus *noun* (*plural* **fungi** (*say* **fung**-I)) a plant without leaves or flowers that grows on other plants or on decayed material, *Mushrooms are fungi.*

funky *adjective* (**funkier, funkiest**) (*informal*) having a strong rhythm.

funnel *noun* 1 a metal chimney on a ship or steam-engine. 2 a tube that is wide at the top and narrow at the bottom to help you pour things into a narrow opening.

funny *adjective* (**funnier, funniest**) 1 that makes you laugh or smile. 2 strange; odd, *a funny smell.* **funnily** *adverb*

fur *noun* 1 the soft hair that covers some animals. 2 animal skin with the fur on it, used for clothing; fabric that looks like animal fur.

furbish *verb* polish or clean; renovate.

furious *adjective* 1 very angry. 2 violent; intense, *furious heat.* **furiously** *adverb*

furl *verb* roll up a sail, flag, or umbrella.

furlough (*say* **ferl**-oh) *noun* leave of absence from duty; a holiday.

furnace *noun* a device in which great heat can be produced, e.g. for melting metals or making glass.

furnish *verb* 1 provide a place with furniture. 2 provide; supply.

furnishings *plural noun* furniture and fitments, curtains, etc.

furniture *noun* tables, chairs, and other movable things that you need in a house or school or office etc.

furore (*say* few-**ror**-ee) *noun* an excited or angry uproar.

furrow[1] *noun* 1 a long cut in the ground made by a plough or other implement. 2 a groove. 3 a deep wrinkle in the skin. 4 an artificial channel for water.

furrow[2] *verb* make furrows in something.

furry *adjective* like fur; covered with fur.

further[1] *adverb* & *adjective* 1 at or to a greater distance; more distant. 2 more; additional, *We made further enquiries.*
further education education for people above school age.
• USAGE: See the note under *farther.*

further[2] *verb* help something to progress, *This success will further your career.*
furtherance *noun*

furthermore *adverb* also; moreover.

furthest *adverb* & *adjective* at or to the greatest distance; most distant.
• USAGE: See the note under *farther.*

furtive *adjective* stealthy; trying not to be seen. **furtively** *adverb*, **furtiveness** *noun*

fury *noun* wild anger; rage.

fuse[1] *noun* a safety device containing a short piece of wire that melts if too much electricity is passed through it.

fuse[2] *verb* (**fused, fusing**) 1 stop working because a fuse has melted, *The lights fused.* 2 blend together, especially through melting.

fuse[3] *noun* a length of material that burns easily, used for setting off an explosive.

fuselage (*say* few-zel-ah*z*h) *noun*
the body of an aircraft.

fusillade (*say* few-zil-**ayd**) *noun* a great
outburst of firing guns or questions etc.

fusion *noun* 1 the action of blending or
uniting things. 2 the uniting of atomic
nuclei, usually releasing energy.

fuss[1] *noun* (*plural* **fusses**) 1 unnecessary
excitement or bustle. 2 an agitated protest,
*They made a fuss about the proposed
building.*

fuss[2] *verb* make a fuss about something.

fussy *adjective* (**fussier, fussiest**) 1 fus-
sing; inclined to make a fuss. 2 choosing
very carefully; hard to please. 3 full of
unnecessary details or decorations, *a fussy
hat.* **fussily** *adverb*, **fussiness** *noun*

fusty *adjective* (**fustier, fustiest**) smelling
stale or stuffy. **fustiness** *noun*

futile (*say* few-tyl) *adjective* useless;
having no result. **futility** *noun*

future[1] *noun* the time that will come; what
is going to happen then.

future[2] *adjective* belonging or referring to
the future.

fuzz *noun* something fluffy or frizzy.

fuzzy *adjective* 1 like fuzz; covered with
fuzz. 2 blurred; not clear. **fuzzily** *adverb*,
fuzziness *noun*

fynbos (*say* **fayn**-bos) *noun* 1 the type of
vegetation found in the coastal areas of the
Cape, often having hard small evergreen
leaves (e.g. ericas, proteas, etc.). 2 a plant or
plants of this type, *a fynbos sale.*

Gg

gabble *verb* (**gabbled, gabbling**) talk so
quickly that it is difficult to know what is
being said.

gable *noun* the pointed part at the top of
an outside wall, between two sloping roofs.
gabled *adjective*

gad *verb* (**gadded, gadding**) **gad about**
gallivant.

gadabout a pleasure-seeking or idle
person.

gadget *noun* any small useful tool.
gadgetry *noun*

gaff *noun* a stock with a metal hook for
landing large fish.

gag[1] *noun* 1 something put into a person's
mouth or tied over it to prevent speaking.
2 a joke.

gag[2] *verb* (**gagged, gagging**) 1 put a gag
on a person. 2 prevent from making comments, *We cannot gag the press.* 3 retch.

gaiety *noun* cheerfulness.

gaily *adverb* in a cheerful way.

gain[1] *verb* 1 get something that you did
not have before; obtain. 2 (of a clock or
watch) become ahead of the correct time.
3 reach; arrive at, *At last we gained the
shore.*

gain on come closer to a person or thing in
chasing them or in a race.

gain[2] *noun* something gained; a profit or
improvement. **gainful** *adjective*

gait *noun* a way of walking or running,
He walked with a shuffling gait.

gala (*say* **gah**-la) *noun* 1 a celebration with
cheerful festivities. 2 a set of sports contests,
a swimming gala.

galaxy *noun* (*plural* **galaxies**) a very large
group of stars. **galactic** *adjective*

gale *noun* a very strong wind.

gall[1] (*say* gawl) *noun* 1 bile. 2 bitterness
of feeling. 3 (*informal*) impudence.

gall[2] (*say* gawl) *noun* a sore spot on an
animal's skin.

gall[3] *verb* 1 rub sore. 2 vex or humiliate
someone.

gallant (*say* **gal**-lant) *adjective* 1 brave;
chivalrous. 2 fine; stately, *our gallant ship.*
gallantly *adverb*, **gallantry** *noun*

galleon *noun* a large Spanish sailing-ship
used in the 16th–17th centuries.

gallery *noun* (*plural* **galleries**) 1 a platform
jutting out from the wall in a church or hall.
2 the highest balcony in a cinema or
theatre. 3 a long room or passage. 4 a room
or building for showing works of art.

galley *noun* (*plural* **galleys**) 1 an ancient
type of ship driven by oars. 2 the kitchen in
a ship or aircraft.

galling (*say* **gawl**-ing) *adjective* vexing;
humiliating.

gallivant *verb* go about in search of pleasure.

gallon *noun* a measure of capacity in the imperial system, 8 pints or about $4\frac{1}{2}$ litres.

gallop[1] *noun* 1 the fastest pace a horse can go. 2 a fast ride on a horse.

gallop[2] *verb* (**galloped, galloping**) go or ride at a gallop.

gallows *noun* a framework with a noose for hanging criminals.

galore *adverb* in plenty; in great numbers, *bargains galore.*

galvanize *verb* (**galvanized, galvanizing**) 1 stimulate into sudden activity. 2 coat iron with zinc to protect it from rust. **galvanization** *noun*

galvanometer *noun* an instrument which measures very small electric currents.

gambit *noun* 1 a kind of opening move in chess. 2 an action or remark intended to gain an advantage, *a conversational gambit.*

gamble[1] *verb* (**gambled, gambling**) 1 bet on the result of a game, race, or other event. 2 take great risks in the hope of gaining something. **gambler** *noun*

gamble[2] *noun* 1 gambling. 2 a risky attempt.

gambol *verb* (**gambolled, gambolling**) jump or skip about in play.

game[1] *noun* 1 a form of play or sport, especially one with rules. 2 a section of a long game such as tennis or whist. 3 a scheme or plan; a trick. 4 wild animals or birds hunted for sport or food. **game farm** a private game reserve where animals are kept for tourists to see as well as for their meat.

game[2] *adjective* 1 able and willing to do something, *She is game for all kinds of tricks.* 2 brave. **gamely** *adverb*

gamekeeper *noun* a person employed to protect game-birds and animals, especially from poachers.

gamete (*say* ga-meet) *noun* a cell able to unite with another in sexual reproduction.

gaming *noun* gambling.

gamma *noun* the third letter of the Greek alphabet (= g), written as Γ, γ. **gamma rays** very short X-rays.

gammon *noun* a kind of ham.

gander *noun* a male goose.

gang[1] *noun* a number of people who do things together.

gang[2] *verb* join in a gang, *gang up.*

gangling *adjective* tall, thin, and awkward-looking.

gangplank *noun* a plank placed so that people can walk into or out of a boat.

gangrene (*say* **gang**-green) *noun* decay of body tissue in a living person.

gangster *noun* a member of a gang of violent criminals.

gangway *noun* 1 a gap left for people to pass between rows of seats or through a crowd. 2 a movable bridge placed so that people can walk into or out of a ship.

gannet *noun* a large sea-bird.

gaol[1] (*say* jayl) *noun* a prison.

gaol[2] *verb* to put into prison. **gaoler** *noun*

gap *noun* 1 a break or opening in something continuous such as a hedge or fence. 2 an interval. 3 a wide difference in ideas, *the generation gap.*

gape *verb* (**gaped, gaping**) 1 have your mouth open. 2 stare with your mouth open. 3 be open wide.

garage (*say* ga-rah*zh*) *noun* 1 a building in which a motor vehicle or vehicles may be kept. 2 an establishment where motor vehicles are repaired or serviced.

garb *noun* special clothing. **garb** *verb*

garbage *noun* rubbish.

garble *verb* (**garbled, garbling**) give a confused account of a story or message so that it is misunderstood.

garden *noun* a piece of ground where flowers, fruit, or vegetables are grown. **gardener** *noun,* **gardening** *noun*

gargantuan (*say* gar-**gan**-tew-an) *adjective* gigantic.

gargle *verb* (**gargled, gargling**) hold a liquid at the back of the mouth and breathe air through it to wash the inside of the throat. **gargle** *noun*

gargoyle *noun* an ugly or comical face or figure carved on a building, especially on a water-spout.

garish (*say* **gair**-ish) *adjective* too bright or highly coloured; gaudy. **garishly** *adverb*

garland *noun* a wreath of flowers worn

or hung as a decoration. **garland** *verb*

garlic *noun* a plant rather like an onion, used for flavouring food.

garment *noun* a piece of clothing.

garner *verb* store up; gather; collect.

garnet *noun* a dark-red stone used as a gem.

garnish[1] *verb* decorate, *The fish was garnished with parsley and lemon slices.*

garnish[2] *noun* something used to decorate food or give it extra flavour.

garrison *noun* 1 troops stationed in a town or fort to defend it. 2 the building they occupy. **garrison** *verb*

garrotte[1] (*say* ga-**rot**) *noun* 1 a metal collar for strangling a person condemned to death, formerly used in Spain. 2 a cord or wire used for strangling a victim.

garrotte[2] *verb* (**garrotted**, **garrotting**) strangle with a garrotte.

garrulous (*say* ga-**rool**-us) *adjective* talkative. **garrulousness** *noun*

garter *noun* a band of elastic to hold up a sock or stocking.

gas[1] *noun* (*plural* **gases**) 1 a substance that (like air) can move freely and is not liquid or solid at ordinary temperatures. 2 a flammable gas used for lighting, heating, or cooking.

gas[2] *verb* (**gassed**, **gassing**) 1 kill or injure with gas, *Thousands of soldiers were gassed in the First World War.* 2 (*informal*) talk idly for a long time.

gas[3] *noun* (*American*) gasoline.

gash *noun* a long deep cut or wound. **gash** *verb*

gasket *noun* a flat ring or strip of soft material for sealing a joint between metal surfaces.

gasoline *noun* (*American*) petrol.

gasometer (*say* gas-**om**-it-er) *noun* a large round tank in which gas is stored.

gasp *verb* 1 breathe in suddenly when you are shocked or surprised. 2 struggle to breathe with your mouth open when you are tired or ill. 3 speak in a breathless way, *'I can't go on,' he gasped.* **gasp** *noun*

gassy *adjective* of, like, or full of gas.

gastric *adjective* of the stomach.

gastronomy (*say* gas-**tron**-om-ee) *noun* the art or science of good eating and drinking. **gastronomic** *adjective*

gastropod *noun* an animal (e.g. a snail) that moves by means of a fleshy 'foot' on its stomach.

gate *noun* 1 a movable barrier, usually on hinges, serving as a door in a wall or fence. 2 the opening it covers, *The bus passed through the school gates.* 3 a barrier for controlling the flow of water in a dam or lock. 4 the number of people attending a soccer match etc., *Today's gate will be given to charity.*

gateau (*say* gat-oh) *noun* a large rich cream cake.

gatecrash *verb* go to a private party without being invited. **gatecrasher** *noun*

gateway *noun* 1 an opening containing a gate. 2 a way to reach something, *The gateway to success.*

gather *verb* 1 come or bring together. 2 collect; obtain gradually, *gather information.* 3 collect as harvest; pluck, *Gather the corn when it is ripe; gather flowers.* 4 understand; learn, *We gather you have been on holiday.* 5 pull cloth into folds by running a thread through it.

gathering *noun* an assembly of people.

gaudy *adjective* too showy and bright. **gaudily** *adverb*, **gaudiness** *noun*

gauge[1] (*say* gayj) *noun* 1 a standard measurement. 2 the distance between a pair of rails on a railway. 3 a measuring-instrument, *a rain gauge.*

gauge[2] *verb* (**gauged**, **gauging**) 1 measure. 2 estimate; form a judgement.

gaunt *adjective* 1 (of a person) lean and haggard. 2 (of a place) grim or desolate-looking. **gauntness** *noun*

gauntlet[1] *noun* a glove with a wide cuff covering the wrist.

gauntlet[2] *noun* **run the gauntlet** have to suffer continuous severe criticism or risk.

gauze *noun* 1 thin transparent woven material. 2 fine wire mesh. **gauzy** *adjective*

gay *adjective* 1 cheerful. 2 brightly coloured. 3 (*informal*) homosexual. **gayness** *noun*

gaze[1] *verb* (**gazed**, **gazing**) look at something steadily for a long time.

gaze[2] *noun* a long steady look, *She grew uncomfortable under his gaze.*

gazelle *noun* a small antelope.

gazette *noun* 1 a newspaper. 2 an official journal, *the Government Gazette.*

GDP *abbreviation* gross domestic product.

gear[1] *noun* 1 a cog-wheel, especially one of a set in a motor vehicle that transmit movement from the engine to the wheels when they are connected. 2 equipment; apparatus, *camping gear.*

gear[2] *verb* **gear up** get ready for something.

gearbox *noun* a case enclosing gears.

gecko *noun* (*plural* **geckoes** or **geckos**) a small lizard with sticky pads on its fingers, found in warm countries.

Geiger counter (*say* **gy**-ger) *noun* an instrument that detects and measures radioactivity.

gel (*say* jel) *noun* a jelly-like substance used for setting hair or as a soap.

gelatine (*say* **jel**-a-teen) *noun* a clear jelly-like substance made by boiling animal tissue and used to make jellies and other foods. **gelatinous** (*say* jil-**at**-in-us) *adjective*

geld *verb* castrate, spay.

gelding *noun* a castrated horse or other male animal.

gelignite (*say* **jel**-ig-nyt) *noun* a kind of explosive.

gem *noun* 1 a precious stone. 2 an excellent person or thing.

gemsbok *noun* a large antelope with long straight horns.

gem squash *noun* a small round vegetable marrow.

gender *noun* 1 a person's sex. 2 the group in which a noun is classed in the grammar of some languages, *English pronouns (e.g. 'he' and 'she') show gender distinctions.*

gene (*say* jeen) *noun* a part of a living cell which controls characteristics (such as the colour of hair or eyes) inherited from parents.

genealogy (*say* jeen-ee-**al**-o-jee) *noun* 1 a statement or diagram showing how people are descended from an ancestor; a pedigree. 2 the study of family history and ancestors. **genealogical**

(*say* jeen-ee-a-**loj**-ik-al) *adjective*

general[1] *adjective* 1 of all or most people or things, *general approval.* 2 not detailed; not exact, *a general account.* 3 chief; head, *the general secretary.*

general dealer a shop with a wide variety of goods for sale.

general election an election of Members of Parliament for the whole country.

general[2] *noun* a senior army officer.

generality *noun* (*plural* **generalities**) 1 being general. 2 a general statement without exact details.

generalize *verb* (**generalized, generalizing**) 1 make a statement that is true of most cases. 2 bring into general use, *The use of this drug is now fairly generalized.* **generalization** *noun*

generally *adverb* 1 usually. 2 in a general sense; without regard to details, *I was speaking generally.*

generate *verb* (**generated, generating**) produce; create.

generation *noun* 1 generating. 2 a single stage in a family, *Three generations were included: children, parents, and grandparents.* 3 all the people born at about the same time.

generator *noun* 1 an apparatus for producing gases or steam. 2 a machine for converting mechanical energy into electricity.

generic (*say* jin-**e**-rik) *adjective* of a whole genus or kind. **generically** *adverb*

generous *adjective* 1 willing to give things or share them. 2 given freely; plentiful, *a generous helping.* 3 kindly and not petty in making judgements. **generously** *adverb*, **generosity** *noun*

genesis *noun* beginning; origin.

genetic (*say* jin-**et**-ik) *adjective* of genes; of characteristics inherited from parents or ancestors. **genetically** *adverb*

genial (*say* **jee**-nee-al) *adjective* kindly and cheerful. **genially** *adverb*, **geniality** (*say* jee-nee-**al**-it-ee) *noun*

genie (*say* **jee**-nee) *noun* (in Arabian tales) a spirit with strange powers.

genital (*say* **jen**-it-al) *adjective* of animal reproduction or reproductive organs.

genitals (*say* **jen**-it-alz) *plural noun* external sexual organs.

genius *noun* (*plural* **geniuses**) **1** an unusually clever person. **2** a very great natural ability.

genocide (*say* **jen**-o-syd) *noun* deliberate extermination of a race of people.

genre (*say* **zh**ahn-ra) *noun* a style of art or literature, *the short story genre.*

genteel (*say* jen-**teel**) *adjective* trying to seem polite and refined. **genteelly** *adverb,* **gentility** (*say* jen-**til**-it-ee) *noun*

gentile *noun* a person who is not Jewish.

gentle *adjective* kind and quiet; not rough or severe. **gently** *adverb,* **gentleness** *noun*

gentleman *noun* (*plural* **gentlemen**) **1** a well-mannered or honourable man. **2** a man of good social position. **3** (in polite use) a man.

genuine *adjective* really what it is said to be; not faked or pretending. **genuinely** *adverb,* **genuineness** *noun*

genus (*say* **jee**-nus) *noun* (*plural* **genera** (*say* **jen**-er-a)) a group of similar animals or plants, *Lions and leopards belong to the same genus.*

geo- *prefix* earth.

geography (*say* jee-**og**-ra-fee) *noun* the study of the earth's surface and of its climate, peoples, and products. **geographer** *noun,* **geographical** *adjective,* **geographically** *adverb*

geology (*say* jee-**ol**-o-jee) *noun* the study of the structure of the earth's crust and its layers. **geological** *adjective,* **geologically** *adverb,* **geologist** *noun*

geometry (*say* jee-**om**-it-ree) *noun* the study of lines, angles, surfaces, and solids in mathematics. **geometric** *adjective,* **geometrical** *adjective,* **geometrically** *adverb*

Georgian (*say* **jor**-jin) *adjective* of the time of the kings George I–IV (1714–1830) or George V–VI (1910–52) of England.

geranium *noun* a garden plant with red, pink, or white flowers.

gerbil (*say* **jer**-bil) *noun* a small brown animal with long hind legs.

geriatric (*say* je-ree-**at**-rik) *adjective* concerned with the care of old people and their health.

germ *noun* **1** a micro-organism, especially one that can cause disease. **2** a tiny living structure from which a plant or animal may develop. **3** part of the seed of a cereal plant, *wheat germ.*

germicide *noun* a substance that kills germs.

germinate *verb* (**germinated, germinating**) begin to grow and develop; put forth shoots. **germination** *noun*

gesticulate (*say* jes-**tik**-yoo-layt) *verb* (**gesticulated, gesticulating**) make expressive movements with hands and arms. **gesticulation** *noun*

gesture (*say* **jes**-cher) *noun* a movement or action that expresses what a person feels. **gesture** *verb*

get *verb* (**got, getting**) This word has many different uses, including **1** obtain or receive, *She got first prize.* **2** become, *Don't get angry!* **3** reach a place, *We got there by midnight.* **4** put or move, *I can't get my shoe on.* **5** prepare, *Will you get the tea?* **6** persuade or order, *Get him to wash up.* **7** catch or suffer from an illness. **8** (*informal*) understand, *Do you get what I mean?*

get away with escape with something; avoid being punished for what you have done.

get by (*informal*) manage.

get on make progress; be friendly with somebody.

get over recover from an illness etc.

get up stand up; get out of your bed in the morning.

get your own back (*informal*) have your revenge.

have got to must.

getaway *noun* an escape after committing a crime.

geyser (*say* **gee**-zer or **gy**-zer) *noun* **1** a natural spring that shoots up columns of hot water. **2** a kind of water-heater.

ghastly *adjective* **1** very unpleasant or bad. **2** looking pale and ill. **ghastliness** *noun*

gherkin (*say* **ger**-kin) *noun* a small cucumber used for pickling.

ghetto (*say* **get**-oh) *noun* (*plural* **ghettos**) a slum area inhabited by a group of people who are treated unfairly in comparison with others.

ghetto-blaster (*informal*) a large portable stereo radio and cassette player.

ghost *noun* the spirit of a dead person. **ghostly** *adjective*

ghoulish (*say* **gool**-ish) *adjective* enjoying things that are grisly or unpleasant. **ghoulishly** *adverb*, **ghoulishness** *noun*

giant *noun* 1 (in fairy-tales) a human-like creature of very great height and size. 2 a person, animal, or plant that is much larger than the usual size. **giantess** *noun*

gibber (*say* **jib**-er) *verb* make quick meaningless sounds, especially when shocked or terrified.

gibberish (*say* **jib**-er-ish) *noun* meaningless speech; nonsense.

gibbet (*say* **jib**-it) *noun* 1 a gallows. 2 an upright post with an arm from which a criminal's body was hung after execution.

gibbon *noun* an ape with very long arms.

gibe (*say* jyb) *noun* & *verb* jeer.

giblets (*say* **jib**-lits) *plural noun* the edible parts of the inside of a bird, taken out before it is cooked.

giddy *adjective* having or causing the feeling that everything is spinning round. **giddily** *adverb*, **giddiness** *noun*

gift *noun* 1 a present. 2 a talent, *She has a gift for music.*

gifted *adjective* talented.

gig *noun* (*informal*) a show when a musician or band plays pop music in public.

gigantic *adjective* very large.

giggle[1] *verb* (**giggled, giggling**) laugh in a silly way.

giggle[2] *noun* 1 a silly laugh. 2 (*informal*) something amusing; a joke.

gild *verb* cover with a thin layer of gold or gold paint.

gills *plural noun* 1 the part of the body through which fishes and certain other water animals breathe while in water. 2 the thin upright parts under the cap of a mushroom.

gilt[1] *noun* a thin gold covering.

gilt[2] *adjective* gilded; gold-coloured.

gimlet *noun* a small tool with a screw-like tip for boring holes.

gimmick *noun* something unusual done or used to attract people's attention.

gin[1] *noun* a colourless alcoholic spirit flavoured with juniper berries.

gin[2] *noun* 1 a kind of trap for catching animals. 2 a machine for separating the fibres of the cotton-plant from its seeds.

gin[3] *verb* (**ginned, ginning**) treat cotton in a gin.

ginger *noun* 1 a flavouring made from the hot-tasting root of a tropical plant. 2 this root. 3 reddish-yellow. **ginger** *adjective*

gingerbread *noun* a ginger-flavoured cake or biscuit.

gingerly *adverb* cautiously.

gipsy *noun* (*plural* **gipsies**) a gypsy.

giraffe *noun* an animal rather like a horse but with a very long neck.

gird *verb* 1 fasten with a belt or band, *He girded on his sword.* 2 prepare for an effort, *Gird yourself for action.*

girder *noun* a metal beam supporting part of a building or a bridge.

girdle *noun* a belt or cord worn round the waist.

girl *noun* 1 a female child. 2 a young woman. **girlhood** *noun*, **girlish** *adjective*

girl-friend *noun* a girl that a boy regularly goes out with.

girt *adjective* girded.

girth *noun* 1 the distance round a thing. 2 a band passing under a horse's body to hold the saddle in place.

gist (*say* jist) *noun* the essential points or general sense of a speech etc.

give *verb* (**gave, given, giving**) 1 cause another person to receive something that you have or can provide. 2 make or perform an action or effort, *She gave a laugh.* 3 be flexible or springy; bend or collapse when pressed. 4 devote or dedicate, *He gave his life to the cause.* **giver** *noun*

give and take exchange words and ideas; be prepared to compromise.

give in acknowledge that you are defeated; yield.

given *adjective* named or stated in advance, *All the people in a given area.*

gizzard *noun* a bird's second stomach, in which food is ground up.

glacé (*say* **glas**-ay) *adjective* iced with sugar; crystallized.

glacial (*say* **glay**-shal) *adjective* icy; of or from ice. **glacially** *adverb*

glacier (*say* **glas**-ee-er) *noun* a river of ice that moves very slowly.

glad *adjective* 1 pleased; expressing joy. 2 giving pleasure, *We brought the glad news.* **gladly** *adverb*, **gladness** *noun* **glad of** grateful for; pleased with.

gladden *verb* make a person glad.

glade *noun* an open space in a forest.

gladiator (*say* **glad**-ee-ay-ter) *noun* a man trained to fight in public shows in ancient Rome. **gladiatorial** (*say* glad-ee-at-**or**-ee-al) *adjective*

glamorize *verb* (**glamorized, glamorizing**) make glamorous or romantic.

glamour *noun* attractiveness; romantic charm. **glamorous** *adjective*

glance *verb* (**glanced, glancing**) 1 look at something briefly. 2 strike something at an angle and slide off it, *The ball glanced off the bat.* **glance** *noun*

gland *noun* an organ of the body that produces substances which are sent into the blood or sent out of the body. **glandular** *adjective*

glare *verb* (**glared, glaring**) 1 shine with an unpleasant dazzling light. 2 stare angrily or fiercely. **glare** *noun*

glasnost *noun* open reporting of news etc. in the former Soviet Union; more open government with information being available more easily.

glass *noun* (*plural* **glasses**) 1 a hard brittle substance that is usually transparent. 2 a container made of glass for drinking from. 3 a mirror, *He looked in the glass to check that his face was clean.* 4 a lens or telescope. **glassy** *adjective*

glasses *plural noun* 1 spectacles. 2 binoculars.

glaze[1] *verb* (**glazed, glazing**) 1 fit or cover with glass. 2 give a shiny surface to something. 3 become glassy.

glaze[2] *noun* a shiny surface or coating, especially on pottery.

glazier (*say* **glay**-zee-er) *noun* a person whose job is to fit glass in windows.

gleam[1] *noun* 1 a beam of soft light, especially one that comes and goes. 2 a small amount of hope, humour, etc.

gleam[2] *verb* send out gleams.

glean *verb* 1 pick up grain left by harvesters. 2 gather bit by bit, *glean some information.* **gleaner** *noun*

glee *noun* lively or triumphant delight. **gleeful** *adjective*, **gleefully** *adverb*

glen *noun* a narrow valley.

glib *adjective* speaking or writing easily but not sincerely or thoughtfully. **glibly** *adverb*, **glibness** *noun*

glide *verb* (**glided, gliding**) 1 fly or move along smoothly. 2 fly without using an engine. **glide** *noun*

glider *noun* an aeroplane that does not use an engine.

glimmer[1] *noun* a faint gleam.

glimmer[2] *verb* gleam faintly.

glimpse[1] *noun* a brief view.

glimpse[2] *verb* (**glimpsed, glimpsing**) catch a glimpse of.

glint[1] *noun* a very brief flash of light.

glint[2] *verb* send out a glint.

glissade (*say* gliss-**ayd**) *verb* (**glissaded, glissading**) glide or slide skilfully, especially down a steep slope.

glisten (*say* **glis**-en) *verb* shine like something wet or polished.

glitter *verb* & *noun* sparkle.

gloat *verb* be full of greedy or unkind pleasure.

global *adjective* 1 of the whole world; world-wide. 2 of or in the whole system. **globally** *adverb* **global warming** the increase in the temperature of the earth's atmosphere as a result of the greenhouse effect.

globe *noun* 1 something shaped like a ball, especially one with a map of the whole world on it. 2 the world, *She has travelled all over the globe.* 3 a hollow round glass object.

globular (*say* **glob**-yoo-ler) *adjective* shaped like a globe.

globule (*say* **glob**-yool) *noun* a small rounded drop.

gloom *noun* a gloomy condition or feeling.

gloomy *adjective* (**gloomier, gloomiest**) 1 almost dark. 2 depressed; depressing; sad.

gloomily *adverb*, **gloominess** *noun*

glorify *verb* (**glorified, glorifying**) **1** give glory or honour. **2** make a thing seem more splendid than it really is. **glorification** *noun*

glorious *adjective* having glory; splendid. **gloriously** *adverb*

glory¹ *noun* **1** fame and honour. **2** praise, *'Glory to God in the highest.'* **3** beauty; magnificence.

glory² *verb* (**gloried, glorying**) rejoice; pride yourself, *They gloried in victory.*

gloss¹ *noun* (*plural* **glosses**) the shine on a smooth surface.

gloss² *verb* make a thing glossy.
gloss over make a fault or mistake etc. seem less serious than it really is.

glossary *noun* (*plural* **glossaries**) a list of difficult words with their meanings explained.

glossy *adjective* (**glossier, glossiest**) shiny. **glossily** *adverb*, **glossiness** *noun*

glove *noun* a covering for the hand, usually with separate divisions for each finger and thumb. **gloved** *adjective*

glow¹ *noun* **1** brightness and warmth without flames. **2** a warm or cheerful feeling, *We felt a glow of pride.*

glow² *verb* produce a glow.

glower (rhymes with *flower*) *verb* stare angrily; scowl.

glow-worm *noun* a kind of beetle whose tail gives out a green light.

glucose *noun* **1** a form of sugar found in the blood and in fruit-juice etc. **2** a simple carbohydrate formed by the process of photosynthesis in plants.

glue¹ *noun* a sticky substance used for joining things. **gluey** *adjective*

glue² *verb* (**glued, gluing**) **1** stick with glue. **2** attach or hold closely, *His ear was glued to the keyhole.*

glum *adjective* sad and gloomy. **glumly** *adverb*, **glumness** *noun*

glut¹ *verb* (**glutted, glutting**) **1** supply with much more than is needed. **2** satisfy fully with food.

glut² *noun* an excessive supply.

gluten (*say* **gloo**-ten) *noun* a sticky protein substance in flour.

glutinous (*say* **gloo**-tin-us) *adjective*

glue-like, sticky.

glutton *noun* a person who eats too much. **gluttonous** *adjective*, **gluttony** *noun*

glycerine (*say* **glis**-er-een) *noun* a thick sweet colourless liquid used in ointments and medicines and in explosives.

gnarled (*say* narld) *adjective* twisted and knobbly, like an old tree.

gnash (*say* nash) *verb* grind teeth together.

gnat (*say* nat) *noun* a tiny fly that bites, also called a muggie.

gnaw (*say* naw) *verb* keep on biting something hard.

gnome (*say* nohm) *noun* a kind of dwarf in fairy-tales, usually living underground.

GNP *abbreviation* gross national product.

gnu (*say* noo) *noun* (*plural* **gnu** or **gnus**) a large ox-like antelope, also called a wildebeest.

go¹ *verb* (**went, gone, going**) This word is used to show **1** movement, especially away from somewhere, *Where are you going?* **2** direction, *The road goes to Durban.* **3** change, *Milk went sour.* **4** progress or result, *The gun went bang.* **5** place, *Plates go on that shelf.* **6** sale, *The house went very cheaply.*

go² *noun* (*plural* **goes**) **1** a turn or try, *May I have a go?* **2** (*informal*) a success, *They made a go of it.* **3** (*informal*) energy; liveliness, *She is full of go.*
on the go active; always working or moving.

goad¹ *noun* a stick with a pointed end for prodding cattle to move onwards.

goad² *verb* stir into action by being annoying, *He goaded me into fighting.*

go-ahead¹ *noun* a signal to proceed.

go-ahead² *adjective* energetic; willing to try new methods.

goal *noun* **1** the place where a ball must go to score a point in soccer, netball, etc. **2** a point scored in this way. **3** an objective.

goalkeeper *noun* the player who stands in the goal to try and keep the ball from entering.

goat *noun* a small animal with horns, kept for its milk.

gobble *verb* (**gobbled, gobbling**) eat quickly and greedily.

gobbledegook *noun* (*informal*) pompous language often used by officials.

go-between *noun* a person who acts as a messenger or negotiator between others.

goblet *noun* a drinking-glass with a stem and a foot.

goblin *noun* a mischievous ugly elf.

God *noun* the creator of the universe in Christian, Jewish, and Muslim belief.

god *noun* a person or thing that is worshipped, *Mars was a Roman god*. **goddess** *noun* (*plural* **goddesses**)

godhead *noun* the divine nature of God.

godly *adjective* (**godlier, godliest**) sincerely religious. **godliness** *noun*

godparent *noun* a person at a child's christening who promises to see that it is brought up as a Christian. **godchild** *noun*, **god-daughter** *noun*, **godfather** *noun*, **godmother** *noun*, **godson** *noun*

godsend *noun* a piece of unexpected good luck.

gogga *noun* (*informal*) an insect or other creepy-crawly.

goggle *verb* (**goggled, goggling**) stare with wide-open eyes.

goggles *plural noun* large spectacles for protecting the eyes from wind, water, dust, etc.

going *present participle* of **go. be going to do something** be ready or likely to do it.

go-kart *noun* a small racing car with an open body.

gold *noun* 1 a precious yellow metal. 2 a deep yellow colour. 3 a gold medal, usually given as first prize, *an Olympic gold*. **gold** *adjective*

golden *adjective* 1 made of gold. 2 coloured like gold. 3 precious; excellent, *a golden opportunity*.

Golden City Johannesburg.

golden wedding the 50th anniversary of a wedding.

goldfield *noun* an area in which gold is found.

goldfish *noun* (*plural* **goldfish**) a small red or orange fish, often kept as a pet.

gold-mine *noun* a place where gold is dug out of the ground.

goldsmith *noun* a person who makes things in gold.

golf *noun* an outdoor game played by hitting a small white ball with a club into a series of holes on a specially prepared ground (a **golf-course** or **golf-links**). **golfer** *noun*, **golfing** *noun*

gondola (*say* **gond**-ol-a) *noun* a boat with high pointed ends used on the canals in Venice, Italy. **gondolier** *noun*

gong *noun* a large metal disc that makes an echoing sound when it is hit.

good[1] *adjective* (**better, best**) 1 having the right qualities; of the kind that people like, *a good book*. 2 kind, *It was good of you to help us*. 3 well-behaved, *Be a good boy*. 4 healthy; giving benefit, *Exercise is good for you*. 5 thorough, *Give it a good clean*. 6 large; considerable, *It's a good distance from the shops*.

Good Friday the Friday before Easter, when Christians commemorate the Crucifixion of Christ.

good[2] *noun* 1 something good, *Do good to others*. 2 benefit, *It's for your own good*. **for good** for ever. **no good** useless.

goodbye *interjection* a word used when you leave somebody or at the end of a phone call.

goodness *noun* 1 being good. 2 the good part of something.

goods *plural noun* 1 things that are bought and sold. 2 things that are carried on trains or trucks.

goodwill *noun* a kindly feeling.

goody *noun* (*plural* **goodies**) (*informal*) 1 something good or attractive, especially to eat. 2 a person of good character. **goody-goody** (*informal*) a self-satisfied person; someone who tries to please others too much.

goose *noun* (*plural* **geese**) a kind of bird with webbed feet, larger than a duck.

gooseberry *noun* (*plural* **gooseberries**) a small yellowish fruit that grows on a bush.

goose-flesh *noun* (also **goose-pimples**) skin that has turned rough with small bumps on it because a person is cold or afraid.

gore[1] *verb* (**gored, goring**) wound by piercing with a horn or tusk.

gore[2] *noun* thickened blood from a cut

or wound.

gorge¹ *noun* **1** a narrow valley with steep sides. **2** the throat or gullet.

gorge² *verb* (**gorged, gorging**) eat greedily; stuff with food.

gorgeous *adjective* magnificent; beautiful. **gorgeously** *adverb*

gorgon *noun* a snake-haired woman in Greek myth who had the power to turn people to stone.

gorilla *noun* a large strong ape.

gorse *noun* a prickly bush with small yellow flowers.

gory *adjective* **1** covered with blood. **2** with much bloodshed, *a gory battle.*

gosh *interjection* (*informal*) an exclamation of surprise.

gosling *noun* a young goose.

gospel *noun* **1** the teachings of Jesus Christ. **2** something you can safely believe. **the Gospels** the first four books of the New Testament, telling of the life and teachings of Jesus Christ.

gossamer *noun* **1** fine cobwebs made by small spiders. **2** any fine delicate material.

gossip¹ *verb* (**gossiped, gossiping**) talk a lot about other people.

gossip² *noun* **1** gossiping talk. **2** a person who enjoys gossiping. **gossipy** *adjective*

got *past tense* of **get. have got** possess, *Have you got a car?*
have got to must.

Gothic *adjective* of the style of building common in Europe in the 12th–16th centuries, with pointed arches and much carving.

gouge (*say* gowj) *verb* (**gouged, gouging**) scoop or force out by pressing.

goulash (*say* goo-lash) *noun* a meat stew seasoned with paprika.

gourd (*say* goord) *noun* **1** the rounded hard-skinned fruit of a climbing plant. **2** the dried skin of the gourd-fruit, used as a cup, bowl, etc.

gourmet (*say* goor-may) *noun* a person who understands and appreciates good food and drink.

gout *noun* a disease that causes painful inflammation of the toes, knees, and fingers. **gouty** *adjective*

govern *verb* be in charge of the public affairs of a country or an organization.

governess *noun* a woman employed to teach children in a private household.

government *noun* **1** the group of people who govern a country. **2** the process of governing, *Four years of weak government had left the economy in ruins.* **governmental** *adjective*

governor *noun* **1** a person who governs a State or a colony etc. **2** a member of the governing body of a school or other institution. **3** the person in charge of a prison.

gown *noun* a loose flowing garment.

GP *abbreviation* general practitioner (a doctor).

grab *verb* (**grabbed, grabbing**) take hold of suddenly or greedily.

grace¹ *noun* **1** beauty of movement or manner or design. **2** goodwill; favour. **3** a short prayer of thanks before or after a meal. **4** the title of a duke, duchess, or archbishop, *His Grace the Archbishop of Cape Town.*

grace² *verb* (**graced, gracing**) bring honour or dignity to something.

graceful *adjective* full of grace. **gracefully** *adverb*, **gracefulness** *noun*

gracious *adjective* kind and pleasant. **graciously** *adverb*, **graciousness** *noun*

grade¹ *noun* a step in a scale of quality or value or rank; a standard.

grade² *verb* (**graded, grading**) arrange in grades.

gradient (*say* gray-dee-ent) *noun* a slope.

gradual *adjective* happening slowly but steadily. **gradually** *adverb*

graduate¹ (*say* grad-yoo-ayt) *verb* (**graduated, graduating**) **1** get a university degree. **2** divide into graded sections; mark with units of measurement. **graduation** *noun*

graduate² (*say* grad-yoo-at) *noun* a person who has a university degree.

graffiti *plural noun* scribblings on a wall.
● USAGE: Strictly speaking, this word should be used with a plural verb because it is a plural noun. However, it is widely used nowadays with a singular verb and most people find this acceptable.

graft¹ *noun* 1 a shoot from one plant or tree fixed into another to form a new growth. 2 a piece of living tissue transplanted by a surgeon to replace what is diseased or damaged, *a skin graft.*

graft² *verb* 1 insert or transplant as a graft. 2 (*informal*) work hard.

grain *noun* 1 a small hard seed or similar particle. 2 cereal plants when they are growing or after being harvested. 3 the pattern of lines made by the fibres in a piece of wood. **grainy** *adjective*

gram *noun* a unit of mass or weight in the metric system.

-gram *suffix* forming nouns meaning something written or drawn etc. (e.g. *diagram, telegram*).

gramadoelas *plural noun* (*informal*) wild places; the most remote parts of the country.

grammar *noun* 1 the rules for using words correctly. 2 a book about these rules.

grammar school a secondary school which concentrates on academic subjects.

grammatical *adjective* of grammar; according to its rules. **grammatically** *adverb*

gramophone *noun* a record-player.

grampus *noun* (*plural* **grampuses**) a large dolphin-like sea animal.

granadilla *noun* a round purple fruit with sweet juicy pulp.

granary *noun* (*plural* **granaries**) a store-house for grain.

grand *adjective* 1 splendid, magnificent. 2 including everything; complete, *The grand total.* **grandly** *adverb*, **grandness** *noun*

grand piano a large piano with the strings fixed horizontally.

grandad *noun* (*informal*) grandfather.

grandchild *noun* (*plural* **grandchildren**) the child of a person's son or daughter.

granddaughter *noun*, **grandson** *noun*

grandeur (*say* grand-yer) *noun* grandness; splendour.

grandfather *noun* the father of a person's father or mother.

grandfather clock a clock in a tall wooden case.

grandiose (*say* grand-ee-ohss) *adjective* imposing; trying to seem grand.

grandma *noun* (*informal*) grandmother.

grandmother *noun* the mother of a person's father or mother.

grandpa *noun* (*informal*) grandfather.

grandparent *noun* a grandfather or grandmother.

grandstand *noun* a building with a roof and rows of seats for spectators at a racecourse or sports ground.

grange *noun* a large country house.

granite *noun* a very hard kind of rock.

granny *noun* (*plural* **grannies**) (*informal*) grandmother.

granny knot a reef-knot with the strings crossed the wrong way.

grant¹ *verb* 1 give or allow what is asked for, *grant a request.* 2 admit; agree that something is true.

take for granted assume that something is true or will always be available.

grant² *noun* something granted, especially a sum of money.

granular *adjective* like grains.

granule *noun* a small grain.

grape *noun* a small green or purple berry that grows in bunches on a vine.

grapefruit *noun* (*plural* **grapefruit**) a large round yellow citrus fruit.

grape-vine *noun* 1 a vine on which grapes grow. 2 a way by which news is passed on unofficially.

graph *noun* a diagram showing how two qualities are related.

graph paper paper printed with small squares, used for drawing graphs.

-graph *suffix* forming nouns and verbs meaning something written or drawn etc. (e.g. *photograph*).

graphic *adjective* 1 of drawing or painting, *a graphic artist.* 2 giving a lively description. **graphically** *adverb*

graphics *plural noun* diagrams, lettering, and drawings.

graphite *noun* a soft black form of carbon used for the lead in pencils, as a lubricant, and in nuclear reactors.

-graphy *suffix* forming names of descriptive sciences (e.g. *geography*) or methods of writing or drawing etc. (e.g. *photography, calligraphy*).

grapnel *noun* a heavy metal device with claws for hooking things.

grapple *verb* (**grappled, grappling**) 1 struggle; wrestle. 2 seize or hold firmly.

grasp *verb* 1 seize and hold firmly. 2 understand. **grasp** *noun*

grasping *adjective* greedy for money or possessions.

grass *noun* (*plural* **grasses**) 1 a plant with green blades and stalks that are eaten by animals. 2 ground covered with grass, *Keep off the grass.* **grassy** *adjective*
grass roots the ordinary people in a political party or other group.

grasshopper *noun* a jumping insect that makes a shrill noise.

grassland *noun* a wide area covered in grass with few trees.

grate[1] *noun* 1 a metal framework that keeps fuel in a fireplace. 2 a fireplace.

grate[2] *verb* (**grated, grating**) 1 shred into small pieces by rubbing on a rough surface. 2 make an unpleasant noise by rubbing. 3 sound harshly or in an irritating way.

grateful *adjective* feeling or showing that you value what was done for you. **gratefully** *adverb*

grater *noun* a device with a jagged surface for grating food.

gratify *verb* (**gratified, gratifying**) 1 give pleasure. 2 satisfy a wish etc., *Please gratify our curiosity.* **gratification** *noun*

grating *noun* a framework of metal or wooden bars placed across an opening.

gratis (*say* **grah**-tiss) *adverb* & *adjective* free of charge, *You can have the leaflet gratis.*

gratitude *noun* being grateful.

gratuitous (*say* gra-**tew**-it-us) *adjective* given or done without payment or without good reason. **gratuitously** *adverb*

gratuity (*say* gra-**tew**-it-ee) *noun* (*plural* **gratuities**) money given in gratitude; a tip.

grave[1] *noun* the place where a corpse is buried.

grave[2] *adjective* serious, solemn. **gravely** *adverb*

gravel *noun* small stones mixed with

coarse sand. **gravelled** *adjective*, **gravelly** *adjective*

graven (*say* **gray**-ven) *adjective* carved.

gravestone *noun* a stone monument over a grave.

graveyard *noun* a burial ground.

gravitate *verb* (**gravitated, gravitating**) move or be attracted towards something.

gravitation *noun* 1 gravitating. 2 the force of gravity. **gravitational** *adjective*

gravity *noun* 1 the force that pulls everything towards the earth. 2 seriousness.

gravy *noun* a hot brown liquid served with meat.

graze[1] *verb* (**grazed, grazing**) 1 feed on growing grass. 2 scrape slightly in passing, *I grazed my elbow on the wall.*

graze[2] *noun* a raw place where skin has been scraped.

grease[1] *noun* melted fat; any thick oily substance.

grease[2] *verb* (**greased, greasing**) put grease on something.

great *adjective* 1 very large; much above average. 2 very important or talented, *a great composer.* 3 (*informal*) very good or enjoyable, *It's great to see you again.* 4 older or younger by one generation, *great-grandfather.* 5 of a chief and his most important wife in traditional African society, *great house.* **greatly** *adverb*, **greatness** *noun*

Great Trek the movement of Boer farmers in the 1830s away from the Cape Colony and British authority, in order to form republics in the northern and eastern parts of South Africa.

grebe (*say* greeb) *noun* a kind of diving bird.

greed *noun* being greedy.

greedy *adjective* wanting more food, money, or other things than you need. **greedily** *adverb*, **greediness** *noun*

green[1] *noun* 1 the colour of growing grass. 2 an area of grass, *the village green.* 3 a person who supports an environmental cause.

green[2] *adjective* 1 of the colour green. 2 inexperienced and likely to make mistakes. 3 supporting the conservation of the environment; environment-friendly, *green products*. **greenness** *noun*

green belt an area kept as open land round a city.

green manure any crop that is grown to be ploughed back into the soil to improve soil structure and fertility.

greenery *noun* green leaves or plants.

greenfly *noun* (*plural* **greenfly**) a small green insect that sucks the juices from plants.

greengrocer *noun* a person who keeps a shop that sells fruit and vegetables. **greengrocery** *noun*

greenhouse *noun* a glass building where plants are protected from cold.

greenhouse effect the warming up of the earth's surface when radiation from the sun is trapped by the atmosphere.

Greenwich Mean Time (*say* **gren**-ich) *noun* the time on the line of longitude which passes through Greenwich in London, England, used as a basis for calculating time throughout the world.

greet *verb* 1 speak to a person who arrives. 2 receive, *They greeted the song with applause.* 3 present itself to, *A strange sight greeted our eyes.*

greeting *noun* 1 words or actions used to greet somebody. 2 good wishes.

gregarious (*say* grig-**air**-ee-us) *adjective* 1 fond of company. 2 living in flocks or communities. **gregariously** *adverb*, **gregariousness** *noun*

gremlin *noun* (*informal*) an imaginary mischief-maker who is blamed for problems which occur in machines etc.

grenade (*say* grin-**ayd**) *noun* a small bomb, usually thrown by hand.

grey *noun* the colour between black and white, like ashes. **grey** *adjective*, **greyness** *noun*

greyhound *noun* a slender dog with smooth hair, used in racing.

grid *noun* a framework or pattern of bars or lines crossing each other.

griddle *noun* a round iron plate for cooking things on.

gridiron *noun* a framework of bars for cooking on.

grief *noun* deep sorrow.
  come to grief suffer a disaster.

grievance *noun* something that people are discontented about.

grieve *verb* (**grieved, grieving**) 1 cause a person grief. 2 feel grief.

grievous (*say* **gree**-vus) *adjective* 1 causing grief. 2 serious. **grievously** *adverb*

griffin *noun* a creature in fables, with an eagle's head and wings on a lion's body.

grill[1] *noun* 1 a heated element on a cooker, for sending heat downwards. 2 food cooked under this, *a mixed grill.* 3 a grille.

grill[2] *verb* 1 cook under a grill. 2 question closely and severely, *The police grilled him for an hour.*

grille *noun* a metal grating covering a window or similar opening.

grim *adjective* (**grimmer, grimmest**) 1 stern; severe. 2 without cheerfulness; unattractive, *a grim prospect.* **grimly** *adverb*, **grimness** *noun*

grimace[1] (*say* **grim**-as or grim-**ayss**) *noun* a twisted expression on the face made in pain or disgust.

grimace[2] *verb* (**grimaced, grimacing**) make a grimace.

grime *noun* dirt clinging to a surface or to the skin. **grimy** *adjective*

grin[1] *noun* a broad smile.

grin[2] *verb* (**grinned, grinning**) smile broadly.

grind (*say* grynd) *verb* (**ground, grinding**) 1 crush into grains or powder. 2 sharpen or smooth by rubbing on a rough surface. 3 rub harshly together, *She ground her teeth in fury.* 4 move with a harsh grating noise, *The bus ground to a halt.* **grinder** *noun*

grindstone *noun* a thick round rough revolving stone for sharpening or grinding things.

grip[1] *verb* (**gripped, gripping**) 1 hold firmly. 2 hold a person's attention, *I was gripped by the play from beginning to end.*

grip[2] *noun* 1 a firm hold. 2 understanding. 3 a handle. 4 (*American*) a suitcase or travel-bag.

gripe *verb* (**griped, griping**) (*informal*) grumble. **gripe** *noun*

grisly *adjective* (**grislier, grisliest**) causing horror or disgust; gruesome.

grist *noun* grain for grinding.
grist to the mill something that can be used to a person's advantage.

gristle *noun* tough rubbery tissue in meat. **gristly** *adjective*

grit[1] *noun* 1 tiny pieces of stone or sand. 2 courage and endurance, *Marathon running takes a lot of grit.* **gritty** *adjective*, **grittiness** *noun*

grit[2] *verb* (**gritted, gritting**) 1 spread with grit, *grit the roads.* 2 clench the teeth when in pain or trouble.

grizzle *verb* (**grizzled, grizzling**) whimper; whine.

grizzled *adjective* streaked with grey hairs.

grizzly *adjective* grey-haired.
grizzly bear a large fierce bear.

groan *verb* 1 make a long deep sound in pain or distress or disapproval. 2 creak loudly under a heavy load. **groan** *noun*, **groaner** *noun*

grocer *noun* a person who keeps a shop that sells food and household supplies. **grocery** *noun* (*plural* **groceries**)

grog *noun* a drink of alcoholic spirits, usually rum, mixed with water.

groggy *adjective* (**groggier, groggiest**) weak and unsteady, especially after illness. **groggily** *adverb*, **grogginess** *noun*

groin *noun* the groove where the thigh joins the trunk of the body.

groom[1] *noun* 1 a person whose job is to look after horses. 2 a bridegroom.

groom[2] *verb* 1 clean and brush (an animal). 2 make neat and trim. 3 train a person for a certain job or position.

groove *noun* a long narrow furrow or channel cut in the surface of something. **grooved** *adjective*

grope *verb* (**groped, groping**) feel about for something you cannot see.

gross[1] (*say* grohss) *adjective* 1 overfed and ugly. 2 having bad manners; vulgar. 3 very obvious or shocking, *gross stupidity.* 4 total; without anything being deducted, *our gross income.* (Compare *net*[3].) **grossly** *adverb*, **grossness** *noun*
gross domestic product the total value

of goods and services produced within a country over a period of time.
gross national product the gross domestic product of a country plus the total income from other countries.

gross[2] *noun* (*plural* **gross**) twelve dozen (144) of something, *ten gross = 1440.*

grotesque (*say* groh-**tesk**) *adjective* very strange; fantastically ugly. **grotesquely** *adverb*, **grotesqueness** *noun*

grotto *noun* (*plural* **grottoes**) a picturesque cave.

ground[1] *past tense* of **grind**.

ground[2] *noun* 1 the solid surface of the earth. 2 a sports field.

ground[3] *verb* 1 run aground. 2 prevent from flying, *All aircraft are grounded because of the fog.* 3 give a good basic training, *Ground them in the rules of spelling.* 4 base, *This theory is grounded on known facts.*

grounding *noun* basic training.

groundless *adjective* without foundation or reasons, *Your fears are groundless.*

grounds *plural noun* 1 the gardens of a large house. 2 solid particles that sink to the bottom, *coffee grounds.* 3 reasons, *There are grounds for suspicion.*

groundsheet *noun* a piece of waterproof material for spreading on the ground.

groundsman *noun* (*plural* **groundsmen**) a person whose job is to look after a sports ground.

groundwork *noun* work that lays the basis for something.

group[1] *noun* a number of people, animals, or things that come together or belong together in some way.
group area under apartheid laws, an area in which only people from a certain race group were allowed to live.

group[2] *verb* put together or come together in a group or groups.

grouse[1] *noun* (*plural* **grouse**) a bird with feathered feet, hunted as game.

grouse[2] *verb* (**groused, grousing**) (*informal*) grumble. **grouse** *noun*, **grouser** *noun*

grove *noun* a group of trees, a small wood.

grovel *verb* (**grovelled, grovelling**) 1 crawl

on the ground, especially in a show of fear or humility. **2** act in an excessively humble way. **groveller** *noun*

grow *verb* (**grew, grown, growing**)
1 become bigger or greater. **2** develop; put out shoots. **3** cultivate; plant and look after, *She grows roses.* **4** become, *He grew rich.* **grower** *noun*

growl *verb* make a deep angry sound. **growl** *noun*

grown-up *noun* an adult person.

growth *noun* **1** the process of growing; development. **2** something that has grown.

grub[1] *noun* **1** a tiny worm-like creature that will become an insect; a larva. **2** (*slang*) food.

grub[2] *verb* (**grubbed, grubbing**) **1** dig up by the roots. **2** rummage.

grubby *adjective* (**grubbier, grubbiest**) rather dirty. **grubbiness** *noun*

grudge[1] *noun* a feeling of resentment or ill will.

grudge[2] *verb* (**grudged, grudging**) resent having to give or allow something.

gruelling *adjective* exhausting.

gruesome *adjective* causing people to feel horror or disgust.

gruff *adjective* having a rough unfriendly voice or manner. **gruffly** *adverb*, **gruffness** *noun*

grumble *verb* (**grumbled, grumbling**) complain in a bad-tempered way. **grumble** *noun*, **grumbler** *noun*

grumpy *adjective* bad-tempered. **grumpily** *adverb*, **grumpiness** *noun*

grunt *verb* **1** make a pig's gruff snort. **2** speak or say gruffly. **grunt** *noun*

grysbok *noun* a small greyish-brown antelope.

guano (*say* **gwah**-noh) *noun* (*plural* **guanos**) a waste matter produced by sea-birds, used as a fertilizer for soil.

guarantee[1] *noun* a formal promise to do something or to repair an object if it breaks or goes wrong.

guarantee[2] *verb* (**guaranteed, guaranteeing**) give a guarantee; promise. **guarantor** *noun*

guard[1] *verb* **1** protect; keep safe. **2** watch over and prevent from escaping.

guard[2] *noun* **1** guarding; protection, *Keep the prisoners under close guard.* **2** someone who guards a person or place. **3** a group of soldiers or police officers etc. acting as a guard. **4** a railway official in charge of a train. **5** a protecting device, *a fire-guard.*

guardian *noun* **1** someone who guards. **2** a person who is legally in charge of a child whose parents cannot look after him or her. **guardianship** *noun*

guava *noun* a pale orange fruit with pink flesh.

guerrilla (*say* ger-il-a) *noun* a person who fights by making surprise attacks as one of a small group.

guess[1] *noun* (*plural* **guesses**) an opinion given without making careful calculations or without certain knowledge.

guess[2] *verb* make a guess. **guesser** *noun*

guest *noun* **1** a person who is invited to visit or stay at another's house. **2** a person staying at a hotel. **3** a person who takes part in another's show as a visiting performer.

guffaw *verb* give a noisy laugh. **guffaw** *noun*

guidance *noun* **1** guiding. **2** advising or advice on problems.

Guide *noun* a member of the Girl Guides Association, an organization for girls.

guide[1] *noun* **1** a person who shows others the way or points out interesting sights. **2** a book giving information about a place or subject.

guide[2] *verb* (**guided, guiding**) act as guide to.

guidebook *noun* a book of information about a place, for travellers or visitors.

guidelines *plural noun* statements that give general advice about something.

guild (*say* gild) *noun* a society of people with similar skills or interests.

guile (rhymes with *mile*) *noun* craftiness.

guillotine[1] (*say* gil-ot-een) *noun* **1** a machine with a heavy blade for beheading criminals. **2** a machine with a long blade for cutting paper or metal. **3** fixing a time for a vote to be taken in Parliament in order to cut short a debate.

guillotine[2] *verb* (**guillotined, guillotining**) cut with a guillotine.

guilt *noun* **1** the fact of having committed an offence. **2** a feeling of being to blame for something that has happened.

guilty *adjective* **1** having done wrong. **2** feeling or showing guilt. **guiltily** *adverb*

guinea-fowl *noun* a dark grey bird with white spots, hunted as game.

guinea-pig *noun* **1** a small furry animal without a tail. **2** a person who is used as the subject of an experiment.

guise (*say as* guys) *noun* an outward disguise or pretence.

guitar *noun* a musical instrument played by plucking its strings. **guitarist** *noun*

gulf *noun* **1** a large area of the sea that is partly surrounded by land. **2** a wide gap; a great difference, *a gulf between the two groups.*

gull *noun* a seagull.

gullet *noun* the tube from the throat to the stomach.

gullible *adjective* easily deceived.

gully *noun* (*plural* **gullies**) a narrow channel that carries water.

gulp¹ *verb* **1** swallow hastily or greedily. **2** make a loud swallowing noise.

gulp² *noun* **1** the act of gulping. **2** a large mouthful of liquid.

gum¹ *noun* the firm flesh in which teeth are rooted.

gum² *noun* **1** a sticky substance produced by some trees and shrubs, used as glue. **2** a sweet made with gum or gelatine. **3** chewing-gum. **4** a gum-tree. **gummy** *adjective*

gum³ *verb* (**gummed, gumming**) cover or stick with gum.

gumboot *noun* a rubber boot.
gumboot dance a mineworkers' dance which is done in rubber boots, usually for tourists.

gumption *noun* (*informal*) common sense.

gum-tree *noun* a eucalyptus.

gun¹ *noun* **1** a weapon that fires shells or bullets from a metal tube. **2** a starting-pistol. **3** a device that forces a substance out of a tube, *a grease-gun.* **gunfire** *noun*, **gunshot** *noun*

gun² *verb* (**gunned, gunning**) shoot with a gun, *They gunned him down.*

gunboat *noun* a small warship.

gunman *noun* (*plural* **gunmen**) a criminal with a gun.

gunner *noun* a person who operates a gun.

gunnery *noun* the making or use of guns.

gunpowder *noun* a kind of explosive.

gunwale (*say* **gun**-al) *noun* the upper edge of a small ship's or boat's side.

gurgle *verb* (**gurgled, gurgling**) make a low bubbling sound. **gurgle** *noun*

guru *noun* (*plural* **gurus**) a teacher or head of a religious sect who has great influence over his or her followers.

gush *verb* **1** flow suddenly or quickly. **2** talk effusively, *a young mother gushing over her baby.* **gush** *noun*

gust¹ *noun* **1** a sudden rush of wind. **2** a burst of rain, smoke, or sound. **gusty** *adjective*, **gustily** *adverb*

gust² *verb* blow in gusts.

gusto *noun* great enjoyment; zest.

gut¹ *noun* the lower part of the digestive system; the intestine.

gut² *verb* (**gutted, gutting**) **1** remove the guts from a dead fish or other animal. **2** remove or destroy the inside of something, *The fire gutted the factory.*

guts *plural noun* **1** the digestive system; the inside parts of a person or thing. **2** (*informal*) courage.

gutter¹ *noun* a long narrow channel at the side of a street, or along the edge of a roof, for carrying away rainwater.

gutter² *verb* (of a candle) burn unsteadily so that melted wax runs down.

guttersnipe *noun* a poor child who plays in the streets in a slum.

guttural (*say* **gut**-er-al) *adjective* throaty, harsh-sounding, *a guttural voice.*

guy¹ *noun* **1** a figure representing Guy Fawkes, burnt on 5 November in memory of the Gunpowder Plot which planned to blow up the parliament of England on that day in 1605. **2** (*informal*) a man.
Guy Fawkes 5 November, when people let off fireworks.

guy² (also **guy-rope**) *noun* a rope used to hold something in place.

guzzle *verb* (**guzzled, guzzling**) eat or drink greedily. **guzzler** *noun*

gym (*say* jim) *noun* (*informal*) 1 a gymnasium. 2 gymnastics.

gymkhana (*say* jim-**kah**-na) *noun* a series of horse-riding contests and other sports events.

gymnasium *noun* a place fitted up for gymnastics.

gymnast *noun* an expert in gymnastics.

gymnastics *plural noun* exercises performed to develop the muscles or to show the performer's agility. **gymnastic** *adjective*

gymnosperm (*say* **jim**-noh-sperm) *noun* a plant that has no flowers and that has seeds unprotected by fruit or pods, e.g. conifers and cycads.

gypsy *noun* (*plural* **gypsies**) a member of a people who live in caravans and wander from place to place.

gyrate (*say* jy-**rayt**) *verb* (**gyrated, gyrating**) revolve; move in circles or spirals. **gyration** *noun*

gyroscope (*say* **jy**-ro-skohp) *noun* a device that keeps steady because of a heavy wheel spinning inside it.

Hh

ha *interjection* an exclamation of triumph or surprise.

haberdashery *noun* dress accessories and small articles used in sewing, e.g. ribbons, buttons, thread.

habit *noun* 1 something that you do without thinking because you have done it so often; a settled way of behaving. 2 the long dress worn by a monk or nun. **habitual** *adjective*, **habitually** *adverb*

habitat *noun* where an animal or plant lives naturally.

habitation *noun* 1 a dwelling. 2 inhabiting a place.

hack[1] *verb* 1 chop or cut roughly. 2 (*informal*) access a computer file without authorization. **hacker** *noun*

hack[2] *noun* a horse for ordinary riding.

hackles *plural noun* **with his** or **her hackles up** angry and ready to fight.

hackneyed *adjective* used so often that it is no longer interesting.

hacksaw *noun* a saw for cutting metal.

haddock *noun* (*plural* **haddock**) a sea-fish like cod but smaller, used as food.

hadedah (*say* **hah**-dee-da) *noun* a large brownish bird which has a loud and harsh call.

hadj *noun* Hajj.

hadji *noun* Hajji.

hadn't (*mainly spoken*) had not.

haemoglobin (*say* heem-a-**gloh**-bin) *noun* the red substance that carries oxygen in the blood.

haemophilia (*say* heem-o-**fil**-ee-a) *noun* a disease that causes people to bleed dangerously from even a slight cut.

haemorrhage (*say* **hem**-er-ij) *noun* bleeding.

hag *noun* an ugly old woman.

haggard *adjective* looking ill or very tired.

haggle *verb* (**haggled, haggling**) argue about a price or agreement.

ha ha *interjection* laughter.

haiku (*say* **hy**-koo) *noun* (*plural* **haiku**) a kind of short poem, usually with three lines and 17 syllables.

hail[1] *noun* frozen drops of rain. **hail** *verb*, **hailstone** *noun*, **hailstorm** *noun*

hail[2] *interjection* an exclamation of greeting.

hail[3] *verb* call out to somebody. **hail from** come from, *He hails from Angola.*

hair *noun* 1 a soft covering that grows on the heads and bodies of people and animals. 2 one of the threads that make up this covering. **hairbrush** *noun*, **haircut** *noun*

keep your hair on (*informal*) do not lose your temper.

split hairs make petty or unimportant distinctions of meaning. **hair-splitting** *noun*

hairdresser *noun* a person whose job is to cut and arrange people's hair.

hairpin *noun* a U-shaped pin for keeping hair in place.

hairpin bend a sharp bend in a road.

hair-raising *adjective* terrifying.

hairy *adjective* **1** with a lot of hair.
2 (*informal*) hair-raising; difficult.

Hajj *noun* the holy journey to Mecca made by Muslims.

Hajji *noun* a Muslim who has made the holy journey to Mecca.

hake *noun* (*plural* **hake**) a sea-fish used as food.

halaal *adjective* keeping to Muslim laws about food, *halaal meat.*

halcyon (*say* **hal**-see-on) *noun* happy and peaceful, *halcyon days.*

hale *adjective* strong and healthy, *hale and hearty.*

half[1] *noun* (*plural* **halves**) one of the two equal parts or amounts into which something is or can be divided.

half[2] *adverb* partly; not completely, *This meat is only half cooked.*

half-baked *adjective* (*informal*) not well planned; foolish.

half-brother *noun* a brother to whom you are related by one parent but not by both parents.

half-hearted *adjective* not very enthusiastic. **half-heartedly** *adverb*

half-sister *noun* a sister to whom you are related by one parent but not by both parents.

half-term *noun* a short holiday in the middle of a term.

half-time *noun* the point or interval halfway through a game.

half-way *adjective* & *adverb* between two others and equally distant from each.

half-witted *adjective* mentally deficient; stupid. **half-wit** *noun*

hall *noun* **1** a space or passage into which the front entrance of a house etc. opens. **2** a very large room or building used for meetings, concerts, etc.

hallelujah *interjection* & *noun* alleluia.

hallmark *noun* an official mark made on gold, silver, and platinum to show its quality.

hallo *interjection* a word used to greet somebody or to attract their attention.

hallow *verb* make a thing holy; honour something as being holy.

Hallowe'en *noun* 31 October, when some people think magical things happen.

hallucination *noun* something you think you can see or hear that is not really there.

halo *noun* (*plural* **haloes**) a circle of light round something, especially round the head of a saint etc. in paintings.

halt[1] *verb* stop.

halt[2] *noun* **1** a stop, *Work came to a halt.* **2** a small stopping-place on a railway.

halter *noun* a rope or strap put round a horse's head so that it can be led or fastened by this.

halva *noun* a kind of confection.

halve *verb* (**halved, halving**) **1** divide into halves. **2** reduce to half its size.

ham *noun* **1** meat from a pig's leg. **2** (*informal*) an actor or performer who is not very good. **3** (*informal*) someone who operates a radio to send and receive messages as a hobby.

hamba *interjection* (*informal*) an expression used to send someone away, 'Go!' **hamba kahle** a traditional farewell, 'Go well.'

hamburger *noun* a flat round cake of minced beef served fried, often in a bread roll.

hamerkop *noun* a kind of wading bird which has a hammer-shaped head.

hamlet *noun* a small village.

hammer[1] *noun* a tool with a heavy metal head used for driving nails in, breaking things, etc.

hammer[2] *verb* **1** hit with a hammer. **2** strike loudly. **3** (*informal*) defeat, *They were hammered by their opposition.*

hammock *noun* a bed made of a strong net or piece of cloth hung by cords.

hamper[1] *noun* a large box-shaped basket with a lid.

hamper[2] *verb* hinder; prevent from moving or working freely.

hamster *noun* a small furry animal with cheek-pouches for carrying grain.

hand[1] *noun* **1** the end part of the arm below the wrist. **2** a pointer on a clock or dial. **3** a worker; a member of a ship's crew, *All hands on deck!* **4** the cards held by one player in a card-game. **5** side or direction, *on the other hand.* **6** control; care, *You are in*

good hands. **7** influence; help, *Give me a hand with these boxes.*
at hand near.
by hand using your hand or hands.
hands down winning easily.
in hand in your possession; being dealt with.
on hand available.
out of hand out of control.
hand² *verb* give or pass something to somebody, *Hand it over.*
handbag *noun* a small bag for holding a purse and personal articles.
handbook *noun* a small book that gives useful facts about something.
handcuff¹ *noun* one of a pair of metal rings linked by a chain, for fastening wrists together.
handcuff² *verb* fasten with handcuffs.
handful *noun* (*plural* **handfuls**) **1** as much as can be carried in one hand. **2** a few people or things. **3** (*informal*) a troublesome person or task.
handicap *noun* **1** a disadvantage, *His lack of education was a handicap.* **2** a physical or mental disability. **handicapped** *adjective*
handicraft *noun* artistic work done with the hands, e.g. woodwork, needlework.
handily *adverb* in a handy way.
handiwork *noun* **1** something made by hand. **2** something done, *Is this mess your handiwork?*
handkerchief *noun* a small square of cloth for wiping the nose or face.
handle¹ *noun* the part of a thing by which it is carried or controlled.
handle² *verb* (**handled**, **handling**) **1** touch or feel something with your hands. **2** deal with; manage, *Will you handle the catering?* **handler** *noun*
handlebar *noun* (also **handlebars**) the bar, with a handle at each end, that steers a bicycle or motor cycle etc.
handrail *noun* a narrow rail for people to hold as a support.
handshake *noun* shaking hands with someone as a greeting etc.
handsome *adjective* **1** good-looking. **2** generous, *a handsome gift.* **handsomely** *adverb*

hands-on *adjective* practical, *hands-on experience.*
handstand *noun* balancing on your hands with your feet in the air.
handwriting *noun* writing done by hand. **handwritten** *adjective*
handy *adjective* (**handier**, **handiest**) **1** convenient; useful. **2** good at using the hands. **handily** *adverb*, **handiness** *noun*
handyman *noun* (*plural* **handymen**) a person who does household repairs or odd jobs.
hang¹ *verb* (**hung**, **hanging**) **1** fix the top or side of something to a hook or nail etc.; be supported in this way. **2** stick wall-paper to a wall. **3** decorate with drapery or hanging ornaments etc., *The tree was hung with lights.* **4** droop; lean, *People hung over the gate.* **5** (with *past tense* & *past participle* **hanged**) execute someone by hanging them from a rope that tightens round the neck.
hang about loiter; not go away.
hang back hesitate to go forward or to do something.
hang on hold tightly; (*informal*) wait.
hang up end a telephone conversation by putting back the receiver.
hang² *noun* the way something hangs.
get the hang of (*informal*) learn how to do or use something.
hangar *noun* a large shed where aircraft are kept.
hanger *noun* a device on which to hang things, *a coat-hanger.*
hang-glider *noun* a framework in which a person can glide through the air. **hang-gliding** *noun*
hangman *noun* (*plural* **hangmen**) **1** a person whose job it is to hang people condemned to death. **2** a game in which players guess the missing letters of a word.
hangover *noun* an unpleasant feeling after drinking too much alcohol.
hank *noun* a coil or piece of wool, thread, etc.
hanker *verb* feel a longing for something.
hanky *noun* (*plural* **hankies**) (*informal*) a handkerchief.

hanslammetjie (*say* **hans**-lam-a-kee) *noun* a lamb without a mother which has been reared by hand, often kept as a pet.

Hanukkah (*say* **hah**-noo-ka) *noun* an eight-day Jewish festival beginning in December.

haphazard *adjective* done or chosen at random, not by planning.

hapless *adjective* having no luck.

happen *verb* 1 take place; occur. 2 do something by chance, *I happened to see him.*

happening *noun* something that happens; an event.

happy *adjective* (**happier, happiest**) pleased; contented; fortunate. **happily** *adverb*, **happiness** *noun*

harangue (*say* ha-**rang**) *verb* (**harangued, haranguing**) make a long speech to somebody. **harangue** *noun*

harass (*say* **ha**-ras) *verb* trouble or annoy somebody often. **harassment** (*say* **ha**-ras-ment) *noun*

harbour[1] *noun* a place where ships can shelter or unload.

harbour[2] *verb* 1 give shelter to somebody, *harbouring a criminal.* 2 keep in your mind, *harbouring a grudge.*

hard[1] *adjective* 1 firm; solid; not soft. 2 difficult, *hard sums.* 3 severe; stern. 4 causing suffering, *hard luck.* 5 using great effort, *a hard worker.* **hardness** *noun*

hard disk a computer storage disk with a large capacity for data.

hard of hearing slightly deaf.

hard up (*informal*) short of money.

hard water water containing minerals that prevent soap from making much lather.

hard[2] *adverb* 1 so as to be hard, *The ground froze hard.* 2 with great effort; intensively, *We worked hard. It is raining hard.* 3 with difficulty, *hard-earned.*

hardboard *noun* stiff board made of compressed wood-pulp.

harden *verb* make or become hard or hardy. **hardener** *noun*

hard-hearted *adjective* unsympathetic.

hardly *adverb* only just; only with difficulty, *She can hardly walk.*

• USAGE: It is incorrect to say 'she can't hardly walk'.

hardship *noun* difficult conditions that cause discomfort or suffering.

hardware *noun* 1 metal implements and tools etc.; machinery. 2 the machinery of a computer. (Compare *software.*)

hardwood *noun* hard heavy wood from deciduous trees, e.g. oak and teak.

hardy *adjective* (**hardier, hardiest**) able to endure cold or difficult conditions. **hardiness** *noun*

hare *noun* an animal like a rabbit but larger.

harem (*say* **har**-eem) *noun* the part of a Muslim palace or house where the women live; the women living there.

hark *verb* listen.

hark back return to an earlier subject.

harlequin *adjective* in mixed colours.

harm[1] *verb* damage; injure.

harm[2] *noun* damage; injury. **harmful** *adjective*, **harmless** *adjective*

harmonic *adjective* of harmony in music.

harmonica *noun* a mouth-organ.

harmonious *adjective* full of harmony.

harmonize *verb* (**harmonized, harmonizing**) make harmonious; produce harmony. **harmonization** *noun*

harmony *noun* (*plural* **harmonies**) 1 a pleasant combination, especially of musical notes. 2 being friendly to each other and not quarrelling.

harness[1] *noun* (*plural* **harnesses**) the straps put round a horse's head and neck for controlling it.

harness[2] *verb* 1 put a harness on a horse. 2 control and use something, *Could we harness the power of the wind?*

harp[1] *noun* a musical instrument made of strings stretched across a frame and plucked by the fingers. **harpist** *noun*

harp[2] *verb* keep on talking about something in a tiresome way, *He is always harping on his misfortunes.*

harpoon *noun* a spear attached to a rope, used for catching whales etc. **harpoon** *verb*

harpsichord *noun* an instrument like a piano but with strings that are plucked (not struck) by a mechanism.

harrow *noun* a heavy device pulled over the ground to break up the soil.

harrowing *adjective* causing horror and distress.

harry *verb* (**harried, harrying**) harass.

harsh *adjective* **1** rough and unpleasant, *harsh weather.* **2** severe; cruel, *harsh punishment.* **harshly** *adverb*, **harshness** *noun*

hart *noun* a male deer. (Compare *hind*[2].)

hartebeest *noun* a large antelope with curving horns.

harvest[1] *noun* **1** the time when farmers gather in the corn, fruit, or vegetables that they have grown. **2** the crop that is gathered in.

harvest[2] *verb* gather in a crop; reap. **harvester** *noun*

hash *noun* a mixture of small pieces of meat and vegetables, usually fried.
make a hash of (*informal*) make a mess of something; bungle.

hashish *noun* a drug made from hemp.

hasn't (*mainly spoken*) has not.

hassle *noun* (*informal*) trouble.

hassock *noun* a small thick cushion for kneeling on in church.

haste *noun* a hurry.
make haste act quickly.

hasten *verb* hurry.

hasty *adjective* hurried; done too quickly. **hastily** *adverb*, **hastiness** *noun*

hat *noun* a shaped covering for the head.
hat trick getting three goals, wickets, victories, etc. one after the other.
keep it under your hat keep it secret.

hatch[1] *noun* (*plural* **hatches**) an opening in a floor, wall, or door, usually with a covering.

hatch[2] *verb* **1** break out of an egg. **2** keep an egg warm until a baby bird comes out. **3** plan, *They hatched a plot.*

hatchback *noun* a car with a sloping back hinged at the top.

hatchet *noun* a small axe.

hate[1] *verb* (**hated, hating**) dislike very strongly.

hate[2] *noun* hatred.

hateful *adjective* arousing hatred.

hatred *noun* strong dislike.

hatter *noun* a person who makes hats.

hau (*say* how) *interjection* an exclamation of surprise, admiration, or distress.

haughty *adjective* proud of yourself and looking down on other people. **haughtily** *adverb*, **haughtiness** *noun*

haul[1] *verb* pull or drag with great effort. **haulage** *noun*

haul[2] *noun* **1** hauling. **2** the amount obtained by an effort; booty, *The robbers made a good haul.* **3** a distance to be covered, *a long haul.*

haunch *noun* (*plural* **haunches**) the buttock and top part of the thigh.

haunt *verb* **1** (of ghosts) appear often in a place or to a person. **2** visit a place often, *She haunted the library.* **3** stay in your mind, *Memories haunt me.*

haustorium *noun* (*plural* **haustoria**) the part of a parasitic plant that it uses to fasten on to its host.

have[1] *verb* (**had, having**) This word has many uses, including **1** possess; own, *We have two dogs.* **2** contain, *This tin has sweets in it.* **3** experience, *He had a shock.* **4** be obliged to do something, *We have to go now.* **5** allow, *I won't have him bullied.* **6** receive; accept, *Will you have a sweet?* **7** get something done, *I'm having my watch mended.* **8** (*informal*) cheat; deceive, *We've been had!*
have somebody on (*informal*) fool him or her.

have[2] *auxiliary verb* used to form the past tense of verbs, e.g. *He has gone.*

haven *noun* a refuge.

haven't (*mainly spoken*) have not.

haversack *noun* a strong bag carried on your back or over your shoulder.

havoc *noun* great destruction or disorder.

hawk[1] *noun* a bird of prey with very strong eyesight.

hawk[2] *verb* carry goods about and try to sell them.

hawker *noun* **1** a person who sells fruit and vegetables in the street or door-to-door. **2** a person who travels about selling goods.

hawthorn *noun* a thorny tree with small red berries.

hay *noun* dried grass for feeding to animals.
hay fever irritation of the nose, throat, and eyes, caused by pollen or dust.

haystack (also **hayrick**) *noun* a large neat pile of hay packed for storing.

haywire *adjective* (*informal*) badly disorganized; out of control.

hazard *noun* 1 a danger; a risk. 2 an obstacle. **hazardous** *adjective*

haze *noun* thin mist.

hazel *noun* 1 a bush with small nuts. 2 a light-brown colour. **hazel-nut** *noun*

hazy *adjective* 1 misty. 2 vague; uncertain. **hazily** *adverb*, **haziness** *noun*

H-bomb *noun* a hydrogen bomb.

he *pronoun* 1 the male person or animal being talked about. 2 a person (male or female), *Before early man learnt how to make metal, he made weapons and tools from stone.*

● USAGE: Many people feel that sense 2 discriminates against women. You should try to use language that includes both men and women. For example, you could write the sentence in a plural form, *Before early people learnt how to make metal, they made weapons and tools from stone.*

head[1] *noun* 1 the part of the body containing the brains, eyes, and mouth. 2 brains; the mind; intelligence, *Use your head!* 3 a talent or ability, *She has a good head for figures.* 4 the side of a coin on which someone's head is shown. 5 a person, *It costs R10 per head.* 6 the top, *a pin-head*; the leading part of something, *at the head of the procession.* 7 the chief; the person in charge; a headteacher. 8 a crisis, *Matters came to a head.*
keep your head stay calm.

head[2] *verb* 1 be at the top or front of something. 2 hit a ball with your head. 3 move in a particular direction, *We headed for the coast.* 4 force someone to turn by getting in front, *head him off.*

headache *noun* 1 a pain in the head. 2 (*informal*) a worrying problem.

head-dress *noun* a covering or decoration for the head.

header *noun* 1 heading the ball in football. 2 a dive or fall with the head first.

heading *noun* a word or words put at the top of a piece of printing or writing.

headland *noun* a promontory.

headlight *noun* a powerful light at the front of a car, engine, etc.

headline *noun* a heading in a newspaper. **the headlines** the main items of news.

headlong *adverb* & *adjective* 1 head first. 2 in a hasty or thoughtless way.

headmaster *noun* the man in charge of a school.

headmistress *noun* (*plural* **headmistresses**) the woman in charge of a school.

head-on *adverb* & *adjective* with the front parts colliding, *a head-on collision.*

headphone *noun* a radio or telephone receiver that fits over the head.

headquarters *noun* or *plural noun* the place from which an organization is controlled.

headstrong *adjective* determined to do as you want.

headteacher *noun* a headmaster or headmistress.

headway *noun* progress, *make headway.*

heal *verb* 1 make or become healthy flesh again, *The wound healed.* 2 (*old use*) cure, *healing the sick.*

health *noun* 1 the condition of a person's body or mind, *His health is bad.* 2 being healthy, *in sickness and in health.*

healthy *adjective* (**healthier**, **healthiest**) 1 being well; free from illness. 2 producing good health, *Fresh air is healthy.* **healthily** *adverb*, **healthiness** *noun*

heap[1] *noun* a pile, especially if untidy. **heaps** *plural noun* (*informal*) a great amount; plenty, *There's heaps of time.*

heap[2] *verb* 1 make into a heap. 2 put on large amounts, *She heaped the plate with food.*

hear *verb* (**heard, hearing**) 1 take in sounds through the ears. 2 receive news or information etc., *Did you hear of their engagement?* **hearer** *noun*
hear! hear! (in a debate) I agree.

hearing *noun* 1 the ability to hear. 2 a chance to be heard; a trial in a lawcourt.

hearing-aid *noun* a device to help a deaf person to hear.

hearsay *noun* something heard, e.g. in a rumour or gossip.

hearse *noun* a vehicle for taking the coffin to a funeral.

heart *noun* 1 the organ of the body that makes the blood circulate. 2 a person's feelings or emotions; sympathy. 3 enthusiasm; courage, *Take heart.* 4 the middle or most important part, *the heart of the matter.* 5 a curved shape representing a heart; a playing-card with red heart shapes on it. **break a person's heart** make him or her very unhappy. **heartbroken** *adjective* **by heart** memorized.

heart attack or **heart failure** a sudden failure of the heart to work properly.

hearten *verb* make a person feel encouraged.

heartfelt *adjective* felt deeply.

hearth *noun* the floor of or near a fireplace.

heartland *noun* the central or most important region.

heartless *adjective* without pity or sympathy.

hearty *adjective* 1 strong; vigorous. 2 enthusiastic; sincere, *hearty congratulations.* 3 (of a meal) large. **heartily** *adverb*, **heartiness** *noun*

heat¹ *noun* 1 hotness or (in scientific use) the form of energy causing this. 2 hot weather. 3 a race or contest to decide who will take part in the final. **heat wave** a long period of hot weather.

heat² *verb* make or become hot.

heater *noun* a device for heating something; a stove.

heath *noun* flat land with low shrubs.

heathen *noun* a person who does not believe in one of the chief religions.

heather *noun* an evergreen plant with small purple, pink, or white flowers.

heave *verb* (**heaved** (in sense 4 **hove**), **heaving**) 1 lift or move something heavy. 2 (*informal*) throw. 3 rise and fall like sea-waves; pant; retch. 4 (of ships) **heave in sight** appear; **heave to** stop without mooring or anchoring, *The ships hove to.* **heave a sigh** utter a deep sigh.

heaven *noun* 1 the place where God and angels are thought to live. 2 a very pleasant place or condition. **the heavens** the sky.

heavenly *adjective* 1 of heaven. 2 in the sky, *Stars are heavenly bodies.* 3 (*informal*) very pleasing.

heavy *adjective* (**heavier, heaviest**) 1 having great weight; difficult to lift or carry. 2 great in amount or force etc., *heavy rain; a heavy penalty.* 3 needing much effort, *heavy work.* 4 full of sadness or worry, *with a heavy heart.* **heavily** *adverb*, **heaviness** *noun*

heavy industry industry producing metal, machines, etc.

heavyweight *noun* 1 a heavy person. 2 a boxer of the heaviest weight. **heavyweight** *adjective*

Hebrew *noun* the language of the Jews in ancient Palestine and modern Israel.

heckle *verb* (**heckled, heckling**) harass a speaker with interruptions and questions. **heckler** *noun*

hectare (*say* **hek**-tair) *noun* a unit of area equal to 10 000 square metres.

hectic *adjective* full of activity.

hecto- *prefix* one hundred (as in *hectogram* = 100 grams).

hector *verb* frighten by bullying talk.

hedge¹ *noun* a row of bushes forming a barrier or boundary.

hedge² *verb* (**hedged, hedging**) 1 surround with a hedge or other barrier. 2 make or trim a hedge. 3 avoid giving a definite answer, *Stop hedging! Are you coming or not?* **hedger** *noun*

hedgehog *noun* a small animal covered with long prickles.

hedgerow *noun* a hedge round a field etc.

heed¹ *verb* pay attention to.

heed² *noun* attention given to something, *take heed.* **heedful** *adjective*, **heedless** *adjective*

hee-haw *noun* a donkey's bray.

heel¹ *noun* 1 the back part of the foot. 2 the part round or under the heel of a sock or shoe etc. **take to your heels** run away.

heel² *verb* lean over to one side; tilt.

heemraad *noun* (*plural* **heemraden**) 1 (in history) a district council which assisted the landdrost in local government. 2 a member of this council.

hefty *adjective* (**heftier, heftiest**) large and strong. **heftily** *adverb*

Hegira (*say* **hej**-ir-a) *noun* the flight of Muhammad from Mecca in AD 622. The Muslim era is reckoned from this date.

heifer (*say* **hef**-er) *noun* a young cow.

height *noun* 1 how high something is; the distance from the base to the top or from head to foot. 2 a high place. 3 the highest or most intense part, *at the height of the holiday season.*

heighten *verb* make or become higher or more intense.

heir (*say as* air) *noun* a person who inherits something.

heir apparent an heir whose right to inherit cannot be cancelled.

heir presumptive an heir whose right to inherit will be cancelled if someone with a stronger right is born.

heiress (*say* **air**-ess) *noun* (*plural* **heiresses**) a female heir, especially to great wealth.

heirloom (*say* **air**-loom) *noun* a valued possession that has been handed down in a family for several generations.

Hejira *noun* Hegira.

helicopter *noun* a kind of aircraft with a large horizontal propeller or rotor.

heliotrope *noun* a plant which turns its small fragrant purple flowers to the sun.

helium (*say* **hee**-lee-um) *noun* a light colourless gas that does not burn.

helix (*say* **hee**-liks) *noun* (*plural* **helices** (*say* **hee**-liss-eez)) a spiral.

hell *noun* 1 a place where wicked people are thought to be punished after they die. 2 a very unpleasant place. 3 (*informal*) an exclamation of anger.

hell for leather (*informal*) at high speed.

hello *interjection* hallo.

helm *noun* the handle or wheel used to steer a ship. **helmsman** *noun*

helmet *noun* a strong covering worn to protect the head.

help[1] *verb* 1 do part of another person's work for him or her. 2 benefit; make something better or easier, *This will help you to sleep.* 3 avoid, *I can't help coughing.* 4 serve food etc. to somebody. **helper** *noun*,

helpful *adjective*, **helpfully** *adverb*

help[2] *noun* 1 helping somebody. 2 a person or thing that helps.

helping *noun* a portion of food.

helpless *adjective* not able to do things. **helplessly** *adverb*, **helplessness** *noun*

helpmate *noun* a helper.

helter-skelter[1] *adverb* in great haste.

helter-skelter[2] *noun* a spiral slide at a fair.

hem[1] *noun* the edge of a piece of cloth that is folded over and sewn down.

hem[2] *verb* (**hemmed, hemming**) put a hem on something.

hem in surround and restrict.

hemisphere *noun* 1 half a sphere. 2 half the earth, *the southern and northern hemispheres.* **hemispherical** *adjective*

hemlock *noun* a poisonous plant; poison made from it.

hemp *noun* 1 a plant that produces coarse fibres from which cloth and ropes are made. 2 a drug made from this plant. **hempen** *adjective*

hen *noun* 1 a female bird. 2 a female fowl.

hence *adverb* 1 henceforth. 2 therefore. 3 (*old use*) from here.

henceforth *adverb* from now on.

henchman *noun* (*plural* **henchmen**) a trusty supporter.

henna *noun* a reddish-brown dye.

hepta- *prefix* seven.

heptagon *noun* a flat shape with seven sides and seven angles. **heptagonal** *adjective*

her[1] *pronoun* the form of *she* used as the object of a verb or after a preposition, *He kissed her. He gave the book to her.*

her[2] *adjective* belonging to her, *her book.*

herald[1] *noun* 1 an official in former times who made announcements and carried messages for a king or queen. 2 a person or thing that heralds something, *The piet-my-vrou is a herald of summer.*

herald[2] *verb* show that something is coming.

heraldry *noun* the study of coats of arms. **heraldic** (*say* hir-**al**-dik) *adjective*

herb *noun* a plant used for flavouring or for making medicine. **herbal** *adjective*

herbaceous (*say* her-**bay**-shus) *adjective*

1 of or like herbs. **2** containing many flowering plants, *a herbaceous border*. **3** (of a soft green perennial plant) producing new stems every season.

herbicide *noun* a substance that is used to kill unwanted vegetation.

herbivorous (*say* her-**biv**-er-us) *adjective* plant-eating. (Compare *carnivorous*.) **herbivore** *noun*

herculean (*say* her-kew-**lee**-an) *adjective* **1** needing great strength or effort, *a herculean task*. **2** as strong as Hercules (a hero in ancient Greek legend).

herd[1] *noun* **1** a group of cattle or other animals that feed together. **2** a mass of people; a mob, *tends to follow the herd*. **herdsman** *noun*

herd[2] *verb* **1** gather or move or send in a herd, *We all herded into the dining-room*. **2** look after a herd of animals.

herder *noun* a person who keeps domesticated animals and moves around to find grazing for them.

here *adverb* in or to this place etc. **here and there** in various places or directions.

hereafter *adverb* from now on; in future.

hereby *adverb* by this act or decree etc.

hereditary *adjective* **1** inherited, *a hereditary disease*. **2** inheriting a position, *Our king is a hereditary monarch*.

heredity (*say* hir-**ed**-it-ee) *noun* inheriting characteristics from parents or ancestors.

heresy (*say* **herri**-see) *noun* (*plural* **heresies**) an opinion that disagrees with the beliefs accepted by the Christian Church or other authority.

heretic (*say* **herri**-tik) *noun* a person who supports a heresy. **heretical** (*say* hi-**ret**-ik-al) *adjective*

heritage *noun* the things that someone has inherited.

hermaphrodite *noun* a person, animal, or plant having both male and female reproductive organs.

hermetically *adverb* so as to be airtight, *The tin is hermetically sealed*.

hermit *noun* a person who lives alone and keeps away from people.

hermitage *noun* a hermit's home.

hermit-crab *noun* a kind of crab that lives in the shell of a whelk or a winkle.

hernia *noun* a condition in which an internal part of the body pushes through another part; a rupture.

hero *noun* (*plural* **heroes**) **1** a man or boy who is admired for doing something very brave or great. **2** the chief male character in a story etc. **heroic** *adjective*, **heroically** *adverb*, **heroism** *noun*

heroin *noun* a very strong drug.

heroine *noun* **1** a woman or girl who is admired for doing something very brave or great. **2** the chief female character in a story etc.

heron *noun* a wading bird with long legs and a long neck.

herring *noun* (*plural* **herring** or **herrings**) a sea-fish used as food.

herring-bone *noun* a zigzag pattern.

hers *possessive pronoun* belonging to her, *Those books are hers*.

● USAGE: It is incorrect to write *her's*.

herself *pronoun* she or her and nobody else. The word is used to refer back to the subject of a sentence (e.g. *She cut herself*) or for emphasis (e.g. *She herself has said it*). **by herself** alone; on her own.

hertz *noun* (*plural* **hertz**) a unit of frequency of electromagnetic waves, = one cycle per second.

hesitant *adjective* hesitating. **hesitantly** *adverb*, **hesitancy** *noun*

hesitate *verb* (**hesitated**, **hesitating**) be slow or uncertain in speaking, moving, etc. **hesitation** *noun*

hessian *noun* sackcloth.

hetero- *prefix* other; different.

heterogeneous (*say* het-er-o-**jeen**-ee-us) *adjective* composed of people or things of different kinds.

heterosexual *adjective* attracted to people of the opposite sex; not homosexual.

hew *verb* (**hewed**, **hewn**, **hewing**) chop or cut with an axe or sword etc.

hexa- *prefix* six.

hexagon *noun* a flat shape with six sides and six angles. **hexagonal** *adjective*

hey *interjection* an exclamation calling attention or expressing surprise or enquiry.

heyday *noun* the time of a thing's greatest success or prosperity.

hi *interjection* an exclamation calling attention or expressing a greeting.

hiatus (*say* hy-**ay**-tus) *noun* (*plural* **hiatuses**) a gap in something that is otherwise continuous.

hibernate *verb* (**hibernated, hibernating**) spend the winter in a state like deep sleep. **hibernation** *noun*

hibiscus *noun* (*plural* **hibiscuses**) a cultivated shrub with large brightly-coloured flowers.

hiccup *noun* 1 a high gulping sound made when your breath is briefly interrupted. 2 a brief hitch, *a hiccup in the process.* **hiccup** *verb* (**hiccuped, hiccuping**)

hickory *noun* (*plural* **hickories**) a tree rather like the walnut tree.

hide[1] *verb* (**hid, hidden, hiding**) 1 keep a person or thing from being seen; conceal. 2 get into a place where you cannot be seen. 3 keep a thing secret.

hide[2] *noun* an animal's skin.

hide-and-seek *noun* a game in which one person looks for others who are hiding.

hidebound *adjective* narrow-minded.

hideous *adjective* very ugly or unpleasant. **hideously** *adverb*

hide-out *noun* a place where somebody hides.

hiding[1] *noun* being hidden, *She went into hiding.* **hiding-place** *noun*

hiding[2] *noun* a thrashing; a beating.

hierarchy (*say* **hyr**-ark-ee) *noun* an organization that ranks people one above another according to the power or authority that they hold.

hieroglyphics (*say* hyr-o-**glif**-iks) *plural noun* pictures or symbols used in ancient Egypt to represent words.

hi-fi *noun* (*informal*) 1 high fidelity. 2 equipment that gives high fidelity.

higgledy-piggledy *adverb* & *adjective* completely mixed up; in great disorder.

high[1] *adjective* 1 reaching a long way upwards, *high hills.* 2 far above the ground or above sea-level, *high clouds.* 3 measuring from top to bottom, *two metres high.* 4 above average level in importance, qual-

ity, amount, etc., *high rank*; *high prices.* 5 (of meat) beginning to go bad. 6 (*informal*) affected by a drug.

high explosive a powerful explosive.

high fidelity reproducing sound with very little distortion.

high road the main road.

high school a secondary school.

high street a town's main street.

high time fully time, *It's high time we left.*

high[2] *adverb* at or to a high level or position etc., *They flew high above us.*

highbrow *adjective* intellectual.

higher *adjective* & *adverb* more high.

higher education education at a university, technikon, or college.

highlands *plural noun* mountainous country. **highland** *adjective*, **highlander** *noun*

highlight[1] *noun* 1 a light area in a painting etc. 2 the most interesting part, *the highlight of the evening.* 3 (*plural*) light streaks in hair made by bleaching.

highlight[2] *verb* draw special attention to something.

highly *adverb* 1 extremely, *highly amusing.* 2 very favourably, *We think highly of her.*

Highness *noun* (*plural* **Highnesses**) the title of a prince or princess.

high-rise *adjective* with many storeys.

high-tech *adjective* making use of advanced technology.

highveld *noun* the mountainous regions and high ground of the former Transvaal.

highway *noun* a main road or route.

highwayman *noun* (*plural* **highwaymen**) a person who robbed travellers on highways in former times.

hijack *verb* seize control of an aircraft or vehicle during a journey. **hijack** *noun*, **hijacker** *noun*

hike *noun* a long walk. **hike** *verb* (**hiked, hiking**), **hiker** *noun*

hilarious *adjective* very funny or merry. **hilariously** *adverb*, **hilarity** *noun*

hill *noun* a piece of land that is higher than the ground around it. **hillside** *noun*, **hilly** *adjective*

hillock *noun* a small hill; a mound.

hilt *noun* the handle of a sword or dagger etc.

to the hilt completely.

him *pronoun* the form of *he* used as the object of a verb or after a preposition, *She kissed him. She gave the book to him.*

himself *pronoun* he or him and nobody else. (Compare *herself.*)

hind[1] *adjective* at the back, *the hind legs.*

hind[2] *noun* a female deer. (Compare *hart.*)

hinder *verb* get in someone's way; make it difficult for a person to do something quickly or for something to happen.
hindrance *noun*

hindmost *adjective* furthest behind.

hindquarters *plural noun* an animal's hind legs and rear parts.

hindsight *noun* looking back on an event with knowledge or understanding that you did not have at the time.

Hindu *noun* (*plural* **Hindus**) a person who believes in Hinduism, which is the main religious and social system of India.

hinge[1] *noun* a joining device on which a lid or door etc. turns when it opens.

hinge[2] *verb* (**hinged, hinging**) 1 fix with a hinge. 2 depend, *Everything hinges on this meeting.*

hint[1] *noun* 1 a slight indication or sugges-tion, *Give me a hint of what you want.* 2 a useful suggestion, *household hints.*

hint[2] *verb* make a hint.

hinterland *noun* the district behind a coast or port etc.

hip[1] *noun* the bony part at the side of the body between the waist and the thigh.

hip[2] *noun* the fruit of the wild rose.

hip[3] *interjection* part of a cheer, *Hip, hip, hooray!*

hippie *noun* (*informal*) a young person who joins with others to live in an unconventional way.

hippo *noun* (*plural* **hippos**) (*informal*) a hippopotamus.

hippopotamus *noun* (*plural* **hippopot-amuses**) a very large animal that lives near water.

hire[1] *verb* (**hired, hiring**) 1 pay to borrow something. 2 lend for payment, *He hires out bicycles.* **hirer** *noun*

hire[2] *noun* hiring, *for hire.*

hire-purchase *noun* buying something by paying in instalments.

hirsute (*say* **herss**-yoot) *adjective* hairy.

his *adjective* & *possessive pronoun* belonging to him, *That is his book. That book is his.*

hiss *verb* make a sound like an *s*, *The snakes were hissing.* **hiss** *noun*

historian *noun* a person who writes or studies history.

historic *adjective* famous or important in history, *a historic town.*

history *noun* (*plural* **histories**) 1 what happened in the past. 2 study of past events. 3 a description of important events. **historical** *adjective*, **historically** *adverb*

hit[1] *verb* (**hit, hitting**) 1 come forcefully against a person or thing; knock or strike. 2 have a bad effect on, *Famine has hit the poor countries.* 3 reach, *I can't hit that high note.*
hit on discover something by chance.

hit[2] *noun* 1 hitting; a knock or stroke. 2 a shot that hits the target. 3 a success; a successful song, show, etc.

hitch[1] *verb* 1 raise or pull with a slight jerk. 2 fasten with a loop or hook etc. 3 hitch-hike.

hitch[2] *noun* 1 a hitching movement. 2 a knot. 3 a difficulty causing delay.

hitch-hike *verb* travel by begging rides in passing vehicles. **hitch-hiker** *noun*

hither *adverb* to or towards this place.

hitherto *adverb* until this time.

HIV *abbreviation* human immuno-deficiency virus, a virus which causes Aids.

hive *noun* 1 a beehive. 2 the bees living in a beehive.
hive of industry a place full of people working busily.

ho *interjection* an exclamation of triumph, surprise, etc.

hoard[1] *noun* a carefully saved store of money, treasure, food, etc.

hoard[2] *verb* store away. **hoarder** *noun*

hoarding *noun* a tall fence covered with advertisements.

hoar-frost *noun* a white frost.

hoarse *adjective* with a rough voice.
hoarsely *adverb*, **hoarseness** *noun*

hoary *adjective* 1 white or grey from

age, *hoary hair.* **2** old, *hoary jokes.*

hoax *verb* deceive somebody as a joke.
hoax *noun,* **hoaxer** *noun*

hob *noun* a flat surface on a cooker or
beside a fireplace, where food etc. can be
cooked or kept warm.

hobble *verb* (**hobbled, hobbling**) limp.

hobby *noun* (*plural* **hobbies**) something
you do for pleasure in your spare time.

hobby-horse *noun* **1** a stick with a horse's
head, used as a toy. **2** a subject that a person
likes to talk about.

hobgoblin *noun* a mischievous or evil
spirit; a bogy.

hob-nob *verb* (**hob-nobbed, hob-
nobbing**) spend time together in a friendly
way, *hob-nobbing with pop stars.*

hobo *noun* (*plural* **hoboes** or **hobos**)
a person without a home or job who walks
from place to place.

hock *noun* the middle joint of an animal's
hind leg.

hockey *noun* a game played by two teams
with curved sticks and a hard ball.

hocus-pocus *noun* trickery.

hoe¹ *noun* a tool for scraping up weeds.

hoe² *verb* (**hoed, hoeing**) scrape or dig with
a hoe.

hoezit *interjection* (*informal*) a greeting,
used especially by young people.

hog¹ *noun* **1** a male pig. **2** (*informal*)
a greedy person.
go the whole hog (*informal*) do something
completely or thoroughly.

hog² *verb* (**hogged, hogging**) (*informal*)
take more than your fair share of something; hoard selfishly.

hoi polloi *noun* the masses; the ordinary
people.

hoist *verb* lift; raise something by using
ropes and pulleys etc.

hokkie *noun* (*informal*) a hutch or other
small structure.

hold¹ *verb* (**held, holding**) This word has
many uses, including **1** have and keep,
especially in your hands. **2** have room
for, *The jug holds two litres.* **3** support,
This plank won't hold my weight. **4** stay
unbroken; continue, *Will the fine weather
hold?* **5** believe; consider, *We shall hold*

you responsible. **6** cause to take place, *hold a
meeting.* **7** restrain; stop, *Hold everything!*
hold forth make a long speech.
hold out last; continue.
hold your tongue (*informal*) stop talking.
hold up hinder; stop and rob somebody by
threats or force.
hold with approve of, *We don't hold with
bullying.*

hold² *noun* **1** holding something; a grasp.
2 something to hold on to for support.
3 the part of a ship where cargo is stored,
below the deck.
get hold of grasp; obtain; make contact
with a person.

holdall *noun* a large portable bag or case.

holder *noun* a person or thing that holds
something.

hold-up *noun* **1** a delay. **2** a robbery with
threats or force.

hole¹ *noun* **1** a hollow place; a gap or
opening. **2** a burrow. **3** (*informal*) an unpleasant place. **4** (*informal*) an awkward
situation. **holey** *adjective*

hole² *verb* (**holed, holing**) **1** make a hole
or holes in something. **2** put into a hole.

holiday *noun* **1** a day or week etc. when
people do not go to work or to school.
2 a time when you go away to enjoy
yourself.

holiness *noun* being holy or sacred.
His Holiness the title of the pope.

hollow¹ *adjective* with an empty space
inside; not solid. **hollowly** *adverb*

hollow² *adverb* completely, *We beat them
hollow.*

hollow³ *noun* a hollow or sunken place.

hollow⁴ *verb* make a thing hollow.

holly *noun* (*plural* **hollies**) an evergreen
bush with shiny prickly leaves and red
berries.

hollyhock *noun* a plant with large flowers
on a very tall stem.

holocaust *noun* an immense destruction,
especially by fire, *the nuclear holocaust.*

holster *noun* a leather case in which a
pistol or revolver is carried.

holy *adjective* (**holier, holiest**) **1** belonging
or devoted to God. **2** consecrated, *holy
water.* **holiness** *noun*

homage *noun* an act or expression of respect or honour, *We paid homage to his achievements.*

home[1] *noun* **1** the place where you live. **2** the place where you were born or where you feel you belong. **3** a place where those who need help are looked after, *an old people's home.* **4** the place to be reached in a race or in certain games.

home economics the study of household management.

home[2] *adjective* **1** of a person's own home or country, *home industries.* **2** played on a team's own ground, *a home match.*

home[3] *adverb* **1** to or at home, *Is she home yet?* **2** to the point aimed at, *Push the bolt home.*

bring something home to somebody make him or her realize it.

home[4] *verb* (**homed, homing**) make for a target, *The missile homed in.*

homeland *noun* any of several former territories in South Africa which were partially independent, set aside for a group of African people by the apartheid government, *the Bophuthatswana homeland.*

homeless *adjective* having no home.

homely *adverb* simple and ordinary, *a homely meal.* **homeliness** *noun*

home-made *adjective* made at home, not bought from a shop.

homesick *adjective* sad because you are away from home. **homesickness** *noun*

homestead *noun* a house, especially a farmhouse, with the land and buildings round it.

homeward *adjective* & *adverb* going towards home. **homewards** *adverb*

homework *noun* school work that a pupil has to do at home.

homicide *noun* the killing of one person by another. **homicidal** *adjective*

homily *noun* (*plural* **homilies**) a lecture about behaviour.

homing *adjective* trained to fly home, *a homing pigeon.*

homo- *prefix* same.

homogeneous (*say* hom-o-**jeen**-ee-us) *adjective* composed of people or things of the same kind.

homograph *noun* a word that is spelt like another but has a different meaning or origin, e.g. *bat* (a flying animal) and *bat* (for hitting a ball).

homonym (*say* **hom**-o-nim) *noun* a homograph or homophone.

homophone *noun* a word with the same sound as another, e.g. *son, sun.*

homosexual *adjective* attracted to people of the same sex. **homosexual** *noun*, **homosexuality** *noun*

honest *adjective* not stealing or cheating or telling lies; truthful. **honestly** *adverb*, **honesty** *noun*

honey *noun* a sweet sticky food made by bees.

honey badger a ratel.

honeycomb *noun* a wax structure of small six-sided sections made by bees to hold their honey and eggs.

honeycombed *adjective* with many holes or tunnels.

honeydew *noun* **1** a sweet sticky substance excreted by aphids on leaves and stems. **2** a kind of melon.

honeymoon *noun* a holiday spent together by a newly-married couple.

honeysuckle *noun* a climbing plant with fragrant yellow or pink flowers.

honk *noun* a loud sound like that made by an old-fashioned car-horn. **honk** *verb*

honorary *adjective* **1** given or received as an honour, *an honorary degree.* **2** unpaid, *the honorary treasurer.*

● USAGE: Do not confuse with *honourable.*

honour[1] *noun* **1** great respect. **2** a person or thing that brings honour, *She is an honour to her school.* **3** honesty and loyalty, *a man of honour.* **4** an award for distinction.

honour[2] *verb* **1** feel or show honour for a person. **2** acknowledge and pay a cheque etc. **3** keep to the terms of an agreement or promise.

honourable *adjective* deserving honour; honest and loyal. **honourably** *adverb*

● USAGE: Do not confuse with *honorary.*

hood *noun* **1** a covering of soft material for the head and neck. **2** a folding roof or cover. **hooded** *adjective*

hoodwink *verb* deceive.

hoof *noun* (*plural* **hoofs** or **hooves**) the horny part of the foot of a horse etc.

hook[1] *noun* a bent or curved piece of metal etc. for hanging things on or for catching hold of something.

hook[2] *verb* 1 catch with a hook. 2 fasten with or on a hook. 3 send a ball in a curving direction.
be hooked on something (*informal*) be addicted to it.

hookah *noun* an oriental tobacco-pipe with a long tube passing through a jar of water.

hooked *adjective* hook-shaped.

hookworm *noun* a kind of parasite.

hooligan *noun* a rough lawless young person. **hooliganism** *noun*

hoop *noun* a ring made of metal or wood.

hoop-la *noun* a game in which people try to throw hoops round objects.

hoopoe *noun* a small brown bird with black and white wings and a large crest which stands up.

hooray *interjection* hurray.

hoot *noun* 1 the sound made by an owl or a vehicle's horn or a steam whistle. 2 a cry of scorn or disapproval, *hoots of derision.* 3 laughter; a cause of this. **hoot** *verb*, **hooter** *noun*

hop[1] *verb* (**hopped, hopping**) 1 jump on one foot. 2 (of an animal) spring from all feet at once. 3 (*informal*) move quickly, *Here's the car – hop in!*
hop it (*informal*) go away.

hop[2] *noun* a hopping movement.

hop[3] *noun* a climbing plant used to give beer its flavour.

hope[1] *noun* 1 a wish for something to happen. 2 a person or thing that gives hope, *You are our only hope.*

hope[2] *verb* (**hoped, hoping**) feel hope; want and expect something.

hopeful *adjective* 1 feeling hope. 2 likely to be good or successful. **hopefully** *adverb*

hopeless *adjective* 1 without hope. 2 very bad at something. **hopelessly** *adverb*, **hopelessness** *noun*

hopper *noun* 1 a V-shaped container with an opening at the bottom. 2 a hopping insect.

hopscotch *noun* a game of hopping into squares drawn on the ground.

horde *noun* a large group or crowd.

horizon *noun* the line where the earth and the sky seem to meet.

horizontal *adjective* level, so as to be parallel to the horizon; going across from left to right. (The opposite is *vertical.*) **horizontally** *adverb*

hormone *noun* a substance that stimulates an organ of the body or of a plant.

horn *noun* 1 a hard substance that grows into a point on the head of a bull, cow, ram, etc. 2 a pointed part. 3 a brass instrument played by blowing. 4 a device for making a warning sound. **horned** *adjective*, **horny** *adjective*

hornet *noun* a large kind of wasp.

hornpipe *noun* a sailors' dance.

horoscope *noun* an astrologer's forecast of future events.

horrendous *adjective* horrifying.

horrible *adjective* horrifying; unpleasant. **horribly** *adverb*

horrid *adjective* horrible. **horridly** *adverb*

horrific *adjective* horrifying. **horrifically** *adverb*

horrify *verb* (**horrified, horrifying**) arouse horror in somebody; shock.

horror *noun* 1 great fear and dislike or dismay. 2 a person or thing causing horror.

hors-d'oeuvre (*say* or-**dervr**) *noun* food served as an appetizer at the start of a meal.

horse *noun* 1 a large four-legged animal used for riding on and for pulling carts etc. 2 a framework for hanging clothes on to dry. 3 a vaulting-horse.
on horseback mounted on a horse.

horse-chestnut *noun* a large tree that produces dark-brown nuts.

horseman *noun* (*plural* **horsemen**) a man who rides a horse, especially a skilled rider. **horsemanship** *noun*

horseplay *noun* rough play.

horsepower *noun* a unit for measuring the power of an engine.

horseradish *noun* a plant which has a strong-tasting root used to make a sauce.

horseshoe *noun* a U-shaped piece of metal nailed to a horse's hoof.

horsewoman *noun* (*plural* **horsewomen**) a woman who rides a horse, especially a skilled rider.

horticulture *noun* the art of cultivating gardens. **horticultural** *adjective*

hose[1] *noun* **1** (also **hose-pipe**) a flexible tube for taking water to something. **2** (*old use*) breeches, *doublet and hose.*

hose[2] *verb* (**hosed, hosing**) water or spray with a hose.

hosiery *noun* (in shops) socks and stockings.

hospice (*say* **hosp**-iss) *noun* **1** a lodging-house for travellers, especially one kept by a religious institution. **2** a nursing home for people who are incurably ill and dying.

hospitable *adjective* welcoming; liking to give hospitality. **hospitably** *adverb*

hospital *noun* a place providing medical and surgical treatment for people who are ill or injured.

hospitality *noun* welcoming people and giving them food and entertainment.

host[1] *noun* **1** a person who has guests and looks after them. **2** an animal or plant that has a parasite.

host[2] *noun* a large number of people or things.

host[3] *noun* the bread consecrated at Holy Communion.

hostage *noun* a person who is held prisoner until the holder gets what he or she wants.

hostel *noun* **1** a lodging-house for travellers, students, or other groups. **2** a large housing block provided in urban areas for employees of mining companies etc.

hostess *noun* a woman who has guests and looks after them.

hostile *adjective* **1** of an enemy. **2** unfriendly, *a hostile glance.* **hostility** *noun*

hot[1] *adjective* (**hotter, hottest**) **1** having great heat or a high temperature. **2** giving a burning sensation when tasted. **3** enthusiastic; excitable, *a hot temper.* **hotly** *adverb*, **hotness** *noun*

hot cross bun a fresh spicy bun marked with a cross, to be eaten on Good Friday.

hot dog a hot sausage in a bread roll.

in hot water (*informal*) in trouble or disgrace.

hot[2] *verb* (**hotted, hotting**) **hot up** (*informal*) make or become hot or hotter or more exciting.

hotel *noun* a building where people pay to have meals and stay for the night.

hotfoot *adverb* in eager haste.

hothead *noun* an impetuous person.

hothouse *noun* a heated greenhouse.

hotplate *noun* a heated surface for cooking food etc. or keeping it hot.

hotpot *noun* a stew.

hound[1] *noun* a dog used in hunting or racing.

hound[2] *verb* chase; harass.

hour *noun* **1** one twenty-fourth part of a day and night; sixty minutes. **2** a time, *Why are you up at this hour?*

hours *plural noun* a fixed period for work, *Office hours are 9 a.m. to 5 p.m.*

hourglass *noun* a glass container with a very narrow part in the middle through which sand runs from the top half to the bottom half, taking one hour.

hourly *adverb* & *adjective* every hour.

house[1] (*say* howss) *noun* **1** a building made for people to live in, usually designed for one family. **2** a building or establishment for a special purpose, *the opera house.* **3** a building for a government assembly; the assembly itself, *the Houses of Parliament.* **4** each of the divisions of a school for sports competitions etc. **5** a family or dynasty, *the royal house of Shaka.*

house[2] (*say* howz) *verb* (**housed, housing**) provide accommodation or room for someone or something.

houseboat *noun* a barge-like boat for living in.

household *noun* all the people who live together in the same house.

householder *noun* a person who owns or rents a house.

housekeeper *noun* a person employed to look after a household.

housekeeping *noun* **1** looking after a household. **2** (*informal*) the money for a household's food and other necessities.

housemaid *noun* a woman servant in a house, especially one who cleans rooms.

house-proud *adjective* very careful to keep a house clean and tidy.

house-trained *adjective* (of an animal) trained to be clean in the house.

house-warming *noun* a party to celebrate moving into a new home.

housewife *noun* (*plural* **housewives**) a woman who does the housekeeping for her family and does not have a full-time paid job. **house-husband** *noun*

housework *noun* the cleaning and cooking etc. done in housekeeping.

housing *noun* 1 accommodation; houses. 2 a stiff cover or guard for a piece of machinery.

housing estate a set of houses planned and built together in one area.

hove *past tense* of **heave** (when used of ships).

hovel *noun* a small shabby house.

hover *verb* 1 stay in one place in the air. 2 wait about near someone or something; linger.

hovercraft *noun* (*plural* **hovercraft**) a vehicle that travels just above the surface of land or water, supported by a strong current of air sent downwards from its engines.

how *adverb* 1 in what way; by what means, *How did you do it?* 2 to what extent or amount etc., *How high can you jump?* 3 in what condition, *How are you?*

how about would you like, *How about a game of soccer?*

how do you do? a formal greeting.

however *adverb* 1 in whatever way; to whatever extent, *You will never catch him, however hard you try.* 2 all the same; nevertheless, *Later, however, he decided to go.*

howl[1] *noun* a long loud sad-sounding cry or sound, such as that made by a dog or wolf.

howl[2] *verb* 1 make a howl. 2 weep loudly.

howler *noun* 1 an animal that howls. 2 (*informal*) a foolish mistake.

howzit *interjection* hoezit.

hub *noun* the central part of a wheel.

hubbub *noun* a loud confused noise of voices.

huddle *verb* (**huddled, huddling**) 1 crowd together into a small space. 2 curl your body closely. **huddle** *noun*

hue[1] *noun* a colour or tint.

hue[2] *noun* **hue and cry** a general outcry of demand, alarm, or protest.

huff[1] *noun* an annoyed or offended mood, *She went away in a huff.* **huffy** *adjective*

huff[2] *verb* blow, *huffing and puffing.*

hug[1] *verb* (**hugged, hugging**) 1 clasp tightly in your arms; embrace. 2 keep close to, *The ship hugged the shore.*

hug[2] *noun* hugging; an embrace.

huge *adjective* extremely large; enormous. **hugely** *adverb*, **hugeness** *noun*

hulk *noun* 1 the body or wreck of an old ship. 2 a large clumsy person or thing. **hulking** *adjective*

hull *noun* the framework of a ship.

hullabaloo *noun* an uproar.

hullo *interjection* hallo.

hum[1] *verb* (**hummed, humming**) 1 sing a tune with your lips closed. 2 make a low continuous sound as some flying insects do.

hum[2] *noun* a humming sound.

human[1] *adjective* of human beings.

human being a creature distinguished from other animals by its better mental development, power of speech, and upright posture.

human[2] *noun* a human being.

humane (*say* hew-**mayn**) *adjective* kind-hearted; merciful. **humanely** *adverb*

humanist *noun* a humanitarian person.

humanitarian *adjective* concerned with people's welfare and the reduction of suffering. **humanitarian** *noun*

humanity *noun* 1 human beings; people. 2 being human. 3 being humane, *show some humanity.*

humanities *plural noun* arts subjects.

humanize *verb* (**humanized, humanizing**) make human or humane. **humanization** *noun*

humble[1] *adjective* 1 modest; not proud or showy. 2 of low rank or importance. **humbly** *adverb*, **humbleness** *noun*

humble[2] *verb* (**humbled, humbling**) make humble.

humbug *noun* 1 deceitful talk or behaviour. **2** a person who tries to win sympathy by deceit. **3** a hard peppermint sweet.

humdrum *adjective* dull and not exciting; commonplace; without variety.

humid (*say* hew-mid) *adjective* (of air) moist. **humidity** *noun*

humiliate *verb* (**humiliated, humiliating**) make a person feel disgraced. **humiliation** *noun*

humility *noun* being humble.

humming-bird *noun* a small tropical bird that makes a humming sound by moving its wings rapidly.

hummock *noun* a hump in the ground.

humorist *noun* a humorous person.

humorous *adjective* full of humour.

humour[1] *noun* **1** being amusing; what makes people laugh. **2** the ability to enjoy comical things, *a sense of humour.* **3** a mood, *in a good humour.*

humour[2] *verb* keep a person contented by doing what he or she wants, *humour your boss.*

hump[1] *noun* **1** a rounded projecting part. **2** an abnormal outward curve at the top of a person's back. **humpback** *noun*, **hump-backed** *adjective*

hump[2] *verb* **1** form a hump. **2** carry something on your back.

humus (*say* hew-mus) *noun* the rich part of the soil, made by decayed plants.

hunch[1] *noun* (*plural* **hunches**) **1** a hump. **2** a feeling that you can guess what will happen. **hunchback** *noun*

hunch[2] *verb* bend into a hump, *He hunched his shoulders.*

hundred *noun* & *adjective* the number 100; ten times ten. **hundredth** *adjective* & *noun*

hundredfold *adjective* & *adverb* one hundred times as much or as many.

hunger *noun* the feeling that you have when you have not eaten for some time; need for food.
hunger strike refusing to eat, as a way of making a protest.

hungry *adjective* (**hungrier, hungriest**) feeling hunger. **hungrily** *adverb*

hunk *noun* a large or clumsy piece.

hunt[1] *verb* **1** chase and kill animals for food

or as a sport. **2** search for something.
hunter *noun*

hunt[2] *noun* **1** hunting. **2** a group of hunters, *The hunt set out across the veld.*

hunter-gatherer *noun* a member of a people who live by hunting animals and collecting plants.

hurdle *noun* **1** an upright frame to be jumped over in hurdling. **2** an obstacle, *a hurdle to economic recovery.*

hurdling *noun* racing in which the runners jump over hurdles. **hurdler** *noun*

hurl *verb* throw something violently.

hurly-burly *noun* a rough bustle of activity.

hurrah (also **hurray**) *interjection* a shout of joy or approval; a cheer.

hurricane *noun* a storm with violent wind.

hurry[1] *verb* (**hurried, hurrying**) **1** move quickly; do something quickly. **2** try to make somebody or something be quick, *A good meal should never be hurried.*
hurried *adjective*, **hurriedly** *adverb*

hurry[2] *noun* hurrying; a need to hurry.

hurt[1] *verb* (**hurt, hurting**) cause pain or damage or injury.

hurt[2] *noun* an injury; harm. **hurtful** *adjective*

hurtle *verb* (**hurtled, hurtling**) move rapidly, *The train hurtled along.*

husband[1] *noun* the man to whom a woman is married.

husband[2] *verb* manage economically and try to save, *husband your strength.*

husbandry *noun* **1** farming, *animal husbandry.* **2** management of resources.

hush[1] *verb* make or become silent or quiet.

hush[2] *noun* silence.

husk *noun* the dry outer covering of some seeds and fruits.

husky[1] *adjective* (**huskier, huskiest**) **1** hoarse. **2** big and strong; burly. **huskily** *adverb*, **huskiness** *noun*

husky[2] *noun* (*plural* **huskies**) a large dog used in the Arctic for pulling sledges.

hustle *verb* (**hustled, hustling**) hurry; bustle. **hustle** *noun*, **hustler** *noun*

hut *noun* a small roughly-made house or shelter.

hutch *noun* (*plural* **hutches**) a box-like cage for a pet rabbit etc.

hyacinth *noun* a fragrant flower that grows from a bulb.

hybrid *noun* 1 a plant or animal produced by combining two different species or varieties. 2 something that combines parts or characteristics of two different things, *a hybrid of Western and African music.*

hydra *noun* a microscopic freshwater animal with a tubular body.

hydrangea (*say* hy-**drayn**-ja) *noun* a shrub with pink, blue, or white flowers growing in large clusters.

hydrant *noun* a special water-tap to which a large hose can be attached for fire-fighting or street-cleaning etc.

hydraulic *adjective* worked by the force of water or other fluid, *hydraulic brakes.*

hydro- *prefix* 1 water (as in *hydroelectric*). 2 (in chemical names) containing hydrogen (as in *hydrochloric*).

hydrochloric acid *noun* a colourless acid containing hydrogen and chlorine.

hydroelectric *adjective* using water-power to produce electricity. **hydroelectricity** *noun*

hydrofoil *noun* a boat designed to skim over the surface of water.

hydrogen *noun* a lightweight gas that combines with oxygen to form water. **hydrogen bomb** a very powerful bomb using energy created by the fusion of hydrogen nuclei.

hydrometer *noun* an instrument used to measure the density of liquids.

hydrophobia *noun* abnormal fear of water, as in someone suffering from rabies.

hydrophyte (*say* **hy**-dro-fyt) *noun* a plant adapted to live in or near water. (Compare *mesophyte* and *xerophyte*.)

hydroponics (*say* hy-droh-**pon**-iks) *noun* growing plants without soil, in water, gravel, etc. which has added nutrients.

hyena *noun* a wild animal that looks like a wolf and makes a shrieking howl.

hygiene (*say* **hy**-jeen) *noun* keeping things clean in order to remain healthy and prevent disease. **hygienic** *adjective*, **hygienically** *adverb*

hymn *noun* a religious song, usually of praise to God. **hymn-book** *noun*

hymnal *noun* a hymn-book.

hyper- *prefix* over or above; excessive.

hyperbola (*say* hy-**per**-bol-a) *noun* a kind of curve.

hyperbole (*say* hy-**per**-bol-ee) *noun* a dramatic exaggeration that is not meant to be taken literally, e.g. 'There were millions of people at the party.'

hypermarket *noun* a very large supermarket.

hyphen *noun* a short dash used to join words or parts of words together (e.g. in *hymn-book*).

hyphenate *verb* (**hyphenated, hyphenating**) join with a hyphen. **hyphenation** *noun*

hypnosis (*say* hip-**noh**-sis) *noun* a condition like a deep sleep in which a person's actions may be controlled by someone else.

hypnotize *verb* (**hypnotized, hypnotizing**) produce hypnosis in somebody. **hypnotism** *noun*, **hypnotic** *adjective*, **hypnotist** *noun*

hypo- *prefix* below; under.

hypochondriac (*say* hy-po-**kon**-dree-ak) *noun* a person who constantly imagines that he or she is ill. **hypochondria** *noun*

hypocrite (*say* **hip**-o-krit) *noun* a person who pretends to be more virtuous than he or she really is. **hypocrisy** (*say* hip-**ok**-riss-ee) *noun*, **hypocritical** *adjective*

hypodermic *adjective* injecting something under the skin, *a hypodermic syringe.*

hypotenuse (*say* hy-**pot**-i-newz) *noun* the side opposite the right angle in a right-angled triangle.

hypothermia *noun* being too cold; the condition in which someone's temperature is below normal.

hypothesis (*say* hy-**poth**-i-sis) *noun* (*plural* **hypotheses**) a suggestion or guess that tries to explain something. **hypothetical** *adjective*

hysterectomy (*say* hist-er-**ek**-tom-ee) *noun* surgical removal of the womb.

hysteria *noun* wild uncontrollable excitement or emotion. **hysterical** *adjective*, **hysterically** *adverb*, **hysterics** *noun*

Ii

I *pronoun* a word used by a person to refer to himself or herself.

ibis (*say* I-bis) *noun* (*plural* **ibises**) a wading bird with a curved bill.

ice[1] *noun* 1 frozen water, a brittle transparent solid substance. 2 an ice-cream.
ice-cap a permanent covering of ice, especially in the polar regions.
ice rink a place made for skating.
ice-skate a boot with a blade beneath, used for skating on ice.

ice[2] *verb* (**iced, icing**) 1 make or become icy. 2 put icing on a cake.

iceberg *noun* a large mass of ice floating in the sea with most of it under water.

ice-breaker *noun* 1 a ship that is able to break through ice. 2 a joke etc. that makes people who have just met relax.

ice-cream *noun* a sweet creamy frozen food.

icicle *noun* a pointed hanging piece of ice formed when dripping water freezes.

icing *noun* a sugary substance for decorating cakes.

icon (*say* I-kon) *noun* 1 a sacred painting or mosaic etc. 2 (in computers) a small symbol or picture on the screen.

icy *adjective* (**icier, iciest**) like ice; very cold. **icily** *adverb*, **iciness** *noun*

ID *abbreviation* identity; identification, *ID document.*

idea *noun* a plan etc. formed in the mind; an opinion.

ideal[1] *adjective* perfect; completely suitable. **ideally** *adverb*

ideal[2] *noun* a person or thing regarded as perfect or worth trying to achieve.

idealist *noun* a person who has high ideals and wishes to achieve them. **idealism** *noun*, **idealistic** *adjective*

idealize *verb* (**idealized, idealizing**) regard or represent a person or thing as perfect. **idealization** *noun*

identical *adjective* exactly the same. **identically** *adverb*

identify *verb* (**identified, identifying**) 1 recognize as being a certain person or thing. 2 treat as being identical, *Don't identify wealth with happiness.* 3 think of yourself as sharing someone's feelings etc., *We can identify with the hero of this play.* **identification** *noun*

identity *noun* (*plural* **identities**) 1 who or what a person or thing is. 2 being identical; sameness. 3 distinctive character.

ideology (*say* I-dee-ol-o-jee) *noun* (*plural* **ideologies**) a set of beliefs and aims, especially in politics, *a socialist ideology.* **ideological** *adjective*

ides (*say* I'dz) *plural noun* the ancient Roman name for the 15th day of March, May, July, and October, and the 13th day of other months.

idiocy *noun* 1 being an idiot. 2 stupid behaviour.

idiom *noun* 1 a phrase that means something different from the meanings of the words in it, e.g. *in hot water* (= in disgrace), *hell for leather* (= at high speed). 2 a special way of using words, e.g. *wash up the dishes* but not *wash up the baby.* **idiomatic** *adjective*, **idiomatically** *adverb*

idiosyncrasy (*say* id-ee-o-**sink**-ra-see) *noun* (*plural* **idiosyncrasies**) one person's own way of behaving or doing something.

idiot *noun* 1 a person who is mentally deficient. 2 (*informal*) a very stupid person. **idiocy** *noun*, **idiotic** *adjective*, **idiotically** *adverb*

idle[1] *adjective* 1 doing no work; lazy. 2 not in use, *The machines were idle.* 3 useless; with no special purpose, *idle gossip.* **idly** *adverb*, **idleness** *noun*

idle[2] *verb* (**idled, idling**) 1 be idle. 2 (of an engine) work slowly. **idler** *noun*

idol *noun* 1 a statue or image that is worshipped as a god. 2 a person who is idolized.

idolatry *noun* 1 worship of idols. 2 idolizing someone. **idolatrous** *adjective*

idolize *verb* (**idolized, idolizing**) admire someone intensely. **idolization** *noun*

idyll (*say* id-il) *noun* a poem describing a peaceful or romantic scene. **idyllic** (*say* id-**il**-ik) *adjective*

i.e. *abbreviation* id est (Latin, = that is), *The world's highest mountain (i.e. Mount Everest) is in the Himalayas.*
• USAGE: Do not confuse with *e.g.*

if *conjunction* **1** on condition that; supposing that, *He will do it if you pay him.* **2** even though, *I'll finish this job if it kills me.* **3** whether, *Do you know if dinner is ready?* **if only** I wish, *If only I were rich!*

igloo *noun* an Eskimo's round house built of blocks of hard snow.

igneous *adjective* formed by the action of a volcano, *igneous rocks.*

ignite *verb* (**ignited, igniting**) **1** set fire to something. **2** catch fire.

ignition *noun* **1** igniting. **2** starting the fuel burning in an engine.

ignoble *adjective* not noble; shameful.

ignominious *adjective* humiliating; with disgrace. **ignominy** *noun*

ignoramus *noun* (*plural* **ignoramuses**) an ignorant person.

ignorant *adjective* not knowing about something or about many things. **ignorantly** *adverb*, **ignorance** *noun*

ignore *verb* (**ignored, ignoring**) take no notice of a person or thing.

iguana (*say* ig-**wah**-na) *noun* a large tree-climbing tropical lizard.

il- *prefix* see **in-**.

ilk *noun* **of that ilk** (*informal*) of that kind.

ill[1] *adjective* **1** unwell; in bad health. **2** bad; harmful, *There were no ill effects.* **ill will** unkind feeling.

ill[2] *adverb* badly, *She was ill-treated.* **ill at ease** uncomfortable; embarrassed.

illegal *adjective* not legal; against the law. **illegally** *adverb*, **illegality** *noun*

illegible *adjective* not legible. **illegibly** *adverb*, **illegibility** *noun*

illegitimate *adjective* not legitimate. **illegitimately** *adverb*, **illegitimacy** *noun*

illicit *adjective* unlawful; not allowed. **illicitly** *adverb*

illiterate *adjective* unable to read or write; uneducated. **illiterately** *adverb*, **illiteracy** *noun*

illness *noun* (*plural* **illnesses**) being ill; a particular form of bad health.

illogical *adjective* not logical; not reasoning correctly. **illogically** *adverb*, **illogicality** *noun*

illuminate *verb* (**illuminated, illuminating**) **1** light something up. **2** decorate streets etc. with lights. **3** decorate a manuscript with coloured designs. **4** clarify or help to explain something, *His lecture illuminated the difficult concept.* **illumination** *noun*

illusion *noun* something unreal or imaginary; a false impression, *The train went so fast that we had the illusion that it was flying.* (Compare *delusion.*) **illusive** *adjective*, **illusory** *adjective*

illusionist *noun* a conjuror.

illustrate *verb* (**illustrated, illustrating**) **1** show something by pictures, examples, etc. **2** put illustrations in a book. **illustrator** *noun*

illustration *noun* **1** a picture in a book etc. **2** illustrating something. **3** an example.

illustrious *adjective* famous; distinguished.

im- *prefix* see **in-**.

image *noun* **1** a picture or statue of a person or thing. **2** the appearance of something as seen in a mirror or through a lens etc. **3** a person or thing that is very much like another, *He is the image of his father.* **4** reputation, *the politician's public image.*

imagery *noun* **1** a writer's or speaker's use of words to produce effects. **2** images; statues.

imaginable *adjective* able to be imagined.

imaginary *adjective* existing only in the imagination; not real.

imagination *noun* the ability to imagine things, especially in a creative or inventive way. **imaginative** *adjective*

imagine *verb* (**imagined, imagining**) form pictures or ideas in your mind.

imam *noun* a Muslim religious leader.

imbalance *noun* lack of balance; disproportion.

imbecile (*say* **imb**-i-seel) *noun* an idiot. **imbecile** *adjective*, **imbecility** *noun*

imbibe *verb* (**imbibed, imbibing**) **1** drink. **2** take ideas etc. into the mind.

imbongi *noun* (*plural* **iimbongi, izibongi, imbongis**) a praise singer, especially to an African chief.

imitate *verb* (imitated, imitating) copy; mimic. **imitation** *noun*, **imitator** *noun*, **imitative** *adjective*

immaculate *adjective* 1 perfectly clean; spotless. 2 without any fault or blemish. **immaculately** *adverb*, **immaculacy** *noun*

immaterial *adjective* 1 having no material body, *as immaterial as a ghost.* 2 unimportant; not mattering, *It is immaterial whether she goes or stays.*

immature *adjective* not mature. **immaturity** *noun*

immediate *adjective* 1 happening or done without any delay. 2 nearest; with nothing or no one between, *our immediate neighbours.* **immediately** *adverb*, **immediacy** *noun*

immemorial *adjective* existing from before what can be remembered or found in histories, *from time immemorial.*

immense *adjective* exceedingly great; huge. **immensely** *adverb*, **immensity** *noun*

immerse *verb* (immersed, immersing) 1 put something completely into a liquid. 2 absorb or involve deeply, *She was immersed in her work.* **immersion** *noun*

immersion heater a device that heats water by means of an electric element immersed in the water in a tank etc.

immigrate *verb* (immigrated, immigrating) come into another country to live there. **immigration** *noun*, **immigrant** *noun*
● USAGE: See the note on *emigrate.*

imminent *adjective* likely to happen at any moment, *an imminent storm.* **imminence** *noun*

immobile *adjective* not moving; immovable. **immobility** *noun*

immobilize *verb* (immobilized, immobilizing) stop a thing from moving or working. **immobilization** *noun*

immodest *adjective* 1 without modesty; indecent. 2 conceited.

immoral *adjective* morally wrong; wicked. **immorally** *adverb*, **immorality** *noun*

immortal *adjective* 1 living for ever; not mortal. 2 famous for all time, *the immortal Shakespeare.* **immortal** *noun*, **immortality** *noun*, **immortalize** *verb*

immovable *adjective* unable to be moved. **immovably** *adverb*

immune *adjective* safe from or protected against something, *immune from* (or *against* or *to*) *infection* etc. **immunity** *noun*

immunize *verb* (immunized, immunizing) make a person immune from a disease etc., e.g. by vaccination. **immunization** *noun*

immutable (*say* i-**mewt**-a-bul) *adjective* unchangeable. **immutably** *adverb*

imp *noun* 1 a small devil. 2 a mischievous child. **impish** *adjective*

impact *noun* 1 a collision; the force of a collision. 2 an influence or effect, *the impact of computers on our lives.*

impair *verb* damage; weaken, *Smoking impairs health.* **impairment** *noun*

impala (*say* im-**pah**-la) *noun* (*plural* impala) a small antelope.

impale *verb* (impaled, impaling) pierce or fix something on a sharp pointed object. **impalement** *noun*

impart *verb* 1 tell, *She imparted the news to her brother.* 2 give, *Lemon imparts a sharp flavour to drinks.*

impartial *adjective* not favouring one side more than the other; not biased; fair. **impartially** *adverb*, **impartiality** *noun*

impassable *adjective* not able to be travelled along or over, *The roads are impassable because of floods.*

impasse (*say* **am**-pahss) *noun* a deadlock.

impassive *adjective* not feeling or not showing emotion. **impassively** *adverb*

impatient *adjective* not patient. **impatiently** *adverb*, **impatience** *noun*

impeach *verb* bring a person to trial for a serious crime against his or her country. **impeachment** *noun*

impeccable *adjective* faultless. **impeccably** *adverb*, **impeccability** *noun*

impede *verb* (impeded, impeding) hinder.

impediment *noun* 1 a hindrance. 2 a defect, *He has an impediment in his speech* (= a lisp or stammer).

impel *verb* (impelled, impelling) 1 urge or drive someone to do something, *Curiosity impelled her to investigate.* 2 drive forward; propel.

impending *adjective* imminent.

impenetrable *adjective* not able to be penetrated.

impenitent *adjective* not penitent; unrepentant.

imperative[1] *adjective* **1** expressing a command. **2** essential, *Speed is imperative.*

imperative[2] *noun* a command; the form of a verb used in making commands (e.g. 'come' in *Come here!*).

imperceptible *adjective* not perceptible; difficult or impossible to see.

imperfect *adjective* not perfect. **imperfectly** *adverb,* **imperfection** *noun* **imperfect tense** a tense of a verb showing a continuous action, e.g. She *was singing.*

imperial *adjective* **1** of an empire or its rulers. **2** of non-metric weights and measures formerly used in Britain. **imperially** *adverb*

imperialism *noun* the policy of extending a country's empire or its influence; colonialism. **imperialist** *noun*

imperious *adjective* commanding; bossy.

impersonal *adjective* **1** not affected by personal feelings; showing no emotion. **2** not referring to a particular person. **impersonally** *adverb* **impersonal verb** a verb used only with 'it', e.g. in *It is raining* or *It is hard to find one.*

impersonate *verb* (**impersonated,** **impersonating**) pretend to be another person. **impersonation** *noun,* **impersonator** *noun*

impertinent *adjective* **1** insolent; not showing proper respect. **2** not pertinent; irrelevant. **impertinently** *adverb,* **impertinence** *noun*

imperturbable *adjective* not excitable; calm. **imperturbably** *adverb*

impervious *adjective* **1** impenetrable, *impervious to water.* **2** not influenced by something, *impervious to criticism.*

impetuous *adjective* **1** hasty; rash. **2** eager; impulsive.

impetus *noun* force or energy of movement.

impi *noun* **1** a tribal army or regiment in former times, *Shaka's impis.* **2** an armed band of fighters.

impiety *noun* lack of reverence.

impious (*say* **imp**-ee-us) *adjective*

impinge *verb* (**impinged, impinging**) make an impact; encroach.

implacable *adjective* not able to be placated; relentless. **implacably** *adverb*

implant *verb* insert; fix something in. **implant** *noun,* **implantation** *noun*

implement[1] *noun* a tool.

implement[2] *verb* put into action, *We shall implement these plans next month.* **implementation** *noun*

implicate *verb* (**implicated, implicating**) involve a person in a crime etc.; show that a person is involved, *His evidence implicates his sister.*

implication *noun* **1** implicating. **2** implying; something that is implied, *The implications of their actions are serious.*

implicit (*say* im-**pliss**-it) *adjective* **1** implied but not stated openly. (Compare *explicit.*) **2** absolute; unquestioning, *She expects implicit obedience.* **implicitly** *adverb*

implore *verb* (**implored, imploring**) beg somebody to do something; entreat.

imply *verb* (**implied, implying**) suggest something without actually saying it. **implication** *noun*

impolite *adjective* not polite.

imponderable *adjective* not able to be estimated.

import[1] *verb* bring in goods etc. from another country.

import[2] *noun* **1** importing; something imported. **2** meaning; importance, *The message was of great import.*

important *adjective* **1** having or able to have a great effect. **2** having great authority or influence. **importantly** *adverb,* **importance** *noun*

impose *verb* (**imposed, imposing**) put; inflict, *It imposes a strain upon us.* **impose on somebody** put an unfair burden on him or her.

imposing *adjective* impressive.

imposition *noun* **1** something imposed; a burden imposed unfairly. **2** imposing something.

impossible *adjective* **1** not possible. **2** (*informal*) very annoying; unbearable,

He really is impossible! **impossibly** *adverb,* **impossibility** *noun*

impostor *noun* a person who dishonestly pretends to be someone else.

imposture *noun* a dishonest pretence.

impotent *adjective* 1 powerless; unable to take action. 2 (of a man) unable to have sexual intercourse. **impotently** *adverb,* **impotence** *noun*

impound *verb* confiscate.

impoverish *verb* 1 make a person poor. 2 make a thing poor in quality, *impoverished soil.* **impoverishment** *noun*

impracticable *adjective* not practicable.

impractical *adjective* not practical; unwise.

imprecise *adjective* not precise.

impregnable *adjective* strong enough to be safe against attack.

impregnate *verb* (**impregnated,** **impregnating**) 1 fertilize; make pregnant. 2 saturate; fill throughout, *The air was impregnated with the scent.* **impregnation** *noun*

impresario *noun* (*plural* **impresarios**) a person who organizes concerts, shows, etc.

impress *verb* 1 cause a person to admire or think something is very good. 2 fix firmly in the mind, *He impressed on them the need for secrecy.* 3 press a mark into something.

impression *noun* 1 an effect produced on the mind, *She made a good impression on the visitors.* 2 a vague idea. 3 an imitation of a person or a sound etc., *He does a humorous impression of the archbishop.* 4 a reprint of a book.

impressionism *noun* a style of painting that gives the general effect of a scene etc. but without details. **impressionist** *noun*

impressive *adjective* making a strong impression; seeming very good.

imprint *noun* a mark pressed into or on something.

imprison *verb* put into prison; keep in confinement. **imprisonment** *noun*

improbable *adjective* unlikely. **improbably** *adverb,* **improbability** *noun*

impromptu *adjective* & *adverb* done without any rehearsal or preparation.

improper *adjective* 1 incorrect; wrong. 2 indecent. **improperly** *adverb,* **impropriety** (*say* im-pro-**pry**-it-ee) *noun* **improper fraction** a fraction in which the numerator is greater than or equal to the denominator.

improve *verb* (**improved, improving**) make or become better. **improvement** *noun*

improvident *adjective* not providing or planning for the future; not thrifty.

improvise *verb* (**improvised, improvising**) 1 compose something impromptu. 2 make something quickly with whatever is available, *They quickly improvised a meal.* **improvisation** *noun*

imprudent *adjective* unwise.

impudent *adjective* impertinent; cheeky. **impudently** *adverb,* **impudence** *noun*

impulse *noun* 1 a sudden desire to do something. 2 a push; impetus. 3 (in physics) a force acting for a very short time, *electrical impulses.*

impulsive *adjective* done or doing things on impulse, not after careful thought. **impulsively** *adverb,* **impulsiveness** *noun*

impundulu *noun* the lightning bird (a bird in African myth that is called up by witches and is often believed to cause crimes).

impunity (*say* im-**pewn**-it-ee) *noun* freedom from punishment or injury.

impure *adjective* not pure. **impurity** *noun*

impute *verb* (**imputed, imputing**) attribute; ascribe. **imputation** *noun*

in[1] *preposition* This word is used to show position or condition, e.g. 1 at or inside; within the limits of something, *in a box, in two hours.* 2 into, *He fell in a puddle.* 3 arranged as; consisting of, *a serial in four parts.* 4 occupied with; a member of, *He is in the army.* 5 by means of, *We paid in cash.* **in all** in total number; altogether.

in[2] *adverb* 1 so as to be in something or inside, *Get in.* 2 inwards, *The top caved in.* 3 at home; indoors, *Is anybody in?* 4 in action; (in cricket) batting; (of a fire) burning. 5 having arrived, *The train is in.* **in for** likely to get, *You're in for a shock.* **in on** (*informal*) aware of or sharing in, *I want to be in on this project.*

in- *prefix* (changing to **il-** before *l*, **im-** before *b, m, p*, **ir-** before *r*) **1** in; into; on; towards (as in *include, invade*). **2** not (as in *incorrect, indirect*).

inability *noun* being unable.

inaccessible *adjective* not accessible.

inaccurate *adjective* not accurate.

inactive *adjective* not active. **inaction** *noun*, **inactivity** *noun*

inadequate *adjective* **1** not enough. **2** not capable enough, *She makes me feel inadequate.* **inadequately** *adverb,* **inadequacy** *noun*

inadvertent *adjective* unintentional.

inadvisable *adjective* not advisable.

inalienable *adjective* that cannot be taken away, *an inalienable right.*

inane *adjective* silly; without sense. **inanely** *adverb,* **inanity** *noun*

inanimate *adjective* **1** not living. **2** not moving.

inappropriate *adjective* not appropriate.

inarticulate *adjective* **1** not able to speak or express yourself clearly, *inarticulate with rage.* **2** not expressed in words, *an inarticulate cry.*

inattention *noun* not being attentive; not listening. **inattentive** *adjective*

inaudible *adjective* not audible. **inaudibly** *adverb,* **inaudibility** *noun*

inaugurate *verb* (**inaugurated, inaugurating**) **1** start or introduce something new and important. **2** install a person in office, *inaugurate a new President.* **inaugural** *adjective,* **inauguration** *noun,* **inaugurator** *noun*

inauspicious *adjective* not auspicious.

inborn *adjective* present in a person or animal from birth, *an inborn ability.*

inbred *adjective* **1** inborn. **2** produced by inbreeding.

inbreeding *noun* breeding from closely related individuals.

incalculable *adjective* not able to be calculated or predicted.

incandescent *adjective* giving out light when heated; shining. **incandescence** *noun*

incantation *noun* a spoken spell or charm; the chanting of this.

incapable *adjective* not able to do something, *incapable of working alone.*

incapacitate *verb* (**incapacitated, incapacitating**) make unable to do something; disable.

incapacity *noun* inability; lack of sufficient strength or power.

incarcerate *verb* (**incarcerated, incarcerating**) shut in; imprison. **incarceration** *noun*

incarnate *adjective* having a body or human form, *a devil incarnate.* **incarnation** *noun*

the Incarnation the embodiment of God in human form as Jesus Christ.

incautious *adjective* rash.

incendiary *adjective* starting or designed to start a fire, *an incendiary bomb.*

incense[1] (*say* **in**-sens) *noun* a substance making a spicy smell when burnt.

incense[2] (*say* in-**sens**) *verb* (**incensed, incensing**) make a person angry.

incentive *noun* something that encourages a person to do something or to work harder.

inception *noun* a beginning.

incessant *adjective* unceasing.

incest *noun* sexual intercourse between two people who are so closely related that they cannot marry each other. **incestuous** *adjective*

inch *noun* (*plural* **inches**) a measure of length in the imperial system, one-twelfth of a foot (about $2\frac{1}{2}$ centimetres).

incidence *noun* the extent or frequency of something, *Study the incidence of the disease.*

incident *noun* an event.

incidental *adjective* happening with something else, *incidental expenses.*

incidentally *adverb* by the way.

incinerate *verb* (**incinerated, incinerating**) destroy something by burning. **incineration** *noun*

incinerator *noun* a device for burning rubbish.

incipient (*say* in-**sip**-ee-ent) *adjective* just beginning, *incipient decay.*

incise *verb* (**incised, incising**) cut or engrave something into a surface.

incision *noun* a cut, especially one made in a surgical operation.

incisive *adjective* clear and sharp, *incisive comments.*

incisor (*say* in-**sy**-zer) *noun* each of the sharp-edged front teeth in the upper and lower jaws.

incite *verb* (**incited, inciting**) urge a person to do something; stir up, *They incited a riot.* **incitement** *noun*

incivility *noun* being uncivil; rudeness.

inclement *adjective* (*formal*) cold, wet, or stormy, *inclement weather.*

inclination *noun* 1 a tendency. 2 a liking or preference, *a musical inclination.* 3 a slope or slant.

incline *verb* (**inclined, inclining**) 1 lean; slope. 2 bend the head or body forward, as in a nod or bow. 3 cause or influence, *Her frank manner inclines me to believe her.* **be inclined** have a tendency, *The door is inclined to bang.*

include *verb* (**included, including**) make or consider something as part of a group of things.

inclusive *adjective* including everything.

incognito (*say* in-kog-**neet**-oh or in-**kog**-nit-oh) *adjective & adverb* with your name or identity concealed, *The film star was travelling incognito.*

incoherent *adjective* not speaking or reasoning in an orderly way.

incombustible *adjective* unable to be set on fire.

income *noun* money received regularly from wages, investments, etc. **income tax** tax charged on income.

incomparable *adjective* without an equal; unsurpassed, *incomparable beauty.*

incompatible *adjective* not compatible.

incompetent *adjective* not competent.

incomplete *adjective* not complete.

incomprehensible *adjective* not able to be understood. **incomprehension** *noun*

inconceivable *adjective* not able to be imagined; most unlikely.

inconclusive *adjective* not conclusive.

incongruous *adjective* unsuitable; not harmonious; out of place. **incongruously** *adverb*, **incongruity** *noun*

inconsiderable *adjective* of small value.

inconsiderate *adjective* not considerate.

inconsistent *adjective* not consistent. **inconsistently** *adverb*, **inconsistency** *noun*

inconsolable *adjective* not able to be consoled; very sad.

inconspicuous *adjective* not conspicuous. **inconspicuously** *adverb*

incontinent *adjective* not able to control excretion. **incontinence** *noun*

incontrovertible *adjective* indisputable.

inconvenience[1] *noun* being inconvenient.

inconvenience[2] *verb* (**inconvenienced, inconveniencing**) cause inconvenience or slight difficulty to someone.

inconvenient *adjective* not convenient.

incorporate *verb* (**incorporated, incorporating**) include something as a part. **incorporation** *noun*

incorporated *adjective* (of a business firm) formed into a legal corporation.

incorrect *adjective* not correct. **incorrectly** *adverb*

incorrigible *adjective* not able to be reformed, *an incorrigible liar.*

incorruptible *adjective* 1 not liable to decay. 2 not able to be bribed.

increase[1] *verb* (**increased, increasing**) make or become larger or more.

increase[2] *noun* increasing; the amount by which a thing increases.

incredible *adjective* unbelievable. **incredibly** *adverb*, **incredibility** *noun*
● USAGE: Do not confuse with *incredulous.*

incredulous *adjective* not believing somebody; showing disbelief. **incredulously** *adverb*, **incredulity** *noun*
● USAGE: Do not confuse with *incredible.*

increment (*say* **in**-krim-ent) *noun* an increase; an added amount.

incriminate *verb* (**incriminated, incriminating**) show a person to have been involved in a crime etc. **incrimination** *noun*

incrustation *noun* encrusting; a crust or deposit formed on a surface.

incubate *verb* (**incubated, incubating**) 1 hatch eggs by keeping them warm.

2 cause bacteria or a disease etc. to develop. **incubation** *noun*

incubator *noun* **1** a device for incubating eggs etc. **2** a device in which a baby born prematurely can be kept warm and supplied with oxygen.

incumbent[1] *adjective* forming an obligation, *It is incumbent on you to warn people of the danger.*

incumbent[2] *noun* a person who holds a particular office or position.

incur *verb* (**incurred, incurring**) bring something on yourself, *incur expense.*

incurable *adjective* not able to be cured. **incurably** *adverb*

incurious *adjective* feeling or showing no curiosity about something.

incursion *noun* a raid or brief invasion.

indaba *noun* **1** a meeting, usually on a serious topic. **2** (*informal*) a concern or problem, *That's her indaba.*

indebted *adjective* owing money or gratitude to someone.

indecent *adjective* not decent; improper. **indecently** *adverb*, **indecency** *noun*

indecipherable *adjective* not able to be deciphered.

indecision *noun* being unable to make up your mind; hesitation.

indecisive *adjective* not decisive.

indeed *adverb* **1** really; truly, *I am indeed surprised*; (used to strengthen a meaning), *very nice indeed.* **2** admittedly, *It is, indeed, his first attempt.*

indefensible *adjective* unable to be defended; unable to be justified.

indefinable *adjective* unable to be defined or described clearly.

indefinite *adjective* not definite; vague. **indefinite article** the word 'a' or 'an'.

indefinitely *adverb* for an indefinite or unlimited time.

indelible *adjective* impossible to rub out or remove. **indelibly** *adverb*

indelicate *adjective* **1** slightly indecent. **2** tactless. **indelicacy** *noun*

indent *verb* **1** make notches or recesses in something. **2** start a line of writing or printing further in from the margin than other lines, *Always indent a quotation of*

more than three lines. **3** place an official order for goods or stores, *Indent for a new office desk.* **indentation** *noun*

indenture *noun* (also **indentures**) an agreement binding an apprentice to work for a certain employer. **indentured** *adjective*

independent *adjective* **1** not dependent; not controlled by any other person or thing. **2** (of a country) governing itself. **3** (of broadcasting) not financed by money from licences. **independently** *adverb*, **independence** *noun*

indescribable *adjective* unable to be described. **indescribably** *adverb*

indestructible *adjective* unable to be destroyed. **indestructibility** *noun*

indeterminate *adjective* not fixed or decided exactly; left vague.

index[1] *noun* **1** (*plural* **indexes**) an alphabetical list of things, especially at the end of a book. **2** a number showing how prices or wages have changed from a previous level. **3** (*plural* **indices**) the exponent of a number. **index finger** the forefinger.

index[2] *verb* make an index to a book etc.; put into an index.

Indian *adjective* **1** of India or its people. **2** of American Indians. **Indian** *noun* **American Indian** a member or descendant of the original inhabitants of the continent of America (other than Eskimos).

indiarubber *noun* a rubber.

indicate *verb* (**indicated, indicating**) **1** point out; make known. **2** be a sign of, *The spoor indicates that a lion was here yesterday.* **indication** *noun*

indicative[1] *adjective* giving an indication.

indicative[2] *noun* the form of a verb used in making a statement (e.g. 'he said' or 'he is coming'), not in a command or question etc.

indicator *noun* **1** a thing that indicates or points to something. **2** a flashing light used to signal that a motor vehicle is turning.

indict (*say* ind-I't) *verb* charge a person with having committed a crime. **indictment** *noun*

indifferent *adjective* **1** not caring about

something; not interested. **2** not very good, *an indifferent cricketer.* **indifferently** *adverb,* **indifference** *noun*

indigenous (*say* in-**dij**-in-us) *adjective* growing or originating in a particular country; native, *The protea is indigenous to South Africa.*

indigent (*say* **in**-dij-ent) *adjective* needy.

indigestible *adjective* difficult or impossible to digest.

indigestion *noun* pain caused by difficulty in digesting food.

indignant *adjective* angry at something that seems unfair or wicked. **indignantly** *adverb,* **indignation** *noun*

indignity *noun* (*plural* **indignities**) treatment that makes a person feel undignified or humiliated; an insult.

indigo *noun* a deep-blue colour.

indirect *adjective* not direct. **indirectly** *adverb*

indiscreet *adjective* **1** not discreet; revealing secrets. **2** incautious; unwise. **indiscreetly** *adverb,* **indiscretion** *noun*

indiscriminate *adjective* showing no discrimination; not making a careful choice. **indiscriminately** *adverb*

indispensable *adjective* not able to be dispensed with; essential. **indispensability** *noun*

indisposed *adjective* **1** slightly unwell. **2** unwilling, *They seem indisposed to help us.* **indisposition** *noun*

indisputable *adjective* undeniable.

indistinct *adjective* not distinct. **indistinctly** *adverb,* **indistinctness** *noun*

indistinguishable *adjective* not distinguishable.

individual[1] *adjective* **1** of or for one person. **2** single; separate, *Count each individual word.* **individually** *adverb*

individual[2] *noun* one person, animal, or plant.

individuality *noun* the things that make one person or thing different from another; distinctive identity.

indivisible *adjective* not able to be divided or separated. **indivisibly** *adverb*

indoctrinate *verb* (**indoctrinated,** **indoctrinating**) fill a person's mind with particular ideas or beliefs, especially so as to make him or her accept them uncritically. **indoctrination** *noun*

indolent *adjective* lazy. **indolently** *adverb,* **indolence** *noun*

indomitable *adjective* not able to be overcome or conquered.

indoor *adjective* used or placed or done etc. inside a building, *indoor games.*

indoors *adverb* inside a building.

indubitable (*say* in-**dew**-bit-a-bul) *adjective* not able to be doubted; certain. **indubitably** *adverb*

induce *verb* (**induced, inducing**) **1** persuade. **2** produce; cause, *Some substances induce sleep.* **induction** *noun*

inducement *noun* an incentive.

indulge *verb* (**indulged, indulging**) allow a person to have or do what he or she wishes. **indulgence** *noun,* **indulgent** *adjective* **indulge in** allow yourself to have or do something that you like.

induna *noun* a person in authority.

industrial *adjective* of industry; working or used in industry. **industrially** *adverb* **industrial action** striking or working to rule. **industrial relations** the relationship between employers and employees. **Industrial Revolution** the expansion of industry by the use of machines in the late 18th and early 19th century.

industrialist *noun* a person who owns or manages an industrial business.

industrialized *adjective* (of a country or district) having many industries. **industrialization** *noun*

industrious *adjective* working hard. **industriously** *adverb*

industry *noun* (*plural* **industries**) **1** making or producing goods etc., especially in factories. **2** being industrious, *She was rewarded for her industry.*

inebriated *adjective* drunk; drunken.

inedible *adjective* not edible.

ineffective *adjective* not effective; inefficient. **ineffectively** *adverb*

ineffectual *adjective* not effectual; not confident, not convincing.

inefficient *adjective* not efficient. **inefficiently** *adverb,* **inefficiency** *noun*

inelegant *adjective* not elegant.
ineligible *adjective* not eligible.
inept *adjective* unsuitable; bungling.
ineptly *adverb*, **ineptitude** *noun*
inequality *noun* (*plural* **inequalities**) not being equal.
inequity *noun* (*plural* **inequities**) unfairness. **inequitable** *adjective*
inert *adjective* not moving; not reacting. **inertly** *adverb*
inertia (*say* in-**er**-sha) *noun* 1 inactivity; being inert or slow to take action.
2 the tendency for a moving thing to keep moving in a straight line.
inescapable *adjective* unavoidable.
inessential *adjective* not essential.
inestimable *adjective* too great or precious to be able to be estimated.
inevitable *adjective* unavoidable; sure to happen. **inevitably** *adverb*, **inevitability** *noun*
inexact *adjective* not exact.
inexcusable *adjective* not excusable.
inexhaustible *adjective* so great that it cannot be used up completely.
inexorable (*say* in-**eks**-er-a-bul) *adjective* relentless; not yielding to requests or entreaties. **inexorably** *adverb*
inexpensive *adjective* not expensive; cheap. **inexpensively** *adverb*
inexperience *noun* lack of experience. **inexperienced** *adjective*
inexpert *adjective* unskilful.
inexplicable *adjective* impossible to explain. **inexplicably** *adverb*
infallible *adjective* never wrong; never failing, *an infallible remedy.* **infallibly** *adverb*, **infallibility** *noun*
infamous (*say* **in**-fam-us) *adjective* having a bad reputation; wicked. **infamously** *adverb*, **infamy** *noun*
infancy *noun* 1 early childhood; babyhood. 2 an early stage of development.
infant *noun* a baby or young child.
infantile *adjective* 1 of an infant. 2 very childish, *infantile behaviour.*
infantry *noun* soldiers who fight on foot. (Compare *cavalry.*)
infatuated *adjective* filled with foolish or unreasoning love. **infatuation** *noun*

infect *verb* pass on a disease or bacteria etc. to a person, animal, or plant.
infection *noun* 1 infecting. 2 an infectious disease or condition.
infectious *adjective* 1 (of a disease) able to be spread by air or water etc. (Compare *contagious.*) 2 quickly spreading to others, *His fear was infectious.*
infer *verb* (**inferred, inferring**) form an opinion by reasoning; conclude, *I infer from your luggage that you are going on holiday.* **inference** *noun*
● USAGE: Do not confuse with *imply.*
inferior *adjective* less good or less important; low or lower in position, quality, etc. **inferiority** *noun*
infernal *adjective* 1 of or like hell, *the infernal regions.* 2 (*informal*) detestable; tiresome, *that infernal noise.* **infernally** *adverb*
inferno *noun* (*plural* **infernos**) a terrifying fire.
infertile *adjective* not fertile. **infertility** *noun*
infest *verb* (of pests) be numerous and troublesome in a place. **infestation** *noun*
infidel (*say* **in**-fid-el) *noun* a person who does not believe in a religion.
infidelity *noun* unfaithfulness.
infiltrate *verb* (**infiltrated, infiltrating**) get into a place or organization gradually and without being noticed. **infiltration** *noun*, **infiltrator** *noun*
infinite *adjective* 1 endless; without a limit. 2 too great to be measured, *infinite care.* **infinitely** *adverb*
infinitesimal *adjective* extremely small. **infinitesimally** *adverb*
infinitive *noun* a form of a verb that does not indicate a particular tense or number or person, in English used with or without *to*, e.g. *go* in 'Let him go' or 'Allow him to go'.
infinity *noun* an infinite number or distance or time.
infirm *adjective* weak, especially from old age or illness. **infirmity** *noun*
infirmary *noun* (*plural* **infirmaries**) 1 a hospital. 2 a place where sick people are cared for in a school or monastery etc.
inflame *verb* (**inflamed, inflaming**)

1 arouse strong feelings or anger in people.
2 cause redness, heat, and swelling in a part
of the body. **inflammation** *noun*, **inflammatory** *adjective*

inflammable *adjective* able to be set on
fire.
• USAGE: This word means the same
as *flammable*; its opposite is *non-
inflammable*.

inflatable *adjective* able to be inflated.

inflate *verb* (**inflated, inflating**) 1 fill with
air or gas and expand. 2 increase too much;
raise prices or wages etc. more than is
justifiable.

inflation *noun* 1 inflating. 2 a general rise
in prices and fall in the purchasing power of
money. **inflationary** *adjective*

inflect *verb* 1 change the ending or form of
a word to show its tense or its grammatical
relation to other words, e.g. *sing* changes to
sang or *sung*, *child* changes to *children*.
2 alter the voice in speaking. **inflection**
noun

inflexible *adjective* not able to be bent or
changed or persuaded. **inflexibly** *adverb*,
inflexibility *noun*

inflict *verb* make a person suffer something, *She inflicted a severe blow on him*.
infliction *noun*

inflow *noun* flowing in; what flows in.

influence[1] *noun* the power to produce
an effect; a person or thing with this
power.

influence[2] *verb* (**influenced, influencing**)
have influence on a person or thing; affect.

influential *adjective* having influence.

influenza *noun* an infectious disease that
causes fever, catarrh, and pain.

influx *noun* a flowing in, especially of
people or things coming in.

inform *verb* give information to somebody.
informant *noun*

informal *adjective* not formal. **informally**
adverb, **informality** *noun*
• USAGE: In this dictionary, words marked
informal are used in talking but not when
you are writing or speaking formally.

informal sector the part of the
economy made up of all unlicensed
businesses, e.g. hawkers, stokvels, etc.

(Compare *formal sector*.)

informal settlement a squatter camp.

information *noun* facts told or heard or
discovered, or put into a computer etc.

informative *adjective* giving a lot of useful
information.

informed *adjective* knowing about
something.

informer *noun* a person who gives
information against someone.

infra- *prefix* below.

infra-red *adjective* below or beyond red in
the spectrum.

infrastructure *noun* the basic facilities
that a country needs to function efficiently,
e.g. roads, sewers, electrical services.

infrequent *adjective* not frequent.

infringe *verb* (**infringed, infringing**) break
a rule or an agreement etc.; violate.
infringement *noun*

infuriate *verb* (**infuriated, infuriating**)
make a person very angry; enrage.
infuriation *noun*

infuse *verb* (**infused, infusing**) 1 add or
inspire with a feeling etc., *infuse them with
courage*; *infuse courage into them*. 2 soak or
steep tea or herbs etc. in a liquid to extract
the flavour. **infusion** *noun*

ingenious *adjective* clever at inventing
things; cleverly made. **ingeniously** *adverb*,
ingenuity *noun*

ingenuous *adjective* naive. **ingenuously**
adverb, **ingenuousness** *noun*
• USAGE: Do not confuse with *ingenious*.

ingot *noun* a lump of gold or silver etc. cast
in a brick shape.

ingrained *adjective* 1 (of dirt) marking a
surface deeply. 2 (of feelings or habits etc.)
firmly fixed.

ingratiate *verb* (**ingratiated, ingratiating**)
ingratiate yourself get yourself into favour.
ingratiation *noun*

ingratitude *noun* lack of gratitude.

ingredient *noun* one of the parts of a
mixture; one of the things used in a recipe.

inhabit *verb* (**inhabited, inhabiting**) live in
a place. **inhabitant** *noun*

inhale *verb* (**inhaled, inhaling**) breathe in.
inhalation *noun*

inharmonious *adjective* not harmonious.

inherent (*say* in-**heer**-ent) *adjective* existing in something as one of its natural or permanent qualities. **inherently** *adverb*, **inherence** *noun*

inherit *verb* (**inherited, inheriting**) 1 receive money, property, or a title etc. when its previous owner dies. 2 get certain qualities etc. from parents or predecessors. **inheritance** *noun*, **inheritor** *noun*

inhibit *verb* (**inhibited, inhibiting**) restrain; hinder; repress. **inhibition** *noun*

inhospitable *adjective* not hospitable.

inhuman *adjective* cruel; without pity or kindness. **inhumanity** *noun*

inhumane *adjective* not humane.

inimitable *adjective* impossible to imitate.

iniquitous *adjective* very unjust. **iniquity** *noun*

initial[1] *noun* the first letter of a word or name.

initial[2] *verb* (**initialled, initialling**) mark or sign something with the initials of your names.

initial[3] *adjective* of the beginning, *the initial stages.* **initially** *adverb*

initiate *verb* (**initiated, initiating**) 1 start something. 2 admit a person as a member of a society or group, often with special ceremonies. **initiation** *noun*, **initiator** *noun*

initiative (*say* in-**ish**-a-tiv) *noun* the power or courage to start a new process; enterprising ability.
take the initiative take action to start something happening.

inject *verb* 1 put a medicine or drug into the body by means of a hollow needle. 2 put liquid into something by means of a syringe etc. 3 add a new quality, *Inject some humour into it.* **injection** *noun*

injudicious *adjective* unwise.

injunction *noun* a command given with authority, e.g. by a lawcourt.

injure *verb* (**injured, injuring**) harm; damage; hurt. **injury** *noun*, **injurious** (*say* in-**joor**-ee-us) *adjective*

injustice *noun* lack of justice; an unjust action or treatment.

ink *noun* a black or coloured liquid used in writing and printing.

inkling *noun* a hint; a slight knowledge or suspicion.

inkosazana *noun* a title of respect used when addressing an unmarried woman.

inkosi *noun* a title of respect used when addressing a man.

inkosikazi *noun* a title of respect used when addressing a married woman.

inky *adjective* 1 stained with ink. 2 black like ink, *inky darkness.*

inland *adjective* & *adverb* in or towards the interior of a country; away from the coast.

in-laws *plural noun* (*informal*) relatives by marriage.

inlay *verb* (**inlaid, inlaying**) set pieces of wood or metal etc. into a surface to form a design. **inlay** *noun*

inlet *noun* 1 a strip of water reaching into the land from a sea or lake. 2 a passage that lets something in (e.g. to a tank).

inmate *noun* one of the occupants of a prison, hospital, or other institution.

inmost *adjective* most inward.

inn *noun* a hotel or public house, especially in the country. **innkeeper** *noun*

innate *adjective* inborn.

inner *adjective* inside; internal; nearer to the centre. **innermost** *adjective*

innings *noun* (*plural* **innings**) the time when a cricket team or player is batting.

innocent *adjective* 1 not guilty. 2 not wicked. 3 harmless, *innocent amusement.* **innocently** *adverb*, **innocence** *noun*

innocuous *adjective* harmless.

innovation *noun* 1 introducing new things or new methods. 2 something newly introduced. **innovative** *adjective*, **innovator** *noun*

innuendo *noun* (*plural* **innuendoes**) an unpleasant insinuation or hint.

innumerable *adjective* countless.

inoculate *verb* (**inoculated, inoculating**) inject or treat with a vaccine or serum as a protection against a disease. **inoculation** *noun*

inoffensive *adjective* harmless.

inordinate *adjective* excessive. **inordinately** *adverb*

inorganic *adjective* not of living organisms; of mineral origin.

input *noun* what is put into something (e.g. data into a computer). **input** *verb*

inquest *noun* an official inquiry to find out how a person died.

inquire *verb* (**inquired, inquiring**) make an investigation. **inquiry** *noun*
• USAGE: It is best to use *enquire* and *enquiry* of asking something, and *inquire* and *inquiry* of investigating.

inquisition *noun* a detailed questioning or investigation. **inquisitor** *noun*
the Inquisition a council of the Roman Catholic Church in the Middle Ages set up to discover and punish heretics.

inquisitive *adjective* always asking questions or trying to look at things; prying. **inquisitively** *adverb*

inroad *noun* an invasion; a raid.
make inroads on or **into** use up large quantities of stores etc.

inrush *noun* (*plural* **inrushes**) a sudden rush in; an influx.

insane *adjective* not sane; mad. **insanely** *adverb*, **insanity** *noun*

insanitary *adjective* unclean and likely to be harmful to health.

insatiable (*say* in-**say**-sha-bul) *adjective* impossible to satisfy, *an insatiable appetite*.

inscribe *verb* (**inscribed, inscribing**) write or carve words etc. on something.

inscription *noun* 1 words or names inscribed on a monument, coin, stone, etc. 2 inscribing.

inscrutable *adjective* enigmatic; impossible to interpret, *an inscrutable smile*.

insect *noun* a small animal with six legs, no backbone, and a body divided into three parts (head, thorax, abdomen).

insecticide *noun* a substance for killing insects.

insectivorous *adjective* feeding on insects and other small invertebrate creatures. **insectivore** *noun*

insecure *adjective* not secure; unsafe. **insecurely** *adverb*, **insecurity** *noun*

inseminate *verb* (**inseminated, inseminating**) insert semen into the womb. **insemination** *noun*

insensible *adjective* 1 unconscious. 2 unaware, *She was insensible of the danger involved.*

insensitive *adjective* not sensitive. **insensitively** *adverb*, **insensitivity** *noun*

inseparable *adjective* 1 not able to be separated. 2 liking to be constantly together, *inseparable friends*. **inseparably** *adverb*

insert *verb* put a thing into something else. **insertion** *noun*

inshore *adverb* & *adjective* near or nearer to the shore.

inside[1] *noun* 1 the inner side, surface, or part. 2 (*informal*) the organs in the abdomen; the stomach and bowels.
inside out with the inside turned to face outwards.

inside[2] *adjective* on or coming from the inside; in or nearest to the middle.

inside[3] *adverb* & *preposition* on or to the inside of something; in, *Come inside. It's inside that box.*

insider *noun* a member of a certain group, especially someone with access to private information.

insidious *adjective* inconspicuous but harmful, *the insidious effects of television on children*. **insidiously** *adverb*

insight *noun* being able to perceive the truth about things; understanding.

insignia *plural noun* emblems; a badge.

insignificant *adjective* not important; not influential. **insignificance** *noun*

insincere *adjective* not sincere. **insincerely** *adverb*, **insincerity** *noun*

insinuate *verb* (**insinuated, insinuating**) 1 hint artfully or unpleasantly. 2 introduce (a person or thing) into a position gradually or craftily, *She insinuated herself into his favour*. **insinuation** *noun*

insipid *adjective* 1 lacking flavour. 2 not lively or interesting. **insipidity** *noun*

insist *verb* be very firm in saying or asking for something. **insistent** *adjective*, **insistence** *noun*

insolent *adjective* very impudent; insulting. **insolently** *adverb*, **insolence** *noun*

insoluble *adjective* 1 impossible to solve, *an insoluble problem*. 2 impossible to dissolve. **insolubility** *noun*

insomnia *noun* being unable to sleep.

insomniac *noun*

inspan *verb* (**inspanned, inspanning**) yoke or harness animals to a wagon or plough etc.

inspect *verb* examine carefully and critically. **inspection** *noun*

inspector *noun* 1 a person whose job is to inspect or supervise things. 2 a police officer ranking next above a sergeant.

inspiration *noun* 1 a sudden brilliant idea. 2 inspiring; an inspiring influence, *Our leader is an inspiration to us all.*

inspire *verb* (**inspired, inspiring**) fill a person with good or useful feelings or ideas, *The applause inspired us with confidence.*

instability *noun* lack of stability.

install *verb* 1 put something in position and ready to use, *They installed air-conditioning.* 2 put a person into an important position with a ceremony, *He was installed as pope.* **installation** *noun*

instalment *noun* each of the parts in which something is given or paid for gradually, *an instalment of a serial.*

instance *noun* an example, *for instance.*

instant¹ *adjective* 1 happening immediately, *instant success.* 2 (of food) designed to be prepared quickly and easily, *instant coffee.* **instantly** *adverb*

instant² *noun* a moment, *not an instant too soon.*

instantaneous *adjective* happening immediately. **instantaneously** *adverb*

instead *adverb* in place of something else; as a substitute.

instep *noun* the top of the foot between the toes and the ankle.

instigate *verb* (**instigated, instigating**) urge; incite; cause something to be done, *instigate a rebellion.* **instigation** *noun*, **instigator** *noun*

instil *verb* (**instilled, instilling**) put ideas into a person's mind gradually.

instinct *noun* a natural tendency or ability, *Birds fly by instinct.* **instinctive** *adjective*, **instinctively** *adverb*

institute¹ *noun* a society or organization; the building used by this.

institute² *verb* (**instituted, instituting**) establish; found; start an inquiry or custom etc.

institution *noun* 1 an institute; a public organization, e.g. a hospital or university. 2 a habit or custom, *the institution of marriage.* 3 instituting something. **institutional** *adjective*

instruct *verb* 1 teach a person a subject or skill. 2 inform, *We are instructed by our clients that you owe them R1 000.* 3 tell a person what he or she must do. **instruction** *noun*, **instructional** *adjective*, **instructor** *noun*

instructive *adjective* giving knowledge.

instrument *noun* 1 a device for producing musical sounds. 2 a tool used for delicate or scientific work. 3 a measuring-device, *the instruments in the cockpit.*

instrumental *adjective* 1 of or using musical instruments. 2 being the means of doing something, *She was instrumental in getting me a job.*

instrumentalist *noun* a person who plays a musical instrument.

insubordinate *adjective* disobedient; rebellious. **insubordination** *noun*

insufferable *adjective* unbearable.

insufficient *adjective* not sufficient.

insular *adjective* of or like an island.

insulate *verb* (**insulated, insulating**) cover or protect something to prevent heat, cold, or electricity etc. from passing in or out. **insulation** *noun*, **insulator** *noun*

insulin *noun* a substance that controls the amount of sugar in the blood.

insult¹ (*say* in-**sult**) *verb* hurt a person's feelings or pride.

insult² (*say* **in**-sult) *noun* an insulting remark or action.

insuperable *adjective* unable to be overcome, *an insuperable difficulty.*

insurance *noun* an agreement to compensate someone for a loss, damage, or injury etc., in return for a payment (called a *premium*) made in advance.

insure *verb* (**insured, insuring**) protect with insurance.

• USAGE: Do not confuse with *ensure.*

insurgent *noun* a rebel. **insurgent** *adjective*

insurmountable *adjective* insuperable.

insurrection *noun* a rebellion.

intact *adjective* not damaged; complete.

intake *noun* 1 taking something in.
2 the number of people or things taken in, *Student intake will increase next year.*

intangible *adjective* not tangible.

integer *noun* a whole number (e.g. 0, 3, 19), not a fraction.

integral (*say* in-tig-ral) *adjective*
1 an essential part of a whole thing, *An engine is an integral part of a car.*
2 whole; complete, *an integral design.*

integrate *verb* (integrated, integrating)
1 make parts into a whole; combine.
2 join together harmoniously into a single community. **integration** *noun*

integrity (*say* in-teg-rit-ee) *noun* honesty.

intellect *noun* the ability to think (contrasted with *feeling* and *instinct*).

intellectual[1] *adjective* 1 of or using the intellect. 2 having a good intellect and a liking for knowledge. **intellectually** *adverb*

intellectual[2] *noun* an intellectual person.

intelligence *noun* 1 being intelligent.
2 information, especially of military value; the people who collect and study this information.

intelligent *adjective* able to learn and understand things; having great mental ability. **intelligently** *adverb*

intelligentsia *noun* intellectual people regarded as a group.

intelligible *adjective* able to be understood. **intelligibly** *adverb*, **intelligibility** *noun*

intend *verb* have something in mind as what you want to do; plan.

intense *adjective* very strong or great. **intensely** *adverb*, **intensity** *noun*

intensify *verb* (intensified, intensifying) make or become more intense. **intensification** *noun*

intensive *adjective* concentrated; thorough; using a lot of effort. **intensively** *adverb*

intent[1] *noun* intention.

intent[2] *adjective* with concentrated attention; very interested. **intently** *adverb*

intention *noun* what a person intends; a purpose or plan.

intentional *adjective* intended; deliberate, not accidental. **intentionally** *adverb*

inter *verb* (interred, interring) bury.

inter- *prefix* between; among.

interact *verb* have an effect upon one another. **interaction** *noun*

interbreed *verb* (interbred, interbreeding) breed with each other; cross-breed.

intercede *verb* (interceded, interceding) intervene on behalf of another person or as a peacemaker. **intercession** *noun*

intercept *verb* stop or catch a person or thing that is going from one place to another. **interception** *noun*

interchange[1] *verb* (interchanged, interchanging) 1 put each of two things into the other's place. 2 exchange, *interchange ideas.* **interchangeable** *adjective*

interchange[2] *noun* 1 interchanging.
2 a road junction designed so that traffic streams do not intersect.

intercom *noun* (*informal*) a system of communication between rooms or compartments, operating rather like a telephone.

intercourse *noun* 1 communication or dealings between people. 2 sexual intercourse (see *sexual*).

intercropping *noun* growing a crop among plants of a different kind, usually in the space between rows.

interdependent *adjective* dependent upon each other.

interdict *noun* a prohibition.

interest[1] *noun* 1 a feeling of wanting to know about or help with something.
2 a thing that interests somebody, *Science fiction is one of my interests.* 3 advantage, *She looks after her own interests.* 4 money paid regularly in return for money lent or deposited.
interest rate the annual interest (sense 4) expressed as a percentage of the sum of money lent or deposited.

interest[2] *verb* arouse a person's interest. **interested** *adjective*, **interesting** *adjective*

interfere *verb* (interfered, interfering)
1 take part in something that has nothing to do with you. 2 get in the way; obstruct, *Don't interfere with Mandla's plans.*
interference *noun*

interim[1] *noun* an interval of time between two events.

interim[2] *adjective* of or in the interim; temporary, *an interim arrangement.*

interior[1] *adjective* inner.

interior[2] *noun* the inside of something; the central or inland part of a country.

interior decorator a person who decorates the insides of houses with paint, curtains, etc.

interject *verb* break in with a remark while someone is speaking.

interjection *noun* 1 an exclamation such as *oh!* or *good heavens!* 2 interjecting; a remark interjected.

interlock *verb* fit into each other.

interloper *noun* an intruder.

interlude *noun* 1 an interval. 2 something happening in an interval or between other events, *a peaceful interlude in the debate.*

intermediary *noun* (*plural* **intermediaries**) a mediator; a go-between.

intermediate *adjective* coming between two things in time, place, or order.

interment *noun* interring; burial.

• USAGE: Do not confuse with *internment.*

interminable *adjective* endless; long and boring. **interminably** *adverb*

intermission *noun* an interval or pause.

intermittent *adjective* happening at intervals; not continuous. **intermittently** *adverb*

intern *verb* imprison in a special camp or area, usually in wartime.

internal *adjective* inside. **internally** *adverb*

internal-combustion engine an engine that produces power by burning fuel inside the engine itself.

international *adjective* of or belonging to more than one country; agreed between nations. **internationally** *adverb*

internment *noun* being interned.

• USAGE: Do not confuse with *interment.*

interpersonal *adjective* between people; social, *interpersonal skills.*

interplanetary *adjective* between planets.

interplay *noun* interaction.

Interpol *abbreviation* International Criminal Police Organization (an international organization of police services which assists members in fighting crime).

interpolate *verb* (**interpolated, interpolating**) 1 interject. 2 insert words; put terms into a mathematical series. **interpolation** *noun*

interpose *verb* (**interposed, interposing**) 1 insert; interject. 2 intervene.

interpret *verb* 1 explain what something means. 2 translate what someone says into another language orally. **interpretation** *noun,* **interpreter** *noun*

interrogate *verb* (**interrogated, interrogating**) question closely or formally. **interrogation** *noun,* **interrogator** *noun*

interrogative *adjective* questioning; expressing a question. **interrogatory** *adjective*

interrupt *verb* prevent from continuing; break in on a person's speech etc. by inserting a remark. **interruption** *noun*

intersect *verb* divide a thing by passing or lying across it; (of lines or roads etc.) cross each other. **intersection** *noun*

intersperse *verb* (**interspersed, interspersing**) insert things here and there in something.

interval *noun* 1 a time between two events or parts of a play etc. 2 a space between two things, *the intervals between seedlings.* **at intervals** with some time or distance between each one.

intervene *verb* (**intervened, intervening**) 1 come between two events, *in the intervening years.* 2 interrupt a discussion or fight etc. to try and stop it or change its result. **intervention** *noun*

interview[1] *noun* a formal meeting with someone to ask him or her questions or to obtain information.

interview[2] *verb* hold an interview with someone. **interviewer** *noun*

intestine *noun* the long tube along which food passes while being absorbed by the body, between the stomach and the anus. **intestinal** *adjective*

intimate[1] (*say* in-tim-at) *adjective* 1 very friendly with someone. 2 private and personal, *intimate thoughts.* 3 detailed, *an intimate knowledge of the country.* **intimately** *adverb,* **intimacy** *noun*

intimate[2] (*say* in-tim-ayt) *verb* (**intimated,**

intimating) tell or hint. **intimation** *noun*

intimidate *verb* (**intimidated**, **intimidating**) frighten a person by threats into doing something. **intimidation** *noun*

into *preposition* used to express **1** movement to the inside, *Go into the house.* **2** change of condition or occupation etc., *It broke into pieces. She went into politics.* **3** (in division) *4 into 20* = 20 divided by 4. **4** (*informal*) interest in something, *She's into chess.*

intolerable *adjective* unbearable. **intolerably** *adverb*

intolerant *adjective* not tolerant. **intolerantly** *adverb*, **intolerance** *noun*

intonation *noun* **1** the tone or pitch of the voice in speaking. **2** intoning.

intone *verb* (**intoned**, **intoning**) recite in a chanting voice.

intoxicate *verb* (**intoxicated**, **intoxicating**) make a person drunk or very excited. **intoxication** *noun*

intra- *prefix* within.

intractable *adjective* unmanageable; difficult to deal with or control. **intractability** *noun*

intransigent *adjective* stubborn. **intransigence** *noun*

intransitive *adjective* (of a verb) used without a direct object after it, e.g. *hear* in *we can hear* (but not in *we can hear you*). (Compare *transitive.*) **intransitively** *adverb*

intravenous (*say* in-tra-**veen**-us) *adjective* into a vein.

intrepid *adjective* fearless; brave. **intrepidly** *adverb*, **intrepidity** *noun*

intricate *adjective* very complicated. **intricately** *adverb*, **intricacy** *noun*

intrigue[1] (*say* in-**treeg**) *verb* (**intrigued**, **intriguing**) **1** plot with someone in an underhand way. **2** interest very much, *The subject intrigues me.*

intrigue[2] *noun* **1** plotting; an underhand plot. **2** (*old use*) a secret love affair.

intrinsic *adjective* belonging naturally in something; inherent, *The concept of ubuntu is intrinsic to African culture.* **intrinsically** *adverb*

intro- *prefix* into; inwards.

introduce *verb* (**introduced**, **introducing**) **1** make a person known to other people. **2** announce a broadcast, speaker, etc. **3** bring something into use or for consideration, *He introduced me to classical music.*

introduction *noun* **1** introducing somebody or something. **2** an explanation put at the beginning of a book or speech etc. **introductory** *adjective*

introspective *adjective* examining your own thoughts and feelings. **introspection** *noun*

introvert *noun* an introspective person. (The opposite is *extrovert.*)

intrude *verb* (**intruded**, **intruding**) come in or join in without being wanted; interfere. **intrusion** *noun*, **intrusive** *adjective*

intruder *noun* **1** someone who intrudes. **2** a burglar.

intuition *noun* the power to know or understand things without having to think hard or without being taught. **intuitive** *adjective*, **intuitively** *adverb*

Inuit (*say* **in**-yoo-it) *noun* (in North America) **1** an Eskimo. **2** the Eskimo language.

inundate *verb* (**inundated**, **inundating**) flood. **inundation** *noun*

inure (*say* in-**yoor**) *verb* (**inured**, **inuring**) accustom, especially to something unpleasant.

invade *verb* (**invaded**, **invading**) **1** attack and enter a country etc. **2** crowd into a place, *Tourists invade Cape Town in summer.* **invader** *noun*

invalid[1] (*say* **in**-va-leed) *noun* a person who is ill or who is weakened by illness.

invalid[2] (*say* in-**val**-id) *adjective* not valid, *This passport is invalid.* **invalidity** *noun*

invalidate *verb* (**invalidated**, **invalidating**) make a thing invalid. **invalidation** *noun*

invaluable *adjective* having a value that is too great to be measured; extremely valuable.

invariable *adjective* not variable; never changing. **invariably** *adverb*

invasion *noun* invading; being invaded.

invective *noun* abusive words.

inveigle (*say* in-**vay**-gul) *verb* (**inveigled**, **inveigling**) entice. **inveiglement** *noun*

invent *verb* **1** be the first person to make or think of a particular thing. **2** make up a false story etc., *invent an excuse*. **invention** *noun*, **inventor** *noun*, **inventive** *adjective*

inventory (*say* in-ven-ter-ee) *noun* (*plural* **inventories**) a detailed list of furniture or goods.

inverse *adjective* reversed; opposite. **inversely** *adverb*

invert *verb* turn something upside down. **inversion** *noun*

inverted commas punctuation marks " " or ' ' put round spoken words.

invertebrate *noun* an animal without a backbone. **invertebrate** *adjective*

invest *verb* **1** use money to make a profit, e.g. by lending it in return for interest to be paid, or by buying stocks and shares or property. **2** give somebody a rank, medal, etc. in a formal ceremony, *invested as governor*. **investment** *noun*, **investor** *noun*

investigate *verb* (**investigated, investigating**) find out as much as you can about something; make a systematic inquiry. **investigation** *noun*, **investigator** *noun*, **investigative** *adjective*

investiture *noun* the process of investing someone with an honour etc.

inveterate *adjective* firmly established; habitual, *an inveterate gambler*.

invidious *adjective* causing resentment because of unfairness.

invigilate *verb* (**invigilated, invigilating**) supervise candidates at an examination. **invigilation** *noun*, **invigilator** *noun*

invigorate *verb* (**invigorated, invigorating**) give a person strength or courage.

invincible *adjective* not able to be defeated; unconquerable. **invincibly** *adverb*, **invincibility** *noun*

invisible *adjective* not visible; not able to be seen. **invisibly** *adverb*, **invisibility** *noun*

invite *verb* (**invited, inviting**) **1** ask a person to come or do something. **2** be likely to cause something to happen, *You are inviting disaster*. **invitation** *noun*

inviting *adjective* attractive; tempting. **invitingly** *adverb*

invoice *noun* a list of goods sent or work done, with the prices charged.

invoke *verb* (**invoked, invoking**) **1** call upon a god in prayer asking for help etc. **2** appeal to for help or protection, *invoke the law*. **invocation** *noun*

involuntary *adjective* not deliberate; unintentional. **involuntarily** *adverb*

involve *verb* (**involved, involving**) **1** have as a part; make a thing necessary, *The job involves hard work*. **2** make someone share in something, *They involved us in their charity work*. **involvement** *noun*

involved *adjective* **1** complicated. **2** concerned; sharing in something, *become involved in charity work*.

invulnerable *adjective* not vulnerable.

inward[1] *adjective* **1** on the inside. **2** going or facing inwards.

inward[2] *adverb* inwards, *an inward-looking person*.

inwards *adverb* towards the inside.

inyanga *noun* a person believed to have the power to heal and to ensure good luck.

iodine *noun* a chemical substance used as an antiseptic.

ion *noun* an electrically charged particle.

ionosphere (*say* I-on-os-feer) *noun* a region of the upper atmosphere, containing ions.

IOU *noun* a written promise to repay a sum of money borrowed.

IQ *abbreviation* intelligence quotient, a number showing how a person's intelligence compares with that of an average person.

ir- *prefix* see **in-**.

irascible (*say* ir-**as**-ib-ul) *adjective* easily becoming angry; irritable.

irate (*say* I-**rayt**) *adjective* angry.

iridescent *adjective* showing rainbow-like colours. **iridescence** *noun*

iris *noun* (*plural* **irises**) **1** a plant with long pointed leaves and large flowers. **2** the coloured part of the eyeball.

irk *verb* annoy.

irksome *adjective* annoying; tiresome.

iron[1] *noun* **1** a hard grey metal. **2** a device with a flat base that is heated for smoothing clothes or cloth. **3** a tool etc. made of iron. **iron** *adjective*

Iron Age the time when tools and weapons were made of iron.

irons *plural noun* fetters.

iron² *verb* smooth clothes or cloth with an iron.

ironic (*say* I-**ron**-ik) *adjective* using irony; full of irony. **ironical** *adjective*, **ironically** *adverb*

ironmonger *noun* a shopkeeper who sells tools and other metal objects. **ironmongery** *noun*

irony (*say* I-ron-ee) *noun* (*plural* **ironies**) **1** saying the opposite of what you mean in order to emphasize it, e.g. saying 'What a lovely day' when it is pouring with rain. **2** an oddly contradictory situation, *The irony of it is that I tripped while telling someone else to be careful.*

irradiation *noun* the treatment of food with small doses of radiation in order to kill bacteria.

irrational *adjective* not rational; illogical. **irrationally** *adverb*

irreducible *adjective* unable to be reduced, *an irreducible minimum.*

irrefutable (*say* ir-**ef**-yoo-ta-bul) *adjective* unable to be refuted.

irregular *adjective* **1** not regular; uneven. **2** against the rules or usual custom. **3** (of troops) not in the regular armed forces. **irregularly** *adverb*, **irregularity** *noun*

irrelevant (*say* ir-**el**-iv-ant) *adjective* not relevant. **irrelevantly** *adverb*, **irrelevance** *noun*

irreparable (*say* ir-**ep**-er-a-bul) *adjective* unable to be repaired or replaced. **irreparably** *adverb*

irreplaceable *adjective* unable to be replaced.

irrepressible *adjective* unable to be repressed. **irrepressibly** *adverb*

irreproachable *adjective* blameless; faultless. **irreproachably** *adverb*

irresistible *adjective* unable to be resisted; very attractive. **irresistibly** *adverb*

irresolute *adjective* feeling uncertain; hesitant. **irresolutely** *adverb*

irrespective *adjective* not taking something into account, *Prizes are awarded to winners, irrespective of age.*

irresponsible *adjective* not showing a proper sense of responsibility. **irresponsibly** *adverb*, **irresponsibility** *noun*

irretrievable *adjective* not able to be retrieved. **irretrievably** *adverb*

irreverent *adjective* not reverent; not respectful. **irreverently** *adverb*, **irreverence** *noun*

irrevocable (*say* ir-**ev**-ok-a-bul) *adjective* unable to be revoked or altered. **irrevocably** *adverb*

irrigate *verb* (**irrigated, irrigating**) supply land with water so that crops etc. can grow. **irrigation** *noun*

irritable *adjective* easily annoyed; bad-tempered. **irritably** *adverb*, **irritability** *noun*

irritate *verb* (**irritated, irritating**) **1** annoy. **2** cause itching. **irritation** *noun*, **irritant** *adjective* & *noun*

irrupt *verb* enter forcibly or violently. **irruption** *noun*

● USAGE: Do not confuse with *erupt.*

isi- *prefix* the language and culture of, e.g. isiXhosa (= Xhosa language and culture).

Islam *noun* the religion of Muslims. **Islamic** *adjective*

island *noun* **1** a piece of land surrounded by water. **2** something resembling an island because it is isolated.

islander *noun* an inhabitant of an island.

isle (*say as* I'll) *noun* (*poetic* & *in names*) an island.

isn't (*mainly spoken*) is not.

iso- *prefix* equal (as in *isobar*).

isobar (*say* I-so-bar) *noun* a line (on a map) connecting places that have the same atmospheric pressure.

isolate *verb* (**isolated, isolating**) place a person or thing apart or alone; separate. **isolation** *noun*

isosceles (*say* I-**soss**-il-eez) *adjective* having two sides equal, *an isosceles triangle.*

isotope *noun* a form of an element that differs from other forms in its nuclear properties but not in its chemical properties.

issue¹ *verb* (**issued, issuing**) **1** come out; go out; flow out. **2** supply; give out,

We issued one blanket to each refugee. **3** put out for sale; publish. **4** send out, *They issued a gale warning.*

issue² *noun* **1** a subject for discussion or concern, *What are the real issues?* **2** a result, *Await the issue of the trial.* **3** something issued, *The Christmas issue of our magazine.* **4** issuing something, *The issue of passports is held up.*

isthmus (*say* **iss**-mus) *noun* (*plural* **isthmuses**) a narrow strip of land connecting two larger pieces of land.

it *pronoun* **1** the thing being talked about. **2** the player who has to catch others in a game. The word is also used **3** in statements about the weather, *It is raining* or about circumstances etc., *It is ten kilometres to the beach.* **4** as an indefinite object, *Run for it!* **5** to refer to a phrase, *It is unlikely that she will fail.*

italic (*say* it-**al**-ik) *adjective* printed with sloping letters (called **italics**) *like this.*

itch¹ *verb* **1** have or feel a tickling sensation in the skin that makes you want to scratch it. **2** long to do something.

itch² *noun* (*plural* **itches**) **1** an itching feeling. **2** a longing, *an itch for adventure.* **itchy** *adjective*, **itchiness** *noun*

item *noun* **1** one thing in a list or group of things. **2** one piece of news in a newspaper or bulletin.

itinerant (*say* it-**in**-er-ant) *adjective* travelling from place to place, *an itinerant preacher.*

itinerary (*say* I-**tin**-er-er-ee) *noun* (*plural* **itineraries**) a list of places to be visited on a journey; a route.

its *possessive pronoun* belonging to it, *The cat hurt its paw.*
● USAGE: Do not put an apostrophe into *its* unless you mean 'it is' or 'it has' (see the next entry).

it's (*mainly spoken*) **1** it is, *It's very hot.* **2** it has, *It's broken all records.*
● USAGE: Do not confuse with *its.*

itself *pronoun* it and nothing else. (Compare *herself.*)
by itself on its own; alone.

ivory *noun* **1** the hard creamy-white substance that forms elephants' tusks.

2 a creamy-white colour.

ivy *noun* (*plural* **ivies**) a climbing evergreen plant with shiny leaves.

izibongo *plural noun* praise poetry.

Jj

ja *interjection* (*informal*) yes.

jab¹ *verb* (**jabbed, jabbing**) poke roughly; push a thing into something.

jab² *noun* **1** a jabbing movement. **2** (*informal*) an injection.

jabber *verb* speak quickly and not clearly; chatter. **jabber** *noun*

jacaranda *noun* a tropical tree with trumpet-shaped blue flowers.

jack¹ *noun* **1** a device for lifting something heavy off the ground. **2** a playing-card with a picture of a young man. **3** a small white ball aimed at in bowls.
jack of all trades someone who can do many different kinds of work.

jack² *verb* lift with a jack.

jackal *noun* a wild animal rather like a dog, which scavenges in packs for food.

jackass *noun* (*plural* **jackasses**) **1** a male donkey. **2** a stupid person.
jackass penguin a penguin with a call like a donkey's bray.

jackdaw *noun* a kind of small crow.

jacket *noun* **1** a short coat, usually reaching to the hips. **2** a cover to keep the heat in a water-tank etc. **3** a paper wrapper for a book. **4** the skin of a potato that is baked without being peeled.

jack-in-the-box *noun* a toy figure that springs out of a box when the lid is lifted.

jackknife *verb* (**jackknifed, jackknifing**) fold one part against another, like a folding knife.

jackpot *noun* an amount of prize-money that increases until someone wins it.

jade *noun* a green stone that is carved to make ornaments.

jaded *adjective* tired and bored.

jagged (*say* **jag**-id) *adjective* having an uneven edge with sharp points.

jaguar *noun* a large fierce South American animal rather like a leopard.

jail *noun* a gaol. **jailer** *noun*

Jain (*say as* jine) *noun* a believer in an Indian religion rather like Buddhism.

jalopy *noun* (*plural* **jalopies**) (*informal*) a dilapidated old car.

jam[1] *noun* 1 a sweet food made of fruit boiled with sugar until it is thick. 2 a lot of people, cars, or logs etc. crowded together so that movement is difficult. 3 (*informal*) a difficult situation, *in a jam*.

jam[2] *verb* (**jammed, jamming**) 1 crowd or squeeze into a space. 2 make or become fixed and difficult to move. 3 push something forcibly, *jam the brakes on*. 4 block a broadcast by causing interference with the transmission.

jamb (*say* jam) *noun* a side-post of a doorway or window-frame.

jamboree *noun* 1 a large party or celebration. 2 a large gathering of Scouts.

Jan Fiskaal *noun* the black and white fiscal shrike or butcher bird, which stores its prey of small lizards etc. by impaling them on barbed wire or thorn bushes.

jangle *verb* (**jangled, jangling**) make a loud harsh ringing sound. **jangle** *noun*

janitor *noun* a caretaker.

jar[1] *noun* a container made of glass or pottery.

jar[2] *verb* (**jarred, jarring**) 1 cause an unpleasant jolt or shock. 2 sound harshly.

jar[3] *noun* a jarring effect.

jargon *noun* special words used by a group of people, *scientists' jargon*.

jasmine *noun* a shrub with yellow or white flowers, often strongly scented.

jaundice *noun* a disease in which the skin becomes yellow.

jaunt *noun* a short trip. **jaunting** *noun*

jaunty *adjective* (**jauntier, jauntiest**) lively and cheerful. **jauntily** *adverb*, **jauntiness** *noun*

javelin *noun* a lightweight spear.

jaw *noun* 1 either of the two bones that form the framework of the mouth. 2 the lower part of the face. 3 something shaped like the jaws or used for gripping things.

jay *noun* a noisy brightly-coloured bird.

jazz *noun* a kind of music with strong rhythm. **jazzy** *adjective*

jealous *adjective* 1 unhappy or resentful because you feel that someone is your rival or is better or luckier than yourself. 2 careful in keeping something, *He is very jealous of his own rights*. **jealously** *adverb*, **jealousy** *noun*

jeans *plural noun* trousers made of strong cotton fabric, especially denim.

jeer *verb* laugh or shout at somebody rudely or scornfully. **jeer** *noun*

jelly *noun* (*plural* **jellies**) 1 a soft transparent food. 2 any soft slippery substance, *petroleum jelly*. **jellied** *adjective*

jellyfish *noun* (*plural* **jellyfish**) a sea animal with a body like jelly.

jemmy *noun* (*plural* **jemmies**) a burglar's crowbar.

jeopardize (*say* jep-er-dyz) *verb* (**jeopardized, jeopardizing**) endanger.

jeopardy (*say* jep-er-dee) *noun* danger.

jerk[1] *verb* make a sudden sharp movement; pull suddenly; move unevenly.

jerk[2] *noun* a jerking movement. **jerky** *adjective*, **jerkily** *adverb*

jerkin *noun* a sleeveless jacket.

jerry-built *adjective* built badly and with poor materials.

jersey *noun* (*plural* **jerseys**) 1 a pullover with sleeves. 2 a plain machine-knitted material used for making clothes.

jest[1] *noun* a joke.

jest[2] *verb* make jokes.

jester *noun* a professional entertainer at a royal court in Europe in the Middle Ages.

Jesuit *noun* a member of the Society of Jesus (a Roman Catholic religious order).

jet[1] *noun* 1 a stream of water, gas, flame, etc. shot out from a narrow opening. 2 a narrow opening from which a jet comes, *the gas jets on the stove*. 3 an aircraft driven by engines that send out a high-speed jet of hot gases at the back.

jet set wealthy and fashionable people.

jet[2] *verb* (**jetted, jetting**) 1 come or send out in a strong stream. 2 (*informal*) travel in a jet aircraft.

jet[3] *noun* 1 a hard black mineral substance. 2 a deep glossy black colour.

jetsam *noun* goods thrown overboard and washed ashore from a ship in distress.

jettison *verb* throw overboard or away; release or drop something from an aircraft or spacecraft in flight.

jetty *noun* (*plural* **jetties**) a small landing-stage.

Jew *noun* a member of a people descended from the ancient tribes of Israel, or a person who believes in the religion of this people. **Jewish** *adjective*

jewel *noun* a precious stone; an ornament containing precious stones. **jewelled** *adjective*

jeweller *noun* a person who sells or makes jewellery.

jewellery *noun* jewels and similar ornaments for wearing.

jib[1] *noun* 1 a triangular sail stretching forward from a ship's front mast. 2 the projecting arm of a crane.

jib[2] *verb* (**jibbed, jibbing**) be reluctant or unwilling to do something.

jiffy *noun* (*informal*) a moment.

jig[1] *noun* 1 a lively jumping dance. 2 a device that holds something in place while you work on it with tools.

jig[2] *verb* (**jigged, jigging**) move up and down quickly and jerkily.

jiggle *verb* (**jiggled, jiggling**) rock or jerk something lightly.

jigsaw *noun* 1 a saw that can cut curved shapes. 2 a jigsaw puzzle.

jigsaw puzzle a picture cut into irregular pieces which are then shuffled and fitted together again for amusement.

jihad *noun* (in Islam) a holy war.

jilt *verb* abandon a boy-friend or girl-friend, especially after promising to marry him or her.

jingle[1] *verb* (**jingled, jingling**) make or cause to make a tinkling sound.

jingle[2] *noun* 1 a jingling sound. 2 a very simple verse or tune.

jitters *plural noun* (*informal*) nervousness. **jittery** *adjective*

job *noun* 1 work that someone does regularly to earn a living. 2 a piece of work to be done. 3 (*informal*) a difficult task, *You'll have a job to lift that box.* 4 (*informal*) a thing; a state of affairs, *It's a good job you're here.*

jobless unemployed.

jockey *noun* (*plural* **jockeys**) a person who rides horses in races.

jocular *adjective* joking. **jocularly** *adverb*, **jocularity** *noun*

jodhpurs (*say* **jod-perz**) *plural noun* trousers for horse-riding, fitting closely from the knee to the ankle.

jog[1] *verb* (**jogged, jogging**) 1 run or trot slowly, especially for exercise. 2 give something a slight push. **jogger** *noun* **jog someone's memory** help him or her to remember something.

jog[2] *noun* 1 a slow run or trot. 2 a slight knock or push.

joggle *verb* (**joggled, joggling**) shake slightly; move jerkily. **joggle** *noun*

jogtrot *noun* a slow steady trot.

join[1] *verb* 1 put or come together; fasten; unite; connect. 2 do something together with others, *We all joined in the chorus.* 3 become a member of a group or organization etc., *join the Navy.* **join up** enlist in the armed forces.

join[2] *noun* a place where things join.

joiner *noun* a person whose job is to make furniture and fitments out of wood. **joinery** *noun*

joint[1] *noun* 1 a join. 2 the place where two bones fit together. 3 a large piece of meat cut ready for cooking.

joint[2] *adjective* shared or done by two or more people, nations, etc., *a joint project*; combined. **jointly** *adverb*

joist *noun* any of the long beams supporting a floor or ceiling.

joke[1] *noun* something said or done to make people laugh.

joke[2] *verb* (**joked, joking**) make jokes.

joker *noun* 1 someone who jokes. 2 an extra playing-card with a jester on it.

jol[1] *verb* (**jolled, jolling**) (*slang*) have fun.

jol[2] *noun* (*slang*) a good time; a party.

jolly[1] *adjective* (**jollier, jolliest**) cheerful; merry. **jollity** *noun*

jolly[2] *adverb* (*informal*) very, *jolly good.*

jolly[3] *verb* (**jollied, jollying**) (*informal*) keep someone in a good humour.

jolt[1] *verb* **1** shake or dislodge with a sudden sharp movement. **2** move along jerkily, e.g. on a rough road. **3** give someone a shock, *She was jolted by the news.*

jolt[2] *noun* **1** a jolting movement. **2** a shock.

jostle *verb* (**jostled, jostling**) push roughly, especially in a crowd.

jot *verb* (**jotted, jotting**) write something quickly, *jot it down.*

jotter *noun* a note-pad or notebook.

joule (*say* jool) *noun* a unit of work or energy.

journal *noun* **1** a newspaper or magazine. **2** a diary.

journalist *noun* a person who writes for a newspaper or magazine. **journalism** *noun*, **journalistic** *adjective*

journey[1] *noun* (*plural* **journeys**) **1** going from one place to another. **2** the distance or time taken to travel somewhere, *two days' journey.*

journey[2] *verb* make a journey.

joust (*say* jowst) *verb* fight on horseback with lances.

jovial *adjective* cheerful and good-humoured. **jovially** *adverb*, **joviality** *noun*

jowl *noun* **1** the jaw or cheek. **2** loose skin on the neck.

joy *noun* **1** a feeling of great pleasure; gladness. **2** a thing that causes joy, *Her work is a joy to mark.* **joyful** *adjective*, **joyfully** *adverb*, **joyfulness** *noun*, **joyous** *adjective*, **joyously** *adverb*

joy-ride *noun* a car ride taken for pleasure, usually without the owner's permission. **joy-riding** *noun*

joystick *noun* **1** the control lever of an aircraft. **2** a device for moving a cursor etc. on a VDU screen.

JSE *abbreviation* Johannesburg Stock Exchange.

jubilant *adjective* rejoicing; triumphant. **jubilantly** *adverb*, **jubilation** *noun*

jubilee (*say* joo-bil-ee) *noun* a special anniversary, *silver* (25th), *golden* (50th), *and diamond* (60th) *jubilee.*

Judaism (*say* joo-day-izm) *noun* the religion of the Jewish people.

judder *verb* shake noisily or violently.

judge[1] *noun* **1** a person appointed to hear cases in a lawcourt and decide what should be done. **2** a person deciding who has won a contest or competition, or the value or quality of something.

judge[2] *verb* (**judged, judging**) **1** act as a judge. **2** form and give an opinion. **3** estimate, *He judged the distance carefully.*

judgement *noun* **1** judging. **2** the decision made by a lawcourt. **3** someone's opinion. **4** the ability to judge wisely, *show good judgement.* **5** something considered as a punishment from God, *It's a judgement on you!*

judicial *adjective* of lawcourts, judges, or judgements. **judicially** *adverb*

judiciary (*say* joo-dish-er-ee) *noun* all the judges in a country.

judicious (*say* joo-dish-us) *adjective* having or showing good sense. **judiciously** *adverb*

judo *noun* a Japanese method of self-defence without using weapons.

juffrou (*say* yu-froh) *noun* a title of respect used when addressing an unmarried woman.

jug *noun* a container for holding and pouring liquids, with a handle and a lip.

juggernaut *noun* a huge lorry.

juggle *verb* (**juggled, juggling**) **1** toss and keep a number of objects in the air, for entertainment. **2** rearrange or alter things skilfully or in order to deceive people. **juggler** *noun*

jugular *adjective* of or in the throat or neck, *the jugular veins.*

juice *noun* **1** the liquid from fruit, vegetables, or other food. **2** a liquid produced by the body, *the digestive juices.* **juicy** *adjective*

juke-box *noun* a machine that plays a record when you put a coin in.

jukskei (*say* yuk-skay) *noun* a game where pegs are thrown at a target on the ground.

jumble[1] *verb* (**jumbled, jumbling**) mix things up into a confused mass.

jumble[2] *noun* a confused mixture of things; a muddle.

jumble sale a sale of second-hand goods.

jumbo *noun* (*plural* **jumbos**) **1** something

very large; a jumbo jet. **2** an elephant.

jumbo jet a very large jet aircraft.

jump¹ *verb* **1** move up suddenly from the ground into the air. **2** go over something by jumping, *jump the fence*. **3** pass over something; miss out part of a book etc. **4** move suddenly in surprise, *You made me jump!* **5** pass quickly to a different place or level.

jump at (*informal*) accept something eagerly.

jump the gun start before you should.

jump the queue not wait your turn.

jump² *noun* **1** a jumping movement. **2** an obstacle to jump over. **3** a sudden rise or change.

jumper *noun* **1** a person or animal that jumps. **2** a jersey.

jumpy *adjective* nervous.

junction *noun* **1** a join. **2** a place where roads or railway lines meet.

juncture *noun* **1** a point of time, especially in a crisis. **2** a join.

jungle *noun* a thick tangled forest, especially in the tropics. **jungly** *adjective*

junior¹ *adjective* **1** younger. **2** for young children, *a junior school*. **3** lower in rank or importance, *junior officers*.

junior² *noun* a junior person.

juniper *noun* an evergreen shrub with prickly leaves and small cones.

junk¹ *noun* rubbish; things of no value.

junk food food that is not nourishing.

junk mail advertisements etc. sent by post to people who have not asked for them.

junk² *noun* a Chinese sailing-boat.

jurisdiction *noun* authority; official power, especially to interpret and apply the law.

juror *noun* a member of a jury.

jury *noun* (*plural* **juries**) a group of people (usually twelve) appointed to give a verdict about a case in a lawcourt.

just¹ *adjective* **1** giving proper consideration to everyone's claims. **2** deserved; right in amount etc., *a just reward*. **justly** *adverb*, **justness** *noun*

just² *adverb* **1** exactly, *It's just what I wanted*. **2** only; simply, *I just wanted to see him*. **3** barely; by only a small amount, *just*

below the knee. **4** at this moment or only a little while ago, *She has just gone*.

justice *noun* **1** being just; fair treatment. **2** legal proceedings, *a court of justice*. **3** a judge or magistrate.

justify *verb* (**justified, justifying**) show that something is fair, just, or reasonable. **justification** *noun*

jut *verb* (**jutted, jutting**) stick out.

jute *noun* fibre from tropical plants, used for making sacks etc.

juvenile *adjective* of or for young people. **juvenile delinquent** a young person who has broken the law.

juxtapose *verb* (**juxtaposed, juxtaposing**) put things side by side. **juxtaposition** *noun*

Kk

kabeljou (*say* **ka**-bel-yoh) *noun* (*plural* **kabeljou**) a sea-fish used as food.

kakiebos (*say* **kah**-kee-bos) *noun* (*plural* **kakiebos** or **kakiebosse**) any of several kinds of weed.

kale *noun* a kind of cabbage.

kaleidoscope (*say* kal-**I**-dos-kohp) *noun* a tube that you look through to see brightly coloured patterns which change as you turn the end of the tube. **kaleidoscopic** *adjective*

kangaroo *noun* an Australian animal that jumps along on its strong hind legs. (See *marsupial*.)

kaolin *noun* fine white clay used in making porcelain and in medicine.

karakul *noun* **1** a kind of sheep which has a dark curled fleece when young. **2** the fur of this young sheep.

karate (*say* ka-**rah**-tee) *noun* a Japanese method of self-defence in which the hands and feet are used as weapons.

kaross *noun* a rug, blanket, etc. of animal skins sewn together.

kayak *noun* a small canoe with a covering that fits round the canoeist's waist.

kebabs *plural noun* small pieces of meat etc. cooked on a skewer.

keel[1] *noun* the long piece of wood or metal along the bottom of a boat.
on an even keel steady.

keel[2] *verb* tilt; overturn, *The ship keeled over.*

keen[1] *adjective* 1 enthusiastic; very interested in or eager to do something, *a keen swimmer.* 2 sharp, *a keen edge.* 3 piercingly cold, *a keen wind.* **keenly** *adverb,* **keenness** *noun*

keen[2] *verb* wail, especially in mourning.

keep[1] *verb* (**kept, keeping**) This word has many uses, including 1 have something and look after it or not get rid of it. 2 stay or cause to stay in the same condition etc., *keep still; keep it hot.* 3 do something continually, *She keeps laughing.* 4 respect and not break, *keep a promise.* 5 make entries in, *keep a diary.*
keep up make the same progress as others; continue something.

keep[2] *noun* 1 maintenance; the food etc. that you need to live, *She earns her keep.* 2 a strong tower in a castle.
for keeps (*informal*) permanently; to keep, *Is this yo-yo mine for keeps?*

keeper *noun* a person who looks after an animal, building, etc., *the park keeper.*

keeping *noun* care; looking after something, *in safe keeping.*
in keeping with conforming to; suiting, *Modern furniture is not in keeping with an old house.*

keepsake *noun* a gift to be kept in memory of the person who gave it.

keg *noun* a small barrel.

kelp *noun* a large seaweed.

kennel *noun* a shelter for a dog.

keratin *noun* a protein found in hair, feathers, hooves, claws, horns, etc.

kerb *noun* the edge of a pavement.

kerchief *noun* (*old use*) 1 a square scarf worn on the head. 2 a handkerchief.

kernel *noun* the part inside the shell of a nut etc.

kestrel *noun* a small falcon.

ketchup *noun* a thick sauce made from tomatoes and vinegar etc.

kettle *noun* a container with a spout and handle, for boiling water in.

kettledrum *noun* a drum consisting of a large metal bowl with skin or plastic over the top.

key *noun* 1 a piece of metal shaped so that it will open a lock. 2 a device for winding up a clock or clockwork toy etc. 3 a small lever to be pressed by a finger, e.g. on a piano or a typewriter. 4 a system of notes in music, *the key of C major.* 5 a fact or clue that explains or solves something, *the key to the mystery.*

keyboard *noun* the set of keys on a piano, computer, etc.

keyhole *noun* the hole through which a key is put into a lock.

keynote *noun* 1 the note on which a key in music is based, *The keynote of C major is C.* 2 the main idea in something said, written, or done; a theme.

keystone *noun* 1 the central wedge-shaped stone in an arch, locking the others together. 2 the main principle of a system, policy, etc.

kgotla (*say* **khot**-la) *noun* (*plural* **makgotla** or **kgotlas**) 1 a meeting-place of a traditional council. 2 the members of this council.

khaki *noun* a dull yellowish-brown colour, used for military uniforms.
khakibos kakiebos.

khaya (*say* **ky**-a) *noun* (*slang*) a house or home.

kibbutz *noun* (*plural* **kibbutzim**) a commune in Israel, especially for farming.

kick[1] *verb* 1 hit or move a person or thing with your foot. 2 move your legs about vigorously. 3 (of a gun) recoil when fired.
kick out get rid of; dismiss.
kick up (*informal*) make a noise or fuss.

kick[2] *noun* 1 a kicking movement. 2 the recoiling movement of a gun. 3 (*informal*) a thrill. 4 (*informal*) an interest or activity, *He's on a health kick.*

kid[1] *noun* 1 a young goat. 2 fine leather made from goat's skin. 3 (*informal*) a child.

kid[2] *verb* (**kidded, kidding**) (*informal*) deceive in fun; tease.

kidnap *verb* (**kidnapped, kidnapping**) abduct, especially in order to obtain a ransom. **kidnapper** *noun*

kidney *noun* (*plural* **kidneys**) either of the

two organs in the body that remove waste products from the blood and excrete urine into the bladder.

kierie (*say* **kee**-ree) *noun* a stick used as a walking-stick or weapon.

kill[1] *verb* **1** make a person or thing die. **2** destroy or put an end to something. **killer** *noun*

kill time occupy time idly while waiting.

kill[2] *noun* **1** killing. **2** the animal or animals killed by a hunter.

kiln *noun* an oven for hardening pottery or bricks, for drying hops, or for burning lime.

kilo *noun* (*plural* **kilos**) a kilogram.

kilo- *prefix* one thousand (as in *kilolitre* = 1 000 litres, *kilohertz* = 1 000 hertz).

kilogram *noun* a unit of mass or weight equal to 1 000 grams.

kilometre (*say* **kil**-o-meet-er or kil-**om**-it-er) *noun* a unit of length equal to 1 000 metres.

kilowatt *noun* a unit of electrical power equal to 1 000 watts.

kilowatt-hour a measure of electrical energy equivalent to a consumption of 1 000 watts for one hour.

kilt *noun* a kind of pleated skirt worn especially by Scotsmen. **kilted** *adjective*

kimono *noun* (*plural* **kimonos**) a long loose Japanese robe.

kin *noun* a person's relatives. **kinsman** *noun*, **kinswoman** *noun*

next of kin a person's closest relative.

kind[1] *noun* a class of similar things or animals; a sort or type.

payment in kind payment in goods not in money.

● USAGE: Correct use is *this kind of thing* or *these kinds of things* (not 'these kind of things').

kind[2] *adjective* friendly and helpful; considerate. **kind-hearted** *adjective*, **kindness** *noun*

kindergarten *noun* a school or class for very young children.

kindle *verb* (**kindled, kindling**) **1** start a flame; set light to something. **2** begin burning.

kindling *noun* small pieces of wood for use in lighting fires.

kindly *adjective* (**kindlier, kindliest**) kind, *a kindly smile*. **kindliness** *noun*

kindred[1] *noun* kin.

kindred[2] *adjective* related; similar, *chemistry and kindred subjects*.

kinetic *adjective* of or produced by movement, *kinetic energy*.

king *noun* **1** a man who is the ruler of a country through inheriting the position. **2** a person or thing regarded as supreme, *the lion is the king of beasts*. **3** the most important piece in chess. **4** a playing-card with a picture of a king. **kingly** *adjective*, **kingship** *noun*

kingdom *noun* **1** a country ruled by a king or queen. **2** any one of the three divisions of the natural world, *the animal, plant, and mineral kingdoms*. **3** the highest category in biological classification.

kingfisher *noun* a small bird with blue feathers that dives to catch fish.

kingklip *noun* a sea-fish used as food.

kink *noun* **1** a short twist in a rope, wire, piece of hair, etc. **2** a peculiarity. **kinky** *adjective*

kiosk *noun* **1** a telephone box. **2** a small hut or stall where newspapers, sweets, etc. are sold.

kipper *noun* a smoked herring.

kiss[1] *noun* (*plural* **kisses**) touching somebody with your lips as a sign of affection. **kiss of life** mouth-to-mouth resuscitation.

kiss[2] *verb* give somebody a kiss.

kist *noun* a chest; a box with a lid.

kit *noun* **1** equipment or clothes for a particular occupation. **2** a set of parts sold ready to be fitted together, *a model car kit*.

kitchen *noun* a room in which meals are prepared and cooked.

kitchenette *noun* a small kitchen.

kite *noun* **1** a light framework covered with cloth, paper, etc. and flown in the wind on the end of a long piece of string. **2** a large hawk.

kith *noun* **kith and kin** friends and relatives.

kitten *noun* a very young cat.

kitty *noun* (*plural* **kitties**) **1** an amount of money that you can win in a card-game.

2 a fund for use by several people.

kiwi (*say* **kee**-wee) *noun* (*plural* **kiwis**) a New Zealand bird that cannot fly.

kleptomania *noun* an uncontrollable tendency to steal things. **kleptomaniac** *noun*

klipspringer *noun* a small mountain antelope.

kloof *noun* a valley, gorge, or ravine.

knack *noun* a special skill.

knacker *noun* a person who buys and slaughters horses and sells the meat and hides.

knapsack *noun* a bag carried on the back by soldiers, hikers, etc.

knave *noun* **1** (*old use*) a dishonest man; a rogue. **2** a jack in playing-cards.

knead *verb* press and stretch something soft (especially dough) with your hands.

knee *noun* the joint in the middle of the leg.

kneecap *noun* the small bone covering the front of the knee-joint.

kneel *verb* (**knelt, kneeling**) be or get yourself in a position on your knees.

knell *noun* the sound of a bell rung solemnly after a death or at a funeral.

knickerbockers *plural noun* loose-fitting short trousers gathered in at the knees.

knickers *plural noun* a woman's or girl's undergarment worn on the lower part of the body.

knick-knack *noun* a small ornament.

knife[1] *noun* (*plural* **knives**) a cutting instrument consisting of a sharp blade set in a handle.

knife[2] *verb* (**knifed, knifing**) stab with a knife.

knight[1] *noun* **1** a man who has been given the rank that allows him to put 'Sir' before his name. **2** a piece in chess, with a horse's head. **3** (in medieval times in Europe) a man of noble rank whose duty was to fight for his king, e.g. King Arthur's knights of the Round Table. **knighthood** *noun*

knight[2] *verb* make someone a knight.

knit *verb* (**knitted** or **knit, knitting**) make something by looping together wool or other yarn, using long needles or a machine. **knitter** *noun*, **knitting-needle** *noun*

knit your brow frown.

knob *noun* **1** the round handle of a door, drawer, etc. **2** a round projecting part. **3** a small lump. **knobbly** *adjective*, **knobby** *adjective*

knobkerrie *noun* a stick with a round knob at one end, used as a club or thrown.

knock[1] *verb* **1** hit a thing hard or so as to make a noise. **2** produce by hitting, *knock a hole in it.* **3** (*informal*) criticize unfavourably, *Stop knocking the government!*

knock off (*informal*) stop working; deduct something from a price.

knock out make a person unconscious, especially by a blow to the head.

knock[2] *noun* the act or sound of knocking.

knocker *noun* a hinged metal device for knocking on a door.

knock-out *noun* **1** knocking somebody out. **2** a contest in which the loser in each round has to drop out. **3** (*informal*) an amazing person or thing, *He's an absolute knock-out!*

knoll *noun* a small round hill; a mound.

knot[1] *noun* **1** a place where a piece of string, rope, or ribbon etc. is twisted round itself or another piece. **2** a tangle; a lump, *Her hair was full of knots.* **3** a round spot on a piece of wood where a branch joined it. **4** a cluster of people or things. **5** a unit for measuring the speed of ships and aircraft, 1 852 metres per hour.

knot[2] *verb* (**knotted, knotting**) **1** tie or fasten with a knot. **2** entangle.

knotty *adjective* (**knottier, knottiest**) **1** full of knots. **2** difficult; puzzling.

know *verb* (**knew, known, knowing**) **1** have something in your mind that you have learnt or discovered. **2** recognize or be familiar with a person or place, *I've known him for years.* **3** understand, *She knows how to please us.*

know-all *noun* a person who behaves as if he or she knows everything.

know-how *noun* skill; ability for a particular job.

knowing *adjective* showing that you know something, *a knowing look.*

knowingly *adverb* **1** in a knowing way. **2** deliberately.

knowledge *noun* 1 knowing. 2 all that a person knows. 3 all that is known.
to my knowledge as far as I know.

knowledgeable *adjective* well-informed.
knowledgeably *adverb*

knuckle[1] *noun* a joint in the finger.

knuckle[2] *verb* (**knuckled, knuckling**)
knuckle down to buckle down to.
knuckle under be submissive.

koala (*say* koh-**ah**-la) *noun* an Australian animal that looks like a small bear.

kob *noun* (*plural* **kob**) a kabeljou.

koeksister *noun* a twisted or plaited doughnut, deep-fried and dipped in syrup.

konfyt (*say* kon-**fayt**) *noun* a fruit preserve; jam.

koppie *noun* a small hill.

Koran (*say* kor-**ahn**) *noun* the sacred book of Islam, written in Arabic, believed by Muslims to contain the words of Allah revealed to the prophet Muhammad.

kosher *adjective* keeping to Jewish laws about food, *kosher meat.*

kraal[1] *noun* 1 an enclosed area for protecting farm animals. 2 a village or settlement.

kraal[2] *verb* drive animals into an enclosed area for protection.

kramat *noun* a tomb or shrine of a Muslim holy person.

krans *noun* (*plural* **kranses** or **kranse**) a cliff face; a steep or overhanging crag.

kreef *noun* (*plural* **kreef**) a rock lobster, also called a crayfish.

kremlin *noun* a citadel in a Russian city.
the Kremlin the government of the former USSR, in Moscow.

krill *noun* a mass of tiny shrimp-like creatures, the chief food of certain whales.

kudos (*say* **kew**-doss) *noun* honour and glory.

kudu *noun* (*plural* **kudu**) a white-striped antelope with spiral horns.

kumquat *noun* a small citrus fruit.

kung fu *noun* a Chinese method of self-defence, rather like karate.

kwa- *prefix* at the place of, e.g. KwaZulu (= in Zululand).

kwashiorkor *noun* a disease caused by a diet lacking in protein.

Ll

laager *noun* (in history) an enclosed area formed by wagons brought together to protect the people inside, and from which these people could fire on attackers.

laatlammetjie (*say* laht-lam-a-kee) *noun* a child who is born long after his or her brothers and sisters.

lab *noun* (*informal*) a laboratory.

label[1] *noun* a small piece of paper, cloth, or metal etc. fixed on or beside something to show what it is or what it costs, or its owner or destination etc.

label[2] *verb* (**labelled, labelling**) put a label on something.

labial (*say* **lay**-bee-al) *adjective* of the lips.

laboratory *noun* (*plural* **laboratories**) a room or building equipped for scientific experiments.

laborious *adjective* 1 needing or using much hard work. 2 explaining something at great length and with obvious effort.
laboriously *adverb*

labour[1] *noun* 1 hard work. 2 a task. 3 workers. 4 the contractions of the womb when a baby is being born.

labour[2] *verb* 1 work hard. 2 explain something laboriously, *Don't labour the point.*

labourer *noun* a person who does hard manual work, especially outdoors.

Labrador *noun* a large black or light-brown dog.

laburnum *noun* a tree with hanging yellow flowers.

labyrinth *noun* a complicated arrangement of paths etc.

lace[1] *noun* 1 net-like material with decorative patterns of holes in it. 2 a piece of thin cord or leather for fastening a shoe etc.
lacy *adjective*

lace[2] *verb* (**laced, lacing**) 1 fasten with a lace. 2 thread a cord etc. through something. 3 add spirits to a drink.

lacerate *verb* (**lacerated, lacerating**) injure flesh by cutting or tearing it; wound.
laceration *noun*

lachrymal (*say* lak-rim-al) *adjective* of tears; producing tears, *lachrymal ducts*.

lack[1] *noun* being without something.

lack[2] *verb* be without, *He lacks courage*.

lackadaisical *adjective* lacking vigour or determination; careless.

lackey *noun* (*plural* **lackeys**) a footman.

laconic *adjective* terse, *a laconic reply*. **laconically** *adverb*

lacquer *noun* a hard glossy varnish. **lacquered** *adjective*

lacrosse *noun* a game using a stick with a net on it to catch and throw a ball.

lactose *noun* a kind of sugar that is found in milk.

lacy *adjective* of or like lace.

lad *noun* a boy; a youth.

ladder[1] *noun* 1 a device with two upright pieces of wood or metal etc. and cross-pieces (*rungs*), for use in climbing. 2 a vertical ladder-like flaw in a stocking etc. where a stitch has become undone.

ladder[2] *verb* cause or have a ladder in a stocking etc.

laden *adjective* carrying a heavy load.

ladle[1] *noun* a large deep spoon with a long handle, used for lifting and pouring liquids.

ladle[2] *verb* (**ladled, ladling**) lift and pour with a ladle.

lady *noun* (*plural* **ladies**) 1 a well-mannered woman. 2 a woman of good social position. 3 (in polite use) a woman. **ladylike** *adjective*, **ladyship** *noun* **Lady** *noun* the title of a noblewoman.

ladybird *noun* a small flying beetle, usually red with black spots.

lag[1] *verb* (**lagged, lagging**) go too slowly and fail to keep up with others.

lag[2] *noun* lagging; a delay.

lag[3] *verb* (**lagged, lagging**) wrap pipes or boilers etc. in insulating material to keep them warm.

lager (*say* lah-ger) *noun* a light beer.

laggard *noun* a person who lags behind.

lagoon *noun* a saltwater lake separated from the sea by sandbanks or reefs.

laid *past tense* of **lay**.

lain *past participle* of **lie**[3].

lair *noun* a sheltered place where a wild animal lives.

laissez-faire (*say* les-say **fair**) *noun* the policy of allowing businesses etc. to operate freely without government control.

laity (*say* lay-it-ee) *noun* lay people, who do not belong to the clergy or other profession.

lake *noun* a large area of water entirely surrounded by land.

lama *noun* a Buddhist priest or monk in Tibet and Mongolia.

lamb *noun* 1 a young sheep. 2 meat from a lamb. **lambswool** *noun*

lame *adjective* 1 unable to walk normally. 2 weak; not convincing, *a lame excuse*. **lamely** *adverb*, **lameness** *noun*

lament[1] *noun* a statement, song, or poem expressing grief or regret.

lament[2] *verb* express grief or regret about something. **lamentation** *noun*

lamentable (*say* lam-in-ta-bul) *adjective* regrettable; deplorable.

lamina *noun* (*plural* **laminae**) the flat surface of a leaf.

laminated *adjective* made of layers joined together.

lamp *noun* a device for producing light from electricity, gas, or oil. **lamplight** *noun*, **lampshade** *noun*

lamppost *noun* a tall post in a street etc., with a lamp at the top.

lamprey *noun* (*plural* **lampreys**) a small eel-like water animal with a sucker mouth.

lance[1] *noun* a long spear.

lance[2] *verb* (**lanced, lancing**) cut open with a surgeon's lancet.

lance-corporal *noun* a soldier ranking between a private and a corporal.

lancet *noun* 1 a pointed two-edged knife used by surgeons. 2 a tall narrow pointed window or arch.

land[1] *noun* 1 the part of the earth's surface not covered by sea. 2 the ground or soil; an area of country, *forest land*. 3 the area occupied by a nation; a country. **land-locked** almost or entirely enclosed by land.

land[2] *verb* 1 arrive or put on land from a ship or aircraft etc. 2 reach the ground after jumping or falling. 3 bring a fish out of the water. 4 obtain, *She landed an excellent job*. 5 arrive or cause to arrive at a certain place

or position etc., *They landed up in gaol.*
6 present with a problem, *He landed me with this task.*

landdrost *noun* the chief magistrate of a district in former times.

landed *adjective* **1** owning land. **2** consisting of land, *landed estates.*

landfill *noun* a place where rubbish is buried under layers of earth.

landing *noun* **1** bringing or coming to land. **2** a place where people can land. **3** the level area at the top of stairs.

landing-stage *noun* a platform on which people and goods are landed from a boat.

landlady *noun* (*plural* **landladies**) **1** a woman who lets rooms to lodgers. **2** a female landlord.

landlord *noun* **1** a person who lets a house, room, or land to a tenant. **2** a person who looks after a public house.

landlubber *noun* (*informal*) a person who is not used to the sea.

landmark *noun* **1** an object that is easily seen in a landscape. **2** an important event in the history of something.

land-mine *noun* an explosive device laid in or on the ground.

landowner *noun* a person who owns a large amount of land.

landscape *noun* the scenery or a picture of the countryside.
landscape gardening laying out a garden to imitate natural scenery.

landslide *noun* **1** a huge mass of soil and rocks sliding down a slope. **2** an overwhelming victory in an election.

landward *adjective* & *adverb* towards the land. **landwards** *adverb*

lane *noun* **1** a narrow road, especially in the country. **2** a strip of road for a single line of traffic. **3** a strip of track or water for one runner, swimmer, etc. in a race.

language *noun* **1** words and their use. **2** the words used in a particular country or by a particular group of people.

languid *adjective* slow because of tiredness, weakness, or laziness. **languidly** *adverb*, **languor** *noun*

languish *verb* **1** become weak or listless and depressed; pine. **2** live in miserable

conditions; be neglected, *languish in gaol.*

lank *adjective* lanky; long and limp.

lanky *adjective* (**lankier, lankiest**) awkwardly thin and tall. **lankiness** *noun*

lanolin *noun* a kind of ointment, made of fat from sheep's wool.

lantern *noun* a transparent case for holding a light and shielding it from the wind.

lap¹ *noun* **1** the level place formed by the front of the legs above the knees when a person is sitting down. **2** going once round a racecourse. **3** one section of a journey, *the last lap.*

lap² *verb* (**lapped, lapping**) **1** fold or wrap round. **2** be a lap ahead of someone in a race.

lap³ *verb* (**lapped, lapping**) **1** take up liquid by moving the tongue, as an animal does. **2** make a gentle splash against something, *Waves lapped the shore.*

lapa *noun* a courtyard or enclosed area surrounded by a wall.

lapel (*say* la-**pel**) *noun* a flap folded back at the front edge of a coat etc.

lappie *noun* (*informal*) a cloth, rag, etc. for cleaning.

lapse¹ *noun* **1** a slight mistake or failure, *a lapse of memory.* **2** a relapse, *a lapse into bad habits.* **3** an amount of time elapsed, *after a lapse of six months.*

lapse² *verb* (**lapsed, lapsing**) **1** pass or slip gradually, *He lapsed into unconsciousness.* **2** be no longer valid, through not being renewed, *My insurance policy has lapsed.*

laptop *noun* a small portable computer that can run off a battery.

lapwing *noun* a peewit.

larceny *noun* stealing possessions.

lard *noun* a white greasy substance prepared from pig-fat and used in cooking. **lardy** *adjective*

larder *noun* a cupboard or small room for storing food.

large *adjective* of more than the ordinary or average size; big. **largeness** *noun*
at large free to roam about, not captured, *The escaped prisoners are still at large*; in general, as a whole, *She is respected by the country at large.*

largely *adverb* to a great extent, *You are*

largely responsible for the accident.

largesse (*say* lar-**jess**) *noun* money or gifts generously given.

lark[1] *noun* a small sandy-brown bird; the skylark.

lark[2] *noun* (*informal*) something amusing; a bit of fun, *We did it for a lark.*

lark[3] *verb* (*informal*) have fun; play, *Stop larking about!*

larney *adjective* (*informal*) smart; posh.

larva *noun* (*plural* **larvae**) an insect in the first stage of its life, after it comes out of the egg. **larval** *adjective*

laryngitis *noun* inflammation of the larynx, causing hoarseness.

larynx (*say* la-rinks) *noun* (*plural* **larynxes**) the part of the throat that contains the vocal cords.

lasagne (*say* la-**zahn**-ya) *noun* pasta in the form of broad sheets, especially as cooked with minced meat and cheese sauce.

laser *noun* a device that makes a very strong narrow beam of light or other electromagnetic radiation.

lash[1] *noun* (*plural* **lashes**) 1 a stroke with a whip etc. 2 the cord or cord-like part of a whip. 3 an eyelash.

lash[2] *verb* 1 strike with a whip; beat violently. 2 move like a whip. 3 tie with cord etc., *Lash the sticks together.*

lass *noun* (*plural* **lasses**) a girl; a young woman. **lassie** *noun*

lassitude *noun* tiredness; listlessness.

lasso[1] *noun* (*plural* **lassoes**) a rope with a sliding noose at the end, used for catching cattle etc.

lasso[2] *verb* (**lassoed, lassoing**) catch with a lasso.

last[1] *adjective & adverb* 1 coming after all others; final. 2 latest; most recent, *last night.* 3 least likely, *She is the last person I'd have chosen.*

the last straw a final thing that makes problems unbearable.

last[2] *noun* 1 a person or thing that is last. 2 the end, *He was brave to the last.*

at last or **at long last** finally; after much delay.

last[3] *verb* 1 continue; go on existing or living or being usable. 2 be enough for,

The food will last us for three days.

last[4] *noun* a block of wood or metal shaped like a foot, used in making and repairing shoes.

lasting *adjective* able to last for a long time.

lastly *adverb* in the last place; finally.

latch[1] *noun* (*plural* **latches**) a small bar fastening a door or gate, lifted by a lever or spring. **latchkey** *noun*

latch[2] *verb* fasten with a latch.

late *adjective & adverb* 1 after the usual or expected time. 2 near the end, *late in the afternoon.* 3 recent, *the latest news.* 4 who has died recently, *the late king.*

of late recently.

lately *adverb* recently.

latent (*say* lay-tent) *adjective* existing but not yet developed or active or visible, *latent heat.*

lateral *adjective* of, at, or towards the side or sides. **laterally** *adverb*

lateral line a sense organ found on the sides of fish, used to sense vibrations and gauge depth.

lateral root a root which grows from the side of a tap root.

latex *noun* (*plural* **latexes**) 1 the milky fluid produced by some trees, especially the rubber tree. 2 an artificial substance like rubber.

lath *noun* a narrow thin strip of wood.

lathe (*say* lay*th*) *noun* a machine for holding and turning pieces of wood while they are being shaped.

lather[1] *noun* a mass of froth.

lather[2] *verb* 1 cover with lather. 2 form a lather.

Latin *noun* the language of the ancient Romans.

Latin America the parts of Central and South America where the main language is Spanish or Portuguese. (These languages were developed from Latin.)

latitude *noun* 1 the distance of a place from the equator, measured in degrees. 2 freedom from restrictions on what people can do or believe, *The teacher allowed his pupils far too much latitude.*

latrine (*say* la-**treen**) *noun* a lavatory in a camp or barracks etc.

latter *adjective* later, *the latter part of the year.*

the latter the second of two people or things just mentioned. (Compare *former.*)

latterly *adverb* lately; recently.

lattice *noun* a framework of crossed laths or bars with spaces between.

laud *verb* (*formal*) praise. **laudatory** (*say* **law**-dat-er-ee) *adjective*

laudable *adjective* praiseworthy. **laudably** *adverb*

laugh[1] *verb* make the sounds that show you think something is funny.

laugh[2] *noun* an act or sound of laughing.

laughable *adjective* deserving to be laughed at.

laughter *noun* the act, sound, or manner of laughing.

launch[1] *verb* **1** send a ship from the land into the water. **2** set a thing moving by throwing or pushing it; send a rocket etc. into space. **3** start into action, *launch an attack.*

launch[2] *noun* (*plural* **launches**) the launching of a ship or spacecraft.

launch pad a platform from which spacecraft etc. are launched.

launch[3] *noun* (*plural* **launches**) a large motor boat.

launder *verb* wash and iron clothes etc.

launderette *noun* a place fitted with washing-machines that people pay to use.

laundry *noun* (*plural* **laundries**) **1** a place where clothes etc. are laundered for customers. **2** clothes etc. sent to or from a laundry.

laureate (*say* **lorri**-at) *adjective* **Poet Laureate** a person appointed to write poems for national occasions.

laurel *noun* an evergreen shrub with smooth shiny leaves.

laurel wreath laurel leaves fastened into a circle and worn on the head in ancient times as a sign of victory.

lava *noun* molten rock that flows from a volcano; the solid rock formed when it cools.

lavatory *noun* (*plural* **lavatories**) **1** a bowl-like fitment in which the body can get rid of its waste matter. **2** a room containing a lavatory.

lavender *noun* **1** a shrub with sweet-smelling purple flowers. **2** light-purple colour.

lavish[1] *adjective* **1** generous. **2** plentiful. **lavishly** *adverb*, **lavishness** *noun*

lavish[2] *verb* give generously, *They lavished praise upon him.*

law *noun* **1** a rule or set of rules that everyone must obey. **2** (*informal*) the police. **3** a scientific statement of something that always happens, *the law of gravity.*

law-abiding *adjective* obeying the law.

lawcourt *noun* a room or building in which a judge or magistrate hears evidence and decides whether someone has broken the law.

lawful *adjective* allowed or accepted by the law. **lawfully** *adverb*

lawless *adjective* **1** not obeying the law. **2** without proper laws, *a lawless country.* **lawlessly** *adverb*, **lawlessness** *noun*

lawn[1] *noun* an area of closely-cut grass in a garden or park.

lawn[2] *noun* very fine cotton material.

lawn-mower *noun* a machine for cutting the grass of lawns.

lawsuit *noun* a dispute or claim etc. brought to a lawcourt for judgement.

lawyer *noun* an expert on law.

lax *adjective* slack; not strict, *discipline was lax.* **laxly** *adverb*, **laxity** *noun*

laxative *noun* a medicine that stimulates the bowels to empty.

lay[1] *verb* (**laid**, **laying**) **1** put something down in a particular place or way. **2** arrange things, especially for a meal, *lay the table.* **3** place, *He laid the blame on his sister.* **4** prepare; arrange, *We laid our plans.* **5** produce an egg.

lay off stop employing somebody for a while; (*informal*) stop doing something.

lay on supply; provide.

lay out arrange or prepare; knock a person unconscious; prepare a corpse for burial.

● USAGE: Do not confuse *lay/laid/laying* = 'put down', with *lie/lay/lain/lying* = 'be in a flat position'. Correct uses are as follows: *Go and lie down; she went and lay down;*

please lay it on the floor. 'Go and lay down' is incorrect.

lay[2] *past tense* of **lie**[3].

lay[3] *noun* (*old use*) a poem meant to be sung; a ballad.

lay[4] *adjective* not belonging to the clergy or other profession, *a lay preacher; lay opinion.*

layabout *noun* a loafer; a person who lazily avoids working for a living.

lay-by *noun* (*plural* **lay-bys**) 1 a place where vehicles can stop beside a main road. 2 a system of purchasing where the customer pays regular instalments to the seller but (in contrast to *hire-purchase*) does not receive the item until it is fully paid for.

layer *noun* a single thickness or coating.

layout *noun* an arrangement of parts of something according to a plan.

layperson *noun* a person who does not have specialized knowledge or training (e.g. as a doctor or lawyer), or who is not ordained as a member of the clergy. **layman** *noun* (*plural* **laymen**), **laywoman** *noun* (*plural* **laywomen**)

laze *verb* (**lazed, lazing**) spend time in a lazy way.

lazy *adjective* (**lazier, laziest**) not wanting to work; doing little work. **lazily** *adverb*, **laziness** *noun*

lead[1] (*say* leed) *verb* (**led, leading**) 1 take or guide, especially by going in front. 2 be winning in a race or contest etc.; be ahead. 3 be a way or route, *This path leads to the beach.* 4 play the first card in a card-game. 5 live or experience, *He leads a dull life.*
lead water (*informal*) irrigate crops by means of sloots and furrows.

lead[2] (*say* leed) *noun* 1 the action of leading; guidance, *Give us a lead.* 2 a leading place or part or position, *She took the lead.* 3 a strap or cord for leading a dog or other animal. 4 an electrical wire attached to something.

lead[3] (*say* led) *noun* 1 a soft heavy grey metal. 2 the writing substance (*graphite*) in a pencil. **lead** *adjective*

leaden (*say* led-en) *adjective* 1 made of lead. 2 heavy and slow. 3 lead-coloured;

dark-grey, *leaden skies.*

leader *noun* a person or thing that leads; a chief. **leadership** *noun*

leaf *noun* (*plural* **leaves**) 1 a flat usually green part of a plant, growing out from its stem, branch, or root. 2 the paper forming one page of a book. 3 a very thin sheet of metal, *gold leaf.* 4 a flap that makes a table larger. **leafy** *adjective*, **leafless** *adjective*
turn over a new leaf make a fresh start and improve your behaviour.

leaflet *noun* 1 a piece of paper printed with information. 2 a small leaf.

league *noun* 1 a group of people or nations who agree to work together. 2 a group of teams who compete against each other for a championship.
in league with working or plotting together.

leak[1] *noun* 1 a hole or crack etc. through which liquid or gas wrongly escapes. 2 the revealing of secret information, *a security leak.* **leaky** *adjective*

leak[2] *verb* 1 get out or let out through a leak. 2 reveal secret information. **leakage** *noun*

lean[1] *adjective* 1 with little or no fat, *lean meat.* 2 thin, *a lean body.*

lean[2] *verb* (**leaned** or **leant, leaning**) 1 bend your body towards or over something. 2 put or be in a sloping position. 3 rest against something.

leaning *noun* a tendency or preference.

leap *verb* (**leaped** or **leapt, leaping**) jump vigorously. **leap** *noun*
leap year a year with an extra day in it (29 February).

leap-frog *noun* a game in which each player jumps with legs apart over another who is bending down.

learn *verb* (**learned** or **learnt, learning**) get knowledge or skill; find out about something.

learned (*say* ler-nid) *adjective* having much knowledge obtained by study.

learner *noun* a person who is learning something.
learner driver a person who is learning to drive a vehicle.

learning *noun* knowledge obtained by study.

lease[1] *noun* an agreement to allow someone to use a building or land etc. for a fixed period in return for payment. **leaseholder** *noun*

lease[2] *verb* (**leased, leasing**) allow or obtain the use of something by lease.

leash *noun* (*plural* **leashes**) a dog's lead.

least[1] *adjective & adverb* very small in amount etc., *the least bit, the least expensive bike.*

least[2] *noun* the smallest amount etc.

leather *noun* material made from animal skins. **leathery** *adjective*

leave[1] *verb* (**left, leaving**) 1 go away from a person or place. 2 stop belonging to a group. 3 cause or allow something to stay where it is or as it is, *You left the door open.* 4 go away without taking something, *I left my book at home.* 5 put something to be collected or passed on, *leave a message.* **leave off** cease. **leave out** omit; not include.

leave[2] *noun* 1 permission. 2 official permission to be away from work; the time for which this permission lasts.

leaven (*say* **lev**-en) *noun* a substance (e.g. yeast) used to make dough rise.

lechery *noun* excessive sexual lust. **lecherous** *adjective*

lectern *noun* a stand to hold a Bible or other large book or notes for reading.

lecture[1] *noun* 1 a talk about a subject to an audience or a class. 2 a long serious warning or rebuke.

lecture[2] *verb* (**lectured, lecturing**) give a lecture. **lecturer** *noun*

led *past tense* of **lead**[1].

ledge *noun* a narrow shelf or similar projecting part.

ledger *noun* an account-book.

lee *noun* the sheltered side or part of something, away from the wind.

leech *noun* (*plural* **leeches**) a small blood-sucking worm that lives in water.

leek *noun* a white vegetable rather like an onion, with broad leaves.

leer *verb* look at someone in an insulting, sly, or unpleasant way. **leer** *noun*

leeward *adjective* on the side sheltered from the wind.

leeway *noun* 1 drift to leeward or off course. 2 extra space or time available. **make up leeway** make up lost time; regain a lost position.

left[1] *adjective & adverb* 1 of or on or towards the left-hand side. 2 (of political groups) in favour of socialist reforms. **left hand** the hand that most people use less than the other, on the same side of the body as the heart. **left-hand** *adjective* **left-handed** *adjective* using the left hand in preference to the right hand.

left[2] *noun* the left-hand side or part etc.

left[3] *past tense* of **leave**[1]. **left-overs** *plural noun* food not eaten.

leg *noun* 1 each of the projecting parts of a person's or animal's body, on which it stands or moves. 2 the part of a garment covering a leg. 3 each of the projecting supports of a chair or other piece of furniture. 4 one part of a journey, *the first leg of our trip.* 5 one of a pair of matches between the same teams.

legacy *noun* (*plural* **legacies**) something left to a person in a will.

legal *adjective* 1 lawful. 2 of the law or lawyers. **legally** *adverb*, **legality** *noun*

legalize *verb* (**legalized, legalizing**) make a thing legal. **legalization** *noun*

legate *noun* an official representative, especially of the pope.

legend *noun* an old story handed down from the past. **legendary** *adjective* (Compare *myth.*)

leggings *plural noun* 1 close-fitting stretch trousers for women or children. 2 a protective outer covering for each leg.

legible *adjective* clear enough to read. **legibly** *adverb*, **legibility** *noun*

legion *noun* 1 a division of the ancient Roman army. 2 a group of soldiers or former soldiers.

legionnaire *noun* a member of an association of former soldiers.

legislate *verb* (**legislated, legislating**) make laws. **legislation** *noun*, **legislator** *noun*

legislative *adjective* making laws, *a legislative assembly.*

legislature *noun* a country's legislative assembly.

legitimate *adjective* **1** lawful. **2** born when parents are married to each other.
legitimately *adverb*, **legitimacy** *noun*
leguaan (*say* **leg**-wahn) *noun* a large amphibious lizard.
legume (*say* **leg**-yewm) *noun* the family of plants that have seeds in pods, e.g. beans and peas. **leguminous** (*say* leg-**yew**-min-us) *adjective*
leisure *noun* time that is free from work, when you can do what you like. **leisured** *adjective*, **leisurely** *adjective*
at leisure having leisure; not hurried.
at your leisure when you have time.
lekker *adjective* (*informal*) good; pleasant.
lemming *noun* a small mouse-like animal of Arctic regions that migrates in large numbers and is said to run headlong into the sea and drown.
lemon *noun* **1** an oval yellow citrus fruit with a sour taste. **2** pale-yellow colour.
lemonade *noun* a lemon-flavoured drink.
lemur (*say* **lee**-mer) *noun* a monkey-like animal.
lend *verb* (**lent, lending**) **1** allow a person to use something of yours for a short time. **2** provide someone with money that they must repay, usually in return for payments (called *interest*). **lender** *noun*
lend a hand help somebody.
length *noun* **1** how long something is. **2** a piece of cloth, rope, wire, etc. cut from a larger piece. **3** the amount of thoroughness in an action, *They went to great lengths to make us comfortable.*
at length after a long time; taking a long time; in detail.
lengthen *verb* make or become longer.
lengthways (also **lengthwise**) *adverb* from end to end; along the longest part.
lengthy *adjective* very long; long and boring. **lengthily** *adverb*
lenient (*say* **lee**-nee-ent) *adjective* merciful; not severe. **leniently** *adverb*, **lenience** *noun*
lens *noun* (*plural* **lenses**) **1** a curved piece of glass or plastic used to focus things. **2** the transparent part of the eye, immediately behind the pupil. **3** a contact lens.
lent *past tense* of **lend**.

lentil *noun* a kind of small bean.
leopard (*say* **lep**-erd) *noun* a large lion-like spotted wild animal, also called a panther.
leopardess *noun*
leotard (*say* **lee**-o-tard) *noun* a close-fitting garment worn by acrobats and dancers etc.
leper *noun* a person who has leprosy.
lepidopterous *adjective* of the group of insects that includes butterflies and moths.
leprechaun (*say* **lep**-rek-awn) *noun* (in Irish folklore) an elf who looks like a little old man.
leprosy *noun* an infectious disease that makes parts of the body waste away.
leprous *adjective*
lesbian *noun* a homosexual woman.
less[1] *adjective* & *adverb* smaller in amount; not so much, *Make less noise. It is less important.*
less[2] *noun* a smaller amount.
less[3] *preposition* minus; deducting, *She earned R800, less tax.*
lessen *verb* make or become less.
lesser *adjective* not so great as the other, *the lesser evil.*
lesson *noun* **1** an amount of teaching given at one time. **2** something to be learnt by a pupil. **3** an example or experience from which you should learn, *Let this be a lesson to you!* **4** a passage from the Bible read aloud as part of a church service.
lest *conjunction* so that something should not happen, *Remind us, lest we forget.*
let *verb* (**let, letting**) **1** allow to do something; not prevent; not forbid, *Let me see it.* **2** cause to, *Let us know what happens.* **3** allow or cause to come or go or pass, *Let me out!* **4** allow someone to use a house or building etc. in return for payment (*rent*). **5** leave, *Let it alone.*
let down deflate; disappoint somebody.
let off cause to explode; excuse somebody from a duty or punishment etc.
let up (*informal*) relax. **let-up** *noun*
lethal (*say* **lee**-thal) *adjective* deadly; causing death. **lethally** *adverb*
lethargy (*say* **leth**-er-jee) *noun* extreme lack of energy or vitality; sluggishness.
lethargic (*say* lith-**ar**-jik) *adjective*
letter *noun* **1** a symbol representing a

sound used in speech. **2** a written message, usually sent by post.

letter-box *noun* **1** a slot in a door, through which letters are delivered. **2** a post-box.

lettering *noun* letters drawn or painted.

lettuce *noun* a garden plant with broad crisp leaves eaten as salad.

leucocyte (*say* **lew**-koh-syt) *noun* a white blood cell.

leukaemia (*say* lew-**kee**-mee-a) *noun* a disease in which there are too many white corpuscles in the blood.

level[1] *adjective* **1** flat; horizontal. **2** at the same height or position etc. as others.
level crossing a place where a road crosses a railway at the same level.

level[2] *noun* **1** height, depth, position, or value etc., *Fix the shelves at eye level.* **2** a level surface. **3** a device that shows whether something is level.
on the level (*informal*) honest.

level[3] *verb* (**levelled, levelling**) **1** make or become level. **2** aim a gun or missile. **3** direct an accusation at a person, *Criticism was levelled against the minister.*

lever[1] *noun* **1** a bar that turns on a fixed point (the *fulcrum*) in order to lift something or force something open. **2** a bar used as a handle to operate machinery etc., *a gear-lever.*

lever[2] *verb* lift or move by means of a lever.

leverage *noun* **1** the action or power of a lever. **2** influence.

leveret *noun* a young hare.

levitation *noun* rising into the air and floating there.

levity *noun* being humorous, especially at an unsuitable time; frivolity.

levy *verb* (**levied, levying**) **1** impose or collect a tax or other payment by the use of authority or force. **2** enrol, *levy an army.*
levy *noun*

lewd *adjective* indecent; obscene. **lewdly** *adverb*, **lewdness** *noun*

lexicography *noun* the process of writing dictionaries. **lexicographer** *noun*

liability *noun* (*plural* **liabilities**) **1** being liable. **2** a debt or obligation. **3** (*informal*) a disadvantage; a handicap.

liable *adjective* **1** likely to do or get

something, *She is liable to colds. The cliff is liable to crumble.* **2** legally responsible for something.

liaise (*say* lee-**ayz**) *verb* (**liaised, liaising**) (*informal*) act as a liaison or go-between.

liaison (*say* lee-**ay**-zon) *noun* **1** communication and co-operation between people or groups. **2** a person who is a link or go-between.

liar *noun* a person who tells lies.

libel[1] (*say* **ly**-bel) *noun* an untrue written, printed, or broadcast statement that damages a person's reputation. (Compare *slander*[1].) **libellous** *adjective*

libel[2] *verb* (**libelled, libelling**) make a libel against someone.

liberal *adjective* **1** giving generously. **2** given in large amounts, *a liberal helping of food.* **3** not strict; tolerant, *a liberal attitude to squatting.* **liberally** *adverb*, **liberality** *noun*

liberalize *verb* (**liberalized, liberalizing**) make less strict. **liberalization** *noun*

liberate *verb* (**liberated, liberating**) set free. **liberation** *noun*, **liberator** *noun*

liberty *noun* freedom.
take liberties behave too casually; be presumptuous.

librarian *noun* a person in charge of or assisting in a library. **librarianship** *noun*

library (*say* **ly**-bra-ree) *noun* (*plural* **libraries**) **1** a place where books are kept for people to use or borrow. **2** a collection of books, records, films, etc.

libretto *noun* (*plural* **librettos**) the words of an opera or other long musical work.

lice *plural* of **louse**.

licence *noun* **1** an official permit to do or use or own something, *a driving-licence.* **2** special freedom to avoid the usual rules or customs.

license *verb* (**licensed, licensing**) give a licence to a person; authorize, *We are licensed to sell tobacco.*

licensee *noun* a person who holds a licence, especially to sell alcohol.

licentious (*say* ly-**sen**-shus) *adjective* breaking the rules of conduct; immoral. **licentiousness** *noun*

lichen (*say* **ly**-ken or **lich**-en) *noun* a dry-looking plant that grows on rocks, walls, trees, etc.

lick[1] *verb* **1** pass the tongue over something. **2** (of a wave or flame) move like a tongue; touch lightly. **3** (*informal*) defeat.

lick[2] *noun* **1** the act of licking. **2** a slight application of paint etc. **3** (*informal*) a fast pace.

lid *noun* **1** a cover for a box or pot etc. **2** an eyelid.

lie[1] *noun* a statement that the person who makes it knows to be untrue.

lie[2] *verb* (**lied, lying**) tell a lie or lies; be deceptive.

lie[3] *verb* (**lay, lain, lying**) **1** be or get in a flat or resting position, *He lay on the grass. The cat has lain here all night.* **2** be or remain, *The island lies near the coast. The machinery lay idle.*

lie low keep yourself hidden.

● USAGE: See the note on **lay**[1].

lie[4] *noun* the way something lies, *the lie of the land.*

liege (*say* leej) *noun* (*old use*) a person entitled to receive feudal service or allegiance (*a liege lord*) or bound to give it (*a liege man*).

lieu (*say* lew) *noun* **in lieu** instead, *He accepted a cheque in lieu of cash.*

lieutenant (*say* lef-**ten**-ant) *noun* **1** an officer in the army or navy. **2** a deputy or chief assistant.

life *noun* (*plural* **lives**) **1** the ability to function and grow; the period between birth and death. **2** living things, *Is there life on Mars?* **3** liveliness, *full of life.* **4** a biography, *I'm reading a life of Smuts.*

lifebelt *noun* a circle of material that will float, used to support someone's body in water.

lifeboat *noun* a boat for rescuing people at sea.

lifebuoy *noun* a device to support someone's body in water.

life-guard *noun* someone whose job is to rescue swimmers who are in difficulty.

life-jacket *noun* a jacket of material that will float, used to support someone's body in water.

lifeless *adjective* **1** without life. **2** unconscious. **lifelessly** *adverb*

lifelike *adjective* looking exactly like a real person or thing.

lifelong *adjective* continuing for the whole of someone's life.

lifetime *noun* the time for which someone is alive.

lift[1] *verb* **1** raise; pick up. **2** rise; go upwards. **3** (*informal*) steal. **4** remove; abolish, *The ban has been lifted.*

lift[2] *noun* **1** the act of lifting. **2** a device for taking people or goods from one floor or level to another in a building. **3** a free ride in somebody else's vehicle.

lift-off *noun* the vertical take-off of a rocket or spacecraft.

ligament *noun* a piece of the tough flexible tissue that holds bones etc. together.

ligature *noun* a thing used in tying something, especially in surgical operations.

light[1] *noun* **1** radiation that stimulates the sense of sight and makes things visible. **2** something that provides light, especially an electric lamp. **3** a flame.

bring or **come to light** make or become known.

light[2] *adjective* **1** full of light; not dark. **2** pale, *light blue.*

light[3] *verb* (**lit** or **lighted, lighting**) **1** start a thing burning; kindle. **2** provide the light.

light up put lights on, especially at dusk; make or become light or bright.

● USAGE: Say *He lit the lamps; the lamps were lit* (not 'lighted'), but *She carried a lighted torch* (not 'a lit torch').

light[4] *adjective* **1** having little weight; not heavy. **2** small in amount or force etc., *light rain; a light punishment.* **3** needing little effort, *light work.* **4** cheerful, not sad, *with a light heart.* **5** not serious or profound, *light music.* **lightly** *adverb*, **lightness** *noun*

light industry industry producing small or light articles.

light[5] *adverb* lightly; with only a small load, *We were travelling light.*

lighten[1] *verb* **1** make or become lighter or brighter. **2** produce lightning.

lighten[2] *verb* make or become lighter or less heavy.

lighter *noun* a device for lighting cigarettes etc.

light-hearted *adjective* cheerful; free from worry; not serious.

lighthouse *noun* a tower with a bright light at the top to guide or warn ships.

lighting *noun* lamps, or the light they provide.

lightning *noun* a flash of bright light produced by natural electricity during a thunderstorm.

lightning bird an impundulu.

lightning conductor a metal rod or wire fixed on a building to divert lightning into the earth.

like lightning with very great speed.

lightweight *noun* **1** a person who is not heavy. **2** a boxer weighing between 57 and 60 kilograms. **lightweight** *adjective*

light-year *noun* the distance that light travels in one year (about 9,6 million million kilometres).

like[1] *verb* (**liked**, **liking**) **1** think a person or thing is pleasant or satisfactory. **2** wish, *I should like to come.*

like[2] *adjective* similar; having some or all of the qualities of another person or thing, *They are as like as two peas.*

like[3] *noun* a similar person or thing, *We shall not see his like again.*

like[4] *preposition* **1** similar to; in the manner of, *He swims like a fish.* **2** in a suitable state for, *It looks like rain.*

likeable *adjective* easy to like; pleasant.

likelihood *noun* being likely; probability.

likely *adjective* (**likelier**, **likeliest**) **1** probable; expected to happen or be true etc., *Rain is likely.* **2** expected to be successful, *a likely lad.*

liken *verb* compare, *He likened the human heart to a pump.*

likeness *noun* (*plural* **likenesses**) **1** being like; a resemblance. **2** a portrait.

likewise *adverb* similarly.

liking *noun* a feeling that you like something, *She has a liking for ice-cream.*

likkewaan (*say* lik-a-vahn) *noun* a leguaan.

lilac *noun* **1** a bush with fragrant purple or white flowers. **2** pale purple.

lilt *noun* a light pleasant rhythm. **lilting** *adjective*

lily *noun* (*plural* **lilies**) a garden plant with trumpet-shaped flowers, growing from a bulb.

limb *noun* **1** a leg, arm, or wing. **2** a projecting part, e.g. a bough of a tree. **out on a limb** isolated; stranded.

limber *verb* **limber up** exercise in preparation for an athletic activity.

limbo *noun* an intermediate state where nothing is happening, *Lack of money has left our plans in limbo.*

lime[1] *noun* a white substance (calcium oxide) used in making cement and as a fertilizer.

lime[2] *noun* a green fruit like a small round lemon. **lime-juice** *noun*

limelight *noun* great publicity.

limerick *noun* a type of comical poem with five lines.

limestone *noun* a kind of rock from which lime (calcium oxide) is obtained.

limit[1] *noun* **1** a line, point, or level where something ends. **2** the greatest amount allowed, *the speed limit.*

limit[2] *verb* **1** keep within certain limits. **2** be a limit to something, *The amount of water available limits the number of animals in the reserve.* **limitation** *noun*

limited *adjective* **1** kept within limits; restricted; small. **2** (after a company name) being a limited company.

limited company (also **limited liability company**) a company whose owners are legally responsible only to a limited amount for its debts.

limousine (*say* lim-oo-**zeen**) *noun* a luxurious car.

limp[1] *verb* walk lamely.

limp[2] *noun* a limping walk.

limp[3] *adjective* **1** not stiff or firm. **2** without strength or energy. **limply** *adverb*, **limpness** *noun*

limpet *noun* a small shellfish that attaches itself firmly to rocks.

limpid *adjective* (of liquids) clear; transparent. **limpidity** *noun*

linchpin *noun* a pin passed through the end of an axle to keep a wheel in position.

line[1] *noun* **1** a long thin mark. **2** a row or series of people or things; a row of words. **3** a length of rope, string, wire, etc. used for a special purpose, *a fishing-line.* **4** a railway; a line of railway track. **5** a system of ships, aircraft, buses, etc. **6** a way of doing things or behaving; a type of business, *She's in the engineering line.*

in line forming a straight line; conforming.

line fish any kind of fish caught with a fishing-line and not by trawling.

line[2] *verb* (**lined, lining**) **1** mark with lines, *Use lined paper.* **2** form into a line or lines, *Line them up.*

line[3] *verb* (**lined, lining**) cover the inside of something, *The jacket was lined with silk.*

lineage (*say* **lin**-ee-ij) *noun* ancestry; a line of descendants from an ancestor.

lineal (*say* **lin**-ee-al) *adjective* of or in a line, especially as a descendant.

linear (*say* **lin**-ee-er) *adjective* **1** of a line; of length. **2** arranged in a line.

linen *noun* **1** cloth made from flax. **2** shirts, sheets, and tablecloths etc. (which were formerly made of linen).

liner *noun* a large ship or aircraft on a regular route, usually carrying passengers.

linesman *noun* (*plural* **linesmen**) an official in soccer or rugby etc. who decides whether the ball has crossed a line.

linger *verb* stay for a long time, as if unwilling to leave; be slow to leave.

lingerie (*say* **lan**-*zh*er-ee) *noun* women's underwear.

linguist *noun* an expert in languages.

linguistics *noun* the study of languages. **linguistic** *adjective*

liniment *noun* embrocation.

lining *noun* a layer that covers the inside of something. (Compare *line*[3].)

link[1] *noun* **1** one ring or loop of a chain. **2** a connection.

link[2] *verb* join things together; connect. **linkage** *noun*

links *noun* or *plural noun* a golf-course.

lino *noun* linoleum.

linocut *noun* a print made from a design cut into a block of thick linoleum.

linoleum *noun* a stiff shiny floor-covering.

linseed *noun* the seed of flax, from which oil is obtained.

lint *noun* a soft material for covering wounds.

lintel *noun* a horizontal piece of wood or stone etc. above a door or other opening.

lion *noun* a large strong flesh-eating animal of the cat family. **lioness** *noun*

lip *noun* **1** either of the two fleshy edges of the mouth. **2** the edge of something hollow, such as a cup or crater. **3** a projecting part at the top of a jug etc., shaped for pouring things.

lip-reading *noun* understanding what a person says by watching the movements of his or her lips, not by hearing.

lip-service *noun* **pay lip-service to something** say that you approve of it but do nothing to support it.

lipstick *noun* a stick of a waxy substance for colouring the lips.

liquefy (*say* **lik**-wee-fy) *verb* (**liquefied, liquefying**) make or become liquid. **liquefaction** *noun*

liqueur (*say* lik-**yoor**) *noun* a strong sweet alcoholic drink.

liquid[1] *noun* a substance (such as water or oil) that flows freely but is not a gas.

liquid[2] *adjective* **1** in the form of a liquid; flowing freely. **2** easily converted into cash, *the firm's liquid assets.* **liquidity** *noun*

liquidate *verb* (**liquidated, liquidating**) **1** pay off or settle a debt. **2** close down a business and divide its value between its creditors. **3** get rid of, especially by killing. **liquidation** *noun,* **liquidator** *noun*

liquidize *verb* (**liquidized, liquidizing**) cause to become liquid; crush into a liquid pulp. **liquidizer** *noun*

liquor *noun* **1** alcoholic drink. **2** juice produced in cooking; liquid in which food has been cooked.

liquorice (*say* **lik**-a-rish) *noun* **1** a black substance used in medicine and as a sweet. **2** the plant from whose root this substance is obtained.

lisp *noun* a fault in speech in which *s* and *z* are pronounced like *th.* **lisp** *verb*

list[1] *noun* a number of names, items, or figures etc. written or printed one after another.

list² *verb* make a list of people or things.

list³ *verb* (of a ship) lean over to one side; tilt. **list** *noun*

listen *verb* pay attention in order to hear something. **listener** *noun*

listless *adjective* too tired to be active or enthusiastic. **listlessly** *adverb*, **listlessness** *noun*

lit *past tense* of **light¹**.

litany *noun* (*plural* **litanies**) a formal prayer with fixed responses.

litchi *noun* a lychee.

literacy *noun* being literate; the ability to read and write.

literal *adjective* meaning exactly what is said, not metaphorical or exaggerated; precise. **literally** *adverb*

literary (*say* lit-er-er-i) *adjective* of literature; interested in literature.

literate *adjective* able to read and write.

literature *noun* books and other writings, especially those considered to have been written well.

lithe *adjective* flexible; supple; agile.

litigant *noun* a person who is involved in a lawsuit.

litigation *noun* a lawsuit; the process of carrying on a lawsuit.

litmus *noun* a blue substance that is turned red by acids and can be turned back to blue by alkalis.

litmus-paper *noun* paper stained with litmus.

litre *noun* a measure of liquid equal to 1 000 cubic centimetres.

litter¹ *noun* 1 rubbish or untidy things left lying about. 2 straw etc. put down as bedding for animals. 3 the young animals born to one mother at one time. 4 a kind of stretcher.

litter² *verb* 1 make a place untidy with litter. 2 spread straw etc. for animals.

little¹ *adjective* (**less**, **least**) small in amount or size or intensity etc.; not great or big or much.

little by little gradually; by a small amount at a time.

little² *adverb* not much, *I eat very little.*

liturgy *noun* (*plural* **liturgies**) a fixed form of public worship used in churches.

liturgical *adjective*

live¹ (rhymes with *give*) *verb* (**lived**, **living**) 1 have life; be alive; stay alive. 2 have your home, *She lives in Bisho.* 3 pass your life in a certain way, *He lived as a hermit.*

live on use something as food; depend on for your living.

live² (rhymes with *hive*) *adjective* 1 alive. 2 burning, *live coals.* 3 carrying electricity. 4 broadcast while it is actually happening, not from a recording.

live wire a wire carrying electricity; a forceful energetic person.

livelihood *noun* a living (= *living* 3).

lively *adjective* (**livelier**, **liveliest**) full of life or action; vigorous and cheerful. **liveliness** *noun*

liven *verb* make or become lively, *liven things up.*

liver *noun* 1 a large organ of the body, found in the abdomen, that processes digested food and produces bile. 2 an animal's liver used as food.

livery *noun* (*plural* **liveries**) 1 a uniform worn by servants in a household. 2 the distinctive colours used by a railway or bus company etc.

livery stables a place where horses are kept for their owner or where horses may be hired.

livestock *noun* farm animals.

livid *adjective* 1 bluish-grey, *a livid bruise.* 2 (*informal*) furiously angry.

living *noun* 1 being alive. 2 the way that a person lives, *a good standard of living.* 3 a way of earning money or providing enough food to support yourself.

living-room *noun* a room for general use during the day.

lizard *noun* a reptile with a rough or scaly skin, four legs, and a long tail.

llama (*say* lah-ma) *noun* a South American animal with woolly fur, like a camel but with no hump.

lo *interjection* (*old use*) see, behold.

load¹ *noun* 1 something carried; a burden. 2 the quantity that can be carried. 3 the total amount of electric current supplied. 4 (*informal*) a large amount, *It's a load of nonsense.*

load² *verb* 1 put a load in or on something. 2 fill heavily. 3 weight with something heavy, *loaded dice.* 4 put a bullet or shell into a gun; put a film into a camera. 5 enter data etc. into a computer.

loaf¹ *noun* (*plural* **loaves**) 1 a shaped mass of bread baked in one piece. 2 minced or chopped meat etc. moulded into an oblong shape.

loaf² *verb* spend time idly; loiter or stand about. **loafer** *noun*

loam *noun* rich soil containing clay, sand, and decayed leaves etc. **loamy** *adjective*

loan¹ *noun* 1 something lent, especially money. 2 lending; being lent, *These books are on loan from the library.*

loan² *verb* lend.
• USAGE: Many people dislike the use of this verb except when it means to lend money. (It is really better to use *lend* in all cases.)

loath (rhymes with *both*) *adjective* unwilling, *I was loath to go.*

loathe (rhymes with *clothe*) *verb* (**loathed, loathing**) feel great hatred and disgust for something; detest. **loathing** *noun*

loathsome *adjective* arousing a feeling of loathing; detestable.

lob¹ *verb* (**lobbed, lobbing**) send a ball in a high curve into the air.

lob² *noun* a lobbed ball.

lobby¹ *noun* (*plural* **lobbies**) 1 an entrance-hall. 2 a group who lobby Members of Parliament etc.

lobby² *verb* (**lobbied, lobbying**) try to influence a Member of Parliament etc. in favour of a special interest.

lobe *noun* a rounded fairly flat part of a leaf or an organ of the body; the rounded soft part at the bottom of an ear. **lobar** *adjective,* **lobed** *adjective*

lobola *noun* the cattle or money paid by a bridegroom to the parents or guardian of his bride.

lobster *noun* a large shellfish with eight legs and two long claws.

lobster-pot *noun* a basket for catching lobsters.

local¹ *adjective* belonging to a particular place or a small area. **locally** *adverb*
local anaesthetic an anaesthetic affecting only the part of the body where it is applied.
local government the organization of the affairs of a town or district etc. by people elected by those who live there.

local² *noun* (*informal*) someone who lives in a particular district.

locality *noun* (*plural* **localities**) a district; a location.

localize *verb* (**localized, localizing**) keep something within a particular area. **localization** *noun*

locate *verb* (**located, locating**) 1 discover where something is, *locate the electrical fault.* 2 situate something in a particular place, *The cinema is located in Main Road.*

location *noun* 1 the place where something is situated. 2 discovering where something is; locating. 3 (*old use*) a township (= *township* 1).
on location filmed in natural surroundings, not in a studio.

loch *noun* a lake in Scotland.

lock¹ *noun* 1 a fastening that is opened with a key or other device. 2 a section of a canal or river fitted with gates and sluices so that boats can be raised or lowered to the level beyond each gate. 3 a wrestling-hold that keeps an opponent's arm or leg from moving. 4 the distance that a vehicle's front wheels can be turned by the steering-wheel.
lock, stock, and barrel completely.

lock² *verb* 1 fasten or secure by means of a lock. 2 store away securely, *lock up your jewellery.* 3 become fixed in one place; jam.

lock³ *noun* a clump of hair.
locks *plural noun* the hair of the head.

locker *noun* a small cupboard or compartment where things can be stowed safely.

locket *noun* a small ornamental case for holding a portrait or lock of hair etc., worn on a chain round the neck.

locksmith *noun* a person whose job is to make and mend locks.

locomotive¹ *noun* a railway engine.

locomotive² *adjective* of movement or the ability to move, *locomotive power.*
locomotion *noun*

locum *noun* a doctor or member of the

clergy who takes the place of another who is temporarily away.

locus (*say* loh-kus) *noun* (*plural* **loci** (*say* loh-sy or loh-ky or loh-kee)) **1** the exact place of something. **2** (in geometry) the path traced by a moving point, or made by points placed in a certain way.

locust *noun* a kind of grasshopper that travels in large swarms which eat all the plants in an area.

locution *noun* a word or phrase.

lodestone *noun* a kind of stone that can be used as a magnet.

lodge[1] *noun* **1** a small house, especially at the gates of a park. **2** a porter's room at the entrance to a college, factory, etc. **3** a large house or hotel, especially in a resort. **4** a beaver's or otter's lair.

lodge[2] *verb* (**lodged, lodging**) **1** stay somewhere as a lodger. **2** provide a person with somewhere to live temporarily, *The refugees were lodged in the community centre.* **3** deposit; be or become fixed, *The ball lodged in the tree.* **lodging-house** *noun*

lodge a complaint complain formally.

lodger *noun* a person who pays to live in another person's house.

lodgings *plural noun* a room or rooms (not in a hotel) rented for living in.

loerie *noun* a lourie.

loft *noun* a room or storage-space under the roof of a house or barn etc.

lofty *adjective* **1** tall. **2** noble. **3** haughty. **loftily** *adverb*, **loftiness** *noun*

log[1] *noun* **1** a large piece of a tree that has fallen or been cut down; a piece cut off this. **2** a detailed record of a ship's voyage, aircraft's flight, etc. kept in a **log-book**. **log cabin** a hut built of logs.

log[2] *verb* (**logged, logging**) enter facts in a log-book.

log in (or **on**), **log out** (or **off**) connect and disconnect a terminal correctly to or from a computer system.

log[3] *noun* a logarithm, *log tables.*

loganberry *noun* (*plural* **loganberries**) a dark-red fruit like a blackberry.

logarithm *noun* one of a series of numbers set out in tables which make it possible to do sums by adding and subtracting instead of multiplying and dividing.

loggerheads *plural noun* **at loggerheads** arguing; quarrelling.

logic *noun* **1** reasoning; a system of reasoning. **2** the principles used in designing a computer; the circuits involved in this.

logical *adjective* using logic; reasoning or reasoned correctly. **logically** *adverb*, **logicality** *noun*

logo (*say* loh-goh or log-oh) *noun* (*plural* **logos**) a printed symbol used by a business company etc. as its emblem.

-logy *suffix* forming nouns meaning a subject of study (e.g. *biology*).

loin *noun* the side and back of the body between the ribs and the hip-bone.

loincloth *noun* a piece of cloth worn round the hips as a garment.

loiter *verb* linger or stand about idly. **loiterer** *noun*

loll *verb* lean lazily against something.

lollipop *noun* a large round hard sweet on a stick.

lolly *noun* (*plural* **lollies**) (*informal*) a lollipop.

ice lolly frozen juice on a small stick.

lone *adjective* solitary.

lonely *adjective* (**lonelier, loneliest**) **1** sad because you are on your own. **2** solitary. **3** far from inhabited places; not often visited or used, *a lonely road.* **loneliness** *noun*

lonesome *adjective* lonely.

long[1] *adjective* **1** measuring a lot or a certain amount from one end to the other. **2** taking a lot of time, *a long holiday.* **3** having a certain length, *The river is 200 kilometres long.*

long division dividing one number by another and writing down all the calculations.

long[2] *adverb* **1** for a long time, *Have you been waiting long?* **2** at a long time before or after, *They left long ago.* **3** throughout a time, *all night long.*

as long as or **so long as** provided that; on condition that.

long[3] *verb* feel a strong desire, *She longed to see him again.*

L

longevity (*say* lon-**jev**-it-ee) *noun* long life.

longhand *noun* ordinary writing, contrasted with shorthand or typing.

longing *noun* a strong desire.

longitude *noun* the distance east or west, measured in degrees, from the Greenwich meridian.

longitudinal *adjective* 1 of longitude. 2 of length; measured lengthwise.

long-suffering *adjective* putting up with things patiently.

long-winded *adjective* talking or writing at great length.

loo *noun* (*informal*) a lavatory.

loofah *noun* a rough sponge made from a dried gourd.

look[1] *verb* 1 use your eyes; turn your eyes in a particular direction. 2 search for something, *Did you look for it?* 3 face in a particular direction, *The room looks north.* 4 have a certain appearance; seem, *You look sad.*

look after protect; attend to somebody's needs; be in charge of something.

look down on despise.

look forward to be waiting eagerly for something you expect.

look into investigate.

look out be careful.

look up search for information about something; improve in prospects, *Things are looking up.*

look up to admire or respect.

look[2] *noun* 1 the act of looking; a gaze or glance. 2 appearance, *I don't like the look of this place.*

looker-on *noun* (*plural* **lookers-on**) a spectator; someone who sees what happens but takes no part in it.

looking-glass *noun* a glass mirror.

look-out *noun* 1 looking out or watching for something. 2 a place from which you can keep watch. 3 a person whose job is to keep watch. 4 a future prospect, *It's a poor look-out for us.* 5 (*informal*) a person's own concern, *If he wastes his money, that's his look-out.*

loom[1] *noun* an apparatus for weaving cloth.

loom[2] *verb* appear suddenly; seem large or close and threatening, *An iceberg loomed up through the fog.*

loony *adjective* (**loonier, looniest**) (*informal*) crazy.

loop[1] *noun* the shape made by a curve crossing itself; a piece of string, ribbon, wire, etc. made into this shape.

loop[2] *verb* 1 make into a loop. 2 enclose in a loop.

loophole *noun* 1 a way of avoiding a law or rule or promise etc. without actually breaking it. 2 a narrow opening in the wall of a fort etc.

loose[1] *adjective* 1 not tight; slack; not firmly fixed, *a loose tooth.* 2 not tied up or shut in, *There's a lion loose!* 3 not packed in a box or packet etc. 4 not exact, *a loose translation.* **loosely** *adverb*, **looseness** *noun*

at a loose end with nothing to do.

loose[2] *verb* (**loosed, loosing**) 1 loosen. 2 untie; release.

● USAGE: Do not confuse with *lose.*

loose-leaf *adjective* with each leaf or page removable, *a loose-leaf notebook.*

loosen *verb* make or become loose or looser.

loot[1] *noun* stolen things; goods taken from an enemy.

loot[2] *verb* 1 rob a place or an enemy, especially in a time of war or disorder. 2 take as loot. **looter** *noun*

lop *verb* (**lopped, lopping**) cut away branches or twigs; cut off.

lope *verb* (**loped, loping**) run with a long jumping stride. **lope** *noun*

lop-eared *adjective* with drooping ears.

lopsided *adjective* with one side lower than the other; uneven.

loquacious (*say* lok-**way**-shus) *adjective* talkative. **loquacity** (*say* lok-**wass**-it-ee) *noun*

loquat (*say* **loh**-kwot) *noun* a small yellow egg-shaped fruit.

lord[1] *noun* 1 a member of the nobility, especially one who is allowed to use the title 'Lord' in front of his name. 2 a master or ruler. **lordly** *adjective*, **lordship** *noun*

the Lord God or Christ.

lord[2] *verb* domineer; behave in a masterful way, *lording it over the whole club.*

lore *noun* a set of traditional facts or beliefs, *San lore*.

lorgnette (*say* lorn-**yet**) *noun* a pair of spectacles held on a long handle.

lorry *noun* (*plural* **lorries**) a large strong motor vehicle for carrying heavy goods etc., also called a truck.

lose *verb* (**lost, losing**) **1** be without something that you once had, especially because you cannot find it. **2** be deprived of something; fail to keep or obtain, *We lost control*. **3** be defeated in a contest or argument etc. **4** cause the loss of, *That fall lost us the game*. **5** (of a clock or watch) become behind the correct time. **loser** *noun*

be lost or **lose your way** not know where you are or which is the right path.

lose your life be killed.

lost cause an idea or policy etc. that is failing.

• USAGE: Do not confuse with *loose*.

loss *noun* (*plural* **losses**) **1** losing something. **2** something lost.

be at a loss be puzzled; not know what to do or say.

lot *noun* **1** a number of people or things. **2** one of a set of objects used in choosing or deciding something by chance, *We drew lots to see who should go first*. **3** a person's share or fate. **4** something for sale at an auction. **5** a piece of land.

the lot or **the whole lot** everything; all.

loth *adjective* loath.

lotion *noun* a liquid for putting on the skin.

lottery *noun* (*plural* **lotteries**) a way of raising money by selling numbered tickets and giving prizes to people who hold winning numbers, which are chosen by a method depending on chance (compare *lot* 2).

lotto *noun* a game like bingo.

lotus *noun* (*plural* **lotuses**) a kind of tropical water-lily.

loud *adjective* **1** easily heard; producing much noise. **2** unpleasantly bright; gaudy, *loud colours*. **loudly** *adverb*, **loudness** *noun*

loudspeaker *noun* a device that changes electrical impulses into sound.

lounge[1] *noun* a sitting-room.

lounge[2] *verb* (**lounged, lounging**) sit or stand lazily; loll.

lourie *noun* a kind of parrot-like bird, often having bright colourful feathers.

louring (rhymes with *flowering*) *adjective* looking dark and threatening, *a louring sky*.

louse *noun* (*plural* **lice**) a small insect that lives as a parasite on animals or plants.

lousy *adjective* (**lousier, lousiest**) **1** full of lice. **2** (*informal*) very bad.

lout *noun* a bad-mannered person.

lovable *adjective* easy to love.

love[1] *noun* **1** great liking or affection. **2** sexual affection or passion. **3** a loved person; a sweetheart. **4** (in games) no score; nil.

in love feeling strong love.

love[2] *verb* (**loved, loving**) feel love for a person or thing. **lover** *noun*, **lovingly** *adverb*

loveless *adjective* without love.

lovelorn *adjective* pining with love, especially when abandoned by a lover.

lovely *adjective* (**lovelier, loveliest**) **1** beautiful. **2** (*informal*) very pleasant or enjoyable. **loveliness** *noun*

lovesick *adjective* languishing with love.

low[1] *adjective* not high. **lowness** *noun*

low[2] *adverb* at or to a low level or position etc., *The plane was flying low*.

low[3] *verb* moo like a cow.

lower[1] *adjective* & *adverb* less high.

lower[2] *verb* make or become lower.

lowlands *plural noun* low-lying country. **lowland** *adjective*, **lowlander** *noun*

lowly *adjective* (**lowlier, lowliest**) humble. **lowliness** *noun*

lowveld *noun* the subtropical low-lying area in the north and north-east of South Africa.

loyal *adjective* always firmly supporting your friends or group or country etc. **loyally** *adverb*, **loyalty** *noun*

loyalist *noun* a person who is loyal to the government during a revolt.

lozenge *noun* **1** a small flavoured tablet, especially as medicine. **2** a diamond shape.

Ltd *abbreviation* Limited.

lubricant *noun* a lubricating substance.

lubricate *verb* (**lubricated, lubricating**) oil or grease something so that it moves smoothly. **lubrication** *noun*

lucid *adjective* 1 clear and easy to understand. 2 sane. **lucidly** *adverb*, **lucidity** *noun*

luck *noun* 1 the way things happen without being planned; chance. 2 good fortune, *It will bring you luck.*

luckless *adjective* unlucky.

lucky *adjective* (**luckier, luckiest**) having or bringing or resulting from good luck. **luckily** *adverb*

lucrative (*say* loo-kra-tiv) *adjective* profitable; producing much money.

lucre (*say* loo-ker) *noun* (*contemptuous*) money.

ludicrous *adjective* ridiculous. **ludicrously** *adverb*

ludo *noun* a game played with dice and counters on a board.

lug[1] *verb* (**lugged, lugging**) drag or carry something heavy.

lug[2] *noun* an ear-like part on an object, by which it may be carried or fixed.

luggage *noun* suitcases and bags etc. holding things for taking on a journey.

lugubrious (*say* lug-oo-bree-us) *adjective* dismal. **lugubriously** *adverb*

lukewarm *adjective* 1 only slightly warm; tepid. 2 not very enthusiastic, *lukewarm applause.*

lull[1] *verb* soothe or calm; send to sleep.

lull[2] *noun* a short period of quiet or inactivity.

lullaby *noun* (*plural* **lullabies**) a song that is sung to send a baby to sleep.

lumbago *noun* pain in the muscles of the loins.

lumbar *adjective* of the loins.

lumber[1] *noun* 1 unwanted furniture etc.; junk. 2 timber.

lumber[2] *verb* 1 encumber. 2 fill up space with junk. 3 move in a heavy clumsy way.

lumberjack *noun* a person whose job is to cut or carry timber.

luminescent *adjective* giving out light. **luminescence** *noun*

luminous *adjective* glowing in the dark. **luminosity** *noun*

lump[1] *noun* 1 a solid piece of something. 2 a swelling. **lumpy** *adjective*

lump sum a single payment, especially one covering a number of items.

lump[2] *verb* put things together as being similar; deal with things together.

lump[3] *verb* **lump it** (*informal*) put up with something you dislike.

lunacy *noun* (*plural* **lunacies**) insanity; madness.

lunar *adjective* of the moon. **lunar month** the period between new moons; four weeks.

lunatic *noun* an insane person. **lunatic** *adjective*

lunch *noun* (*plural* **lunches**) a meal eaten in the middle of the day. **lunch** *verb*

luncheon *noun* (*formal*) lunch.

lung *noun* either of the two parts of the body, in the chest, used in breathing.

lunge *verb* (**lunged, lunging**) thrust the body forward suddenly. **lunge** *noun*

lupin *noun* a garden plant with tall spikes of flowers.

lurch[1] *verb* stagger; lean suddenly to one side. **lurch** *noun*

lurch[2] *noun* **leave somebody in the lurch** leave somebody in difficulties.

lure *verb* (**lured, luring**) tempt a person or animal into a trap; entice. **lure** *noun*

lurid (*say* lewr-id) *adjective* 1 in very bright colours; gaudy. 2 sensational and shocking, *the lurid details of the murder.* **luridly** *adverb*, **luridness** *noun*

lurk *verb* wait where you cannot be seen.

luscious (*say* lush-us) *adjective* delicious. **lusciously** *adverb*, **lusciousness** *noun*

lush *adjective* 1 growing thickly and strongly, *lush grass.* 2 luxurious. **lushly** *adverb*, **lushness** *noun*

lust *noun* powerful desire. **lustful** *adjective*

lustre *noun* brightness; brilliance. **lustrous** *adjective*

lusty *adjective* (**lustier, lustiest**) strong and vigorous. **lustily** *adverb*, **lustiness** *noun*

lute *noun* a musical instrument rather like a guitar.

luxuriant *adjective* growing abundantly. ● USAGE: Do not confuse with *luxurious.*

luxuriate *verb* (**luxuriated, luxuriating**) enjoy something as a luxury, *luxuriating in the warm sunshine.*

luxury *noun* (*plural* **luxuries**) 1 something expensive that you enjoy but do not really need. 2 expensive and comfortable surroundings. **luxurious** *adjective*, **luxuriously** *adverb*

lychee (*say* lee-chee) *noun* a small sweet white fruit in a thin reddish shell.

lying *present participle* of **lie**² and **lie**³.

lymph (*say* limf) *noun* a colourless fluid from the flesh or organs of the body, containing white blood-cells. **lymphatic** *adjective*

lynch *verb* join together to execute or punish someone violently without a proper trial.

lynx *noun* (*plural* **lynxes**) a wild animal like a very large cat with thick fur and very sharp sight, also called a rooikat.

lyre *noun* an ancient musical instrument like a small harp, popular in Europe in the 14th–17th centuries.

lyric (*say* lirrik) *noun* 1 a short poem that expresses thoughts and feelings. 2 the words of a song. **lyrical** *adjective*, **lyrically** *adverb*

Mm

ma *noun* (*informal*) mother.

ma'am (*say* mam) *noun* madam.

maas *noun* thick naturally soured milk.

mac *noun* (*informal*) a mackintosh.

macabre (*say* mak-**ah**br) *adjective* gruesome.

macadam *noun* layers of broken stone rolled flat to make a firm road-surface. **macadamized** *adjective*

macaroni *noun* flour-paste (*pasta*) formed into tubes.

macaroon *noun* a small sweet cake or biscuit made with ground almonds.

macaw *noun* a brightly coloured parrot.

mace *noun* an ornamental staff carried or placed in front of an official.

mach (*say* mahk) *noun* **mach number** the ratio of the speed of a moving object to the speed of sound, *mach one is the speed of sound.*

machete (*say* ma-**shet**-ee) *noun* a broad heavy knife used as a tool or weapon.

machiavellian (*say* mak-ee-a-**vel**-ee-an) *adjective* very cunning or deceitful.

machinations (*say* mash-in-**ay**-shonz) *plural noun* clever schemes or plots.

machine¹ *noun* something with parts that work together to do a job.

machine² *verb* (**machined, machining**) make something with a machine, *a machined component.* **machinist** *noun*

machine-gun *noun* a gun that can keep firing bullets quickly one after another.

machinery *noun* 1 machines. 2 mechanism. 3 an organized system for doing something, *the machinery of Parliament.*

macho (*say* **mach**-oh) *adjective* showing off masculine strength.

mackerel *noun* (*plural* **mackerel**) a seafish used as food.

mackintosh *noun* (*plural* **mackintoshes**) a raincoat.

macrocosm *noun* 1 the universe. 2 a large complete structure. (Compare *microcosm*.)

mad *adjective* (**madder, maddest**) 1 having something wrong with the mind; insane. 2 extremely foolish. 3 very keen, *He is mad about football.* 4 (*informal*) very excited or annoyed. **madly** *adverb*, **madness** *noun*, **madman** *noun*

like mad (*informal*) with great speed, energy, or enthusiasm.

madam *noun* a word used when speaking politely to a woman, *Can I help you, madam?*

madcap *noun* a wildly impulsive person.

madden *verb* make a person mad or angry.

madonna *noun* a picture or statue of the Virgin Mary.

madrigal *noun* a song for several voices singing different parts together.

maelstrom (*say* **mayl**-strom) *noun* a great whirlpool.

maestro (*say* **my**-stroh) *noun* (*plural* **maestros**) a master, especially a musician.

magazine *noun* 1 a paper-covered

publication that comes out regularly, with articles or stories etc. by a number of writers. **2** the part of a gun that holds the cartridges. **3** a store for weapons and ammunition or for explosives. **4** a device that holds film for a camera or slides for a projector.

magenta (*say* ma-**jen**-ta) *noun* a colour between bright red and purple.

maggot *noun* the larva of some kinds of fly. **maggoty** *adjective*

Magi (*say* **mayj**-I) *plural noun* the 'wise men' from the East who brought offerings to the infant Jesus at Bethlehem.

magic *noun* the art or pretended art of making things happen by secret or unusual powers. **magic** *adjective*, **magical** *adjective*, **magically** *adverb*

magician *noun* a person who is skilled in magic; a wizard.

magisterial *adjective* **1** of a magistrate. **2** masterful; full of authority; imperious.

magistrate *noun* an official who hears and judges minor cases in a local court. **magistracy** *noun*

magma *noun* a molten substance beneath the earth's crust.

magnanimous (*say* mag-**nan**-im-us) *adjective* generous and forgiving; not petty-minded. **magnanimously** *adverb*, **magnanimity** *noun*

magnate *noun* a wealthy influential person, especially in business.

magnesia *noun* a white powder that is a compound of magnesium, used in medicine.

magnesium *noun* a silvery-white metal that burns with a very bright flame.

magnet *noun* a piece of iron or steel etc. that can attract iron and that points north and south when it is hung up. **magnetism** *noun*

magnetic *adjective* having the powers of a magnet. **magnetically** *adverb*

magnetize *verb* (**magnetized, magnetizing**) **1** make into a magnet. **2** attract like a magnet. **magnetization** *noun*

magneto (*say* mag-**neet**-oh) *noun* (*plural* **magnetos**) a small electric generator using magnets.

magnificent *adjective* **1** grand or splendid in appearance etc. **2** excellent, *a magnificent achievement*. **magnificently** *adverb*, **magnificence** *noun*

magnify *verb* (**magnified, magnifying**) **1** make something look or seem bigger than it really is. **2** (*old use*) praise, *My soul doth magnify the Lord*. **magnification** *noun*, **magnifier** *noun*

magnifying glass a lens that magnifies things.

magnitude *noun* **1** largeness; size. **2** importance.

magnolia *noun* a tree with large white or pale-pink flowers.

magnum *noun* a large bottle containing about 1,5 litres of wine or spirits.

magpie *noun* a noisy bird with black and white feathers.

maharajah *noun* the title of certain Indian princes.

mah-jong *noun* a Chinese game for four people, played with pieces called tiles.

mahogany *noun* a hard brown wood.

maid *noun* **1** a female servant. **2** (*old use*) a girl. **maidservant** *noun*

maiden[1] *noun* (*old use*) a girl. **maidenhood** *noun*

maiden[2] *adjective* **1** not married, *a maiden aunt*. **2** first, *a maiden voyage*.

maiden name a woman's family name before she married.

maiden over a cricket over in which no runs are scored.

mail[1] *noun* letters or parcels etc. sent by post.

mail order ordering goods by post.

mail[2] *verb* send by post.

mail[3] *noun* armour made of metal rings joined together, *a suit of chain-mail*.

maim *verb* injure a person so that part of his or her body is useless.

main[1] *adjective* principal; most important; largest.

main[2] *noun* the main pipe or cable in a public system carrying water, gas, or (usually called **mains**) electricity to a building.

mainland *noun* the main part of a country or continent, not the islands round it.

mainly *adverb* chiefly; almost completely.

mainstay *noun* the chief support.

maintain *verb* 1 cause something to continue; keep in existence. 2 keep a thing in good condition, *Her car is well-maintained.* 3 provide money for a person to live on. 4 state that something is true, *maintain his innocence.* **maintenance** *noun*

maisonette *noun* 1 a small house. 2 part of a house used as a separate dwelling.

maize *noun* a tall kind of corn with large seeds on cobs, also called mealie(s).

majestic *adjective* stately and dignified; imposing. **majestically** *adverb*

majesty *noun* (*plural* **majesties**) 1 the title of a king or queen, *His Majesty the King.* 2 being majestic.

major[1] *adjective* 1 greater; very important, *major roads.* 2 of the musical scale that has a semitone after the 3rd and 7th notes. (Compare *minor.*)

major[2] *noun* 1 an army officer ranking next above a captain. 2 the main subject or course studied by a student.

majority *noun* (*plural* **majorities**) 1 the greatest part of a group of people or things. (Compare *minority.*) 2 the difference between numbers of votes, *She had a majority of 25 over her opponent.* 3 the age at which a person becomes an adult according to the law (now 18, formerly 21 years of age), *He attained his majority.*

make[1] *verb* (**made, making**) 1 bring something into existence, especially by putting things together. 2 gain or earn, *She makes R30 000 a year.* 3 cause or compel, *Make him repeat it.* 4 achieve, *The swimmer just made the shore.* 5 reckon, *What do you make the time?* 6 perform an action etc., *make an effort.* 7 arrange for use, *make the beds.* 8 cause to be successful or happy, *Her visit made my day.*

make do manage with something that is not what you really want.

make for go towards.

make love have sexual intercourse; (*old use*) embrace a lover.

make off go away quickly.

make out manage to see, hear, or understand something; pretend.

make up build or put together; invent a story etc.; compensate for something; put on make-up.

make up your mind decide.

make[2] *noun* 1 making; how something is made. 2 a brand of goods; something made by a particular firm.

make-believe *noun* pretending; imagining things.

maker *noun* the person or firm that has made something.

makeshift *adjective* improvised or used because you have nothing better, *We used a box as a makeshift table.*

make-up *noun* 1 cosmetics. 2 the way something is made up. 3 a person's character, *a generous make-up.*

makgotla *plural* of **kgotla**.

makhulu (*say* ma-**koo**-loo) *adjective* (*informal*) big; important.

mal- *prefix* bad; badly (as in *malnourished*).

maladjusted *adjective* not fitting well with his or her own circumstances.

maladministration *noun* bad administration, especially of business affairs.

malady *noun* (*plural* **maladies**) an illness or disease.

malapropism *noun* a comical confusion of words that sound the same or similar, e.g. using *hooligan* instead of *hurricane.*

malaria *noun* a feverish disease spread by mosquitoes. **malarial** *adjective*

malcontent *noun* a discontented person.

male[1] *adjective* 1 of the sex that reproduces by fertilizing egg-cells produced by the female. 2 of men, *a male voice choir.*

male[2] *noun* a male person, animal, or plant.

malediction (*say* mal-id-**ik**-shon) *noun* a curse.

malefactor (*say* **mal**-if-ak-ter) *noun* a wrongdoer.

malevolent (*say* ma-**lev**-ol-ent) *adjective* wishing to harm people. **malevolently** *adverb*, **malevolence** *noun*

malformed *adjective* faultily formed.

malfunction *noun* faulty functioning.

malice *noun* a desire to harm others or to tease. **malicious** *adjective*, **maliciously** *adverb*

malign[1] (*say* mal-**I**'n) *adjective* 1 harmful, *a malign influence*. 2 showing malice. **malignity** (*say* mal-**ig**-nit-ee) *noun*

malign[2] *verb* say unpleasant and untrue things about somebody.

malignant *adjective* 1 (of a tumour) growing uncontrollably. 2 full of ill will. **malignantly** *adverb*, **malignancy** *noun*

malinger *verb* pretend to be ill in order to avoid work. **malingerer** *noun*

mall *noun* 1 a covered or sheltered walk. 2 an enclosed shopping centre.

malleable *adjective* 1 able to be pressed or hammered into shape. 2 easy to influence; adaptable. **malleability** *noun*

mallet *noun* 1 a large hammer, usually made of wood. 2 an implement with a long handle, used in croquet or polo for striking the ball.

malnutrition *noun* not having enough food to eat. **malnourished** *adjective*

malpractice *noun* wrongdoing.

malt *noun* dried barley used in brewing, making vinegar, etc. **malted** *adjective*

maltreat *verb* ill-treat. **maltreatment** *noun*

mama *noun* 1 mother. 2 an older woman, *the mama on the bus*.

mamba *noun* a fast-moving poisonous snake.

mamlambo *noun* a water snake in African myth that has magical powers.

mammal *noun* any animal of which the female can feed her babies with her own milk. **mammalian** (*say* mam-**ay**-lee-an) *adjective*

mammoth[1] *noun* an extinct elephant with a hairy skin and curved tusks.

mammoth[2] *adjective* huge.

man[1] *noun* (*plural* **men**) 1 a grown-up male human being. 2 an individual person. 3 mankind. (See note on usage at *he*.) 4 a piece used in chess etc.

man[2] *verb* (**manned, manning**) supply with people to work something, *Man the pumps!*

manacle[1] *noun* a fetter or handcuff.

manacle[2] *verb* (**manacled, manacling**) fasten with manacles.

manage *verb* (**managed, managing**) 1 be able to do something difficult, *He managed to do the sum*. 2 control; be in charge of a shop, factory, etc. **manageable** *adjective*

management *noun* 1 managing. 2 managers; the people in charge.

manager *noun* a person who manages something. **manageress** *noun*, **managerial** (*say* man-a-**jeer**-ee-al) *adjective*

mandarin *noun* 1 an important official. 2 a kind of small orange.

mandate *noun* authority given to someone to carry out a certain task or policy, *An elected government has a mandate to govern the country*.

mandatory *adjective* obligatory; compulsory.

mandible *noun* 1 a jaw, especially the lower one. 2 either part of a bird's beak or the similar part in insects etc. (Compare *maxilla*.)

mandolin *noun* a musical instrument rather like a guitar.

mane *noun* the long hair on a horse's or lion's neck.

manful *adjective* brave. **manfully** *adverb*

manganese *noun* a hard brittle metal.

mange *noun* a skin disease of dogs etc. **mangy** *adjective*

manger *noun* a trough in a stable etc., for horses or cattle to feed from.

mangle[1] *noun* a wringer. **mangle** *verb*

mangle[2] *verb* (**mangled, mangling**) damage something by crushing or cutting it roughly.

mango *noun* (*plural* **mangoes**) a tropical fruit with yellow pulp and a large fibrous stone.

mangrove *noun* a tropical tree growing in mud and swamps, with many tangled roots above the ground.

manhandle *verb* (**manhandled, manhandling**) treat or push roughly.

manhole *noun* a space or opening, usually with a cover, by which a person can get into a sewer or boiler etc. to inspect or repair it.

manhood *noun* 1 the condition of being a man. 2 qualities traditionally associated with men.

mania *noun* 1 violent madness. 2 great enthusiasm, *a mania for sport*. **manic** *adjective*

maniac *noun* a person with mania.

manicure *noun* care and treatment of the hands and nails. **manicure** *verb*, **manicurist** *noun*

manifest¹ *adjective* clear and obvious. **manifestly** *adverb*

manifest² *verb* show a thing clearly. **manifestation** *noun*

manifesto *noun* (*plural* **manifestos**) a public statement of a group's or person's policy or principles.

manifold *adjective* of many kinds; very varied.

manioc *noun* cassava; the flour made from this.

manipulate *verb* (**manipulated, manipulating**) handle or arrange something cleverly or cunningly. **manipulation** *noun*, **manipulator** *noun*

mankind *noun* human beings in general. (See note on usage at *he*.)

manly *adjective* considered suitable for a man; strong, brave. **manliness** *noun*

manner *noun* 1 the way something happens or is done. 2 a person's way of behaving. 3 sort, *all manner of things*. **manners** *plural noun* how a person behaves with other people; politeness.

mannerism *noun* a person's habit or way of doing something.

mannish *adjective* like a man.

manoeuvre¹ (*say* man-**oo**-ver) *noun* a difficult or skilful or cunning action.

manoeuvre² *verb* (**manoeuvred, manoeuvring**) make a manoeuvre. **manoeuvrable** *adjective*

man-of-war *noun* (*plural* **men-of-war**) a warship.

manometer (*say* ma-**nom**-i-ter) *noun* an instrument that measures gas or liquid pressure.

manor *noun* a large important house (*manor house*) in the country; the land belonging to it. **manorial** *adjective*

manpower *noun* the number of people who are working or needed or available for work on something.

mansion *noun* a large stately house.

manslaughter *noun* killing a person unlawfully but without meaning to.

mantelpiece *noun* a shelf above a fireplace.

mantilla *noun* a lace veil worn by Spanish women over the hair and shoulders.

mantis *noun* (*plural* **mantis** or **mantises**) an insect that preys on other insects and holds its forelegs like hands folded in prayer.

mantle *noun* a cloak.

manual¹ *adjective* of or done with the hands, *manual work*. **manually** *adverb*

manual² *noun* a handbook.

manufacture *verb* (**manufactured, manufacturing**) 1 make goods, especially in a factory etc. 2 invent a story or evidence. **manufacture** *noun*, **manufacturer** *noun*

manure *noun* fertilizer, especially dung.

manuscript *noun* something written or typed but not printed.

many¹ *adjective* (**more, most**) great in number; numerous, *many people*.

many² *noun* many people or things, *Many were found*.

map¹ *noun* a diagram of part or all of the earth's surface or of the sky.

map² *verb* (**mapped, mapping**) make a map of an area. **map out** plan the details of something.

maple *noun* a tree with broad leaves, often having a sugary sap.

mar *verb* (**marred, marring**) spoil.

marabou (*say* **ma**-ra-boo) *noun* a large stork.

maraca *noun* a gourd filled with beans that is shaken rhythmically as a musical instrument.

marathon *noun* a long-distance race for runners, usually of 42 kilometres.

marauding *adjective* going about in search of plunder or prey. **marauder** *noun*

marble *noun* 1 a small glass ball used in games. 2 a kind of limestone polished and used in sculpture or building.

march¹ *verb* 1 walk with regular steps. 2 make somebody walk somewhere, *He marched them up the hill.* **marcher** *noun*

march² *noun* (*plural* **marches**) 1 marching. 2 music suitable for marching to.

mare *noun* a female horse or donkey.

margarine (*say* mar-ja-**reen**) *noun*

a substance used like butter, made from animal or vegetable fats.

marge *noun* (*informal*) margarine.

margin *noun* **1** an edge or border. **2** the blank space between the edge of a page and the writing or pictures etc. on it. **3** the difference between two scores or prices etc., *She won by a narrow margin.*

marginal *adjective* **1** of or in a margin, *marginal notes.* **2** very slight, *a marginal difference.* **marginally** *adverb*

marginal seat a constituency where a Member of Parliament was elected with only a small majority and may be defeated in the next election.

marigold *noun* a yellow or orange garden flower.

marijuana (*say* ma-ri-**hwah**-na) *noun* a drug made from hemp, also called dagga.

marimba *noun* a kind of xylophone.

marina *noun* a harbour for yachts, motor boats, etc.

marinade *noun* a flavoured liquid in which meat or fish is soaked before being cooked. **marinade** or **marinate** *verb*

marine[1] (*say* ma-**reen**) *adjective* of or concerned with the sea.

marine[2] *noun* a member of the troops who are trained to serve at sea as well as on land.

mariner (*say* ma-rin-er) *noun* a sailor.

marionette *noun* a puppet worked by strings or wires.

marital *adjective* of marriage.

maritime *adjective* **1** of the sea or ships. **2** found near the sea, *the maritime cities of South Africa.*

mark[1] *noun* **1** a spot, dot, line, or stain etc. on something. **2** a number or letter etc. put on a piece of work to show its quality. **3** a distinguishing feature, *The horse had a mark on its leg.* **4** a symbol. **5** a target; the normal standard, *way off the mark.* **6** the position from which you start a race, *On your marks!*

mark[2] *verb* **1** put a mark on something. **2** give a mark to a piece of work; correct. **3** pay attention to something, *Mark my words!* **4** keep close to an opposing player in football etc. **marker** *noun*

mark time march on one spot without moving forward; occupy your time without making progress.

mark[3] *noun* a German unit of money.

marked *adjective* noticeable, *a marked improvement.* **markedly** *adverb*

market[1] *noun* **1** a place where things are bought and sold, usually from stalls in the open air. **2** demand for things; trade, *the free market system.* **market-place** *noun*

market research the study of consumers' needs and preferences.

market[2] *verb* (**marketed, marketing**) offer things for sale. **marketable** *adjective*

marksman *noun* (*plural* **marksmen**) an expert in shooting at a target. **marksman-ship** *noun*

mark-up *noun* the difference between the selling price and the cost price of a product or service, often expressed as a percentage.

marmalade *noun* jam made from oranges, lemons, or other citrus fruit.

marmoset *noun* a kind of small monkey.

maroon[1] *verb* abandon or isolate somebody in a deserted place; strand.

maroon[2] *noun* dark red.

marquee (*say* mar-**kee**) *noun* a large tent used for a party or exhibition etc.

marriage *noun* **1** the state of being married. **2** a wedding.

marrow *noun* **1** a large gourd eaten as a vegetable. **2** the soft substance inside bones.

marry *verb* (**married, marrying**) **1** become a person's husband or wife. **2** unite a man and woman legally for the purpose of living together.

marsh *noun* (*plural* **marshes**) an area of very wet ground. **marshy** *adjective*

marshal[1] *noun* **1** an official who supervises a contest or ceremony etc. **2** an officer of very high rank, *a Field Marshal.*

marshal[2] *verb* (**marshalled, marshalling**) **1** arrange neatly. **2** usher; escort.

marshmallow *noun* a soft spongy sweet.

marsupial (*say* mar-**soo**-pee-al) *noun* an animal such as a kangaroo or wallaby. The female has a pouch on the front of its body in which its babies are carried.

martial *adjective* of war; warlike.

martial arts fighting sports, such as judo and karate.

martial law government of a country by the armed forces during a crisis.

martin *noun* a bird rather like a swallow.

martinet *noun* a very strict person.

martyr[1] *noun* a person who is killed or suffers because of his or her beliefs. **martyrdom** *noun*

martyr[2] *verb* kill or torment someone as a martyr.

marula *noun* a subtropical tree with plum-like fruits.

marvel[1] *noun* a wonderful thing.

marvel[2] *verb* (**marvelled, marvelling**) be filled with wonder.

marvellous *adjective* wonderful.

Marxism *noun* the Communist theories of the German writer Karl Marx (1818–83). **Marxist** *noun*

marzipan *noun* a soft sweet food made of ground almonds and sugar.

masala *noun* a mixture of curry spices.

mascara *noun* a cosmetic for darkening the eyelashes.

mascot *noun* a person, animal, or thing that is believed to bring good luck.

masculine *adjective* of or like men; considered suitable for men. **masculinity** *noun*

mash[1] *verb* crush into a soft mass.

mash[2] *noun* 1 a soft mixture of cooked grain or bran etc. 2 (*informal*) mashed potatoes.

mask[1] *noun* a covering worn over the face to disguise or protect it.

mask[2] *verb* 1 cover with a mask. 2 disguise; screen; conceal, *mask the unpleasant smell with perfume.*

masochist (*say* mas-ok-ist) *noun* a person who enjoys things that seem painful or tiresome. **masochism** *noun*

mason *noun* a person who builds or works with stone; a bricklayer.

masonry *noun* 1 the stone parts of a building; stonework. 2 a mason's work.

masquerade[1] *noun* a pretence.

masquerade[2] *verb* (**masqueraded, masquerading**) pretend to be something, *He masqueraded as a policeman.*

mass[1] *noun* (*plural* **masses**) 1 a large amount. 2 a heap or other collection of matter. 3 (in scientific use) the quantity of matter that a thing contains. In non-scientific use this is called *weight.*

mass production manufacturing goods in large quantities. **mass-produced** *adjective*

the masses *plural noun* the ordinary people.

mass[2] *verb* collect into a mass.

mass[3] *noun* (*plural* **masses**) the Communion service in a Roman Catholic church.

massacre *noun* the killing of a large number of people. **massacre** *verb*

massage (*say* mas-ahzh) *verb* (**massaged, massaging**) rub and press the body to make it less stiff or less painful. **massage** *noun*, **masseur** *noun*, **masseuse** *noun*

massive *adjective* large and heavy; huge.

mast *noun* a tall pole that holds up a ship's sails or a flag or an aerial.

master[1] *noun* 1 a man who is in charge of something. 2 a male teacher. 3 a great artist, composer, sportsman, etc. 4 something from which copies are made, *the master tape.* 5 **Master** a title put before a boy's name.

Master of Arts a person who has taken the next degree after Bachelor of Arts.

master[2] *verb* 1 learn a subject or a skill thoroughly. 2 overcome; bring under control.

masterful *adjective* 1 domineering. 2 very skilful, *a masterful pilot.* **masterfully** *adverb*

masterly *adjective* very skilful, *a masterly display of aerobatics.*

mastermind[1] *noun* 1 a very clever person. 2 the person who is planning and organizing a scheme etc.

mastermind[2] *verb* plan and organize a scheme etc.

masterpiece *noun* 1 an excellent piece of work. 2 a person's best piece of work.

mastery *noun* complete control or thorough knowledge or skill in something.

masticate *verb* (**masticated, masticating**) chew food. **mastication** *noun*

mastiff *noun* a large kind of dog.

masturbate *verb* (**masturbated, masturbating**) excite yourself by fingering your genitals. **masturbation** *noun*

mat *noun* 1 a small carpet; a doormat. 2 a small piece of material put on a table to protect the surface.

matador *noun* a bullfighter who fights on foot.

match¹ *noun* (*plural* **matches**) a small thin stick with a head made of a substance that gives a flame when rubbed on something rough. **matchbox** *noun*, **matchstick** *noun*

match² *noun* (*plural* **matches**) 1 a game or contest between two teams or players. 2 one person or thing that matches another. 3 a marriage.

match³ *verb* 1 be equal or similar to another person or thing. 2 put teams or players to compete against each other. 3 find something that is similar or corresponding.

matchboard *noun* a piece of board that fits into a groove in a similar piece.

matchmaker *noun* a person who arranges marriages or tries to bring couples together.

mate¹ *noun* 1 a companion or friend. 2 one of a mated pair, *the lion's mate.* 3 an officer on a merchant ship.

mate² *verb* (**mated, mating**) 1 come or put together so as to have offspring. 2 put together as a pair or as corresponding.

mate³ *noun* & *verb* (in chess) checkmate.

material¹ *noun* 1 anything used for making something else. 2 cloth; fabric.

material² *adjective* of physical objects, needs, etc. rather than those of the mind or spirit, *material comforts.*

materialism *noun* regarding possessions as very important. **materialist** *noun*, **materialistic** *adjective*

materialize *verb* (**materialized, materializing**) 1 become visible; appear, *The ghost didn't materialize.* 2 become a fact; happen, *The trip did not materialize.* **materialization** *noun*

maternal *adjective* 1 of a mother. 2 motherly. **maternally** *adverb*

maternity *noun* 1 motherhood. 2 having a baby.

matey *adjective* friendly; sociable.

mathematics *noun* the study of numbers, measurements, and shapes. **mathematical** *adjective*, **mathematically** *adverb*, **mathematician** *noun*

maths *noun* (*informal*) mathematics.

matinée *noun* an afternoon performance at a theatre or cinema.

matins *noun* the church service of morning prayer.

matriarch (*say* **may**-tree-ark) *noun* a woman who is head of a family or tribe. (Compare *patriarch.*) **matriarchal** *adjective*, **matriarchy** *noun*

matric *noun* 1 matriculation. 2 a person in a matriculation class, *this year's matrics.*

matriculate *verb* (**matriculated, matriculating**) pass the matriculation exam.

matriculation *noun* a school-leaving examination that must be passed to gain entrance to higher education.

matrimony *noun* marriage. **matrimonial** *adjective*

matrix (*say* **may**-triks) *noun* (*plural* **matrices**) an array of mathematical quantities etc. in rows and columns.

matron *noun* 1 a woman in charge of the nursing staff in a hospital or of nursing in a school etc. 2 a mature married woman. **matronly** *adjective*

matt *adjective* not shiny, *matt paint.*

matted *adjective* tangled into a mass.

matter¹ *noun* 1 something you can touch or see, not spirit or mind or qualities etc. 2 things of a certain kind, *printed matter.* 3 something to be thought about or done, *It's a serious matter.* 4 a quantity, *in a matter of minutes.*
no matter it does not matter.
what is the matter? what is wrong?

matter² *verb* be important, *It matters to me.*

matter-of-fact *adjective* keeping to facts; not imaginative or emotional.

matting *noun* rough material for covering floors.

mattress *noun* (*plural* **mattresses**) soft or springy material in a fabric covering, used on or as a bed.

mature¹ *adjective* fully grown or

developed; grown-up. **maturely** *adverb,*
maturity *noun*

mature² *verb* (**matured, maturing**) make or
become mature.

maudlin *adjective* sentimental in a silly or
tearful way.

maul *verb* injure by handling or clawing,
He was mauled by a lion.

mausoleum (*say* maw-sol-**ee**-um) *noun*
a magnificent tomb.

mauve *noun* pale purple.

maverick *noun* a person who belongs to
a group but often disagrees with its beliefs.

maw *noun* the jaws, mouth, or stomach of
a hungry or fierce animal.

maxilla *noun* (*plural* **maxillae**) the upper
jaw; a similar part in a bird or insect etc.
(Compare *mandible*.)

maxim *noun* a short saying giving a general
truth or rule of behaviour, e.g. 'Waste not,
want not'.

maximize *verb* (**maximized, maximizing**)
increase something to a maximum.

maximum *noun* (*plural* **maxima**) the
greatest possible number or amount.
(The opposite is *minimum*.)

may¹ *auxiliary verb* (*past tense* **might**) used
to express **1** permission, *You may go now.*
2 possibility, *It may be true.* **3** wish, *Long
may she reign.* **4** uncertainty, *whoever it
may be.*

• USAGE: *Can* is also used to express
permission ('You can go now'), but *may*
is preferred in formal English.

may² *noun* hawthorn blossom.

maybe *adverb* perhaps; possibly.

mayday *noun* an international radio signal
calling for help.

mayfly *noun* an insect that lives for only
a short time, in spring.

mayhem *noun* violent confusion or
damage, *The mob caused mayhem.*

mayonnaise *noun* a creamy sauce made
from eggs, oil, vinegar, etc.

mayor *noun* the person in charge of the
council in a town or city. **mayoral** *adjective,*
mayoress *noun*

maze *noun* a network of paths, especially
one designed as a puzzle in which to try and
find your way.

mbaqanga *noun* a jazz music style.

me *pronoun* the form of *I* used as the object
of a verb or after a preposition.

meadow *noun* a field of grass.

meagre *adjective* scanty in amount.

meal¹ *noun* food served and eaten at one
sitting. **mealtime** *noun*

meal² *noun* coarsely-ground grain. **mealy**
adjective

mealie *noun* maize.

mealie meal finely-ground maize used to
make porridge; porridge made from this.

mealiepap mealie meal porridge.

mealie rice dried maize kernels that are
ground and used as a substitute for rice.

mealy-mouthed *adjective* too polite.

mean¹ *verb* (**meant, meaning**) **1** have as
an equivalent, *'Maybe' means 'perhaps'.*
2 have as a purpose; intend, *I mean to win.*
3 indicate, *Dark clouds mean rain.*

mean² *adjective* **1** not generous; miserly.
2 unkind; spiteful, *a mean trick.* **3** poor in
quality or appearance, *a mean little house.*
meanly *adverb,* **meanness** *noun*

mean³ *noun* a middle point or condition.

mean⁴ *adjective* average.

meander (*say* mee-**an**-der) *verb* take
a winding course; wander. **meander** *noun*

meaning *noun* what something means.
meaningful *adjective,* **meaningless**
adjective

means¹ *noun* a way of achieving something or producing a result, *We transport
our goods by means of bakkies.*

by all means certainly.

by no means not at all.

means² *plural noun* money or other
wealth.

means test an inquiry into how much
money etc. a person has, in order to decide
whether he or she is entitled to get help
from public funds.

meantime *noun* the time between two
events or while something else is happening, *in the meantime.*

meanwhile *adverb* in the time between
two events or while something else is
happening.

measles *noun* an infectious disease that
causes small red spots on the skin.

measly *adjective* (*informal*) very small.

measure[1] *verb* (**measured, measuring**) 1 find how big or heavy something is by comparing it with a unit of standard size or weight. 2 be a certain size, *The carpet measures 2 metres by 3 metres.* **measurable** *adjective*, **measurement** *noun*

measure[2] *noun* 1 a unit used for measuring, *A kilometre is a measure of length.* 2 a device used in measuring, *a tape-measure.* 3 the size or quantity of something. 4 the rhythm of poetry; time in music. 5 something done for a particular purpose; a law, *We took measures to stop vandalism.*

meat *noun* animal flesh used as food. **meaty** *adjective*

mebos (*say* **mee**-bos) *noun* a confection of minced dried apricots, usually coated in sugar.

mechanic *noun* a person who uses or repairs machinery.

mechanical *adjective* 1 of machines; produced or worked by machines. 2 automatic; done or doing things without thought. **mechanically** *adverb*

mechanics *noun* 1 the study of movement and force. 2 the study or use of machines.

mechanism *noun* 1 the moving parts of a machine. 2 the way a machine works.

mechanized *adjective* equipped with machines. **mechanization** *noun*

medal *noun* a piece of metal shaped like a coin, star, or cross, given to a person for bravery or for achieving something.

medallion *noun* a large medal.

medallist *noun* a winner of a medal.

meddle *verb* (**meddled, meddling**) 1 interfere. 2 tinker, *Don't meddle with it.* **meddler** *noun*, **meddlesome** *adjective*

media *plural* of **medium** *noun* **the media** newspapers, radio, and television, which convey information and ideas to the public. (See *medium*[2] 2.)
● USAGE: This word is a plural. Say *The media are* (not 'is') *very influential.* It is incorrect to speak of one of them (e.g. television) as 'this media'.

medial *adjective* in the middle; average.

median[1] *adjective* in the middle.

median[2] *noun* 1 a median point or line. 2 a median number or position.

mediate *verb* (**mediated, mediating**) negotiate between the opposing sides in a dispute. **mediation** *noun*, **mediator** *noun*

medical *adjective* connected with the treatment of disease. **medically** *adverb*

medicament *noun* a medicine or ointment etc.

medicated *adjective* treated with a medicinal substance. **medication** *noun*

medicine *noun* 1 a substance, usually swallowed, used to try to cure a disease. 2 the study and treatment of diseases. **medicinal** (*say* med-**iss**-in-al) *adjective*, **medicinally** *adverb*

medieval (*say* med-ee-**ee**-val) *adjective* of the Middle Ages, about AD 1000 to 1400.

mediocre (*say* mee-dee-**oh**-ker) *adjective* not very good; of only medium quality; middling. **mediocrity** *noun*

meditate *verb* (**meditated, meditating**) think deeply and quietly. **meditation** *noun*, **meditative** *adjective*

Mediterranean *adjective* of the Mediterranean Sea (which lies between Europe and Africa) or the countries round it, *Mediterranean food.*

medium[1] *adjective* of middle size or degree or quality etc.; moderate.

medium[2] *noun* (*plural* **media**) 1 a middle size or degree or quality etc. 2 a thing in which something exists, moves, or is expressed, *Air is the medium in which sound travels. Television is used as a medium for advertising.* (See *media*.) 3 the substance used to make a work of art, *the medium of bronze.* 4 (with plural **mediums**) a person who claims to be able to communicate with the dead.

medley *noun* (*plural* **medleys**) an assortment or mixture of things.

meek *adjective* quiet and obedient. **meekly** *adverb*, **meekness** *noun*

meercat (also **meerkat**) *noun* a small animal like a mongoose.

meet[1] *verb* (**met, meeting**) 1 come together from different places; come face to face. 2 come into contact; touch. 3 go to receive an arrival, *We will meet your train.* 4 pay a

bill or the cost of something. **5** deal with,
meet the problem head-on.

meet² *noun* a gathering of people for sport,
especially athletics.

meet³ *adjective* (*old use*) suitable; proper.

meeting *noun* coming together; a number
of people who have come together for a
discussion, contest, etc.

mega- *prefix* **1** large; great (as in *megaphone*). **2** one million (as in *megahertz* =
one million hertz).

megalomania *noun* an exaggerated idea
of your own importance. **megalomaniac**
noun

megaphone *noun* a funnel-shaped device
for amplifying a person's voice.

meiosis (*say* my-**oh**-sis) *noun* a type of cell
division that results in cells with half the
chromosome number of the parent cell.
(Compare *mitosis*.) **meiotic** *adjective*

melamine *noun* a strong kind of plastic.

melancholy¹ *adjective* sad; gloomy.

melancholy² *noun* sadness; gloom.

mêlée (*say* **mel**-ay) *noun* **1** a confused
fight. **2** a muddle.

melktert *noun* a tart made with milk and
eggs.

mellow¹ *adjective* **1** not harsh; soft and rich
in flavour, colour, or sound. **2** kindly and
genial. **mellowness** *noun*

mellow² *verb* make or become mellow.

melodious *adjective* full of melody.

melodrama *noun* a play full of dramatic
excitement and emotion. **melodramatic**
adjective

melody *noun* (*plural* **melodies**) a tune,
especially a pleasing one.

melon *noun* a large sweet fruit with a
yellow, brown, or green skin.

melt *verb* **1** make or become liquid by
heating. **2** disappear slowly. **3** soften,
His heart melted at the sight of her tears.

member *noun* **1** a person or thing that
belongs to a particular society or group.
2 a part of something. **membership** *noun*

membrane *noun* a thin skin or similar
covering. **membranous** *adjective*

memento *noun* (*plural* **mementoes**)
a souvenir.

memo (*say* **mem**-oh) *noun* (*plural*

memos) (*informal*) a memorandum.

memoir (*say* **mem**-wahr) *noun*
a biography.

memoirs *plural noun* an autobiography.

memorable *adjective* worth remembering;
easy to remember. **memorably** *adverb*

memorandum *noun* (*plural* **memoranda**)
a written note, especially to remind yourself
of something.

memorial *noun* something to remind
people of a person or event, *a war
memorial.* **memorial** *adjective*

memorize *verb* (**memorized, memorizing**)
get something into your memory.

memory *noun* (*plural* **memories**) **1** the
ability to remember things. **2** something
that you remember, *childhood memories.*
3 the part of a computer where information
is stored.

menace¹ *noun* **1** a threat or danger.
2 a troublesome person or thing.

menace² *verb* (**menaced, menacing**)
threaten with harm or danger.

menagerie *noun* a small zoo.

mend¹ *verb* **1** repair. **2** make or become
better; improve. **mender** *noun*

mend² *noun* a repair.

mendacious (*say* men-**day**-shus)
adjective untruthful; telling lies.
mendaciously *adverb*, **mendacity** *noun*

mendicant *noun* a beggar.

meneer *noun* a title of respect used when
addressing a man.

menial¹ (*say* **meen**-ee-al) *adjective* lowly;
needing little or no skill, *menial tasks.*
menially *adverb*

menial² *noun* a person who does menial
work; a servant.

meningitis *noun* a disease causing
inflammation of the membranes
(*meninges*) round the brain and spinal cord.

meniscus (*say* men-**is**-kus) *noun* (*plural*
menisci (*say* men-**is**-I)) (in physics) the
curved surface of a liquid in a container.

menopause *noun* the time of life when
a woman finally ceases to menstruate.

menstruate *verb* (**menstruated, men-
struating**) bleed from the womb about
once a month, as normally happens to girls
and women from their teens until middle

age. **menstruation** *noun,* **menstrual** *adjective*

mental *adjective* 1 of or in the mind. 2 (*informal*) mad. **mentally** *adverb*

mentality *noun* (*plural* **mentalities**) a person's mental ability or attitude.

menthol *noun* a solid white peppermint-flavoured substance.

mention[1] *verb* speak or write about a person or thing briefly; refer to.

mention[2] *noun* mentioning something.

mentor *noun* a trusted adviser; a counsellor.

menu (*say* **men**-yoo) *noun* 1 a list of the food available in a restaurant or served at a meal. 2 a list of things, shown on a screen, from which you decide what you want a computer to do.

mercantile *adjective* trading; of trade.

mercenary[1] *adjective* working only for money or some other reward.

mercenary[2] *noun* (*plural* **mercenaries**) a soldier hired to serve in a foreign army.

merchandise *noun* goods for sale.

merchant *noun* a person involved in trade. **merchant navy** ships involved in trade; people who work on them.

merciful *adjective* showing mercy. **mercifully** *adverb*

merciless *adjective* showing no mercy; cruel. **mercilessly** *adverb*

mercurial *adjective* 1 of mercury. 2 having sudden changes of mood.

mercury *noun* a heavy silvery metal (also called *quicksilver*) that is usually liquid, used in thermometers. **mercuric** *adjective*

mercy *noun* (*plural* **mercies**) 1 kindness or pity shown in not punishing or harming a wrongdoer or enemy etc. 2 something to be thankful for.

mere *adjective* not more than, *He's a mere child.*

merely *adverb* only; simply.

merest *adjective* very small, *the merest trace of colour.*

merge *verb* (**merged, merging**) combine; blend.

merger *noun* the combining of two business companies etc. into one.

meridian *noun* a line on a map or globe from the North Pole to the South Pole. The meridian that passes through Greenwich is shown on maps as 0° longitude.

meringue (*say* mer-**ang**) *noun* a crisp cake made from egg-white and sugar.

merino *noun* (*plural* **merinos**) a kind of sheep with fine soft wool.

merit[1] *noun* a quality that deserves praise; excellence. **meritorious** *adjective*

merit[2] *verb* (**merited, meriting**) deserve.

mermaid *noun* a mythical sea-creature with a woman's body but with a fish's tail instead of legs. **merman** *noun*

merry *adjective* (**merrier, merriest**) cheerful and lively. **merrily** *adverb*, **merriment** *noun*

merry-go-round *noun* a circular revolving ride at fun-fairs.

mesembryanthemum (*say* mee-zem-bree-**an**-the-mum) *noun* a kind of plant which has fleshy leaves and bright flowers that open in the sun.

mesh[1] *noun* 1 the open spaces in a net, sieve, or other criss-cross structure. 2 material made like a net; network.

mesh[2] *verb* (of gears) engage.

mesmerize *verb* hypnotize; fascinate or hold a person's attention completely. **mesmerism** *noun*

mesophyte (*say* **mee**-zoh-fyt) *noun* a plant adapted to live in conditions where there is a moderate amount of water. (Compare *hydrophyte* and *xerophyte*.)

mess[1] *noun* (*plural* **messes**) 1 a dirty or untidy condition or thing. 2 a difficult or confused situation; trouble. 3 (in the armed forces) a dining-room. **make a mess of** bungle.

mess[2] *verb* 1 make a thing dirty or untidy. 2 bungle; spoil by muddling, *They messed up our plans.* **mess about** behave stupidly; potter. **mess with** interfere or tinker with.

message *noun* a piece of information etc. sent from one person to another.

messenger *noun* a person who carries a message.

Messiah (*say* mis-I-a) *noun* 1 the saviour expected by the Jews. 2 Jesus Christ, who Christians believe was this saviour.

Messianic *adjective*

messy *adjective* dirty; untidy. **messily** *adverb*, **messiness** *noun*

metabolism (*say* mit-**ab**-ol-izm) *noun* the process by which food is built up into living material in a plant or animal, or used to supply it with energy. **metabolic** *adjective*, **metabolize** *verb*

metal *noun* a hard mineral substance (e.g. gold, silver, copper, iron) that melts when it is heated. **metallic** *adjective*

metallurgy (*say* mit-**al**-er-jee) *noun* the study of metals; the craft of making and using metals. **metallurgical** *adjective*, **metallurgist** *noun*

metamorphic *adjective* formed or changed by heat or pressure, *Marble is a metamorphic rock.*

metamorphosis (*say* met-a-**mor**-fo-sis) *noun* (*plural* **metamorphoses**) a change of form or character. **metamorphose** *verb*

metaphor *noun* using a word or phrase in a way that is not literal, e.g. 'The pictures of starving people *touched our hearts*'. **metaphorical** *adjective*, **metaphorically** *adverb*

mete *verb* (**meted, meting**) **mete out** deal out; allot, *mete out punishment.*

meteor (*say* **meet**-ee-er) *noun* a piece of rock or metal that moves through space and burns up when it enters the earth's atmosphere.

meteoric (*say* meet-ee-**o**-rik) *adjective* 1 of meteors. 2 like a meteor in brilliance or sudden appearance, *a meteoric career.*

meteorite *noun* a meteor that has landed on the earth.

meteorology *noun* the study of the conditions of the atmosphere, especially in order to forecast the weather. **meteorological** *adjective*, **meteorologist** *noun*

meter *noun* a device for measuring something, e.g. the amount supplied, *a gas meter.* **meter** *verb*

methane (*say* **mee**-thayn) *noun* an inflammable gas found in marshy areas and in coal-mines.

method *noun* 1 a procedure or way of doing something. 2 methodical behaviour; orderliness.

methodical *adjective* doing things in an orderly or systematic way. **methodically** *adverb*

meths *noun* (*informal*) methylated spirit.

methylated spirit (also **spirits**) *noun* a liquid fuel made from alcohol.

meticulous *adjective* very careful and exact. **meticulously** *adverb*

metre *noun* 1 a unit of length in the metric system. 2 rhythm in poetry, *the sonnet's metre of ten syllables per line.*

metric *adjective* 1 of the metric system. 2 of metre in poetry. **metrically** *adverb*

metric system a measuring system based on decimal units (the metre, litre, and gram).

metrical *adjective* of or in rhythmic metre, not prose, *metrical psalms.*

metronome *noun* a device that makes a regular clicking noise to help a person keep in time when practising music.

metropolis *noun* the chief city of a country or region. **metropolitan** *adjective*

mettle *noun* courage; strength of character. **mettlesome** *adjective*

be on your mettle be determined to show your courage or ability.

mevrou (*say* me-**froh**) *noun* a title of respect used when addressing a married or older woman.

mew *verb* make a cat's cry. **mew** *noun*

mews *noun* a group of what were once stables, rebuilt or converted into garages or small houses.

Mfecane *noun* the large and widespread movements of people in South Africa in the early 19th century, often as a result of wars.

miaow *verb* & *noun* mew.

miasma (*say* mee-**az**-ma) *noun* unpleasant or unhealthy air.

mica *noun* a mineral substance used to make electrical insulators.

micro- *prefix* very small (as in *microfilm*).

microbe *noun* a micro-organism.

microbiology *noun* the study of micro-organisms.

microchip *noun* a very small piece of silicon etc. made to work like a complex wired electric circuit.

microcomputer *noun* a very small computer.

microcosm *noun* a world in miniature; something regarded as resembling something else on a very small scale. (Compare *macrocosm*.)

microfilm *noun* a length of film on which written or printed material is photographed in greatly reduced size.

microlight *noun* a kind of hang-glider with a motor.

micro-organism *noun* a microscopic creature, e.g. a bacterium or virus.

microphone *noun* an electrical device that picks up sound waves for recording, amplifying, or broadcasting.

microprocessor *noun* a miniature computer (or a unit of this) consisting of one or more microchips.

microscope *noun* an instrument with lenses that magnify tiny objects or details.

microscopic *adjective* 1 extremely small; too small to be seen without the aid of a microscope. 2 of a microscope.

microwave *noun* 1 a very short electromagnetic wave. 2 a microwave oven. **microwave oven** an oven that uses microwaves to heat food very quickly.

mid *adjective* in the middle of; middle.

midday *noun* the middle of the day; noon.

middle[1] *noun* 1 the place or part of something that is at the same distance from all its sides or edges or from both its ends. 2 someone's waist.

middle[2] *adjective* 1 placed or happening in the middle. 2 moderate in size or rank etc. **Middle Ages** the period in history from about AD 1000 to 1400. **middle class** the class of people between the very rich and the working class, including business and professional people. **Middle East** the countries from Egypt to Iran inclusive.

middleman *noun* (*plural* **middlemen**) 1 a trader who buys from a producer and sells to a consumer. 2 an intermediary.

middling *adjective* & *adverb* moderately good; moderately.

midge *noun* a small insect like a gnat.

midget *noun* an extremely small person or thing. **midget** *adjective*

midnight *noun* twelve o'clock at night.

midriff *noun* the front part of the body just above the waist.

midshipman *noun* (*plural* **midshipmen**) a sailor ranking next above a cadet.

midst *noun* the middle of something.

midsummer *noun* the middle of summer, about 22 December in the southern hemisphere.

midway *adverb* half-way.

midwife *noun* (*plural* **midwives**) a person trained to look after a woman who is giving birth to a baby. **midwifery** *noun*

mielie *noun* a mealie.

mien (*say* meen) *noun* a person's manner.

might[1] *noun* great strength or power.

might[2] *auxiliary verb* used 1 as the past tense of *may*[1], *We told her she might go.* 2 to express possibility, *It might be true.*

mighty *adjective* very strong or powerful. **mightily** *adverb*, **mightiness** *noun*

migraine (*say* mee-grayn) *noun* a severe kind of headache.

migrant *noun* a person or animal that migrates or has migrated.

migrate *verb* (**migrated**, **migrating**) 1 leave one place or country and settle in another. 2 (of birds or animals) move periodically from one area to another. **migration** *noun*, **migratory** *adjective*

mike *noun* (*informal*) a microphone.

mild *adjective* 1 gentle; not harsh or severe. 2 not strongly flavoured, *mild mustard*. **mildly** *adverb*, **mildness** *noun*

mildew *noun* a tiny fungus that forms a white coating on things kept in damp conditions. **mildewed** *adjective*

mile *noun* a measure of distance in the imperial system, about 1,6 kilometres.

mileage *noun* the number of miles travelled.

milestone *noun* 1 a stone of a kind that used to be fixed beside a road to mark the distance between towns. 2 an important event in life or history.

milieu (*say* meel-yer) *noun* (*plural* **milieux** or **milieus**) environment; surroundings.

militant *adjective* eager to fight or be

aggressive. **militant** *noun*, **militancy** *noun*

militarism *noun* belief in the use of military strength and methods. **militarist** *noun*, **militaristic** *adjective*

military *adjective* of soldiers or the armed forces.

militate *verb* (**militated, militating**) have a strong effect or influence, *The weather militated against the success of our plans.*
● USAGE: Do not confuse with *mitigate.*

militia (*say* mil-**ish**-a) *noun* a military force, especially one raised from civilians.

milk¹ *noun* **1** a white liquid that female mammals produce in their bodies to feed their babies. **2** the milk of cows, used as food by human beings. **3** a milky liquid, e.g. that in a coconut.

milk tooth a temporary tooth in young mammals.

milk² *verb* get the milk from a cow or other animal.

milkman *noun* (*plural* **milkmen**) a person who delivers milk to customers' houses.

milky *adjective* like milk; white.

Milky Way the broad bright band of stars formed by our galaxy.

mill¹ *noun* **1** machinery for grinding corn to make flour; a building containing this machinery. **2** a grinding machine, *a coffee-mill.* **3** a factory for processing certain materials, *a paper-mill.*

mill² *verb* **1** grind or crush in a mill. **2** cut markings round the edge of a coin. **3** move in a confused crowd, *The animals were milling around.* **miller** *noun*

millennium *noun* (*plural* **millenniums**) a period of 1 000 years.

millet *noun* a kind of cereal with tiny seeds.

milli- *prefix* **1** one thousand (as in *milli-pede*). **2** one-thousandth (as in *milligram, millilitre, millimetre*).

milliner *noun* a person who makes or sells women's hats. **millinery** *noun*

million *noun* & *adjective* one thousand thousand (1 000 000). **millionth** *adjective* & *noun*
● USAGE: Say *a few million*, not 'a few millions'.

millionaire *noun* an extremely rich person.

millipede *noun* a small crawling creature like a centipede, with many legs, also called a songololo.

millstone *noun* **1** either of a pair of large circular stones between which corn is ground. **2** a heavy responsibility.

milt *noun* a male fish's sperm.

mime *noun* acting with movements of the body, not using words. **mime** *verb*

mimic¹ *verb* (**mimicked, mimicking**) imitate. **mimicry** *noun*

mimic² *noun* a person who mimics others, especially to amuse people.

mimosa *noun* a tropical tree or shrub with small ball-shaped flowers.

minaret *noun* the tall tower of a mosque.

mince¹ *verb* (**minced, mincing**) **1** cut into very small pieces in a machine. **2** walk in an affected way. **mincer** *noun*

not to mince matters speak bluntly.

mince² *noun* minced meat.

mincemeat *noun* a sweet mixture of currants, raisins, apple, etc. used in pies.

mince pie *noun* a pie containing mince-meat.

mind¹ *noun* **1** the ability to think, feel, understand, and remember, originating in the brain. **2** a person's thoughts and feelings or opinion, *I changed my mind.*

mind² *verb* **1** look after, *He was minding the baby.* **2** be careful about, *Mind the step.* **3** be sad or upset about something; object to, *We don't mind waiting.* **minder** *noun*

mindful *adjective* taking thought or care, *She was mindful of her reputation.*

mindless *adjective* without intelligence.

mine¹ *possessive pronoun* belonging to me.

mine² *noun* **1** a place where coal, metal, precious stones, etc. are dug out of the ground. **2** an explosive placed in or on the ground or in the sea etc. to destroy people or things that come close to it.

mine dump a large hill of waste material from mining activities.

mine³ *verb* (**mined, mining**) **1** dig from a mine. **2** lay explosive mines in a place.

minefield *noun* an area where explosive mines have been laid.

miner *noun* a person who works in a mine.

mineral *noun* **1** a hard inorganic substance found in the ground. **2** a cold fizzy nonalcoholic drink.

mineralogy (*say* min-er-**al**-o-jee) *noun*
the study of minerals. **mineralogist** *noun*

minestrone (*say* mini-**stroh**-nee) *noun*
an Italian soup containing vegetables and
pasta.

minesweeper *noun*　a ship used to clear
explosive mines from the sea.

mingle *verb*　(**mingled, mingling**) mix.

mini- *prefix*　miniature; very small.

miniature[1] *adjective*　very small; copying
something on a very small scale.

miniature[2] *noun*　1 a very small portrait.
2 a small-scale model.

minibus *noun*　(*plural* **minibuses**) a small
bus.
　minibus taxi a minibus that carries
passengers on a regular route.

minicomputer *noun*　a small computer.

minim *noun*　a note in music, lasting half as
long as a semibreve.

minimize *verb*　(**minimized, minimizing**)
reduce something to a minimum.

minimum *noun*　(*plural* **minima**) the lowest
possible number or amount. (The opposite
is *maximum.*) **minimal** *adjective*

minion *noun*　(*contemptuous*) a very
obedient assistant or servant.

minister[1] *noun*　1 a person in charge of a
government department. 2 a member of
the clergy. **ministerial** *adjective*

minister[2] *verb*　attend to people's needs.

ministry *noun*　(*plural* **ministries**)
1 a government department, *the Ministry
of Defence.* 2 the work of the clergy.

mink *noun*　1 an animal rather like a stoat.
2 this animal's valuable brown fur.

minnow *noun*　a tiny freshwater fish.

minor *adjective*　1 less important; not very
important. 2 of the musical scale that has a
semitone after the second note. (Compare
major.)

minority *noun*　(*plural* **minorities**) 1 the
smallest part of a group of people or things.
2 a small group that is different from others.
(Compare *majority.*)

minstrel *noun*　a travelling singer and
musician in the Middle Ages in Europe.

mint[1] *noun*　1 a plant with fragrant leaves
that are used for flavouring things.

2 peppermint; a sweet flavoured with this.

mint[2] *noun*　the place where a country's
coins are made.

mint[3] *adjective*　clean and new or unused.

mint[4] *verb*　make coins.

minuet *noun*　a slow stately dance.

minus[1] *preposition*　with the next number
or thing subtracted, *Ten minus four equals
six (10 − 4 = 6).*

minus[2] *adjective*　less than zero, *temperatures of minus ten degrees* (−10°).

minute[1] (*say* **min**-it) *noun*　1 one-sixtieth
of an hour. 2 a very short time; a moment.
3 a particular time, *Come here this minute!*
4 one-sixtieth of a degree (used in
measuring angles).
　minutes *plural noun* a written summary
of what was said at a meeting.

minute[2] (*say* my-**newt**) *adjective*　1 very
small, *a minute insect.* 2 very detailed,
a minute examination. **minutely** *adverb*

minx *noun*　(*plural* **minxes**) a cheeky or
mischievous girl.

miracle *noun*　something wonderful and
good that happens, especially something
believed to have a supernatural or divine
cause. **miraculous** *adjective*, **miraculously**
adverb

mirage (*say* mi-**rah**zh) *noun*　an illusion;
something that seems to be there but is not,
especially when a lake seems to appear in a
desert.

mire *noun*　swampy ground; mud.

mirror[1] *noun*　a device or surface of
reflecting material, usually glass.

mirror[2] *verb*　reflect in or like a mirror.

mirth *noun*　merriment; laughter. **mirthful**
adjective, **mirthless** *adjective*

mis *noun*　1 manure that has been dried for
fuel. 2 a mixture of cow-dung and water
formerly used for spreading on floors.
　misvloer a floor made of dried dung.

mis- *prefix*　badly; wrongly.
(Compare *amiss.*)

misadventure *noun*　a piece of bad luck.

misanthropy *noun*　dislike of people. **mis-
anthropist** *noun*, **misanthropic** *adjective*

misapprehend *verb*　misunderstand.
　misapprehension *noun*

misappropriate *verb*　take something

dishonestly. **misappropriation** *noun*

misbehave *verb* behave badly.
misbehaviour *noun*

miscalculate *verb* calculate incorrectly.
miscalculation *noun*

miscarriage *noun* 1 the birth of a baby
before it has developed enough to live.
2 failure to achieve the right result,
a miscarriage of justice.

miscellaneous (*say* mis-el-**ay**-nee-us)
adjective of various kinds; mixed.
miscellany (*say* mis-**el**-an-ee) *noun*

mischance *noun* misfortune.

mischief *noun* naughty or troublesome
behaviour; trouble caused by this.
mischievous *adjective,* **mischievously**
adverb

misconception *noun* a mistaken idea.

misconduct *noun* bad behaviour.

misconstrue *verb* (**misconstrued,**
misconstruing) misinterpret. **mis-
construction** *noun*

miscreant (*say* **mis**-kree-ant) *noun*
a wrongdoer; a villain.

misdeed *noun* a wrong or improper
action.

misdemeanour (*say* mis-de-**mee**-ner)
noun a misdeed; an unlawful act.

miser *noun* a person who hoards money
and spends as little as possible. **miserly**
adjective, **miserliness** *noun*

miserable *adjective* 1 full of misery; very
unhappy, poor, or uncomfortable.
2 disagreeable; unpleasant, *miserable
weather.* **miserably** *adverb*

misery *noun* (*plural* **miseries**) 1 great
unhappiness or discomfort or suffering.
2 (*informal*) a discontented or disagreeable
person.

misfire *verb* (**misfired, misfiring**) fail to
fire; fail to function correctly or to have the
required effect, *The joke misfired.*

misfit *noun* 1 a person who does not fit in
well with other people or who is not well
suited to his or her work. 2 a garment that
does not fit.

misfortune *noun* bad luck; an unlucky
event or accident.

misgiving *noun* a feeling of doubt or slight
fear or mistrust.

misguided *adjective* mistaken.

mishap (*say* **mis**-hap) *noun* an unlucky
accident.

misinterpret *verb* interpret incorrectly.
misinterpretation *noun*

misjudge *verb* (**misjudged, misjudging**)
judge wrongly; form a wrong opinion or
estimate. **misjudgement** *noun*

mislay *verb* (**mislaid, mislaying**) lose
something for a short time.

mislead *verb* (**misled, misleading**) give
somebody a wrong idea; deceive.

mismanagement *noun* bad management.

misnomer *noun* an unsuitable name
for something.

misogynist (*say* mis-**oj**-in-ist) *noun* a
person who hates women. **misogyny** *noun*

misplace *verb* (**misplaced, misplacing**)
place wrongly. **misplacement** *noun*

misprint *noun* a mistake in printing.

mispronounce *verb* pronounce incorrectly. **mispronunciation** *noun*

misquote *verb* (**misquoted, misquoting**)
quote incorrectly. **misquotation** *noun*

misread *verb* read or interpret incorrectly.

misrepresent *verb* represent in a false or
misleading way. **misrepresentation** *noun*

misrule *noun* bad government.

Miss *noun* (*plural* **Misses**) a title put
before a girl's or unmarried woman's name.

miss[1] *verb* 1 fail to hit, reach, catch, see,
hear, or find something. 2 be sad because
someone or something is not with you, *She
misses her mother.* 3 notice that something
has gone.

miss[2] *noun* (*plural* **misses**) missing
something, *Was that shot a hit or a miss?*

misshapen *adjective* badly shaped.

missile *noun* a weapon or other object for
firing or throwing at a target.

missing *adjective* 1 lost; not in the proper
place. 2 absent.

mission *noun* 1 an important job that
somebody is sent to do or feels he or she
must do. 2 a place or building where
missionaries work.

missionary *noun* (*plural* **missionaries**)
a person who is sent to another country
to spread the Christian faith.

mist *noun* 1 damp cloudy air near the

ground. **2** condensed water-vapour on a window, mirror, etc.

mistake¹ *noun* something done wrongly; an incorrect opinion.

mistake² *verb* (**mistook, mistaken, mistaking**) **1** misunderstand, *Don't mistake my meaning.* **2** choose or identify wrongly, *We mistook her for her sister.*

mistaken *adjective* incorrect; unwise.

mistime *verb* (**mistimed, mistiming**) do or say something at a wrong time.

mistletoe *noun* a plant with white berries that grows as a parasite on trees.

mistreat *verb* treat badly.

mistress *noun* (*plural* **mistresses**) **1** a woman who is in charge of something. **2** a woman teacher. **3** a woman who is a man's lover but not his wife.

mistrust *verb* feel no trust in somebody or something. **mistrust** *noun*

misty *adjective* full of mist; not clear. **mistily** *adverb*, **mistiness** *noun*

misunderstand *verb* (**misunderstood, misunderstanding**) get a wrong idea or impression of something.

misuse *verb* (**misused, misusing**) **1** use incorrectly. **2** treat badly. **misuse** *noun*

mite *noun* **1** a tiny spider-like creature found in food, *cheese-mites.* **2** a very small amount. **3** a small child.

mitigate *verb* (**mitigated, mitigating**) make a thing less intense or less severe. **mitigation** *noun*
mitigating circumstances facts that may partially excuse wrongdoing.
• USAGE: Do not confuse with *militate.*

mitosis (*say* my-**toh**-sis) *noun* a type of cell division that results in two cells each having the same number of chromosomes as the parent cell. (Compare *meiosis.*) **mitotic** *adjective*

mitre¹ *noun* **1** the tall tapering hat worn by a bishop. **2** a mitred join.

mitre² *verb* (**mitred, mitring**) join two tapered pieces of wood or cloth etc. so that they form a right angle.

mitten *noun* a kind of glove without separate parts for the fingers.

mix¹ *verb* **1** put different things together so that the substances etc. are no longer distinct; blend; combine. **2** (of a person) get together with others. **mixer** *noun*
mix up mix thoroughly; confuse.

mix² *noun* (*plural* **mixes**) a mixture.

mixed *adjective* containing two or more kinds of things or people.
mixed blessing something that has disadvantages as well as advantages.

mixture *noun* **1** something made of different things mixed together. **2** the process of mixing.

mizzen-mast *noun* the mast nearest to the stern on a three-masted ship.

mnemonic (*say* nim-**on**-ik) *noun* a verse or saying that helps you to remember something.

moan *verb* **1** make a long low sound of pain or suffering. **2** grumble. **moan** *noun*

moat *noun* a deep wide ditch round a castle, usually filled with water. **moated** *adjective*

mob¹ *noun* **1** a large disorderly crowd; a rabble. **2** a gang.

mob² *verb* (**mobbed, mobbing**) crowd round somebody.

mobile¹ *adjective* moving easily. **mobility** *noun*
mobile home a large caravan permanently parked and used for living in.

mobile² *noun* a decoration for hanging up so that its parts move in currents of air.

mobilize *verb* (**mobilized, mobilizing**) assemble people or things for a particular purpose, especially for war. **mobilization** *noun*

moccasin *noun* a soft leather shoe.

mock¹ *verb* **1** make fun of a person or thing. **2** imitate; mimic. **mockery** *noun*

mock² *adjective* sham; imitation, not real, *a mock battle.*

mock-up *noun* a model of something, made in order to test or study it.

mode *noun* **1** the way a thing is done. **2** what is fashionable.

model¹ *noun* **1** a copy of an object, usually on a smaller scale. **2** a particular design, *the latest model of that car.* **3** a person who poses for an artist or displays clothes by wearing them. **4** a person or thing that is worth copying.

model[2] *verb* (**modelled, modelling**)
1 make a model of something. 2 make
according to a model, *modelled after the
original.* 3 work as an artist's model or a
fashion model.

modem (*say* **moh**-dem) *noun* a device that
links a computer and a telephone line so
that data can be transmitted to and from
the computer.

moderate[1] *adjective* medium; not
extremely small or great or hot etc.,
a moderate climate. **moderately** *adverb*

moderate[2] (*say* **mod**-er-ayt) *verb* (**mod-
erated, moderating**) make or become
moderate. **moderation** *noun*
in moderation in moderate amounts.

modern *adjective* of the present or recent
times; in fashion now. **modernity** *noun*

modernize *verb* (**modernized, moderniz-
ing**) make a thing more modern.
modernization *noun*

modest *adjective* 1 not vain; not boasting.
2 moderate; not showy or splendid. 3 rather
shy; decorous. **modestly** *adverb*, **modesty**
noun

modicum *noun* a small amount.

modify *verb* (**modified, modifying**)
1 change something slightly. 2 qualify a
word by describing it, *Adjectives modify
nouns.* **modification** *noun*

modulate *verb* (**modulated, modulating**)
1 adjust; regulate. 2 vary in pitch or tone
etc., *The actor spoke in a well-modulated
voice.* **modulation** *noun*

module *noun* 1 an independent part of a
spacecraft, building, etc. 2 a unit; a section
of a course of study. **modular** *adjective*

moegoe (*say* **muu**-khu) *noun* (*informal*)
a person who is easily deceived; a fool.

mogul (*say* **moh**-gul) *noun* (*informal*)
an important or influential person.

mohair *noun* fine silky wool from an
angora goat.

moist *adjective* slightly wet; damp.
moistly *adverb*, **moistness** *noun*

moisten *verb* make or become moist.

moisture *noun* water in the air or making
a thing moist.

molar *noun* any of the wide teeth at the
back of the jaw, used in chewing.

molasses *noun* syrup from raw sugar.

mole[1] *noun* 1 a small furry animal that
burrows under the ground. 2 a person who
secretly gives confidential information to
an enemy or rival.

mole[2] *noun* a small dark spot on skin.

molecule *noun* the smallest part into
which a substance can be divided without
changing its chemical nature; a group of
atoms. **molecular** *adjective*

molehill *noun* a small pile of earth thrown
up by a burrowing mole.

molest *verb* pester. **molestation** *noun*

mollify *verb* (**mollified, mollifying**) make
a person less angry. **mollification** *noun*

mollusc *noun* an invertebrate with a soft
body and usually a hard shell, e.g. a snail.

molten *adjective* melted; made liquid by
great heat.

mom *noun* (*informal*) mother.

moment *noun* 1 a very short time.
2 a particular time, *Call me the moment she
arrives.* 3 importance, *These are matters
of great moment.*

momentary *adjective* lasting for only a
moment. **momentarily** *adverb*

momentous (*say* mo-**ment**-us) *adjective*
very important.

momentum *noun* amount or force of
movement, *The stone gathered momentum
as it rolled downhill.*

mompara *noun* (*informal*) a fool.

monarch *noun* a king, queen, emperor,
or empress ruling a country. **monarchic**
adjective

monarchy *noun* (*plural* **monarchies**)
a country ruled by a monarch. **monarchist**
noun

monastery *noun* (*plural* **monasteries**)
a building where monks live and work.
(Compare *nunnery.*) **monastic** *adjective*

monetary *adjective* of money.

money *noun* 1 coins and banknotes.
2 wealth.

mongoose *noun* (*plural* **mongooses**)
a small tropical carnivorous animal that can
kill snakes.

mongrel (*say* **mung**-rel) *noun* a dog of
mixed breeds.

monitor[1] *noun* 1 a device for watching or

testing how something is working. **2** a pupil who is given a special responsibility in a school. **3** a visual display unit.

monitor[2] *verb* watch or test how something is working.

monk *noun* a member of a community of men who live according to the rules of a religious organization. (Compare *nun*.)

monkey *noun* (*plural* **monkeys**)
1 an animal with long arms, hands with thumbs, and often a tail. **2** a mischievous person.
monkeys' wedding (*informal*) rain and sunshine at the same time.

mono- *prefix* one; single.

monochrome *adjective* done in one colour or in black and white.

monocle *noun* an eyeglass for one eye.

monocotyledon (*say* mo-noh-kot-a-**lee**-den) *noun* a flowering plant which has one cotyledon.

monoculture *noun* growing a single crop.

monogamy *noun* the custom of being married to only one person at a time. (Compare *polygamy*.) **monogamous** *adjective*

monogram *noun* a design made up of a letter or letters, especially a person's initials. **monogrammed** *adjective*

monograph *noun* a scholarly book or article on one particular subject.

monolith *noun* a large single upright block of stone.

monolithic *adjective* **1** consisting of monoliths. **2** single and huge, *a monolithic monument.*

monologue *noun* a speech by one person.

monoplane *noun* a type of aeroplane with only one set of wings.

monopolize *verb* (**monopolized, monopolizing**) take the whole of something for yourself, *One girl monopolized my attention.* **monopolization** *noun*

monopoly *noun* (*plural* **monopolies**) complete possession or control of something by one group, *The company had a monopoly in supplying electricity.*

monorail *noun* a railway that uses a single rail, not a pair of rails.

monosyllable *noun* a word with only one syllable. **monosyllabic** *adjective*

monotheism (*say* mon-oth-ee-izm) *noun* belief that there is only one god. **monotheist** *noun*

monotone *noun* a level unchanging tone of voice in speaking or singing.

monotonous *adjective* boring because it does not change. **monotonously** *adverb*, **monotony** *noun*

monoxide *noun* an oxide with one atom of oxygen.

monsoon *noun* **1** a strong wind in and near the Indian Ocean, bringing heavy rain in summer. **2** the rainy season brought by this wind.

monster[1] *noun* **1** a large frightening creature. **2** a huge thing, *a monster of a wave.*

monster[2] *adjective* huge.

monstrosity *noun* (*plural* **monstrosities**) a monstrous thing.

monstrous *adjective* **1** like a monster; huge. **2** very shocking; outrageous.

month *noun* each of the twelve parts into which a year is divided.

monthly *adjective* & *adverb* happening or done once a month.

monument *noun* a statue, building, or column etc. put up as a memorial of some person or event.

monumental *adjective* **1** of or as a monument. **2** extremely great; huge, *a monumental struggle.*

moo *verb* make the low deep sound of a cow. **moo** *noun*

mood *noun* the way someone feels, *She is in a cheerful mood.*

moody *adjective* gloomy or sullen; likely to become bad-tempered suddenly. **moodily** *adverb*, **moodiness** *noun*

moon[1] *noun* **1** the natural satellite of the earth that can be seen in the sky at night. **2** a satellite of any planet. **moonbeam** *noun*, **moonlight** *noun*, **moonlit** *adjective*

moon[2] *verb* go about in a dreamy or listless way.

moor[1] *noun* an area of rough land with bushes but no trees. **moorland** *noun*

moor[2] *verb* fasten a boat etc. to a fixed object by means of a cable.

moorhen *noun* a small water-bird.

moose *noun* (*plural* **moose**) a North American elk.

moot[1] *adjective* debatable; undecided, *That's a moot point.*

moot[2] *verb* put forward an idea for discussion.

mop[1] *noun* **1** a bunch or pad of soft material fastened on the end of a stick, used for cleaning floors etc. **2** a thick mass of hair.

mop[2] *verb* (**mopped, mopping**) clean or wipe with a mop etc.; wipe away.

mopane (*say* mo-**pah**-nee) *noun* a tropical bush or tree with leaves that are eaten by cattle, buck, etc.

mopane worm an edible caterpillar that feeds on mopane leaves.

mope *verb* (**moped, moping**) be sad.

moped (*say* **moh**-ped) *noun* a bicycle worked by a motor.

moraine *noun* a mass of stones and earth etc. carried down by a glacier.

moral[1] *adjective* **1** connected with what is right and wrong in behaviour. **2** virtuous, *a moral person.* **morally** *adverb*, **morality** *noun*

moral support encouragement.

moral[2] *noun* a lesson in right behaviour taught by a story or event.

morals *plural noun* standards of behaviour; virtuousness.

morale (*say* mor-**ahl**) *noun* confidence; the state of someone's spirits, *Morale was high after the victory.*

moralize *verb* (**moralized, moralizing**) talk or write about right and wrong behaviour. **moralist** *noun*

morass *noun* (*plural* **morasses**) **1** a marsh or bog. **2** a confused situation.

moratorium *noun* a temporary ban.

morbid *adjective* **1** thinking about gloomy or unpleasant things. **2** unhealthy. **morbidly** *adverb*, **morbidity** *noun*

more[1] *adjective* (comparative of **much** and **many**) greater in amount etc.

more[2] *noun* a greater amount.

more[3] *adverb* **1** to a greater extent, *more beautiful.* **2** again, *once more.*

more or less about; approximately.

morena (*say* mo-**re**-na) *noun* a term of respect used when addressing a man.

moreover *adverb* besides; in addition to what has been said.

morgen *noun* (*plural* **morgen**) a Dutch unit of land area, 0,856 hectares (this was the area that a team of oxen could plough in one morning).

Mormon *noun* a member of a religious group founded in the USA.

morn *noun* (*poetic*) morning.

morning *noun* the early part of the day, before noon or before lunchtime.

morning star the planet Venus, which can be seen in the east before sunrise.

morocco *noun* a kind of leather originally made in Morocco from goatskins.

morogo (*say* mo-ro-kho) *noun* a plant like spinach that is grown as a food crop.

moron *noun* (*informal*) a very stupid person.

morose *adjective* sullen and gloomy. **morosely** *adverb*, **moroseness** *noun*

morphia (also **morphine**) (*say* mor-feen) *noun* a drug made from opium, used to lessen pain.

morrow *noun* (*poetic*) the following day.

Morse code *noun* a signalling code using short and long sounds or flashes of light (dots and dashes) to represent letters.

morsel *noun* a small piece of food; a small amount.

mortal[1] *adjective* **1** that can die, *All of us are mortal.* **2** causing death; fatal, *a mortal wound.* **3** deadly, *mortal enemies.* **mortally** *adverb*, **mortality** *noun*

mortal[2] *noun* a person who is not immortal.

mortar *noun* **1** a mixture of sand, cement, and water used in building to stick bricks together. **2** a hard bowl in which substances are pounded with a pestle. **3** a short cannon.

mortar-board *noun* an academic cap with a stiff square top.

mortgage[1] (*say* mor-gij) *noun* an arrangement to borrow money to buy a house, with the house as security for the loan.

mortgage[2] *verb* (**mortgaged, mortgaging**) offer a house etc. as security in return for a loan.

mortify *verb* (**mortified, mortifying**) humiliate a person greatly. **mortification** *noun*

mortise *noun* a hole made in a piece of wood for another piece to be joined to it. **mortise lock** a lock set into a door.

mortuary *noun* a place where dead bodies are kept before being buried.

mosaic (*say* mo-**zay**-ik) *noun* a picture or design made from small coloured pieces of stone or glass.

mosbolletjie (*say* **mos-bol**-a-kee) *noun* a bun that is made with fermenting grape juice, which causes the dough to rise.

moskonfyt (*say* **mos**-kon-**fayt**) *noun* a thick syrup made from boiling fermenting grapes.

mosque (*say* mosk) *noun* a building where Muslims worship.

mosquito *noun* (*plural* **mosquitoes**) a kind of gnat that sucks blood.

moss *noun* (*plural* **mosses**) a plant that grows in damp places and has no flowers. **mossy** *adjective*

mossie *noun* a sparrow.

most¹ *adjective* (superlative of **much** and **many**) greatest in amount etc., *Most people came by bus.*

most² *noun* the greatest amount, *Most of the food was eaten.*

most³ *adverb* **1** to the greatest extent; more than any other, *most beautiful.* **2** very; extremely, *most impressive.*

mostly *adverb* mainly.

motel *noun* a hotel providing accommodation for motorists and their cars.

moth *noun* an insect rather like a butterfly, that usually flies at night.

mother¹ *noun* a female parent. **motherhood** *noun*

mother² *verb* look after someone in a motherly way.
Mother's Day the day on which people often give presents to their mothers.

mother-in-law *noun* (*plural* **mothers-in-law**) the mother of a married person's husband or wife.

motherly *adjective* kind and gentle like a mother. **motherliness** *noun*

mother-of-pearl *noun* a pearly substance

lining the shells of mussels etc.

motif *noun* a repeated design or theme.

motion¹ *noun* **1** moving; movement. **2** a formal statement to be discussed and voted on at a meeting.

motion² *verb* signal by a gesture, *She motioned him to sit beside her.*

motionless *adjective* not moving.

motivate *verb* (**motivated, motivating**) give a person a motive or incentive to do something. **motivation** *noun*

motive¹ *noun* what makes a person do something, *a motive for murder.*

motive² *adjective* producing movement, *The engine provides motive power.*

motley *adjective* **1** multicoloured. **2** made up of various sorts of things, *a motley crew of teachers, pupils, and dogs.*

motor¹ *noun* a machine providing power to drive machinery etc.; an engine.

motor² *verb* go or take someone in a car.

motorcade *noun* a procession of cars.

motorist *noun* a person who drives a car.

motorized *adjective* equipped with a motor or with motor vehicles.

motorway *noun* a wide road for fast long-distance traffic.

mottled *adjective* marked with spots or patches of colour.

motto *noun* (*plural* **mottoes**) **1** a short saying used as a guide for behaviour, *Their motto is 'Who dares, wins'.* **2** a short verse or riddle etc. found inside a cracker.

mould¹ *noun* a hollow container of a particular shape, in which a liquid or soft substance is put to set into this shape.

mould² *verb* make something have a particular shape or character.

mould³ *noun* a fine furry growth of very small fungi. **mouldy** *adjective*

moulder *verb* rot away; decay into dust.

moult *verb* shed feathers, hair, or skin etc. while a new growth forms.

mound *noun* a pile of earth or stones etc.; a small hill.

mount¹ *verb* **1** climb or go up; ascend. **2** get on a horse or bicycle etc. **3** increase in amount, *Our costs mounted.* **4** place or fix in position for use or display, *Mount your photos in an album.*

mount[2] *noun* **1** a mountain, *Mount Kilimanjaro*. **2** something on which an object is mounted. **3** a horse etc. for riding.

mountain *noun* **1** a very high hill, especially one over 305 metres high. **2** a large heap or pile or quantity, *a mountain of letters*. **mountainous** *adjective*

mountain bike a bicycle which has a strong but light frame, fat tyres, and many gears, suited for riding on rough terrain.

mountaineer *noun* a person who climbs mountains. **mountaineering** *noun*

mounted *adjective* serving on horseback, *mounted police*.

mourn *verb* be sad, especially because someone has died. **mourner** *noun*

mournful *adjective* sad; sorrowful. **mournfully** *adverb*

mouse *noun* (*plural* **mice**) **1** a small animal with a long thin tail and a pointed nose. **2** a small hand-held device connected to a computer, used to control the cursor. **mousetrap** *noun*, **mousy** *adjective*

mousebird *noun* a small grey crested fruit-eating bird with a long tail.

mousse (*say* mooss) *noun* **1** a creamy pudding flavoured with fruit or chocolate. **2** a frothy creamy substance.

moustache (*say* mus-**tahsh**) *noun* hair allowed to grow on a man's upper lip.

mouth[1] *noun* **1** the opening through which food is taken into the body. **2** the place where a river enters the sea. **3** an opening or outlet, *the mouth of the cave*. **mouthful** *noun*

mouth-to-mouth resuscitation breathing into an unconscious person's lungs through the mouth in order to restore consciousness.

mouth[2] *verb* form words carefully with your lips, especially without saying them aloud.

mouth-organ *noun* a small musical instrument that you play by blowing and sucking while passing it along your lips.

mouthpiece *noun* **1** the part of a musical or other instrument that you put to your mouth. **2** (*informal*) a person, newspaper, etc. that expresses the opinions of another person or other people.

movable *adjective* able to be moved.

move[1] *verb* (**moved, moving**) **1** take or go from one place to another; change a person's or thing's position. **2** affect a person's feelings, *Their sad story moved us deeply*. **3** put forward a formal statement (a *motion*) to be discussed and voted on at a meeting. **mover** *noun*

move[2] *noun* **1** moving; a movement. **2** a player's turn to move a piece in chess etc., *It's your move*.

get a move on (*informal*) hurry up.

on the move moving; making progress.

movement *noun* **1** the action of moving or being moved. **2** a group of people working together to achieve something, *the environmental movement*. **3** one of the main divisions of a symphony or other long musical work.

movie *noun* (*informal*) a cinema film.

mow *verb* (**mowed, mown, mowing**) cut down grass etc. **mower** *noun*

mow down knock down and kill.

MP *abbreviation* Member of Parliament.

Mr (*say* **mist**-er) *noun* (*plural* **Messrs**) a title put before a man's name.

Mrs (*say* **mis**-iz) *noun* (*plural* **Mrs**) a title put before a married woman's name.

Ms (*say* miz) *noun* a title put before a woman's name.

Mt *abbreviation* mount or mountain.

much[1] *adjective* (**more, most**) existing in a large amount, *much noise*.

much[2] *noun* a large amount of something.

much[3] *adverb* **1** greatly; considerably, *much to my surprise*. **2** approximately, *It is much the same*.

muck[1] *noun* **1** farmyard manure. **2** (*informal*) dirt; filth. **mucky** *adjective*

muck[2] *verb* make dirty, mess.

muck about (*informal*) mess about.

muck up (*informal*) mess up; spoil.

mucous (*say* **mew**-kus) *adjective* like mucus; covered with mucus, *a mucous membrane*.

mucus (*say* **mew**-kus) *noun* the moist sticky substance on the inner surface of the throat etc.

mud *noun* wet soft earth. **muddy** *adjective*, **muddiness** *noun*

muddle[1] *verb* (**muddled, muddling**) mix things up; confuse. **muddler** *noun*

muddle[2] *noun* a muddled condition or thing; confusion; disorder.

mudguard *noun* a curved cover over the top part of the wheel of a bicycle etc. to protect the rider from the mud and water thrown up by the wheel.

muesli (*say* **mooz**-lee) *noun* a food made of mixed cereals, dried fruit, nuts, etc.

muezzin (*say* moo-**ez**-in or mew-**ez**-in) *noun* a person who calls Muslims to prayer.

muff[1] *noun* a short tube-shaped piece of warm material into which the hands are pushed from opposite ends.

muff[2] *verb* (*informal*) bungle.

muffin *noun* 1 a kind of spongy cake eaten toasted and buttered. 2 a similar round cake made from batter or dough.

muffle *verb* (**muffled, muffling**) 1 cover or wrap something to protect it or keep it warm. 2 deaden the sound of something, *a muffled scream.*

muffler *noun* a warm scarf.

mufti *noun* ordinary clothes worn by someone who usually wears a uniform.

mug[1] *noun* 1 a kind of large cup, usually used without a saucer. 2 (*informal*) a fool; a person who is easily deceived. 3 (*informal*) a person's face.

mug[2] *verb* (**mugged, mugging**) attack and rob somebody in the street. **mugger** *noun*

muggie *noun* 1 a gnat. 2 any small flying insect that irritates you.

muggy *adjective* unpleasantly warm and damp, *muggy weather.* **mugginess** *noun*

mulberry *noun* (*plural* **mulberries**) a purple or white fruit rather like a blackberry.

mulch *noun* a layer of compost, grass, leaves, etc. that is spread around or over a plant to enrich or insulate the soil. **mulch** *verb*

mule *noun* an animal that is the offspring of a donkey and a mare, known for being stubborn. **mulish** *adjective*

mull[1] *verb* heat wine or beer with sugar and spices, as a drink, *mulled ale.*

mull[2] *verb* think about something carefully; ponder, *mull it over.*

mullet *noun* a kind of fish used as food.

multi- *prefix* many (as in *multicoloured* = with many colours).

multifarious (*say* multi-**fair**-ee-us) *adjective* of many kinds; very varied.

multilateral *adjective* (of an agreement or treaty) made between three or more people or countries etc.

multimillionaire *noun* a person with a fortune of several millions.

multinational *adjective* (of a business company) working in several countries.

multiple[1] *adjective* having many parts.

multiple[2] *noun* a number that contains another number (a *factor*) an exact amount of times without remainder, *8 and 12 are multiples of 4.*

multiplicity *noun* a great variety.

multiply *verb* (**multiplied, multiplying**) 1 take a number a given quantity of times, *Five multiplied by four equals twenty* ($5 \times 4 = 20$). 2 make or become many; increase. **multiplication** *noun*, **multiplier** *noun*

multiracial *adjective* consisting of people of many different races.

multitude *noun* a great number of people or things. **multitudinous** *adjective*

mum[1] *noun* (*informal*) mother.

mum[2] *adjective* (*informal*) silent, *keep mum.*

mum[3] *verb* (**mummed, mumming**) act in a mime. **mummer** *noun*

mumble *verb* (**mumbled, mumbling**) speak indistinctly and not be easy to hear. **mumble** *noun*, **mumbler** *noun*

mumbo-jumbo *noun* talk or ceremony that has no real meaning.

mummy[1] *noun* (*plural* **mummies**) (*informal*) mother.

mummy[2] *noun* (*plural* **mummies**) a corpse treated with preservatives before being buried, as was the custom in ancient Egypt. **mummify** *verb*

mumps *noun* an infectious disease that causes the neck to swell painfully.

munch *verb* chew vigorously.

mundane *adjective* 1 ordinary, not exciting. 2 concerned with practical matters, not ideals.

municipal (*say* mew-**nis**-ip-al) *adjective* of a town or city.

municipality *noun* (*plural* **municipalities**) a town or city that has its own local government (see *local*).

munificent *adjective* extremely generous. **munificently** *adverb*, **munificence** *noun*

munitions *plural noun* military weapons and ammunition etc.

mural[1] *adjective* of or on a wall.

mural[2] *noun* a wall-painting.

murder[1] *verb* kill a person unlawfully and deliberately. **murderer** *noun*, **murderess** *noun*

murder[2] *noun* the murdering of somebody. **murderous** *adjective*

murky *adjective* dark and gloomy. **murk** *noun*, **murkiness** *noun*

murmur *verb* 1 make a low continuous sound. 2 speak in a soft voice. **murmur** *noun*

muscle *noun* 1 a band or bundle of fibrous tissue that can contract and relax and so produce movement in parts of the body. 2 the power of muscles; strength. **muscular** *adjective*, **muscularity** *noun* **muscular dystrophy** a disease that weakens the muscles.

muse *verb* (**mused, musing**) think deeply about something; ponder; meditate.

museum *noun* a place where interesting objects, especially antiquities, are displayed for people to see.

mush *noun* soft pulp. **mushy** *adjective*

mushroom[1] *noun* an edible fungus with a stem and a dome-shaped top.

mushroom[2] *verb* grow or appear suddenly in large numbers, *Blocks of flats mushroomed in the city.*

music *noun* 1 pleasant or interesting sounds made by instruments or by the voice. 2 printed or written instructions for making music. **music centre** a device that combines a radio, tape-recorder, CD player, etc.

musical[1] *adjective* 1 of or with music; producing music. 2 good at music; interested in music. **musically** *adverb*

musical[2] *noun* a play or film containing a lot of songs.

musician *noun* someone who plays a musical instrument.

musk *noun* a strong-smelling substance used in perfumes. **musky** *adjective*

musket *noun* a kind of gun with a long barrel, formerly used by soldiers.

musketeer *noun* a soldier armed with a musket.

Muslim *noun* a person who follows the religious teachings of Muhammad (who lived in about AD 570–632), set out in the Koran.

muslin *noun* very thin cotton cloth.

mussel *noun* a shellfish often used as food.

must *auxiliary verb* used to express 1 necessity or obligation, *You must go.* 2 certainty, *You must be joking!*

mustang *noun* a wild horse of Mexico and California.

mustard *noun* a yellow paste or powder used to give food a hot taste. **mustard and cress** small green plants eaten in salads.

muster[1] *verb* assemble; gather together.

muster[2] *noun* an assembly of people or things. **pass muster** be up to the required standard.

mustn't (*mainly spoken*) must not.

musty *adjective* smelling or tasting mouldy or stale. **mustiness** *noun*

mutable (*say* mew-ta-bul) *adjective* able or likely to change. **mutability** *noun*

mutation *noun* a change or alteration in the form of something.

mute[1] *adjective* 1 silent; not speaking; not able to speak. 2 not pronounced, *The g in 'gnat' is mute.* **mutely** *adverb*, **muteness** *noun*

mute[2] *noun* a person who cannot speak.

mute[3] *verb* (**muted, muting**) make a thing quieter or less intense.

muti (*say* **moo**-tee) *noun* 1 the medicines, charms, or herbs used in traditional healing or in witchcraft. 2 any kind of medicine.

mutilate *verb* (**mutilated, mutilating**) damage something by breaking or cutting off part of it. **mutilation** *noun*

mutineer *noun* a person who mutinies.

mutiny[1] *noun* (*plural* **mutinies**) rebellion

against authority; refusal by members of the armed forces to obey orders.

mutinous *adjective*, **mutinously** *adverb*

mutiny² *verb* (**mutinied, mutinying**) take part in a mutiny.

mutter *verb* 1 speak in a low voice. 2 grumble. **mutter** *noun*

mutton *noun* meat from a sheep.

mutual (*say* mew-tew-al) *adjective* given to each other; felt by each for the other, *mutual affection*. **mutually** *adverb*

mutualism *noun* a kind of symbiosis in which both partners benefit from the relationship.

muzzle¹ *noun* 1 an animal's nose and mouth. 2 a cover put over an animal's nose and mouth so that it cannot bite. 3 the open end of a gun.

muzzle² *verb* (**muzzled, muzzling**) 1 put a muzzle on an animal. 2 silence; prevent a person from expressing opinions.

my *adjective* belonging to me.

mycelium (*say* my-see-lee-um) *noun* (*plural* **mycelia**) the body of a fungus.

mynah *noun* a kind of starling that talks.

myriad (*say* mirri-ad) *adjective* innumerable.

myriads *plural noun* a very great number, *myriads of gnats*.

myrrh (*say* mer) *noun* a substance used in perfumes and incense and medicine.

myrtle *noun* an evergreen shrub with dark leaves and white flowers.

myself *pronoun* I or me and nobody else. (Compare *herself*.)

mysterious *adjective* full of mystery; puzzling. **mysteriously** *adverb*

mystery *noun* (*plural* **mysteries**) something that cannot be explained or understood; something puzzling.

mystic¹ *adjective* 1 having a spiritual meaning. 2 mysterious and filling people with wonder. **mystical** *adjective*, **mystically** *adverb*, **mysticism** *noun*

mystic² *noun* a person who seeks to obtain spiritual contact with God by deep religious meditation.

mystify *verb* (**mystified, mystifying**) puzzle; bewilder. **mystification** *noun*

mystique (*say* mis-**teek**) *noun* an air of mystery or mystical power.

myth (*say* mith) *noun* 1 an old story containing ideas about ancient times or about supernatural beings. (Compare *legend*.) 2 an untrue story or belief, *the myth of love at first sight*.

mythical *adjective* imaginary; found in myths, *a mythical animal*.

mythology *noun* myths; the study of myths. **mythological** *adjective*

myxomatosis (*say* miks-om-at-**oh**-sis) *noun* a disease that kills rabbits.

Nn

N. *abbreviation* north; northern.

naartjie (*say* **nah**-chee) *noun* a citrus fruit rather like an orange, but smaller and sweeter.

nab *verb* (**nabbed, nabbing**) (*informal*) catch or arrest (a wrongdoer); seize.

nag¹ *verb* (**nagged, nagging**) 1 pester a person by keeping on criticizing, complaining, or asking for things. 2 keep on hurting, *a nagging pain*.

nag² *noun* (*informal*) a horse.

nagana *noun* a disease of cattle, horses, etc. that is carried by the tsetse fly.

Nagmaal (*say* nakh-mahl) *noun* the Holy Communion of the Dutch Reformed Church, a time for large gatherings of people.

nail¹ *noun* 1 the hard covering over the end of a finger or toe. 2 a small sharp piece of metal hammered in to fasten pieces of wood etc. together.

nail² *verb* 1 fasten with a nail or nails. 2 catch; arrest.

naive (*say* ny-**eev**) *adjective* showing a lack of experience or good judgement; innocent and unsophisticated. **naively** *adverb*, **naivety** *noun*

naked *adjective* without any clothes or coverings on. **nakedly** *adverb*, **nakedness** *noun*

the naked eye the eye when it is not helped by a telescope or microscope etc.

Namaqualand daisy *noun* a plant which grows in dry and barren places and bears bright flowers after good rains.

name¹ *noun* 1 the word or words by which a person, animal, place, or thing is known. 2 a reputation.

name² *verb* (**named, naming**) 1 give a name to. 2 state the name or names of.

nameless *adjective* without a name.

namely *adverb* that is to say, *My two favourite subjects are sciences, namely chemistry and biology.*

namesake *noun* a person or thing with the same name as another.

nanny *noun* (*plural* **nannies**) a nurse who looks after young children.

nanny-goat *noun* a female goat. (Compare *billy-goat.*)

nap¹ *noun* a short sleep.
catch a person napping catch a person unprepared for something or not alert.

nap² *noun* short raised fibres on the surface of cloth or leather.

napalm (*say* **nay**-pahm) *noun* a substance made of petrol, used in some incendiary bombs.

napkin *noun* 1 a piece of cloth or paper used to keep your clothes clean or to wipe your lips or fingers; a serviette, *a table-napkin.* 2 a piece of cloth or other fabric put round a baby's bottom.

nappy *noun* (*plural* **nappies**) a baby's napkin.

narcissus *noun* (*plural* **narcissi**) a garden flower like a daffodil.

narcotic *noun* a drug that makes a person sleepy or unconscious. **narcotic** *adjective*, **narcosis** *noun*

narrate *verb* (**narrated, narrating**) tell a story; give an account of something. **narration** *noun*, **narrator** *noun*

narrative *noun* a spoken or written account of something.

narrow¹ *adjective* 1 not wide; not broad. 2 uncomfortably close; with only a small margin of safety, *a narrow escape.* **narrowly** *adverb*

narrow² *verb* make or become narrower.

narrow-minded *adjective* not tolerant of other people's beliefs and ways.

nasal *adjective* 1 of the nose. 2 sounding as if the breath comes out through the nose, *a nasal voice.* **nasally** *adverb*

nasturtium (*say* na-**ster**-shum) *noun* a garden plant with round leaves and red, yellow, or orange flowers.

nasty *adjective* 1 unpleasant. 2 unkind. **nastily** *adverb*, **nastiness** *noun*

natal (*say* **nay**-tal) *adjective* of birth; from birth.

nation *noun* a large community of people most of whom have the same ancestors, language, history, and customs, and who usually live in the same part of the world under one government. **national** *adjective* & *noun*, **nationally** *adverb*

nationalist *noun* 1 a person who is very patriotic. 2 a person who wants his or her country to be independent and not to form part of another country. **nationalism** *noun*, **nationalistic** *adjective*

nationality *noun* (*plural* **nationalities**) the condition of belonging to a particular nation, *What is his nationality?*

nationalize *verb* (**nationalized, nationalizing**) put an industry etc. under public ownership. **nationalization** *noun*

native¹ *noun* a person born in a particular place, *He is a native of America.*

native² *adjective* 1 belonging to a person because of the place of his or her birth, *my native country.* 2 natural; belonging to a person by nature, *native ability.*
native American an American Indian.

nativity *noun* a person's birth.
the Nativity the birth of Jesus Christ.

natty *adjective* (**nattier, nattiest**) neat and trim; dapper. **nattily** *adverb*

natural¹ *adjective* 1 produced or done by nature, not by people or machines. 2 normal; not surprising. 3 (of a note in music) neither sharp nor flat. **naturally** *adverb*, **naturalness** *noun*
natural history the study of plants and animals.

natural² *noun* 1 a person who is naturally good at something, *She's a natural when it comes to athletics.* 2 a natural note in music.

naturalist *noun* an expert in natural history.

naturalize *verb* (**naturalized, naturalizing**)
1 give a person full rights as a citizen of a country although they were not born there. **2** cause a plant or animal to grow or live naturally in a country that is not its own. **naturalization** *noun*

nature *noun* **1** everything in the world that was not made by people. **2** the qualities and characteristics of a person or thing, *She has a loving nature.* **3** a kind or sort of thing, *He likes things of that nature.*

naught *noun* (*old use*) nothing.

naughty *adjective* behaving badly; disobedient. **naughtily** *adverb*, **naughtiness** *noun*

nausea (*say* naw-zee-a) *noun* a feeling of sickness or disgust. **nauseous** *adjective*, **nauseating** *adjective*

nautical *adjective* of ships or sailors. **nautical mile** a measure of distance used in navigating, 1,852 kilometres.

naval *adjective* of a navy.

nave *noun* the main central part of a church (the other parts are the chancel, aisles, and transepts).

navel *noun* the small hollow in the centre of the abdomen, where the umbilical cord was attached.

navigable *adjective* **1** suitable for ships to sail in, *a navigable river.* **2** able to be steered. **navigability** *noun*

navigate *verb* (**navigated, navigating**)
1 sail in or through a river or sea etc., *The ship navigated the Suez Canal.* **2** make sure that a ship, aircraft, or vehicle is going in the right direction. **navigation** *noun*, **navigator** *noun*

navy *noun* (*plural* **navies**) **1** a country's warships; the people trained to use them. **2** (also **navy blue**) very dark blue, the colour of naval uniform.

nay *adverb* (*old use*) no.

Nazi (*say* **nah**-tsee) *noun* (*plural* **Nazis**) a member of the National Socialist Party in Germany in Hitler's time, with Fascist - beliefs. **Nazism** *noun*

NB *abbreviation* take note that (Latin *nota bene* = note well).

NCO *abbreviation* non-commissioned officer.

NE *abbreviation* north-east; north-eastern.

near¹ *adverb* & *adjective* not far away.

near² *preposition* not far away from, *near the shops.*

near³ *verb* come near to, *The ship neared the harbour.*

nearby¹ *adjective* near, *a nearby house.*

nearby² *adverb* (also **near by**) not far away, *They live nearby/near by.*

nearly *adverb* **1** almost, *We have nearly finished.* **2** closely, *They are nearly related.*

neat *adjective* **1** simple and clean and tidy. **2** skilful, *a neat solution to the problem.* **3** undiluted, *neat whisky.* **neatly** *adverb*, **neatness** *noun*

neaten *verb* make or become neat.

nebula *noun* (*plural* **nebulae**) a bright or dark patch in the sky, caused by a distant galaxy or a cloud of dust or gas.

nebulous *adjective* indistinct; vague, *nebulous ideas.*

necessary *adjective* not able to be done without; essential. **necessarily** *adverb*

necessitate *verb* (**necessitated, necessitating**) make a thing necessary.

necessity *noun* (*plural* **necessities**) need; something necessary.

neck *noun* **1** the part of the body that joins the head to the shoulders. **2** the part of a garment round the neck. **3** a narrow part of something, especially of a bottle.

necklace¹ *noun* **1** an ornament worn round the neck. **2** a tyre soaked or filled with petrol, placed around the neck of someone and set alight.

necklace² *verb* (**necklaced, necklacing**) kill someone using a necklace (= *necklace 2*).

necklet *noun* **1** a necklace. **2** a small fur worn round the neck.

necktie *noun* a strip of material worn passing under the collar of a shirt and knotted in front.

nectar *noun* **1** a sweet liquid collected by bees from flowers. **2** a delicious drink.

nectarine (*say* nek-ta-reen) *noun* a kind of peach with a smooth skin.

nectary *noun* (*plural* **nectaries**) the nectar-producing part of a plant.

née (*say* nay) *adjective* born (used in giving a woman's maiden name if she has changed it through marriage), *Mrs Smith*, *née Jones*.

need[1] *verb* **1** be without something you should have; require, *We need two more chairs.* **2** (as an *auxiliary verb*) have to do something, *You need not answer.*

need[2] *noun* **1** something needed; a necessary thing. **2** a situation where something is necessary, *There is no need to cry.* **3** great poverty or hardship. **needful** *adjective*, **needless** *adjective*

needle *noun* **1** a very thin pointed piece of steel used in sewing. **2** something long and thin and sharp, *a knitting-needle.* **3** the pointer of a meter or compass.

needlework *noun* sewing or embroidery.

needy *adjective* very poor; lacking things necessary for life. **neediness** *noun*

ne'er *adverb* (*poetic*) never.

nefarious (*say* nif-**air**-ee-us) *adjective* wicked.

negate *verb* (**negated, negating**) **1** make a thing ineffective. **2** disprove. **negation** *noun*

negative[1] *adjective* **1** that says 'no', *a negative answer.* **2** not definite; not positive, *a negative attitude.* **3** less than nought; minus. **4** of the kind of electric charge carried by electrons. **negatively** *adverb*

● USAGE: The opposite of sense 1 is *affirmative*, and of senses 2, 3, 4 *positive.*

negative[2] *noun* **1** something negative. **2** a photograph on film with the dark parts light and the light parts dark, from which a positive print (with the dark and light or colours correct) can be made.

neglect[1] *verb* **1** not look after or attend to a person or thing. **2** not do something; forget, *He neglected to shut the door.*

neglect[2] *noun* neglecting; being neglected. **neglectful** *adjective*

negligence (*say* **neg**-li-jens) *noun* lack of proper care or attention; carelessness. **negligent** *adjective*, **negligently** *adverb*

negligible *adjective* not big enough or important enough to be worth bothering about.

negotiable *adjective* **1** able to be changed after being discussed, *The salary is negoti-*

able. **2** (of a cheque) able to be changed for cash or transferred to another person.

negotiate *verb* (**negotiated, negotiating**) **1** bargain or discuss with others in order to reach an agreement. **2** arrange after discussion, *They negotiated a treaty.* **3** get over an obstacle or difficulty. **negotiation** *noun*, **negotiator** *noun*

neigh *verb* make the high-pitched cry of a horse. **neigh** *noun*

neighbour *noun* a person who lives next door or near to another. **neighbouring** *adjective*, **neighbourly** *adjective*

neighbourhood *noun* the surrounding district or area.

neighbourhood watch an organized system in which ordinary people help the police to combat crime in their area.

neither[1] (*say* **ny**-*th*er or **nee**-*th*er) *adjective* & *pronoun* not either.

● USAGE: Correct use is *Neither of them likes it. Neither he nor his children like it.* Use a singular verb (e.g. *likes*) unless one of its subjects is plural (e.g. *children*).

neither[2] *adverb* & *conjunction* **neither ... nor** not one thing and not the other, *She neither knew nor cared.*

● USAGE: Say *I don't know that either* (not 'neither').

nek *noun* a narrow ridge or saddle that connects two hills or mountains.

nemesis (*say* **nem**-i-sis) *noun* retribution; justifiable punishment that comes upon somebody who hoped to escape it.

neo- *prefix* new.

neolithic (*say* nee-o-**lith**-ik) *adjective* of the later part of the Stone Age.

neon *noun* a gas that glows when electricity passes through it, used in glass tubes to make illuminated signs.

nephew *noun* the son of a person's brother or sister.

nepotism (*say* **nep**-ot-izm) *noun* showing favouritism to relatives in appointing them to jobs.

nerve[1] *noun* **1** any of the fibres in the body that carry messages to and from the brain, so that parts of the body can feel and move. **2** courage; calmness in a dangerous situation, *Don't lose your nerve.* **3** (*informal*) impudence, *Oliver Twist had the nerve to ask for more.*

nerves *plural noun* nervousness.

nerve[2] *verb* (**nerved, nerving**) give strength or courage to someone.

nervous *adjective* **1** easily upset or agitated; excitable. **2** slightly afraid; timid. **3** of the nerves, *a nervous illness.*
nervously *adverb*, **nervousness** *noun*

nervy *adjective* nervous.

nest[1] *noun* **1** a structure or place in which a bird lays its eggs and feeds its young. **2** a place where some small creatures (e.g. mice, wasps) live. **3** a set of similar things that fit inside each other, *a nest of tables.*

nest[2] *verb* **1** have or make a nest. **2** fit inside something.

nest-egg *noun* a sum of money saved up for future use.

nestle *verb* (**nestled, nestling**) curl up comfortably.

nestling *noun* a bird that is too young to leave the nest.

net[1] *noun* **1** material made of pieces of thread, cord, or wire etc. joined together in a criss-cross pattern with holes between. **2** something made of this.

net[2] *verb* (**netted, netting**) cover or catch with a net.

net[3] *adjective* remaining when nothing more is to be deducted, *The net weight, without the box, is 100 grams.* (Compare *gross.*)

net[4] *verb* (**netted, netting**) obtain or produce as net profit.

netball *noun* a game in which two teams try to throw a ball into a high net hanging from a ring.

nether *adjective* lower, *the nether regions.*

netting *noun* a piece of net.

nettle[1] *noun* a wild plant with leaves that sting when they are touched.

nettle[2] *verb* (**nettled, nettling**) annoy or provoke someone.

network *noun* **1** a net-like arrangement of connected lines or parts, *a road network.* **2** a group of people, businesses, etc. that exchange information. **3** (*American*) a group of broadcasting stations that broadcast the same programmes at the same

time. **4** a system of computers linked together.

neuralgia (*say* newr-**al**-ja) *noun* pain along a nerve.

neurology *noun* the study of nerves and their diseases. **neurological** *adjective*, **neurologist** *noun*

neuron (*say* **new**-ron) *noun* a nerve cell.

neurotic (*say* newr-**ot**-ik) *adjective* always very worried about something.

neuter *adjective* neither masculine nor feminine.

neutral *adjective* **1** not supporting either side in a war or quarrel. **2** not very distinctive, *a neutral colour such as grey.* **3** (in chemistry) neither acid nor alkaline. **4** (of electricity) without an electric charge; neither positive nor negative. **neutrally** *adverb*, **neutrality** *noun*

neutral gear a gear that is not connected to the driving parts of an engine.

neutralize *verb* (**neutralized, neutralizing**) make a thing neutral or ineffective. **neutralization** *noun*

neutron *noun* a particle with no electric charge.

never *adverb* at no time; not ever; not at all.

nevertheless *adverb & conjunction* in spite of this; although this is a fact.

new[1] *adjective* not existing before; just made, invented, discovered, or received etc. **newly** *adverb*, **newness** *noun*
New Year's Day 1 January.

new[2] *adverb* newly, *new-born; new-laid.*

newcomer *noun* a person who has arrived recently.

newel *noun* the upright post to which the handrail of a stair is fixed, or that forms the centre pillar of a winding stair.

newfangled *adjective* disliked because it is new in method or style.

newly *adverb* **1** recently. **2** in a new way.

news *noun* **1** information about recent events; a broadcast report of this. **2** a piece of new information.

newsagent *noun* a shopkeeper who sells newspapers.

newsletter *noun* an informal printed report that is sent regularly to members of a club, society, etc.

newspaper *noun* 1 a daily or weekly publication on large sheets of paper, containing news reports, articles, etc. 2 the sheets of paper forming a newspaper, *Wrap it in newspaper.*

newsy *adjective* (*informal*) full of news.

newt *noun* a small animal rather like a lizard, that lives near or in water.

newton *noun* a unit of force.

next[1] *adjective* nearest; coming immediately after, *on the next day.*
next door in the next house or room.

next[2] *adverb* in the next place; on the next occasion, *What happens next?*

nib *noun* the pointed metal part of a pen.

nibble *verb* (**nibbled, nibbling**) take small quick or gentle bites.

nice *adjective* 1 pleasant; kind; satisfactory. 2 precise; careful, *Dictionaries make nice distinctions between meanings of words.*
nicely *adverb*, **niceness** *noun*

nicety (*say* **ny**-sit-ee) *noun* (*plural* **niceties**) 1 precision. 2 a small detail or difference pointed out.

niche (*say* neesh) *noun* 1 a small recess, especially in a wall, *The vase stood in a niche.* 2 a suitable place or position, *She found her niche in the drama club.*

nick[1] *noun* 1 a small cut or notch. 2 (*informal*) condition, *in good nick.*
in the nick of time only just in time.

nick[2] *verb* 1 make a nick in something. 2 (*informal*) steal. 3 (*informal*) catch; arrest.

nickel *noun* a silvery-white metal.

nickname *noun* a name given to a person instead of his or her real name.

nicotine *noun* a poisonous substance found in tobacco.

nictitate (*say* **nik**-tl-tayt) *verb* (**nictitated, nictitating**) (in biology) close and open the eyes; blink or wink.
nictitating membrane a membrane which protects the eye in some animals.

niece *noun* the daughter of a person's brother or sister.

niggardly *adjective* mean; stingy.
niggardliness *noun*

niggle *verb* (**niggled, niggling**) fuss over details or very small faults.

nigh *adverb* & *preposition* (*old use*) near.

night *noun* 1 the dark hours between sunset and sunrise. 2 a particular night or evening, *the first night of the play.*
night school an educational institution that provides classes in the evening.
night-time the part of the day when it is dark.

nightdress *noun* a loose garment worn in bed.

nightfall *noun* the coming of darkness at the end of the day.

nightie *noun* (*informal*) a nightdress.

nightingale *noun* a small brown bird that sings sweetly.

nightly *adjective* & *adverb* happening every night.

nightmare *noun* a frightening dream.
nightmarish *adjective*

nil *noun* nothing; nought.

nimble *adjective* able to move quickly; agile. **nimbly** *adverb*

nimbus *noun* (*plural* **nimbi** or **nimbuses**) a large grey rain-cloud.

nine *noun* & *adjective* the number 9; one more than eight. **ninth** *adjective* & *noun*

ninepins *noun* the game of skittles played with nine objects.

nineteen *noun* & *adjective* the number 19; one more than eighteen. **nineteenth** *adjective* & *noun*

ninety *noun* & *adjective* (*plural* **nineties**) the number 90; nine times ten. **ninetieth** *adjective* & *noun*

nip[1] *verb* (**nipped, nipping**) 1 pinch or bite quickly. 2 (*informal*) go quickly.

nip[2] *noun* 1 a quick pinch or bite. 2 sharp coldness, *There's a nip in the air.*

nipple *noun* a small projecting part, especially at the front of a person's breast.

nippy *adjective* (**nippier, nippiest**) (*informal*) 1 quick; nimble. 2 cold.

nit *noun* a parasitic insect; its egg.

nit-picking *noun* pointing out very small faults.

nitric acid (*say* **ny**-trik) *noun* a very strong colourless acid containing nitrogen.

nitrogen (*say* **ny**-tro-jen) *noun* a gas that makes up about four-fifths of the air.

nitwit *noun* (*informal*) a stupid person. **nitwitted** *adjective*

nkosazana *noun* inkosazana.

nkosi *noun* inkosi.

nkosikazi *noun* inkosikazi.

no[1] *adjective* not any, *We have no money.* **no man's land** an area that does not belong to anybody. **no one** no person; nobody.

no[2] *adverb* 1 used to deny or refuse something, *Will you come? No.* 2 not at all, *She is no better.*

No. (also **no.**) *abbreviation* (*plural* **Nos.** or **nos.**) number.

nobility *noun* (*plural* **nobilities**) 1 a class of nobles; an aristocracy. 2 nobleness of character or mind.

noble[1] *adjective* 1 of high social rank; aristocratic. 2 having a very good character or qualities, *a noble king.* 3 stately; impressive, *a noble building.* **nobly** *adverb*, **nobleness** *noun*

noble[2] *noun* a person of high social rank. **nobleman** *noun*, **noblewoman** *noun*

nobody *pronoun* no person; no one.

nocturnal *adjective* of or in the night; active at night, *nocturnal animals.* (Compare *diurnal.*)

nocturne *noun* a piece of music with the quiet dreamy feeling of night.

nod *verb* (**nodded, nodding**) 1 move the head up and down, especially as a way of agreeing with somebody or as a greeting. 2 be drowsy. **nod** *noun*

node *noun* a swelling like a small knob.

nodule *noun* a small node.

noise *noun* a sound, especially one that is loud or unpleasant. **noisy** *adjective*, **noisily** *adverb*, **noiseless** *adjective*

noisome (*say* **noi**-sum) *adjective* smelling unpleasant; harmful.

nomad *noun* a member of a people moving from place to place looking for pasture for their animals. **nomadic** *adjective*

nominal *adjective* 1 in name, *He is the nominal ruler, but the real power is held by the generals.* 2 small, *We charged them only a nominal fee.* **nominally** *adverb*

nominate *verb* (**nominated, nominating**) name a person or thing to be appointed or chosen. **nomination** *noun*, **nominator** *noun*

nominee *noun* a person who is nominated.

non- *prefix* not.

nonagenarian *noun* a person aged between 90 and 99.

nonchalant (*say* non-shal-ant) *adjective* calm and casual; showing no anxiety or excitement. **nonchalantly** *adverb*, **nonchalance** *noun*

non-commissioned *adjective* not holding a commission, *Non-commissioned officers include corporals and sergeants.*

non-committal *adjective* not committing yourself; not showing what you think.

nonconformist *noun* a person who does not keep to accepted rules, customs, etc.

nondescript *adjective* having no special or distinctive qualities and therefore difficult to describe.

none[1] *pronoun* 1 not any. 2 no one, *None can tell.*

● USAGE: It is better to use a singular verb (e.g. *None of them is here*), but the plural is not incorrect (e.g. *None of them are here*).

none[2] *adverb* not at all, *He is none too bright.*

nonentity (*say* non-**en**-tit-ee) *noun* (*plural* **nonentities**) an unimportant person.

non-existent *adjective* not existing; unreal.

non-fiction *noun* writings that are not fiction; books about real people and things and true events.

nonplus *verb* (**nonplussed, nonplussing**) puzzle someone completely.

nonsense *noun* 1 words put together in a way that does not mean anything. 2 stupid ideas or behaviour. **nonsensical** (*say* non-**sens**-ik-al) *adjective*

non-stop *adjective* 1 not stopping, *non-stop chatter.* 2 not stopping between two main stations, *a non-stop train.*

noodles *plural noun* pasta made in narrow strips or rings, used in soups etc.

nook *noun* a sheltered corner; a recess.

noon *noun* twelve o'clock midday.

noose *noun* a loop in a rope that gets smaller when the rope is pulled.

nor *conjunction* and not, *She cannot do it; nor can I.*

norm *noun* a standard or average type, amount, level, etc.

normal *adjective* **1** usual or ordinary. **2** natural and healthy; without a physical or mental illness. **normally** *adverb*, **normality** *noun*

north[1] *noun* **1** the direction to the left of a person who faces east. **2** the northern part of a country, city, etc.

north[2] *adjective* & *adverb* towards or in the north. **northerly** *adjective*, **northern** *adjective*, **northerner** *noun*, **northernmost** *adjective*

north-east *noun, adjective* & *adverb* midway between north and east. **north-easterly** *adjective*, **north-eastern** *adjective*

northward *adjective* & *adverb* towards the north. **northwards** *adverb*

north-west *noun, adjective* & *adverb* midway between north and west. **north-westerly** *adjective*, **north-western** *adjective*

Nos. (also **nos.**) *plural* of **No.** or **no.**

nose[1] *noun* **1** the part of the face that is used for breathing and for smelling things. **2** the front end or part.

nose[2] *verb* (**nosed, nosing**) **1** push the nose into or near something. **2** go forward cautiously, *Ships nosed through the ice.*

nosebag *noun* a bag containing fodder, for hanging on a horse's head.

nosedive *noun* a steep downward dive, especially of an aircraft. **nosedive** *verb*

nosegay *noun* a small bunch of flowers.

nostalgia (*say* nos-**tal**-ja) *noun* sentimental remembering or longing for the past. **nostalgic** *adjective*, **nostalgically** *adverb*

nostril *noun* either of the two openings in the nose.

nosy *adjective* (**nosier, nosiest**) inquisitive. **nosily** *adverb*, **nosiness** *noun*

not *adverb* used to change the meaning of something to its opposite.

notable *adjective* worth noticing; remarkable; famous. **notably** *adverb*, **notability** *noun*

notation *noun* a system of symbols representing numbers, quantities, musical notes, etc.

notch[1] *noun* (*plural* **notches**) a small V-shape cut into a surface.

notch[2] *verb* cut a notch or notches in. **notch up** score.

note[1] *noun* **1** something written down as a reminder or as a comment or explanation. **2** a short letter. **3** a banknote, *a R100 note.* **4** a single sound in music. **5** any of the black or white keys on a piano etc. (see *key* 3). **6** a sound or quality that indicates something, *a note of warning.* **7** notice; attention, *Take note.*

note[2] *verb* (**noted, noting**) **1** make a note about something; write down. **2** notice; pay attention to, *Note what we say.*

notebook *noun* a book with blank pages on which to write notes.

noted *adjective* famous; well-known.

notepaper *noun* paper for writing letters.

nothing[1] *noun* **1** no thing; not anything. **2** no amount; nought.

for nothing without payment, free; without a result.

nothing[2] *adverb* not at all; in no way, *It's nothing like as good.*

notice[1] *noun* **1** something written or printed and displayed for people to see. **2** attention, *It escaped my notice.* **3** information that something is going to happen; warning that you are about to end an agreement or a person's employment etc., *We gave him a month's notice.*

notice[2] *verb* (**noticed, noticing**) see; become aware of something.

noticeable *adjective* easily seen or noticed. **noticeably** *adverb*

notice-board *noun* a board on which notices may be displayed.

notifiable *adjective* that must be reported.

notify *verb* (**notified, notifying**) inform, *Notify the police.* **notification** *noun*

notion *noun* an idea, especially one that is vague or incorrect.

notional *adjective* guessed and not definite. **notionally** *adverb*

notorious *adjective* well-known for something bad. **notoriously** *adverb*, **notoriety** (*say* noh-ter-**I**-it-ee) *noun*

notwithstanding *preposition* in spite of.

nougat (*say* noo-gah) *noun* a chewy sweet made from nuts, sugar or honey, and egg-white.

nought (*say* nawt) *noun* 1 the figure 0. 2 nothing.

noun *noun* a word that stands for a person, place, or thing. **Common nouns** are words such as *boy, dog, river, sport, table,* which are used of a whole kind of people or things; **proper nouns** are words such as *Catherine, Drakensberg,* and *Ulundi* which name a particular person or thing.

nourish *verb* keep a person, animal, or plant alive and well by means of food. **nourishment** *noun*

novel[1] *noun* a story that fills a whole book.

novel[2] *adjective* of a new and unusual kind, *a novel experience.* **novelty** *noun*

novelist *noun* a person who writes novels.

novice *noun* a beginner.

now[1] *adverb* 1 at this time. 2 by this time. 3 immediately, *You must go now.* 4 I wonder or am telling you, *Now why didn't I think of that?*
now and again or **now and then** sometimes; occasionally.

now[2] *conjunction* as a result of or at the same time as something, *Now that you have come, we'll start.*

now[3] *noun* this moment, *They will be at home by now.*

nowadays *adverb* at the present time, as contrasted with years ago.

nowhere[1] *adverb* not anywhere.

nowhere[2] *noun* no place, *Nowhere is as beautiful as Cape Town.*

noxious *adjective* unpleasant and harmful.

nozzle *noun* the spout of a hose or pipe etc.

nuance (*say* new-ahns) *noun* a slight difference or shade of meaning.

nub *noun* 1 a small knob or lump. 2 the central point of a problem.

nuclear *adjective* 1 of a nucleus. 2 using the energy that is created by reactions in the nuclei of atoms.
nuclear family a family consisting only of mother, father, and children.

nucleus *noun* (*plural* **nuclei**) 1 the part in the centre of something, round which other things are grouped. 2 the central part of an atom or of a seed or a biological cell.

nude *adjective* not wearing any clothes; naked. **nudity** *noun*

nudge *verb* (**nudged, nudging**) 1 poke a person gently with your elbow. 2 push slightly or gradually. **nudge** *noun*

nudist *noun* a person who believes that going naked is enjoyable and good for the health. **nudism** *noun*

nugget *noun* a rough lump of gold or platinum found in the earth.

nuisance *noun* an annoying person or thing.

null *adjective* not valid, *null and void.*

nullify *verb* (**nullified, nullifying**) make a thing null. **nullification** *noun*

numb[1] *adjective* unable to feel or move. **numbly** *adverb*, **numbness** *noun*

numb[2] *verb* make numb.

number[1] *noun* 1 a symbol or word indicating how many; a numeral or figure. 2 a numeral given to a thing to identify it, *a telephone number.* 3 a quantity of people or things, *the number of people present.* 4 one issue of a magazine or newspaper. 5 a song or piece of music.

number[2] *verb* 1 mark with numbers. 2 count. 3 amount to, *The crowd numbered 10 000.*

numberless *adjective* too many to count.

numeral *noun* a symbol that represents a certain number; a figure.

numerate *adjective* having a good basic knowledge of mathematics. **numeracy** *noun*

numeration *noun* numbering.

numerator *noun* the number above the line in a fraction, showing how many parts are to be taken, e.g. 2 in $^2/_3$. (Compare *denominator.*)

numerical (*say* new-**merri**-kal) *adjective* of a number or series of numbers, *in numerical order.* **numerically** *adverb*

numerous *adjective* many.

numismatics (*say* new-miz-**mat**-iks) *noun* the study of coins. **numismatist** *noun*

nun *noun* a member of a community of women who live according to the rules of a religious organization. (Compare *monk.*)

nunnery *noun* (*plural* **nunneries**) a convent for nuns. (Compare *monastery.*)

nuptial *adjective* of marriage; of a wedding. **nuptials** *plural noun* a wedding.

nurse[1] *noun* **1** a person trained to look after people who are ill or injured. **2** a woman employed to look after young children.

nurse[2] *verb* (**nursed, nursing**) **1** look after someone who is ill or injured. **2** hold carefully. **3** feed a baby.

nursing home a small hospital or home for invalids.

nursemaid *noun* a young woman employed to look after young children.

nursery *noun* (*plural* **nurseries**) **1** a place where young children are looked after or play. **2** a place where young plants are grown for sale or transplantation.

nursery rhyme a simple rhyme or song of the kind that young children like.

nursery school a school for children below primary school age.

nurture[1] *verb* (**nurtured, nurturing**) **1** nourish. **2** train and educate; bring up.

nurture[2] *noun* nurturing; nourishment.

nut *noun* **1** a fruit with a hard shell. **2** a kernel. **3** a small piece of metal with a hole in the middle, for screwing on to a bolt. **4** (*informal*) a mad or eccentric person. **nutty** *adjective*

nutcrackers *plural noun* pincers for cracking nuts.

nutmeg *noun* the hard seed of a tropical tree, grated and used in cooking.

nutrient (*say* new-tree-ent) *noun* a nourishing substance. **nutrient** *adjective*

nutriment (*say* new-trim-ent) *noun* nourishing food.

nutrition (*say* new-trish-on) *noun* nourishment; the study of what nourishes people. **nutritional** *adjective*, **nutritionally** *adverb*

nutritious (*say* new-trish-us) *adjective* nourishing; giving good nourishment. **nutritiousness** *noun*

nutritive (*say* new-trit-iv) *adjective* nourishing.

nutshell *noun* the shell of a nut. **in a nutshell** stated very briefly.

nuzzle *verb* (**nuzzled, nuzzling**) rub gently

with the nose.

NW *abbreviation* north-west; north-western.

nyala (*say* nyah-la) *noun* (*plural* **nyala**) a kind of antelope that lives in wooded areas.

nylon *noun* a synthetic lightweight very strong cloth or fibre.

nymph (*say* nimf) *noun* **1** (in myths) a young goddess living in the sea or woods etc. **2** the young stage of an insect which does not undergo complete metamorphosis.

Oo

O *interjection* oh.

oaf *noun* (*plural* **oafs**) a stupid lout.

oak *noun* a large deciduous tree with seeds called acorns. **oaken** *adjective*

oar *noun* a pole with a flat blade at one end, used for rowing a boat. **oarsman** *noun*, **oarsmanship** *noun*, **oarswoman** *noun*

oasis (*say* oh-ay-sis) *noun* (*plural* **oases**) a fertile place in a desert, with a spring or well of water.

oath *noun* **1** a solemn promise to do something or that something is true, appealing to God or a holy person as witness. **2** use of the name of God in anger or to emphasize something.

oatmeal *noun* ground oats.

oats *plural noun* a cereal used as food.

ob- *prefix* (changing to **oc-** before *c*, **of-** before *f*, **op-** before *p*) **1** to; towards (as in *observe*). **2** against (as in *opponent*). **3** in the way; blocking (as in *obstruct*).

obedient *adjective* doing what you are told; willing to obey. **obediently** *adverb*, **obedience** *noun*

obeisance (*say* o-bay-sans) *noun* a deep bow or curtsy.

obelisk *noun* a tall pillar set up as a monument.

obese (*say* o-beess) *adjective* very fat. **obesity** (*say* o-beess-it-ee) *noun*

obey *verb* do what you are told to do by a person, law, etc.

obituary *noun* (*plural* **obituaries**)
a printed notice of a person's death, often
with a short account of his or her life.

object[1] (*say* ob-jikt) *noun* **1** something
that can be seen or touched. **2** a purpose
or intention. **3** (in grammar) the word or
words naming who or what is acted upon by
a verb or by a preposition, e.g. *him* in *the
dog bit him* and *against him*.

object[2] (*say* ob-jekt) *verb* say that you are
not in favour of something or do not agree;
protest. **objector** *noun*

objection *noun* **1** objecting to something.
2 a reason for objecting, *Her main objection
to the plan is that it would take too long.*

objectionable *adjective* unpleasant; not
liked. **objectionably** *adverb*

objective[1] *noun* what you are trying to
reach or do; an aim.

objective[2] *adjective* **1** real; actual, *Dreams
have no objective existence.* **2** not influenced
by personal feelings or opinions, *an objective account of the quarrel.* (Compare *subjective.*) **objectively** *adverb*, **objectivity** *noun*

obligation *noun* **1** being obliged to do
something. **2** what you are obliged to do;
a duty, *parental obligations.*

under an obligation owing gratitude to
someone who has helped you.

obligatory (*say* ob-lig-a-ter-ee) *adjective*
compulsory, not optional.

oblige *verb* (**obliged**, **obliging**) **1** compel.
2 help and please someone, *Can you oblige
me with a loan?*

be obliged to someone feel gratitude to
a person who has helped you.

obliging *adjective* polite and helpful.

oblique (*say* ob-leek) *adjective* **1** slanting.
2 not saying something straightforwardly,
an oblique reply. **obliquely** *adverb*

obliterate *verb* (**obliterated**, **obliterating**)
blot out; destroy and remove all traces of
something. **obliteration** *noun*

oblivion *noun* **1** being forgotten, *Her films
sank into oblivion after her death.* **2** being
oblivious.

oblivious *adjective* unaware of something,
oblivious to the danger.

oblong *adjective* rectangular in shape and
longer than it is wide (like a page of this

book). **oblong** *noun*

obnoxious *adjective* very unpleasant;
objectionable.

oboe *noun* a high-pitched woodwind
instrument. **oboist** *noun*

obscene (*say* ob-**seen**) *adjective* indecent
in a repulsive or very offensive way.
obscenely *adverb*, **obscenity** *noun*

obscure[1] *adjective* **1** difficult to see or to
understand; not clear. **2** not famous, *an
obscure poet.* **obscurely** *adverb*, **obscurity**
noun

obscure[2] *verb* (**obscured**, **obscuring**)
make a thing obscure; darken or conceal,
Clouds obscured the sun.

obsequious (*say* ob-**seek**-wee-us) *adjective*
respectful in an excessive or sickening
way. **obsequiously** *adverb*, **obsequious-
ness** *noun*

observance *noun* obeying or keeping a
law, custom, religious festival, etc.

observant *adjective* quick at observing or
noticing things. **observantly** *adverb*

observation *noun* **1** observing; watching.
2 a comment or remark.

observatory *noun* (*plural* **observatories**)
a building with telescopes etc. for observation of the stars or weather.

observe *verb* (**observed**, **observing**)
1 see and notice; watch carefully. **2** obey
a law, *observe the crayfish quota.* **3** keep or
celebrate a custom or religious festival etc.
4 make a remark. **observer** *noun*

obsess *verb* occupy a person's thoughts
continually. **obsession** *noun*, **obsessive**
adjective

obsolescent *adjective* becoming obsolete;
going out of use or fashion. **obsolescence**
noun

obsolete *adjective* not used any more;
out of date.

obstacle *noun* something that stands in
the way or obstructs progress.

obstetrics *noun* the branch of medicine
and surgery that deals with the birth of
babies.

obstinate *adjective* keeping firmly to your
own ideas or ways, even though they may
be wrong. **obstinately** *adverb*, **obstinacy**
noun

obstreperous (*say* ob-**strep**-er-us) *adjective* noisy and unruly.

obstruct *verb* stop a person or thing from getting past; hinder. **obstruction** *noun*, **obstructive** *adjective*

obtain *verb* get; come into possession of something by buying, taking, or being given it. **obtainable** *adjective*

obtrude *verb* (**obtruded**, **obtruding**) force yourself or your ideas on someone; be obtrusive. **obtrusion** *noun*

obtrusive *adjective* obtruding; unpleasantly noticeable. **obtrusiveness** *noun*

obtuse *adjective* stupid. **obtusely** *adverb*, **obtuseness** *noun*

obtuse angle an angle of more than 90° but less than 180°. (Compare *acute*.)

obverse *noun* the side of a coin or medal showing the head or chief design (the other side is the *reverse*).

obvious *adjective* easy to see or understand. **obviously** *adverb*

oc- *prefix* see **ob-**.

occasion[1] *noun* 1 the time when something happens. 2 a special event, *a memorable occasion*. 3 a suitable time; an opportunity.

occasion[2] *verb* cause.

occasional *adjective* 1 happening at intervals. 2 for special occasions, *occasional music*. **occasionally** *adverb*

Occident (*say* **ok**-sid-ent) *noun* the West as opposed to the Orient. **occidental** *adjective*

occult *adjective* 1 mysterious; supernatural, *occult powers*. 2 secret except when people have special knowledge.

occupant *noun* someone who occupies a place. **occupancy** *noun*

occupation *noun* 1 an activity that keeps a person busy; a job. 2 occupying.

occupational *adjective* of or caused by an occupation, *an occupational disease*. **occupational therapy** creative work designed to help people to recover from certain illnesses.

occupy *verb* (**occupied**, **occupying**) 1 live in a place; inhabit. 2 fill a space or position, *His clothes occupy most of the cupboard*. 3 capture enemy territory and place troops there. 4 keep somebody busy; fill with activity. **occupier** *noun*

occur *verb* (**occurred**, **occurring**) 1 happen; come into existence as an event or process. 2 be found to exist, *These plants occur in ponds*. 3 come into a person's mind, *An idea occurred to me*.

occurrence *noun* 1 occurring. 2 an incident or event; a happening, *a regular occurrence*.

ocean *noun* the seas that surround the continents of the earth, especially one of the large named areas of this, *the Pacific Ocean*. **oceanic** *adjective*

ocelot (*say* **oss**-il-ot) *noun* a leopard-like animal of Central and South America.

ochre (*say* **oh**-ker) *noun* 1 a mineral used as a pigment. 2 pale brownish-yellow.

o'clock *adverb* by the clock, *Lunch is at one o'clock*.

octa- (also **octo-**) *prefix* eight.

octagon *noun* a flat shape with eight sides and eight angles. **octagonal** *adjective*

octave *noun* the interval of eight steps between one musical note and the next note of the same name above or below it.

octet *noun* a group of eight instruments or singers.

octo- *prefix* see **octa-**.

octogenarian *noun* a person aged between 80 and 89.

octopus *noun* (*plural* **octopuses**) a sea animal with eight long tentacles.

ocular *adjective* of or for the eyes; visual.

oculist *noun* a doctor who treats diseases of the eye.

odd *adjective* 1 strange; unusual. 2 not an even number; not able to be divided exactly by 2. 3 left over from a pair or set, *I've got one odd sock*. 4 of various kinds; not regular, *odd jobs*. **oddly** *adverb*, **oddness** *noun*, **oddity** *noun*

oddments *plural noun* small things of various kinds.

odds *plural noun* the chances that a certain thing will happen; a measure of this, *When the odds are 10 to 1, you will win R10 if you bet R1*.

odds and ends oddments.

ode *noun* a poem addressed to a person or thing.

odious (*say* oh-dee-us) *adjective* hateful. **odiously** *adverb*, **odiousness** *noun*

odium (*say* oh-dee-um) *noun* general hatred or disgust felt towards a person or actions.

odour *noun* a smell. **odorous** *adjective*, **odourless** *adjective*

odyssey (*say* od-iss-ee) *noun* (*plural* **odysseys**) a long adventurous journey, named after the *Odyssey*, a Greek poem telling of the wanderings of Odysseus.

o'er *preposition* & *adverb* (*poetic*) over.

oesophagus (*say* ee-sof-a-gus) *noun* (*plural* **oesophagi**) the gullet.

of *preposition* (used to indicate relationships) **1** belonging to, *the mother of the child*. **2** concerning; about, *news of the disaster*. **3** made from, *built of stone*. **4** from, *north of the town*.

of- *prefix* see **ob-**.

off¹ *preposition* **1** not on; away or down from, *He fell off the ladder*. **2** not taking or wanting, *She is off her food*. **3** deducted from, *R10 off the price*.

off² *adverb* & *adjective* **1** away or down from something, *His hat blew off*. **2** not working; not happening, *The heating is off*. **3** to the end; completely, *Finish it off*. **4** as regards money or supplies, *How are you off for cash?* **5** behind or at the side of a stage, *There were noises off*. **6** (of food) beginning to go bad.

offal *noun* the organs of an animal (e.g. liver, kidneys) sold as food.

offence *noun* **1** an illegal action. **2** a feeling of annoyance or resentment, *Don't take offence*.

offend *verb* **1** cause offence to someone; hurt a person's pride. **2** do wrong, *offend against the law*. **offender** *noun*

offensive¹ *adjective* **1** causing offence; insulting. **2** disgusting, *an offensive smell*. **3** used in attacking, *offensive weapons*. **offensively** *adverb*, **offensiveness** *noun*

offensive² *noun* an attack. **take the offensive** be the first to attack.

offer¹ *verb* (**offered**, **offering**) **1** present something so that people can accept it if they want to. **2** say that you are willing to do or give something or to pay a certain amount.

offer² *noun* **1** offering something. **2** an amount offered.

offering *noun* what is offered.

offhand *adjective* **1** without preparation. **2** casual; curt. **offhanded** *adjective*

office *noun* **1** a room or building used for business, especially for clerical work or for a special department; the people who work there. **2** a government department, *the President's Office*. **3** an important job or position.
be in office hold an official position.

officer *noun* **1** a person who is in charge of others, especially in the armed forces. **2** an official, *an officer of the court*. **3** a member of the police.

official¹ *adjective* **1** done or said by someone with authority. **2** of officials. **officially** *adverb*

official² *noun* a person who holds a position of authority.

officiate *verb* (**officiated**, **officiating**) be in charge of a meeting, event, etc.

officious *adjective* too ready to give orders; bossy. **officiously** *adverb*

offing *noun* **in the offing** not far away; likely to happen.

off-licence *noun* a shop with a licence to sell alcohol to be drunk somewhere else.

off-line *adjective* (of a device or a process) not connected to or controlled by a computer. (Compare *on-line*.)

offload *verb* **1** unload. **2** get rid of something.

off-sales *noun* an off-licence.

off-season *noun* the time of the year which is least busy in business, travel, etc., *off-season hotel rates*.

offset *verb* (**offset**, **offsetting**) counterbalance or make up for something, *Defeats are offset by successes*.

offshoot *noun* **1** a side-shoot on a plant. **2** something which has developed from something else.

offshore *adjective* **1** from the land towards the sea, *an offshore breeze*. **2** in the sea some distance from the shore, *an offshore island*.

offside *adjective* & *adverb* (of a player in

soccer etc.) in a position where the rules do not allow him or her to play the ball.

offspring *noun* (*plural* **offspring**) a person's child or children; the young of an animal.

off-stage *adjective* & *adverb* not on the stage; not visible to the audience, *an off-stage explosion.*

oft *adverb* (*old use*) often.

often *adverb* many times; in many cases.

ogle *verb* (**ogled, ogling**) stare at someone whom you find attractive.

ogre *noun* 1 a cruel giant in fairy-tales. 2 a terrifying person.

oh *interjection* an exclamation of pain, surprise, delight, etc., or used for emphasis, *Oh yes I will!*

ohm *noun* a unit of electrical resistance.

oil[1] *noun* 1 a thick slippery liquid that will not dissolve in water. 2 a kind of petroleum used as fuel. **oil-well** *noun*

oil rig a structure with equipment used for drilling for oil under the ground or under the sea.

oil[2] *verb* put oil on something, especially to make it work smoothly.

oil-colour *noun* paint made with oil.

oilfield *noun* an area where oil is found.

oil-painting *noun* a painting done with oil-colours.

oilskin *noun* cloth made waterproof by treatment with oil.

oily *adjective* of or like oil; covered or soaked with oil. **oiliness** *noun*

ointment *noun* a cream or slippery paste for putting on sore skin and cuts.

OK (also **okay**) *adverb* & *adjective* (*informal*) all right.

okapi (*say* oh-**kah** pee) *noun* (*plural* **okapi** or **okapis**) an animal like a giraffe but with a shorter neck and a striped body.

old *adjective* 1 not new; born or made or existing from a long time ago. 2 of a particular age, *I'm ten years old.* 3 former; original, *in its old place.* 4 (*informal*, used casually or for emphasis), *good old Peter!* **oldness** *noun*

olden *adjective* (*old use*) of former times.

old-fashioned *adjective* of the kind that was usual a long time ago.

oleander (*say* oh-lee-**an**-der) *noun* a poisonous flowering shrub with pink, red, or white flowers.

olfactory *adjective* of the sense of smell.

oligarchy *noun* (*plural* **oligarchies**) a country ruled by a small group of people. **oligarch** *noun*, **oligarchic** *adjective*

olive *noun* 1 an evergreen tree with a small bitter fruit. 2 this fruit, from which an oil (*olive oil*) is made. 3 a shade of green like an unripe olive.

olive-branch *noun* something done or offered that shows you want to make peace.

Olympic Games (also **Olympics**) *plural noun* a series of international sports contests held every fourth year in a different part of the world.

ombudsman *noun* (*plural* **ombudsmen**) an official whose job is to investigate complaints against government organizations etc.

omega (*say* oh-**meg**-a) *noun* the last letter of the Greek alphabet, a long *o*, written Ω, ω.

omelette *noun* eggs beaten together and cooked in a pan, often with a filling.

omen *noun* an event regarded as a sign of what is going to happen.

ominous *adjective* seeming as if trouble is coming. **ominously** *adverb*

omission *noun* 1 omitting. 2 something that has been omitted or not done.

omit *verb* (**omitted, omitting**) 1 miss something out. 2 fail to do something, *omit to close the door.*

omni- *prefix* all.

omnibus *noun* (*plural* **omnibuses**) 1 (*old use*) a bus. 2 a book containing several stories or books that were previously published separately.

omnipotent (*say* om-**ni**-poh-tent) *adjective* having unlimited power or very great power.

omniscient (*say* om-**ni**-see-ent) *adjective* knowing everything. **omniscience** *noun*

omnivorous (*say* om-**niv**-er-us) *adjective* feeding on all kinds of food. (Compare *carnivorous, herbivorous.*)

on[1] *preposition* 1 supported by; covering; added or attached to, *the sign on the door.*

2 close to; towards, *The army advanced on Mafikeng.* **3** during; at the time of, *on my birthday.* **4** by reason of, *Arrest him on suspicion.* **5** concerning, *a book on butterflies.* **6** in a state of; using or showing, *The house was on fire.*

on² *adverb* **1** so as to be on something, *Put it on.* **2** further forward, *Move on.* **3** working; in action, *Is the heater on?*
  on and off not continually.

once¹ *adverb* **1** for one time or on one occasion only, *They came only once.* **2** formerly, *They once lived here.*

once² *noun* one time, *Once is enough.*

once³ *conjunction* as soon as, *You can go once I have taken your names.*

oncoming *adjective* approaching; coming towards you, *oncoming traffic.*

one¹ *adjective* single; individual; united.

one² *noun* **1** the smallest whole number, 1. **2** a person or thing alone.
  one another each other.

one³ *pronoun* a person; any person, *One likes to help.* **oneself** *pronoun*

onerous (*say* on-er-us) *adjective* burdensome.

one-way *adjective* where traffic is allowed to travel in one direction only.

onion *noun* a round vegetable with a strong flavour. **oniony** *adjective*

on-line *adjective* (of a device or a process) connected to and controlled by a computer, *on-line theatre bookings.* (Compare *off-line.*)

onlooker *noun* a spectator.

only¹ *adjective* being the one person or thing of a kind; sole, *my only wish.*
  only child a child who has no brothers or sisters.

only² *adverb* no more than; and that is all, *There are only three cakes left.*

only³ *conjunction* but then; however, *He makes promises, only he never keeps them.*

onomatopoeia (*say* on-om-at-o-pee-a) *noun* the formation of words that imitate what they stand for, e.g. *cuckoo, plop.*
  onomatopoeic *adjective*

onrush *noun* an onward rush.

onset *noun* **1** a beginning, *the onset of winter.* **2** an attack.

onshore *adjective* from the sea towards the land, *an onshore breeze.*

onslaught *noun* a fierce attack.

onto *preposition* to a position on; in contact with.

onus (*say* oh-nus) *noun* the duty or responsibility of doing something.

onward *adverb* & *adjective* going forward; further on. **onwards** *adverb*

onyx *noun* a stone rather like marble, with different colours in layers.

oom *noun* a title of respect used when addressing an older man.

ooze¹ *verb* (**oozed, oozing**) **1** flow out slowly; trickle. **2** allow something to flow out slowly, *The wound oozed blood.*

ooze² *noun* mud at the bottom of a river or sea.

op- *prefix* see **ob-**.

opal *noun* a kind of stone with a rainbow sheen. **opalescent** *adjective*

opaque (*say* o-payk) *adjective* not transparent; not translucent.

open¹ *adjective* **1** allowing people or things to go in and out; not closed or covered; not blocked up. **2** spread out; unfolded, *had the map open on the table.* **3** not limited; not restricted, *an open championship.* **4** letting in visitors or customers. **5** with wide spaces between solid parts, *an open weave.* **6** honest; frank; not secret or secretive, *Be open about the danger.* **7** not decided, *an open mind.* **openness** *noun*
  In the open air not inside a house or building. **open-air** *adjective*

open² *verb* **1** make or become open or more open. **2** begin. **opener** *noun*

opencast *adjective* (of a mine) worked by removing layers of earth from the surface, not underground.

opening *noun* **1** a space or gap; a place where something opens. **2** the beginning of something. **3** an opportunity.

openly *adverb* without secrecy.

opera¹ *noun* a play in which all or most of the words are sung. **operatic** *adjective*

opera² *plural* of **opus.**

operate *verb* (**operated, operating**) **1** make something work. **2** be in action; work, *The* *new council operates more efficiently than the old one.* **3** perform a surgical operation on somebody. **operable** *adjective*

operation *noun* **1** operating; working. **2** a piece of work. **3** something done to the body to take away or repair a part of it. **4** a planned military activity. **operational** *adjective*

operative *adjective* **1** working; functioning. **2** of surgical operations.

operator *noun* a person who works something, especially a telephone switch-board or exchange.

operetta *noun* a short light opera.

ophthalmic (*say* off-**thal**-mik) *adjective* of or for the eyes.

opinion *noun* what you think of something; a belief or judgement.

opinion poll an estimate of what people think, made by questioning a sample of them.

opinionated *adjective* having strong opinions and holding them obstinately.

opium *noun* a drug made from the juice of certain poppies, used in medicine.

opossum *noun* a small furry marsupial that lives in trees, with different kinds in America and Australia.

opponent *noun* a person or group opposing another in a contest or war.

opportune *adjective* **1** (of time) suitable for a purpose. **2** done or happening at a suitable time, *an opportune question.* **opportunely** *adverb*

opportunist *noun* a person who is quick to seize opportunities.

opportunity *noun* (*plural* **opportunities**) a time or set of circumstances that are suitable for doing a particular thing.

oppose *verb* (**opposed, opposing**) **1** argue or fight against; resist. **2** contrast, *'Soft' is opposed to 'hard'.*

opposite[1] *adjective* **1** placed on the other or further side; facing, *on the opposite side of the road.* **2** moving away from or towards each other, *The trains were travelling in opposite directions.* **3** completely different, *opposite characters.*

opposite[2] *noun* an opposite person or thing.

opposite[3] *adverb* in an opposite position or direction, *I'll sit opposite.*

opposite[4] *preposition* opposite to, *They live opposite the school.*

opposition *noun* **1** opposing something; resistance. **2** the people who oppose something.

the Opposition the chief political party opposing the one that is in power.

oppress *verb* **1** govern or treat somebody cruelly or unjustly. **2** weigh down with worry or sadness. **oppression** *noun,* **oppressive** *adjective,* **oppressor** *noun*

opt *verb* choose.

opt out decide not to join in.

optic *adjective* of the eye or sight.

optics *noun* the study of sight and of light as connected with this.

optical *adjective* of sight; aiding sight, *optical instruments.* **optically** *adverb*

optical illusion a deceptive appearance that makes you see something wrongly.

optician *noun* a person who makes or sells spectacles etc.

ophthalmic optician someone who is qualified to test people's eyesight and prescribe spectacles etc.

optimist *noun* a person who expects that things will turn out well. (Compare *pessimist.*) **optimism** *noun,* **optimistic** *adjective,* **optimistically** *adverb*

optimum *adjective* best; most favourable. **optimum** *noun,* **optimal** *adjective*

option *noun* **1** the right or power to choose something. **2** something chosen or that may be chosen, *a range of options.*

optional *adjective* that you can choose, not compulsory. **optionally** *adverb*

opulent *adjective* **1** wealthy; rich. **2** plentiful. **opulently** *adverb,* **opulence** *noun*

opus (*say* **oh**-pus) *noun* (*plural* **opera**) **1** a numbered musical composition, *Beethoven opus 15.* **2** a work of art.

or *conjunction* used to show that there is a choice or an alternative, *Do you want a sandwich or a biscuit?*

oracle *noun* **1** a shrine where the ancient Greeks consulted one of their gods for advice or a prophecy. **2** a wise adviser. **oracular** (*say* or-**ak**-yoo-ler) *adjective*

oracy (*say* or-a-see) *noun* the ability to express yourself well in speaking.

oral *adjective* 1 spoken, not written. 2 of or using the mouth, *oral hygiene.* **orally** *adverb*

orange *noun* 1 a round juicy citrus fruit with reddish-yellow peel. 2 a reddish-yellow colour.

orangeade *noun* an orange-flavoured drink.

orang-utan *noun* a large ape of Borneo and Sumatra.

oration *noun* a long formal speech.

orator *noun* a person who makes speeches. **oratory** *noun*, **oratorical** *adjective*

oratorio *noun* (*plural* **oratorios**) a piece of music for voices and an orchestra, usually on a religious subject.

orb *noun* a sphere or globe.

orbit[1] *noun* 1 the curved path taken by something moving round a planet etc. in space. 2 the range of someone's influence or control. **orbital** *adjective*

orbit[2] *verb* (**orbited, orbiting**) move in an orbit round something, *The spacecraft orbited the earth.*

orchard *noun* a piece of ground planted with fruit-trees.

orchestra *noun* a large group of people playing various musical instruments together. **orchestral** *adjective*

orchestrate *verb* (**orchestrated, orchestrating**) 1 compose or arrange music for an orchestra. 2 co-ordinate things deliberately, *They orchestrated their campaigns.* **orchestration** *noun*

orchid *noun* a kind of flower, often with brilliant colours and unevenly shaped petals.

ordain *verb* 1 appoint a person ceremonially to perform spiritual duties in the Christian Church. 2 declare authoritatively; decree, *ordained by fate.*

ordeal *noun* something very hard to endure.

order[1] *noun* 1 a command. 2 a request for something to be supplied. 3 the way things are arranged, *in alphabetical order.* 4 a neat arrangement; a proper arrangement or condition, *in working order.* 5 obedience to rules or laws, *law and order.* 6 a kind or sort,

She showed courage of the highest order. 7 a special group; a religious organization, *an order of monks.*

in order that or **in order to** for the purpose of.

order[2] *verb* 1 command. 2 ask for something to be supplied. 3 put into order; arrange neatly.

orderly[1] *adjective* 1 arranged neatly or well; methodical. 2 well-behaved; obedient. **orderliness** *noun*

orderly[2] *noun* (*plural* **orderlies**) 1 a soldier whose job is to assist an officer. 2 an assistant in a hospital.

ordinal number *noun* a number showing a thing's position in a series, e.g. *first, fifth, twentieth.* (Compare *cardinal.*)

ordinance *noun* a command; a decree.

ordinary *adjective* normal; usual; not special. **ordinarily** *adverb*

ordination *noun* ordaining or being ordained as a member of the clergy.

ordnance *noun* military equipment.

ore *noun* rock with metal or other useful substances in it, *iron ore.*

organ *noun* 1 a musical instrument from which sounds are produced by air forced through pipes, played by keys and pedals. 2 a part of the body with a particular function, *the digestive organs.*

organdie *noun* a kind of thin fabric, usually stiffened.

organelle (*say* or-gan-**el**) *noun* any of the small structures found in the cytoplasm of a cell, e.g. the nucleus, chloroplasts, etc.

organic *adjective* 1 of organs of the body, *organic diseases.* 2 of or formed from living things, *organic matter.* 3 (of food) produced without chemical fertilizers or pesticides etc. **organically** *adverb*

organism *noun* a living thing; an individual animal or plant.

organist *noun* a person who plays the organ.

organization *noun* 1 an organized group of people. 2 the organizing of something. **organizational** *adjective*

organize *verb* (**organized, organizing**) 1 plan and prepare something, *We organized a picnic.* 2 form people into a group

to work together. **3** put things in order.
organizer *noun*

orgasm *noun* the climax of sexual excitement.

orgy *noun* (*plural* **orgies**) **1** a wild party.
2 an extravagant activity, *an orgy of spending.*

oribi *noun* (*plural* **oribi** or **oribis**) a small
antelope that has straight horns.

Orient *noun* the East; oriental countries.
(Compare *Occident.*)

orient *verb* orientate.

oriental *adjective* of the countries east of
the Mediterranean Sea, especially China
and Japan.

orientate *verb* (**orientated**, **orientating**)
place something or face in a certain
direction. **orientation** *noun*

orienteering *noun* the sport of finding
your way across rough country with a map
and compass.

orifice (*say* o-rif-iss) *noun* an opening.

origami (*say* o-rig-**ah**-mee) *noun* folding
paper into decorative shapes.

origin *noun* the start of something; the
point or cause from which something
began.

original *adjective* **1** existing from the start;
earliest, *the original inhabitants.* **2** new in its
design etc., not a copy. **3** producing new
ideas; inventive. **originally** *adverb*, **originality** *noun*

originate *verb* (**originated**, **originating**)
1 cause to begin; create. **2** have its origin,
The quarrel originated in rivalry. **origination** *noun*, **originator** *noun*

ornament[1] *noun* a decoration.
ornamental *adjective*

ornament[2] *verb* decorate with things.
ornamentation *noun*

ornate *adjective* elaborately ornamented.
ornately *adverb*

ornithology *noun* the study of birds.
ornithologist *noun*, **ornithological**
adjective

orphan *noun* a child whose parents are
dead. **orphaned** *adjective*

orphanage *noun* a home for orphans.

ortho- *prefix* right; straight; correct.

orthodontics *noun* the treatment of
irregularities in the teeth and jaws. **orthodontic** *adjective*, **orthodontist** *noun*

orthodox *adjective* holding beliefs that are
correct or generally accepted. **orthodoxy**
noun

Orthodox Church the Christian Churches
of eastern Europe.

orthopaedics (*say* orth-o-**pee**-diks) *noun*
the treatment of deformities and injuries
to bones and muscles. **orthopaedic**
adjective

oscillate *verb* (**oscillated**, **oscillating**)
1 move to and fro like a pendulum; vibrate.
2 waver; vary. **oscillation** *noun*, **oscillator**
noun

osier (*say* oh-zee-er) *noun* a willow with
flexible twigs used in making baskets.

osmosis *noun* the passing of fluid through
a porous partition into another more
concentrated fluid.

ostensible *adjective* pretended; used to
conceal the true reason, *Their ostensible
reason for travelling was to visit friends.*
ostensibly *adverb*

ostentatious *adjective* making a showy
display of something to impress people.
ostentatiously *adverb*, **ostentation** *noun*

osteopath *noun* a person who treats
certain diseases etc. by manipulating a
patient's bones and muscles. **osteopathy**
noun, **osteopathic** *adjective*

ostracize *verb* (**ostracized**, **ostracizing**)
exclude; ignore someone completely.
ostracism *noun*

ostrich *noun* (*plural* **ostriches**) **1** a large
long-legged bird that can run very fast but
cannot fly. **2** a person who refuses to
recognize an unpleasant truth.

other[1] *adjective* **1** different, *some other
tune.* **2** remaining, *Try the other shoe.*
3 additional, *my other friends.* **4** just recent
or past, *I saw him the other day.*

other[2] *noun* & *pronoun* the other person or
thing, *Where are the others?*

otherwise *adverb* **1** if things happen
differently; if you do not, *Write it down,
otherwise you'll forget.* **2** in other ways, *It
rained, but otherwise the holiday was good.*
3 differently, *We could not do otherwise.*

otter *noun* a fish-eating animal with

webbed feet, a flat tail, and thick brown fur, living near water.

ottoman *noun* 1 a long padded seat. 2 a storage box with a padded top.

ought *auxiliary verb* expressing duty (*We ought to feed them*), rightness or advisability (*You ought to take more exercise*), or probability (*At this speed, we ought to be there by noon*).

oughtn't (*mainly spoken*) ought not.

ouma *noun* 1 grandmother. 2 old woman.

ounce *noun* a unit of weight in the imperial system, equal to about 28 grams.

oupa *noun* 1 grandfather. 2 old man.

our *adjective* belonging to us.

ours *possessive pronoun* belonging to us, *These seats are ours.*

- USAGE: It is incorrect to write *our's*.

ourselves *pronoun* we or us and nobody else. (Compare *herself*.)

oust *verb* drive out; expel; eject from a position or employment etc.

out *adverb* 1 away from or not in a particular place or position or state etc.; not at home. 2 into the open; into existence or sight etc., *The sun came out.* 3 not in action or use etc.; (of a batsman) having had the innings ended; (of a fire) not burning. 4 to or at an end; completely, *sold out; tired out.* 5 without restraint; boldly; loudly, *Speak out!*

be out for or **out to** be seeking or wanting, *They are out to make trouble.*

out of date old-fashioned; not valid any more.

out of doors in the open air.

out of the way remote; unusual.

out- *prefix* 1 out of; away from (as in *outcast*). 2 external; separate (as in *outhouse*). 3 more than; so as to defeat or exceed (as in *outdo*).

out-and-out *adjective* thorough; complete, *an out-and-out villain.*

outback *noun* the remote inland districts of Australia.

outboard motor *noun* a motor fitted to the outside of a boat's stern.

outbreak *noun* the start of a disease or war or anger etc.

outburst *noun* the bursting out of anger or laughter etc.

outcast *noun* a person who has been rejected by family, friends, or society.

outcome *noun* the result of what happens or has happened.

outcrop *noun* a piece of rock from a lower level that sticks out on the surface of the ground.

outcry *noun* (*plural* **outcries**) 1 a loud cry. 2 a strong protest.

outdated *adjective* out of date.

outdistance *verb* (**outdistanced, outdistancing**) get far ahead of someone in a race etc.

outdo *verb* (**outdid, outdone, outdoing**) do better than another person etc.

outdoor *adjective* done or used outdoors.

outdoors *adverb* in the open air.

outer *adjective* outside; external; nearer to the outside. **outermost** *adjective*

outfit *noun* 1 a set of clothes worn together. 2 a set of equipment.

outflow *noun* 1 flowing out; what flows out. 2 a pipe for liquid flowing out.

outgoing *adjective* 1 going out. 2 sociable and friendly.

outgoings *plural noun* expenditure.

outgrow *verb* (**outgrew, outgrown, outgrowing**) 1 grow out of clothes or habits etc. 2 grow faster or larger than another person or thing.

outgrowth *noun* something that grows out of another thing, *Feathers are outgrowths on a bird's skin.*

outhouse *noun* a small building (e.g. a shed or barn) that belongs to a house but is separate from it.

outing *noun* a journey for pleasure.

outlandish *adjective* looking or sounding strange or foreign.

outlast *verb* last longer than something else.

outlaw[1] *noun* a person who is punished by being excluded from legal rights and the protection of the law.

outlaw[2] *verb* 1 make a person an outlaw. 2 declare something to be illegal; forbid.

outlay *noun* what is spent on something.

outlet *noun* 1 a way for something to get out. 2 a market for goods.

outline[1] *noun* 1 a line round the outside of something, showing its boundary or shape. 2 a summary, *an outline of the plot.*

outline[2] *verb* (**outlined, outlining**) 1 make an outline of something. 2 summarize.

outlive *verb* (**outlived, outliving**) live or last longer than another person etc.

outlook *noun* 1 a view on which people look out. 2 a person's mental attitude to something. 3 future prospects, *a better outlook for gold mining.*

outlying *adjective* far from a centre; remote, *the outlying districts.*

outmoded *adjective* out of date.

outnumber *verb* be more numerous than another group.

out-patient *noun* a person who visits a hospital for treatment but does not stay there.

outpost *noun* a distant settlement.

output *noun* the amount produced.

outrage[1] *noun* 1 something that shocks people by being very wicked or cruel. 2 great anger. **outrageous** *adjective*, **outrageously** *adverb*

outrage[2] *verb* (**outraged, outraging**) shock and anger people greatly.

outrider *noun* a person riding on horseback or on a motor cycle as an escort.

outrigger *noun* a projecting framework attached to a boat, e.g. to prevent a canoe from capsizing.

outright[1] *adverb* 1 completely; entirely, not gradually. 2 frankly, *We told him this outright.*

outright[2] *adjective* thorough; complete, *an outright fraud.*

outrun *verb* (**outran, outrun, outrunning**) 1 run faster or further than another. 2 go on for longer than it should, *The play outran its popularity.*

outset *noun* the beginning, *from the outset of his career.*

outside[1] *noun* the outer side, surface, or part.

outside[2] *adjective* 1 on or coming from the outside, *the outside edge.* 2 greatest possible, *the outside price.* 3 remote; unlikely, *an outside chance.*

outside[3] *adverb* on or to the outside; outdoors, *Leave it outside. It's cold outside.*

outside[4] *preposition* on or to the outside of, *Leave it outside the door.*

outsider *noun* 1 a person who does not belong to a certain group. 2 a horse or person thought to have no chance of winning a race or competition.

outsize *adjective* much larger than average.

outskirts *plural noun* the outer parts or districts, especially of a town.

outspan *verb* (**outspanned, outspanning**) unharness the animals pulling a wagon; break a wagon journey. **outspan** *noun*

outspoken *adjective* speaking or spoken very frankly.

outspread *adjective* spread out.

outstanding *adjective* 1 extremely good or distinguished. 2 conspicuous. 3 not yet paid or dealt with, *an outstanding debt.*

outstretched *adjective* stretched out.

outstrip *verb* (**outstripped, outstripping**) 1 outrun. 2 surpass.

outvote *verb* (**outvoted, outvoting**) defeat by a majority of votes.

outward *adjective* 1 going outwards. 2 on the outside. **outwardly** *adverb*, **outwards** *adverb*

outweigh *verb* be greater in weight or importance than something else.

outwit *verb* (**outwitted, outwitting**) deceive somebody by being crafty.

ova *plural* of **ovum.**

oval *adjective* shaped like a 0, rounded and longer than it is broad. **oval** *noun*

ovary *noun* (*plural* **ovaries**) 1 either of the two organs in which ova or egg-cells are produced in a woman's or female animal's body. 2 part of the pistil in a plant, from which fruit is formed.

ovation *noun* enthusiastic applause.

oven *noun* a closed space in which things are cooked or heated.

over[1] *preposition* 1 above. 2 more than, *It's over a kilometre away.* 3 concerning, *They quarrelled over money.* 4 across the top of; on or to the other side of, *They rowed the boat over the lake.* 5 during, *We can talk over dinner.* 6 in superiority or preference to, *their victory over the Boks.*

over² *adverb* 1 out and down from the top or edge; from an upright position, *He fell over.* 2 so that a different side shows, *Turn it over.* 3 at or to a place; across, *Walk over to our house.* 4 remaining, *There is nothing left over.* 5 all through; thoroughly, *Think it over.* 6 at an end, *The lesson is over.*
over and over many times; repeatedly.

over³ *noun* a series of six balls bowled in cricket.

over- *prefix* 1 over (as in *overturn*). 2 too much; too (as in *over-anxious*).

overall *adjective* including everything; total, *the overall cost.*

overalls *plural noun* a garment worn over other clothes to protect them.

overarm *adjective & adverb* with the arm lifted above shoulder level and coming down in front of the body.

overawe *verb* (**overawed, overawing**) overcome a person with awe.

overbalance *verb* (**overbalanced, overbalancing**) lose balance and fall over; cause to lose balance.

overbearing *adjective* domineering.

overblown *adjective* (of a flower) too fully open; past its best.

overboard *adverb* from in or on a ship into the water, *She jumped overboard.*

overcast *adjective* covered with cloud.

overcoat *noun* a warm outdoor coat.

overcome *verb* (**overcame, overcome, overcoming**) 1 win a victory over somebody; defeat. 2 make a person helpless, *He was overcome by the fumes.* 3 find a way of dealing with a problem etc.

overcrowd *verb* crowd too many people into a place or vehicle etc.

overdo *verb* (**overdid, overdone, overdoing**) 1 do something too much. 2 cook food for too long.

overdose *noun* too large a dose of a drug.

overdraft *noun* the amount by which a bank account is overdrawn.

overdraw *verb* (**overdrew, overdrawn, overdrawing**) draw more money from a bank account than the amount you have in it.

overdue *adjective* late; not paid or arrived etc. by the proper time.

overestimate *verb* (**overestimated, overestimating**) estimate too highly.

overflow *verb* flow over the edge or limits of something. **overflow** *noun*

overgraze *verb* (**overgrazed, overgrazing**) (of livestock) feed on grassland so heavily that the vegetation is damaged and the ground becomes liable to erosion.

overgrown *adjective* covered with weeds or unwanted plants.

overhang *verb* (**overhung, overhanging**) jut out over something. **overhang** *noun*

overhaul *verb* 1 examine something thoroughly and repair it if necessary. 2 overtake. **overhaul** *noun*

overhead *adjective & adverb* 1 above the level of your head. 2 in the sky.
overheads *plural noun* the expenses of running a business.

overhear *verb* (**overheard, overhearing**) hear something accidentally or without the speaker intending you to hear it.

overjoyed *adjective* filled with great joy.

overland *adjective & adverb* travelling over the land, not by sea or air.

overlap *verb* (**overlapped, overlapping**) 1 lie across part of something. 2 happen partly at the same time, *The two parties overlapped.* **overlap** *noun*

overlay¹ *verb* (**overlaid, overlaying**) cover with a layer; lie on top of something.

overlay² *noun* a thing laid over another.

overlie *verb* (**overlay, overlain, overlying**) be or lie over something.

overlook *verb* 1 not notice or consider something. 2 not punish an offence. 3 have a view over something.

overlord *noun* a supreme lord.

overnight *adjective & adverb* of or during a night, *an overnight stop in Beaufort West.*

overpower *verb* overcome.

overpowering *adjective* very strong.

overrate *verb* (**overrated, overrating**) have too high an opinion of something.

overreach *verb* **overreach yourself** fail through being too ambitious.

override *verb* (**overrode, overridden, overriding**) 1 overrule. 2 be more important than, *Safety overrides all other considerations.*

overripe *adjective* too ripe.

overrule *verb* (**overruled, overruling**) reject a suggestion etc. by using your authority, *We voted for having a picnic but the principal overruled the idea.*

overrun *verb* (**overran, overrun, overrunning**) 1 spread over and occupy or harm something, *Mice overran the place.* 2 go on for longer than it should, *The broadcast overran its time.*

overseas *adverb* across or beyond the sea; abroad.

oversee *verb* (**oversaw, overseen, overseeing**) superintend. **overseer** *noun*

overshadow *verb* 1 cast a shadow over something. 2 make a person or thing seem unimportant in comparison.

overshoot *verb* (**overshot, overshooting**) go beyond a target or limit, *The plane overshot the runway.*

oversight *noun* a mistake made by not noticing something.

oversleep *verb* (**overslept, oversleeping**) sleep for longer than you intended.

overspill *noun* what spills over; the extra population of a town, who take homes in nearby districts.

overstep *verb* (**overstepped, overstepping**) go beyond a limit.

overt *adjective* done or shown openly, *overt hostility.* **overtly** *adverb*

overtake *verb* (**overtook, overtaken, overtaking**) 1 pass a moving vehicle or person etc. 2 catch up with someone, *overtaken by bad weather.*

overtax *verb* 1 tax too heavily. 2 put too heavy a burden or strain on someone.

overthrow[1] *verb* (**overthrew, overthrown, overthrowing**) cause the downfall of, *They overthrew the king.*

overthrow[2] *noun* 1 overthrowing; downfall. 2 throwing a ball too far.

overtime *noun* time spent working outside the normal hours; payment for this.

overtone *noun* an extra quality, *There were overtones of envy in his speech.*

overture *noun* 1 a piece of music written as an introduction to an opera, ballet, etc.

2 a friendly attempt to start a discussion, *They made overtures of peace.*

overturn *verb* 1 turn over or upside-down. 2 upset; overthrow.

overweight *adjective* too heavy.

overwhelm *verb* 1 bury or drown beneath a huge mass. 2 overcome completely.

overwork *verb* 1 work or cause to work too hard. 2 use too often, *'Nice' is an overworked word.* **overwork** *noun*

overwrought *adjective* very upset and nervous or worried.

oviparous (*say* oh-**vi**-pa-rus) *adjective* egg-laying.

ovoid *adjective* egg-shaped.

ovoviviparous (*say* oh-voh-vi-**vi**-pa-rus) *adjective* producing living young from an egg that hatches inside the body of the mother.

ovulate *verb* (**ovulated, ovulating**) produce an ovum from an ovary.

ovum (*say* oh-vum) *noun* (*plural* **ova**) a female cell that can develop into a new individual when fertilized.

owe *verb* (**owed, owing**) 1 have a duty to pay or give something to someone, especially money. 2 have something because of the action of another person or thing, *They owed their lives to the pilot's skill.*

owing to because of; caused by.

owl *noun* a bird of prey with large eyes, usually flying at night.

own[1] *adjective* belonging to yourself or itself.

get your own back get revenge.

on your own alone.

own[2] *verb* 1 possess; have something as your property. 2 acknowledge; admit, *I own that I made a mistake.*

own up (*informal*) confess; admit guilt.

owner *noun* the person who owns something. **ownership** *noun*

ox *noun* (*plural* **oxen**) a large animal kept for its meat and for pulling carts.

oxide *noun* a compound of oxygen and one other element.

oxidize *verb* (**oxidized, oxidizing**) 1 combine or cause to combine with oxygen.

2 coat with an oxide. **oxidation** *noun*

oxtail *noun* the tail of an ox, used to make soup or stew.

oxygen *noun* a colourless odourless tasteless gas that exists in the air and is essential for living things.

oyster *noun* a kind of shellfish whose shell sometimes contains a pearl.

ozone *noun* a form of oxygen with a sharp smell.

ozone-friendly not containing substances that could damage the ozone layer.

ozone hole an area of the ozone layer which has been destroyed or damaged.

ozone layer a layer of ozone high in the atmosphere, protecting the world from harmful amounts of the sun's rays.

Pp

p. *abbreviation* (*plural* **pp.**) page.

pa *noun* (*informal*) father.

pace¹ *noun* **1** one step in walking, marching, or running. **2** speed, *an increased pace.*

pace² *verb* (**paced, pacing**) **1** walk with slow or regular steps. **2** measure a distance in paces, *pace it out.*

pacemaker *noun* **1** a person who sets the pace for another in a race. **2** an electrical device to keep the heart beating.

pacific (*say* pa-**sif**-ik) *adjective* peaceful; making or loving peace. **pacifically** *adverb*

pacifist (*say* **pas**-if-ist) *noun* a person who believes that war is always wrong. **pacifism** *noun*

pacify *verb* (**pacified, pacifying**) make peaceful or calm. **pacification** *noun*

pack¹ *noun* **1** a bundle; a collection of things wrapped or tied together. **2** a set of playing-cards (usually 52). **3** a group of hounds or wolves etc. **4** a group of people; a group of Brownies or Cub Scouts. **5** a large amount, *a pack of lies.* **6** a mass of pieces of ice floating in the sea, *pack-ice.*

pack² *verb* **1** put things into a suitcase, bag, or box etc. in order to move or store them. **2** crowd together; fill tightly.

pack off send a person away.

send a person packing dismiss him or her.

package *noun* **1** a parcel or packet. **2** a package deal. **packaging** *noun*

package deal a number of things offered or accepted together.

package tour a holiday with everything arranged and included in the price.

packet *noun* a small parcel.

pact *noun* an agreement; a treaty.

pad¹ *noun* **1** a soft thick mass of material, used e.g. to protect or stuff something. **2** a device worn to protect the leg in cricket and other games. **3** a set of sheets of paper fastened together at one edge. **4** the soft fleshy part under an animal's foot or the end of a finger or toe. **5** a flat surface from which spacecraft are launched or where helicopters take off and land.

pad² *verb* (**padded, padding**) put a pad on or in something.

pad³ *verb* (**padded, padding**) walk softly.

padding *noun* material used to pad things.

paddle¹ *verb* (**paddled, paddling**) walk about in shallow water. **paddle** *noun*

paddle² *noun* a short oar with a broad blade; something shaped like this.

paddle³ *verb* (**paddled, paddling**) move a boat along with a paddle or paddles; row gently.

paddock *noun* a small field where horses are kept.

paddy *noun* (*plural* **paddies**) a field where rice is grown. **paddy-field** *noun*

padkos (*say* **putt**-kos) *noun* food that is packed for a journey.

padlock *noun* a detachable lock with a metal loop that passes through a ring or chain etc.

padre (*say* **pah**-dray) *noun* (*informal*) a chaplain in the armed forces.

paean (*say* **pee**-an) *noun* a song of praise or triumph.

paediatrics (*say* peed-ee-**at**-riks) *noun* the study of children's diseases. **paediatric** *adjective*, **paediatrician** *noun*

pagan (*say* **pay**-gan) *adjective* & *noun* heathen.

page¹ *noun* a piece of paper that is part of a book or newspaper etc.; one side of this.

page² *noun* a boy or man employed to go on errands or be an attendant.

pageant *noun* 1 a play or entertainment about historical events and people. 2 a procession of people in costume as an entertainment. **pageantry** *noun*

pagoda (*say* pag-**oh**-da) *noun* a Buddhist tower, or a Hindu temple shaped like a pyramid, in India and the Far East.

paid *past tense* of **pay¹**. **put paid to** (*informal*) put an end to someone's activity or hope etc.

pail *noun* a bucket.

pain¹ *noun* 1 an unpleasant feeling caused by injury or disease. 2 suffering in the mind. **painful** *adjective*, **painfully** *adverb*, **painless** *adjective*
take pains make a careful effort with work etc. **painstaking** *adjective*

pain² *verb* cause pain to someone.

paint¹ *noun* a liquid substance put on something to colour it. **paintbox** *noun*, **paintbrush** *noun*

paint² *verb* 1 put paint on something. 2 make a picture with paints.

painter¹ *noun* a person who paints.

painter² *noun* a rope used to tie up a boat.

painting *noun* a painted picture.

pair¹ *noun* 1 a set of two things or people; a couple. 2 something made of two joined parts, *a pair of scissors*.

pair² *verb* put together as a pair.

pal *noun* (*informal*) a friend.

palace *noun* a mansion where a king, queen, or other important person lives.

palaeolithic (*say* pal-ee-oh-**lith**-ik) *adjective* of the early part of the Stone Age.

palatable *adjective* tasting pleasant.

palate *noun* 1 the roof of the mouth. 2 a person's sense of taste.
• USAGE: Do not confuse with *palette* and *pallet.*

palatial (*say* pa-**lay**-shal) *adjective* like a palace; large and splendid.

pale¹ *adjective* 1 almost white, *a pale face.* 2 not bright in colour or light, *pale green; the pale moonlight.* **palely** *adverb*, **paleness** *noun*

pale² *noun* a boundary.
beyond the pale beyond the limits of good

taste or behaviour etc.

palette *noun* a board on which an artist mixes colours ready for use.
• USAGE: Do not confuse with *palate* and *pallet.*

paling *noun* a fence made of wooden posts or railings; one of its posts.

palisade *noun* a fence of pointed sticks or boards.

pall¹ (*say* pawl) *noun* 1 a cloth spread over a coffin. 2 a dark covering, *A pall of smoke lay over the town.*

pall² (*say* pawl) *verb* become uninteresting or boring to someone.

pallbearer *noun* a person helping to carry the coffin at a funeral.

pallet *noun* 1 a mattress stuffed with straw. 2 a hard narrow bed.
• USAGE: Do not confuse with *palate* and *palette.*

palliate *verb* (**palliated, palliating**) make a thing less serious or less severe. **palliation** *noun*, **palliative** *adjective* & *noun*

pallid *adjective* pale, especially because of illness. **pallor** *noun*

palm¹ *noun* 1 the inner part of the hand, between the fingers and the wrist. 2 a palm-tree.

palm² *verb* pick up something secretly and hide it in the palm of your hand.
palm off deceive a person into accepting something.

palmistry *noun* fortune-telling by looking at the creases in the palm of a person's hand. **palmist** *noun*

palm-tree *noun* a tropical tree with large leaves and no branches.

palpable *adjective* 1 able to be touched or felt. 2 obvious, *a palpable lie.* **palpably** *adverb*

palpitate *verb* (**palpitated, palpitating**) 1 (of the heart) beat hard and quickly. 2 (of a person) quiver with fear or excitement. **palpitation** *noun*

palsy (*say* **pawl**-zee) *noun* paralysis.

paltry (*say* **pol**-tree) *adjective* very small and almost worthless, *a paltry amount.*

pampas *noun* wide grassy plains in South America.

pampas-grass *noun* a tall ornamental

grass with feathery flowers.

pamper *verb* treat very kindly and indulgently; coddle.

pamphlet *noun* a leaflet or booklet giving information on a subject.

pan[1] *noun* **1** a wide container with a flat base, used for cooking etc. **2** something shaped like this. **3** the bowl of a lavatory. **4** a shallow lake which dries out easily.

pan[2] *verb* (**panned, panning**) **1** wash small stones, gravel, etc. in order to find gold or other minerals. **2** (*informal*) criticize severely, *The play was panned by the critics.* **3** move a film or video camera from side to side to get a panoramic view.

pan- *prefix* **1** all (as in *panorama*). **2** of the whole of a continent or group etc. (as in *pan-African*).

panacea (*say* pan-a-**see**-a) *noun* a cure for all kinds of diseases or troubles.

panama *noun* a hat made of a fine straw-like material.

pancake *noun* a thin round cake of batter fried on both sides.

pancreas (*say* **pan**-kree-as) *noun* a gland near the stomach, producing insulin and digestive juices.

panda *noun* a large bear-like black-and-white animal found in China.

pandemonium *noun* uproar.

pander *verb* **pander to** indulge someone by providing things, *Don't pander to his taste for sweet things!*

pane *noun* a sheet of glass in a window.

panegyric (*say* pan-i-**ji**rrik) *noun* a piece of praise; a eulogy.

panel *noun* **1** a long flat piece of wood, metal, etc. that is part of a door, wall, piece of furniture, etc. **2** a group of people appointed to discuss or decide something. **panelled** *adjective*, **panelling** *noun* **panel-beater** a person who beats out the metal panels of vehicles to repair them.

pang *noun* a sudden sharp pain.

panga (*say* **pan**-ga) *noun* a knife with a broad blade used for cutting cane or bush, or as a weapon.

panic[1] *noun* sudden uncontrollable fear. **panic-stricken** *adjective*, **panicky** *adjective*

panic[2] *verb* (**panicked, panicking**) fill or be filled with panic.

pannier *noun* a large bag or basket hung on one side of a bicycle or horse etc.

panoply *noun* (*plural* **panoplies**) a splendid array.

panorama *noun* a view or picture of a wide area. **panoramic** *adjective*

pansy *noun* (*plural* **pansies**) a small brightly coloured garden flower with velvety petals.

pant *verb* take short quick breaths, usually after running or working hard.

pantaloons *plural noun* wide trousers.

pantechnicon *noun* a kind of large lorry, used for carrying furniture etc.

panther *noun* a leopard, especially a black one.

panties *plural noun* (*informal*) short underpants worn by women and girls.

pantihose *noun* (*plural* **pantihose**) women's tights.

pantile *noun* a curved tile for a roof.

pantomime *noun* **1** a Christmas entertainment based on a fairy-tale. **2** mime.

pantry *noun* (*plural* **pantries**) **1** a room where china, glasses, cutlery, etc. are kept. **2** a larder.

pants *plural noun* (*informal*) **1** trousers. **2** underpants; knickers.

pap *noun* **1** (*say* pap) soft food suitable for babies. **2** (*say* pup) porridge, usually of mealie meal.

papa *noun* (*old use*) father.

papacy (*say* **pay**-pa-see) *noun* the position of pope.

papal (*say* **pay**-pal) *adjective* of the pope.

paper[1] *noun* **1** a substance made in thin sheets from wood, rags, etc. and used for writing or printing or drawing on or for wrapping things. **2** a newspaper. **3** wallpaper. **4** a document, *confidential papers.*

paper[2] *verb* cover with wallpaper.

paperback *noun* a book with a thin flexible cover.

papier mâché (*say* pap-yay **mash**-ay) *noun* paper made into pulp and moulded to make models, ornaments, etc.

paprika (*say* **pap**-rik-a) *noun* red pepper.

papyrus (*say* pap-**I**-rus) *noun* (*plural* **papyri**) **1** a kind of paper made from the stems of a plant like a reed, used in ancient Egypt. **2** a document written on this paper.

par *noun* an average or normal amount or condition.

para-¹ *prefix* **1** beside (as in *parallel*). **2** beyond (as in *paradox*).

para-² *prefix* protecting (as in *parasol*).

parable *noun* a story told to teach people something, especially one of those told by Jesus Christ.

parabola (*say* pa-**rab**-ol-a) *noun* a curve like the path of an object thrown into the air and falling down again. **parabolic** *adjective*

parachute *noun* an expanding device on which people or things can float slowly to the ground from an aircraft. **parachuting** *noun*, **parachutist** *noun*

parade¹ *noun* **1** a procession that displays people or things. **2** an assembly of troops for inspection, drill, etc.; a ground for this. **3** a public square or promenade.

parade² *verb* (**paraded**, **parading**) **1** move in a parade. **2** assemble for a parade.

paradise *noun* **1** heaven; a heavenly place. **2** the Garden of Eden.

paradox *noun* (*plural* **paradoxes**) a statement that seems to contradict itself but which contains a truth, e.g. 'More haste, less speed'. **paradoxical** *adjective*, **paradoxically** *adverb*

paraffin *noun* a kind of oil used as fuel.

paragon *noun* a person or thing that seems to be perfect.

paragraph *noun* one or more sentences on a single subject, forming a section of a piece of writing and beginning on a new line, usually away from the margin of the page.

parakeet *noun* a kind of small parrot.

parallax *noun* what seems to be a change in the position of something when you look at it from a different place.

parallel¹ *adjective* **1** (of lines etc.) always at the same distance from each other, like the rails on which a train runs. **2** similar; corresponding, *When petrol prices rise there is a parallel rise in bus fares.* **parallelism** *noun*

parallel² *noun* **1** a line etc. that is parallel to another. **2** a line of latitude. **3** something similar or corresponding. **4** a comparison, *draw a parallel between the situations.*

parallel³ *verb* (**paralleled**, **paralleling**) find or be a parallel to something.

parallelogram *noun* a quadrilateral with its opposite sides equal and parallel.

paralyse *verb* (**paralysed**, **paralysing**) **1** cause paralysis in a person etc. **2** make something be unable to move, *paralysed with fear.*

paralysis *noun* being unable to move, especially because of a disease or an injury to the nerves. **paralytic** (*say* pa-ra-**lit**-ik) *adjective*

paramedic *noun* a person whose job it is to assist and support doctors. **paramedical** *adjective*

parameter (*say* pa-**ram**-it-er) *noun* a quantity or quality etc. that is variable and affects other things (which depend on it) by its changes, *parameters of time and money.* ● USAGE: Do not confuse with *perimeter.*

paramilitary *adjective* organized like a military force but not part of the armed services.

paramount *adjective* more important than anything else, *Secrecy is paramount.*

paranoia *noun* an abnormal mental condition in which a person has delusions or suspects and distrusts people. **paranoid** *adjective*

parapet *noun* a low wall along the edge of a balcony, bridge, roof, etc.

paraphernalia *noun* numerous pieces of equipment, possessions, etc.

paraphrase *verb* (**paraphrased**, **paraphrasing**) give the meaning of something by using different words. **paraphrase** *noun*

parasite *noun* an animal or plant that lives in or on another, from which it gets its food. **parasitic** *adjective*

parasol *noun* a lightweight umbrella used to shade yourself from the sun.

paratroops *plural noun* troops trained to come down from aircraft by parachute. **paratrooper** *noun*

parboil *verb* boil food until it is partly cooked.

parcel¹ *noun* something wrapped up to be sent by post or carried.

parcel[2] *verb* (**parcelled, parcelling**) **1** wrap up as a parcel. **2** divide into portions, *parcel out the work.*

parched *adjective* very dry or thirsty.

parchment *noun* a kind of heavy paper, originally made from animal skins.

pardon[1] *noun* forgiveness.

pardon[2] *verb* **1** forgive. **2** excuse somebody kindly, *Pardon my asking, but haven't we met before?* **pardonable** *adjective*, **pardonably** *adverb*

pare (*say as* pair) *verb* (**pared, paring**) **1** trim by cutting away the edges; peel. **2** reduce gradually, *We had to pare down our expenses.*

parent *noun* **1** a father or mother; a living thing that has produced others of its kind. **2** a source from which others are derived, *the parent company.* **parenthood** *noun*, **parenting** *noun*, **parental** (*say* pa-**rent**-al) *adjective*

parentage *noun* descent from parents; lineage; ancestry.

parenthesis (*say* pa-**ren**-thi-sis) *noun* (*plural* **parentheses**) **1** something extra that is inserted in a sentence, usually between brackets or dashes. **2** either of the pair of brackets (like these) used to mark off words from the rest of a sentence. **parenthetical** *adjective*

pariah (*say* pa-ry-a) *noun* an outcast.

parish *noun* (*plural* **parishes**) a district with its own church. **parishioner** *noun*

parity *noun* equality.

park[1] *noun* **1** a large garden or recreation ground for public use. **2** a large area enclosed by fences etc. where wild animals are kept, *lion park.*
car park an area where cars may be parked.
national park an area with valuable natural resources protected by the government for public use.

park[2] *verb* leave a vehicle somewhere for a time.

parka *noun* a warm jacket with a hood.

parley *verb* (**parleyed, parleying**) hold a discussion with someone. **parley** *noun*

parliament *noun* the assembly that makes a country's laws. **parliamentary** *adjective*

parliamentarian *noun* a person who is good at debating things in parliament.

parlour *noun* (*old use*) a sitting-room.

parochial (*say* per-**oh**-kee-al) *adjective* **1** of a parish. **2** local; interested only in your own area, *a narrow parochial attitude.*

parody[1] *noun* (*plural* **parodies**) an imitation that makes fun of a person or thing.

parody[2] *verb* (**parodied, parodying**) make or be a parody of a person or thing.

parole *noun* the release of a prisoner before the end of his or her sentence on condition of good behaviour, *He was on parole.*

paroxysm (*say* **pa**-roks-izm) *noun* a spasm; a sudden outburst of rage, laughter, etc.

parquet (*say* **par**-kay) *noun* wooden blocks arranged in a pattern to make a floor.

parrot *noun* a brightly-coloured tropical bird that can learn to repeat words etc.

parry *verb* (**parried, parrying**) **1** turn aside an opponent's weapon or blow by using your own to block it. **2** avoid an awkward question skilfully.

parse *verb* (**parsed, parsing**) state what is the grammatical form and function of a word or words in a sentence.

parsimonious *adjective* stingy; very sparing in the use of something. **parsimony** *noun*

parsley *noun* a plant with crinkled green leaves used to flavour and decorate food.

parsnip *noun* a plant with a pointed pale-yellow root used as a vegetable.

parson *noun* a rector or vicar; (*informal*) a member of the clergy.

parsonage *noun* a rectory or vicarage.

part[1] *noun* **1** some but not all of a thing or number of things; anything that belongs to something bigger. **2** the character played by an actor or actress. **3** the words spoken by a character in a play. **4** one side in an agreement or in a dispute or quarrel.
part of speech any of the groups into which words are divided in grammar (noun, pronoun, adjective, verb, adverb, preposition, conjunction, interjection).
take in good part not be offended at something.
take part join in an activity.

part[2] *verb*　separate; divide.
　part with give away or get rid of something.
partake *verb* (**partook, partaken, partak-ing**) 1 participate. 2 eat or drink something, *We all partook of the food.*
part-exchange *noun*　giving something that you own, as part of the price of what you are buying.
partial *adjective*　1 of a part; not complete, not total, *a partial eclipse.* 2 biased; unfair. **partially** *adverb*, **partiality** *noun*
　be partial to be fond of something.
participate *verb* (**participated, participat-ing**) take part or have a share in something. **participant** *noun*, **participation** *noun*, **participator** *noun*
participle *noun*　a word formed from a verb (e.g. *gone, going; guided, guiding*) and used with an auxiliary verb to form certain tenses (e.g. *It has gone. It is going*) or the passive (e.g. *We were guided to our seats*), or as an adjective (e.g. *a guided missile; a guiding light*). The **past participle** (e.g. *gone, guided*) describes a completed action or past condition. The **present participle** (which ends in *-ing*) describes a continuing action or condition.
particle *noun*　a very small portion or amount.
particoloured *adjective*　partly of one colour and partly of another; variegated.
particular[1] *adjective*　1 of this one and no other; individual, *This particu-lar stamp is very rare.* 2 special, *Take particular care of it.* 3 giving some-thing close attention; choosing carefully, *He is very particular about his clothes.* **particularly** *adverb*
particular[2] *noun*　a single fact; a detail.
　in particular especially, *We liked this one in particular*; special, *We did nothing in particular.*
parting *noun*　1 leaving; separation. 2 a line where hair is combed away in different directions.
partisan *noun*　1 a strong supporter of a party or group etc. 2 a member of an organization resisting the authorities in a conquered country.
partition[1] *noun*　1 a thin wall that divides a room or space. 2 dividing something into parts.
partition[2] *verb*　1 divide into parts, *partition the defeated country.* 2 divide a room or space by means of a partition.
partly *adverb*　to some extent but not completely.
partner[1] *noun*　one of a pair of people who do something together, e.g. in business or dancing or playing a game. **partnership** *noun*
partner[2] *verb*　be a person's partner; put together as partners.
partook *past tense* of **partake**.
partridge *noun*　a game-bird with brown feathers.
part-time *adjective* & *adverb*　working for only some of the normal hours. **part-timer** *noun*
party *noun* (*plural* **parties**) 1 a gathering of people to enjoy themselves, *a birthday party.* 2 a group working or travelling together. 3 an organized group of people with similar political beliefs, *the Democratic Party.* 4 a person who is involved in an action or lawsuit etc., *the guilty party.*
pascal *noun*　a unit of pressure.
pas de deux (*say* pah der **der**) *noun*　a dance (e.g. in a ballet) for two persons.
pass[1] *verb* (**passed, passing**) 1 go past something; go onwards. 2 cause to move, *Pass the cord through the ring.* 3 give or transfer to another person, *Pass the butter to your father.* 4 be successful in a test or examination. 5 approve or accept, *They passed a law.* 6 occupy time. 7 happen, *We heard what passed when they met.* 8 disappear. 9 utter, *Pass a remark.* 10 let your turn go by at cards or in a competition etc., *Pass!*
　pass out complete your military training; faint.
pass[2] *noun* (*plural* **passes**) 1 passing something. 2 a permit to go in or out of a place. 3 a route through a gap in a range of mountains. 4 a critical state of affairs, *Things have come to a pretty pass!* 5 a permit or identity document which Africans were required to carry in former times.
passable *adjective*　1 able to be passed.

2 satisfactory but not especially good, *a passable performance.* **passably** *adverb*

passage *noun* **1** a way through something; a corridor. **2** a journey by sea or air. **3** a section of a piece of writing or music. **4** passing, *the passage of time.* **passageway** *noun*

passbook *noun* a special notebook in which a bank or building society writes down how much a customer has paid in or drawn out.

passenger *noun* a person who is driven or carried in a car, train, ship, or aircraft etc.

passer-by *noun* (*plural* **passers-by**) a person who happens to be going past something.

passion *noun* **1** strong emotion. **2** great enthusiasm or liking, *a passion for biltong.* **the Passion** the sufferings of Jesus Christ at the Crucifixion.

passionate *adjective* full of passion. **passionately** *adverb*

passion-fruit *noun* a granadilla.

passive *adjective* **1** acted upon and not active; not resisting or fighting against something. **2** (of a form of a verb) used when the subject of the sentence receives the action, e.g. *was hit* in 'She was hit on the head'. (Compare *active.*) **passively** *adverb*, **passiveness** *noun*, **passivity** *noun*

Passover *noun* a Jewish religious festival commemorating the freeing of the Jews from slavery in Egypt.

passport *noun* an official document that entitles the person holding it to travel abroad.

password *noun* a secret word or phrase used to distinguish friends from enemies.

past¹ *adjective* of the time before now, *during the past week.*

past² *noun* past times or events.

past³ *preposition* **1** beyond, *Walk past the school.* **2** after, *It is past midnight.* **past it** (*informal*) too old to be able to do something.

pasta *noun* an Italian food consisting of a dried paste made from flour and shaped into macaroni, spaghetti, etc.

paste¹ *noun* **1** a soft and moist or gluey substance. **2** a hard glassy substance used to make imitation gems.

paste² *verb* (**pasted, pasting**) **1** stick by using paste. **2** coat something with paste.

pastel *noun* **1** a crayon that is like chalk. **2** a light delicate colour.

pastern *noun* the part of a horse's foot between the fetlock and the hoof.

pasteurize *verb* (**pasteurized, pasteurizing**) purify milk by heating and then cooling it.

pastille *noun* a small flavoured sweet for sucking.

pastime *noun* something done to make time pass pleasantly; a recreation.

pastor *noun* a member of the clergy who is in charge of a church or congregation.

pastoral *adjective* **1** of country life, *a pastoral scene.* **2** of a pastor or a pastor's duties.

pastry *noun* (*plural* **pastries**) **1** dough made with flour, fat, and water, rolled flat and baked. **2** something made of pastry, *Danish pastries.*

pasture¹ *noun* land covered with grass etc. that cattle, sheep, or horses can eat.

pasture² *verb* (**pastured, pasturing**) put animals to graze in a pasture.

pasty¹ (*say* **pas**-tee) *noun* (*plural* **pasties**) pastry with a filling of meat, fruit, or jam etc., baked without a dish to shape it.

pasty² (*say* **pay**-stee) *adjective* **1** like paste. **2** looking pale and unhealthy.

pat¹ *verb* (**patted, patting**) tap gently with the open hand or with something flat.

pat² *noun* **1** a patting movement or sound. **2** a small piece of butter or other soft substance. **a pat on the back** praise.

patch¹ *noun* (*plural* **patches**) **1** a piece of material or metal etc. put over a hole or damaged place. **2** an area that is different from its surroundings, *a damp patch.* **3** a piece of ground, *the cabbage patch.* **4** a small area or piece of something, *There are patches of fog.* **not a patch on** (*informal*) not nearly as good as.

patch² *verb* **1** put a patch on something. **2** piece things together. **patch up** repair something roughly; settle a quarrel.

patchwork *noun* needlework in which small pieces of different cloth are sewn edge to edge.

patchy *adjective* occurring in patches; uneven. **patchily** *adverb*, **patchiness** *noun*

pate *noun* (*old use*) the head.

pâté (*say* pat-ay) *noun* paste made of meat or fish.

patent[1] (*say* pat-ent or **pay**-tent) *noun* the official right given to an inventor to make or sell his or her invention and to prevent other people from copying it.

patent[2] (*say* pay-tent) *adjective* 1 protected by a patent, *patent medicines*. 2 obvious. **patently** *adverb*

patent leather glossy leather.

patent[3] *verb* get a patent for something.

patentee (*say* pay-ten-**tee** or pat-en-**tee**) *noun* a person who holds a patent.

paternal *adjective* 1 of a father. 2 fatherly. **paternally** *adverb*

paternalistic *adjective* treating people in a paternal way, providing for their needs but giving them no responsibility. **paternalism** *noun*

paternity *noun* 1 fatherhood. 2 being the father of a particular baby, *He acknowledged paternity of the child.*

path *noun* 1 a narrow way along which people or animals can walk. 2 a line or direction along which a person or thing moves, *the path of the storm.*

pathetic *adjective* 1 arousing pity or sadness. 2 miserably inadequate or useless, *a pathetic attempt.* **pathetically** *adverb*

pathology *noun* the study of diseases of the body. **pathological** *adjective*, **pathologist** *noun*

pathos (*say* pay-thoss) *noun* a quality that arouses pity or sadness.

patience *noun* 1 being patient. 2 a card-game for one person.

patient[1] *adjective* 1 able to wait or put up with annoyances without becoming angry. 2 able to persevere. **patiently** *adverb*

patient[2] *noun* a person who has treatment from a doctor or dentist etc.

patio *noun* (*plural* **patios**) a paved area beside a house.

patriarch (*say* pay-tree-ark) *noun* 1 a man who is head of a family or tribe. 2 a bishop of high rank in certain Churches. **patriarchal** *adjective*

patrician *noun* an ancient Roman noble. (Compare *plebeian*.) **patrician** *adjective*

patriot (*say* pay-tree-ot or pat-ree-ot) *noun* a person who loves his or her country and supports it loyally. **patriotic** *adjective*, **patriotically** *adverb*, **patriotism** *noun*

patrol[1] *verb* (**patrolled**, **patrolling**) walk or travel regularly over an area so as to guard it and see that all is well.

patrol[2] *noun* 1 a patrolling group of people, ships, aircraft, etc. 2 a group of Scouts or Guides.

on patrol patrolling.

patron (*say* pay-tron) *noun* 1 someone who supports a person or cause with money or encouragement. 2 a regular customer. **patronage** (*say* pat-ron-ij) *noun*

patron saint a saint who is thought to protect a particular place or activity.

patronize (*say* pat-ron-I'z) *verb* (**patronized**, **patronizing**) 1 be a patron or supporter of something. 2 treat someone in a condescending way.

patter[1] *noun* 1 a series of light tapping sounds. 2 the quick talk of a comedian, conjuror, salesperson, etc.

patter[2] *verb* make light tapping sounds.

pattern *noun* 1 an arrangement of lines, shapes, or colours etc. 2 a thing to be copied in order to make something, *a dress pattern*. 3 an excellent example; a model.

patty *noun* (*plural* **patties**) a small pie or pasty.

paucity *noun* scarcity; fewness, *a paucity of books.*

paunch *noun* a large belly.

pauper *noun* a person who is very poor.

pause[1] *noun* a temporary stop in speaking or doing something.

pause[2] *verb* (**paused**, **pausing**) make a pause.

pave *verb* (**paved**, **paving**) lay a hard surface on a road or path etc. **paving-stone** *noun*

pave the way prepare for something.

pavement *noun* a paved path along the side of a street.

pavilion *noun* 1 a building for use by players and spectators etc. 2 an ornamental building or shelter used for dances, concerts, exhibitions, etc.

paw[1] *noun* the foot of an animal that has claws.

paw[2] *verb* touch with a hand or foot.

pawl *noun* a bar with a catch that fits into the notches of a ratchet.

pawn[1] *noun* 1 any of the least valuable pieces in chess. 2 a person whose actions are controlled by somebody else.

pawn[2] *verb* leave something with a pawn-broker as security for a loan.

pawnbroker *noun* a shopkeeper who lends money to people in return for objects that they leave as security. **pawnshop** *noun*

pawpaw *noun* an orange-coloured tropical fruit used as food.

pay[1] *verb* (**paid, paying**) 1 give money in return for goods or services. 2 give what is owed, *pay your debts; pay the rent.* 3 be profitable or worth while, *It pays to advertise.* 4 give or express, *pay attention; pay them a visit; pay compliments.* 5 suffer a penalty, *You'll pay for this!* 6 let out a rope by loosening it gradually. **payer** *noun*
pay up pay fully; pay what is asked.

pay[2] *noun* payment; wages.

payable *adjective* that must be paid.

PAYE *abbreviation* pay-as-you-earn, a method of collecting income tax by deducting it from wages before these are paid to people who earn them.

payee *noun* a person to whom money is paid or is to be paid.

paymaster *noun* an official who pays troops or workers etc.

payment *noun* 1 paying. 2 money paid.

PE *abbreviation* physical education.

pea *noun* the small round green seed of a climbing plant, growing inside a pod and used as a vegetable.

peace *noun* 1 a condition in which there is no war, violence, or disorder. 2 quietness; calm. **peaceful** *adjective*, **peacefully** *adverb*, **peacefulness** *noun*

peaceable *adjective* peaceful; not quarrelsome. **peaceably** *adverb*

peach *noun* (*plural* **peaches**) 1 a round soft juicy fruit with a pinkish or yellowish skin and a large stone. 2 (*informal*) a beauty.

peacock *noun* a male bird with a long brightly-coloured tail that it can spread out like a fan. **peahen** *noun*

peak[1] *noun* 1 a pointed top, especially of a mountain. 2 the highest or most intense part of something, *Traffic reaches its peak at 5 p.m.* 3 the part of a cap that sticks out in front. **peaked** *adjective*

peak[2] *verb* reach its highest point.

peaky *adjective* looking pale and ill.

peal[1] *noun* 1 the loud ringing of a bell or set of bells. 2 a loud burst of thunder or laughter.

peal[2] *verb* sound in a peal.

peanut *noun* a small round nut that grows in a pod in the ground.
peanut butter roasted peanuts crushed into a paste.

pear *noun* a juicy fruit that gets narrower near the stalk.

pearl *noun* 1 a small shiny white ball found in the shells of some oysters and used as a jewel. 2 something shaped like this. **pearly** *adjective*
pearl barley grains of barley made small by grinding.

peasant *noun* (in some countries) a person who works on a farm. **peasantry** *noun*

peat *noun* rotted plant material that can be dug out of the ground and used as fuel or in gardening. **peaty** *adjective*

pebble *noun* a small round stone. **pebbly** *adjective*

pecan (*say* pee-kan) *noun* a smooth nut with an edible kernel.

peccadillo *noun* (*plural* **peccadilloes**) an unimportant offence.

peck[1] *verb* 1 bite or eat something with the beak. 2 kiss lightly.

peck[2] *noun* a pecking movement.

peck[3] *noun* a measure of grain or fruit etc. in the imperial system, *4 pecks = 1 bushel.*

peckish *adjective* (*informal*) hungry.

pectin *noun* a substance found in ripe fruits, causing jam to set firmly.

pectoral *adjective* of the chest or breast, *pectoral muscles.*

peculiar *adjective* **1** strange; unusual.
2 special, *This point is of peculiar interest.*
3 restricted, *This custom is peculiar to this country.* **peculiarly** *adverb,* **peculiarity** *noun*

pecuniary *adjective* of money, *pecuniary aid.*

pedagogue (*say* **ped**-a-gog) *noun* a teacher who teaches in a pedantic way.

pedal[1] *noun* a lever pressed by the foot to operate a bicycle, car, machine, etc. or in certain musical instruments.

pedal[2] *verb* (**pedalled, pedalling**) use a pedal; move or work something by means of pedals.

pedant *noun* a pedantic person.

pedantic *adjective* being very careful and strict about exact meanings and facts etc. in learning. **pedantically** *adverb*

peddle *verb* (**peddled, peddling**) **1** sell goods as a pedlar. **2** sell drugs illegally.

pedestal *noun* the raised base on which a statue or pillar etc. stands.
put someone on a pedestal admire him or her greatly.

pedestrian *noun* a person who is walking.

pedigree *noun* a list of a person's or animal's ancestors, especially to show how well an animal has been bred.

pediment *noun* a wide triangular part decorating the top of a building.

pedlar *noun* a person who goes from house to house selling small things.

peek *verb & noun* peep.

peel[1] *noun* the skin of certain fruits and vegetables.

peel[2] *verb* **1** remove the peel or covering from something. **2** come off in strips or layers, *the paint peeled in the sun.* **3** lose a covering or skin.

peelings *plural noun* strips of skin peeled from potatoes etc.

peep *verb* **1** look quickly or secretly. **2** look through a narrow opening. **3** show slightly or briefly, *The moon peeped out from behind the clouds.* **peep** *noun,* **peep-hole** *noun*

peer[1] *verb* look at something closely or with difficulty.

peer[2] *noun* **1** a noble. **2** someone who is equal to another in rank or merit etc., *She had no peer.* **peeress** *noun*

peerage *noun* **1** peers. **2** the rank of peer, *He was raised to the peerage.*

peerless *adjective* without an equal; superb.

peeved *adjective* (*informal*) annoyed.

peevish *adjective* irritable.

peewit *noun* a kind of plover, named after its cry.

peg[1] *noun* a piece of wood or metal or plastic for fastening things together or for hanging things on.

peg[2] *verb* (**pegged, pegging**) **1** fix with pegs. **2** keep wages or prices at a fixed level.
peg away work diligently; persevere.

pejorative (*say* pij-**orra**-tiv) *adjective* derogatory; insulting.

pelican *noun* a large bird with a pouch in its long beak for storing fish.

pellagra *noun* a disease that results from an inadequate diet, which causes the skin to crack.

pellet *noun* a tiny ball of metal, food, paper, etc.

pell-mell *adverb & adjective* in a hasty untidy way.

pelmet *noun* an ornamental strip of wood or material etc. above a window, especially to conceal a curtain rail.

pelt[1] *verb* **1** throw a lot of things at someone. **2** run fast. **3** rain very hard.

pelt[2] *noun* an animal skin, especially with the fur still on it.

pelvis *noun* (*plural* **pelvises**) the round framework of bones at the lower end of the spine. **pelvic** *adjective*

pen[1] *noun* a device with a point for writing with ink.

pen[2] *noun* an enclosure for cattle, sheep, hens, or other animals.

pen[3] *verb* (**penned, penning**) shut into a pen or other enclosed space.

pen[4] *noun* a female swan. (Compare *cob.*)

penal (*say* **peen**-al) *adjective* of punishment; used for punishment.

penalize *verb* (**penalized, penalizing**) punish; put a penalty on someone.
penalization *noun*

penalty *noun* (*plural* **penalties**)

1 a punishment. **2** a point or advantage given to one side in a game when a member of the other side has broken a rule.

penance *noun* something done to show penitence.

pence *plural noun* see **penny**.

pencil[1] *noun* a device for drawing or writing, made of a thin stick of graphite or coloured chalk etc. enclosed in a cylinder of wood or metal.

pencil[2] *verb* (**pencilled, pencilling**) write, draw, or mark with a pencil.

pendant *noun* an ornament worn hanging on a cord or chain round the neck.

pendent *adjective* hanging.

pending[1] *preposition* **1** until, *Please take charge, pending his return.* **2** during, *pending these discussions.*

pending[2] *adjective* waiting to be decided or settled, *judgement is pending.*

pendulous *adjective* hanging down.

pendulum *noun* a weight hung so that it can swing to and fro, especially in the works of a clock.

penetrable *adjective* able to be penetrated.

penetrate *verb* (**penetrated, penetrating**) make or find a way through or into something; pierce. **penetration** *noun,* **penetrative** *adjective*

pen-friend *noun* a friend to whom you write without meeting.

penguin *noun* a black and white sea-bird of the southern hemisphere that cannot fly but uses its wings as flippers for swimming.

penicillin *noun* an antibiotic obtained from mould.

peninsula *noun* a piece of land that is almost surrounded by water. **peninsular** *adjective*

penis (*say* peen-iss) *noun* (*plural* **penises**) the part of the body with which a male urinates and has sexual intercourse.

penitence *noun* regret for having done wrong. **penitent** *adjective,* **penitently** *adverb*

penknife *noun* (*plural* **penknives**) a small folding knife.

pennant *noun* a long pointed flag.

penniless *adjective* having no money; very poor.

penny *noun* (*plural* **pennies** for separate coins, **pence** for a sum of money) a British coin worth $1/100$ of a pound.

penny-pincher a mean person.

penny whistle a tin whistle with six finger holes.

pension[1] *noun* an income consisting of regular payments made by a government or firm to someone who is retired, widowed, or disabled.

pension[2] *verb* pay a pension to someone.

pensioner *noun* a person who receives a pension.

pensive *adjective* thinking deeply; thoughtful. **pensively** *adverb*

pent *adjective* shut in, *pent in* or *up.*

penta- *prefix* five.

pentagon *noun* a flat shape with five sides and five angles. **pentagonal** (*say* pent-**ag**-on-al) *adjective*

the Pentagon a five-sided building in Washington, headquarters of the leaders of the American armed forces.

pentameter *noun* a line of verse with five rhythmic beats.

pentathlon *noun* an athletic contest consisting of five events.

penthouse *noun* a flat at the top of a tall building.

penultimate *adjective* last but one.

penumbra *noun* an area that is partly but not fully shaded, e.g. during an eclipse.

penurious (*say* pin-**yoor**-ee-us) *adjective* **1** in great poverty. **2** mean; stingy. **penury** (*say* **pen**-yoor-ee) *noun*

peony *noun* (*plural* **peonies**) a plant with large round red, pink, or white flowers.

people[1] *plural noun* human beings; persons, especially those belonging to a particular country, area, or group etc.

people[2] *noun* a community or nation, *a warlike people; the English-speaking peoples.*

people[3] *verb* fill a place with people; populate.

pep *noun* (*informal*) vigour; energy.

pepper[1] *noun* **1** a hot-tasting powder used to flavour food. **2** a bright green, red, or yellow vegetable. **peppery** *adjective*

pepper[2] *verb* **1** sprinkle with pepper.

2 pelt with small objects, *peppered with bullets*.

peppercorn *noun* the dried black berry from which pepper is made.

peppermint *noun* **1** a kind of mint used for flavouring. **2** a sweet flavoured with this mint.

per *preposition* for each, *The charge is R10 per person*.

per annum for each year; yearly.

per capita for each person, *per capita income*.

per cent for or in every hundred, *three per cent* (3%).

per- *prefix* **1** through (as in *perforate*). **2** thoroughly (as in *perturb*). **3** away entirely; towards badness (as in *pervert*).

perambulate *verb* (**perambulated, perambulating**) walk through or round an area. **perambulation** *noun*

perambulator *noun* a baby's pram.

perceive *verb* (**perceived, perceiving**) see; notice.

percentage *noun* the amount per cent (see *per*); a proportion or part.

perceptible *adjective* able to be perceived. **perceptibly** *adverb*, **perceptibility** *noun*

perception *noun* perceiving.

perceptive *adjective* quick to notice things.

perch[1] *noun* (*plural* **perches**) **1** a place where a bird sits or rests. **2** a seat high up.

perch[2] *verb* rest or place on a perch.

percipient *adjective* perceptive. **percipience** *noun*

percolate *verb* (**percolated, percolating**) flow through small holes or spaces. **percolation** *noun*

percolator *noun* a pot for making coffee, in which boiling water percolates through coffee grounds.

percussion *noun* the striking of one thing against another. **percussive** *adjective* **percussion instruments** musical instruments (e.g. drum, cymbals) played by being struck or shaken.

perdition *noun* eternal damnation.

peregrination *noun* travelling about; a journey.

peregrine *noun* a kind of falcon.

peremptory *adjective* giving commands; imperious.

perennial[1] *adjective* lasting for many years; keeping on recurring. **perennially** *adverb*

perennial[2] *noun* a plant that lives for many years.

perestroika (*say* peri-**stroik**-a) *noun* restructuring, especially of the former Soviet economy.

perfect[1] (*say* **per**-fikt) *adjective* **1** so good that it cannot be made any better. **2** complete, *a perfect stranger*. **perfectly** *adverb*

perfect tense a tense of a verb showing a completed action, e.g. He *has arrived*.

perfect[2] (*say* per-**fekt**) *verb* make a thing perfect. **perfection** *noun*

to perfection perfectly.

perfectionist *noun* a person who likes everything to be done perfectly.

perfidious *adjective* treacherous; disloyal. **perfidiously** *adverb*, **perfidy** *noun*

perforate *verb* (**perforated, perforating**) **1** make tiny holes in something, especially so that it can be torn off easily. **2** pierce. **perforation** *noun*

perforce *adverb* by necessity; unavoidably.

perform *verb* **1** do something in front of an audience, *perform a play*. **2** do something, *perform an operation*. **performance** *noun*, **performer** *noun*

performing arts drama, music, dance, etc.

perfume *noun* **1** a pleasant smell. **2** a liquid for giving something a pleasant smell; scent. **perfume** *verb*, **perfumery** *noun*

perfunctory *adjective* done without much care or interest, *a perfunctory glance*. **perfunctorily** *adverb*

pergola *noun* an arch formed by climbing plants growing over trellis-work.

perhaps *adverb* it may be; possibly.

peri- *prefix* around (as in *perimeter*).

perianth (*say* **per**-ee-anth) *noun* the outer part of a flower.

peril *noun* danger. **perilous** *adjective*, **perilously** *adverb*

perimeter *noun* **1** the outer edge or boundary of something. **2** the distance round the edge.

• USAGE: Do not confuse with *parameter*.

period *noun* 1 a length of time. 2 the time when a woman menstruates. 3 (in punctuation) a full stop. **periodic** *adjective*

periodical[1] *adjective* periodic; at set times. **periodically** *adverb*

periodical[2] *noun* a magazine published at regular intervals (e.g. monthly).

periphery (*say* per-**if**-er-ee) *noun* the part at the edge or boundary. **peripheral** *adjective*

periscope *noun* a device with a tube and mirrors by which a person in a trench or submarine etc. can see things that are otherwise out of sight.

perish *verb* 1 die; be destroyed. 2 rot, *The rubber ring has perished.* 3 (*informal*) make a person etc. feel very cold. **perishable** *adjective*

peristalsis (*say* per-ee-**stal**-sis) *noun* the involuntary muscular contractions which move food through the digestive system.

periwinkle[1] *noun* a trailing plant with blue or white flowers.

periwinkle[2] *noun* a winkle.

perjure *verb* (**perjured, perjuring**) **perjure yourself** commit perjury.

perjury *noun* telling a lie while you are on oath to speak the truth.

perk[1] *verb* raise the head quickly or cheerfully.
perk up make or become more cheerful.

perk[2] *noun* (*informal*) a perquisite.

perky *adjective* lively and cheerful. **perkily** *adverb*

perlemoen (*say* per-le-**moon**) *noun* a large edible shellfish.

perm *noun* a permanent wave. **perm** *verb*

permanent *adjective* lasting for always or for a very long time. **permanently** *adverb*, **permanence** *noun*
permanent wave treatment of the hair to give it long-lasting waves.

permeable *adjective* able to be permeated by fluids etc. **permeability** *noun*

permeate *verb* (**permeated, permeating**) spread into every part of something; pervade, *Smoke had permeated the hall.* **permeation** *noun*

permissible *adjective* allowable.

permission *noun* the right to do something, given by someone in authority; authorization.

permissive *adjective* permitting things; allowing much freedom to do things.

permit[1] (*say* per-**mit**) *verb* (**permitted, permitting**) give permission or consent or a chance to do something; allow.

permit[2] (*say* **per**-mit) *noun* written or printed permission to do something or go somewhere.

permutation *noun* 1 changing the order of a set of things. 2 a changed order, *3, 1, 2 is a permutation of 1, 2, 3.*

pernicious *adjective* very harmful.

peroration *noun* an elaborate ending to a speech.

perpendicular *adjective* upright; at a right angle (90°) to a line or surface.

perpetrate *verb* (**perpetrated, perpetrating**) commit or be guilty of, *perpetrate a crime or an error.* **perpetration** *noun*, **perpetrator** *noun*

perpetual *adjective* lasting for a long time; continual. **perpetually** *adverb*

perpetuate *verb* (**perpetuated, perpetuating**) make a thing perpetual; cause to be remembered for a long time, *The statue will perpetuate her memory.* **perpetuation** *noun*

perpetuity *noun* being perpetual.
in perpetuity for ever.

perplex *verb* bewilder or puzzle somebody. **perplexity** *noun*

perquisite (*say* per-**kwiz**-it) *noun* something extra given to a worker, *Use of the firm's car is a perquisite of this job.*

persecute *verb* (**persecuted, persecuting**) be continually cruel to somebody, especially because you disagree with his or her beliefs; harass. **persecution** *noun*, **persecutor** *noun*

persevere *verb* (**persevered, persevering**) go on doing something even though it is difficult. **perseverance** *noun*

persist *verb* 1 continue firmly or obstinately, *She persists in breaking the rules.* 2 continue to exist, *The custom persists in some countries.* **persistent** *adjective*, **persistently** *adverb*, **persistence** *noun*, **persistency** *noun*

person *noun* 1 a human being; a man, woman, or child. 2 (in grammar) any of the three groups of personal pronouns and forms taken by verbs. The **first person** (= *I, me, we, us*) refers to the person(s) speaking; the **second person** (= *thou, thee, you*) refers to the person(s) spoken to; the **third person** (= *he, him, she, her, it, they, them*) refers to the person(s) spoken about.
in person being actually present oneself, *She was there in person.*

personable *adjective* having a pleasant appearance.

personage *noun* a person; someone important.

personal *adjective* 1 belonging to, done by, or concerning a particular person. 2 criticizing a person, *making personal remarks.* **personally** *adverb*
● USAGE: Do not confuse with *personnel.*

personality *noun* (*plural* **personalities**) 1 a person's character, *She has a cheerful personality.* 2 a well-known person.

personify *verb* (**personified, personifying**) represent a quality or idea etc. as a person, *Justice is often personified as a blindfolded woman holding a pair of scales.* **personification** *noun*

personnel *noun* the people employed by a firm, armed services, etc.
● USAGE: Do not confuse with *personal.*

perspective *noun* the impression of depth and space in a picture or scene.
in perspective giving a well-balanced view of things.

perspicacious *adjective* perceptive. **perspicacity** *noun*

perspire *verb* (**perspired, perspiring**) sweat. **perspiration** *noun*

persuade *verb* (**persuaded, persuading**) cause a person to believe or agree to do something. **persuasion** *noun*, **persuasive** *adjective*

pert *adjective* cheeky. **pertly** *adverb*, **pertness** *noun*

pertain *verb* be relevant to something, *evidence pertaining to the crime.*

pertinacious *adjective* persistent and determined. **pertinaciously** *adverb*, **pertinacity** *noun*

pertinent *adjective* pertaining; relevant. **pertinently** *adverb*, **pertinence** *noun*

perturb *verb* worry someone. **perturbation** *noun*

peruse (*say* per-**ooz**) *verb* (**perused, perusing**) read something carefully. **perusal** *noun*

pervade *verb* (**pervaded, pervading**) spread all through something; permeate. **pervasion** *noun*, **pervasive** *adjective*

perverse *adjective* obstinately doing something different from what is reasonable or required. **perversely** *adverb*, **perversity** *noun*

pervert[1] (*say* per-**vert**) *verb* 1 turn something from the right course of action, *By false evidence they perverted the course of justice.* 2 cause a person to behave wickedly or abnormally.

pervert[2] (*say* per-**vert**) *noun* a person who behaves wickedly or abnormally.

pessimist *noun* a person who expects that things will turn out badly. (Compare *optimist.*) **pessimism** *noun*, **pessimistic** *adjective*, **pessimistically** *adverb*

pest *noun* 1 a destructive insect or animal, such as a locust or a mouse. 2 a nuisance, *Don't be such a pest!*

pester *verb* keep annoying someone by frequent questions or requests.

pesticide *noun* a substance for killing harmful insects etc.

pestiferous *adjective* troublesome.

pestilence *noun* a deadly epidemic.

pestilential *adjective* troublesome.

pestle *noun* a tool with a heavy rounded end for pounding substances in a mortar.

pet[1] *noun* 1 a tame animal kept for companionship and amusement. 2 a person treated as a favourite, *teacher's pet.*

pet[2] *verb* (**petted, petting**) treat or fondle affectionately.

petal *noun* any of the separate coloured outer parts of a flower.

peter *verb* **peter out** become gradually less and cease to exist.

petiole *noun* the thin stalk that joins a leaf to the stem of a plant.

petite (*say* pe-**teet**) *adjective* having a small and dainty figure.

P philosophy

petition[1] *noun* a formal request for something, especially a written one signed by many people.
petition[2] *verb* request by a petition.
petitioner *noun*
petrel *noun* a kind of sea-bird.
petrify *verb* (**petrified, petrifying**) 1 paralyse someone with terror, surprise, etc.
2 change into a stony mass, *petrified forests*.
petrifaction *noun*
petroglyph *noun* a rock-carving.
petrol *noun* a liquid made from petroleum, used as fuel for engines.
petroleum *noun* an oil found underground that is refined to make fuel (e.g. petrol, paraffin) or for use in dry-cleaning etc.
petticoat *noun* a woman's or girl's dress-length undergarment.
pettifogging *adjective* & *noun* paying too much attention to unimportant details.
petting *noun* affectionate treatment or fondling.
pettish *adjective* peevish.
petty *adjective* (**pettier, pettiest**) unimportant; trivial, *petty regulations*. **pettily** *adverb*, **pettiness** *noun*
petty cash cash kept by an office for small payments.
petty officer an NCO in the navy.
petulant *adjective* peevish. **petulantly** *adverb*, **petulance** *noun*
petunia *noun* a garden plant with funnel-shaped flowers.
pew *noun* a long wooden seat, usually fixed in rows, in a church.
pewter *noun* a grey alloy of tin and lead.
pH *noun* a measure of the alkali or acid level of a solution or substance.
phalanx *noun* (*plural* **phalanxes**) a number of people or soldiers in a close formation.
phantasm *noun* a phantom.
phantom *noun* a ghost; something that is not real.
Pharaoh (*say* **fair**-oh) *noun* the title of the king of ancient Egypt.
pharmaceutical (*say* farm-as-**yoot**-ik-al) *adjective* of pharmacy; of medicines.
pharmacist *noun* a person who is trained in pharmacy; a pharmaceutical chemist.

pharmacology (*say* farm-a-**kol**-o-jee) *noun* the study of medicinal drugs.
pharmacological *adjective*, **pharmacologist** *noun*
pharmacy *noun* (*plural* **pharmacies**)
1 a shop selling medicines; a dispensary.
2 the process of preparing medicines.
pharynx (*say* **fa**-rinks) *noun* the cavity at the back of the mouth and nose.
phase[1] *noun* a stage in the progress or development of something.
phase[2] *verb* (**phased, phasing**) do something in stages, *a phased withdrawal*.
pheasant (*say* **fez**-ant) *noun* a game-bird with a long tail.
phenomenal *adjective* amazing; remarkable. **phenomenally** *adverb*
phenomenon *noun* (*plural* **phenomena**) an event or fact, especially one that is remarkable.
• USAGE: Note that *phenomena* is a plural; it is incorrect to say 'this phenomena' or 'these phenomenas'.
phial *noun* a small glass bottle.
phil- *prefix* see **philo-**.
philander *verb* flirt. **philanderer** *noun*
philanthropy *noun* love of humankind, especially as shown by kind and generous acts that benefit large numbers of people. **philanthropist** *noun*, **philanthropic** *adjective*
philately (*say* fil-**at**-il-ee) *noun* stamp-collecting. **philatelist** *noun*
philharmonic *adjective* (in names of orchestras etc.) devoted to music.
philistine (*say* **fil**-ist-I'n) *noun* a person who dislikes art, poetry, etc.
philo- *prefix* (becoming **phil-** before vowels and *h*) fond of; lover of (as in *philosophy*).
philology *noun* the study of languages. **philological** *adjective*, **philologist** *noun*
philosopher *noun* an expert in philosophy.
philosophical *adjective* 1 of philosophy.
2 calm and not upset, *Be philosophical about losing*. **philosophically** *adverb*
philosophy *noun* (*plural* **philosophies**)
1 the study of truths about life, morals, etc.
2 a set of ideas or principles or beliefs, *a capitalist philosophy*.

phlegm (*say* flem) *noun* thick mucus that forms in the throat and lungs when someone has a bad cold.

phlegmatic (*say* fleg-**mat**-ik) *adjective* not easily excited or worried; sluggish. **phlegmatically** *adverb*

phloem (*say* **floh**-em) *noun* a kind of tissue in plants that transports food substances from the leaves to the rest of the plant.

phobia (*say* **foh**-bee-a) *noun* great or abnormal fear of something.

phoenix (*say* **feen**-iks) *noun* (*plural* **phoenixes**) a mythical bird that was said to burn itself to death in a fire and be born again from the ashes.

phone¹ *noun* a telephone.

phone² *verb* (**phoned, phoning**) telephone.

phone-in *noun* a broadcast in which people phone the studio and take part.

phonetic (*say* fon-**et**-ik) *adjective* of speech-sounds. **phonetically** *adverb* **phonetics** the study of speech-sounds and their production.

phoney *adjective* (*informal*) sham; not genuine.

phosphate *noun* a substance containing phosphorus.

phosphorescent (*say* fos-fer-**ess**-ent) *adjective* luminous. **phosphorescence** *noun*

phosphorus *noun* a chemical substance that glows in the dark.

photo *noun* (*plural* **photos**) a photograph.

photo- *prefix* light (as in *photograph*).

photocopy *noun* (*plural* **photocopies**) a copy of a document or page etc. made by photographing it on a specially prepared surface. **photocopy** *verb*, **photocopier** *noun*

photoelectric *adjective* using the electrical effects of light.

photogenic *adjective* looking attractive in photographs.

photograph¹ *noun* a picture made by the effect of light or other radiation on film or special paper.

photograph² *verb* take a photograph of a person or thing. **photographer** *noun*

photography *noun* taking photographs.

photographic *adjective*

photosynthesis *noun* the process by which green plants use sunlight to turn carbon dioxide and water into food (carbohydrates), giving off oxygen.

phrase¹ *noun* **1** a group of words that form a unit in a sentence or clause, e.g. *in the garden* in 'The film star was in the garden'. **2** a short section of a tune.

phrase² *verb* (**phrased, phrasing**) **1** put something into words. **2** divide music into phrases.

phraseology (*say* fray-zee-**ol**-o-jee) *noun* wording; the way something is worded.

physical *adjective* **1** of the body. **2** of things that you can touch or see, *the physical world*. **3** of physics. **physically** *adverb*

physical education or **physical training** gymnastics or other exercises done to keep the body healthy.

physician *noun* a doctor, especially one who is not a surgeon.

physicist (*say* **fiz**-i-sist) *noun* an expert in physics.

physics (*say* **fiz**-iks) *noun* the study of the properties of matter and energy (e.g. heat, light, sound, movement).

physiognomy (*say* fiz-ee-**on**-o-mee) *noun* the features of a person's face.

physiology (*say* fiz-ee-**ol**-o-jee) *noun* the study of the body and its parts and how they function. **physiological** *adjective*, **physiologist** *noun*

physiotherapy (*say* fiz-ee-o-th'e-ra-pee) *noun* the treatment of a disease or weakness by massage, exercises, etc. **physiotherapist** *noun*

physique (*say* fiz-**eek**) *noun* a person's build.

pianist *noun* a person who plays the piano.

piano *noun* (*plural* **pianos**) a large musical instrument with a keyboard.

piazza (*say* pee-**at**-sa) *noun* a public square or market-place.

piccolo *noun* (*plural* **piccolos**) a small high-pitched flute.

pick¹ *verb* **1** separate a flower or fruit from its plant, *We picked apples*. **2** choose; select carefully, *She picked the chocolate cake for* *tea.* **3** pull bits off or out of something. **4** open a lock by using something pointed, not with a key.

pick a quarrel deliberately provoke a quarrel with somebody.

pick holes in find fault with.

pick on keep criticizing or harassing a particular person.

pick someone's pocket steal from it.

pick up lift, take up; collect; take someone into a vehicle; manage to hear something; get better, recover.

pick[2] *noun* **1** choice, *take your pick.* **2** the best of a group.

pick[3] *noun* **1** a pickaxe. **2** a plectrum.

pickaxe *noun* a heavy pointed tool with a long handle, used for breaking up hard ground etc.

picket[1] *noun* **1** a striker or group of strikers who try to persuade other people not to go into a place during a strike. **2** a group of sentries. **3** a pointed post as part of a fence.

picket[2] *verb* (**picketed, picketing**) act as a picket; place people as pickets.

pickle[1] *noun* **1** a strong-tasting food made of pickled vegetables. **2** (*informal*) a mess.

pickle[2] *verb* (**pickled, pickling**) preserve in vinegar or salt water.

pickpocket *noun* a thief who picks people's pockets (see *pick*[1]).

pick-up *noun* **1** the part of a record-player holding the stylus. **2** an open truck for carrying small loads.

picnic[1] *noun* a meal eaten in the open air away from home.

picnic[2] *verb* (**picnicked, picnicking**) have a picnic. **picnicker** *noun*

pictorial *adjective* with or using pictures. **pictorially** *adverb*

picture[1] *noun* **1** a representation of a person or thing made by painting, drawing, or photography. **2** a film at the cinema. **3** how something seems; an impression, *an accurate picture of events.*

picture[2] *verb* (**pictured, picturing**) **1** show in a picture. **2** imagine, *picture the situation.*

picturesque *adjective* **1** forming an attractive scene, *a picturesque village.* **2** vividly described; expressive, *picturesque language.* **picturesquely** *adverb*

pidgin *noun* a simplified form of a language used between people who speak different languages.

pie *noun* a baked dish of meat, fish, or fruit covered with pastry.

piebald *adjective* with patches of black and white, *a piebald donkey.*

piece[1] *noun* **1** a part or portion of something; a fragment. **2** a separate thing or example, *a fine piece of work.* **3** something written, composed, or painted etc., *a piece of music.* **4** any of the objects used to play a game on a board, *a chess-piece.*

piece[2] *verb* (**pieced, piecing**) put pieces together to make something.

piecemeal *adjective & adverb* done or made one piece at a time.

pier *noun* **1** a long structure built out into the sea for people to walk on. **2** a pillar supporting a bridge or arch.

pierce *verb* (**pierced, piercing**) make a hole through something; penetrate.

piercing *adjective* **1** very loud. **2** penetrating; very strong, *a piercing wind.*

pietà (*say* pee-ye-**ta**) *noun* a painting or sculpture of the Virgin Mary, holding the body of the dead Christ on her lap or in her arms.

piet-my-vrou (*say* **peet**-may-froh) *noun* a migratory cuckoo with a distinctive call which signals the beginning of summer.

piety *noun* piousness.

piffle *noun* (*informal*) nonsense.

pig *noun* **1** a fat animal with short legs and a blunt snout, kept for its meat. **2** (*informal*) someone greedy, dirty, or unpleasant. **piggy** *adjective & noun*

pigeon *noun* a bird with a fat body and a small head.

pigeon-hole *noun* a small compartment above a desk etc., used for holding letters or papers.

piggery *noun* (*plural* **piggeries**) a place where pigs are bred or kept.

piggyback *adverb* carried on somebody else's back or shoulders. **piggyback** *noun*

piggy bank *noun* a money-box often

made in the shape of a hollow pig.

pig-headed *adjective* obstinate.

pig-iron *noun* iron that has been processed in a smelting-furnace.

piglet *noun* a young pig.

pig-lily *noun* an arum lily.

pigment *noun* a substance that
colours something. **pigmented** *adjective*,
pigmentation *noun*

pigsty *noun* (*plural* **pigsties**) a partly-
covered pen for pigs.

pigtail *noun* a plait of hair worn hanging
at the back of the head.

pike *noun* 1 a heavy spear. 2 (*plural* **pike**)
a large freshwater fish.

pilchard *noun* a small sea-fish.

pile[1] *noun* 1 a number of things on top of
one another. 2 (*informal*) a large quantity;
a lot of money. 3 a tall building.

pile[2] *verb* (**piled, piling**) put things into
a pile; make a pile.

pile[3] *noun* a heavy beam made of metal,
concrete, or timber driven into the ground
to support something.

pile[4] *noun* a raised surface on fabric,
made of upright threads, *a carpet with
a thick pile.*

pilfer *verb* steal small things. **pilferer**
noun, **pilferage** *noun*

pilgrim *noun* a person who travels
to a holy place for religious reasons.
pilgrimage *noun*

pill *noun* a small solid piece of medicinal
substance for swallowing.
the pill a contraceptive pill.

pillage *verb* (**pillaged, pillaging**) plunder.
pillage *noun*

pillar *noun* a tall stone or wooden post.

pillar-box *noun* a post-box standing in
a street.

pillion *noun* a seat behind the driver on
a motor cycle.

pillory[1] *noun* (*plural* **pillories**) a wooden
framework with holes for a person's head
and hands, in which offenders were formerly made to stand and be ridiculed and
scorned by the public as a punishment.

pillory[2] *verb* (**pilloried, pillorying**)
1 put into a pillory. 2 expose a person to
public ridicule, and scorn, *He was pilloried*

in the newspapers for what he had done.

pillow[1] *noun* a cushion for a person's
head to rest on, especially in bed.

pillow[2] *verb* rest the head on a pillow etc.

pillowcase (also **pillowslip**) *noun* a cloth
cover for a pillow.

pilot[1] *noun* 1 a person who works the
controls for flying an aircraft. 2 a person
qualified to steer a ship in and out of a
port or through a difficult stretch of water.
3 a guide.

pilot[2] *verb* (**piloted, piloting**) 1 be pilot
of an aircraft or ship. 2 guide; steer.

pilot[3] *adjective* testing on a small scale
how something will work, *a pilot scheme.*

pilot-light *noun* 1 a small flame that
lights a larger burner on a gas cooker etc.
2 an electric indicator light.

pimple *noun* a small round raised spot
on the skin. **pimply** *adjective*

pin[1] *noun* 1 a short thin piece of metal
with a sharp point and a rounded head,
used to fasten pieces of cloth or paper etc.
together. 2 a pointed device for fixing or
marking something.
pins and needles a prickling feeling.

pin[2] *verb* (**pinned, pinning**) 1 fasten with
a pin or pins. 2 make a person or thing
unable to move, *He was pinned under the
wreckage.* 3 fix, *They pinned the blame on her.*

pinafore *noun* an apron.

pinball *noun* a game in which small metal
balls are shot across a sloping board and
score points by striking pins and other
obstacles.

pincer *noun* the claw of a shellfish such
as a lobster.

pincers *plural noun* a tool with two parts
that are pressed together for gripping and
holding things.

pinch[1] *verb* 1 squeeze tightly or painfully
between two things, especially between
the finger and thumb. 2 (*informal*) steal.
3 (*informal*) arrest.

pinch[2] *noun* (*plural* **pinches**) 1 a pinching movement. 2 difficulty; stress or pressure of circumstances, *They began to feel
the pinch.* 3 the amount that can be held
between the tips of the thumb and forefinger, *a pinch of salt.*

at a pinch in time of difficulty.

pincushion *noun* 1 a small pad into which pins are stuck to keep them ready for use. 2 a kind of protea which has long stamens like pins.

pine[1] *noun* an evergreen tree with needle-shaped leaves.

pine[2] *verb* (**pined, pining**) feel an intense longing; become weak through longing for somebody or something.

pineapple *noun* a large tropical fruit with a tough prickly skin and yellow flesh.

ping *noun* a short sharp ringing sound.

ping-pong *noun* table tennis.

pinion[1] *noun* a bird's wing, especially the outer end.

pinion[2] *verb* 1 clip a bird's wings to prevent it from flying. 2 hold or fasten a person's arms or legs so as to prevent movement.

pinion[3] *noun* a small cog-wheel that engages with another or with a rod (called a *rack*).

pink[1] *adjective* pale red. **pinkness** *noun*

pink[2] *noun* 1 pink colour. 2 a garden plant with fragrant flowers, often pink or white.

pink[3] *verb* 1 pierce slightly. 2 cut a zigzag edge on cloth.

pinnacle *noun* 1 a pointed ornament on a roof. 2 a peak.

pin-point[1] *adjective* exact; precise, *with pin-point accuracy.*

pin-point[2] *verb* find or identify something precisely.

pinprick *noun* a small annoyance.

pin-stripe *noun* a very narrow stripe. **pin-striped** *adjective*

pint *noun* a measure of capacity in the imperial system, one-eighth of a gallon (0,57 litres).

pin-up *noun* (*informal*) a picture of an attractive or famous person for pinning on a wall.

pioneer *noun* one of the first people to go to a place or do or investigate something. **pioneer** *verb*

pious *adjective* very religious; devout. **piously** *adverb*, **piousness** *noun*

pip[1] *noun* 1 a small hard seed of an apple, pear, orange, etc. 2 one of the spots on playing-cards, dice, or dominoes. 3 a short high-pitched sound, *She heard the six pips of the time-signal on the radio.*

pip[2] *verb* (**pipped, pipping**) (*informal*) defeat.

pipe[1] *noun* 1 a tube through which water or gas etc. can flow from one place to another. 2 a short narrow tube with a bowl at one end in which tobacco can burn for smoking. 3 a tube forming a musical instrument or part of one. **the pipes** bagpipes.

pipe[2] *verb* (**piped, piping**) 1 send something along pipes. 2 transmit music or other sound by wire or cable. 3 play music on a pipe or the bagpipes. 4 trim or ornament with piping. **pipe down** (*informal*) be quiet.

pipe-dream *noun* an impossible wish.

pipeline *noun* a pipe for carrying oil or water etc. a long distance. **in the pipeline** in the process of being made or organized.

piper *noun* a person who plays a pipe or bagpipes.

pipette *noun* a small glass tube used in a laboratory, usually filled by suction.

piping[1] *noun* 1 pipes; a length of pipe. 2 a long narrow pipe-like fold or line decorating something.

piping[2] *adjective* shrill, *a piping voice.* **piping hot** very hot.

pippin *noun* a kind of apple.

piquant (*say* **pee**-kant) *adjective* pleasantly sharp and appetizing or stimulating, *a piquant smell.* **piquancy** *noun*

pique (*say* peek) *noun* a feeling of hurt pride. **pique** *verb*

piranha (*say* pi-**rah**-na) *noun* a small South American freshwater fish that attacks and eats live animals.

pirate *noun* 1 a person on a ship who robs other ships at sea or makes a plundering raid on the shore. 2 someone who produces or publishes or broadcasts without authorization, *a pirate radio station.* **piratical** *adjective*, **piracy** *noun*

pirouette (*say* pir-oo-**et**) *noun* a spinning movement of the body made while balanced on the point of the toe or on one foot. **pirouette** *verb*

pistachio *noun* (*plural* **pistachios**) a nut with an edible green kernel.

pistil *noun* the part of a flower that produces the seed, consisting of the ovary, style, and stigma.

pistol *noun* a small hand-gun.

piston *noun* a disc or cylinder that fits inside a tube in which it moves up and down as part of an engine or pump etc.

pit[1] *noun* **1** a deep hole or depression. **2** a coal-mine. **3** the part of a racecourse where racing-cars are refuelled and repaired during a race.

pit[2] *verb* (**pitted, pitting**) **1** make pits or depressions in something, *The ground was pitted with holes.* **2** put somebody in competition with somebody else, *She was pitted against the champion.*

pitch[1] *noun* (*plural* **pitches**) **1** a piece of ground marked out for cricket, football, or another game. **2** the highness or lowness of a voice or a musical note. **3** intensity; strength, *Excitement was at fever pitch.* **4** the steepness of a slope, *the pitch of the roof.*

pitch[2] *verb* **1** throw; fling. **2** fix a tent etc. **3** fall heavily. **4** move up and down on a rough sea. **5** set something at a particular level, *They pitched their hopes high.* **6** (of a bowled ball in cricket) strike the ground.

pitched battle a battle between troops in prepared positions; a vigorous argument etc.

pitched roof a sloping roof.

pitch in (*informal*) start working or eating vigorously.

pitch[3] *noun* a black sticky substance rather like tar.

pitch-black or **pitch-dark** *adjective* very black or very dark.

pitchblende *noun* a mineral ore (uranium oxide) from which radium is obtained.

pitcher *noun* a large jug.

pitchfork[1] *noun* a large fork with two prongs, used for lifting hay.

pitchfork[2] *verb* **1** lift with a pitchfork. **2** put a person somewhere suddenly.

piteous *adjective* causing pity. **piteously** *adverb*

pitfall *noun* an unsuspected danger or difficulty.

pith *noun* the spongy substance in the stems of certain plants or lining the rind of oranges etc.

pithy *adjective* **1** like pith; containing much pith. **2** short and full of meaning, *pithy comments.*

pitiable *adjective* pitiful.

pitiful *adjective* arousing pity; pathetic. **pitifully** *adverb*

pitiless *adjective* showing no pity. **pitilessly** *adverb*

pittance *noun* a very small allowance of money.

pituitary (*say* pit-**yew**-it-ree) *noun* (*plural* **pituitaries**) a small gland at the base of the brain that produces growth hormones.

pity[1] *noun* **1** the feeling of being sorry because someone is in pain or trouble. **2** a cause for regret, *It's a pity that you can't come.*

take pity on feel sorry for someone and help them.

pity[2] *verb* (**pitied, pitying**) feel pity for someone.

pivot[1] *noun* a point or part on which something turns or swings. **pivotal** *adjective*

pivot[2] *verb* (**pivoted, pivoting**) turn or place something to turn on a pivot.

pixie *noun* a small fairy; an elf.

pizza (*say* **peets**-a) *noun* an Italian food consisting of a layer of dough baked with a savoury topping of cheese, tomatoes, etc.

pizzicato (*say* pits-i-**kah**-toh) *adjective* & *adverb* plucking the strings of a musical instrument.

placard *noun* a poster; a notice.

placate *verb* (**placated, placating**) pacify; conciliate. **placatory** *adjective*

place[1] *noun* **1** a particular part of space, especially where something belongs; an area; a position. **2** a seat, *Save me a place.* **3** a job; employment. **4** a building; a home, *Come round to our place.* **5** a duty or function, *It's not my place to interfere.*

6 a point in a series of things, *In the first place, the date is wrong.*

in place in the right position; suitable.

out of place in the wrong position; unsuitable.

place² *verb* (**placed, placing**) put something in a particular place. **placement** *noun*

placenta *noun* a piece of body tissue that forms in the womb during pregnancy and supplies the foetus with nourishment.

placid *adjective* calm and peaceful; not easily made anxious or upset. **placidly** *adverb*, **placidity** *noun*

plagiarize (*say* play-jee-er-I'z) *verb* (**plagiarized, plagiarizing**) copy and use someone else's writings or ideas etc. as if they were your own. **plagiarism** *noun*, **plagiarist** *noun*

plague¹ *noun* **1** a dangerous illness that spreads very quickly. **2** a large number of pests, *a plague of locusts.*

plague² *verb* (**plagued, plaguing**) pester; annoy.

plaice *noun* (*plural* **plaice**) a flat edible sea-fish.

plaid (*say* plad) *noun* cloth with a tartan or similar pattern.

plain¹ *adjective* **1** not decorated; not elaborate; not flavoured. **2** not beautiful. **3** easy to see or hear or understand, *plain language.* **4** frank; straightforward. **plainly** *adverb*, **plainness** *noun*

plain clothes civilian clothes worn instead of a uniform, e.g. by police.

plain² *noun* a large area of flat country.

plaintiff *noun* the person who brings a complaint against somebody else to a law-court. (Compare *defendant.*)

plaintive *adjective* sounding sad.

plait¹ (*say* plat) *verb* weave three or more strands to form one length.

plait² *noun* something plaited.

plan¹ *noun* **1** a way of doing something thought out in advance. **2** a drawing showing the arrangement of parts of something. **3** a map of a town or district.

plan² *verb* (**planned, planning**) make a plan for something. **planner** *noun*

plane¹ *noun* **1** an aeroplane. **2** a tool for making wood smooth by scraping its surface. **3** a flat or level surface.

plane² *verb* (**planed, planing**) smooth wood with a plane.

plane³ *adjective* flat; level, *a plane surface.*

plane⁴ *noun* a tall tree with broad leaves.

planet *noun* any of the heavenly bodies that move in an orbit round the sun, *The main planets are Mercury, Venus, Earth, Mars, Jupiter, Saturn, Uranus, Neptune, and Pluto.* **planetary** *adjective*

plank *noun* a long flat piece of wood.

plankton *noun* microscopic plants and animals that float in the sea, lakes, etc.

plant¹ *noun* **1** a living thing that cannot move and that makes its food from chemical substances, *Flowers, trees, and shrubs are plants.* **2** a small plant, not a tree or shrub. **3** a factory or its equipment. **4** (*informal*) something planted to deceive people (see *plant²* 3).

plant² *verb* **1** put something in soil for growing. **2** fix firmly in place, *The pole was planted in the ground.* **3** place something where it will be found, usually to mislead people or cause trouble. **planter** *noun*

plantation *noun* **1** a large area of land where cotton, tobacco, or tea etc. is planted. **2** a group of planted trees.

plaque (*say* plak) *noun* **1** a flat piece of metal or porcelain fixed on a wall as an ornament or memorial. **2** a filmy substance that forms on teeth and gums, where bacteria can live.

plasma *noun* the colourless liquid part of blood, carrying the corpuscles.

plaster¹ *noun* **1** a mixture of lime, sand, and water etc. for covering walls and ceilings. **2** plaster of Paris. **3** a piece of sticking-plaster.

plaster of Paris a white paste used for making moulds or for casts round a broken limb etc.

plaster² *verb* **1** cover with plaster. **2** cover thickly; daub, *plastered with mud.*

plastic¹ *noun* a strong light synthetic substance that can be moulded into a permanent shape.

plastic² *adjective* **1** made of plastic.

2 soft and easy to mould, *Clay is a plastic substance.* **plasticity** *noun*

plastic surgery surgery to repair deformed or injured parts of the body.

platanna *noun* a clawed toad.

plate¹ *noun* **1** an almost flat usually circular object from which food is eaten or served. **2** a thin flat sheet of metal, glass, or other hard material. **3** an illustration on special paper in a book. **plateful** *noun*

plate² *verb* (**plated, plating**) **1** coat metal with a thin layer of gold, silver, tin, etc. **2** cover with sheets of metal.

plateau (*say* **plat**-oh) *noun* (*plural* **plateaux** or **plateaus** (*say* **plat**-ohz)) a flat area of high land.

platform *noun* **1** a flat surface that is above the level of the ground or the rest of the floor, e.g. in a hall or beside a railway line at a station. **2** the policy that a political party puts forward when there is an election. **3** the thick sole of a shoe.

platinum *noun* a valuable silver-coloured metal that does not tarnish.

platitude *noun* a very ordinary remark. **platitudinous** *adjective*

platoon *noun* a small group of soldiers.

platteland *noun* country districts; rural areas.

platter *noun* a flat dish or plate.

platypus *noun* (*plural* **platypuses**) an Australian animal with a beak like that of a duck, that lays eggs like a bird but is a mammal and suckles its young.

plaudits *plural noun* applause; expressions of approval.

plausible *adjective* seeming to be honest or worth believing but perhaps deceptive, *a plausible excuse.* **plausibly** *adverb*, **plausibility** *noun*

play¹ *verb* **1** take part in a game or other amusement. **2** make music or sound with a musical instrument, tape-recorder, etc. **3** perform a part in a play or film. **player** *noun*

play down give people the impression that something is not important.

play up (*informal*) be mischievous.

play² *noun* **1** a story acted on a stage or on radio or television. **2** playing.

playback *noun* playing back something that has been recorded.

playful *adjective* wanting to play; full of fun; not serious. **playfully** *adverb*, **playfulness** *noun*

playground *noun* a piece of ground for children to play on.

playgroup *noun* a group of very young children who play together regularly, supervised by adults.

playing-card *noun* each of a set of cards (usually 52) used for playing games.

playing-field *noun* a field used for outdoor games.

playmate *noun* a person you play games with.

plaything *noun* a toy.

playtime *noun* the time when young schoolchildren may go out to play.

playwright *noun* a dramatist.

plaza (*say* **plah**-za) *noun* an outdoor square.

plea *noun* **1** a request; an appeal, *a plea for mercy.* **2** an excuse, *He stayed at home on the plea of a headache.* **3** a formal statement of 'guilty' or 'not guilty' made in a lawcourt by someone accused of a crime.

plead *verb* make a plea.

pleasant *adjective* pleasing; giving pleasure. **pleasantly** *adverb*, **pleasantness** *noun*

pleasantry *noun* (*plural* **pleasantries**) being humorous; a humorous remark.

please *verb* (**pleased, pleasing**) **1** make a person feel satisfied or glad. **2** (used to make a request or an order polite), *Please ring the bell.* **3** like; think suitable, *Do as you please.*

pleasurable *adjective* causing pleasure.

pleasure *noun* **1** a feeling of satisfaction or gladness; enjoyment. **2** something that pleases you.

pleat *noun* a flat fold made by doubling cloth upon itself. **pleated** *adjective*

plebeian (*say* plib-**ee**-an) *noun* a member of the common people in ancient Rome. (Compare *patrician.*) **plebeian** *adjective*

plebiscite (*say* **pleb**-iss-it) *noun* a referendum.

plectrum *noun* (*plural* **plectra**) a small

piece of metal or bone etc. for plucking the strings of a musical instrument.

pledge¹ *noun* 1 a solemn promise. 2 a thing handed over as security for a loan or contract.

pledge² *verb* (**pledged, pledging**) 1 promise solemnly. 2 hand something over as security.

plein (*say as* plane) *noun* a square or plaza.

plenary (*say* **pleen**-er-ee) *adjective* attended by all members, *a plenary session of the council.*

plenipotentiary (*say* plen-i-pot-**en**-sher-ee) *adjective* having full authority to make decisions on behalf of a government, *Our ambassador has plenipotentiary power.* **plenipotentiary** *noun*

plentiful *adjective* quite enough in amount; abundant. **plentifully** *adverb*

plenty¹ *noun* quite enough; as much as is needed or wanted.

plenty² *adverb* (*informal*) quite; fully, *It's plenty big enough.*

pleurisy (*say* **ploor**-i-see) *noun* inflammation of the membrane round the lungs.

pliable *adjective* easy to bend or influence; flexible. **pliability** *noun*

pliant *adjective* pliable.

pliers *plural noun* pincers that have jaws with flat surfaces for gripping things.

plight¹ *noun* a difficult situation, *the plight of the street child.*

plight² *verb* (*old use*) pledge.

plimsoll *noun* a canvas sports-shoe with a rubber sole.

Plimsoll line *noun* a mark on a ship's side showing how deeply it may legally go down in the water when loaded.

plinth *noun* a block or slab forming the base of a column or a support for a statue or vase etc.

plod *verb* (**plodded, plodding**) 1 walk slowly and heavily. 2 work slowly but steadily. **plodder** *noun*

plop *noun* the sound of something dropping into water. **plop** *verb*

plot¹ *noun* 1 a secret plan. 2 the story in a play, novel, or film. 3 a small piece of land.

plot² *verb* (**plotted, plotting**) 1 make a secret plan. 2 make a chart or graph of something, *We plotted the ship's route on our map.*

plough¹ *noun* a farming implement for turning the soil over.

plough² *verb* 1 turn over soil with a plough. 2 go through something with great effort or difficulty, *He ploughed through the book.* **ploughman** *noun* **plough back** reinvest profits in the business that produced them.

ploughshare *noun* the cutting-blade of a plough.

plover (*say* **pluv**-er) *noun* a kind of wading bird.

ploy *noun* a cunning manoeuvre to gain an advantage; a ruse, *a sales ploy.*

pluck¹ *verb* 1 pick a flower or fruit. 2 pull the feathers off a bird. 3 pull something up or out, *plucked from the icy river.* 4 pull a string (e.g. on a guitar) and let it go again. **pluck up courage** summon up courage and overcome fear.

pluck² *noun* 1 courage; bravery. 2 plucking; a pull.

plucky *adjective* (**pluckier, pluckiest**) showing pluck; brave. **pluckily** *adverb*

plug¹ *noun* 1 something used to stop up a hole. 2 a device that fits into a socket to connect wires to a supply of electricity. 3 (*informal*) a piece of publicity for something.

plug² *verb* (**plugged, plugging**) 1 stop up a hole. 2 (*informal*) publicize something, *the advertisement plugs the new model.* **plug in** put a plug into an electrical socket.

plum *noun* 1 a soft juicy fruit with a pointed stone in the middle. 2 (*old use*) a dried grape or raisin used in cooking, *plum pudding.* 3 reddish-purple colour. 4 (*informal*) something good, *a plum job.*

plumage (*say* **ploom**-ij) *noun* a bird's feathers.

plumb¹ *verb* 1 measure how deep something is. 2 get to the bottom of a matter, *We could not plumb the mystery.* 3 fit with a plumbing system.

plumb² *adjective* exactly upright; vertical, *The wall was plumb.*

plumb[3] *adverb* (*informal*) exactly, *It fell plumb in the middle.*

plumber *noun* a person who fits and mends plumbing.

plumbing *noun* 1 the water-pipes, water-tanks, and drainage-pipes in a building. 2 the work of a plumber.

plumb-line *noun* a cord with a weight on the end, used to find how deep something is or whether a wall etc. is vertical.

plume[1] *noun* 1 a large feather. 2 something shaped like a feather, *a plume of smoke.*

plume[2] *verb* (**plumed, pluming**) preen.

plumed *adjective* ornamented with plumes, *a plumed helmet.*

plummet[1] *noun* a plumb-line or the weight on its end.

plummet[2] *verb* (**plummeted, plummeting**) drop downwards quickly.

plump[1] *adjective* slightly fat; rounded. **plumpness** *noun*

plump[2] *verb* drop or fall quickly. **plump for** (*informal*) choose.

plunder[1] *verb* rob a person or place forcibly or systematically; loot. **plunderer** *noun*

plunder[2] *noun* 1 plundering. 2 goods etc. that have been plundered; loot.

plunge[1] *verb* (**plunged, plunging**) 1 go or push forcefully into something; dive. 2 fall or go downwards suddenly. 3 go or force into action etc., *They plunged the world into war.* **plunger** *noun*

plunge[2] *noun* plunging; a dive. **take the plunge** start a bold course of action.

plural *noun* the form of a noun or verb used when it stands for more than one person or thing, *The plural of 'child' is 'children'.* (Compare *singular.*) **plural** *adjective*, **plurality** *noun*

plus *preposition* with the next number or thing added, *two plus two equals four* (2 + 2 = 4).

plush *noun* a thick velvety cloth used in furnishings. **plushy** *adjective*

plutocrat *noun* a person who is powerful because of his or her wealth. **plutocracy** *noun*

plutonium *noun* a radioactive substance used in nuclear weapons and reactors.

ply[1] *noun* 1 a thickness or layer of wood or cloth etc. 2 a strand in yarn, *4-ply wool.*

ply[2] *verb* (**plied, plying**) 1 use or wield a tool or weapon. 2 work at, *Tailors plied their trade.* 3 keep offering, *They plied her with food* or *with questions.* 4 go regularly, *The boat plies between the two harbours.* 5 drive or wait about looking for custom, *Taxis are allowed to ply for hire.*

plywood *noun* strong thin board made of layers of wood glued together.

p.m. *abbreviation* post meridiem (Latin = after noon).

pneumatic (*say* new-**mat**-ik) *adjective* filled with or worked by compressed air, *a pneumatic drill.* **pneumatically** *adverb*

pneumonia (*say* new-**moh**-nee-a) *noun* inflammation of one or both lungs.

PO *abbreviation* 1 Post Office. 2 postal order.

poach *verb* 1 cook an egg (removed from its shell) in or over boiling water. 2 cook fish or fruit etc. in a small amount of liquid. 3 steal game or fish from someone else's land or water. 4 take unfairly, *One club was poaching members from another.* **poacher** *noun*

pocket[1] *noun* 1 a small bag-shaped part, especially in a garment. 2 a person's supply of money, *The expense is beyond my pocket.* 3 an isolated part or area, *small pockets of rain.* 4 a bag or sack containing vegetables, with a mass of 10 kg or more, *a pocket of potatoes.* **pocketful** *noun* **be out of pocket** have spent more money than you have gained.

pocket[2] *adjective* small enough to carry in a pocket, *a pocket calculator.*

pocket[3] *verb* (**pocketed, pocketing**) put something into a pocket.

pocket-money *noun* money given to a child to spend as he or she likes.

pod *noun* a long seed-container of the kind found on a pea or bean plant.

podgy *adjective* (**podgier, podgiest**) short and fat.

podium (*say* **poh**-dee-um) *noun* (*plural* **podia**) a platform or pedestal.

poem *noun* a composition in verse.

poet *noun* a person who writes poems.
poetess *noun*

poetry *noun* poems. **poetic** *adjective*,
poetical *adjective*, **poetically** *adverb*

pogrom *noun* an organized massacre.

poignant (*say* **poin**-yant) *adjective*
very distressing; affecting the feelings,
poignant memories. **poignancy** *noun*

poinsettia *noun* a plant that has large
scarlet bracts.

point¹ *noun* 1 the narrow or sharp end of
something. 2 a dot or other punctuation
mark. 3 a particular place or time, *At this
point she was winning*. 4 a detail; a characteristic, *He has his good points*. 5 the
important or essential idea, *Keep to the
point!* 6 purpose; value, *There is no point
in hurrying*. 7 an electrical socket.
8 a device for changing a train from one
track to another.
point of view a way of looking at or thinking of something.

point² *verb* 1 aim; direct, *She pointed a
gun at me*. 2 show where something is,
especially by holding out a finger etc.
towards it. 3 fill in the parts between
bricks with mortar or cement.
point out draw attention to something.

point-blank¹ *adjective* 1 aimed or fired
from close to the target. 2 direct; straightforward, *a point-blank refusal*.

point-blank² *adverb* in a point-blank
manner, *He refused point-blank*.

point-duty *noun* being stationed at a
road junction to control the movement
of traffic.

pointed *adjective* 1 with a point at
the end. 2 clearly directed at a person,
a pointed remark. **pointedly** *adverb*

pointer *noun* 1 a stick, rod, or mark etc.
used to point at something. 2 a dog that
points with its muzzle towards birds that
it scents. 3 an indication or hint.

pointless *adjective* without a point; with
no purpose. **pointlessly** *adverb*

poise¹ *verb* (**poised, poising**) balance.

poise² *noun* 1 balance; the way something is poised. 2 a dignified self-confident
manner.

poison¹ *noun* a substance that can harm
or kill a living thing. **poisonous** *adjective*

poison² *verb* 1 give poison to; kill with
poison. 2 put poison in something,
a poisoned apple. 3 corrupt; fill with prejudice, *He poisoned their minds*. **poisoner**
noun

poke¹ *verb* (**poked, poking**) 1 prod; jab.
2 push out or forward; stick out. 3 search,
I was poking about in the attic.
poke fun at ridicule.

poke² *noun* a poking movement; a prod.

poker¹ *noun* a stiff metal rod for poking
a fire.

poker² *noun* a card-game in which
players bet on who has the best cards.

poky *adjective* (**pokier, pokiest**) small and
cramped, *poky little rooms*.

polar *adjective* 1 of or near the North Pole
or South Pole. 2 of either pole of a magnet.
polarity *noun*
polar bear a white bear living in Arctic
regions.

polarize *verb* (**polarized, polarizing**)
1 keep vibrations of light-waves etc. to a
single direction. 2 set at opposite extremes
of feeling, *Opinions had polarized*.
polarization *noun*

pole¹ *noun* a long slender rounded piece
of wood or metal.

pole² *noun* 1 a point on the earth's surface that is as far north (**North Pole**) or as
far south (**South Pole**) as possible. 2 either
of the ends of a magnet. 3 either terminal
of an electric cell or battery.

polecat *noun* an animal of the weasel
family with an unpleasant smell.

pole-star *noun* the star above the North
Pole.

pole-vault *noun* a jump over a high bar
done with the help of a long pole.

polemic (*say* pol-**em**-ik) *noun* an attack
in words against someone's opinion or
actions. **polemical** *adjective*

police¹ *noun* the people whose job is to
catch criminals and make sure that the
law is kept. **policeman** *noun*, **police
officer** *noun*, **policewoman** *noun*

police² *verb* (**policed, policing**) keep
order in a place by means of police.

policy¹ *noun* (*plural* **policies**) the aims or plan of action of a person or group.

policy² *noun* (*plural* **policies**) a document stating the terms of a contract of insurance.

polio *noun* poliomyelitis.

poliomyelitis (*say* poh-lee-oh-my-il-**I**-tiss) *noun* a disease that can cause paralysis.

polish¹ *verb* **1** make a thing smooth and shiny by rubbing. **2** make a thing better by making corrections and alterations, *She polished her essay.* **polisher** *noun* **polish off** finish off.

polish² *noun* (*plural* **polishes**) **1** a substance used in polishing. **2** a shine. **3** elegance of manner, *He lacks polish.*

polite *adjective* having good manners. **politely** *adverb*, **politeness** *noun*

politic (*say* pol-it-ik) *adjective* prudent.

political *adjective* connected with the governing of a country, city, or county. **politically** *adverb*

politician *noun* a person who is involved in politics.

politics *noun* political matters.

polka *noun* a lively dance for couples.

poll¹ (*say as* pole) *noun* **1** voting or votes at an election. **2** an opinion poll (see *opinion*). **3** (*old use*) the head. **poll tax** a tax on each person.

poll² *verb* **1** vote at an election. **2** receive a stated number of votes. **polling-booth** *noun*, **polling-station** *noun*

pollarded *adjective* (of trees) with the tops trimmed so that young shoots start to grow thickly there.

polled *adjective* (of cattle) with the horns trimmed.

pollen *noun* powder produced by the anthers of flowers, containing male cells for fertilizing other flowers.

pollinate *verb* (**pollinated, pollinating**) fertilize with pollen. **pollination** *noun*

pollster *noun* a person who conducts an opinion poll.

pollute *verb* (**polluted, polluting**) make a place or thing dirty or impure. **pollutant** *noun*, **pollution** *noun*

polo *noun* a game rather like hockey, with players on horseback.

polo neck a high round turned-over collar. **polo-necked** *adjective*

poltergeist *noun* a ghost or spirit that throws things about noisily.

poly- *prefix* many (as in *polygon*).

polyanthus *noun* (*plural* **polyanthuses**) a kind of cultivated primrose.

polychromatic (also **polychrome**) *adjective* having many colours.

polyester *noun* a kind of synthetic substance.

polygamy (*say* pol-**ig**-a-mee) *noun* the system of having more than one wife or husband at a time. **polygamous** *adjective*

polyglot *adjective* knowing or using several languages.

polygon *noun* a shape with many sides, *Hexagons and octagons are polygons.* **polygonal** *adjective*

polyhedron *noun* a solid shape with many sides.

polymer *noun* a substance whose molecule is formed from a large number of simple molecules combined.

polyp (*say* pol-ip) *noun* **1** a tiny creature with a tube-shaped body. **2** a small abnormal growth on a mucous membrane in the body.

polystyrene *noun* a kind of plastic used for insulating or packing things.

polytheism (*say* pol-ith-ee-izm) *noun* belief in more than one god. **polytheist** *noun*

polythene *noun* a lightweight plastic used to make bags, wrappings, etc.

pomegranate *noun* a tropical fruit with many seeds.

pommel *noun* **1** a knob on the handle of a sword. **2** the raised part at the front of a saddle.

pomp *noun* stately and splendid ceremonial.

pompon *noun* a ball of coloured threads used as a decoration.

pompous *adjective* full of great dignity and self-importance. **pompously** *adverb*, **pomposity** *noun*

pond *noun* a small lake.

ponder *verb* think deeply and seriously; muse.

ponderous *adjective* **1** heavy and awkward. **2** laborious, *He writes in a ponderous style.* **ponderously** *adverb*

pondok *noun* a rough hut; a hovel.

pont *noun* a flat-bottomed ferry boat used to transport cars, passengers, etc. across a river, worked on chains or ropes.

pontiff *noun* **1** the pope. **2** a bishop; a chief priest.

pontifical *adjective* **1** of a pontiff. **2** speaking or writing pompously. **pontifically** *adverb*

pontificate *verb* (**pontificated, pontificating**) speak or write pompously. **pontification** *noun*

pontoon¹ *noun* a boat or float used to support a bridge (a **pontoon bridge**) over a river.

pontoon² *noun* **1** a card-game in which players try to get cards whose value totals 21. **2** a score of 21 from two cards in this game.

pony *noun* (*plural* **ponies**) a small horse.

pony-tail *noun* a bunch of long hair tied at the back of the head.

poodle *noun* a dog with thick curly hair.

pooh *interjection* an exclamation of contempt.

pool¹ *noun* **1** a pond. **2** a puddle. **3** a swimming-pool.

pool² *noun* **1** the fund of money staked in a gambling game. **2** a group of things shared by several people, *a pool car.*

pool³ *verb* put money or things together for sharing.

poop *noun* the stern of a ship.

poor *adjective* **1** have very little money or other resources. **2** not good; inadequate, *a poor piece of work.* **3** unfortunate; deserving pity, *Poor thing!* **poorness** *noun*

poorly *adverb* **1** in a poor way, *She was poorly dressed.* **2** rather ill.

poort *noun* a narrow pass through mountains or hills.

pop¹ *noun* **1** a small explosive sound. **2** a fizzy drink.

pop² *verb* (**popped, popping**) **1** make a pop. **2** (*informal*) put or go quickly, *Pop down to the shop.*

pop³ *noun* modern popular music.

popcorn *noun* maize heated to burst and form fluffy balls.

pope *noun* the bishop of Rome, leader of the Roman Catholic Church.

pop-eyed *adjective* with bulging eyes.

popgun *noun* a toy that shoots a cork etc. with a popping sound.

poplar *noun* a tall slender tree.

poplin *noun* a plain woven cotton material.

poppadam *noun* a thin crisp biscuit made of lentil-flour and eaten with curry.

poppy *noun* (*plural* **poppies**) a plant with showy flowers, often red.

populace *noun* the general public.

popular *adjective* **1** liked or enjoyed by many people. **2** of or for the general public, *the popular press.* **popularly** *adverb*, **popularity** *noun*

popularize *verb* (**popularized, popularizing**) make a thing generally liked or known. **popularization** *noun*

populate *verb* (**populated, populating**) supply with a population; inhabit.

population *noun* a group of living things of the same type living in the same area; inhabitants.

population density the total number of a group living in one specific area.

porcelain *noun* the finest kind of china.

porch *noun* (*plural* **porches**) a shelter outside the entrance to a building.

porcupine *noun* a small animal covered with long prickles.

pore¹ *noun* a tiny opening on the skin through which moisture can pass in or out.

pore² *verb* (**pored, poring**) **pore over** study with close attention, *He was poring over his books.*

pork *noun* meat from a pig.

pornography (*say* porn-og-ra-fee) *noun* obscene pictures or writings. **pornographic** *adjective*

porous *adjective* allowing liquid or air to pass through. **porosity** *noun*

porphyry (*say* por-fir-ee) *noun* a kind of rock containing crystals of minerals.

porpoise (*say* por-pus) *noun* a sea-animal rather like a small whale, with a blunt rounded snout.

porridge *noun* a food made by boiling oatmeal or mealie meal to a thick paste.

port¹ *noun* 1 a harbour. 2 a place where goods pass in and out of a country by ship or aircraft. 3 the left-hand side of a ship or aircraft when you are facing forward. (Compare *starboard.*)

port² *noun* a strong sweet wine.

portable *adjective* able to be carried.

portal *noun* a doorway or gateway.

portcullis *noun* (*plural* **portcullises**) a strong heavy vertical grating that can be lowered in grooves to block the gateway to a castle.

portend *verb* foreshadow; be a sign that something will happen, *Dark clouds portend a storm.*

portent *noun* an omen; a sign that something will happen. **portentous** *adjective*

porter¹ *noun* a person whose job is to carry luggage or other goods.

porter² *noun* a person whose job is to look after the entrance to a large building.

portfolio *noun* (*plural* **portfolios**) 1 a case for holding documents or drawings. 2 a government minister's special responsibility.

porthole *noun* a small window in the side of a ship or aircraft (formerly a hole for pointing a ship's cannon through).

portico *noun* (*plural* **porticoes**) a roof supported on columns, usually forming a porch to a building.

portion¹ *noun* a part or share given to somebody.

portion² *verb* divide into portions, *Portion it out.*

portly *adjective* (**portlier, portliest**) stout and dignified. **portliness** *noun*

portmanteau (*say* port-**mant**-oh) *noun* a trunk that opens into two equal parts for holding clothes etc.

portmanteau word a word made from the sounds and meanings of two others, e.g. *motel* (from *motor + hotel*).

portrait *noun* a picture of a person or animal.

portray *verb* 1 make a picture of a person or scene etc. 2 describe or show, *The play portrays the king as a kindly man.*

portrayal *noun*

pose¹ *noun* 1 a position or posture of the body, e.g. for a portrait or photograph. 2 a pretence; unnatural behaviour to impress people.

pose² *verb* (**posed, posing**) 1 take up a pose. 2 put someone into a pose. 3 pretend, *She posed as a famous singer.* 4 put forward, *It poses several problems for us.*

poser *noun* 1 a puzzling question or problem. 2 a person who poses.

posh *adjective* (*informal*) very smart; high-class; luxurious.

position¹ *noun* 1 the place where something is or should be. 2 the way a person or thing is placed or arranged, *in a sitting position.* 3 a situation or condition, *I am in no position to help you.* 4 paid employment; a job. **positional** *adjective*

position² *verb* place a person or thing in a certain position.

positive¹ *adjective* 1 definite; certain, *We have positive proof that he is guilty.* 2 agreeing; saying 'yes', *We received a positive reply.* 3 greater than nought. 4 of the kind of electric charge that lacks electrons. 5 (of an adjective or adverb) in the simple form, not comparative or superlative, *The positive form is 'big', the comparative is 'bigger', the superlative is 'biggest'.* **positively** *adverb*

● USAGE: The opposite of senses 1–4 is *negative.*

positive² *noun* a photograph with the light and dark parts or colours as in the thing photographed. (Compare *negative.*)

positron *noun* a particle of matter with a positive electric charge.

posse (*say* **poss**-ee) *noun* a strong group, especially one that helps a sheriff.

possess *verb* 1 have or own something. 2 control someone's thoughts or behaviour, *I don't know what possessed you to do such a thing!* **possessor** *noun*

possessed *adjective* seeming to be controlled by strong emotion or an evil spirit, *He fought like a man possessed.*

possession *noun* 1 something you possess or own. 2 possessing.

possessive *adjective* 1 wanting to possess and keep things for yourself. 2 showing that somebody owns something, *a possessive pronoun* (see *pronoun*).

possibility *noun* (*plural* **possibilities**) 1 being possible. 2 something that may exist or happen etc.

possible *adjective* able to exist, happen, be done, or be used.

possibly *adverb* 1 in any way, *I can't possibly do it.* 2 perhaps.

possum *noun* an opossum.

post[1] *noun* 1 an upright piece of wood, concrete, or metal etc. set in the ground. 2 the starting-point or finishing-point of a race, *He was left at the post.*

post[2] *verb* put up a notice or poster etc. to announce something.

post[3] *noun* 1 the collecting and delivering of letters, parcels, etc. 2 these letters and parcels etc.

post office a building or room where postal business is carried on.

post[4] *verb* put a letter or parcel etc. into a post-box or post office for collection.

keep me posted keep me informed.

post[5] *noun* 1 a position of paid employment; a job. 2 the place where someone is on duty, *a sentry-post.* 3 a place occupied by soldiers, traders, etc.

last post a military bugle-call sounded at sunset and at military funerals etc.

post[6] *verb* place someone on duty, *We posted sentries.*

post- *prefix* after (as in *post-war*).

postage *noun* the charge for sending something by post.

postage stamp a stamp for sticking on things to be posted, showing the amount paid.

postal *adjective* of or by the post.

postal order a document bought from a post office for sending money by post.

post-box *noun* a box into which letters are put for collection.

postcard *noun* a card for sending messages by post without an envelope.

postcode *noun* a group of letters and numbers included in an address to help in sorting the post.

poster *noun* a large sheet of paper announcing or advertising something, for display in a public place.

posterior[1] *adjective* situated at the back of something. (The opposite is *anterior*.)

posterior[2] *noun* the buttocks.

posterity *noun* future generations of people.

postern *noun* a small entrance at the back or side of a fortress etc.

post-haste *adverb* with great speed or haste.

posthumous (*say* **poss**-tew-mus) *adjective* happening after a person's death.

postilion (*say* poss-**til**-yon) *noun* a person riding one of the horses pulling a carriage.

postman *noun* (*plural* **postmen**) a person who delivers or collects letters etc.

postmark *noun* an official mark put on something sent by post to show where and when it was posted.

post-mortem *noun* an examination of a dead body to discover the cause of death.

postpone *verb* (**postponed, postponing**) fix a later time for something, *They postponed the meeting for a fortnight.* **postponement** *noun*

postscript *noun* something extra added at the end of a letter (after the writer's signature) or at the end of a book.

postulant *noun* a person who applies to be admitted to an order of monks or nuns.

postulate[1] *verb* (**postulated, postulating**) assume that something is true and use it in reasoning. **postulation** *noun*

postulate[2] *noun* something postulated.

posture[1] *noun* the way a person stands, sits, or walks; a pose.

posture[2] *verb* (**postured, posturing**) pose, especially to impress people.

post-war *adjective* of the time after a war.

posy *noun* (*plural* **posies**) a small bunch of flowers.

pot[1] *noun* 1 a deep usually round container. 2 (*informal*) a lot of something, *She has got pots of money.*

go to pot (*informal*) lose quality; be ruined.

take pot luck (*informal*) take whatever is available.

pot² *verb* (**potted, potting**) **1** put into a pot. **2** abridge, *a potted version of the story.*

pot³ *noun* (*informal*) marijuana.

potash *noun* potassium carbonate, so called because it was first obtained from vegetable ashes washed in a pot.

potassium *noun* a soft silvery-white metal substance that is essential for living things.

potato *noun* (*plural* **potatoes**) a starchy white tuber growing underground, used as a vegetable.

potent (*say* **poh**-tent) *adjective* powerful. **potency** *noun*

potentate (*say* **poh**-ten-tayt) *noun* a powerful monarch or ruler.

potential¹ (*say* po-**ten**-shal) *adjective* capable of happening or being used or developed, *a potential winner.* **potentially** *adverb*, **potentiality** *noun*

potential energy a body's ability to do work by virtue of its position relative to others, stresses within itself, electric charge, etc.

potential² *noun* an ability or resources etc. available for use or development.

pot-hole *noun* **1** a deep natural hole in the ground. **2** a hole in a road.

pot-holing *noun* exploring underground pot-holes. **pot-holer** *noun*

potion *noun* a liquid for drinking as a medicine etc.

potjie (*say* **poy**-kee) *noun* a three-legged iron pot.

potjiekos food cooked in a potjie over a fire.

pot-pourri (*say* **poh**-poor-ee) *noun* a scented mixture of dried petals and spices.

potter¹ *noun* a person who makes pottery.

potter² *verb* work or move about in a leisurely way.

pottery *noun* (*plural* **potteries**) **1** cups, plates, ornaments, etc. made of baked clay. **2** a place where a potter works.

pouch *noun* (*plural* **pouches**) **1** a small bag. **2** something shaped like a bag.

pouffe (*say* poof) *noun* a low padded stool.

poultice *noun* a soft hot dressing put on a sore or inflamed place.

poultry *noun* birds (e.g. chickens, geese, turkeys) kept for their eggs and meat.

pounce *verb* (**pounced, pouncing**) jump or swoop down quickly on something. **pounce** *noun*

pound¹ *noun* **1** a unit of money in Britain and some other countries. **2** a unit of weight in the imperial system, equal to 16 ounces or about 454 grams.

pound² *noun* **1** a place where stray animals are taken. **2** a public enclosure for vehicles officially removed.

pound³ *verb* **1** hit something often, especially so as to crush it. **2** run or go heavily, *pounding along.* **3** thump, *My heart was pounding.*

pour *verb* **1** flow; cause to flow. **2** rain heavily, *It poured all day.* **3** come or go in large amounts, *Letters poured in.* **pourer** *noun*

pout *verb* push out your lips when you are annoyed or sulking. **pout** *noun*

poverty *noun* being poor.

powder¹ *noun* **1** a mass of fine dry particles of something. **2** a medicine or cosmetic etc. made as a powder. **3** gunpowder, *Keep your powder dry.* **powdery** *adjective*

powder² *verb* **1** put powder on something. **2** make into powder.

power *noun* **1** strength; energy; vigour. **2** the ability to do something; authority. **3** a powerful country, person, or organization. **4** mechanical or electrical energy; the electricity supply, *There was a power failure after the storm.* **5** (in mathematics) the product of a number multiplied by itself a given number of times, *The third power of* $2 = 2 \times 2 \times 2 = 8$. **6** (in physics) the rate of energy output, *A machine with a power of one watt can do one joule of work in one second.* **powered** *adjective*, **powerless** *adjective*

powerful *adjective* having great power, strength, or influence. **powerfully** *adverb*

powerhouse *noun* **1** a power-station.

2 a person or thing of great energy.

power-station *noun* a building where electricity is produced.

pp. *abbreviation* pages.

practicable *adjective* able to be done.

practical *adjective* **1** able to do useful things, *a practical person.* **2** likely to be useful, *a very practical invention.* **3** actually doing something, *She has had practical experience.* **practicality** *noun*

practical joke a trick played on somebody.

practically *adverb* **1** in a practical way. **2** almost, *I've practically finished.*

practice *noun* **1** practising, *Have you done your piano practice?* **2** actually doing something; action, not theory, *It works well in practice.* **3** the professional business of a doctor, dentist, lawyer, etc. **4** a habit or custom, *It is his practice to work until midnight.*

out of practice no longer skilful because you have not practised recently.

● USAGE: See the note on *practise.*

practise *verb* (**practised, practising**) **1** do something repeatedly in order to become better at it. **2** do something actively or habitually, *Practise what you preach.* **3** work as a doctor, dentist, or lawyer.

● USAGE: Note the spelling; *practice* is a noun, *practise* is a verb.

practised *adjective* experienced; expert.

practitioner *noun* a professional worker, especially a doctor.

pragmatic *adjective* treating things in a practical way, *Take a pragmatic approach to the problem.* **pragmatically** *adverb*, **pragmatism** *noun*, **pragmatist** *noun*

prairie *noun* a large area of flat grass-covered land in North America.

praise¹ *verb* (**praised, praising**) **1** say that somebody or something is very good. **2** honour God in words.

praise² *noun* words that praise somebody or something. **praiseworthy** *adjective*

praise name the clan name of a group of African families, *Mandela is called Madiba, his praise name.*

praise poetry the poetry chanted by a praise singer.

praise singer someone who chants in honour of a chief and the chief's ancestors.

pram *noun* a four-wheeled carriage for a baby, pushed by a person walking.

prance *verb* (**pranced, prancing**) move about in a lively or happy way.

prank *noun* a piece of mischief; a practical joke. **prankster** *noun*

prattle *verb* (**prattled, prattling**) chatter like a young child. **prattle** *noun*

prawn *noun* an edible shellfish like a large shrimp.

pray *verb* **1** talk to God. **2** ask earnestly for something; entreat. **3** (*formal*) please, *Pray be seated.*

prayer *noun* praying; words used in praying.

pre- *prefix* before (as in *prehistoric*).

preach *verb* give a religious or moral talk. **preacher** *noun*

preamble *noun* the introduction to a speech or book or document etc.

pre-arranged *adjective* arranged beforehand. **pre-arrangement** *noun*

precarious (*say* pri-**kair**-ee-us) *adjective* not very safe or secure. **precariously** *adverb*

precaution *noun* something done to prevent future trouble or danger. **precautionary** *adjective*

precede *verb* (**preceded, preceding**) come or go in front of or before a person or thing.

precedence (*say* **press**-i-dens) *noun* priority; a first or earlier place.

precedent (*say* **press**-i-dent) *noun* a previous case that is taken as an example to be followed.

precept (*say* **pree**-sept) *noun* a rule for action or conduct; an instruction.

precinct (*say* **pree**-sinkt) *noun* **1** the area round a place, especially round a cathedral. **2** a part of a town where traffic is not allowed, *a shopping precinct.*

precious¹ *adjective* **1** very valuable. **2** greatly loved. **preciousness** *noun*

precious² *adverb* (*informal*) very, *We have precious little time.*

precipice *noun* a very steep place, such

as the face of a cliff.

precipitate[1] *verb* (**precipitated, precipitating**) 1 make something happen suddenly or soon, *The insult precipitated a quarrel.* 2 throw or send down; cause to fall, *The push precipitated him through the window.* 3 cause a solid substance to separate chemically from a solution. **precipitation** *noun*

precipitate[2] *noun* a substance precipitated from a solution.

precipitate[3] *adjective* hurried; hasty, *a precipitate departure.*

precipitous *adjective* like a precipice; steep. **precipitously** *adverb*

précis (*say* **pray**-see) *noun* (*plural* **précis** (*say* **pray**-seez)) a summary.

precise *adjective* exact; clearly stated. **precisely** *adverb*, **precision** *noun*

preclude *verb* (**precluded, precluding**) prevent.

precocious (*say* prik-**oh**-shus) *adjective* developed or having abilities earlier than is usual, *a precocious child.* **precociously** *adverb*, **precocity** *noun*

preconceived *adjective* (of an idea) formed in advance, before full information is available. **preconception** *noun*

precursor *noun* a forerunner.

predator (*say* **pred**-a-ter) *noun* an animal that hunts or preys upon others. **predatory** *adjective*

predecessor (*say* **pree**-dis-ess-er) *noun* an earlier person or thing, e.g. an ancestor or the former holder of a job.

predestine *verb* (**predestined, predestining**) destine beforehand. **predestination** *noun*

predicament (*say* prid-**ik**-a-ment) *noun* a difficult or unpleasant situation.

predicate *noun* the part of a sentence that says something about the subject, e.g. 'is short' in *life is short.*

predicative (*say* prid-**ik**-a-tiv) *adjective* forming part of the predicate, e.g. *old* in *The dog is old.* (Compare *attributive.*) **predicatively** *adverb*

predict *verb* forecast; prophesy. **predictable** *adjective*, **prediction** *noun*, **predictor** *noun*

predispose *verb* (**predisposed, predisposing**) cause a tendency; influence in advance, *We are predisposed to pity the refugees.* **predisposition** *noun*

predominate *verb* (**predominated, predominating**) be the largest or most important or most powerful. **predominant** *adjective*, **predominance** *noun*

pre-eminent *adjective* excelling others; outstanding. **pre-eminently** *adverb*, **pre-eminence** *noun*

preen *verb* 1 (of a bird) smooth its feathers with its beak. 2 (of a person) smarten. **preen yourself** congratulate yourself.

prefab *noun* (*informal*) a prefabricated building.

prefabricated *adjective* made in sections ready to be assembled on a site. **prefabrication** *noun*

preface (*say* **pref**-as) *noun* an introduction at the beginning of a book or speech. **preface** *verb*

prefect *noun* a school pupil given authority to help to keep order.

prefer *verb* (**preferred, preferring**) 1 like one person or thing more than another. 2 put forward, *They preferred charges of forgery against him.* **preference** *noun*

preferable (*say* **pref**-er-a-bul) *adjective* liked better; more desirable. **preferably** *adverb*

preferential (*say* pref-er-**en**-shal) *adjective* being favoured above others, *preferential treatment.*

preferment *noun* promotion.

prefix *noun* (*plural* **prefixes**) a word or syllable joined to the front of a word to change or add to its meaning, as in *dis*order, *out*stretched, *un*happy.

pregnant *adjective* having a baby developing in the womb. **pregnancy** *noun*

prehensile *adjective* (of an animal's foot or tail etc.) able to grasp things.

prehistoric *adjective* belonging to very ancient times, before written records of events were made. **prehistory** *noun*

prejudice *noun* a fixed opinion formed without examining the facts fairly. **prejudiced** *adjective*

prelate (*say* **prel**-at) *noun* an important member of the clergy.

preliminary *adjective* coming before an important action or event and preparing for it.

prelude *noun* 1 a thing that introduces or leads up to something else. 2 a short piece of music.

premature *adjective* too early; coming before the usual or proper time. **prematurely** *adverb*

premeditated *adjective* planned beforehand, *a premeditated crime.*

premier[1] (*say* **prem**-ee-er) *adjective* first in importance, order, or time.

premier[2] *noun* 1 (**Premier**) the chief minister of the legislative body of a province. 2 a prime minister.

première (*say* prem-**yair**) *noun* the first public performance of a play or film.

premises *plural noun* a building and its grounds.

premiss (*say* **prem**-iss) *noun* (*plural* **premisses**) a statement used as the basis for a piece of reasoning.

premium *noun* 1 an amount or instalment paid to an insurance company. 2 an extra payment; a bonus.
at a premium above the normal price; highly valued.

premonition *noun* a presentiment.

preoccupied *adjective* having your thoughts completely busy with something. **preoccupation** *noun*

prep *noun* homework.
prep school a preparatory school.

preparation *noun* 1 preparing. 2 something prepared.

preparatory *adjective* preparing for something.
preparatory school a school that prepares pupils for a higher school.

prepare *verb* (**prepared**, **preparing**) make ready; get ready.
be prepared to be ready and willing to do something.

preponderate *verb* (**preponderated**, **preponderating**) be more than others or more powerful. **preponderance** *noun*, **preponderant** *adjective*

preposition *noun* a word used with a noun or pronoun to show place, position, time, or means, e.g. *at* home, *in* the hall, *on* Sunday, *by* train.

prepossessing *adjective* attractive, *Its appearance is not very prepossessing.*

preposterous *adjective* very absurd; outrageous.

prerequisite *noun* something required as a condition or in preparation for something else, *The ability to swim is a prerequisite for learning to sail.* **prerequisite** *adjective*

prerogative *noun* a right or privilege that belongs to one person or group.

Presbyterian (*say* prez-bit-**eer**-ee-an) *noun* a member of a Church that is governed by people called *elders* or *presbyters* who are chosen by the congregation.

presbytery *noun* 1 a group of presbyters. 2 the house of a Roman Catholic priest.

pre-school *adjective* of the time before a child is old enough to attend school.

prescribe *verb* (**prescribed**, **prescribing**) 1 advise a person to use a particular medicine or treatment etc. 2 say what should be done.
• USAGE: Do not confuse with *proscribe.*

prescription *noun* 1 a doctor's written order for a medicine. 2 the medicine prescribed. 3 prescribing.

presence *noun* being present in a place, *Your presence is required.*
presence of mind the ability to act quickly and sensibly in an emergency.

present[1] *adjective* 1 in a particular place, *No one else was present.* 2 belonging or referring to what is happening now; existing now, *the present principal.*

present[2] *noun* present times or events.

present[3] *noun* something given or received without payment; a gift.

present[4] (*say* priz-**ent**) *verb* 1 give, especially with a ceremony, *Who is to present the prizes?* 2 introduce someone to another person or to an audience. 3 put on a play or other entertainment. 4 show, *She presents a cheerful face to the world.* 5 cause, *Writing a dictionary*

presents many problems. **presentation**
noun, **presenter** *noun*

presentable *adjective* fit to be presented
to someone; looking good.

presentiment *noun* a feeling that something is about to happen; a foreboding.

presently *adverb* 1 soon, *I shall be with
you presently.* 2 now, *the person who is
presently in charge.*

preserve[1] *verb* (**preserved, preserving**)
keep something safe or in good condition.
preserver *noun,* **preservation** *noun,*
preservative *adjective* & *noun*

preserve[2] *noun* 1 jam. 2 an activity that
belongs to a particular person or group,
Skateboarding is a teenage preserve.

preside *verb* (**presided, presiding**) be in
charge of a meeting etc.

president *noun* 1 the person in charge of
a club, society, or council etc. 2 the head
of a republic. **presidency** *noun,* **presidential** *adjective*

press[1] *verb* 1 put weight or force steadily
on something; squeeze. 2 make something
by pressing. 3 flatten; smooth; iron.
4 urge; make demands, *They pressed for
an increase in wages.*

press[2] *noun* (*plural* **presses**) 1 the action
of pressing something. 2 a device for
pressing things. 3 a device for printing
things. 4 a firm that prints or publishes
books etc., *Oxford University Press.*
5 newspapers; journalists.
press conference an interview with
a group of journalists.

press-gang *noun* (in history) a group
of men whose job was to force people
to serve in the army or navy.

pressure *noun* 1 continuous pressing.
2 the force with which something presses.
3 an influence that persuades or compels
you to do something, *peer pressure.*

pressurize *verb* (**pressurized, pressuriz-
ing**) 1 keep a compartment at the same air-
pressure all the time. 2 try to compel a person to do something. **pressurization** *noun*

prestige (*say* pres-**teej**) *noun* good
reputation. **prestigious** *adjective*

presumably *adverb* according to what
you may presume.

presume *verb* (**presumed, presuming**)
1 suppose; assume something to be true.
2 take the liberty of doing something; venture, *May we presume to advise you?*
presumption *noun*

presumptive *adjective* presuming
something.
heir presumptive see *heir.*

presumptuous *adjective* too bold or
confident. **presumptuously** *adverb*

presuppose *verb* (**presupposed, presupposing**) suppose or assume something beforehand. **presupposition** *noun*

pretence *noun* 1 pretending. 2 a pretext.
false pretences pretending to be something that you are not, in order to deceive
people.

pretend *verb* 1 behave as if something is
true or real when you know that it is not,
either in play or so as to deceive people.
2 put forward a claim, *I don't pretend to
be an expert.* **pretender** *noun*

pretension *noun* 1 a doubtful claim.
2 pretentious or showy behaviour.

pretentious *adjective* 1 showy; ostentatious. 2 claiming to have great merit or
importance. **pretentiously** *adverb,*
pretentiousness *noun*

pretext *noun* a reason put forward
to conceal the true reason.

pretty[1] *adjective* (**prettier, prettiest**)
attractive in a delicate way. **prettily**
adverb, **prettiness** *noun*

pretty[2] *adverb* quite, *It's pretty cold.*

prevail *verb* 1 be the most frequent or
general, *The prevailing wind is from the
south-west.* 2 be victorious, *good sense
prevailed.*

prevalent (*say* **prev**-a-lent) *adjective*
most frequent or common; widespread.
prevalence *noun*

prevaricate *verb* (**prevaricated, pre-
varicating**) say something that is not
actually a lie but is evasive or misleading.
prevarication *noun*

prevent *verb* 1 stop something from happening. 2 stop a person from doing something. **preventable** *adjective,* **prevention**
noun, **preventive** or **preventative** *adjective*
& *noun*

preview *noun* a showing of a film or play etc. before it is shown to the general public.

previous *adjective* coming before this; preceding. **previously** *adverb*

prey[1] (*say as* pray) *noun* an animal that is hunted or killed by another for food; a victim.
bird or **beast of prey** one that kills and eats other birds or four-footed animals.

prey[2] *verb* **prey on** hunt or take as prey; cause to worry, *The problem preyed on his mind.*

price[1] *noun* 1 the amount of money for which something is bought or sold. 2 what must be given or done in order to achieve something, *the price of fame.*

price[2] *verb* (**priced, pricing**) decide the price of something.

priceless *adjective* 1 very valuable. 2 (*informal*) very amusing.

prick *verb* 1 make a tiny hole in something. 2 hurt somebody with a pin or needle etc. **prick** *noun*
prick out remove seedlings from seed-beds and transplant them into small containers or into holes pricked in the soil.
prick up your ears start listening suddenly.

prickle[1] *noun* 1 a small thorn. 2 a sharp-pointed projection on a hedgehog or cactus etc. 3 a feeling that something is pricking you. **prickly** *adjective*
prickly pear a cactus with a prickly fruit shaped like a pear; the fruit from this cactus.

prickle[2] *verb* (**prickled, prickling**) feel or cause a pricking feeling.

pride[1] *noun* 1 being proud. 2 something that makes you feel proud, *The team's victory was the pride of the country.* 3 a group of lions.
pride of place the most important or most honoured position.

pride[2] *verb* (**prided, priding**) **pride yourself on** be proud of.

priest *noun* 1 a member of the clergy. 2 a person who conducts religious ceremonies. **priestess** *noun*, **priesthood** *noun*, **priestly** *adjective*

prig *noun* a self-righteous person. **priggish** *adjective*

prim *adjective* (**primmer, primmest**) formal and correct in manner; disliking anything rough or rude. **primly** *adverb*, **primness** *noun*

primacy (*say* pry-ma-see) *noun* 1 being the first or most important. 2 the position of primate (= archbishop).

prima donna (*say* preem-a) *noun* (*plural* **prima donnas**) 1 the chief female singer in an opera. 2 a temperamental and self-important person.

primary *adjective* first; most important. (Compare *secondary.*) **primarily** (*say* pry-mer-il-ee) *adverb*
primary colours the colours from which all others can be made by mixing (red, yellow, and blue for paint; red, green, and violet for light).
primary consumer an animal that feeds on plants.
primary production the extraction of raw materials from the earth or the sea.
primary school a school for the first stage of a child's education.

primate (*say* pry-mat) *noun* 1 an animal of the group that includes human beings, apes, and monkeys. 2 an archbishop.

prime[1] *adjective* 1 chief; most important, *the prime cause.* 2 excellent; first-rate, *prime beef.*
prime minister the leader of a government.
prime number a number (e.g. 2, 3, 5, 7, 11) that can be divided exactly only by itself and one.

prime[2] *noun* the best time or stage of something, *in the prime of life.*

prime[3] *verb* (**primed, priming**) 1 prepare something for use or action, *prime a bomb.* 2 put a coat of liquid on something to prepare it for painting. 3 equip a person with information.

primer *noun* 1 a liquid for priming a surface. 2 an elementary textbook.

primeval (*say* pry-mee-val) *adjective* of the earliest times of the world.

primitive *adjective* of or at an early stage of development or civilization; not complicated or sophisticated.

primogeniture *noun* being a first-born child; the custom by which an eldest child inherits all his or her parents' property.

primordial *adjective* primeval.

primrose *noun* a pale-yellow flower that blooms in spring.

prince *noun* 1 the son of a king or queen. 2 a man or boy in a royal family. **princely** *adjective*

princess *noun* (*plural* **princesses**) 1 the daughter of a king or queen. 2 a woman or girl in a royal family. 3 the wife of a prince.

principal[1] *adjective* chief; most important. **principally** *adverb*

principal[2] *noun* 1 the head of a college or school. 2 a sum of money that is invested or lent, *Interest is paid on the principal.*
• USAGE: Do not confuse with *principle* (which is never used of a person).

principality *noun* a country ruled by a prince.

principle *noun* 1 a general truth, belief, or rule, *She taught me the principles of geometry.* 2 a rule of conduct, *Cheating is against his principles.*
in principle in general, not in details.
on principle because of your principles of behaviour.
• USAGE: See the note on *principal.*

print[1] *verb* 1 put words or pictures on paper by using a machine. 2 write with letters that are not joined together. 3 press a mark or design etc. on a surface. 4 make a picture from the negative of a photograph. **printer** *noun*
printed circuit an electric circuit made by pressing thin metal strips on to a surface.

print[2] *noun* 1 printed lettering or words. 2 a mark made by something pressing on a surface, *a fingerprint.* 3 a printed picture, photograph, or design.
printmaking the process of making prints by means of engraving, etching, linocuts, woodcuts, etc.

printout *noun* information etc. produced in printed form by a computer or teleprinter.

prior[1] *adjective* earlier or more important than something else.

prior[2] *noun* a monk who is the head of a religious house or order. **prioress** *noun*

priority *noun* (*plural* **priorities**) 1 being earlier or more important than something else; precedence. 2 something considered more important than other things, *Safety is a priority.*

priory *noun* (*plural* **priories**) a religious house governed by a prior or prioress.

prise *verb* (**prised, prising**) lever something out or open, *Prise the lid off the crate.*

prism (*say* prizm) *noun* 1 a solid shape with ends that are triangles or polygons which are equal and parallel. 2 a glass prism that breaks up light into the colours of the rainbow. **prismatic** *adjective*

prison *noun* a place where criminals are kept as a punishment.

prisoner *noun* 1 a person kept in prison. 2 a captive.

pristine *adjective* ancient and unspoilt; original, *in its pristine form.*

private[1] *adjective* 1 belonging to a particular person or group, *private property.* 2 confidential, *private talks.* 3 secluded. 4 not holding public office, *a private citizen.* 5 independent; not organized by a government, *private school; a private detective.* **privately** *adverb*, **privacy** (*say* priv-a-see) *noun*
in private where only particular people can see or hear; not in public.
private sector the part of the economy that is not controlled by the government. (Compare *public sector.*)

private[2] *noun* a soldier of the lowest rank.

privation *noun* loss or lack of something; lack of necessities.

privatize *verb* (**privatized, privatizing**) transfer a nationalized industry etc. to a private organization. **privatization** *noun*

privet *noun* an evergreen shrub with small leaves, used to make hedges.

privilege *noun* a special right or advantage given to one person or group. **privileged** *adjective*

privy *adjective* (*old use*) hidden; secret.
be privy to be sharing in the secret of someone's plans etc.

prize[1] *noun* an award given to the winner of a game or competition etc.

prize[2] *verb* (**prized, prizing**) value something greatly.

pro *noun* (*plural* **pros**) (*informal*) a professional.

pro- *prefix* 1 favouring or supporting (as in *pro-government*). 2 deputizing or substituted for (as in *pronoun*). 3 onwards; forwards (as in *proceed*).

pro and con for and against.
  pros and cons reasons for and against something.

probable *adjective* likely to happen or be true. **probably** *adverb*, **probability** *noun*

probate *noun* the official process of proving that a person's will is valid.

probation *noun* the testing of a person's character and abilities. **probationary** *adjective*
  on probation being supervised by an official (a **probation officer**) instead of being sent to prison.

probationer *noun* a person at an early stage of training, e.g. as a nurse.

probe[1] *noun* 1 an instrument for exploring something. 2 an investigation, *a probe into corruption at the highest levels*.

probe[2] *verb* (**probed, probing**) 1 explore with a probe. 2 investigate.

probity (*say* **proh**-bit-ee) *noun* honesty.

problem *noun* 1 something difficult to deal with or understand. 2 something that has to be done or answered, *a maths problem*. **problematic** or **problematical** *adjective*

proboscis (*say* pro-**boss**-iss) *noun* (*plural* **proboscises**) 1 a long flexible snout. 2 an insect's long mouth-part.

procedure *noun* an orderly way of doing something.

proceed *verb* 1 go forward or onward. 2 continue; go on with an action, *She proceeded to explain the plan*.

proceedings *plural noun* 1 things that happen; activities. 2 a lawsuit.

proceeds *plural noun* the money made from a sale or show etc.; profit.

process[1] (*say* **proh**-sess) *noun* (*plural* **processes**) 1 a series of actions for making or doing something. 2 a series of changes that happen naturally, *the process of ageing*.

process[2] *verb* put something through a manufacturing or other process, *processed cheese*.

process[3] (*say* pro-**sess**) *verb* go in procession.

procession *noun* a number of people or vehicles etc. moving steadily forward following each other.

processor *noun* a machine that processes things.

proclaim *verb* announce officially or publicly. **proclamation** *noun*

procrastinate *verb* (**procrastinated, procrastinating**) put off doing something. **procrastination** *noun*, **procrastinator** *noun*

procreate *verb* (**procreated, procreating**) produce offspring by the natural process of reproduction. **procreation** *noun*

procure *verb* (**procured, procuring**) obtain; acquire. **procurement** *noun*

prod *verb* (**prodded, prodding**) 1 poke. 2 stimulate into action. **prod** *noun*

prodigal *adjective* wasteful; extravagant. **prodigally** *adverb*, **prodigality** *noun*

prodigious *adjective* wonderful; enormous. **prodigiously** *adverb*

prodigy *noun* (*plural* **prodigies**) 1 a person with wonderful abilities. 2 a wonderful thing.

produce[1] *verb* (**produced, producing**) 1 make or create something; bring into existence. 2 bring out so that it can be seen, *He produced a rabbit from a hat*. 3 organize the performance of a play, making of a film, etc. 4 extend a line further, *Produce the base of the triangle*. **producer** *noun*

produce[2] (*say* **prod**-yooss) *noun* things produced, especially by farmers.

product *noun* 1 something produced. 2 the result of multiplying two numbers. (Compare *quotient*.)

production *noun* 1 producing. 2 the thing or amount produced.
  production line a sequence of mechanical or manual operations involved in producing a commodity.

productive *adjective* producing a lot of things.

productivity *noun* a measure of the efficiency of production, *High labour productivity means each worker is producing a lot of output.*

profane[1] *adjective* irreverent; blasphemous. **profanely** *adverb*, **profanity** *noun*

profane[2] *verb* (**profaned, profaning**) treat irreverently.

profess *verb* 1 declare. 2 claim; pretend, *She professed interest in our work.* **professedly** *adverb*

profession *noun* 1 an occupation that needs special education and training, *The professions include being a doctor, nurse, or lawyer.* 2 a declaration, *They made professions of loyalty.*

professional *adjective* 1 of a profession. 2 doing a certain kind of work as a full-time job for payment, not as an amateur, *a professional golfer.* **professional** *noun*, **professionally** *adverb*

professor *noun* a university lecturer of the highest rank. **professorship** *noun*

proffer *verb* & *noun* offer.

proficient *adjective* doing something properly because of training or practice; skilled. **proficiency** *noun*

profile *noun* 1 a side view of a person's face. 2 a short description of a person's character or career.
keep a low profile not make yourself noticeable.

profit[1] *noun* 1 the extra money obtained by selling something for more than it cost to buy or make. 2 an advantage gained by doing something. **profitable** *adjective*, **profitably** *adverb*

profit[2] *verb* (**profited, profiting**) get a profit.

profiteer *noun* a person who makes a great profit unfairly. **profiteering** *noun*

profligate *adjective* wasteful; unrestrained. **profligacy** *noun*

profound *adjective* 1 very deep or intense, *We take a profound interest in it.* 2 showing or needing great study. **profoundly** *adverb*, **profundity** *noun*

profuse *adjective* lavish; plentiful.

profusely *adverb*, **profuseness** *noun*, **profusion** *noun*

progenitor *noun* an ancestor.

progeny (*say* proj-in-ee) *noun* offspring; descendants.

prognosis (*say* prog-**noh**-sis) *noun* (*plural* **prognoses**) a forecast or prediction, especially about a disease. **prognostication** *noun*

program[1] *noun* a series of coded instructions for a computer to carry out.

program[2] *verb* (**programmed, programming**) prepare a computer by means of a program. **programmer** *noun*

programme *noun* 1 a list of planned events; a leaflet giving details of a play, concert, etc. 2 a show, play, or talk etc. on radio or television.

progress[1] (*say* **proh**-gress) *noun* 1 forward movement; an advance. 2 a development or improvement, *scientific progress.*

progress[2] (*say* pro-**gress**) *verb* make progress. **progression** *noun*, **progressive** *adjective*

prohibit *verb* (**prohibited, prohibiting**) forbid; ban, *Smoking is prohibited.* **prohibition** *noun*

prohibitive *adjective* 1 prohibiting. 2 (of prices) so high that people will not buy things.

project[1] (*say* **proj**-ekt) *noun* 1 a plan or scheme. 2 the task of finding out as much as you can about something and writing about it.

project[2] (*say* pro-**jekt**) *verb* 1 stick out. 2 throw outwards, *project your voice on stage.* 3 show a picture on a screen. **projection** *noun*

projectile *noun* a missile.

projectionist *noun* a person who works a projector.

projector *noun* a machine for showing films or photographs on a screen.

proletariat (*say* proh-lit-**air**-ee-at) *noun* working people.

proliferate *verb* (**proliferated, proliferating**) increase rapidly in numbers. **proliferation** *noun*

prolific *adjective* producing much fruit or

many flowers or other things. **prolifically** *adverb*

prologue (*say* proh-log) *noun* an introduction to a poem or play etc.

prolong *verb* make a thing longer or make it last for a long time. **prolongation** *noun*

prom *noun* (*informal*) 1 a promenade. 2 a promenade concert.

promenade (*say* prom-in-**ahd**) *noun* 1 a place suitable for walking, especially beside the sea-shore. 2 a leisurely walk. **promenade** *verb*

promenade concert a concert where part of the audience may stand or walk about.

prominent *adjective* 1 sticking out; projecting. 2 conspicuous, *The tree occupies a prominent position in the garden.* 3 important, *a prominent politician.* **prominently** *adverb*, **prominence** *noun*

promiscuous *adjective* 1 indiscriminate. 2 having many casual sexual relationships. **promiscuously** *adverb*, **promiscuity** *noun*

promise¹ *noun* 1 a statement that you will definitely do or not do something. 2 an indication of future success or good results, *Her work shows promise.*

promise² *verb* (**promised, promising**) make a promise.

promising *adjective* likely to be good or successful, *a promising pianist.*

promontory *noun* (*plural* **promontories**) a piece of high land that sticks out into a sea or lake.

promote *verb* (**promoted, promoting**) 1 move a person to a higher rank or position. 2 help the progress or sale of something. **promoter** *noun*, **promotion** *noun*

prompt¹ *adjective* 1 without delay, *a prompt reply.* 2 punctual. **promptly** *adverb*, **promptness** *noun*, **promptitude** *noun*

prompt² *verb* 1 cause or encourage a person to do something. 2 remind an actor or speaker of words when he or she has forgotten them. **prompter** *noun*

promulgate *verb* (**promulgated, promulgating**) make known to the public; proclaim. **promulgation** *noun*

prone *adjective* lying face downwards. (The opposite is *supine.*)

be prone to be likely to do or suffer something, *He is prone to jealousy.*

prong *noun* a spike of a fork. **pronged** *adjective*

pronoun *noun* a word used instead of a noun. **Demonstrative pronouns** are *this, that, these, those;* **interrogative pronouns** are *who? what? which?,* etc.; **personal pronouns** are *I, me, we, us, thou, thee, you, ye, he, him, she, her, it, they, them;* **possessive pronouns** are *mine, yours, theirs,* etc.; **reflexive pronouns** are *myself, yourself,* etc.; **relative pronouns** are *who, what, which, that.*

pronounce *verb* (**pronounced, pronouncing**) 1 say a sound or word in a particular way, *'Two' is pronounced like 'too'.* 2 declare formally, *I now pronounce you husband and wife.*

pronounced *adjective* noticeable, *She walks with a pronounced limp.*

pronouncement *noun* a declaration.

pronunciation *noun* 1 the way a word is pronounced. 2 the way a person pronounces words.

● USAGE: Note the spelling; this word should not be written or spoken as 'pronounciation'.

proof¹ *noun* 1 a fact or thing that shows something is true. 2 a printed copy of a book or photograph etc. made for checking before other copies are printed.

proof² *adjective* able to resist something or not be penetrated, *a bullet-proof jacket.*

prop¹ *noun* a support, especially one made of a long piece of wood or metal.

prop² *verb* (**propped, propping**) support something by leaning it against something else.

propaganda *noun* publicity intended to make people believe something.

propagate *verb* (**propagated, propagating**) 1 breed; reproduce. 2 send out or transmit sound, light, etc. **propagation** *noun*, **propagator** *noun*

propel *verb* (**propelled, propelling**) push something forward.

propellant *noun* a substance that propels things, *Liquid fuel is the propellant used in these rockets.*

propeller *noun* a device with blades that spin round to drive an aircraft or ship.

propensity *noun* (*plural* **propensities**) a tendency.

proper *adjective* **1** suitable; right, *the proper way to hold a bat.* **2** respectable, *prim and proper.* **3** (*informal*) complete; great, *You're a proper nuisance!* **properly** *adverb*

proper fraction a fraction in which the numerator is less than the denominator, e.g. $^3/_5$.

proper noun the name of one person or thing, e.g. *Tshepo, Pretoria, Namibia.*

property *noun* (*plural* **properties**) **1** a thing or things that belong to somebody. **2** a building or someone's land. **3** a quality or characteristic, *It has the property of becoming soft when heated.*

prophecy (*say* **pro**-fi-see) *noun* (*plural* **prophecies**) **1** a statement that prophesies something. **2** the action of prophesying.

prophesy (*say* **pro**-fi-sy) *verb* (**prophesied, prophesying**) forecast; foretell.

prophet *noun* **1** a person who makes prophecies. **2** a religious teacher who is believed to be inspired by God. **prophetess** *noun*, **prophetic** *adjective*

the Prophet Muhammad, who founded the Muslim faith.

propinquity *noun* nearness.

propitiate (*say* pro-**pish**-ee-ayt) *verb* (**propitiated, propitiating**) win a person's favour or forgiveness. **propitiation** *noun*, **propitiatory** *adjective*

propitious (*say* pro-**pish**-us) *adjective* favourable.

proponent (*say* prop-**oh**-nent) *noun* the person who puts forward a proposal.

proportion *noun* **1** a part or share of a whole thing. **2** a ratio. **3** the correct relationship in size, amount, or importance between two things. **proportional** *adjective*, **proportionally** *adverb*, **proportionate** *adjective*

proportions *plural noun* size, *a ship of large proportions.*

proportional representation a system in which each political party has a number of Members of Parliament in proportion to the number of votes for all its candidates.

propose *verb* (**proposed, proposing**) **1** suggest an idea or plan etc. **2** ask a person to marry you. **proposal** *noun*

proposition *noun* **1** a suggestion. **2** a statement. **3** (*informal*) an undertaking; a matter, *a difficult proposition.*

propound *verb* put forward an idea for consideration.

proprietary (*say* pro-**pry**-it-er-ee) *adjective* **1** made or sold by one firm; branded, *proprietary medicines.* **2** of an owner or ownership.

proprietor *noun* the owner of a shop or business. **proprietress** *noun*

propriety (*say* pro-**pry**-it-ee) *noun* (*plural* **proprieties**) **1** being proper. **2** correct behaviour.

propulsion *noun* propelling something.

prosaic *adjective* plain or dull and ordinary. **prosaically** *adverb*

proscribe *verb* (**proscribed, proscribing**) forbid by law.

● USAGE: Do not confuse with *prescribe.*

prose *noun* writing or speech that is not in verse.

prosecute *verb* (**prosecuted, prosecuting**) **1** make someone go to a lawcourt to be tried for a crime. **2** perform; carry on, *prosecuting their trade.* **prosecution** *noun*, **prosecutor** *noun*

proselyte *noun* a person who has been converted to the Jewish faith or from one religion, opinion, etc. to another.

prosody (*say* **pross** od-ee) *noun* the study of verse and its structure.

prospect[1] *noun* **1** a possibility, *There is no prospect of success.* **2** a wide view.

prospect[2] (*say* pro-**spekt**) *verb* explore in search of something, *prospecting for gold.* **prospector** *noun*

prospective *adjective* expected to be or to happen; possible, *prospective customers.*

prospectus *noun* (*plural* **prospectuses**) a booklet describing and advertising a school, business company, etc.

prosper *verb* be successful.

prosperous *adjective* successful; rich. **prosperity** *noun*

prostitute *noun* a person who takes part in sexual acts for payment. **prostitution** *noun*

prostrate[1] *adjective* lying face downwards.

prostrate[2] *verb* (**prostrated, prostrating**) cause to be prostrate. **prostration** *noun*

protagonist *noun* 1 the main character in a play. 2 a person leading a movement, cause, etc., *a leading protagonist of feminism.*

protea *noun* a kind of evergreen shrub, many of which have distinctive flowers.

protect *verb* keep safe from harm or injury. **protection** *noun*, **protective** *adjective*, **protector** *noun*

protectorate *noun* a country that is under the official protection of a stronger country.

protégé (*say* **prot**-ezh-ay) *noun* a person who is given helpful protection or encouragement by another.

protein *noun* a substance that is found in all living things and is an essential part of the food of animals.

Protestant *noun* a member of any of the western Christian Churches separated from the Roman Catholic Church.

protest[1] (*say* **proh**-test) *noun* a statement or action showing that you disapprove of something.

protest[2] (*say* pro-**test**) *verb* 1 make a protest. 2 declare firmly, *They protested their innocence.* **protestation** *noun*

proto- *prefix* first.

protocol *noun* etiquette connected with people's rank.

proton *noun* a particle of matter with a positive electric charge.

prototype *noun* the first model of something, from which others are copied or developed.

protract *verb* prolong in time; lengthen. **protraction** *noun*

protractor *noun* a device for measuring angles, usually a semicircle marked off in degrees.

protrude *verb* (**protruded, protruding**) project; stick out. **protrusion** *noun*

protuberance *noun* a protuberant part.

protuberant *adjective* sticking out from a surface.

proud *adjective* 1 very pleased with yourself or with someone else who has done well. 2 causing pride, *This is a proud moment for us.* 3 full of self-respect and independence, *They were too proud to ask for help.* **proudly** *adverb*

prove *verb* (**proved, proving**) 1 show that something is true. 2 turn out, *The forecast proved to be correct.* **provable** *adjective*

proven (*say* **proh**-ven) *adjective* proved, *a man of proven ability.*

provender *noun* fodder; food.

proverb *noun* a short well-known saying that states a truth, e.g. 'Many hands make light work'.

proverbial *adjective* 1 of or in a proverb. 2 well-known.

provide *verb* (**provided, providing**) 1 make something available; supply. 2 prepare for something, *Try to provide against emergencies.* **provider** *noun*

provided *conjunction* on condition, *You can stay provided that you help.*

providence *noun* 1 being provident. 2 God's or nature's care and protection.

provident *adjective* wisely providing for the future; thrifty.

providential *adjective* happening very luckily. **providentially** *adverb*

providing *conjunction* provided.

province *noun* 1 a section of a country. 2 the area of a person's special knowledge or responsibility, *Teaching you to swim is not my province.* **provincial** *adjective* **the provinces** the parts of a country outside its capital city.

provision *noun* 1 providing something. 2 a statement in a document, *the provisions of the treaty.*
provisions *plural noun* supplies of food and drink.

provisional *adjective* arranged or agreed upon temporarily but possibly to be altered later. **provisionally** *adverb*

proviso (*say* prov-**I**-zoh) *noun* (*plural* **provisos**) a stipulation.

provoke *verb* (**provoked, provoking**) 1 make a person angry. 2 arouse;

stimulate, *The joke provoked laughter.*
provocation *noun,* **provocative** *adjective*

prow *noun* the front end of a ship.

prowess *noun* great ability or daring.

prowl *verb* move about quietly or cautiously. **prowl** *noun,* **prowler** *noun*

proximity *noun* 1 nearness. 2 the part near something, *in the proximity of the station.*

proxy *noun* (*plural* **proxies**) a person authorized to represent or act for another person.

prude *noun* a person who is easily shocked. **prudish** *adjective,* **prudery** *noun*

prudent *adjective* careful, not rash or reckless. **prudently** *adverb,* **prudence** *noun,* **prudential** *adjective*

prune[1] *noun* a dried plum.

prune[2] *verb* (**pruned, pruning**) cut off unwanted parts of a tree or bush etc. so that it will grow better.

pry *verb* (**pried, prying**) look or ask inquisitively.

PS *abbreviation* postscript.

psalm (*say* sahm) *noun* a religious song, especially one from the Book of Psalms in the Bible. **psalmist** *noun*

pseudo- (*say* s'**yood**-oh) *prefix* false; pretended.

pseudonym *noun* a false name used by an author.

psychedelic (*say* sy-ki-**del**-ik) *adjective* 1 (of a drug) producing hallucinations. 2 (*informal*) having very bright vivid colours or sounds.

psychiatrist (*say* sy-**ky**-a-trist) *noun* a doctor who treats mental illnesses. **psychiatry** *noun,* **psychiatric** *adjective*

psychic (*say* **sy**-kik) *adjective* 1 of powers or events that seem to be supernatural. 2 of the mind or soul. **psychical** *adjective*

psycho- *prefix* of the mind.

psychoanalysis *noun* investigation of a person's mental processes, especially in psychotherapy.

psychology *noun* the study of the mind and how it works. **psychological** *adjective,* **psychologist** *noun*

psychotherapy *noun* treatment of mental illness by psychological methods.

PT *abbreviation* physical training.

PTA *abbreviation* parent-teacher association.

pterodactyl (*say* te-ro-**dak**-til) *noun* an extinct reptile with wings.

PTO *abbreviation* please turn over.

pub *noun* (*informal*) a public house.

puberty (*say* **pew**-ber-tee) *noun* the time when a young person is developing physically into an adult.

pubic (*say* **pew**-bik) *adjective* of the lower front part of the abdomen.

public[1] *adjective* belonging to or known by everyone, not private. **publicly** *adverb*
public house a building licensed to serve alcoholic drinks to the public.
public relations all activities and practices which lead to better understanding between an organization and those with whom it comes into contact.
public sector the part of the economy that is controlled by the government. (Compare *private sector.*)
public service civil service.

public[2] *noun* all the people.
in public openly, not in private.

publican *noun* the person in charge of a public house.

publication *noun* 1 publishing. 2 a published book or newspaper etc.

publicity *noun* public attention; doing things (e.g. advertising) to draw people's attention to something.

publicize *verb* (**publicized, publicizing**) bring something to people's attention; advertise.

publish *verb* 1 have something printed and sold to the public. 2 announce something in public. **publisher** *noun*

puce *noun* brownish-purple colour.

puck *noun* a hard rubber disc used in ice hockey.

pucker *verb* wrinkle.

pudding *noun* 1 a food made in a soft mass, especially in a mixture of flour and other ingredients, *Christmas pudding.* 2 the sweet course of a meal.

puddle *noun* a shallow patch of liquid, especially of rainwater on a road.

pudgy *adjective* podgy.

puerile (*say* **pew**-er-I'll) *adjective* silly and

childish. **puerility** *noun*

puff¹ *noun* 1 a short blowing of breath, wind, or smoke etc. 2 a soft pad for putting powder on the skin. 3 a cake of very light pastry filled with cream.

puff² *verb* 1 blow out puffs of smoke etc. 2 breathe with difficulty; pant. 3 inflate or swell something, *He puffed out his chest.*

puff-adder *noun* a poisonous snake that inflates the upper part of its body.

puffin *noun* a sea-bird with a large striped beak.

puffy *adjective* puffed out; swollen. **puffiness** *noun*

pug *noun* a small dog with a flat face like a bulldog.

pugilist (*say* pew-jil-ist) *noun* a boxer.

pugnacious *adjective* wanting to fight; aggressive. **pugnaciously** *adverb*, **pugnacity** *noun*

pull *verb* 1 make a thing come towards or after you by using force on it. 2 move by a driving force, *The car pulled out into the road.* **pull** *noun*

pull a face make a strange face.

pull off achieve something.

pull somebody's leg tease him or her.

pull through recover from an illness.

pull yourself together become calm or sensible.

pullet *noun* a young hen.

pulley *noun* (*plural* **pulleys**) a wheel with a rope, chain, or belt over it, used for lifting or moving heavy things.

pullover *noun* a knitted garment (with no fastenings) for the top half of the body.

pulmonary (*say* pul-mon-er-ee) *adjective* of the lungs.

pulp *noun* 1 the soft moist part of fruit. 2 any soft moist mass. **pulpy** *adjective*

pulpit *noun* a small enclosed platform for the preacher in a church or chapel.

pulsate *verb* (**pulsated, pulsating**) expand and contract rhythmically; vibrate. **pulsation** *noun*

pulse¹ *noun* 1 the rhythmical movement of the arteries as blood is pumped through them by the beating of the heart, *The pulse can be felt in a person's wrists.* 2 a throb, *the pulse of the music.*

pulse² *verb* (**pulsed, pulsing**) throb.

pulse³ *noun* the edible seed of peas, beans, lentils, etc.

pulverize *verb* (**pulverized, pulverizing**) crush into powder. **pulverization** *noun*

puma (*say* pew-ma) *noun* a large brown animal of western America, also called a cougar or mountain lion.

pumice *noun* a kind of porous stone used for rubbing stains from the skin or as powder for polishing things.

pummel *verb* (**pummelled, pummelling**) keep on hitting something.

pump¹ *noun* a device that pushes air or liquid into or out of something, or along pipes.

pump² *verb* 1 move air or liquid with a pump. 2 (*informal*) question a person to obtain information.

pump up inflate.

pump³ *noun* 1 a plimsoll. 2 a lightweight shoe.

pumpkin *noun* a very large round fruit with a hard skin.

pun *noun* a joking use of a word sounding the same as another, e.g. 'Deciding where to bury him was a *grave* decision'.

punch¹ *verb* 1 hit with a fist. 2 make a hole in something.

punch² *noun* (*plural* **punches**) 1 a hit with a fist. 2 a device for making holes in paper, metal, leather, etc. 3 vigour, *her speech lacked punch.*

punch line words that give the climax of a joke or story.

punch³ *noun* a drink made by mixing wine or spirits and fruit-juice in a bowl.

punch-up *noun* (*informal*) a fight.

punctilious *adjective* very careful about details; conscientious. **punctiliously** *adverb*, **punctiliousness** *noun*

punctual *adjective* doing things exactly at the time arranged; not late. **punctually** *adverb*, **punctuality** *noun*

punctuate *verb* (**punctuated, punctuating**) 1 put punctuation marks into something. 2 put in at intervals, *His speech was punctuated with cheers.*

punctuation *noun* 1 marks such as commas, full stops, and brackets put into

a piece of writing to make it easier to read.
2 the action of punctuating.

puncture[1] *noun* a small hole made by
something sharp, especially in a tyre.

puncture[2] *verb* (**punctured, puncturing**)
make a puncture in something.

pundit *noun* a person who is an authority
on something.

pungent (*say* **pun**-jent) *adjective*
1 having a strong taste or smell.
2 (of remarks) sharp. **pungently** *adverb*,
pungency *noun*

punish *verb* make a person suffer because
he or she has done something wrong.
punishable *adjective*, **punishment** *noun*

punitive (*say* **pew**-nit-iv) *adjective*
inflicting punishment.

punk *noun* (*informal*) a hooligan or petty
criminal.

punnet *noun* a small container for soft
fruit such as strawberries.

punt[1] *noun* a flat-bottomed boat, usually
moved by pushing a pole against the bottom of a river while standing in the punt.

punt[2] *verb* move a punt with a pole.

punt[3] *verb* kick a football after dropping it
from your hands and before it touches the
ground.

punt[4] *verb* gamble; bet on a horse-race.
punter *noun*

puny (*say* **pew**-nee) *adjective* small or
undersized; feeble.

pup *noun* 1 a puppy. 2 a young seal.

pupa (*say* **pew**-pa) *noun* (*plural* **pupae**)
an insect in the stage of development
between a larva and an adult.

pupate (*say* pew-**payt**) *verb* (**pupated,
pupating**) become a pupa. **pupation** *noun*

pupil *noun* 1 someone who is being
taught by another person. 2 the opening
in the centre of the eye.

puppet *noun* 1 a kind of doll that can be
made to move by fitting it over your hand
or working it by strings or wires. 2 a person whose actions are controlled by someone else. **puppetry** *noun*

puppy *noun* (*plural* **puppies**) a young
dog.

purchase[1] *verb* (**purchased, purchasing**)
buy. **purchaser** *noun*

purchase[2] *noun* 1 something bought.
2 buying. 3 a firm hold to pull or raise
something.

purdah *noun* the Muslim or Hindu custom of keeping women from the sight of
men or strangers.

pure *adjective* 1 not mixed with anything
else; clean. 2 mere; nothing but, *pure nonsense*. **purely** *adverb*, **pureness** *noun*

purée (*say* **pewr**-ay) *noun* fruit or vegetables made into pulp.

purgative *noun* a strong laxative.

purgatory *noun* (in Roman Catholic
belief) a place or condition in which souls
are purified by punishment.

purge[1] *verb* (**purged, purging**) get rid of
unwanted people or things.

purge[2] *noun* 1 purging. 2 a purgative.

purify *verb* (**purified, purifying**) make
a thing pure. **purification** *noun*, **purifier**
noun

purist *noun* a person who likes things to
be exactly right, especially in people's use
of words.

Puritan *noun* a Protestant in the 16th and
17th centuries who wanted simpler
religious ceremonies and strictly moral
behaviour.

puritan *noun* a person with very strict
morals. **puritanical** *adjective*

purity *noun* pureness.

purl[1] *noun* a knitting-stitch that makes
a ridge towards the knitter. **purl** *verb*

purl[2] *verb* (of a stream) ripple with
a murmuring sound.

purloin *verb* take something without
permission.

purple *noun* deep reddish-blue colour.

purport[1] (*say* per-**port**) *verb* claim,
The letter purports to be from the council.
purportedly *adverb*

purport[2] (*say* **per**-port) *noun* meaning.

purpose *noun* 1 what you intend to do;
a plan or aim. 2 determination. **purpose-
ful** *adjective*, **purposefully** *adverb*
on purpose by intention, not by accident.

purposely *adverb* on purpose.

purr *verb* make the low murmuring sound
that a cat does when it is pleased. **purr**
noun

purse[1] *noun* a small pouch for carrying money.

purse[2] *verb* (**pursed, pursing**) draw into folds, *She pursed up her lips.*

purser *noun* a ship's officer in charge of accounts.

pursuance *noun* performing or carrying out an intention etc., *in pursuance of my duties.*

pursue *verb* (**pursued, pursuing**) 1 chase in order to catch or kill. 2 continue with something; work at, *We are pursuing our enquiries.* **pursuer** *noun*

pursuit *noun* 1 the action of pursuing. 2 a regular activity.

purvey *verb* (**purveyed, purveying**) supply food etc. as a trade. **purveyor** *noun*

pus *noun* a thick yellowish substance produced in inflamed or infected tissue, e.g. in an abscess or boil.

push[1] *verb* 1 make a thing go away from you by using force on it. 2 move yourself by using force, *He pushed in front of me.* 3 try to force someone to do or use something; urge. **pusher** *noun*

push off (*informal*) go away.

push[2] *noun* (*plural* **pushes**) a pushing movement or effort.

at a push if necessary but only with difficulty.

push-chair *noun* a folding chair on wheels, in which a child can be pushed along.

pushy *adjective* unpleasantly self-confident and eager to do things.

pusillanimous (*say* pew-zil-**an**-im-us) *adjective* timid; cowardly.

puss *noun* (*informal*) a cat.

pussy *noun* (*plural* **pussies**) (*informal*) a cat.

pussy willow a willow with furry catkins.

pustule *noun* a pimple containing pus.

put *verb* (**put, putting**) This word has many uses, including 1 move a person or thing to a place or position, *Put the lamp on the table.* 2 cause a person or thing to do or experience something or be in a certain condition, *Put the light on. Put her in a good mood.* 3 express in words,

She put it tactfully.

be hard put have difficulty in doing something.

put off postpone; dissuade; stop someone wanting something, *The smell puts me off.*

put out stop a fire from burning or a light from shining; annoy or inconvenience, *Our lateness has put her out.*

put up build; raise; give someone a place to sleep; provide, *Who will put up the money?*

put up with endure; tolerate.

putrefy (*say* pew-trif-I) *verb* (**putrefied, putrefying**) decay; rot. **putrefaction** *noun*

putrid (*say* **pew**-trid) *adjective* 1 decomposed; rotting. 2 smelling bad.

putt *verb* hit a golf-ball gently towards the hole. **putt** *noun*, **putter** *noun*, **putting-green** *noun*

putty *noun* a soft paste that sets hard, used for fitting the glass into a window-frame.

putu *noun* a stiff porridge made from mealie meal.

puzzle[1] *noun* 1 a difficult question; a problem. 2 a game or toy that sets a problem or difficult task. 3 a jigsaw puzzle.

puzzle[2] *verb* (**puzzled, puzzling**) 1 give someone a problem so that they have to think hard. 2 think patiently about how to solve something. **puzzlement** *noun*

pygmy (*say* **pig**-mee) *noun* (*plural* **pygmies**) 1 a very small person or thing. 2 a member of a dwarf people of Africa and parts of Asia.

pyjamas *plural noun* a loose jacket and trousers worn in bed.

pylon *noun* a tall framework made of strips of steel, supporting electric cables.

pyramid *noun* 1 a structure with a square base and with sloping sides that meet in a point at the top. 2 an ancient Egyptian tomb shaped like this. **pyramidal** (*say* pir-**am**-id-al) *adjective*

pyre *noun* a pile of wood etc. for burning a dead body as part of a funeral ceremony.

python *noun* a large snake that squeezes its prey so as to suffocate it.

Qq

QED *abbreviation* quod erat demonstrandum (Latin = which was the thing that had to be proved).

quack[1] *verb* make the harsh cry of a duck. **quack** *noun*

quack[2] *noun* a person who falsely claims to have medical skill or have remedies to cure diseases.

quad (*say* kwod) *noun* **1** a quadrangle. **2** a quadruplet.

quadrangle *noun* a rectangular courtyard with large buildings round it.

quadrant *noun* a quarter of a circle.

quadri- *prefix* four.

quadrilateral *noun* a flat geometric shape with four couples.

quadruped *noun* an animal with four feet.

quadruple[1] *adjective* **1** four times as much or as many. **2** having four parts.

quadruple[2] *verb* (**quadrupled, quadrupling**) make or become four times as much or as many.

quadruplet *noun* each of four children born to the same mother at one time.

quadruplicate *noun* each of four things that are exactly alike.

quaff (*say* kwof) *verb* drink.

quagga (*say* **kwa**-kha) *noun* an extinct zebra-like wild ass.

quagmire *noun* a bog or marsh.

quail[1] *noun* (*plural* **quail** or **quails**) a bird related to the partridge.

quail[2] *verb* flinch; feel or show fear.

quaint *adjective* attractive through being unusual or old-fashioned. **quaintly** *adverb*, **quaintness** *noun*

quake *verb* (**quaked, quaking**) tremble; shake with fear.

Quaker *noun* a member of a religious group called the Society of Friends, founded by George Fox in Britain in the 17th century.

qualify *verb* (**qualified, qualifying**) **1** make or become able to do something through having certain qualities or training, or by passing a test. **2** make a statement less extreme, limit its meaning, *qualified approval*. **3** (of an adjective) add meaning to a noun. **qualification** *noun*

quality *noun* (*plural* **qualities**) **1** how good or bad something is. **2** a characteristic; something that is special in a person or thing.

qualm (*say* kwahm) *noun* a misgiving; a scruple.

quandary *noun* (*plural* **quandaries**) a difficult situation where you are uncertain what to do.

quantity *noun* (*plural* **quantities**) **1** how much there is of something; how many things there are of one sort. **2** a large amount, *It's cheaper to buy goods in quantity.*

quantum *noun* (*plural* **quanta**) a quantity or amount.

quarantine *noun* keeping a person or animal isolated in case they have a disease which could spread to others.

quarrel[1] *noun* an angry disagreement.

quarrel[2] *verb* (**quarrelled, quarrelling**) have a quarrel. **quarrelsome** *adjective*

quarry[1] *noun* (*plural* **quarries**) an open place where stone or slate is dug or cut out of the ground.

quarry[2] *verb* (**quarried, quarrying**) dig or cut from a quarry.

quarry[3] *noun* (*plural* **quarries**) an animal etc. being hunted or pursued.

quart *noun* a liquid measure in the imperial system, equal to two pints, a quarter of a gallon (0,946 litres).

quarter[1] *noun* **1** each of four equal parts into which a thing is or can be divided. **2** three months, one-fourth of a year. **3** a district or region, *People came from every quarter.* **4** mercy towards an enemy, *They gave no quarter.* **quarters** *plural noun* lodgings. **at close quarters** very close together.

quarter[2] *verb* **1** divide something into quarters. **2** put soldiers etc. into lodgings.

quarterdeck *noun* the part of a ship's upper deck nearest the stern, usually reserved for the officers.

quarterly[1] *adjective* & *adverb* happening or produced once in every three months.

quarterly[2] *noun* (*plural* **quarterlies**) a quarterly magazine etc.

quartet *noun* 1 a group of four musicians. 2 a piece of music for four musicians. 3 a set of four people or things.

quartz *noun* a hard mineral.

quash *verb* cancel or annul something, *The judges quashed his conviction.*

quasi- (*say* **kwayz**-I) *prefix* seeming to be something but not really so, *a quasi-scientific explanation.*

quatrain *noun* a stanza with four lines.

quaver[1] *verb* tremble; quiver.

quaver[2] *noun* 1 a quavering sound. 2 a note in music lasting half as long as a crotchet.

quay (*say* kee) *noun* a landing-place where ships can be tied up for loading and unloading; a wharf. **quayside** *noun*

queasy *adjective* feeling slightly sick. **queasily** *adverb*, **queasiness** *noun*

queen *noun* 1 a woman who is the ruler of a country through inheriting the position. 2 the wife of a king. 3 a female bee or ant that produces eggs. 4 an important piece in chess. 5 a playing-card with a picture of a queen on it. **queenly** *adjective*
queen mother a king's widow who is the mother of the present king or queen.

queer[1] *adjective* 1 strange; eccentric. 2 slightly ill or faint. **queerly** *adverb*, **queerness** *noun*

queer[2] *verb* **queer a person's pitch** spoil his or her chances beforehand.

quell *verb* suppress; subdue.

quench *verb* 1 satisfy your thirst by drinking. 2 put out a fire or flame.

quern *noun* a hand-operated device for grinding corn or pepper.

querulous (*say* **kwe**-rew-lus) *adjective* complaining peevishly. **querulously** *adverb*

query (*say* **kweer**-ee) *noun* (*plural* **queries**) 1 a question. 2 a question mark.

quest *noun* a search, *the quest for gold.*

question[1] *noun* 1 a sentence asking something. 2 a problem to be discussed or solved, *Parliament debated the question of capital punishment.* 3 doubt, *Whether we shall win is open to question.*
in question being discussed or disputed,

His honesty is not in question.
out of the question impossible.
question mark the punctuation mark (?) placed after a question.

question[2] *verb* 1 ask someone questions. 2 say that you are doubtful about something. **questioner** *noun*

questionable *adjective* causing doubt; not certainly true or honest or advisable.

questionnaire *noun* a list of questions.

queue[1] (*say* kew) *noun* a line of people or vehicles waiting for something.

queue[2] *verb* (**queued, queuing**) wait in a queue.

quibble[1] *noun* a petty objection.

quibble[2] *verb* (**quibbled, quibbling**) make petty objections.

quiche (*say* keesh) *noun* an open tart with a savoury filling.

quick *adjective* 1 taking only a short time to do something. 2 done in a short time, *have a quick swim.* 3 able to notice or learn or think quickly. 4 (*old use*) alive, *the quick and the dead.* **quickly** *adverb*, **quickness** *noun*

quicken *verb* 1 make or become quicker. 2 stimulate; make or become livelier.

quicksand *noun* an area of loose wet sand which is so deep that heavy objects sink into it.

quicksilver *noun* mercury.

quiescent (*say* kwee-**ess**-ent) *adjective* inactive; quiet. **quiescence** *noun*

quiet[1] *adjective* 1 silent, *Be quiet!* 2 with little sound; not loud or noisy. 3 calm; without disturbance; peaceful, *a quiet life.* 4 (of colours) not bright. **quietly** *adverb*, **quietness** *noun*

quiet[2] *noun* quietness.

quieten *verb* make or become quiet.

quiff *noun* an upright tuft of hair.

quill *noun* 1 a large feather. 2 a pen made from a large feather. 3 one of the spines on a porcupine.

quilt[1] *noun* a padded bed-cover.

quilt[2] *verb* line material with padding and fix it with lines of stitching.

quin *noun* a quintuplet.

quince *noun* a hard pear-shaped fruit used for making jam.

quincentenary *noun* the 500th anniversary of something.

quinine (*say* kwin-**een**) *noun* a bittertasting medicine used to cure malaria.

quintessence *noun* 1 the essence of something. 2 a perfect example of a quality, *She is the quintessence of generosity.*

quintet *noun* 1 a group of five musicians. 2 a piece of music for five musicians.

quintuplet *noun* each of five children born to the same mother at one time.

quip *noun* a witty remark.

quirk *noun* 1 a peculiarity of a person's behaviour. 2 a trick of fate.

quit *verb* (**quitted** or **quit, quitting**) 1 leave; abandon. 2 (*informal*) stop doing something. **quitter** *noun*

quite *adverb* 1 completely; entirely, *I am quite all right.* 2 somewhat; rather, *She is quite a good swimmer.* 3 really, *It's quite a change.*

quits *adjective* even or equal after retaliating or paying someone.

quiver[1] *noun* a container for arrows.

quiver[2] *verb* tremble. **quiver** *noun*

quixotic (*say* kwiks-**ot**-ik) *adjective* very chivalrous and unselfish, often to an impractical extent. **quixotically** *adverb*

quiz[1] *noun* (*plural* **quizzes**) a series of questions, especially as an entertainment or competition.

quiz[2] *verb* (**quizzed, quizzing**) question someone closely.

quizzical *adjective* 1 in a questioning way. 2 gently amused. **quizzically** *adverb*

quoit (*say* koit) *noun* a ring thrown at a peg in the game of **quoits**.

quorum *noun* the smallest number of people needed to make a meeting of a committee etc. valid.

quota *noun* 1 a fixed share that must be given or received or done. 2 a limited amount, *a strict import quota.*

quotation *noun* 1 quoting. 2 something quoted. 3 a statement of the price. **quotation marks** inverted commas (see *invert*).

quote *verb* (**quoted, quoting**) 1 repeat words that were first written or spoken by someone else. 2 mention something as proof. 3 state the price of goods or services that you can supply.

quoth *verb* (*old use*) said.

quotient (*say* **kwoh**-shent) *noun* the result of dividing one number by another. (Compare *product.*)

Rr

rabbi (*say* **rab**-I) *noun* (*plural* **rabbis**) a Jewish religious leader.

rabbit *noun* a furry animal with long ears that digs burrows.

rabble *noun* a disorderly crowd; a mob.

rabid (*say* **rab**-id) *adjective* 1 fanatical, *a rabid tennis fan.* 2 suffering from rabies.

rabies (*say* **ray**-beez) *noun* a fatal disease that affects dogs, cats, etc. and can infect people.

race[1] *noun* 1 a competition to be the first to reach a particular place or to do something. 2 a strong fast current of water, *the tidal race.*

race[2] *verb* (**raced, racing**) 1 compete in a race. 2 move very fast. **racer** *noun*

race[3] *noun* a very large group of people thought to have the same ancestors and with physical characteristics (e.g. colour of skin and hair, shape of eyes and nose) that differ from those of other groups. **racial** *adjective*

race relations relationships between people of different races in the same country.

racecourse *noun* a place where horse-races are run.

racialism (*say* **ray**-shal-izm) *noun* racism. **racialist** *noun*

racism (*say* **ray**-sizm) *noun* 1 belief that a particular race of people is better than others. 2 hostility towards people of other races. **racist** *noun*

rack[1] *noun* 1 a framework used as a shelf or container. 2 a bar or rail with cogs into which the cogs of a gear or wheel etc. fit. 3 an ancient device for torturing people by stretching them.

rack[2] *verb* torment, *He was racked with pain.*
rack your brains think hard in trying to solve a problem.

rack[3] *noun* destruction, *The place has gone to rack and ruin.*

racket[1] *noun* a bat with strings stretched across a frame, used in tennis and similar games.

racket[2] *noun* 1 a loud noise; a din. 2 a dishonest business; a swindle, *a drugs racket.*

racketeer *noun* a person involved in a dishonest business. **racketeering** *noun*

racoon *noun* an American animal with a bushy tail.

racy *adjective* lively in style, *She gave a racy account of her travels.*

radar *noun* a system or apparatus that uses radio waves to show on a screen etc. the position of objects that cannot be seen because of darkness, fog, distance, etc.

radial *adjective* 1 of rays or radii. 2 having spokes or lines that radiate from a central point. **radially** *adverb*

radiant *adjective* 1 radiating light or heat etc.; radiated. 2 looking very bright and happy. **radiantly** *adverb*, **radiance** *noun*
radiant energy energy transmitted by radiation.

radiate *verb* (**radiated, radiating**) 1 send out light, heat, or other energy in rays. 2 spread out from a central point like the spokes of a wheel.

radiation *noun* 1 the process of radiating. 2 light, heat, or other energy radiated. 3 radioactivity.

radiator *noun* 1 a device that gives out heat, especially a metal case that is heated electrically or through which steam or hot water flows. 2 a device that cools the engine of a motor vehicle.

radical[1] *adjective* 1 basic; thorough, *radical changes.* 2 wanting to make great reforms, *a radical politician.* **radically** *adverb*

radical[2] *noun* a person who wants to make great reforms.

radicle *noun* a root that forms in the seed of a plant.

radio *noun* (*plural* **radios**) 1 the process of sending and receiving sound or pictures by means of electromagnetic waves without a connecting wire, *radio signals.* 2 an apparatus for receiving sound (a *receiver*) or sending it out (a *transmitter*) in this way. 3 sound-broadcasting, *community radio.*

radio- *prefix* 1 of rays or radiation. 2 of radio.

radioactive *adjective* having atoms that break up and send out radiation which produces electrical and chemical effects and penetrates things. **radioactivity** *noun*

radiography *noun* the production of X-ray photographs. **radiographer** *noun*

radiology *noun* the study of X-rays and similar radiation. **radiologist** *noun*

radish *noun* (*plural* **radishes**) a small hard round red vegetable, eaten raw in salads.

radium *noun* a radioactive substance found in pitchblende.

radius *noun* (*plural* **radii**) 1 a straight line from the centre of a circle or sphere to the circumference; the length of this line. 2 a range or distance from a central point, *The school takes pupils living within a radius of ten kilometres.*

raffia *noun* soft fibre from the leaves of a kind of palm-tree.

raffish *adjective* looking disreputable.

raffle[1] *noun* a kind of lottery, usually to raise money for a charity.

raffle[2] *verb* (**raffled, raffling**) offer something as a prize in a raffle.

raft *noun* a flat floating structure made of wood etc., used as a boat.

rafter *noun* any of the long sloping pieces of wood that hold up a roof.

rag[1] *noun* 1 an old or torn piece of cloth. 2 a piece of ragtime music.
rag trade (*informal*) the clothing business.

rag[2] *noun* a carnival held by students to collect money for charity.

rag[3] *verb* (**ragged, ragging**) (*informal*) tease.

ragamuffin *noun* a person in ragged dirty clothes.

rage[1] *noun* 1 great or violent anger. 2 a craze, *Skateboarding was all the rage.*

rage[2] *verb* (**raged, raging**) 1 be very angry.

2 be violent or noisy, *A storm was raging.*

ragged *adjective* **1** torn or frayed.
2 wearing torn clothes. **3** jagged. **4** irregular; uneven, *a ragged performance.*

ragtime *noun* a kind of jazz music.

raid¹ *noun* **1** a sudden attack. **2** a surprise visit by police etc. to arrest people or seize illegal goods.

raid² *verb* make a raid on a place. **raider** *noun*

rail¹ *noun* **1** a level or sloping bar for hanging things on or forming part of a fence, banisters, etc. **2** a long metal bar forming part of a railway track.
by rail on a train.

rail² *verb* protest angrily.

railings *plural noun* a fence made of metal bars.

railway *noun* **1** the parallel metal bars that trains travel on. **2** a system of transport using rails.

raiment *noun* (*old use*) clothing.

rain¹ *noun* drops of water that fall from the sky. **rainy** *adjective*

rain² *verb* **1** fall as rain or like rain. **2** send down like rain, *They rained blows on him.*

rainbow *noun* a curved band of colours seen in the sky when the sun shines through rain.

raincoat *noun* a waterproof coat.

raindrop *noun* a single drop of rain.

rainfall *noun* the amount of rain that falls in a particular place or time.

rainforest *noun* a dense tropical forest that has high rainfall throughout the year.

raise *verb* (**raised, raising**) **1** move something to a higher place or an upright position. **2** increase the amount or level of something. **3** collect; manage to obtain, *They raised R200 for the SPCA.* **4** bring up young children or animals, *raise a family.* **5** rouse; cause, *She raised a laugh with her joke.* **6** put forward, *We raised objections.* **7** end a siege.

raisin *noun* a dried grape.

raj (*say* rahj) *noun* the period of Indian history when the country was ruled by Britain.

rajah *noun* an Indian king or prince. (Compare *ranee.*)

rake¹ *noun* a gardening tool with a row of short spikes fixed to a long handle.

rake² *verb* (**raked, raking**) **1** gather or smooth with a rake. **2** search. **3** gather; collect, *raking it in.*
rake up collect; remind people of an old scandal etc., *Don't rake that up.*

rake³ *noun* a man who lives an irresponsible and immoral life.

rakish (*say* ray-kish) *adjective* like a rake (= *rake³*); jaunty.

rally¹ *noun* (*plural* **rallies**) **1** a large meeting to support something or share an interest. **2** a competition to test skill in driving, *the Dakar Rally.* **3** a series of strokes in tennis before a point is scored.
4 a recovery.

rally² *verb* (**rallied, rallying**) **1** bring or come together for a united effort, *They rallied support. People rallied round.*
2 revive; recover strength.

RAM *abbreviation* random-access memory (in a computer), with contents that can be retrieved or stored directly without having to read through items already stored.

ram¹ *noun* **1** a male sheep. **2** a device for ramming things.

ram² *verb* (**rammed, ramming**) push one thing hard against another.

Ramadan (also **Ramadaan**) *noun* the ninth month of the Muslim year, when Muslims fast between sunrise and sunset.

ramble¹ *noun* a long walk in the country.

ramble² *verb* (**rambled, rambling**) **1** go for a ramble; wander. **2** talk or write a lot without keeping to the subject, *a rambling account of the plot.* **rambler** *noun*

ramifications *plural noun* **1** the branches of a structure. **2** the many effects of a plan or action, *Budget cuts will have widespread ramifications.*

ramkietjie (*say* ram-kee-kee) *noun* a home-made guitar, often made out of a tin can and wire.

ramp¹ *noun* a slope joining two different levels.

ramp² *noun* a swindle.

rampage *verb* (**rampaged, rampaging**) rush about wildly or destructively. **rampage** *noun*

rampant *adjective* **1** growing or increasing unrestrained, *Disease was rampant in the poorer districts.* **2** (of an animal on coats of arms) standing upright on a hind leg, *a lion rampant.*

rampart *noun* a wide bank of earth built as a fortification; a wall on top of this.

ramrod *noun* a straight rod formerly used for ramming an explosive into a gun.

ramshackle *adjective* badly made and rickety, *a ramshackle hut.*

ranch *noun* (*plural* **ranches**) a large cattle-farm in America.

rancid *adjective* smelling or tasting unpleasant like stale fat.

rancour (*say* **rank**-er) *noun* bitter resentment or ill will. **rancorous** *adjective*

Rand *noun* the most important gold-mining area of Gauteng.

rand *noun* a unit of money (= 100 cents).

random[1] *noun* **at random** using no particular order or method, *In bingo, numbers are chosen at random.*

random[2] *adjective* done or taken at random, *a random sample.*

ranee (*say* **rah**-nee) *noun* a rajah's wife or widow.

range[1] *noun* **1** a line or series of things, *a range of mountains.* **2** the limits between which things exist or are available; an extent, *a wide range of goods.* **3** the distance that a gun can shoot, an aircraft can travel, a sound can be heard, etc. **4** a place with targets for shooting-practice. **5** a large open area of grazing-land or hunting-ground. **6** a kitchen fireplace with ovens.

range[2] *verb* (**ranged, ranging**) **1** exist between two limits; extend, *Prices ranged from R1 to R50.* **2** arrange. **3** move over a wide area; wander, *Elephants ranged across the southern areas.*

ranger *noun* someone who looks after or patrols a park, forest, etc.

rank[1] *noun* **1** a position in a series of different levels, *He holds the rank of sergeant.* **2** a place where taxis stand to await customers. **3** a line of people or things.
the rank and file ordinary people.

rank[2] *verb* **1** arrange in a rank or ranks. **2** have a certain rank or place, *She ranks among the greatest novelists.*

rank[3] *adjective* **1** growing too thickly and coarsely. **2** smelling very unpleasant. **3** unmistakably bad, *rank injustice.* **rankly** *adverb*, **rankness** *noun*

rankle *verb* (**rankled, rankling**) cause lasting annoyance or resentment.

ransack *verb* **1** search thoroughly or roughly. **2** rob or pillage a place.

ransom[1] *noun* money that has to be paid for a prisoner to be set free.
hold to ransom hold someone captive or in your power and demand ransom.

ransom[2] *verb* **1** free someone by paying a ransom. **2** get a ransom for someone.

rant *verb* speak loudly and violently.

rap[1] *verb* (**rapped, rapping**) **1** knock loudly. **2** (*informal*) reprimand. **3** (*informal*) chat. **4** speak rhymes with a backing of rock music.

rap[2] *noun* **1** a rapping movement or sound. **2** (*informal*) blame; punishment, *take the rap.* **3** (*informal*) a chat. **4** rhymes spoken with a backing of rock music.

rapacious (*say* ra-**pay**-shus) *adjective* greedy; plundering. **rapaciously** *adverb*, **rapacity** *noun*

rape[1] *noun* the act of having sexual intercourse with a person without her or his consent.

rape[2] *verb* (**raped, raping**) commit rape on a person. **rapist** *noun*

rape[3] *noun* a plant grown as food for farm animals and for its seed from which oil is obtained.

rapid *adjective* quick; swift. **rapidly** *adverb*, **rapidity** *noun*

rapids *plural noun* part of a river where the water flows very quickly.

rapier *noun* a thin lightweight sword.

rapport (*say* ra-**por**) *noun* a close relationship in which people communicate well and understand each other.

rapt *adjective* very intent and absorbed; enraptured. **raptly** *adverb*

rapture *noun* very great delight.
rapturous *adjective*, **rapturously** *adverb*

rare *adjective* **1** unusual; not often found

or happening. 2 (of air) thin; below normal pressure. **rarely** *adverb*, **rareness** *noun*, **rarity** *noun*

rarefied *adjective* 1 (of air) thin; rare. 2 (of an idea etc.) very subtle.

rascal *noun* a dishonest or mischievous person; a rogue. **rascally** *adjective*

rash[1] *adjective* doing something or done without thinking of the possible risks or effects, *a rash decision*. **rashly** *adverb*, **rashness** *noun*

rash[2] *noun* (*plural* **rashes**) an outbreak of spots or patches on the skin.

rasher *noun* a slice of bacon.

rasp[1] *noun* 1 a file with sharp points on its surface. 2 a rough grating sound.

rasp[2] *verb* 1 scrape roughly. 2 make a rough grating sound or effect.

raspberry *noun* (*plural* **raspberries**) a small soft red fruit.

Rastafarian *noun* a member of a religious group that started in Jamaica.

rat *noun* 1 an animal like a large mouse. 2 an unpleasant or treacherous person. **rat race** a continuous struggle for success in a career, business, etc.

ratchet *noun* a row of notches on a bar or wheel in which a device (a *pawl*) catches to prevent it running backwards.

rate[1] *noun* 1 speed, *The train travelled at a great rate.* 2 a measure of cost, value, etc., *Postage rates went up.* 3 quality; standard, *first-rate.* 4 a tax paid by businesses and householders to the local authority, calculated on the value of land and buildings occupied.
at any rate anyway.

rate[2] *verb* (**rated, rating**) 1 put a value on something. 2 regard as, *He rated me among his friends.*

ratel (*say* **rah**-til) *noun* a kind of animal like a badger.

rather *adverb* 1 slightly; somewhat, *It's rather dark.* 2 more willingly; preferably, *I would rather not go.* 3 more exactly, *He is lazy rather than stupid.*

ratify *verb* (**ratified, ratifying**) confirm or agree to something officially, *They ratified the treaty.* **ratification** *noun*

rating *noun* 1 the way something is rated.

2 a sailor who is not an officer.

ratio (*say* **ray**-shee-oh) *noun* (*plural* **ratios**) 1 the relationship between two numbers, given by the quotient, *The ratio of 2 to 10 = 2:10 = $^2/_{10}$ = $^1/_5$.* 2 proportion, *Mix flour and butter in the ratio of two to one* (= two measures of flour to one measure of butter).

ration[1] *noun* an amount allowed to one person.

ration[2] *verb* share something out in fixed amounts.

rational *adjective* 1 reasonable; sane. 2 able to reason, *Plants are not rational.* **rationally** *adverb*, **rationality** *noun*

rationalize *verb* (**rationalized, rationalizing**) 1 make a thing logical and consistent, *Attempts to rationalize English spelling have failed.* 2 invent a reasonable explanation of something, *She rationalized her meanness by calling it economy.* 3 make an industry etc. more efficient by reorganizing it. **rationalization** *noun*

rattle[1] *verb* (**rattled, rattling**) 1 make a series of short sharp hard sounds. 2 say something quickly, *She rattled off the poem.* 3 (*informal*) make a person nervous or flustered.

rattle[2] *noun* 1 a rattling sound. 2 a device or baby's toy that rattles.

rattlesnake *noun* a poisonous American snake with a tail that rattles.

rattling *adjective* 1 that rattles. 2 vigorous; brisk, *a rattling pace.*

ratty *adjective* (*informal*) bad-tempered.

raucous (*say* **raw**-kus) *adjective* loud and harsh, *a raucous voice.*

ravage *verb* (**ravaged, ravaging**) do great damage to something; devastate. **ravages** *plural noun*

rave *verb* (**raved, raving**) 1 talk wildly or angrily or madly. 2 talk rapturously about something, *She raved about the concert.* **rave** *noun*

ravel *verb* (**ravelled, ravelling**) tangle.

raven *noun* a large black bird with a hoarse cry.

ravenous *adjective* very hungry. **ravenously** *adverb*

ravine (*say* ra-**veen**) *noun* a deep narrow gorge or valley.

ravish *verb* **1** (*old use*) rape. **2** enrapture.

ravishing *adjective* very beautiful.

raw *adjective* **1** not cooked. **2** in the natural state; not yet processed, *raw materials.* **3** without experience, *raw recruits.* **4** with the skin removed, *a raw wound.* **5** cold and damp, *a raw morning.* **rawness** *noun*

raw deal (*informal*) unfair treatment.

ray[1] *noun* **1** a thin line of light, heat, or other radiation. **2** each of a set of lines or parts extending from a centre.

ray[2] *noun* a large sea-fish.

rayon *noun* a synthetic fibre or cloth made from cellulose.

raze *verb* (**razed, razing**) destroy a building or town completely, *raze it to the ground.*

razor *noun* a device with a very sharp blade, especially one used for shaving.

razzmatazz *noun* (*informal*) showy publicity.

RC *abbreviation* Roman Catholic.

re- *prefix* **1** again (as in *rebuild*). **2** back again, to an earlier condition (as in *reopen*). **3** in return; to each other (as in *react*). **4** against (as in *rebel*). **5** away or down (as in *recede*).

reach[1] *verb* **1** go as far as; arrive at a place or thing. **2** stretch out your hand to get or touch something. **reachable** *adjective*

reach[2] *noun* (*plural* **reaches**) **1** the distance a person or thing can reach. **2** a distance you can easily travel, *We live within reach of the sea.* **3** a straight stretch of a river or canal.

react *verb* have a reaction.

reaction *noun* **1** an effect or feeling etc. produced in one person or thing by another. **2** a chemical change caused when substances act upon each other.

reactionary *adjective* opposed to progress or reform.

reactor *noun* an apparatus for producing nuclear power in a controlled way.

read *verb* (**read** (*say as* red), **reading**) **1** look at something written or printed and understand it or say it aloud. **2** (of a computer) copy, search, or extract data. **3** indicate; register, *The thermometer reads 20° Celsius.* **readable** *adjective*

reader *noun* **1** a person who reads.

2 a book that helps you learn to read.

readily (*say* red-il-ee) *adverb* **1** willingly. **2** easily; without any difficulty.

ready[1] *adjective* (**readier, readiest**) able or willing to do something or be used immediately; prepared. **readiness** *noun*

at the ready ready for use or action.

ready[2] *adverb* beforehand, *This meat is ready cooked.* **ready-made** *adjective*

real *adjective* **1** existing; true; not imaginary. **2** genuine; not an imitation, *real pearls.*

realism *noun* seeing or showing things as they really are. **realist** *noun*, **realistic** *adjective*, **realistically** *adverb*

reality *noun* (*plural* **realities**) what is real; something real.

realize *verb* (**realized, realizing**) **1** be fully aware of something; accept something as true. **2** make a hope or plan etc. happen, *She realized her ambition to become a racing driver.* **3** obtain money in exchange for something by selling it, *How much did you realize on those paintings?* **realization** *noun*

really *adverb* truly; certainly; in fact.

realm (*say* relm) *noun* **1** a kingdom. **2** an area of knowledge, interest, etc., *in the realms of science.*

ream *noun* 500 (originally 480) sheets of paper.

reams *plural noun* a large quantity of writing or paper.

reap *verb* **1** cut down and gather corn when it is ripe. **2** obtain as the result of something done, *They reaped great benefit from their training.* **reaper** *noun*

reappear *verb* appear again.

rear[1] *noun* the back part, *the rear of the house.*

rear[2] *adjective* placed at the rear.

rear[3] *verb* **1** bring up young children or animals. **2** raise itself on hind legs, *The horse reared in fright.* **3** raise one's head, *The cobra reared its hood.*

rearguard *noun* troops protecting the rear of an army.

rearrange *verb* (**rearranged, rearranging**) arrange in a different way or order. **rearrangement** *noun*

reason[1] *noun* **1** a cause or explanation of

something. **2** reasoning; common sense, *Listen to reason.*

● USAGE: Do not use the phrase *the reason is* with the word *because* (which means the same thing). Correct usage is *We cannot come. The reason is that we both have flu* (not 'The reason is because . . .').

reason² *verb* **1** use your ability to think and draw conclusions. **2** try to persuade someone by giving reasons, *We reasoned with the rebels.*

reasonable *adjective* **1** ready to use or listen to reason; sensible; logical. **2** fair; moderate; not expensive, *reasonable prices.* **reasonably** *adverb*

reassure *verb* (**reassured, reassuring**) restore someone's confidence by removing doubts and fears. **reassurance** *noun*

rebate *noun* a reduction in the amount to be paid; a partial refund.

rebel¹ (*say* rib-el) *verb* (**rebelled, rebelling**) refuse to obey someone in authority, especially the government; fight against the rulers of your own country.

rebel² (*say* reb-el) *noun* someone who rebels. **rebellion** *noun*, **rebellious** *adjective*

rebirth *noun* a return to life or activity; a revival of something.

rebound *verb* bounce back after hitting something. **rebound** *noun*

rebuff *noun* an unkind refusal; a snub. **rebuff** *verb*

rebuild *verb* (**rebuilt, rebuilding**) build something again after it has been destroyed.

rebuke *verb* (**rebuked, rebuking**) speak severely to a person who has done wrong. **rebuke** *noun*

rebut *verb* (**rebutted, rebutting**) refute; disprove. **rebuttal** *noun*

recalcitrant *adjective* disobedient. **recalcitrance** *noun*

recall¹ *verb* **1** ask a person to come back. **2** bring back into the mind; remember.

recall² *noun* recalling.

recant *verb* withdraw something you have said. **recantation** *noun*

recap *verb* (**recapped, recapping**) (*informal*) recapitulate. **recap** *noun*

recapitulate *verb* (**recapitulated, recapitulating**) state again the main points of what has been said. **recapitulation** *noun*

recapture *verb* (**recaptured, recapturing**) capture again; recover. **recapture** *noun*

recede *verb* (**receded, receding**) go back from a certain point, *The floods receded.*

receipt (*say* ris-eet) *noun* **1** a written statement that money has been paid or something has been received. **2** receiving something.

receive *verb* (**received, receiving**) **1** take or get something that is given or sent. **2** greet someone who comes, *The princess was received by the Premier.*

receiver *noun* **1** a person or thing that receives something. **2** a person who buys and sells stolen goods. **3** an official who takes charge of a bankrupt person's property. **4** a radio or television set that receives broadcasts. **5** the part of a telephone that receives the sound and is held to a person's ear.

recent *adjective* not long past; happening or made a short time ago. **recently** *adverb*, **recency** *noun*

receptacle *noun* something for holding or containing what is put into it.

reception *noun* **1** the way a person or thing is received. **2** a formal party to receive guests, *a wedding reception.* **3** a place in a hotel or office etc. where visitors are received and registered.

receptionist *noun* a person whose job is to receive and direct visitors, patients, etc.

receptive *adjective* quick or willing to receive ideas etc.

recess (*say* ris-ess) *noun* (*plural* **recesses**) **1** an alcove. **2** a time when work or business is stopped for a while.

recession *noun* **1** receding from a point. **2** a reduction in trade or prosperity.

recharge *verb* (**recharged, recharging**) charge again. **rechargeable** *adjective*

recipe (*say* ress-ip-ee) *noun* instructions for preparing or cooking food.

recipient *noun* a person who receives something.

reciprocal¹ (*say* ris-ip-rok-al) *adjective* given and received; mutual, *reciprocal help.*

reciprocally *adverb*, **reciprocity** *noun*

reciprocal[2] *noun* a reversed fraction, $^3/_2$ is the reciprocal of $^2/_3$.

reciprocate *verb* (**reciprocated, reciprocating**) give and receive; do the same thing in return, *She did not reciprocate his love*. **reciprocation** *noun*

recital *noun* 1 reciting something. 2 a musical entertainment given by one performer or group.

recitative (*say* res-it-a-**teev**) *noun* a speech sung to music in an oratorio or opera.

recite *verb* (**recited, reciting**) say a poem etc. aloud from memory. **recitation** *noun*

reckless *adjective* rash; heedless. **recklessly** *adverb*, **recklessness** *noun*

reckon *verb* 1 calculate; count up. 2 have as an opinion; feel confident, *I reckon we shall win*.

reclaim *verb* 1 claim or get something back. 2 make a thing usable again, *reclaimed land*. **reclamation** *noun*

recline *verb* (**reclined, reclining**) lean or lie back.

recluse *noun* a person who lives alone and avoids mixing with people.

recognize *verb* (**recognized, recognizing**) 1 know who someone is or what something is because you have seen that person or thing before. 2 realize, *We recognize the truth of what you said*. 3 accept something as genuine, welcome, or lawful etc., *Nine countries recognized the island's new government*. **recognition** *noun*, **recognizable** *adjective*

recollect *verb* remember. **recollection** *noun*

recommend *verb* say that a person or thing would be a good one to do a job or achieve something. **recommendation** *noun*

recompense *verb* (**recompensed, recompensing**) repay or reward someone; compensate. **recompense** *noun*

reconcile *verb* (**reconciled, reconciling**) 1 make people who have quarrelled become friendly again. 2 persuade a person to put up with something, *Making friends reconciled her to the new school*. 3 make

things agree, *I cannot reconcile what you say with what you do*. **reconciliation** *noun*

recondition *verb* overhaul and repair.

reconnaissance (*say* rik-**on**-i-sans) *noun* an exploration of an area, especially in order to gather information about it for military purposes.

reconnoitre *verb* (**reconnoitred, reconnoitring**) make a reconnaissance of an area.

reconsider *verb* consider something again and perhaps change an earlier decision. **reconsideration** *noun*

reconstitute *verb* (**reconstituted, reconstituting**) put together again; reconstruct; reorganize.

reconstruct *verb* 1 construct or build something again. 2 create or act past events again, *Police reconstructed the robbery*. **reconstruction** *noun*

record[1] (*say* **rek**-ord) *noun* 1 information kept in a permanent form, e.g. written or printed. 2 a disc on which sound has been recorded. 3 facts known about a person's past life or career etc., *She has a good school record*. 4 the best performance in a sport etc., or the most remarkable event of its kind, *He holds the record for the high jump*.

record[2] (*say* rik-**ord**) *verb* 1 put something down in writing or other permanent form. 2 store sounds or scenes (e.g. television pictures) on a disc or tape etc. so that you can play or show them later.

recorder *noun* 1 a kind of flute held downwards from the player's mouth. 2 a person or thing that records something.

record-player *noun* a device for reproducing sound from records.

recount *verb* give an account of, *We recounted our adventures*.

re-count *verb* count something again.

recoup (*say* ri-**koop**) *verb* recover the cost of an investment etc. or of a loss.
● USAGE: Note that this word does not mean *recuperate*.

recourse *noun* a source of help.
have recourse to go to a person or thing for help.

recover *verb* 1 get something back again after losing it; regain. 2 get well again after being ill or weak. **recovery** *noun*

recreation *noun* **1** refreshing your mind or body after work through an enjoyable pastime. **2** a game or hobby etc. that is an enjoyable pastime. **recreational** *adjective*

recrimination *noun* an angry retort or accusation made against a person who has criticized or blamed you.

recrudescence (*say* rek-roo-**dess**-ens) *noun* a fresh outbreak of a disease or trouble etc.

recruit[1] *noun* **1** a person who has just joined the armed forces. **2** a new member of a society or group etc.

recruit[2] *verb* enlist recruits. **recruitment** *noun*

rectangle *noun* a shape with four sides and four right angles. **rectangular** *adjective*

rectify *verb* (**rectified, rectifying**) correct or put something right. **rectification** *noun*

rectilinear *adjective* with straight lines, *Squares and triangles are rectilinear figures.*

rectitude *noun* moral goodness; rightness of behaviour or procedure.

rector *noun* **1** a member of the clergy in charge of a parish. **2** the head of some universities, colleges, etc.

rectory *noun* (*plural* **rectories**) the house of a rector.

rectum *noun* the last part of the large intestine, ending at the anus.

recumbent *adjective* lying down.

recuperate *verb* (**recuperated, recuperating**) get better after an illness. **recuperation** *noun*

recur *verb* (**recurred, recurring**) happen again; keep on happening. **recurrent** *adjective*, **recurrence** *noun*

recycle *verb* (**recycled, recycling**) convert waste material into a form in which it can be reused.

red[1] *adjective* (**redder, reddest**) **1** of the colour of blood or a colour rather like this. **2** of Communists or socialists; favouring Communism or socialism. **redness** *noun*
red herring something that draws attention away from the main subject; a misleading clue.
red tape use of too many rules and forms in official business.

red[2] *noun* **1** red colour. **2** a Communist or socialist.
in the red in debt (debts were entered in red in account-books).

redden *verb* make or become red.

reddish *adjective* rather red.

redeem *verb* **1** buy something back; pay off a debt. **2** save a person from damnation, *Christians believe that Christ redeemed us all.* **3** make up for faults, *His one redeeming feature is his kindness.* **redeemer** *noun*, **redemption** *noun*

redevelop *verb* (**redeveloped, redeveloping**) develop land etc. in a different way. **redevelopment** *noun*

red-handed *adjective* while actually committing a crime, *She was caught red-handed.*

redhead *noun* a person with reddish hair.

redolent (*say* red-ol-ent) *adjective* **1** having a strong smell, *redolent of onions.* **2** full of memories, *a castle redolent of romance.*

redoubtable *adjective* formidable.

redound *verb* come back as an advantage or disadvantage, *This will redound to our credit.*

redress[1] *verb* set right; rectify, *redress the balance.*

redress[2] *noun* redressing; compensation, *You should seek redress for this damage.*

reduce *verb* (**reduced, reducing**) **1** make or become smaller or less. **2** force someone into a condition or situation, *He was reduced to borrowing the money.* **reduction** *noun*

redundant *adjective* not needed, especially for a particular job. **redundancy** *noun*

reebok *noun* a small antelope, either red or grey.

re-echo *verb* (**re-echoed, re-echoing**) echo; go on echoing.

reed *noun* **1** a tall plant that grows in water or marshy ground. **2** a thin strip that vibrates to make the sound in a clarinet, saxophone, oboe, etc.

reedy *adjective* **1** full of reeds. **2** (of a voice) having a thin high tone like a reed instrument. **reediness** *noun*

reef[1] *noun* **1** a ridge of rock or sand etc.,

especially one near the surface of the sea.
2 a vein of metal ore; the bedrock around
this.
the Reef the urban and industrial area
of gold-mining around Johannesburg.
reef² *verb* shorten a sail by drawing in a
strip (called a *reef*) at the top or bottom to
reduce the area exposed to the wind.
reef-knot *noun* a symmetrical double knot
that is very secure.
reek *verb* smell strongly or unpleasantly.
reek *noun*
reel¹ *noun* **1** a long or round object on
which thread, wire, camera film, etc. is
wound. **2** the thread, wire, film, etc. wound
round this, *a reel of film.*
reel² *verb* **1** wind something on to or off
a reel. **2** stagger.
reel off say something quickly.
re-elect *verb* elect again.
re-enter *verb* enter again.
re-examine *verb* examine again.
ref *noun* (*informal*) a referee.
refectory *noun* (*plural* **refectories**) the
dining-room of a monastery etc.
refer *verb* (**referred, referring**) pass a
problem etc. to someone else, *My doctor
referred me to a specialist.* **referral** *noun*
refer to mention; speak about, *I wasn't
referring to you;* look in a book etc. for
information, *We referred to our dictionary.*
referee¹ *noun* someone appointed to see
that people keep to the rules of a game.
referee² *verb* (**refereed, refereeing**) act as
a referee; umpire.
reference *noun* **1** referring to something,
There was no reference to recent events.
2 a direction to a book or page or file
etc. where information can be found.
3 a testimonial.
in or **with reference to** concerning; about.
reference book a book (such as a dictionary
or encyclopaedia) that gives information
systematically.
reference library a library where books can
be used but not taken away.
referendum *noun* (*plural* **referendums**)
voting by all the people of a country (not by
Parliament) to decide whether something
shall be done. It is also called a *plebiscite.*

refill *verb* fill again. **refill** *noun*
refine *verb* (**refined, refining**) **1** purify.
2 improve something, especially by making
small changes.
refined *adjective* **1** purified, *refined sugar.*
2 cultured; with good manners.
refinement *noun* **1** the action of refining.
2 being refined. **3** something added to
improve a thing, *editorial refinements.*
refinery *noun* (*plural* **refineries**) a factory
for refining something, *an oil refinery.*
reflect *verb* **1** send back light, heat, or
sound etc. from a surface. **2** form an image
of something as a mirror does. **3** think
something over; consider. **4** be influenced
by something, *Prices reflect the cost of
producing things.* **reflection** *noun,*
reflective *adjective,* **reflector** *noun*
reflex *noun* (*plural* **reflexes**) a movement
or action done without any conscious
thought.
reflex angle an angle of more than 180°.
reflexive *adjective* referring back.
reflexive pronoun any of the pronouns
myself, herself, himself, etc. (as in 'She cut
herself'), which refer back to the subject of
the verb.
reflexive verb a verb where the subject and
the object are the same person or thing, as
in 'She *cut herself*', 'The cat *washed itself*'.
reform¹ *verb* make or become better by
removing faults. **reformer** *noun,* **reform-
ative** *adjective,* **reformatory** *adjective*
reform² *noun* **1** reforming. **2** a change
made in order to improve something.
reformation *noun* reforming.
the Reformation a religious movement
in Europe in the 16th century to reform
certain teachings and practices of the
Church, which resulted in the establishment of the Reformed or Protestant
Churches.
refract *verb* bend a ray of light at the point
where it enters water or glass etc. at an
angle. **refraction** *noun,* **refractor** *noun,*
refractive *adjective*
refractory *adjective* **1** difficult to control;
stubborn. **2** (of substances) resistant to heat.
refrain¹ *verb* stop yourself from doing
something, *Refrain from talking.*

refrain[2] *noun* the chorus of a song.

refresh *verb* make a tired person etc. feel fresh and strong again.

refreshment *noun* refreshing.
refreshments *plural noun* drinks and snacks.

refrigerate *verb* (**refrigerated, refrigerating**) make a thing extremely cold, especially in order to preserve it and keep it fresh.
refrigeration *noun*

refrigerator *noun* a cabinet or room in which food is stored at a very low temperature.

refuel *verb* (**refuelled, refuelling**) supply a ship or aircraft with more fuel.

refuge *noun* a place where a person is safe from pursuit or danger.

refugee *noun* a person who has had to leave home and seek refuge somewhere, e.g. because of war or persecution or famine.

refund[1] *verb* pay money back.

refund[2] *noun* money paid back.

refurbish *verb* freshen something up; redecorate.

refuse[1] (*say* ri-**fewz**) *verb* (**refused, refusing**) say that you are unwilling to do or give or accept something. **refusal** *noun*

refuse[2] (*say* **ref**-yooss) *noun* waste material, *Trucks collected the refuse.*

refute *verb* (**refuted, refuting**) prove that a person or statement etc. is wrong.
refutation *noun*
  ● USAGE: This word is sometimes used incorrectly as if it meant 'reject' or 'say that something is not true'.

regain *verb* **1** get something back after losing it. **2** reach a place again.

regal (*say* **ree**-gal) *adjective* of or by a monarch; fit for a king or queen.

regale (*say* rig-**ayl**) *verb* (**regaled, regaling**) feed or entertain well, *They regaled us with stories.*

regalia *plural noun* the emblems of royalty or rank, *The royal regalia include the crown, sceptre, and orb.*

regard[1] *verb* **1** look or gaze at. **2** think of in a certain way; consider to be, *We regard the matter as serious.*

regard[2] *noun* **1** a gaze. **2** consideration; heed, *You acted without regard to people's* safety. **3** respect, *We have a great regard for her.*

regards *plural noun* kind wishes sent in a message, *Give him my regards.*
with regard to concerning.

regarding *preposition* concerning, *There are laws regarding drugs.*

regardless *adverb* without considering something, *Do it, regardless of the cost.*

regatta *noun* a meeting for boat or yacht races.

regency *noun* being a regent.

regenerate *verb* (**regenerated, regenerating**) give new life or strength to something. **regeneration** *noun*

regent *noun* a person appointed to rule a country while the monarch is too young or unable to rule.

reggae (*say* **reg**-ay) *noun* a West Indian style of music with a strong beat.

regime (*say* ray-**zheem**) *noun* a system of government or organization, *a military regime.*

regiment *noun* an army unit, usually divided into battalions or companies.
regimental *adjective*

region *noun* an area; a part of a country or of the world, *in tropical regions.* **regional** *adjective*, **regionally** *adverb*
in the region of near, *The cost will be in the region of R100.*

register[1] *noun* **1** an official list of things or names etc. **2** a book in which information about school attendances is recorded. **3** a device that records the amount of something automatically, *a cash register.* **4** the range of a voice or musical instrument.

register office an office where marriages are performed and records of births, marriages, and deaths are kept.

register[2] *verb* **1** list something in a register. **2** indicate; show, *The thermometer registered 100°.* **3** make an impression on someone's mind, *Her warning didn't seem to register with you at all.* **4** pay extra for a letter or parcel to be sent with special care.
registration *noun*

registrar *noun* an official whose job is to keep written records or registers.

registry *noun* (*plural* **registries**) a place where registers are kept.

registry office (*informal*) a register office.

regression *noun* 1 a backward movement. 2 reversion; returning to an earlier condition. **regressive** *adjective*

regret[1] *noun* a feeling of sorrow or disappointment about something that has happened or been done. **regretful** *adjective,* **regretfully** *adverb*

regret[2] *verb* (**regretted, regretting**) feel regret about something. **regrettable** *adjective,* **regrettably** *adverb*

regular *adjective* 1 always happening or doing something at certain times. 2 even; symmetrical, *regular teeth.* 3 normal; standard; correct, *the regular procedure.* 4 of a country's permanent armed services, *a regular soldier.* **regularly** *adverb,* **regularity** *noun*

regulate *verb* (**regulated, regulating**) 1 adjust. 2 control, *Council attempts to regulate informal trading have failed.* **regulator** *noun*

regulation *noun* 1 regulating. 2 a rule or law.

regurgitate *verb* (**regurgitated, regurgitating**) bring swallowed food up again into the mouth. **regurgitation** *noun*

rehabilitation *noun* restoring a person to a normal life or a building etc. to a good condition. **rehabilitate** *verb*

rehash *verb* (*informal*) repeat something without changing it very much.

rehearse *verb* (**rehearsed, rehearsing**) practice something before performing to an audience. **rehearsal** *noun*

reign[1] *verb* 1 rule a country as king or queen. 2 be supreme; be the strongest influence, *Silence reigned.*

reign[2] *noun* the time when someone reigns, *the reign of Shaka.*

reimburse *verb* (**reimbursed, reimbursing**) repay. **reimbursement** *noun*

rein *noun* a strap used to guide a horse.

reincarnation *noun* being born again into a new body.

reindeer *noun* (*plural* **reindeer**) a kind of deer that lives in Arctic regions.

reinforce *verb* (**reinforced, reinforcing**) strengthen by adding extra people or supports etc.

reinforcement *noun* 1 reinforcing. 2 something that reinforces. **reinforcements** *plural noun* extra troops or ships etc. sent to strengthen a force.

reinstate *verb* (**reinstated, reinstating**) put a person or thing back into a former position. **reinstatement** *noun*

reiterate *verb* (**reiterated, reiterating**) say something again and again. **reiteration** *noun*

reject *verb* 1 refuse to accept a person or thing. 2 throw away; discard. **rejection** *noun*

rejoice *verb* (**rejoiced, rejoicing**) feel or show great joy.

rejoin *verb* 1 join again. 2 answer; retort.

rejoinder *noun* an answer; a retort.

rejuvenate *verb* (**rejuvenated, rejuvenating**) make a person seem young again. **rejuvenation** *noun*

relapse *verb* (**relapsed, relapsing**) return to a previous condition; become worse after improving. **relapse** *noun*

relate *verb* (**related, relating**) 1 narrate. 2 connect or compare one thing with another, *Economic growth is related to foreign investment.* 3 behave happily towards people or animals, *Some people cannot relate to animals.*

related *adjective* belonging to the same family.

relation *noun* 1 a relative. 2 the way one thing is related to another.

relationship *noun* 1 how people or things are related. 2 how people get on with each other, *a relationship of mutual distrust.*

relative[1] *noun* a person who is related to another.

relative[2] *adjective* connected or compared with something; compared with the average, *They live in relative comfort.* **relatively** *adverb*

relative pronoun see *pronoun.*

relax *verb* 1 become less strict or stiff. 2 stop working; rest. **relaxation** *noun*

relay[1] *verb* pass on a message or broadcast.

relay[2] *noun* 1 a fresh group taking the place of another, *The paramedics worked in* *relays.* **2** a relay race. **3** a device for relaying a broadcast.

relay race a race between teams in which each person covers part of the distance.

release[1] *verb* (**released, releasing**) **1** set free; unfasten. **2** let a thing fall or fly or go out. **3** make a film or record etc. available to the public.

release[2] *noun* **1** being released. **2** something released. **3** a device that unfastens something.

relegate *verb* (**relegated, relegating**) **1** put into a less important place. **2** put a sports team into a lower division of a league. **relegation** *noun*

relent *verb* become less severe or more merciful.

relentless *adjective* not relenting; pitiless. **relentlessly** *adverb*

relevant *adjective* connected with what is being discussed or dealt with. (The opposite is *irrelevant.*) **relevance** *noun*

reliable *adjective* able to be relied on; trustworthy. **reliably** *adverb*, **reliability** *noun*

reliance *noun* relying; trust. **reliant** *adjective*

relic *noun* something that has survived from an earlier time.

relief *noun* **1** the ending or lessening of pain, trouble, boredom, etc. **2** something that gives relief or help, *Relief supplies were sent to the refugees.* **3** a person who takes over a turn of duty when another finishes. **4** a method of making a design etc. that stands out from a surface.

relief map a map that shows hills and valleys by shading or moulding.

relieve *verb* (**relieved, relieving**) give relief to a person or thing.

relieve of take something from a person, *The thief relieved him of his wallet.*

religion *noun* what people believe about God or gods, and how they worship.

religious *adjective* **1** of religion. **2** believing firmly in a religion and taking part in its customs. **religiously** *adverb*

relinquish *verb* give up; let go. **relinquishment** *noun*

relish[1] *noun* **1** great enjoyment, *She ate with relish.* **2** something tasty that adds flavour to plainer food.

relish[2] *verb* enjoy greatly.

reluctant *adjective* unwilling; not keen. **reluctantly** *adverb*, **reluctance** *noun*

rely *verb* (**relied, relying**) **rely on** trust a person or thing to help or support you.

remain *verb* **1** be there after other parts have gone or been dealt with; be left over. **2** continue to be in the same place or condition; stay.

remainder *noun* **1** the remaining part or people or things. **2** the number left after subtraction or division.

remains *plural noun* **1** all that is left over after other parts have been removed or destroyed. **2** ancient ruins or objects; relics. **3** a dead body.

remand *verb* send back a prisoner into custody while further evidence is sought. **remand** *noun*

remark[1] *noun* something said; a comment.

remark[2] *verb* **1** make a remark; say. **2** notice, *worthy of remark.*

remarkable *adjective* unusual; extraordinary. **remarkably** *adverb*

remedial *adjective* helping to cure an illness or deficiency.

remedy[1] *noun* (*plural* **remedies**) something that cures or relieves a disease etc. or that puts a matter right.

remedy[2] *verb* (**remedied, remedying**) be a remedy for something; put right.

remember *verb* **1** keep something in your mind. **2** bring something back into your mind. **remembrance** *noun*

remind *verb* help or cause a person to remember something. **reminder** *noun*

reminisce (*say* rem-in-**iss**) *verb* (**reminisced, reminiscing**) think or talk about things that you remember. **reminiscence** *noun*, **reminiscent** *adjective*

remiss *adjective* negligent; careless about doing what you ought to do.

remit *verb* (**remitted, remitting**) **1** send, especially money. **2** forgive; reduce or cancel a punishment etc., *remit a prison sentence.* **3** make or become less intense; slacken, *We must not remit our efforts.* **remission** *noun*

remittance *noun* 1 sending money. 2 the money sent.

remnant *noun* a part or piece left over from something.

remonstrate *verb* (remonstrated, remonstrating) make a protest, *We remonstrated with him about his behaviour.*

remorse *noun* deep regret for having done wrong. **remorseful** *adjective*, **remorsefully** *adverb*

remorseless *adjective* relentless.

remote *adjective* 1 far away. 2 some but very little; unlikely, *a remote chance.* **remotely** *adverb*, **remoteness** *noun* **remote control** controlling something from a distance, usually by electricity or radio.

removable *adjective* able to be removed.

removal *noun* removing or moving something.

remove¹ *verb* (removed, removing) take something away or off.

remove² *noun* a distance or degree away from something, *That is several removes from the truth.*

remunerate *verb* (remunerated, remunerating) pay or reward someone. **remuneration** *noun*, **remunerative** *adjective*

Renaissance (*say* ren-ay-sans) *noun* the revival of classical styles of art and literature in Europe in the 14th–16th centuries.

renal (*say* reen-al) *adjective* of the kidneys.

rend *verb* (rent, rending) rip; tear.

render *verb* 1 give or perform something, *render help to the victims.* 2 cause to become, *The shock rendered us speechless.*

rendezvous (*say* rond-ay-voo) *noun* (*plural* **rendezvous** (*say* rond-ay-vooz)) a meeting with somebody; a place arranged for this.

renegade (*say* ren-ig-ayd) *noun* a person who deserts a group or religion etc.

renew *verb* 1 restore something to its original condition or replace it with something new. 2 begin or make or give again, *We renewed our request.* **renewal** *noun*

renewable *adjective* able to be renewed. **renewable resource** a resource that can be replaced by natural processes, *Plants and*

animals are renewable resources.

rennet *noun* a substance used to curdle milk in making cheese.

renounce *verb* (renounced, renouncing) give up; reject. **renunciation** *noun*

renovate *verb* (renovated, renovating) repair a thing and make it look new. **renovation** *noun*

renown *noun* fame. **renowned** *adjective*

rent¹ *noun* a regular payment for the use of something, especially a house that belongs to another person.

rent² *verb* have or allow the use of something in return for rent.

rent³ *past tense* of **rend**.

rent⁴ *noun* a torn place; a split.

rental *noun* rent (= **rent¹**).

renunciation *noun* renouncing something.

rep *noun* (*informal*) a representative (= *representative¹* 2).

repair¹ *verb* put something into good condition after it has been damaged or broken etc. **repairable** *adjective*

repair² *noun* repairing; repaired.

repair³ *verb* (*formal*) go, *The guests repaired to the dining-room.*

reparation *noun* compensation; amends.

repartee *noun* a witty reply.

repast *noun* (*formal*) a meal.

repatriate *verb* (repatriated, repatriating) send a person back to his or her own country. **repatriation** *noun*

repay *verb* (repaid, repaying) pay back, especially money. **repayable** *adjective*, **repayment** *noun*

repeal *verb* cancel a law officially. **repeal** *noun*

repeat¹ *verb* say or do the same thing again. **repeatedly** *adverb*

repeat² *noun* 1 the action of repeating. 2 something that is repeated.

repel *verb* (repelled, repelling) 1 drive away; repulse, *repel the attack.* 2 disgust somebody. **repellent** *adjective* & *noun*

repent *verb* be sorry for what you have done. **repentance** *noun*, **repentant** *adjective*

repercussion *noun* a result or reaction produced indirectly by something.

repertoire (*say* rep-er-twahr) *noun*
a stock of songs or plays etc. that a person
or company knows and can perform.

repertory *noun* a repertoire.
repertory company or **theatre** a company
or theatre giving performances of various
plays for short periods.

repetition *noun* repeating; something
repeated. **repetitious** *adjective*

repetitive *adjective* full of repetitions.
repetitively *adverb*

replace *verb* (**replaced, replacing**) **1** put a
thing back in its place. **2** take the place of
another person or thing, *Will computers
ever replace workers?* **3** put a new or
different thing in place of something,
replace the battery. **replacement** *noun*

replay *verb* play a sports match or a
recording again. **replay** *noun*

replenish *verb* fill again; add a new supply
of something. **replenishment** *noun*

replete *adjective* **1** well supplied. **2** feeling
full after eating.

replica *noun* an exact copy.

reply[1] *noun* (*plural* **replies**) something
said or written to deal with a question,
letter, etc.; an answer.

reply[2] *verb* (**replied, replying**) give a reply
to; answer.

report[1] *verb* **1** describe something that has
happened or that you have done or studied.
2 make a complaint or accusation against
somebody. **3** go and tell somebody that you
have arrived or are ready for work.

report[2] *noun* **1** a description or account of
something. **2** a regular statement of how
someone has worked or behaved, e.g. at
school. **3** an explosive sound.

reporter *noun* a person whose job is to
collect and report news for a newspaper,
radio or television programme, etc.

repose[1] *noun* rest; sleep.

repose[2] *verb* (**reposed, reposing**) rest or
lie somewhere.

repository *noun* (*plural* **repositories**)
a place where things are stored.

repossess *verb* take back goods which
have been sold on credit, after the buyer has
failed to pay for them in the time expected.

reprehensible *adjective* deserving blame

or rebuke.

represent *verb* **1** show a person or thing in
a picture or play etc. **2** symbolize; stand
for, *In Roman numerals, V represents 5.*
3 be an example or equivalent of something, *The program represents the new
generation of software.* **4** help someone
by speaking or doing something on their
behalf. **representation** *noun*

representative[1] *noun* **1** a sample or
specimen of a class of person or thing.
2 a company's travelling salesperson who
visits shops etc. to get orders. **3** a delegate or
substitute.

representative[2] *adjective* **1** representing
others. **2** typical of a group, *a representative
sample.*

repress *verb* keep down; restrain; suppress.
repression *noun*, **repressive** *adjective*

reprieve[1] *noun* postponement or cancellation of a punishment etc., especially the
death penalty.

reprieve[2] *verb* (**reprieved, reprieving**)
give a reprieve to.

reprimand[1] *noun* a rebuke, especially
a formal or official one.

reprimand[2] *verb* give someone a reprimand.

reprisal *noun* an act of revenge.

reproach *verb* rebuke. **reproach** *noun*,
reproachful *adjective*, **reproachfully**
adverb

reproduce *verb* (**reproduced, reproducing**) **1** cause to be seen or heard or happen
again. **2** make a copy of something.
3 produce offspring. **reproduction** *noun*,
reproductive *adjective*

reprove *verb* (**reproved, reproving**)
rebuke; reproach. **reproof** *noun*

reptile *noun* a cold-blooded scaly animal
that has a backbone and very short legs or
no legs at all, e.g. a snake, lizard, crocodile,
or tortoise.

republic *noun* a country that has a
president, especially one who is elected,
and an elected government. (Compare
monarchy.) **republican** *adjective*

repudiate *verb* (**repudiated, repudiating**)
reject; deny. **repudiation** *noun*

repugnant *adjective* distasteful; objectionable. **repugnance** *noun*

repulse *verb* (**repulsed, repulsing**) 1 drive away; repel. 2 reject an offer etc.; rebuff.

repulsion *noun* 1 repelling; repulsing. 2 a feeling of disgust. (The opposite is *attraction*.)

repulsive *adjective* 1 disgusting. 2 repelling things. (The opposite is *attractive*.) **repulsively** *adverb*, **repulsiveness** *noun*

reputable (*say* rep-yoo-ta-bul) *adjective* having a good reputation; respected. **reputably** *adverb*

reputation *noun* what people say about a person or thing.

repute *noun* reputation.

reputed *adjective* said or thought to be something, *This is reputed to be the best hotel*. **reputedly** *adverb*

request¹ *verb* ask for a thing; ask a person to do something.

request² *noun* 1 asking for something. 2 a thing asked for.

requiem (*say* rek-wee-em) *noun* a special Mass for someone who has died; music for the words of this.

require *verb* (**required, requiring**) 1 need. 2 make somebody do something; oblige, *Drivers are required to pass a test*.

requirement *noun* what is required; a need.

requisite¹ (*say* rek-wiz-it) *adjective* required; needed.

requisite² *noun* a thing needed for something.

requisition *verb* take something over for official use.

rescue¹ *verb* (**rescued, rescuing**) save from danger, harm, etc.; bring away from captivity. **rescuer** *noun*

rescue² *noun* the action of rescuing.

research¹ (*say* ri-**serch** or **ree**-serch) *noun* careful study or investigation to discover facts or information.

research² (*say* ri-**serch** or **ree**-serch) *verb* do research into something.

resemblance *noun* likeness.

resemble *verb* (**resembled, resembling**) be like another person or thing.

resent *verb* feel indignant about or insulted by something. **resentful** *adjective*, **resentfully** *adverb*, **resentment** *noun*

reservation *noun* 1 reserving.

2 something reserved, *theatre reservations*. 3 an area of land kept for a special purpose. 4 a limit on how far you agree with something, *I believe most of his story, but I have some reservations*.

reserve¹ *verb* (**reserved, reserving**) 1 keep or order something for a particular person or a special use. 2 postpone, *reserve judgement*.

reserve² *noun* 1 a person or thing kept ready to be used if necessary. 2 an area of land kept for a special purpose, *a nature reserve*. 3 shyness; keeping your thoughts and feelings private.

reserved *adjective* (of a person) showing reserve of manner (see *reserve²* 3).

reservoir (*say* **rez**-er-vwar) *noun* a place where water is stored, especially an artificial lake.

reshuffle *noun* a rearrangement, especially an exchange of jobs between members of a group, *a Cabinet reshuffle*. **reshuffle** *verb*

reside *verb* (**resided, residing**) live in a particular place; dwell.

residence *noun* 1 a place where a person lives. 2 residing.

resident *noun* a person living or residing in a particular place. **resident** *adjective*

residential *adjective* containing people's homes, *a residential area*.

residue *noun* what is left over. **residual** *adjective*

resign *verb* give up your job or position. **resignation** *noun*

be resigned or **resign yourself to something** accept that you must put up with it.

resilient *adjective* 1 springy. 2 recovering quickly from illness or trouble. **resilience** *noun*

resin *noun* a sticky substance that comes from plants or is manufactured, used in varnish, plastics, etc. **resinous** *adjective*

resist *verb* oppose; fight or act against something. **resistance** *noun*, **resistant** *adjective*

resistor *noun* a device that increases the resistance to an electric current.

resolute *adjective* showing great determination. **resolutely** *adverb*

resolution *noun* 1 being resolute. 2 something you have resolved to do, *New Year resolutions.* 3 a formal decision made by a committee etc. 4 the solving of a problem etc.

resolve¹ *verb* (**resolved, resolving**) 1 decide firmly or formally. 2 solve a problem etc. 3 overcome doubts or disagreements, *resolve their differences.*

resolve² *noun* 1 something you have decided to do; a resolution. 2 great determination.

resonant *adjective* resounding; echoing. **resonance** *adjective*

resort¹ *verb* turn to or make use of something, *They resorted to violence.*

resort² *noun* 1 a place where people go for relaxation or holidays. 2 resorting, *without resort to cheating.*

the last resort something to be tried when everything else has failed.

resound *verb* fill a place with sound; echo.

resounding *adjective* very great; outstanding, *a resounding victory.*

resource *noun* 1 something that can be used; an asset, *The country's natural resources include coal and oil.* 2 an ability; ingenuity.

resourceful *adjective* clever at finding ways of doing things. **resourcefully** *adverb*, **resourcefulness** *noun*

respect¹ *noun* 1 admiration for a person's or thing's good qualities. 2 politeness; consideration, *Have respect for people's feelings.* 3 a detail or aspect, *In this respect he is like his sister.* 4 reference, *The rules with respect to bullying are quite clear.*

respect² *verb* have respect for a person or thing.

respectable *adjective* 1 having good manners and character etc. 2 fairly good, *a respectable score.* **respectably** *adverb*, **respectability** *noun*

respectful *adjective* showing respect. **respectfully** *adverb*

respecting *preposition* concerning.

respective *adjective* of or for each individual, *We went to our respective rooms.* **respectively** *adverb*

respiration *noun* 1 breathing. 2 (in biology) in living organisms, the taking in of oxygen and the release of energy and carbon dioxide after carbohydrates are broken down. **respiratory** *adjective*

respirator *noun* 1 a device that fits over a person's nose and mouth to purify air before it is breathed. 2 an apparatus for giving artificial respiration.

respire *verb* (**respired, respiring**) breathe.

respite *noun* an interval of rest, relief, or delay.

resplendent *adjective* brilliant with colour or decorations.

respond *verb* 1 reply. 2 react.

respondent *noun* the person answering.

response *noun* 1 a reply. 2 a reaction.

responsibility *noun* (*plural* **responsibilities**) 1 being responsible. 2 something for which a person is responsible, *Looking after the dog is your responsibility.*

responsible *adjective* 1 looking after a person or thing and having to take the blame if something goes wrong. 2 reliable; trustworthy. 3 with important duties, *a responsible job.* 4 causing something, *His carelessness was responsible for their deaths.* **responsibly** *adverb*

responsive *adjective* responding well.

rest¹ *noun* 1 a time of sleep or freedom from work as a way of regaining strength. 2 a support, *an arm-rest.* 3 an interval of silence between notes in music.

rest² *verb* 1 have a rest; be still. 2 allow to rest, *Sit down and rest your feet.* 3 support; be supported. 4 be left without further investigation etc., *And there the matter rests.*

rest³ *noun* **the rest** the remaining part; the others.

rest⁴ *verb* remain, *Rest assured, it will be a success.*

rest with be left to someone to deal with, *It rests with you to suggest a date.*

restaurant *noun* a place where you can buy a meal and eat it.

restful *adjective* giving rest or a feeling of rest.

restitution *noun* 1 restoring something. 2 compensation, *making restitution for the past.*

restive *adjective* restless or impatient because of delay, boredom, etc.

restless *adjective* unable to rest or keep still. **restlessly** *adverb*

restore *verb* (**restored, restoring**) put something back to its original place or condition. **restoration** *noun*

restrain *verb* hold a person or thing back; keep under control. **restraint** *noun*

restrict *verb* limit. **restriction** *noun*, **restrictive** *adjective*

result[1] *noun* 1 something produced by an action or condition etc.; an effect or consequence. 2 the score or situation at the end of a game, competition, or race etc. 3 the answer to a sum or calculation.

result[2] *verb* 1 happen as a result. 2 have a particular result, *Increased productivity results in higher profits.* **resultant** *adjective*

resume *verb* (**resumed, resuming**) 1 begin again after stopping for a while. 2 take or occupy again, *After the interval we resumed our seats.* **resumption** *noun*

résumé (*say* **rez**-yoo-may) *noun* a summary.

resurgence *noun* a rise or revival of something, *a resurgence of interest in grammar.*

resurrect *verb* bring back into use or existence, *resurrect an old custom.*

resurrection *noun* 1 coming back to life after being dead. 2 the revival of something.

resuscitate *verb* (**resuscitated, resuscitating**) revive a person from unconsciousness or a custom etc. from disuse. **resuscitation** *noun*

retail[1] *verb* 1 sell goods to the general public. 2 tell what happened; recount; relate. **retailer** *noun*

retail[2] *noun* selling to the general public. (Compare *wholesale.*)

retain *verb* 1 continue to have something; keep in your possession or memory etc. 2 hold something in place.

retainer *noun* 1 an amount of money paid to someone in advance so that they will be available to provide a service when required, *a retainer of R500 per month.* 2 (*old use*) an attendant of a person of high rank.

retaliate *verb* (**retaliated, retaliating**) repay an injury or insult etc. with a similar one; counter-attack. **retaliation** *noun*

retard *verb* slow down or delay the progress or development of something. **retarded** *adjective*, **retardation** *noun*

retch *verb* strain your throat as if being sick.

retention *noun* retaining; keeping. **retentive** *adjective*

reticent (*say* **ret**-i-sent) *adjective* not telling people what you feel or think; discreet. **reticence** *noun*

retina *noun* a layer of membrane at the back of the eyeball, sensitive to light.

retinue *noun* a group of people accompanying an important person.

retire *verb* (**retired, retiring**) 1 give up your regular work because you are getting old. 2 retreat, *retire from the fray.* 3 go to bed or to your private room. **retirement** *noun*

retiring *adjective* shy; avoiding company.

retort[1] *noun* 1 a quick or witty or angry reply. 2 a glass bottle with a long downward-bent neck, used in distilling liquids. 3 a receptacle used in making steel etc.

retort[2] *verb* make a quick, witty, or angry reply.

retrace *verb* (**retraced, retracing**) go back over something, *We retraced our steps and returned to the station.*

retract *verb* 1 pull back or in, *The snail retracts its horns.* 2 withdraw, *She refused to retract her threat.* **retraction** *noun*, **retractable** *adjective*, **retractile** *adjective*

retreat[1] *verb* go back after being defeated or to avoid danger or difficulty etc.; withdraw.

retreat[2] *noun* 1 retreating. 2 a quiet place to which someone can withdraw.

retrench *verb* reduce the amount of something; economize. **retrenchment** *noun*

retribution *noun* a deserved punishment.

retrieve *verb* (**retrieved, retrieving**) get something back; rescue. **retrievable** *adjective*, **retrieval** *noun*

retriever *noun* a kind of dog that is often trained to retrieve game.

retro- *prefix* back; backward (as in *retrograde*).

retrograde *adjective* **1** going backwards.
2 becoming less good.

retrogress *verb* **1** move backwards.
2 deteriorate. **retrogression** *noun*,
retrogressive *adjective*

retrospect *noun* a survey of past events.
in retrospect when you look back at what
has happened.

retrospective *adjective* **1** looking back on
the past. **2** applying to the past as well as the
future, *The law could not be made retro-*
spective. **retrospection** *noun*

return[1] *verb* **1** come back or go back.
2 bring, give, put, or send back.

return[2] *noun* **1** returning. **2** something
returned. **3** profit, *He gets a good return*
on his savings. **4** a return ticket.

return match a second match played
between the same teams.

return ticket a ticket for a journey to a place
and back again.

reunion *noun* **1** reuniting. **2** a meeting of
people who have not met for some time,
a school reunion.

reunite *verb* (**reunited, reuniting**) unite
again after being separated.

reuse[1] *verb* (**reused, reusing**) use again.
reusable *adjective*

reuse[2] *noun* using again.

rev[1] *verb* (**revved, revving**) (*informal*)
make an engine run quickly, especially
when starting.

rev[2] *noun* (*informal*) a revolution of an
engine.

Rev. *abbreviation* Reverend.

reveal *verb* let something be seen or
known.

reveille (*say* riv-**al**-ee) *noun* a military
waking-signal sounded on a bugle or
drums.

revel *verb* (**revelled, revelling**) **1** take great
delight in something. **2** hold revels.
reveller *noun*
revels *plural noun* noisy festivities.

revelation *noun* **1** revealing. **2** something
revealed, especially something surprising.

revelry *noun* revelling; revels.

revenge[1] *noun* harming somebody in
return for harm that they have caused.

revenge[2] *verb* (**revenged, revenging**)
avenge; take vengeance.

revenue *noun* **1** income; the items that
make up income for a person, business,
etc., *sales and advertising revenue*.
2 a country's income from taxes etc., used
for paying public expenses.

reverberate *verb* (**reverberated, rever-**
berating) resound; re-echo. **reverberation**
noun

revere (*say* riv-**eer**) *verb* (**revered, rever-**
ing) respect deeply or with reverence.

reverence *noun* a feeling of awe and deep
or religious respect.

reverend *noun & adjective* **1** deserving to
be treated with reverence. **2** (**Reverend**) the
title of a member of the clergy, *the Reverend*
Frank Mbeki.
● USAGE: Do not confuse with *reverent*.

reverent *adjective* feeling or showing
reverence. **reverently** *adverb*
● USAGE: Do not confuse with *reverend*.

reverie (*say* **rev**-er-ee) *noun* a day-dream.

revers (*say* riv-**eer**) *noun* (*plural* **revers**
(*say* riv-**eerz**)) a folded-back part of a
garment, as in a lapel.

reversal *noun* reversing.

reverse[1] *adjective* opposite in direction,
order, or manner etc.

reverse gear a gear that allows a vehicle
to be driven backwards.

reverse[2] *noun* **1** the reverse side, order,
manner, etc. **2** a piece of misfortune, *They*
suffered several reverses.
in reverse the opposite way round.

reverse[3] *verb* (**reversed, reversing**) **1** turn
in the opposite direction or order etc.; turn
something inside out or upside down.
2 move backwards. **3** cancel a decision
or decree. **reversible** *adjective*

revert *verb* return to a former condition,
habit, or subject etc. **reversion** *noun*

review[1] *noun* **1** an inspection or survey.
2 a published description and opinion of
a book, film, play, etc.

review[2] *verb* make a review of something.
reviewer *noun*
● USAGE: Do not confuse with *revue*.

revile *verb* (**reviled, reviling**) criticize
angrily. **revilement** *noun*

revise *verb* (**revised, revising**) **1** go over

work that you have already done, especially in preparing for an examination. **2** alter or correct something, *She revised her earlier impression of him.* **revision** *noun*

revive *verb* (**revived, reviving**) come or bring back to life, strength, activity, or use etc. **revival** *noun*

revoke *verb* (**revoked, revoking**) withdraw or cancel a decree or licence etc.

revolt[1] *verb* **1** rebel. **2** disgust somebody.

revolt[2] *noun* **1** a rebellion. **2** a feeling of disgust.

revolting *adjective* disgusting.

revolution *noun* **1** a rebellion that overthrows the government. **2** a complete change, *the revolution brought about by industrialization.* **3** revolving; rotation; one complete turn of a wheel, engine, etc.

revolutionary *adjective* **1** involving a great change. **2** of a political revolution.

revolutionize *verb* (**revolutionized, revolutionizing**) make a great change in something.

revolve *verb* (**revolved, revolving**) turn or keep on turning round.

revolver *noun* a pistol with a revolving mechanism that makes it possible to fire it a number of times without reloading.

revue *noun* an entertainment consisting of a number of items.

● USAGE: Do not confuse with *review.*

revulsion *noun* strong disgust.

reward[1] *noun* something given in return for a useful action or a merit.

reward[2] *verb* give a reward to someone.

rewrite *verb* (**rewrote, rewritten, rewriting**) write something again or differently.

rhapsody (*say* rap-so-dee) *noun* (*plural* **rhapsodies**) **1** a statement of great delight about something. **2** a romantic piece of music. **rhapsodize** *verb*

rhebok *noun* a reebok.

rheostat *noun* a device that is used to control an electric current by varying the resistance.

rhetoric (*say* ret-er-ik) *noun* **1** the act of using words impressively, especially in public speaking. **2** affected or exaggerated expressions used because they sound impressive. **rhetorical** *adjective,*

rhetorically *adverb*

rhetorical question something put as a question so that it sounds dramatic, not to get an answer, e.g. 'Who cares?' (= nobody cares).

rheumatism *noun* a disease that causes pain and stiffness in joints and muscles. **rheumatic** *adjective,* **rheumatoid** *adjective*

rhino *noun* (*plural* **rhino** or **rhinos**) (*informal*) a rhinoceros.

rhinoceros *noun* (*plural* **rhinoceros** or **rhinoceroses**) a large heavy animal with a horn or two horns on its nose.

rhizome *noun* an underground stem which bears both roots and shoots.

rhododendron *noun* an evergreen shrub with large trumpet-shaped flowers.

rhombus *noun* (*plural* **rhombuses**) a quadrilateral with equal sides but no right angles, like the diamond on playing-cards.

rhubarb *noun* a plant with thick reddish stalks that are used as fruit.

rhyme[1] *noun* **1** a similar sound in the endings of words, e.g. *bat/fat/mat, batter/fatter/matter.* **2** a poem with rhymes. **3** a word that rhymes with another.

rhyme[2] *verb* (**rhymed, rhyming**) form a rhyme; have rhymes.

rhythm *noun* a regular pattern of beats, sounds, or movements. **rhythmic** *adjective,* **rhythmical** *adjective,* **rhythmically** *adverb*

rib *noun* **1** each of the curved bones round the chest. **2** a curved part that looks like a rib or supports something, *the ribs of an umbrella.* **ribbed** *adjective*

ribald (*say* rib-ald) *adjective* funny in a vulgar or disrespectful way. **ribaldry** *noun*

riband *noun* a ribbon.

ribbok *noun* a reebok.

ribbon *noun* **1** a narrow strip of silk or nylon etc. used for decoration or for tying something. **2** a long narrow strip of inked material used in a typewriter etc.

rice *noun* the white seeds of a plant that is grown in marshes in hot countries, used as food.

rich *adjective* **1** having a lot of money or property or resources etc.; wealthy. **2** full of goodness, quality, etc. **3** costly; luxurious, *rich fabrics.* **richly** *adverb,* **richness** *noun*

riches *plural noun* wealth.

rick[1] *noun* a large neat stack of hay or straw.

rick[2] *verb* sprain; wrench.

rickets *noun* a disease caused by lack of vitamin D, causing deformed bones.

rickety *adjective* unsteady.

rickshaw *noun* a two-wheeled carriage pulled by one or more people.

ricochet (*say* rik-osh-ay) *verb* (**ricocheted, ricocheting**) bounce off something; rebound, *The bullets ricocheted off the wall.* **ricochet** *noun*

rid *verb* (**rid, ridding**) make a person or place free from something unwanted, *He rid the town of rats.* **riddance** *noun* **get rid of** cause to go away.

riddle[1] *noun* a puzzling question, especially as a joke.

riddle[2] *noun* a coarse sieve.

riddle[3] *verb* (**riddled, riddling**) 1 pass gravel etc. through a riddle. 2 pierce with many holes, *They riddled the target with bullets.*

ride[1] *verb* (**rode, ridden, riding**) 1 sit on a horse, bicycle, etc. and be carried along on it. 2 travel in a car, bus, train, etc. 3 float or be supported on something, *The ship rode the waves.*

ride[2] *noun* riding; a journey on a horse, bicycle, etc. or in a vehicle.

rider *noun* 1 someone who rides. 2 an extra comment or statement.

ridge *noun* a long narrow part higher than the rest of something. **ridged** *adjective*

ridgeback *noun* a large dog with a ridge of hair growing along its spine.

ridicule *verb* (**ridiculed, ridiculing**) make fun of a person or thing. **ridicule** *noun*

ridiculous *adjective* so silly that it makes people laugh or despise it. **ridiculously** *adverb*

riempie *noun* a narrow strip of soft leather used to make chair seats, stools, etc. **riempiestoel** a chair made with riempies.

rife *adjective* widespread; happening frequently, *Crime was rife in the town.*

riff-raff *noun* the rabble; disreputable people.

rifle[1] *noun* a long gun with spiral grooves (called *rifling*) inside the barrel that make the bullet spin and so travel more accurately.

rifle[2] *verb* (**rifled, rifling**) search and rob, *They rifled his desk.*

rift *noun* 1 a crack or split. 2 a disagreement that separates friends.

rift-valley *noun* a steep-sided valley formed where the land has sunk.

rig[1] *verb* (**rigged, rigging**) 1 provide a ship with ropes, spars, sails, etc. 2 set something up quickly or out of makeshift materials. **rig out** provide with clothes or equipment. **rig-out** *noun*

rig[2] *noun* 1 a framework supporting the machinery for drilling an oil-well. 2 the way a ship's masts and sails etc. are arranged.

rigging *noun* the ropes etc. that support a ship's mast and sails.

right[1] *adjective* 1 of the right-hand side. 2 correct; true, *the right answer.* 3 morally good; fair; just, *Is it right to cheat?* 4 (of political groups) not in favour of socialist reforms. **rightly** *adverb*, **rightness** *noun*

right angle an angle of 90°.

right hand the hand that most people use more than the left, on the side of the body opposite the left hand. **right-hand** *adjective*

right-handed *adjective* using the right hand in preference to the left hand.

right[2] *adverb* 1 on or towards the right-hand side, *Turn right.* 2 straight, *Go right on.* 3 completely, *Go right round it.* 4 exactly, *right in the middle.* 5 rightly, *You did right to tell me.* **right away** immediately.

right[3] *noun* 1 the right-hand side or part etc. 2 what is morally good or fair or just. 3 something that people are allowed to do or have, *People over 18 have the right to vote in elections.*

right[4] *verb* make a thing right or upright, *They righted the boat.*

righteous *adjective* doing what is right; virtuous. **righteously** *adverb*, **righteousness** *noun*

rightful *adjective* deserved; proper, *in her rightful place.* **rightfully** *adverb*

rigid *adjective* 1 stiff; firm; not bending,

a rigid support. **2** strict, *rigid rules.* **rigidly** *adverb*, **rigidity** *noun*

rigmarole *noun* **1** a long rambling statement. **2** a complicated procedure.

rigorous *adjective* strict; severe. **rigorously** *adverb*

rigour *noun* **1** strictness; severity. **2** harshness of weather or conditions, *the rigours of winter.*

rile *verb* (**riled, riling**) (*informal*) annoy.

rill *noun* a very small stream.

rim *noun* the outer edge of a cup, wheel, or other round object.

rimmed *adjective* edged.

rind *noun* the tough skin on bacon, cheese, or fruit.

rinderpest *noun* a disease that affects cattle.

ring[1] *noun* **1** a circle. **2** a thin circular piece of metal worn on a finger. **3** the space where a circus performs. **4** a square area in which a boxing-match or wrestling-match takes place.

ring[2] *verb* put a ring round something; encircle.

ring[3] *verb* (**rang, rung, ringing**) **1** cause a bell to sound. **2** make a loud clear sound like that of a bell. **3** be filled with sound, *The hall rang with cheers.* **4** telephone, *Please ring me tomorrow.* **ringer** *noun*

ring[4] *noun* **1** the act or sound of ringing. **2** a telephone call.

ringleader *noun* a person who leads others in rebellion, mischief, crime, etc.

ringlet *noun* a tube-shaped curl.

ringmaster *noun* the person in charge of a performance in a circus ring.

rink *noun* a place made for skating.

rinkhals *noun* a large poisonous spitting cobra.

rinse *verb* (**rinsed, rinsing**) **1** wash something lightly. **2** wash in clean water to remove soap. **rinse** *noun*

riot[1] *noun* wild or violent behaviour by a crowd of people.

riot[2] *verb* (**rioted, rioting**) take part in a riot.

riotous *adjective* **1** disorderly; unruly. **2** boisterous, *riotous laughter.*

rip[1] *verb* (**ripped, ripping**) **1** tear roughly. **2** rush.

rip off (*informal*) swindle. **rip-off** *noun*

rip[2] *noun* a torn place.

ripe *adjective* **1** ready to be harvested or eaten. **2** ready and suitable, *The time is ripe for revolution.* **3** mature; advanced, *She lived to a ripe old age.* **ripeness** *noun*

ripen *verb* make or become ripe.

riposte (*say* rip-**ost**) *noun* **1** a quick counterstroke in fencing. **2** a quick retort.

ripple[1] *noun* a small wave or series of waves.

ripple[2] *verb* (**rippled, rippling**) form ripples.

rise[1] *verb* (**rose, risen, rising**) **1** go upwards. **2** get up from lying, sitting, or kneeling; get out of bed. **3** come to life again after death, *Christ is risen.* **4** rebel, *They rose in revolt against the tyrant.* **5** (of a river) begin its course. **6** (of the wind) begin to blow more strongly.

rise[2] *noun* **1** the action of rising; an upward movement. **2** an increase in amount etc. or in wages. **3** an upward slope. **give rise to** cause.

rising *noun* a revolt.

risk[1] *noun* a chance of danger or loss.

risk[2] *verb* take the chance of damaging or losing something.

risky *adjective* (**riskier, riskiest**) full of risk.

rissole *noun* a fried cake of minced meat or fish.

rite *noun* a religious ceremony; a solemn ritual. **rite of passage** an event that marks a new stage in someone's life, e.g. marriage.

ritual *noun* the series of actions used in a religious or other ceremony. **ritual** *adjective*, **ritually** *adverb*

rival[1] *noun* a person or thing that competes with another or tries to do the same thing. **rivalry** *noun*

rival[2] *verb* (**rivalled, rivalling**) be a rival of a person or thing.

riven *adjective* split; torn apart.

river *noun* a large stream of water flowing in a natural channel.

rivet[1] *noun* a strong nail or bolt for holding pieces of metal together. The end opposite the head is flattened to form another head when it is in place.

rivet² *verb* (**riveted, riveting**) 1 fasten with rivets. 2 hold firmly, *He stood riveted to the spot.* 3 fascinate, *The concert was riveting.* **riveter** *noun*

rivulet *noun* a small stream.

roach *noun* (*plural* **roach**) a small freshwater fish.

road *noun* 1 a level way with a hard surface made for traffic to travel on. 2 a way or course, *the road to success.* **roadside** *noun*, **roadway** *noun*

roadworthy *adjective* safe to be used on roads.

roam *verb* wander. **roam** *noun*

roan *adjective* (of a horse) brown or black with many white hairs.

roar¹ *noun* a loud deep sound like that made by a lion.

roar² *verb* make a roar.
 a roaring trade brisk selling of something.

roast¹ *verb* 1 cook meat etc. in an oven or by exposing it to heat. 2 make or be very hot, *It was roasting on the beach.*

roast² *adjective* roasted, *roast beef.*

roast³ *noun* meat for roasting; roast meat.

rob *verb* (**robbed, robbing**) take or steal from somebody, *She robbed me of my watch.* **robber** *noun*, **robbery** *noun*

robe¹ *noun* a long loose garment.

robe² *verb* (**robed, robing**) dress in a robe or ceremonial robes.

robin *noun* a small brown bird with a red breast.

robot *noun* 1 a machine that looks and acts like a person. 2 a machine operated by remote control. 3 a traffic light.

robust *adjective* strong; vigorous. **robustly** *adverb*, **robustness** *noun*

rock¹ *noun* 1 a large stone or boulder. 2 the hard part of the earth's crust, under the soil. 3 a hard sweet usually shaped like a stick.
 rock lobster a crayfish, also called a kreef.
 rock painting a picture drawn on cave walls in former times.

rock² *verb* 1 move gently backwards and forwards while supported on something. 2 shake violently, *The earthquake rocked the city.*

rock³ *noun* 1 a rocking movement. 2 rock music.

rock music popular music with a heavy beat.

rocker *noun* 1 a thing that rocks something or is rocked. 2 a rocking-chair.
 off your rocker (*informal*) mad.

rockery *noun* (*plural* **rockeries**) a mound or bank in a garden, where plants are made to grow between large rocks.

rocket¹ *noun* 1 a firework that shoots high into the air. 2 a structure that flies by expelling burning gases, used to send up a missile or a spacecraft. **rocketry** *noun*

rocket² *verb* (**rocketed, rocketing**) move quickly upwards or away.

rocking-chair *noun* a chair that can be rocked by a person sitting in it.

rocking-horse *noun* a model of a horse that can be rocked by a child sitting on it.

rocky¹ *adjective* (**rockier, rockiest**) like rock; full of rocks, *rocky ground.*

rocky² *adjective* (**rockier, rockiest**) unsteady, *a rocky start.* **rockiness** *noun*

rod *noun* 1 a long thin stick or bar. 2 a stick with a line attached for fishing.

rodent *noun* an animal that has large front teeth for gnawing things, *Rats, porcupines, and squirrels are rodents.*

rodeo (*say* roh-**day**-oh) *noun* (*plural* **rodeos**) a display of cowboys' skill in riding, controlling horses, etc.

roe¹ *noun* a mass of eggs or reproductive cells in a fish's body.

roe² *noun* (*plural* **roes** or **roe**) a kind of small deer. The male is called a **roebuck**.

rogue *noun* 1 a dishonest person. 2 a mischievous person. **roguery** *noun*

roguish *adjective* playful.

roister *verb* make merry noisily.

role *noun* a performer's part in a play or film etc.

roll¹ *verb* 1 move along by turning over and over, like a ball or wheel. 2 form something into the shape of a cylinder or ball. 3 flatten something by rolling a rounded object over it, *roll out pastry.* 4 rock from side to side. 5 pass steadily, *The years rolled on.* 6 make a long vibrating sound, *The thunder rolled.*

roll² *noun* 1 a cylinder made by rolling something up. 2 a small individual portion

of bread baked in a rounded shape.
3 an official list of names. **4** a long vibrating
sound, *a drum roll.*

roll-call *noun* the calling of a list of names
to check that everyone is present.

roller *noun* **1** a cylinder for rolling over
things, or on which something is wound.
2 a long swelling sea-wave.

roller-coaster *noun* a switchback at
a fair etc.

roller-skate *noun* a framework with
wheels, fitted under a shoe so that the
wearer can roll smoothly over the ground.
roller-skating *noun*

rollicking *adjective* boisterous and full
of fun.

rolling-pin *noun* a heavy cylinder for
rolling over pastry to flatten it.

rolling-stock *noun* railway engines and
carriages and wagons etc.

ROM *abbreviation* read-only memory
(in a computer), with contents that can
be searched or copied but not changed.

Roman *adjective* **1** of ancient or modern
Rome or its people. **2** Roman Catholic.
Roman *noun*

Roman candle a tubular firework that
sends out coloured fire-balls.

Roman Catholic of the Church that has the
pope (bishop of Rome) as its leader;
a member of this Church.

Roman numerals letters that represent
numbers (I = 1, V = 5, X = 10, etc.), used by
the ancient Romans.

romance (*say* ro-**manss**) *noun* **1** tender
feelings, experiences, and qualities connected with love. **2** a love story. **3** a love
affair. **4** an imaginative story about the
adventures of heroes, *a romance of King
Arthur's court.* **5** a feeling of excitement and
adventure, *the romance of travel.* **romantic**
adjective, **romantically** *adverb*

romp *verb* play in a lively way. **romp** *noun*

rompers *plural noun* a young child's
garment covering the trunk of the body.

rondavel (*say* ron-**dah**-vil) *noun* a circular
building with one room and a cone-shaped
roof.

rondo *noun* (*plural* **rondos**) a piece of
music whose first part recurs several times.

rood *noun* a crucifix in a church, especially
one placed on top of a screen (the **rood-
screen**) separating the nave from the
chancel.

roof *noun* (*plural* **roofs**) **1** the part that
covers the top of a building, shelter, or
vehicle. **2** the upper part of the mouth.

rooibos (*say* **roy**-bos) *noun* an evergreen
shrub with leaves used to make a health tea.

rooikat (*say* **roy**-kat) *noun* (*plural* **rooikats**
or **rooikatte**) a lynx.

rooikrans (*say* **roy**-krans) *noun* an alien
tree introduced to provide fodder, shade,
etc., now difficult to control.

rook[1] *noun* a black crow that nests in large
groups.

rook[2] *verb* (*informal*) swindle; charge
people an unnecessarily high price.

rook[3] *noun* a chess piece shaped like
a castle.

rookery *noun* (*plural* **rookeries**) a place
where many rooks nest.

room *noun* **1** a part of a building with its
own walls and ceiling. **2** enough space,
Is there room for me? **roomful** *noun*

roomy *adjective* (**roomier, roomiest**)
containing plenty of room; spacious.

roost[1] *noun* a place where birds perch
or settle for sleep.

roost[2] *verb* perch; settle for sleep.

rooster *noun* a cockerel.

root[1] *noun* **1** that part of a plant that grows
under the ground and absorbs water and
nourishment from the soil. **2** a source or
basis, *The love of money is the root of all evil.*
3 a number in relation to the number it
produces when multiplied by itself, *9 is the
square root of 81 (9 × 9 = 81).*
take root grow roots; become established.

root[2] *verb* **1** take root; cause something to
take root. **2** fix firmly, *Fear rooted us to the
spot.*
root out get rid of something.

root[3] *verb* rummage; (of an animal) turn up
ground in search of food.

rope[1] *noun* a strong thick cord made of
twisted strands of fibre.
show someone the ropes show him or her
how to do something.

rope[2] *verb* (**roped, roping**) fasten with a rope.

rope in persuade a person to take part in something.

rosary *noun* (*plural* **rosaries**) a string of beads for keeping count of a set of prayers as they are said.

rose[1] *noun* 1 a shrub that has showy flowers often with thorny stems. 2 deep pink colour. 3 a sprinkling-nozzle with many holes, e.g. on a watering-can or hose-pipe.

rose[2] *past tense* of **rise**[1].

roseate *adjective* deep pink; rosy.

rosebud *noun* the bud of a rose.

rosemary *noun* an evergreen shrub with fragrant leaves.

rosette *noun* a large circular badge or ornament.

roster[1] *noun* a list showing people's turns to be on duty etc.

roster[2] *verb* place on a roster.

rostrum *noun* (*plural* **rostra**) a platform for one person.

rosy *adjective* (**rosier**, **rosiest**) 1 deep pink. 2 hopeful; cheerful, *a rosy future*. **rosiness** *noun*

rot[1] *verb* (**rotted**, **rotting**) go soft or bad and become useless; decay.

rot[2] *noun* 1 rotting; decay. 2 (*informal*) nonsense.

rota (*say* **roh**-ta) *noun* a list of people to do things or of things to be done in turn.

rotate *verb* (**rotated**, **rotating**) 1 go round like a wheel; revolve. 2 arrange or happen in a series; take turns at doing something, *Crops are rotated every season*. **rotation** *noun*, **rotary** *adjective*, **rotatory** *adjective*

rote *noun* **by rote** from memory or by routine, without full understanding of the meaning, *We learn our tables by rote*.

roti *noun* (*plural* **rotis**) an Indian flat bread.

rotor *noun* a rotating part of a machine or helicopter.

rotten *adjective* 1 rotted, *rotten apples*. 2 (*informal*) worthless; unpleasant. **rottenness** *noun*

rotter *noun* (*informal*) a dishonourable person.

rotund *adjective* rounded; plump. **rotundity** *noun*

rotunda *noun* a building or room built to a circular plan, especially one with a dome.

rouble (*say* **roo**-bul) *noun* the unit of money in Russia.

rouge (*say* roozh) *noun* a reddish cosmetic for colouring the cheeks. **rouge** *verb*

rough[1] *adjective* 1 not smooth; uneven. 2 not gentle or careful; violent, *a rough push*. 3 not exact, *a rough guess*. **roughly** *adverb*, **roughness** *noun*

rough[2] *verb* **rough it** do without ordinary comforts.

rough out draw or plan something roughly.

rough up (*informal*) treat a person violently.

roughage *noun* fibre in food, which helps digestion.

roughen *verb* make or become rough.

roulette (*say* roo-**let**) *noun* a gambling game where players bet on where the ball in a rotating disc will come to rest.

round[1] *adjective* 1 shaped like a circle or ball or cylinder; curved. 2 full; complete, *a round dozen*. 3 returning to the start, *a round trip*. **roundness** *noun*

in round figures approximately, without giving exact units.

round[2] *adverb* 1 in a circle or curve; round something, *Go round to the back of the house*. 2 in every direction, *Hand the cakes round*. 3 in a new direction, *Turn your chair round*. 4 to someone's house or office etc., *Go round after dinner*. 5 into being conscious again, *Has she come round from the anaesthetic yet?*

round about near by; approximately.

round[3] *preposition* 1 on all sides of, *Put a fence round the field*. 2 in a curve or circle at an even distance from, *The earth moves round the sun*. 3 to all parts of, *Show them round the house*. 4 on the further side of, *The shop is round the corner*.

round[4] *noun* 1 a round object. 2 a series of meetings, discussions, etc., *the next round of wage talks*. 3 a series of visits made by a doctor, postman, etc. 4 one section or stage in a competition, *Winners go on to the next round*. 5 a shot or volley of shots from a gun; ammunition for this. 6 a song in which people sing the same words but start at

different times. **7** a whole slice of bread;
a sandwich made with two slices of bread.

round[5] *verb* **1** make or become round.
2 travel round, *The car rounded the corner.*
round off finish something.
round up gather people or animals
together. **round-up** *noun*

roundabout[1] *noun* **1** a road junction
where traffic has to pass round a circular
structure in the road. **2** a merry-go-round.

roundabout[2] *adjective* indirect; not using
the shortest way of going or of saying or
doing something, *I heard the news in a
roundabout way.*

rounders *noun* a game in which players try
to hit a ball and run round a circuit.

roundly *adverb* **1** thoroughly; severely,
We were roundly told off for being late.
2 in a rounded shape.

rouse *verb* (**roused, rousing**) **1** make or
become awake. **2** cause to become active
or excited.

rousing *adjective* loud, *three rousing
cheers.*

rout[1] *verb* defeat and chase away an enemy.
rout *noun*

rout[2] *verb* root (= *root*[2]).

route (*say as* root) *noun* the way taken to
get to a place.

routine (*say* roo-**teen**) *noun* a regular way
of doing things. **routinely** *adverb*

rove *verb* (**roved, roving**) roam. **rover**
noun

row[1] (rhymes with *go*) *noun* a line of people
or things.

row[2] (rhymes with *go*) *verb* make a boat
move by using oars. **rower** *noun*, **rowing-
boat** *noun*

row[3] (rhymes with *cow*) *noun* (*informal*)
1 a loud noise. **2** a quarrel. **3** a scolding.

rowdy *adjective* (**rowdier, rowdiest**) noisy
and disorderly. **rowdiness** *noun*

rowlock (*say* **rol**-ok) *noun* a device on the
side of a boat, keeping an oar in place.

royal *adjective* of or connected with a king
or queen. **royally** *adverb*

royalty *noun* (*plural* **royalties**) **1** being
royal. **2** a royal person or persons, *in the
presence of royalty.* **3** a payment made to an
author or composer etc. for each copy of a

work sold or for each performance.

RSVP *abbreviation* please reply (French =
répondez s'il vous plaît).

rub *verb* (**rubbed, rubbing**) move something backwards and forwards while
pressing it on something else. **rub** *noun*
rub out remove something by rubbing.

rubber *noun* **1** a strong elastic substance
used for making tyres, balls, hoses, etc.
2 a piece of rubber for rubbing out pencil
or ink marks. **rubbery** *adjective*
rubberduck an inflatable rubber boat that
has an outboard motor.

rubbish *noun* **1** things that are worthless
or not wanted. **2** nonsense.

rubble *noun* broken pieces of brick or
stone.

rubicund *adjective* ruddy; red-faced.

ruby *noun* (*plural* **rubies**) a red jewel.

ruck *noun* a dense crowd.

rucksack *noun* a bag on straps for carrying
on the back.

ructions *plural noun* (*informal*) protests
and noisy argument.

rudder *noun* a hinged upright piece at the
back of a ship or aircraft, used for steering.

ruddy *adjective* red and healthy-looking,
a ruddy complexion.

rude *adjective* **1** impolite. **2** indecent;
improper. **3** roughly made; crude, *a rude
shelter.* **4** vigorous; hearty, *in rude health.*
rudely *adverb*, **rudeness** *noun*

rudimentary *adjective* **1** of rudiments;
elementary. **2** not fully developed, *Penguins
have rudimentary wings.*

rudiments (*say* **rood**-i-ments) *plural noun*
the elementary principles of a subject,
Learn the rudiments of chemistry.

rue *verb* (**rued, ruing**) regret, *I rue the day
I started this!*

rueful *adjective* regretful. **ruefully** *adverb*

ruff *noun* **1** a starched pleated frill worn
round the neck in the 16th century in
Europe. **2** a collar-like ring of feathers or fur
round a bird's or animal's neck.

ruffian *noun* a violent lawless person.
ruffianly *adjective*

ruffle[1] *verb* (**ruffled, ruffling**) **1** disturb the
smoothness of a thing. **2** upset or annoy
someone, *Don't let him ruffle you.*

ruffle² *noun* a gathered ornamental frill.

rug *noun* **1** a thick mat for the floor. **2** a piece of thick fabric used as a blanket.

rugby *noun* (also **Rugby football**) a kind of ball game using an oval ball that players may carry or kick.

rugged *adjective* **1** having an uneven surface or outline; craggy. **2** sturdy.

rugger *noun* (*informal*) rugby.

ruin¹ *noun* **1** severe damage or destruction to something. **2** a building that has fallen down.

ruin² *verb* damage a thing so severely that it is useless; destroy. **ruination** *noun*

ruinous *adjective* **1** causing ruin. **2** in ruins; ruined.

rule¹ *noun* **1** something that people have to obey. **2** ruling; governing, *under Dutch rule.* **3** a carpenter's ruler.
as a rule usually; more often than not.

rule² *verb* (**ruled, ruling**) **1** govern; reign. **2** make a decision, *The referee ruled that it was a foul.* **3** draw a straight line with a ruler or other straight edge.

ruler *noun* **1** a person who governs. **2** a strip of wood, metal, or plastic with straight edges, used for measuring and drawing straight lines.

ruling *noun* a judgement.

rum *noun* a strong alcoholic drink made from sugar or molasses.

rumble *verb* (**rumbled, rumbling**) make a deep heavy continuous sound like thunder. **rumble** *noun*

ruminant¹ *adjective* ruminating.

ruminant² *noun* an animal that chews the cud (see *cud*).

ruminate *verb* (**ruminated, ruminating**) **1** chew the cud. **2** meditate; ponder, *ruminating on recent events.* **rumination** *noun*, **ruminative** *adjective*

rummage *verb* (**rummaged, rummaging**) turn things over or move them about while looking for something. **rummage** *noun*

rummy *noun* a card-game in which players try to form sets or sequences of cards.

rumour¹ *noun* information that spreads to a lot of people but may not be true.

rumour² *verb* **be rumoured** be spread as a rumour.

rump *noun* the hind part of an animal.

rumple *verb* (**rumpled, rumpling**) crumple; make a thing untidy.

rumpus *noun* (*plural* **rumpuses**) (*informal*) an uproar; an angry protest.

run¹ *verb* (**ran, run, running**) **1** move with quick steps so that both or all feet leave the ground at each stride. **2** go or travel; flow, *Tears ran down his cheeks.* **3** produce a flow of liquid, *Run some water into it.* **4** work or function, *The engine was running smoothly.* **5** manage; organize, *She runs a grocery shop.* **6** compete in a contest, *He ran for President.* **7** extend, *A fence runs round the estate.* **8** go or take in a vehicle, *I'll run you to the station.*
run away leave a place secretly or quickly.
run into collide with; happen to meet.
run out have used up your stock of something; knock over the wicket of a running batsman.
run over knock down or crush with a moving vehicle.

run² *noun* **1** the action of running; a time spent running, *Go for a run.* **2** a point scored in cricket or baseball. **3** a continuous series of events, etc., *She had a run of good luck.* **4** an enclosure for animals, *a chicken run.* **5** a track, *a ski-run.*
on the run running away from pursuit or capture.

runaway¹ *noun* someone who has run away.

runaway² *adjective* **1** having run away or out of control, *a runaway bus.* **2** won easily, *a runaway victory.*

rung¹ *noun* a cross-piece in a ladder.

rung² *past participle* of **ring³**.

runner *noun* **1** a person or animal that runs, especially in a race. **2** a stem that grows away from a plant and roots itself. **3** a groove, rod, or roller for a thing to move on; each of the long strips under a sledge. **4** a long narrow strip of carpet or covering. **runner bean** a kind of climbing bean.

runner-up *noun* (*plural* **runners-up**) someone who comes second in a competition.

running¹ *present participle* of **run**. **in the running** competing and with a chance of winning.

running[2] *adjective* continuous; consecutive; without an interval, *It rained for four days running.*

runny *adjective* flowing like liquid; producing a flow of liquid.

run-off *noun* water that does not enter the soil but flows away during rainfall, irrigation, etc.

runway *noun* a long hard surface on which aircraft take off and land.

rupee *noun* the unit of money in India, Pakistan, and other countries.

rupture *verb* (**ruptured, rupturing**) break; burst. **rupture** *noun*

rural *adjective* of or like the countryside.

rusbank *noun* a settle with riempies on the back and seat.

ruse *noun* a deception or trick.

rush[1] *verb* 1 hurry. 2 move or flow quickly. 3 attack or capture by rushing, *They rushed the rebels' stronghold.*

rush[2] *noun* (*plural* **rushes**) 1 a hurry. 2 a sudden movement towards something. 3 a sudden great demand for something, *a rush on yo-yos.*

rush[3] *noun* (*plural* **rushes**) a plant with a thin stem that grows in marshy places.

rush-hour *noun* the time when traffic is busiest.

rusk *noun* a kind of biscuit, especially for feeding babies.

russet *noun* reddish-brown colour.

rust[1] *noun* 1 a red or brown substance that forms on iron or steel exposed to damp and corrodes it. 2 reddish-brown colour.

rust[2] *verb* make or become rusty.

rustic *adjective* 1 rural. 2 made of rough timber or branches, *a rustic bridge.*

rusticate *verb* (**rusticated, rusticating**) settle in the country. **rustication** *noun*

rustle *verb* (**rustled, rustling**) 1 make a sound like paper being crumpled. 2 (*American*) steal horses or cattle, *cattle rustling.* **rustle** *noun*, **rustler** *noun* **rustle up** (*informal*) produce, *rustle up a meal.*

rusty *adjective* (**rustier, rustiest**) 1 coated with rust. 2 weakened by lack of use or practice, *My Afrikaans is a bit rusty.* **rustiness** *noun*

rut *noun* 1 a deep track made by wheels in soft ground. 2 a settled and usually dull way of life, *We are getting into a rut.* **rutted** *adjective*

ruthless *adjective* pitiless; merciless; cruel. **ruthlessly** *adverb*, **ruthlessness** *noun*

rye *noun* a cereal used to make bread, biscuits, etc.

Ss

S. *abbreviation* south; southern.

sabbath *noun* a weekly day for rest and prayer, Saturday for Jews, Sunday for Christians.

SABC *abbreviation* South African Broadcasting Corporation.

sable *noun* 1 a kind of dark fur. 2 (*poetic*) black.

sabotage *noun* deliberate damage or disruption to hinder an enemy, employer, etc. **sabotage** *verb*, **saboteur** *noun*

sabre *noun* 1 a heavy sword with a curved blade. 2 a light fencing-sword.

SABS *abbreviation* South African Bureau of Standards.

sac *noun* a bag-shaped part in an animal or plant.

saccharin (*say* sak-er-in) *noun* a very sweet substance used as a substitute for sugar.

saccharine (*say* sak-er-een) *adjective* unpleasantly sweet, *a saccharine smile.*

sachet (*say* sash-ay) *noun* a small sealed bag or packet holding a scented substance or a single portion of something.

sack[1] *noun* a large bag made of strong material. **sacking** *noun* **the sack** (*informal*) dismissal from a job, *He got the sack.*

sack[2] *verb* (*informal*) dismiss someone from a job.

sack[3] *verb* plunder a captured town in a violent destructive way. **sack** *noun*

sacrament *noun* an important Christian religious ceremony such as baptism or Holy Communion.

sacred *adjective* holy; of God or a god.

sacrifice[1] *noun* **1** giving something that you think will please a god. **2** giving up a thing you value, so that something good may happen. **3** a thing sacrificed, *The sacrifice, a goat, was brought into the courtyard.* **sacrificial** *adjective*

sacrifice[2] *verb* (**sacrificed, sacrificing**) give something as a sacrifice.

sacrilege (*say* sak-ril-ij) *noun* disrespect or damage to something people regard as sacred. **sacrilegious** *adjective*

sacrosanct *adjective* sacred or respected and therefore not to be harmed.

sad *adjective* (**sadder, saddest**) unhappy; showing or causing sorrow. **sadly** *adverb*, **sadness** *noun*

sadden *verb* make a person sad.

saddle[1] *noun* **1** a seat for putting on the back of a horse or other animal. **2** the seat of a bicycle. **3** a ridge of high land between two peaks.

saddle[2] *verb* (**saddled, saddling**) put a saddle on a horse etc.

sadist (*say* say-dist) *noun* a person who enjoys hurting other people. **sadism** *noun*, **sadistic** *adjective*

sadza *noun* a stiff porridge, usually made from mealie meal.

s.a.e. *abbreviation* stamped addressed envelope.

safari *noun* (*plural* **safaris**) an expedition to see or hunt wild animals.

safari park a park where wild animals are kept to be seen by visitors travelling in vehicles.

safari suit a lightweight suit with long or short trousers and a bush jacket.

safe[1] *adjective* free from risk or danger; not dangerous. **safely** *adverb*, **safeness** *noun*, **safety** *noun*

safe sex sexual activity in which special care is taken to prevent the spread of Aids and other sexually-transmitted diseases.

safe[2] *noun* a strong cupboard or box in which valuables can be locked safely.

safeguard[1] *noun* a protection.

safeguard[2] *verb* protect.

safety-pin *noun* a U-shaped pin with a clip fastening over the point.

saffron *noun* **1** deep yellow colour. **2** a kind of crocus with orange-coloured stigmas. **3** these stigmas dried and used to colour or flavour food.

sag *verb* (**sagged, sagging**) go down in the middle because something heavy is pressing on it; droop. **sag** *noun*

saga (*say* sah-ga) *noun* a long story with many episodes.

sagacious (*say* sa-gay-shus) *adjective* shrewd and wise. **sagaciously** *adverb*, **sagacity** *noun*

sage[1] *noun* a kind of herb.

sage[2] *adjective* wise. **sagely** *adverb*

sage[3] *noun* a wise and respected person.

sago *noun* a starchy white food used to make puddings.

sail[1] *noun* **1** a large piece of strong cloth attached to a mast etc. to catch the wind and make a ship or boat move. **2** a short voyage. **3** an arm of a windmill.

sail[2] *verb* **1** travel in a ship or boat. **2** start a voyage, *We sail at noon.* **3** control a ship or boat. **4** move quickly and smoothly. **sailing-ship** *noun*

sailor *noun* a person who sails; a member of a ship's crew or of a navy.

saint *noun* a holy or very good person. **saintly** *adverb*, **saintliness** *noun*

sake *noun* **for the sake of** so as to help or please a person, get a thing, etc.

salaam *noun* a low bow with the right hand on the forehead.

salad *noun* a mixture of vegetables eaten raw or cold.

salamander *noun* a lizard-like animal formerly thought to live in fire.

salami *noun* a spiced sausage.

salary *noun* (*plural* **salaries**) a regular wage, usually for a year's work, paid in monthly instalments. **salaried** *adjective*

sale *noun* **1** selling. **2** a time when things are sold at reduced prices.

salesperson *noun* (*plural* **salespersons** or **salespeople**) a person employed to sell goods. **salesman** *noun* (*plural* **salesmen**), **saleswoman** *noun* (*plural* **saleswomen**)

salient[1] (*say* say-lee-ent) *adjective*

1 projecting. 2 most noticeable, *the salient features of the plan.*

salient² *noun* a part of a fortification or battle-line that juts out.

saline *adjective* containing salt.

salinization *noun* the process in which soils become too salty and therefore infertile, *Poor irrigation and the accumulation of fertilizers increase the danger of salinization.*

saliva *noun* the natural liquid in a person's or animal's mouth. **salivary** *adjective*

salivate (*say* sal-iv-ayt) *verb* (**salivated, salivating**) form saliva. **salivation** *noun*

sallow *adjective* slightly yellow, *a sallow complexion.* **sallowness** *noun*

sally¹ *noun* (*plural* **sallies**) 1 a sudden rush forward. 2 an excursion. 3 a lively or witty remark, *sallies of humour.*

sally² *verb* (**sallied, sallying**) make a sudden attack or an excursion.

salmon (*say* sam-on) *noun* (*plural* **salmon**) a large edible fish with pink flesh.

salmonella (*say* sal-mon-el-a) *noun* a bacterium that can cause food-poisoning and various diseases.

salomi (*say* sa-loh-mee) *noun* a roti spread with a curried filling and rolled up.

salon *noun* 1 a large elegant room. 2 a room or shop where a hairdresser etc. receives customers.

saloon *noun* 1 a car with a hard roof. 2 a room where people can sit, drink, etc.

salt¹ *noun* 1 sodium chloride, the white substance that gives sea-water its taste and is used for flavouring food. 2 a chemical compound of a metal and an acid. **salty** *adjective*

salts *plural noun* a substance that looks like salt, especially a laxative.

salt² *verb* flavour or preserve food with salt.

salt-cellar *noun* a small dish or perforated pot holding salt for use at meals.

salubrious *adjective* good for people's health. **salubrity** *noun*

salutary *adjective* beneficial; having a good effect, *She gave us some salutary advice.*

salutation *noun* a greeting.

salute¹ *verb* (**saluted, saluting**) 1 raise your right hand to your forehead as a sign of respect. 2 greet, *saluted her with a smile.* 3 say that you respect or admire something, *We salute this achievement.*

salute² *noun* 1 the act of saluting. 2 the firing of guns as a sign of greeting or respect.

salvage *verb* (**salvaged, salvaging**) save or rescue something so that it can be used again. **salvage** *noun*

salvation *noun* 1 saving from loss or damage etc. 2 (in Christian teaching) saving the soul from sin and its consequences.

salve¹ *noun* 1 a soothing ointment. 2 something that soothes.

salve² *verb* (**salved, salving**) soothe a person's conscience or wounded pride.

salver *noun* a small tray, usually of metal.

salvo *noun* (*plural* **salvoes**) a volley of shots or of applause.

sambal *noun* a spiced relish that is served as a side dish with curries.

same *adjective* of one kind, exactly alike or equal; not changing; not different. **sameness** *noun*

samoosa *noun* a fried pastry in the shape of a triangle, which has a filling of spiced meat or vegetables.

samovar *noun* a Russian tea-urn.

samp *noun* coarsely ground maize kernels.

sampan *noun* a small flat-bottomed boat used in China.

sample¹ *noun* a small amount that shows what something is like; a specimen.

sample² *verb* (**sampled, sampling**) take a sample of something.

sampler *noun* a piece of embroidery worked in various stitches to show skill in needlework.

sanatorium *noun* a hospital for treating chronic diseases (e.g. tuberculosis) or convalescents.

sanctify *verb* (**sanctified, sanctifying**) make holy or sacred. **sanctification** *noun*

sanctimonious *adjective* making a show of being virtuous or pious.

sanction[1] *noun* 1 permission; authorization. 2 action taken against a nation that is considered to have broken an international law etc., *Sanctions against that country include refusing to trade with it.*

sanction[2] *verb* permit; authorize.

sanctity *noun* being sacred; holiness.

sanctuary *noun* (*plural* **sanctuaries**) 1 a safe place; a refuge. 2 a sacred place; the part of a church where the altar stands.

sanctum *noun* a person's private room.

sand[1] *noun* the tiny particles that cover the ground in deserts, sea-shores, etc. **sands** *plural noun* a sandy area.

sand[2] *verb* smooth or polish with sandpaper or some other rough material. **sander** *noun*

sandal *noun* a lightweight shoe with straps over the foot. **sandalled** *adjective*

sandalwood *noun* a scented wood from a tropical tree.

sandbag *noun* a bag filled with sand, used to build defences.

sandbank *noun* a bank of sand under water.

SANDF *abbreviation* South African National Defence Force.

sandpaper *noun* strong paper coated with sand or a similar substance, rubbed on rough surfaces to make them smooth.

sandstone *noun* rock made of compressed sand.

sandwich[1] *noun* (*plural* **sandwiches**) two or more slices of bread with jam, meat, or cheese etc. between them.

sandwich[2] *verb* put a thing between two other things.

sandy *adjective* 1 like sand; covered with sand. 2 yellowish-red, *sandy hair.* **sandiness** *noun*

sane *adjective* 1 having a healthy mind; not mad. 2 sensible. **sanely** *adverb*, **sanity** *noun*

sangoma *noun* a traditional healer; a person believed to be able to foretell the future and remove evil spirits.

sanguinary *adjective* bloodstained.

sanguine (*say* **sang**-gwin) *adjective* hopeful; optimistic.

sanitary *adjective* 1 free from germs and dirt; hygienic. 2 of sanitation.
sanitary towel an absorbent pad worn during menstruation.

sanitation *noun* arrangements for drainage and the disposal of sewage.

sanity *noun* being sane.

Sanskrit *noun* the ancient language of the Hindus in India.

sap[1] *noun* the liquid inside a plant, carrying food to all its parts.

sap[2] *verb* (**sapped, sapping**) take away a person's strength gradually.

sapling *noun* a young tree.

sapphire *noun* a bright-blue jewel.

saprophyte (*say* **sap**-roh-fyt) *noun* a plant or micro-organism that lives on dead or decaying organic substances.

Saracen *noun* an Arab or Muslim of the time of the Crusades.

sarcastic *adjective* saying amusing or contemptuous things that hurt someone's feelings; using irony. **sarcastically** *adverb*, **sarcasm** *noun*

sarcophagus *noun* (*plural* **sarcophagi**) a stone coffin, often decorated with carvings.

sardine *noun* a small sea-fish, usually sold in tins, packed tightly in oil.

sardonic *adjective* funny in a grim or sarcastic way. **sardonically** *adverb*

sari *noun* (*plural* **saris**) a length of cloth worn wrapped round the body as a garment, especially by Indian women and girls.

sarong *noun* a strip of cloth worn around the waist by men and women of Malaya and Java.

sartorial *adjective* of clothes.

sash *noun* (*plural* **sashes**) a strip of cloth worn round the waist or over one shoulder.

sash window *noun* a window that slides up and down.

satanic (*say* sa-**tan**-ik) *adjective* of or like Satan, the Devil in Jewish and Christian teaching.

satchel *noun* a bag worn on the shoulder or over the back, especially for carrying books to and from school.

sate *verb* (**sated, sating**) satiate.

sateen *noun* a cotton material that looks like satin.

satellite *noun* 1 a planet or spacecraft etc. that moves in an orbit round a planet, *The moon is a satellite of the earth.* 2 a country that is under the influence of a more powerful country; a hanger-on.

satiate (*say* say-shee-ayt) *verb* (**satiated, satiating**) satisfy an appetite or desire etc. fully; glut.

satiety (*say* sat-I-it-ee) *noun* being or feeling satiated.

satin *noun* a silky material that is shiny on one side. **satiny** *adjective*

satire *noun* using humour or exaggeration to make fun of a person or thing; a play or poem etc. that does this. **satirical** *adjective*, **satirically** *adverb*, **satirist** *noun*, **satirize** *verb*
• USAGE: Do not confuse with *satyr*.

satisfaction *noun* 1 satisfying. 2 being satisfied and pleased because of this. 3 something that satisfies a desire etc., *the satisfaction of a job well done.*

satisfactory *adjective* good enough; sufficient. **satisfactorily** *adverb*

satisfy *verb* (**satisfied, satisfying**) 1 give a person etc. what is needed or wanted. 2 make someone feel certain; convince, *The firefighters were satisfied that the fire was out.*

satsuma *noun* a kind of mandarin orange originally grown in Japan.

saturate *verb* (**saturated, saturating**) 1 make a thing very wet. 2 make something take in as much as possible of a substance or goods etc., *saturate the market with inferior goods.* **saturation** *noun*

saturnine *adjective* looking gloomy and forbidding, *a saturnine face.*

satyagraha (*say* sat-**ya**-grah-ha) *noun* a political struggle that uses non-violent means, such as that practised by Mahatma Gandhi and his followers.

satyr (*say* sat-er) *noun* (in Greek myths) a woodland god with a man's body and a goat's ears, tail, and legs.
• USAGE: Do not confuse with *satire*.

sauce *noun* 1 a thick liquid served with food to add flavour. 2 (*informal*) being cheeky; impudence.

saucepan *noun* a metal cooking-pan with a handle at the side.

saucer *noun* a small shallow object on which a cup etc. is placed.

saucy *adjective* (**saucier, sauciest**) cheeky; impudent. **saucily** *adverb*, **sauciness** *noun*

sauna *noun* a room or compartment filled with steam, used as a kind of bath (originally in Finland).

saunter *verb* walk slowly and casually. **saunter** *noun*

sausage *noun* a tube of skin or plastic stuffed with minced meat and other filling.

savage¹ *adjective* wild and fierce; cruel. **savagely** *adverb*, **savageness** *noun*, **savagery** *noun*

savage² *noun* a savage person.

savannah *noun* (also **savanna**) a grassy plain in a hot country, with few or no trees.

save¹ *verb* (**saved, saving**) 1 keep safe; free a person or thing from danger or harm. 2 keep something, especially money, so that it can be used later. 3 avoid wasting something, *This will save time.* 4 (in sports) prevent an opponent from scoring. **save** *noun*, **saver** *noun*

save² *preposition* except, *All the trains save one were late.*

savings *plural noun* money saved.

saviour *noun* a person who saves someone.
our Saviour Jesus Christ.

savour¹ *noun* the taste or smell of something.

savour² *verb* 1 taste or smell. 2 enjoy; relish.

savoury¹ *adjective* 1 tasty but not sweet. 2 having an appetizing taste or smell.

savoury² *noun* (*plural* **savouries**) a savoury dish.

saw¹ *noun* a tool with a zigzag edge for cutting wood or metal etc.

saw² *verb* (**sawed, sawn, sawing**) 1 cut with a saw. 2 move to and fro as a saw does.

saw[3] *past tense* of **see**[1].

sawdust *noun* powder that comes from wood cut by a saw.

sawmill *noun* a mill where timber is cut into planks etc. by machinery.

sawyer *noun* a person whose job is to saw timber.

saxophone *noun* a brass wind instrument with a reed in the mouthpiece. **saxophonist** *noun*

say[1] *verb* (**said, saying**) **1** speak or express something in words. **2** give an opinion, *What do you say about corporal punishment?*

say[2] *noun* the power to decide something, *I have no say in the matter.*

saying *noun* a well-known phrase or proverb or other statement.

scab *noun* **1** a hard crust that forms over a cut or graze while it is healing. **2** (*informal*) a blackleg. **scabby** *adjective*

scabbard *noun* the sheath of a sword or dagger.

scabies (*say* skay-beez) *noun* a contagious skin-disease that causes itching.

scaffold *noun* **1** a platform on which criminals are executed. **2** scaffolding.

scaffolding *noun* a structure of poles or tubes and planks making platforms for workers to stand on while building or repairing a house etc.

scald *verb* **1** burn yourself with very hot liquid or steam. **2** heat milk until it is nearly boiling. **3** clean pans etc. with boiling water. **scald** *noun*

scale[1] *noun* **1** a series of units, degrees, or qualities etc. for measuring something. **2** a series of musical notes going up or down in a fixed pattern. **3** proportion; ratio, *The scale of this map is one centimetre to the kilometre.* **4** the relative size or importance of something, *They entertain friends on a large scale.*

scale[2] *verb* (**scaled, scaling**) **1** climb, *She scaled the ladder.* **2** alter or arrange something in proportion to something else, *Scale your spending according to your income!*

scale[3] *noun* **1** each of the thin overlapping parts on the outside of fish, snakes, etc.; a thin flake or part like this. **2** a hard substance formed in a kettle or boiler by hard water, or on teeth.

scale[4] *verb* (**scaled, scaling**) remove scales or scale from something, *The fish was cleaned and scaled.*

scale[5] *noun* the pan of a balance. **scales** *plural noun* a device for weighing things.

scallop *noun* **1** a shellfish with two hinged fan-shaped shells. **2** each curve in an ornamental wavy border, *large scallops in a flower bed.* **scalloped** *adjective*

scallywag *noun* (*slang*) a rascal.

scalp[1] *noun* the skin on the top of the head.

scalp[2] *verb* cut or tear the scalp from.

scalpel *noun* a small straight knife used by a surgeon or artist.

scaly *adjective* covered in scales or scale.

scamp *noun* a rascal.

scamper *verb* run hurriedly. **scamper** *noun*

scampi *plural noun* large prawns.

scamto *noun* an African township jargon.

scan *verb* (**scanned, scanning**) **1** look at every part of something. **2** glance at something. **3** count the beats of a line of poetry; be correct in rhythm, *This line doesn't scan.* **4** sweep a radar or electronic beam over an area in search of something. **scan** *noun*, **scanner** *noun*

scandal *noun* **1** something shameful or disgraceful. **2** gossip about people's faults and wrongdoing, *Have you heard the latest scandal?* **scandalous** *adjective*

scandalize *verb* (**scandalized, scandalizing**) shock a person by something considered shameful or disgraceful.

scandalmonger *noun* a person who invents or gossips about scandal.

Scandinavian *adjective* of Scandinavia (= Norway, Sweden, and Denmark; sometimes also Finland and Iceland). **Scandinavian** *noun*

scansion *noun* the scanning of verse.

scant *adjective* scanty.

scanty *adjective* (**scantier, scantiest**) small in amount or extent; meagre, *a scanty harvest.* **scantily** *adverb*, **scantiness** *noun*

scapegoat *noun* a person who is made to bear the blame or punishment for what others have done.

scar[1] *noun* the mark left by a cut or burn etc. after it has healed.

scar[2] *verb* (**scarred, scarring**) make a scar or scars on skin etc.

scar[3] *noun* a steep craggy place.

scarab *noun* an ancient Egyptian ornament or symbol carved in the shape of a beetle.

scarce *adjective* not enough to supply people; rare. **scarcity** *noun*
make yourself scarce (*informal*) go away; keep out of the way.

scarcely *adverb* only just; only with difficulty, *She could scarcely walk.*

scare[1] *verb* (**scared, scaring**) frighten.

scare[2] *noun* a fright; alarm. **scary** *adjective*

scarecrow *noun* a figure of a person dressed in old clothes, set up to frighten birds away from crops.

scarf *noun* (*plural* **scarves**) a strip of material worn round the neck or head.

scarlet *adjective* & *noun* bright red.
scarlet fever an infectious fever producing a scarlet rash.

scarp *noun* a steep slope on a hill.

scathing (*say* **skayth**-ing) *adjective* severely criticizing a person or thing.

scatter *verb* throw or send or move in various directions.

scatterbrain *noun* a careless forgetful person. **scatterbrained** *adjective*

scavenge *verb* (**scavenged, scavenging**) 1 search for useful things amongst rubbish. 2 (of a bird or animal) search for decaying flesh as food. **scavenger** *noun*

scenario (*say* si-**nah**-ree-oh) *noun* (*plural* **scenarios**) a summary of the plot of a play etc.
● USAGE: Note that this word does not mean the same as *scene*.

scene *noun* 1 the place where something happens, *the scene of the crime.* 2 a part of a play or film. 3 a view as seen by a spectator, *a pleasant country scene.* 4 an angry or noisy outburst, *He made a scene about the money.* 5 stage scenery.

scenery *noun* 1 the natural features of a landscape. 2 things put on a stage to make it look like a place.

scenic *adjective* having fine natural scenery, *a scenic road along the coast.*

scent[1] *noun* 1 a pleasant smell. 2 a liquid perfume. 3 an animal's smell that other animals can detect.

scent[2] *verb* 1 discover something by its scent; detect. 2 put scent on something; make fragrant. **scented** *adjective*

sceptic (*say* **skep**-tik) *noun* a sceptical person.

sceptical (*say* **skep**-tik-al) *adjective* not believing things. **sceptically** *adverb*, **scepticism** *noun*

sceptre *noun* a rod carried by a king or queen as a symbol of sovereignty.

schedule[1] (*say* **shed**-yool) *noun* a programme or timetable of planned events or work.

schedule[2] *verb* (**scheduled, scheduling**) put into a schedule; plan.

schematic (*say* skee-**mat**-ik) *adjective* in the form of a diagram or chart.

scheme[1] *noun* a plan of action.

scheme[2] *verb* (**schemed, scheming**) make plans; plot. **schemer** *noun*

scherzo (*say* **skairts**-oh) *noun* (*plural* **scherzos**) a lively piece of music.

schism (*say* skizm or sizm) *noun* the splitting of a group into two opposing sections because they disagree about something important.

schizophrenia (*say* skit-zo-**free**-nee-a) *noun* a kind of mental illness in which a person finds it more and more difficult to relate to others and to the real world. **schizophrenic** *adjective* & *noun*

scholar *noun* 1 a person who has studied a subject thoroughly. 2 a person who has been awarded a scholarship. **scholarly** *adjective*

scholarship *noun* 1 a grant of money given to someone to help to pay for his or her education. 2 scholars' knowledge or methods; advanced study.

scholastic *adjective* of schools or education; academic.

school[1] *noun* 1 a place where teaching is

done, especially of pupils aged 5–18.
2 the pupils in a school. **3** the time when
teaching takes place in a school, *School
begins at 8 a.m.* **4** a group of people who
have the same beliefs or style of work etc.,
the impressionist school of painting.
schoolboy *noun,* **schoolchild** *noun,*
schoolgirl *noun,* **schoolmaster** *noun,*
schoolmistress *noun,* **schoolroom** *noun,*
schoolteacher *noun*
school² *verb* train, *She was schooling her
horse for the competition.*
school³ *noun* a shoal of fish or whales
etc.
schooling *noun* training; education,
especially in a school.
schooner (*say* skoon-er) *noun* a sailing-
ship with two or more masts and with
sails rigged along its length, not crosswise.
sciatica (*say* sy-**at**-ik-a) *noun* pain in the
sciatic nerve (a large nerve in the hip and
thigh).
science *noun* the study of chemistry,
physics, plants and animals, etc.
science fiction stories about imaginary
scientific discoveries or space travel and
life on other planets.
scientific *adjective* **1** of science or scientists. **2** studying things systematically and
testing ideas carefully. **scientifically** *adverb*
scientist *noun* an expert in science;
someone who studies science.
sci-fi (*say* sy-fy) *abbreviation* (*informal*)
science fiction.
scimitar *noun* a curved oriental sword.
scintillate *verb* (**scintillated, scintillating**)
sparkle; be brilliant. **scintillation** *noun*
scion (*say* sy-on) *noun* a descendant,
especially of a noble family.
scissors *plural noun* a cutting-
instrument used with one hand, with
two blades pivoted so that they can close
against each other.
scoff *verb* jeer; speak contemptuously.
scoffer *noun*
scold *verb* rebuke; find fault with
someone angrily. **scolding** *noun*
scone (*say* skon) *noun* a soft flat cake,
usually eaten with butter.
scoop¹ *noun* **1** a kind of deep spoon

for serving ice-cream etc. **2** a deep shovel
for lifting grain, sugar, etc. **3** a scooping
movement. **4** an important piece of news
published by only one newspaper.
scoop² *verb* lift or hollow something out
with a scoop.
scoot *verb* run or go away quickly.
scooter *noun* **1** a kind of lightweight
motor cycle. **2** a board for riding on, with
wheels and a long handle.
scope *noun* **1** opportunity to work, *This
job gives scope for your musical abilities.*
2 the range or extent of a subject.
scorch *verb* **1** make something go brown
by burning it slightly. **2** (*informal*) travel
very fast, *scorching along.*
scorching *adjective* (*informal*) very hot.
score¹ *noun* **1** the number of points or
goals made in a game; a result. **2** twenty,
'Three score years and ten' means $3 \times 20 +
10 = 70$ *years.* **3** written or printed music.
4 a reason, *We refused to go on the score
of cost.*
score² *verb* (**scored, scoring**) **1** get a
point or goal in a game. **2** keep a count of
the score. **3** mark with lines or cuts, *rocks
scored by wind-driven sand.* **4** write out a
musical score. **scorer** *noun*
scorn¹ *noun* contempt. **scornful**
adjective, **scornfully** *adverb*
scorn² *verb* treat or refuse scornfully.
scorpion *noun* a small animal that has
eight legs, two of which form claws, and
a long tail that can bend over its body to
give a poisonous sting.
scotch *verb* put an end to an idea or
rumour etc.
scot-free *adjective* without harm or
punishment.
scour¹ *verb* **1** rub something until it is
clean and bright. **2** clear a channel or pipe
by the force of water flowing through it.
scourer *noun*
scour² *verb* search thoroughly.
scourge¹ (*say* skerj) *noun* **1** a whip for
flogging people. **2** something that inflicts
suffering or punishment.
scourge² *verb* (**scourged, scourging**)
1 flog with a whip. **2** cause suffering or
punishment.

Scout *noun* a member of the Scout Association, an organization for boys.

scout[1] *noun* someone sent out to collect information.

scout[2] *verb* act as a scout; search an area thoroughly.

scowl[1] *noun* a bad-tempered frown.

scowl[2] *verb* make a scowl.

Scrabble *noun* (*trade mark*) a game played on a board, in which words are built up from single letters.

scrabble *verb* (**scrabbled, scrabbling**) 1 scratch or claw at something with the hands or feet. 2 grope or struggle to get something.

scraggy *adjective* thin and bony.

scram *verb* (*informal*) go away.

scramble[1] *verb* (**scrambled, scrambling**) 1 move quickly and awkwardly. 2 struggle to do or get something, *Players scrambled for possession of the ball.* 3 (of aircraft or their crew) hurry and take off quickly. 4 cook eggs by mixing them up and heating them in a pan. 5 mix things together. 6 alter a telephone signal so that it cannot be used without a special receiver. **scrambler** *noun*

scramble[2] *noun* 1 a climb or walk over rough ground. 2 a struggle to do or get something. 3 a motor-cycle race over rough ground.

scrap[1] *noun* 1 a small piece. 2 rubbish; waste material, especially metal that is suitable for reprocessing.

scrap[2] *verb* (**scrapped, scrapping**) get rid of something that is useless or unwanted.

scrap[3] *noun* (*informal*) a fight.

scrap[4] *verb* (**scrapped, scrapping**) (*informal*) fight.

scrapbook *noun* a book that has blank pages for sticking pictures, cuttings, etc. in.

scrape[1] *verb* (**scraped, scraping**) 1 clean or smooth or damage something by passing something hard over it. 2 remove by scraping, *Scrape the mud off your shoes.* 3 pass with difficulty, *We scraped through.* 4 get something by great effort or care, *They scraped together enough money for a holiday.* **scraper** *noun*

scrape[2] *noun* 1 a scraping movement

or sound. 2 a mark etc. made by scraping. 3 an awkward situation caused by mischief or foolishness.

scrappy *adjective* made of scraps or bits or disconnected things. **scrappiness** *noun*

scratch[1] *verb* 1 mark or cut the surface of a thing with something sharp. 2 rub the skin with fingernails or claws because it itches. 3 withdraw from a race or competition, *The horse was scratched from the race.*

scratch[2] *noun* (*plural* **scratches**) 1 a mark made by scratching. 2 the action of scratching. **scratchy** *adjective* **start from scratch** start from the beginning or with nothing prepared. **up to scratch** up to the proper standard.

scrawl[1] *noun* untidy handwriting.

scrawl[2] *verb* write in a scrawl.

scrawny *adjective* scraggy.

scream[1] *noun* 1 a loud cry of pain, fear, anger, or excitement. 2 a loud piercing sound. 3 (*informal*) a very amusing person or thing, *She's a scream.*

scream[2] *verb* make a scream.

scree *noun* a mass of loose stones on the side of a mountain.

screech *noun* a harsh high-pitched scream or sound. **screech** *verb*

screed *noun* a very long piece of writing.

screen[1] *noun* 1 a thing that protects, hides, or divides something. 2 a surface on which films or television pictures are shown. 3 a windscreen.

screen[2] *verb* 1 protect, hide, or divide with a screen. 2 show a film or television pictures on a screen. 3 examine carefully, e.g. to check whether a person is suitable for a job or whether a substance is present in something. 4 sift gravel etc.

screw[1] *noun* 1 a metal pin with a spiral ridge (the *thread*) round it, holding things together by being twisted in. 2 a twisting movement. 3 something twisted, *a screw of paper.* 4 a propeller, especially for a ship or motor boat.

screw[2] *verb* 1 fasten with a screw or screws. 2 twist.

screwdriver *noun* a tool for turning screws.

scribble *verb* (**scribbled, scribbling**)
1 write quickly or untidily or carelessly.
2 make meaningless marks. **scribble** *noun*

scribe *noun* 1 a person who made copies of writings before printing was invented. 2 a professional religious scholar in former times. **scribal** *adjective*

scrimmage *noun* a confused struggle.

scrimp *verb* skimp, *scrimp and save.*

script *noun* 1 handwriting. 2 a manuscript. 3 the text of a play, film, broadcast talk, etc.

scripture *noun* sacred writings, especially the Bible.

scroll[1] *noun* 1 a roll of paper or parchment used for writing on. 2 a spiral design.

scroll[2] *verb* move a display on a computer screen in order to view new material.

scrotum (*say* **skroh**-tum) *noun* the pouch of skin behind the penis, containing the testicles. **scrotal** *adjective*

scrounge *verb* (**scrounged, scrounging**) (*informal*) cadge. **scrounger** *noun*

scrub[1] *verb* (**scrubbed, scrubbing**) 1 rub with a hard brush, especially to clean something. 2 (*informal*) cancel. **scrub** *noun*

scrub[2] *noun* low trees and bushes; land covered with these.

scrubby *adjective* undersized and shabby or wretched.

scruff *noun* the back of the neck.

scruffy *adjective* shabby and untidy. **scruffily** *adverb*, **scruffiness** *noun*

scrum *noun* 1 (also **scrummage**) a group of players from each side in rugby who push against each other and try to heel out the ball which is thrown between them. 2 a crowd pushing against each other.

scrumptious *adjective* delicious.

scrunch *verb* crunch.

scruple[1] *noun* a feeling of doubt or hesitation when your conscience tells you that an action would be wrong.

scruple[2] *verb* (**scrupled, scrupling**) have scruples, *He would not scruple to betray us.*

scrupulous *adjective* 1 very careful and conscientious. 2 strictly honest or honourable. **scrupulously** *adverb*

scrutinize *verb* (**scrutinized, scrutinizing**) examine or look at something carefully. **scrutiny** *noun*

scuba-diving *noun* swimming underwater using an aqualung.

scud *verb* (**scudded, scudding**) move fast, *Clouds scudded across the sky.*

scuff *verb* 1 drag your feet while walking. 2 scrape with your foot; mark or damage something by doing this.

scuffle[1] *noun* a confused fight or struggle.

scuffle[2] *verb* (**scuffled, scuffling**) take part in a scuffle.

scull[1] *noun* a small or lightweight oar.

scull[2] *verb* row with sculls.

scullery *noun* (*plural* **sculleries**) a room where dishes etc. are washed up.

sculptor *noun* a person who makes sculptures.

sculpture *noun* making shapes by carving wood or stone or casting metal; a shape made in this way. **sculpture** *verb*

scum *noun* 1 froth or dirt on top of a liquid. 2 worthless people.

scupper[1] *noun* an opening in a ship's side to let water drain away.

scupper[2] *verb* 1 sink a ship deliberately. 2 (*informal*) wreck, *It scuppered our plans.*

scurf *noun* flakes of dry skin. **scurfy** *adjective*

scurrilous *adjective* 1 very insulting. 2 vulgar. **scurrilously** *adverb*

scurry *verb* (**scurried, scurrying**) run with short steps; hurry.

scurvy *noun* a disease caused by lack of vitamin C in food.

scut *noun* the short tail of a rabbit etc.

scutter *verb* scurry.

scuttle[1] *noun* a bucket or container for coal in a house.

scuttle[2] *verb* (**scuttled, scuttling**) scurry; hurry away.

scuttle[3] *noun* a small opening with a lid in a ship's deck or side.

scuttle[4] *verb* (**scuttled, scuttling**) sink a ship deliberately by letting water into it.

scythe[1] *noun* a tool with a long curved blade for cutting grass or corn.

scythe[2] *verb* (**scythed**, **scything**) cut with a scythe.

SE *abbreviation* south-east; south-eastern.

se- *prefix* 1 apart; aside (as in *secluded*). 2 without (as in *secure*).

sea *noun* 1 the salt water that covers most of the earth's surface; a part of this. 2 a lake, *the Sea of Galilee*. 3 a large area of something, *a sea of faces*.
at sea on the sea; not knowing what to do.
sea anemone a sea-creature with short tentacles round its mouth.
sea change a dramatic change.

seaboard *noun* the coast.

seafaring *adjective* & *noun* working or travelling on the sea. **seafarer** *noun*

seafood *noun* fish or shellfish from the sea eaten as food.

seagull *noun* a sea-bird with long wings.

sea-horse *noun* a small fish with a head rather like a horse's head.

seal[1] *noun* a sea-animal with thick fur or bristles, that eats fish.

seal[2] *noun* 1 a piece of metal with an engraved design for pressing on a soft substance to leave an impression. 2 this impression. 3 something designed to close an opening and prevent air or liquid etc. from getting in or out. 4 a small decorative sticker, *Christmas seals*.

seal[3] *verb* 1 close something by sticking two parts together. 2 close securely; stop up, *The jar must be properly sealed*. 3 press a seal on something.
seal off prevent people getting to an area.

sea-level *noun* the level of the sea half-way between high and low tide.

sealing-wax *noun* a substance that is soft when heated but hardens when cooled, used for sealing documents or for marking with a seal.

sea-lion *noun* a kind of large seal.

seam *noun* 1 the line where two edges of cloth or wood etc. join. 2 a layer of coal etc. in the ground.

seaman *noun* (*plural* **seamen**) a sailor.

seamanship *noun* skill in seafaring.

seamy *adjective* **seamy side** the less attractive side or part, *Police see a lot of the seamy side of life*.

seance (*say* say-ahns) *noun* a spiritualist meeting.

seaplane *noun* an aeroplane that can land on and take off from water.

seaport *noun* a port on the coast.

sear *verb* scorch or burn the surface of something.

search *verb* look very carefully in a place etc. in order to find something. **search** *noun*, **searcher** *noun*

searchlight *noun* a light with a strong beam that can be turned in any direction.

seascape *noun* a picture or view of the sea. (Compare *landscape*.)

seasick *adjective* sick because of the movement of a ship. **seasickness** *noun*

seaside *noun* a place by the sea where people go for holidays.

season[1] *noun* 1 each of the four main parts of the year (spring, summer, autumn, winter). 2 the time of year when something happens, *the cricket season*.
in season available and ready for eating, *Apples are in season in the autumn*; (of a female animal) ready to mate.

season[2] *verb* 1 give extra flavour to food by adding salt, pepper, or other strong-tasting substances. 2 dry and treat timber etc. to make it ready for use.

seasonable *adjective* suitable for the season, *Hot weather is seasonable in summer*. **seasonably** *adverb*

seasonal *adjective* of or for a season; happening in a particular season, *Fruit-picking is seasonal work*. **seasonally** *adverb*

seasoning *noun* a substance used to season food.

season-ticket *noun* a ticket that can be used as often as you like throughout a period of time.

seat[1] *noun* 1 a thing made or used for sitting on. 2 the right to be a member of a council, committee, parliament, etc., *She won the seat ten years ago*. 3 the buttocks; the part of a skirt or trousers covering these. 4 the place where something is based or located, *London is the seat of the British government*.

seat² *verb* **1** place in or on a seat. **2** have seats for, *The theatre seats 3 000 people.*

seat-belt *noun* a strap to hold a person securely in a seat.

sea-urchin *noun* a sea-animal with a shell covered in sharp spikes.

seaward *adjective* & *adverb* towards the sea. **seawards** *adverb*

seaweed *noun* a plant or plants that grow in the sea.

seaworthy *adjective* (of a ship) fit for a sea voyage. **seaworthiness** *noun*

secant *noun* **1** a line cutting a curve at one or more points. **2** (in a right-angled triangle) the ratio of the hypotenuse to the shorter side adjacent to an acute angle.

secateurs *plural noun* clippers held in the hand for pruning plants.

secede (*say* sis-**seed**) *verb* (**seceded, seceding**) withdraw from being a member of an organization of states or a religious body. **secession** *noun*

secluded *adjective* screened or sheltered from view. **seclusion** *noun*

second¹ *adjective* **1** next after the first. **2** another, *a second chance.* **3** less good, *second quality.* **secondly** *adverb*
second nature behaviour that has become automatic or a habit, *Lying is second nature to him.*
second sight the ability to foresee the future.

second² *noun* **1** a person or thing that is second. **2** an attendant of a fighter in a boxing-match, duel, etc. **3** a thing that is of second (not the best) quality. **4** one-sixtieth of a minute of time or of a degree used in measuring angles.

second³ *verb* **1** assist someone. **2** support a proposal, motion, etc. **seconder** *noun*

second⁴ (*say* sik-**ond**) *verb* transfer a person temporarily to another job or department etc. **secondment** *noun*

secondary *adjective* **1** coming after or from something. **2** less important. **3** (of education etc.) for children in standards 6 to 10, *a secondary school.* (Compare *primary.*)
secondary colours colours made by mixing two primary colours.

secondary consumer an animal that eats primary consumers (herbivores).

secondary production the process of turning raw materials into finished goods through manufacturing, construction, etc.

second-hand *adjective* **1** bought or used after someone else has owned it. **2** selling used goods, *a second-hand shop.*

secret¹ *adjective* **1** that must not be told or shown to other people. **2** not known by everybody. **3** working secretly, *a secret agent.* **secretly** *adverb*, **secrecy** *noun*

secret² *noun* something secret.

secretariat *noun* an administrative department of a large organization such as the United Nations.

secretary (*say* sek-rit-ree) *noun* (*plural* **secretaries**) **1** a person whose job is to help with letters, answer the telephone, and make business arrangements for a person or organization. **2** the chief assistant of a government minister or ambassador. **secretarial** *adjective*
secretary bird a bird which has long legs and prominent feathers behind the ears.

secrete (*say* sik-**reet**) *verb* (**secreted, secreting**) **1** hide something. **2** produce a substance in the body, *Saliva is secreted in the mouth.* **secretion** *noun*

secretive (*say* **seek**-rit-iv) *adjective* liking or trying to keep things secret. **secretively** *adverb*, **secretiveness** *noun*

sect *noun* a group whose beliefs differ from those of others in the same religion; a faction.

sectarian (*say* sekt-**air**-ee-an) *adjective* belonging to or supporting a sect.

section *noun* **1** a part of something. **2** a cross-section. **sectional** *adjective*

sector *noun* **1** one part of an area. **2** a part of something, *the private sector of industry.*

secular *adjective* of worldly affairs, not of spiritual or religious matters.

secure¹ *adjective* **1** safe, especially against attack. **2** certain not to slip or fail. **3** reliable, *a secure investment.* **securely** *adverb*

secure² *verb* (**secured, securing**) **1** make a thing secure. **2** obtain,

We secured two tickets for the show.

security *noun* (*plural* **securities**)
1 being secure; safety. 2 precautions against theft or spying etc., *a security system.* 3 something given as a guarantee that a promise will be kept or a debt repaid. 4 investments such as stocks and shares.

sedan-chair *noun* an enclosed chair for one person, mounted on two horizontal poles and carried by two people, used in the 17th–18th centuries.

sedate *adjective* calm and dignified. **sedately** *adverb*, **sedateness** *noun*

sedative (*say* sed-a-tiv) *noun* a medicine that makes a person calm. **sedation** *noun*

sedentary (*say* sed-en-ter-ee) *adjective* done sitting down, *sedentary work.*

sedge *noun* a grass-like plant growing in marshes or near water.

sediment *noun* fine particles of solid matter that float in liquid or sink to the bottom of it.

sedimentary *adjective* formed from particles that have settled on a surface, *sedimentary rocks.*

sedition *noun* making people rebel against the authority of the State. **seditious** *adjective*

seduce *verb* (**seduced, seducing**)
1 persuade a person to have sexual intercourse. 2 attract or lead astray by offering temptations. **seducer** *noun*, **seduction** *noun*, **seductive** *adjective*

sedulous *adjective* diligent and persevering. **sedulously** *adverb*

see[1] *verb* (**saw, seen, seeing**) 1 perceive with the eyes. 2 meet or visit somebody, *See a doctor about your cough.* 3 understand, *She saw what I meant.* 4 imagine, *Can you see yourself as a teacher?* 5 consider, *I will see what can be done.* 6 make sure, *See that the windows are shut.* 7 discover, *See who is at the door.* 8 escort, *See her to the door.*

see through not be deceived by something.

see to attend to.

see[2] *noun* the district of which a bishop or archbishop is in charge, *the see of Johannesburg.*

seed[1] *noun* (*plural* **seeds** or **seed**)
1 a fertilized part of a plant, capable of growing into a new plant. 2 (*old use*) descendants. 3 a seeded player.

seed[2] *verb* 1 plant or sprinkle seeds in something. 2 name the best players and arrange for them not to play against each other in the early rounds of a tournament.

seed-bed *noun* a specially prepared piece of ground where seedlings are grown before they are transplanted.

seedling *noun* a very young plant growing from a seed.

seedy *adjective* (**seedier, seediest**)
1 full of seeds. 2 shabby and disreputable. **seediness** *noun*

seeing *conjunction* considering, *Seeing that we have all finished, let's go.*

seek *verb* (**sought, seeking**) search for; try to find or obtain.

seem *verb* give the impression of being something, *She seems worried about her work.* **seemingly** *adverb*

seemly *adjective* (of behaviour etc.) proper; suitable. **seemliness** *noun*

seep *verb* ooze slowly out or through something. **seepage** *noun*

seer *noun* a prophet.

seersucker *noun* fabric woven with a puckered surface.

see-saw *noun* a plank balanced in the middle so that two people can sit, one on each end, and make it go up and down.

seethe *verb* (**seethed, seething**)
1 bubble and surge like water boiling. 2 be very angry or excited.

segment *noun* a part that is cut off or separates naturally from other parts, *the segments of an orange.* **segmented** *adjective*

segregate *verb* (**segregated, segregating**) 1 separate people of different religions, races, etc. 2 isolate a person or thing. **segregation** *noun*

seine (*say* sayn) *noun* a fishing-net with weights at the bottom edge and floats at the top.

seismic (*say* sy-zmik) *adjective* of earthquakes or other vibrations of the earth.

seismograph (*say* sy-zmo-grahf) *noun* an instrument for measuring the strength of earthquakes.

seize *verb* (**seized, seizing**) **1** take hold of a person or thing suddenly or forcibly. **2** take eagerly, *Seize your chance!* **3** have a sudden effect on, *Panic seized us.*
seize up become jammed, especially because of friction or overheating.

seizure *noun* **1** seizing. **2** a sudden fit, as in epilepsy or a heart attack.

seldom *adverb* rarely; not often.

select[1] *verb* choose a person or thing.
selection *noun*, **selector** *noun*

select[2] *adjective* **1** carefully chosen, *a select group of pupils.* **2** (of a club etc.) choosing its members carefully; exclusive.

selective *adjective* choosing or chosen carefully. **selectively** *adverb*, **selectivity** *noun*

self *noun* (*plural* **selves**) **1** a person as an individual. **2** a person's particular nature, *She has recovered and is her old self again.* **3** a person's own advantage, *He always puts self first.*

self- *prefix* **1** of or to or done by yourself or itself. **2** automatic (as in *self-loading*).
self-addressed addressed to yourself.
self-assured self-confident.
self-catering catering for yourself (instead of having meals provided).
self-centred selfish.
self-confident confident of your own abilities.
self-conscious embarrassed or unnatural because you know that people are watching you.
self-contained complete in itself.
self-control the ability to control your own behaviour.
self-controlled having self-control.
self-defence defending yourself.
self-denial deliberately going without things you would like to have.
self-employed working independently, not for an employer.
self-evident obvious and not needing proof or explanation.
self-important pompous.

self-interest your own advantage.
self-possessed calm and dignified.
self-raising (of flour) making cakes rise without needing to have baking-powder etc. added.
self-respect your own proper respect for yourself.
self-righteous smugly sure that you are behaving virtuously.
self-satisfied very pleased with yourself.
self-seeking selfishly trying to benefit yourself.
self-service where customers help themselves to things and pay a cashier for what they have taken.
self-sufficient able to provide what you need without help from others.
self-willed obstinately doing what you want; stubborn.

selfish *adjective* doing what you want and not thinking of other people; keeping things for yourself. **selfishly** *adverb*, **selfishness** *noun*

selfless *adjective* unselfish.

selfsame *adjective* the very same.

sell[1] *verb* (**sold, selling**) exchange something for money. **seller** *noun*
sell out sell all your stock of something; (*informal*) betray someone.

sell[2] *noun* **1** the manner of selling something. **2** (*informal*) a deception.

selvage *noun* an edge of cloth woven so that it does not unravel.

selves *plural* of **self**.

semaphore *noun* a system of signalling by holding the arms in positions that indicate letters of the alphabet.

semblance *noun* an outward appearance.

semen (*say* **seem**-en) *noun* a white liquid produced by males and containing sperm.

semi- *prefix* half; partly.

semibreve *noun* the longest musical note normally used, equal to two minims in length.

semicircle *noun* half a circle.
semicircular *adjective*

semicolon *noun* a punctuation mark (;) used to mark a break that is more than that marked by a comma.

semiconductor *noun* a substance that can conduct electricity but not as well as most metals do.

semi-detached *adjective* (of a house) joined to another house on one side only.

semifinal *noun* a match or round whose winner will take part in the final.

seminar *noun* a meeting for advanced discussion and research on a subject.

seminary *noun* (*plural* **seminaries**) a training college for priests or rabbis.

semiquaver *noun* a note in music, equal to half a quaver in length.

Semitic (*say* sim-**it**-ik) *adjective* of the Semites, the group of people that includes the Jews and Arabs. **Semite** (*say* **see**-my't) *noun*

semitone *noun* half a tone in music.

semolina *noun* hard round grains of wheat used to make milk puddings and pasta.

senate *noun* 1 the governing council in ancient Rome. 2 the upper house of a par- liament, usually with members nominated by political parties. **senator** *noun*

send *verb* (**sent, sending**) 1 make a per- son or thing go somewhere. 2 cause to become, *It sent them mad.* **sender** *noun*

send for order a person or thing to come or be brought to you.

send up (*informal*) make fun of something by imitating it.

senile (*say* **seen**-I'll) *adjective* suffering from weakness of the body or mind because of old age. **senility** *noun*

senior[1] *adjective* 1 older in age. 2 higher in rank. 3 for older children, *a senior school.* **seniority** *noun*

senior[2] *noun* 1 a person who is older or higher in rank than you are, *He is my senior.* 2 a member of a senior school.

senna *noun* the dried pods or leaves of a tropical tree, used as a laxative.

sensation *noun* 1 a feeling, *a sensation of warmth.* 2 a very excited condition; something causing this, *The news caused a great sensation.* **sensational** *adjective*, **sensationally** *adverb*

sensationalism *noun* deliberate use of dramatic words or style etc. to arouse

excitement. **sensationalist** *noun*

sense[1] *noun* 1 the ability to see, hear, smell, touch, or taste things. 2 the ability to feel or appreciate something; aware- ness, *a sense of humour.* 3 the power to think or make wise decisions, *She hasn't got the sense to come in out of the rain.* 4 meaning, *The word 'run' has many senses.*

senses *plural noun* sanity, *He is out of his senses.*

make sense have a meaning; be a sensible idea.

sense[2] *verb* (**sensed, sensing**) 1 feel; get an impression, *I sensed that she did not like me.* 2 detect something, *This device senses radioactivity.* **sensor** *noun*

senseless *adjective* 1 stupid; not showing good sense. 2 unconscious.

sensibility *noun* (*plural* **sensibilities**) sensitiveness; feeling, *The criticism hurt the artist's sensibilities.*

● USAGE: Note that this word does not mean 'being sensible' or 'having good sense'.

sensible *adjective* 1 wise; having or show- ing good sense. 2 aware, *We are sensible of the honour you have done us.* **sensibly** *adverb*

sensitive *adjective* 1 receiving impres- sions quickly and easily, *sensitive fingers.* 2 easily hurt or offended, *She is very sens- itive about her height.* 3 affected by some- thing. *Photographic paper is sensitive to light.* **sensitively** *adverb*, **sensitivity** *noun*

sensitize *verb* (**sensitized, sensitizing**) make a thing sensitive to something.

sensory *adjective* of the senses; receiving sensations, *sensory nerves.*

sensual *adjective* of the senses; pleasing the body, *sensual pleasures.*

sensuous *adjective* giving pleasure to the senses, especially by being beautiful or delicate.

sentence[1] *noun* 1 a group of words that express a complete thought and form a statement, question, exclamation, or com- mand. 2 the punishment announced to a convicted person in a lawcourt.

sentence[2] *verb* (**sentenced, sentencing**) give someone a sentence in a lawcourt, *The judge sentenced him to a year in prison.*

sententious *adjective* giving moral advice in a pompous way.

sentient *adjective* capable of feeling and perceiving things, *sentient beings.*

sentiment *noun* 1 an opinion. 2 sentimentality.

sentimental *adjective* showing or arousing tenderness or romantic feeling or foolish emotion. **sentimentally** *adverb*, **sentimentality** *noun*

sentinel *noun* a sentry.

sentry *noun* (*plural* **sentries**) a soldier guarding something.

sepal *noun* each of the leaves forming the calyx of a bud.

separable *adjective* able to be separated.

separate[1] *adjective* not joined to anything; on its own; not shared. **separately** *adverb*

separate[2] *verb* (**separated, separating**) 1 make or keep separate; divide. 2 become separate. 3 stop living together as a married couple. **separation** *noun*, **separator** *noun*

sepia *noun* reddish-brown.

sepsis *noun* a septic condition.

septet *noun* 1 a group of seven musicians. 2 a piece of music for seven musicians.

septic *adjective* infected with harmful bacteria that cause pus to form.

sepulchral (*say* sep-**ul**-kral) *adjective* 1 of a sepulchre. 2 (of a voice) sounding deep and hollow.

sepulchre (*say* sep-ul-ker) *noun* a tomb.

sequel *noun* 1 a book or film etc. that continues the story of an earlier one. 2 something that follows or results from an earlier event.

sequence *noun* 1 the following of one thing after another; the order in which things happen. 2 a series of things.

sequestrate *verb* (**sequestrated, sequestrating**) confiscate. **sequestration** *noun*

sequin *noun* a tiny bright disc sewn on clothes etc. to decorate them. **sequinned** *adjective*

seraph *noun* (*plural* **seraphim** or **seraphs**) a kind of angel.

seraphic (*say* ser-**af**-ik) *adjective* angelic, *a seraphic smile.* **seraphically** *adverb*

serenade[1] *noun* a song or tune played by a lover to his lady.

serenade[2] *verb* (**serenaded, serenading**) sing or play a serenade to someone.

serene *adjective* calm and cheerful. **serenely** *adverb*, **serenity** *noun*

serf *noun* a farm labourer who worked for a landowner in the Middle Ages in Europe. **serfdom** *noun*

serge *noun* a kind of strong woven fabric.

sergeant (*say* sar-jent) *noun* a soldier or police officer who is in charge of others.

sergeant-major *noun* a soldier who is one rank higher than a sergeant.

serial *noun* a story or film etc. that is presented in separate parts.

serialize *verb* (**serialized, serializing**) produce a story or film etc. as a serial. **serialization** *noun*

series *noun* (*plural* **series**) a number of things following or connected with each other.

serious *adjective* 1 solemn and thoughtful; not smiling. 2 sincere; not casual; not light-hearted, *a serious attempt.* 3 causing anxiety, not trivial, *a serious accident.* **seriously** *adverb*, **seriousness** *noun*

sermon *noun* a talk given by a preacher, especially as part of a religious service.

serpent *noun* a snake.

serpentine *adjective* twisting and curving like a snake, *a serpentine road.*

serrated *adjective* having a notched edge.

serried *adjective* arranged in rows close together, *serried ranks of troops.*

serum (*say* seer-um) *noun* the thin pale-yellow liquid that remains from blood when the rest has clotted; this fluid used medically.

servant *noun* a person whose job is to work or serve in someone else's house.

serve[1] *verb* (**served, serving**) 1 work for a person or organization or country etc. 2 sell things to people in a shop. 3 give out food to people at a meal. **4** spend time in something; undergo, *He served a prison sentence.* **5** be suitable for something, *This will serve our purpose.* **6** start play in tennis etc. by hitting the ball. **server** *noun*

it serves you right you deserve it.

serve² *noun* a service in tennis etc.

service¹ *noun* **1** working for a person or organization or country etc. **2** something that helps people or supplies what they want, *a bus service.* **3** the army, navy, or air force, *the armed services.* **4** a religious ceremony. **5** providing people with goods, food, etc., *quick service.* **6** a set of dishes and plates etc. for a meal, *a dinner service.* **7** the servicing of a vehicle or machine etc. **8** the action of serving in tennis etc.

service² *verb* (**serviced**, **servicing**) **1** repair or keep a vehicle or machine etc. in working order. **2** supply with services.

serviceable *adjective* usable; suitable for ordinary use or wear.

serviceman *noun* (*plural* **servicemen**) a member of the armed services. **servicewoman** *noun* (*plural* **servicewomen**)

serviette *noun* a piece of cloth or paper used to keep your clothes or hands clean at a meal.

servile *adjective* of or like a slave; slavish. **servility** *noun*

servitude *noun* the condition of being obliged to work for someone else and having no independence; slavery.

session *noun* **1** a meeting or series of meetings, *The President will open the next session of Parliament.* **2** a time spent doing one thing, *a recording session.*

set¹ *verb* (**set**, **setting**) This word has many uses, including **1** put or fix, *Set the vase on the table. Set a date for the wedding.* **2** make or become firm or hard, *Leave the jelly to set.* **3** give someone a task, *This sets us a problem.* **4** put into a condition, *Set them free.* **5** go down below the horizon, *The sun was setting.*

set about start doing something; (*informal*) attack somebody.

set off begin a journey; start something happening; cause to explode.

set out begin a journey; display or make known.

set sail begin a voyage.

set to begin doing something vigorously; begin fighting or arguing.

set up place in position; establish, *set up house*; cause or start, *set up a din.*

set² *noun* **1** a group of people or things that belong together. **2** a radio or television receiver. **3** the way something is placed, *the set of her jaw.* **4** a badger's burrow. **5** the scenery or stage for a play or film. **6** a group of games in a tennis match.

set-back *noun* something that stops progress or slows it down.

set square *noun* a device shaped like a right-angled triangle, used in drawing lines parallel to each other etc.

settee *noun* a long soft seat with a back and arms.

setter *noun* a dog of a long-haired breed that can be trained to stand rigid when it scents game.

setting *noun* **1** the way or place in which something is set, *The setting of the play is Sophiatown in the 1950s.* **2** music for the words of a song etc.

settle¹ *verb* (**settled**, **settling**) **1** arrange; decide or solve something, *That settles the problem.* **2** make or become calm or comfortable or orderly; stop being restless, *Stop chattering and settle down!* **3** go and live somewhere, *They settled in Canada.* **4** sink; come to rest on something, *Dust had settled on his books.* **5** pay a bill or debt. **settler** *noun*

settle² *noun* a long wooden seat with a high back and arms.

settlement *noun* **1** settling something. **2** the way something is settled, *a divorce settlement.* **3** a small number of people or houses established in a new area.

set-up *noun* (*informal*) the way something is organized or arranged.

seven *noun* & *adjective* the number 7; one more than six. **seventh** *adjective* & *noun*

seventeen *noun* & *adjective* the number 17; one more than sixteen. **seventeenth** *adjective* & *noun*

seventy *noun* & *adjective* (*plural* **seventies**) the number 70; seven times ten. **seventieth** *adjective* & *noun*

sever *verb* (**severed, severing**) cut or break off. **severance** *noun*

several *adjective* & *noun* more than two but not many.

severally *adverb* separately.

severe *adjective* **1** strict; not gentle or kind. **2** intense; forceful, *severe gales.* **3** very plain, *a severe style of dress.* **severely** *adverb*, **severity** *noun*

sew *verb* (**sewed, sewn** or **sewed, sewing**) **1** join things together by using a needle and thread. **2** work with a needle and thread or with a sewing-machine.

sewage (*say* soo-ij) *noun* liquid waste matter carried away in drains.

sewer (*say* soo-er) *noun* a drain for carrying away sewage.

sewerage *noun* **1** a system of sewers. **2** sewage.

sewing-machine *noun* a machine for sewing things.

sex *noun* (*plural* **sexes**) **1** each of the two groups (*male* and *female*) into which living things are placed according to their functions in the process of reproduction. **2** the instinct that causes people to be attracted to one another. **3** sexual intercourse, *modern attitudes to sex.*

sexism *noun* discrimination against people of a particular sex, especially women. **sexist** *adjective* & *noun*

sextant *noun* an instrument for measuring the angle of the sun and stars, used for finding your position when navigating.

sextet *noun* **1** a group of six musicians. **2** a piece of music for six musicians.

sexton *noun* a person whose job is to take care of a church and churchyard.

sextuplet *noun* each of six children born to the same mother at one time.

sexual *adjective* **1** of sex or the sexes. **2** (of reproduction) happening by the fusion of male and female cells. **sexually** *adverb*, **sexuality** *noun*

sexual intercourse the coming together of two people to make love, by the male putting his penis into the female's vagina.

sexy *adjective* (**sexier, sexiest**) (*informal*) **1** sexually attractive. **2** concerned with sex.

SF *abbreviation* science fiction.

shabby *adjective* (**shabbier, shabbiest**) **1** in a poor or worn-out condition; dilapidated. **2** poorly dressed. **3** unfair; dishonourable, *a shabby trick.* **shabbily** *adverb*, **shabbiness** *noun*

shack *noun* a roughly-built hut.

shackle[1] *noun* an iron ring for fastening a prisoner's wrist or ankle to something.

shackle[2] *verb* (**shackled, shackling**) put shackles on a prisoner.

shad *noun* (*plural* **shad** or **shads**) an edible sea-fish which spawns in fresh water.

shade[1] *noun* **1** slight darkness produced where something blocks the sun's light. **2** a device that reduces or shuts out bright light, *a sun-shade.* **3** a colour; how light or dark a colour is. **4** a slight difference, *The word had several shades of meaning.* **5** a ghost.

shade[2] *verb* (**shaded, shading**) **1** shelter something from bright light. **2** make part of a drawing darker than the rest.

shadoof (also **shaduf**) *noun* a simple device used in Egypt to get water from a river in order to irrigate crops.

shadow[1] *noun* **1** the dark shape that falls on a surface when something is between the surface and a light. **2** an area of shade. **shadowy** *adjective*

shadow[2] *verb* **1** cast a shadow on something. **2** follow a person secretly.

shady *adjective* (**shadier, shadiest**) **1** giving shade, *a shady tree.* **2** in the shade, *a shady place.* **3** not completely honest; disreputable, *a shady deal.*

shaft *noun* **1** a long slender rod or straight part, *the shaft of an arrow.* **2** a ray of light. **3** a deep narrow hole, *a mine-shaft.*

shaggy *adjective* (**shaggier, shaggiest**) **1** having long rough hair or fibre. **2** rough, thick, and untidy, *shaggy hair.*

shah *noun* the former ruler of Iran.

shake[1] *verb* (**shook, shaken, shaking**) **1** move quickly up and down or from side to side. **2** disturb; shock; upset, *The news shook us.* **3** tremble; be unsteady, *His voice* *was shaking.* **shaker** *noun*

shake hands clasp a person's right hand with yours in greeting or parting or as a sign of agreement.

shake² *noun* **1** shaking; a shaking movement. **2** (*informal*) a moment, *I'll be there in two shakes.* **shaky** *adjective*, **shakily** *adverb*

shale *noun* a kind of stone that splits easily into layers.

shall *auxiliary verb* **1** used with *I* and *we* to express the ordinary future tense, e.g. *I shall arrive tomorrow*, and in questions, e.g. *Shall I shut the door?* (but *will* is used with other words, e.g. *they will arrive*; *will you shut the door?*). **2** used with words other than *I* and *we* in promises, e.g. *Cinderella, you shall go to the ball!* (but *I will go* = I promise or intend to go).

● USAGE: If you want to be strictly correct, keep to the rules given here, but nowadays many people use *will* after *I* and *we* and it is not usually regarded as wrong.

shallot *noun* a kind of small onion.

shallow *adjective* **1** not deep, *shallow water.* **2** not capable of deep feelings, *a shallow character.* **shallowness** *noun*

shallows *plural noun* a shallow part of a stretch of water.

sham¹ *noun* something that is not genuine; a pretence. **sham** *adjective*

sham² *verb* (**shammed, shamming**) pretend.

shaman (*say* **shay**-man or **shah**-man) *noun* a person who is believed to be able to communicate with the spirit world in some religions.

shamble *verb* (**shambled, shambling**) walk or run in a lazy or awkward way.

shambles *noun* a scene of great disorder or bloodshed.

shame¹ *noun* **1** a feeling of great sorrow or guilt because you have done wrong. **2** something you regret, *It's a shame that it rained.* **shameful** *adjective*, **shamefully** *adverb*

shame² *verb* (**shamed, shaming**) make a person feel ashamed.

shamefaced *adjective* looking ashamed.

shameless *adjective* not feeling or looking ashamed. **shamelessly** *adverb*

shampoo¹ *noun* **1** a liquid substance for washing the hair. **2** a substance for cleaning a carpet etc. or washing a car.

shampoo² *verb* wash or clean with a shampoo.

shandy *noun* (*plural* **shandies**) a mixture of beer and lemonade or some other soft drink.

shank *noun* **1** the leg, especially the part from knee to ankle. **2** a long narrow part, *the shank of a pin.*

shan't (*mainly spoken*) shall not.

shantung *noun* soft Chinese silk.

shanty¹ *noun* (*plural* **shanties**) a shack. **shanty town** a settlement consisting of shanties.

shanty² *noun* (*plural* **shanties**) a sailors' song with a chorus.

shape¹ *noun* **1** a thing's outline; the appearance an outline produces. **2** proper form or condition, *Get it into shape.*

shape² *verb* (**shaped, shaping**) **1** make into a particular shape. **2** develop, *It's shaping up nicely.*

shapeless *adjective* having no definite shape.

shapely *adjective* (**shapelier, shapeliest**) having an attractive shape.

share¹ *noun* **1** a part given to one person or thing out of something that is being divided. **2** each of the equal parts forming a business company's capital, giving the person who holds it the right to receive a portion (a *dividend*) of the company's profits. **shareholder** *noun*

share² *verb* (**shared, sharing**) **1** give portions of something to two or more people. **2** have or use or experience something that others have too, *share a room*; *share the responsibility.*

shark *noun* a large sea-fish with sharp teeth.

sharp¹ *adjective* **1** with an edge or point that can cut or make holes. **2** quick at noticing or learning things, *sharp eyes.* **3** steep or pointed; not gradual, *a sharp bend.* **4** forceful; severe, *a sharp frost.* **5** distinct; loud and shrill, *a sharp cry.*

6 slightly sour. **7** (in music) one semitone higher than the natural note, *C sharp*.
sharply *adverb*, **sharpness** *noun*
sharp practice dishonest or barely honest dealings in business.
sharp² *adverb* **1** sharply, *turn sharp right*. **2** punctually, *at six o'clock sharp*. **3** (in music) above the correct pitch, *You were singing sharp*.
sharp³ *noun* (in music) a note one semitone higher than the natural note.
sharpen *verb* make or become sharp.
sharpener *noun*
sharpshooter *noun* a skilled marksman.
shatter *verb* **1** break violently into small pieces. **2** destroy, *It shattered our hopes*. **3** upset greatly, *We were shattered by the news*.
shave¹ *verb* (**shaved, shaving**) **1** scrape growing hair off the skin. **2** cut or scrape a thin slice off something, *She shaved off a small amount from the block of wood*.
shaver *noun*
shave² *noun* the act of shaving the face.
close shave (*informal*) a narrow escape.
shavings *plural noun* thin strips shaved off a piece of wood or metal.
shawl *noun* a large piece of material worn round the shoulders or head or wrapped round a baby.
she *pronoun* the female person or animal being talked about.
sheaf *noun* (*plural* **sheaves**) **1** a bundle of corn-stalks tied together. **2** a bundle of arrows, papers, etc. held together.
shear *verb* (**sheared, shorn** or **sheared, shearing**) cut or trim; cut the wool off a sheep. **shearer** *noun*
● USAGE: Do not confuse with *sheer*.
shears *plural noun* a cutting-tool shaped like a very large pair of scissors and worked with both hands.
sheath *noun* a close-fitting cover; a cover for the blade of a knife or sword etc.
sheathe *verb* (**sheathed, sheathing**) **1** put into a sheath, *He sheathed his sword*. **2** put a close covering on something.
shebeen *noun* a place that sells home-brewed beer and other alcoholic drinks to the public.

shed¹ *noun* a simply-made building used for storing things or sheltering animals, or as a workshop.
shed² *verb* (**shed, shedding**) **1** let something fall or flow, *The tree shed its leaves. We shed tears*. **2** give off, *A heater sheds warmth*.
sheen *noun* a shine; a gloss.
sheep *noun* (*plural* **sheep**) an animal that eats grass and has a thick fleecy coat, kept in flocks for its wool and its meat.
sheep-dog *noun* a dog trained to guard and herd sheep.
sheepish *adjective* bashful; embarrassed.
sheepishly *adverb*, **sheepishness** *noun*
sheepshank *noun* a knot used to shorten a rope.
sheer¹ *adjective* **1** complete; thorough, *sheer stupidity*. **2** vertical, with almost no slope, *a sheer drop*. **3** (of material) very thin; transparent.
sheer² *verb* swerve; move sharply away.
● USAGE: Do not confuse with *shear*.
sheet¹ *noun* **1** a large piece of lightweight material used on a bed in pairs for a person to sleep between. **2** a whole flat piece of paper, glass, or metal. **3** a wide area of water, ice, flame, etc.
sheet² *noun* a rope or chain fastening a sail.
sheikh (*say* shayk) *noun* the leader of an Arab tribe or village.
shelf *noun* (*plural* **shelves**) **1** a flat piece of wood, metal, or glass etc. fixed to a wall or in a piece of furniture so that things can be placed on it. **2** a flat level surface that sticks out; a ledge.
shell¹ *noun* **1** the hard outer covering of a nut, egg, snail, tortoise, etc. **2** the walls or framework of a building, ship, etc. **3** a metal case filled with explosive, fired from a large gun.
shell² *verb* **1** take something out of its shell. **2** fire explosive shells at something.
shell out (*informal*) pay out money.
shellfish *noun* (*plural* **shellfish**) a sea-animal that has a shell.
shelter¹ *noun* **1** something that protects people from rain, wind, danger, etc. **2** protection, *Seek shelter from the rain*.

shelter² *verb* **1** provide with shelter.
2 protect. **3** find a shelter, *They sheltered under the trees.*

shelve *verb* (**shelved, shelving**) **1** put things on a shelf or shelves. **2** fit a wall or cupboard etc. with shelves. **3** postpone or reject a plan etc. **4** slope, *The bed of the river shelves steeply.*

shepherd¹ *noun* a person whose job is to look after sheep. **shepherdess** *noun* **shepherd's pie** cottage pie.

shepherd² *verb* guide or direct people.

sherbet *noun* a fizzy sweet powder or drink.

sheriff *noun* a law officer, whose duties vary in different countries.

sherry *noun* (*plural* **sherries**) a kind of strong wine.

shield¹ *noun* **1** a large piece of metal, wood, etc. carried to protect the body. **2** a model of a triangular shield used as a trophy, *She won the school's chess shield.* **3** a protection.

shield² *verb* protect from harm or from being discovered.

shift¹ *verb* **1** move; change. **2** manage, *Learn to shift for yourself.*

shift² *noun* **1** a change of position or condition etc. **2** a group of workers who start work as another group finishes; the time when they work, *the night shift.* **3** a straight dress.

shifty *adjective* evasive, not straight-forward; untrustworthy. **shiftily** *adverb*, **shiftiness** *noun*

shilling *noun* a former British coin.

shilly-shally *verb* (**shilly-shallied**; **shilly-shallying**) be unable to make up your mind.

shimmer *verb* shine with a quivering light, *The sea shimmered in the moonlight.* **shimmer** *noun*

shin¹ *noun* the front of the leg between the knee and the ankle.

shin² *verb* (**shinned, shinning**) climb by using the arms and legs, not on a ladder.

shine¹ *verb* (**shone** (in sense 4 **shined**), **shining**) **1** give out or reflect light; be bright. **2** be excellent, *He doesn't shine in maths.* **3** aim a light, *Shine your torch on*

it. **4** polish, *Have you shined your shoes?*

shine² *noun* **1** brightness. **2** a polish.

shingle *noun* pebbles on a beach.

shiny *adjective* (**shinier, shiniest**) shining; glossy.

ship¹ *noun* a large boat, especially one that goes to sea.

ship² *verb* (**shipped, shipping**) send goods etc. by ship; transport.

shipment *noun* **1** the process of shipping goods. **2** the amount shipped.

shipping *noun* **1** ships, *South Africa's shipping.* **2** transporting goods by ship.

shipshape *adjective* in good order; tidy.

shipwreck *noun* the wrecking of a ship. **shipwrecked** *adjective*

shipyard *noun* a ship-building yard; a dock.

shirk *verb* avoid a duty or work etc. selfishly or unfairly. **shirker** *noun*

shirr *verb* gather cloth into folds by rows of threads run through it.

shirt *noun* a loose-fitting garment of cotton or silk etc. for the top half of the body.

shirty *adjective* (*informal*) annoyed.

shiver¹ *verb* tremble with cold or fear. **shiver** *noun*, **shivery** *adjective*

shiver² *verb* shatter into pieces.

shoal¹ *noun* a large number of fish swimming together.

shoal² *noun* a shallow place; an underwater sandbank.

shock¹ *noun* **1** a sudden unpleasant surprise. **2** great weakness caused by pain or injury etc. **3** the effect of a violent shake or knock, *the shock of the explosion.* **4** an effect caused by electric current passing through the body.

shock² *verb* **1** give someone a shock; surprise or upset a person greatly. **2** seem very improper or scandalous to a person.

shock³ *noun* a bushy mass of hair.

shod *past tense* of **shoe**.

shoddy *adjective* (**shoddier, shoddiest**) of poor quality; badly made or done, *shoddy work.* **shoddily** *adverb*, **shoddiness** *noun*

shoe¹ *noun* **1** a strong covering for the

foot. **2** a horseshoe. **3** something shaped
or used like a shoe, *a brake shoe*.
shoelace *noun*, **shoemaker** *noun*
be in somebody's shoes be in his or her
situation.
on a shoe-string with only a small
amount of money.
shoe² *verb* (**shod, shoeing**) fit with
a shoe or shoes.
shoehorn *noun* a curved piece of stiff
material for easing your heel into the back
of a shoe.
shongololo *noun* a songololo.
shoo *interjection* a word used to frighten
animals away. **shoo** *verb*
shoot¹ *verb* (**shot, shooting**) **1** fire a gun
or missile etc. **2** hurt or kill by shooting.
3 move or send very quickly, *The car shot
past us*. **4** kick or hit a ball at a goal.
5 (of a plant) put out buds or shoots.
6 slide the bolt of a door into or out of
its fastening. **7** film or photograph something, *They shot the film in Mauritius*.
shooting star a meteor.
shoot² *noun* **1** a young branch or new
growth of a plant. **2** an expedition for
shooting animals, *a tiger shoot*.
shop¹ *noun* **1** a building or room where
goods or services are on sale to the public.
2 a workshop. **3** talk that is about your
own work or job, *She is always talking
shop*.
shop steward a trade-union official who
represents his or her fellow workers.
shop² *verb* (**shopped, shopping**) go and
buy things at shops. **shopper** *noun*
shopkeeper *noun* a person who owns
or manages a shop.
shoplifter *noun* a person who steals
goods from a shop after entering as a
customer. **shoplifting** *noun*
shopping *noun* **1** buying goods in shops.
2 the goods bought, *put the shopping in
the car*.
shore¹ *noun* the land along the edge
of a sea or of a lake.
shore² *verb* (**shored, shoring**) prop
something up with a piece of wood etc.
shorn *past participle* of **shear**.
short¹ *adjective* **1** not long; occupying

a small distance or time, *a short walk*.
2 not tall, *a short person*. **3** not enough;
not having enough of something, *We are
short of water*. **4** curt. **5** (of pastry) rich and
crumbly because it contains a lot of fat.
shortness *noun*
for short as an abbreviation, *Modiehi
is called Modi for short*.
short circuit a fault in an electrical circuit
in which current flows along a shorter
route than the normal one.
short cut a route or method that is
quicker than the usual one.
short division dividing one number
by another without writing down the
calculations.
short for an abbreviation of, *'Modi' is short
for Modiehi*.
short² *adverb* suddenly, *She stopped
short*.
shortage *noun* lack or scarcity of
something; insufficiency.
shortbread *noun* a rich sweet biscuit
of butter, flour, and sugar.
shortcake *noun* shortbread.
shortcoming *noun* a fault or failure
to reach a good standard.
shorten *verb* make or become shorter.
shorthand *noun* a set of special signs for
writing words down as quickly as people
say them.
shortly *adverb* **1** in a short time; soon,
They will arrive shortly. **2** in a few words.
3 curtly.
shorts *plural noun* trousers with legs that
do not reach to the knee.
short-sighted *adjective* unable to see
distant things clearly.
short-tempered *adjective* easily
becoming angry.
shot¹ *past tense* of **shoot**.
shot² *noun* **1** the firing of a gun or missile
etc.; the sound of this. **2** something fired
from a gun; lead pellets for firing from
small guns. **3** a person judged by skill in
shooting, *She's a good shot*. **4** a heavy
metal ball thrown as a sport. **5** a stroke
in tennis, cricket, billiards, etc. **6** a photograph; a filmed scene. **7** an attempt,
Have a shot at the crossword.

shot[3] *adjective* (of fabric) woven so that different colours show at different angles, *shot silk.*

shotgun *noun* a gun for firing small shot at close range.

should *auxiliary verb* used to express 1 obligation or duty, = ought to, *You should have told me.* 2 something expected, *They should be here by ten o'clock.* 3 a possible event, *if you should happen to see him.* 4 with *I* and *we* to make a polite statement, *I should like to come* or in a conditional clause, *If they had supported us we should have won.*
● USAGE: In sense 4, although *should* is strictly correct, many people nowadays use *would* and this is not regarded as wrong.

shoulder[1] *noun* 1 the part of the body between the neck and the arm, foreleg, or wing. 2 a side that juts out, *the shoulder of the bottle.*

shoulder[2] *verb* 1 take something on your shoulder or shoulders. 2 push with your shoulder, *shoulder the crowd aside.* 3 accept responsibility or blame.

shoulder-blade *noun* either of the two large flat bones at the top of your back.

shouldn't (*mainly spoken*) should not.

shout[1] *noun* a loud cry or call.

shout[2] *verb* give a shout; call loudly.

shove *verb* (**shoved, shoving**) push roughly. **shove** *noun*
shove off (*informal*) go away.

shovel[1] *noun* a tool like a spade with the sides turned up, used for lifting coal, earth, snow, etc.

shovel[2] *verb* (**shovelled, shovelling**) 1 move or clear with a shovel. 2 scoop or push roughly, *He was shovelling food into his mouth.*

show[1] *verb* (**showed, shown, showing**) 1 allow or cause something to be seen, *Show me your new bike.* 2 make a person understand; demonstrate, *Show me how to use it.* 3 guide, *Show him in.* 4 treat in a certain way, *She showed us much kindness.* 5 be visible, *That scratch won't show.* 6 prove your ability to someone, *We'll show them!*

show off show something proudly; try to impress people.
show up make or be clearly visible; reveal a fault etc.; (*informal*) arrive.

show[2] *noun* 1 a display or exhibition, *a flower show.* 2 an entertainment. 3 (*informal*) something that happens or is done, *He runs the whole show.*
give the show away reveal a secret.
good show! well done!

show-down *noun* a final test or confrontation.

shower[1] *noun* 1 a brief fall of rain or snow. 2 a lot of small things coming or falling like rain, *a shower of stones.* 3 a device or cabinet for spraying water to wash a person's body; a wash in this.

shower[2] *verb* 1 fall or send things in a shower. 2 wash under a shower.

showery *adjective* (of weather) with many showers.

show-jumping *noun* a competition in which riders make their horses jump over fences and other obstacles. **show-jumper** *noun*

showman *noun* (*plural* **showmen**) 1 a person who presents entertainments. 2 someone who is good at attracting attention. **showmanship** *noun*

showroom *noun* a room where goods are displayed for people to look at.

showy *adjective* (**showier, showiest**) likely to attract attention; brightly or highly decorated. **showily** *adverb*, **showiness** *noun*

shrapnel *noun* pieces of metal scattered from an exploding shell.

shred[1] *noun* 1 a tiny piece torn or cut off something. 2 a small amount, *There is not a shred of evidence.*

shred[2] *verb* (**shredded, shredding**) cut into shreds. **shredder** *noun*

shrew *noun* 1 a small mouse-like animal. 2 a bad-tempered woman who is constantly scolding people. **shrewish** *adjective*

shrewd *adjective* having common sense and good judgement; clever. **shrewdly** *adverb*, **shrewdness** *noun*

shriek[1] *noun* a shrill cry or scream.

shriek² *verb* give a shriek.

shrift *noun* **short shrift** curt treatment.

shrill *adjective* sounding very high and piercing. **shrilly** *adverb*, **shrillness** *noun*

shrimp *noun* **1** a small shellfish, pink when boiled. **2** a small person. ·

shrimping *noun* fishing for shrimps.

shrine *noun* an altar, chapel, or other sacred place.

shrink *verb* (**shrank, shrunk, shrinking**) **1** make or become smaller. **2** move back to avoid something. **3** avoid doing something because of fear, conscience, embarrassment, etc. **shrinkage** *noun*
shrink-wrap enclose something in plastic film that covers it tightly.

shrive *verb* (**shrove, shriven, shriving**) (*old use*) (of a priest) hear a person's confession and give absolution.

shrivel *verb* (**shrivelled, shrivelling**) make or become dry and wrinkled.

shroud¹ *noun* **1** a cloth in which a dead body is wrapped. **2** each of a set of ropes supporting a ship's mast.

shroud² *verb* **1** wrap in a shroud. **2** cover or conceal, *The town was shrouded in mist.*

shrub *noun* a woody plant smaller than a tree; a bush. **shrubby** *adjective*

shrubbery *noun* (*plural* **shrubberies**) an area planted with shrubs.

shrug *verb* (**shrugged, shrugging**) raise your shoulders as a sign that you do not care, do not know, etc. **shrug** *noun*

shrunken *adjective* having shrunk.

shudder *verb* **1** shiver violently with horror, fear, or cold. **2** make a strong shaking movement, *The ground shuddered as the earthquake struck.* **shudder** *noun*

shuffle *verb* (**shuffled, shuffling**) **1** walk without lifting the feet from the ground. **2** slide playing-cards over each other to get them into random order. **3** shift; rearrange, *She shuffled the photos around, looking for the one she wanted.* **shuffle** *noun*

shun *verb* (**shunned, shunning**) avoid.

shunt *verb* move a train or wagons on to another track; divert. **shunt** *noun*, **shunter** *noun*

shut *verb* (**shut, shutting**) **1** move a door, lid, or cover etc. so that it blocks an opening; make or become closed. **2** bring or fold parts together, *Shut the book.*
shut down stop work; stop business.
shut up shut securely; (*informal*) stop talking or making a noise.

shutter *noun* **1** a panel or screen that can be closed over a window. **2** the device in a camera that opens and closes to let light fall on the film. **shuttered** *adjective*

shuttle¹ *noun* **1** a holder carrying the weft-thread across a loom in weaving. **2** a train, bus, or aircraft that makes frequent short journeys between two points. **3** a space shuttle (see *space*).

shuttle² *verb* (**shuttled, shuttling**) move, travel, or send backwards and forwards.

shuttlecock *noun* a small rounded piece of cork or plastic with a crown of feathers, struck to and fro by players in badminton etc.

shy¹ *adjective* (**shyer, shyest**) afraid to meet or talk to other people; timid. **shyly** *adverb*, **shyness** *noun*

shy² *verb* (**shied, shying**) move suddenly in alarm, *The horse shied at the sound.*

shy³ *verb* (**shied, shying**) throw a stone etc.

shy⁴ *noun* (*plural* **shies**) a throw.

SI *abbreviation* the international system of units of measurement (French = Système International).

Siamese *adjective* of Siam (now called Thailand) or its people. **Siamese** *noun*
Siamese cat a cat with short pale fur with darker face, ears, tail, and feet.
Siamese twins twins who are born with their bodies joined together.

sibilant¹ *adjective* having a hissing sound, *a sibilant whisper.*

sibilant² *noun* a speech-sound that sounds like hissing, e.g. *s, sh.*

sibling *noun* a brother or sister.

sibyl *noun* a prophetess in ancient Greece or Rome.

sick *adjective* **1** ill; physically or mentally unwell. **2** vomiting or likely to vomit, *I feel sick.* **3** (*informal*) (of a joke etc.) cruel or offensive, *sick humour.*
sick of tired of.

sicken *verb* **1** begin to be ill. **2** make or become distressed or disgusted, *Vandalism sickens us all.* **sickening** *adjective*

sickle *noun* **1** a tool with a narrow curved blade, used for cutting corn etc. **2** something shaped like this blade, e.g. the crescent moon.

sickly *adjective* **1** often ill; unhealthy. **2** making people feel sick, *a sickly smell.* **3** weak, *a sickly smile.*

sickness *noun* **1** illness. **2** a disease. **3** vomiting.

side¹ *noun* **1** a surface, especially one joining the top and bottom of something. **2** a line that forms part of the boundary of a triangle, square, etc. **3** either of the two halves into which something can be divided by a line down its centre. **4** the part near the edge and away from the centre. **5** the place or region next to a person or thing, *He stood at my side.* **6** one aspect or view of something, *Study all sides of the problem.* **7** one of two groups or teams etc. who oppose each other. **on the side** as a sideline. **side by side** next to each other.

side² *adjective* at or on a side, *the side door.*

side³ *verb* (**sided, siding**) take a person's side in an argument, *She sided with her son.*

sideboard *noun* a long piece of furniture with drawers and cupboards for china etc. and a flat top.

side-car *noun* a small compartment for a passenger, fixed to the side of a motor cycle.

sidelight *noun* **1** a light at the side of a vehicle or ship. **2** light from one side.

sideline *noun* **1** something done in addition to the main work or activity. **2** a line at the side of a football pitch etc.; the area just outside this.

sidelong *adjective* towards one side; sideways, *a sidelong glance.*

sidereal (*say* sid-**eer**-ee-al) *adjective* of or measured by the stars.

side-show *noun* a small entertainment forming part of a large one, e.g. at a fair.

sideways *adverb* & *adjective* **1** to or from one side, *Move it sideways.* **2** with one side facing forwards, *We sat sideways in the bus.*

siding *noun* a short railway line by the side of a main line.

sidle *verb* (**sidled, sidling**) walk in a shy or nervous manner.

siege *noun* the besieging of a place. **lay siege to** begin besieging.

sienna *noun* a kind of clay used in making brownish paints.

sierra *noun* a range of mountains with sharp peaks, in Spain or parts of America.

siesta (*say* see-**est**-a) *noun* an afternoon rest.

sieve¹ (*say* siv) *noun* a device made of mesh or perforated metal or plastic, used to separate the smaller or soft parts of something from the larger or hard parts.

sieve² *verb* (**sieved, sieving**) put something through a sieve.

sift *verb* **1** sieve. **2** examine and analyse facts or evidence etc. carefully. **sifter** *noun*

sigh¹ *noun* a sound made by breathing out heavily when you are sad, tired, relieved, etc.

sigh² *verb* make a sigh.

sight¹ *noun* **1** the ability to see. **2** a thing that can be seen or is worth seeing, *Our roses are a wonderful sight.* **3** an unsightly thing, *You do look a sight in those clothes!* **4** a device looked through to help aim a gun or telescope etc. **at sight** or **on sight** as soon as a person or thing has been seen. **in sight** visible; clearly near, *Victory was in sight.*

sight² *verb* **1** see or observe something. **2** aim a gun or telescope etc.

sightless *adjective* blind.

sight-reading *noun* playing or singing music at sight, without preparation.

sightseeing *noun* visiting interesting places in a town etc. **sightseer** *noun*

sign¹ *noun* **1** something that shows that a thing exists, *There are signs of decay.* **2** a mark, device, or notice etc. that gives a special meaning, *a road sign.* **3** an action or movement giving information or a command etc. **4** any of the twelve divisions of the zodiac, represented by a symbol.

sign language a system of communication using gestures rather than words.

sign² *verb* **1** make a sign or signal. **2** write your signature on something; accept a contract etc. by doing this.

signal¹ *noun* **1** a device, gesture, or sound etc. that gives information or a command; a message made up of such things. **2** a sequence of electrical impulses or radio waves.

signal² *verb* (**signalled, signalling**) make a signal to somebody, *The police officer signalled that the car should stop*. **signaller** *noun*

signal³ *adjective* remarkable, a *signal success*. **signally** *adverb*

signal-box *noun* a building from which railway signals are controlled.

signalman *noun* (*plural* **signalmen**) a person who controls railway signals.

signatory *noun* (*plural* **signatories**) a person who signs an agreement etc.

signature *noun* a person's name written by himself or herself.

signature tune a special tune always used to announce a particular programme, performer, etc.

signet *noun* a seal with an engraved design, especially one set in a person's ring (a **signet-ring**).

significant *adjective* **1** having a meaning; full of meaning. **2** important, *a significant event*. **significantly** *adverb*, **significance** *noun*

signification *noun* meaning.

signify *verb* (**signified, signifying**) **1** be a sign or symbol of; mean. **2** indicate, *She signified her approval*. **3** be important; matter, *It doesn't signify, so please ignore it*.

signpost *noun* a sign at a road junction etc. showing the names and distances of places down each road.

Sikh (*say as* seek) *noun* a member of an Indian religion believing in one God and accepting some Hindu and some Islamic beliefs. **Sikhism** *noun*

silage *noun* fodder made from green crops stored in a silo.

silence¹ *noun* absence of sound or talk.

silence² *verb* (**silenced, silencing**) make a person or thing silent.

silencer *noun* a device for reducing the sound made by a gun or a vehicle's exhaust system etc.

silent *adjective* without any sound; not speaking. **silently** *adverb*

silhouette (*say* sil-oo-et) *noun* a dark shadow seen against a light background. **silhouette** *verb*

silica *noun* a hard white mineral that is a compound of silicon.

silicon *noun* a substance found in many rocks, used in making transistors, chips for microprocessors, etc.

silicone *noun* a compound of silicon used in paints, varnish, artificial rubber, and lubricants.

silk *noun* a fine soft thread or cloth made from the fibre produced by silkworms for making their cocoons. **silken** *adjective*, **silky** *adjective*

silkworm *noun* the caterpillar of a kind of moth, which feeds on mulberry leaves and spins itself a cocoon.

sill *noun* a strip of stone, wood, or metal underneath a window or door.

silly *adjective* (**sillier, silliest**) foolish; unwise. **silliness** *noun*

silo (*say* sy-loh) *noun* (*plural* **silos**) **1** a pit or tower for storing green crops (see *silage*) or corn or cement etc. **2** an underground place for storing a missile ready for firing.

silt¹ *noun* **1** sediment laid down by a river or sea etc. **2** a kind of soil particle bigger than a clay particle but smaller than a sand particle.

silt² *verb* block or clog or become blocked with silt, *The harbour had silted up*.

silvan *adjective* of the woods; having woods, rural.

silver¹ *noun* **1** a shiny white precious metal. **2** the colour of silver. **3** coins or objects made of silver or silver-coloured metal. **4** a silver medal, usually given as second prize, *She won a silver at the Games*. **silvery** *adjective*

silver[2] *adjective* **1** made of silver.
2 coloured like silver.
silver tree a tree of the protea family that has silver-grey leaves.
silver wedding the 25th anniversary of a wedding.
silver[3] *verb* make or become silvery.
simian *adjective* like a monkey.
similar *adjective* nearly the same as another person or thing; of the same kind. **similarly** *adverb*, **similarity** *noun*
simile (*say* sim-il-ee) *noun* a comparison of one thing with another, e.g. *He is as strong as a horse. We ran like the wind.*
similitude *noun* similarity.
simmer *verb* boil very gently.
simmer down calm down.
simper *verb* smile in a silly affected way. **simper** *noun*
simple *adjective* **1** easy, *a simple question.* **2** not complicated or elaborate; plain, not showy, *a simple cottage.* **3** without much sense or intelligence. **4** not of high rank; ordinary, *a simple working person.* **simplicity** *noun*
simpleton *noun* a foolish person.
simplify *verb* (**simplified, simplifying**) make a thing simple or easy to understand. **simplification** *noun*
simply *adverb* **1** in a simple way, *Explain it simply.* **2** without doubt; completely, *It's simply marvellous.* **3** only; merely, *It's simply a question of time.*
simulate *verb* (**simulated, simulating**) **1** reproduce the appearance or conditions of something; imitate, *This device simulates a space flight.* **2** pretend, *They simulated fear.* **simulation** *noun*, **simulator** *noun*
simultaneous (*say* sim-ul-**tay**-nee-us) *adjective* happening at the same time. **simultaneously** *adverb*
sin[1] *noun* the breaking of a religious or moral law; a very bad action.
sin[2] *verb* (**sinned, sinning**) commit a sin. **sinner** *noun*
since[1] *conjunction* **1** from the time when, *Where have you been since I last saw you?* **2** because, *Since we have missed the bus, we must walk home.*
since[2] *preposition* from a certain time,

She has been here since Christmas.
since[3] *adverb* between then and now, *He ran away and hasn't been seen since.*
sincere *adjective* without pretence; truly felt or meant, *my sincere thanks.* **sincerely** *adverb*, **sincerity** *noun*
Yours sincerely see *yours.*
sine *noun* (in a right-angled triangle) the ratio of the length of a side opposite one of the acute angles to the length of the hypotenuse.
sinecure (*say* sy-nik-yoor) *noun* a paid job that requires no work.
sinew *noun* **1** a tendon. **2** strength; muscular power. **sinewy** *adjective*
sinful *adjective* guilty of sin; wicked. **sinfully** *adverb*, **sinfulness** *noun*
sing *verb* (**sang, sung, singing**) **1** make musical sounds with the voice. **2** perform a song. **3** make a humming or whistling sound. **singer** *noun*
singe (*say* sinj) *verb* (**singed, singeing**) burn something slightly.
single[1] *adjective* **1** one only; not double or multiple. **2** suitable for one person, *single beds.* **3** separate, *We sold every single thing.* **4** not married. **5** for the journey to a place but not back again, *a single ticket.* **singly** *adverb*
single file a line of people one behind the other.
single[2] *noun* **1** a single person or thing. **2** a single ticket. **3** a record with one short piece of music on each side.
single[3] *verb* (**singled, singling**) **single out** pick out or distinguish from other people or things.
single-handed *adjective* without help.
single-minded *adjective* with your mind set on one purpose only.
singlet *noun* a man's garment worn under or instead of a shirt; a vest.
singsong[1] *adjective* having a monotonous tone or rhythm, *a singsong voice.*
singsong[2] *noun* **1** informal singing by a gathering of people. **2** a singsong tone.
singular[1] *noun* the form of a noun or verb used when it stands for only one person or thing, *The singular is 'man', the plural is 'men'.*

singular² *adjective* **1** of the singular.
2 uncommon; extraordinary, *a woman
of singular courage.* **singularly** *adverb,*
singularity *noun*

sinister *adjective* looking evil or harmful;
wicked.

sink¹ *verb* (**sank, sunk, sinking**) **1** go or
cause to go under the surface or to the
bottom of the sea etc., *The ship sank.
They sank the ship.* **2** go or fall slowly
downwards, *He sank to his knees.* **3** dig or
drill, *They sank a well.* **4** invest money in
something.
sinkhole an area of ground that has sunk,
often as a result of underground mining.
sink in become understood.

sink² *noun* a fixed basin with a drainpipe
and usually a tap or taps to supply water.

Sintu *adjective* of African languages, *Sintu
languages.*
• USAGE: *Sintu* is preferred to *Bantu* by
some people.

sinuous *adjective* with many bends or
curves.

sinus (*say* sy-nus) *noun* (*plural* **sinuses**)
a hollow part in the bones of the skull,
connected with the nose, *My sinuses are
blocked.*

sip *verb* (**sipped, sipping**) drink in small
mouthfuls. **sip** *noun*

siphon¹ *noun* **1** a pipe or tube in the form
of an upside-down U, arranged so that
liquid is forced up it and down to a lower
level. **2** a bottle containing soda-water
which is released through a tube.

siphon² *verb* flow or draw out through
a siphon.

sir *noun* **1** a word used when speaking
politely to a man, *Please sir, may I go?*
2 **Sir** the title given to a knight or baronet,
Sir John Moore.

sire *noun* **1** the male parent of a horse
or dog etc. (Compare *dam².*) **2** a word
formerly used when speaking to a king.

siren *noun* **1** a device that makes a long
loud sound as a signal. **2** a dangerously
attractive woman (named after the Sirens
in Greek legend, women who by their
sweet singing lured seafarers to shipwreck
on the rocks).

sirloin *noun* beef from the upper part of
the loin.

sirocco *noun* a hot dry wind that reaches
southern Europe from Africa.

sisal (*say* sy-sal) *noun* fibre from a
tropical plant, used for making ropes.

sisi *noun* a word used when speaking
politely to a woman.

sissy *noun* (*plural* **sissies**) (*informal*)
a timid or cowardly person.

sister *noun* **1** a daughter of the same parents as another person. **2** a woman who is
a fellow member of an association etc.
3 a nun. **4** a female hospital nurse in
charge of others. **sisterhood** *noun,*
sisterly *adjective*

sister-in-law *noun* (*plural* **sisters-in-law**)
the sister of a married person's husband
or wife; the wife of a person's brother.

sit *verb* (**sat, sitting**) **1** rest with the body
supported on the buttocks; occupy a seat,
We were sitting in the front row. **2** seat;
cause someone to sit. **3** (of birds) perch;
stay on the nest to hatch eggs. **4** be a candidate for an examination. **5** be situated;
stay, *Those shoes sat in my cupboard for
years.* **6** (of Parliament or a lawcourt etc.)
be assembled for business. **sitter** *noun*

sitar *noun* an Indian musical instrument
that is like a guitar.

site¹ *noun* the place where something
happens or happened or is built etc.,
a building-site.

site² *verb* (**sited, siting**) provide with
a site; locate.

sitting-room *noun* a room with comfortable chairs for sitting in.

situated *adjective* in a particular place or
situation.

situation *noun* **1** a position, with its surroundings. **2** a state of affairs at a certain
time, *The police faced a difficult situation.*
3 a job, *situations vacant.*

six *noun* & *adjective* (*plural* **sixes**) the
number 6; one more than five. **sixth**
adjective & *noun*
at sixes and sevens in disorder.

sixteen *noun* & *adjective* the number 16;
one more than fifteen. **sixteenth** *adjective*
& *noun*

sixty *noun* & *adjective* (*plural* **sixties**) the number 60; six times ten. **sixtieth** *adjective* & *noun*

size[1] *noun* **1** the measurements or extent of something. **2** any of the series of standard measurements in which certain things are made, *a size eight shoe.*

size[2] *verb* (**sized, sizing**) arrange things according to their size.
size up estimate the size of something; (*informal*) form an opinion or judgement about a person or thing.

size[3] *noun* a gluey substance used to glaze paper or stiffen cloth etc.

size[4] *verb* (**sized, sizing**) treat with size.

sizeable *adjective* large; fairly large.

sizzle *verb* (**sizzled, sizzling**) make a crackling or hissing sound.

sjambok (*say* sham-bok) *noun* a heavy whip made of hide or plastic. **sjambok** *verb* (**sjambokked, sjambokking**)

skate[1] *noun* **1** a boot with a steel blade attached to the sole, used for sliding smoothly over ice. **2** a roller-skate.

skate[2] *verb* (**skated, skating**) move on skates. **skater** *noun*

skate[3] *noun* (*plural* **skate**) a large flat edible sea-fish.

skateboard *noun* a small board with wheels, used for riding on (as a sport) while standing. **skateboarding** *noun*

skein *noun* a coil of yarn or thread.

skeleton *noun* **1** the framework of bones of the body. **2** the shell or other hard part of a crab etc. **3** a framework, e.g. of a building. **skeletal** *adjective*

skelm[1] *noun* (*informal*) a rascal.

skelm[2] *adjective* (*informal*) cunning; underhand.

sketch[1] *noun* (*plural* **sketches**) **1** a rough drawing or painting. **2** a short account of something. **3** a short amusing play.

sketch[2] *verb* make a sketch.

sketchy *adjective* rough and not detailed or careful.

skew[1] *adjective* askew; slanting.

skew[2] *verb* make a thing askew.

skewer *noun* a long pin pushed through meat to hold it together while it is being cooked. **skewer** *verb*

ski[1] (*say* skee) *noun* (*plural* **skis**) each of a pair of long narrow strips of wood, metal, or plastic fixed under the feet for moving quickly over snow.

ski[2] *verb* (**ski'd, skiing**) travel on skis. **skier** *noun*

skid[1] *verb* (**skidded, skidding**) slide accidentally.

skid[2] *noun* **1** a skidding movement. **2** a runner on a helicopter, for use in landing.

skilful *adjective* having or showing great skill. **skilfully** *adverb*

skill *noun* the ability to do something well.

skilled *adjective* **1** skilful. **2** (of work or a worker) requiring or having skill or special training.

skim *verb* (**skimmed, skimming**) **1** remove something from the surface of a liquid; take the cream off milk. **2** move quickly over a surface or through the air. **3** read something quickly.

skimmel *adjective* grey, dappled, or roan. **skimmelperd** a grey, dappled, or roan horse.

skimp *verb* supply or use less than is needed, *Don't skimp on the food.*

skimpy *adjective* (**skimpier, skimpiest**) scanty; too small.

skin[1] *noun* **1** the flexible outer covering of a person's or animal's body. **2** an outer layer or covering, e.g. of a fruit. **3** a skin-like film formed on the surface of a liquid.

skin[2] *verb* (**skinned, skinning**) take the skin off something.

skinder (*say* skin-ner or skin-der) *noun* (*informal*) gossip. **skinder** *verb*

skin-diving *noun* swimming under water with flippers and breathing-apparatus but without a diving-suit. **skin-diver** *noun*

skinflint *noun* a miserly person.

skinhead *noun* a youth with very closely cropped hair.

skinny *adjective* (**skinnier, skinniest**) **1** very thin. **2** (*informal*) miserly.

skip[1] *verb* (**skipped, skipping**) **1** move along lightly, especially by hopping on each foot in turn. **2** jump with a skipping-rope. **3** go quickly from one subject to another. **4** miss something out, *You can* *skip chapter six.*

skip[2] *noun* a skipping movement.

skip[3] *noun* a large metal container for taking away builders' rubbish etc.

skipper *noun* a captain.

skipping-rope *noun* a rope, usually with a handle at each end, that is swung over your head and under your feet as you jump.

skirmish *noun* (*plural* **skirmishes**) a small fight or conflict. **skirmish** *verb*

skirt[1] *noun* a woman's or girl's garment that hangs down from the waist.

skirt[2] *verb* go round the edge of something.

skirting *noun* (also **skirting-board**) a narrow board round the wall of a room, close to the floor.

skit *noun* a parody, *He wrote a skit on 'Hamlet'.*

skittish *adjective* frisky.

skittle *noun* a wooden pin that people try to knock down by bowling a ball in the game of **skittles**.

skive *verb* (**skived, skiving**) (*slang*) dodge work etc. **skiver** *noun*

skoffel *verb* (**skoffeled, skoffeling**) cultivate or hoe the ground to clear it of weeds.

skolly *noun* (*plural* **skollies**) a hooligan; a member of a criminal gang.

skulk *verb* loiter stealthily.

skull *noun* the framework of bones of the head.

skunk *noun* a black furry American animal that can spray a bad-smelling fluid.

sky[1] *noun* (*plural* **skies**) the space above the earth, appearing blue in daylight on fine days.

sky[2] *verb* (**skied, skying**) hit a ball very high.

skylark *noun* a lark that sings while it hovers high in the air.

skylight *noun* a window in a roof.

skyline *noun* 1 the horizon, where earth and sky appear to meet. 2 the outline of buildings etc. against the sky.

skyscraper *noun* a very tall building.

slab *noun* a thick flat piece.

slack[1] *adjective* 1 not pulled tight.

2 not busy; not working hard. **slackly** *adverb*, **slackness** *noun*

slack[2] *verb* avoid work. **slacker** *noun*

slacken *verb* make or become slack.

slacks *plural noun* trousers for informal occasions.

slag *noun* waste material separated from metal in smelting.

slag-heap *noun* a mound of waste matter from a mine etc.

slain *past participle* of **slay**.

slake *verb* (**slaked, slaking**) quench, *slake your thirst.*

slam *verb* (**slammed, slamming**) 1 shut loudly. 2 hit violently. **slam** *noun*

slander[1] *noun* a spoken statement that damages a person's reputation and is untrue. (Compare *libel*[1].) **slanderous** *adjective*

slander[2] *verb* make a slander against someone. **slanderer** *noun*

slang[1] *noun* words that are used very informally to add vividness or humour to what is said. **slangy** *adjective*

slang[2] *verb* speak insultingly to somebody.

slant *verb* 1 slope. 2 present news or information etc. from a particular point of view. **slant** *noun*

slap *verb* (**slapped, slapping**) 1 hit with the palm of the hand or with something flat. 2 put forcefully or carelessly, *We slapped paint on the walls.* **slap** *noun*

slapdash *adjective* hasty and careless.

slapstick *noun* comedy with people hitting each other, falling over, etc.

slash[1] *verb* 1 make large cuts in something; cut or strike with a long sweeping movement. 2 reduce greatly, *Prices were slashed.*

slash[2] *noun* (*plural* **slashes**) a slashing cut.

slasto *noun* (*trade mark*) a material that is used to make flooring blocks and tiles.

slat *noun* each of the thin strips of wood or metal or plastic arranged so that they overlap and form a screen, e.g. in a Venetian blind.

slate[1] *noun* 1 a kind of grey rock that is easily split into flat plates. 2 a piece of this rock used in covering a roof or (formerly) for writing on. **slaty** *adjective*

slate² *verb* (**slated, slating**) 1 cover a roof with slates. 2 (*informal*) criticize severely; reprimand.

slattern *noun* a slovenly woman. **slatternly** *adjective*

slaughter *verb* 1 kill an animal for food. 2 kill people or animals ruthlessly or in great numbers. **slaughter** *noun*

slaughterhouse *noun* a place where animals are killed for food.

slave¹ *noun* a person who is owned by another and obliged to work for him or her without being paid. **slavery** *noun*

slave² *verb* (**slaved, slaving**) work very hard.

slave-driver *noun* a person who makes others work very hard.

slaver (*say* **slav**-er or **slay**-ver) *verb* have saliva flowing from the mouth, *a slavering dog.*

slavish *adjective* like a slave; showing no independence or originality.

slay *verb* (**slew, slain, slaying**) kill.

sled *noun* (*American*) a sledge.

sledge *noun* a vehicle for travelling over snow, with strips of metal or wood instead of wheels. **sledging** *noun*

sledge-hammer *noun* a very large heavy hammer.

sleek *adjective* smooth and shiny.

sleep¹ *noun* the condition or time of rest in which the eyes are closed, the body relaxed, and the mind unconscious. **sleepy** *adjective*, **sleepily** *adverb*, **sleepiness** *noun*

sleep² *verb* (**slept, sleeping**) have a sleep. **sleeping sickness** a disease caused by a parasite spread by tsetse flies.

sleeper *noun* 1 someone who is asleep. 2 each of the wooden or concrete beams on which the rails of a railway rest. 3 a railway carriage with beds or berths for passengers to sleep in; a place in this.

sleepless *adjective* unable to sleep.

sleep-walker *noun* a person who walks about while asleep. **sleep-walking** *noun*

sleet *noun* a mixture of rain and snow or hail.

sleeve *noun* 1 the part of a garment that covers the arm. 2 the cover of a record. **up your sleeve** hidden but ready for you to use.

sleeveless *adjective* without sleeves.

sleigh (*say as* slay) *noun* a sledge, especially a large one pulled by horses. **sleighing** *noun*

sleight (*say as* slight) *noun* **sleight of hand** skill in using the hands to do conjuring tricks etc.

slender *adjective* slim. **slenderness** *noun*

sleuth (*say* slooth) *noun* a detective.

slew *past tense* of **slay**.

slice¹ *noun* 1 a thin piece cut off something. 2 a portion.

slice² *verb* (**sliced, slicing**) 1 cut into slices. 2 cut from a larger piece, *Slice the top off the egg.* 3 cut cleanly, *The knife sliced through the apple.*

slick¹ *adjective* 1 quick and clever or cunning. 2 slippery, *a slick surface.*

slick² *noun* 1 a large patch of oil floating on water. 2 a slippery place.

slide¹ *verb* (**slid, sliding**) 1 move or cause to move smoothly on a surface. 2 move quietly or secretly, *The thief slid behind a bush.*

slide² *noun* 1 a sliding movement. 2 a smooth surface or structure on which people or things can slide. 3 a photograph that can be projected on a screen. 4 a small glass plate on which things are placed to be examined under a microscope. 5 a fastener to keep hair tidy.

slight¹ *adjective* very small; not serious or important. **slightly** *adverb*, **slightness** *noun*

slight² *verb* insult a person by treating him or her without respect.

slim¹ *adjective* (**slimmer, slimmest**) 1 thin and graceful. 2 small, *a slim chance.* **slimness** *noun*

slim² *verb* (**slimmed, slimming**) make yourself thinner. **slimmer** *noun*

slime *noun* unpleasant wet slippery stuff. **slimy** *adjective*, **sliminess** *noun*

sling¹ *noun* 1 a loop or band placed round something to support or lift it.

2 a looped strap used to throw a stone etc.

sling[2] *verb* (**slung, slinging**) **1** support or lift with a sling. **2** (*informal*) throw, *sling it over the fence.*

slink *verb* (**slunk, slinking**) move in a stealthy or guilty way. **slinky** *adjective*

slip[1] *verb* (**slipped, slipping**) **1** slide accidentally; lose your balance by sliding. **2** move or put quickly and quietly, *Slip it in your pocket. We slipped away from the party.* **3** escape from, *The dog slipped its leash. It slipped my memory.*

slip up make a mistake.

slip[2] *noun* **1** an accidental slide or fall. **2** a mistake. **3** a small piece of paper. **4** a petticoat. **5** a pillowcase. **6** a cutting taken from a plant for grafting or planting. **give someone the slip** escape or avoid him or her skilfully.

slipper *noun* a soft comfortable shoe to wear indoors.

slippery *adjective* smooth or wet so that it is difficult to stand on or hold. **slipperiness** *noun*

slipshod *adjective* careless; not systematic.

slip-slops *plural noun* sandals with no backs; (rubber) sandals with a thong between the toes.

slit[1] *noun* a narrow straight cut or opening.

slit[2] *verb* (**slitted, slitting**) make a slit or slits in something.

slither *verb* slip or slide unsteadily.

sliver (*say* sliv-er) *noun* a thin strip of wood or glass etc.

slobber *verb* slaver; dribble.

slog *verb* (**slogged, slogging**) **1** hit hard. **2** work or walk hard and steadily. **slog** *noun,* **slogger** *noun*

slogan *noun* a phrase used to advertise something or to sum up the aims of a campaign etc., *Their slogan was 'Ban the bomb!'*

sloop *noun* a small sailing-ship with one mast.

sloot *noun* **1** an artificial water channel. **2** a natural water course or dry ditch.

slop *verb* (**slopped, slopping**) spill liquid over the edge of its container.

slops *plural noun* slopped liquid; liquid waste matter.

slope[1] *verb* (**sloped, sloping**) lie or turn at an angle; slant.

slope[2] *noun* **1** a sloping surface. **2** the amount by which something slopes.

sloppy *adjective* (**sloppier, sloppiest**) **1** liquid and splashing easily. **2** careless; slipshod, *sloppy work.* **3** weakly sentimental, *a sloppy story.* **sloppily** *adverb,* **sloppiness** *noun*

slosh *verb* (*informal*) splash; slop; pour liquid carelessly.

slot *noun* a narrow opening to put things in. **slotted** *adjective*

sloth (rhymes with *both*) *noun* **1** laziness. **2** a South American animal that lives in trees and moves very slowly. **slothful** *adjective*

slot-machine *noun* a machine worked by putting a coin in the slot.

slouch *verb* stand, sit, or move in a lazy awkward way, not with an upright posture. **slouch** *noun*

slough[1] (rhymes with *cow*) *noun* a swamp or marshy place.

slough[2] (*say* sluf) *verb* shed, *A snake sloughs its skin periodically.*

slovenly (*say* **sluv**-en-lee) *adjective* carelessly; untidy. **slovenliness** *noun*

slow[1] *adjective* **1** not quick; taking more time than is usual. **2** showing a time earlier than the correct time, *Your watch is slow.* **slowly** *adverb,* **slowness** *noun*

slow[2] *adverb* slowly, *Go slow.*

slow[3] *verb* go more slowly; cause to go more slowly, *The storm slowed us down.*

sludge *noun* thick mud.

slug *noun* **1** a small slimy animal like a snail without a shell. **2** a pellet for firing from a gun.

sluggard *noun* a slow or lazy person.

sluggish *adjective* slow-moving; not alert or lively.

sluice[1] (*say* slooss) *noun* **1** a sliding barrier for controlling a flow of water. **2** a channel carrying off water.

sluice[2] *verb* (**sluiced, sluicing**) **1** wash with a flow of water. **2** let out water.

slum *noun* an area of dirty overcrowded houses.

slumber *noun & verb* sleep. **slumberer** *noun*, **slumberous** or **slumbrous** *adjective*

slump[1] *verb* fall heavily or suddenly.

slump[2] *noun* a sudden great fall in prices or trade.

slur[1] *verb* (**slurred, slurring**) 1 pronounce words indistinctly by running the sounds together. 2 mark with a slur in music.

slur[2] *noun* 1 a slurred sound. 2 discredit, *It casts a slur on his reputation.* 3 a curved line placed over notes in music to show that they are to be sung or played smoothly without a break.

slush *noun* partly melted snow on the ground. **slushy** *adjective*

sly *adjective* (**slyer, slyest**) 1 unpleasantly cunning or secret. 2 mischievous, *a sly smile.* **slyly** *adverb*, **slyness** *noun*

smack[1] *noun* a slap; a hard hit.

smack[2] *verb* slap; hit hard. **smack your lips** close and then part them noisily in enjoyment.

smack[3] *adverb* (*informal*) with a smack; directly, *The ball went smack through the window.*

smack[4] *noun* a slight flavour of something; a trace, *a smack of dishonesty.*

smack[5] *verb* have a slight flavour or trace, *His manner smacks of conceit.*

smack[6] *noun* a small sailing-boat used for fishing etc.

small *adjective* not large; less than the usual size. **smallness** *noun* **the small of the back** the smallest part of the back (at the waist).

small-minded *adjective* selfish; petty.

smallpox *noun* a former contagious disease with spots that often left bad scars on the skin.

smart[1] *adjective* 1 neat and elegant; dressed well. 2 clever. 3 forceful; brisk, *She ran at a smart pace.* **smartly** *adverb*, **smartness** *noun*

smart[2] *verb* feel a stinging pain. **smart** *noun*

smarten *verb* make or become smarter.

smash[1] *verb* 1 break noisily into pieces. 2 hit or move with great force. 3 destroy or defeat completely, *Police smashed the car theft syndicate.*

smash[2] *noun* (*plural* **smashes**) 1 the action or sound of smashing. 2 a collision. 3 a disaster. **smash hit** (*informal*) something very successful.

smashing *adjective* (*informal*) excellent; beautiful. **smasher** *noun*

smattering *noun* a slight knowledge of a subject or a foreign language.

smear *verb* 1 rub something greasy or sticky or dirty on a surface. 2 try to damage someone's reputation, *a smear campaign.* **smear** *noun*, **smeary** *adjective*

smell[1] *verb* (**smelt, smelling**) 1 be aware of something by means of the sense-organs of the nose, *I can smell smoke.* 2 give out a smell.

smell[2] *noun* 1 something you can smell; a quality in something that makes people able to smell it. 2 an unpleasant quality of this kind. 3 the ability to smell things, *a good sense of smell.* **smelly** *adjective*

smelt *verb* melt ore to get the metal it contains.

smile[1] *noun* an expression on the face that shows pleasure or amusement, with the lips stretched and turning upwards at the ends.

smile[2] *verb* (**smiled, smiling**) give a smile.

smirch *verb* 1 soil. 2 disgrace or dishonour a reputation. **smirch** *noun*

smirk[1] *noun* a self-satisfied smile.

smirk[2] *verb* give a smirk.

smite *verb* (**smote, smitten, smiting**) hit hard. **be smitten with** be affected by a disease or desire or fascination etc.

smith *noun* a person who makes things out of metal; a blacksmith.

smithereens *plural noun* (*informal*) small fragments.

smithy *noun* a blacksmith's workshop.

smitten *past participle* of **smite**.

smock[1] *noun* an overall shaped like a very long shirt.

smock[2] *verb* stitch into close gathers with embroidery. **smocking** *noun*

smog *noun* a mixture of smoke and fog.

smoke[1] *noun* **1** the mixture of gas and solid particles given off by a burning substance. **2** a period of smoking tobacco, *He wanted a smoke.* **smoky** *adjective*

smoke[2] *verb* (**smoked, smoking**) **1** give out smoke. **2** have a lighted cigarette, cigar, or pipe between your lips and draw its smoke into your mouth; do this as a habit. **3** preserve meat or fish by treating it with smoke, *smoked haddock.* **smoker** *noun*

smokeless *adjective* without smoke. **smokeless zone** an area in which it is illegal to create smoke and where only smokeless fuel may be used.

smokescreen *noun* **1** a mass of smoke used to hide the movement of troops. **2** something that conceals what is happening.

smooth[1] *adjective* **1** having a surface without any lumps, wrinkles, roughness, etc. **2** moving without bumps or jolts etc., *a smooth ride.* **3** not harsh, *a smooth flavour.* **smoothly** *adverb*, **smoothness** *noun*

smooth[2] *verb* make a thing smooth.

smote *past tense* of **smite**.

smother *verb* **1** suffocate. **2** cover thickly, *The buns were smothered in sugar.* **3** restrain; conceal, *She smothered a smile.*

smoulder *verb* **1** burn slowly without a flame. **2** continue to exist inwardly, *Their anger smouldered.*

smous (*say* smohss) *noun* a pedlar who travels from place to place selling goods, *a fish smous.*

smudge[1] *noun* a dirty mark made by rubbing something. **smudgy** *adjective*

smudge[2] *verb* (**smudged, smudging**) make a smudge on something; become smudged.

smug *adjective* self-satisfied. **smugly** *adverb*, **smugness** *noun*

smuggle *verb* (**smuggled, smuggling**) bring something into a country etc. secretly or illegally. **smuggler** *noun*

smut *noun* **1** a small piece of soot or dirt. **2** indecent talk or pictures etc. **smutty** *adjective*

snack *noun* a small meal; food eaten between meals.

snag *noun* **1** a difficulty. **2** a sharp projection. **3** a tear in material that has been caught on something sharp.

snail *noun* a small animal with a soft body and a shell.

snail's pace a very slow pace.

snake *noun* a reptile with a long narrow body and no legs. **snaky** *adjective*

snap[1] *verb* (**snapped, snapping**) **1** break suddenly or with a sharp sound. **2** bite suddenly or quickly. **3** say something quickly and angrily. **4** take something or move quickly. **5** take a snapshot of something.

snap[2] *noun* **1** the action or sound of snapping. **2** a snapshot. **3 Snap** a card-game in which players shout 'Snap!' when they see two similar cards.

snap[3] *adjective* sudden, *a snap decision.*

snapdragon *noun* a plant with flowers that have a mouth-like opening.

snappy *adjective* **1** snapping at people. **2** quick; lively, *a snappy tune.* **snappily** *adverb*

snapshot *noun* an informal photograph.

snare[1] *noun* a trap for catching birds or animals.

snare[2] *verb* (**snared, snaring**) catch in a snare.

snarl[1] *verb* **1** growl angrily. **2** speak in a bad-tempered way, *'Go away!' she snarled.* **snarl** *noun*

snarl[2] *verb* make or become tangled or jammed, *Traffic was snarled up.*

snatch *verb* seize; take quickly.

sneak[1] *verb* **1** move quietly and secretly. **2** (*informal*) take secretly, *He sneaked a biscuit from the tin.* **3** (*informal*) tell tales.

sneak[2] *noun* a tell-tale. **sneaky** *adjective*, **sneakily** *adverb*

sneer *verb* speak or behave in a scornful way. **sneer** *noun*

sneeze *verb* (**sneezed, sneezing**) send out air suddenly and uncontrollably through the nose and mouth in order to get rid of something irritating the nostrils. **sneeze** *noun*

not to be sneezed at (*informal*) worth having.

sniff *verb* **1** make a sound by drawing in air through the nose. **2** smell something, *The dog sniffed the bone.* **sniff** *noun*, **sniffer** *noun*

sniffle *verb* (**sniffled, sniffling**) sniff slightly; keep on sniffing. **sniffle** *noun*

snigger *verb* giggle slyly. **snigger** *noun*

snip *verb* (**snipped, snipping**) cut with scissors or shears in small quick cuts. **snip** *noun*

snipe[1] *noun* (*plural* **snipe**) a marsh-bird with a long beak.

snipe[2] *verb* (**sniped, sniping**) shoot at people from a hiding-place. **sniper** *noun*

snippet *noun* a small piece of news, information, etc.

snivel *verb* (**snivelled, snivelling**) cry or complain in a whining way.

snob *noun* a person who despises those who have not got wealth, power, or particular tastes or interests. **snobbery** *noun*, **snobbish** *adjective*

snoek *noun* (*plural* **snoek**) a large fish with very sharp serrated teeth found off the Cape coast.

snooker *noun* a game played with cues and 21 balls on a special cloth-covered table.

snoop *verb* (*informal*) pry. **snooper** *noun*

snooze *noun* a nap. **snooze** *verb*

snore *verb* (**snored, snoring**) breathe very noisily while sleeping. **snore** *noun*

snorkel *noun* a tube through which a person swimming under-water can take in air. **snorkelling** *noun*

snort *verb* make a rough sound by breathing forcefully through the nose. **snort** *noun*

snout *noun* an animal's projecting nose, or nose and jaws.

snow[1] *noun* frozen drops of water that fall from the sky in small white flakes.

snow[2] *verb* send down snow.

be snowed under be overwhelmed with a mass of letters or work etc.

snowball *noun* snow pressed into a ball for throwing. **snowballing** *noun*

snowdrop *noun* a small white flower that blooms in early spring.

snowflake *noun* a flake of snow.

snowman *noun* (*plural* **snowmen**) a figure made of snow.

snow-plough *noun* a vehicle or device for clearing a road or railway track etc. by pushing snow aside.

snowstorm *noun* a storm in which snow falls.

snow-white *adjective* pure white.

snowy *adjective* **1** with snow falling, *snowy weather.* **2** covered with snow, *snowy roofs.* **3** pure white.

snub[1] *verb* (**snubbed, snubbing**) treat in a scornful or unfriendly way.

snub[2] *noun* scornful or unfriendly treatment.

snub-nosed *adjective* having a short thick nose.

snuff[1] *noun* powdered tobacco for taking into the nose by sniffing.

snuff[2] *verb* put out a candle by covering or pinching the flame. **snuffer** *noun*

snuffle *verb* (**snuffled, snuffling**) sniff in a noisy way. **snuffle** *noun*

snug *adjective* (**snugger, snuggest**) cosy. **snugly** *adverb*, **snugness** *noun*

snuggle *verb* (**snuggled, snuggling**) press closely and comfortably; nestle.

so[1] *adverb* **1** in this way; to such an extent, *Why are you so cross?* **2** very, *Cricket is so boring.* **3** also, *I was wrong but so were you.*

or so or about that number.

so far up to now.

so long! (*informal*) goodbye.

so what? (*informal*) that is not important.

so[2] *conjunction* for that reason, *They threw me out, so I came here.*

soak *verb* make a person or thing very wet. **soak** *noun*

soak up take in a liquid in the way that a sponge does.

so-and-so *noun* (*plural* **so-and-so's**) a person or thing that need not be named.

soap[1] *noun* a substance used with water for washing and cleaning things. **soapy** *adjective*

soap[2] *verb* put soap on something.

soar *verb* **1** rise high in the air. **2** rise very high, *Prices were soaring.*

sob *verb* (**sobbed, sobbing**) make a gasping sound when crying. **sob** *noun*

sober[1] *adjective* **1** not intoxicated. **2** serious and calm. **3** (of colour) not bright. **soberly** *adverb*, **sobriety** (*say* so-bry-it-ee) *noun*

sober[2] *verb* make or become sober.

so-called *adjective* named in what may be the wrong way, *This so-called gentleman slammed the door.*

soccer *noun* football.

sociable *adjective* liking to be with other people; friendly. **sociably** *adverb*, **sociability** *noun*

social *adjective* **1** living in a community, not alone, *Bees are social insects.* **2** of life in a community, *social science.* **3** concerned with people's welfare, *social worker.* **4** helping people to meet each other, *a social club.* **5** sociable. **socially** *adverb*

social security money and other assistance provided by the government for those in need through being ill, disabled, unemployed, etc.

social services welfare services provided by the government, including schools, hospitals, and pensions.

socialism *noun* a political system where wealth is shared equally between people, and the main industries and trade etc. are controlled by the government. (Compare *capitalism.*)

socialist *noun* a person who believes in socialism.

society *noun* (*plural* **societies**) **1** a community; people living together in a group or nation. **2** a group of people organized for a particular purpose, *the school dramatic society.* **3** company; companionship, *We enjoy the society of our friends.*

sociology (*say* soh-see-**ol**-o-jee) *noun* the study of human society and social behaviour. **sociological** *adjective*, **sociologist** *noun*

sock[1] *noun* a short stocking reaching only to the ankle or below the knee.

sock[2] *verb* (*informal*) hit hard; punch, *He socked me on the jaw.* **sock** *noun*

socket *noun* **1** a hollow into which something fits, *a tooth-socket.* **2** a device into which an electric plug or bulb is put to make a connection.

sod *noun* a piece of turf.

soda *noun* **1** a compound of sodium used in washing, cooking, etc. **2** soda-water.

soda-water *noun* water made fizzy with carbon dioxide, used in drinks.

sodden *adjective* made very wet.

sodium *noun* a soft white metal.

sofa *noun* a kind of settee.

soft *adjective* **1** not hard or firm; easily pressed. **2** smooth, not rough or stiff, *soft fur.* **3** gentle; not loud, *soft music.* **softly** *adverb*, **softness** *noun*

soft drink a drink that is not alcoholic.

softball *noun* a form of baseball using a softer and larger ball.

soften *verb* make or become soft or softer. **softener** *noun*

software *noun* computer programs, data, etc. (Compare *hardware.*)

soggy *adjective* (**soggier, soggiest**) very wet and heavy, *soggy ground.*

soil[1] *noun* **1** the loose earth in which plants grow. **2** territory, *on South African soil.* **soil erosion** the removal of layers of topsoil caused by wind, rain, etc.

soil[2] *verb* make a thing dirty.

sojourn[1] (*say* **soj**-ern) *verb* stay at a place temporarily.

sojourn[2] *noun* a temporary stay.

solace (*say* **sol**-as) *verb* (**solaced, solacing**) comfort someone who is unhappy or disappointed. **solace** *noun*

solar *adjective* of or from the sun. **solar power** electricity produced by harnessing the energy of the sun's rays. **solar system** the sun and the planets that revolve round it.

solder *noun* a soft alloy that is melted to join pieces of metal together. **solder** *verb*

soldier *noun* a member of an army.

sole[1] *noun* **1** the bottom surface of a foot or shoe. **2** an edible flat-fish.

sole[2] *verb* (**soled, soling**) put a sole on a shoe.

sole[3] *adjective* single; only, *She was the sole survivor.* **solely** *adverb*

solemn *adjective* 1 not smiling; not cheerful. 2 dignified; formal. **solemnly** *adverb*, **solemnity** *noun*

solemnize *verb* (**solemnized, solemnizing**) celebrate a festival; perform a marriage ceremony. **solemnization** *noun*

solenoid *noun* a coil of wire that becomes magnetic when an electric current is passed through it.

sol-fa *noun* a system of syllables (*doh, ray, me, fah, soh, la, te*) used to represent the notes of the musical scale.

solicit *verb* (**solicited, soliciting**) ask for; try to obtain, *solicit votes* or *solicit for votes.* **solicitation** *noun*

solicitor *noun* a lawyer who advises clients, prepares legal documents, etc.

solicitous *adjective* anxious and concerned about a person's comfort, welfare, etc. **solicitously** *adverb*, **solicitude** *noun*

solid¹ *adjective* 1 not hollow; with no space inside. 2 keeping its shape; not liquid or gas. 3 continuous, *for two solid hours.* 4 firm or strongly made; not flimsy, *a solid foundation.* 5 showing solidarity; unanimous, *solid support.* **solidly** *adverb*, **solidity** *noun*

solid² *noun* 1 a solid thing; solid food. 2 a shape that has three dimensions (length, width, and height or depth).

solidarity *noun* 1 being solid. 2 unity and support for each other because of agreement in opinions, interests, etc.

solidify *verb* (**solidified, solidifying**) make or become solid.

soliloquy (*say* sol-**il**-ok-wee) *noun* (*plural* **soliloquies**) a speech in which a person speaks his or her thoughts aloud without addressing anyone. **soliloquize** *verb*

solitaire *noun* 1 a game for one person, in which marbles are moved on a special board until only one is left. 2 a diamond or other precious stone set by itself. 3 patience (see *patience* 2).

solitary *adjective* 1 alone, without companions. 2 single, *a solitary example.* 3 lonely, *a solitary valley.*

solitude *noun* being solitary.

solo *noun* (*plural* **solos**) something sung, played, danced, or done by one person.

solo *adjective* & *adverb*, **soloist** *noun*

solstice (*say* sol-stiss) *noun* either of the two times in each year when the sun is at its furthest point north or south of the equator.
summer solstice about 22 December (in the southern hemisphere).
winter solstice about 21 June (in the southern hemisphere).

soluble *adjective* 1 able to be dissolved. 2 able to be solved. **solubility** *noun*

solution *noun* 1 a liquid in which something is dissolved. 2 the answer to a problem or puzzle.

solve *verb* (**solved, solving**) find the answer to a problem or puzzle.

solvent¹ *adjective* 1 having enough money to pay all your debts. 2 able to dissolve another substance. **solvency** *noun*

solvent² *noun* a liquid used for dissolving something.

sombre *adjective* dark and gloomy.

sombrero (*say* som-**brair**-oh) *noun* (*plural* **sombreros**) a hat with a very wide brim.

some¹ *adjective* 1 a few; a little, *some apples*; *some sugar.* 2 an unknown person or thing, *Some fool left the door open.* 3 about, *We waited some 20 minutes.*
some time at some point in time, *Come and see me some time* (not 'sometime'). *They left some time ago.*

some² *pronoun* a certain number or amount that is less than the whole, *Some of them were late.*

somebody *pronoun* some person.

somehow *adverb* in some way.

someone *pronoun* somebody.

somersault *noun* a movement in which you turn head over heels before landing on your feet. **somersault** *verb*

something *noun* some thing.
something like rather like, *It's something like a rabbit*; approximately, *It cost something like R10.*

sometime *adjective* former, *her sometime friend.* (Compare *some time* in the entry for *some*.)

sometimes *adverb* at some times but not always, *We sometimes walk to school.*

somewhat *adverb* to some extent, *He was somewhat annoyed.*

somewhere *adverb* in or to some place.

somnambulist *noun* a sleep-walker.

somnolent *adjective* sleeping; sleepy. **somnolence** *noun*

son *noun* a boy or man who is someone's child.

son-in-law *noun* (*plural* **sons-in-law**) a daughter's husband.

sonar *noun* a device for finding objects under water by the reflection of sound-waves.

sonata *noun* a musical composition for one instrument or two, in several movements.

song *noun* 1 a tune for singing. 2 singing, *He burst into song.*
a song and dance (*informal*) a great fuss.
for a song bought or sold very cheaply.

songbird *noun* a bird that sings sweetly.

songololo *noun* a millipede that has a hard jointed armour and that coils itself up when alarmed.

songster *noun* 1 a singer. 2 a songbird.

sonic *adjective* of sound or sound-waves.

sonnet *noun* a kind of poem with 14 lines.

sonny *noun* (*informal*) boy, young man, *Come on, sonny!*

sonorous (*say* **sonn**-er-us) *adjective* giving a loud deep sound; resonant.

soon *adverb* 1 in a short time from now. 2 not long after something.
as soon as willingly, *I'd just as soon stay here.*
as soon as at the moment that.
sooner or later at some time in the future.

soot *noun* the black powder left by smoke in a chimney or on a building etc. **sooty** *adjective*

soothe *verb* (**soothed, soothing**) calm; ease pain or distress. **soothingly** *adverb*

soothsayer *noun* a prophet.

sop *noun* 1 a piece of bread dipped in liquid before being eaten or cooked. 2 something unimportant given to pacify or bribe a troublesome person.

sophisticated *adjective* 1 of or accustomed to fashionable life and its ways.
2 complicated, *a sophisticated machine.* **sophistication** *noun*

sophistry (*say* **sof**-ist-ree) *noun* (*plural* **sophistries**) a piece of reasoning that is clever but false or misleading.

soporific *adjective* causing sleep.

sopping *adjective* very wet; drenched.

soppy *adjective* 1 very wet. 2 (*informal*) sentimental in a sickly way.

soprano *noun* (*plural* **sopranos**) a woman, girl, or boy with a high singing-voice.

sorcerer *noun* a wizard. **sorceress** *noun*, **sorcery** *noun*

sordid *adjective* 1 dirty; squalid. 2 dishonourable; selfish and mercenary, *sordid motives.* **sordidly** *adverb*, **sordidness** *noun*

sore[1] *adjective* 1 painful; smarting. 2 (*informal*) annoyed; offended. 3 serious; distressing, *in sore need.* **soreness** *noun*

sore[2] *noun* a sore place.

sorely *adverb* seriously; very, *I was sorely tempted to run away.*

sorghum *noun* a crop of edible grains, produced in warm climates.

sorrel[1] *noun* a herb with sharp-tasting leaves.

sorrel[2] *noun* a reddish-brown horse.

sorrow[1] *noun* unhappiness or regret caused by loss or disappointment. **sorrowful** *adjective*, **sorrowfully** *adverb*

sorrow[2] *verb* feel sorrow; grieve.

sorry *adjective* (**sorrier, sorriest**) 1 feeling pity, regret, or sympathy. 2 wretched, *His clothes were in a sorry state.*

sort[1] *noun* 1 a group of things or people that are similar; a kind or variety. 2 (*informal*) a person, *He's quite a good sort.*
out of sorts slightly unwell or depressed.
sort of (*informal*) rather; to some extent, *I sort of expected it.*
● USAGE: Correct use is *this sort of thing* or *these sorts of things* (not 'these sort of things').

sort[2] *verb* arrange things in groups according to their size, kind, etc. **sorter** *noun*
sort out disentangle; select; (*informal*) deal with and punish someone.

sortie *noun* 1 an attack by troops coming out of a besieged place. 2 an attacking expedition by a military aircraft.

SOS *noun* (*plural* **SOSs**) an urgent appeal for help.

sosatie *noun* a number of meat pieces that have been spiced and placed on a skewer for grilling.

soul *noun* 1 the invisible part of a person that is believed to go on living after the body has died. 2 a person's mind and emotions etc. 3 a person, *There isn't a soul about.*

soulful *adjective* having or showing deep feeling. **soulfully** *adverb*

sound[1] *noun* 1 vibrations that travel through the air and can be detected by the ear; the sensation they produce. 2 sound reproduced in a film etc. 3 a mental impression, *We don't like the sound of her plans.*

sound barrier the resistance of the air to objects moving at nearly supersonic speed.

sound[2] *verb* 1 produce or cause to produce a sound. 2 give an impression when heard, *He sounds angry.* 3 test by noting the sounds heard, *A doctor sounds a patient's lungs with a stethoscope.*

sound[3] *verb* test the depth of water beneath a ship.

sound out try to find out what a person thinks or feels about something.

sound[4] *adjective* 1 in good condition; not damaged. 2 healthy; not diseased. 3 reasonable; correct, *Her ideas are sound.* 4 reliable; secure, *a sound investment.* 5 thorough; deep, *a sound sleep.* **soundly** *adverb*, **soundness** *noun*

sound[5] *noun* a strait.

soundtrack *noun* the sound that goes with a cinema film.

soup *noun* liquid food made from stewed bones, meat, fish, vegetables, etc.
in the soup (*informal*) in trouble.

sour[1] *adjective* 1 tasting sharp like unripe fruit. 2 stale and unpleasant, not fresh, *sour milk.* 3 bad-tempered. **sourly** *adverb*, **sourness** *noun*

sour fig a plant grown on dunes to bind the sand; its edible fruit.

sour[2] *verb* make or become sour.

source *noun* the place from which something comes.

sousboontjies *plural noun* beans in a sweet and sour sauce.

souse *verb* (**soused**, **sousing**) 1 soak; drench. 2 soak fish in pickle.

south[1] *noun* 1 the direction to the right of a person who faces east. 2 the southern part of a country, city, etc.

south[2] *adjective* & *adverb* towards or in the south. **southerly** (*say* **su**th-er-lee) *adjective*, **southern** *adjective*, **southerner** *noun*, **southernmost** *adjective*

South African War *noun* one of the wars between British and colonial troops and burgher republican forces: 1880–81 (the first war) and 1899–1902 (the second war).

south-east *noun, adjective* & *adverb* midway between south and east. **south-easterly** *adjective*, **south-eastern** *adjective*

southeaster *noun* the wind that blows most frequently during the summer at the Cape.

southward *adjective* & *adverb* towards the south. **southwards** *adverb*

south-west *noun, adjective* & *adverb* midway between south and west. **south-westerly** *adjective*, **south-western** *adjective*

souvenir (*say* soo-ven-**eer**) *noun* something that you keep to remind you of a person, place, or event.

sou'wester *noun* a waterproof hat with a wide flap at the back.

sovereign[1] *noun* a king or queen who is the ruler of a country; a monarch. **sovereignty** *noun*

sovereign[2] *adjective* 1 supreme, *sovereign power.* 2 having sovereign power; independent, *sovereign states.*

Soviet *adjective* of the former USSR.

sow[1] (rhymes with *go*) *verb* (**sowed**, **sown** or **sowed**, **sowing**) put seeds into the ground so that they will grow into plants. **sower** *noun*

sow[2] (rhymes with *cow*) *noun* a female pig.

soya bean *noun* a kind of bean from which edible oil and flour are made.

spa *noun* a health resort where there is a spring of water containing mineral salts.

space¹ *noun* 1 the whole area outside the earth, where the stars and planets are. 2 an area or volume, *This table takes too much space.* 3 an empty area; a gap, *a space between two words.* 4 an interval of time, *within the space of an hour.*
space shuttle a spacecraft for repeated use to and from outer space.

space² *verb* (**spaced, spacing**) arrange things with spaces between, *Space them out.*

spacecraft *noun* (*plural* **spacecraft**) a vehicle for travelling in outer space.

spaceman *noun* (*plural* **spacemen**) an astronaut. **spacewoman** *noun* (*plural* **spacewomen**)

spaceship *noun* a spacecraft.

spacious *adjective* providing a lot of space; roomy. **spaciousness** *noun*

spade¹ *noun* a tool with a long handle and a wide blade for digging.

spade² *noun* a playing-card with black shapes like upside-down hearts on it, each with a short stem.

spaghetti *noun* pasta made in long thin sticks.

span¹ *noun* 1 the length from end to end or across something. 2 the distance from the tip of the thumb to the tip of the little finger when the hand is spread out. 3 the part between two uprights of an arch or bridge. 4 the length of a period of time, *over a span of twenty years.*

span² *verb* (**spanned, spanning**) reach across, *A bridge spans the river.*

spangle *noun* a small piece of glittering material. **spangled** *adjective*

spaniel *noun* a kind of dog with long ears and silky fur.

spank *verb* smack a person on the bottom as a punishment.

spanking *adjective* (*informal*) brisk; lively, *at a spanking pace.*

spanner *noun* a tool for gripping and turning the nut on a bolt etc.

spanspek *noun* a cantaloup.

spar¹ *noun* a strong pole used for a mast or boom etc. on a ship.

spar² *verb* (**sparred, sparring**) 1 practise boxing. 2 quarrel or argue.

spare¹ *verb* (**spared, sparing**) 1 afford to give something, *Can you spare a moment?* 2 be merciful towards someone; not hurt or harm a person or thing. 3 use or treat economically, *No expense will be spared. Spare the rod and spoil the child!*

spare² *adjective* 1 not used but kept ready in case it is needed; extra, *a spare wheel.* 2 thin; lean. **sparely** *adverb*, **spareness** *noun*
spare time time not needed for work.

sparing (*say* **spair**-ing) *adjective* economical; grudging. **sparingly** *adverb*

spark¹ *noun* 1 a tiny glowing particle. 2 a flash produced electrically.

spark² *verb* give off a spark or sparks.

sparking-plug *noun* (also **spark-plug**) a device that makes a spark to ignite the fuel in an engine.

sparkle *verb* (**sparkled, sparkling**) 1 shine with tiny flashes of light. 2 show brilliant wit or liveliness.

sparkler *noun* a sparking firework.

sparrow *noun* a small brown bird.

sparse *adjective* thinly scattered; not numerous, *a sparse population.* **sparsely** *adverb*, **sparseness** *noun*

spartan *adjective* simple and without comfort or luxuries.

spasm *noun* 1 a sudden involuntary movement of a muscle. 2 a sudden brief spell of activity etc., *a spasm of artistic inspiration.*

spasmodic *adjective* in spasms; happening or done at irregular intervals. **spasmodically** *adverb*

spastic *noun* & *adjective* 1 (a person) suffering from cerebral palsy with spasm of the muscles. 2 spasmodic.
• USAGE: Many people dislike the term *spastic.* To avoid offence, say *She suffers from cerebral palsy* rather than *She is a spastic.*

spat¹ *past tense* of **spit¹**.

spat² *noun* a short gaiter.

spate *noun* a sudden flood or rush.

spathe (rhymes with *bathe*) *noun* a large petal-like part of a flower, round a central spike.

spatial *adjective* of or in space.

spatter *verb* scatter in small drops; splash. **spatter** *noun*

spatula *noun* a tool like a knife with a broad blunt flexible blade, used for spreading things.

spawn[1] *noun* 1 the eggs of fish, frogs, toads, or shellfish. 2 the thread-like matter from which fungi grow.

spawn[2] *verb* 1 put out spawn; produce from spawn. 2 produce something in great quantities, *The drama festival spawned many would-be critics.*

spay *verb* sterilize a female animal by removing the ovaries.

spaza (*say* spah-za) *noun* (also **spaza shop**) an informal shop, often located in the trader's own home.

speak *verb* (**spoke, spoken, speaking**) 1 say something; talk. 2 talk or be able to talk in another language, *Do you speak Zulu?*
speak up speak more loudly; give your opinion.

speaker *noun* 1 a person who is speaking; someone who makes a speech. 2 a loudspeaker.
the Speaker the person who controls the debates in Parliament or a similar assembly.

spear[1] *noun* a weapon for throwing or stabbing, with a long shaft and a pointed tip.

spear[2] *verb* pierce with a spear or with something pointed.

spearmint *noun* mint used in cookery and for flavouring chewing-gum.

special *adjective* 1 of a particular kind; for some purpose, not general, *special training.* 2 exceptional, *Take special care of it.*

specialist *noun* an expert in one subject, *a skin specialist.*

speciality *noun* (*plural* **specialities**) a special quality or product; something in which a person specializes.

specialize *verb* (**specialized,** specializing) give particular attention or study to one subject or thing, *She specialized in biology.* **specialization** *noun*

specially *adverb* in a special way; for a special purpose.

species (*say* spee-sheez or spee-seez) *noun* (*plural* **species**) 1 a group of animals or plants that are very similar. 2 a kind or sort, *a species of sledge.*

specific *adjective* definite; precise; of or for a particular thing, *The money was given for a specific purpose.* **specifically** *adverb*
specific gravity the weight of something as compared with the same volume of water or air.

specify *verb* (**specified, specifying**) name or list things precisely, *The recipe specified cream, not milk.* **specification** *noun*

specimen *noun* 1 a sample. 2 an example, *a fine specimen of an oak-tree.*

specious (*say* spee-shus) *adjective* seeming good but lacking real merit, *specious reasoning.*

speck *noun* a small spot or particle.

speckle *noun* a small spot or mark. **speckled** *adjective*

specs *plural noun* (*informal*) spectacles.

spectacle *noun* 1 an impressive sight or display. 2 a ridiculous sight, *You're making a spectacle of yourself.*
spectacles *plural noun* a pair of lenses set in a frame, worn in front of the eyes to help the wearer to see clearly. **spectacled** *adjective*

spectacular *adjective* impressive.

spectator *noun* a person who watches a game, show, incident, etc.

spectre *noun* a ghost. **spectral** *adjective*

spectrum *noun* (*plural* **spectra**) 1 the bands of colours seen in a rainbow. 2 a wide range of things, ideas, etc., *a spectrum of opinions.*

speculate *verb* (**speculated, speculating**) 1 form opinions without having any definite evidence. 2 make investments in the hope of making a profit but risking a loss.

speculation *noun,* **speculator** *noun,*
speculative *adjective*

sped *past tense* of **speed**².

speech *noun* (*plural* **speeches**)
1 the action or power of speaking. 2 words
spoken; a talk to an audience.

speechless *adjective* unable to speak
because of great emotion.

speed¹ *noun* 1 a measure of the time in
which something moves or happens.
2 quickness; swiftness.
at speed quickly.

speed² *verb* (**sped** (in senses 3 and 4
speeded), **speeding**) 1 go quickly,
The train sped by. 2 send quickly, *to speed
you on your way.* 3 travel too fast. 4 make
or become quicker, *This will speed things
up.*

speedboat *noun* a fast motor-boat.

speedometer *noun* a device in a vehicle,
showing its speed.

speedway *noun* a track for motor-cycle
racing.

speedy *adjective* (**speedier**, **speediest**)
quick; swift. **speedily** *adverb*

speleology (*say* spel-ee-**ol**-o-jee) *noun*
the exploration and study of caves.

spell¹ *noun* a saying or action etc.
supposed to have magical power.

spell² *noun* 1 a period of time, *a dry spell.*
2 a period of a certain work or activity etc.,
have a spell of baby-sitting.

spell³ *verb* (**spelt**, **spelling**) 1 put letters in
the right order to make a word or words.
2 have as a result, *Wet weather spells ruin
for crops.* **speller** *noun*

spellbound *adjective* entranced as if by
a magic spell.

spend *verb* (**spent**, **spending**)
1 use money to pay for things. 2 use up,
Don't spend too much time on it. 3 pass
time, *We spent a holiday in Namibia.*

spendthrift *noun* a person who spends
money extravagantly and wastefully.

sperm *noun* (*plural* **sperms** or **sperm**)
the male cell that fuses with an ovum.

spew *verb* 1 vomit. 2 cast out in a stream,
The volcano spewed out lava.

sphere *noun* 1 a perfectly round solid
shape; the shape of a ball. 2 a field of

action or interest etc., *That country was
in Russia's sphere of influence.* **spherical**
adjective

spheroid *noun* a sphere-like but not
perfectly spherical solid.

sphinx *noun* (*plural* **sphinxes**)
a stone statue with the body of a lion and
a human head, especially the huge one
(almost 5 000 years old) in Egypt.

spice *noun* a substance used to flavour
food, often made from dried parts of
plants. **spicy** *adjective*

spick and span *adjective* neat and clean.

spider *noun* a small animal with eight
legs that spins webs to catch insects on
which it feeds. **spidery** *adjective*

spike¹ *noun* 1 a pointed piece of metal;
a sharp point. 2 a long narrow projecting
part, *spikes of grass.* **spiky** *adjective*

spike² *verb* (**spiked**, **spiking**) 1 put spikes
on something. 2 pierce with a spike.
spike a person's guns spoil his or her
plans.

spill¹ *verb* (**spilt** or **spilled**, **spilling**)
1 let something fall out of a container.
2 become spilt, *The coins came spilling
out.* **spillage** *noun*

spill² *noun* 1 spilling. 2 a fall.

spill³ *noun* a thin strip of wood or rolled
paper used to carry a flame, e.g. to light a
pipe.

spin¹ *verb* (**spun**, **spinning**) 1 turn round
and round quickly. 2 make raw wool or
cotton into threads by pulling and twisting
its fibres. 3 (of a spider or silkworm) make
a web or cocoon out of threads from its
body.
spin a yarn tell a story.
spin out cause to last a long time.

spin² *noun* 1 a spinning movement.
2 a short excursion in a vehicle, *a spin
round the peninsula.*

spinach *noun* a vegetable with
dark-green leaves.

spinal *adjective* of the spine.

spindle *noun* 1 a thin rod on which
thread is wound. 2 a pin or bar that turns
round or on which something turns.

spindly *adjective* thin and long or tall.

spin-drier *noun* a machine in which

washed clothes are spun round and round to dry them.

spindrift *noun* spray blown along the surface of the sea.

spine *noun* 1 the line of bones down the middle of the back. 2 a thorn or prickle. 3 the back part of a book where the pages are joined together.

spine-chilling *adjective* frightening and exciting at the same time. **spine-chiller** *noun*

spineless *adjective* 1 without a backbone. 2 lacking in determination or strength of character.

spinet *noun* a small harpsichord.

spinney *noun* (*plural* **spinneys**) a small wood; a thicket.

spinning-wheel *noun* a household device for spinning fibre into thread.

spin-off *noun* (*plural* **spin-offs**) a by-product.

spinster *noun* a woman who has not married.

spiny *adjective* full of spines; prickly.

spiral[1] *adjective* going round and round a central point and becoming gradually closer to it or further from it; twisting continually round a central line or cylinder etc. **spirally** *adverb*

spiral[2] *noun* a spiral line or course.

spiral[3] *verb* (**spiralled, spiralling**) move in a spiral.

spire *noun* a tall pointed part on top of a church tower.

spirit[1] *noun* 1 the soul. 2 a person's mood or mind and feelings, *He was in good spirits.* 3 a ghost; a supernatural being. 4 courage; liveliness, *She answered with spirit.* 5 a kind of quality in something, *the romantic spirit of the book.* 6 a strong distilled alcoholic drink.

spirit[2] *verb* carry off quickly and secretly, *They spirited her away.*

spirited *adjective* brave; lively.

spiritual[1] *adjective* 1 of the human soul; not physical. 2 of the Church or religion. **spiritually** *adverb*, **spirituality** *noun*

spiritual[2] *noun* a religious folk-song, especially of black people in America.

spiritualism *noun* the belief that the

spirits of dead people communicate with living people. **spiritualist** *noun*

spirituous *adjective* containing a lot of alcohol; distilled, *spirituous liquors.*

spit[1] *verb* (**spat** or **spit, spitting**) 1 send out drops of liquid etc. forcibly from the mouth, *He spat at me.* 2 fall lightly, *It's spitting with rain.*

spit[2] *noun* saliva; spittle. **spitting image** an exact likeness.

spit[3] *noun* 1 a long thin metal spike put through meat to hold it while it is being roasted. 2 a narrow strip of land sticking out into the sea.

spite *noun* a desire to hurt or annoy somebody. **spiteful** *adjective*, **spitefully** *adverb*, **spitefulness** *noun* **in spite of** not being prevented by, *We went out in spite of the rain.*

spitfire *noun* a fiery-tempered person.

spittle *noun* saliva, especially that spat out.

spittoon *noun* a receptacle for people to spit into.

splash[1] *verb* 1 make liquid fly about in drops. 2 (of liquid) be splashed, *Tea splashed on the table.* 3 wet by splashing, *The bus splashed us.*

splash[2] *noun* (*plural* **splashes**) 1 the action or sound or mark of splashing. 2 a striking display or effect, *the interview created quite a splash.*

splatter *verb* splash noisily.

splay *verb* spread or slope apart.

spleen *noun* 1 an organ of the body, close to the stomach, that helps to keep the blood in good condition. 2 bad temper; spite, *He vented his spleen on us.*

splendid *adjective* 1 magnificent; full of splendour. 2 excellent, *a splendid achievement.* **splendidly** *adverb*

splendour *noun* a brilliant display or appearance.

splice *verb* (**spliced, splicing**) 1 join pieces of rope etc. by twisting their strands together. 2 join pieces of film or wood etc. by overlapping the ends.

splint[1] *noun* a straight piece of wood or metal etc. tied to a broken arm or leg to hold it firm.

splint² *verb* hold with a splint.

splinter¹ *noun* a thin sharp piece of wood, glass, stone, etc. broken off a larger piece.

splinter² *verb* break into splinters.

split¹ *verb* (**split**, **splitting**) 1 break into parts; divide. 2 (*informal*) reveal a secret.

split² *noun* 1 the splitting or dividing of something. 2 a place where something has split, *a split in her skirt*.

the splits an acrobatic position in which the legs are stretched widely in opposite directions.

splutter *verb* 1 make a quick series of spitting sounds. 2 speak quickly but not clearly, *Stop spluttering; I can't hear what you're saying!* **splutter** *noun*

spoil¹ *verb* (**spoilt** or **spoiled**, **spoiling**) 1 damage something and make it useless or unsatisfactory. 2 make someone selfish by always letting them have what they want.

spoil² *noun* (also **spoils**) plunder or other things gained by a victor, *the spoils of war*.

spoil-sport *noun* a person who spoils other people's enjoyment of things.

spoke¹ *noun* each of the bars or rods that go from the centre of a wheel to its rim.

spoke² *past tense* of **speak**.

spokesperson *noun* (*plural* **spokespersons** or **spokespeople**) a person who speaks on behalf of a group of people. **spokesman** *noun* (*plural* **spokesmen**), **spokeswoman** *noun* (*plural* **spokeswomen**)

spoliation *noun* pillaging.

sponge¹ *noun* 1 a sea-creature with a soft porous body. 2 the skeleton of this creature, or a piece of a similar substance, used for washing or padding things. 3 a soft lightweight cake or pudding. **spongy** *adjective*

sponge² *verb* (**sponged**, **sponging**) 1 wipe or wash something with a sponge. 2 (*informal*) live by cadging from people, *He sponged on his friends*. **sponger** *noun*

sponsor¹ *noun* someone who provides money or help etc. for a person or thing, or who gives money to a charity in return for something achieved by another

person. **sponsorship** *noun*

sponsor² *verb* be a sponsor for a person or thing.

spontaneous (*say* spon-**tay**-nee-us) *adjective* happening or done naturally; not forced or suggested by someone else. **spontaneously** *adverb*, **spontaneity** *noun*

spoof *noun* (*informal*) a hoax; a parody.

spook *noun* (*informal*) a ghost. **spooky** *adjective*, **spookiness** *noun*

spool *noun* a rod or cylinder on which something is wound.

spoon¹ *noun* a small device with a rounded bowl on a handle, used for lifting things to the mouth or for stirring or measuring things. **spoonful** *noun* (*plural* **spoonfuls**)

spoon² *verb* take or lift something with a spoon.

spoonerism *noun* an accidental exchange of the initial letters of two words, e.g. by saying *a boiled sprat* instead of *a spoiled brat*.

spoor *noun* the track left by an animal or person.

sporadic *adjective* happening or found at irregular intervals; scattered. **sporadically** *adverb*

spore *noun* a tiny reproductive cell of a plant such as a fungus or fern.

sport¹ *noun* 1 an athletic activity; a game or pastime, especially outdoors. 2 games of this kind, *Are you keen on sport?* 3 (*informal*) a person who behaves fairly and generously, *Come on, be a sport!* **sports car** an open low-built fast car. **sports coat** or **jacket** a man's jacket for informal wear (not part of a suit).

sport² *verb* 1 play; amuse yourself. 2 wear, *She sported a beaded earring in one ear*.

sporting *adjective* 1 connected with sport; interested in sport. 2 behaving fairly and generously.

a sporting chance a reasonable chance of success.

sportive *adjective* playful.

sportsperson *noun* (*plural* **sportspersons** or **sportspeople**) a person who takes part in sport, especially professionally. **sportsman** *noun* (*plural* **sportsmen**), **sportsmanship** *noun*, **sportswoman** *noun* (*plural* **sportswomen**)

spot¹ *noun* 1 a small round mark. 2 a pimple. 3 a small amount, *We had a spot of trouble.* 4 a place, *a shady spot.* 5 a drop, *a few spots of rain.* **on the spot** without delay or change of place; under pressure to take action, *This really puts him on the spot!*

spot² *verb* (**spotted, spotting**) 1 mark with spots. 2 (*informal*) notice, *We spotted her in the crowd.* 3 watch for and take note of, *train-spotting.* **spotter** *noun*

spotless *adjective* perfectly clean.

spotlight *noun* a strong light that can shine on one small area.

spotty *adjective* marked with spots.

spouse *noun* a person's husband or wife.

spout¹ *noun* 1 a pipe or similar opening from which liquid can pour. 2 a jet of liquid.

spout² *verb* 1 come or send out as a jet of liquid. 2 (*informal*) speak for a long time.

sprain *verb* injure a joint by twisting it. **sprain** *noun*

sprat *noun* a small edible fish.

sprawl *verb* 1 sit or lie with the arms and legs spread out loosely. 2 spread out loosely or untidily, *Shacks sprawled along the highway.* **sprawl** *noun*

spray¹ *verb* scatter tiny drops of liquid over something.

spray² *noun* 1 tiny drops of liquid sprayed. 2 a device for spraying liquid.

spray³ *noun* 1 a single shoot with its leaves and flowers. 2 a small bunch of flowers.

spread¹ *verb* (**spread, spreading**) 1 open or stretch something out to its full size, *The bird spread its wings.* 2 make something cover a surface, *We spread jam on the bread.* 3 become longer or wider, *The stain was spreading.* 4 make or become more widely known or felt or distributed etc., *We spread the news. Panic spread.*

spread² *noun* 1 the action or result of spreading. 2 a thing's breadth or extent, *the spread of the suburb.* 3 a paste for spreading on bread. 4 (*informal*) a huge meal.

spread-eagle *verb* (**spread-eagled, spread-eagling**) spread out a person's body with arms and legs stretched out.

spree *noun* (*informal*) a lively outing.

sprig *noun* a small branch; a shoot.

sprightly *adjective* (**sprightlier, sprightliest**) lively; full of energy.

spring¹ *verb* (**sprang, sprung, springing**) 1 jump; move quickly or suddenly, *He sprang to his feet.* 2 originate; arise, *The trouble has sprung from carelessness.* 3 present or produce suddenly, *They sprang a surprise on us.*

spring² *noun* 1 a springy coil or bent piece of metal. 2 a springing movement. 3 a place where water comes up naturally from the ground. 4 the season when most plants begin to grow.

springboard *noun* a springy board from which people jump in diving and gymnastics.

springbok *noun* (*plural* **springbok** or **springboks**) a gazelle that runs with high jumping movements.

spring-clean *verb* clean a house thoroughly in springtime.

springtime *noun* the season of spring.

springy *adjective* (**springier, springiest**) able to spring back easily after being bent or squeezed. **springiness** *noun*

sprinkle *verb* (**sprinkled, sprinkling**) make tiny drops or pieces fall on something. **sprinkler** *noun*

sprinkling *noun* a few here and there.

sprint *verb* run very fast for a short distance. **sprint** *noun*, **sprinter** *noun*

sprite *noun* an elf, fairy, or goblin.

sprocket *noun* each of the row of teeth round a wheel, fitting into links on a chain.

sprout¹ *verb* start to grow; put out shoots.

sprout² *noun* 1 a shoot of a plant. 2 a Brussels sprout.

spruce¹ *noun* a kind of fir-tree.

spruce² *adjective* neat and trim; smart.

spruce³ *verb* (**spruced, sprucing**) smarten, *Spruce yourself up.*

spruit *noun* a water course that is often filled only after rain.

spry *adjective* (**spryer**, **spryest**) active; nimble; lively.

spud *noun* (*informal*) a potato.

spume *noun* froth; foam.

spur[1] *noun* **1** a sharp device worn on the heel of a rider's boot to urge a horse to go faster. **2** a stimulus or incentive. **3** a projecting part.

on the spur of the moment on an impulse; without planning.

spur[2] *verb* (**spurred**, **spurring**) urge on; encourage.

spurious *adjective* not genuine.

spurn *verb* reject scornfully.

spurt[1] *verb* **1** gush out. **2** increase your speed suddenly, *The horse spurted ahead.*

spurt[2] *noun* **1** a sudden gush. **2** a sudden increase in speed or effort.

sputter *verb* splutter. **sputter** *noun*

spy[1] *noun* (*plural* **spies**) someone who works secretly to find out things about another country, person, etc.

spy[2] *verb* (**spied**, **spying**) **1** be a spy; keep watch secretly. **2** see; notice, *She spied a house.*

squabble *verb* (**squabbled**, **squabbling**) quarrel; bicker. **squabble** *noun*

squad *noun* a small group of people working or being trained together.

squadron *noun* part of an army, navy, or air force.

squalid *adjective* dirty and unpleasant. **squalidly** *adverb*, **squalor** *noun*

squall[1] *noun* **1** a sudden storm or gust of wind. **2** a baby's loud cry.

squall[2] *verb* (of a baby) cry loudly.

squander *verb* spend money or time etc. wastefully.

square[1] *noun* **1** a flat shape with four equal sides and four right angles. **2** an area surrounded by buildings, *Greenmarket Square.* **3** the number produced by multiplying something by itself, *9 is the square of 3 (9 = 3 × 3).*

square[2] *adjective* **1** having the shape of a square. **2** forming a right angle, *The desk has square corners.* **3** equal; even, *The teams are all square with six points each.* **4** honest; fair, *a square deal.* **5** (*informal*) old-fashioned. **squarely** *adverb*,

squareness *noun*

square meal a good satisfying meal.

square metre etc., the area of a surface with sides that are one metre etc. long.

square root the number that gives a particular number if it is multiplied by itself, *3 is the square root of 9 (3 × 3 = 9).*

square[3] *verb* (**squared**, **squaring**) **1** make a thing square. **2** multiply a number by itself, *5 squared is 25.* **3** match; make or be consistent, *His story doesn't square with yours.* **4** (*informal*) bribe.

square-rigged *adjective* with the sails set across the ship, not lengthways.

squash[1] *verb* **1** press something so that it loses its shape; crush. **2** pack tightly. **3** suppress; quash, *squash the proposal.*

squash[2] *noun* (*plural* **squashes**) **1** a crowded condition. **2** a fruit-flavoured soft drink. **3** a game played with rackets and a soft ball in a special indoor court.

squash[3] *noun* (*plural* **squashes**) a kind of gourd used as a vegetable.

squat[1] *verb* (**squatted**, **squatting**) **1** sit on your heels; crouch. **2** live in an unoccupied house or on unoccupied land without permission. **squat** *noun*, **squatter** *noun*

squatter camp an area that is occupied mainly by shacks.

squat[2] *adjective* short and fat.

squaw *noun* an American Indian woman or wife.

squawk *verb* make a loud harsh cry. **squawk** *noun*

squeak *verb* make a short high-pitched cry or sound. **squeak** *noun*, **squeaky** *adjective*, **squeakily** *adverb*

squeal *verb* make a long shrill cry or sound. **squeal** *noun*

squeamish *adjective* easily disgusted or shocked. **squeamishness** *noun*

squeeze[1] *verb* (**squeezed**, **squeezing**) **1** press from opposite sides; press something so as to get liquid out of it. **2** force into or through a place, *We squeezed through a gap in the hedge.* **squeezer** *noun*

squeeze[2] *noun* **1** the action of squeezing. **2** a drop of liquid squeezed out, *Add a* *squeeze of lemon.* **3** a time when money is difficult to get or borrow.

squelch *verb* make a sound like someone treading in thick mud. **squelch** *noun*

squib *noun* a small firework that hisses and then explodes.

squid *noun* a sea-animal with eight short tentacles and two long ones.

squiggle *noun* a short curly line.

squint *verb* **1** be cross-eyed. **2** peer; look with half-shut eyes at something. **squint** *noun*

squire *noun* **1** a man who owns land in a country district. **2** (in history) a man who was an assistant to a knight, before becoming a knight himself.

squirm *verb* wriggle.

squirrel *noun* a small animal with a bushy tail and red or grey fur, living in trees.

squirt *verb* send or come out in a jet of liquid.

St. *abbreviation* **1** Saint. **2** Street.

stab¹ *verb* (**stabbed, stabbing**) pierce or wound with something sharp.

stab² *noun* **1** the action of stabbing. **2** a sudden sharp pain, *She felt a stab of fear.* **3** (*informal*) an attempt, *I'll have a stab at it.*

stability *noun* being stable.

stabilize *verb* (**stabilized, stabilizing**) make or become stable. **stabilization** *noun*, **stabilizer** *noun*

stable¹ *adjective* steady; firmly fixed. **stably** *adverb*

stable² *noun* a building where horses are kept.

stable door a door divided horizontally into two parts.

stable³ *verb* (**stabled, stabling**) put or keep in a stable.

staccato *adverb* & *adjective* (in music) played with each note short and separate.

stack¹ *noun* **1** a neat pile. **2** a haystack. **3** (*informal*) a large amount, *a stack of work.* **4** a single tall chimney; a group of chimneys.

stack² *verb* pile things up.

stadium *noun* a sports ground surrounded by seats for spectators.

staff¹ *noun* **1** the people who work in an office, shop, etc. **2** the teachers in a school or college. **3** a stick or pole used as a weapon or support or as a symbol of authority. **4** (*plural* **staves**) a set of five horizontal lines on which music is written.

staff² *verb* provide with a staff of people.

stag *noun* a male deer.

stage¹ *noun* **1** a platform for performances in a theatre or hall. **2** a point or part of a process, journey, etc., *the final stage.*

stage² *verb* (**staged, staging**) **1** present a performance on a stage. **2** organize, *We decided to stage a protest.*

stage-coach *noun* a horse-drawn coach that formerly ran regularly from one point to another along the same route.

stagger *verb* **1** walk unsteadily. **2** shock deeply; amaze, *We were staggered at the price.* **3** arrange things so that they do not coincide, *Please stagger your holidays so that there is always someone here.* **stagger** *noun*

stagnant *adjective* not flowing or not changing, *a pool of stagnant water.*

stagnate *verb* (**stagnated, stagnating**) **1** be stagnant. **2** be dull through lack of activity or variety. **stagnation** *noun*

staid *adjective* steady and serious in manner; sedate.

stain¹ *noun* **1** a dirty mark on something. **2** a blemish on someone's character or past record. **3** a liquid used for staining things.

stain² *verb* **1** make a stain on something. **2** colour with a liquid that sinks into the surface.

stainless *adjective* without a stain. **stainless steel** steel that does not rust easily.

stair *noun* each of the fixed steps in a series that lead from one level or floor to another in a building.

staircase *noun* a flight of stairs.

stake¹ *noun* **1** a thick pointed stick to be driven into the ground. **2** the post to which people used to be tied for execution by being burnt alive. **3** an amount of money bet on something. **4** an investment that gives a person a share or interest in an enterprise.

at stake being risked.

stake² *verb* (**staked**, **staking**) 1 fasten, support, or mark out with stakes. 2 bet or risk money etc. on an event.

stake a claim claim or obtain a right to something.

stalactite *noun* a stony spike hanging like an icicle from the roof of a cave.

stalagmite *noun* a stony spike standing like a pillar on the floor of a cave.

stale *adjective* not fresh. **staleness** *noun*

stalemate *noun* 1 a drawn position in chess when a player cannot make a move without putting his or her king in check. 2 a deadlock; a draw in a contest that was held to decide something.

stalk¹ *noun* a stem of a plant etc.

stalk² *verb* 1 track or hunt stealthily. 2 walk in a stiff or dignified way, *He stalked off in a huff.*

stall¹ *noun* 1 a stand from which things are sold. 2 a place for one animal in a stable or shed. 3 a seat in the part of a theatre (*the stalls*) nearest the stage.

stall² *verb* 1 stop suddenly, *The car engine stalled.* 2 put an animal into a stall.

stall³ *verb* delay things deliberately so as to avoid having to take action.

stallion *noun* a male horse.

stalwart *adjective* sturdy; strong and faithful, *my stalwart supporters.*

stamen *noun* the part of a flower bearing pollen.

stamina *noun* strength and ability to endure things for a long time.

stammer *verb* keep repeating the same syllables when you speak. **stammer** *noun*

stamp¹ *noun* 1 a postage stamp; a small piece of gummed paper with a special design on it. 2 a small device for pressing words or marks on something; the words or marks made by this. 3 a distinctive characteristic, *His story bears the stamp of truth.*

stamp² *verb* 1 bang a foot heavily on the ground. 2 walk with loud heavy steps. 3 stick a stamp on something. 4 press a mark or design etc. on something.

stamp out put out a fire etc. by stamping; stop something, *stamp out cruelty.*

stampede *noun* a sudden rush by animals or people. **stampede** *verb*

stampmealies *plural noun* samp.

stance *noun* the way a person or animal stands; an attitude.

stanchion *noun* an upright bar or post forming a support.

stand¹ *verb* (**stood**, **standing**) 1 be on your feet without moving, *We were standing at the back of the hall.* 2 set or be upright; place, *We stood the vase on the table.* 3 stay the same, *My offer still stands.* 4 be a candidate for election, *She stood for Parliament.* 5 tolerate; endure, *I can't stand that noise.* 6 provide and pay for, *I'll stand you a drink.*

it stands to reason it is reasonable or obvious.

stand by be ready for action.

stand for represent; tolerate.

stand up for support; defend.

stand up to resist bravely; stay in good condition in hard use.

stand² *noun* 1 something made for putting things on, *a music-stand.* 2 a stall where things are sold or displayed. 3 a grandstand. 4 a stationary condition or position, *He took his stand near the door.* 5 resistance to attack, *We made a stand.* 6 a piece of land in an urban area.

standard¹ *noun* 1 how good something is, *a high standard of work.* 2 a thing used to measure or judge something else, *an internationally-recognized standard.* 3 a special flag, *the royal standard.* 4 an upright support.

a standard lamp a lamp on an upright pole that stands on the floor.

standard of living a measure of how wealthy people are, sometimes estimated by measuring the average national income.

standard² *adjective* 1 of the usual or average quality or kind. 2 regarded as the best and widely used, *the standard book on spiders.*

standard unit a kind of measurement from which other units are derived, e.g.

the metre is the standard unit of length.

standardize *verb* (**standardized, standardizing**) make things be of a standard size, quality, etc. **standardization** *noun*

standpoint *noun* a point of view.

standstill *noun* a stop; an end to movement or activity.

stanza *noun* a verse of poetry.

staple[1] *noun* 1 a small piece of metal pushed through papers and clenched to fasten them together. 2 a U-shaped nail. **staple** *verb*, **stapler** *noun*

staple[2] *adjective* main; usual, *Rice is their staple food.* **staple** *noun*

star[1] *noun* 1 a heavenly body that is seen as a speck of light in the sky at night. 2 a shape with rays from it; an asterisk; a mark of this shape showing that something is good, *a five-star hotel.* 3 a famous performer; one of the chief performers in a play or show etc.

star[2] *verb* (**starred, starring**) 1 perform or present as a star in a show etc. 2 mark with an asterisk or star symbol.

starboard *noun* the right-hand side of a ship or aircraft when you are facing forward. (Compare *port*[1].)

starch[1] *noun* (*plural* **starches**) 1 a white carbohydrate in bread, potatoes, etc. 2 this or a similar substance used to stiffen clothes. **starchy** *adjective*

starch[2] *verb* stiffen with starch.

stardom *noun* being a star performer.

stare *verb* (**stared, staring**) look at something intensely. **stare** *noun*

starfish *noun* (*plural* **starfish** or **starfishes**) a sea-animal shaped like a star with five points.

stark[1] *adjective* 1 complete; unmistakable, *stark nonsense.* 2 desolate; without cheerfulness, *the stark lunar landscape.* **starkly** *adverb*, **starkness** *noun*

stark[2] *adverb* completely, *stark naked.*

starlight *noun* light from the stars.

starling *noun* a noisy black bird with speckled feathers.

starry *adjective* full of stars.

start[1] *verb* 1 begin or cause to begin. 2 begin a journey, *She started out at dawn.* 3 make a sudden movement because of

pain or surprise. **starter** *noun*

start[2] *noun* 1 the beginning; the place where a race starts. 2 an advantage that someone starts with, *We gave the young ones ten minutes' start.* 3 a sudden movement, *The dog's barking gave us a start.*

startle *verb* (**startled, startling**) surprise or alarm someone.

starve *verb* (**starved, starving**) 1 suffer or die from lack of food; cause to do this. 2 (*informal*) be very hungry. **starvation** *noun*

state[1] *noun* 1 the quality of a person's or thing's characteristics or circumstances; condition. 2 a grand style, *She arrived in state.* 3 an organized community under one government; such a community forming part of a federal republic. 4 a country's government, *Help for the flood victims was provided by the state.* 5 **the States** the United States of America. 6 (*informal*) an excited or upset condition, *Don't get into a state about the robbery.*

state[2] *verb* (**stated, stating**) express something in spoken or written words.

stately *adjective* (**statelier, stateliest**) dignified; imposing; grand. **stateliness** *noun*

statement *noun* 1 words stating something. 2 a formal account of facts, *The witness made a statement to the police.* 3 a written report of a financial account, *a bank statement.*

statesperson *noun* a person who is important or skilled in governing a country. **statesman** *noun* (*plural* **statesmen**), **statesmanship** *noun*, **stateswoman** *noun* (*plural* **stateswomen**)

static *adjective* not moving; not changing. **static electricity** electricity that is present in something, not flowing as current.

station[1] *noun* 1 a place where a person or thing stands or is stationed; a position. 2 a stopping-place on a railway with buildings for passengers and goods. 3 a building equipped for people who serve the public or for certain activities, *the police station.* 4 a broadcasting establishment with its own frequency.

station[2] *verb* put someone in a certain place for a purpose, *He was stationed at the door to take the tickets.*

stationary *adjective* not moving, *The car was stationary when the van hit it.*
- USAGE: Do not confuse with *stationery.*

stationer *noun* a shopkeeper who sells stationery.

stationery *noun* paper, envelopes, and other articles used in writing or typing.
- USAGE: Do not confuse with *stationary.*

station-wagon *noun* a car with a door or doors at the back, and rear seats that can be removed or folded away.

statistic *noun* a piece of information expressed as a number, *These statistics show that the population has doubled.* **statistical** *adjective,* **statistically** *adverb* **statistics** *noun* the study of information based on the numbers of things.

statistician (*say* stat-is-**tish**-an) *noun* an expert in statistics.

statuary *noun* statues.

statue *noun* a model made of stone or metal etc. to look like a person or animal.

statuesque (*say* stat-yoo-**esk**) *adjective* like a statue in stillness or dignity.

statuette *noun* a small statue.

stature *noun* 1 the natural height of the body. 2 greatness because of ability or achievement.

status (*say* **stay**-tus) *noun* (*plural* **statuses**) 1 a person's or thing's position or rank in relation to others. 2 high rank or prestige.

status quo (*say* stay-tus **kwoh**) *noun* the state of affairs as it is now, or as it was before a change.

statute *noun* a law passed by a parliament. **statutory** *adjective*

staunch[1] *adjective* firm and loyal, *our staunch supporters.* **staunchly** *adverb*

staunch[2] *verb* 1 stop the flow of, *staunch the bleeding.* 2 stop or control the flow of blood from, *staunch a wound.*

stave[1] *noun* 1 each of the curved strips of wood forming the side of a cask or tub. 2 a staff in music (see *staff*[1] 4).

stave[2] *verb* (**staved** or **stove, staving**) dent or break a hole in something, *The collision stove in the front of the ship.*

stave off keep something away, *We staved off the disaster.*

stay[1] *verb* 1 continue to be in the same place or condition; remain. 2 spend time in a place as a visitor. 3 satisfy temporarily, *We stayed our hunger with a sandwich.* 4 pause. 5 show endurance in a race or task.

stay put (*informal*) remain in place.

stay[2] *noun* 1 a time spent somewhere, *We made a short stay in Swaziland.* 2 a postponement, *a stay of execution.*

stay[3] *noun* a support, especially a rope or wire holding up a mast etc.

stead *noun* **in a person's** or **thing's stead** instead of this person or thing. **stand a person in good stead** be very useful to him or her.

steadfast *adjective* firm and not changing, *a steadfast refusal.*

steady *adjective* (**steadier, steadiest**) 1 not shaking or moving; firm. 2 regular; continuing the same, *a steady pace.* **steadily** *adverb,* **steadiness** *noun*

steak *noun* a thick slice of meat or fish.

steal *verb* (**stole, stolen, stealing**) 1 take and keep something that does not belong to you; take secretly or dishonestly. 2 move secretly or without being noticed, *He stole out of the room.*

stealthy (*say* **stelth**-ee) *adjective* (**stealthier, stealthiest**) quiet and secret, so as not to be noticed. **stealth** *noun,* **stealthily** *adverb,* **stealthiness** *noun*

steam[1] *noun* 1 the gas or vapour that comes from boiling water; this used to drive machinery. 2 energy, *She ran out of steam.* **steamy** *adjective*

steam[2] *verb* 1 give out steam. 2 cook or treat by steam, *steamed vegetables.* 3 move by the power of steam, *The ship steamed down the river.*

steam-engine *noun* an engine driven by steam.

steamer *noun* 1 a steamship. 2 a container in which things are steamed.

steamroller *noun* a heavy vehicle with a large roller used to flatten surfaces when making roads.

steamship *noun* a ship driven by steam.

steed *noun* (*poetical*) a horse.

steel *noun* 1 a strong metal made from iron and carbon. 2 a steel rod for sharpening knives. **steely** *adjective*

steel band a band of musicians playing calypso-style music with instruments usually made from oil-drums.

steenbok *noun* a small antelope which often lives in rocky areas.

steenbras *noun* a sea-fish used as food.

steep¹ *adjective* 1 sloping very sharply, not gradually. 2 (*informal*) unreasonably high, *a steep price.* **steeply** *adverb*, **steepness** *noun*

steep² *verb* soak thoroughly; saturate.

steepen *verb* make or become steeper.

steeple *noun* a church tower with a spire on top.

steeplechase *noun* a race across country or over hedges or fences.

steeplejack *noun* a person who climbs tall chimneys or steeples to do repairs.

steer¹ *verb* make a car, ship, or bicycle etc. go in the direction you want; guide. **steerer** *noun*

steer² *noun* a young bull kept for its beef.

steering-wheel *noun* a wheel for steering a car, boat, etc.

stellar *adjective* of a star or stars.

stem¹ *noun* 1 the main central part of a tree, shrub, or plant. 2 a thin part on which a leaf, flower, or fruit is supported. 3 a thin upright part; the thin part of a wineglass between the bowl and the foot. 4 the main part of a verb or other word, to which endings are attached. 5 the front part of a ship, *from stem to stern.*

stem² *verb* (**stemmed**, **stemming**) **stem from** arise from; have as its source.

stem³ *verb* (**stemmed**, **stemming**) stop the flow of something.

stench *noun* (*plural* **stenches**) a very unpleasant smell.

stencil¹ *noun* a piece of card, metal, or plastic with pieces cut out of it, used to produce a picture, design, etc.

stencil² *verb* (**stencilled**, **stencilling**) produce or decorate with a stencil.

stentorian *adjective* very loud, *a stentorian voice.*

step¹ *noun* 1 a movement made by lifting the foot and setting it down. 2 the sound or rhythm of stepping, *We heard hurried steps outside.* 3 a level surface for placing the foot on in climbing up or down. 4 each of a series of things done in some process or action, *The first step is to find somewhere to practise.*

steps *plural noun* a step-ladder.

in step stepping in time with others in marching or dancing; in agreement.

watch your step be careful.

step² *verb* (**stepped**, **stepping**) tread; walk.

step in intervene.

step on it (*informal*) hurry.

step up increase something.

step- *prefix* related through remarriage of one parent.

stepchild *noun* (*plural* **stepchildren**) a child that a person's husband or wife has from an earlier marriage. **stepbrother, stepdaughter, stepsister, stepson** *nouns*

stepfather *noun* a man who is married to your mother but was not your natural father.

step-ladder *noun* a folding ladder with flat treads.

stepmother *noun* a woman who is married to your father but was not your natural mother.

steppe *noun* a grassy plain with few trees, especially in Russia.

stepping-stone *noun* 1 each of a line of stones put into a shallow stream so that people can walk across. 2 a means or stage of progress to an end.

stereo¹ *adjective* stereophonic.

stereo² *noun* (*plural* **stereos**) 1 stereophonic sound or recording. 2 a stereophonic radio, tape-recorder, etc.

stereophonic *adjective* using sound that comes from two different directions so as to give a natural effect.

stereoscopic *adjective* giving the effect of being three-dimensional, e.g. in photographs.

stereotype *noun* a standardized character; a fixed idea etc., *The stereotype of a hero is one who is tall, strong, brave, and good-looking.*

sterile *adjective* 1 not fertile; barren. 2 free from germs. **sterility** *noun*

sterilize *verb* (**sterilized, sterilizing**) 1 make a thing free from germs, e.g. by heating it. 2 make a person or animal unable to reproduce. **sterilization** *noun*, **sterilizer** *noun*

sterling[1] *noun* British money.

sterling[2] *adjective* 1 genuine, *sterling silver.* 2 excellent; of great worth, *her sterling qualities.*

stern[1] *adjective* strict and severe, not lenient or kindly. **sternly** *adverb*, **sternness** *noun*

stern[2] *noun* the back part of a ship.

steroid *noun* a substance of a kind that includes certain hormones and other natural secretions.

stethoscope *noun* a device used for listening to sounds in a person's body, e.g. heart-beats and breathing.

stevedore *noun* a person employed in loading and unloading ships.

stew[1] *verb* cook slowly in liquid.

stew[2] *noun* a dish of stewed food, especially meat and vegetables. **in a stew** (*informal*) very worried or agitated.

steward *noun* 1 a person whose job is to look after the passengers on a ship or aircraft. 2 an official who looks after something. **stewardess** *noun*

stick[1] *noun* 1 a long thin piece of wood. 2 a walking-stick. 3 the implement used to hit the ball in hockey, polo, etc. 4 a long thin piece of something, *a stick of rock.*

stick[2] *verb* (**stuck, sticking**) 1 push a thing into something, *Stick a pin in it.* 2 fix or be fixed by glue or as if by this, *Stick stamps on the parcel.* 3 become fixed and unable to move, *The boat stuck on a sandbank.* 4 (*informal*) stay, *We must stick together.* 5 (*informal*) endure; tolerate, *I can't stick this job any longer!* 6 (*informal*) impose a task on someone, *We were stuck with the clearing up.*

stick out come or push out from a surface; stand out from the surrounding area; be very noticeable.

stick to remain faithful to a friend or promise etc.; keep to and not alter, *He stuck to his story.*

stick up for (*informal*) stand up for.

sticker *noun* an adhesive label or sign for sticking to something.

sticking-plaster *noun* a strip of adhesive material for covering cuts.

stickleback *noun* a small fish with sharp spines on its back.

stickler *noun* a person who insists on something, *a stickler for punctuality.*

sticky *adjective* (**stickier, stickiest**) 1 able or likely to stick to things. 2 (of weather) hot and humid, causing perspiration. 3 (*informal*) unpleasant, *He'll come to a sticky end.* 4 (*informal*) uncooperative, *She was very sticky about giving me leave.* **stickily** *adverb*, **stickiness** *noun*

stiff *adjective* 1 not bending or moving or changing its shape easily. 2 not fluid; hard to stir, *a stiff dough.* 3 difficult, *a stiff examination.* 4 formal in manner; not friendly. 5 strong, *a stiff breeze.* **stiffly** *adverb*, **stiffness** *noun*

stiffen *verb* make or become stiff. **stiffener** *noun*

stifle *verb* (**stifled, stifling**) 1 suffocate. 2 suppress, *She stifled a yawn.*

stigma *noun* 1 a mark of disgrace; a stain on a reputation. 2 the part of a pistil that receives the pollen in pollination.

stigmatize *verb* (**stigmatized, stigmatizing**) brand as something disgraceful, *He was stigmatized as a coward.*

stile *noun* an arrangement of steps or bars for people to climb over a fence.

stiletto *noun* (*plural* **stilettos**) a dagger with a narrow blade. **stiletto heel** a high pointed shoe-heel.

still[1] *adjective* 1 not moving, *still water.* 2 silent. 3 not fizzy. **stillness** *noun*

still[2] *adverb* 1 without moving, *Stand still.* 2 up to this or that time, *He was still there.* 3 in a greater amount or degree, *You can do still better.* 4 nevertheless, *They've lost. Still, they tried, and that was good.*

still life a painting of lifeless things such as ornaments and fruit.

still[3] *verb* make or become still.

still[4] *noun* an apparatus for distilling alcohol or other liquid.

stillborn *adjective* born dead.

stilted *adjective* stiffly formal.

stilts *plural noun* 1 a pair of poles with supports for the feet so that the user can walk high above the ground. 2 posts for supporting a house etc. above marshy ground.

stimulant *noun* something that stimulates.

stimulate *verb* (**stimulated**, **stimulating**) make more lively or active; excite or interest. **stimulation** *noun*

stimulus *noun* (*plural* **stimuli**) something that stimulates or produces a reaction.

sting[1] *noun* 1 a sharp-pointed part of an animal or plant that can cause a wound. 2 a painful wound caused by this part.

sting[2] *verb* (**stung**, **stinging**) 1 wound or hurt with a sting. 2 feel a sharp pain. 3 stimulate sharply, *I was stung into answering rudely.* 4 (*informal*) cheat a person by over-charging; extort money from someone.

stingy (*say* stin-jee) *adjective* (**stingier**, **stingiest**) mean, not generous; giving or given in small amounts. **stingily** *adverb*, **stinginess** *noun*

stink[1] *noun* 1 an unpleasant smell. 2 (*informal*) an unpleasant fuss or protest, *Their behaviour caused quite a stink.*

stink[2] *verb* (**stank** or **stunk**, **stunk**, **stinking**) have an unpleasant smell.

stinkwood *noun* the wood from several indigenous trees that is valued for furniture, souvenirs, etc.

stint[1] *noun* 1 a fixed amount of work to be done. 2 limitation of a supply or effort, *They gave help without stint.*

stint[2] *verb* limit; be niggardly, *Don't stint them of food.*

stipend (*say* sty-pend) *noun* a salary.

stipple *verb* (**stippled**, **stippling**) paint, draw, or engrave in small dots.

stipulate *verb* (**stipulated**, **stipulating**) insist on something as part of an agreement. **stipulation** *noun*

stir[1] *verb* (**stirred**, **stirring**) 1 mix a liquid or soft mixture by moving a spoon etc. round and round in it. 2 move slightly; start to move, *The tortoise stirred with the first warmth of spring.* 3 excite; stimulate, *They stirred up trouble.*

stir[2] *noun* 1 the action of stirring. 2 a disturbance; excitement, *The news caused a stir.*

stir-fry *verb* fry food rapidly while stirring. **stir-fry** *noun*

stirrup *noun* a metal part that hangs from each side of a horse's saddle, for a rider to put his or her foot in.

stitch[1] *noun* (*plural* **stitches**) 1 a loop of thread made in sewing or knitting. 2 a method of arranging the threads, *cross-stitch.* 3 a sudden sharp pain in the side of the body, caused by running.

stitch[2] *verb* sew or fasten with stitches.

stoat *noun* a kind of weasel also called an ermine.

stock[1] *noun* 1 a number of things kept ready to be sold or used. 2 livestock. 3 a line of ancestors, *a man of Swazi stock.* 4 liquid made by stewing meat, fish, or vegetables, used for making soup etc. 5 a garden flower with a sweet smell. 6 shares in a business company's capital (see *share*[1] 2). 7 the main stem of a tree or plant. 8 the base, holder, or handle of an implement etc. 9 a kind of cravat.

Stock Exchange a place where stocks and shares are bought and sold.

stock[2] *verb* 1 keep goods in stock. 2 provide a place with a stock of something, *The parents stocked the tuck-shop with cakes.*

stockade *noun* a fence made of stakes.

stockbroker *noun* a broker who deals in stocks and shares.

stock-car *noun* an ordinary car strengthened for use in races where deliberate bumping is allowed.

stockfish *noun* (*plural* **stockfish**) hake.

stocking *noun* a garment covering the foot and part or all of the leg.

stockist *noun* a shopkeeper who stocks a certain kind of goods.

stockpile *noun* a large stock of things kept in reserve. **stockpile** *verb*

stocks *plural noun* a wooden framework with holes for a seated person's legs, used like the pillory.

stock-still *adjective* quite still.

stocky *adjective* (**stockier, stockiest**) short and solidly built, *a stocky man.*

stodge *noun* stodgy food.

stodgy *adjective* (**stodgier, stodgiest**) 1 (of food) heavy and filling. 2 dull and boring, *a stodgy book.* **stodginess** *noun*

stoep (*say* stup or stoop) *noun* a raised platform or veranda around or at the front of a house.

stoical (*say* stoh-ik-al) *adjective* bearing pain or difficulties etc. calmly without complaining. **stoically** *adverb,* **stoicism** *noun*

stoke *verb* (**stoked, stoking**) put fuel in a furnace or on a fire. **stoker** *noun*

stokvel (*say* stok-fel) *noun* a savings club or syndicate for the pooling of funds, mutual support, and investment, often organized through parties held at members' homes in rotation.

stole[1] *noun* a wide piece of material worn round the shoulders.

stole[2] *past tense* of **steal.**

stolid *adjective* not excitable; not feeling or showing emotion. **stolidly** *adverb,* **stolidity** *noun*

stoma *noun* (*plural* **stomas** or **stomata**) a tiny opening in the surface of a leaf that allows gases and water to pass in and out of the plant.

stomach[1] *noun* 1 the part of the body where food starts to be digested. 2 the abdomen.

stomach[2] *verb* endure; tolerate.

stompie *noun* (*informal*) a cigarette butt.

stone[1] *noun* 1 a piece of rock. 2 stones or rock as material, e.g. for building. 3 a jewel. 4 the hard case round the kernel of plums, cherries, etc.

Stone Age the time when tools and weapons were made of stone.

stone[2] *verb* (**stoned, stoning**) 1 throw stones at somebody. 2 remove the stones from fruit.

stone- *prefix* completely, *stone-cold.*

stony *adjective* 1 full of stones. 2 like stone; hard. 3 not answering, *a stony silence.*

stony-broke *adjective* (*informal*) having spent all your money.

stooge *noun* (*informal*) 1 a comedian's assistant, used as a target for jokes. 2 an assistant who does dull or routine work.

stool *noun* a movable seat without arms or a back; a footstool.

stoop *verb* 1 bend your body forwards and down. 2 lower yourself, *He would not stoop to cheating.* **stoop** *noun*

stop[1] *verb* (**stopped, stopping**) 1 bring or come to an end; not continue working or moving. 2 stay. 3 prevent or obstruct something, *Don't stop her going out.* 4 fill a hole, especially in a tooth. **stoppage** *noun*

stop[2] *noun* 1 stopping; a pause or end. 2 a place where a bus or train etc. regularly stops. 3 a punctuation mark, especially a full stop. 4 a lever or knob that controls pitch in a wind instrument or allows organ-pipes to sound.

stopcock *noun* a valve controlling the flow of liquid or gas in a pipe.

stopgap *noun* a temporary substitute.

stopper *noun* a plug for closing a bottle etc.

stop-press *noun* late news put into a newspaper after printing has started.

stop-watch *noun* a watch that can be started and stopped when you wish, used for timing races etc.

storage *noun* the storing of things.

store[1] *noun* 1 a stock of things kept for future use; a place where these are kept. 2 a shop, especially a large one.

in store being stored; going to happen, *There's a surprise in store for you.*

set store by something value it greatly.

store[2] *verb* (**stored, storing**) keep things until they are needed.

storey *noun* (*plural* **storeys**) one whole floor of a building.

stork *noun* a large bird with long legs and a long beak.

storm[1] *noun* 1 a very strong wind usually with rain, lightning, etc. 2 a violent attack or outburst, *a storm of protest*. **stormy** *adjective*

storm in a teacup a great fuss over something unimportant.

storm[2] *verb* 1 move or behave violently or angrily, *She stormed out of the room.* 2 attack or capture by a sudden assault, *They stormed the castle.*

story *noun* (*plural* **stories**) 1 an account of a real or imaginary event. 2 the plot of a play or novel etc. 3 (*informal*) a lie, *Don't tell stories!*

stout[1] *adjective* 1 rather fat. 2 thick and strong. 3 brave, *a stout heart.* **stoutly** *adverb*, **stoutness** *noun*

stout[2] *noun* a kind of dark beer.

stove[1] *noun* 1 a device containing an oven or ovens. 2 a device for heating a room.

stove[2] *past tense* of **stave**[2].

stow *verb* pack or store something away. **stowage** *noun*

stow away hide on a ship or aircraft so as to travel without paying. **stowaway** *noun*

straddle *verb* (**straddled, straddling**) be astride; sit or stand across something, *A long bridge straddles the river.*

straggle *verb* (**straggled, straggling**) 1 grow or spread in an untidy way. 2 lag behind; wander on your own, *The pupils straggled along behind their teacher.* **straggler** *noun*, **straggly** *adjective*

straight[1] *adjective* 1 going continuously in one direction; not curving or bending. 2 tidy; in proper order. 3 honest; frank, *a straight answer.* **straightness** *noun*

straight[2] *adverb* 1 in a straight line or manner. 2 directly; without delay, *Go straight home.*

straight away immediately.

straighten *verb* make or become straight.

straightforward *adjective* 1 easy, not complicated. 2 honest; frank, *She answered in a straightforward way.*

strain[1] *verb* 1 stretch tightly. 2 injure or weaken something by stretching or working it too hard. 3 make a great effort, *He strained to lift the boulder.* 4 put something through a sieve or filter to separate liquid from solid matter.

strain[2] *noun* 1 straining; the force of straining. 2 an injury caused by straining. 3 something that uses up strength, patience, resources, etc., *Population growth puts a strain on the environment.* 4 exhaustion. 5 a part of a tune.

strain[3] *noun* 1 a breed or variety of animals, plants, etc.; a line of descent. 2 an inherited characteristic, *There's an artistic strain in the family.*

strainer *noun* a device for straining liquids, *a tea-strainer.*

strait[1] *adjective* (*old use*) narrow; restricted.

● USAGE: Do not confuse with *straight.*

strait[2] *noun* a narrow stretch of water connecting two seas.

straits *plural noun* 1 a strait, *the Straits of Gibraltar.* 2 a difficult condition, *We were in dire straits when we lost our money.*

straitened *adjective* restricted; made narrow.

in straitened circumstances short of money.

strait-jacket *noun* a strong jacket-like garment put round a violent person to restrain his or her arms.

strait-laced *adjective* very prim and proper.

strand[1] *noun* 1 each of the threads or wires etc. twisted together to form a rope, yarn, or cable. 2 a single thread. 3 a lock of hair.

strand[2] *noun* a shore.

strand[3] *verb* 1 run or cause to run on to sand or rocks in shallow water. 2 leave in a difficult or helpless position, *We were stranded when our car broke down.*

strandloper *noun* a person who lived near the coast and gathered seafood in former times.

strandwolf *noun* (*plural* **strandwolwe**) a brown hyena which scavenges along the sea-shore.

strange *adjective* unusual; not known or seen or experienced before. **strangely** *adverb*, **strangeness** *noun*

stranger *noun* **1** a person you do not know. **2** a person who is in a place or company that he or she does not know, *a stranger to urban ways.*

strangle *verb* (**strangled, strangling**) kill by squeezing the throat to prevent breathing. **strangler** *noun*

strangulate *verb* (**strangulated, strangulating**) strangle; squeeze so that nothing can pass through. **strangulation** *noun*

strap¹ *noun* a flat strip of leather or cloth etc. for fastening things or holding them in place.

strap² *verb* (**strapped, strapping**) fasten with a strap or straps; bind.

strapping *adjective* tall and healthy-looking, *a strapping girl.*

strata *plural* of **stratum.**

stratagem *noun* a cunning method of achieving something; a trick.

strategic *adjective* **1** of strategy. **2** giving an advantage. **strategical** *adjective,* **strategically** *adverb*

strategist *noun* an expert in strategy.

strategy *noun* (*plural* **strategies**) **1** a plan or policy to achieve something, *our economic strategy.* **2** the planning of a war or campaign. (Compare *tactics.*)

stratified *adjective* arranged in strata. **stratification** *noun*

stratosphere *noun* a layer of the atmosphere between about 10 and 60 kilometres above the earth's surface.

stratum (*say* **strah**-tum or **stray**-tum) *noun* (*plural* **strata**) a layer.

• USAGE: The word *strata* is a plural. It is incorrect to say 'a strata' or 'this strata'; correct use is *this stratum* or *these strata.*

straw *noun* **1** dry cut stalks of corn. **2** a narrow tube for drinking through.

strawberry *noun* (*plural* **strawberries**) a small red juicy fruit.

stray¹ *verb* leave a group or proper place and wander; get lost.

stray² *adjective* that has strayed, *a stray cat.* **stray** *noun*

streak¹ *noun* **1** a long thin line or mark. **2** a trace, *a streak of cruelty.* **streaky** *adjective*

streak² *verb* **1** mark with streaks.

2 move very quickly. **3** (*informal*) run naked through a public place.

stream¹ *noun* **1** water flowing in a channel; a brook or river. **2** a flow of liquid or of things or people. **3** a group in which children of similar ability are placed in a school.

stream² *verb* **1** move in or like a stream. **2** produce a stream of liquid, *Her face streamed with sweat.* **3** arrange schoolchildren in streams according to their ability.

streamer *noun* a long narrow ribbon or strip of paper etc.

streamline *verb* (**streamlined, streamlining**) **1** give something a smooth shape that helps it to move easily through air or water. **2** organize something so that it works more efficiently, *streamlining the civil service.*

street *noun* a road with houses beside it in a city or village.

strength *noun* how strong a person or thing is; being strong.

strengthen *verb* make or become stronger.

strenuous *adjective* needing or using great effort. **strenuously** *adverb*

stress¹ *noun* (*plural* **stresses**) **1** a force that acts on something, e.g. by pressing, pulling, or twisting it; strain. **2** emphasis, especially the extra force with which you pronounce part of a word or phrase.

stress² *verb* put a stress on something; emphasize.

stretch¹ *verb* **1** pull something or be pulled so that it becomes longer or wider or larger. **2** be continuous, *The wall stretches right round the property.* **3** push out your arms and legs etc.

stretch² *noun* (*plural* **stretches**) **1** the action of stretching. **2** a continuous period of time or area of land or water.

stretcher *noun* a framework for carrying a sick or injured person.

strew *verb* (**strewed, strewn** or **strewed, strewing**) scatter things over a surface.

striated (*say* stry-**ay**-tid) *adjective* marked with lines or ridges. **striation** *noun*

stricken *adjective* overcome or strongly

affected by an illness, grief, fear, etc.

strict *adjective* **1** demanding obedience and good behaviour, *a strict teacher.* **2** complete; exact, *the strict truth.* **strictly** *adverb*, **strictness** *noun*

stricture *noun* **1** criticism. **2** a rule that restricts behaviour or action, *the strictures of religion.*

stride[1] *verb* (**strode, stridden, striding**) **1** walk with long steps. **2** stand astride something.

stride[2] *noun* **1** a long step when walking or running. **2** progress, *an important stride in the fight against crime.*

get into your stride settle into a fast and steady pace of working.

strident (*say* **stry**-dent) *adjective* loud and harsh. **stridently** *adverb*, **stridency** *noun*

strife *noun* a conflict; fighting or quarrelling.

strike[1] *verb* (**struck, striking**) **1** hit. **2** attack suddenly. **3** produce by pressing or stamping something, *They are striking some special coins.* **4** light a match by rubbing it against a rough surface. **5** sound, *The clock struck ten.* **6** make an impression on someone's mind, *She strikes me as truthful.* **7** find gold or oil etc. by digging or drilling. **8** stop work until the people in charge agree to improve wages or conditions etc. **9** go in a certain direction, *We struck north through the forest.*

strike off or **out** cross out.

strike up begin playing or singing; start a friendship etc.

strike[2] *noun* **1** a hit. **2** an attack. **3** a stoppage of work, as a way of making a protest (see sense 8 of the verb). **4** a sudden discovery of gold or oil etc.

on strike (of workers) striking.

striker *noun* **1** a person or thing that strikes something. **2** a worker who is on strike. **3** a soccer, hockey, etc. player whose function is to try to score goals.

striking *adjective* **1** that strikes. **2** noticeable, *The Minister's absence was striking.* **strikingly** *adverb*

string[1] *noun* **1** cord used to fasten or tie things; a piece of this or similar material. **2** a piece of wire or cord etc. stretched and vibrated to produce sounds in a musical instrument. **3** a line or series of things, *a string of buses.*

strings *plural noun* stringed instruments.

string[2] *verb* (**strung, stringing**) **1** fit or fasten with string. **2** thread on a string. **3** remove the tough fibre from beans.

string out spread out in a line; cause something to last a long time.

stringed *adjective* (of musical instruments) having strings.

stringent (*say* **strin**-jent) *adjective* strict, *There are stringent rules.* **stringently** *adverb*, **stringently** *noun*

stringy *adjective* **1** like string. **2** containing tough fibres, *New cultivars of mangoes are no longer stringy.*

strip[1] *verb* (**stripped, stripping**) **1** take a covering or layer off something. **2** undress. **3** deprive a person of something, *He was stripped of his title.* **stripper** *noun*

strip[2] *noun* a long narrow piece or area.

strip cartoon a comic strip (see *comic*).

stripe *noun* **1** a long narrow band of colour. **2** a strip of cloth worn on the sleeve of a uniform to show the wearer's rank. **striped** *adjective*, **stripy** *adjective*

stripling *noun* a youth.

strip-tease *noun* an entertainment in which a person slowly undresses.

strive *verb* (**strove, striven, striving**) **1** try hard to do something. **2** carry on a conflict.

strobe *noun* (short for **stroboscope**) a light that flashes on and off continuously.

stroke[1] *noun* **1** a hit; a movement or action. **2** the sound made by a clock striking. **3** a sudden illness that often causes paralysis.

stroke[2] *verb* (**stroked, stroking**) move your hand gently along something. **stroke** *noun*

stroll *verb* **1** walk in a leisurely way. **2** beg or scavenge. **stroll** *noun*

stroller *noun* **1** a person who walks in a leisurely way. **2** a homeless child who lives by begging or scavenging.

strong[1] *adjective* **1** having great power, energy, effect, flavour, etc. **2** not easy to break, damage, or defeat. **3** having a certain number of members, *an army 5 000 strong.* **strongly** *adverb*

strong² *adverb* strongly, *going strong.*

stronghold *noun* a fortified place.

strontium *noun* a soft silvery metal.

strop¹ *noun* a strip of leather or canvas on which a razor is sharpened.

strop² *verb* (**stropped, stropping**) sharpen on a strop.

strove *past tense* of **strive.**

structure *noun* 1 something that has been constructed or built. 2 the way something is constructed or organized. **structural** *adjective*, **structurally** *adverb*

struggle¹ *verb* (**struggled, struggling**) 1 move your arms, legs, etc. in trying to get free. 2 make strong efforts to do something, *They struggled to swim back to the beach against the current.* 3 try to overcome an opponent or a problem etc.

struggle² *noun* the action of struggling.

strum *verb* (**strummed, strumming**) 1 sound a guitar by running your fingers across its strings. 2 play badly or casually on a musical instrument.

strut¹ *verb* (**strutted, strutting**) walk proudly or stiffly.

strut² *noun* 1 a bar of wood or metal strengthening a framework. 2 a strutting walk.

strychnine (*say* strik-neen) *noun* a bitter poisonous substance.

stub¹ *noun* 1 a short stump left when the rest has been used or worn down. 2 a counterfoil, *the stub of the cheque.*

stub² *verb* (**stubbed, stubbing**) bump your toe painfully.
stub out put out a cigarette by pressing it against something hard.

stubble *noun* 1 the short stalks of corn left in the ground after the harvest is cut. 2 short hairs growing after shaving.

stubborn *adjective* obstinate. **stubbornly** *adverb*, **stubbornness** *noun*

stubby *adjective* short and thick.

stucco *noun* plaster or cement used for coating walls and ceilings, often moulded into decorations. **stuccoed** *adjective*

stuck-up *adjective* (*informal*) conceited; snobbish.

stud¹ *noun* 1 a small curved lump or knob. 2 a device like a button on a stalk, used to fasten a detachable collar to a shirt.

stud² *verb* (**studded, studding**) set or decorate with studs etc., *The necklace was studded with jewels.*

stud³ *noun* horses kept for breeding.

student *noun* a person who studies a subject, especially at a college or university.

studio *noun* (*plural* **studios**) 1 the room where a painter or photographer etc. works. 2 a place where cinema films are made. 3 a room from which radio or television broadcasts are made or recorded.

studious *adjective* 1 keen on studying. 2 deliberate, *with studious politeness.* **studiously** *adverb*, **studiousness** *noun*

study¹ *verb* (**studied, studying**) 1 spend time learning about something. 2 look at something carefully, *We studied the map.*

study² *noun* (*plural* **studies**) 1 the process of studying. 2 a subject studied; a piece of research, *a study on spiders.* 3 a room where someone studies. 4 a piece of music for playing as an exercise.

stuff¹ *noun* 1 a substance or material. 2 things, *Leave your stuff outside.* 3 (*informal*) valueless matter, *stuff and nonsense!*

stuff² *verb* 1 fill tightly. 2 fill with stuffing. 3 push a thing into something, *He stuffed the catapult into his pocket.* 4 (*informal*) eat greedily.

stuffing *noun* 1 material used to fill the inside of something; padding. 2 a savoury mixture put into meat or poultry etc. before cooking.

stuffy *adjective* (**stuffier, stuffiest**) 1 badly ventilated; without fresh air. 2 with blocked breathing passages, *a stuffy nose.* 3 formal; boring. **stuffily** *adverb*, **stuffiness** *noun*

stultify *verb* (**stultified, stultifying**) prevent from being effective, *Their stubbornness stultified the discussions.* **stultification** *noun*

stumble *verb* (**stumbled, stumbling**)
1 trip and lose your balance. 2 speak or
do something hesitantly or uncertainly,
He stumbled through his speech. **stumble**
noun
stumble across or **on** find accidentally.
stumbling-block *noun* an obstacle;
something that causes difficulty.
stump[1] *noun* 1 the bottom of a tree-trunk
left in the ground when the rest has fallen
or been cut down. 2 something left when
the main part is cut off or worn down.
3 each of the three upright sticks of a
wicket in cricket.
stump[2] *verb* 1 walk stiffly or noisily.
2 put a batsman out by knocking the bails
off the stumps while he or she is out of the
crease. 3 (*informal*) be too difficult for
somebody, *The question stumped him.*
stumpnose *noun* a sea-fish used as food.
stumpy *adjective* short and thick.
stumpiness *noun*
stun *verb* (**stunned, stunning**) 1 knock
a person unconscious. 2 daze or shock,
She was stunned by the news.
stunt[1] *verb* prevent a thing from growing
or developing normally, *a stunted tree.*
stunt[2] *noun* something unusual or difficult done as a performance or to attract
attention.
stupefy *verb* (**stupefied, stupefying**)
make a person dazed. **stupefaction** *noun*
stupendous *adjective* amazing; tremendous. **stupendously** *adverb*
stupid *adjective* not clever or thoughtful;
without reason or common sense.
stupidly *adverb*, **stupidity** *noun*
stupor (*say* stew-per) *noun* a dazed
condition.
sturdy *adjective* (**sturdier, sturdiest**)
strong and vigorous or solid. **sturdily**
adverb, **sturdiness** *noun*
sturgeon *noun* (*plural* **sturgeon**) a large
edible fish.
stutter *verb* & *noun* stammer.
sty[1] *noun* (*plural* **sties**) a pigsty.
sty[2] (also **stye**) *noun* (*plural* **sties** or
styes) a sore swelling on an eyelid.
style[1] *noun* 1 the way something is done,
made, said, or written etc. 2 elegance,

a woman with style. 3 the part of a pistil
that supports the stigma in a plant.
stylistic *adjective*
style[2] *verb* (**styled, styling**) design or
arrange something, especially in a fashionable style. **stylist** *noun*
stylish *adjective* in a fashionable style.
suave (*say* swahv) *adjective* smoothly
polite. **suavely** *adverb*, **suavity** *noun*
sub *noun* (*informal*) 1 a submarine.
2 a subscription. 3 a substitute.
sub- *prefix* (often changing to **suc-**,
suf-, **sum-**, **sup-**, **sur-**, **sus-** before certain
consonants) 1 under (as in *submarine*).
2 subordinate, secondary (as in *sub-
section*).
subaltern *noun* an army officer ranking
below a captain.
subconscious *adjective* of our own
mental activities of which we are not fully
aware. **subconscious** *noun*
subcontinent *noun* a large mass of land
not large enough to be called a continent,
the Indian subcontinent.
subdivide *verb* (**subdivided, subdivid-
ing**) divide again or into smaller parts.
subdivision *noun*
subdue *verb* (**subdued, subduing**)
1 overcome; bring under control.
2 make quieter or gentler, *subdued
lighting.*
subject[1] *noun* 1 the person or thing
being talked about or written about etc.
2 something that is studied. 3 (in grammar) the word or words naming who or
what does the action of a verb, e.g. '*the
book*' in *the book fell off the table.*
4 someone who is ruled by a particular
king, government, etc.
subject[2] *adjective* ruled by a king or
government etc.; not independent.
subject to having to obey; liable to,
Aircraft are subject to delays during fog;
depending upon, *Our decision is subject
to your approval.*
subject[3] (*say* sub-jekt) *verb* 1 make a person or thing undergo something, *They
subjected him to torture.* 2 bring a country
under your control. **subjection** *noun*
subjective *adjective* 1 existing in a

person's mind and not produced by things outside it. **2** depending on a person's own taste or opinions etc. (Compare *objective*.)

subjugate *verb* (**subjugated, subjugating**) bring under your control; conquer. **subjugation** *noun*

subjunctive *noun* the form of a verb used to indicate what is imagined or wished or possible. There are only a few cases where it is commonly used in English, e.g. '*were*' in *if I were you* and '*bless*' in *God bless Africa*.

sublet *verb* (**sublet, subletting**) let to another person a house etc. that is let to you by a landlord.

sublime *adjective* **1** noble; impressive. **2** extreme; not caring about the consequences, *with sublime carelessness*.

submarine¹ *adjective* under the sea, *We laid a submarine cable*.

submarine² *noun* a ship that can travel under water.

submerge *verb* (**submerged, submerging**) go under or put under water or other liquid. **submergence** *noun*, **submersion** *noun*

submissive *adjective* willing to obey.

submit *verb* (**submitted, submitting**) **1** let someone have authority over you; surrender. **2** put forward for consideration, testing, etc., *Submit your plans to the committee*. **submission** *noun*

subnormal *adjective* below normal.

subordinate¹ *adjective* less important; lower in rank.
subordinate clause a clause that is not the main clause in a sentence, e.g. *when it rang* in *She answered the phone when it rang*.

subordinate² *noun* a person working under someone's authority or control.

subordinate³ *verb* (**subordinated, subordinating**) treat as being less important than another person or thing. **subordination** *noun*

suborn *verb* bribe; incite someone secretly.

sub-plot *noun* a secondary plot in a play etc.

subpoena¹ (*say* sub-**peen**-a) *noun*

an official document ordering a person to appear in a lawcourt.

subpoena² *verb* (**subpoenaed, subpoenaing**) summon by a subpoena.

subscribe *verb* (**subscribed, subscribing**) **1** contribute money; pay regularly so as to be a member of a society, get a periodical, have the use of a telephone, etc. **2** sign, *subscribe your name*. **3** say that you agree, *We cannot subscribe to this theory*. **subscriber** *noun*, **subscription** *noun*

subsequent *adjective* coming after in time or order; later. **subsequently** *adverb*

subservient *adjective* under someone's power; submissive. **subservience** *noun*

subset *noun* (in mathematics) a set of which all the elements are contained in another set.

subside *verb* (**subsided, subsiding**) **1** sink. **2** become less intense, *Her fear subsided*. **subsidence** *noun*

subsidiary *adjective* **1** less important; secondary. **2** (of a business) controlled by another, *a subsidiary company*.

subsidize *verb* (**subsidized, subsidizing**) pay a subsidy to a person or firm etc.

subsidy *noun* (*plural* **subsidies**) money paid to an industry etc. that needs help, or to keep down the price at which its goods etc. are sold to the public.

subsist *verb* exist; keep yourself alive, *We subsisted on nuts*. **subsistence** *noun*
subsistence farm a farm that produces only enough food etc. for the farmer and his or her family to live on, but not enough to sell. (Compare *commercial farm*.)

subsoil *noun* soil lying just below the surface layer.

subsonic *adjective* not as fast as the speed of sound. (Compare *supersonic*.)

substance *noun* **1** matter of a particular kind. **2** the main or essential part of something, *We agree with the substance of your report but not with its details*.

substantial *adjective* **1** of great size, value, or importance, *a substantial fee*. **2** solidly built, *substantial houses*. **3** actually existing. **substantially** *adverb*

substantiate *verb* (**substantiated, sub-**

stantiating) produce evidence to prove something. **substantiation** *noun*

substation *noun* a subsidiary station for distributing electric current.

substitute[1] *noun* a person or thing that acts or is used instead of another.

substitute[2] *verb* (**substituted, substituting**) put or use a person or thing as a substitute. **substitution** *noun*

subterfuge *noun* a deception.

subterranean *adjective* underground.

subtitle *noun* 1 a subordinate title. 2 words shown on the screen during a film, e.g. to translate a foreign language.

subtle (*say* sut-el) *adjective* 1 slight and delicate, *a subtle perfume*. 2 ingenious; not immediately obvious, *a subtle joke*. **subtly** *adverb*, **subtlety** *noun*

subtotal *noun* the total of part of a group of figures.

subtract *verb* deduct; take away a part, quantity, or number from a greater one. **subtraction** *noun*

subtropical *adjective* of regions that border on the tropics.

suburb *noun* a district with houses that is outside the central part of a city. **suburban** *adjective*, **suburbia** *noun*

subvert *verb* get someone to be disloyal to their government, religion, standards of behaviour, etc.; overthrow a government etc. in this way. **subversion** *noun*, **subversive** *adjective*

subway *noun* an underground passage.

suc- *prefix* see **sub-**.

succeed *verb* 1 be successful. 2 come after another person or thing; gain the right to a title, *Who will succeed him as President? She succeeded to the throne.*

success *noun* (*plural* **successes**) 1 doing or getting what you wanted or intended. 2 a person or thing that does well, *The show was a great success.*

successful *adjective* having success; being a success. **successfully** *adverb*

succession *noun* 1 a series of people or things, *a succession of defeats*. 2 the process of following in order, *the succession of the months*. 3 succeeding to the throne; the right of doing this.

successive *adjective* following one after another, *on five successive days*. **successively** *adverb*

successor *noun* a person or thing that succeeds another.

succinct (*say* suk-**sinkt**) *adjective* concise. **succinctly** *adverb*

succour (*say* suk-er) *noun* & *verb* help.

succulent *adjective* juicy.

succumb (*say* suk-**um**) *verb* give way to something overpowering.

such *adjective* 1 of the same kind; similar, *Cabbage, broccoli, and all such foods are nutritious*. 2 of the kind described, *There's no such person*. 3 so great or intense, *It gave me such a fright!*

such-and-such *adjective* particular but not now named, *He promises to come at such-and-such a time but is always late.*

suchlike *adjective* (*informal*) of that kind.

suck *verb* 1 take in liquid or air through almost-closed lips. 2 squeeze something in your mouth by using your tongue, *sucking a toffee*. 3 draw in, *The canoe was sucked into the whirlpool*. **suck** *noun*

suck up to (*slang*) flatter someone in the hope of winning their favour.

sucker *noun* 1 a thing that sucks something. 2 something that can stick to a surface by suction. 3 a shoot coming up from a root or underground stem. 4 (*slang*) a person who is easily deceived.

suckle *verb* (**suckled, suckling**) feed on milk at the mother's breast or udder.

suckling *noun* a child or animal that has not yet been weaned.

suction *noun* 1 sucking. 2 producing a vacuum so that things are sucked into the empty space, *Vacuum cleaners work by suction.*

sudden *adjective* happening or done quickly or without warning. **suddenly** *adverb*, **suddenness** *noun*

suds *plural noun* froth on soapy water.

sue *verb* (**sued, suing**) start a lawsuit to claim money from somebody.

suede (*say* swayd) *noun* leather with one side rubbed to make it velvety.

suet *noun* hard fat from cattle and sheep, used in cooking.

suf- *prefix* see **sub-**.

suffer *verb* **1** feel pain or sadness.
2 experience something bad, *suffer damage*. **3** (*old use*) allow; tolerate, *Suffer the children to come unto me*. **sufferer** *noun*, **suffering** *noun*

sufferance *noun* **on sufferance** allowed but only reluctantly.

suffice *verb* (**sufficed, sufficing**) be enough for someone's needs.

sufficient *adjective* enough. **sufficiently** *adverb*, **sufficiency** *noun*

suffix *noun* (*plural* **suffixes**) a letter or set of letters joined to the end of a word to make another word (e.g. in forget*ful*, lion*ess*, rust*y*) or a form of a verb (e.g. sing*ing*; wait*ed*).

suffocate *verb* (**suffocated, suffocating**) **1** make it difficult or impossible for someone to breathe. **2** suffer or die because breathing is prevented. **suffocation** *noun*

suffrage *noun* the right to vote in political elections.

suffragette *noun* a woman who campaigned in Britain in the early 20th century for women to have the right to vote.

suffuse *verb* (**suffused, suffusing**) spread through or over something, *A blush suffused her cheeks*.

sugar *noun* a sweet food obtained from the juices of various plants (e.g. sugar-cane, sugar-beet). **sugar** *verb*, **sugary** *adjective*

sugarbird *noun* a kind of bird with a long beak and tail that feeds on insects and nectar.

sugarbush (also **suikerbos**) *noun* any of various kinds of protea which have nectar in large amounts (used in former times to make syrup).

suggest *verb* **1** give somebody an idea that you think is useful. **2** cause an idea or possibility to come into the mind. **suggestion** *noun*, **suggestive** *adjective*

suggestible *adjective* easily influenced by people's suggestions.

suicide *noun* **1** killing yourself deliberately, *commit suicide*. **2** a person who deliberately kills himself or herself. **suicidal** *adjective*

suit¹ *noun* **1** a matching jacket and trousers, or a jacket and skirt, that are meant to be worn together. **2** clothing for a particular activity, *a diving-suit*. **3** any of the four sets of cards (clubs, hearts, diamonds, spades) in a pack of playing-cards. **4** a lawsuit.

suit² *verb* **1** be suitable or convenient for a person or thing. **2** make a person look attractive, *Red suits you*.

suitable *adjective* satisfactory or right for a particular person, purpose, or occasion etc. **suitably** *adverb*, **suitability** *noun*

suitcase *noun* a rectangular container for carrying clothes, usually with a hinged lid and a handle.

suite (*say as* sweet) *noun* **1** a set of furniture, *a bedroom suite*. **2** a set of rooms. **3** a set of short pieces of music.

suitor *noun* a man who is courting a woman.

sulk *verb* be silent and bad-tempered because you are not pleased. **sulks** *plural noun*, **sulky** *adjective*, **sulkily** *adverb*, **sulkiness** *noun*

sullen *adjective* sulking and gloomy. **sullenly** *adverb*, **sullenness** *noun*

sully *verb* (**sullied, sullying**) soil or stain something; blemish, *The scandal sullied his reputation*.

sulphur *noun* a yellow chemical used in industry and in medicine. **sulphurous** *adjective*

sulphuric acid *noun* a strong colourless acid containing sulphur.

sultan *noun* the ruler of certain Muslim countries.

sultana *noun* **1** a raisin without seeds. **2** a sultan's mother, wife, or daughter.

sultry *adjective* hot and humid, *sultry weather*. **sultriness** *noun*

sum¹ *noun* **1** a total. **2** a problem in arithmetic. **3** an amount of money.

sum² *verb* (**summed, summing**) **sum up** summarize, especially at the end of a talk etc.; form an opinion of a person, *sum him up*.

sum- *prefix* see **sub-**.

summarize *verb* (**summarized, summarizing**) make or give a summary of something.

summary¹ *noun* (*plural* **summaries**) a statement of the main points of something said or written.

summary² *adjective* **1** brief. **2** done or given hastily, without delay, *summary punishment.* **summarily** *adverb*

summer *noun* the warm season between spring and autumn. **summery** *adjective*

summer-house *noun* a small building providing shade in a garden or park.

summit *noun* **1** the top of a mountain or hill. **2** a meeting between the leaders of powerful countries, *a summit conference.*

summon *verb* **1** order someone to come or appear. **2** request firmly, *She summoned the rebels to surrender.*
summon up gather or prepare, *Can you summon up the energy to get out of bed?*

summons *noun* (*plural* **summonses**) a command to appear in a lawcourt.

sump *noun* a metal case that holds oil round an engine.

sumptuous *adjective* splendid and expensive-looking. **sumptuously** *adverb*

sun¹ *noun* **1** the large ball of fire round which the earth travels. **2** light and warmth from the sun, *Go and sit in the sun.*

sun² *verb* (**sunned, sunning**) warm something in the sun, *sunning ourselves on the beach.*

sunbathe *verb* (**sunbathed, sunbathing**) expose your body to the sun.

sunbeam *noun* a ray of sun.

sunbird *noun* a kind of bird that feeds on nectar, the male of which has bright feathers.

sunburn *noun* redness of the skin caused by the sun. **sunburnt** *adjective*

sundae (*say* sun-day) *noun* a mixture of ice-cream and fruit, nuts, cream, etc.

sunder *verb* (*poetical*) break apart; sever.

sundial *noun* a device that shows the time by a shadow on a dial.

sundown *noun* sunset.

sundries *plural noun* various small things.

sundry *adjective* various; several.
all and sundry everyone.

sunflower *noun* a very tall flower with golden petals round a dark centre.

sun-glasses *plural noun* dark glasses to protect your eyes from strong sunlight.

sunken *adjective* sunk deeply into a surface, *Their cheeks were pale and sunken.*

sunlight *noun* light from the sun. **sunlit** *adjective*

sunny *adjective* (**sunnier, sunniest**) **1** full of sunshine. **2** cheerful, *She was in a sunny mood.* **sunnily** *adverb*

sunrise *noun* the rising of the sun; dawn.

sunset *noun* the setting of the sun.

sunshade *noun* a parasol or other device to protect people from the sun.

sunshine *noun* sunlight with no cloud between the sun and the earth.

sunspot *noun* **1** a dark place on the sun's surface. **2** (*informal*) a sunny place.

sunstroke *noun* illness caused by being in the sun too long.

sup *verb* (**supped, supping**) **1** drink liquid in sips or spoonfuls. **2** eat supper.

sup- *prefix* see **sub-**.

super *adjective* (*informal*) excellent; superb.

super- *prefix* **1** over; on top (as in *superstructure*). **2** of greater size or quality etc. (as in *supermarket*). **3** extremely (as in *superabundant*). **4** beyond (as in *supernatural*).

superannuation *noun* a pension; regular payments made by an employee towards his or her pension.

superb *adjective* magnificent; excellent. **superbly** *adverb*

supercilious *adjective* haughty and scornful. **superciliously** *adverb*

superficial *adjective* on the surface; not deep or thorough. **superficially** *adverb*, **superficiality** *noun*

superfluous *adjective* more than is needed. **superfluity** *noun*

superhuman *adjective* **1** beyond ordinary human ability, *superhuman strength.* **2** higher than human; divine.

superimpose *verb* (**superimposed, superimposing**) place a thing on top of something else. **superimposition** *noun*

superintend *verb* supervise. **superintendent** *noun*

superior[1] *adjective* **1** higher in position or rank, *She is your superior officer.* **2** better than another person or thing. **3** conceited, *a superior attitude.* **superiority** *noun*

superior[2] *noun* a person or thing that is superior to another.

superlative[1] *adjective* of the highest degree or quality, *superlative skill.* **superlatively** *adverb*

superlative[2] *noun* the form of an adjective or adverb that expresses 'most', *The superlative of 'great' is 'greatest'.* (Compare *positive* and *comparative*.)

superman *noun* (*plural* **supermen**) a man with superhuman powers. **superwoman** (*plural* **superwomen**)

supermarket *noun* a large self-service shop that sells food and other goods.

supernatural *adjective* not belonging to the natural world, *supernatural beings such as ghosts.*

superphosphate *noun* a chemical fertilizer that contains phosphorus.

superpower *noun* one of the most powerful nations in the world.

supersede *verb* (**superseded, superseding**) take the place of something, *Cars superseded horse-drawn carriages.*

supersonic *adjective* faster than the speed of sound. (Compare *subsonic*.)

superstition *noun* a belief or action that is not based on reason or evidence, e.g. the belief that it is unlucky to walk under a ladder. **superstitious** *adjective*

superstructure *noun* a structure that rests on something else; a building as distinct from its foundations.

supertanker *noun* a very large tanker.

supervene *verb* (**supervened, supervening**) happen and interrupt or change something, *The country was prosperous until an earthquake supervened.*

supervise *verb* (**supervised, supervising**) be in charge of a person or thing and inspect what is done. **supervision** *noun*, **supervisor** *noun*, **supervisory** *adjective*

supine (*say* soop-I'n) *adjective* **1** lying face upwards. (The opposite is *prone*.) **2** not taking action.

supper *noun* a meal eaten in the evening.

supplant *verb* take the place of a person or thing that has been ousted.

supple *adjective* bending easily; flexible. **supplely** *adverb*, **suppleness** *noun*

supplement[1] *noun* **1** something added as an extra. **2** an extra section added to a book or newspaper, *the colour supplement.* **supplementary** *adjective*

supplement[2] *verb* add to something, *She supplements her pocket-money by working on Saturdays.*

suppliant (*say* sup-lee-ant) *noun* a person who asks humbly for something.

supplicate *verb* (**supplicated, supplicating**) beg humbly; beseech. **supplication** *noun*

supply[1] *verb* (**supplied, supplying**) give or sell or provide what is needed or wanted. **supplier** *noun*

supply[2] *noun* (*plural* **supplies**) **1** an amount of something that is available for use when needed, *a regular supply of milk.* **2** the action of supplying something; the thing supplied.

supply and demand (in economics) the quantity of a product available and required, as factors regulating its price.

support[1] *verb* **1** keep a person or thing from falling or sinking. **2** give strength, help, or encouragement to someone, *Support your local team.* **3** provide with the necessities of life, *She has two children to support.* **supporter** *noun*, **supportive** *adjective*

support[2] *noun* **1** the action of supporting. **2** a person or thing that supports.

suppose *verb* (**supposed, supposing**) think that something is likely to happen or be true. **supposedly** *adverb*, **supposition** *noun*

be supposed to be expected to do something; have as a duty.

suppress *verb* **1** put an end to something forcibly or by authority, *Troops suppressed the rebellion.* **2** keep something from being known or seen, *They suppressed the truth.* **suppression** *noun*, **suppressor** *noun*

supreme *adjective* highest in rank; most important; greatest, *supreme courage.* **supremely** *adverb*, **supremacy** *noun*

sur-1 *prefix* see **sub-**.

sur-2 *prefix* = super- (as in *surcharge, surface*).

surcharge *noun* an extra charge.

sure1 *adjective* 1 convinced; feeling no doubt. 2 certain to happen or do something, *Our team is sure to win.* 3 reliable; undoubtedly true. **sureness** *noun*
for sure definitely.
make sure find out exactly; make something happen or be true, *Make sure the door is locked.*

sure2 *adverb* (*informal*) surely.
sure enough certainly; in fact.

surely *adverb* 1 in a sure way; certainly; securely. 2 it must be true; I feel sure, *Surely we met last year?*

surety *noun* (*plural* **sureties**) 1 a guarantee. 2 a person who promises to pay a debt or fulfil a contract etc. if another person fails to do so.

surf *noun* the white foam of waves breaking on a rock or shore.

surface1 *noun* 1 the outside of something. 2 any of the sides of an object, especially the top part. 3 an outward appearance, *On the surface he was a kindly man.*

surface2 *verb* (**surfaced, surfacing**) 1 put a surface on a road, path, etc. 2 come up to the surface from under water.

surfboard *noun* a board used in surfing.

surfeit (*say* ser-fit) *noun* too much of something. **surfeited** *adjective*

surfing *noun* balancing yourself on a board that is carried to the shore on the waves. **surfer** *noun*

surge *verb* (**surged, surging**) move forwards or upwards like waves. **surge** *noun*

surgeon *noun* a doctor who treats disease or injury by cutting or repairing the affected parts of the body.

surgery *noun* (*plural* **surgeries**) 1 the place where a doctor or dentist etc. regularly gives advice and treatment to patients. 2 the time when patients can visit the doctor etc., *surgery hours.* 3 the work of a surgeon. **surgical** *adjective*, **surgically** *adverb*

surly *adjective* (**surlier, surliest**) bad-tempered and unfriendly. **surliness** *noun*

surmise *noun* a guess. **surmise** *verb*

surmount *verb* 1 overcome a difficulty. 2 get over an obstacle. 3 be on top of something, *The church tower is surmounted by a steeple.*

surname *noun* the name held by all members of a family.

surpass *verb* do or be better than all others; excel.

surplice *noun* a loose white garment worn over a cassock by clergy and choir at a religious service.

surplus *noun* (*plural* **surpluses**) an amount left over after spending or using all that was needed.

surprise1 *noun* 1 something unexpected. 2 the feeling caused by something that was not expected.

surprise2 *verb* (**surprised, surprising**) 1 be a surprise to somebody. 2 come upon or attack somebody unexpectedly. **surprisingly** *adverb*

surrealism *noun* a style of painting that shows strange shapes like those seen in dreams and fantasies. **surrealist** *noun*, **surrealistic** *adjective*

surrender *verb* 1 give yourself up to an enemy. 2 hand something over to another person, especially when compelled to do so. **surrender** *noun*

surreptitious (*say* su-rep-**tish**-us) *adjective* stealthy. **surreptitiously** *adverb*

surrogate (*say* **su**-rog-at) *noun* 1 somebody or something acting for or used in place of another; a substitute. 2 a deputy.

surround *verb* come or be all round a person or thing; encircle.

surroundings *plural noun* the things or conditions round a person or thing.

surveillance (*say* ser-**vay**-lans) *noun* a close watch kept on a person or thing, *Police kept him under surveillance.*

survey1 (*say* **ser**-vay) *noun* 1 a general look at something. 2 an inspection of an area, building, etc.

survey2 (*say* ser-**vay**) *verb* make a survey

of something; inspect. **surveyor** *noun*

survive *verb* (**survived, surviving**) stay alive; go on living or existing after someone has died or after a disaster. **survival** *noun*, **survivor** *noun*

sus- *prefix* see **sub-**.

susceptible (*say* sus-**ept**-ib-ul) *adjective* likely to be affected by something, *She is susceptible to colds.* **susceptibility** *noun*

suspect[1] (*say* sus-**pekt**) *verb* 1 think that a person is not to be trusted or has committed a crime; distrust. 2 have a feeling that something is likely or possible, *I suspect that you're right.*

suspect[2] (*say* sus-**pekt**) *noun* a person who is suspected of a crime etc. **suspect** *adjective*

suspend *verb* 1 hang something up. 2 postpone; stop something temporarily. 3 deprive a person of a job or position etc. for a time.

suspender *noun* a fastener to hold up a sock or stocking by its top.

suspense *noun* an anxious or uncertain feeling while waiting for something to happen or become known.

suspension *noun* suspending. **suspension bridge** a bridge supported by cables.

suspicion *noun* 1 suspecting a person or thing; being suspected; distrust. 2 a slight belief, *I have a suspicion that he's planning something.*

suspicious *adjective* feeling or causing suspicion. **suspiciously** *adverb*

sustain *verb* 1 support. 2 keep someone alive. 3 keep something happening. 4 undergo; suffer, *We sustained a defeat.*

sustainable *adjective* 1 (of farming) that produces crops and animals without using up or damaging natural resources. 2 (of a resource) that can be used at a certain level without permanently depleting it; renewable.

sustenance *noun* food; nourishment.

suture (*say* **soo**-cher) *noun* surgical stitching of a cut.

suzerainty (*say* **soo**-zer-en-tee) *noun* 1 the partial control of a weaker country by a stronger one. 2 the power of an overlord in feudal times.

svelte *adjective* slim and graceful.

SW *abbreviation* south-west; south-western.

swab[1] (*say* swob) *noun* a mop or pad for cleaning or wiping something.

swab[2] *verb* (**swabbed, swabbing**) clean or wipe with a swab.

swaddle *verb* (**swaddled, swaddling**) wrap in warm clothes or blankets etc.

swag *noun* loot.

swagger *verb* walk or behave in a conceited way; strut. **swagger** *noun*

swain *noun* (*old use*) 1 a country lad. 2 a suitor.

swallow[1] *verb* 1 make something go down your throat. 2 believe something that ought not to be believed, *Did you really swallow all that nonsense?* **swallow** *noun*
swallow up take in and cover; engulf, *She was swallowed up in the crowd.*

swallow[2] *noun* a small bird with a forked tail and pointed wings which migrates north in winter.

swamp[1] *noun* a marsh. **swampy** *adjective*

swamp[2] *verb* 1 flood. 2 overwhelm with a great mass or number of things.

swan *noun* a large usually white swimming bird with a long neck.

swank[1] *verb* (*informal*) boast; swagger.

swank[2] *noun* (*informal*) 1 swanking; boasting. 2 a boastful person.

swan-song *noun* a person's last performance or work.

swap *verb* (**swapped, swapping**) (*informal*) exchange. **swap** *noun*

swarm[1] *noun* a large number of insects or birds etc. flying or moving about together.

swarm[2] *verb* 1 gather or move in a swarm. 2 be crowded or overrun with insects, people, etc.

swarm[3] *verb* climb by gripping with the hands or arms and legs.

swarthy *adjective* having a dark complexion. **swarthiness** *noun*

swashbuckling *adjective* swaggering aggressively.

swastika *noun* an ancient symbol

formed by a cross with its ends bent at right angles, adopted by the Nazis as their sign.

swat *verb* (**swatted, swatting**) hit or crush a fly etc. **swatter** *noun*

swathe *verb* (**swathed, swathing**) wrap in layers of bandages, paper, or clothes etc.

sway *verb* **1** swing gently; move from side to side. **2** influence, *His speech swayed the crowd.* **sway** *noun*

swear *verb* (**swore, sworn, swearing**) **1** make a solemn promise, *She swore to tell the truth.* **2** make a person take an oath, *We swore him to secrecy.* **3** use curses or coarse words in anger or surprise etc. **swear-word** *noun*

swear by have great confidence in something.

sweat¹ (*say* swet) *noun* moisture given off by the body through the pores of the skin; perspiration. **sweaty** *adjective*

sweat² *verb* give off sweat; perspire.

sweater *noun* a jersey or pullover.

swede *noun* a large yellow kind of turnip.

sweep¹ *verb* (**swept, sweeping**) **1** clean or clear with a broom or brush etc. **2** move or remove quickly, *The floods swept away the bridge.* **3** go smoothly, quickly, or proudly, *She swept out of the room.* **sweeper** *noun*

sweep² *noun* **1** the process of sweeping, *Give this room a good sweep.* **2** a chimney-sweep. **3** a sweepstake.

sweeping *adjective* general; wide-ranging, *He made sweeping changes.*

sweepstake *noun* a kind of lottery used in gambling on the result of a horse-race etc.

sweet¹ *adjective* **1** tasting as if it contains sugar; not bitter. **2** very pleasant, *a sweet smell.* **3** (*informal*) charming. **sweetly** *adverb*, **sweetness** *noun*

sweet corn the seeds of maize.

sweet pea a climbing plant with fragrant flowers.

sweet² *noun* **1** a small shaped piece of sweet food made with sugar, chocolate, etc. **2** a pudding; the sweet course in a meal. **3** a beloved person.

sweetbread *noun* an animal's pancreas used as food.

sweeten *verb* make or become sweet. **sweetener** *noun*

sweetheart *noun* a person you love very much.

sweetmeat *noun* a sweet.

swell¹ *verb* (**swelled, swollen** or **swelled, swelling**) make or become larger in size or amount or force.

have a swelled head (*slang*) be conceited.

swell² *noun* **1** the process of swelling. **2** the rise and fall of the sea's surface.

swell³ *adjective* (*American*) (*informal*) very good.

swelling *noun* a swollen place.

swelter *verb* feel uncomfortably hot.

swerve *verb* (**swerved, swerving**) turn to one side suddenly. **swerve** *noun*

swift¹ *adjective* quick; rapid. **swiftly** *adverb*, **swiftness** *noun*

swift² *noun* a small bird rather like a swallow.

swig *verb* (**swigged, swigging**) (*slang*) drink; swallow. **swig** *noun*

swill¹ *verb* pour water over or through something; wash or rinse.

swill² *noun* **1** the process of swilling, *Give it a swill.* **2** a sloppy mixture of waste food given to pigs.

swim¹ *verb* (**swam, swum, swimming**) **1** move the body through the water; be in the water for pleasure. **2** cross by swimming, *She swam the Channel.* **3** float. **4** be covered with or full of liquid, *Our eyes were swimming in tears.* **5** feel dizzy, *His head swam.* **swimmer** *noun*, **swimming-costume** *noun*

swim² *noun* the action of swimming, *We went for a swim.*

swimming-bath (also **swimming-pool**) *noun* an artificial pool for swimming in.

swindle *verb* (**swindled, swindling**) cheat a person in business etc. **swindle** *noun*, **swindler** *noun*

swine *noun* (*plural* **swine**) **1** a pig. **2** a very unpleasant person or thing.

swing¹ *verb* (**swung, swinging**) **1** move to and fro while hanging; move or turn in a curve, *The door swung open.* **2** change from one opinion or mood etc. to another.

swing² *noun* **1** a swinging movement.
2 a seat hung on chains or ropes etc. so
that it can be moved backwards and forwards. **3** the amount by which votes or
opinions etc. change from one side to
another, *Voters have swung to the right.*
4 a kind of jazz music..
in full swing full of activity; working fully.
swingeing (*say* **swin**-jing) *adjective*
1 (of a blow) very powerful. **2** huge in
amount, *a swingeing increase in taxes.*
swipe *verb* (**swiped, swiping**) (*informal*)
1 hit hard. **2** steal something. **swipe** *noun*
swirl *verb* move round quickly in circles;
whirl. **swirl** *noun*
swish¹ *verb* move with a hissing sound.
swish *noun*
swish² *adjective* (*informal*) smart;
fashionable.
switch¹ *noun* (*plural* **switches**) **1** a device
that is pressed or turned to start or stop
something working, especially by electricity. **2** a change of opinion, policy, or
methods. **3** a mechanism for moving the
points on a railway track. **4** a flexible rod
or whip.
switch² *verb* **1** turn something on or off
by means of a switch. **2** change or transfer
or divert something.
switchback *noun* a railway at a funfair,
with steep slopes up and down alternately.
switchboard *noun* a panel with switches
etc. for making telephone connections or
operating electric circuits.
swivel *verb* (**swivelled, swivelling**) turn
round. **swivel** *noun*
swollen *past participle* of **swell**.
swoon *verb* faint. **swoon** *noun*
swoop *verb* come down with a rushing
movement; make a sudden attack. **swoop**
noun
swop *verb* (**swopped, swopping**) swap.
sword (*say* sord) *noun* a weapon with a
long pointed blade fixed in a handle or
hilt. **swordsman** *noun*
swot *verb* (**swotted, swotting**) (*informal*)
study hard. **swot** *noun*
sycamore *noun* a kind of maple-tree.
sycophant (*say* **sik**-o-fant) *noun* a person

who tries to win people's favour by flattering them. **sycophantic** *adjective*, **syco-
phantically** *adverb*, **sycophancy** *noun*
syl- *prefix* see **syn-**.
syllable *noun* a word or part of a word
that has one sound when you say it,
*'Cat' has one syllable, 'el-e-phant' has three
syllables.* **syllabic** *adjective*
syllabus *noun* (*plural* **syllabuses**) a summary of the things to be studied by a class
or for an examination etc.
sylph *noun* a slender girl or woman.
sym- *prefix* see **syn-**.
symbiosis (*say* sim-by-**oh**-sis) *noun*
(*plural* **symbioses**) a close relationship
between two different kinds of living
things for mutual benefit.
symbol *noun* **1** a thing that suggests
something, *The dove is a symbol of peace.*
2 a mark or sign with a special meaning
(e.g. +, −, and ÷ in mathematics).
symbolic *adjective*, **symbolical** *adjective*,
symbolically *adverb*
symbolize *verb* (**symbolized, symboliz-
ing**) make or be a symbol of something.
symbolism *noun* the use of symbols to
represent things.
symmetrical *adjective* able to be divided
into two halves which are exactly the same
but the opposite way round, *Wheels and
butterflies are symmetrical.* **symmetrically**
adverb, **symmetry** *noun*
sympathize *verb* (**sympathized,
sympathizing**) show or feel sympathy.
sympathizer *noun*
sympathy *noun* (*plural* **sympathies**)
1 the sharing or understanding of other
people's feelings, opinions, etc. **2** a feeling
of pity or tenderness towards someone
who is hurt, sad, or in trouble. **sym-
pathetic** *adjective*, **sympathetically**
adverb
symphony *noun* (*plural* **symphonies**)
a long piece of music for an orchestra.
symphonic *adjective*
symptom *noun* a sign that a disease or
condition exists, *Red spots are a symptom
of measles.* **symptomatic** *adjective*
syn- *prefix* (changing to **syl-** or **sym-** before certain consonants) **1** with, together

(as in *synchronize*). **2** alike (as in *synonym*).

synagogue (*say* **sin**-a-gog) *noun* a place where Jews meet for worship.

synchronize (*say* **sink**-ron-I'z) *verb* (**synchronized, synchronizing**) **1** make things happen at the same time, *synchronized swimming*. **2** make watches or clocks show the same time. **3** happen at the same time, *remarkably synchronized events*. **synchronization** *noun*

syncopate (*say* **sink**-o-payt) *verb* (**syncopated, syncopating**) change the strength of beats in a piece of music. **syncopation** *noun*

syndicate *noun* a group of people or firms who work together in business.

syndrome *noun* a set of symptoms.

synod (*say* **sin**-od) *noun* a council of senior members of the clergy.

synonym (*say* **sin**-o-nim) *noun* a word that means the same or almost the same as another word, *'Large' and 'great' are synonyms of 'big'*. **synonymous** (*say* sin-**on**-im-us) *adjective*

synopsis (*say* sin-**op**-sis) *noun* (*plural* **synopses**) a summary.

syntax (*say* **sin**-taks) *noun* the way words are arranged to make phrases or sentences. **syntactic** *adjective*, **syntactically** *adverb*

synthesis (*say* **sin**-thi-sis) *noun* (*plural* **syntheses**) combining different things to make something. **synthesize** *verb*

synthesizer *noun* an electronic musical instrument that can make a large variety of sounds.

synthetic *adjective* artificially made; not natural. **synthetically** *adverb*

syringe *noun* a device for sucking in a liquid and squirting it out.

syrup *noun* a thick sweet liquid. **syrupy** *adjective*

system *noun* **1** a set of parts, things, or ideas that are organized to work together, *the digestive system*. **2** a way of doing something, *a new system of training motor-cyclists*.

systematic *adjective* methodical; carefully planned. **systematically** *adverb*

Tt

tab *noun* a small flap or strip that sticks out.

tabby *noun* (*plural* **tabbies**) a grey or brown cat with dark stripes.

tabernacle *noun* (in the Bible) the portable shrine used by the ancient Jews during their wanderings in the desert.

table[1] *noun* **1** a piece of furniture with a flat top supported on legs. **2** a list of facts or figures arranged in order; a list of the results of multiplying a number by other numbers, *multiplication tables*.

table[2] *verb* (**tabled, tabling**) put forward a proposal etc. for discussion in Parliament, or in a meeting etc.

tableau (*say* **tab**-loh) *noun* (*plural* **tableaux** (*say* **tab**-lohz)) a dramatic or picturesque scene, especially one posed on a stage by a group of people who do not speak or move.

tablecloth *noun* a cloth for covering a table, especially at meals.

table d'hôte (*say* tahbl **doht**) *noun* a restaurant meal served at a fixed inclusive price. (Compare *à la carte*.)

tablespoon *noun* a large spoon for serving food. **tablespoonful** *noun*

tablet *noun* **1** a pill. **2** a solid piece of soap. **3** a flat piece of stone or wood etc. with words carved or written on it.

tabloid *noun* a newspaper with pages that are half the size of larger newspapers.

taboo[1] *noun* (*plural* **taboos**) a custom that forbids people to touch, do, use, or talk about a certain thing.

taboo[2] *adjective* not to be touched, done, used, or spoken about, *Talking about sex is still taboo in some communities*.

tabor (*say* **tay**-ber) *noun* a small drum.

tabular *adjective* arranged in a table or in columns.

tabulate *verb* (**tabulated, tabulating**) arrange information or figures in a table or list. **tabulation** *noun*

tabulator *noun* a device on a typewriter

or computer that automatically sets the positions for columns.

tachograph (*say* **tak**-o-grahf) *noun* a device that automatically records the speed and travelling-time of a motor vehicle in which it is fitted.

tacit (*say* **tas**-it) *adjective* implied or understood without being put into words; silent, *tacit approval.*

taciturn (*say* **tas**-i-tern) *adjective* saying very little. **taciturnity** *noun*

tack[1] *noun* 1 a short nail with a flat top. 2 a tacking stitch. 3 (in sailing) the direction taken when tacking.

tack[2] *verb* 1 nail down with tacks. 2 fasten material together with long stitches. 3 sail a zigzag course so as to use what wind there is.

tack on (*informal*) add an extra thing.

tack[3] *noun* harness, saddles, etc.

tackie *noun* a laced canvas shoe with rubber soles.

tackle[1] *verb* (**tackled, tackling**) 1 try to do something that needs doing. 2 try to get the ball from someone else in a game of rugby or hockey etc.

tackle[2] *noun* 1 equipment, especially for fishing. 2 a set of ropes and pulleys. 3 the action of tackling someone.

tacky *adjective* sticky, not quite dry, *The paint is still tacky.* **tackiness** *noun*

tact *noun* skill in not offending people. **tactful** *adjective*, **tactfully** *adverb*, **tactless** *adjective*, **tactlessly** *adverb*

tactics *noun* the method of arranging troops etc. skilfully for a battle, or of doing things to achieve something. **tactical** *adjective*, **tactically** *adverb*, **tactician** *noun*

● USAGE: *Strategy* is a general plan for a whole campaign, *tactics* is for one part of this.

tactile *adjective* of or using the sense of touch.

tadpole *noun* a young frog or toad that has developed from the egg and lives entirely in water.

taffeta *noun* a stiff silky material.

tag[1] *noun* 1 a label tied on or stuck into something. 2 a metal or plastic point at the end of a shoelace.

tag[2] *verb* (**tagged, tagging**) 1 label something with a tag. 2 add as an extra thing, *A postscript was tagged on to her letter.* 3 (*informal*) go with other people, *Her brother tagged along.*

tag[3] *noun* a game in which one person chases the others.

tail[1] *noun* 1 the part that sticks out from the rear end of the body of a bird, fish, or animal. 2 the part at the end or rear of something. 3 the side of a coin opposite the head, *Heads or tails?*

tail[2] *verb* 1 remove stalks etc. from fruit, *top and tail gooseberries.* 2 (*informal*) follow a person or thing.

tail off become fewer, smaller, or slighter etc.; cease gradually.

tailless *adjective* without a tail.

tailor[1] *noun* a person who makes clothes, especially men's clothes.

tailor[2] *verb* 1 make or fit clothes. 2 adapt or make something for a special purpose, *a dictionary tailored for South African schools.*

taint[1] *noun* a small amount of decay, pollution, or a bad quality that spoils something.

taint[2] *verb* give something a taint.

take *verb* (**took, taken, taking**) This word has many uses, including 1 get something into your hands or possession or control etc., *take this cup*; *we took many prisoners.* 2 make use of, *take a taxi* or indulge in, *take a holiday.* 3 carry or convey, *Take this parcel to the post.* 4 perform or deal with, *When do you take your music exam?* 5 study or teach a subject, *Who takes you for maths?* 6 make an effort, *take trouble* or experience a feeling, *Don't take offence.* 7 accept; endure, *I'll take a risk.* 8 require, *It takes a strong person to lift this.* 9 write down, *take notes.* 10 make a photograph. 11 subtract, *take 4 from 10.* 12 assume, *I take it that you agree.* **taker** *noun*

take after be like a parent etc.

take in deceive somebody.

take leave of say goodbye to.

take off (of an aircraft) leave the ground and become airborne. **take-off** *noun*

take on begin to employ someone; play

or fight against someone; (*informal*) show
that you are upset.

take over take control. **take-over** *noun*
take place happen; occur.
take up start something; occupy space
or time etc.; accept an offer.

take-away *noun* a place that sells cooked
meals for customers to take away; a meal
from this.

takings *plural noun* money received.

takkie *noun* a tackie.

talcum powder *noun* a scented powder
put on the skin to make it feel smooth
and dry.

tale *noun* a story.

talent *noun* a special or very great ability.
talented *adjective*

talisman *noun* (*plural* **talismans**)
an object supposed to bring good luck.

talk[1] *verb* speak; have a conversation.
talker *noun*

talk[2] *noun* 1 talking; a conversation.
2 an informal lecture, *He gave a talk
about Aids.*

talkative *adjective* talking a lot.

tall *adjective* 1 higher than the average,
a tall tree. 2 measured from the bottom
to the top, *It is 10 metres tall.* **tallness**
noun

tall story (*informal*) a story that is hard
to believe.

tallow *noun* animal fat used to make
candles, soap, lubricants, etc.

tally[1] *noun* (*plural* **tallies**) the total
amount of a debt or score.

tally[2] *verb* (**tallied, tallying**) correspond or
agree with something else, *Does your list
tally with mine?*

talon *noun* a strong claw.

tambookie grass *noun* a tall grass used
for mats and thatching.

tamboti (*say* tam-**boo**-a-tee) *noun*
a hardwood tree that grows in the bushveld; the wood from this tree.

tambourine *noun* a circular musical
instrument with metal discs round it,
tapped or shaken to make it jingle.

tame[1] *adjective* 1 (of animals) gentle and
not afraid of people; not wild or dangerous. 2 not exciting; dull. **tamely** *adverb*,

tameness *noun*

tame[2] *verb* (**tamed, taming**) make an
animal become tame. **tamer** *noun*

tam-o'-shanter *noun* a beret with a wide
top.

tamp *verb* pack or ram down tightly.

tamper *verb* meddle or interfere with
something.

tampon *noun* a plug of absorbent
material, used especially to absorb blood
during menstruation.

tan[1] *noun* 1 light-brown colour. 2 brown
colour in skin that has been exposed to sun.

tan[2] *verb* (**tanned, tanning**) 1 make or
become brown by exposing skin to the
sun. 2 make an animal's skin into leather
by treating it with chemicals.

tandem *noun* a bicycle for two riders, one
behind the other.

tandoori *noun* food spiced and cooked in
a clay oven (a *tandoor*).

tang *noun* a strong flavour or smell.

tangent *noun* 1 a straight line that
touches the outside of a curve or circle.
2 (in a right-angled triangle) the ratio of
the sides (other than the hypotenuse)
opposite and adjacent to an angle.

tangerine *noun* a kind of small orange.

tangible *adjective* able to be touched;
real. **tangibly** *adverb*, **tangibility** *noun*

tangle *verb* (**tangled, tangling**) make or
become twisted into a confused mass.
tangle *noun*

tango *noun* (*plural* **tangos**) a ballroom
dance with gliding steps.

tank *noun* 1 a large container for a liquid
or gas. 2 a heavy armoured vehicle used
in war.

tankard *noun* a large mug for drinking
from, usually made of silver or pewter.

tanker *noun* 1 a large ship for carrying oil.
2 a large lorry for carrying a liquid.

tanner *noun* a person who tans animal
skins into leather. **tannery** *noun*

tannie *noun* (*informal*) auntie; a word
used by a child when speaking politely to
an older woman.

tannin *noun* a substance obtained
from the bark or fruit of various trees
(also found in tea), used in tanning

and dyeing things.

tantalize *verb* (**tantalized, tantalizing**) tease or torment a person by showing him or her something good but keeping it out of reach (in Greek mythology, Tantalus was punished by being made to stand near water and fruit which moved away when he tried to reach them).

tantamount *adjective* equivalent, *The principal's request was tantamount to a command.*

tantrum *noun* an outburst of bad temper.

tap¹ *noun* a device for letting out liquid or gas in a controlled flow.

tap root a long root that grows deep into the soil.

tap² *verb* (**tapped, tapping**) 1 take liquid out of something, especially through a tap. 2 obtain supplies or information etc. from a source, *tap the tourist potential of this country.* 3 fix a device to a telephone cable etc. so that you can overhear conversations on it.

tap³ *noun* 1 a quick light hit; the sound of this. 2 tap-dancing.

tap⁴ *verb* (**tapped, tapping**) hit a person or thing quickly and lightly.

tap-dancing *noun* dancing with shoes that make elaborate tapping sounds on the floor. **tap-dance** *noun*, **tap-dancer** *noun*

tape¹ *noun* 1 a narrow strip of cloth, paper, plastic, etc. 2 a narrow plastic strip coated with a magnetic substance and used for making recordings. 3 a tape-recording. 4 a tape-measure.

tape² *verb* (**taped, taping**) 1 fix, cover, or surround something with tape. 2 record something on magnetic tape.

get or **have something taped** (*informal*) know or understand it; be able to deal with it.

tape-measure *noun* a long strip marked in centimetres or inches for measuring things.

taper¹ *verb* make or become narrower gradually.

taper² *noun* a very thin candle.

tape-recorder *noun* a device for recording sounds or computer data on magnetic tape and reproducing them.

tape-recording *noun*

tapestry *noun* (*plural* **tapestries**) a piece of strong cloth with pictures or patterns woven or embroidered on it.

tapeworm *noun* a long flat worm that can live as a parasite in the intestines of people and animals.

tapioca *noun* a starchy substance in hard white grains obtained from cassava, used for making puddings.

tapir (*say* **tay**-per) *noun* a pig-like animal with a long flexible snout.

tar¹ *noun* a thick black liquid made from coal or wood etc. and used in making roads.

tar² *verb* (**tarred, tarring**) coat something with tar.

tarantula *noun* a large kind of spider found in southern Europe and in tropical countries.

tardy *adjective* (**tardier, tardiest**) slow; late. **tardily** *adverb*, **tardiness** *noun*

target¹ *noun* something aimed at; a thing that someone tries to hit or reach.

target² *verb* (**targeted, targeting**) aim at or have as a target.

tariff *noun* a list of prices or charges.

tarmac *noun* an area surfaced with tarmacadam, especially on an airfield.

tarmacadam *noun* a mixture of tar and broken stone, used for making a hard surface on roads, paths, playgrounds, etc.

tarnish *verb* 1 make or become less shiny, *The silver had tarnished.* 2 spoil; blemish, *The scandal tarnished his reputation.* **tarnish** *noun*

tarpaulin *noun* a large sheet of waterproof canvas.

tarragon *noun* a plant with leaves that are used to flavour salads, vinegar, etc.

tarry¹ (*say* **tar**-ee) *adjective* of or like tar.

tarry² (*say* **ta**-ree) *verb* (**tarried, tarrying**) (*old use*) linger.

tart¹ *noun* 1 a pie containing fruit or sweet filling. 2 a piece of pastry with jam etc. on top.

tart² *adjective* 1 sour. 2 sharp in manner, *a tart reply.* **tartly** *adverb*, **tartness** *noun*

tartan *noun* a pattern with coloured

stripes crossing each other, especially one associated with a Scottish clan.

tartar[1] *noun* a person who is fierce or difficult to deal with.

tartar[2] *noun* a hard chalky deposit that forms on teeth.

tartlet *noun* a small pastry tart.

task *noun* a piece of work to be done. **take a person to task** rebuke him or her. **task force** a group specially organized for a particular task.

taskmaster *noun* a person imposing tasks on others, *a hard taskmaster.*

tassel *noun* a bundle of threads tied together at the top and used to decorate something. **tasselled** *adjective*

taste[1] *verb* (**tasted, tasting**) 1 take a small amount of food or drink to try its flavour. 2 be able to perceive flavours. 3 have a certain flavour, *It tastes of garlic.*

taste[2] *noun* 1 the feeling caused in the tongue by something placed on it. 2 the ability to taste things. 3 the ability to enjoy beautiful things or to choose what is suitable, *Her choice of clothes shows her good taste.* 4 a liking, *He always had a taste for camping.* 5 a very small amount of food or drink, *Would you like a taste of this soup?*

tasteful *adjective* showing good taste. **tastefully** *adverb,* **tastefulness** *noun*

tasteless *adjective* 1 having no flavour. 2 showing poor taste. **tastelessly** *adverb,* **tastelessness** *noun*

tasty *adjective* (**tastier, tastiest**) having a strong pleasant taste.

tattered *adjective* badly torn; ragged.

tatters *plural noun* rags; badly torn pieces, *My coat was in tatters.*

tattle *verb* (**tattled, tattling**) gossip. **tattle** *noun*

tattoo[1] *verb* mark a person's skin with a picture or pattern by using a needle and some dye.

tattoo[2] *noun* a tattooed mark.

tattoo[3] *noun* 1 a drumming or tapping sound. 2 an entertainment consisting of military music, marching, etc.

tatty *adjective* 1 ragged; shabby and untidy. 2 cheap and gaudy. **tattily**

adverb, **tattiness** *noun*

taunt *verb* jeer at or insult someone. **taunt** *noun*

taut *adjective* stretched tightly. **tautly** *adverb,* **tautness** *noun*

tauten *verb* make or become taut.

tautology *noun* (*plural* **tautologies**) saying the same thing again in different words, e.g. *You can get the book free for nothing* (where *free* and *for nothing* mean the same).

tavern *noun* an inn or public house.

tawdry *adjective* cheap and gaudy. **tawdriness** *noun*

tawny *adjective* brownish-yellow.

tax[1] *noun* (*plural* **taxes**) 1 money that people or business firms have to pay to the government, to be used for public purposes. 2 a strain or burden, *The long walk was a tax on his strength.*

tax[2] *verb* 1 put a tax on something. 2 charge someone a tax, *She is taxed on her income.* 3 pay the tax on something, *I have taxed the car up to June.* 4 put a strain or burden on a person or thing, *Will it tax your strength?* 5 accuse, *I taxed him with leaving the door open.* **taxable** *adjective,* **taxation** *noun*

taxi[1] *noun* (*plural* **taxis**) a vehicle that carries passengers for payment, usually with a meter (*taximeter*) to record the fare payable. **taxi-cab** *noun*

taxi[2] *verb* (**taxied, taxiing**) (of an aircraft) move along the ground or water, especially before or after flying.

taxidermist *noun* a person who prepares and stuffs the skins of animals in a lifelike form. **taxidermy** *noun*

taxpayer *noun* a person who pays tax.

TB *abbreviation* tuberculosis.

tea *noun* 1 a drink made by pouring hot water on the dried leaves of an evergreen shrub (the *tea-plant*). 2 these dried leaves. 3 a meal in the afternoon or evening at which tea is served. **teacup** *noun,* **tea-leaf** *noun,* **tea-table** *noun,* **teatime** *noun*

tea-bag *noun* a small bag holding about a teaspoonful of tea.

teach *verb* (**taught, teaching**) 1 give a person knowledge or skill; train. 2 give lessons, especially in a particular subject. **3** show someone what to do or avoid, *That will teach you not to meddle!*

teachable *adjective* able to be taught.

teacher *noun* a person who teaches others, especially in a school.

tea-cloth *noun* **1** a tea-towel. **2** a cloth for a tea-table.

teak *noun* the hard strong wood of an evergreen Asian tree.

teal *noun* (*plural* **teal**) a kind of duck.

team[1] *noun* **1** a set of players forming one side in certain games and sports. **2** a set of people working together. **3** two or more animals harnessed to pull a vehicle or a plough etc.

team[2] *verb* put together in a team; combine.

teapot *noun* a pot with a lid and a handle, for making and pouring tea.

tear[1] (*say* teer) *noun* a drop of the water that comes from the eyes when a person cries. **tear-drop** *noun* **in tears** crying.

tear[2] (*say* tair) *verb* (**tore, torn, tearing**) **1** pull something apart, away, or into pieces. **2** become torn, *Newspaper tears easily.* **3** run or travel hurriedly, *motor bikes tearing down the road.*

tear[3] *noun* a split made by tearing.

tearful *adjective* in tears; crying easily. **tearfully** *adverb*

tear-gas *noun* a gas that makes people's eyes water painfully.

tease[1] *verb* (**teased, teasing**) **1** amuse yourself by deliberately annoying or making fun of someone. **2** pick threads apart into separate strands.

tease[2] *noun* a person who often teases others.

teaser *noun* a difficult problem.

teaspoon *noun* a small spoon for stirring tea etc. **teaspoonful** *noun*

teat *noun* **1** a nipple through which a baby sucks milk. **2** the cap of a baby's feeding-bottle.

tea-towel *noun* a cloth for drying washed dishes, cutlery, etc.

Tech (*say* tek) *noun* (*informal*) a technical college or technikon.

technical *adjective* **1** concerned with technology. **2** of a particular subject and its methods, *the technical terms of chemistry.* **technically** *adverb*

technical college a college where technical subjects are taught.

technicality *noun* (*plural* **technicalities**) **1** being technical. **2** a technical word or phrase; a special detail, *Make sure you understand the technicalities of the contract before signing it.*

technician *noun* a skilled mechanic.

technikon *noun* a college where technical subjects are taught.

technique *noun* the method of doing something skilfully.

technology *noun* (*plural* **technologies**) the study of machinery, engineering, and how things work. **technological** *adjective,* **technologist** *noun*

teddy-bear *noun* a soft furry toy bear.

tedious *adjective* annoyingly slow or long; boring. **tediously** *adverb,* **tediousness** *noun,* **tedium** *noun*

tee *noun* **1** the flat area from which golfers strike the ball at the start of play for each hole. **2** a small piece of wood or plastic on which the ball is placed for being struck.

teem *verb* **1** be full of something, *The river was teeming with fish.* **2** rain very hard; pour.

teenage *adjective* of teenagers.

teenaged *adjective* in your teens.

teenager *noun* a person in his or her teens.

teens *plural noun* the time of life between 13 and 19 years of age.

teeny *adjective* (**teenier, teeniest**) (*informal*) tiny.

teeter *verb* stand or move unsteadily.

teething *noun* (of a baby) having its first teeth beginning to grow through the gums.

teetotal *adjective* never drinking alcohol. **teetotaller** *noun*

tele- *prefix* far; at a distance (as in *telescope*).

telecommunications *plural noun* communications over a long distance, e.g. by telephone, telegraph, radio, or television.

telegram *noun* a message sent by telegraph.

telegraph *noun* a way of sending messages by using electric current along wires or by radio. **telegraphic** *adjective*, **telegraphy** *noun*

telepathy (*say* til-**ep**-ath-ee) *noun* communication of thoughts from one person's mind to another without speaking, writing, or gestures. **telepathic** *adjective*

telephone[1] *noun* a device or system using electric wires or radio etc. to enable one person to speak to another who is some distance away.

telephone[2] *verb* (**telephoned, telephoning**) speak to a person on the telephone.

telephonist (*say* til-**ef**-on-ist) *noun* a person who operates a telephone switchboard.

telescope[1] *noun* an instrument using lenses to magnify distant objects. **telescopic** *adjective*

telescope[2] *verb* (**telescoped, telescoping**) 1 make or become shorter by sliding overlapping sections into each other. 2 compress or condense so as to take less space or time.

televise *verb* (**televised, televising**) broadcast something by television.

television *noun* 1 a system using radio waves to reproduce a view of scenes, events, or plays etc. on a screen. 2 an apparatus for receiving these pictures. 3 televised programmes, *children's television.*

telex *noun* a system for sending printed messages by telegraphy. **telex** *verb*

tell *verb* (**told, telling**) 1 make a thing known to someone, especially by words. 2 speak, *Tell the truth.* 3 order, *Tell them to wait.* 4 reveal a secret, *Promise you won't tell.* 5 decide; distinguish, *Can you tell the difference between butter and margarine?* 6 produce an effect, *The strain began to tell on him.* 7 count, *There are ten of them, all told.*

tell off (*informal*) reprimand.

tell tales report what someone has done.

teller *noun* 1 a person employed to receive and pay out money in a bank etc. 2 a person who counts votes etc. 3 a person who tells, especially stories.

telling *adjective* having a strong effect, *a very telling reply.*

tell-tale[1] *noun* a person who tells tales.

tell-tale[2] *adjective* revealing or indicating something, *There was a tell-tale spot of jam on her chin.*

temerity (*say* tim-**erri**-tee) *noun* rashness; boldness.

temper[1] *noun* 1 a person's mood, *He is in a good temper.* 2 an angry mood, *She was in a temper.*

lose your temper lose your calmness and become angry.

temper[2] *verb* 1 harden or strengthen metal etc. by heating and cooling it. 2 moderate or soften the effects of something, *tempering justice with mercy.*

temperament *noun* a person's nature as shown in the way he or she usually behaves, *a nervous temperament.*

temperamental *adjective* 1 of a person's temperament. 2 likely to become excitable or moody suddenly. **temperamentally** *adverb*

temperance *noun* 1 moderation; self-restraint. 2 drinking little or no alcohol.

temperate *adjective* neither extremely hot nor extremely cold, *temperate zones of the world.*

temperature *noun* 1 how hot or cold a person or thing is. 2 an abnormally high temperature of the body, *Do you have a temperature?*

tempest *noun* a violent storm.

tempestuous *adjective* stormy; full of commotion.

temple[1] *noun* a building devoted to the worship, or regarded as the dwelling place, of a god or gods.

temple[2] *noun* the part of the head between the forehead and the ear.

tempo *noun* (*plural* **tempos**) the speed or rhythm of something, especially of a piece of music.

temporary *adjective* lasting for a limited

time only; not permanent. **temporarily** (*say* **tem**-per-er-il-ee) *adverb*

temporize *verb* (**temporized, temporizing**) avoid giving a definite answer, in order to postpone something.

tempt *verb* try to persuade or attract someone, especially into doing something wrong or unwise. **temptation** *noun*, **tempter** *noun*, **temptress** *noun*

ten *noun* & *adjective* the number 10; one more than nine.

tenable *adjective* able to be held, *a tenable theory; the job is tenable for one year only.*

tenacious (*say* ten-**ay**-shus) *adjective* holding or clinging firmly to something. **tenaciously** *adverb*, **tenacity** *noun*

tenant *noun* a person who rents a house, building, or land etc. from a landlord. **tenancy** *noun*

tend[1] *verb* have a certain tendency, *Prices tend to rise.*

tend[2] *verb* look after, *Shepherds were tending their sheep.*

tendency *noun* (*plural* **tendencies**) the way a person or thing is likely to behave, *She has a tendency to be lazy.*

tender[1] *adjective* 1 easy to chew; not tough or hard. 2 easily hurt or damaged; sensitive; delicate, *tender plants.* 3 gentle and loving, *a tender smile.* **tenderly** *adverb*, **tenderness** *noun*

tender[2] *verb* offer something formally, *He tendered his resignation.*

tender[3] *noun* a formal offer to supply goods or carry out work at a stated price, *The council asked for tenders to build a school.*

legal tender kinds of money that are legal for making payments, *Are one rand notes still legal tender?*

tender[4] *noun* 1 a truck attached to a steam locomotive to carry its coal and water. 2 a small boat carrying stores or passengers to and from a larger one.

tendon *noun* a strong strip of tissue that joins muscle to bone.

tendril *noun* 1 a thread-like part by which a climbing plant clings to a support. 2 a thin curl of hair etc.

tenement *noun* a large house or building divided into flats or rooms that are let to separate tenants.

tenet (*say* **ten**-it) *noun* a firm belief held by a person or group.

tennis *noun* a game played with rackets and a ball on a court with a net across the middle.

tenon *noun* a projecting piece of wood etc. shaped to fit into a mortise.

tenor *noun* a male singer with a high voice.

tense[1] *noun* the form of a verb that shows when something happens, e.g. he *came* (**past tense**), he *comes* or *is coming* (**present tense**), he *will come* (**future tense**).

tense[2] *adjective* 1 tightly stretched. 2 with muscles tight because you are nervous or excited. **tensely** *adverb*, **tenseness** *noun*

tense[3] *verb* (**tensed, tensing**) make or become tense.

tensile *adjective* 1 of tension, *the tensile strength of cable.* 2 able to be stretched.

tension *noun* 1 pulling so as to stretch something; being stretched. 2 tenseness; the condition when feelings are tense. 3 voltage, *high-tension cables.*

tent *noun* a shelter made of canvas or other material.

tentacle *noun* a long flexible part of the body of certain animals (e.g. snails, octopuses), used for feeling or grasping things or for moving.

tentative *adjective* cautious; trying something out, *a tentative suggestion.* **tentatively** *adverb*

tenterhooks *plural noun* on **tenterhooks** tense and anxious.

tenth *adjective* & *noun* next after the ninth.

tenuous *adjective* very slight or thin, *tenuous threads.*

tenure (*say* **ten**-yoor) *noun* the holding of office or of land, accommodation, etc.

tepee (*say* **tee**-pee) *noun* a wigwam.

tepid *adjective* only slightly warm; lukewarm, *tepid water.*

term[1] *noun* 1 the period of weeks when

a school or college is open. **2** a definite period, *a term of imprisonment*. **3** a word or expression, *technical terms*.

terms *plural noun* a relationship between people, *They are on friendly terms*; conditions offered or accepted, *peace terms*.

term² *verb* name; call by a certain term, *This music is termed jazz*.

termagant *noun* a shrewish bullying woman.

terminable *adjective* able to be terminated.

terminal¹ *noun* **1** the place where something ends; a terminus. **2** a building where air passengers arrive or depart. **3** a place where a wire is connected in an electric circuit or battery etc. **4** a device for sending information to a computer, or for receiving it.

terminal² *adjective* **1** of or at the end or boundary of something. **2** of or in the last stage of a fatal disease, *terminal cancer*. **terminally** *adverb*

terminate *verb* (**terminated, terminating**) end; stop finally. **termination** *noun*

terminology *noun* the technical terms of a subject. **terminological** *adjective*

terminus *noun* (*plural* **termini**) the end of something; the last station on a railway or bus route.

termite *noun* a small insect that is very destructive to timber.

tern *noun* a sea-bird with long wings.

terrace *noun* **1** a level area on a slope or hillside for cultivation. **2** a paved area beside a house. **3** a row of houses joined together. **terraced** *adjective*

terracotta *noun* **1** a kind of pottery. **2** the brownish-red colour of flowerpots.

terra firma *noun* dry land; the ground, *I was glad to be back on terra firma after the bumpy flight*.

terrain *noun* a stretch of land, *hilly terrain*.

terrapin *noun* an edible freshwater turtle of North America.

terrestrial *adjective* **1** of the earth. **2** of land; living on land.

terrible *adjective* very bad; distressing. **terribly** *adverb*

terrier *noun* a kind of small lively dog.

terrific *adjective* (*informal*) **1** very great, *a terrific storm*. **2** excellent. **terrifically** *adverb*

terrify *verb* (**terrified, terrifying**) fill someone with terror.

territory *noun* (*plural* **territories**) an area of land, especially one that belongs to a country or person. **territorial** *adjective*

terror *noun* **1** very great fear. **2** a terrifying person or thing.

terrorist *noun* a person who uses violence for political purposes. **terrorism** *noun*

terrorize *verb* (**terrorized, terrorizing**) fill someone with terror; control or compel someone by frightening them. **terrorization** *noun*

terse *adjective* concise; curt. **tersely** *adverb*, **terseness** *noun*

tertiary (*say* ter-sher-ee) *adjective* of the third stage of something; coming after secondary.

tertiary consumer an animal that feeds on secondary consumers.

tertiary education education at a university, technikon, etc.

tertiary production the distribution of goods and the provision of services.

tessellate *verb* (**tessellated, tessellating**) fit shapes into a pattern without overlapping. **tessellation** *noun*

test¹ *noun* **1** a short examination; a way of discovering the qualities or abilities etc. of a person or thing. **2** (*informal*) a test match.

test match a cricket or rugby match between teams from different countries.

test² *verb* make a test of a person or thing, *test their driving skills*. **tester** *noun*

testament *noun* **1** a written statement. **2** either of the two main parts of the Bible, the Old Testament or the New Testament.

testator *noun* a person who has made a will.

testicle *noun* either of the two glands in the scrotum where semen is produced.

testify *verb* (**testified, testifying**) give evidence; swear that something is true.

testimonial *noun* **1** a letter describing

someone's abilities, character, etc.
2 a gift presented to someone as a mark of respect.

testimony *noun* (*plural* **testimonies**) evidence; what someone testifies.

test-tube *noun* a tube of thin glass with one end closed, used for experiments in chemistry etc.

testy *adjective* easily annoyed; irritable.

tetanus *noun* a disease that makes the muscles become stiff, caused by bacteria.

tête-à-tête (*say* tayt-ah-**tayt**) *noun* a private conversation, especially between two people.

tether[1] *verb* tie an animal so that it cannot move far.

tether[2] *noun* a rope for tethering an animal.
at the end of your tether unable to endure something any more.

tetra- *prefix* four.

tetrahedron *noun* a solid with four sides (e.g. a pyramid with a triangular base).

text *noun* **1** the words of something written or printed. **2** a sentence from the Bible used as the subject of a sermon etc.

textbook *noun* a book that teaches you about a subject.

textiles *plural noun* kinds of cloth; fabrics.

texture *noun* the way that the surface of something feels.

than *conjunction* compared with another person or thing, *His sister is taller than he is* or *taller than him.*

thank *verb* tell someone that you are grateful to him or her.
thank you I thank you.

thankful *adjective* grateful. **thankfully** *adverb*

thankless *adjective* not likely to win thanks from people, *a thankless task.*

thanks *plural noun* **1** statements of gratitude. **2** (*informal*) thank you.
thanks to as a result of; because of, *Thanks to your help, we succeeded.*

thanksgiving *noun* an expression of gratitude, especially to God.

that[1] *adjective & pronoun* (*plural* **those**)

the one there, *That book is mine. Whose is that?*

that[2] *adverb* to such an extent, *I'll come that far but no further.*

that[3] *relative pronoun* which, who, or whom, *This is the book that I wanted. We liked the people that we met on holiday.*

that[4] *conjunction* used to introduce a wish, reason, result, etc., *I hope that you are well. The puzzle was so hard that no one could solve it.*

thatch[1] *noun* straw, grass, palm leaves, reeds, etc. used to make a roof.

thatch[2] *verb* make a roof with thatch.
thatcher *noun*

thaw[1] *verb* melt; stop being frozen.

thaw[2] *noun* the process of thawing; weather that thaws ice.

the *adjective* (called the *definite article*) a particular one; that or those.

theatre *noun* **1** a building where plays etc. are performed to an audience. **2** a special room where surgical operations are done, *the operating-theatre.*

theatrical *adjective* of plays or acting.
theatrically *adverb*

theatricals *plural noun* performances of plays etc.

thee *pronoun* (*old use*) the form of *thou* used as the object of a verb or after a preposition.

theft *noun* stealing.

their *adjective* **1** belonging to them, *Their coats are over there.* **2** (*informal*) belonging to a person, *Somebody has left their coat on the bus.*

theirs *possessive pronoun* belonging to them, *These coats are theirs.*
● USAGE: It is incorrect to write *their's.*

them *pronoun* the form of *they* used as the object of a verb or after a preposition, *We saw them.*

theme *noun* **1** the subject about which a person speaks, writes, or thinks. **2** a melody.

themselves *pronoun* they or them and nobody else. (Compare *herself.*)

then *adverb* **1** at that time, *We were younger then.* **2** after that; next, *Make the tea, then pour it out.* **3** in that case, *If this* *is yours, then this must be mine.*

thence *adverb* from that place.

theology *noun* the study of religion.
 theological *adjective*, **theologian** *noun*

theorem *noun* a mathematical statement that can be proved by reasoning.

theoretical *adjective* based on theory not on experience. **theoretically** *adverb*

theorize *verb* (**theorized, theorizing**) form a theory or theories.

theory *noun* (*plural* **theories**) **1** an idea or set of ideas put forward to explain something. **2** ideas (contrasted with *practice*), *different theories about how to bring up children.* **3** the principles of a subject, *music theory.*

therapeutic (*say* therra-**pew**-tik) *adjective* treating or curing a disease etc., *Exercise can have a therapeutic effect.*

therapy *noun* treatment to cure a disease etc.

there *adverb* **1** in or to that place etc. **2** used to call attention to something, *There's a good boy!* or to introduce a sentence where the verb comes before its subject, *There was plenty to eat.*

thereabouts *adverb* near there.

thereafter *adverb* from then or there onwards.

thereby *adverb* by that means; because of that.

therefore *adverb* for that reason.

therm *noun* a unit for measuring heat, especially from gas.

thermal *adjective* **1** of heat; worked by heat. **2** hot, *thermal springs.*

thermo- *prefix* heat.

thermodynamics *noun* the science dealing with the relation between heat and other forms of energy.

thermometer *noun* a device for measuring temperature.

Thermos *noun* (*trade mark*) a kind of vacuum flask.

thermostat *noun* a device that automatically keeps the temperature of a room or device steady. **thermostatic** *adjective*, **thermostatically** *adverb*

thesaurus (*say* thi-**sor**-us) *noun* (*plural* **thesauri**) a kind of dictionary containing sets of words grouped according to their meaning.

these *plural* of **this**.

thesis *noun* (*plural* **theses**) a theory put forward, especially a long essay written by a candidate for a university degree.

they *pronoun* **1** the people or things being talked about. **2** people in general, *They say the show is a great success.* **3** (*informal*) he or she; a person, *I am never angry with anyone unless they deserve it.*

they're (*mainly spoken*) they are.
 ● USAGE: Do not confuse with *their* and *there*.

thick *adjective* **1** measuring a lot or a certain amount between opposite surfaces, *a thick book.* **2** (of a line) broad, not fine. **3** crowded with things; dense, *a thick forest; thick fog.* **4** fairly stiff, *thick cream.* **5** (*informal*) stupid. **thickly** *adverb*, **thickness** *noun*

thicken *verb* make or become thicker.

thicket *noun* a number of shrubs and small trees etc. growing close together.

thickset *adjective* having a stocky or burly body.

thief *noun* (*plural* **thieves**) a person who steals things. **thievish** *adjective*, **thievery** *noun*, **thieving** *noun*

thigh *noun* the part of the leg between the hip and the knee.

thimble *noun* a small metal or plastic cap worn on the end of the finger to push the needle in sewing.

thin¹ *adjective* (**thinner, thinnest**) **1** not thick; not fat. **2** feeble, *a thin excuse.* **thinly** *adverb*, **thinness** *noun*

thin² *verb* (**thinned, thinning**) make or become less thick. **thinner** *noun*

thine *adjective* & *possessive pronoun* (*old use*) belonging to thee.

thing *noun* an object; that which can be seen, touched, thought about, etc.

think *verb* (**thought, thinking**) **1** use your mind; form connected ideas. **2** have as an idea or opinion, *We think we shall win.* **thinker** *noun*

third¹ *adjective* next after the second. **thirdly** *adverb*

third² *noun* **1** the third person or thing. **2** one of three equal parts of something.

Third World *noun* the developing countries of Asia, Africa, and South America (originally called 'third' because they were not considered to be politically connected with either the USA or the USSR).

thirst *noun* **1** a feeling of dryness in the mouth and throat, causing a desire to drink. **2** a strong desire, *a thirst for adventure.* **thirsty** *adjective,* **thirstily** *adverb*

thirteen *noun & adjective* the number 13; one more than twelve. **thirteenth** *adjective & noun*

thirty *noun & adjective* (*plural* **thirties**) the number 30; three times ten. **thirtieth** *adjective & noun*

this[1] *adjective & pronoun* (*plural* **these**) the one here, *This house is ours. Whose is this?*

this[2] *adverb* to such an extent, *I'm surprised he got this far.*

thistle *noun* a prickly wild plant with purple, white, or yellow flowers.

thistledown *noun* the very light fluff on thistle seeds.

thither *adverb* (*old use*) to that place.

thong *noun* a narrow strip of leather etc. used for fastening things.

thorax *noun* (*plural* **thoraxes**) the part of the body between the head or neck and the abdomen. **thoracic** *adjective*

thorn *noun* **1** a small pointed growth on the stem of a plant. **2** a thorny tree or shrub.

thorny *adjective* (**thornier, thorniest**) **1** having many thorns. **2** like a thorn. **3** difficult, *a thorny problem.*

thorough *adjective* **1** done or doing things carefully and in detail. **2** complete in every way, *a thorough mess.* **thoroughly** *adverb,* **thoroughness** *noun*

thoroughbred *adjective* bred of pure or pedigree stock. **thoroughbred** *noun*

thoroughfare *noun* a public road or path that is open at both ends.

those *plural* of **that**.

thou *pronoun* (*old use,* in speaking to one person) you.

though[1] *conjunction* in spite of the fact that; even if, *We must look for it, though we probably shan't find it.*

though[2] *adverb* however, *She's right, though.*

thought[1] *noun* **1** something that you think; an idea or opinion. **2** the process of thinking, *She was deep in thought.*

thought[2] *past tense* of **think**.

thoughtful *adjective* **1** thinking a lot. **2** showing thought for other people's needs; considerate. **thoughtfully** *adverb,* **thoughtfulness** *noun*

thoughtless *adjective* **1** careless, not thinking of what may happen. **2** inconsiderate. **thoughtlessly** *adverb,* **thoughtlessness** *noun*

thousand *noun & adjective* the number 1 000; ten hundred. **thousandth** *adjective & noun*

● USAGE: Say *a few thousand* (not 'a few thousands').

thrall *noun* slavery; servitude, *in thrall.*

thrash *verb* **1** beat with a stick or whip; keep hitting very hard. **2** defeat someone thoroughly. **3** move violently, *The crocodile thrashed its tail.*

thread[1] *noun* **1** a thin length of any substance. **2** a length of spun cotton, wool, or nylon etc. used for making cloth or in sewing or knitting. **3** the spiral ridge round a screw.

thread[2] *verb* **1** put a thread through the eye of a needle. **2** pass a strip of film etc. through or round something. **3** put beads on a thread.

threadbare *adjective* (of cloth) with the surface worn away so that the threads show.

threat *noun* **1** a warning that you will punish, hurt, or harm a person or thing. **2** a sign of something undesirable, *the threat of drought.* **3** a person or thing causing danger.

threaten *verb* **1** make threats against someone. **2** be a threat or danger to a person or thing, *High crime rates threaten the stability of the country.*

three *noun & adjective* the number 3; one more than two.

three-dimensional *adjective* having three dimensions (length, width, and height or depth).

thresh *verb* beat corn so as to separate the grain from the husks.

threshold *noun* 1 a slab of stone or board etc. forming the bottom of a doorway; the entrance. 2 the beginning, *We are on the threshold of a great discovery.*

thrice *adverb* (*old use*) three times.

thrift *noun* being economical with money or resources. **thrifty** *adjective*, **thriftily** *adverb*

thrill[1] *noun* a feeling of excitement.

thrill[2] *verb* feel or cause someone to feel a thrill.

thriller *noun* an exciting story, play, or film, usually about crime.

thrips *noun* (*plural* **thrips**) a small winged insect that feeds by sucking plant juices.

thrive *verb* (**thrived** or **throve**, **thriving**) grow strongly; prosper or be successful.

throat *noun* 1 the tube in the neck that takes food and drink down into the body. 2 the front of the neck.

throaty *adjective* 1 produced deep in the throat, *a throaty chuckle.* 2 hoarse. **throatily** *adverb*

throb *verb* (**throbbed**, **throbbing**) beat or vibrate with a strong rhythm, *My heart throbbed.* **throb** *noun*

throes *plural noun* severe pangs of pain. **in the throes of** (*informal*) struggling with, *We are in the throes of exams.*

thrombosis *noun* the formation of a clot of blood in the body.

throne *noun* a special chair for a king, queen, or bishop at ceremonies.

throng[1] *noun* a crowd of people.

throng[2] *verb* crowd, *People thronged the streets.*

throttle[1] *noun* a device controlling the flow of fuel to an engine; an accelerator.

throttle[2] *verb* (**throttled**, **throttling**) strangle.
throttle back or **down** reduce the speed of an engine by partially closing the throttle.

through[1] *preposition* 1 from one end or side to the other end or side of, *climb through the window.* 2 by means of; because of, *We lost it through carelessness.* 3 at the end of; having finished success-

fully, *She is through her exam.*

through[2] *adverb* 1 through something, *We squeezed through.* 2 with a telephone connection made, *I'll put you through to the president.* 3 finished, *Wait till I'm through with these papers.*

through[3] *adjective* 1 going through something, *No through road.* 2 going all the way to a destination, *a through train.*

throughout *preposition* & *adverb* all the way through.

throve *past tense* of **thrive**.

throw *verb* (**threw**, **thrown**, **throwing**) 1 send a person or thing through the air. 2 put carelessly or hastily, *Don't throw your clothes into the suitcase.* 3 move part of your body quickly, *He threw his head back.* 4 cause to be in a certain condition etc., *It threw us into confusion.* 5 move a switch or lever so as to operate it. 6 shape a pot on a potter's wheel. **throw** *noun*, **thrower** *noun*

throw away put something out as being useless or unwanted; waste, *You threw away an opportunity.*

thrum *verb* (**thrummed**, **thrumming**) sound monotonously; strum. **thrum** *noun*

thrush[1] *noun* (*plural* **thrushes**) a songbird with a speckled breast.

thrush[2] *noun* a disease causing tiny white patches in the mouth and throat.

thrust *verb* (**thrust**, **thrusting**) push hard. **thrust** *noun*

thud *verb* (**thudded**, **thudding**) make the dull sound of a heavy knock or fall. **thud** *noun*

thug *noun* a violent ruffian. **thuggery** *noun*

thumb[1] *noun* the short thick finger set apart from the other four.
be under a person's thumb be completely under his or her influence.

thumb[2] *verb* turn the pages of a book etc. quickly with your thumb.
thumb a lift hitch-hike.

thumbscrew *noun* a former instrument of torture for squeezing the thumb.

thump *verb* 1 hit or knock something heavily. 2 punch. 3 thud. **thump** *noun*

thunder¹ *noun* **1** the loud noise that goes with lightning. **2** a similar noise, *thunders of applause.* **thunderous** *adjective,* **thunderstorm** *noun,* **thundery** *adjective*

thunder² *verb* **1** sound with thunder. **2** make a noise like thunder; speak loudly.

thunderbolt *noun* a lightning-flash thought of as a destructive missile.

thunderstruck *adjective* amazed.

thus *adverb* **1** in this way, *Hold the wheel thus.* **2** therefore; as a result of this.

thwart *verb* frustrate.

thy *adjective* (*old use*) belonging to thee.

thyme (*say as* time) *noun* a herb with fragrant leaves.

thyroid gland *noun* a large gland at the front of the neck.

thyself *pronoun* (*old use*) thou or thee and nobody else. (Compare *herself.*)

tiara (*say* tee-**ar**-a) *noun* a woman's jewelled crescent-shaped ornament worn like a crown.

tic *noun* an unintentional twitch of a muscle, especially of the face.

tick¹ *noun* **1** a small mark put by something to show that it is correct or has been checked. **2** a regular clicking sound, especially that made by a clock or watch. **3** (*informal*) a moment.

tick² *verb* **1** put a tick by something. **2** make the sound of a tick.

tick off (*informal*) reprimand someone.

tick³ *noun* a small blood-sucking animal.

ticket *noun* **1** a printed piece of paper or card that allows a person to travel on a bus or train, see a show, etc. **2** a label showing a thing's price.

tickle *verb* (**tickled, tickling**) **1** touch a person's skin lightly so as to cause a slight tingling feeling. **2** (of a part of the body) have a slight tingling or itching feeling. **3** amuse or please somebody.

ticklish *adjective* **1** likely to laugh or wriggle when tickled. **2** awkward; difficult, *a ticklish situation.*

tidal *adjective* of or affected by tides. **tidal wave** a huge sea-wave.

tiddler *noun* (*informal*) a very small fish.

tide¹ *noun* **1** the regular rise and fall in the level of the sea which usually happens

twice a day. **2** (*old use*) a time or season, *Christmas-tide.*

tide² *verb* (**tided, tiding**) **tide a person over** provide him or her with what is needed, for a short time.

tidings *plural noun* news.

tidy¹ *adjective* (**tidier, tidiest**) **1** with everything in its right place; orderly. **2** (*informal*) fairly large, *It costs a tidy amount.* **tidily** *adverb,* **tidiness** *noun*

tidy² *verb* (**tidied, tidying**) make a thing tidy.

tie¹ *verb* (**tied, tying**) **1** fasten with string, ribbon, etc. **2** arrange something into a knot or bow. **3** make the same score as another competitor.

tie² *noun* **1** a necktie. **2** a result when two or more competitors have equal scores.

tier (*say* teer) *noun* each of a series of rows or levels etc. placed one above the other. **tiered** *adjective*

tiff *noun* a slight quarrel.

tiger *noun* a large wild animal of the cat family, with yellow and black stripes.

tight *adjective* **1** fitting very closely. **2** firmly fastened. **3** fully stretched; tense. **4** in short supply, *Money is tight at the moment.* **5** stingy, *He is very tight with his money.* **6** (*slang*) drunk. **tightly** *adverb,* **tightness** *noun*

tighten *verb* make or become tighter.

tightrope *noun* a tightly stretched rope high above the ground, on which acrobats perform.

tights *plural noun* a garment that fits tightly over the feet, legs, and lower part of the body.

tigress *noun* a female tiger.

tile *noun* a thin piece of baked clay or other hard material, used in rows for covering roofs, walls, or floors. **tiled** *adjective*

till¹ *preposition* & *conjunction* until.

• USAGE: It is better to use *until* rather than *till* when the word stands first in a sentence (e.g. *Until last year we had never been abroad*) or when you are speaking or writing formally.

till² *noun* a drawer or box for money in a shop; a cash register.

till³ *verb* cultivate land.

tiller *noun* a handle used to turn a boat's rudder.

tilt[1] *verb* move into a sloping position.

tilt[2] *noun* a sloping position.
at full tilt at full speed or force.

tilth *noun* the condition of tilled soil, *Make a fine tilth before planting seeds.*

timber *noun* 1 wood for building or making things. 2 a wooden beam.

timbered *adjective* made of wood or with a wooden framework, *timbered houses.*

timbre (*say* tambr) *noun* the quality of a voice or musical sound.

time[1] *noun* 1 all the years of the past, present, and future; the continuous existence of the universe. 2 a particular point or portion of time, *What time is it?* 3 an occasion, *the first time I saw him.* 4 a period suitable or available for something, *Is there time for a cup of tea?* 5 a system of measuring time, *Greenwich Mean Time.* 6 (in music) rhythm depending on the number and accentuation of beats in the bar. 7 (in mathematics) **times** multiplied by, *Five times three is 15* ($5 \times 3 = 15$).
in time not late; eventually.
on time punctual.

time[2] *verb* (**timed, timing**) 1 measure how long something takes. 2 arrange when something is to happen, *The match is timed for 3.30.* **timer** *noun*

timeless *adjective* not affected by the passage of time; eternal.

time-limit *noun* a fixed amount of time within which something must be done.

timely *adjective* happening at a suitable or useful time, *a timely warning.*

timetable *noun* a list showing the times when things will happen, e.g. when buses or trains will arrive and depart, or when school lessons will take place.

timid *adjective* easily frightened. **timidly** *adverb,* **timidity** *noun*

timing *noun* the way something is timed.

timorous *adjective* timid.

timpani *plural noun* kettledrums.

tin[1] *noun* 1 a silvery-white metal. 2 a metal container for food.

tin[2] *verb* (**tinned, tinning**) seal food in a tin to preserve it.

tincture *noun* 1 a solution of medicine in alcohol. 2 a slight trace of something.

tinder *noun* any dry substance that catches fire easily.

tine *noun* a point or prong of a fork, harrow, or antler.

tinge *verb* (**tinged, tingeing**) colour something slightly; tint. **tinge** *noun*

tingle *verb* (**tingled, tingling**) have a slight pricking or stinging feeling. **tingle** *noun*

tinker[1] *noun* (*old use*) a person travelling about to mend pots and pans etc.

tinker[2] *verb* work at something casually, trying to improve or mend it.

tinkle *verb* (**tinkled, tinkling**) make a gentle ringing sound. **tinkle** *noun*

tinny *adjective* of tin; like tin.

tinsel *noun* strips of glittering material used for decoration.

tint[1] *noun* a shade of colour, especially a pale one.

tint[2] *verb* colour something slightly.

tiny *adjective* (**tinier, tiniest**) very small.

tip[1] *noun* the part right at the top or end of something.

tip[2] *verb* (**tipped, tipping**) put a tip on something.

tip[3] *noun* 1 a small present of money given to someone who has helped you. 2 a small but useful piece of advice; a hint, *useful tips on saving water.* 3 a slight push.

tip[4] *verb* (**tipped, tipping**) 1 give a person a tip. 2 name as a likely winner, *Which team would you tip to win the championship?* **tipper** *noun*

tip[5] *verb* (**tipped, tipping**) 1 tilt; topple. 2 empty rubbish somewhere.

tip[6] *noun* 1 the action of tipping something. 2 a place where rubbish etc. is tipped.

tipple *verb* (**tippled, tippling**) drink alcohol. **tipple** *noun,* **tippler** *noun*

tipsy *adjective* drunk.

tiptoe *verb* (**tiptoed, tiptoeing**) walk on your toes very quietly or carefully.
on tiptoe walking or standing on your toes.

tiptop *adjective* (*informal*) excellent; very best, *in tiptop condition.*

tirade (*say* ty-**rayd**) *noun* a long angry or violent speech.

tire *verb* (**tired, tiring**) make or become tired.

tired *adjective* feeling that you need to sleep or rest.
tired of having had enough of something and impatient or bored with it.

tiresome *adjective* annoying.

tissue *noun* 1 tissue-paper. 2 a paper handkerchief. 3 a group of cells in a plant or animal that are similar to one another and have a similar function, *bone-tissue*.

tissue-paper *noun* very thin soft paper used for wrapping and packing things.

tit¹ *noun* a kind of small bird.

tit² *noun* **tit for tat** something equal given in return; retaliation.

titanic (*say* ty-**tan**-ik) *adjective* huge.

titbit *noun* a nice little piece of something, e.g. of food, gossip, or information.

tithe *noun* one-tenth of a year's output from a farm etc., formerly paid as tax to support the clergy and church.

titillate *verb* (**titillated, titillating**) stimulate something pleasantly. **titillation** *noun*

titivate *verb* (**titivated, titivating**) put the finishing touches to something; smarten up. **titivation** *noun*

title *noun* 1 the name of a book, film, song, etc. 2 a word used to show a person's rank or position, e.g. *Dr, Lord, Mrs*. 3 a championship in sport, *the world heavyweight title*. 4 a legal right to something.

titled *adjective* having a title as a noble.

titter *verb* & *noun* giggle.

TNT *abbreviation* trinitrotoluene, a powerful explosive.

to¹ *preposition* This word is used to show 1 direction or arrival at a position, *We walked to school. She rose to power.* 2 limit, *from noon to two o'clock.* 3 comparison, *We won by six goals to three.* 4 receiving or being affected by something, *Give it to me. Be kind to animals.*

to² used before a verb to form an infinitive, *I want to see him* or to show purpose etc.,

He does that to annoy us or alone when the verb is understood, *We meant to go but forgot to.*

to³ *adverb* 1 to or in the proper or closed position or condition, *Push the door to.* 2 into a state of activity, *We set to and cleaned the kitchen.*
to and fro backwards and forwards.

toad *noun* a frog-like animal that lives chiefly on land.

toadstool *noun* a fungus (usually poisonous) with a round top on a stalk.

toady *verb* (**toadied, toadying**) flatter someone so as to make them want to like or help you. **toady** *noun*

toast¹ *verb* 1 heat bread etc. to make it brown and crisp. 2 warm something in front of a fire etc. 3 drink in honour of someone.

toast² *noun* 1 toasted bread. 2 the call to drink in honour of someone; the person honoured in this way, *The team was the toast of the whole country.*

toaster *noun* an electrical device for toasting bread.

tobacco *noun* the dried leaves of certain plants prepared for smoking or making snuff.

tobacconist *noun* a shopkeeper who sells cigarettes, cigars, etc.

toboggan *noun* a small sledge used for sliding downhill. **tobogganing** *noun*

today¹ *noun* this present day, *Today is Monday.*

today² *adverb* on this day, *Have you seen him today?*

toddler *noun* a young child who has only recently learnt to walk. **toddle** *verb*

toddy *noun* a sweetened drink made with spirits and hot water.

to-do *noun* a fuss; a commotion.

toe *noun* 1 any of the separate parts (five in humans) at the end of each foot. 2 the part of a shoe or sock etc. that covers the toes.

toffee *noun* a sticky sweet made from heated butter and sugar.

toga (*say* **toh**-ga) *noun* a long loose garment worn by people in ancient Rome.

together *adverb* with another person or

thing; with each other, *They went to the party together.*

toggle *noun* a short piece of wood or metal etc. used like a button.

toil[1] *verb* **1** work hard. **2** move slowly and with difficulty, *The old man toiled up the hill.* **toiler** *noun*

toil[2] *noun* hard work.

toilet *noun* **1** a lavatory. **2** the process of washing, dressing, and tidying yourself.

toilet-paper *noun* paper for use in a lavatory.

token *noun* **1** a piece of metal or plastic bought for use instead of money, *milk tokens.* **2** a voucher or coupon that can be exchanged for goods. **3** a sign or signal of something, *a token of our friendship.*

tokoloshe (*say* to-ko-**lo**-shee) *noun* a troublesome and often evil spirit in African myth.

toktokkie *noun* **1** a large black beetle which makes a knocking sound. **2** a children's game of knocking on doors and running away.

tolerable *adjective* able to be tolerated. **tolerably** *adverb*

tolerant *adjective* tolerating things, especially other people's behaviour, beliefs, etc. **tolerantly** *adverb*, **tolerance** *noun*

tolerate *verb* (**tolerated, tolerating**) allow something without protesting or interfering. **toleration** *noun*

toll[1] (rhymes with *hole*) *noun* **1** a charge made for using a road, bridge, etc. **2** loss or damage caused, *The death toll in the earthquake is rising.*

toll[2] (rhymes with *hole*) *verb* ring a bell slowly. **toll** *noun*

tom *noun* a male cat. **tomcat** *noun*

tomahawk *noun* a small axe used by American Indians.

tomato *noun* (*plural* **tomatoes**) a soft round red or yellow fruit eaten as a vegetable.

tomb (*say* toom) *noun* a place where someone is buried; a monument built over this.

tombola *noun* a kind of lottery.

tomboy *noun* a girl who enjoys rough noisy games etc.

tombstone *noun* a memorial stone set up over a grave.

tome *noun* a large heavy book.

tommy-gun *noun* a small machine-gun.

tomorrow *noun* & *adverb* the day after today.

tom-tom *noun* a drum with a low sound; a small drum beaten with the hands.

ton *noun* **1** a unit of weight in the imperial system equal to 2 240 pounds or about 1 016 kilograms. **2** a large amount, *There's tons of room.* **metric ton** 1 000 kilograms.

tone[1] *noun* **1** a sound in music or of the voice. **2** each of the five larger intervals between notes in a musical scale (the smaller intervals are *semitones*). **3** a shade of a colour. **4** the quality or character of something, *a cheerful tone.* **tonal** *adjective*, **tonally** *adverb*

tone[2] *verb* (**toned, toning**) give a particular tone of sound or colour to something. **tone down** make a thing quieter or less bright or less harsh. **tone in** harmonize in colour, *Her new shoes tone in well with her dress.* **tone up** make a thing brighter or stronger.

tongs *plural noun* a tool with two arms joined at one end, used to pick up or hold things.

tongue *noun* **1** the long soft muscular part that moves about inside the mouth. **2** a language, *an African tongue.* **3** a projecting strip or flap. **4** a pointed flame.

tongue-tied *adjective* too shy to speak.

tongue-twister *noun* something that is difficult to say quickly and correctly, e.g. 'She sells sea shells'.

tonic *noun* **1** a medicine etc. that makes a person healthier or stronger. **2** a keynote in music. **tonic** *adjective*

tonight *noun* & *adverb* this evening or night.

tonnage *noun* the amount a ship or ships can carry, expressed in tons.

tonne *noun* a metric ton (1 000 kilograms).

tonsil *noun* either of two small masses of soft tissue at the sides of the throat.

tonsillitis *noun* inflammation of the tonsils.

too *adverb* 1 also, *Take the others too.* 2 more than is wanted or allowed etc., *That's too much sugar for me.*

● USAGE: It is incorrect to say *I like chocolate too much.* The correct form is *I like chocolate very much.*

tool *noun* an object that helps you to do a particular job, *A saw is a tool for cutting wood or metal.*

toot *noun* a short sound produced by a horn. **toot** *verb*

tooth *noun* (*plural* **teeth**) 1 any of the hard white bony parts that are rooted in the gums, used for biting and chewing things. 2 each of a row of sharp parts or projections, *the teeth of a saw.* **toothache** *noun*, **toothbrush** *noun*, **toothed** *adjective*

fight tooth and nail fight very fiercely.

toothpaste *noun* a paste for cleaning your teeth.

toothpick *noun* a small pointed piece of wood etc. for removing bits of food from between your teeth.

toothy *adjective* having large teeth.

top[1] *noun* 1 the highest part of something. 2 the upper surface. 3 the covering or stopper of a bottle, jar, etc. 4 a garment for the upper part of the body.

on top of in addition to something.

top[2] *adjective* highest, *at top speed.*

top hat a man's tall stiff black or grey hat worn with formal clothes.

top[3] *verb* (**topped, topping**) 1 put a top on something. 2 be at the top of something, *She tops the list.* 3 remove the top of something, *top and tail the beans.*

top up fill up something that is half empty.

top[4] *noun* a toy that can be made to spin on its point.

topaz *noun* a kind of gem, often yellow.

top-dress *verb* apply fertilizer on the top of the soil instead of ploughing it in. **top-dressing** *noun*

top-heavy *adjective* too heavy at the top and likely to overbalance.

topic *noun* a subject to write, learn, or talk about.

topical *adjective* connected with things that are happening now, *a topical film.* **topically** *adverb*, **topicality** *noun*

topless *adjective* not wearing any clothes on the top half of the body.

topmost *adjective* highest.

topography (*say* top-**og**-ra-fee) *noun* the position of the rivers, mountains, roads, buildings, etc. in a place. **topographical** *adjective*

topple *verb* (**toppled, toppling**) 1 fall over; totter and fall. 2 cause to fall; overthrow, *The rebellion toppled the military regime.*

topsoil *noun* the top layer of soil which has important nutrients in it that help plants to grow.

topsy-turvy *adverb* & *adjective* upside-down; muddled.

torch *noun* (*plural* **torches**) 1 a small electric lamp for carrying in the hand. 2 a stick with burning material on the end, used as a light.

toreador (*say* **t**orree-a-dor) *noun* a bull-fighter.

torment[1] *verb* 1 cause a person to suffer greatly. 2 tease; keep annoying someone. **tormentor** *noun*

torment[2] *noun* great suffering.

tornado (*say* tor-**nay**-doh) *noun* (*plural* **tornadoes**) a violent storm or whirlwind.

torpedo[1] *noun* (*plural* **torpedoes**) a long tubular missile that can be sent under water to destroy ships.

torpedo[2] *verb* (**torpedoed, torpedoing**) attack or destroy with a torpedo.

torpid *adjective* slow-moving, not lively. **torpidly** *adverb*, **torpidity** *noun*, **torpor** *noun*

torrent *noun* 1 a rushing stream; a great flow. 2 a great downpour. **torrential** *adjective*

torrid *adjective* very hot and dry.

torsion *noun* twisting, especially of one end of a thing while the other is held in a fixed position.

torso *noun* (*plural* **torsos**) the trunk of the human body.

tortoise *noun* a slow-moving animal with a shell over its body.

tortoiseshell (*say* tort-a-shell) *noun*
1 the mottled brown and yellow shell of certain turtles, used for making combs etc.
2 a cat or butterfly with mottled brown colouring.

tortuous *adjective* full of twists and turns. **tortuosity** *noun*

torture *verb* (**tortured, torturing**) make a person feel great pain or worry. **torture** *noun*, **torturer** *noun*

toss *verb* 1 throw, especially up into the air. 2 spin a coin to decide something according to which side of it is upwards after it falls. 3 move restlessly or unevenly from side to side. **toss** *noun*

toss-up *noun* 1 the tossing of a coin.
2 an even chance.

tot[1] *noun* 1 a small child. 2 a small amount of spirits, *a tot of rum.*

tot[2] *verb* (**totted, totting**) **tot up** (*informal*) add up.

total[1] *adjective* 1 including everything, *the total amount.* 2 complete, *total darkness.* **totally** *adverb*

total[2] *noun* the amount you get by adding everything together.

total[3] *verb* (**totalled, totalling**) 1 reckon up the total. 2 amount to something, *debts totalling R3 million.*

totalitarian *adjective* using a form of government where people are not allowed to form rival political parties.

totality *noun* 1 being total. 2 a total.

totem-pole *noun* a pole carved or painted by American Indians with the emblems (*totems*) of their tribes or families.

totter *verb* walk unsteadily; wobble. **tottery** *adjective*

toucan (*say* too-kan) *noun* a tropical American bird with a huge beak.

touch[1] *verb* 1 put your hand or fingers etc. on something lightly. 2 be or come together so that there is no space between. 3 hit gently. 4 move or meddle with something, *Don't touch those papers!* 5 reach, *The thermometer touched 30° Celsius.* 6 arouse sympathy etc. in someone, *The sad story touched our hearts.* 7 (*slang*) persuade someone to give

or lend money.

touch and go an uncertain situation.

touch down (of an aircraft) land; (in rugby) touch the ball on the ground behind the goal-line.

touch up improve something by making small additions or changes.

touch[2] *noun* (*plural* **touches**) 1 the action of touching. 2 the ability to feel things by touching them. 3 a small amount; a small thing done, *the finishing touches.*
4 a special skill or style of workmanship, *She hasn't lost her touch.* 5 communication with someone, *We lost touch with him.*
6 the part of a football field outside the playing area.

touchable *adjective* able to be touched.

touchdown *noun* the action of touching down.

touching *adjective* arousing kindly feelings such as pity or sympathy.

touchstone *noun* a test by which the quality of something is judged.

touchy *adjective* (**touchier, touchiest**) easily offended. **touchily** *adverb*, **touchiness** *noun*

tough *adjective* 1 strong; difficult to break or damage. 2 difficult to chew. 3 firm; stubborn; rough or violent, *tough criminals.* 4 difficult, *a tough job.* **toughly** *adverb*, **toughness** *noun*

toughen *verb* make or become tough.

tour[1] *noun* 1 a journey visiting several places. 2 a series of matches, performances, etc. in different places, *next year's netball tour to the Eastern Cape.*

tour[2] *verb* make a tour.

tourist *noun* a person who makes a tour or visits a place for pleasure. **tourism** *noun*

tournament *noun* a series of contests.

tourniquet (*say* toor-nik-ay) *noun* a strip of material etc. pulled tightly round an arm or leg to stop bleeding from an artery.

tousle *verb* (**tousled, tousling**) ruffle someone's hair.

tout[1] (rhymes with *scout*) *verb* try to obtain orders for goods or services etc.

tout[2] *noun* a person who touts things, *ticket touts.*

tow[1] (rhymes with *go*) *verb* pull something along behind you. **tow** *noun*

tow[2] (rhymes with *go*) *noun* short light-coloured fibres of flax or hemp.

toward *preposition* towards.

towards *preposition* **1** in the direction of, *She walked towards the sea.* **2** in relation to; regarding, *He behaved kindly towards his children.* **3** as a contribution to, *Put the money towards a new bicycle.* **4** near, *towards four o'clock.*

towel *noun* a piece of absorbent cloth for drying things. **towelling** *noun*

tower[1] *noun* a tall narrow building.

tower[2] *verb* be very high; be taller than others, *Skyscrapers towered over the city.*

town *noun* a place with many houses, shops, offices, and other buildings.

town hall a building with offices for the local council and usually a hall for public events.

township *noun* **1** an urban area which was set aside for African people under apartheid. **2** an urban area which is new or going to be developed.

tow-path *noun* a path beside a canal or river, originally for use when a horse was towing a barge etc.

toxic *adjective* poisonous; caused by poison. **toxicity** *noun*

toxicology *noun* the study of poisons. **toxicologist** *noun*

toxin *noun* a poisonous substance, especially one formed in the body by germs.

toy[1] *noun* a thing to play with.

toy[2] *adjective* **1** made as a toy. **2** (of a dog) of a very small breed kept as a pet, *a toy poodle.*

toy[3] *verb* **toy with** handle a thing or consider an idea casually.

toyi-toyi *verb* (**toyi-toyied, toyi-toying**) dance defiantly and even aggressively, usually during political demonstrations. **toyi-toyi** *noun*

toyshop *noun* a shop that sells toys.

trace[1] *noun* **1** a mark left by a person or thing; a sign, *There was no trace of the thief.* **2** a very small amount.

trace[2] *verb* (**traced, tracing**) **1** copy a picture or map etc. by drawing over it on transparent paper. **2** follow the traces of a person or thing; find. **tracer** *noun*

trace[3] *noun* each of the two straps or ropes etc. by which a horse pulls a cart. **kick over the traces** (of a person) become disobedient or reckless.

traceable *adjective* able to be traced.

tracery *noun* a decorative pattern of holes in stone, e.g. in a church window.

trachea (*say* tra-**kee**-a) *noun* (*plural* **tracheae** or **tracheas**) the windpipe.

track[1] *noun* **1** a mark or marks left by a moving person or thing. **2** a rough path made by being used. **3** a road or area of ground specially prepared for something (e.g. racing). **4** a set of rails for trains or trams etc. **5** a section of a CD or along the length of a magnetic tape etc. **6** a continuous band round the wheels of a tank or tractor etc.

keep track of keep yourself informed about where something is or what someone is doing.

track suit a warm loose suit of the kind worn by athletes etc. before and after contests or for jogging.

track[2] *verb* **1** follow the tracks left by a person or animal. **2** follow or observe something as it moves. **tracker** *noun* **track down** find by searching.

tract[1] *noun* **1** an area of land. **2** a series of connected parts along which something passes, *the digestive tract.*

tract[2] *noun* a pamphlet containing a short essay, especially about religion.

traction *noun* pulling a load.

traction-engine *noun* a steam or diesel engine for pulling a heavy load along a road or across a field etc.

tractor *noun* a motor vehicle for pulling farm machinery or other heavy loads.

trade[1] *noun* **1** buying, selling, or exchanging goods. **2** business of a particular kind; the people working in this. **3** an occupation, especially a skilled craft.

trade mark a firm's registered emblem or name used to distinguish its goods etc. from those of other firms.

trade union (*plural* **trade unions**) a group

of workers organized to help and protect workers in their own trade.

trade² *verb* (**traded**, **trading**) buy, sell, or exchange things. **trader** *noun*
trade in give a thing as part of the payment for something new, *He traded in his motor cycle for a car.*

tradesman *noun* (*plural* **tradesmen**) a person employed in trade, especially one who sells or delivers goods. **tradespeople** *plural noun*, **tradeswoman** *noun* (*plural* **tradeswomen**)

tradition *noun* 1 the passing down of beliefs or customs etc. from one generation to another. 2 something passed on in this way. **traditional** *adjective*, **traditionally** *adverb*
traditional leader a king, chief, etc. who is the leader of an indigenous people (often an inherited position).
traditional weapon a weapon which has a cultural significance for a group of people, e.g. the assegai for the Zulus.

traffic¹ *noun* 1 vehicles, ships, or aircraft moving along a route. 2 trading, especially when it is illegal or wrong, *drug traffic.*
traffic warden an official who assists police to control the movement and parking of vehicles.

traffic² *verb* (**trafficked**, **trafficking**) trade. **trafficker** *noun*

traffic light (also **traffic lights**) *noun* an automatic signal controlling road traffic especially at junctions by coloured lights.

tragedian (*say* tra-**jee**-dee-an) *noun* 1 a person who writes tragedies. 2 an actor in tragedies.

tragedy *noun* (*plural* **tragedies**) 1 a play with unhappy events or a sad ending. 2 a very sad event.

tragic *adjective* 1 very sad; causing sadness. 2 of tragedies, *a great tragic actor.* **tragically** *adverb*

trail¹ *noun* 1 a track, scent, or other sign left where something has passed. 2 a path or track made through a wild region.

trail² *verb* 1 follow the trail of something; track. 2 drag or be dragged along behind;

lag behind. 3 hang down or float loosely.

trailer *noun* 1 a truck or other container pulled along by a vehicle. 2 a short piece from a film or television programme, shown in advance to advertise it.

train¹ *noun* 1 a railway engine pulling a line of carriages or trucks that are linked together. 2 a number of people or animals moving in a line, *a camel train.* 3 a series of things, *a train of events.* 4 part of a long dress or robe that trails on the ground at the back.

train² *verb* 1 give a person instruction or practice so that he or she becomes skilled. 2 practise, *She was training for the race.* 3 make something grow in a particular direction. 4 aim a gun etc., *Train that gun on the bridge.*

trainee *noun* a person being trained.

trainer *noun* 1 a person who trains people or animals. 2 a soft rubber-soled shoe of the kind worn for running or by athletes etc. while exercising.

traipse *verb* (**traipsed**, **traipsing**) trudge.

trait (*say as* tray) *noun* a characteristic, *personality traits.*

traitor *noun* a person who betrays his or her country or friends. **traitorous** *adjective*

trajectory *noun* (*plural* **trajectories**) the path taken by a moving object such as a bullet or rocket.

tram *noun* a public passenger vehicle running on rails in the road.

tramlines *plural noun* 1 rails for a tram. 2 the pair of parallel lines at the side of a tennis court.

tramp¹ *noun* 1 a person without a home or job who walks from place to place. 2 a long walk, *have a tramp across the veld.* 3 the sound of heavy footsteps.

tramp² *verb* 1 walk with heavy footsteps. 2 walk for a long distance.

trample *verb* (**trampled**, **trampling**) tread heavily on something; crush something by treading on it.

trampoline *noun* a large piece of canvas joined to a frame by springs, used for jumping on in acrobatics.

trance *noun* a dreamy or unconscious condition rather like sleep.

tranquil *adjective* calm and quiet.
tranquilly *adverb*, **tranquillity** *noun*

tranquillizer *noun* a medicine used
to make a person feel calm.

trans- *prefix* across; through; beyond.

transact *verb* carry out business.
transaction *noun*

transatlantic *adjective* across or on the
other side of the Atlantic Ocean.

transcend *verb* go beyond something;
surpass.

transcribe *verb* (**transcribed, transcrib-
ing**) copy or write something out.
transcription *noun*

transcript *noun* a written copy.

transept *noun* the part that is at right
angles to the nave in a cross-shaped
church.

transfer[1] *verb* (**transferred, transferring**)
1 move a person or thing to another place.
2 hand over, *transfer ownership of the
house*. **transferable** *adjective*, **transfer-
ence** *noun*

transfer[2] *noun* 1 the transferring of a
person or thing. 2 a picture or design that
can be transferred on to another surface.

transfigure *verb* (**transfigured, transfig-
uring**) change the appearance of something greatly. **transfiguration** *noun*

transfix *verb* 1 pierce and fix with something pointed. 2 make a person or animal
unable to move because of fear or surprise
etc.

transform *verb* change the form or
appearance or character of a person or
thing. **transformation** *noun*

transformer *noun* a device used to
change the voltage of an electric current.

transfusion *noun* putting blood taken
from one person into another person's
body. **transfuse** *verb*

transgress *verb* break a rule or law etc.
transgression *noun*

transient *adjective* passing away quickly;
not lasting. **transience** *noun*

transistor *noun* 1 a tiny semiconductor
device controlling a flow of electricity.
2 (also **transistor radio**) a radio receiver
using transistors. **transistorized**
adjective

transit *noun* the process of travelling
across or through, *goods in transit*.

transition *noun* the process of changing
from one condition or style etc. to
another. **transitional** *adjective*

transitive *adjective* (of a verb) used with a
direct object after it, e.g. *change* in *change
your shoes* (but not in *change into dry
shoes*). Compare *intransitive*. **transitively**
adverb

transitory *adjective* existing for a time
but not lasting.

translate *verb* (**translated, translating**)
put something into another language.
translatable *adjective*, **translation** *noun*,
translator *noun*

transliterate *verb* (**transliterated,
transliterating**) put letters or words into
letters of a different alphabet. **translitera-
tion** *noun*

translucent (*say* tranz-**loo**-sent) *adjective*
allowing light to shine through but not
transparent.

transmigration *noun* 1 migration.
2 the passing of a person's soul into
another body after his or her death.

transmission *noun* 1 transmitting something. 2 a broadcast, *a direct transmission
from Parliament*. 3 the gears by which
power is transmitted from the engine to
the wheels of a vehicle.

transmit *verb* (**transmitted, transmitting**)
1 send or pass on from one person or
place to another. 2 send out a signal or
broadcast etc. **transmitter** *noun*

transmutation *noun* the process of
changing or being changed from one form
or substance into another.

transom *noun* 1 a horizontal bar of wood
or stone dividing a window or separating
a door from a window above it. 2 a small
window above a door.

transparency *noun* (*plural* **transparen-
cies**) 1 being transparent. 2 a transparent
photograph that can be projected on to a
screen.

transparent *adjective* able to be seen
through.

transpire *verb* (**transpired, transpiring**)
1 (of information) become known; leak

out. **2** (of plants) give off watery vapour from leaves etc. **transpiration** *noun*

transplant[1] *verb* **1** remove a plant and put it to grow somewhere else. **2** transfer a part of the body to another person or animal, *a heart transplant.* **transplantation** *noun*

transplant[2] *noun* **1** the process of transplanting. **2** something transplanted.

transport[1] *verb* take a person, animal, or thing from one place to another. **transportation** *noun*, **transporter** *noun*

transport[2] *noun* the action or means of transporting people, animals, or things.

transpose *verb* (**transposed, transposing**) **1** change the position or order of something. **2** put a piece of music into a different key. **transposition** *noun*

transverse *adjective* lying across something. **transversely** *adverb*

trap[1] *noun* **1** a device for catching and holding animals. **2** an arrangement for capturing, detecting, or cheating someone. **3** a device for collecting water etc. or preventing it from passing. **4** a two-wheeled carriage pulled by a horse.

trap[2] *verb* (**trapped, trapping**) catch or hold in a trap. **trapper** *noun*

trapdoor *noun* a door in a floor, ceiling, or roof.

trapeze *noun* a bar hanging from two ropes as a swing for acrobats.

trapezium *noun* a quadrilateral in which two opposite sides are parallel and the other two are not.

trapezoid *noun* a quadrilateral in which no sides are parallel.

trappings *plural noun* **1** ornamental accessories or equipment etc., e.g. for officials. **2** ornamental harness for a horse.

trash *noun* rubbish; nonsense. **trashy** *adjective*

trauma (*say* traw-ma) *noun* a shock that produces a lasting effect on a person's mind. **traumatic** *adjective*, **traumatize** *verb*

travail *noun* (*old use*) hard or laborious work. **travail** *verb*

travel *verb* (**travelled, travelling**) move from place to place. **travel** *noun*,

traveller *noun*

traverse *verb* (**traversed, traversing**) go across something. **traversal** *noun*

travesty *noun* (*plural* **travesties**) a bad or ridiculous form of something, *His story is a travesty of the truth.*

trawl *verb* fish by dragging a large net along the sea-bed.

trawler *noun* a boat used in trawling.

tray *noun* **1** a flat piece of wood, metal, or plastic, usually with raised edges, for carrying cups, plates, food, etc. **2** an open container for holding letters etc. in an office.

treacherous *adjective* **1** betraying someone; disloyal. **2** not to be trusted. **treacherously** *adverb*, **treachery** *noun*

treacle *noun* a thick sticky liquid produced when sugar is purified. **treacly** *adjective*

tread[1] *verb* (**trod, trodden, treading**) walk or put your foot on something.

tread[2] *noun* **1** a sound or way of walking. **2** the top surface of a stair; the part you put your foot on. **3** the part of a tyre that touches the ground.

treadle *noun* a lever that you press with your foot to turn a wheel that works a machine.

treadmill *noun* a wide mill-wheel turned by the weight of people or animals treading on steps fixed round its edge.

treason *noun* the action of betraying your country. **treasonable** *adjective*, **treasonous** *adjective*

treasure[1] *noun* **1** a store of precious metals or jewels. **2** a precious thing or person.
treasure trove gold or silver etc. found hidden and with no known owner.

treasure[2] *verb* (**treasured, treasuring**) value greatly something that you have.

treasurer *noun* a person in charge of the money of a club, society, etc.

treasure-hunt *noun* a game in which people try to find a hidden object.

treasury *noun* (*plural* **treasuries**) a place where money and valuables are kept.
the Treasury the government department in charge of a country's income.

treat¹ *verb* **1** behave in a certain way towards a person or thing. **2** deal with a subject etc., *The issue is treated at a later stage of the book.* **3** give medical care in order to cure a person or animal.
4 put something through a chemical or other process, *The fabric has been treated to make it waterproof.* **5** pay for someone else's food, drink, or entertainment, *I'll treat you to an ice-cream.*

treat² *noun* **1** something special that gives pleasure. **2** the process of treating someone to food, drink, or entertainment.

treatise *noun* a book or long essay on a subject.

treatment *noun* the process or manner of dealing with a person, animal, or thing.

treaty *noun* (*plural* **treaties**) a formal agreement between two or more countries.

treble¹ *adjective* three times as much or as many.

treble² *noun* **1** a treble amount.
2 a person with a high-pitched or soprano voice.

treble³ *verb* (**trebled, trebling**) make or become three times as much or as many.

tree *noun* a tall plant with a single very thick hard stem or trunk that is usually without branches for some distance above the ground.

trefoil *noun* a plant with three small leaves (e.g. clover).

trek¹ *noun* **1** a long hard walk or ride.
2 a long hard journey overland lasting several days or weeks.
trekboer (in former times) a farmer who did not settle in one place, but moved around with his animals to find new grazing.
trek fishing fishing with a trek net.
trek net a large fishing-net used from boats and from the shore, with floats along the top edge and weights at the base.

trek² *verb* (**trekked, trekking**) make a trek.

trellis *noun* (*plural* **trellises**) a framework with crossing bars of wood or metal etc. to support climbing plants.

tremble *verb* (**trembled, trembling**) shake gently, especially with fear. **tremble** *noun*

tremendous *adjective* **1** very large; huge. **2** (*informal*) excellent. **tremendously** *adverb*

tremor *noun* a shaking or trembling movement.

tremulous *adjective* trembling from nervousness or weakness. **tremulously** *adverb*

trench¹ *noun* (*plural* **trenches**) a long narrow hole cut in the ground.

trench² *verb* dig a trench or trenches.

trenchant *adjective* strong and effective, *trenchant criticism.*

trend *noun* the general direction in which something is going.

trendy *adjective* (**trendier, trendiest**) (*informal*) fashionable; following the latest trends. **trendily** *adverb*, **trendiness** *noun*

trepidation *noun* fear and anxiety; nervousness.

trespass¹ *verb* **1** go on someone's land or property unlawfully. **2** (*old use*) do wrong; sin. **trespasser** *noun*

trespass² *noun* (*plural* **trespasses**) (*old use*) wrongdoing; sin.

tress *noun* (*plural* **tresses**) a lock of hair.

trestle *noun* each of a set of supports on which a board is rested to form a table. **trestle-table** *noun*

tri- *prefix* three (as in *triangle*).

trial *noun* **1** testing a thing to see how good it is. **2** a test of qualities or ability.
3 the trying of a person in a lawcourt.
4 an annoying person or thing; a hardship. **on trial** being tried.

triangle *noun* **1** a flat shape with three sides and three angles. **2** a percussion instrument made from a metal rod bent into a triangle. **triangular** *adjective*

tribe *noun* **1** a group of families living in one area as a community, ruled by a chief.
2 a set of people. **tribal** *adjective*, **tribally** *adverb*, **tribesman** *noun*, **tribespeople** *plural noun*, **tribeswoman** *noun*

tribulation *noun* great troubles.

tribunal (*say* try-bew-nal) *noun* a committee appointed to hear evidence and give judgements when there is a dispute.

tribune *noun* an official chosen by the people in ancient Rome.

tributary *noun* (*plural* **tributaries**) a river or stream that flows into a larger one or into a lake.

tribute *noun* **1** something said, done, or given to show respect or admiration. **2** payment that one country or ruler was formerly obliged to pay to a more powerful one.

trice *noun* (*old use*) **in a trice** in a moment.

trick¹ *noun* **1** a crafty or deceitful action; a practical joke. **2** a skilful action, especially one done for entertainment. **3** one round of a card-game such as whist.

trick² *verb* **1** deceive or cheat someone by a trick. **2** decorate, *The building was tricked out with little flags.*

trickery *noun* the use of tricks.

trickle *verb* flow or move slowly. **trickle** *noun*

trickster *noun* a person who tricks or cheats people.

tricky *adjective* (**trickier**, **trickiest**) **1** difficult; needing skill, *a tricky job.* **2** cunning; deceitful. **trickiness** *noun*

tricolour (*say* **trik**-ol-er) *noun* a flag with three coloured stripes, e.g. the national flag of France or Ireland.

tricycle *noun* a vehicle like a bicycle but with three wheels.

trident *noun* a spear with three prongs for spearing fish, carried by the Roman god Neptune as a symbol of his power over the sea.

triennial (*say* try-**en**-ee-al) *adjective* happening every third year.

trier *noun* a person who tries hard.

trifle¹ *noun* **1** a pudding made of sponge-cake covered in custard, fruit, cream, etc. **2** a very small amount. **3** something that has very little importance or value, *a mere trifle.*

trifle² *verb* (**trifled**, **trifling**) behave frivolously; toy with something.

trifling *adjective* trivial.

trigger¹ *noun* a lever that is pulled to fire a gun.

trigger² *verb* **trigger off** start something happening.

trigonometry (*say* trig-on-**om**-it-ree)

noun the calculation of distances and angles by using triangles.

trilateral *adjective* **1** having three sides. **2** of three people or groups, *trilateral negotiations.*

trilby *noun* (*plural* **trilbies**) a man's soft felt hat.

trill *verb* make a quivering musical sound. **trill** *noun*

trillion *noun* **1** a million million million. **2** (*American*) a million million.

trilogy *noun* (*plural* **trilogies**) a group of three stories, poems, or plays etc. about the same people or things.

trim¹ *adjective* neat and orderly. **trimly** *adverb*, **trimness** *noun*

trim² *verb* (**trimmed**, **trimming**) **1** cut the edges or unwanted parts off something. **2** ornament a piece of clothing etc., *trim with lace.* **3** arrange sails to suit the wind. **4** balance a boat or aircraft evenly by arranging the people or cargo in it.

trim³ *noun* **1** condition, *in good trim.* **2** cutting or trimming, *Your beard needs a trim.* **3** ornamentation. **4** the balance of a boat or aircraft.

Trinity *noun* God regarded as three persons (Father, Son, and Holy Spirit).

trinket *noun* a small ornament or piece of jewellery.

trio *noun* (*plural* **trios**) **1** a group of three people or things. **2** a group of three musicians or singers. **3** a piece of music for three musicians.

trip¹ *verb* (**tripped**, **tripping**) **1** catch your foot on something and fall; cause a person to do this. **2** move with quick light steps. **3** operate a switch.
trip up stumble; make a slip or blunder; cause a person to do this.

trip² *noun* **1** a journey or excursion. **2** the action of tripping; a stumble.

tripartite *adjective* having three parts; involving three groups, *tripartite talks.*

tripe *noun* **1** part of an ox's stomach used as food. **2** (*slang*) nonsense.

triple¹ *adjective* **1** consisting of three parts. **2** involving three people or groups, *a triple alliance.* **3** three times as much or as many. **triply** *adverb*

triple² *verb* (**tripled, tripling**) treble.

triplet *noun* each of three children or animals born to the same mother at one time.

triplicate *noun* **in triplicate** as three identical copies.

tripod (*say* **try**-pod) *noun* a stand with three legs, e.g. to support a camera.

tripper *noun* a person who is making a pleasure-trip.

trireme (*say* **try**-reem) *noun* an ancient warship with three banks of oars.

trisect *verb* divide into three equal parts. **trisection** *noun*

trite (rhymes with *kite*) *adjective* commonplace; hackneyed, *a few trite remarks.*

triumph¹ *noun* **1** a great success or victory; a feeling of joy at this. **2** a celebration of a victory. **triumphal** *adjective*, **triumphant** *adjective*, **triumphantly** *adverb*

triumph² *verb* **1** be successful or victorious. **2** rejoice in success or victory.

triumvirate *noun* a ruling group of three people.

trivet *noun* an iron stand for a pot or kettle etc., placed over a fire.

trivia *plural noun* unusual, often unimportant, facts about something.

trivial *adjective* of only small value or importance. **trivially** *adverb*, **triviality** *noun*

troglodyte *noun* a person living in a cave in ancient times.

troika *noun* a group of three people working together, e.g. as political leaders of a country.

troll (rhymes with *hole*) *noun* (in Scandinavian mythology) a supernatural being, either a giant or a friendly but mischievous dwarf.

trolley *noun* (*plural* **trolleys**) **1** a small table on wheels or castors. **2** a small cart or truck.

trombone *noun* a large brass musical instrument with a sliding tube.

troop¹ *noun* **1** an organized group of soldiers, Scouts, etc. **2** a number of people moving along together.

troops *plural noun* armed forces.

troop² *verb* move along as a group or in large numbers, *They all trooped in.*

trooper *noun* a soldier in the cavalry or in an armoured unit.

trophy *noun* (*plural* **trophies**) a prize or souvenir for a victory or other success.

tropic *noun* a line of latitude about $23^1/_2°$ north of the equator (**tropic of Cancer**) or $23^1/_2°$ south of the equator (**tropic of Capricorn**). **tropical** *adjective*
the tropics the region between these two latitudes.

troposphere *noun* the layer of the atmosphere extending about 10 kilometres upwards from the earth's surface.

trot¹ *verb* (**trotted, trotting**) **1** (of a horse) run, going faster than when walking but more slowly than when cantering. **2** (*informal*) go, *Trot round to the chemist.*
trot out (*informal*) produce, *He trotted out the usual excuses.*

trot² *noun* a trotting run.
on the trot (*informal*) one after the other without a break, *She worked for ten days on the trot.*

troth (rhymes with *both*) *noun* (*old use*) loyalty; a solemn promise.

trotter *noun* an animal's foot as food, *pigs' trotters.*

troubadour (*say* **troo**-bad-oor) *noun* a poet and singer in southern France in the 11th–13th centuries.

trouble¹ *noun* **1** difficulty, inconvenience, or distress. **2** a cause of any of these.
take trouble take great care in doing something.

trouble² *verb* (**troubled, troubling**) **1** cause trouble to someone. **2** give yourself trouble or inconvenience etc., *Don't trouble to reply.*

troublesome *adjective* causing trouble or annoyance.

trough (*say* trof) *noun* **1** a long narrow open container, especially one holding water or food for animals. **2** a channel for liquid. **3** the low part between two waves or ridges. **4** a long region of low air-pressure.

trounce *verb* (**trounced, trouncing**)

1 thrash. 2 defeat someone heavily.

troupe (*say as* troop) *noun* a company of actors or other performers.

trousers *plural noun* a garment worn over the lower half of the body, with a separate part for each leg.

trousseau (*say* troo-soh) *noun* a bride's collection of clothing etc. to begin married life.

trout *noun* (*plural* **trout**) a freshwater fish that is caught as a sport and for food.

trowel *noun* 1 a small garden tool with a curved blade for lifting plants or scooping things. 2 a small tool with a flat blade for spreading mortar etc.

troy weight *noun* a system of weights used for precious metals and gems.

truant *noun* a child who stays away from school without permission. **truancy** *noun* **play truant** be a truant.

truce *noun* an agreement to stop fighting for a while.

truck[1] *noun* 1 a lorry. 2 an open container on wheels for transporting loads; an open railway-wagon. 3 a cart.

truck[2] *noun* dealings, *I'll have no truck with fortune-tellers!*

truculent (*say* truk-yoo-lent) *adjective* defiant and aggressive. **truculently** *adverb*, **truculence** *noun*

trudge *verb* (**trudged**, **trudging**) walk slowly and heavily.

true *adjective* (**truer**, **truest**) 1 representing what has happened or exists, *a true story*. 2 genuine, not false, *He was the true heir*. 3 accurate, *Her aim was true*. 4 loyal; faithful, *Be true to your friends*. **trueness** *noun*

truffle *noun* 1 a soft sweet made with chocolate. 2 a fungus that grows underground and is valued as food because of its rich flavour.

truism *noun* a statement that is obviously true, especially one that is hackneyed, e.g. 'Nothing lasts for ever'.

truly *adverb* 1 truthfully. 2 sincerely; genuinely, *We are truly grateful*. 3 accurately. 4 loyally; faithfully.

Yours truly see *yours*.

trump[1] *noun* a playing-card of a suit that

ranks above the others for one game.

trump[2] *verb* defeat a card by playing a trump.

trump up invent an excuse or an accusation etc.

trumpery *adjective* showy but worthless, *trumpery ornaments*.

trumpet[1] *noun* 1 a metal wind instrument with a narrow tube that widens near the end. 2 something shaped like this.

trumpet[2] *verb* (**trumpeted**, **trumpeting**) 1 blow a trumpet. 2 (of an elephant) make a loud sound with its trunk. 3 shout or announce something loudly. **trumpeter** *noun*

truncate *verb* (**truncated**, **truncating**) shorten something by cutting off its top or end. **truncation** *noun*

truncheon *noun* a short thick stick carried as a weapon, especially by police.

trundle *verb* (**trundled**, **trundling**) roll along heavily, *A bus trundled up. He was trundling a wheelbarrow.*

trunk *noun* 1 the main stem of a tree. 2 an elephant's long flexible nose. 3 a large box with a hinged lid for transporting or storing clothes etc. 4 the human body except for the head, arms, and legs.

trunks *plural noun* shorts worn by men and boys for swimming, boxing, etc.

trunk-road *noun* an important main road.

truss[1] *noun* (*plural* **trusses**) 1 a framework of beams or bars supporting a roof or bridge etc. 2 a bundle of hay etc.

truss[2] *verb* 1 tie up a person or thing securely. 2 support a roof or bridge etc. with trusses.

trust[1] *verb* 1 believe that a person or thing is good, truthful, or strong. 2 entrust. 3 hope, *I trust that you are well.* **trust to** rely on, *trusting to luck.*

trust[2] *noun* 1 the belief that a person or thing can be trusted. 2 responsibility; being trusted, *Being a prefect is a position of trust*. 3 money legally entrusted to a person with instructions about how to use it. **trustful** *adjective*, **trustfully** *adverb*, **trustworthy** *adjective*

trustee *noun* a person who looks after

money entrusted to him or her.

trusty *adjective* (*old use*) trustworthy; reliable, *my trusty sword.*

truth *noun* 1 something that is true. 2 the quality of being true, *How much truth is there in that story?*

truthful *adjective* 1 telling the truth, *a truthful boy.* 2 true, *a truthful account of what happened.* **truthfully** *adverb,* **truthfulness** *noun*

try[1] *verb* (**tried, trying**) 1 attempt. 2 test something by using or doing it, *Try sleeping on your back.* 3 examine the accusations against someone in a lawcourt. 4 be a strain on, *Very small print tries your eyes.*

try on put on clothes etc. to see if they fit.

try[2] *noun* (*plural* **tries**) 1 an attempt. 2 (in rugby) putting the ball down behind the opponents' goal-line so as to score points.

trying *adjective* putting a strain on someone's patience; annoying.

tsar (*say* zar) *noun* the title of the former ruler of Russia.

tsessebe *noun* (*plural* **tsessebe**) a reddish antelope similar to a hartebeest.

tsetse (*say* tet-see) *noun* a tropical fly that can transmit sleeping sickness to people whom it bites.

T-shirt *noun* a short-sleeved shirt shaped like a T.

tsotsi *noun* a young and violent criminal, often dressed in a flashy way.

tub *noun* a round open container holding liquid, ice-cream, soil for plants, etc.

tuba (*say* tew-ba) *noun* a large brass wind instrument with a deep tone.

tubby *adjective* (**tubbier, tubbiest**) short and fat. **tubbiness** *noun*

tube *noun* 1 a long hollow piece of metal, plastic, rubber, glass, etc., especially for liquids or air etc. to pass along. 2 a container made of flexible material with a screw-cap, *a tube of toothpaste.* 3 the underground railway in London.

tuber *noun* a short thick rounded root (e.g. of a dahlia) or underground stem (e.g. of a potato) that produces buds from which new plants will grow.

tuberculosis *noun* a disease of people and animals, producing small swellings in the parts affected by it, especially in the lungs. **tubercular** *adjective*

tubing *noun* tubes; a length of tube.

tubular *adjective* shaped like a tube.

tuck[1] *verb* 1 push a loose edge into something so that it is hidden or held in place. 2 put something away in a small space, *Tuck this in your pocket.*

tuck in (*informal*) eat heartily.

tuck[2] *noun* 1 a flat fold stitched in a garment. 2 (*informal*) food, especially sweets and cakes etc. that children enjoy. **tuck-shop** *noun*

tuft *noun* a bunch of threads, grass, hair, or feathers etc. growing close together. **tufted** *adjective*

tug[1] *verb* (**tugged, tugging**) 1 pull hard or suddenly. 2 tow.

tug[2] *noun* 1 a hard or sudden pull. 2 a small powerful boat used for towing others.

tug of war a contest between two teams pulling a rope from opposite ends.

tuition *noun* teaching.

tula *interjection* (*informal*) be quiet.

tulip *noun* a large cup-shaped flower on a tall stem growing from a bulb.

tulle (*say* tewl) *noun* a very fine silky net material used for veils, wedding-dresses, etc.

tumble *verb* (**tumbled, tumbling**) 1 fall. 2 cause to fall. 3 move or push quickly and carelessly. **tumble** *noun*

tumble to (*informal*) realize what something means.

tumbledown *adjective* falling into ruins.

tumbler *noun* 1 a drinking-glass with no stem or handle. 2 a part of a lock that is lifted when a key is turned to open it.

tummy *noun* (*plural* **tummies**) (*informal*) the stomach.

tumour (*say* tew-mer) *noun* an abnormal lump growing on or in the body.

tumult (*say* tew-mult) *noun* an uproar; a state of confusion and agitation.

tumultuous (*say* tew-**mul**-tew-us) *adjective* making a tumult; noisy.

tun *noun* a large cask or barrel.

tuna (*say* tew-na) *noun* (*plural* **tuna**) a large edible sea-fish with pink flesh.

tundra *noun* the vast level Arctic regions of Europe, Asia, and America where there are no trees and the subsoil is always frozen.

tune[1] *noun* a short piece of music; a pleasant series of musical notes. **tuneful** *adjective*, **tunefully** *adverb*
in tune at the correct musical pitch.

tune[2] *verb* (**tuned, tuning**) 1 put a musical instrument in tune. 2 adjust a radio or television set to receive a certain channel. 3 adjust an engine so that it runs smoothly. **tuner** *noun*

tungsten *noun* a grey metal used to make a kind of steel.

tunic *noun* 1 a jacket worn as part of a uniform. 2 a garment reaching from the shoulders to the hips or knees.

tunnel[1] *noun* an underground passage.

tunnel[2] *verb* (**tunnelled, tunnelling**) make a tunnel.

tunny *noun* (*plural* **tunnies**) a tuna.

turban *noun* a covering for the head made by wrapping a strip of cloth round a cap.

turbid *adjective* (of water, etc.) muddy, not clear. **turbidly** *adverb*, **turbidity** *noun*

turbine *noun* a machine or motor driven by a flow of water, steam, or gas.

turbo-jet *noun* a jet engine or aircraft with turbines.

turbulent *adjective* 1 moving violently and unevenly, *turbulent seas*. 2 unruly, *a turbulent crowd*. **turbulently** *adverb*, **turbulence** *noun*

tureen *noun* a deep dish with a lid, from which soup is served at the table.

turf[1] *noun* short grass and the earth round its roots.
the turf the course on which a horse-race is run; horse-racing generally.

turf[2] *verb* cover ground with turf.
turf out (*slang*) throw out.

turgid (*say* ter-jid) *adjective* swollen and not flexible.

turkey *noun* (*plural* **turkeys**) a large bird kept for its meat.

turmeric *noun* a spice used in curry etc.
or for yellow dye.

turmoil *noun* a disturbance; confusion.

turn[1] *verb* 1 move round; move to a new direction. 2 change in appearance etc.; become, *He turned pale.* 3 make something change, *You can turn milk into butter.* 4 move a switch or tap etc. to control something, *Turn that radio off.* 5 pass a certain time, *It has turned midnight.* 6 shape something on a lathe.
turn down fold down; reduce the flow or sound of something; reject, *We offered her a job but she turned it down.*
turn out send out, expel; empty something, especially to search or clean it; happen; prove to be, *The visitor turned out to be my uncle.*
turn up appear or arrive; increase the flow or sound of something.

turn[2] *noun* 1 the action of turning; a turning movement. 2 a change; the point where something turns. 3 an opportunity or duty etc. that comes to each person etc. in succession, *It's your turn to wash up.* 4 a short performance in an entertainment. 5 (*informal*) an attack of illness; a nervous shock, *It gave me a nasty turn.*
good turn a helpful action.
in turn in succession; one after another.

turncoat *noun* a person who changes his or her principles or beliefs.

turner *noun* a person who makes things on a lathe. **turnery** *noun*

turning *noun* a place where one road meets another, forming a corner.

turning-point *noun* a point where an important change takes place.

turnip *noun* a plant with a large round white root used as a vegetable.

turnover *noun* 1 the amount of money received by a firm selling things. 2 the rate at which goods are sold or workers leave and are replaced. 3 a small pie made by folding pastry over fruit, jam, etc.

turnpike *noun* (*old use*) a toll-gate; a road with toll-gates.

turnstile *noun* a revolving gate that admits one person at a time.

turntable *noun* a circular revolving platform or support, e.g. for turning a railway locomotive around at the end of a track.

turpentine *noun* a kind of oil used for thinning paint, cleaning paintbrushes, etc.

turpitude *noun* wickedness.

turps *noun* (*informal*) turpentine.

turquoise *noun* 1 a sky-blue or greenish-blue colour. 2 a blue jewel.

turret *noun* 1 a small tower on a castle or other building. 2 a revolving structure containing a gun. **turreted** *adjective*

turtle *noun* a sea-animal that looks like a tortoise.
turn turtle capsize.

turtle-dove *noun* a wild dove.

tusk *noun* a long pointed tooth projecting outside the mouth of an elephant, walrus, etc.

tussle¹ *noun* a struggle; a conflict.

tussle² *verb* (**tussled, tussling**) take part in a tussle.

tussock *noun* a tuft or clump of grass.

tutor *noun* 1 a teacher who teaches one person or small group, not in a school. 2 a teacher of students in a college or university.

tutu (*say* **too**-too) *noun* a ballet-dancer's short stiff frilled skirt.

TV *abbreviation* television.

twaddle *noun* nonsense.

twain *noun & adjective* (*old use*) two.

twang *verb* 1 play a guitar etc. by plucking its strings. 2 make a sharp sound like that of a wire when plucked. **twang** *noun*

tweak *verb* pinch and twist or pull something sharply. **tweak** *noun*

tweed *noun* thick woollen twill, often woven of mixed colours.

tweet *noun* the chirping sound made by a small bird.

tweezers *plural noun* small pincers for picking up or pulling very small things.

twelve *noun & adjective* the number 12; one more than eleven. **twelfth** *adjective & noun*

twenty *noun & adjective* (*plural* **twenties**) the number 20; two times ten. **twentieth** *adjective & noun*

twice *adverb* 1 two times; on two occasions. 2 double the amount.

twiddle *verb* (**twiddled, twiddling**) twirl or finger something in an idle way; twist something quickly to and fro. **twiddle** *noun*, **twiddly** *adjective*

twig¹ *noun* a small shoot on a branch or stem of a tree or shrub.

twig² *verb* (**twigged, twigging**) (*informal*) realize what something means.

twilight *noun* dim light from the sky just after sunset or just before sunrise.

twill *noun* material woven so that there is a pattern of diagonal lines.

twin¹ *noun* 1 either of two children or animals born to the same mother at one time. 2 either of two things that are exactly alike, *an aircraft with twin engines.*

twin² *verb* (**twinned, twinning**) put things together as a pair.

twine¹ *noun* strong thin string.

twine² *verb* (**twined, twining**) twist or wind together or round something.

twinge *noun* a sudden pain; a pang.

twinkle *verb* (**twinkled, twinkling**) sparkle. **twinkle** *noun*

twirl *verb* twist quickly. **twirl** *noun*

twist¹ *verb* 1 pass threads or strands round something or round each other. 2 turn the ends of something in opposite directions. 3 turn round or from side to side, *The road twisted through the hills.* 4 bend something out of its proper shape. 5 give false meaning to words intentionally, *The journalist twisted the Minister's speech.* **twister** *noun*

twist² *noun* a twisting movement or action. **twisty** *adjective*

twit¹ *verb* (**twitted, twitting**) taunt.

twit² *noun* (*slang*) a silly person.

twitch *verb* pull or move with a slight jerk. **twitch** *noun*

twitter *verb* make quick chirping sounds. **twitter** *noun*

two *noun & adjective* (*plural* **twos**) the number 2; one more than one.
be in two minds be undecided about something.

tycoon *noun* a rich and influential business person.

tying *present participle* of **tie**¹.

type¹ *noun* 1 a kind or sort. 2 letters or figures etc. designed for use in printing.

type[2] *verb* (**typed, typing**) write something by using a typewriter.

typescript *noun* a typewritten document.

typewriter *noun* a machine with keys that are pressed to print letters or figures etc. on a piece of paper. **typewritten** *adjective*

typhoid fever *noun* a serious infectious disease with fever, caused by harmful bacteria in food or water etc.

typhoon *noun* a violent hurricane in the western Pacific or East Asian seas.

typhus *noun* an infectious disease causing fever, weakness, and a rash.

typical *adjective* 1 having the qualities of a particular type of person or thing, *a typical school playground*. 2 usual in a particular person or thing, *He worked with typical carefulness*. **typically** *adverb*

typify (*say* tip-if-I) *verb* (**typified, typifying**) be a typical example of something.

typist *noun* a person who types.

typography (*say* ty-**pog**-ra-fee) *noun* the style or appearance of the letters and figures etc. in printed material.

tyrannize (*say* tirran-I'z) *verb* (**tyrannized, tyrannizing**) rule or behave like a tyrant.

tyranny (*say* tirran-ee) *noun* (*plural* **tyrannies**) 1 government by a tyrant. 2 the way a tyrant behaves towards people, *Is there no end to the military regime's tyrannies?* **tyrannical** *adjective*, **tyrannous** *adjective*

tyrant (*say* ty-rant) *noun* a person who rules cruelly and unjustly; someone who insists on being obeyed.

tyre *noun* a covering of rubber fitted round a wheel to make it grip the road and run more smoothly.

Uu

ubiquitous (*say* yoo-**bik**-wit-us) *adjective* found everywhere, *The ubiquitous television aerials spoil the view.* **ubiquity** *noun*

U-boat *noun* a German submarine of the kind used in the Second World War.

ubuntu *noun* generosity; compassion, *Ubuntu is our humaneness, our ability to care.*

udder *noun* the bag-like part of a cow, ewe, female goat, etc. from which milk is taken.

UFO *abbreviation* (also **ufo**) (*plural* **UFOs** or **ufos**) unidentified flying object.

ugly *adjective* (**uglier, ugliest**) 1 unpleasant to look at; not beautiful. 2 hostile and threatening, *The crowd was in an ugly mood.* **ugliness** *noun*

UHF *abbreviation* ultra-high frequency (between 300 and 3 000 megahertz).

UK *abbreviation* United Kingdom.

ukulele (*say* yoo-kul-**ay**-lee) *noun* a small guitar with four strings.

ulcer *noun* an open sore. **ulcerated** *adjective*, **ulceration** *noun*

ulterior *adjective* beyond what is obvious or stated, *an ulterior motive.*

ultimate *adjective* furthest in a series of things; final, *Our ultimate destination is Cairo.* **ultimately** *adverb*

ultimatum (*say* ul-tim-**ay**-tum) *noun* a final demand; a statement that unless something is done by a certain time action will be taken or war will be declared.

ultra- *prefix* 1 beyond (as in *ultraviolet*). 2 extremely; excessively (as in *ultramodern*).

ultramarine *noun* deep bright blue.

ultrasonic *adjective* (of sound) beyond the range of human hearing.

ultraviolet *adjective* (of light-rays) beyond the violet end of the spectrum.

umama *noun* a word used when speaking politely to an elderly woman.

umber *noun* a kind of brown pigment.

umbilical (*say* um-**bil**-ik-al) *adjective* of the navel.

umbilical cord the tube through which a baby receives nourishment before it is born, connecting its body with the mother's womb.

umbrage *noun* **take umbrage** take offence.

umbrella *noun* 1 a circular piece of material stretched over a folding frame with a central stick used as a handle, or a central pole, opened to protect the user from rain or sun. **2** a general protection, *Police operated under the umbrella of the security forces.*

umnumzana *noun* a word used when speaking politely to a man.

umpire¹ *noun* a referee in cricket, tennis, and some other games.

umpire² *verb* (**umpired**, **umpiring**) act as an umpire.

UN *abbreviation* United Nations.

un- *prefix* **1** not (as in *uncertain*). **2** (before a verb) reversing the action (as in *unlock* = release from being locked). NOTE Many words beginning with this prefix are not listed here if their meaning is obvious.

unable *adjective* not able to do something.

unaccountable *adjective* **1** unable to be explained. **2** not accountable for what you do. **unaccountably** *adverb*

unadulterated *adjective* pure; not mixed with things that are less good.

unaided *adjective* without help.

unanimous (*say* yoo-**nan**-im-us) *adjective* with everyone agreeing, *a unanimous decision.* **unanimously** *adverb,* **unanimity** (*say* yoo-nan-**im**-it-ee) *noun*

unassuming *adjective* modest; not arrogant or pretentious.

unavoidable *adjective* not able to be avoided.

unaware *adjective* not aware.

unawares *adverb* unexpectedly; without noticing.

unbearable *adjective* not able to be endured. **unbearably** *adverb*

unbeatable *adjective* unable to be defeated or surpassed.

unbeaten *adjective* not defeated; not surpassed.

unbecoming *adjective* not making a person look attractive; not suitable.

unbeknown *adjective* (*informal*) without someone knowing about it, *Unbeknown to us, they were working for our enemies.*

unbelievable *adjective* not able to be believed; incredible. **unbelievably** *adverb*

unbend *verb* (**unbent**, **unbending**) **1** change or become changed from a bent

position. **2** relax and become friendly.

unbiased *adjective* not biased.

unbidden *adjective* not commanded; not invited.

unblock *verb* remove an obstruction from something.

unborn *adjective* not yet born.

unbridled *adjective* unrestrained.

unbroken *adjective* not broken; not interrupted.

unburden *verb* remove a burden from the person etc. carrying it. **unburden yourself** tell someone what you know.

uncalled-for *adjective* not justified; impertinent.

uncanny *adjective* (**uncannier**, **uncanniest**) **1** strange and rather frightening. **2** extraordinary, *They forecast the exam results with uncanny accuracy.* **uncannily** *adverb,* **uncanniness** *noun*

unceremonious *adjective* without proper formality or dignity.

uncertain *adjective* **1** not certain. **2** not reliable, *His aim is rather uncertain.* **uncertainly** *adverb,* **uncertainty** *noun* **in no uncertain terms** clearly and forcefully.

uncharitable *adjective* making unkind judgements of people or actions. **uncharitably** *adverb*

uncle *noun* **1** the brother of your father or mother; your aunt's husband. **2** a word used by children when speaking politely to a man.

unclothed *adjective* naked.

uncomfortable *adjective* not comfortable. **uncomfortably** *adverb*

uncommon *adjective* not common; unusual.

uncompromising (*say* un-**komp**-rom-I-zing) *adjective* not allowing a compromise; inflexible.

unconcerned *adjective* **1** not caring about something; not worried. **2** not involved, not taking part in something, *She is quite unconcerned with feminist issues.*

unconditional *adjective* without any conditions; absolute, *unconditional surrender.* **unconditionally** *adverb*

unconscious *adjective* not conscious; not aware of things. **unconsciously** *adverb*, **unconsciousness** *noun*

uncontrollable *adjective* unable to be controlled or stopped. **uncontrollably** *adverb*

uncooperative *adjective* not co-operative.

uncouple *verb* (**uncoupled, uncoupling**) disconnect.

uncouth (*say* un-**koo**th) *adjective* rude and awkward in manner; boorish.

uncover *verb* 1 remove the covering from something. 2 reveal; expose, *They uncovered a plot to kill the king*.

unction *noun* 1 anointing with oil, especially in a religious ceremony. 2 unctuousness.

unctuous (*say* unk-tew-us) *adjective* having an oily manner; polite in an exaggerated way. **unctuously** *adverb*, **unctuousness** *noun*

undecided *adjective* 1 not yet settled; not certain, *The result of the election is still undecided*. 2 not having made up your mind yet.

undeniable *adjective* impossible to deny; undoubtedly true. **undeniably** *adverb*

under[1] *preposition* 1 below; beneath, *Hide it under the desk*. 2 less than, *under 5 years old*. 3 governed or controlled by, *The country prospered under his rule*. 4 in the process of; undergoing, *The road is under repair*. 5 using, *He writes under the name of 'Lewis Carroll'*. 6 according to the rules of, *This is permitted under our agreement*.
under way moving on water; in progress.

under[2] *adverb* in or to a lower place or level or condition, *Slowly the diver went under*.

under[3] *adjective* lower, *the under layers*.

under- *prefix* 1 below, beneath (as in *underwear*). 2 lower; subordinate (as in *under-manager*). 3 not enough; incompletely (as in *undercooked*).

underarm *adjective & adverb* 1 moving the hand and arm forward and upwards. 2 in or for the armpit.

undercarriage *noun* an aircraft's landing-wheels and their supports.

underclothes *plural noun* underwear. **underclothing** *noun*

undercover *adjective* done or doing things secretly, *an undercover agent*.

undercurrent *noun* 1 a current that is below the surface or below another current. 2 an underlying feeling or influence, *an undercurrent of fear*.

undercut *verb* (**undercut, undercutting**) 1 cut away the part below something. 2 sell something for a lower price than someone else sells it.

underdog *noun* a person or team etc. that is expected to lose a contest or struggle.

underdone *adjective* not thoroughly done; undercooked.

underestimate *verb* (**underestimated, underestimating**) make too low an estimate of a person or thing.

underfoot *adverb* on the ground; under your feet.

undergarment *noun* a piece of underwear.

undergo *verb* (**underwent, undergone, undergoing**) experience or endure something; be subjected to, *The new aircraft underwent intensive tests*.

undergraduate *noun* a student at a university who has not yet taken a degree.

underground[1] *adjective & adverb* 1 under the ground. 2 done or working in secret, *an underground organization*.

underground[2] *noun* a railway that runs through tunnels under the ground.

undergrowth *noun* bushes and other plants growing closely, especially under trees.

underhand *adjective* done or doing things in a sly or secret way.

underlie *verb* (**underlay, underlain, underlying**) 1 be or lie under something. 2 be the basis or explanation of something.

underline *verb* (**underlined, underlining**) 1 draw a line under a word etc. 2 emphasize something.

underling *noun* a subordinate.

underlying *adjective* 1 lying under something, *the underlying rocks*. **2** forming the basis or explanation of something, *the underlying causes of the trouble*.

undermine *verb* (**undermined, undermining**) **1** make a hollow or tunnel beneath something, especially one causing weakness at the base. **2** weaken something gradually.

underneath *preposition & adverb* below; beneath; under.

underpants *plural noun* an undergarment covering the lower part of the body, worn under clothes.

underpass *noun* (*plural* **underpasses**) a road that goes underneath another.

underpay *verb* (**underpaid, underpaying**) pay someone too little.

underprivileged *adjective* having less than the normal standard of living or rights in a community.

underrate *verb* (**underrated, underrating**) have too low an opinion of a person or thing.

undersell *verb* (**undersold, underselling**) sell at a lower price than another person.

undersigned *adjective* who has or have signed at the bottom of this document, *We, the undersigned, wish to protest*.

undersized *adjective* of less than the normal size.

understand *verb* (**understood, understanding**) **1** know what something means or how it works or why it exists. **2** know and tolerate a person's ways, *We understand each other*. **3** have been told, *I understand that you're leaving today*. **4** take something for granted, *Your expenses will be paid, that's understood*.

understandable *adjective,* **understandably** *adverb*

understanding *noun* **1** the power to understand or think; intelligence. **2** sympathy; tolerance. **3** agreement in opinion or feeling, *a better understanding between nations*.

understatement *noun* an incomplete or very restrained statement of facts or truth, *To say they disagreed is an understatement; they had a violent quarrel*.

understudy[1] *noun* (*plural* **understudies**)

an actor who studies a part in order to be able to play it if the usual performer is absent.

understudy[2] *verb* (**understudied, understudying**) be an understudy for an actor or part.

undertake *verb* (**undertook, undertaken, undertaking**) agree or promise to do something.

undertaker *noun* a person whose job is to arrange funerals and burials or cremations.

undertaking *noun* **1** work etc. undertaken. **2** a promise or guarantee. **3** the business of an undertaker.

undertone *noun* **1** a low or quiet tone, *They spoke in undertones*. **2** an underlying quality or feeling etc., *His letter has a threatening undertone*.

undertow *noun* a current below that of the surface of the sea and moving in the opposite direction.

underwater *adjective & adverb* placed, used, or done beneath the surface of water.

underwear *noun* clothes worn next to the skin, under indoor clothing.

underweight *adjective* not heavy enough.

underwent *past tense* of **undergo**.

underworld *noun* **1** (in myths and legends) the place for the spirits of the dead, under the earth. **2** the people who are regularly engaged in crime.

underwrite *verb* (**underwrote, underwritten, underwriting**) guarantee to finance something, or to pay for any loss or damage etc. **underwriter** *noun*

undesirable *adjective* not desirable; objectionable. **undesirably** *adverb*

undignified *adjective* not dignified.

undo *verb* (**undid, undone, undoing**) **1** unfasten; unwrap. **2** cancel the effect of something, *He has undone all our careful work*.

undoubted *adjective* certain; not regarded as doubtful. **undoubtedly** *adverb*

undress *verb* take clothes off.

undue *adjective* excessive; too great. **unduly** *adverb*

undulate *verb* (**undulated, undulating**) move like a wave or waves; have a wavy appearance. **undulation** *noun*

undying *adjective* everlasting.

unearth *verb* 1 dig something up; uncover by digging. 2 find something by searching, *His investigation unearthed corruption at the highest levels.*

unearthly *adjective* 1 not earthly; supernatural; strange and frightening. 2 (*informal*) very early or inconvenient, *We had to get up at an unearthly hour.*

uneasy *adjective* 1 uncomfortable. 2 worried; worrying about something. **uneasily** *adverb*, **uneasiness** *noun*

uneatable *adjective* not fit to be eaten.

uneconomic *adjective* not profitable.

unemployed *adjective* without a job. **unemployment** *noun*

unending *adjective* not coming to an end.

unequal *adjective* not equal. **unequalled** *adjective*, **unequally** *adverb*

unerring (*say* un-**er**-ing) *adjective* making no mistake, *unerring accuracy.*

uneven *adjective* 1 not level; not regular. 2 unequal. **unevenly** *adverb*, **unevenness** *noun*

unexampled *adjective* unprecedented; exceptional, *an unexampled opportunity.*

unexceptionable *adjective* not in any way objectionable.
● USAGE: Do not confuse with *unexceptional.*

unexceptional *adjective* not exceptional; quite ordinary.
● USAGE: Do not confuse with *unexceptionable.*

unexpected *adjective* not expected. **unexpectedly** *adverb*, **unexpectedness** *noun*

unfair *adjective* not fair; unjust. **unfairly** *adverb*, **unfairness** *noun*

unfaithful *adjective* not faithful; disloyal.

unfamiliar *adjective* not familiar. **unfamiliarity** *noun*

unfasten *verb* open the fastenings of something.

unfavourable *adjective* not favourable. **unfavourably** *adverb*

unfeeling *adjective* 1 not able to feel things. 2 not caring about other people's feelings; unsympathetic.

unfit[1] *adjective* 1 unsuitable. 2 not in perfect health.

unfit[2] *verb* (**unfitted, unfitting**) make a person or thing unsuitable.

unfold *verb* 1 open; spread out. 2 make or become known slowly, *as the story unfolds.*

unforeseen *adjective* not foreseen; unexpected.

unforgettable *adjective* not able to be forgotten.

unforgivable *adjective* not able to be forgiven.

unfortunate *adjective* 1 unlucky. 2 unsuitable; regrettable, *an unfortunate remark.* **unfortunately** *adverb*

unfounded *adjective* not based on facts.

unfreeze *verb* (**unfroze, unfrozen, unfreezing**) thaw; cause something to thaw.

unfriendly *adjective* not friendly. **unfriendliness** *noun*

unfrock *verb* dismiss a person from being a priest.

unfurl *verb* unroll; spread out.

unfurnished *adjective* without furniture.

ungainly *adjective* awkward-looking; clumsy; ungraceful. **ungainliness** *noun*

ungodly *adjective* 1 not giving reverence to God; not religious. 2 (*informal*) outrageous; very inconvenient, *She woke me at an ungodly hour.* **ungodliness** *noun*

ungovernable *adjective* uncontrollable.

ungracious *adjective* not kindly; not courteous. **ungraciously** *adverb*

ungrateful *adjective* not grateful. **ungratefully** *adverb*

unguarded *adjective* 1 not guarded. 2 without thought or caution; indiscreet, *He said this in an unguarded moment.*

unguent (*say* **ung**-went) *noun* an ointment or lubricant.

unhappy *adjective* 1 not happy; sad. 2 unfortunate; unsuitable. **unhappily** *adverb*, **unhappiness** *noun*

unhealthy *adjective* not healthy. **unhealthiness** *noun*

unheard-of *adjective* never known or

done before; extraordinary.

unhinge *verb* (**unhinged, unhinging**)
cause a person's mind to become
unbalanced.

uni- *prefix* one; single (as in *unicorn*).

unicorn *noun* (in legends) an animal that
is like a horse with one long straight horn
growing from its forehead.

uniform[1] *noun* special clothes showing
that the wearer is a member of a certain
organization, school, etc.

uniform[2] *adjective* always the same; not
varying, *The desks are of uniform size.*
uniformly *adverb*, **uniformity** *noun*

uniformed *adjective* wearing a uniform.

unify *verb* (**unified, unifying**) make into
one thing; unite. **unification** *noun*

unilateral *adjective* of or done by one
person or group or country etc.

unimpeachable *adjective* completely
trustworthy, *unimpeachable honesty.*

uninhabitable *adjective* not suitable for
habitation.

uninhabited *adjective* not inhabited.

uninhibited *adjective* not inhibited;
having no inhibitions.

uninterested *adjective* not interested;
showing or feeling no concern.
• USAGE: See the note on *disinterested.*

union *noun* 1 the joining of things together; uniting. 2 a trade union (see *trade*).
Union Jack the British flag.

unionist *noun* 1 a member of a trade
union. 2 a person who wishes to unite one
country with another.

unique (*say* yoo-**neek**) *adjective* being the
only one of its kind, *This jewel is unique.*
uniquely *adverb*

unison *noun* **in unison** with all sounding
or singing the same tune etc. together, or
speaking in chorus; in agreement.

unit *noun* 1 an amount used as a standard
in measuring or counting things, *Centimetres are units of length; cents are units
of money.* 2 a group, device, piece of furniture, etc. regarded as a single thing but
forming part of a larger group or whole,
an army unit; a sink unit.

unite *verb* (**united, uniting**) join together;
make or become one thing.

unity *noun* 1 being united; being in
agreement. 2 something whole that is
made up of parts. 3 (in mathematics) the
number one.

universal *adjective* of or including or
done by everyone or everything.
universally *adverb*

universe *noun* everything that exists,
including the earth and living things and
all the heavenly bodies.

university *noun* (*plural* **universities**)
a place where people go to study at an
advanced level after leaving school.

unjust *adjective* not fair; not just.

unkempt *adjective* looking untidy or
neglected.

unkind *adjective* not kind. **unkindly**
adverb, **unkindness** *noun*

unknown *adjective* not known.

unleaded (*say* un-**led**-ed) *adjective*
(of petrol) not containing added lead.

unleash *verb* set free from a leash; let
loose.

unleavened (*say* un-**lev**-end) *adjective*
(of bread) made without yeast or other
substances that would make it rise.

unless *conjunction* except when; if . . .
not, *We cannot go unless we are invited.*

unlike[1] *preposition* not like, *Unlike me,
she enjoys cricket.*

unlike[2] *adjective* not alike; different,
The two children are very unlike.

unlikely *adjective* (**unlikelier, unlikeliest**)
not likely to happen or be true.

unlimited *adjective* not limited; very great
or very many.

unload *verb* remove the load of things
carried by a ship, aircraft, vehicle, etc.

unlock *verb* open something by undoing
a lock.

unlucky *adjective* not lucky; having or
bringing bad luck. **unluckily** *adverb*

unmanageable *adjective* unable to be
managed.

unmarried *adjective* not married.

unmask *verb* 1 remove a person's mask.
2 reveal what a person or thing really is.

unmentionable *adjective* too bad to be
spoken of.

unmistakable *adjective* not able to be

mistaken for another person or thing.
unmistakably *adverb*

unmitigated *adjective* absolute,
an unmitigated disaster.

unnatural *adjective* not natural; not
normal. **unnaturally** *adverb*

unnecessary *adjective* not necessary;
more than is necessary.

unnerve *verb* (**unnerved, unnerving**)
cause someone to lose courage or
determination.

unoccupied *adjective* not occupied.

unofficial *adjective* not official.
unofficially *adverb*

unpack *verb* take things out of a suitcase,
bag, box, etc.

unparalleled *adjective* having no parallel
or equal.

unparliamentary *adjective* impolite;
abusive.
● USAGE: It is a rule of debates in
Parliament that speakers must be polite
to each other. Impolite language is
'unparliamentary'.

unpick *verb* undo the stitching of
something.

unpleasant *adjective* not pleasant.
unpleasantly *adverb*, **unpleasantness**
noun

unpopular *adjective* not popular.

unprecedented (*say* un-**press**-id-en-tid)
adjective that has never happened before.

unprejudiced *adjective* impartial.

unprepared *adjective* not prepared
beforehand; not ready, not equipped.

unprepossessing *adjective* not attractive; not making a good impression.

unprincipled *adjective* without good
moral principles; unscrupulous.

unprintable *adjective* too rude or
indecent to be printed.

unprofessional *adjective* not professional; not worthy of a member of a
profession.

unprofitable *adjective* not producing a
profit or advantage. **unprofitably** *adverb*

unqualified *adjective* 1 not officially
qualified to do something. 2 not limited,
We gave it our unqualified approval.

unravel *verb* (**unravelled, unravelling**)
1 disentangle. 2 undo something that is
knitted. 3 investigate and solve a mystery
etc.

unready *adjective* not ready; hesitating.

unreal *adjective* not real, existing in the
imagination only. **unreality** *noun*

unreasonable *adjective* 1 not reasonable.
2 excessive; unjust, *unreasonable
demands.* **unreasonably** *adverb*

unreel *verb* unwind from a reel.

unrelieved *adjective* without anything to
vary it, *unrelieved gloom.*

unremitting *adjective* not stopping, not
relaxing; persistent.

unrequited (*say* un-ri-**kwy**-tid) *adjective*
(of love) not returned or rewarded.

unreserved *adjective* 1 not reserved.
2 without restriction; complete, *unreserved
loyalty.* **unreservedly** *adverb*

unrest *noun* 1 restlessness; trouble
caused because people are dissatisfied.
2 civil disorder; riot, *an unrest area.*

unripe *adjective* not yet ripe.

unrivalled *adjective* having no equal;
better than all others.

unroll *verb* open something that has been
rolled up.

unruly *adjective* difficult to control;
disorderly. **unruliness** *noun*

unsavoury *adjective* unpleasant;
disgusting.

unscathed *adjective* uninjured.

unscrew *verb* undo something that has
been screwed up.

unscrupulous *adjective* having no
scruples about wrongdoing.

unseat *verb* throw a person from horseback or from a seat on a bicycle etc.

unseemly *adjective* not seemly;
improper.

unseen[1] *adjective* not seen; invisible.

unseen[2] *noun* a passage for translation
without previous preparation.

unselfish *adjective* not selfish.

unsettled *adjective* not settled; not calm;
likely to change.

unshakeable *adjective* not able to be
shaken; firm.

unsightly *adjective* not pleasant to look
at; ugly. **unsightliness** *noun*

unskilled *adjective* not having or not needing special skill or training.

unsociable *adjective* not sociable.

unsocial *adjective* not social.
unsocial hours time spent working when most people are free.

unsolicited *adjective* not asked for.

unsound *adjective* not sound; damaged, unhealthy, unreasonable, or unreliable.

unspeakable *adjective* too bad to be described; very objectionable.

unstable *adjective* not stable; likely to change or become unbalanced.

unsteady *adjective* not steady.

unstinted *adjective* given generously.

unstuck *adjective* **come unstuck** cease to stick; (*informal*) fail, go wrong.

unsuccessful *adjective* not successful.

unsuitable *adjective* not suitable.

untenable *adjective* not tenable.

unthinkable *adjective* too bad or too unlikely to be worth considering.

unthinking *adjective* thoughtless.

untidy *adjective* (**untidier, untidiest**) not tidy. **untidily** *adverb*, **untidiness** *noun*

untie *verb* (**untied, untying**) undo something that has been tied.

until *preposition* & *conjunction* up to a particular time or event.
● USAGE: See the note on *till*[1].

untimely *adjective* happening too soon or at an unsuitable time.

unto *preposition* (*old use*) to.

untold *adjective* **1** not told. **2** too much or too many to be counted, *untold wealth* or *wealth untold*.

untoward *adjective* inconvenient; awkward, *if nothing untoward happens*.

untraceable *adjective* unable to be traced.

untrue *adjective* not true.

untruth *noun* an untrue statement; a lie. **untruthful** *adjective*, **untruthfully** *adverb*

unused *adjective* **1** (*say* un-**yoozd**) not yet used, *an unused stamp*. **2** (*say* un-**yoost**) not accustomed, *He is unused to eating meat.*

unusual *adjective* not usual; exceptional; strange. **unusually** *adverb*

unutterable *adjective* too great to be described, *unutterable joy.*

unvarnished *adjective* **1** not varnished. **2** plain and straightforward, *the unvarnished truth.*

unveil *verb* **1** remove a veil or covering from something. **2** reveal, *The government's anti-crime measures were unveiled this morning.*

unwanted *adjective* not wanted.

unwarrantable *adjective* not justifiable. **unwarrantably** *adverb*

unwarranted *adjective* not justified; not authorized.

unwary *adjective* not cautious. **unwarily** *adverb*, **unwariness** *noun*

unwell *adjective* not in good health.

unwholesome *adjective* not wholesome.

unwieldy *adjective* awkward to move or control because of its size, shape, or weight. **unwieldiness** *noun*

unwilling *adjective* not willing. **unwillingly** *adverb*

unwind *verb* (**unwound, unwinding**) **1** unroll. **2** (*informal*) relax after a time of work or strain.

unwise *adjective* not wise; foolish. **unwisely** *adverb*

unwitting *adjective* **1** unaware. **2** unintentional. **unwittingly** *adverb*

unwonted (*say* un-**wohn**-tid) *adjective* not customary; not usual, *She spoke with unwonted rudeness.* **unwontedly** *adverb*

unworn *adjective* not yet worn.

unworthy *adjective* not worthy.

unwrap *verb* (**unwrapped, unwrapping**) open something that is wrapped.

up[1] *adverb* **1** to or in a higher place or position or level, *Prices went up.* **2** so as to be upright, *Stand up.* **3** out of bed, *It's time to get up.* **4** completely, *Eat up your carrots.* **5** finished, *Your time is up.* **6** (*informal*) happening, *Something is up.*
up against close to; (*informal*) faced with difficulties, dangers, etc.
ups and downs ascents and descents; alternate good and bad luck.
up to until; busy with or doing something; capable of; needed from, *It's up to us to help her.*

up to date modern; fashionable; giving recent information etc.
• USAGE: Use hyphens when this is used as an adjective before a noun, e.g. *up-to-date information* (but *The information is up to date*).

up² *preposition* upwards through or along or into, *Water came up the pipes.*

upbraid *verb* (*formal*) reproach.

upbringing *noun* the way someone is trained during childhood.

update *verb* (**updated, updating**) bring a thing up to date.

upheaval *noun* a sudden violent change or disturbance.

uphill¹ *adverb* up a slope.

uphill² *adjective* 1 going up a slope. 2 difficult, *It was uphill work.*

uphold *verb* (**upheld, upholding**) 1 support, keep something from falling. 2 support a decision or belief etc.

upholster *verb* put covers, padding, and springs etc. on furniture. **upholstery** *noun*

upkeep *noun* keeping something in good condition; the cost of this.

uplands *plural noun* the higher parts of a country or region. **upland** *adjective*

upon *preposition* on.

upper *adjective* higher in place or rank etc.

uppermost¹ *adjective* highest.

uppermost² *adverb* on or to the top or the highest place, *Keep the painted side uppermost.*

upright¹ *adjective* 1 vertical; erect. 2 strictly honest or honourable.

upright² *noun* a post or rod etc. placed upright, especially as a support.

uprising *noun* a rebellion; a revolt.

uproar *noun* an outburst of noise or excitement or anger.

uproarious *adjective* very noisy.

uproot *verb* 1 remove a plant and its roots from the ground. 2 make someone leave the place where he or she has lived for a long time.

upset¹ *verb* (**upset, upsetting**) 1 overturn; knock something over. 2 make a person unhappy. 3 disturb the normal working of

something, *Strikes upset the train time-table.*

upset² *noun* upsetting something; being upset.

upshot *noun* an outcome.

upside-down *adverb & adjective* 1 with the upper part underneath instead of on top. 2 in great disorder; very untidy.

upstairs *adverb & adjective* to or on a higher floor.

upstart *noun* a person who has risen suddenly to a high position, especially one who then behaves arrogantly.

upstream *adjective & adverb* in the direction from which a stream flows.

uptake *noun* (*informal*) understanding, *She is quick on the uptake.*

uptight *adjective* (*informal*) tense and nervous or annoyed.

upward *adjective & adverb* going towards what is higher. **upwards** *adverb*

uranium *noun* a heavy radioactive grey metal used as a source of nuclear energy.

urban *adjective* of a town or city.

urbane *adjective* having smoothly polite manners. **urbanely** *adverb*, **urbanity** *noun*

urbanize *verb* (**urbanized, urbanizing**) change a place into a town-like area. **urbanization** *noun*

urchin *noun* 1 a poorly dressed or mischievous child. 2 a sea-urchin.

urge¹ *verb* (**urged, urging**) 1 try to persuade a person to do something. 2 drive people or animals onward.

urge² *noun* a strong desire.

urgent *adjective* needing to be done or dealt with immediately. **urgently** *adverb*, **urgency** *noun*

urinate (*say* yoor-in-ayt) *verb* (**urinated, urinating**) pass urine out of your body. **urination** *noun*

urine (*say* yoor-in) *noun* waste liquid that collects in the bladder and is passed out of the body. **urinary** *adjective*

urn *noun* 1 a large metal container with a tap, in which water is heated. 2 a container shaped like a vase, usually with a foot; a container for holding the ashes of a cremated person.

US *abbreviation* United States (of America).

us *pronoun* the form of *we* used when it is the object of a verb or after a preposition.

USA *abbreviation* United States of America.

usable *adjective* able to be used.

usage *noun* 1 use; the way something is used. 2 the way words are used in a language, *South African usage often differs from American usage.*

use¹ (*say* yooz) *verb* (**used, using**) perform an action or job with something, *Use soap for washing.* **user** *noun*
used to was or were accustomed to, *We used to go by train.*
user-friendly easy for the user to operate, *a user-friendly ATM.*
use up use all of something.

use² (*say* yooss) *noun* 1 the action of using something; being used. 2 the purpose for which something is used, *The device has more than one use.* 3 the quality of being useful, *It's of no use to me.*

used *adjective* not new; second-hand.

useful *adjective* able to be used a lot or to do something that needs doing. **usefully** *adverb*, **usefulness** *noun*

useless *adjective* not useful; producing no effect, *Their efforts were useless.* **uselessly** *adverb*, **uselessness** *noun*

usher¹ *noun* a person who shows people to their seats in a public hall or church etc. **usherette** *noun*

usher² *verb* lead in or out; escort someone as an usher.

USSR *abbreviation* (in history) Union of Soviet Socialist Republics.

usual *adjective* such as happens or is done or used etc. always or most of the time. **usually** *adverb*

usurp (*say* yoo-**zerp**) *verb* take power or a position or right etc. wrongfully or by force. **usurpation** *noun*, **usurper** *noun*

usury (*say* **yoo**-zher-ee) *noun* the lending of money at an excessively high rate of interest. **usurer** *noun*

utensil (*say* yoo-**ten**-sil) *noun* a device or container, especially one for use in the house, *cooking utensils.*

uterus (*say* **yoo**-ter-us) *noun* the womb.

utilitarian *adjective* designed to be useful rather than decorative or luxurious; practical.

utility *noun* (*plural* **utilities**) 1 usefulness. 2 a useful thing. 3 a service provided for the public, e.g. a water or electricity supply.

utilize *verb* (**utilized, utilizing**) use; find a use for something. **utilization** *noun*

utmost *adjective* extreme; greatest, *Look after it with the utmost care.* **utmost** *noun*

Utopia (*say* yoo-**toh**-pee-a) *noun* an imaginary place or state of things where everything is perfect. **Utopian** *adjective*

utter¹ *verb* say or speak; make a sound with your mouth. **utterance** *noun*

utter² *adjective* complete; absolute, *utter misery.* **utterly** *adverb*

uttermost *adjective* & *noun* utmost.

U-turn *noun* 1 a U-shaped turn made in a vehicle so that it then travels in the opposite direction. 2 a complete change of policy.

Vv

vacant *adjective* 1 empty; not filled or occupied. 2 without expression; blank, *a vacant stare.* **vacantly** *adverb*, **vacancy** *noun*

vacate *verb* (**vacated, vacating**) leave or give up a place or position.

vacation (*say* vak-**ay**-shon) *noun* 1 a holiday, especially between the terms at a university. 2 vacating a place etc.

vaccinate (*say* **vak**-sin-ayt) *verb* (**vaccinated, vaccinating**) inoculate someone with a vaccine. **vaccination** *noun*

vaccine (*say* **vak**-seen) *noun* a substance used to immunize a person against a disease.

vacillate (*say* **vass**-il-ayt) *verb* (**vacillated, vacillating**) keep changing your mind; waver. **vacillation** *noun*

vacuole *noun* a space within the cytoplasm of a cell, enclosed by a membrane and usually containing fluid.

vacuous (*say* vak-yoo-us) *adjective* empty-headed; without expression, *a vacuous stare*. **vacuously** *adverb*, **vacuousness** *noun*, **vacuity** *noun*

vacuum *noun* 1 a completely empty space; a space without any air in it. 2 (*informal*) a vacuum cleaner. **vacuum** *verb*

vacuum cleaner an electrical device that sucks up dust and dirt etc.

vacuum flask a container with double walls that have a vacuum between them, used for keeping liquids hot or cold.

vagabond *noun* a wanderer; a vagrant.

vagary (*say* **vay**-ger-ee) *noun* (*plural* **vagaries**) an impulsive change or whim, *the vagaries of fashion*.

vagina (*say* va-**jy**-na) *noun* the passage that leads from the vulva to the womb in female mammals.

vagrant (*say* **vay**-grant) *noun* a person with no settled home or regular work; a tramp. **vagrancy** *noun*

vague *adjective* not definite; not clear. **vaguely** *adverb*, **vagueness** *noun*

vain *adjective* 1 conceited, especially about your appearance. 2 useless, *They made vain attempts to save her*. **vainly** *adverb*

in vain with no result; uselessly.

valance *noun* a short curtain round the frame of a bed or above a window.

vale *noun* a valley.

valediction (*say* val-id-**ik**-shon) *noun* saying farewell. **valedictory** *adjective*

valentine *noun* 1 a card sent on St. Valentine's day (14 February) to the person you love. 2 the person to whom you send this card.

valet (*say* **val**-ay or **val**-it) *verb* 1 work as a man's servant looking after his clothes etc. 2 clean or clean out a car, *car valeting service*. **valet** *noun*

valetudinarian *noun* a person who is excessively concerned about keeping healthy.

valiant *adjective* brave; courageous. **valiantly** *adverb*

valid *adjective* 1 legally able to be used or

accepted, *This passport is out of date and not valid*. 2 (of reasoning) sound and logical. **validity** *noun*

valley *noun* (*plural* **valleys**) 1 a long low area between hills. 2 an area through which a river flows, *the Nile valley*.

valour *noun* bravery. **valorous** *adjective*

valuable *adjective* worth a lot of money; of great value. **valuably** *adverb*

valuables *plural noun* valuable things.

value¹ *noun* 1 the amount of money etc. that is considered to be the equivalent of something, or for which it can be exchanged. 2 how useful or important something is, *They learnt the value of regular exercise*.

value² *verb* (**valued**, **valuing**) 1 think that something is valuable. 2 estimate the value of a thing, *The necklace was valued at R500*. **valuation** *noun*, **valuer** *noun*

valueless *adjective* having no value.

valve *noun* 1 a device for controlling the flow of gas or liquid through a pipe or tube. 2 each piece of the shell of oysters etc. **valvular** *adjective*

vamp¹ *noun* the front part of a shoe that goes over the foot.

vamp² *verb* 1 make from odds and ends, *We'll vamp something up*. 2 improvise a musical accompaniment.

vampire *noun* a ghost or revived corpse supposed to leave a grave at night and suck blood from living people.

van¹ *noun* 1 a covered vehicle for carrying goods or horses etc. or prisoners. 2 a railway carriage for luggage or goods, or for the use of the guard.

van² *noun* the vanguard; the forefront.

vandal *noun* a person who deliberately breaks or damages things. **vandalism** *noun*

vandalize *verb* (**vandalized**, **vandalizing**) damage things as a vandal.

vane *noun* 1 a weather-vane. 2 the blade of a propeller, sail of a windmill, or other device that acts on or is moved by wind or water.

vanguard *noun* 1 the leading part of an army or fleet. 2 the first people to adopt a fashion or idea etc.

vanilla *noun* a flavouring obtained from the pods of a tropical plant.

vanish *verb* disappear completely.

vanity *noun* conceit; being vain.

vanquish *verb* conquer.

vantage-point *noun* a place from which you have a good view of something.

vapid *adjective* not lively, not interesting.

vaporize *verb* (**vaporized**, **vaporizing**) change or be changed into vapour. **vaporization** *noun*, **vaporizer** *noun*

vapour *noun* a visible gas to which some substances can be converted by heat; steam or mist.

variable¹ *adjective* varying; changeable. **variably** *adverb*, **variability** *noun*

variable² *noun* something that varies or can vary; a variable quantity.

variance *noun* the amount by which things differ.

at variance differing; conflicting.

variant *adjective* differing from something, *'Gipsy' is a variant spelling of 'gypsy'.* **variant** *noun*

variation *noun* **1** varying; the amount by which something varies. **2** a different form of something.

varicose *adjective* (of veins) permanently swollen.

varied *adjective* of different sorts; full of variety.

variegated (*say* vair-ig-ay-tid) *adjective* with patches of different colours. **variegation** *noun*

variety *noun* (*plural* **varieties**) **1** a quantity of different kinds of things. **2** the quality of not always being the same; variation, *a life full of variety*. **3** a particular kind of something, *There are several varieties of spaniel*. **4** an entertainment that includes short performances of various kinds.

various *adjective* **1** of several kinds; unlike one another, *for various reasons*. **2** several, *We met various people.* **variously** *adverb*

varnish¹ *noun* (*plural* **varnishes**) a liquid that dries to form a hard shiny usually transparent coating.

varnish² *verb* coat something with varnish.

varsity *noun* (*plural* **varsities**) (*informal*) university.

vary *verb* (**varied**, **varying**) **1** make or become different; change. **2** be different.

vascular *adjective* consisting of tubes or similar vessels for circulating blood, sap, or water in animals or plants, *the vascular system*.

vase *noun* an open usually tall container used for holding cut flowers or as an ornament.

Vaseline *noun* (*trade mark*) petroleum jelly for use as an ointment.

vassal *noun* a humble servant or subordinate.

vast *adjective* very great, especially in area, *a vast expanse of water*. **vastly** *adverb*, **vastness** *noun*

VAT *abbreviation* value added tax, a tax on goods and services.

vat *noun* a very large container for holding liquid.

vaudeville (*say* vawd-vil) *noun* a kind of variety entertainment.

vault¹ *verb* jump over something, especially while supporting yourself on your hands or with the help of a pole.

vault² *noun* **1** a vaulting jump. **2** an arched roof. **3** an underground room used to store things. **4** a room for storing money or valuables. **5** a burial chamber.

vaulted *adjective* having an arched roof.

vaulting-horse *noun* a padded structure for vaulting over in gymnastics.

vaunt *verb* & *noun* (*old use* or *poetical*) boast.

VDU *abbreviation* visual display unit.

veal *noun* calf's flesh used as food.

vector *noun* (in mathematics) a quantity that has size and direction (e.g. velocity, = speed in a certain direction). **vectorial** *adjective*

Veda (*say* vay-da or vee-da) *noun* the most ancient and sacred literature of the Hindus. **Vedic** *adjective*

veer *verb* change direction; swerve.

vegetable *noun* a plant that can be used as food.

vegetarian *noun* a person who does not eat meat. **vegetarianism** *noun*

vegetate *verb* (**vegetated, vegetating**) live a dull or inactive life.

vegetation *noun* 1 plants that are growing. 2 vegetating.

vegetative propagation *noun* the asexual reproduction of plants from any plant part, e.g. cuttings, buds, suckers.

vehement (*say* vee-im-ent) *adjective* showing strong feeling, *a vehement refusal.* **vehemently** *adverb,* **vehemence** *noun*

vehicle *noun* a device for transporting people or goods on land or in space.

veil[1] *noun* a piece of thin material worn to cover the face or head.

take the veil become a nun.

veil[2] *verb* cover with a veil or as if with a veil; conceal partially.

vein *noun* 1 any of the tubes that carry blood from all parts of the body to the heart. (Compare *artery.*) 2 a line or streak on a leaf, rock, insect's wing, etc. 3 a long deposit of mineral or ore in the middle of a rock. 4 a mood or manner, *She spoke in a serious vein.*

veld (*say* felt) *noun* an area of open country; a landscape, grassland, etc. which has a particular vegetation or ecology, *sweet veld.*

veldcraft knowledge about the veld and how to manage it.

veldkos food (e.g. bulbs, insects, small animals) gathered from the veld.

veld-cornet *noun* a field-cornet.

vellies *plural noun* (*informal*) velskoens.

vellum *noun* smooth parchment or writing-paper.

velocity *noun* (*plural* **velocities**) speed.

velour (*say* vil-**oor**) *noun* a thick velvety material.

velskoen *noun* (*plural* **velskoens** or **velskoene**) a rough suede ankle-boot or shoe, often with a light rubber sole.

velvet *noun* a woven material with very short soft furry fibres on one side. **velvety** *adjective*

venal (*say* **veen**-al) *adjective* able to be bribed. **venality** *noun*

venation *noun* the way in which the veins in a leaf are arranged.

vend *verb* offer something for sale.

vendetta *noun* a feud.

vending-machine *noun* a slot-machine where small articles can be obtained.

vendor *noun* a seller.

veneer *noun* 1 a thin layer of good wood covering the surface of a cheaper wood in furniture etc. 2 an outward show of some good quality, *a veneer of politeness.*

venerable *adjective* worthy of being venerated, especially because of great age.

venerate *verb* (**venerated, venerating**) honour with great respect or reverence. **veneration** *noun*

venereal (*say* vin-**eer**-ee al) *adjective* of sexual intercourse; caused by sexual intercourse with an infected person, *venereal diseases.*

venetian blind *noun* a window blind consisting of horizontal strips that can be adjusted to let light in or shut it out.

vengeance *noun* revenge.

with a vengeance very strongly or effectively.

vengeful *adjective* seeking vengeance. **vengefully** *adverb,* **vengefulness** *noun*

venial (*say* **veen**-ee-al) *adjective* (of sins or faults) pardonable, not serious.

venison *noun* deer's flesh as food.

venom *noun* 1 the poisonous fluid produced by snakes, scorpions, etc. 2 very bitter feeling towards somebody; hatred, *Her words dripped venom.* **venomous** *adjective*

vent[1] *noun* an opening in something, especially to let out smoke or gas etc.

give vent to express your feelings etc. openly.

vent[2] *verb* 1 make a vent in something. 2 give vent to feelings, *He vented his anger on the ball.*

ventilate *verb* (**ventilated, ventilating**) let air move freely in and out of a room etc. **ventilation** *noun,* **ventilator** *noun*

ventral *adjective* of or on the abdomen, *This fish has a ventral fin.*

ventriloquist *noun* an entertainer who makes his or her voice sound as if it comes from another source. **ventriloquism** *noun*

venture[1] *noun* something you decide to do that is risky.

venture[2] *verb* (**ventured**, **venturing**) risk; dare to do or say something or to go somewhere, *We ventured out into the snow.*

venturesome *adjective* ready to take risks; daring.

venue (*say* **ven**-yoo) *noun* the place where a meeting, sports match, etc. is held.

veracity (*say* ver-**as**-it-ee) *noun* truth. **veracious** (*say* ver-**ay**-shus) *adjective*

veranda *noun* a terrace with a roof along the side of a house.

verb *noun* a word or phrase which shows an action, an event, or a state, e.g. *bring, happen, sleep.*

verbal *adjective* **1** of or in words; spoken, not written, *a verbal statement.* **2** of verbs. **verbally** *adverb*

verbatim (*say* ver-**bay**-tim) *adverb & adjective* in exactly the same words, *He copied his friend's essay verbatim.*

verbose *adjective* using more words than are needed. **verbosely** *adverb*, **verbosity** (*say* ver-**boss**-it-ee) *noun*

verdant *adjective* (of grass or fields) green.

verdict *noun* a judgement or decision made after considering something, especially that made by a jury.

verdigris (*say* **verd**-i-gree) *noun* green rust on copper or brass.

verdure *noun* green vegetation; its greenness.

verge[1] *noun* **1** the extreme edge or brink of something. **2** a strip of grass along the edge of a road or path etc.

verge[2] *verb* (**verged**, **verging**) **verge on** border on something; be close to.

verger *noun* a person who is caretaker and attendant in a church.

verify *verb* (**verified**, **verifying**) check or show that something is true or correct. **verifiable** *adjective*, **verification** *noun*

verisimilitude *noun* an appearance of being true or lifelike.

veritable *adjective* real; rightly named, *a veritable villain.* **veritably** *adverb*

verity *noun* (*plural* **verities**) truth.

verkramp *adjective* narrow-minded; conservative. (Compare *verlig*.)

verlig *adjective* broad-minded; open to new ideas. (Compare *verkramp*.)

vermicelli (*say* verm-i-**sel**-ee) *noun* pasta made in long thin threads.

vermilion *noun & adjective* bright red.

vermin *plural noun* **1** pests (e.g. foxes, rats, mice) regarded as harmful to domestic animals, crops, or food. **2** unpleasant or parasitic insects, e.g. lice. **verminous** *adjective*

vernacular (*say* ver-**nak**-yoo-ler) *noun* the language of a country or district, as distinct from an official or formal language.

vernal *adjective* of the season of spring.

verruca (*say* ver-**oo**-ka) *noun* a kind of wart on the sole of the foot.

versatile *adjective* able to do or be used for many different things. **versatility** *noun*

verse *noun* **1** writing arranged in short lines, usually with a particular rhythm and often with rhymes. **2** a group of lines forming a unit in a poem or hymn. **3** each of the short numbered sections of a chapter in the Bible.

versed *adjective* **versed in** experienced or skilled in something.

version *noun* **1** a particular person's account of something that happened. **2** a translation, *modern versions of the Bible.* **3** a special or different form of something, *the latest version of this car.*

versus *preposition* against; competing with, *Chiefs versus Pirates.*

vertebra *noun* (*plural* **vertebrae**) each of the bones that form the backbone.

vertebrate *noun* an animal that has a backbone. (The opposite is *invertebrate*.)

vertex *noun* (*plural* **vertices** (*say* **ver**-tis-eez)) the highest point (*apex*) of a cone or triangle, or of a hill etc.

vertical *adjective* at right angles to something horizontal; upright. **vertically** *adverb*

vertigo *noun* a feeling of dizziness and loss of balance, especially when you are very high up.

verve (*say* verv) *noun* enthusiasm; liveliness.

very[1] *adverb* 1 to a great amount or intensity; extremely, *It was very cold.* 2 (used to emphasize something), *on the very next day*; *the very last drop.*

very[2] *adjective* 1 exact; actual, *It's the very thing we need.* 2 extreme, *at the very end.*

vespers *plural noun* a church service held in the evening.

vessel *noun* 1 a ship or boat. 2 a container, especially for liquid. 3 a tube carrying blood or other liquid in the body of an animal or plant.

vest[1] *noun* an undergarment covering the trunk of the body.

vest[2] *verb* 1 confer something as a right, *The power to make laws is vested in Parliament.* 2 (*old use*) clothe.

vested interest a right that benefits a person or group and is securely held by them.

vestibule *noun* 1 an entrance hall or lobby. 2 a church porch.

vestige *noun* a trace; a very small amount, especially of something that formerly existed. **vestigial** *adjective*

vestment *noun* a ceremonial garment, especially one worn by clergy or choir at a service.

vestry *noun* (*plural* **vestries**) a room in a church where vestments are kept and where clergy and choir put these on.

vet[1] *noun* a person trained to give medical and surgical treatment to animals.

vet[2] *verb* (**vetted, vetting**) check a thing to see if it has any mistakes or faults.

vetch *noun* a plant of the pea family, often used for fodder.

veteran *noun* a person who has had long service or experience in something.

veteran car a car that is at least seventy years old.

veterinary (*say* vet-rin-ree) *adjective* of the medical and surgical treatment of animals, *a veterinary surgeon.*

vetkoek (*say* fet-kuuk) *noun* (*plural* **vetkoek**) a cake of deep-fried dough with various fillings.

veto[1] (*say* vee-toh) *noun* (*plural* **vetoes**) 1 a refusal to let something happen.

2 the right to prohibit something, *the presidential veto.*

veto[2] *verb* (**vetoed, vetoing**) refuse or prohibit something.

vex *verb* annoy; cause somebody worry. **vexation** *noun,* **vexatious** *adjective*

vexed question a problem that is difficult or much discussed.

VHF *abbreviation* very high frequency.

via (*say* vy-a) *preposition* through, *The train goes from Cape Town to Johannesburg via Matjiesfontein.*

viable *adjective* able to exist successfully; practicable. **viability** *noun*

viaduct *noun* a long bridge, usually with many arches, carrying a road or railway over a valley or low ground. (Compare *aqueduct.*)

vial *noun* a small glass bottle.

viands (*say* vy-andz) *plural noun* food.

vibrant *adjective* vibrating; lively.

vibraphone *noun* a musical instrument like a xylophone with metal bars under which there are tiny electric fans making a vibrating effect.

vibrate *verb* (**vibrated, vibrating**) 1 shake very quickly to and fro. 2 make a throbbing sound. **vibration** *noun*

vicar *noun* a member of the clergy who is in charge of a parish.

vicarage *noun* the house of a vicar.

vicarious (*say* vik-**air**-ee-us) *adjective* felt by imagining you share someone else's activities, *We felt a vicarious thrill by watching people skiing.*

vice[1] *noun* 1 evil; wickedness. 2 an evil or bad habit; a bad fault, *Laziness is a nasty vice.*

vice[2] *noun* a device for gripping something and holding it firmly while you work on it.

vice- *prefix* 1 authorized to act as a deputy or substitute (as in *vice-captain, vice-president*). 2 next in rank to someone (as in *vice-admiral*).

vicinity *noun* the area near or round something.

vicious *adjective* evil; brutal; dangerously wicked or strong. **viciously** *adverb,* **viciousness** *noun*

vicious circle a situation where a problem

produces an effect which itself produces the original problem or makes it worse.

vicissitude (*say* viss-**iss**-i-tewd) *noun* a change of circumstances, *the vicissitudes of love.*

victim *noun* someone who is injured, killed, robbed, etc.

victimize *verb* (**victimized, victimizing**) make a victim of someone; punish a person unfairly. **victimization** *noun*

victor *noun* the winner.

Victorian *adjective* of the time of Queen Victoria of England (1837–1901). **Victorian** *noun*

victory *noun* (*plural* **victories**) success won against an opponent in a battle, contest, or game. **victorious** *adjective*

victualler (*say* **vit**-ler) *noun* a person who supplies victuals. **licensed victualler** a person who holds the licence of a public house.

victuals (*say* **vit**-alz) *plural noun* food; provisions.

video *noun* (*plural* **videos**) **1** recorded or broadcast pictures. **2** (*informal*) a video recorder. **3** (*informal*) a film etc. recorded on a videotape. **video recorder** a device for recording a television programme etc. on magnetic tape for playing back later.

videotape *noun* magnetic tape suitable for recording television programmes.

vie *verb* (**vied, vying**) compete; carry on a rivalry, *vying with each other.*

view[1] *noun* **1** what can be seen from one place; beautiful scenery. **2** sight; range of vision, *The ship sailed into view.* **3** an opinion, *She has strong views about politics.* **in view of** because of. **on view** displayed for inspection. **with a view to** with the hope or intention of.

view[2] *verb* **1** look at something. **2** consider, *He viewed it with suspicion.* **viewer** *noun*

viewpoint *noun* a point of view.

vigil (*say* **vij**-il) *noun* staying awake to keep watch or to pray, *a long vigil.*

vigilant (*say* **vij**-il-ant) *adjective* watchful.

vigilantly *adverb*, **vigilance** *noun*

vigilante (*say* vij-il-**an**-tee) *noun* a member of a group who organize themselves, without authority, to try to prevent crime and disorder in a small area.

vigorous *adjective* full of vigour. **vigorously** *adverb*

vigour *noun* strength; energy; liveliness.

Viking *noun* a Scandinavian trader and pirate operating in northern and western Europe in the 8th–10th centuries.

vile *adjective* **1** extremely disgusting. **2** very bad or wicked. **vilely** *adverb*, **vileness** *noun*

vilify (*say* **vil**-if-I) *verb* (**vilified, vilifying**) say unpleasant things about a person or thing. **vilification** *noun*

villa *noun* a house.

village *noun* a group of houses and other buildings in a country district, smaller than a town. **villager** *noun*

villain *noun* a wicked person; a criminal. **villainous** *adjective*, **villainy** *noun*

villein (*say* **vil**-in) *noun* a tenant in feudal times in medieval Europe.

vim *noun* (*informal*) vigour.

vindicate *verb* (**vindicated, vindicating**) **1** clear a person of blame or suspicion etc. **2** prove something to be true or worth while, *Subsequent events vindicated her suspicions.* **vindication** *noun*

vindictive *adjective* showing a desire for revenge. **vindictively** *adverb*, **vindictiveness** *noun*

vine *noun* a climbing or trailing plant whose fruit is the grape.

vinegar *noun* a sour liquid used to flavour food or in pickling.

vineyard (*say* **vin**-yard) *noun* a plantation of vines producing grapes for making wine.

vintage *noun* **1** the harvest of a season's grapes; the wine made from this. **2** the period from which something comes. **vintage car** a car made between 1917 and 1930.

vinyl (*say* **vy**-nil) *noun* a kind of plastic.

viola[1] (*say* vee-**oh**-la) *noun* a musical instrument like a violin but slightly larger and with a lower pitch.

viola² (*say* **vy**-ol-a) *noun* a plant of the kind that includes violets and pansies.

violate *verb* (**violated, violating**) 1 break a promise, law, or treaty etc. 2 break into somewhere; treat a person or place without respect, *violate someone's privacy.* **violation** *noun*, **violator** *noun*

violence *noun* force that does harm or damage. **violent** *adjective*, **violently** *adverb*

violet *noun* 1 a small plant that often has purple flowers. 2 purple.

violin *noun* a musical instrument with four strings, played with a bow. **violinist** *noun*

VIP *abbreviation* very important person.

viper *noun* a small poisonous snake.

virago (*say* vir-**ah**-goh) *noun* (*plural* **viragos**) a fierce or bullying woman.

virgin¹ *noun* a person, especially a woman, who has never had sexual intercourse. **virginal** *adjective*, **virginity** *noun*

virgin² *adjective* 1 of a virgin. 2 spotless. 3 not yet touched, *virgin snow.*

virile (*say* **vir**-I'l) *adjective* having masculine strength or vigour. **virility** *noun*

virology *noun* the study of viruses. **virological** *adjective*, **virologist** *noun*

virtual *adjective* being something in effect though not in form, *His silence was a virtual admission of guilt.* **virtually** *adverb*

virtue *noun* 1 moral goodness; a particular form of this, *Honesty is a virtue.* 2 a good quality; an advantage, *The car's main virtue is its economy.* **virtuous** *adjective*, **virtuously** *adverb* **in virtue of** because of.

virtuoso (*say* ver-tew-**oh**-soh) *noun* (*plural* **virtuosos** or **virtuosi**) a person with outstanding skill, especially in singing or playing music. **virtuosity** *noun*

virulent (*say* **vir**-oo-lent) *adjective* 1 strongly poisonous or harmful, *a virulent disease.* 2 bitterly hostile, *virulent criticism.* **virulence** *noun*

virus *noun* (*plural* **viruses**) 1 a very tiny living thing, smaller than a bacterium, that can cause disease in living things. 2 a hidden code in a computer program

that destroys or corrupts data in a computer system.

visa (*say* **vee**-za) *noun* an official mark put on someone's passport by officials of a foreign country to show that the holder has permission to enter that country.

visage (*say* **viz**-ij) *noun* a person's face.

vis-à-vis (*say* veez-ah-**vee**) *adverb* & *preposition* 1 in a position facing one another; opposite to. 2 as compared with.

viscera (*say* **vis**-er-a) *plural noun* the intestines and other internal organs of the body.

viscid (*say* **vis**-id) *adjective* thick and gluey. **viscidity** *noun*

viscose (*say* **vis**-kohs) *noun* fabric made from viscous cellulose.

viscount (*say* **vy**-kownt) *noun* a nobleman ranking below an earl and above a baron. **viscountess** *noun*

viscous (*say* **visk**-us) *adjective* thick and gluey, not pouring easily. **viscosity** *noun*

visible *adjective* able to be seen or noticed, *The ship was visible on the horizon.* **visibly** *adverb*, **visibility** *noun*

● USAGE: Do not confuse with *visual.*

vision *noun* 1 the ability to see; sight. 2 something seen in a person's imagination or in a dream. 3 foresight and wisdom in planning things. 4 a person or thing that is beautiful to see. 5 the picture on a television screen, *We apologize for the poor vision in some areas.*

visionary¹ *adjective* 1 imaginary; fanciful. 2 having vision or foresight.

visionary² *noun* (*plural* **visionaries**) a person with visionary ideas.

visit¹ *verb* 1 go to see a person or place. 2 stay somewhere for a while. **visitor** *noun*

visit² *noun* the action of visiting.

visitant *noun* 1 a visitor, especially a supernatural one. 2 a bird that is a visitor to an area while migrating.

visitation *noun* an official visit, especially to inspect something.

visor (*say* **vy**-zer) *noun* 1 the part of a helmet that covers the face. 2 a shield to protect the eyes from bright light or sunshine.

vista *noun* a long view.

visual *adjective* of or used in seeing; of sight. **visually** *adverb*

visual aids pictures and films etc. used as an aid in teaching.

visual display unit a device that looks like a television screen and displays data being received from a computer or fed into it.
● USAGE: Do not confuse with *visible*.

visualize *verb* (**visualized, visualizing**) form a mental picture of something. **visualization** *noun*

vital *adjective* 1 connected with life; necessary for life to continue, *vital functions such as breathing*. 2 essential; very important, *a vital part of the plan*. **vitally** *adverb*

vitality *noun* liveliness; energy.

vitalize *verb* (**vitalized, vitalizing**) put life or vitality into something.

vitamin (*say* vit-a-min or vy-ta-min) *noun* any of a number of substances that are present in various foods and are essential to keep people and animals healthy.

vitiate (*say* vish-ee-ayt) *verb* (**vitiated, vitiating**) spoil something by making it imperfect. **vitiation** *noun*

vitreous (*say* vit-ree-us) *adjective* like glass in being hard, transparent, or brittle, *vitreous enamel*.

vitriol (*say* vit-ree-ol) *noun* 1 sulphuric acid or one of its compounds. 2 savage criticism. **vitriolic** *adjective*

vituperation *noun* abusive words.

viva (*say* vee-va) *interjection* a cry or salute meaning 'long live!', *Viva Mandela!*

vivacious (*say* viv-ay-shus) *adjective* happy and lively. **vivaciously** *adverb*, **vivacity** *noun*

vivid *adjective* 1 bright and strong or clear, *vivid colours; a vivid description*. 2 active and lively, *a vivid imagination*. **vividly** *adverb*, **vividness** *noun*

viviparous (*say* vi-vi-pa-rus) *adjective* producing living young which develop inside the mother's body.

vivisection *noun* doing surgical experiments on live animals.

vixen *noun* a female fox.

vizier (*say* viz-eer) *noun* (in former times) an important Muslim official.

vlaktes *plural noun* plains; flat land.

vlei (*say* flay) *noun* a lake or swamp.

vlek (*say* flek) *verb* (**vlekked, vlekking**) gut or clean a fish, carcass, etc.

vocabulary *noun* (*plural* **vocabularies**) 1 a list of words with their meanings. 2 the words known to a person or used in a particular book or subject etc., *She has a wide vocabulary*.

vocal *adjective* of or producing or using the voice. **vocally** *adverb*

vocal cords two strap-like membranes in the throat that can be made to vibrate and produce sounds.

vocalist *noun* a singer, especially in a pop group.

vocation *noun* 1 a person's job or occupation. 2 a strong desire to do a particular kind of work, or feeling of being called by God to do something. **vocational** *adjective*

vociferate (*say* vo-sif-er-ayt) *verb* (**vociferated, vociferating**) say something loudly or noisily. **vociferation** *noun*

vociferous (*say* vo-sif-er-us) *adjective* making an outcry; shouting.

vodka *noun* a strong alcoholic drink very popular in Russia.

voetstoots *adjective & adverb* (of a thing sold) as it stands, *The car was sold voetstoots;* (of a sale) at the buyer's risk, *a voetstoots clause*.

vogue *noun* the current fashion.

voice[1] *noun* 1 sounds formed by the vocal cords and uttered by the mouth, especially in speaking, singing, etc. 2 the ability to speak or sing, *She has lost her voice*. 3 an opinion expressed. 4 the right to express an opinion or desire, *I have no voice in this matter*.

voice[2] *verb* (**voiced, voicing**) say something, *We voiced our opinions*.

void[1] *adjective* 1 empty. 2 having no legal validity, *null and void*.

void[2] *noun* an empty space.

voile (*say* voil) *noun* a very thin almost transparent material.

volatile (*say* vol-a-tyl) *adjective* 1 evaporating quickly, *a volatile liquid*.

2 changing quickly from one mood or interest to another. **volatility** *noun*

volcano *noun* (*plural* **volcanoes**) a mountain with an opening at the top from which lava and hot gases etc. flow. **volcanic** *adjective*

vole *noun* a small animal rather like a rat.

volition *noun* using your own will in choosing to do something, *She left of her own volition.*

volk *noun* people; nation. **Volksraad** the legislative assembly of Afrikaner republics in former times.

volley[1] *noun* (*plural* **volleys**) **1** a number of bullets or shells etc. fired at the same time. **2** hitting back the ball in tennis etc. before it touches the ground.

volley[2] *verb* send or hit something in a volley or volleys.

volley-ball *noun* a game in which two teams hit a large ball to and fro over a net with their hands.

volt *noun* a unit for measuring electric force.

voltage *noun* electric force measured in volts.

voluble *adjective* talking very much. **volubly** *adverb*, **volubility** *noun*

volume *noun* **1** the amount of space filled by something. **2** an amount or quantity, *The volume of work has increased.* **3** the strength or power of sound. **4** a book, especially one of a set.

voluminous (*say* vol-**yoo**-min-us) *adjective* **1** bulky; large and full, *a voluminous skirt.* **2** numerous; filling many volumes, *a voluminous writer.*

voluntary[1] *adjective* **1** done or doing something willingly, not by being compelled. **2** unpaid, *a voluntary position in the organization.* **voluntarily** *adverb*

voluntary[2] *noun* (*plural* **voluntaries**) an organ solo, often improvised, played before or after a church service.

volunteer[1] *verb* give or offer something of your own accord.

volunteer[2] *noun* a person who volunteers to do something, e.g. to serve in the armed forces.

voluptuous *adjective* giving a luxurious or sensual feeling, *voluptuous furnishings.*

vomit *verb* bring up food etc. from the stomach and out through the mouth; be sick. **vomit** *noun*

voodoo *noun* a form of witchcraft and magical rites, especially in the West Indies.

Voortrekker *noun* a person who took part in the Great Trek.

voracious (*say* vor-**ay**-shus) *adjective* greedy; devouring things eagerly. **voraciously** *adverb*, **voracity** *noun*

vortex *noun* (*plural* **vortices**) a whirlpool or whirlwind.

vote[1] *verb* (**voted**, **voting**) show which person or thing you prefer by putting up your hand, making a mark on a paper, etc. **voter** *noun*

vote[2] *noun* **1** the action of voting. **2** the right to vote.

votive *adjective* given in fulfilment of a vow, *votive offerings at the shrine.*

vouch *verb* **vouch for** guarantee that something is true or certain, *I will vouch for his honesty.*

voucher *noun* a piece of paper that can be exchanged for certain goods or services; a receipt.

vouchsafe *verb* (**vouchsafed**, **vouchsafing**) grant something in a gracious or condescending way, *She did not vouchsafe a reply.*

vow[1] *noun* a solemn promise, especially to God or a saint.

vow[2] *verb* make a vow.

vowel *noun* any of the letters a, e, i, o, u, and sometimes y, which represent sounds in which breath comes out freely. (Compare *consonant.*)

voyage[1] *noun* a long journey on water or in space.

voyage[2] *verb* (**voyaged**, **voyaging**) make a voyage. **voyager** *noun*

vrot *adjective* (*slang*) rotten.

vuka *interjection* wake up!

vula *interjection* open; open up!

vulcanize *verb* (**vulcanized**, **vulcanizing**) treat rubber with sulphur to strengthen it. **vulcanization** *noun*

vulgar *adjective* rude; without good manners. **vulgarly** *adverb*, **vulgarity** *noun*

vulgar fraction a fraction shown by numbers above and below a line (e.g. $^2/_3$, $^5/_8$), not a decimal fraction.

vulnerable *adjective* able to be hurt or harmed or attacked. **vulnerability** *noun*

vulture *noun* a large bird that feeds on dead animals.

vulva *noun* the outer parts of the female genitals.

vygie (*say* **fay**-khee) *noun* a brightly-coloured flowering plant which has fleshy leaves.

vying *present participle* of **vie**.

Ww

W. *abbreviation* west; western.

wad[1] (*say* wod) *noun* a pad or bundle of soft material or pieces of paper etc.

wad[2] *verb* (**wadded, wadding**) pad something with soft material.

waddle *verb* (**waddled, waddling**) walk with short steps, swaying from side to side. **waddle** *noun*

wade *verb* (**waded, wading**) walk through water or mud etc. **wader** *noun*

wafer *noun* a kind of thin biscuit.

waffle[1] (*say* wof-el) *noun* a small cake made of batter and eaten hot.

waffle[2] (*say* wof-el) *noun* (*informal*) vague wordy talk or writing. **waffle** *verb*

waft (*say* woft) *verb* carry or float gently through the air or over water.

wag[1] *verb* (**wagged, wagging**) move quickly to and fro. **wag** *noun*

wag[2] *noun* a person who makes jokes.

wage[1] *noun* (also **wages** *plural noun*) a regular payment to someone in return for his or her work.

wage[2] *verb* (**waged, waging**) carry on a war or campaign.

wager (*say* way-jer) *noun* & *verb* bet.

waggle *verb* (**waggled, waggling**) wag. **waggle** *noun*

wagon *noun* 1 a cart with four wheels, pulled by a horse or an ox. 2 an open railway truck, e.g. for coal. 3 a trolley for carrying food etc.

wagoner *noun* the driver of a horse-drawn wagon.

wagtail *noun* a small bird with a long tail that it moves up and down.

waif *noun* a homeless and helpless person, especially a child.

wail *verb* make a long sad cry. **wail** *noun*

wainscoting *noun* wooden panelling on the wall of a room.

waist *noun* the narrow part in the middle of the body.

waistcoat *noun* a short close-fitting jacket without sleeves, worn over a shirt and under a jacket.

wait[1] *verb* 1 stay somewhere or postpone an action until something happens; pause. 2 be postponed, *This question must wait until our next meeting.* 3 wait on people. **wait on** hand food and drink to people at a meal; be an attendant to someone.

wait[2] *noun* an act or time of waiting, *We had a long wait for the train.*

waiter *noun* a man employed to serve people with food. **waitress** *noun*

waiting-list *noun* a list of people waiting for something to become available.

waiting-room *noun* a room provided for people who are waiting for something.

waive *verb* (**waived, waiving**) not insist on having something, despite having a legal or official right to it, *He waived a claim to his mother's painting.*
● USAGE: Do not confuse with *wave*.

wake[1] *verb* (**woke, woken, waking**) 1 stop sleeping, *Wake up! I woke when I heard the bell.* 2 cause someone to stop sleeping, *You have woken the baby.*

wake[2] *noun* (in Ireland) festivities held in connection with a funeral.

wake[3] *noun* 1 the track left on the water by a moving ship. 2 currents of air left behind a moving aircraft. **in the wake of** following.

wakeful *adjective* unable to sleep.

waken *verb* wake.

walk[1] *verb* move along on your feet at an ordinary speed. **walker** *noun*

walk[2] *noun* 1 a journey on foot. 2 the manner of walking, *I recognize her* *walk.* **3** a path or route for walking.

walk of life a person's occupation or social level.

walkabout *noun* an informal stroll among a crowd by an important visitor.

walkie-talkie *noun* (*informal*) a small portable radio transmitter and receiver.

walking-stick *noun* a stick for use as a support while walking.

walk-over *noun* an easy victory.

wall[1] *noun* **1** a continuous upright structure, usually made of brick or stone, forming one of the sides of a building or room or supporting something or enclosing an area. **2** the outside part of something, *the wall of an artery.*

wall[2] *verb* enclose or block with a wall.

wallaby *noun* (*plural* **wallabies**) a kind of small kangaroo.

wallet *noun* a small flat folding case for holding banknotes, documents, etc.

wallflower *noun* a garden plant with fragrant flowers, blooming in spring.

wallop *verb* (**walloped, walloping**) (*slang*) thrash. **wallop** *noun*

wallow *verb* **1** roll about in water, mud, etc. **2** get great pleasure by being surrounded by something, *wallowing in luxury.* **wallow** *noun*

wallpaper *noun* paper used to cover the inside walls of rooms.

walnut *noun* an edible nut with a wrinkled surface.

walrus *noun* (*plural* **walruses**) a large Arctic sea-animal with two long tusks.

waltz[1] *noun* (*plural* **waltzes**) a dance with three beats to a bar.

waltz[2] *verb* dance a waltz.

wan (*say* wonn) *adjective* pale from being ill or tired. **wanly** *adverb*, **wanness** *noun*

wand *noun* a thin rod, especially one used by a magician.

wander[1] *verb* **1** go about without trying to reach a particular place. **2** leave the right path or direction; stray. **wanderer** *noun*

wander[2] *noun* a wandering journey.

wanderlust *noun* a strong desire to travel.

wane *verb* (**waned, waning**) **1** (of the moon) show a bright area that becomes gradually smaller after being full. (The op-

posite is *wax.*) **2** become less or smaller, *His popularity waned.* **wane** *noun*

wangle *verb* (**wangled, wangling**) (*slang*) get or arrange something by using trickery, special influence, etc. **wangle** *noun*

want[1] *verb* **1** wish to have something. **2** need, *Your hair wants cutting.* **3** be without something; lack. **4** be without the necessaries of life, *Waste not, want not.*

want[2] *noun* **1** a wish to have something. **2** lack or need of something, *The plants died from want of water.*

wanted *adjective* (of a suspected criminal) that the police wish to find or arrest.

wanton (*say* **wonn**-ton) *adjective* irresponsible; without a motive, *wanton damage.*

war *noun* **1** fighting between nations or groups, especially using armed forces. **2** a serious struggle or effort against crime, disease, poverty, etc.

at war engaged in a war.

warble *verb* (**warbled, warbling**) sing with a trilling sound, as some birds do. **warble** *noun*

warbler *noun* a kind of small bird.

ward[1] *noun* **1** a room with beds for patients in a hospital. **2** a child looked after by a guardian. **3** an area electing a councillor to represent it.

ward[2] *verb* **ward off** keep something away.

warden *noun* an official who is in charge of a hostel, college, etc., or who supervises something.

warder *noun* an official in charge of prisoners in a prison.

wardrobe *noun* **1** a cupboard to hang clothes in. **2** a stock of clothes or costumes.

ware *noun* manufactured goods of a certain kind, *hardware*; *silverware.*

wares *plural noun* goods offered for sale.

warehouse *noun* a large building where goods are stored.

warfare *noun* war; fighting.

warhead *noun* the head of a missile or torpedo etc., containing explosives.

warlike *adjective* **1** fond of making war. **2** of or for war.

warm[1] *adjective* **1** fairly hot; not cold

or cool. **2** loving; enthusiastic, *a warm welcome.* **warmly** *adverb,* **warmness** *noun,* **warmth** *noun*

warm² *verb* make or become warm.

warm-blooded *adjective* having blood that remains warm permanently.

warn *verb* tell someone about a danger etc. that may affect them, or about what they should do, *I warned you to take your raincoat.* **warning** *noun*

warp¹ (*say* worp) *verb* **1** bend out of shape, e.g. by dampness. **2** distort a person's ideas etc., *Jealousy warped his mind.*

warp² *noun* **1** a warped condition. **2** the lengthwise threads in weaving, crossed by the weft.

warrant¹ *noun* a document that authorizes a person to do something (e.g. to search a place) or to receive something.

warrant² *verb* **1** justify, *Nothing can warrant such rudeness.* **2** guarantee, *I'll warrant that you'll regret it.*

warranty *noun* a guarantee.

warren *noun* **1** a piece of ground where there are many burrows in which rabbits live and breed. **2** a building or place with many winding passages.

warring *adjective* occupied in war.

warrior *noun* a person who fights in battle; a soldier.

warship *noun* a ship for use in war.

wart *noun* a small hard lump on the skin, caused by a virus.

warthog *noun* a wild pig which has curved tusks and lumps on its face.

wartime *noun* a time of war.

wary (*say* wair-ee) *adjective* cautious; looking carefully for possible danger or difficulty. **warily** *adverb,* **wariness** *noun*

wash¹ *verb* **1** clean something with water or other liquid. **2** be washable, *Cotton washes easily.* **3** flow against or over something, *Waves washed over the deck.* **4** carry along by a moving liquid, *A wave washed him overboard.* **5** (*informal*) be accepted or believed, *That excuse won't wash.*

wash out (*informal*) cancel something.

wash up wash dishes and cutlery etc. after use. **washing-up** *noun*

wash² *noun* (*plural* **washes**) **1** the action of washing. **2** clothes etc. being washed. **3** the disturbed water or air behind a moving ship or aircraft. **4** a thin coating of colour.

washable *adjective* able to be washed without becoming damaged.

washbasin *noun* a small sink for washing your hands etc.

washer *noun* **1** a small ring of rubber or metal etc. placed between two surfaces (e.g. under a bolt or screw) to fit them tightly together. **2** a washing-machine.

washing *noun* clothes etc. being washed.

washing-machine *noun* a machine for washing clothes etc.

wash-out *noun* (*informal*) a complete failure.

wasn't (*mainly spoken*) was not.

wasp *noun* a stinging insect with black and yellow stripes round its body.

wastage *noun* loss of something by waste.

waste¹ *verb* (**wasted, wasting**) **1** use something in an extravagant way or without getting enough results. **2** fail to use something, *You wasted an opportunity.* **3** make or become gradually weaker or useless, *She wasted away through illness.*

waste² *adjective* **1** left over or thrown away because it is not wanted. **2** not used; not usable, *waste land.*

lay waste destroy the crops and buildings etc. of a district.

waste³ *noun* **1** the action of wasting a thing, not using it well, *a waste of time.* **2** things that are not wanted or not used. **3** an area of waste land, *the wastes of the Sahara Desert.* **wasteful** *adjective,* **wastefully** *noun,* **wastefulness** *noun*

wastrel (*say* way-strel) *noun* a person who wastes his or her life and does nothing useful.

watch¹ *verb* **1** look at a person or thing for some time. **2** be on guard or ready for something to happen, *Watch for the robot to turn green.* **3** take care of something. **watcher** *noun*

watch² *noun* (*plural* **watches**) **1** the action of watching. **2** a turn of being on duty in a ship. **3** a device like a small clock, usually worn on the wrist.

watchful *adjective* watching closely; alert. **watchfully** *adverb*, **watchfulness** *noun*

watchman *noun* (*plural* **watchmen**) a person employed to look after an empty building etc., especially at night.

watchword *noun* a word or phrase that sums up a group's policy; a slogan, *Our watchword is 'safety first'.*

water¹ *noun* **1** a colourless odourless tasteless liquid that is a compound of hydrogen and oxygen. **2** a lake or sea etc. **3** the tide, *at high water.* **4** urine; sweat; saliva.

water² *verb* **1** sprinkle or supply something with water. **2** produce tears or saliva, *It makes my mouth water.*

water down dilute.

waterblommetjie *noun* a plant that grows in water, with small flowers, often eaten in a mutton stew, *waterblommetjie bredie.*

water-closet *noun* a lavatory with a pan that is flushed by water.

water-colour *noun* **1** paint made with pigment and water (not oil). **2** a painting done with this kind of paint.

watercress *noun* a kind of cress that grows in water.

waterfall *noun* a stream flowing over the edge of a cliff or large rock.

watering-can *noun* a container with a long spout, for watering plants.

water-lily *noun* a plant that grows in water, with broad floating leaves and large flowers.

waterlogged *adjective* completely soaked or swamped in water.

watermark *noun* **1** a mark showing how high a river or tide rises or how low it falls. **2** a design that can be seen in some kinds of paper when they are held up to the light.

watermelon *noun* a large dark-green melon with red flesh and black seeds.

waterproof *adjective* that keeps out water. **waterproof** *verb*

watershed *noun* **1** a line of high land from which streams flow down on each side. **2** a turning-point in the course of events, *The election was a watershed in our history.*

water-skiing *noun* skimming over the surface of water on a pair of flat boards (**water-skis**) while being towed by a motor boat.

waterspout *noun* a column of water formed when a whirlwind draws up a whirling mass of water from the sea.

water-table *noun* the level below which the ground is saturated with water.

watertight *adjective* **1** made or fastened so that water cannot get in or out. **2** that cannot be changed or set aside or proved to be untrue, *a watertight excuse.*

waterway *noun* a river or canal that ships can travel on.

waterworks *noun* a place with pumping machinery etc. for supplying water to a district.

watery *adjective* **1** of or like water. **2** full of water, *watery eyes.* **3** containing too much water, *watery orange juice.*

watsonia (*say* wot-**soh**-nee-a) *noun* an indigenous plant which has bright flowers.

watt *noun* a unit of electric power.

wattage *noun* electric power measured in watts.

wattle¹ *noun* **1** sticks and twigs woven together to make fences, walls, etc. **2** an alien tree with golden flowers.

wattle² *noun* a red fold of skin hanging from the throat of turkeys and some other birds.

wave¹ *noun* **1** a ridge moving along the surface of the sea etc. or breaking on the shore. **2** a wave-like curve, e.g. in hair. **3** the wave-like movement by which heat, light, sound, or electricity etc. travels. **4** the action of waving.

wave² *verb* (**waved, waving**) **1** move loosely to and fro or up and down. **2** move your hand to and fro as a signal or greeting etc. **3** make a thing wavy. **4** be wavy, *Her hair waves naturally.*

● USAGE: Do not confuse with *waive.*

waveband *noun* the wavelengths between certain limits.

wavelength *noun* the size of a soundwave or electromagnetic wave.

wavelet *noun* a small wave.

waver *verb* 1 be unsteady; move unsteadily. 2 hesitate; be uncertain.

wavy *adjective* full of waves or curves. **wavily** *adverb*, **waviness** *noun*

wax[1] *noun* (*plural* **waxes**) 1 a soft substance that melts easily, used to make candles, crayons, and polish. 2 beeswax. **waxy** *adjective*

wax[2] *verb* coat or polish something with wax.

wax[3] *verb* 1 (of the moon) show a bright area that becomes gradually larger. (The opposite is *wane*.) 2 become stronger or more important.

waxbill *noun* a kind of small seed-eating bird.

waxen *adjective* 1 made of wax. 2 like wax.

waxwork *noun* a model of a person etc. made in wax.

way[1] *noun* 1 a line of communication between places, e.g. a path or road. 2 a route or direction. 3 a distance to be travelled, *It's a long way to Durban.* 4 how something is done; a method or style. 5 a respect, *It's a good idea in some ways.* 6 a condition or state, *Things were in a bad way.*

get or **have your own way** make people let you do what you want.

give way collapse; let somebody else move first; yield.

in the way forming an obstacle or hindrance.

no way (*informal*) that is impossible!

under way see *under*.

way[2] *adverb* (*informal*) far, *That is way beyond what we can afford.*

wayfarer *noun* a traveller, especially someone who is walking.

waylay *verb* (**waylaid, waylaying**) lie in wait for a person or people, especially so as to talk to them or rob them.

wayside *noun* the land beside a road or path.

wayward *adjective* disobedient; wilfully doing what you want.

WC *abbreviation* water-closet.

we *pronoun* a word used by a person to refer to himself or herself and another or others.

weak *adjective* not strong; easy to break, bend, defeat, etc. **weakness** *noun*

weaken *verb* make or become weaker.

weakling *noun* a weak person or animal.

weakly[1] *adverb* in a weak manner.

weakly[2] *adjective* sickly; not strong.

weal *noun* a ridge raised on the flesh by a cane or whip etc.

wealth *noun* 1 much money or property; riches. 2 a large quantity, *The book has a wealth of illustrations.*

wealthy *adjective* (**wealthier, wealthiest**) having wealth; rich. **wealthiness** *noun*

wean *verb* make a baby take food other than its mother's milk.

weapon *noun* something used to do harm in a battle or fight. **weaponry** *noun*

wear *verb* (**wore, worn, wearing**) 1 have something on your body as clothes, ornaments, etc. 2 damage something by rubbing or using it often; become damaged in this way, *The carpet has worn thin.* 3 last while in use, *It has worn well.* **wearable** *adjective*, **wearer** *noun*

wear off be removed by wear or use; become less intense.

wear on pass gradually, *The night wore on.*

wear out use or be used until it becomes weak or useless; exhaust.

wearisome *adjective* causing weariness.

weary[1] *adjective* (**wearier, weariest**) 1 tired. 2 tiring, *It's weary work.* **wearily** *adverb*, **weariness** *noun*

weary[2] *verb* (**wearied, wearying**) tire.

weasel *noun* a small fierce animal with a slender body and reddish-brown fur.

weather[1] *noun* the rain, snow, wind, sunshine etc. at a particular time or place. **under the weather** feeling ill or depressed.

weather[2] *verb* 1 expose something to the effects of the weather. 2 come through something successfully, *The ship weathered the storm.*

weathercock (also **weather-vane**) *noun* a pointer, often shaped like a cockerel, that turns in the wind and shows from which direction it is blowing.

weave[1] *verb* (**wove, woven, weaving**)
1 make material or baskets etc. by passing crosswise threads or strips under and over lengthwise ones. 2 put a story together, *She wove a thrilling tale.* 3 (*past tense & past participle* **weaved**) twist and turn, *He weaved through the traffic.*

weave[2] *noun* a style of weaving, *a loose weave.*

weaver *noun* 1 a person who weaves. 2 a kind of bird which builds elaborate nests.

web *noun* 1 a cobweb. 2 a network, *Food webs are made up of a number of food chains.*

webbed (also **web-footed**) *adjective* having toes joined by pieces of skin, *Ducks have webbed feet; they are web-footed.*

wed *verb* (**wedded, wedding**) 1 marry. 2 unite two different things.

wedding *noun* the ceremony when a man and woman get married.

wedge[1] *noun* 1 a piece of wood or metal etc. that is thick at one end and thin at the other. It is pushed between things to force them apart or prevent something from moving. 2 a wedge-shaped thing.

wedge[2] *verb* (**wedged, wedging**) 1 keep something in place with a wedge. 2 pack tightly together, *Ten of us were wedged in the lift.*

wedlock *noun* the condition of being married; matrimony.

wee *adjective* (*Scottish*) little.

weed[1] *noun* 1 a wild plant that grows where it is not wanted. 2 a person with a thin weak body.

weed[2] *verb* remove weeds from the ground.

weeds *plural noun* the black clothes formerly worn by a widow in mourning.

weedy *adjective* (**weedier, weediest**) 1 full of weeds. 2 thin and weak.

week *noun* a period of seven days, especially from Sunday to the following Saturday.

weekday *noun* a day other than Sunday or other than Saturday and Sunday.

weekend *noun* Saturday and Sunday.

weekly *adjective* & *adverb* happening or done once a week.

weeny *adjective* (*informal*) tiny.

weep *verb* (**wept, weeping**) 1 shed tears; cry. 2 ooze moisture in drops. **weep** *noun*, **weepy** *adjective*

weeping *adjective* (of a tree) having drooping branches, *a weeping willow.*

weevil *noun* a kind of small beetle.

weft *noun* the crosswise threads in weaving, passing through the warp.

weigh *verb* 1 measure the weight of something. 2 have a certain weight. 3 be important; have influence, *Her evidence weighed with the jury.*

weigh anchor raise the anchor and start a voyage.

weigh down keep something down by its weight; depress or trouble somebody.

weigh up estimate; assess.

weight[1] *noun* 1 how heavy something is; an object's mass expressed as a number according to a scale of units. (Compare *mass*[1] 3.) 2 a piece of metal of known weight, especially one used on scales to weigh things. 3 a heavy object. 4 importance; influence, *Her opinion carried weight.* **weighty** *adjective*, **weightless** *adjective*

weight[2] *verb* put a weight on something.

weir (*say* weer) *noun* a small dam across a river or canal to control the flow of water.

weird *adjective* very strange; uncanny. **weirdly** *adverb*, **weirdness** *noun*

welcome[1] *noun* a greeting or reception, especially a kindly one.

welcome[2] *adjective* 1 that you are glad to receive or see, *a welcome gift.* 2 gladly allowed, *You are welcome to come.*

welcome[3] *verb* (**welcomed, welcoming**) show that you are pleased when a person or thing arrives.

weld *verb* 1 join pieces of metal or plastic by heating and pressing or hammering them together. 2 unite people or things into a whole.

welfare *noun* people's health, happiness, and comfort.

Welfare State a country that looks after

the welfare of its people by social services run by the government.

well[1] *noun*   **1** a deep hole dug to bring up water or oil from underground. **2** a deep space, e.g. containing a staircase.

well[2] *verb*   rise or flow up, *Tears welled up in our eyes.*

well[3] *adverb*   (**better, best**) **1** in a good or suitable way, *She swims well.* **2** thoroughly, *Polish it well.* **3** easily; probably, *This may well be our last chance.*

well off fairly rich; in a good situation.

well[4] *adjective*   **1** in good health, *He is not well.* **2** satisfactory, *All is well.*

well-being *noun*   good health, happiness, and comfort.

wellingtons *plural noun*   rubber or plastic waterproof boots. **wellies** *plural noun* (*informal*)

well-known *adjective*   **1** known to many people. **2** known thoroughly.

well-mannered *adjective*   having good manners.

wellnigh *adverb*   almost.

well-read *adjective*   having read much literature.

well-to-do *adjective*   fairly rich.

welsh *verb*   cheat someone by avoiding paying what you owe them or by breaking an agreement. **welsher** *noun*

welt *noun*   **1** a strip or border. **2** a weal.

welter[1] *verb*   (of a ship) be tossed to and fro by waves.

welter[2] *noun*   a confused mixture.

welwitschia *noun*   a kind of plant with long leathery leaves found in the Namib Desert.

wen *noun*   a large but harmless tumour on the head or neck.

wench *noun*   (*plural* **wenches**) (*old use*) a girl or young woman.

wend *verb*   **wend your way** go.

weren't (*mainly spoken*)   were not.

werewolf *noun*   (*plural* **werewolves**) (in legends) a person who sometimes changes into a wolf.

west[1] *noun*   **1** the direction where the sun sets, opposite east. **2** the western part of a country, city, etc.

west[2] *adjective*   **1** situated in the west,

the west coast. **2** coming from the west, *a west wind.*

west[3] *adverb*   towards the west, *We sailed west.*

westerly *adjective*   to or from the west.

western[1] *adjective*   of or in the west.

western[2] *noun*   a film or story about cowboys or American Indians in western North America.

westward *adjective* & *adverb*   towards the west. **westwards** *adverb*

wet[1] *adjective*   (**wetter, wettest**) **1** soaked or covered in water or other liquid. **2** not yet dry, *wet paint.* **3** rainy, *wet weather.* **wetly** *adverb*, **wetness** *noun*

wet[2] *verb*   (**wetted, wetting**) make a thing wet.

whack *verb*   hit hard, especially with a stick. **whack** *noun*

whale *noun*   a very large sea-animal. **a whale of a** (*informal*) very good or great, *We had a whale of a time.*

whaler *noun*   a person or ship that hunts whales. **whaling** *noun*

wharf (*say* worf) *noun*   a quay where ships are loaded and unloaded.

what[1] *adjective*   used to ask the amount or kind of something, *What kind of bike have you got?* or to say how strange or great a person or thing is, *What a fool you are!*

what[2] *pronoun*   **1** what thing or things, *What did you say?* **2** the thing that, *This is what you must do.*

what's what (*informal*) which things are important or useful.

whatever[1] *pronoun*   **1** anything or everything, *Do whatever you like.* **2** no matter what, *Keep calm, whatever happens.*

whatever[2] *adjective*   of any kind or amount, *Take whatever books you need. There is no doubt whatever.*

wheat *noun*   a cereal plant from which flour is made. **wheaten** *adjective*

wheedle *verb*   (**wheedled, wheedling**) coax.

wheel[1] *noun*   **1** a round device that turns on a shaft that passes through its centre. **2** a horizontal revolving disc on which clay is made into a pot.

wheel[2] *verb*   **1** push a bicycle or trolley etc.

along on its wheels. **2** move in a curve or circle; change direction and face another way, *He wheeled round in astonishment.*

wheelbarrow *noun* a small cart with one wheel at the front and legs at the back, pushed by handles.

wheelchair *noun* a chair on wheels for a person who cannot walk.

wheeze *verb* (**wheezed, wheezing**) make a hoarse whistling sound as you breathe. **wheeze** *noun*, **wheezy** *adjective*

whelk *noun* a shellfish that looks like a snail.

whelp *noun* a young dog; a pup.

when¹ *adverb* at what time; at which time, *When can you come to tea?*

when² *conjunction* **1** at the time that, *The bird flew away when I moved.* **2** although; considering that, *Why do you smoke when you know it's dangerous?*

whence *adverb* & *conjunction* from where; from which.

whenever *conjunction* at whatever time; every time, *Whenever I see it, I smile.*

where¹ *adverb* & *conjunction* in or to what place or that place, *Where did you put it? Leave it where it is.*

where² *pronoun* what place, *Where does she come from?*

whereabouts *adverb* in or near what place. **whereabouts** *plural noun*

whereas *conjunction* but in contrast, *Some people enjoy sport, whereas others hate it.*

whereby *adverb* by which.

wherefore *adverb* (*old use*) why.

whereupon *conjunction* after which; and then.

wherever *adverb* in or to whatever place.

whet *verb* (**whetted, whetting**) **whet your appetite** stimulate it.
● USAGE: Do not confuse with *wet.*

whether *conjunction* as one possibility; if, *I don't know whether to believe her or not.*

whetstone *noun* a shaped stone for sharpening tools.

whey (*say as* way) *noun* the watery liquid left when milk forms curds.

which¹ *adjective* what particular, *Which way did he go?*

which² *pronoun* **1** what person or thing, *Which is your desk?* **2** the person or thing referred to, *The film, which is a western, will be shown on Saturday.*

whichever *pronoun* & *adjective* no matter which; any which, *Take whichever you like.*

whiff *noun* a puff or slight smell of smoke, gas, etc.

while¹ *conjunction* **1** during the time that; as long as, *Whistle while you work.* **2** although; but, *She is dark, while her sister is fair.*

while² *noun* a period of time; the time spent on something, *a long while.*

while³ *verb* (**whiled, whiling**) **while away** pass time, *We whiled away the afternoon on the river.*

whilst *conjunction* while.

whim *noun* a sudden wish to do or have something.

whimper *verb* cry or whine softly. **whimper** *noun*

whimsical *adjective* impulsive and playful. **whimsically** *adverb*, **whimsicality** *noun*

whine *verb* (**whined, whining**) **1** make a long high miserable cry or a shrill sound. **2** complain in a petty or feeble way. **whine** *noun*

whinge *verb* (**whinged, whingeing**) (*informal*) complain; grumble.

whinny *verb* (**whinnied, whinnying**) neigh gently or happily. **whinny** *noun*

whip¹ *noun* **1** a cord or strip of leather fixed to a handle and used for hitting people or animals. **2** an official of a political party in Parliament. **3** a pudding made of whipped cream and fruit or flavouring.

whip² *verb* (**whipped, whipping**) **1** hit with a whip. **2** beat cream until it becomes thick. **3** move or take suddenly, *He whipped out a gun.* **4** (*informal*) steal something.
whip up arouse people's feelings etc., *She whipped up support for her plans.*

whippet *noun* a small dog rather like a greyhound, used for racing.

whirl *verb* turn or spin very quickly. **whirl** *noun*

whirlpool *noun* a whirling current of water.

whirlwind *noun* a strong wind that whirls round a central point.

whirr *verb* make a continuous buzzing sound. **whirr** *noun*

whisk[1] *verb* 1 move or brush away quickly and lightly. 2 beat eggs etc. until they are frothy.

whisk[2] *noun* 1 a device for whisking things. 2 a whisking movement.

whisker *noun* 1 a hair of those growing on a man's face, forming a beard or moustache if not shaved off. 2 a long bristle growing near the mouth of a cat etc. **whiskery** *adjective*

whisky *noun* (*plural* **whiskies**) a strong alcoholic drink.

whisper *verb* 1 speak very softly. 2 talk secretly. **whisper** *noun*

whist *noun* a card-game usually for four people.

whistle[1] *verb* (**whistled, whistling**) make a shrill or musical sound, especially by blowing through your lips. **whistler** *noun*

whistle[2] *noun* 1 a whistling sound. 2 a device that makes a shrill sound when air or steam is blown through it.

whit *noun* the least possible amount, *not a whit better.*

white[1] *noun* 1 the very lightest colour, like snow or salt. 2 the transparent substance (*albumen*) round the yolk of an egg, turning white when cooked.

white[2] *adjective* 1 of the colour white. 2 very pale from the effects of illness or fear etc. **whiteness** *noun*

white coffee coffee with milk.

white-collar (of people) doing clerical or professional work, rather than work requiring physical labour. (Compare *blue-collar.*)

white elephant a useless possession.

white flag a symbol of surrender.

white horses waves in the sea with white tops on them.

white lie a harmless or small lie.

White Paper a government report which provides information about a matter that is to be debated by Parliament.

whitebait *noun* (*plural* **whitebait**) a small silvery-white fish.

white-eye *noun* a small bird which has white rings around its eyes.

white-hot *adjective* extremely hot; so hot that heated metal looks white.

whiten *verb* make or become whiter.

whitewash *noun* a white liquid containing lime or powdered chalk, used for painting walls and ceilings etc. **whitewash** *verb*

whither *adverb* & *conjunction* (*old use*) to what place.

whiting *noun* (*plural* **whiting**) a small edible sea-fish with white flesh.

whittle *verb* (**whittled, whittling**) 1 shape wood by trimming thin slices off the surface. 2 reduce something by removing various things from it, *whittle down the cost.*

whiz *verb* (**whizzed, whizzing**) 1 move very quickly. 2 sound like something rushing through the air.

who *pronoun* which person or people; the particular person or people, *This is the boy who stole the apples.*

whoa *interjection* a command to a horse to stop or stand still.

whoever *pronoun* 1 any or every person who. 2 no matter who.

whole[1] *adjective* complete; not injured or broken.

whole number a number without fractions.

whole[2] *noun* 1 the full amount. 2 a complete thing.

on the whole considering everything; mainly.

wholemeal *adjective* made from the whole grain of wheat etc.

wholesale[1] *noun* selling goods in large quantities to be resold by others. (Compare *retail.*) **wholesaler** *noun*

wholesale[2] *adjective* & *adverb* 1 on a large scale; including everybody or everything, *wholesale destruction.* 2 in the wholesale trade.

wholesome *adjective* good for health; healthy, *wholesome food.* **wholesomeness** *noun*

wholly *adverb* completely; entirely.

whom *pronoun* the form of *who* used when it is the object of a verb or comes after a preposition, as in *the boy whom I saw* or *to whom we spoke*.

whoop (*say* woop) *noun* a loud cry of excitement. **whoop** *verb*

whoopee *interjection* a cry of joy.

whooping cough (*say* hoop-ing) *noun* an infectious disease that causes spasms of coughing and gasping for breath.

whopper *noun* (*slang*) something very large.

whopping *adjective* (*slang*) very large or remarkable, *a whopping lie*.

whorl *noun* 1 a coil or curved shape. 2 a ring of leaves or petals.

who's (*mainly spoken*) who is; who has.
• USAGE: Do not confuse with *whose*.

whose *pronoun* belonging to what person or persons; of whom; of which, *Whose house is that?*
• USAGE: Do not confuse with *who's*.

why *adverb* for what reason or purpose; the particular reason on account of which, *This is why I came.*

wick *noun* 1 the string that goes through the middle of a candle and is lit. 2 the strip of material that you light in a lamp or heater etc. that uses oil.

wicked *adjective* 1 morally bad or cruel. 2 very bad; severe, *a wicked blow.* 3 mischievous, *a wicked smile.* **wickedly** *adverb*, **wickedness** *noun*

wicker *noun* thin canes or osiers woven together to make baskets or furniture etc. **wickerwork** *noun*

wicket *noun* 1 a set of three stumps and two bails used in cricket. 2 the part of a cricket ground between or near the wickets.

wicket-gate *noun* a small gate used to save opening a much larger one.

wicket-keeper *noun* the fielder in cricket who stands behind the batsman's wicket.

wide¹ *adjective* 1 measuring a lot from side to side; not narrow. 2 measuring from side to side, *The cloth is one metre wide.* 3 covering a great range, *a wide knowledge of birds.* 4 fully open, *staring with wide*

eyes. 5 far from the target, *The shot was wide of the mark.* **widely** *adverb*, **wideness** *noun*

wide² *adverb* 1 widely. 2 completely; fully, *wide awake.* 3 far from the target, *The shot went wide.*

widen *verb* make or become wider.

widespread *adjective* existing in many places or over a wide area.

widow *noun* a woman whose husband has died. **widowed** *adjective*

widower *noun* a man whose wife has died.

width *noun* how wide something is; wideness.

wield *verb* hold something and use it.

wife *noun* (*plural* **wives**) the woman to whom a man is married.

wig *noun* a covering made of real or artificial hair, worn on the head.

wiggle *verb* (**wiggled**, **wiggling**) move from side to side; wriggle. **wiggle** *noun*

wigwam *noun* a tent formerly used by American Indians, made by fastening skins or mats over poles.

wild *adjective* 1 living or growing in its natural state, not looked after by people. 2 not cultivated, *a wild landscape.* 3 not civilized, *the Wild West.* 4 not controlled; very violent or excited. 5 very foolish or unreasonable, *these wild ideas.* **wildly** *adverb*, **wildness** *noun*

wildebeest *noun* (*plural* **wildebeest**, **wildebeeste**, **wildebeests**) a gnu.

wilderness *noun* (*plural* **wildernesses**) a wild uncultivated area; a desert.

wildlife *noun* wild animals.

wile *noun* a piece of trickery.

wilful *adjective* 1 obstinately determined to do what you want, *a wilful child.* 2 deliberate, *wilful murder.* **wilfully** *adverb*, **wilfulness** *noun*

will¹ *auxiliary verb* used to express the future tense, questions, or promises.
• USAGE: See the entry for *shall.*

will² *noun* 1 the mental power to decide and control what you do. 2 a desire; a chosen decision, *I went to the party against my will.* 3 determination, *They set to work with a will.* 4 a person's attitude towards others, *full of good will.* **5** a written statement of how a person's possessions are to be disposed of after his or her death.

at will as you like, *You can come and go at will.*

will³ *verb* use your will-power; influence something by doing this, *I was willing you to win!*

willing *adjective* ready and happy to do what is wanted. **willingly** *adverb*, **willingness** *noun*

will-o'-the-wisp *noun* **1** a flickering spot of light seen on marshy ground. **2** an elusive person or hope.

willow *noun* a tree or shrub with flexible branches, usually growing near water.

will-power *noun* strength of mind to control what you do.

willy-nilly *adverb* whether you want to or not.

wilt *verb* lose freshness or strength; droop.

wily (*say* **wy**-lee) *adjective* cunning; crafty. **wiliness** *noun*

wimple *noun* a piece of cloth folded round the head and neck, worn by some nuns.

win¹ *verb* (**won, winning**) **1** be victorious in a battle, game, or contest. **2** get or achieve something by a victory or by using effort or skill etc., *She won the prize.*

win² *noun* a victory.

wince *verb* (**winced, wincing**) make a slight movement because of pain or embarrassment etc.

winch¹ *noun* (*plural* **winches**) a device for lifting or pulling things, using a rope or cable etc. that winds on to a revolving drum or wheel.

winch² *verb* lift or pull with a winch.

wind¹ (rhymes with *tinned*) *noun* **1** a current of air. **2** gas in the stomach or intestines that makes you feel uncomfortable. **3** breath used for a purpose, e.g. for running or speaking. **4** the wind instruments of an orchestra.

get or **have the wind up** (*slang*) feel frightened.

wind instrument a musical instrument played by blowing, e.g. a trumpet.

wind² *verb* cause a person to be out of breath, *The climb had winded us.*

wind³ (rhymes with *find*) *verb* (**wound, winding**) **1** go or turn something in twists, curves, or circles. **2** wind up a watch or clock etc. **winder** *noun*

wind up make a clock or watch work by tightening its spring; close a business; (*informal*) end up in a place or condition, *He wound up in gaol.*

windbag *noun* (*informal*) a person who talks at great length.

wind-break *noun* a row of trees etc. which protects people and crops from the wind.

windfall *noun* **1** a fruit blown off a tree by the wind. **2** a piece of unexpected good luck, especially a sum of money.

windlass *noun* (*plural* **windlasses**) a device for pulling or lifting things (e.g. a bucket from a well), with a rope or cable that is wound round an axle by turning a handle.

windmill *noun* a mill worked by the wind that turns projecting parts (*sails*).

window *noun* **1** an opening in a wall or roof etc. to let in light and often air, usually filled with glass. **2** the glass in this opening. **3** (in computers) a defined area on a VDU screen in which a part of a file or image can be displayed.

windpipe *noun* the tube by which air passes from the throat to the lungs.

windscreen *noun* the window at the front of a motor vehicle.

windsurfing *noun* surfing on a board that has a sail fixed to it, also called boardsailing.

windward *adjective* facing the wind, *the windward side of the ship.*

windy *adjective* with much wind.

wine *noun* **1** an alcoholic drink made from grapes or other plants. **2** dark red colour.

wing¹ *noun* **1** each of a pair of projecting parts of a bird, bat, or insect, used in flying. **2** each of a pair of long flat projecting parts that support an aircraft while it flies. **3** a projecting part at one end or side of something; **the wings** the sides of a theatre stage out of sight of the audience.

4 the part of a motor vehicle's body above a wheel. **5** a player at either end of the forward line in football or hockey etc. **6** a section of a political party, with more extreme opinions than the others, *the left and right wing factions.*
on the wing flying.
take wing fly away.
wing² *verb* **1** fly; travel by means of wings, *The bird winged its way home.* **2** wound a bird in the wing or a person in the arm.
winged *adjective* having wings.
wingless *adjective* without wings.
wink¹ *verb* **1** close and open your eye quickly, especially as a signal to someone. **2** (of a light) flicker; twinkle.
wink² *noun* **1** the action of winking. **2** a very short period of sleep, *I didn't sleep a wink.*
winkle¹ *noun* a kind of edible shellfish.
winkle² *verb* (**winkled, winkling**)
winkle out extract; prise a thing out.
winner *noun* **1** a person or animal etc. that wins. **2** something very successful, *Her latest book is a winner.*
winnings *plural noun* money won.
winnow *verb* toss or fan grain etc. so that the loose dry outer part is blown away.
winsome *adjective* charming.
winter¹ *noun* the coldest season of the year, between autumn and spring. **wintry** *adjective*
winter² *verb* spend the winter somewhere.
wipe *verb* (**wiped, wiping**) dry or clean something by rubbing it. **wiper** *noun*
wipe out cancel, *wipe out the debt;* destroy something completely.
wire¹ *noun* **1** a strand or thin flexible rod of metal. **2** a fence etc. made from wire. **3** a piece of wire used to carry electric current.
wire² *verb* (**wired, wiring**) **1** fasten or strengthen with wire. **2** fit or connect with wires to carry electric current.
wireless *noun* (*plural* **wirelesses**) (*old use*) **1** radio. **2** a radio set.
wiry *adjective* **1** like wire. **2** lean and strong.
wisdom *noun* **1** being wise. **2** wise sayings.

wisdom tooth a molar tooth that may grow at the back of the jaw of a person aged about 20 or more.
wise¹ *adjective* knowing or understanding many things; judging well. **wisely** *adverb*
wise² *noun* (*old use* or as a *suffix*) manner or direction, *It is in no wise better; otherwise; clockwise; crosswise.*
wish¹ *verb* **1** feel or say that you would like to have or do something or would like something to happen. **2** say that you hope someone will get something, *Wish me luck!*
wish² *noun* (*plural* **wishes**) **1** something you wish for; a desire. **2** the action of wishing, *Make a wish when you blow out the candles.*
wishbone *noun* a forked bone between the neck and breast of a bird (sometimes pulled apart by two people; the person who gets the bigger part can make a wish).
wishful *adjective* desiring something.
wishful thinking believing something because you want it to be true.
wisp *noun* **1** a few strands of hair or bits of straw etc. **2** a small streak of smoke or cloud etc. **wispy** *adjective*
wistaria (*say* wist-**air**-ee-a) *noun* a climbing plant with hanging blue, purple, or white flowers.
wistful *adjective* sadly longing for something. **wistfully** *adverb*, **wistfulness** *noun*
wit *noun* **1** intelligence; cleverness, *Use your wits.* **2** a clever kind of humour. **3** a witty person.
at your wits' end not knowing what to do.
witch *noun* (*plural* **witches**) a person, especially a woman, who uses magic to do things. **witchcraft** *noun*
with *preposition* used to indicate **1** being in the company or care etc. of, *Come with me.* **2** having, *a man with a beard.* **3** using, *Hit it with a hammer.* **4** because of, *shaking with laughter.* **5** feeling or showing, *We heard it with pleasure.* **6** towards, concerning, *I was angry with him.* **7** in opposition to; against, *Don't argue with your father.* **8** being separated from, *We had to part with it.*
withdraw *verb* (**withdrew, withdrawn,**

withdrawing) 1 take back or away; remove, *She withdrew money from the bank.* **2** go away from a place or people, *The troops withdrew from the frontier.* **withdrawal** *noun*

wither *verb* **1** shrivel; wilt. **2** cause to shrivel or wilt. **3** make a person feel subdued or snubbed.

withers *plural noun* the ridge between a horse's shoulder-blades.

withhold *verb* (**withheld, withholding**) refuse to give or allow something (e.g. information or permission).

within *preposition & adverb* inside; not beyond something.

without[1] *preposition* **1** not having, *without food.* **2** free from, *without fear.* **3** (*old use*) outside, *without the city wall.*

without[2] *adverb* outside, *We looked at the house from within and without.*

withstand *verb* (**withstood, withstanding**) endure something successfully; resist.

withy *noun* (*plural* **withies**) a thin flexible branch for tying bundles etc.

witness[1] *noun* (*plural* **witnesses**) **1** a person who sees or hears something happen, *There were no witnesses to the accident.* **2** a person who gives evidence in a lawcourt.

witness[2] *verb* **1** be a witness of something. **2** sign a document to confirm that it is genuine.

witted *adjective* having wits of a certain kind, *quick-witted.*

witticism *noun* a witty remark.

wittingly *adverb* intentionally.

witty *adjective* (**wittier, wittiest**) clever and amusing; full of wit. **wittily** *adverb*, **wittiness** *noun*

wizard *noun* **1** a male witch; a magician. **2** a person with amazing abilities, *a computer wizard.* **wizardry** *noun*

wizened (*say* **wiz**-end) *adjective* full of wrinkles, *a wizened face.*

wobble *verb* (**wobbled, wobbling**) stand or move unsteadily; shake slightly. **wobble** *noun,* **wobbly** *adjective*

woe *noun* **1** sorrow. **2** misfortune. **woeful** *adjective,* **woefully** *adverb*

woebegone *adjective* looking unhappy.

woema (*say* **vu**-ma) *noun* (*slang*) energy; power.

wok *noun* a Chinese cooking-pan shaped like a large bowl.

wolf[1] *noun* (*plural* **wolves**) a fierce wild animal of the dog family.

wolf[2] *verb* eat something greedily.

woman *noun* (*plural* **women**) a grown-up female human being. **womanhood** *noun,* **womanly** *adjective*

womb (*say* woom) *noun* the hollow organ in a female's body where babies develop before they are born, also called a uterus.

wombat *noun* an Australian animal rather like a small bear.

wonder[1] *noun* **1** a feeling of surprise and admiration or curiosity. **2** something that causes this feeling; a marvel. **no wonder** it is not surprising.

wonder[2] *verb* **1** feel that you want to know; try to form an opinion, *We are still wondering what to do next.* **2** feel wonder.

wonderful *adjective* marvellous; surprisingly good, excellent. **wonderfully** *adverb*

wonderment *noun* a feeling of wonder.

wondrous *adjective* (*old use*) wonderful.

wont[1] (*say* wohnt) *adjective* (*old use*) accustomed, *He was wont to dress in rags.*

wont[2] *noun* a habit or custom, *He was dressed in rags, as was his wont.*

won't (*mainly spoken*) will not.

woo *verb* **1** (*old use*) court a woman. **2** seek someone's favour. **wooer** *noun*

wood *noun* **1** the substance of which trees are made. **2** many trees growing close together.

woodcut *noun* an engraving made on wood; a print made from this.

wooded *adjective* covered with growing trees.

wooden *adjective* **1** made of wood. **2** stiff and showing no expression or liveliness. **woodenly** *adverb*

woodland *noun* wooded country.

woodlouse *noun* (*plural* **woodlice**) a small crawling creature with seven pairs of legs, living in rotten wood or damp soil etc.

woodpecker *noun* a bird that taps

tree-trunks with its beak to find insects.

woodwind *noun* wind instruments that are usually made of wood, e.g. the clarinet and oboe.

woodwork *noun* 1 making things out of wood. 2 things made out of wood.

woodworm *noun* the larva of a kind of beetle that bores into wooden furniture etc.

woody *adjective* 1 like wood; consisting of wood. 2 full of trees.

wool *noun* 1 the thick soft hair of sheep and goats etc. 2 thread or cloth made from this.

woollen *adjective* made of wool.

woollens *plural noun* woollen clothes.

woolly *adjective* 1 covered with wool or wool-like hair. 2 like wool; woollen. 3 not thinking clearly; vague or confused, *woolly ideas.* **woolliness** *noun*

word¹ *noun* 1 a set of sounds or letters that has a meaning, and when written or printed has no spaces between the letters. 2 a promise, *He kept his word.* 3 a command or spoken signal, *Run when I give the word.* 4 a message; information, *We sent word of our safe arrival.*

word for word in exactly the same words.

word of honour a solemn promise.

word processor a kind of computer or program used for editing and printing words entered using the keyboard.

word² *verb* express something in words, *Word the question carefully.*

wording *noun* the way something is worded.

word-perfect *adjective* having memorized every word perfectly.

wordy *adjective* using too many words; not concise.

work¹ *noun* 1 something you have to do that needs effort or energy, *Digging is hard work.* 2 the use of effort or energy to do something (contrasted with *play* or *recreation*). 3 a job; employment. 4 something produced by work, *The teacher marked our work.*

at work working.

out of work having no work; unable to find paid employment.

work of art a fine picture, building, etc.

work² *verb* 1 do work. 2 have a job; be employed, *She works in a bank.* 3 act or operate correctly or successfully, *Is the lift working?* 4 make something act; operate, *Can you work the lift?* 5 shape or press etc., *Work the mixture into a paste.* 6 make a way; pass, *The grub works its way into timber.*

working class people who work for wages, especially in manual or industrial work.

work out find an answer by thinking or calculating; have a particular result.

work up make people become excited; arouse.

workable *adjective* usable; practicable.

worker *noun* 1 a person who works. 2 a member of the working class. 3 a bee or ant etc. that does the work in a hive or colony but does not produce eggs.

workman *noun* (*plural* **workmen**) a person employed to do manual labour; a worker.

workmanship *noun* a person's skill in working; the result of this.

workshop *noun* a place where things are made or mended.

work-shy *adjective* avoiding work; lazy.

world *noun* 1 the earth with all its countries and peoples. 2 the universe. 3 the people or things belonging to a certain activity, *the world of sport.* 4 a very great amount, *It will do him a world of good. She is worlds better today.*

worldly *adjective* 1 of life on earth, not spiritual. 2 interested only in money, pleasure, etc. **worldliness** *noun*

worm¹ *noun* 1 an animal with a long small soft rounded or flat body and no backbone or limbs. 2 an unimportant or unpleasant person. **wormy** *adjective*

worm² *verb* move by wriggling or crawling.

wormwood *noun* a woody plant with a bitter taste.

worried *adjective* feeling or showing worry.

worry¹ *verb* (**worried, worrying**) 1 be troublesome to someone; make a person feel slightly afraid. **2** feel anxious. **3** hold something in the teeth and shake it, *The dog was worrying a rat.* **worrier** *noun*

worry^2 *noun* (*plural* **worries**) **1** the condition of worrying; being uneasy. **2** something that makes a person worry.

worse *adjective & adverb* more bad or more badly; less good or less well.

worsen *adjective* make or become worse.

worship^1 *verb* (**worshipped, worshipping**) **1** give praise or respect to God or a god. **2** love or respect a person or thing greatly. **worshipper** *noun*

worship^2 *noun* **1** worshipping; religious ceremonies. **2** a title of respect for a mayor or certain magistrates, *his worship the mayor.*

worst *adjective & adverb* most bad or most badly; least good or least well.

worsted *noun* a kind of woollen material.

worth^1 *adjective* **1** having a certain value, *This stamp is worth R100.* **2** deserving something; good or important enough for something, *That book is worth reading.* **worth while** worth the time or effort needed, *The job was not worth while.*
● USAGE: Use *worthwhile* when it comes before the noun (e.g. *a worthwhile job*).

worth^2 *noun* value; usefulness.

worthless *adjective* having no value; useless. **worthlessness** *noun*

worthwhile *adjective* important or good enough to do; useful, *a worthwhile job.*
● USAGE: See *worth* for the use of *worth while.*

worthy *adjective* having great merit; deserving respect or support, *a worthy cause.* **worthiness** *noun*

worthy of deserving, *This charity is worthy of your support.*

would *auxiliary verb* used **1** as the past tense of *will*^{1}, *We said we would do it,* in questions, *Would you like to come?* and polite requests, *Would you come in, please?* **2** with *I* and *we* and the verbs *like, prefer, be glad,* etc. (e.g. *I would like to come, we would be glad to help*), where the strictly correct use is *should.* **3** of something to be expected, *That's just what*

he would do!
● USAGE: See the note on *should* 4.

would-be *adjective* wanting or pretending to be, *a would-be comedian.*

wouldn't (*mainly spoken*) would not.

wound^1 (*say* woond) *noun* **1** an injury done by a cut, stab, or hit. **2** a hurt to a person's feelings.

wound^2 *verb* **1** cause a wound to a person or animal. **2** hurt a person's feelings.

wound^3 (*say* wownd) *past tense* of **wind**^{3}.

wraith *noun* a ghost.

wrangle *verb* (**wrangled, wrangling**) have a noisy argument or quarrel. **wrangle** *noun*, **wrangler** *noun*

wrap^1 *verb* (**wrapped, wrapping**) put paper or cloth etc. round something as a covering.

wrap^2 *noun* a shawl, coat, or cloak etc. worn for warmth.

wrapper *noun* a piece of paper etc. wrapped round something.

wrath (rhymes with *cloth*) *noun* anger. **wrathful** *adjective*, **wrathfully** *adverb*

wreak (*say as* reek) *verb* inflict, *Fog wreaked havoc with the flow of traffic.*

wreath (*say* reeth) *noun* **1** flowers or leaves etc. fastened into a circle, *wreaths of holly.* **2** a curving line of mist or smoke, *wreaths of mist.*

wreathe (*say* reeth) *verb* (**wreathed, wreathing**) **1** surround or decorate with a wreath. **2** cover, *Their faces were wreathed in smiles.* **3** move in a curve, *Smoke wreathed upwards.*

wreck^1 *verb* damage something, especially a ship, so badly that it cannot be used again.

wreck^2 *noun* **1** a wrecked ship or building or car etc. **2** a person who is left very weak, *a nervous wreck.* **3** the wrecking of something, *The wreck of the Birkinhead occurred on the Eastern Cape coast in 1852.*

wreckage *noun* the pieces of a wreck.

wren *noun* a very small brown bird.

wrench^1 *verb* twist or pull something violently.

wrench^2 *noun* (*plural* **wrenches**) **1** a wrenching movement. **2** pain caused by parting, *Leaving home was a great* *wrench.* **3** an adjustable tool rather like a spanner, used for gripping and turning bolts, nuts, etc.

wrest *verb* force or wrench something away, *We wrested his sword from him.*

wrestle *verb* (**wrestled, wrestling**) **1** fight by grasping your opponent and trying to throw him or her to the ground. **2** struggle with a problem etc. **wrestle** *noun*, **wrestler** *noun*

wretch *noun* (*plural* **wretches**) **1** a person who is very unhappy. **2** a person who is disliked; a rascal.

wretched *adjective* **1** miserable; unhappy. **2** shabby. **3** not satisfactory; causing a nuisance, *This wretched car won't start.* **wretchedly** *adverb*, **wretchedness** *noun*

wriggle *verb* (**wriggled, wriggling**) move with short twisting movements. **wriggle** *noun*, **wriggly** *adjective*

wriggle out of avoid work or blame etc. cunningly.

wring *verb* (**wrung, wringing**) **1** twist and squeeze a wet thing to get water etc. out of it. **2** squeeze firmly or forcibly. **3** get something by a great effort, *We wrung a promise out of him.* **wring** *noun*

wringing wet so wet that water can be squeezed out of it.

wringer *noun* a device with a pair of rollers for squeezing water out of washed clothes etc.

wrinkle[1] *noun* a small crease; a small furrow or ridge in the skin.

wrinkle[2] *verb* (**wrinkled, wrinkling**) make wrinkles in something; form wrinkles.

wrist *noun* the joint that connects the hand and arm.

wrist-watch *noun* a watch for wearing on the wrist.

writ (*say* rit) *noun* a formal written command issued by a lawcourt etc. **Holy Writ** the Bible.

write *verb* (**wrote, written, writing**) **1** put letters or words etc. on paper or another surface. **2** be the author or composer of something, *write books* or *music.* **3** send a letter to somebody. **writer** *noun*, **writing** *noun*

writhe *verb* (**writhed, writhing**) **1** twist your body because of pain. **2** wriggle. **3** suffer because of great shame, *writhing with embarrassment.*

wrong[1] *adjective* **1** incorrect; not true, *the wrong answer.* **2** morally bad; unfair; unjust, *It is wrong to cheat.* **3** not working properly, *There's something wrong with the engine.* **wrongly** *adverb*, **wrongness** *noun*

wrong[2] *adverb* wrongly, *You guessed wrong.*

wrong[3] *noun* something morally wrong; a wrong action; an injustice.

in the wrong having done or said something wrong.

wrong[4] *verb* do wrong to someone; treat a person unfairly.

wrongdoer *noun* a person who does wrong. **wrongdoing** *noun*

wrongful *adjective* unfair; unjust; illegal. **wrongfully** *adverb*

wrought *adjective* (of metal) worked by being beaten out or shaped by hammering or rolling etc., *wrought iron.*

wry *adjective* (**wryer, wryest**) **1** twisted or bent out of shape. (Compare *awry.*) **2** showing disgust or disappointment or mockery, *a wry smile.* **wryly** *adverb*, **wryness** *noun*

Xx

xenophobia (*say* zen-o-**foh**-bee-a) *noun* strong dislike of foreigners.

xerophyte (*say* **zeer**-oh-fyt) *noun* a plant adapted to live in dry conditions. (Compare *hydrophyte* and *mesophyte.*)

Xerox (*say* **zeer**-oks) *noun* (*trade mark*) a photocopy made by a special process. **xerox** *verb*

Xmas *noun* Christmas.

X-ray[1] *noun* a photograph or examination of the inside of something, especially a part of the body, made by a kind of radiation (called *X-rays*) that can penetrate solid things.

X-ray[2] *verb* make an X-ray of something.

xylem (*say* **zy**-lem) *noun* a kind of plant tissue made of long thin cells. Xylem tissue transports water and mineral salts from the roots to the rest of the plant.

xylophone (*say* **zy**-lo-fohn) *noun* a musical instrument made of wooden bars that you hit with small hammers.

Yy

yacht (*say* yot) *noun* 1 a sailing-boat used for racing or cruising. 2 a private ship. **yachting** *noun*, **yachtsman** *noun*, **yachtswoman** *noun*

yak *noun* an ox with long hair, found in central Asia.

yam *noun* the edible starchy tuber of a tropical plant.

Yank *noun* (*informal*) a Yankee.

yank *verb* (*informal*) pull something strongly and suddenly. **yank** *noun*

Yankee *noun* an American, especially of the northern USA.

yap *verb* (**yapped, yapping**) bark shrilly. **yap** *noun*

yard[1] *noun* 1 a measure of length in the imperial system, 36 inches or about 91 centimetres. 2 a long pole stretched out from a mast to support a sail.

yard[2] *noun* an enclosed area beside a building or used for a certain kind of work, *a timber yard.*

yardstick *noun* a standard by which something is measured.

yarn *noun* 1 thread spun by twisting fibres together, used in knitting etc. 2 (*informal*) a tale or story.

yarrow *noun* a wild plant with strong-smelling flowers.

yashmak *noun* a veil worn in public by Muslim women in some countries.

yawl *noun* a kind of sailing-boat or fishing-boat.

yawn *verb* 1 open the mouth wide and breathe in deeply when feeling sleepy or bored. 2 form a wide opening, *A pit yawned in front of us.* **yawn** *noun*

ye *pronoun* (*old use*, in speaking to two or more people) you.

yea (*say* yay) *adverb* (*old use*) yes.

year *noun* 1 the time the earth takes to go right round the sun, about 365 $\frac{1}{4}$ days. 2 the time from 1 January to 31 December. **yearly** *adjective* & *adverb*

yearling *noun* an animal between one and two years old.

yearn *verb* long for something.

yeast *noun* a substance that causes alcohol and carbon dioxide to form as it develops, used in making beer and wine and in baking bread etc.

yebo *interjection* (*informal*) yes; an expression indicating agreement.

yell *verb* give a loud cry; shout. **yell** *noun*

yellow[1] *noun* the colour of egg yolks and ripe lemons.

yellow[2] *adjective* 1 of yellow colour. 2 (*informal*) cowardly. **yellowness** *noun*

yellowtail *noun* (*plural* **yellowtail**) a large edible sea-fish with a yellow tail.

yellowwood *noun* a large evergreen tree, whose wood is prized for furniture.

yelp *verb* give a shrill bark or cry. **yelp** *noun*

yen[1] *noun* (*plural* **yen**) a unit of money in Japan.

yen[2] *noun* a longing.

yeoman (*say* **yoh**-man) *noun* (*plural* **yeomen**) (*old use*) a man who owns and runs a small farm. **yeomanry** *noun*

yes *adverb* used to agree to something (= the statement is correct) or as an answer (= I am here).

yesterday *noun* & *adverb* the day before today.

yesterday, today, and tomorrow a shrub which bears purple, mauve, and white flowers at the same time.

yet[1] *adverb* 1 up to this time; by this time, *The post hasn't come yet.* 2 eventually, *I'll get even with him yet!* 3 in addition; even, *She became yet more excited.*

yet[2] *conjunction* nevertheless, *It is strange, yet it is true.*

yeti *noun* (*plural* **yetis**) a very large animal thought to live in the Himalayas, sometimes called the 'Abominable Snowman'.

yew *noun* an evergreen tree with dark-green needle-like leaves and red berries.

yield¹ *verb* **1** surrender; do what is asked or ordered; give way, *He yielded to persuasion.* **2** produce as a crop or as profit etc.

yield² *noun* the amount yielded or produced, *What is the yield of wheat per hectare?*

yodel *verb* (**yodelled, yodelling**) sing or shout with the voice continually going from a low note to a high note and back again. **yodeller** *noun*

yoga (*say* **yoh**-ga) *noun* a Hindu system of meditation and self-control.

yoghurt (*say* **yog**-ert or **yoh**-gert) *noun* milk thickened by the action of certain bacteria, giving it a sharp taste.

yoke¹ *noun* **1** a curved piece of wood put across the necks of animals pulling a cart or plough etc. **2** a shaped piece of wood fitted across a person's shoulders, with a pail or load hung at each end. **3** a close-fitting upper part of a garment, from which the rest hangs.

yoke² *verb* (**yoked, yoking**) harness or join by means of a yoke.

yokel (*say* **yoh**-kel) *noun* a country bumpkin.

yolk (rhymes with *coke*) *noun* the round yellow part inside an egg.

Yom Kippur (*say* yom kip-**oor**) *noun* the Day of Atonement, a solemn Jewish religious festival, a day of fasting and repentance.

yon *adjective & adverb* (*dialect*) yonder.

yonder *adjective & adverb* over there.

yore *noun* **of yore** of long ago, *in days of yore.*

you *pronoun* **1** the person or people being spoken to, *Who are you?* **2** anyone; everyone; one, *You can't tell what will happen next.*

young¹ *adjective* having lived or existed for only a short time; not old.

young² *noun* children or young animals or birds, *The penguin was feeding its young.*

youngster *noun* a young person; a child.

your *adjective* belonging to you.

you're (*mainly spoken*) you are.

yours *possessive pronoun* belonging to you. **Yours faithfully, Yours sincerely, Yours truly** ways of ending a letter before you sign it. (*Yours faithfully* and *Yours truly* are more formal than *Yours sincerely.*)
● USAGE: It is incorrect to write *your's.*

yourself *pronoun* (*plural* **yourselves**) you and nobody else. (Compare *herself.*)

youth *noun* **1** being young; the time when you are young. **2** a young man. **3** young people. **youthful** *adjective*, **youthfulness** *noun*

youth club a club providing leisure activities for young people.

yowl *verb & noun* wail; howl.

yo-yo *noun* (*plural* **yo-yos**) a toy consisting of two round pieces of wood or plastic which are made to rise and fall when the player pulls on an attached string.

yule *noun* (*old use*) the Christmas festival, also called **yule-tide.**

Zz

zap *verb* (**zapped, zapping**) (*slang*) **1** attack or destroy something forcefully. **2** move suddenly, *We zapped around the new shopping centre in our lunch break.*

zeal *noun* enthusiasm; keenness. **zealous** (*say* **zel**-us) *adjective*, **zealously** *adverb*

zealot (*say* **zel**-ot) *noun* a zealous person; a fanatic.

zebra (*say* **zeb**-ra) *noun* an animal of the horse family, with black and white stripes all over its body.

zebra crossing a place for pedestrians to cross a road safely, marked with broad white stripes.

zebu (*say* **zee**-bew) *noun* an ox with a humped back, found in India, East Asia, and Africa.

zenith *noun* **1** the part of the sky directly above you. **2** the highest point, *His power was at its zenith.*

zephyr (*say* **zef**-er) *noun* a soft gentle wind.

zero *noun* (*plural* **zeros**) **1** nought; the
figure 0; nothing. **2** the point marked 0
on a thermometer etc.
  zero hour the time when something is
  planned to start.

zest *noun* great enjoyment or interest.
zestful *adjective*, **zestfully** *adverb*

zigzag[1] *noun* a line or route that turns
sharply from side to side.

zigzag[2] *verb* (**zigzagged, zigzagging**)
move in a zigzag.

zinc *noun* **1** a white metal. **2** (*informal*)
galvanized iron, *a zinc roof.*

zip[1] *noun* **1** a zip-fastener. **2** a sharp
sound like a bullet going through the air.
3 liveliness; vigour. **zippy** *adjective*

zip[2] *verb* (**zipped, zipping**) **1** fasten with a
zip-fastener. **2** move quickly with a sharp
sound.

zip-fastener (also **zipper**) *noun* a fastener
consisting of two strips of material, each
with rows of small teeth that interlock
when a sliding tab brings them together.

zither *noun* a musical instrument with
many strings stretched over a shallow
box-like body.

zodiac (*say* **zoh**-dee-ak) *noun* a strip
of sky where the sun, moon, and main
planets are found, divided into twelve
equal parts (called **signs of the zodiac**),
each named after a constellation.

zone *noun* an area of a special kind or for
a particular purpose.

zoo *noun* (*plural* **zoos**) a place where wild
animals are kept so that people can look at
them or study them.

zoology (*say* **zoh-ol**-o-jee) *noun* the study
of animals. **zoological** *adjective*, **zoologist**
noun

zoom *verb* **1** move very quickly, especially
with a buzzing sound. **2** rise quickly, *Prices
had zoomed.* **zoom** *noun*
  zoom lens a camera lens that can be
  adjusted continuously to focus on things
  that are close up or far away.

zoophyte (*say* **zoh**-oh-fyt) *noun* a plant-
like animal, e.g. a sea anemone, a coral, or
a sponge.

zygote *noun* a cell formed by the union
of two gametes in sexual reproduction.

Spelling

It can be difficult to find a word in the dictionary if you are not sure how the first sound is written. (See the section on pronunciation, page xvi, for an explanation of the sounds.)

If the first sound of the word is:	the word may begin with:	If the first sound of the word is:	the word may begin with:
b	bu (as in *build, buy*)	ah	aa (as in *aardvark, aardwolf*)
f	ph (as in *phone, pheasant*)		ar (as in *artist, arson*)
g	gh (as in *ghost, ghetto*)	air	ar (as in *arum lily*)
	gu (as in *guess, guard*)	ay	ai (as in *aid, aim*)
gw	gu (as in *guava*)		ei (as in *eight, eina*)
h	wh (as in *who, whole*)	e	a (as in *any*)
j	g (as in *gem squash, gentle*)	ee	ea (as in *each*)
			ei (as in *Eid*)
k	c (as in *cattle, crayfish*)	i	e (as in *enjoy*)
	ch (as in *choir, character*)	I	ai (as in *aisle, aikona*)
kh	g (as in *gogga, gramadoelas*)		ei (as in *either, eiderdown*)
	kg (as in *kgotla*)	o	ho (as in *honour, honest*)
kw	qu (as in *queen, quagga*)		au (as in *aunt*)
n	gn (as in *gnome, gnu*)	oh	oa (as in *oats*)
	kn (as in *know, knobkerrie*)	or	au (as in *author, audio*)
	pn (as in *pneumatic*)		aw (as in *awful, awning*)
r	wr (as in *write, wren*)		oa (as in *oar*)
s	c (as in *cent, cycad*)	ur	ea (as in *early*)
	ps (as in *psychology, psychic*)		ir (as in *irk*)
		uu	u (as in *ubuntu, umama*)
sh	ch (as in *chassis, chic*)	y	eu (as in *eutrophication*)
	sj (as in *sjambok*)		j (as in *Jan Fiskaal, jukskei*)

Spelling of nouns

Plurals

Add **-s** to the noun (e.g. *dog/dogs, band/bands, car/cars, toy/toys, shoes/shoes*).

EXCEPTIONS:
- Add **-es** to the noun if it ends in **-ch** (e.g. *sandwich/sandwiches*), **-o** (e.g. *potato/potatoes*), **-sh** (e.g. *wish/wishes*), **-ss** (e.g. *mass/masses*), and **-x** (e.g. *box/boxes*).
- Change **-y** to **-ies** if the noun ends with a consonant plus **-y** (e.g. *cry/cries, lily/lilies*).
- Many nouns have irregular plural forms (e.g. *mouse/mice, goose/geese, woman/women*). Irregular plural forms are given in the entries for nouns in the dictionary.

The -ing form

Verbs can be made into nouns by adding **-ing** (e.g. *sing/singing*).

EXCEPTIONS:
- If the verb ends in a consonant plus **-e** (e.g. *love, write, gobble*), the **-e** is replaced by **-ing** (e.g. *loving, writing, gobbling*).
- If the verb ends in **-ie** (e.g. *die, tie*), the **-ie** is replaced by **-ying** (e.g. *dying, tying*).
- If the verb is a short word with one written vowel followed by one written consonant on the end, the last letter is doubled (e.g. *bat/batting, fib/fibbing, let/letting*). But verbs ending in **-w** or **-y** (e.g. *bow, say*) do not have the last letter doubled, nor do verbs with the vowel sound written using two letters (e.g. *clear, doubt, meet*).
- The last letter is also doubled in longer words if the last vowel is stressed (e.g. *forget/forgetting, begin/beginning*), as well as in verbs ending in **-el** which have the first syllable stressed (e.g *travel/travelling*).

Spelling of adjectives

Comparative and superlative forms

If the adjective ends in a consonant, **-er** and **-est** are added (e.g. *dark/darker/darkest, loud/louder/loudest, small/smaller/smallest*).

If the adjective ends in **-e**, **-r** and **-st** are added (e.g. *white/whiter/whitest, lame/lamer/lamest, free/freer/freest*).

EXCEPTIONS:
- If the adjective ends in a consonant plus **-y**, **-y** is replaced by **-ier** and **-iest** (e.g. *gloomy/gloomier/gloomiest, flabby/flabbier/flabbiest*).

- If the adjective is a short word with one written vowel followed by one written consonant on the end, the last letter is doubled (e.g. *big/bigger/biggest, slim/slimmer/slimmest*). But adjectives ending in **-w** or **-y** (e.g. *raw, grey*) do not have the last letter doubled, nor do adjectives with the vowel sound written using two letters (e.g. *dear, sour, sweet*).
- Longer adjectives do not change their spelling to form the comparative or the superlative. Add **more** and **most** to these words (e.g. *intelligent/more intelligent/most intelligent*).
- Many adjectives have irregular comparative and superlative forms (e.g. *far/further/furthest, good/better/best*). Irregular forms are given in the entries for adjectives in the dictionary.

Spelling of verbs

Present tense (3rd person singular)

Add **-s** to the verb (e.g. *dances, walks, thinks, eats*).

EXCEPTIONS:
- Add **-es** to the verb if it ends in **-ch** (e.g. *clutch/clutches*), **-o** (e.g. *do/does*), **-sh** (e.g. *wish/wishes*), **-ss** (e.g. *kiss/kisses*), and **-x** (e.g. *fix/fixes*).
- Change **-y** to **-ies** if the noun ends with a consonant plus **-y** (e.g. *cry/cries, carry/carries*).

Present participle (used in continuous tenses)

See the note on the **-ing** form on page 524.

Past tense

Add **-ed** to the verb (e.g. *walked, cooked, washed*).

EXCEPTIONS:
- Add **-d** if the verb ends in **-e** (e.g. *loved, gobbled, moved*).
- If the verb ends in a consonant plus **-y** (e.g. *carry/cry*), the **-y** is replaced by **-ied** (e.g. *carried/cried*).
- If the verb is a short word with one written vowel followed by one written consonant on the end, the last letter is doubled (e.g. *bat/batted, fib/fibbed, pet/petted*). But verbs ending in **-w** or **-y** (e.g. *bow/bowed*) do not have the last letter doubled, nor do verbs with the vowel sound written using two letters (e.g. *clear/cleared, doubt/doubted*).
- The last letter is also doubled in longer words if the last vowel is stressed (e.g. *propel/propelled*), as well as in verbs ending in **-el** which have the first syllable stressed (e.g. *travel/travelled*).

Verbs

Tenses of regular verbs

The past   *Example*

Past perfect   It had rained.
Past perfect continuous   It had been raining.
Past (simple)   It rained.
Past continuous   It was raining.

The present

Present perfect   It has rained.
Present perfect continuous   It has been raining.
Present (simple)   It rains.
Present continuous   It is raining.

The future

Future (simple)   It will rain.
Future continuous   It will be raining.
Future perfect   It will have rained.
Future perfect continuous   It will have been raining.

Tenses of irregular verbs

Many verbs have irregular past tense and past participle forms.
This list contains all irregular verbs found in the dictionary.

Infinitive form	Past tense	Past participle
abide	abided, abode	abided, abode
arise	arose	arisen
awake	awoke	awoken
be	was/were	been
bear	bore	borne
beat	beat	beaten
become	became	become
befall	befell	befallen
beget	begot, begat	begotten
begin	began	begun
behold	beheld	beheld
bend	bent	bent

Infinitive form	Past tense	Past participle
beseech	besought, beseeched	besought, beseeched
beset	beset	beset
bet	bet, betted	bet, betted
bid	bid, bade	bidden, bid
bind	bound	bound
bite	bit	bitten
bleed	bled	bled
bless	blessed	blessed
blow	blew	blown
break	broke	broken
breed	bred	bred
bring	brought	brought
broadcast	broadcast	broadcast
build	built	built
burn	burnt, burned	burnt, burned
burst	burst	burst
bust	bust, busted	bust, busted
buy	bought	bought
cast	cast	cast
catch	caught	caught
chide	chided, chid	chided, chidden
choose	chose	chosen
cleave	cleaved, clove, cleft	cleaved, cloven, cleft
cling	clung	clung
come	came	come
cost	cost, costed	cost, costed
creep	crept	crept
cut	cut	cut
deal	dealt	dealt
dig	dug	dug
dive	dived, dove	dived
do	did	done
draw	drew	drawn
dream	dreamt, dreamed	dreamt, dreamed
drink	drank	drunk
drive	drove	driven
dwell	dwelt, dwelled	dwelt
eat	ate	eaten
fall	fell	fallen
feed	fed	fed
feel	felt	felt
fight	fought	fought
find	found	found
flee	fled	fled
fling	flung	flung
fly	flew	flown
forbear	forbore	forborne

Infinitive form	Past tense	Past participle
forbid	forbade	forbidden
forecast	forecast, forecasted	forecast, forecasted
foresee	foresaw	foreseen
foretell	foretold	foretold
forget	forgot	forgotten
forgive	forgave	forgiven
forgo	forwent	forgone
forsake	forsook	forsaken
freeze	froze	frozen
get	got	got
give	gave	given
go	went	gone
grind	ground	ground
grow	grew	grown
hang	hung, hanged	hung, hanged
have	had	had
hear	heard	heard
heave	heaved, hove	heaved, hove
hew	hewed	hewed, hewn
hide	hid	hidden
hit	hit	hit
hold	held	held
hurt	hurt	hurt
inlay	inlaid	inlaid
input	input, inputted	input, inputted
keep	kept	kept
kneel	knelt, kneeled	knelt, kneeled
knit	knitted, knit	knitted, knit
know	knew	known
lay	laid	laid
lead	led	led
lean	leant, leaned	leant, leaned
leap	leaped, leapt	leaped, leapt
learn	learnt, learned	learnt, learned
leave	left	left
lend	lent	lent
let	let	let
lie[3]	lay	lain
light	lit, lighted	lit, lighted
lose	lost	lost
make	made	made
mean	meant	meant
meet	met	met
mislay	mislaid	mislaid
misread	misread	misread
(*say* mis-**reed**)	(*say* mis-**red**)	(*say* mis-**red**)
mistake	mistook	mistaken

Infinitive form	Past tense	Past participle
misunderstand	misunderstood	misunderstood
mow	mowed	mowed, mown
offset	offset	offset
outdo	outdid	outdone
outgrow	outgrew	outgrown
outrun	outran	outrun
overcome	overcame	overcome
overdo	overdid	overdone
overdraw	overdrew	overdrawn
overhang	overhung	overhung
overhear	overheard	overheard
overlay	overlaid	overlaid
override	overrode	overridden
overrun	overran	overrun
oversee	oversaw	overseen
overshoot	overshot	overshot
oversleep	overslept	overslept
overtake	overtook	overtaken
overthrow	overthrew	overthrown
partake	partook	partaken
pay	paid	paid
plead	pleaded	pleaded
prove	proved	proven
put	put	put
quit	quit	quit
read (*say* reed)	read (*say* red)	read (*say* red)
rebuild	rebuilt	rebuilt
rend	rent	rent
rid	rid	rid
ride	rode	ridden
ring	rang	rung
rise	rose	risen
run	ran	run
saw	sawed	sawn
say	said	said
see	saw	seen
seek	sought	sought
sell	sold	sold
send	sent	sent
set	set	set
sew	sewed	sewn, sewed
shake	shook	shaken
shear	sheared	shorn, sheared
shed	shed	shed
shine	shone, shined	shone, shined
shoe	shod	shod
shoot	shot	shot

Infinitive form	Past tense	Past participle
show	showed	shown, showed
shrink	shrank, shrunk	shrunk
shut	shut	shut
sing	sang	sung
sink	sank	sunk
sit	sat	sat
slay	slew	slain
sleep	slept	slept
slide	slid	slid
sling	slung	slung
slink	slunk	slunk
slit	slit	slit
smell	smelt, smelled	smelt, smelled
smite	smote	smitten
sow	sowed	sown, sowed
speak	spoke	spoken
speed	sped, speeded	sped, speeded
spell	spelt, spelled	spelt, spelled
spend	spent	spent
spill	spilt, spilled	spilt, spilled
spin	spun	spun
spit	spat	spat
split	split	split
spoil	spoilt, spoiled	spoilt, spoiled
spread	spread	spread
spring	sprang	sprung
stand	stood	stood
stave	staved, stove	staved, stove
steal	stole	stolen
stick	stuck	stuck
sting	stung	stung
stink	stank, stunk	stank, stunk
strew	strewed	strewed, strewn
stride	strode	—
strike	struck	struck
string	strung	strung
strive	strove, strived	striven
sublet	sublet	sublet
swear	swore	sworn
sweep	swept	swept
swell	swelled	swollen, swelled
swim	swam	swum
swing	swung	swung
take	took	taken
teach	taught	taught
tear	tore	torn
tell	told	told

Infinitive form	Past tense	Past participle
think	thought	thought
throw	threw	thrown
thrust	thrust	thrust
tread	trod	trodden, trod
unbend	unbent	unbent
undercut	undercut	undercut
undergo	underwent	undergone
underlie	underlay	underlain
underpay	underpaid	underpaid
undersell	undersold	undersold
understand	understood	understood
undertake	undertook	undertaken
underwrite	underwrote	underwritten
undo	undid	undone
unfreeze	unfroze	unfrozen
unwind	unwound	unwound
uphold	upheld	upheld
upset	upset	upset
wake	woke	woken
waylay	waylaid	waylaid
wear	wore	worn
weave	wove, weaved	woven, weaved
wed	wedded, wed	wedded, wed
weep	wept	wept
wet	wet, wetted	wet, wetted
win	won	won
wind³ (*say* wI'nd)	wound (*say* wownd)	wound (*say* wownd)
withdraw	withdrew	withdrawn
withhold	withheld	withheld
withstand	withstood	withstood
wring	wrung	wrung
write	wrote	written

Prefixes and suffixes

Prefixes

A prefix is placed at the beginning of a word to alter its meaning or to form a new word. The following prefixes have entries in their alphabetical places in the dictionary:

a-	at-	demi-	hetero-	mono-	peri-	suf-
ab-	auto-	di-	hexa-	multi-	philo-	sum-
abs-	be-	dia-	homo-	neo-	photo-	sup-
ac-	bene-	dif-	hydro-	non-	poly-	super-
ad-	bi-	dis	hyper-	ob-	post-	supra-
aero-	bio-	dys-	hypo-	oc-	pre-	sur-
af-	cat-	e-	il-	oct-	pro-	sus-
ag-	cata-	ef-	im-	octa-	proto-	syl-
al-	cath-	electro-	in-	octo-	pseudo-	sym-
ama-	centi-	em-	infra-	of-	psycho-	syn-
ambi-	circum-	en-	inter-	off-	quadri-	tele-
amphi-	co-	epi-	intra-	omni-	quasi-	tetra-
an-	col-	equi-	intro-	on-	radio-	thermo-
ana-	com-	eu-	isi-	op-	re-	trans-
Anglo-	con-	ex-	kilo-	ortho-	retro-	tri-
ante-	contra-	extra-	mal-	out-	se-	ultra-
anti-	cor-	for-	mega-	over-	self-	un-
ap-	counter-	fore-	micro-	pan-	semi-	uni-
apo-	de-	geo-	milli-	para-	step-	vice-
ar-	deca-	hecto-	mini-	penta-	sub-	
arch-	deci-	hepta-	mis-	per-	suc-	

Suffixes

A suffix is placed at the end of a word to form another word or to form a plural, past tense, comparative, superlative, etc.

-able, **-ible**, **-ble**, and **-uble** form adjectives (e.g. *readable*, *legible*). The corresponding nouns end in **-bility** (e.g. *readability*, *legibility*).

-arch and **-archy** form nouns meaning 'ruler' or 'ruling' (e.g. *monarch*, *monarchy*).

-arian forms nouns and adjectives (e.g. *vegetarian*) showing membership of a group.

-ary forms adjectives (e.g. *contrary*, *primary*) or nouns (e.g. *dictionary*, *January*).

-ate forms (1) adjectives (e.g. *passionate*), (2) nouns showing status or function (e.g. *magistrate*) or (in scientific use)

nouns meaning salts of certain acids
(e.g. *nitrate* compare -**ite**), (3) verbs
(e.g. *create, fascinate*).

-**ation** forms nouns, often from verbs
(e.g. *creation, organization, starvation*).

-**ble** see -**able**.

-**cide** forms nouns meaning 'killing'
or 'killer' (e.g. *homicide*).

-**cle** see -**cule**.

-**cracy** and -**crat** form nouns meaning
'government' or 'ruling' or 'ruler'
(e.g. *democracy, democrat*).

-**cule** and -**cle** form diminutives
(e.g. *molecule* = little mass, *particle* =
little part).

-**cy** forms nouns showing rank, office,
territory, or condition (e.g. *kingdom,
freedom*).

-**ed** can form a past participle of a verb
(e.g. *paint/painted*), or an adjective
(e.g. *diseased*).

-**ee** forms nouns meaning 'person affected
by or described as' (e.g. *absentee,
employee, refugee*).

-**er** and -**ier** can form the comparative of
adjectives and adverbs (e.g. *high/higher,
lazy/lazier*).

-**er** and -**or** can form nouns meaning
'a person or thing that does something'
(e.g. *farmer, computer, sailor*).

-**esque** forms adjectives meaning 'like'
or 'in the style of' (e.g. *picturesque*).

-**ess** forms feminine nouns (e.g. *lioness,
princess*).

-**est** and -**iest** can form the superlative of
adjectives and adverbs (e.g. *high/highest,
lazy/laziest*).

-**ette** forms diminutives which mean 'little'
(e.g. *cigarette, kitchenette*).

-**faction** forms nouns (e.g. *satisfaction*)
from verbs that end in -**fy**.

-**ferous** and -**iferous** form nouns meaning
'carrying' or 'providing' (e.g. *carboniferous*).

-**fold** forms adjectives and adverbs
meaning 'multiplied by' (e.g. *twofold,
fourfold, manifold*).

-**ful** forms (1) adjectives meaning 'full of'
or 'having this quality' (e.g. *beautiful,*

truthful), (2) nouns meaning 'the
amount required to fill something'
(e.g. *handful*).

-**fy** forms verbs meaning 'make' or 'bring
into a certain condition' (e.g. *beautify,
purify*).

-**gen** forms nouns in scientific use meaning
'producing' or 'produced' (e.g. *oxygen,
hydrogen*).

-**gon** forms nouns meaning 'having a
certain number of angles (and sides)'
(e.g. *hexagon*).

-**gram** forms nouns meaning something
written or drawn etc. (e.g. *photograph*).

-**graphy** forms names of descriptive
sciences (e.g. *geography*) or methods
of writing and drawing etc. (e.g.
photography).

-**hood** forms nouns meaning condition
or quality (e.g. *childhood*).

-**ible** see -**able**.

-**ic** forms (1) adjectives, some of which are
used as nouns (e.g. *comic, domestic,
public*), (2) names of arts (e.g. *music,
magic*).

-**ical** forms adjectives from or similar
to words ending in -**ic** (e.g. *comical,
musical*).

-**ician** forms nouns meaning 'person
skilled in something' (e.g. *musician*).

-**icity** forms nouns (e.g. *publicity*) from
words ending in -**ic**.

-**ics** forms nouns which are plural in form
but are often used with a singular verb
(e.g. *mathematics, gymnastics*).

-**ie** see -**y**.

-**ier** see -**er**.

-**iest** see -**est**.

-**iferous** see -**ferous**.

-**ification** forms nouns of action (e.g.
purification) from verbs that end in -**fy**.

-**ing** forms nouns and adjectives showing
the action of a verb (e.g. *hearing, tasting,
telling*).

-**ion**, -**sion**, and -**tion** form nouns meaning
'condition or action' (e.g. *dominion,
dimension, attraction, pollution*).

-**ise** see -**ize**.

-ish forms adjectives meaning (1) 'of a certain nature' (e.g. *foolish*), (2) 'rather' (e.g. *greenish, yellowish*).

-ism forms nouns showing action from verbs ending in **-ize** (e.g. *baptism, criticism*) or condition (e.g. *heroism*).

-ist forms nouns meaning 'person who does something or believes in or supports something' (e.g. *cyclist, Communist*).

-ite (in scientific use) forms names of minerals (e.g. *anthracite*), explosives (e.g. *dynamite*), and salts of certain acids (e.g. *nitrite*; compare **-ate**).

-itis forms nouns meaning 'inflammation of' (e.g. *tonsillitis*).

-ive forms adjectives, chiefly from verbs (e.g. *active, explosive*).

-ize or **-ise** form verbs meaning 'bring or come into a certain condition' (e.g. *civilize*), 'treat in a certain way' (e.g. *pasteurize*), or 'have a certain feeling' (e.g. *sympathize*).

-king forms diminutives (e.g. *lambkin* = little lamb).

-less forms adjectives meaning 'without' (e.g. *colourless*) or 'unable to be...' (e.g. *countless*).

-ling forms nouns meaning 'having a certain quality' (e.g. *weakling*) or diminutives meaning 'little' (e.g. *duckling*).

-logical forms adjectives (e.g. *biological*) from nouns ending in **-logy**.

-logist forms nouns meaning 'an expert in or student of something' (e.g. *biologist*).

-logy forms nouns meaning 'a subject of study' (e.g. *biology, zoology*).

-ly forms (1) adjectives (e.g. *friendly, heavenly, sickly*), (2) adverbs from adjectives (e.g. *boldly, sweetly, thoroughly*).

-most forms superlative adjectives (e.g. *hindmost, uppermost*).

-ness forms nouns from adjectives (e.g. *kindness, poorness*).

-oid forms adjectives and nouns meaning 'having a certain form' (e.g. *ovoid*).

-or see **-er**.

-pathy forms nouns meaning 'feeling or suffering something' (e.g. *sympathy, telepathy*).

-phobia forms nouns meaning 'fear or great dislike of something' (e.g. *hydrophobia*).

-ship forms nouns meaning 'condition' (e.g. *friendship, hardship*), position (e.g. *chairmanship*) or skill (e.g. *seamanship*).

-sion see **-ion**.

-some forms adjectives meaning 'quality or manner' (e.g. *handsome, quarrelsome*).

-teen is a form of 'ten' added to numbers from three to nine to form *thirteen* to *nineteen*.

-tion see **-ion**.

-tude forms nouns meaning 'quality or condition' (e.g. *altitude, solitude*).

-uble see **-able**.

-vore forms nouns and **-vorous** forms adjectives meaning 'eating or feeding on something' (e.g. *carnivore, carnivorous*).

-ward forms adjectives and adverbs showing direction (e.g. *backward, forward, homeward*).

-ways forms adverbs showing direction or manner (e.g. *sideways*).

-wise forms adverbs meaning 'in this manner or direction' (e.g. *otherwise, clockwise*).

-y and **-ie** form names showing fondness, or diminutives (e.g. *daddy, pussy*).

Punctuation and writing

This section shows you how to use punctuation in written English.
It also helps you to write down a conversation and shows you how
to set out formal and informal letters.

Full stop (.)

A full stop is used
- at the end of a sentence that is not a
  question or an exclamation:
  *I knocked at the door. There was no reply.
  I knocked again.*
- sometimes in abbreviations:
  Jan.   e.g.   a.m.

Comma (,)

Commas indicate a slight pause and are
used to divide a sentence into several parts
so that it is easier to follow its meaning.
They are used
- to separate words in a list, though they
  are often omitted before *and* and *or*:
  *a bouquet of red, pink, and white roses
  tea, coffee, milk or hot chocolate*
- to separate phrases or clauses:
  *If you keep calm, take your time,
  concentrate and think ahead, then
  you're likely to pass your driving test.
  Worn out after all the excitement of the
  party, the children soon fell asleep.*
- before and after a clause or phrase that
  gives additional, but not essential,
  information about the noun it follows:
  *Mount Everest, the world's highest
  mountain, was first climbed in 1953.
  The Drakensberg Mountains, which are
  very popular with walkers, are situated
  between Lesotho and KwaZulu/Natal.*
  (No commas are used before and after a
  clause that defines the noun it follows:
  *The mountains that separate Lesotho
  from KwaZulu/Natal are called the
  Drakensberg.)*

- to separate main clauses, especially long
  ones, linked by a conjunction such as
  and, as, but, for, or:
  *We had been looking forward to our
  camping holiday all year, but
  unfortunately it rained every day.*
- to separate an introductory word or
  phrase, or an adverb or adverbial phrase
  that applies to the whole sentence, from
  the rest of the sentence:
  *Oh, so that's where it was!
  As it happens, however, I never saw her
  again.
  By the way, did you hear what happened
  to Sue's car?*
- to separate a tag question from the rest
  of the sentence:
  *It's quite expensive, isn't it?
  You live in Johannesburg, right?*
- before or after 'he said', etc. when
  writing down conversation:
  'Come back soon,' she said.
- before a short quotation:
  *It was the British Prime Minister Disraeli
  who said, 'Little things affect little
  minds'.*
- in decimal fractions:
  Fifty centimetres can be written as 0,5 m.

Colon (:)

A colon is used
- to introduce a list of items:
  *These are our options: we go by train and
  leave before the end of the show, or we
  take the car and see it all.*
- in formal writing, before a clause or
  phrase that gives more information

about the main clause:

The garden had been neglected for a long time: it was overgrown and full of weeds.

(A semicolon or a full stop, but not a comma, may be used instead of a colon here.)

Semicolon (;)

A semicolon is used

- instead of a comma to separate parts of a sentence that already contain commas:
She was determined to succeed whatever the cost; she would achieve her aim, whoever might suffer on the way.
- in formal writing, to separate two main clauses, especially those not joined by a conjunction:
The sun was already low in the sky; it would soon be dark.

Question mark (?)

A question mark is used

- at the end of a direct question:
Where's the car? You're leaving already?
(A question mark is not used at the end of an indirect question: *He asked if I was leaving.*)

Exclamation mark (!)

An exclamation mark is used at the end of a sentence expressing surprise, joy, anger, shock, or some other strong emotion:
'That's marvellous!' 'Never!' she cried.

Apostrophe (')

An apostrophe is used

- with *s* to indicate that a thing or person belongs to somebody:
my friend's brother   the waitress's apron
King James's crown/King James' crown
the students' books   the women's coats
- in short forms, to indicate that letters have been omitted:
I'm (I am)
they'd (they had/they would)
the summer of '97 (1997)

- sometimes with *s* to form the plural of a letter, a figure, or an abbreviation:
roll your r's
during the 1990's
MP's in favour of the motion

Hyphen (-)

A hyphen is used

- to form a compound from two or more other words:
hard-hearted
fork-lift truck
mother-to-be
to form a compound from a prefix and a proper name:
pre-Raphaelite
pro-American
when writing compound numbers between 21 and 99 in words:
seventy-three
thirty-one
- sometimes to separate a prefix ending in a vowel from a word beginning with the same vowel:
co-operate
pre-eminent
- after the first section of a word that is divided between one line and the next:
decide what to do in order to avoid mis-takes of this kind in the future

Dash (–)

A dash is used

- in informal English, instead of a colon or semicolon, to indicate that what follows is a summary or conclusion of what has gone before:
Men were shouting, women were screaming, children were crying – it was chaos.
You've admitted that you lied to me – how can I trust you again?
- singly or in pairs to separate a comment or an afterthought from the rest of the sentence:
He knew nothing at all about it – or so he said.

Dots (…)

Three dots (also called an ellipsis) are used to indicate that words have been omitted, especially from a quotation or at the end of a conversation:

… challenging the view that South Africa … had not changed all that fundamentally.

Slash (/)

A slash or oblique is used

- to separate alternative words or phrases:
  have a pudding and/or cheese
  single/married/widowed/divorced (delete as applicable)
- to indicate the end of a line of poetry where the lines are not set separately:
  Wordsworth's famous lines, 'I wandered lonely as a cloud/That floats on high o'er vales and hills…'

Quotation marks (' "")

Quotation marks or inverted commas are used

- to enclose words and punctuation in direct speech:
  'Why on earth did you do that?' he asked.
  'I'll fetch it,' she replied.
- to draw attention to a word that is unusual for the context, for example a slang expression, or to a word that is being used for special effect, such as irony:
  He told me in no uncertain terms to 'get lost'.
  Thousands were imprisoned in the name of 'national security'.
- to enclose the titles of articles, books, poems, plays, etc.:
  Serote's 'Alexandria'
  I was watching 'Junior Topsport'.
- around short quotations or sayings:
  Do you know the origin of the saying:
  'A little learning is a dangerous thing'?

Brackets ()

Brackets (also called parentheses) are used

- to separate extra information or a comment from the rest of a sentence:
  The Nile River (6 670 km) is the longest river in Africa.
  He thinks that modern music (i.e. anything written after 1900) is rubbish.
- to enclose cross-references:
  This moral ambiguity is a feature of Shakespeare's later works (see Chapter Eight).
- around numbers or letters in text:
  Our objectives are (1) to increase output, (2) to improve quality and (3) to maximize profits.

Italics

In handwritten text italics are indicated by underlining. Italics are used

- to show emphasis:
  I'm not going to do it – *you* are.
  … proposals which we cannot accept under any circumstances
- to indicate the titles of books, plays, etc.:
  Paton's *Cry the Beloved Country*
  a letter in *The Star*
  the title role in Shakespeare's *Macbeth*
- for foreign words or phrases:
  the camel thorn tree (*Acacia erioloba*)
  The men were drinking *utshwala*, a traditional beer brewed from maize.

Quoting conversation

When you write down a conversation, you normally begin a new paragraph for each new speaker. Quotation marks enclose the words spoken:

'You're sure of this?' I asked.
He nodded grimly.
'I'm certain.'

Verbs used to indicate direct speech, for example, *he said, she complained*, are separated by commas from the words spoken, unless a question mark or an exclamation mark is used:

'That's all I know,' said Nick.
Nick said, 'That's all I know.'
'Why?' asked Nick.

Writing letters

In a letter to a friend, you write your address, or a short form of it, at the top right of the letter, and then the date. You do not need to put the name and address of the person you are writing to.

In a formal letter, you put your own address in the top right-hand corner, and then the date. You put the name and address of the person you are writing to below and to the left of this. Compare the layout and style of the following letters:

---

26 Windmill Road
Claremont
7700

The Information Officer
Zimbabwe Tourist Board
PO Box 7181
Cape Town
8000

Dear Sir/Madam
I hope to have a holiday in Zimbabwe this summer with my family.

Could you please send me a list of campsites in the area, and information about the facilities they offer.

My son and daughter would like to go horse riding: could you therefore also send me a list of riding centres that cater for children aged between 11 and 14? Thank you very much.
Yours faithfully

Rachel Bam

---

26 Windmill Road
Claremont
7700

22 March

Dear Barbara,
How are you and Tom? It seems ages since we saw you. I hope your new job is going well. David and I are both fine, and Lizzie is getting on well at her new school.

I'm writing now because I'm coming to Stellenbosch next Tuesday for a meeting, and I wondered if we could meet for a pizza or something afterwards. Alternatively, I could just call round at your house for a little while on my way home. The meeting should be over by 5.30 at the latest. Let me know what suits you. It would be lovely to see you if you have time.

Love from
Rachel

Numbers

Using numbers

Compound numbers

- You can find the numbers from one to twenty, and also *thirty, forty, fifty*, etc., in the main part of the dictionary. These are used to make compound numbers up to one hundred. In compound numbers, we put a hyphen between the words:
  thirty-five   sixty-seven
- Numbers over 10 are often written in figures.
- Ordinal numbers such as *fifth, ninth*, and *thirtieth* are also given in the dictionary. Compound ordinal numbers up to one hundred are formed by adding the ordinals *first, second, third*, etc. to *twenty, thirty, sixty*, etc.:
  twenty-first   eighty-seventh
- When ordinal numbers are written in figures, the last two letters of the written ordinal must be added:
  21st   22nd   23rd   24th   25th etc.
  Dates, however, can be written as:
  19 May 1997   19th May 1997

Numbers over 100

- For numbers over 100, we say *six hundred and forty-two, seven hundred and ninety*, etc. using *and* to link the hundreds and the tens. In a more mathematical context, we might say the individual figures instead:
  three two nine   five six zero
- Numbers between 100 and 199 can be written or spoken as *one hundred and four* or *a hundred and four*. We say *one hundred and four*, etc. when we want to be precise. In informal contexts, or when we are giving only an approximate number or amount, we say *a hundred and four*. Compare:
  The total cost was one hundred and sixty-three rand and five cents.
  The bill came to about a hundred and sixty rand.

Numbers over 1 000

- We can say and write numbers over 1 000 in two ways. For 1 200, for example, we can say *one thousand two hundred* or, more informally, *twelve hundred*.
- For numbers between 1 000 and 1099, we can use *a* instead of *one* before *thousand*:
  one thousand and sixty
  a thousand and sixty
  However, if there are any hundreds in the number we would normally say:
  one thousand two hundred and sixty
- Larger numbers are usually said as:
  twenty-eight thousand, one hundred and forty-four
  A comma is used after the thousands when a number is written in words. When the number is written in figures, a space is used:
  28 144
  Numbers over a million are written in a similar way:
  2 600 830
  two million, six hundred thousand, eight hundred and thirty
- Long numbers which do not stand for a quantity, such as bank account and telephone numbers, are usually grouped into twos, threes, fours or fives:
  My credit card number is:
  0432 9999 4567 9876
  Dial 01865 56767 for more information.
  Each number is said individually.

Zero

English has several names for the figure 0. *Zero* is the most precise word and is also the most common in American English. *Nought, nothing* and *o* (*say* oh) are used in informal English. In both British and American English, *o* is used to represent 0 when saying bank account or telephone numbers.

Fractions

- Common fractions, written as $^1/_2$, $^1/_4$, $^1/_3$, are generally said as *a half, a quarter*, or *a third*. *One* may be used instead of *a* for emphasis. For other fractions which are more commonly used in a technical or mathematical context, we say *one twelfth, one sixteenth*, etc. Fractions such as $^2/_3$, $^3/_4$ and $^7/_{10}$ are said as *two thirds, three quarters*, and *seven tenths*.
- When a fraction is used before a noun phrase, the word *of* is inserted:
a fifth of the annual turnover
a quarter of all women
When *half* is used in this way, *a* is omitted, and *of* may also be left out:
Half (of) the members voted against increasing subscriptions.
- If a fraction is used with an uncountable or a singular noun, the verb is generally singular:
A quarter of the money has already been spent.
Two thirds of the area is flooded.
If the noun is singular but represents a group of people, the verb may be singular or plural:
A third of the population is/are in favour of the change.
If the noun is countable, the verb is plural:
Three quarters of all graduates find jobs within six months.
- When a fraction follows a whole number we link them with *and*: $2^1/_4$ is said as *two and a quarter*, $3^5/_{16}$ is said as *three and five sixteenths*.

More complex fractions, such as $^7/_{256}$, $^{31}/_{144}$, and $^{19}/_{56}$ are said as *seven over two five six, thirty-one over one four four*, and *nineteen over fifty-six*.

Percentages

- Percentages are written in words as *twenty-five per cent* and in figures as 25%.
- When they are used with a noun phrase as the subject of a sentence, the verb is singular or plural according to the pattern described for fractions:
90% of the land is cultivated.
Eighty per cent of the workforce is/are against the strike.
65% of children play computer games.

Decimals

In South Africa, a comma is used when writing decimals. We also say *comma* when speaking the number.

If there is more than one figure after the decimal comma, we say each separately:
26,23   twenty-six comma two three
3,142   three comma one four two
In numbers less than one, for example 0,15, we say *zero comma one five, comma one five* or, sometimes, *nought comma one five*.

Numbers in time

Telling the time

- The twelve-hour system is used for most purposes. Morning, afternoon, or evening is not specified when this is obvious:
'What time is it, please?'
'It's six o'clock.'
- There is often more than one way of saying the time:
eleven thirty
half past eleven
half eleven (informal)

The time can be expressed in different ways:
— *It's (a) quarter to eight.*
It's seven forty-five.
— *It's (a) quarter past one.*
It's one fifteen.
— *It's ten (minutes) past six.*
It's six ten.
— *It's five (minutes) to four.*
It's three fifty-five.
The word *minutes* can be omitted after 5, 10, 20, and 25, but it is almost always used after other numbers:
It's eighteen minutes past nine.
- In a formal context, or when the time of day is not obvious, morning or evening is specified. We often use *a.m.* meaning *in the morning* and *p.m.* meaning *in the afternoon* or *in the evening*:
Students should assemble at the main gate at 5 p.m.
He came round at three o'clock in the morning!
- The twenty-four hour clock is used for timetables and in some official letters and notices. Times are spoken as:
0300   (o) three hundred hours
1345   thirteen forty-five
2305   twenty-three o five
There are two ways of saying midnight:
0000   zero hundred hours
2400   twenty-four hundred hours

Duration

- The length of time something takes is expressed in hours, minutes, and, where appropriate, seconds:
Cover the pan and simmer gently for one and a half hours.
He took just two minutes to knock out his opponent.
When *half* is used alone without another number, it does not have *a* before it or *of* after it:
The journey takes half an hour.
Abbreviations are often used in written English:
Allow 4–5 hrs for the paint to dry.
The fastest time was 12 mins 26 secs.

Numbers in measurement

The metric system of measurement is used in South Africa.

Length and height

- We talk about something being a particular measurement long, wide, high, or thick:
The garden is 50 metres long.
He had a three-centimetre scar on his leg.
The road rises to 2 288 m above sea level.
The ice was several centimetres thick.
- When we are describing people, we talk about how tall they are:
She's 1,63 metres tall.

Distance and speed

- Distance by road is measured in kilometres:
It is 42 kilometres to Durban.
The signpost said: 'Durban 42'.
- When describing speed, we talk about kilometres per hour (kph), kilometres per second, etc. In informal English, *per* is often replaced by *a* or *an*:
A speed limit of 50 kph
a hundred-kilometre-an-hour chase
Light travels at 299 792 kilometres per second.
- Distance in sport is usually measured in metres:
the women's 800 metres freestyle

Dimension

- We often state the size of something in terms of its length and width, and sometimes also its height and depth. We say *by* but write 'x' between each of the measurements:
The box measures 800 by 400 by 400 (millimetres) (800 x 400 x 400 mm).

Area

- Land used for farming or as part of an estate is measured in hectares:
a 2 000 hectare farm

- Regions or areas of a country are usually measured in square kilometres:

  The lake covers an area of more than 350 square kilometres.

  Population density is only 24 people per square kilometre (24/km²).
- Smaller areas are measured in square metres:

  15 square metres of carpet (e.g. 5 m x 3 m)

  As in the above examples, *square* is used immediately after a number when giving a measurement of area.

  When *square* follows both a number and a unit of measurement, the number indicates the length of each of the sides of something. Compare the previous example with:

  a carpet 15 metres square (15 m x 15 m)

Mass

- Food is usually measured in kilograms or grams:

  Could I have 200 grams of smoked ham, please and half a kilogram of Cheddar?

  net weight 175 g (on a packet of biscuits)
- A person's weight and heavy items are both measured in kilograms (informally kilos):

  My brother weighs 83 kilograms.

  a 40 kg sack of gravel

  Our baggage allowance is only 20 kilos.

Capacity

- We buy milk, fruit juice, and many other liquids in litres:

  a one-litre carton of milk

  half a litre of cooking oil

  5 litres of paint
- Petrol and diesel are sold in litres.
- Small amounts of liquid are usually measured in millilitres in a scientific context, or in cookery:

  100 ml sulphuric acid

  Add 250 ml milk and beat thoroughly.

Weights and measures

Metric measures

Length		
	10 millimetres (mm)	= 1 centimetre (cm)
	100 centimetres	= 1 metre (m)
	1 000 metres	= 1 kilometre (km)

Area		
	100 square metres (m²)	= 1 are
	100 ares	= 1 hectare (ha)
	100 hectares	= 1 square kilometre (km²)

Weight		
	1 000 milligrams (mg)	= 1 gram (g)
	1 000 grams	= 1 kilogram (kg)
	1 000 kilograms	= 1 tonne

Capacity		
	10 millilitres (ml)	= 1 centilitre (cl)
	100 centilitres	= 1 litre (l)
	10 litres	= 1 decalitre (dal)

SI units

The International System of Units (Système International d'Unités — SI) is an internationally agreed system of measurement that uses seven base units, with two supplementary units.

All other SI units are derived from the seven base units. In addition, multiples and sub-multiples (fractions of units) are expressed by the use of approved prefixes.

Units

	Physical quantity	Name	Symbol
Base units	length	metre	m
	mass	kilogram	kg
	time	second	s
	electric current	ampere	A
	thermodynamic temperature	kelvin	K
	luminous intensity	candela	cd
	amount of substance	mole	mol
Supplementary units	plane angle	radian	rad
	solid angle	steradian	sr

Prefixes

Multiple	Prefix	Symbol	Sub-multiple	Prefix	Symbol
10	deca-	da	10^{-1}	deci-	d
10^2	hecto-	h	10^{-2}	centi-	c
10^3	kilo-	k	10^{-3}	milli-	m
10^6	mega-	M	10^{-6}	micro-	μ
10^9	giga-	G	10^{-9}	nano-	n
10^{12}	tera-	T	10^{-12}	pico-	p
10^{15}	peta-	P	10^{-15}	femto-	f
10^{18}	exa-	E	10^{-18}	atto-	a

Abbreviations and acronyms

@	at
AC/a.c.	alternating current
a/c	account
AD	Anno Domini (in the year of Our Lord)
ad lib.	*ad libitum* (at pleasure)
Admin.	Administration
Adv.	Advocate
ad val.	*ad valorem* (according to value)
Afr.	Afrikaans/Afrikaner
AGM	annual general meeting
AI	artificial insemination
Aids	acquired immunodeficiency syndrome
alt.	altitude
a.m.	*ante meridiem* (before noon)
a/o	account of
app.	appendix
appro.	approval
Apr.	April
Assoc.	Association
asst.	assistant
ATM	automatic teller machine
Att.-Genl.	Attorney-General
Aug.	August
AWOL	absent without official leave
b.	born/née; bowled
bal.	balance
BC	before Christ
b/d	brought down
B/E	Bill of Exchange
b.f.	brought forward
B/L	bill of lading (for ship's cargo)
bn	billion
B/P	bill payable
B/R	bill receivable
Bros	Brothers
C	Celsius
c	cent(s)
c/ca	circa (about)
CAD	computer-aided design
c. and b.	caught and bowled
caps.	capital letters
C/B	credit balance
CBD	central business district
cc	cubic centimetre(s)
CC/cc	close corporation
c/d	carried down
CD	compact disc
CE	chief executive
cf./cp.	confer (compare)
cg	centigram(s)
ch(ap)	chapter
CID	Criminal Investigation Department
c.i.f.	cost, insurance, freight
cl	centilitre(s)
cm	centimetre(s)
C/N	credit note
Co	company
c/o	care of
COD	cash on delivery
COL	cost of living
con.	contra (against)
contd.	continued
Co-op.	Co-operative Society
cor	corner
Cr.	credit/creditor
cu(b.)	cubic
cum div.	*cum dividendo* (with dividend)
CV	curriculum vitae
CWO	cash with order
cwt	hundredweight
D	Roman 500
dB	decibels
Dec.	December
dept.	department
dg	decigram(s)
Dg	decagram(s)
DG	Director-General
dict.	dictionary

dip.	diploma	GMT	Greenwich Mean Time
dist.	district	GNP	gross national product
div.	division	govt.	government
div.	dividend(s)	GP	general practitioner
DIY	do-it-yourself	GPO	general post office
Dl	decalitre(s)		
dm	decimetre(s)	h	*hora* (hour)
Dm	decametre(s)	ha	hectare(s)
D/N	debit note	HE	His/Her Excellency
do.	ditto (the same)	hg	hectogram(s)
doz.	dozen	HIV	human immunodeficiency
Dr	Doctor		virus
Dr.	debit/debtor	hl	hectolitre(s)
		hm	hectometre(s)
E.	east	h.p.	horsepower
E&OE	errors and omissions excepted	HP	hire purchase
ECG	electrocardiogram	HQ	headquarters
Ed.	editor		
ed.	edition	ibid	*ibidem* (in the same place)
e.g.	*exempli gratia* (for example)	ICU	intensive care unit
elec.	electrical, electricity	id.	*idem* (the same)
encl.	enclosure	IDB	illicit diamond buying
ESP	extra-sensory perception	i.e.	*id est* (that is)
Esq.	Esquire	illus.	illustrated
est.	established	IMF	International Monetary Fund
et al	*et alii* (and others)	inc.	incorporated
etc.	*etcetera* (and so forth)	incl.	inclusive
exam.	examination	infra **dig.**	*infra dignitatem* (beneath one's
Exc.	Excellency		dignity)
ex off.	*ex officio* (by virtue of his/her	inst.	instant (this month)
	office)	int. al.	*inter alia* (amongst other
			things)
F	Fahrenheit	intro.	introduction
f.a.s.	free alongside ship	inv.	invoice
FBI	Federal Bureau of	IOU	I owe you
	Investigation	IQ	intelligence quotient
Feb.	February	ISBN	International Standard Book
fig.	figure		Number
Finrand	financial rand	ital.	italics
FM	frequency modulation		
f.o.b.	free on board	Jan.	January
fol.	folio	JSE	Johannesburg Stock Exchange
fol.	following	Jul.	July
f.o.r.	free on rail	jun.	junior (the younger)
forex	foreign exchange	Jun.	June
Fri.	Friday		
		kg	kilogram(s)
g	gram(s)	kl	kilolitre(s)
GDP	gross domestic product	km	kilometre(s)

km/h	kilometres per hour
kPa	kilopascal(s)
kW	kilowatt(s)
l	litre(s)
L	Roman 50
lab.	laboratory
l.b.w.	leg before wicket
l.c.	lower case
lex./dict.	lexicon/dictionary
lib.	library
lit.	literature
loc. cit	*loco citato* (at the place cited)
Ltd	Limited
m	metre(s)
M	Roman 1 000
Mar.	March
matric.	matriculation
MC	master of ceremonies
MD	managing director
memo.	memorandum
Messrs.	*Messieurs* (gentlemen)
mg	milligram(s)
mil.	military
min.	minute
ml	millilitre(s)
mm	millimetre(s)
MOH	medical officer of health
Mon.	Monday
MP	military police
MP	Member of Parliament
Mr	Mister
Mrs	Mistress
MS	manuscript
Ms	Mizz
Mt.	Mount
mus.	music(al)
N.	north
n.	*natus* (born)
n.a./NA	not applicable
NB	*nota bene* (mark well)
NE	north-east
neg.	negative
No.	*numero* (number)
n.o.	not out
Nov.	November
num.	numeral
o/a	on account
o.b.	on board
ob.	*obiit* (died)
Oct.	October
O/D	overdraft
OK	all correct
op.	*opus* (work)
op. cit.	*opere citato* (in the work cited)
p.	page
par.	paragraph
PAYE	pay as you earn
P/B	private bag
PC	personal computer
p.c.	per cent
pd.	paid
p.d.	*per diem* (per day)
PI	private investigator
pl.	plural
PM	Prime Minister
p.m.	*post meridiem* (after noon)
P/N	promissory note
PO	post office
POW	prisoner(s) of war
pp.	pages
pref.	preface; prefix
Pres.	president
PRO	public relations officer
pro.	professional
Prof.	Professor
pro tem.	*pro tempore* (for the time being)
Prov.	province/provincial
PS	*post scriptum* (postscript)
PTO	please turn over
Pty Ltd	Proprietary Limited
PWV	Pretoria, Witwatersrand, Vereeniging area
q.e.	*quod est* (which is)
QED	*quod erat demonstrandum* (that which had to be demonstrated)
q.t.	quietly
R	rand(s)
R	radius
R/D	refer to drawer
re	regarding
recap.	recapitulate

ref.	reference
rem.	remarks
resp.	respectively
Rev.	Reverend
RIP	*requiescat in pace* (rest in peace)
r/min	revolutions per minute
RSVP	*répondez s'il vous plaît* (please reply)
Rt. Hon.	Right Honourable
Rt. Rev.	Right Reverend
S.	south
SA	South Africa
SAA	South African Airways
SAAF	South African Air Force
SABC	South African Broadcasting Corporation
SABS	South African Bureau of Standards
SANDF	South African National Defence Force
Sapa	South African Press Association
SAPS	South African Police Services
Sat.	Saturday
sec.	second(s)
Sen.	Senate/Senator
sen.	senior (the eldest)
Sept.	September
SG	specific gravity
sing.	singular
sitcom	situation comedy
SOS	last signal for help
sq.	square
SRC	Students' Representative Council
St.	Saint
Std.	Standard
Sun.	Sunday
t	ton(s)
t.	*tare* (own weight)
TB	tuberculosis
tech.	technical
tel.	telephone
temp.	temperature
Thur.	Thursday
Tues.	Tuesday
TV	television

u.c.	upper case
UFO	unidentified flying object
UN	United Nations
Univ.	University
v./vs.	versus (against)
V	Roman 5
VAT	value added tax
VD	venereal disease
vet.	veterinary surgeon
vid.	*vide* (see, look)
VIP	very important person
viz.	*videlicet* (namely)
vol.	volume
W.	west
w.	week
w.c.	water closet
Wed.	Wednesday
wpm	words per minute
x	multiplication sign
X	Roman 10
Xmas	Christmas
Your Hon.	Your Honour

South African languages and peoples

South Africa is a multilingual country. The eleven official languages are listed below:

Language	People
Afrikaans	Afrikaners
English	English
isiNdebele	amaNdebele
isiXhosa	amaXhosa
isiZulu	amaZulu
Sepedi (Northern Sotho)	Bapedi
Sesotho	Basotho
Setswana	Batswana
Siswati	amaSwazi
Tshivenda	Bavenda, Vhavenda
Xitsonga	Vatsonga

Some peoples of South Africa not listed above:

amaBhaca
amaGaika
amaGcaleka
amaMfengu
amaMpondo
amaThembu
Barolong
Hlubi
Griqua
Khoikhoi
Nama
San
Shangaan
Shona

Chemical elements

Element	Symbol	Atomic number	Element	Symbol	Atomic number
actinium	Ac	89	indium	In	49
aluminium	Al	13	iodine	I	53
americium	Am	95	iridium	Ir	77
antimony	Sb	51	iron	Fe	26
argon	Ar	18	krypton	Kr	36
arsenic	As	33	lanthanum	La	57
astatine	At	85	lawrencium	Lr	103
barium	Ba	56	lead	Pb	82
berkelium	Bk	97	lithium	Li	3
beryllium	Be	4	lutetium	Lu	71
bismuth	Bi	83	magnesium	Mg	12
boron	B	5	manganese	Mn	25
bromine	Br	35	mendelevium	Md	101
cadmium	Cd	48	mercury	Hg	80
caesium	Cs	55	molybdenum	Mo	42
calcium	Ca	20	neodymium	Nd	60
californium	Cf	98	neon	Ne	10
carbon	C	6	neptunium	Np	93
cerium	Ce	58	nickel	Ni	28
chlorine	Cl	17	niobium	Nb	41
chromium	Cr	24	nitrogen	N	7
cobalt	Co	27	nobelium	No	102
copper	Cu	29	osmium	Os	76
curium	Cm	96	oxygen	O	8
dysprosium	Dy	66	palladium	Pd	46
einsteinium	Es	99	phosphorus	P	15
erbium	Er	68	platinum	Pt	78
europium	Eu	63	plutonium	Pu	94
fermium	Fm	100	polonium	Po	84
fluorine	F	9	potassium	K	19
francium	Fr	87	praseodymium	Pr	59
gadolinium	Gd	64	promethium	Pm	61
gallium	Ga	31	protactinium	Pa	91
germanium	Ge	32	radium	Ra	88
gold	Au	79	radon	Rn	86
hafnium	Hf	72	rhenium	Re	75
hahnium	Ha	105	rhodium	Rh	45
helium	He	2	rubidium	Rb	37
holmium	Ho	67	ruthenium	Ru	44
hydrogen	H	1	rutherfordium	Rf	104

Element	Symbol	Atomic number
samarium	Sm	62
scandium	Sc	21
selenium	Se	34
silicon	Si	14
silver	Ag	47
sodium	Na	11
strontium	Sr	38
sulphur	S	16
tantalum	Ta	73
technetium	Tc	43
tellurium	Te	52
terbium	Tb	65
thallium	Tl	81
thorium	The	90
thulium	Tm	69
tin	Sn	50
titanium	Ti	22
tungsten	w	74
uranium	U	92
vanadium	V	23
xenon	Xe	54
ytterbium	Yb	70
yttrium	Y	39
zinc	Zn	30
zirconium	Zr	40

NOTES